Principles of Marketing
Second European Edition

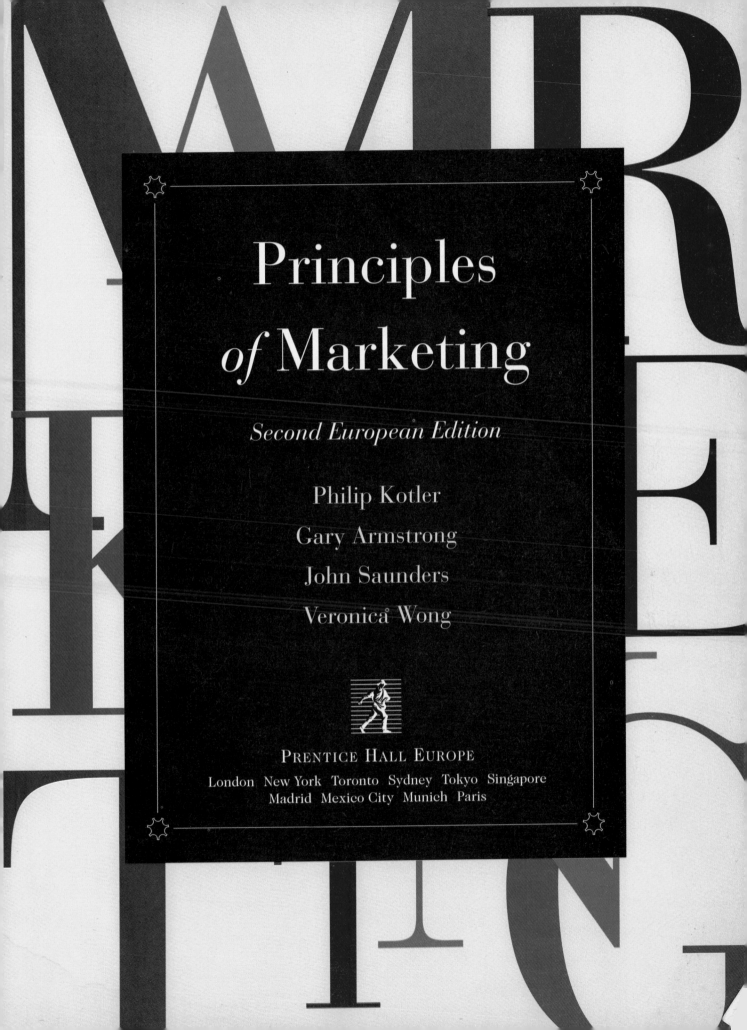

Principles *of* Marketing

Second European Edition

Philip Kotler

Gary Armstrong

John Saunders

Veronica Wong

PRENTICE HALL EUROPE

London New York Toronto Sydney Tokyo Singapore
Madrid Mexico City Munich Paris

Acquisitions Editor: Julia Helmsley
Development Editor: Andrew Goss
Permissions Manager: Sara Jillings
Production Editor: Ian Stoneham
Manufacturing Manager: Richard Lamprecht
Marketing Manager: Scott Dustan

Original eighth edition entitled *Principles of Marketing*
published by Prentice Hall Inc.
A Simon & Schuster Company
Upper Saddle River
New Jersey, USA
Copyright © 1999 by Prentice Hall Inc.

First European Edition published 1996
Second European Edition published 1999 by Prentice Hall Europe
Authorised for sale only in Europe, the Middle East and Africa

Copyright © Prentice Hall Europe 1996, 1999

Text and cover design: Design Deluxe, Bath, Avon
Typeset in 10pt Caslon 224 Book by Goodfellow and Egan, Cambridge

Printed and bound in Italy by Rotolito Lombarda, Milan

British Library Cataloguing in Publication Data

A catalogue record for this book is available from the British Library

ISBN 0-13-262254-8

1 2 3 4 5   03 02 01 00 99

To Wong and Bridget

Contents

Part Two
The Marketing Setting 140

Part Three
Core Strategy 374

Part Four
Product 556

Part Five
Price 676

Chapter 16
Pricing Considerations and Approaches 678

Part Six
Promotion 752

Part Seven
Place 890

Preface

Markets are changing fast. New markets are emerging, trading blocks are extending and communications channels about products and selling them are changing at a revolutionary pace. The signs of this change are everywhere in this text. Many people will use *Principles of Marketing* alongside its associated CD-ROM, *Interactive Marketing*. An increasing number of references are now Website addresses that anyone can access from their PC. Yet amid this turmoil some issues remain the same. Products change continuously, but the great brands shine through like storm-swept lighthouses: Coca-Cola, Nokia, Sony, BMW, Saab and Shell, to name but a few.

Marketing is changing to meet the changing world. Marketing remains the business activity that identifies an organization's customer needs and wants, determines which target markets it can serve best and designs appropriate products, services and programmes to serve these markets. However, marketing is much more than an isolated business function – it is a philosophy that guides the entire organization. The goal of marketing is to create customer satisfaction profitably by building valued relationships with customers. The marketing people cannot accomplish this goal by themselves. They must work closely with other people in their company and with other organizations in their value chain, to provide superior value to customers. Thus, marketing calls upon everyone in the organization to 'think customer' and to do all that they can to help create and deliver superior customer value and satisfaction. As Professor Stephen Burnett says: 'In a truly great marketing organization, you can't tell who's in the marketing department. Everyone in the organization has to make decisions based on the impact on the consumer.'

Marketing is not solely advertising or selling. Real marketing is less about selling and more about knowing what to make! Organizations gain market leadership by understanding customer needs and finding solutions that delight through superior value, quality and service. No amount of advertising or selling can compensate for a lack of customer satisfaction. Marketing is also about applying that same process of need fulfilment to groups other than the final consumer. Paying customers are only one group of stakeholders in our society, so it is important to reach out to others sharing our world.

Marketing is all around us. 'We are all customers now', notes the author Peter Mullen, 'in every area of customer inter-relationship from the supply and consumption of education and health care to the queue in the Post Office and the ride in an Inter-City express train, and in every financial transaction from the buying of biscuits to the purchase of a shroud.' Marketing is not only for manufacturing companies, wholesalers and retailers, but for all kinds of individuals and organizations. Lawyers, accountants and doctors use marketing to manage demand for their services. So do hospitals, museums and performing arts groups. No politician can get the needed votes, and no resort the needed tourists, without developing and carrying out marketing plans. *Principles of Marketing* helps students learn and apply the basic concepts and practices of modern marketing as used in a wide variety of settings: in product and service firms, consumer and business markets, profit and non-profit organizations, domestic and global companies, and small and large businesses.

People in these organizations need to know how to define and segment markets and how to position themselves by developing need-satisfying products and services for their chosen target segments. They must know how to price their offerings attractively and affordably, and how to choose and manage the marketing channel that delivers these products and services to customers. They need to know how to advertise and promote their products and services, so that customers will know about and want them. All of these demand a broad range of skills to sense, serve and satisfy consumers.

People need to understand marketing from the point of view of consumers and citizens. Someone is always trying to sell us something, so we need to recognize the methods they use. When they are seeking jobs, people have to market themselves. Many will start their careers within a sales force, in retailing, in advertising, in research or in one of the many other marketing areas.

Principles of Marketing provides a comprehensive introduction to marketing, taking a practical and managerial approach. It is rich in real-world illustrative examples and applications, showing the major decisions that marketing managers face in their efforts to balance the organization's objectives and resources against the needs and opportunities in the global marketplace.

Recognizing Europe's internationalism, illustrative examples and cases are drawn not from Europe alone, but also from North America, Japan, China, other countries in south-east Asia, and Africa. Some examples and cases concentrate on national issues, but many are pan-European and global cases that have an exciting international appeal. Although they cover many markets and products, the brands and customers used have been chosen to align closely with the experiences or aspirations of readers. Some examples are about global brands, such as Nike, Calvin Klein and Mercedes, while others cover interesting markets ranging from jeans and beer to executive jets, mine sweepers and Zoo Doo.

Principles of Marketing describes and discusses the stories that reveal the drama of modern marketing: Nike's powerful marketing; BMW's entry into the off-road market; the Swatchmobile; Levi Strauss & Co.'s startling success in finding new ways to grow globally; Apple Computers' and KFC's invasion of Japan; Qantas's struggle in the south-east Asian airline market; 3M's legendary emphasis on new-product development; MTV's segmentation of the European music market; Virgin's lifestyle marketing; B & B's Euro-segmentation; EuroDisney's disastrous adventure; Nestlé's difficulty with pressure groups and adverse publicity; Stena Sealink's quest for cross-channel passengers against Le Shuttle and Eurostar. These and dozens of other illustrative examples throughout each chapter reinforce the key concepts and techniques and bring marketing to life.

Its clear writing style, contemporary approach, extensive use of practical illustrative examples, and fresh and colourful design make this text easy to read, lively and an enjoyable learning experience.

The Second European Edition

Following extensive market research throughout Europe, this Second European Edition of *Principles of Marketing* provides significant improvements in content and structure, illustrative examples and case material, pedagogical features and text design.

Content and Structure

The content and structure have been changed to meet the needs of the user and take in new market developments. Chapter 3 is shortened to give a tighter introduction to strategic marketing planning while introducing the concepts developed in subsequent chapters. Other chapters reflect recent marketing developments. Two related changes are the coverage of key account management in chapter 8 and an extended coverage of relationship marketing in chapter 11. Competitive strategy is expanded upon in chapter 12 paying particular attention to making more money from markets.

During recent years manufacturers' brands have come under increasing attack as companies try to lever more out of the brands they own. These developments receive increased attention in chapter 13. Finally, chapters 21 and 22 on the place dimension of the marketing mix are radically changed to gather new ideas on direct and on-line marketing.

The overall structure is clearer, grouping chapters into seven parts each with a two-page introduction. Within this framework an extended second part, on the marketing setting, covers the marketing environment, buyer behaviour and how marketing research is used as an investigative tool.

Case Studies

A total of 51 case studies are now provided in this text. There are 11 new cases in this Second Edition, and of those retained from the First Edition, many have been revised and updated. There are now three distinct types: preview cases, chapter end case studies and part overview cases.

To improve consistency and the flexibility of case material to meet the needs of a range of different abilities, each of these cases now end with six questions, many of which have been reworked. These are graded by their level of difficulty; there are two questions for each of the three levels:

● Questions 1 and 2 (basic): direct issues arising from the case

● Questions 3 and 4 (intermediate): more penetrating issues which require the application of principles

● Questions 5 and 6 (advanced): demanding issues which require decision-making abilities

To familiarize yourself with the main features you will encounter throughout the text, a Guided Tour is provided on pages xx–xxi.

Supplements and Web-site

A successful marketing course requires more than a well-written textbook. Today's classroom requires a dedicated teacher and a fully integrated teaching system. *Principles of Marketing* is supported by an extensive, innovative and high-quality range of teaching and learning materials.

Supplements

Lecturer's Resource Manual/CD-ROM
    This comprehensive and helpful teaching resource, prepared by T.C. Melewar, comprises:

- Chapter overviews.
- Teaching tips.
- Class exercises.
- Teaching/discussion notes for all the cases.
- Answers to all the chapter-end 'Discussing the Issues' questions and 'Applying the Concepts' exercises.
- CD-ROM containing over 100 full-colour PowerPoint slides of the key figures and tables from the text.

● *Web-site*

This market-leading, fully functional Web-site has been specially commissioned and designed to accompany this Second European Edition. The site is regularly maintained and updated, and comprises a number of innovative interactive features for both students and lecturers. Lecturers may also download the Resource Manual and PowerPoint slides.

This companion Web-site can be accessed via the Prentice Hall Europe Web-site at http://www.prenhall.co.uk. For further details and to apply for an access password to certain areas of the site, please contact your local sales representative or the PHE marketing department at the following address:

Prentice Hall Europe, Campus 400, Maylands Avenue, Hemel Hempstead, Hertfordshire HP2 7EZ, UK. Telephone: + (0)1442 881900; Fax: +1442 882265.

Acknowledgements

No book is the work only of its authors. We owe much to the pioneers of marketing who first identified its major issues and developed its concepts and techniques. Our thanks go to our colleagues at the J.L. Kellogg Graduate School of Management, Northwestern University; the Kenan-Flagler Business School, University of North Carolina; and Aston, Loughborough and Warwick Business Schools for ideas, encouragement and suggestions. Thanks also to all our friends in the Academy of Marketing, the European Marketing Academy, Informs, the American Marketing Association and the Chartered Institute of Marketing, who have stimulated and advised us over the years. It has been an honour to work with so many people who have helped pioneer marketing in Europe.

Special thanks to Chris Stagg of Aston Business School, who has helped with many parts of the book; Marion Aitkenhead, who after the briefest of retirements gave us indispensable help in organizing our work; Andy Hirst of Loughborough Business School, who helped with many of the cases; T.C. Melewar of Warwick University for his patience and work in revising the Lecturer's Resource Manual; and Fatimah Moran, Stephen Cleary, Alan Hawley and Ken Randall at Staffordshire University for their work on the Interactive Marketing software. We also owe particular thanks to our many colleagues who share our international vision and have contributed such an outstanding set of international cases to this book: Pontus Alenroth, Pedro Quelhas Brito, Roberto Alvarez del Blanco, Robert Bjornstrom, Sue Bridgewater, Brenda Cullen, Peter Doyle, Colin Egan, Joakim Eriksson, Anton Hartmann-Olesen, Benoit Heilbrunn, Thomas Helgesson, Hapenga M. Kabeta, Sylvie Laforet, Richard Lynch, Peter McKiernan, Damien McLoughlin, Alkis Magdalinos, Malin Nilsson, Franscesc Parés, Verena A. Priemer, Jeff Rapaport, Lluís G. Renart, Javier Sarda, Anki Sjostrom and Anneli Zell.

Many reviewers at other colleges provided valuable comments and suggestions. We are indebted to the following colleagues: Chris Blackburn, Oxford Brookes University; D. Brownlie, University of Stirling; Drs H.D. and H.A. Cabooter, Hogeschool Venlo; Auorey Gilmore, University of Ulster at Jordanstown; Dr Constantine S. Katsikeas, Cardiff Business School, University of Wales; Tore Kristensen, IOA – Copenhagen Business School; Damien McLoughlin, Dublin City University; Professor M.T.G. Meulenberg, Agricultural University; Blain Meyrick, Coventry University; Elaine O'Brien, University of Strathclyde; Adrian Palmer, De Montfort University; David Shipley, Trinity College, Dublin; Chris Simango, University of Northumbria at Newcastle; M. van den Bosch, HEAO – Arnhem; Richard Varey, Sheffield Hallam University; and Helen R. Woodruffe, University of Salford.

We remain grateful to the numerous teachers who helped develop the First Edition, and to those listed below who provided comments and suggestions during the market research for this Second Edition:

R. Rosen, University of Portsmouth
A. Kuss, Freie Universität Berlin
S. Mitchell, Cheltenham & Gloucester College
S. Al-Hasan, University of Wales
G. Morgan, Sheffield Hallam University
D. Rose, University of Derby
J. Woods, Croydon College
J. Pilling, Highbury College of Technology
C. Griffiths, University of Brighton
M. Jonsson, Karlskrona/Ronneby University
A. Cunningham, Shannon College
D. Gilbert, University of Surrey
M. York, University of North London
P. Nonhuf, Hogeschool Nord-Nederland
C. Dennis, Brunel University
P. Whittaker, Paisley University
J. Lopez-Sintas, Universidade Autonoma de Barcelona
J. Brannigan, University of Aberdeen
S. Andersson, Universiteit Linkoping
A Pyne, University of Luton
G. Wootten, Hogeschool West-Brabant
M. Higgins, Keele University
T. Desbordes, ESC Paris
D. Marshall, University of Edinburgh
M. Baoring, Jonkoping University
P. Murphy, Dundee University
M. de Juan Vigary, Universidade de Alicante

J. Bon, ESC Paris
P. Britto, Universidade de Porto
S. Laverick, University of Derby
J. Gavaghan, Tralee RTC
A. Vickerstaff, Nottingham Trent University
R. Chetin, Bilkent University
C. Blackburn, Oxford Brookes University
P. Camp, Hogeschool Arnhem and Nijmegen
M. Manktelow, University of Wolverhampton
K. MacGettigan, Letterkenny RTC
P. Bjork, Svenska Handelschogskolen
L. Peters, University of East Anglia
B. Oney, University of Lefke
L. Murphy, Dundalk RTC
T. Helgesson, Hogskolan Halmstad
M. Raposo, Universidade de Beira Interior
M. Carberry-Long, De Montfort University
S. Hogan, University of Brighton
P. Hellman, Vaantaa Polytechnic/Mercuria
B. Ardley, Norwich City College
L. Varnham, Brunel University
M. van den Bosch, HEAO Arnhem
H. Mathias Thjymye, Handelschoyskolen
I. Fraser, University of Glasgow
K. Howlett, North Hertfordshire College
E. Shaw, University of Glasgow
F. Betts, University of Buckingham
G. Clarke, De Montfort University

We also owe a great deal to the people at Prentice Hall Europe who helped to develop and produce this Second Edition: Marketing Editor, Julia Helmsley provided encouragement, calming words, sound advice and a steadying hand; Andy Goss, Senior Development Editor, Chris Bessant was our very patient and professional copy editor; Ian Stoneham, Production Editor, did a very fine job of guiding the book smoothly through production.

PHILIP KOTLER
GARY ARMSTRONG
JOHN SAUNDERS
VERONICA WONG

Guided Tour

LEARNING OBJECTIVES: Bullet-points which highlight the core coverage in terms of the learning outcomes you should acquire after reading each chapter.

PREVIEW CASE: Combines both a practical illustrative overview of the chapter material, and a short problem-based case study (including graded questions) which should be attempted after you have read each chapter.

MARKETING HIGHLIGHT: Integrated throughout each chapter, these provide additional illustrative examples and/or discussion of more advanced marketing techniques and concepts.

KEY TERMS: Emboldened in the text with a concise definition in the margin to highlight the key concepts and techniques in each chapter.

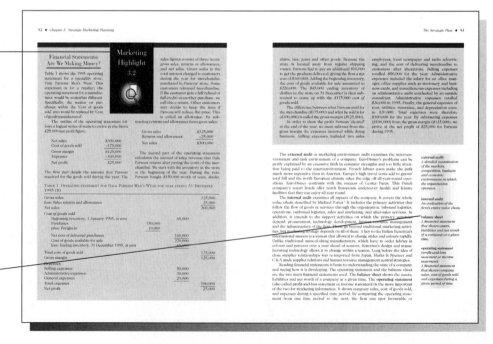

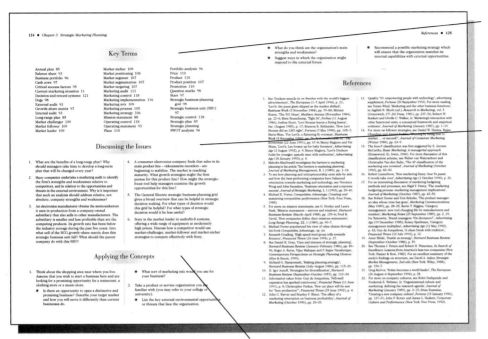

KEY TERMS LIST: An alphabetical listing of the key terms in each chapter, including a page reference, to assist rapid revision of the key concepts and techniques.

DISCUSSING THE ISSUES: Short questions that encourage you to review and/or critically discuss your understanding of the main topics in each chapter, either individually or in a group.

APPLYING THE CONCEPTS: Practical exercises that encourage you to develop and apply your understanding of the main topics in each chapter, either individually or in a group.

CASE STUDY: Each chapter ends with a practical problem-based illustration, including graded questions. Each of these case studies is more substantive and challenging than a chapter-opening preview case.

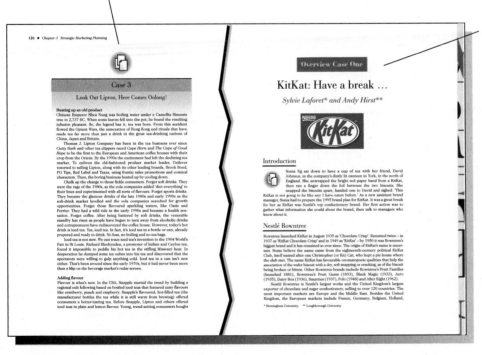

OVERVIEW CASE: Each part of the text ends with a comprehensive and practical problem-based illustration, including graded questions. Each of these cases integrates concepts and techniques from preceding chapters, allowing you to apply your understanding within a broader business context.

About the Authors

PHILIP KOTLER is S. C. Johnson & Son Distinguished Professor of International Marketing at the J. L. Kellogg Graduate School of Management, Northwestern University. He received his master's degree at the University of Chicago and his PhD at MIT, both in Economics. Dr Kotler is author of *Marketing Management: Analysis, Planning, Implementation and Control* (Prentice Hall). He has authored several other successful books and he has written over 100 articles for leading journals. He is the only three-time winner of the Alpha Kappa Psi award for the best annual article in the *Journal of Marketing*. Dr Kotler's numerous major honours include the Paul D. Converse Award given by the American Marketing Association to honour 'outstanding contributions to the science of marketing' and the Stuart Henderson Britt Award as Marketer of the Year. In 1985, he was named the first recipient of two major awards: the Distinguished Marketing Educator of the Year Award, given by the American Marketing Association and the Philip Kotler Award for Excellence in Health Care Marketing. Dr Kotler has served as a director of the American Marketing Association. He has consulted with many major US and foreign companies on marketing strategy.

GARY ARMSTRONG is Professor and Chair of Marketing in the Kenan-Flagler Business School at the University of North Carolina at Chapel Hill. He received his PhD in marketing from Northwestern University. Dr Armstrong has contributed numerous articles to leading research journals and consulted with many companies on marketing strategy. But Dr Armstrong's first love is teaching. He has been very active in Kenan-Flagler's undergraduate business programme and he has received several campus-wide and business schools teaching awards. He is the only repeat recipient of the School's highly regarded Award for Excellence in Undergraduate Teaching, which he won for the third time in 1993.

JOHN SAUNDERS Bachelor of Science (Loughborough), Master of Business Administration (Cranfield), Doctor of Philosophy (Bradford), Fellow of the British Academy of Management, Fellow of the Chartered Institute of Marketing, Fellow of the Royal Society of Arts, is Professor of Marketing and Head of *Aston Business School*, Birmingham. Previously, he worked for the Universities of Loughborough, Warwick, Bradford, Huddersfield and Hawaii, for the Hawker Siddeley Group and British Aerospace. He is past editor of the *International Journal of Research in Marketing*, is an assistant editor of the *British Journal of Management*, President of the *European Marketing Academy*, a member of the *British Academy of Management's* fellowship committee and the *Chartered Institute of Marketing's*. His publications include *The Marketing Initiative*, co-authorship of *Competitive Positioning* and *Principles of Marketing: the European Edition*. He has published over sixty refereed journal articles including publications in the *Journal of Marketing, Journal of Marketing Research, Marketing Science, International Journal of Research in Marketing, Journal of International Business Studies, Journal of Product Innovation Management* and *Journal of Business Research*.

VERONICA WONG, BSc, MBA (Bradford), PhD (CNAA), FRSA is a Reader in marketing at Warwick Business School. Dr Wong was born in Malaysia where she studied until her first degree. She has also taught in Malaysia and worked for Ciba Geigy. Dr Wong has worked with a wide range of international firms and government bodies concerned with product innovation and its management, including Britain's Department of Trade and Industry (DTI) Innovation Advisory Unit. She wrote the DTI's manual on *Identifying and Exploiting New Market Opportunities*. She has also published over fifty papers in refereed conferences and journals, including the *Journal of International Business Studies*, the *Journal of Product Innovation Management* and the *European Journal of Marketing*.

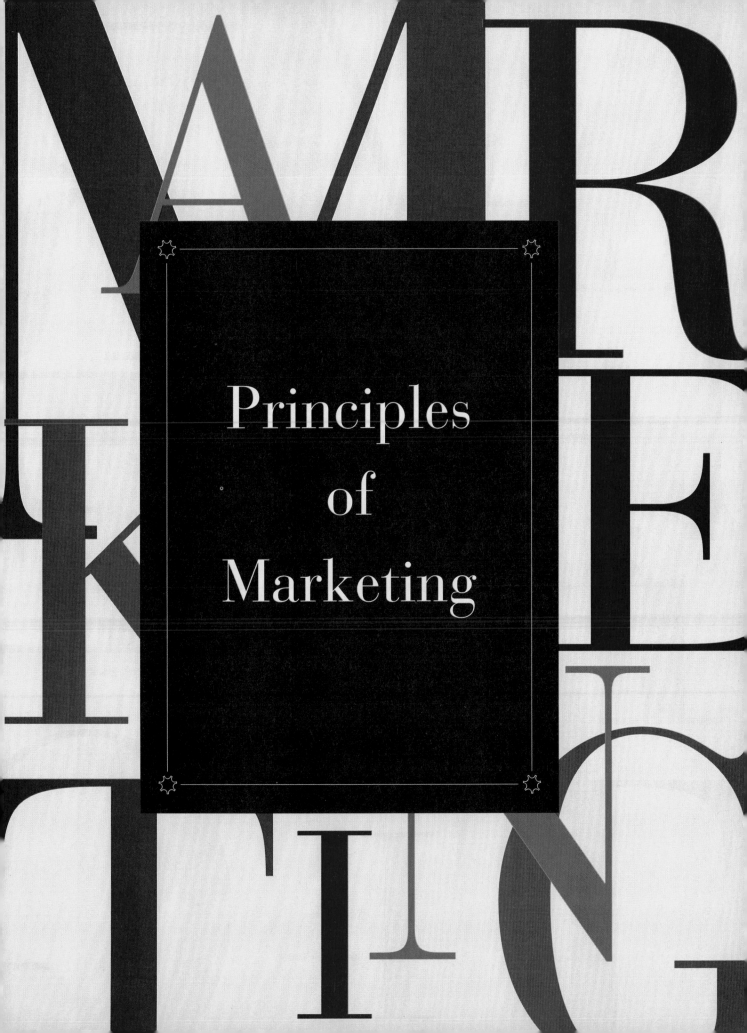

Principles

of

Marketing

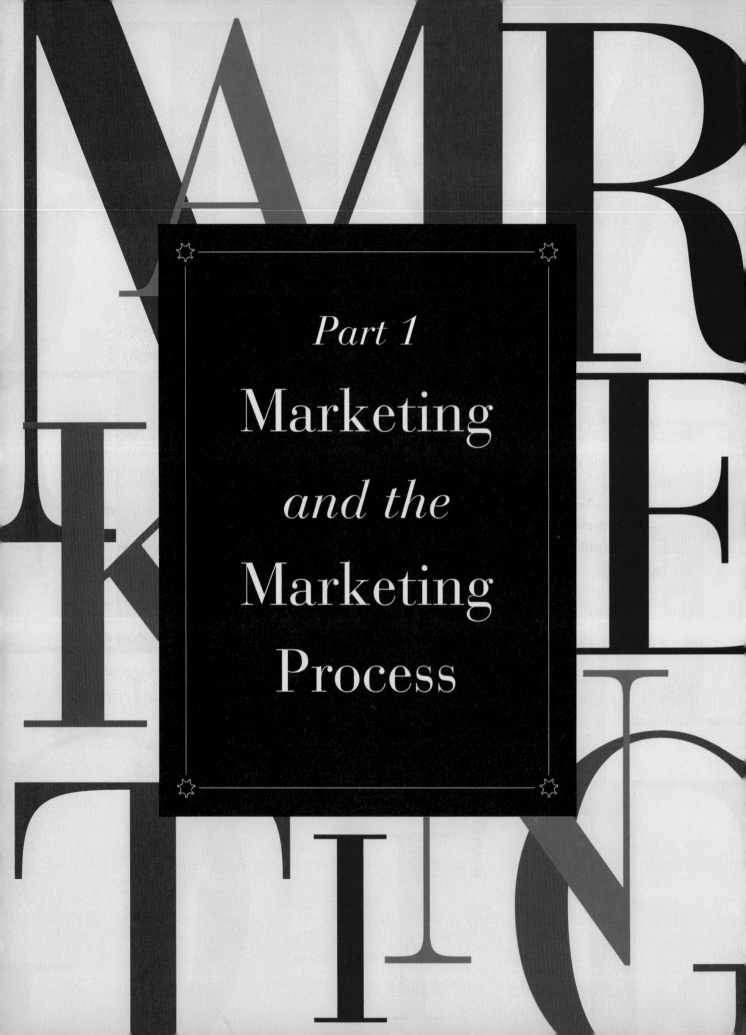

Part 1

Marketing and the Marketing Process

Part Introduction

PART ONE OF *PRINCIPLES OF MARKETING* examines marketing's role in society and the organizations that use it.

Chapter 1 shows how marketing is everywhere. It also tells how marketing has grown as the belief that organizations do best by caring for their customers. This understanding is expanded in Chapter 2, which looks beyond buying and selling to examine marketing's role and responsibilities in society. Together these chapters examine marketing as 'the place where the selfish interests of the manufacturer coincide with the interest of society', as the advertising guru David Ogilvy put it.

Chapter 3 takes the discussion from what marketing does to how marketing is done. In developing the strategic marketing planning process, it looks at how marketing fits with other business activities and how it is organized. Most importantly, it introduces the marketing activities appearing elsewhere in *Principles of Marketing* and shows how they combine to make modern marketing.

1

Marketing in a
Changing World:
Satisfying Human Needs

CHAPTER OBJECTIVES

After reading this chapter, you should be able to:

- Define *marketing* and discuss its core concepts.
- Define *marketing management* and examine how marketers *manage demand* and *build profitable customer relationships*.
- Compare the five *marketing management philosophies*, and express the basic ideas of demand management and the creation of *customer value* and *satisfaction*.
- Analyse the key *marketing challenges* facing marketers heading *into the next century*.

Preview Case

Nike

THE 'SWOOSH' – IT'S EVERYWHERE! JUST for fun, try counting the swooshes whenever you pick up the sports pages, watch a tennis match or basketball game, or tune into a televised golf match. Nike has built the ubiquitous swoosh (which represents the wing of Nike, the Greek goddess of victory) into one of the best-known brand symbols on the planet. The symbol is so well known that the company routinely runs ads without even mentioning the Nike name. In fact, you may be surprised to find that your latest pair of

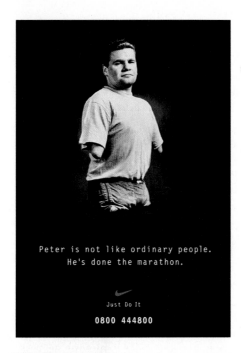

Peter is not like ordinary people.
He's done the marathon.

Just Do It

0800 444800

Nike's inspirational pre-Olympic campaign in 1996, using disabled athlete Peter Hull, is not just about running a marathon. Here, Nike forces people to reconsider stereotyped ideas.

Photography: Tim O'Sullivan
Advertising Agency: Simons Palmer

Nike shoes, or your Nike hat or T-shirt, carries no brand identification at all other than the swoosh.

The power of its brand and logo speaks loudly to Nike's superb marketing skills. The company's now-proven strategy of building superior products around popular athletes has changed the face of sports marketing for ever. Nike spends hundreds of millions of dollars each year on big-name endorsements, splashy promotional events and lots of attention-getting ads. Over the years, Nike has associated itself with some of the biggest names in sports. No matter what your sport, the chances are good that one of your favourite athletes wears the Nike swoosh.

Nike knows, however, that good marketing runs much deeper than promotional hype and promises. Good marketing means consistently delivering real value to customers. Nike's initial success resulted from the technical superiority of its running and basketball shoes, pitched to serious athletes who were frustrated by the lack of innovation in athletic equipment. To this day, Nike leads the industry in product development and innovation.

But Nike gives its customers more than just good athletic gear. As the company notes on its Web page (www.nike.com): 'Nike has always known the truth – it's not so much the shoes but where they take you.' Beyond shoes, apparel and equipment, Nike markets a way of life, a sports culture, a 'Just do it!' attitude. When you lace up your Nikes, you link yourself, in at least some small way, with all that Nike and its athletes have come to represent – a genuine passion for sports, a maverick disregard for convention, hard work and serious sports performance. Through Nike, you share a little of Michael Jordan's intense competitiveness, Tiger Woods' cool confidence, Jackie Joyner-Kersee's gritty endurance, Ken Griffey, Jr's selfless consistency or Michael Johnson's blurring speed. Nike is athletes, athletes are sports, *Nike is sports.*

Nike's marketers build relationships – between Nike, its athletes and customers. For example, a recent ad in a tennis magazine shows only a Nike tennis shoe with the red swoosh and a freephone number. Readers who call the number hear tennis favourite Jim Courier talking drums with his favourite drummer, Randy Goss of Toad the Wet Sprocket. Call the number in a similar basketball ad and you'll overhear a humorous phone conversation in which Father Guido Sarducci tries to get Michael Jordan to invest in his newest invention, edible bicycles.

Nike seems to care as much about its customers' lives as their bodies. It doesn't just promote sales, it promotes *sports* for the benefit of all. For example, its 'If you let me play' campaign lends strong support to women's sports and the many benefits of sports participation for girls and young women. Nike also invests in a wide range of lesser-known sports, even though they provide less lucrative marketing opportunities. Such actions establish Nike not just as a producer of good athletic gear, but as a good and caring *company*.

Taking care of customers has paid off handsomely for Nike. Over the past decade, Nike's revenues have grown at an incredible annual rate of 21 per cent; annual return to investors has averaged 47 per cent. Over 1996 alone, total revenues increased by 36 per cent. Nike, with 27 per cent share, twice that of nearest competitor Reebok, flat-out dominates the world's athletic footwear market.

Nike founder and chief executive Phil Knight has brashly predicted that Nike will double its sales within the next five years. To meet this ambitious goal in the face of a maturing US footwear market, Nike is moving aggressively into new product categories, sports and regions of the world. In only a few years, Nike's sports apparel business has grown explosively, now accounting for nearly a quarter of Nike's $8 billion in yearly sales. And Nike is slapping its familiar swoosh logo on everything from sunglasses and footballs to batting gloves and hockey sticks. Nike has recently invaded a dozen new sports, including baseball, golf, ice and street hockey, inline skating, wall climbing, and hiking and other outdoor endeavours.

Still, to meet its goals, much of Nike's growth will have to come from overseas. And to dominate globally, Nike must dominate in football, the world's most popular sport. Nike has previously all but ignored the multibillion dollar world football market, which currently accounts for only 3 per cent of its sales. Now, soccer is Nike's top priority. In typical fashion, Nike has set World Cup 2002 as its deadline for becoming the world's no. 1 supplier of football boots, clothing and equipment.

Elbowing its way to the top by 2002 won't be easy. World football has long been dominated by Adidas, which claims an 80 per cent global market share in football gear. Nike will have to build in just a few years what Adidas has built over the past fifty. Employing classic in-your-face marketing tactics, Nike is spending hundreds of millions of dollars in an all-out assault on competitors. Its open-wallet spending has dazzled the football world and its vast resources are rapidly changing the economics of the game. For example, it recently paid a record-setting $200 million over ten years to snatch sponsorship of the World Cup champions, Brazil's national team, from Umbro.

Still, winning in worldwide football, or in anything else Nike does, will take more than just writing fat cheques. Some Nike watchers fear that Nike's massive global expansion, coupled with its entry into new sports and products, will result in a loss of focus and overexposure of the Nike brand name. They worry that the swoosh could suddenly become unhip. To prevent this, Nike will have to deliver worldwide a consistent image of superior quality, innovation and value compared to its rivals. It will have to earn respect on a country-by-country basis and become a part of the cultural fabric of each new market.

Competitors can only hope that Nike will overreach, but few are counting on it. For now, most can only sit back and marvel at Nike's marketing prowess. As for football, rival Puma sees Nike's tactics as heavy handed but has little doubt that Nike's superb marketing will prevail. Its president states flatly, 'Nike will control the soccer world.'[1]

QUESTIONS

You should attempt these questions only after completing your reading of this chapter

1. What do you understand by the term 'marketing'?
2. What would you consider to be Nike's 'superb marketing skills'?
3. Why does Nike require these skills to compete in the marketplace?
4. Why does Nike spend hundred of millions of dollars on promoting its brand and logo?
5. Who are Nike's consumers? What might their needs be?
6. Show how marketing principles and practices will enable Nike to satisfy these needs, bearing in mind the diverse range of product and geographic markets the company operates in.

Introduction

Many large and small organizations seek success. A myriad factors contribute to making a business successful – strategy, dedicated employees, good information systems, excellent implementation. However, today's successful companies at all levels have one thing in common – like Nike they are strongly customer-focused and heavily committed to marketing. These companies share an absolute dedication to sensing, serving and satisfying the needs of customers in well-defined target markets. They motivate everyone in the organization to deliver high quality and superior value for their customers, leading to high levels of customer satisfaction. These organizations know that if they take care of their customers, market share and profits will follow.

Marketing, more than any other business function, deals with customers. Creating customer value and satisfaction are at the very heart of modern marketing thinking and practice. Although we will explore more detailed definitions of marketing later in this chapter, perhaps the simplest definition is this one: Marketing is the delivery of customer satisfaction at a profit. The goal of marketing is to attract new customers by promising superior value, and to keep current customers by delivering satisfaction.

Many people think that only large companies operating in highly developed economies use marketing, but some marketing is critical to the success of every organization, whether large or small, domestic or global. In the business sector, marketing first spread most rapidly in consumer packaged-goods companies, consumer durables companies and industrial equipment companies. Within the past few decades, however, consumer service firms, especially airline, insurance and financial services companies, have also adopted modern marketing practices. Business groups such as lawyers, accountants, physicians and architects, too,

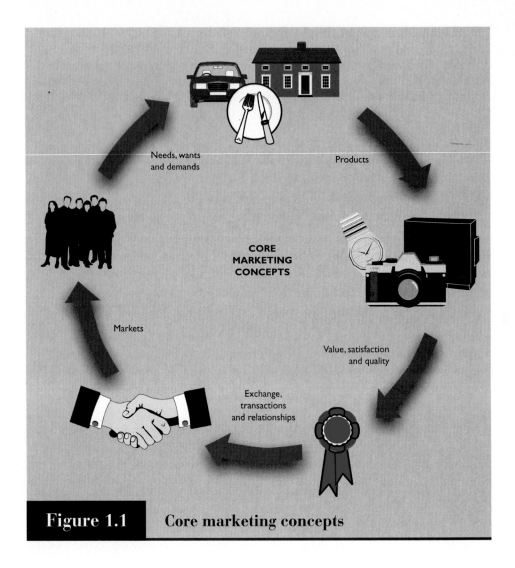

Figure 1.1   **Core marketing concepts**

Needs, wants and demands

Products

CORE MARKETING CONCEPTS

Value, satisfaction and quality

Markets

Exchange, transactions and relationships

have begun to take an interest in marketing and to advertise and to price their services aggressively.

Marketing has also become a vital component in the strategies of many *non-profit* organizations, such as schools, charities, churches, hospitals, museums, performing arts groups and even police departments. We will explore the growth of non-profit marketing later in this chapter.

Today, marketing is practised widely all over the world. Most countries in North and South America, western Europe and Asia have well-developed marketing systems. Even in eastern Europe and the former Soviet republics, where marketing has long had a bad name, dramatic political and social changes have created new opportunities for marketing. Business and government leaders in most of these nations are eager to learn everything they can about modern marketing practices.

You already know a lot about marketing – it's all around you. You see the results of marketing in the abundance of products that line the store shelves in your nearby shopping mall. You see marketing in the advertisements that fill your TV screen, magazines and mailbox. At home, at school, where you work, where you play – you are exposed to marketing in almost everything you do. Yet, there is much more to marketing than meets the consumer's casual eye. Behind it all is a massive network of people and activities competing for your attention and money.

The remaining pages of this book will give you a more complete and formal introduction to the basic concepts and practices of today's marketing. In this chapter, we begin by defining marketing and its core concepts, describing the major philosophies of marketing thinking and practice, and discussing some of the major new challenges that marketers now face.

What is Marketing?

What does the term *marketing* mean? Marketing must be understood not in the old sense of making a sale – 'selling' – but in the new sense of satisfying customer needs. Many people think of marketing only as selling and advertising. And no wonder, for every day we are bombarded with television commercials, newspaper ads, direct mail and sales calls. Someone is always trying to sell us something. It seems that we cannot escape death, taxes or selling!

Therefore, you may be surprised to learn that selling and advertising are only the tip of the marketing iceberg. Although they are important, they are only two of many marketing functions, and often not the most important ones. If the marketer does a good job of identifying customer needs, develops products that provide superior value, distributes and promotes them effectively, these goods will sell very easily.

Everyone knows something about 'hot' products. When Sony designed its first Walkman cassette and disc players, when Nintendo first offered its improved video game console, and when The Body Shop introduced animal-cruelty-free cosmetics and toiletries, these manufacturers were swamped with orders. They had designed the 'right' products: not 'me-too' products, but ones offering new benefits. Peter Drucker, a leading management thinker, has put it this way: 'The

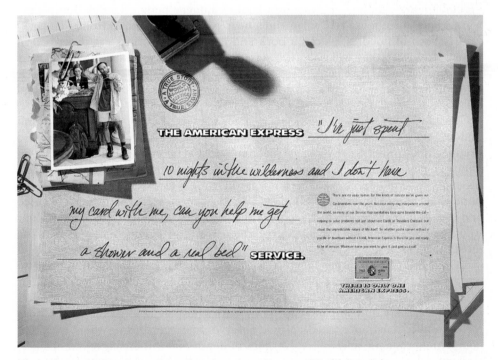

This ad assures card members that American Express World Service representatives go beyond the call of duty to solve their unexpected problems.

aim of marketing is to make selling superfluous. The aim is to know and understand the customer so well that the product or service fits ... and sells itself.'[2]

This does not mean that selling and advertising are unimportant. Rather, it means that they are part of a larger marketing mix – a set of marketing tools that work together to affect the marketplace. We define **marketing** as: *a social and managerial process by which individuals and groups obtain what they need and want through creating and exchanging products and value with others*.[3] To explain this definition, we examine the following important terms: *needs*, *wants* and *demands*; *products*; *value* and *satisfaction*; *exchange*, *transactions* and *relationships*; and *markets*. Figure 1.1 shows that these core marketing concepts are linked, with each concept building on the one before it.

Needs, Wants and Demands

The most basic concept underlying marketing is that of human needs. A **human need** is a state of felt deprivation. Humans have many complex needs. These include basic *physical* needs for food, clothing, warmth and safety; *social* needs for belonging and affection; and *individual* needs for knowledge and self-expression. These needs are not invented by marketers, they are a basic part of the human make-up. When a need is not satisfied, a person will do one of two things:

1. look for an object that will satisfy it; or
2. try to reduce the need.

People in industrial societies may try to find or develop objects that will satisfy their desires. People in less developed societies may try to reduce their desires and satisfy them with what is available.

Human wants are the form taken by human needs as they are shaped by culture and individual personality. A hungry person in Bahrain may want a vegetable curry, mango chutney and lassi. A hungry person in Eindhoven may want a ham and cheese roll, salad and a beer. A hungry person in Hong Kong may want a bowl of noodles, char siu pork and jasmine tea. Wants are described in terms of objects that will satisfy needs. As a society evolves, the wants of its members expand. As people are exposed to more objects that arouse their interest and desire, producers try to provide more want-satisfying products and services.

People have narrow, basic needs (e.g. for food or shelter), but almost unlimited wants. However, they also have limited resources. Thus they want to choose products that provide the most satisfaction for their money. When backed by an ability to pay – that is, buying power – wants become **demands**. Consumers view products as bundles of benefits and choose products that give them the best bundle for their money. Thus a Honda Civic means basic transportation, low price and fuel economy. A Mercedes means comfort, luxury and status. Given their wants and resources, people demand products with the benefits that add up to the most satisfaction.

Outstanding marketing companies go to great lengths to learn about and understand their customers' needs, wants and demands. They conduct consumer research, focus groups and customer clinics. They analyze customer complaint, inquiry, warranty and service data. They train salespeople to be on the look-out for unfulfilled customer needs. They observe customers using their own and competing products, and interview them in depth about their likes and dislikes. Understanding customer needs, wants and demands in detail provides important input for designing marketing strategies.

marketing
A social and managerial process by which individuals and groups obtain what they need and want through creating and exchanging products and value with others.

human need
A state of felt deprivation.

human want
The form that a human need takes as shaped by culture and individual personality.

demands
Human wants that are backed by buying power.

Products and Services

People satisfy their needs and wants with products. A **product** is anything that can be offered to a market to satisfy a need or want. Usually, the word *product* suggests a physical object, such as a car, a television set or a bar of soap. However, the concept of product is not limited to physical objects – anything capable of satisfying a need can be called a product. In addition to tangible goods, products include **services**, which are activities or benefits offered for sale that are essentially intangible and do not result in the ownership of anything. Examples are banking, airline, hotel and household appliance repair services. Broadly defined, products also include other entities such as *persons, places, organizations, activities* and *ideas*. Consumers decide which entertainers to watch on television, which political party to vote for, which places to visit on holiday, which organizations to support through contributions and which ideas to adopt. Thus the term *product* covers physical goods, services and a variety of other vehicles that can satisfy consumers' needs and wants. If at times the term *product* does not seem to fit, we could substitute other terms such as *satisfier, resource* or *offer*.

Many sellers make the mistake of paying more attention to the physical products they offer than to the benefits produced by these products. They see themselves as selling a product rather than providing a *solution* to a need. The importance of physical goods lies not so much in owning them as in the benefits they provide. We don't buy food to look at, but because it satisfies our hunger. We don't buy a microwave to admire, but because it cooks our food. A manufacturer of drill bits may think that the customer needs a drill bit, but what the customer *really* needs is a hole. These sellers may suffer from 'marketing myopia'.[4] They are so taken with their products that they focus only on existing wants and lose sight of underlying customer needs. They forget that a physical product is only a tool to solve a consumer problem. These sellers have trouble if a new product comes along that serves the need better or less expensively. The customer with the same *need* will *want* the new product.

Value, Satisfaction and Quality

Consumers usually face a broad array of products and services that might satisfy a given need. How do they choose among these many products? Consumers make buying choices based on their perceptions of the value that various products and services deliver.

The guiding concept is **customer value**. Customer value is the difference between the values the customer gains from owning and using a product and the costs of obtaining the product. For example, Federal Express customers gain a number of benefits. The most obvious is fast and reliable package delivery. However, when using Federal Express, customers may also receive some status and image values. Using Federal Express usually makes both the package sender and the receiver feel more important. When deciding whether to send a package via Federal Express, customers will weigh these and other values against the money, effort and psychic costs of using the service. Moreover, they will compare the value of using Federal Express against the value of using other shippers – UPS, DHL, the postal service – and select the one that gives them the greatest delivered value.

Customers often do not judge product values and costs accurately or objectively. They act on *perceived* value. Customers perceive the firm to provide faster, more reliable delivery and are hence prepared to pay the higher prices that

product
Anything that can be offered to a market for attention, acquisition, use or consumption that might satisfy a want or need. It includes physical objects, services, persons, places, organizations and ideas.

service
Any activity or benefit that one party can offer to another which is essentially intangible and does not result in ownership of anything.

customer value
The consumer's assessment of the product's overall capacity to satisfy his or her needs.

customer satisfaction
The extent to which a product's perceived performance matches a buyers expectations. If the product's performance falls short of expectations, the buyer is disatisfied. If performance matches or exceeds expectations the buyer is satisfied or delighted.

total quality management (TQM)
Programmes designed to constantly improve the quality of products, service and marketing processes

Federal Express charges. **Customer satisfaction** depends on a product's perceived performance in delivering value relative to a buyer's expectations. If the product's performance falls short of the customer's expectations, the buyer is dissatisfied. If performance matches expectations, the buyer is satisfied. If performance exceeds expectations, the buyer is delighted. Outstanding marketing companies go out of their way to keep their customers satisfied. Satisfied customers make repeat purchases, and they tell others about their good experiences with the product. The key is to match customer expectations with company performance. Smart companies aim to *delight* customers by promising only what they can deliver, then delivering *more* than they promise.[5]

Customer satisfaction is closely linked to quality. In recent years, many companies have adopted **total quality management** (TQM) programmes, designed constantly to improve the quality of their products, services and marketing processes. Quality has a direct impact on product performance, and hence on customer satisfaction.

In the narrowest sense, quality can be defined as 'freedom from defects'. But most customer-centred companies go beyond this narrow definition of quality. Instead, they define quality in terms of customer satisfaction. For example, Motorola, a company that pioneered total quality efforts in the United States, stresses that 'Quality has to do something for the customer … Our definition of a defect is "if the customer doesn't like it, it's a defect".' Customer-focused definitions of quality suggest that a company has achieved total quality only when its products or services meet or exceed customer expectations. Thus, the fundamental aim of today's *total quality* movement has become *total customer satisfaction*. Quality begins with customer needs and ends with customer satisfaction.

Today, consumer-behaviourists have gone far beyond narrow economic assumptions about how consumers form value judgements and make product choices. We will look at modern theories of consumer-choice behaviour in Chapter 7. In Chapter 11, we will examine more fully customer satisfaction, value and quality.

Exchange, Transactions and Relationships

exchange
The act of obtaining a desired object from someone by offering something in return.

Marketing occurs when people decide to satisfy needs and wants through exchange. **Exchange** is the act of obtaining a desired object from someone by offering something in return. Exchange is only one of many ways people can obtain a desired object. For example, hungry people can find food by hunting, fishing or gathering fruit. They could beg for food or take food from someone else. Finally, they could offer money, another good or a service in return for food.

As a means of satisfying needs, exchange has much in its favour. People do not have to prey on others or depend on donations. Nor must they possess the skills to produce every necessity for themselves. They can concentrate on making things they are good at making and trade them for needed items made by others. Thus exchange allows a society to produce much more than it would with any alternative system.

Exchange is the core concept of marketing. For an exchange to take place, several conditions must be satisfied. Of course, at least two parties must participate and each must have something of value to offer the other. Each party must also want to deal with the other party and each must be free to accept or reject the other's offer. Finally, each party must be able to communicate and deliver.

These conditions simply make exchange *possible*. Whether exchange actually *takes place* depends on the parties coming to an agreement. If they agree, we must conclude that the act of exchange has left both of them better off or, at least, not worse off. After all, each was free to reject or accept the offer. In this sense, exchange creates value just as production creates value. It gives people more consumption choices or possibilities.

Whereas exchange is the core concept of marketing, a transaction is marketing's unit of measurement. A **transaction** consists of a trading of values between two parties. In a transaction, we must be able to say that one party gives *X* to another party and gets *Y* in return. For example, you pay a retailer £300 for a television set or the hotel £90 a night for a room. This is a classic *monetary transaction*, but not all transactions involve money. In a barter transaction, you might trade your old refrigerator in return for a neighbour's second-hand television set.

transaction
A trade between two parties that involves at least two things of value, agreed-upon conditions, a time of agreement and a place of agreement.

Going Back to Barter

Marketing Highlight 1.1

With today's high prices, many companies are returning to the primitive but time-honoured practice of barter – trading goods and services that they make or provide for other goods and services that they need. The European barter market is estimated to be worth up to $200 million a year and forecasts put the value at nearly $1 billion by the year 2000. On a global scale, companies barter more than $275 billion worth of goods and services a year, and the practice is growing rapidly.

Companies use barter to increase sales, unload extra goods and save cash. For example, companies are offering television programmes to broadcasters in exchange for air-time: Unilever owns the European rights to the TV game shows, *Wheel of Fortune* and *Jeopardy*, which it barters to stations all over Europe. Others like PepsiCo traded Pepsi-Cola and pizza parlours to the Russians for ships and Stolichnaya vodka, while Pierre Cardin served as a consultant to China in exchange for silks and cashmeres, and Turnkey Contracts and Consultancy, a Singapore company, was paid in Burmese logs for the construction of an International Business Centre in Burma's capital city, Rangoon.

As a result of this increase in barter activity, many kinds of speciality company have appeared to help other companies with their bartering. Retail-trade exchanges and trade clubs arrange barter for small retailers. Larger corporations use trade consultants and brokerage firms. Media brokerage houses provide advertising in exchange for products, and international barter is often handled by counter-trade organizations.

Barter has become especially important in today's global markets, where it now accounts for as much as 40 per cent of all world trade. The present world currency shortage means that more and more companies are being forced to trade for goods and services rather than cold, hard cash. International barter transactions can be very complex. For example, a trader for SGD International, a New York-based bartering company, arranged the following series of exchanges:

[The trader] supplied a load of latex rubber to a Czech company in exchange for 9,000 metres of finished carpeting. He then traded the carpeting for hotel room credits. The rooms were traded to a Japanese company for electronic equipment, which [the trader] bartered away for convention space. The final [exchange] came when he swapped the convention space for ad space that his company used.

SOURCES: 'TV barters for the future', *The European* (25–31 March 1994); Victor Mallet, 'Barter proves best for business, Burma style', *Financial Times* (8 February 1994), p. 8; Quote from Cyndee Miller, 'Worldwide money crunch fuels more international barter', *Marketing News* (2 March 1992), p. 5; also see Arthur Bragg, 'Bartering comes of age', *Sales and Marketing Management* (January 1988), pp. 61–3; Joe Mandese, 'Marketers swap old product for ad time, space', *Advertising Age* (14 October 1991), p. 3.

A *barter transaction* can also involve services as well as goods: for example, when a lawyer writes a will for a doctor in return for a medical examination (see Marketing Highlight 1.1). A transaction involves at least two things of value, conditions that are agreed upon, a time of agreement and a place of agreement.

In the broadest sense, the market tries to bring about a response to some offer. The response may be more than simply 'buying' or 'trading' goods and services. A political candidate, for instance, wants a response called 'votes', a church wants 'membership', and a social-action group wants 'idea acceptance'. Marketing consists of actions taken to obtain a desired response from a target audience towards some product, service, idea or other object.

relationship marketing
The process of creating, maintaining and enhancing strong, value-laden relationships with customers and other stakeholders.

Transaction marketing is part of the larger idea of **relationship marketing**. Smart marketers work at building long-term relationships with valued customers, distributors, dealers and suppliers. They build strong economic and social ties by promising and consistently delivering high-quality products, good service and fair prices. Increasingly, marketing is shifting from trying to maximize the profit on each individual transaction to maximizing mutually beneficial relationships with consumers and other parties. In fact, ultimately, a company wants to build a unique company asset called a *marketing network*. A marketing network consists of the company and all of its supporting stakeholders: customers, employees, suppliers, distributors, retailers, ad agencies, and others with whom it has built mutually profitable business relationships. Increasingly, competition is not between companies but rather between whole networks, with the prize going to the company that has built the best network. The operating principle is simple: build a good network of relationships with key stakeholders, and profits will follow.[6] Chapter 11 will explore relationship marketing and its role in creating and maintaining customer satisfaction.

Markets

market
The set of all actual and potential buyers of a product or service.

The concept of exchange leads to the concept of a market. A **market** is the set of actual and potential buyers of a product. These buyers share a particular need or want that can be satisfied through exchange. Thus, the size of a market depends on the number of people who exhibit the need, have resources to engage in exchange, and are willing to offer these resources in exchange for what they want.

Originally the term *market* stood for the place where buyers and sellers gathered to exchange their goods, such as a village square. Economists use the term to refer to a collection of buyers and sellers who transact in a particular product class, as in the housing market or the grain market. Marketers, however, see the sellers as constituting an industry and the buyers as constituting a market. The relationship between the *industry* and the *market* is shown in Figure 1.2. The sellers and the buyers are connected by four flows. The sellers send products, services and communications to the market; in return, they receive money and information. The inner loop shows an exchange of money for goods; the outer loop shows an exchange of information.

Modern economies operate on the principle of division of labour, where each person specializes in producing something, receives payment, and buys needed things with this money. Thus, modern economies abound in markets. Producers go to resource markets (raw material markets, labour markets, money markets), buy resources, turn them into goods and services, and sell them to intermediaries, who sell them to consumers. The consumers sell their labour, for which they receive income to pay for the goods and services they buy. The government is another market that plays several roles. It buys goods from resource, producer and intermediary markets; it pays them; it taxes these markets (including

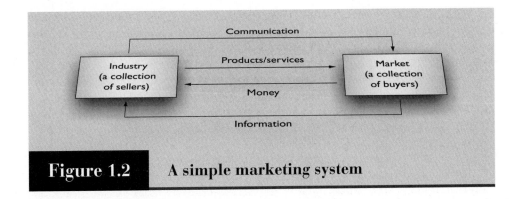

Figure 1.2   **A simple marketing system**

consumer markets); and it returns needed public services. Thus each nation's economy and the whole world economy consist of complex interacting sets of markets that are linked through exchange processes.

In advanced societies, markets need not be physical locations where buyers and sellers interact. With modern communications and transportation, a merchant can easily advertise a product on a late evening television programme, take orders from thousands of customers over the phone, and mail the goods to the buyers on the following day without having had any physical contact with them.

Businesspeople use the term *markets* to cover various groupings of customers. They talk about *need markets* (such as health seekers); *product markets* (such as teens or the baby boomers); and *geographic markets* (such as western Europe or the United States). Or they extend the concept to cover non-customer groupings. For example, a *labour market* consists of people who offer their work in return for wages or products. Various institutions, such as employment agencies and job-counselling firms, will grow up around a labour market to help it function better. The *money market* is another important market that emerges to meet the needs of people so that they can borrow, lend, save and protect money. The *donor market* has emerged to meet the financial needs of non-profit organizations.

Marketing

The concept of markets finally brings us full circle to the concept of marketing. Marketing means managing markets to bring about exchanges for the purpose of satisfying human needs and wants. Thus, we return to our definition of marketing as a process by which individuals and groups obtain what they need and want by creating and exchanging products and value with others.

Exchange processes involve work. Sellers must search for buyers, identify their needs, design good products and services, promote them, and store and deliver them. Activities such as product development, research, communication, distribution, pricing and service are core marketing activities.

Although we normally think of marketing as being carried on by sellers, buyers also carry out marketing activities. Consumers do 'marketing' when they search for the goods they need at prices they can afford. Company purchasing agents do 'marketing' when they track down sellers and bargain for good terms. A *sellers' market* is one in which sellers have more power and buyers must be the more active 'marketers'. In a *buyers' market*, buyers have more power and sellers have to be more active 'marketers'.

Figure 1.3 shows the main elements in a modern marketing system. In the usual situation, marketing involves serving a market of end users in the face of

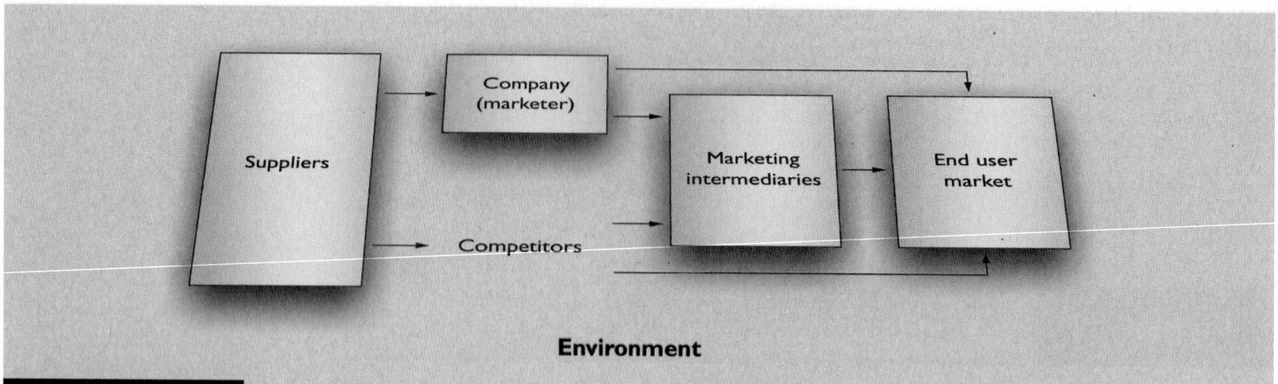

Figure 1.3 **Main actors and forces in a modern marketing system**

competitors. The company and the competitors send their respective products and messages directly to consumers or through marketing intermediaries to the end users. All of the actors in the system are affected by major environmental forces – demographic, economic, physical, technological, political/legal, social/cultural. We will address these forces that affect marketing decisions in Chapter 4.

Each party in the system adds value for the next level. Thus, a company's success depends not only on its own actions, but also on how well the entire value chain serves the needs of final consumers. IKEA cannot fulfil its promise of low prices unless its suppliers provide merchandise at low costs. And Toyota cannot deliver high quality to car buyers unless its dealers provide outstanding service.

Marketing Management

marketing management
The analysis, planning, implementation and control of programmes designed to create, build and maintain beneficial exchanges with target buyers for the purpose of achieving organisational objectives.

We define **marketing management** as the analysis, planning, implementation and control of programmes designed to create, build and maintain beneficial exchanges with target buyers for the purpose of achieving organizational objectives. Thus, marketing management involves managing demand, which in turn involves managing customer relationships.

Demand Management

Most people think of marketing management as finding enough customers for the company's current output, but this is too limited a view. The organization has a desired level of demand for its products. At any point in time, there may be no demand, adequate demand, irregular demand or too much demand, and marketing management must find ways to deal with these different demand states. Marketing management is concerned not only with finding and increasing demand, but also with changing or even reducing it.

demarketing
Marketing to reduce demand temporarily or permanently – the aim is not to destroy demand but only to reduce or shift it.

For example, Disney World is badly overcrowded in the summertime and power companies sometimes have trouble meeting demand during peak usage periods. In these and other cases of excess demand, the needed marketing task, called **demarketing**, is to reduce demand temporarily or permanently. The aim of demarketing is not to destroy demand, but only to reduce or shift it. Thus, marketing management seeks to affect the level, timing and nature of demand in a way that helps the organization achieve its objectives. Simply put, marketing management is *demand management.*

● *Building Profitable Customer Relationships*

Managing demand means managing customers. A company's demand comes from two groups: new customers and repeat customers. Traditional marketing theory and practice have focused on attracting new customers and making the sale. Today, however, the emphasis is shifting. Beyond designing strategies to *attract* new customers and create *transactions* with them, companies are now going all out to *retain* current customers and build lasting customer *relationships*.

Why the new emphasis on keeping customers? In the past, companies facing an expanding economy and rapidly growing markets could practise the 'leaky bucket' approach to marketing. Growing markets meant a plentiful supply of new customers. Companies could attract new customers without worrying about losing old customers. However, companies today are facing some new marketing realities. Changing demographics, a slow-growth economy, more sophisticated competitors and overcapacity in many industries – all of these factors mean that there are fewer new customers to go around. Many companies are now fighting for shares of flat or fading markets. Thus, the costs of attracting new customers are rising. In fact, it costs five times as much to attract a new customer as it does to keep a current customer satisfied.[7]

Companies are also realizing that losing a customer means more than losing a single sale – it means losing the entire stream of purchases that the customer would make over a lifetime of patronage. For example, the *customer lifetime value* of a Ford customer might well exceed £250,000. Thus, working to retain customers makes good economic sense. A company can lose money on a specific transaction, but still benefit greatly from a long-term relationship.

Attracting new customers remains an important marketing management task. However, the focus today is shifting towards retaining current customers and building profitable, long-term relationships with them. The key to customer retention is superior customer value and satisfaction.

Marketing Management Philosophies

We describe marketing management as carrying out tasks to achieve desired exchanges with target markets. What *philosophy* should guide these marketing efforts? What weight should be given to the interests of the organization, customers and society? Very often these interests conflict. Invariably, the organization's marketing management philosophy influences the way it approaches its buyers.

There are five alternative concepts under which organizations conduct their marketing activities: the *production, product, selling, marketing* and *societal marketing* concepts.

The Production Concept

The **production concept** holds that consumers will favour products that are available and highly affordable, and that management should therefore focus on improving production and distribution efficiency. This concept is one of the oldest philosophies that guides sellers.

production concept
The philosophy that consumers will favour products that are available and highly affordable, and that management should therefore focus on improving production and distribution efficiency.

The production concept is a useful philosophy in two types of situation. The first occurs when the demand for a product exceeds the supply. Here, management should look for ways to increase production. The second situation occurs when the product's cost is too high and improved productivity is needed to bring it down. For example, Henry Ford's whole philosophy was to perfect the production of the Model T so that its cost could be reduced and more people could afford it. He joked about offering people a car of any colour as long as it was black. Today, Texas Instruments (TI) follows this philosophy of increased production and lower costs in order to bring down prices. The company won a big share of the hand-calculator market with this philosophy. However, companies operating under a production philosophy run a big risk of focusing too narrowly on their own operations. When TI used the same strategy in the digital watch market, it failed. Although TI's watches were priced low, customers did not find them very attractive. In its drive to bring down prices, TI lost sight of something else that its customers wanted – namely, *attractive*, affordable digital watches.

The Product Concept

product concept
The idea that consumers will favour products that offer the most quality, performance and features, and that the organization should therefore devote its energy to making continuous product improvements.

Another important concept guiding sellers, the **product concept**, holds that consumers will favour products that offer the most quality, performance and innovative features, and that an organization should thus devote energy to making continuous product improvements. Some manufacturers believe that if they can build a better mousetrap, the world will beat a path to their door.[8] But they are often rudely shocked. Buyers may well be looking for a better solution to a mouse problem, but not necessarily for a better mousetrap. The solution might be a chemical spray, an exterminating service or something that works better than a mousetrap. Furthermore, a better mousetrap will not sell unless the manufacturer designs, packages and prices it attractively; places it in convenient distribution channels; and brings it to the attention of people who need it and convinces them that it is a better product. A product orientation leads to obsession with technology because managers believe that technical superiority is the key to business success.

The product concept also can lead to 'marketing myopia'. For instance, railway management once thought that users wanted *trains* rather than *transportation* and overlooked the growing challenge of airlines, buses, trucks and cars. Building bigger and better trains would not satisfy consumers' demand for transportation, but creating other forms of transportation and extending choice would.

The Selling Concept

selling concept
The idea that consumers will not buy enough of the organization's products unless the organization undertakes a large-scale selling and promotion effort.

Many organizations follow the **selling concept**, which holds that consumers will not buy enough of the organization's products unless it undertakes a large-scale selling and promotion effort. The concept is typically practised with *unsought goods* – those that buyers do not normally think of buying, such as encyclopaedias and funeral plots. These industries must be good at tracking down prospects and convincing them of product benefits.

The selling concept is also practised in the non-profit area. A political party, for example, will vigorously sell its candidate to voters as a fantastic person for the job. The candidate works hard at selling him or herself – shaking hands, kissing babies, meeting donors and making speeches. Much money also has to be spent on radio and television advertising, posters and mailings. Candidate flaws are

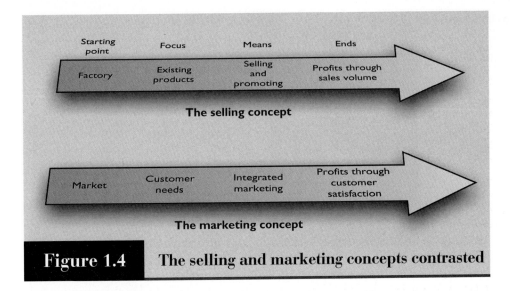

Starting point	Focus	Means	Ends
Factory	Existing products	Selling and promoting	Profits through sales volume

The selling concept

| Market | Customer needs | Integrated marketing | Profits through customer satisfaction |

The marketing concept

Figure 1.4   **The selling and marketing concepts contrasted**

often hidden from the public because the aim is to get the sale, not to worry about consumer satisfaction afterwards.

Most firms practise the selling concept when they have overcapacity. Their aim is to sell what they make rather than make what the market wants. Thus marketing based on hard selling carries high risks. It focuses on short-term results – creating sales transactions – rather than on building long-term, profitable relationships with customers. It assumes that customers who are coaxed into buying the product will like it. Or, if they don't like it, they may forget their disappointment and buy it again later. These are usually poor assumptions to make about buyers. Most studies show that dissatisfied customers do not buy again. Worse yet, while the average satisfied customer tells three others about good experiences, the average dissatisfied customer tells ten others his or her bad experiences.[9]

The Marketing Concept

The **marketing concept** holds that achieving organizational goals depends on determining the needs and wants of target markets and delivering the desired satisfactions more effectively and efficiently than competitors do. Surprisingly, this concept is a relatively recent business philosophy.

The selling concept and the marketing concept are frequently confused. Figure 1.4 compares the two concepts. The selling concept takes an *inside-out* perspective. It starts with the factory, focuses on the company's existing products and calls for heavy selling and promotion to obtain profitable sales. It focuses on customer conquest – getting short-term sales with little concern about who buys or why. In contrast, the marketing concept takes an *outside-in* perspective. It starts with a well-defined market, focuses on customer needs, co-ordinates all the marketing activities affecting customers and makes profits by creating long-term customer relationships based on customer value and satisfaction. Under the marketing concept, companies produce what consumers want, thereby satisfying consumers and making profits.

Many successful and well-known global companies have adopted the marketing concept. IKEA, Marks & Spencer, Procter & Gamble, Marriott, Nordström and McDonald's follow it faithfully (see Marketing Highlight 1.2). Toyota, the highly successful Japanese car manufacturer, is also a prime example of an organization that takes a customer- and marketing-oriented view of its business.

marketing concept
The marketing management philosophy which holds that achieving organizational goals depends on determining the needs and wants of target markets and delivering the desired satisfactions more effectively and efficiently than competitors do.

McDonald's Applies the Marketing Concept

McDonald's Corporation, the American fast-food hamburger retailer, is a master global marketer. With over 18,000 outlets in more than 90 countries and more than $23 billion in annual worldwide sales, McDonald's opens a new restaurant every three hours somewhere in the world. Credit for this performance belongs to a strong marketing orientation: McDonald's knows how to serve people and adapt to changing consumer wants.

Before McDonald's appeared, Americans could get hamburgers in restaurants or diners. But consumers often encountered poor-quality hamburgers, slow and unfriendly service, unattractive décor, unclean conditions and a noisy atmosphere. In 1955 Ray Kroc, a 52-year-old salesman of milkshake-mixing machines, became excited about a string of seven fast-food restaurants owned by Richard and Maurice McDonald. He bought the chain for $2.7 million and expanded it by selling franchises, and the number of restaurants grew rapidly. As times changed, so did McDonald's. It expanded its sit-down sections, improved the décor, launched a breakfast menu, added new food items and opened new outlets in busy, high-traffic areas.

Kroc's marketing philosophy is captured in McDonald's motto of 'QSC & V', which stands for quality, service, cleanliness and value. Customers enter a spotlessly clean restaurant, walk up to a friendly counter-person, quickly receive a good-tasting meal, and eat it there or take it out. There are no jukeboxes or telephones to create a teenage hang-out. Nor are there any cigarette machines – McDonald's is a family affair, appealing strongly to children.

McDonald's has mastered the art of serving consumers and it carefully teaches the basics to its employees and franchisees. All franchisees take training courses at McDonald's 'Hamburger

McDonald's delivers "quality, service, cleanliness, and value" to customers around the world, here in the world's largest McDonald's in Beijing.

University' in Elk Grove Village, Illinois. McDonald's monitors product and service quality through continuous customer surveys and puts great energy into improving hamburger production methods in order to simplify operations, bring down costs, speed up service and bring greater value to customers. Beyond these efforts, each McDonald's restaurant works to become a part of its neighbourhood through community involvement and service projects.

In its restaurants outside the United States, McDonald's carefully customizes its menu and service to local tastes and customs. For instance, McDonald's India offers products developed especially for the Indian market – particularly vegetarians. It serves only mutton, chicken, fish and vegetable products, not beef, pork and their by-products. Big Mac in India is called Maharaja Mac! It serves corn soup and teriyaki burgers in Japan, pasta salads in Rome, and wine and live piano music with its McNuggets in Paris. When McDonald's opened its first restaurant in Moscow, the company had to overcome enormous hurdles to meet its high standards for consumer satisfaction in this new market. It had to educate suppliers, employees and even consumers about the time-tested McDonald's way of doing things. Technical experts with special strains of disease-resistant seed were brought in from Canada to teach Russian farmers how to grow russet Burbank potatoes for French fries, and the company built its own pasteurizing plant to ensure a plentiful supply of fresh milk. It trained Russian managers at Hamburger University and subjected each of 630 new employees to hours of training on such essentials as cooking meat patties,

assembling Filet-O-Fish sandwiches and giving service with a smile. McDonald's even had to train consumers, most of whom had never seen a fast-food restaurant. Customers waiting in line were shown videos telling them everything from how to order and pay at the counter to how to handle a Big Mac. And in its usual way, McDonald's began immediately to build community involvement. On opening day, it held a kick-off party for 700 Muscovite orphans and donated the day's proceeds to the Moscow Children's Fund. As a result, the new Moscow restaurant got off to a very successful start. About 50,000 customers swarmed through the restaurant during its first day of business.

Riding on its success in Moscow, McDonald's continues to expand its worldwide presence. The 28,000 square-foot restaurant in Beijing has 29 cash registers and seats 700 people.

Thus, McDonald's focus on consumers has made it the world's largest food-service organization. The company's huge success has been reflected in the increased value of its stock over the years: 250 shares of McDonald's stock purchased for less than $6,000 in 1965 would be worth well over a million dollars today!

SOURCES: Scott Hume, 'McDonald's Fred Turner: making all the right moves', *Advertising Age* (1 January 1990), pp. 6, 17; Gail McKnight, 'Here comes Bolshoi Mac', *USA Today Weekend* (26–8 January 1990), pp. 4–5; Rosemarie Boyle, 'McDonald's gives Soviets something worth waiting for', *Advertising Age* (19 March 1990), p. 61; 'Food draws raves, prices don't at Beijing McDonald's opening', *Durham Herald-Sun* (12 April 1992), p. B12; Laura Mazur, *Marketing Business* (September 1997), p. 35.

Toyota openly publicizes its intent on getting deep into the hearts and minds of its customers, to establish precisely what they want and subsequently find ways to fulfil their wishes. In Japan, Toyota has built the Amlux, a 14-storey building resembling a blue and black striped rocket, which it uses to attract millions of visitors. These could be potential customers or people with ideas on how the company should respond to consumers' vehicle requirements. These visitors are allowed to spend as much time as they want designing their own vehicles on computer/ TV screen in the vehicle-design studio. There is a two-way information centre where visitors obtain specific information about the company, its dealers or products. The visitors are also allowed to expound, at length, on what they think Toyota should be doing or making. Meanwhile, Toyota's attentive note-taking staff ensure that the entire Amlux complex is dedicated to involving potential customers who can give them close insights into how their car needs can be satisfied.

In marketing-led organizations, real customer focus has to work from the top down and the bottom up, and it has to be totally accepted by the whole workforce. This organization-wide belief ensures that customer retention becomes a priority and all staff are committed to building lasting relationships with the customer. To achieve successful implementation of the marketing concept, the organization therefore focuses on how best to tap and channel the knowledge and understanding, the motivation, the inspiration and the imagination of all staff to deliver products and services that meet exactly what the customer requires from the organization.

Many companies claim to practise the marketing concept, but do not. They have the *forms* of marketing – such as a marketing director, product managers, marketing plans and marketing research – but this does not mean that they are *market-focused* and *customer-driven* companies. The question is whether they are finely tuned to changing customer needs and competitor strategies. Formerly great western companies – Philips, General Motors, IBM, General Electric Company – all lost substantial market share because they failed to adjust their marketing strategies to the changing marketplace. Years of hard work are needed to turn a sales-oriented company into a marketing-oriented company. The goal is to build customer satisfaction into the very fabric of the firm. Customer satisfaction is no longer a fad. As one marketing analyst notes: 'It's becoming a way of life … as embedded into corporate cultures as information technology and strategic planning.'[10]

However, the marketing concept does not mean that a company should try to give *all* consumers *everything* they want. Marketers must balance creating more value for customers against making profits for the company: As one marketing expert notes, 'The purpose of marketing is not to *maximise* customer satisfaction. The shortest definition of marketing I know is "meeting needs profitably". The purpose of marketing is to generate customer value [at a profit]. The truth is [that the relationship with a customer] will break up if value evaporates. You've got to continue to generate more value for the consumer but not give away the house. It's a very delicate balance.'[11]

The Societal Marketing Concept

societal marketing concept
The idea that the organization should determine the needs, wants and interests of target markets and deliver the desired satisfactions more effectively and efficiently than competitors in a way that maintains or improves the consumer's and society's well-being.

The **societal marketing concept** holds that the organization should determine the needs, wants and interests of target markets. It should then deliver the desired satisfactions more effectively and efficiently than competitors in a way that maintains or improves the consumer's *and the society's* well-being. The societal marketing concept is the newest of the five marketing management philosophies.

The societal marketing concept questions whether the pure marketing concept is adequate in an age of environmental problems, resource shortages, world-wide economic problems and neglected social services. It asks if the firm that senses, serves and satisfies individual wants is always doing what's best for consumers and society in the long run. According to the societal marketing concept, the pure marketing concept overlooks possible conflicts between short-run consumer *wants* and long-run consumer *welfare*.

Consider the Coca-Cola Company. Most people see it as a highly responsible corporation producing fine soft drinks that satisfy consumer tastes. Yet certain consumer and environmental groups have voiced concerns that Coke has little nutritional value, can harm people's teeth, contains caffeine and adds to the litter problem with disposable bottles and cans.

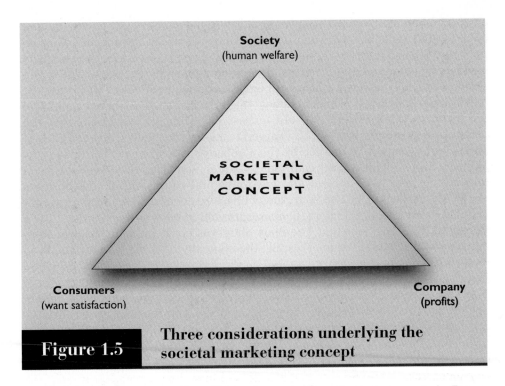

Society
(human welfare)

SOCIETAL
MARKETING
CONCEPT

Consumers
(want satisfaction)

Company
(profits)

| **Figure 1.5** | **Three considerations underlying the societal marketing concept** |

Such concerns and conflicts led to the societal marketing concept. As Figure 1.5 shows, the societal marketing concept calls upon marketers to balance three considerations in setting their marketing policies: company profits, consumer wants and society's interests. Originally, most companies based their marketing decisions largely on short-run company profit. Eventually, they began to recognize the long-run importance of satisfying consumer wants, and the marketing concept emerged. Now many companies are beginning to think of society's interests when making their marketing decisions.

One such company is the international corporation Johnson & Johnson, which stresses community and environmental responsibility. J & J's concern for societal interests is summarized in a company document called 'Our Credo', which stresses honesty, integrity and putting people before profits. Under this credo, Johnson & Johnson would rather take a big loss than ship a bad batch of one of its products. And the company supports many community and employee programmes that benefit its consumers and workers, and the environment. J & J's chief executive puts it this way: 'If we keep trying to do what's right, at the end of the day we believe the marketplace will reward us.'[12]

Consider the tragic tampering case in which eight people died from swallowing cyanide-laced capsules of Tylenol, a Johnson & Johnson brand. Although J & J believed that the pills had been altered in only a few stores, not in the factory, it quickly recalled all of its product. The recall cost the company $240 million in earnings. In the long run, however, the company's swift recall of Tylenol strengthened consumer confidence and loyalty, and Tylenol remains the leading brand of pain reliever in the US market. In this and other cases, J & J management has found that doing what's right benefits both consumers and the company. Says the chief executive: 'The Credo should not be viewed as some kind of social welfare program – it's just plain good business.'[13] Thus over the years, Johnson & Johnson's dedication to consumers and community service has made it one of America's most admired companies, *and* one of the most profitable.

Increasingly, firms also have to meet the expectations of society as a whole. For example, society expects businesses genuinely to uphold basic ethical and environmental standards. Not only should they have ethics and environmental policies, they must also back these with actions. Consider, for instance, the bad publicity The Body Shop received during the early 1990s when the company came under attack in 1992 over its environmental standards. Some critics who researched the company's ethical and environmental practices charged that the high standards which it claims to uphold might be less genuine than it would like the world to think. The critics also expressed a broader concern – that the company persistently appears to exaggerate its involvement in worthy causes. Such charges cannot be ignored by the company's management, particularly its founder, Anita Roddick, and chairman, Gordon Roddick, who have long been involved in promoting ethical and environmental causes within the business world. Any tarnishing of The Body Shop's image removes the organization's point of differentiation and, therefore, increases its vulnerability to competition.[14] As a riposte to the allegations that The Body Shop was not living up to its own standards on issues such as animal testing, the company took the lead in the UK to undertake an ethical auditing exercise. At the beginning of 1996 it published its first Values Report, a massive affair spanning five volumes and over 300 pages of data and feedback from stakeholders – suppliers, customers, employees, shareholders and others representing the public at large – in three main areas: environment, social policy and animal protection.

Marketing Challenges into the Next Century

Marketing operates within a dynamic global environment. Every decade calls upon marketing managers to think afresh about their marketing objectives and practices. Rapid changes can quickly make yesterday's winning strategies out of date. As management thought-leader Peter Drucker once observed, a company's winning formula for the last decade will probably be its undoing in the next decade.

What are the marketing challenges as we head into the twenty-first century? Today's companies are wrestling with changing customer values and orientations, increased global competition, environmental decline, economic stagnation and a host of other economic, political and social problems. In the European Union (EU), as the concept of nationally separate markets vaporizes, competition among sellers will further intensify. There is increasing pressure on individual firms within member countries to adjust to evolving deregulation and advancement of universal trading standards within the single market. However, these problems also provide marketing opportunities.

We now look more deeply into several key trends and forces that are changing the marketing landscape and challenging marketing strategy: the growth of non-profit marketing, the information technology boom, rapid globalization, the changing world economy and the call for more socially responsible actions.

Growth of Non-Profit Marketing

In the past, marketing has been most widely applied in the business sector. In recent years, however, marketing also has become a major component in the strategies of many non-profit organizations, such as colleges, charities, churches, hospitals, museums, performing arts groups and even police departments. Consider the following examples:

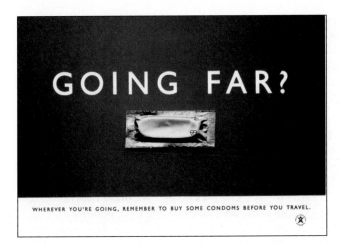

Government agencies such as England's Health Education Authority have successfully used marketing tools to reach target audiences.

Faced with the daunting task of selling the single currency to European citizens, many of whom appeared disturbed by the economic sacrifices involved, the European Commission turned to marketing and media experts to develop a strategy to promote the 'euro'. Pan-European advertising campaigns were also launched to reinforce national initiatives to influence public opinion in favour of replacing national currencies.[15]

To stem the falling number of church-goers, many of Britain's church groups are seeking more effective ways to attract members and maintain financial support. Increasingly, and despite the controversy, preachers are using the press, television and radio to advertise religion to the general public. They are conducting marketing research to better understand member needs and are redesigning their 'service offerings' accordingly. Some evangelical groups are even starting their own radio and television stations. The Vatican has been known to have appointed the advertising agency, Saatchi and Saatchi, to run a £2.5m television campaign.[16]

Over the past decade, many charities have moved on from tin-rattling and tombolas to employing some of the most sophisticated marketing tools, to win support for their causes. For example, the Royal Society for the Protection of Birds (RSPB) is Europe's largest wildlife conservation charity, dealing with issues as wide-ranging as biodiversity, protection of wildlife sites, and marine life. The charity hired a marketing agency to run an awareness advertising campaign for them, which aimed to take their membership up to one million in 1997. They also tied in the campaign with direct marketing activity. One of the objectives is to reach a younger audience than the RSPB's traditional 55+, the 30-somethings, who get more worried about the environment when they have kids of their own. The campaign used a message that suggested birds are a barometer of the health of the environment.

Many longstanding non-profit organizations – the YMCA, the Red Cross, the Salvation Army, the Girl Scouts – are striving to modernize their missions and 'products' to attract more members and donors.[17]

Finally, government agencies have shown an increased interest in marketing. For example, various government agencies are now designing

Charities such as Save the Children also use marketing techniques to attract donors.

Save the Children ❣ 0171-703 5400

> *social marketing campaigns* to encourage energy conservation and concern for the environment, or to discourage smoking, excessive drinking and drug use.[18]

The continued growth of non-profit and public sector marketing presents new and exciting challenges for marketing managers.

The Information Technology Boom

The explosive growth in computer, telecommunications and information technology has had a major impact on the way companies bring value to their customers. The technology boom has created exciting new ways to learn about and track customers, create products and services tailored to meet customer needs, distribute products more efficiently and effectively, and communicate with customers in large groups or one-to-one. For example, through videoconferencing, marketing researchers at a company's headquarters in New York can look in on focus groups in Chicago or Paris without ever stepping on to a plane. With only a few clicks of a mouse button, a direct marketer can tap into online data services to learn anything from what car you drive to what you read to what flavour of ice cream you prefer.

Using today's vastly more powerful computers, marketers create detailed databases and use them to target individual customers with offers designed to meet their specific needs and buying patterns. With a new wave of communication and advertising tools – ranging from cell phones, fax machines and CD-ROMS to interactive TV and video kiosks at airports and shopping malls – marketers can zero in on selected customers with carefully targeted messages. Through electronic commerce, customers can design, order and pay for products and services – all without ever leaving home. From virtual reality displays that test new products to online virtual stores that sell them, the boom in computer, telecommunications and information technology is affecting every aspect of marketing.

● *The Internet*

internet (the Net)
A vast global computer network that enables computers, with the right software and a modem (a telecommunications device that sends data across telephone lines), to be linked together so that their users can obtain or share information and interact with other users.

Perhaps the most dramatic new technology surrounds the development of the Information Superhighway and its backbone, the **Internet**. The Internet is a vast and burgeoning global Web of computer networks, with no central management or ownership. It was created during the late 1960s by the US Department of Defense, initially to link government labs, contractors and military installations. Today, the Internet links computer users of all types around the world. Anyone with a PC and modem – or TV and set-top 'Web box' – and the right software can browse the Internet to obtain or share information on almost any subject and to interact with other users.[19] Companies are using the Internet to link employees in remote offices, distribute sales information more quickly, build closer relationships with customers and suppliers, and sell and distribute their products more efficiently and effectively. Internet usage surged in the 1990s with the development of the user-friendly World Wide Web. More than 50 million people surf the Internet each month, up from just 1 million people in late 1994. There may be as many as 4–6 million Web sites worldwide, and these numbers are growing explosively.[20] The advent of the World Wide Web has given companies access to millions of new customers at a fraction of the cost of print and television advertising. Companies of all types are now attempting to snare new customers in the Web. For example:

> Car makers like Toyota (www.Toyota.com) use the Internet to develop relationships with owners, as well as to sell cars. Its site offers product information, dealer services and locations, leasing information and much more. For example, visitors to the site can view any of seven lifestyle magazines – *alt.Terrain*, *A Man's Life*, *Women's Web Weekly*, *Sportzine*, *Living Arts*, *Living Home* and *Car Culture* – designed to appeal to Toyota's well-educated, above-average-income target audience.

> Sports fans can cosy up with Nike by logging on to www.nike.com, where they can check out the latest Nike products, explore the company's history, down-load Michael Jordan's latest stats, or keep up with Tiger Woods' latest movements. Through its Web page, in addition to its mass-media presence, Nike relates with customers in a more personal, one-to-one way.

> The Ty Web site (www.ty.com) builds relationships with children who collect Beanie Babies by offering extra information, including the 'birth date' of the 50-plus toys, highlights on special Beanie Babies each month, promotion of newly developed Beanie Babies, and even a role of honour section that includes a child's photo and grades. Is it effective? In less than a year, based on the counter on the site, Ty.com received over 266 million visitors.

> The very small retail chain Next Stop North Pole (NSNP) sells only penguin-related products – T-shirts, plush toys, porcelain reproductions, books and others. A search for 'penguins' on the Web yields Pete & Barbara's Penguin Page ('the best source for information about penguins'), which contains a link to the NSNP Web site. The Web site contains pages from the store's direct-mail catalogue and a link to its e-mail mailbox, where visitors can request the full printed catalogue. The Internet gives tiny Next Stop North Pole access to consumers around the world at very little cost.[21]

It seems that almost every business, from garage-based start-ups to established giants, is setting up shop on the Internet. All are racing to explore and exploit the Web's possibilities for marketing, shopping and browsing for information. However, for all its potential, the Internet does have drawbacks. It's yet to be seen how many of the millions of Web browsers will become actual buyers. Although the value of a Web site is difficult to measure, the actuality is that few companies have made any money from their Internet efforts. And the Web poses security problems. Companies that link their internal computer networks to the outside world expose their systems to possible attacks by vandals. Similarly, consumers are wary about sending credit card account numbers or other confidential information that may be intercepted in cyberspace and misused. Finally, using the Web can be costly. For companies to make the most of the Internet, they must invest heavily in leased telephone lines, powerful computers and other technologies, and Internet specialists.

However, given the lightning speed at which Internet technology and applications are developing, it's unlikely that these drawbacks will deter the millions of businesses and consumers who are logging on to the Net each day. 'Marketers aren't going to have a choice about being on Internet,' says Midori Chan, vice president of creative services at Interse, which helped put Windham Hill Records and Digital Equipment Corp. on the Internet. 'To not be on the Internet ... is going to be like not having a phone.'[22] We will examine these online marketing developments more fully in Chapter 22.

Rapid Globalization

The world economy has undergone radical change during the past two decades. Geographical and cultural distances have shrunk with the advent of jet planes, fax machines, global computer and telephone hook-ups, world television satellite and cable broadcasts, and other technical advances. This has allowed companies greatly to expand their geographical market coverage, purchasing and manufacturing. Many companies are trying to create a global structure to move ideas swiftly around the world. The picture is one of a vastly more complex marketing environment for both companies and consumers.

Today, almost every company, large or small, is touched in some way by global competition. European and US firms, for example, are being challenged at home by the skilful marketing of Japanese and other Asian multinationals. Companies like Toyota, Honda, Fujitsu, Sony and Samsung have often outperformed their western competitors in overseas markets. Similarly, western companies in a wide range of industries have found new opportunities abroad. Glaxo, Asea Brown Boveri, Coca-Cola, IKEA, Toys 'Я' Us, Club Mediterranean and many others have developed global operations, making and selling their products worldwide (see Marketing Highlight 1.3). Many companies are moving aggressively to take advantage of international marketing opportunities.

Today, companies are not only trying to sell more of their locally produced goods in international markets; they are also buying or making more components

Many US companies are finding new global opportunities. Looking for growth, MTV tries to repeat its phenomenal American success abroad, here in Hungary.

Taking Advantage of Global Opportunities

Marketing Highlight 1.3

The following are just a few of the countless examples of western companies taking advantage of international marketing opportunities:

IKEA, the Swedish home furnishings retailer, grew from one store in 1958 to more than 130 stores, stretched over 28 countries, by the late 1990s. IKEA's European expansion has hit the fortunes of traditional furniture retailers and manufacturers in supposedly staid furniture markets. Some have not survived the onslaught. [The UK's Habitat] was later acquired by IKEA. IKEA has successfully spread into the North American, Far Eastern and Australian markets. It practises its four-pronged philosophy – attention to product quality, value (low prices and 'more for your money'), innovative style and service – which it has successfully transferred to markets worldwide. Over the years, IKEA has built, and capitalized on, its 'affordable Swedish style' mass market positioning. IKEA's international expansion has raised its fortunes in what competition claims to be a traditionally dull and fragmented market. IKEA has proven that, with the right marketing approach, fortunes can be grown even in staid, old markets.

Toys 'Я' Us spent several years slogging through the swamps of Japanese bureaucracy before it was allowed to open the very first large US discount store in Japan, the world's no. 2 toy market behind the United States. The entry of this foreign giant has Japanese toy makers and retailers edgy. The typical small Japanese toy store stocks only 1,000 to 2,000 items, whereas Toys 'Я' Us stores carry as many as 15,000. And the discounter will probably offer toys at prices 10–15 per cent below those of competitors. The opening of the first Japanese store was 'astonishing', attracting more than 60,000 visitors in the first three days. The retailer appears to be benefiting from profound social change in Japan. According to one source, 'Japan's absentee, workaholic salaryman father is increasingly becoming a relic, and his successor is taking life easier, spending more time with his family.

Japanese families now spend more time together ... On Sunday they ... go out to lunch and then browse at a big store like Toys 'Я' Us ... Toys 'Я' Us has made shopping a form of leisure in Japan.' Japanese retailers will have their hands full. Toys 'Я' Us began with just five European stores in 1985 but now has over 80 and growing. European sales, now over $800 million, are growing at triple the rate of total company sales.

After ten years of relentless growth in America, Music Television's (MTV) home market has become saturated. However, the US music video network is exploding abroad. For example, it's a monster hit in Europe. Set up in 1990, MTV Europe now reaches 27 countries and 59 million homes, almost a million more than US MTV. The network is aggressively pan-European – its programming and advertising are the same throughout Europe and they are all in English. It has almost single-handedly created a Euro-language of simplified English. MTV meets the common concerns of teenagers worldwide, broadcasting news and socially conscious programming, such as features on the plight of European immigrants and notes on global warming. MTV Europe has convinced advertisers that a true 'Euroconsumer' exists. It delivers advertising from companies such as Levi Strauss, Procter & Gamble, Apple Computer and Pepsi-Cola to a huge international audience. The company also operates MTV Asia, MTV Latino and MTV Japan. In all, MTV reaches more than 240 million homes in 63 territories around the world.

Sources: For these and other examples, see J. Reynolds, 'IKEA: a competitive company with style', *Retail and Distribution Management*, 16, 3 (1988); Helen Jones, 'IKEA's global strategy is a winning formula', *Marketing Week* (15 March 1997), p. 22; 'MTV: rock on', *The Economist* (3 August 1991), p. 66; 'Teens: the most global market of all', *Fortune* (16 May 1994), pp. 90–7; Robert Neff, 'Guess who's selling Barbies in Japan now?', *Business Week* (9 December 1991), pp. 72–6; Patrick Oster, 'Toys 'Я' Us making Europe its playpen', *Business Week* (20 January 1992), pp. 88–91; Julie Skur Hill, 'Toys 'Я' Us seeks global growth', *Advertising Age* (30 March 1992), p. 33; Kevin Cote, 'Toys 'Я' Us grows in Europe', *Advertising Age* (27 April 1992), pp. 1–16.

and obtaining supplies abroad. Increasingly, international firms have to co-ordinate functional operations across borders and to increase efficiency. Consequently, many domestically purchased goods and services are 'hybrids', with design, material purchases, manufacturing and marketing taking place in several countries. British consumers who decide to 'buy British' might reasonably decide to avoid Sony televisions and purchase Amstrad's. Imagine their surprise when they learn that the Amstrad TV was actually made from parts and components imported from the Far East, whereas the Sony product was assembled in the United Kingdom from British-made parts.

Luxury cars are another case in point. Japanese luxury car makers such as Honda (the Acura) and Toyota (the Lexus) have moved some production to America. The German Mercedes is building sport-utility vehicles at its American assembly plant in Alabama. Rival, BMW's factory in South Carolina, already makes several versions of the 3-series as well as the Z3 coupé for export to dozens of markets around the world – including Germany. Buyers, who want high quality and low price, are now prepared to accept American-built luxury cars.[23]

Thus managers in countries around the world are asking: Just what is global marketing? How does it differ from domestic marketing? How do global competitors and forces affect our business? To what extent should we 'go global'? The technological and marketing resources needed to conquer world markets in sectors such as telecommunications, airlines, cars and media, are forcing companies to seek partners. Many companies are forming strategic alliances with foreign companies, even competitors, who serve as suppliers or marketing partners. The past few years have produced some surprising alliances between competitors such as Mazda and Ford, France Telecom, Deutsche Telecom and Sprint, General Electric and Matsushita, Philips and Siemens, and Daimler Benz and United Technologies of the United States. And Microsoft and Dow Jones have teamed up to develop software for global financial markets. Winning companies in the decade ahead may well be those that have built the best global partnerships and networks.[24] We will examine global marketing management issues in greater detail in Chapter 5.

The Changing World Economy

A sluggish world economy has resulted in more difficult times for both consumers and marketers. Around the world, people's needs are greater than ever, but in many areas, people lack the means to pay for needed goods. Markets, after all, consist of people with needs *and* purchasing power. In many cases, the latter is currently lacking. In the developed western and Asian economies, although wages have risen, real buying power has declined, especially for the less skilled members of the workforce. Many households have managed to maintain their buying power only because both spouses work. However, many workers have lost their jobs as manufacturers have automated to improve productivity or 'downsized' to cut costs.

Current economic conditions create both problems and opportunities for marketers. Some companies are facing declining demand and see few opportunities for growth. Others, however, are developing new solutions to changing consumer problems. Stronger businesses have recognized and taken advantage of recent developments in communications and related technologies. These developments have raised customers' expectations of product quality, performance and durability. They no longer accept or tolerate shoddy products. Power and control have also shifted from brand manufacturers to channel members, which have become as sophisticated at marketing and exploiting technology as producers themselves. Many are finding ways to offer consumers 'more for less', like Sweden's IKEA and America's Toys 'Я' Us. Heavy discounters are emerging to offer consumers quality merchandise at everyday low prices. These days, customers want value and more value. Increasingly, marketers must deliver offerings that delight, not merely satisfy, customers. Toyota has succeeded in doing that: its highly acclaimed Lexus luxury line offers consumers all the technology (gadgetry) and comfort they can ever dream of, and, at about £44,000, is considered exceptionally good value for money, compared to rival offerings in its class.

The Call for More Ethics and Social Responsibility

A third factor in today's marketing environment is the increased call for companies to take responsibility for the social and environmental impact of their actions. Corporate ethics has become a hot topic in almost every business arena, from the corporate boardroom to the business school classroom. And few companies can ignore the renewed and very demanding environmental movement.

The ethics and environmental movements will place even stricter demands on companies in the future. In the former Eastern bloc and many Asian countries, air, water and soil pollution has added to our environmental concerns. These and other governments across the world must consider how to handle such problems as the destruction of rain forests, global warming, endangered species and other environmental threats. The pressure is on businesses to 'clean up' our environment. Clearly, in the future, companies will be held to an increasingly high standard of environmental responsibility in their marketing and manufacturing activities.[25]

More specifically, in the EU, the continuing trend towards tougher environmental rules should drive non-conformers out of business, while others who are committed to 'cleaning up' or 'greening' their practices and operations will emerge the stronger. Specialist industries for environmental goods and services (e.g. paper, bottle and tyre recyclers) have expanded quickly in recent years. As they say, 'there is money in Europe's muck'.[26]

In Chapter 2 we will take a closer look at marketing ethics and social responsibility.

The New Marketing Landscape

The past decade taught business firms everywhere a humbling lesson. Domestic companies learned that they can no longer ignore global markets and competitors. Successful firms in mature industries learned that they cannot overlook emerging markets, technologies and management approaches. Companies of every sort learned that they cannot remain inwardly focused, ignoring the needs of their customers.

Prominent western multinationals of the 1970s which floundered at marketing, including Philips, Volvo, General Motors and RCA, are all struggling to revive their fortunes today. They failed to understand their changing marketplace, their customers and the need to provide value. Today, General Motors is still trying to figure out why so many consumers around the world have switched to Japanese and European cars. In the consumer electronics industry, Philips has lost its way, losing share to Japanese competitors that have been more successful in turning expensive technologies into mass consumer products. Volvo, which has long capitalized on its safety positioning, has, of late, lost this unique selling point to other car manufacturers, which have turned the safety benefit into a universal feature: many large European and Japanese car producers now offer, as standard features, driver and passenger airbags, anti-lock braking system and other safety devices. RCA, inventor of so many new products, never quite mastered the art of marketing and now puts its name on products largely imported from Asia.

As we move into the twenty-first century, companies must become customer-oriented and market driven in all that they do. It is not enough to be product or technology driven – too many companies still design their products without customer input, only to find them rejected in the marketplace. It is not enough to be good at winning new customers – too many companies forget about customers after the sale, only to lose their future business. Not surprisingly, we are now seeing a flood of books with titles such as *The Customer Driven Company*, *Customers for Life*, *Turning Lost Customers Into Gold*, *Customer Bonding*, *Sustaining Knock Your Socks Off Service* and *The Loyalty Effect*.[27] These books emphasize that the key to success on the rapidly changing marketing landscape will be a strong focus on the marketplace and a total marketing commitment to providing value to customers.

Summary

Today's successful companies share a strong focus and a heavy commitment to marketing. Modern marketing seeks to attract new customers by promising superior value, and to keep current customers by delivering satisfaction. Sound marketing is critical to the success of all organizations, whether large or small, for-profit or non-profit, domestic or global.

Many people think of marketing as only selling or advertising. But marketing combines many activities – marketing research, product development, distribution, pricing, advertising, personal selling and others – designed to sense, serve and satisfy consumer needs while meeting the organization's goals. Marketing operates within a dynamic global environment. Rapid changes can quickly make yesterday's winning strategies obsolete. In the twenty-first century, marketers will face many new challenges and opportunities. To be successful, companies will have to be strongly market focused.

We define marketing as *a social and managerial process by which individuals and groups obtain what they need and want through creating and exchanging products and value with others*. The core concepts of marketing are *needs*, *wants* and *demands*; *products* and *services*; *value*, *satisfaction* and *quality*; *exchange*, *transactions* and *relationships*; and *markets*. Wants are the form assumed by human needs when shaped by culture and individual personality. When backed by buying power, wants become demands. People satisfy their needs, wants and demands with products and services. A product is anything that can be offered to a market to satisfy a need, want or demand. Products also include services and other entities such as persons, places, organizations, activities and ideas.

In deciding which products and services to buy, consumers rely on their perception of relative value. *Customer value* is the difference between the values the customer gains from owning and using a product and the costs of obtaining and using the product. *Customer satisfaction* depends on a product's perceived performance in delivering value relative to a buyer's expectations. Customer satisfaction is closely linked to *quality*, leading many companies to adopt *total quality management (TQM)* practices. Marketing occurs when people satisfy their needs, wants and demands through exchange. Beyond creating short-term exchanges, marketers need to build long-term relationships with valued customers, distributors, dealers and suppliers.

Marketing management is the analysis, planning, implementation and control of programmes designed to create, build and maintain beneficial exchanges with target buyers for the purpose of achieving organizational objectives. It involves more than simply finding enough customers for the company's current output. Marketing is at times also concerned with changing or even reducing demand. Managing demand means managing customers. Beyond designing strategies to *attract* new customers and create *transactions* with them, today's companies are focusing on *retaining* current customers and building lasting relationships through offering superior customer value and satisfaction.

Marketing management can be guided by five different philosophies. The *production concept* holds that consumers favour products that are available and highly affordable; management's task is to improve production efficiency and bring down prices. The *product concept* holds that consumers favour products that offer the most quality, performance and innovative features; thus, little promotional effort is required. The *selling concept* holds that consumers will not buy enough of the organization's products unless it undertakes a large-scale selling and promotion effort. The *marketing concept* holds that achieving organizational goals depends on determining the needs and wants of target markets and delivering the desired satisfactions more effectively and efficiently than competitors do. The *societal marketing* concept holds that the company should determine the needs, wants and interests of target markets. Generating customer satisfaction *and* long-run societal well-being are the keys to achieving both the company's goals and its responsibilities.

We also analyzed the major challenges facing marketers heading into the twenty-first century. Companies are wrestling with changing customer values and orientations, a sluggish world economy, the growth of non-profit marketing; the information technology boom, including the Internet; rapid globalization, including increased global competition; and a host of other economic, political and social challenges. These challenges are intensified by a demand that marketers conduct all of their business with an emphasis on *more ethics* and *social responsibility*. Taken together, these changes define *a new marketing landscape*. Companies that succeed in this environment will have a strong focus on the changing marketplace and a total commitment to using the tools of marketing to provide real value to customers.

Key Terms

Customer satisfaction 12
Customer value 11
Demands 10
Demarketing 16
Exchange 12
Human need 10
Human want 10

Internet 26
Market 14
Marketing 10
Marketing concept 19
Marketing management 16
Product 11
Product concept 18

Production concept 17
Relationship marketing 14
Selling concept 18
Service 11
Societal marketing concept 22
Total quality management 12
Transaction 13

Discussing the Issues

1. Discuss why you should study marketing.
2. As the Preview Case implies, the marketing efforts of organizations seek to fulfil consumer needs. How genuine are the needs targeted by Nike's marketing efforts? Critically evaluate the role that marketing plays in satisfying human desires.

3. Many people dislike or fear certain products and would not 'demand' them at any price. How might a health-care marketer manage the *negative* demand for such products as colon-cancer screenings?

4. What is the single biggest difference between the marketing concept and the production, product and selling concepts? Which concepts are easiest to apply in the short run? Which concept can offer the best long-term success?

5. Using examples covered in the chapter – e.g., Nike (Preview Case), McDonald's (Marketing Highlight 1.2) and IKEA, MTV and Toys 'R' Us (Marketing Highlight 1.3) – discuss the key challenges facing companies as they approach the twenty-first century. What actions might they take to ensure they continue to survive and thrive in the new marketing landscape?

6. According to economist Milton Friedman, 'Few trends could so thoroughly undermine the very foundations of our free society as the acceptance by corporate officials of a social responsibility other than to make as much money for their stockholders as possible.' Do you agree or disagree with Friedman's statement? What are some drawbacks of the societal marketing concept?

Applying the Concepts

1. Go to McDonald's and order a meal. Note the questions you are asked, and observe how special orders are handled. Next go to a restaurant on your college or university campus and order a meal. Note the questions you are asked here, and observe whether special orders are handled the same way as they are at McDonald's.

   ● Did you observe any significant differences in how orders are handled?

   ● Consider the differences you saw. Do you think the restaurants have different marketing management philosophies? Which is closest to the marketing concept? Is one closer to the selling or production concept?

   ● What are the advantages of closely following the marketing concept? Are there any disadvantages?

2. Take a trip to a shopping mall. Find the directory sign. List five major categories of store, such as department stores, shoe stores, bookstores, women's clothing shops and restaurants. List the competing stores in each category, walk past them and quickly observe their merchandise and style. Look at the public spaces of the mall, and note how they are decorated. Watch the shoppers in the mall.

   ● Are the competing stores really unique, or could one pretty much substitute for another? What does this say about the overall goals that the mall is fulfilling?

   ● Consider the attitudes of the shoppers you saw. Did some apparently find shopping a pleasure, while others found it a bother?

   ● A major goal for marketing is to maximize consumer satisfaction. Discuss the extent to which the mall serves this goal.

References

1. Quotes from Linda Himelstein, 'The swoosh heard "round the world"', *Business Week* (12 May 1997), p. 76; and Jeff Jensen, 'Marketer of the Year', *Advertising Age* (16 December 1996), pp. 1, 16. See also Himelstein, 'The soul of a new Nike,' *Business Week* (17 June 1996), p. 70; Gary Hamel, 'Killer strategies that make shareholders rich', *Fortune* (23 June 1997), pp. 70–83; John Wyatt, 'Is it time to jump on Nike?', *Fortune* (26 May 1997), pp. 185–6; Patrick Harverson, 'Showing a clean pair of heels', *Financial Times* (17/18 January 1998), p. 6; Nike's World Wide Web page at www.nike.com.

2. Peter F. Drucker, *Management: Tasks, responsibilities, practices* (New York: Harper & Row, 1973), pp. 64–5.

3. Here are some other definitions: 'Marketing is the performance of business activities that direct the flow of goods and services from producer to consumer or user.' 'Marketing is selling goods that don't come back to people that do.' 'Marketing is getting the right goods and services to the right people at the right place at the right time at the right price with the right communication and promotion.' 'Marketing is the creation and delivery of a standard of living.' 'Marketing is the creation of time, place and possession utilities.' The American Marketing Association approved the definition: 'Marketing is the process of planning and executing the conception, pricing, promotion, and distribution of ideas, goods, and services to create exchanges that satisfy individual and organizational objectives.' As you can see, there is no single, universally agreed definition of marketing.

There are definitions that emphasize marketing as a process, a concept or philosophy of business, or an orientation. The diversity of views adopted by authors is reflected in the wide selection of marketing definitions in common use. See Michael J. Baker, *Macmillan Dictionary of Marketing and Advertising*, 2nd edn (London: Macmillan, 1990), pp. 148–9.

4. See Theodore Levitt's classic article, 'Marketing myopia', *Harvard Business Review* (July–August 1960), pp. 45–56; Dhananjayan Kashyap, 'Marketing myopia revisited: a look through the "colored glass of a client"', *Marketing and Research Today* (August 1996), pp. 197–201.

5. Richard A. Spreng, Scott B. MacKenzie and Richard W. Olshavsky, 'A reexamination of the determinants of customer satisfaction,' *Journal of Marketing* (July 1996), pp. 15–32; Thomas A. Stewart, 'A satisfied customer isn't enough,' *Fortune* (21 July 1997), pp. 112–13.

6. See James C. Anderson, Hakan Hakansson and Jan Johanson, 'Dyadic business relationships within a business network context,' *Journal of Marketing* (October 1994), pp. 1–15.

7. Kevin J. Clancy and Robert S. Schulman, 'Breaking the mold', *Sales and Marketing Management* (January 1994), pp. 82–4; Thomas O. Jones and W. Earl Sasser, 'Why satisfied customers defect', *Harvard Business Review* (November–December 1995), pp. 88–99.

8. Ralph Waldo Emerson offered this advice: 'If a man … makes a better mousetrap … the world will beat a path to his door.' Several companies, however, have built better mousetraps yet failed. One was a laser mousetrap costing $1,500. Contrary to popular assumptions, people do not automatically learn about new products, believe product claims, or willingly pay higher prices.

9. Barry Farber and Joyce Wycoff, 'Customer service: evolution and revolution', *Sales and Marketing Management* (May 1991), p. 47.

10. See Bernard J. Jaworski and Ajay K. Kohli, 'Market orientation: antecedents and consequences', *Journal of Marketing* (July 1993), pp. 53–70; E.K. Valentin, 'The marketing concept and the conceptualization of market strategy', *Journal of Marketing Theory and Practice* (Fall 1996), pp. 16–27.

11. Thomas E. Caruso, 'Kotler: future marketers will focus on customer data base to compete globally', *Marketing News* (8 June 1992), pp. 21–2.

12. See 'Leaders of the most admired', *Fortune* (29 January 1990), pp. 40–54; Edward A. Robinson, 'America's most admired companies', *Fortune* (3 March 1997), pp. 68–75.

13. *Fortune* (29 January 1990), p. 54.

14. Andrew Jack and Neil Buckley, 'Halo slips on the raspberry bubbles', *Financial Times* (27–28 August 1994), p. 8.

15. Victor Smart, 'Brussels ask admen how to sell the euro', *The European* (18–24 January 1996), p. 1.

16. Martin Wroe, 'Ministries, missions and markets', *Marketing Business* (October 1993), pp. 8–11.

17. For more examples, see Philip Kotler and Karen Fox, *Strategic Marketing for Educational Institutions* (Englewood Cliffs, NJ: Prentice Hall, 1985); Norman Shawchuck, Philip Kotler, Bruce Wren and Gustav Rath, *Marketing for Congregations: Choosing to serve people more effectively* (Nashville, TN: Abingdon Press, 1993); Joanne Scheff and Philip Kotler, 'How the arts can prosper', *Harvard Business Review* (January–February 1996), pp. 56–62.

18. Philip Kotler and Eduardo Roberto, *Social Marketing: Strategies for changing public behaviour* (New York: Free Press, 1990).

19. For more on the basics of using the Internet, see Raymond D. Frost and Judy Strauss, *The Internet: A new marketing tool* (Upper Saddle River, NJ: Prentice Hall, 1997).

20. Amy Cortese, 'A census in cyberspace', *Business Week* (5 May 1997), p. 84. For the most recent statistics, check the results of an ongoing survey of Internet usage conducted by CommerceNet and Nielsen Media Research, www.commerce.net/nielsen/.

21. Pete & Barbara's Penguin Page is located at http://ourworld.compuserve.com/homepages/Peter_and_Barbara_Barham/.

22. See John Deighton, 'The future of interactive', *Harvard Business Review* (November–December 1996), pp. 151–62; Debora Spar and Jeffrey Bussgang, 'The Net', *Harvard Business Review* (May–June 1996), pp. 125–33.

23. 'Luxury cars in America', *The Economist* (8 July 1995), pp. 81, 84; Justin Martin, 'Mercedes: "Made in Alabama"', *Fortune* (7 July 1997), pp. 74–9.

24. For more on strategic alliances, see Jordan D. Lewis, *Partnerships for Profit: Structuring and managing strategic alliances* (New York: Free Press, 1990); Peter Lorange and Johan Roos, *Strategic Alliances: Formation, implementation and evolution* (Cambridge, MA: Blackwell, 1992); Frederick E. Webster, Jr, 'The changing role of marketing in the corporation', *Journal of Marketing* (October 1992), pp. 1–17.

25. Stuart L. Hart, 'Beyond greening: strategies for a sustainable world', *Harvard Busines Review* (January–February 1997), pp. 67–76.

26. 'The money in Europe's muck', *The Economist* (20 November 1993), pp. 109–10.

27. Richard C. Whitely, *The Customer Driven Company* (Reading, MA: Addison-Wesley, 1991); Charles Sewell, *Customers for Life: How to turn the one-time buyer into a lifetime customer* (New York: Pocket Books, 1990); Joan K. Cannie, *Turning Lost Customers into Gold: And the art of achieving zero defections* (New York: Amacom, 1993); Richard Cross and Janet Smith, *Customer Bonding: The five-point system for maximizing customer loyalty* (Chicago, IL: NTC Business Books, 1994); Ron Zemke and Thomas K. Connellan, *Sustaining Knock Your Socks Off Service* (New York: Amacom, 1993); Frederick F. Reicheld, *The Loyalty Effect* (Boston: Harvard Business School Press, 1996).

Case 1

Amphitrion: Your Ultimate Host in Greece
Alkis S. Magdalinos

AROUND THE END OF OCTOBER 1993, Constantinos Mitsiou, owner and manager of the Greek Amphitrion group of companies, was wondering if he should launch a special tour for teenagers. What he had in mind was a tour lasting 14 days that would incorporate most of the natural beauty spots of Greece, as well as numerous historic and archaeological sites. He had already concluded a tentative agreement with a couple of professors who would act as guides and worked out a preliminary itinerary, but now he was not sure if he should continue with the idea.

Amphitrion, which started as a travel agency in 1957, was now a large travel and shipping business – 'your ultimate hosts in Greece'. The head office of Amphitrion is in Constitution Square, a prestigious business area in the centre of Athens. It also has branches in Tokyo, Washington, DC, and Toronto as well as other Greek offices in Athens, Crete and Piraeus. The largest part of the touring business was for executives and employees of businesses who bought their tickets from the agency branch of the business. These clients also bought family holidays and travel. In 1993 the biggest part of the clientele was middle and senior executives and, sometimes, their secretaries and assistants. Only some 10 per cent of sales came from 'drop-ins', people who casually dropped in at one of Amphitrion's travel offices.

Mr Mitsiou had first started thinking about his teenager tour after a meeting with other agents at an International Convention, in Milan, in September 1993. He had had a discussion with a travel agent from Rome, who told him about a similar exercise he had organized successfully during the last holiday season. He was already thinking of repeating the tour in Greece. He also told Mr Mitsiou that both parents and teenagers looked forward to such tours, since it allowed them to have separate holidays. The best time for the tours was between July and August when schools were on holiday. Parents accepted the idea of the tour if the agent could guarantee proper supervision and the calibre of the people acting as guides.

When Mr Mitsiou came back to Athens he repeated the idea to his friends Joan and George Lykidis, and asked them whether they would like to act as guides for the tour. Mr Lykidis was the headteacher of one of Athens' largest schools and a professor of history. Both Mr and Mrs Lykidis were enthusiastic about the idea and were eager to take it on.

Mr Mitsiou did not know if anyone else in Greece had started such a tour. However, he knew that for some years a professor at a well-known school had organized tours of Europe for students from private schools. The activity had developed into a profitable summer business. As far as Mr Mitsiou knew, the tours were always successful and sold out each year. The teacher used no special advertising for his tours, getting most of his business from former students who had been on the tour themselves and who now sent their children.

The tours Mr Mitsiou had in mind would focus on Greece, including its local colour as well as the important historic and archaeological sites around the country. Characteristically, Mr Mitsiou said the nature of the tour had occurred to him after reading letters from parents and professors in the daily press. These complained about the theoretical way Greek history was taught at school. To Mr Mitsiou, it was obvious from the letters that parents and students wanted a tour visiting the sites they had studied so drily in their history classes. Parents definitely looked forward to giving their children a well-organized tour, in which they would visit all these places and in which, with proper guidance, the entire history of their ancestry would be revealed to them.

Mr Mitsiou also knew very well that teenagers would not like it if the whole of the itinerary comprised only visits to museums, and to historic and archaeological sites. He would therefore give them a chance to enjoy the beautiful seashores and beaches; to go into towns and villages; and to have fun at tavernas and discos and enjoy some dancing and entertainment.

After considerable thought, he developed the following itinerary:

Day 1   Departure from Athens , Thermopylae, Tempi, Mount Olympus, Thessaloniki overnight.

Day 2   Morning free. Afternoon visit Eptapyrgio, Old City, St Demetrious Church, International Fairgrounds, night at a disco, stay overnight at Eptapyrgio.

Day 3   Depart for Philippi, visit sites of interest at Kavala, stay overnight on Thasos Island.

Day 4   Swimming at Golden Beach, Makrynammos, visit Necropolis Museum, return to Kavala, stay overnight.

Day 5   Depart for Polygyros, Agion Oros, swimming at Chalkidiki Beach, overnight in Thessaloniki, go to a disco.

Day 6   Leave for ancient Pella, Vergina, Tomb of Philippos, Grevena, Metsovo, stay overnight.

Day 7   Ioannina, visit Vella Monastery, Ali Pasha Island in Ioannina lake, old town, stay overnight.

Day 8   Dodoni, Arta, Agrinio, Missolonghi, visit sites, Aetolikon, the lagoon, fishing ponds at Tholi, overnight in Missolonghi.

Day 9   Depart for Patras, visit sites, leave for Kyllini, swimming, stay overnight.

Day 10   Leave for Olympia, visit archaeological grounds, overnight in Vityna.

Day 11   Leave for Tripolis, Sparta, visit the museum, Mystras, Gythio, Diros caves, Gerolimena for swimming, overnight in Areopolis.

Day 12   Departure for Kalamata, Pylos, Methoni, swimming, return to Kalamata, afternoon free, disco, stay overnight.

Day 13   Leave for Tripolis, Nafplio, Tolo, swimming, Tyrins, Argos, Mycenae, Nemea, overnight in Korinth.

Day 14   Ancient Korinth, Sykion, Kiato, Nerantza for swimming, return to Athens.

Mr Mitsiou knew that tours of this type could be cancelled at the last moment, which would mean that money would have to be refunded. If that happened, the total spending on the promotion of the tour would amount to a loss of about Dr266,000. In addition, money had to be paid two months in advance to secure good rooms, especially at places with only one hotel, and this would be a significant sum that would have to be written off if the tour did not go ahead. By Mr Mitsiou's calculation, advertising and other expenses would bring the loss to about Dr1,000,000 if the whole tour were cancelled.

With a group of 40 participants on tour, his total cost came to Dr2,260,000. From this he expected to clear 7 per cent profit. If he had more people on the tour, the profits would be greater; but George Lykidis had already said that more than 40 teenagers would be impossible to supervise properly.

It was important not to cancel the tour in the first year once it had been advertised. Word of mouth was the best way of attracting tour members, particularly as a result of previous members telling their friends. So he decided he would go ahead with as few as 20 participants, even though that meant he would make a loss. By charging more, he could make money with only 20 participants, but he did not think that he could charge more than Dr60,450 per person in the first year. When he had organized tours in the past, he had used subagents who required a 5 per cent commission. In this project, however, his margins were so small that he would not use subagents.

Soon after he had finished working out the plans for the tour, Mr Mitsiou met a friend, a very renowned lawyer, who had two sons in their teens. The lawyer said that he would never let his sons go on such a tour. He added that such tours treated teenagers like sheep. Anyhow teenagers had no interest in history, no matter what newspapers said to the contrary. His idea was to give his boys some money and a couple of tickets, and to allow them to travel for as long as the money lasted. For that age group, guides were not important, and it was best to give such teenagers the chance to prove that they were responsible and could travel on their own. This worried Mr Mitsiou, since he always trusted his friend's opinions. He started to reconsider his planned tour and to think of other ways to make the tour look more attractive.

QUESTIONS

1. Has Mr Mitsiou taken a marketing-oriented approach to developing his teenage tour idea? What elements of marketing orientation, if any, are missing?

2. Is the teenage tour idea financially attractive? Does it fit the strengths of the Amphitrion Group? Is it a market that the company naturally understands?

3. Would the tour have been attractive to you as a teenager? Would this Greek tour be attractive to teenagers in your country?

4. Would you have found a similar tour of your own country attractive? Would your parents find it attractive? Who is the customer in this case and what do they want?

5. Is running a tour the only way to see if it would be successful or not? How else do you think its appeal could be tested?

6. How could the tour be changed to be more appealing and less risky?

2

Marketing and Society:

Social Responsibility and Marketing Ethics

CHAPTER OBJECTIVES

After reading this chapter, you should be able to:

● List and respond to the social criticisms of marketing.

● Define *consumerism* and *environmentalism* and explain how they affect marketing strategies.

● Describe the principles of socially responsible marketing.

● Explain the role of ethics in marketing.

Preview Case

Brown & Williamson Tobacco: 'Keeping Smokers Addicted'

IT HAS LONG BEEN KNOWN that tobacco companies control nicotine levels in their cigarettes. In the 1940s, nicotine and tar levels in cigarettes were more than three times today's levels. Manufacturers have gradually reduced them through refinements in the processing technique to satisfy demand for smoother and lighter cigarettes. A new battle started between the US Food and Drug Administration (FDA) and tobacco companies in June 1994. At the centre of the debate was damning evidence presented to Congress which suggested that US tobacco companies had been deliberately manipulating the amount of nicotine in cigarettes to keep the nation's 46 million smokers addicted.

On 21 June 1994, a House of Representatives subcommittee heard allegations that Brown & Williamson (B & W) Tobacco, a US subsidiary of Britain's BAT Industries, had secretly developed a genetically engineered tobacco called Y-1 that contained more than twice the amount of nicotine found in normal tobacco plants. Mr David Kessler, head of the US FDA, informed the committee that B & W had earlier denied breeding tobacco plants for high or low nicotine content. Yet the company had several million pounds of Y-1 tobacco stored in US warehouses and had been using it in five local brands of cigarettes.

Kessler suggested that US tobacco manufacturers had deliberately 'spiked' their products to keep smokers addicted. It is difficult to prove this. However, he said that it is sufficient to show that cigarette companies have the ability to control nicotine levels in their products, allowing them to remain at addictive levels. Such evidence could be used to implicate B & W in the Y-1 row to push his case for bringing tobacco under his agency's control. He has previously threatened to regulate cigarettes as drugs if he could show that manufacturers intend consumers to buy them to satisfy an addiction. The discovery of the Y-1 high-nicotine tobacco proved beyond doubt that tobacco firms were manipulating and controlling nicotine concentration in their products.

B & W defended the allegations. First, it accused Kessler of blowing the issue out of proportion. Second, it stressed the fact that Y-1 is nothing secret and just one of a variety of local and foreign tobaccos it used to give the unique 'recipe' of ingredients that went into each brand. 'Y-1 was a blending tool for flavour', B & W said.

Tobacco companies argue that they cannot eliminate nicotine altogether from their products as it is an essential contributor to cigarette flavour. Smokers no longer enjoy cigarettes when the nicotine level falls below a certain point. So, it is important to adjust the level of nicotine and other flavour-enhancers to provide what cigarettes consumers like. Mr Walker Merriman, vice-president of the Tobacco Institute, said that 'consumer preference' was the specific reason for having any particular level of nicotine and tar in any particular cigarette. Low-nicotine brands have commanded very low market share, while no-nicotine brands had failed through lack of demand.

In reality, Kessler is more concerned now with two issues: whether cigarettes are addictive, and if manufacturers intend them to be addictive. If so, on either issue, the FDA may be able to bring them under its jurisdiction as a drug. Kessler can then force the tobacco industry gradually to reduce nicotine levels in their products and so wean smokers away from the habit. The industry position is that cigarettes are *not* a drug, as defined in the 1938 Federal Food, Drug and Cosmetic Act, because they 'do not intend to affect the structure or any function of the body'. Furthermore, manufacturers argue that smoking cannot be addictive because 50 per cent or more of American citizens today who have ever smoked have quit – over 90 per cent of them without professional help. Critics of Kessler's policy say that there is a risk that smokers would smoke even more cigarettes to compensate for the loss of nicotine intake, which raises smokers' exposure to another serious health risk – the carcinogenic ingredients of cigarettes. Besides, this policy would boost industry profits.

One debate is whether tobacco companies like B & W are knowingly manipulating nicotine levels in their products with intent to cause addiction. If so, such socially irresponsible behaviour arguably must be controlled. On past record, it will take a long time to reach the point at which the FDA will bring the tobacco industry under its control. But things are stirring up fast. The race is already on to sue America's tobacco giants. In February 1995, a New Orleans court ruled that every American ever addicted to nicotine – or the relations of any nicotine-dependent-but-now-dead American – could sue the tobacco companies. Four American states also began to sue for the cost of treating smokers!

These events in the United States trivialize the tobacco advertising debate in Europe. The emergence of medical evidence suggesting that smoking is a health hazard has triggered reactions from anti-smoking groups, who argue that smoking should be at least discouraged, if not banned outright. Over the 1980s, lobbying by anti-smoking campaigners throughout Europe led to enforcement of tighter restrictions, notably on tobacco advertising. Those who rage against the evil of cigarette advertising assume that it is creating droves of new smokers. Tobacco firms argue that the assumption is doubtful, claiming that there is no evidence that advertising has much effect on total consumption. It is true that, according to one study, advertising bans in Norway, Finland, Canada and New Zealand helped to reduce cigarette consumption. But studies in other countries, such as Italy and Sweden, have shown that bans were followed by increases in smoking. Ironically, some argue that a ban would have one drawback: it would end the health warnings that now accompany tobacco advertising.

Current restrictions are already tight. Cigarette companies are prohibited from advertising on television in many European markets. To stave off more draconian legislation, they have agreed: to stop advertising in the cinema or on posters near schools; to reduce advertising on shop fronts; to stop using celebrities in their advertising; and to avoid any hint that smoking brings social or sexual success. Yet, tobacco adverts are not quite dead! Advertisers often resort to the use of cryptic pictures, like *red* motorcycles – the clue that told consumers to rush out and buy 'Marlboro' (red is the Marlboro brand colour).

In search of new customers, cigarette manufacturers are targeting females. In France, Spain, Germany and Britain, between a quarter and a third of smokers are women. In Sweden, they form a majority of smokers. In some countries, like India and Hong Kong, women-only brands have been launched. In the Baltic states, there are massive advertising campaigns tempting women and there is a big increase in the number of women smoking. Worse, tobacco firms are preying on children. Their aggressive campaigns in the less developed Far Eastern countries, with fewer consumer protection laws, are also cause for concern.[1]

QUESTIONS

You should attempt these questions only after completing your reading of this chapter.

1. Is advertising of hazardous products ethical? Tobacco firms claim that they advertise not to expand demand for cigarettes, but merely to maintain their market share against competitors' brands. Is this a bogus or friendly argument?

2. Should tobacco firms take greater responsibility for communicating the health hazards of smoking, and discouraging the habit?

3. Can society expect the industry to regulate its own actions and practise socially responsible marketing?

4. Can customers and society, at large, be left to develop their own sense

of personal responsibility – to avoid harmful products – even if firms
don't? Discuss.

5. Should legislators be the ultimate force that protects innocent
    consumers from unsavoury marketing?

6. In the interest of consumer safety and well-being, should tobacco firms
    circumvent current rules?

Introduction

Responsible marketers discover what consumers want and respond with the right
products, priced to give good value to buyers and profit to the producer. The
marketing concept is a philosophy of customer service and mutual gain. Its practice leads the economy by an invisible hand to satisfy the many and changing
needs of millions of consumers. But does social responsibility and morality have
any role to play? Or is it incompatible with commercial survival in a competitive
global marketplace?

Those are the sort of questions that used to be asked only in classrooms and
communes. But in an era when the consumer is wiser to much more of a
company's practice, and when there are increasingly wide concerns about environmental issues, animal testing and human rights, the need for social responsibility and sound ethics in marketing has become crucial if customers' demands
are to be fulfilled. How companies behave in the broadest sense is beginning to
have an impact on how people view their products and services. Walkers Snack
Foods successfully avoided serious damage to its brand value following the
discovery of glass fragments in a packet of crisps last November. Although it was
discovered that a broken lens on the production line may have contaminated no
more than five or six packets, the company immediately withdrew the entire
offending line – totalling 9 million packets of crisps. Press statements were drafted
and within 24 hours the company had a consumer helpline running. As we saw in
Chapter 1, another example of a socially responsible act is Johnson & Johnson's
very speedy recall of contaminated Tylenol capsules from store shelves to prevent
further possibilities of consumer injury. The 'Tylenol scare' was a serious public
issue and caused great consumer concern in markets where the drug was sold.
However, in taking responsible action, the brand value remained undamaged in
the long run and sales revived when the problem was resolved.

However, not all marketers follow the marketing concept. In fact, some
companies use questionable marketing practices, and some marketing actions
that seem innocent in themselves strongly affect the larger society. Consider,
again, the sale of sensitive products such as cigarettes. Ordinarily, companies
should be free to sell cigarettes, and smokers should be free to buy them. But this
transaction affects the public interest. First, the smoker may be shortening his or
her own life. Second, smoking places a burden on the smoker's family and on
society at large. Third, other people around the smoker may have to inhale the
smoke and may suffer discomfort and harm. This is not to say that cigarettes
should be banned, although the anti-smoking lobbyists would welcome that.
Rather, it shows that private transactions may involve larger questions of public
policy. In practice, the answers are by no means always clear cut. It may be
ethical for tobacco firms to stop peddling cigarettes altogether, but this, while
seen by absolute moralists as 'the right thing' to do, will lead to companies'

demise, job losses and the repercussions of increased unemployment on the wider community.

Marketers face difficult decisions when choosing to serve customers profitably, on the one hand, and seeking to maintain a close fit between consumers' wants or desires and societal welfare, on the other. In this chapter, we discuss marketing in the context of society, the need for integrity, social responsibility and sound ethics, and the dilemmas that marketing people face. We begin with a look at the impact of private marketing practices on individual consumers and society as a whole, and examine the social criticisms of marketing. Next we discuss consumerism, environmentalism and regulation, and the way they affect marketing strategies. We address two questions: What steps have private citizens taken to curb marketing ills? What steps have legislators and government agencies taken to curb marketing ills? This leads to an overview of responsible or enlightened marketing and marketing ethics. Finally, we conclude with a set of principles for public policy towards marketing: consumer and producer freedom, avoiding harm, meeting basic needs, economic efficiency, innovation, and consumer education, information and protection.

Social Criticisms of Marketing

Marketing receives much criticism. Some of this criticism is justified; much is not.[2] Social critics claim that certain marketing practices hurt individual consumers, society as a whole and other business firms.

Marketing's Impact on Individual Consumers

Consumers have many concerns about how well marketing and businesses, as a whole, serve their interests. Consumer advocates, government agencies and other critics have accused marketing of harming consumers through high prices, deceptive practices, high-pressure selling, shoddy or unsafe products, planned obsolescence and poor service to disadvantaged consumers.

● *High Prices*

Many critics charge that marketing practices raise the cost of goods and cause prices to be higher than they would be if clever marketing were not applied. They point to three factors: *high costs of distribution, high advertising and promotion costs*, and *excessive mark-ups*.

HIGH COSTS OF DISTRIBUTION. A long-standing charge is that greedy intermediaries mark up prices beyond the value of their services. Critics charge either that there are too many intermediaries, or that intermediaries are inefficient and poorly run, provide unnecessary or duplicate services, and practise poor management and planning. As a result, distribution costs too much and consumers pay for these excessive costs in the form of higher prices.

How do retailers answer these charges? They argue, first, that intermediaries do work which would otherwise have to be done by manufacturers or consumers. Second, the rising mark-up reflects improved services that consumers themselves want – more convenience, larger stores and more assortment, longer store opening hours, return privileges and others. Third, the costs of operating stores keep rising, forcing retailers to raise their prices. Fourth, retail competition is so intense that margins are actually quite low: for example, after taxes, supermarket chains are typically left with barely 1 per cent profit on their sales. If some resellers try to charge too much relative to the value they add, other resellers will step in with lower prices. Low-price stores and other discounters pressure their competitors to operate efficiently and keep their prices down.

HIGH ADVERTISING AND PROMOTION COSTS.   Modern marketing is also accused of pushing up prices because of heavy advertising and sales promotion. For example, a dozen tablets of a heavily promoted brand of aspirin sell for the same price as 100 tablets of less promoted brands. Differentiated products – cosmetics, detergents, toiletries – include promotion and packaging costs that can amount to 40 per cent or more of the manufacturer's price to the retailer. Critics charge that much of the packaging and promotion adds only psychological value to the product rather than real functional value. Retailers use additional promotion – advertising, displays and competitions – that add even more to retail prices.

Marketers answer these charges in several ways. First, consumers *want* more than the merely functional qualities of products. They also want psychological benefits – they want to feel wealthy, beautiful or special. Consumers can usually buy functional versions of products at lower prices, but are often willing to pay more for products that also provide desired psychological benefits. Second, branding gives buyers confidence. A brand name implies a certain quality and consumers are willing to pay for well-known brands even if they cost a little more. Third, heavy advertising is needed to inform millions of potential buyers of the merits of a brand. If consumers want to know what is available on the market, they must expect manufacturers to spend large sums of money on advertising. Fourth, heavy advertising and promotion may be necessary for a firm to match competitors' efforts. The business would lose 'share of mind' if it did not match competitive spending. At the same time, companies are cost conscious about promotion and try to spend their money wisely. Finally, heavy sales promotion is needed from time to time because goods are produced ahead of demand in a mass-production economy. Special incentives have to be offered in order to sell inventories.

EXCESSIVE MARK-UPS.   Critics also charge that some companies mark up goods excessively. They point to the drug industry, where a pill costing 5p to make may cost the consumer 40p to buy. Or to the pricing tactics of perfume manufacturers, who take advantage of customers' ignorance of the true worth of a 50 gram bottle of Joy perfume, while preying on their desire to fulfil emotional needs.

Marketers argue that most businesses try to deal fairly with consumers because they want repeat business. Most consumer abuses are unintentional. When shady marketers do take advantage of consumers, they should be reported to industry watchdogs and to other consumer-interest or consumer-protection groups. Marketers also stress that consumers often don't understand the reason for high mark-ups. For example, pharmaceutical mark-ups must cover the costs of purchasing, promoting and distributing existing medicines, plus the high research and development costs of finding new medicines.

● *Deceptive Practices*

Marketers are sometimes accused of deceptive practices that lead consumers to believe they will get more value than they actually do. Deceptive marketing practices fall into three groups: *deceptive pricing, promotion* and *packaging*. Deceptive pricing includes practices such as falsely advertising 'factory' or 'whole-

WITHDRAWN

If an ad misleads, we're here to stamp it out.
Advertising Standards Authority
2 Torrington Place London WC1E 7HW 0171 580 5555 http://www.asa.org.uk ASA

The ASA advertises its services to those its seeks to protect – the consumer.

sale' prices or a large price reduction from a phoney high retail list price. Deceptive promotion includes practices such as overstating the product's features or performance, luring the customer to the store for a bargain that is out of stock, or running rigged contests. Deceptive packaging includes exaggerating package contents through subtle design, not filling the package to the top, using misleading labelling, or describing size in misleading terms.

Deceptive practices have led to legislation and other consumer-protection actions. Positive steps have already been taken, for example, with regard to European directives aimed at the cosmetic industry. Council Directive 93/35/EEC of 14 June 1993 introduced far-reaching changes to cosmetic laws. The legislation controls the constituents of cosmetic products and their associated instructions and warnings about use, and specifies requirements relating to the marketing of cosmetic products, which cover product claims, labelling, information on packaging and details about the product's intended function. Where a product claims to remove 'unsightly cellulite' or make the user look '20 years younger', proofs must be documented and made available to the enforcement authorities. These laws also require clear details specifying where animal testing has been carried out on both the finished product and/or its ingredients. The EU has recognized increased public resistance to animal testing and has proposed a limited ban on animal testing for cosmetic ingredients from 1 January 1998. Similar directives are found to regulate industry practices in the United States. The Federal Trade Commission (FTC), which has the power to regulate 'unfair or deceptive acts or practices', has published several guidelines listing deceptive practices. The toughest problem is defining what is 'deceptive'. For example, some years ago, Shell Oil advertised that Super Shell petrol with platformate gave more mileage than did the same fuel without platformate. Now this was true, but what Shell did not say is that almost *all* petrol includes platformate. Its defence was that it had never claimed that platformate was found only in Shell petroleum fuel. But even though the message was literally true, the FTC felt that the ad's *intent* was to deceive.

Marketers argue that most companies avoid deceptive practices because such practices harm their business in the long run. If consumers do not get what they expect, they will switch to more reliable products. In addition,

We Have Ways of Making You Buy!

Marketing Highlight 2.1

Britain's life assurance industry was severely criticized for mis-selling, offering poor value to customers who surrender their policies early, and exploiting customers' ignorance – in short, for breaking the rules!

In the early 1990s LAUTRO, the body that regulated the selling of life insurance, fined at least a dozen life assurance companies a total of nearly £1million for failing to ensure that potential customers were fully informed about different policies. Those singled out included Scottish Widows, Guardian Royal Exchange, General Accident, Commercial Union and Norwich Union.

In June 1994, the Office of Fair Trading (OFT), a government watchdog, published its report on 60 of the United Kingdom's largest life insurers. It criticized firms for poor 'surrender values' – many household names, the symbols of probity and financial solidity, were short-changing customers who cashed in long-term policies early. London & Manchester, London Life, MGM, Refuge, Royal Life, Tunbridge Wells, Abbey Life, Allied Dunbar, Confederation Life, Cornhill Insurance, Irish Life, Midland Life and Reliance Mutual were all found to offer *zero* surrender value at the end of the first year for two types of policy investigated by the OFT. So, if a customer cancelled a £100 a month, ten-year savings plan after only one year, she got no money back from the insurer. There were also wide disparities in the surrender values of life insurance policies, although such information was seldom disclosed to buyers.

What is all the fuss about, though? Why should companies be penalized because their investors want to cash in earlier on long-term savings plans? Regulators believe that life insurers had exploited customers' ignorance and vulnerability, selling them products that generated big profits for the sellers, but were unsuited to the buyer. In many cases, insurers were accused of filling the pockets of salespeople, senior managers and, in the case of limited companies, the shareholders,

by extracting fat commission from high-pressure selling schemes that customers did not really want or need. Sales 'tricks' were not unusual in the industry. For example, some salespeople sent letters to married women, talking about their company and appending a blank form with a piece of paper telling the woman: 'This is what you get when your husband dies.'

Although the surrender values offered by the insurers in later years were reasonable, the Securities and Investments Board suggested that one-quarter to one-third of all policies were cashed in during the first two years alone. A number of companies actually profited from early lapse rates, and many people holding policies with companies which have relatively high lapse rates were actually worse off than if they had no policy at all. Lapses are insurers' profits!

The insurance companies' response is that customers have the product literature to help them assess their policies. The OFT argues that the idea that customers could understand readily the surrender values of their policies simply by reading the product literature is quite false. 'These things are not only obscure to the average consumer but to the informed consumer as well,' says John Mills, head of the OFT's consumer policy division.

So, what fuels this pervasive practice in the industry? One answer is that not nearly as many people would have bought life insurance if the products had not been actively sold to them. Another is that few consumers have the expertise to compare the costs and benefits of different policies. What consumers buy is all about how quickly the sales rep gets to them and how persuasive he or she is.

Although many independent financial advisers ensure that clients get good value for money from respectable insurers, there are many others who are forced to sell poor-quality products, because they are trapped in a commission structure that requires them to sell or starve.

One insurance sales representative says: 'You would see that some prospective clients might have to struggle to pay the premiums, but because your livelihood depended on it, you would play on their emotions to try to sell them something.' Another salesperson commented: 'We were licensed to give best advice, but it wasn't. A superior product offered by another company would not be mentioned.' Salespeople argue that they were often put under increasing pressure and encouraged by a range of incentives, some of them fairly obvious, such as bottles of whisky and holidays in the Bahamas. There were bizarre punishments for those that did badly: at one branch of a big insurer, the worst performer over the previous month would be told to walk around the building for a day dressed in ladies' underwear.

Regulators and watchdogs now address two key issues: what customers are told about products and the people selling them; and self-regulation versus government (statutory) regulation. The OFT introduced disclosure rules in January 1995. Salespeople must now inform the consumer how much commission they take for selling a given policy and need to spend hours with customers filling in forms with personal details. Predictably, independent financial advisers protest that disclosure will force many of them out of business. After years of deliberately confusing consumers with jargon, blinding them with technical language and pressurizing to do the deal, the industry has lost the public's trust. Bad publicity on mis-selling has also affected industry-wide sales. To compound the industry's problems, new entrants, including Direct Line, Marks & Spencer and Virgin Direct, began to sell life insurance and pension products over the phone from the mid-1990s. Not only are these helping to drive prices down, but their image as the new 'clean' competitors from outside the industry, which truly apply 'customer first' marketing philosophy, is helping to wake the industry up. They are doing the traditional insurance companies no end of good.

The moral of the story is clear. Using trickery or vigorous sales approaches to pressure customers unfairly into buying financial products (or any product or service) that they either do not need or would do better to buy elsewhere, does not make sound marketing sense. Consumers become disenchanted or disillusioned or withdraw consumption altogether. High-pressure selling usually backfires on the aggressive sellers. You cannot sell something nobody wants, no matter how you push it!

SOURCES: Alison Smith, 'Standard Life's surrender bonus', *Financial Times* (21 November 1994), p. 22; Alison Smith, 'OFT names insurers offering zero first year surrender value', *Financial Times* (9–10 July 1994), p. 1; Alison Smith, 'Back from the brink', *Financial Times* (23 June 1994), p. 16; Norma Cohen, 'Life insurers criticised for poor surrender values', 'Your lapses are their profits', *Financial Times* (18–19 June 1994), pp. I, III; Peter Marsh, 'We have ways of making you buy', *Financial Times* (14 June 1994), p. 18; Peter Marsh, 'When he dies, my dear, all this will be yours', *Financial Times* (11–12 June 1994), pp. I, XII; 'All life's troubles', *The Economist* (17 July 1993), pp. 76–7; Sean Brierley, 'A matter of life and death', *Marketing Week* (28 June 1995); Andrew Duffy, 'Great British pensions disaster', *Business Age* (5 July 1995), pp. 40–3; Alan Mitchell, 'Swimming with the sharks', *Marketing Business* (September 1997), pp. 26–30.

consumers usually protect themselves from deception. Most consumers recognize a marketer's selling intent and are careful when they buy, sometimes to the point of not believing completely true product claims. Theodore Levitt claims that some advertising puffery is bound to occur – and that it may even be desirable:

There is hardly a company that would not go down in ruin if it refused to provide fluff, because nobody will buy pure functionality ... Worse, it denies ... man's honest needs and values ... Without distortion, embellishment and elaboration, life would be drab, dull, anguished and at its existential worst ...[3]

● *High-Pressure Selling*

Salespeople are sometimes accused of high-pressure selling that persuades people to buy goods they had no thought of buying. It is often said that cars, financial services, property and home improvement plans are *sold*, not *bought*. Salespeople are trained to deliver smooth, canned talks to entice purchase. They sell hard because commissions and sales contests promise big prizes to those who sell the most.

Marketers know that buyers can often be talked into buying unwanted or unneeded things. A key question is whether industry self-regulatory or trading standards bodies, consumer-protection laws and consumer-interest groups are sufficiently effective in checking and curbing unsavoury sales practices. In this modern era, it is encouraging to note that one or more of these can work to the advantage of consumers. Or, where malpractices are pervasive, regulators will catch out wrongdoers, who will invariably pay the penalties for irresponsible marketing. This is evident in the case of the mis-selling of pensions and life assurance policies in the UK market (see Marketing Highlight 2.1).

● *Shoddy or Unsafe Products*

Another criticism is that products lack the quality they should have. One complaint is that products are not made well. Such complaints have been lodged against products and services ranging from home appliances, cars and clothing to home and car repair services.

A second complaint is that some products deliver little benefit. In an attempt to persuade customers to buy their brand rather than any other, manufacturers sometimes make claims that are not fully substantiated. In the United Kingdom, for example, the Independent Television Commission (ITC) introduced new rules covering the advertising of medicines and treatments, health claims, and nutrition and dietary supplements, including slimming products. The move, which follows the publication of new advertising rules by the Advertising Standards Authority, brings the ITC in line with public and private sector opinion, and recent European Union legislation governing the advertising and sales of these products. Health claims for food, for example, must now be fully substantiated. Creative ads must guard against encouraging overindulgence in products such as confectionery, so advertisers must pay attention to health implications.[4]

In markets where many brands are promising a wide array of product benefits, consumers are often left confused. In fact, consumers often end up paying more for product benefits that do not exist (see Marketing Highlight 2.2).

A third complaint concerns product safety. Product safety has been a problem for several reasons, including manufacturer indifference, increased production complexity, poorly trained labour and poor quality control. Consider the following cases of costly and image-damaging crises brought upon vehicle manufacturers:

> In 1990, consumer activists declared the Daihatsu Sportrak as 'potentially unstable' and Suzuki was urged to recall tens of thousands of similar cars. This problem pales by comparison with that faced by the Ford Pinto, which became the symbol of automotive disaster when several people died during the 1970s in fuel tank fires allegedly linked to a design fault. More recently, Chrysler issued one of the largest product recall notices in the history of the motoring industry, calling back 900,000 vehicles, ranging from pick-ups to a selection of 'people carriers' including the

Marketing Highlight 2.2

'Shopper's Friend' Brand Benefit Claims

The Consumers' Association (CA) in the United Kingdom, an independent, self-appointed organization, seeks to police the goods and services offered by consumer-products manufacturers and business sectors, and aims to improve the quality of people's purchasing decisions. It carries out independent research and tests on all sorts of consumer goods and services, ranging from soap powders, kettles and motor cars to free-range turkeys, holidays and insurance policies, and then rates these based on 'value for money' and effectiveness criteria. Its public face, *Which?* magazine, is an important channel used to provide consumers with a counterpoint to the persuasive marketing of consumer goods and services. *Which?* forms the 'mouthpiece' of the Association, playing the role of 'shopper's friend' by offering unbiased views on brand features, quality and/or performance, and advice on 'best buy' and 'good value' purchases. Generally, the criteria for any investigation are: How many people will it affect? How important an issue is it? Can the CA do anything about it?

Here is an example of a toothpaste test reported in one issue of the CA's *Which?* magazine. The test sought to substantiate the oral health, including medicinal (e.g. relief from the pain of sensitive teeth), claims made in toothpaste advertising. The report lists the main claims made for toothpastes and picks out the brands that the test team believes can substantiate their claims and those which cannot.

Three main types of 'claim' are: (1) prevention of gum disease/anti-plaque property; (2) protection of sensitive teeth; and (3) tartar control. To substantiate claims, the test team turns to (a) evidence from clinical trials and (b) evidence of 'availability of actives': that is, that the effective ingredient has not been inactivated by any of the other chemicals in the toothpaste. Unsubstantiated claims are ones where the manufacturer did not provide the test team with evidence either of suitable clinical trials on the particular toothpaste or of 'availability of actives'. This means not that the toothpaste is ineffective, but that the test panel has not seen enough proof that the manufacturer can substantiate its dental health claim(s).

Table 1 shows results for the manufacturers' and own-label brands of toothpaste tested.

The CA asserts that no manufacturer should make claims for its products, on packaging or in advertising, unless they can be substantiated by evidence of a reasonable standard. It draws attention to recommended toothpaste brands, but highlights the fact that many expensive toothpastes marked for sensitive teeth do not contain fluoride, so will not offer protection against decay.

Consumer-interest bodies like the CA help to improve buyers' decisions by offering impartial information and guidance on all kinds of purchasing decision. The CA uses expert panels and professionals, together with its own teams of testers and evaluators, to conduct product evaluations. Testing criteria for products and services are always described in full. Where appropriate, accreditation bodies' results are also consulted and compared with its own test results. Not surprisingly, the CA has made many enemies of manufacturers and businesses that fail to deliver good value to customers. Aggrieved companies often raise questions about the CA's impartiality and accountability.

Manufacturers that achieve poor product ratings are invariably given the option to challenge the test results. Many use these findings to direct product-improvement efforts and make positive changes in their products. The CA's printed mission is to 'empower people to make informed consumer decisions' and improve the quality of goods and services. If these goals are truly achieved, then the role of consumer bodies that have the consumer at heart is more important now – in the era of consumerism – than ever before. Brand owners beware! Friend or foe, 'shopper's friend', vigilant as ever, is here to stay.

SOURCES: Consumers' Association, 'Toothpaste', *Which?* (July 1992), pp. 372–5; Tom O'Sullivan, 'Shopper's friend counters enemies', *Marketing Week* (10 February 1995), pp. 22–3.

TABLE 1 CLAIM VERSUS PERFORMANCE OF TOOTHPASTE

	IS CLAIM SUBSTANTIATED BY TOOTHPASTE PERFORMANCE?	
CLAIMS MADE	YES	NO
Prevention of gum disease	Colgate Gum Protection Formula Mentadent P	Aqua Fresh Triple Protection Asda Anti-Plaque Boots Anti-Plaque Boots Total Care Co-op Anti-Plaque Gateway Fresh Breath Anti-Plaque Gibbs SR Macleans Anti-Plaque Oral B Zendium Tesco Dental Care Minty Blue Gel Waitrose Plaque-Control Superdrug Oral Health Gum Health Formula
Protection of sensitive teeth	Asda Sensitive Boots Formula Gateway Fresh Breath Formula Macleans Sensitive Mentadent S Safeway Sensitive Sainsbury's Oral Health Sensitive Teeth Tesco Sensitive Teeth Formula Sensodyne Original and Mint Sensodyne F Waitrose Sensitive	Boots Formula F
Tartar control	Colgate Tartar Control Formula Crest Tartar Control Crest Ultra Protection Mentadent P Sainsbury's Oral Health Tartar Control Tesco Dental Care Anti-Tartar	Safeway Tartar Control Superdrug Oral Health Tartar Control

Voyager, Wrangler and Jeep Cherokee models, for a variety of reasons in seven different recalls. One of the biggest recalls in 1997, according to figures from the British vehicle inspectorate, was one undertaken by VW, asking 150,000 Golf and Vento saloon owners to have their car checked for wiring faults. In 1996, VW also recalled 350,000 of its models worldwide because of a potentially faulty electric cable, as well as some 950,000 Golfs, Jettas, Passats and Corrados because of problems, including a cooling system fault, which could potentially damage engines and injure passengers. Early in 1997, Vauxhall called in more than 39,000 Vectras to check loose fuel pipes. Even Rolls-Royce was forced to check some of its Bentley Continental T sports coupés (at £220,000 apiece) because of concerns that airbags were firing unexpectedly.[5]

For years now, consumer protection groups or associations in many countries have regularly tested products for safety, and have reported hazards found in tested products, such as electrical dangers in appliances, and injury risks from lawn mowers and faulty car design. The testing and reporting activities of these organizations have helped consumers make better buying decisions and have encouraged businesses to eliminate product flaws. Marketers may sometimes face dilemmas when seeking to balance consumer needs and ethical considerations. For example, no amount of test results can guarantee product safety in cars if consumers value speed and power more than safety features. Buyers might choose a less expensive chain saw without a safety guard, although society or a government regulatory agency might deem it irresponsible and unethical for the manufacturer to sell it.

However, most responsible manufacturers *want* to produce quality goods. The way a company deals with product quality and safety problems can damage or help its reputation. Companies selling poor-quality or unsafe products risk damaging conflicts with consumer groups. Moreover, unsafe products can result in product liability suits and large awards for damages. Consumers who are unhappy with a firm's products may avoid its other products and talk other consumers into doing the same. More fundamentally, today's marketers know that self-imposed, high ethical standards, which accompany customer-driven quality, result in customer satisfaction, which in turn creates profitable customer relationships.

● *Planned Obsolescence*

Critics have charged that some producers follow a programme of **planned obsolescence**, causing their products to become obsolete before they need replacement. In many cases, producers have been accused of continually changing consumer concepts of acceptable styles in order to encourage more and earlier buying. An obvious example is constantly changing clothing fashions. Producers have also been accused of holding back attractive functional features, then introducing them later to make older models obsolete. Critics claim that this practice is frequently found in the consumer electronics and computer industry. The Japanese camera, watch and consumer electronics companies frustrate consumers because rapid and frequent model replacement has created difficulties in obtaining spare parts for old models; dealers refuse to repair outdated models and planned obsolescence rapidly erodes basic product values. Finally, producers have been accused of using materials and components that will break, wear, rust or rot sooner than they should. For example, many drapery manufacturers are using a higher percentage of rayon in their curtains. They argue that rayon reduces the price of the curtains and has better holding power. Critics claim that using more rayon causes the curtains to fall apart sooner. European consumers have also found, to their annoyance, how rapidly certain European brands of toasters rust – for an appliance that rarely gets into contact with water, this is an amazing technological feat!

Marketers respond that consumers *like* style changes; they get tired of the old goods and want a new look in fashion or a new design in cars. No one has to buy the new look, and if too few people like it, it will simply fail. Companies frequently withhold new features when they are not fully tested, when they add more cost to the product than consumers are willing to pay, and for other good reasons. But they do so at the risk that a competitor will introduce the new feature and steal the market. Moreover, companies often put in new materials to lower their costs and prices. They do not design their products to break down earlier, because they do not want to lose their customers to other brands. Thus, much so-called

Planned obsolescence
A *strategy of causing products to become obsolete before they actually need replacement.*

planned obsolescence is the working of the competitive and technological forces in a free society – forces that lead to ever-improving goods and services.

● *Poor Service to Disadvantaged Consumers*

Finally, marketing has been accused of poorly serving disadvantaged consumers. Critics claim that the urban poor often have to shop in smaller stores that carry inferior goods and charge higher prices. Marketing's eye on profits also means that disadvantaged consumers are not viable segments to target. The high-income consumer is the preferred target.

Clearly, better marketing systems must be built in low-income areas – one hope is to get large retailers to open outlets in low-income areas. Moreover low-income people clearly need consumer protection. Consumer-protection agencies should take action against suppliers who advertise false values, sell old merchandise as new, or charge too much for credit. Offenders who deliver poor value should be expected to compensate customers, as in the case of many UK pensions providers, who were required to meet mis-selling compensation targets following the disclosure of malpractices by an Office of Fair Trading (OFT) investigation.

We now turn to social critics' assessment of how marketing affects society as a whole.

Marketing's Impact on Society as a Whole

The marketing system as we – in Europe and other developed economies outside North America – are experiencing it, has been accused of adding to several 'evils' in our society at large. Advertising has been a special target. It has been blamed for creating false wants, nurturing greedy aspirations and inculcating too much materialism in our society.

● *False Wants and Too Much Materialism*

Critics have charged that, in advanced nations such as the USA, the marketing system urges too much interest in material possessions. People are judged by what they *own* rather than by what they *are*. To be considered successful, people must own a smart-looking house or apartment in a prime residential site, expensive cars and the latest designer label clothes and consumer electronics.

> Consider, for example, the training-shoe market. These days, training shoes have gone the same way as cameras, watches and mobile phones: functionality is useless without 'techno-supremacy' and high style. Take Nike's Air Max Tailwind which features: 'flexi-laces' which stretch to give foot comfort; 'interactive eyestay' for one-movement tightening and adjusting; 'mesh upper' made of lightweight synthetic leather for cooler feet; 'plastic air pockets' filled with sulphur hexafluoride for added cushioning; 'flexible grooves' in the arch of the shoe to allow natural foot movements and give support and 'waffle soles' with grooved treads for traction and support! So sophisticated has it become that it is no longer even enough to say that you have a pair of Nikes. Its famous tick logo is now more globally visible than the crucifix, so your Nikes had better be a very rare variety and/or very expensive if you expect to seriously impress. Alternatively, you could go for a limited edition Adidas or something slightly underground like DC skate shoes.[6]

Is there a similar enchantment with money in Europe? Asia? The rest of the world? It is neither feasible nor appropriate for this chapter to indulge readers in an extensive debate on cross-cultural similarities and dissimilarities in materialistic tendencies and behaviour, and whether marketing is the root cause of these desires. Rather, we acknowledge the phenomenon of the 'yuppie generation' that emerged in the 1980s, symbolizing a new materialistic culture that looked certain to stay. In the 1990s, although many social scientists noted a reaction against the opulence and waste of the 1980s and a return to more basic values and social commitment, our infatuation with material things continues. For example, when asked in a recent poll what they value most in their lives, subjects listed enjoyable work (86 per cent), happy children (84 per cent), a good marriage (69 per cent) and contributions to society (66 per cent). However, when asked what most symbolizes success, 85 per cent said money and the things it will buy.[7]

Critics view this interest in material things not as a natural state of mind, but rather as a matter of false wants created by marketing. Businesses stimulate people's desires for goods through the force of advertising, and advertisers use the mass media to create materialistic models of the good life. People work harder to earn the necessary money. Their purchases increase the output of the nation's industry, and industry, in turn, uses the advertising media to stimulate more desire for its industrial output. Thus marketing is seen as creating false wants that benefit industry more than they benefit consumers.

However, these criticisms overstate the power of business to create needs. People have strong defences against advertising and other marketing tools. Marketers are most effective when they appeal to existing wants rather than when they attempt to create new ones. Furthermore, people seek information when making important purchases and often do not rely on single sources. Consumers ultimately display rational buying behaviour: even minor purchases that may be affected by advertising messages lead to repeat purchases only if the product performs as promised. Finally, the high failure rate of new products shows that companies are not always able to control demand.

On a deeper level, our wants and values are influenced not only by marketers, but also by family, peer groups, religion, ethnic background and education. If societies are highly materialistic, these values arose out of basic socialization processes that go much deeper than business and mass media could produce alone. The importance of wealth and material possessions to the overseas Chinese, for example, is explained more by cultural and socialization factors than by sustained exposure to western advertising influences.

● *Too Few Social Goods*

Business has been accused of overselling private goods at the expense of public goods. As private goods increase, they require more public services that are usually not forthcoming. For example, an increase in car ownership (private good) requires more roads, traffic control, parking spaces and police services (public goods). The overselling of private goods results in 'social costs'. For cars, the social costs include excessive traffic congestion, air pollution, and deaths and injuries from car accidents.

A way must be found to restore a balance between private and public goods. One option is to make producers bear the full social costs of their operations. For example, the government could require car manufacturers to build cars with additional safety features and better pollution-control systems. Car makers would then raise their prices to cover extra costs. If buyers found the price of some cars too high, however, the producers of these cars would disappear, and demand would move to those producers that could support both the private and social costs.

● *Cultural Pollution*

Critics charge the marketing system with creating *cultural pollution*. Our senses are being assaulted constantly by advertising. Commercials interrupt serious programmes; pages of ads obscure printed matter; billboards mar beautiful scenery. These interruptions continuously pollute people's minds with messages of materialism, sex, power or status. Although most people do not find advertising overly annoying (some even think it is the best part of television programming), some critics call for sweeping changes.

Marketers answer the charges of 'commercial noise' with the following arguments. First, they hope that their ads reach primarily the target audience. But because of mass-communication channels, some ads are bound to reach people who have no interest in the product and are therefore bored or annoyed. People who buy magazines slanted towards their interests – such as *Vogue* or *Fortune* – rarely complain about the ads because the magazines advertise products of interest. Second, ads make much of television and radio free, and keep down the costs of magazines and newspapers. Most people think commercials are a small price to pay for these benefits.

● *Too Much Political Power*

Another criticism is that business wields too much political power. 'Oil', 'tobacco', 'pharmaceuticals', 'financial services' and 'alcohol' have the support of important politicians and civil servants, who look after an industry's interests against the public interest. Advertisers are accused of holding too much power over the mass media, limiting their freedom to report independently and objectively.

The setting up of citizens' charters and greater concern for consumer rights and protection in the 1990s will see improvements, not regression, in business accountability. Fortunately, many powerful business interests once thought to be untouchable have been tamed in the public interest. For example, in the United States, Ralph Nader, consumerism campaigner, caused legislation that forced the car industry to build more safety into its cars, and the Surgeon General's Report resulted in cigarette companies putting health warnings on their packages. Moreover, because the media receive advertising revenues from many different advertisers, it is easier to resist the influence of one or a few of them. Too much business power tends to result in counterforces that check and offset these powerful interests.

Let us now take a look at the criticisms that business critics have levelled at companies' marketing practices.

Marketing's Impact on Other Businesses

Critics also charge that companies' marketing practices can harm other companies and reduce competition. Three problems are involved: acquisition of competitors, marketing practices that create barriers to entry, and unfair competitive marketing practices.

Critics claim that firms are harmed and competition reduced when companies expand by acquiring competitors rather than by developing their own new products. In the car industry alone there has been a spate of acquisitions over the past decade: General Motors bought the British sports-car maker, Lotus; Ford acquired 75 per cent of Britain's Aston Martin, which makes hand-built, high-

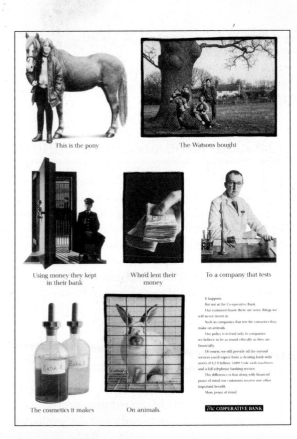

This is the pony

The Watsons bought

Using money they kept in their bank

Who'd lent their money

To a company that tests

The cosmetics it makes

On animals.

In this innovative ad, the Co-operative Bank reflects its unspoken and unwritten culture – it professes that it will not do business with organizations that are environmentally or politically unsound.

and able to buy. Certain groups who lack purchasing power may go without needed goods and services, causing harm to their physical or psychological well-being. While preserving the principle of producer and consumer freedom, marketers should support economic and political actions to solve this problem. The marketing system should strive to meet the basic needs of all people, and all people should share to some extent in the standard of living it creates.[23]

The Principle of Economic Efficiency

The marketing system strives to supply goods and services efficiently. The extent to which a society's needs and wants can be satisfied depends on how efficiently its scarce resources are used. For marketing to work efficiently, the system needs competition. An open market allows for competition, free flow of goods, freedom of information and informed buyers. These make a market efficient. To make profits, competitors must watch their costs carefully while developing products, prices and marketing programmes that serve buyer needs. Buyers get the most satisfaction by finding out about different competing products, prices and qualities, and choosing carefully. The presence of active competition and well-informed buyers keeps quality high and prices low. But, more importantly, competition brings out the best in products and services. Producers that strive to offer the best value can expect to thrive.

The Principle of Innovation

The marketing system encourages genuine innovation to reduce production and distribution costs, and to develop new products to meet changing consumer needs. Much innovation is really imitation of other brands, with a slight difference to provide a selling point. The consumer may face ten very similar brands in a product class. But an effective marketing system encourages real product innovation and sustainable differentiation to meet the wants of different market segments.

The Principle of Consumer Education and Information

An effective marketing system invests heavily in consumer education and information to increase long-run consumer satisfaction and welfare. The principle of economic efficiency requires this investment, especially in cases where products are confusing because of their numbers and conflicting claims. Ideally, companies will provide enough information about their products. But consumer groups, regulatory agencies and government can also give out information and ratings. They should encourage more access to the media for the arguments for or against consumption of goods or services, where neither businesses nor customers are behaving responsibly.

The Principle of Consumer Protection

Consumer education and information cannot do the whole job of protecting consumers. The marketing system must also provide consumer protection. Modern products are so complex that even trained consumers cannot evaluate them with confidence. Consumers do not know whether a mobile phone gives off cancer-causing radiation, whether a new car has safety flaws, or whether a new drug product has dangerous side-effects. A government agency has to review and judge the safety levels of various foods, drugs, toys, appliances, fabrics, cars and housing. Similarly, it has to assess the integrity or professionalism of service providers like banks, insurance companies, doctors and police forces. Consumers may buy products but fail to understand the environmental consequences, so consumer protection also covers production and marketing activities that might harm the environment. Finally, consumer protection prevents deceptive practices and high-pressure selling techniques where consumers would be defenceless.

These seven principles are based on the assumption that marketing's goal is not just to maximize company profits or total consumption or consumer choice, but rather to balance that with maximization of life quality. Life quality means meeting basic needs, having available many good products, and enjoying the natural and cultural environment. Properly managed, the marketing system can help to create and deliver a higher quality of life to people around the world. The very implementation of the marketing philosophy can therefore be seen as a productive activity, not a destructive evil. Responsible marketing works.

Summary

A marketing system should sense, serve and satisfy consumer needs and improve the quality of consumers' lives. In working to meet consumer needs, marketers may take some actions that are not to everyone's liking or benefit. Marketing managers should be aware of the main *criticisms of marketing*.

Marketing's *impact on individual consumer welfare* has been criticized for its *high prices, deceptive practices, high-pressure selling, shoddy or unsafe products, planned obsolescence* and *poor service to disadvantaged consumers*. Marketing's *impact on society* has been criticized for *creating false wants* and *too much materialism, too few social goods, cultural pollution* and *too much political power*. Critics have also criticized marketing's *impact on other businesses* for *harming competitors* and *reducing competition* through acquisitions, practices that create barriers to entry, and unfair competitive marketing practices.

Concerns about the marketing system have led to *citizen and public actions to regulate marketing*. *Consumerism* is an organized social movement intended to strengthen the rights and power of consumers relative to sellers. Alert marketers view it as an opportunity to serve consumers better by providing more consumer information, education and protection.

Environmentalism is an organized social movement seeking to minimize the harm done to the environment and quality of life by marketing practices. It calls for curbing consumer wants when their satisfaction would create too much environmental cost. Citizen action has led to the passage of many laws to protect consumers in the area of product safety, truth in packaging, truth in lending and truth in advertising.

Many companies originally opposed these social movements and laws, but most of them now recognize a need for positive consumer information, education and protection. Some companies have followed a policy of enlightened marketing based on the principles of *consumer orientation, innovation, value creation, social mission* and *societal marketing*. Increasingly, companies are responding to the need to provide company policies and guidelines to help their employees deal with questions of *marketing ethics*. Although there are many questions concerning marketing and social responsibility, companies are urged to consider seven principles for public policy towards modern, responsible marketing: *consumer and producer freedom; curbing potential harm; meeting basic needs; economic efficiency; innovation; consumer education and information*; and *consumer protection*.

Key Terms

Consumer-oriented marketing 61
Consumerism 56
Deficient products 64
Desirable products 64
Enlightened marketing 61

Environmentalism 57
Innovative marketing 62
Planned obsolescence 51
Pleasing products 64
Salutary products 64

Sense-of-mission marketing 63
Societal marketing 63
Value marketing 62

Discussing the Issues

1. Consider the following example. The great Disney animation revival, which began with *The Little Mermaid* in 1989, reached a peak with the 1994 blockbuster *Lion King*, which took $770 million at the box office worldwide. Since then, each new release has done less well. Analysts say a backlash is

developing against Disney's hard sell. Parents are put off by the marketing blitz and the cost of the extras – the T-shirt, the video, the toys, all the rest of it – that follow each new release. 'When you come out to the cinema foyer you are barraged with Disney products,' parents complain. Disney's expensive marketing campaigns leave parents feeling crammed and committed to spending on a host of knick-knacks that their children demand after seeing the movie. Is it right or wrong for the company to use merchandising to market its films? Why? Why not?

2. Does marketing *create* barriers to entry or *reduce* them? Describe how a small local manufacturer of household cleaning products could use advertising to compete with the market leader, which holds a dominant share of the product sector.

3. There is evidence to suggest that laws are more effective than voluntary actions to protect our environment (for example, see Marketing Highlight 2.3). If you were a marketing manager at a chemical company, which would you prefer: government regulations on acceptable levels of air and water pollution, or a voluntary industry code suggesting target levels of emissions? Why?

4. The issue of ethics provides special challenges for international marketers as business standards and practices vary a great deal from one country to the next. Should a company adapt its ethical standards to compete effectively in countries with different standards? (Bribes, use of child labour, positive discrimination against female workers and members from ethic minorities might be useful examples of values/practices which vary across countries/cultures in different corners of the globe and can be used to focus your discussion.)

5. Compare the marketing concept with the principle of societal marketing. Do you think marketers should adopt the societal marketing concept? Why or why not?

6. If you had the power to change our marketing system in any way feasible, what improvements would you make? What improvements can you make as a consumer or marketing practitioner?

Applying the Concepts

1. Changes in consumer attitudes, especially the growth of consumerism and environmentalism, have led to more societal marketing – and to more marketing that is *supposedly* good for society, but is actually close to deception.

   ● List three examples of marketing campaigns that you feel are genuine societal marketing. If possible, find examples of advertising or packaging that supports these campaigns.

   ● Find three examples of deceptive or borderline imitations of societal marketing. How are you able to tell which campaigns are genuine and which are not?

   ● What remedies, if any, would you recommend for this problem?

2. Consider the case of Scandinavian employers' hostility towards the SAS frequent-flyers programme (Marketing Highlight 2.6) and discuss the following:

   ● Should airlines reward regular customers with bonus points?

   ● Should employees' private use of airline bonus points gained on business trips constitute an abuse of business perks?

   ● Where do we draw the line between a legal inducement offered by the supplier of a product or service to cultivate loyal customers, and an unethical ploy to bribe customers and encourage unnecessary purchase and usage? And, who should police unsavoury practices?

   ● Thinking about other countries in Europe/Asia/North America, to your knowledge, is personal use of airline bonus points accumulated on business trips deemed unlawful?

   ● How universal are different country authorities' treatment of frequent-flyer inducements for business travellers?

References

1. See 'The return of the smoke-free cigarette', *The Economist* (26 October 1996), p. 111; David Brierley, 'A woman's place is in the pub, smoking', *The European* (20–6 June 1996), p. 29; Richard Tomkins, 'Addiction or taste in battle for smokers' allegiance', *Financial Times* (23 June 1994), p. 6; 'The race is on to sue America's tobacco giants', *The Economist* (25 February 1995), p. 7; 'Tobacco adverts', *The Economist* (5 February 1994), pp. 33–4. For more discussion about the gains and losses in a total ban on tobacco advertising, see David Short, 'Winners and losers in the tobacco advertising war', *The European* (24–30 June 1994), p. 25; Stephanie Bentley, 'Stubbing out advertising', *Marketing Week* (5 January 1996), pp. 18–21; 'Chewing up tobacco', *The Economist* (20 September 1997), p. 106.

2. See Steven H. Star, 'Marketing and its discontents', *Harvard Business Review* (November–December 1989), pp. 148–54.

3. Excerpts from Theodore Levitt, 'The morality(?) of advertising', *Harvard Business Review* (July–August 1970), pp. 84–92.

4. 'ITC unveils new rules on food, drugs', *Marketing Week* (3 February 1995), p. 9.

5. 'When quality control breaks down', *The European* (6–12 November 1997), p. 29. For more discussion on managing product recalls, see N. Craig Smith, Robert J. Thomas and John A. Quelch, 'A strategic approach to managing product recalls', *Harvard Business Review* (September–October 1996), pp. 102–12.

6. Stephanie Theobold, 'The art of wearing trainers', *The European* (21 August 1997), p. 50.

7. See Anne B. Fisher, 'A brewing revolt against the rich', *Fortune* (17 December 1990), pp. 89–94; Norval D. Glenn, 'What does family mean?', *American Demographics* (June 1992), pp. 30–7.

8. 'America's new king of Europe's roads', *The Economist* (9 March 1991), pp. 79–81; Kieren Cooke, 'Suharto family a driving force at Lamborghini', *Financial Times* (11 February 1994), p. 28.

9. Peter Doyle, *Marketing Management and Strategy*, 1st edn (New York: Prentice Hall, 1994), p. 148.

10. For more details, see Paul N. Bloom and Stephen A. Greyser, 'The maturing of consumerism', *Harvard Business Review* (November–December 1981), pp. 130–9; Robert J. Samualson, 'The aging of Ralph Nader', *Newsweek* (16 December 1985), p. 57; Douglas A. Harbrecht, 'The second coming of Ralph Nader', *Business Week* (6 March 1989), p. 28.

11. Michael Lindemann, 'Green light begins to flash for recyclable cars in Germany', *Financial Times* (3 August 1994), p. 2.

12. For more details on the 'green' debate, see INRA, *Europeans and the Environment in 1992*, report produced for the Commission of the European Communities Directorate General XVII: Energy (Brussels, 1992); R. Schuster, *Environmentally Oriented Consumer Behaviour in Europe* (Hamburg: Kovac, 1992); R. Worcester, *Public and Elite Attitudes to Environmental Issues* (London: MORI, 1993); 'A survey of the global environment', *The Economist* (30 May 1992); Paul Abrahams, 'Chemicals and the environment', survey, *Financial Times* (18 June 1993); Ian Hamilton Fazey, 'Paints and the environment', survey, *Financial Times* (8 April 1994); Noble Robinson, Ralph Earle III and Ronand A. N. McLean, 'Transnational corporations and global environmental policy', *Prism* (Cambridge, MA: Arthur D. Little Inc.; First Quarter, 1994), pp. 51–63.

13. Robinson *et al.*, 'Transnational corporations and global environmental policy', op. cit., p. 56.

14. Dorothy Mackenzie, 'Greener than thou', *Marketing Business* (April 1992), pp. 10–13; Roland Rowell and Jane Hancock, 'Legal make-up', *Marketing Business* (November 1993), pp. 42–3; 'Putting a price on being green', *Marketing Business* (December 1989), pp. 18–19; W. Hopfenbeck, *The Green Management Revolution* (New York: Prentice Hall, 1992); K. Peattie, *Green Marketing* (London: Pitman, 1992).

15. 'Richardson Sheffield, a very British success', *The Economist* (4 March 1989), p. 86.

16. Nathan Yates, 'Now recycle your room', *The European Magazine* (24–30 April 1997), p. 13.

17. Alan Mitchell, 'Changing channels', *Marketing Business* (February 1995), pp. 10–13.

18. Alexander Jarrett, 'Doing the right thing', *Marketing Business* (August 1996), pp. 12–16; Sam King, 'Bidders float ideas for Brent Spar's future', *The European*, (22 August 1996), p. 5.

19. 'Who will listen to Mr Clean?', *The Economist* (2 August 1997), p. 58.

20. 'Good takes on greed', *The Economist* (17 February 1990), pp. 87–9.

21. See Susan Norgan, *Marketing Management: A European perspective* (Wokingham, Berks: Addison-Wesley, 1994), p. 49.

22. From 'Ethics as a practical matter', a message from David R. Whitman, chairman of the board of Whirlpool Corporation, as reprinted in Ricky E. Griffin and Ronald J. Ebert, *Business* (Englewood Cliffs, NJ: Prentice Hall, 1989), pp. 578–9. For more discussion, see Shelby D. Hunt, Van R. Wood and Lawrence B. Chonko, 'Corporate ethical values and organizational commitment in marketing', *Journal of Marketing* (July 1989), pp. 79–90.

23. For more discussion on how businesses can contribute to society's well-being and enhance living standards, see 'Business in the community: annual report 1997', *Financial Times* (4 December 1997).

Case 2

Nestlé: Singled Out Again and Again

'during the first few months, the mother's milk will always be the most natural nutriment, and every mother able to do so, should herself suckle her children.'

Henri Nestlé, 1869

In July 1994 the corporate affairs department at Nestlé UK's headquarters in Croydon were bracing themselves for another burst of adverse publicity. At the forthcoming General Synod of the Church of England to take place at York University, an Oxford diocesan motion would call for a continued ban on Nescafé by the Church. They also wanted the Church Commissioners to disinvest their £1.1 million in Nestlé. The Church's much publicized boycott of Nescafé first occurred, amid much ridicule, in 1991, as a protest against the use of breast milk substitutes in the Third World countries. In the aftermath of the 1991 vote, Nescafé claimed that its sales increased, although many churchgoers said they stopped using the brand-leading coffee. The 1994 protest would be one of many the company had faced from activist protesters in the last 20 years although, according to Nestlé, the protesters' complaints had no foundation.

Nestlé SA, whose headquarters are in Vevey, Switzerland, is the world's largest food company, with annual worldwide sales of SFr57.5 billion. The company produces in 494 factories operating in 69 countries. Numerous Nestlé brands are quite familiar: Nestlé's chocolates, Nesquik, Nescafé, Crosse & Blackwell, Libby, Perrier, Friskies and many others. Over 100 years ago Henri Nestlé invented manufactured baby food 'to save a child's life' and the company have been suppliers ever since. Then, in the late 1970s and early 1980s, Nestlé came under heavy fire from health professionals, who charged the company with encouraging Third World mothers to give up breast feeding and use a company-prepared formula. In 1974 the British charity, War on Want, published a pamphlet, *The Baby Killer*, that criticized Unigate and Nestlé's ill-advised marketing efforts in Africa. While War on Want criticized the entire infant formula industry, the German-based Third World Action Group issued a German 'translation' of the original pamphlet retitled *Nestlé Kills Babies*, which singled out Nestlé for 'unethical and immoral behaviour'. The pamphlets generated much publicity – the general public became both aware and concerned about the issue. Enraged at the protest, Nestlé sued the activists for defamation. The two-year case kept media attention on the issue. 'We won the legal case, but it was a public-relations disaster,' commented a Nestlé executive.

In 1977, two American social-interest groups, the Interfaith Center on Corporate Responsibility and the Infant Formula Action Coalition (INFACT), spearheaded a worldwide boycott against Nestlé. The campaign continued despite the fact that many organizations rejected the boycott. The US United

Methodist Church concluded that the activists were guilty of 'substantial and sometimes gross misrepresentation', of 'inflammatory rhetoric', and of using 'wildly exaggerated figures'. The boycott was called off in 1984 when the activists accepted that the company was complying with an infant formula marketing code adopted by the World Health Organization (WHO). Since then, church, university, local government and other action groups periodically rediscover the controversy and create publicity by calling for a boycott.

In 1991 the main accusation was the use of sophisticated promotional techniques to persuade hundreds of thousands of poverty-stricken, poorly educated mothers that formula feeding was better for their children. One issue predominated: the donation of free or low-cost supplies of infant formula to maternity wards and hospitals in developing countries. Formula feeding is not usually a wise practice in such countries. Because of poor living conditions and habits, people cannot or do not clean bottles properly and often mix formula with impure water. Furthermore, income level does not permit many families to buy sufficient quantities of formula. Protesters particularly hit out at several industry practices, keeping Nestlé as their target:

● Promotional baby booklets ignoring or de-emphasizing breast feeding.

● Misleading advertising encouraging mothers to bottle feed their babies and showing breast feeding to be old-fashioned and inconvenient.

● Gifts and samples inducing mothers to bottle feed their infants.

● Posters and pamphlets in hospitals.

● Endorsements of bottle feeding by milk nurses.

● Formula so expensive that poor customers dilute to non-nutritious levels.

The WHO code eliminates all promotional efforts, requiring companies to serve primarily as passive 'order takers'. It prohibits advertising, samples and direct contact with consumers. Contacts with professionals (such as doctors) occur only if professionals seek such contact. Manufacturers can package products with some form of visual corporate identity, but they cannot picture babies. The WHO code effectively allows almost no marketing. However, the code contains only *recommended* guidelines. They become *mandatory* only if individual governments adopt national codes through their own regulatory mechanisms.

WHO allows the donation of free or low-cost supplies of infant formulas for infants who cannot be breast-fed. However, because of protests the International Association of Infant Food Manufacturers (IFM) is working with WHO and UNICEF to secure country-by-country agreements with countries to end free and low-cost supplies. By the end of 1994, only one small developing country had not agreed to the change.

Nestlé itself has a policy on low-cost supplies in developing countries, as follows:

● Where there is government agreement, Nestlé will strictly apply the terms of that agreement.

● Where there is no agreement Nestlé, in co-operation with others, will be active in trying to secure early government action.

● Where other companies break an agreement, Nestlé will work with IFM and governments to stop the breach.

● Nestlé will take disciplinary measures against any Nestlé personnel or distributors who deliberately violate Nestlé policy.

Nestlé continues to sell infant formula and display the Nestlé name on almost all its brands. This contrasts with some companies using furtive branding to hide common ownership. Given the repeated public relations problems that Nestlé faces, why does it not take unilateral action in ending free supplies? Since the Third World infant formula market is so small compared with Nestlé's worldwide interests, why bother with it? Part of the answer is in Henri Nestlé's desire 'to save a child's life'. The European Commission's directive on baby food concludes that infant formula is 'the only processed foodstuff that wholly satisfies the nutritional requirements of infants' first four to six months of life'.

Few mothers in countries with very high infant mortality rates use anything other than breast milk. However, Kenya is probably typical of what happens when mothers do supplement breast milk with something else:

- 33 per cent use uji, a local food made from maize.
- 33 per cent use cow's milk.
- 28 per cent use water.
- 14 per cent use glucose.
- 11 per cent use milk powder, of which some is infant formula.
- 3 per cent use tea.

A study in the Ivory Coast shows the sort of problems that arise when Nestlé withdraws unilaterally. Other companies replaced the supplies to the affluent private nurseries, but supplies for mothers in need collapsed. As a result, two premature babies fed on ordinary powdered milk did not survive, and the main hospital was not able to 'afford to buy enough to feed abandoned babies or those whose mothers are ill'.

QUESTIONS

1. Was and is Nestlé's and the other IFM members' marketing of infant formula 'unethical and immoral'?

2. Is it the case that ethical standards should be the responsibility of organizations such as WHO and UNESCO, and that the sole responsibility of firms is to work within the bounds set?

3. Is Nestlé just unlucky or did its actions precipitate its being singled out by activists? Is the activists' focus on Nestlé unjust and itself dangerous? What accounts for Nestlé's continuing in the infant formula market despite the protests?

4. Did Nestlé benefit from confronting the activists directly in court and winning? Should firms ever confront activists directly? What other forms of action are available to the company? Should firms withdraw from legitimate markets because of the justified or unjustified actions of pressure groups?

5. The WHO code is a recommendation to government. Is it Nestlé's responsibility to operate according to the national legislation of any given country, or to follow WHO's recommendations to that country? Do international bodies setting international standards, such as WHO and UNICEF, have a moral responsibility to make those standards clearly understood by all parties and to demand action by national governments to enact them?

6. How should Nestlé respond to the threats from the General Synod in 1994? Since Nestlé claimed sales increased after the Nescafé boycott in 1991, should they just ignore the problem?

SOURCES: 'A boycott over infant formula', *Business Week* (23 April 1979), pp. 137–40; John Sparks, 'The Nestlé controversy – anatomy of a boycott', Public Policy Education Fund, Inc. (June 1981); 'Infant formula protest teaches Nestlé a tactical lesson', *Marketing News* (10 June 1983), p. 1; Robert F. Hartley, *Marketing Mistakes* (Chichester, UK: Wiley, 1986); European Commission, Commission Directive on Infant Formula and Follow-on Formula, 91/321/EEC; The Associated Press, Abidjan, Ivory Coast (16 April 1991); UNICEF, *The State of the World's Children* (1992); RBL, *Survey of Baby Feeding in Kenya* (1992); Philip Kotler and Gary Armstrong, 'Nestlé: under fire again', in id. *Principles of Marketing* (London: Prentice Hall, 1994); Nestlé, *Nestlé and Baby Milk* (1994); Andrew Brown, 'Synod votes to end Nestlé boycott after passionate debate', *Independent* (12 July 1994), 'Church boycott of Nescafé ends', *The Times* (12 July 1994); Damion Thompson, 'Synod rejects disestablishment move', *Daily Telegraph* (12 July 1994); 'Clear conscience for Nescafé drinkers', *Church Times* (17 July 1994); Sylvie Laforet and John Saunders, 'The management of brand portfolios: how the pros do it', *Journal of Advertising Research* (September–October 1994), pp. 64–76.

3

Strategic Marketing Planning

CHAPTER OBJECTIVES

After reading this chapter, you should be able to:

- Explain company-wide strategic planning and its principal steps.
- Describe how companies develop mission statements and objectives.
- Explain how companies evaluate and develop their business portfolios.
- Explain marketing's role in strategic planning.
- Describe the marketing management process and the brand plan.
- Show how marketing organizations are changing.

Preview Case

Levi's Strategic Marketing and Planning

Bavarian immigrant to America, Levi-Strauss, carted a load of heavy fabric to California to make tents during the gold rush. He found that the gold seekers needed trousers more than tents, so he used the fabric to make canvas trousers. His blue jeans are now a worldwide institution. Levi-Strauss & Co. still dominates the jeans industry. From the 1950s to the 1970s, as the baby boom caused an explosion in the number of young people, Levi-Strauss & Co. and other jeans makers experienced heady 10–15 per cent annual sales growth, with little or no strategic or marketing planning effort. Selling jeans was easy – Levi concentrated on simply trying to make enough jeans to satisfy a seemingly insatiable market. However, by the early 1980s, demographics had caught up with the jeans industry. Its best customers, the

baby-boomers, were ageing, and their tastes were changing with their waist-lines – they bought fewer jeans and wore them longer. Meanwhile, the 18- to 24-year-old segment, the group traditionally most likely to buy jeans, was shrinking. Thus Levi found itself fighting for share in a fading jeans market.

At first, despite the declining market, Levi-Strauss & Co. stuck closely to its basic jeans business. It sought growth through mass-marketing strategies, substantially increasing its advertising and selling through mass retailers like Sears and J.C. Penney. When these tactics failed and profits continued to plummet, Levi tried diversification into faster-growing fashion and speciality apparel businesses. It hastily added more than 75 new lines, including Ralph Lauren's Polo line (high fashion); the David Hunter line (classic men's sportswear); the Perry Ellis Collection (men's, women's and children's casual sportswear); Tourage SSE (fashionable men's wear); Frank Shorter Sportswear (athletic wear); and many others. By 1984 Levi had diversified into a muddled array of businesses ranging from its true blue jeans to men's hats, ski-wear and even denim maternity wear. As one analyst reported at the time in *Inc.* magazine:

> For years, Levi prospered with one strategy: chase the demand for blue jeans. Then came the designer jeans craze – and Levi became unstitched. The company diversified into fashion. It slapped its famous name on everything from running suits to women's polyester pants. The results were disastrous: profits collapsed by 79 per cent last year, and the company slashed about 5,000 jobs.

In 1985, in an effort to turn around an ailing Levi-Strauss & Co., new management implemented a bold new strategic plan, beginning with a drastic reorganization. It sold most of the ill-fated fashion and speciality apparel businesses and took the company back to what it had always done best – making and selling jeans. For starters, Levi rejuvenated its flagship product, the classic button-fly, shrink-to-fit 501 jeans. It invested $38 million in the now-classic 501 blues' advertising campaign, a series of hip, documentary-style reality ads. Never before had a company spent so much on a single item of clothing. At the time, many analysts questioned this strategy. As one put it: 'That's just too much to spend on one lousy pair of jeans.' However, the 501 blues campaign spoke for all of the company's products. It reminded consumers of Levi's strong tradition and refocused the company on its basic, blue jeans heritage. During the next six years, the campaign would more than double the sales of 501s.

Building on this solid-blue base, Levi began to add new products. For example, it successfully added prewashed, stonewashed and brightly coloured jeans to its basic line. In late 1986, Levi introduced Dockers, casual and comfortable cotton trousers targeted at the ageing male baby-boomers. A natural extension of the jeans business, the new line had even broader appeal than anticipated. Not only did adults buy Dockers, so did their children. In the few years since its introduction, the Dockers line has become a $1 billion-a-year success. Levi's has continued to develop new products for the ageing boomers. In 1992 it introduced 550 and 560 loose-fitting jeans – 'a loose interpretation of the original' – for men who have outgrown the company's slimmer-cut 501s.

In addition to introducing new products, Levi-Strauss & Co. also stepped up its efforts to develop new markets. In 1991, for example, it developed jeans designed especially for women and launched an innovative five-month, $12 million 'Jeans for Women' advertising campaign, featuring renderings of the female form in blue jeans by four female artists.

But Levi's most dramatic turnaround has been in its international markets. In 1985 Levi almost sold its then stumbling and unprofitable foreign operations. Since then, however, the company has turned what was a patchwork of foreign licensees into a well-co-ordinated team of worldwide subsidiaries. Levi is now a truly global apparel maker. Its strategy is to 'think globally, act locally'. It operates a closely co-ordinated worldwide marketing, manufacturing and distribution system. Twice a year, Levi brings together managers from around the world to share product and advertising ideas, and to search for those that have global appeal. For example, the Dockers line originated in Argentina, but has now become a worldwide best seller. However, within its global strategy, Levi encourages local units to tailor products and programmes to their home markets. For example, in Brazil, it developed the Feminina line of curvaceously cut jeans that provide the ultratight fit that Brazilian women favour. Levi's European Docker division now plans to conquer Europe from its Swedish base. In doing so it has created the world's biggest advertisement, a 480 square metre banner hung on Stockholm's up-market NK department store.

In most markets abroad, Levi-Strauss & Co. boldly plays up its deep American roots. For example, James Dean is a central figure in almost all Levi advertising in Japan. Indonesian ads show Levi-clad teenagers driving around Dubuque, Iowa, in 1960s convertibles. And almost all foreign ads feature English-language dialogue. However, whereas Americans usually think of their Levis as basic knockaround wear, most European and Asian consumers view them as up-market fashion statements. The prices match the snob appeal – a pair of Levi 501 jeans selling for $30 in the United States costs $63 in Tokyo and $88 in Paris, creating lush profit margins.

Levi's aggressive and innovative global marketing efforts have produced stunning results. As the domestic market continues to shrink, foreign sales have accounted for most of Levi's growth. Overseas markets now yield 39 per cent of the company's total revenues and 60 per cent of its profits. Perhaps more impressive, its foreign business is growing at 32 per cent per year, five times the growth rate of its domestic business. Levi continues to look for new international market opportunities. For example, the first Romanian shop officially to sell Levi's jeans recently opened to large crowds, and Levi is now racing competitors to reach jeans-starved consumers in eastern Europe and the former Soviet republics. Dramatic strategic and marketing planning actions have transformed Levi-Strauss into a vigorous and profitable company, one better matched to its changing market opportunities. Since its 1985 turnaround, Levi's sales have grown more than 31 per cent and its profits have increased fivefold. Thus, by building a strong base in its core jeans business, coupled with well-planned product and market development, Levi has found ways to grow profitably despite the decline in the domestic jeans market. As one company observer suggests, Levi has learned that 'with the right mix of persistence and smarts, [planning new products and] cracking new markets can seem as effortless as breaking in a new pair of Levi's stonewashed jeans'.[1]

QUESTIONS

1. What stimulated Levi to diversify away from its homeland in the American blue jeans market?

2. With its focus on the global blue jeans market, is Levi likely to face the same pressure for diversification again?

3. Conduct a SWOT (strengths, weaknesses, opportunities and threats) analysis of Levi and comment upon its implications for the company.

4. Use the 'product/market expansion grid' to plot the moves made by Levi during the case. In which quadrants was Levi least successful and why? In which was it most successful and why?

5. Suggest a 'mission statement' for Levi that would help the company focus on its strengths.

6. Considering Levi's international subsidiaries as 'strategic business units', what do you imagine Levi's 'BCG growth-share matrix' to look like? What global strategies does the matrix suggest?

Introduction

All companies need strategies to meet changing markets. No one strategy is best for all companies. Each company must find the way that makes most sense, given its situation, opportunities, objectives and resources. Marketing plays an important role in strategic planning. It provides information and other inputs to help prepare the strategic plan. Strategic planning is also the first stage of marketing planning and defines marketing's role in the organization. The strategic plan guides marketing, which must work with other departments in the organization to achieve strategic objectives.

Here we look at the three stages of strategic market planning: first, the strategic plan and its implications for marketing; secondly, the marketing process; and thirdly, ways of putting the plan into action.

Strategic Planning

Overview of Planning

Many companies operate without formal plans. In new companies, managers are sometimes too busy for planning. In small companies, managers may think that only large corporations need planning. In mature companies, many managers argue that they have done well without formal planning, so it cannot be very important. They may resist taking the time to prepare a written plan. They may argue that the marketplace changes too fast for a plan to be useful – that it would end up collecting dust.[2]

Yet formal planning can yield many benefits for all types of company, large and small, new and mature. It encourages systematic thinking. It forces the company to sharpen its objectives and policies, leads to better co-ordination of company efforts, and provides clearer performance standards for control. The argument that planning is less useful in a fast-changing environment makes little sense. The opposite is true: sound planning helps the company to anticipate and respond quickly to environmental changes, and to prepare better for sudden developments. The best-performing companies plan, but plan in a way that does not suppress entrepreneurship.[3]

Companies usually prepare annual plans, long-range plans and strategic plans:

- The **annual plan** is a short-term plan that describes the current situation, company objectives, the strategy for the year, the action programme, budgets and controls.

- The **long-range plan** describes the primary factors and forces affecting the organization during the next several years. It includes the long-term objectives, the main marketing strategies used to attain them and the resources required. This long-range plan is reviewed and updated each year so that the company always has a current long-range plan. The company's annual and long-range plans deal with current businesses and how to keep them going.

- The **strategic plan** involves adapting the firm to take advantage of opportunities in its constantly changing environment. It is the process of developing and maintaining a strategic fit between the organization's goals and capabilities and its changing marketing opportunities.

Strategic planning sets the stage for the marketing plan. It starts with its overall purpose and mission. These guide the formation of measurable corporate objectives. A corporate audit then gathers information on the company, its competitors, its market and the general environment in which the firm competes. A SWOT analysis gives a summary of the strengths and weaknesses of the company together with the opportunities and threats it faces. Next, headquarters decides what portfolio of businesses and products is best for the company and how much support to give each one. This helps to provide the strategic objectives that guide the company's various activities. Then each business and product unit develops detailed marketing and other functional plans to support the company-wide plan. Thus marketing planning occurs at the business-unit, product and market levels. It supports company strategic planning with more detailed planning for specific marketing opportunities. For instance Nestlé, the world's largest

annual plan
A short-term plan that describes the company's current situation, its objectives, the strategy, action programme and budgets for the year ahead and controls.

long-range plan
A plan that describes the principal factors and forces affecting the organization during the next several years, including long-term objectives, the chief marketing strategies used to attain them and the resources required.

strategic plan
A plan that describes how a firm will adapt to take advantage of opportunities in its constantly changing environment, thereby maintaining a strategic fit between the firm's goals and capabilities and its changing market opportunities.

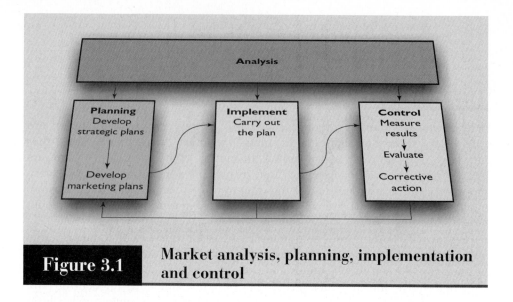

Figure 3.1 **Market analysis, planning, implementation and control**

food manufacturer, develops an overall strategic plan at its headquarters in Vevey, Switzerland. Below that, each strategic group, such as confectionery, develops subordinate strategic plans. These feed into the strategic plan's national operations. At each level, marketing and other functional plans will exist. At the final level, brand plans cover the marketing of brands such as Kit Kat, Lion and Quality Street in national markets.

The Planning Process

Putting plans into action involves four stages: analysis, planning, implementation and control. Figure 3.1 shows the relationship between these functions that are common to strategic planning, marketing planning or the planning for any other function.

ANALYSIS. Planning begins with a complete analysis of the company's situation. The company must analyse its environment to find attractive opportunities and to avoid environmental threats. It must analyze company strengths and weaknesses, as well as current and possible marketing actions, to determine which opportunities it can best pursue. Analysis feeds information and other inputs to each of the other stages.

PLANNING. Through strategic planning, the company decides what it wants to do with each business unit. Marketing planning involves deciding marketing strategies that will help the company attain its overall strategic objectives. Marketing, product or brand plans are at the centre of this.

IMPLEMENTATION Implementation turns strategic plans into actions that will achieve the company's objectives. People in the organization that work with others both inside and outside the company implement marketing plans.

CONTROL. Control consists of measuring and evaluating the results of plans and activities, and taking corrective action to make sure objectives are being achieved. Analysis provides information and evaluations needed for all the other activities.

The Strategic Plan

The strategic plan contains several components: the mission, the strategic objectives, the strategic audit, SWOT analysis, portfolio analysis, objectives and strategies. All of these feed from and feed into marketing plans.

The Mission

A mission states the purpose of a company. Firms often start with a clear mission held within the mind of their founder. Then, over time, the mission fades as the company acquires new products and markets. A mission may be clear, but forgotten by some managers. An extreme case of this was the Anglican Church Commissioners, who thought they had the 'Midas touch' when they started speculating on the international property market. They found out that markets go down as well as up and lost a third of the Church's ancient wealth in the process. Other problems can occur when the mission may remain clear, but no longer fits the environment. The Levi preview shows that company struggling with this problem.

When an organization is drifting, the management must renew its search for purpose. It must ask: What business are we in? What do consumers value? What are we in business for? What sort of business are we? What makes us special? These simple-sounding questions are among the most difficult that the company will ever have to answer. Successful companies continuously raise these questions and answer them. Asking such basic questions is a sign of strength, not uncertainty.

Company mission: 3M states its mission not as making office products, but as creating innovations that 'make your work – make your life – simpler, more efficient, more productive.'

mission statement
A statement of the organizations purpose – what it wants to accomplish in the wider environment.

Many organizations develop formal mission statements that answer these questions. A **mission statement** is a statement of the organization's purpose – what it wants to accomplish in the larger environment. A clear mission statement acts as an 'invisible hand' that guides people in the organization, so that they can work independently and yet collectively towards overall organizational goals.

Traditionally, companies have defined their business in product terms ('we manufacture furniture'), or in technological terms ('we are a chemical-processing firm'). But mission statements should be *market-oriented*.

WHAT BUSINESS ARE WE IN? Asking this question helps. Market definitions of a business are better than product or technological definitions. Products and technologies eventually become outdated, but basic market needs may last for ever. A market-oriented mission statement defines the business based on satisfying basic customer needs. Thus Rolls-Royce is in the power business, not the aero-engine business. Visa's business is not credit cards, but allowing customers to exchange value – to exchange assets, such as cash on deposit or equity in a home, for virtually anything, anywhere in the world. Creative 3M does more than just make adhesives, scientific equipment and healthcare products; it solves people's problems by putting innovation to work for them.

WHO ARE OUR CUSTOMERS? This is a probing question. Who are the customers of Rolls-Royce's new Trent aero-engine? At one level it is the airframers, like Boeing and European Airbus. If Rolls-Royce can get an airframer to launch a new aircraft with a Rolls-Royce engine, this saves development costs and makes early orders likely. Is it the airline or leasing companies that eventually buy the engines? They will certainly have to sell to them as well. Is it the pilot, the service crew or even the passenger? Unlike the competition, Rolls-Royce has a brand name that is synonymous with prestige and luxury.

WHAT ARE WE IN BUSINESS FOR? This is a hard question for non-profit-making organizations. Do universities exist to educate students or to train them for industry? Is the pursuit of knowledge by the faculty the main reason for their existence? If so, is good research of economic value or is pure research better?

WHAT SORT OF BUSINESS ARE WE? This question guides the strategy and structure of organizations. Companies aiming at *cost leadership* seek efficiency. These firms, like Aldi or KwikSave, run simple, efficient organizations with careful cost control. These contrast with *differentiators*, like Sony, who aim to make profits by inventing products, such as the Walkman, whose uniqueness gives a competitive edge. *Focused* companies concentrate upon being the best at serving a well-defined target market. They succeed by tailoring their products or services to customers they know well. In Britain, Coutts & Co., a National Westminster Bank subsidiary, does this by providing 'personal banking' to the very wealthy. Michael Porter[4] describes a fourth option that occurs if firms do not define how they are to do business: *stuck in the middle*.

Management should avoid making its mission too narrow or too broad. A lead-pencil manufacturer that says it is in the communication equipment business is stating its mission too broadly. A mission should be:

● *Realistic.* Singapore International Airlines is excellent, but it would be deluding itself if its mission were to become the world's largest airline.

● *Specific.* It should fit the company and no other. Many mission statements exist for public-relations purposes, so lack specific, workable guidelines. The statement 'We want to become the leading company in this industry by producing the highest-quality products with the best service at the lowest prices' sounds good, but it is full of generalities and contradictions. Such motherhood statements will not help the company make tough decisions.

● Based on *distinctive competences*. Bang & Olufsen has the technology to build microcomputers, but an entry into that market would not take advantage of its core competences in style, hi-fi and exclusive distribution.

● *Motivating*. It should give people something to believe in. It should get a 'Yeah!', not a yawn or a 'Yuck!'. A company's mission should not say 'making more sales or profits' – profits are only a reward for undertaking a useful activity. A company's employees need to feel that their work is significant and that it contributes to people's lives. Contrast the missions of the two computer giants IBM and Apple. When IBM sales were $50 billion, president John Akers said that IBM's goal was to become a $100 billion company by the end of the century. Meanwhile, Apple's long-term goal has been to put computer power into the hands of every person. Apple's mission is much more motivating than IBM's.

Visions guide the best missions. A vision is a contagious dream, a widely communicated statement or slogan that captures the needs of the time. Sony's

Marketing Highlight 3.1

Eastman Kodak Asks: 'What Business Are We In?'

Eastman Kodak is one of many firms now asking: 'What business are we in?' It is one of many companies that diversified in the 1980s. Originally a photographic products company, it entered the attractive pharmaceuticals and consumer healthcare industry by acquisition and alliances. Then, in the late 1980s, tough competition and tight economic conditions saw its fortunes decline. Its debt burden went up and its imaging business lacked money for investment. Like IBM, the company was a troubled giant.

In early 1994 George Fisher, the company's new chair, launched a new plan that would take Kodak back to its imaging roots. George Eastman had started the company in 1880 and it had grown to be the world's biggest photographic company using silver-halide technology. This time the proposed technology was digital imaging – a business that was a small fraction of current sales and a loss maker. Silver-halide offered little opportunity for development, but digital imaging was on track for the much discussed 'information highway'. It offers the chance to take images from any source, manipulate them electronically, store them digitally (on PCs or CDs), transmit them, and display them on everything from photographic paper to TVs.

Kodak wanted to sell its pharmaceuticals and consumer health-care divisions and reinvest the proceeds in its imaging business. The move would also lighten the group's $7 billion debt. Three divisions went up for sale: Stirling Winthrop (drugs and consumer health care), L & F products (personal care and household products), and the Clinical Diagnostics division. The sales raised $16.4 billion, almost a quarter of Kodak's 1993 revenue.

After the sale, Kodak was left with its imaging business and Health Sciences division. Health Sciences' X-ray film and electronic diagnostics businesses were central to Kodak's imaging strategy. Steps would be taken to protect and develop Kodak's traditional film products and especially its position in the rapidly developing market for digital electronic imaging, where its technology was the standard in multimedia applications.

Kodak is already coming under increasing pressure in the conventional silver-halide-based photographic markets. People in the developed world are buying more and better cameras, but not more films. Fuji is competing hard on price, and own-label films are undercutting Kodak's prices by 40 per cent. Unlike many market leaders, Kodak has joined the price cutters and launched Funtime, priced 20 per cent lower than Kodak Gold. New markets in the East are growing fast, but these are very price sensitive and bootlegging abounds.

The move into digital imaging is a gamble. So far Kodak has little to show for the millions of dollars it has invested in digital-imaging technology. Its Photo-CD system, which uses CDs to store images, was a flop in the consumer market. Only a few hundred were sold in 1993. Kodak's digital camera also has problems: the black-and-white model costs over $8,000 and produces poorer pictures than a 35 mm camera.

Joint ventures make Kodak's prospects look better. A new digital camera from Apple Computer, using Kodak technology, may be on the market soon. It will cost a tenth of Kodak's product. Microsoft and Silicon Graphics are already using Kodak's digital-imaging technology. Fisher says he is talking to several potential part-ners about longer-term ventures: 'We have to work with companies that are much stronger in software and telecoms than we are.' With these ventures, the digital-imaging group expects to move into profit in two to three years. Will it? The 'electronic highways' to carry the digital pictures of little Jimmy do not exist yet. Also, there is still a price and quality gulf between silver-halide and digital imaging. The gap will eventually narrow, but expect it to close only slowly. Whenever a new technology takes on an old one, competition usually finds ways of squeezing unexpected performance out of the old dog.

Kodak missed out on video technology by concentrating on conventional films. It dominated the 16 mm-video film market that almost disappeared overnight when video cameras arrived. Its effort in digital imaging recognizes that its business is imaging, not silver-halide film.

SOURCES: Patrick Harveson, 'Eastman Kodak prepare for a new image', *Financial Times* (4 May 1993), p. 29; Patrick Harveson, 'Kodak to return to core with drug sale', *Financial Times* (4 May 1994), p. 23; Chris Butler and Tony Patey, 'Drug firms on the trail of US partners', *The European* (6–12 May 1994), p. 15; 'Picture imperfect', *The Economist* (28 May 1994), pp. 87–8.

president, Akio Morita, wanted everyone to have access to 'personal portable sound', and his company created the Walkman. Richard Branson thought 'flying should be fun', so he founded Virgin Airlines. Thomas Monaghan wanted to deliver hot pizza to any home within 30 minutes, and he created Domino's Pizza.

The company's mission statement should provide a vision and direction for the company for the next 10–20 years. They do not change every few years in response to each new turn in the environment. Still, a company must redefine its mission if that mission has lost credibility or no longer defines an optimal course for the company.[5] Marketing Highlight 3.1 describes how recent events have caused Eastman Kodak to think carefully about its mission. The hostile environment in the early 1990s caused Siemens, the German electronic giant, to review its strategy. Its seven core statements (Figure 3.2) provided strong communications and drove its strategy, structure and style of management.

From Mission to Strategic Objectives

The company's mission needs to be turned into strategic objectives to guide management. Each manager should have objectives and be responsible for reaching them. For example, its fertilizer business unit is one of International

Strategy	Competitive strength	Achieve a sustained leading position worldwide
Identity	Progress	Technological, social and marketing competences focused on progress
Entrepreneurial style	Will to lead	Agree on clear objectives and vigorously transform them into competitive advantage
Managers	Entrepreneurship	Managers and employees think and act as if it were their own company
Executive decision making	Speed	Faster decision making through integrated business functions
New organization	Close to the customer	Marketing-oriented business functions create entrepreneurial freedom
Strength	Systems integration	Integrate competitive products into problem-solving systems

Figure 3.2   Siemens' seven core statements

Minerals & Chemical Corporation's many activities. The fertilizer division does not say that its mission is to produce fertilizer. Instead, it says that its mission is to 'increase agricultural productivity'. This mission leads to a hierarchy of objectives, including business objectives and marketing objectives. The mission of increasing agricultural productivity leads to the company's business objective of researching new fertilizers that promise higher yields. Unfortunately, research is expensive and requires improved profits to plough back into research programmes. So improving profits becomes another key business objective. Profits are improved by increasing sales or reducing costs. Sales increase by improving the company's share of the domestic market, or by entering new foreign markets, or both. These goals then become the company's current marketing objectives. The objective to 'increase our market share' is not as useful as the objective to 'increase our market share to 15 per cent in two years'. The mission states the philosophy and direction of a company, whereas the strategic objectives are measurable goals.

Strategic Audit

'Knowledge is power': so stated Francis Bacon, the sixteenth-century philosopher, while according to the ancient Chinese strategist Sun Zi, 'The leader who does not want to buy information is inconsiderate and can never win.' The strategic audit covers the gathering of this vital information. It is the intelligence used to build the detailed objectives and strategy of a business. It has two parts: the external and internal audit.

Financial Statements: Are We Making Money?

Marketing Highlight 3.2

Table 1 shows the 1995 operating statement for a speciality store, Dale Parsons Men's Wear. This statement is for a retailer; the operating statement for a manufacturer would be somewhat different. Specifically, the section on purchases within the 'Cost of goods sold' area would be replaced by 'Cost of goods manufactured'.

The outline of the operating statement follows a logical series of steps to arrive at the firm's $25,000 net profit figure:

Net sales	$300,000
Cost of goods sold	−175,000
Gross margin	$125,000
Expenses	−100,000
Net profit	$25,000

The first part details the amount that Parsons received for the goods sold during the year. The sales figures consist of three items: gross sales, returns or allowances, and net sales. *Gross sales* is the total amount charged to customers during the year for merchandise purchased in Parsons' store. Some customers returned merchandise. If the customer gets a full refund or full credit on another purchase, we call this a return. Other customers may decide to keep the item if Parsons will reduce the price. This is called an allowance. By subtracting returns and allowances from gross sales:

Gross sales	$325,000
Returns and allowances	−25,000
Net sales	$300,000

The second part of the operating statement calculates the amount of sales revenue that Dale Parsons retains after paying the costs of the merchandise. We start with the inventory in the store at the beginning of the year. During the year, Parsons bought $150,000 worth of suits, slacks,

TABLE 1 OPERATING STATEMENT FOR DALE PARSONS MEN'S WEAR FOR YEAR ENDING 31 DECEMBER 1995 ($)

Gross sales			325,000
less: Sales returns and allowances			25,000
Net sales			300,000
Cost of goods sold			
Beginning inventory, 1 January 1995, at cost		60,000	
Purchases	150,000		
plus: Freight-in	10,000		
Net cost of delivered purchases		160,000	
Cost of goods available for sale		220,000	
less: Ending inventory, 31 December 1995, at cost		45,000	
Total cost of goods sold			175,000
Gross margin			125,000
Expenses			
Selling expenses:		50,000	
Administrative expenses:		30,000	
General expenses:		20,000	
Total expenses			100,000
Net profit			25,000

shirts, ties, jeans and other goods. Because the store is located away from regular shipping routes, Parsons had to pay an additional $10,000 to get the products delivered, giving the firm a net cost of $160,000. Adding the beginning inventory, the cost of goods available for sale amounted to $220,000. The $45,000 ending inventory of clothes in the store on 31 December is then subtracted to come up with the $175,000 *cost of goods sold*.

The difference between what Parsons paid for the merchandise ($175,000) and what he sold it for ($300,000) is called the *gross margin* ($125,000).

In order to show the profit Parsons 'cleared' at the end of the year, we must subtract from the gross margin the expenses incurred while doing business. *Selling expenses* included two sales employees, local newspaper and radio advertising, and the cost of delivering merchandise to customers after alterations. Selling expenses totalled $50,000 for the year. *Administrative expenses* included the salary for an office manager, office supplies such as stationery and business cards, and miscellaneous expenses including an administrative audit conducted by an outside consultant. Administrative expenses totalled $30,000 in 1995. Finally, the *general expenses* of rent, utilities, insurance, and depreciation came to $20,000. Total expenses were therefore $100,000 for the year. By subtracting expenses ($100,000) from the gross margin ($125,000), we arrive at the *net profit* of $25,000 for Parsons during 1995.

The **external audit** or marketing environment audit examines the macroenvironment and task environment of a company. EuroDisney's problems can be partly explained by an excessive faith in company strengths and too little attention being paid to the macroenvironment. French labour costs make the park much more expensive than in America, Europe's high travel costs add to guests' total bill and the north European climate takes the edge off all-year-round operations. EuroDisney contrasts with the success of Center Parcs. This Dutch company's resort hotels offer north Europeans undercover health and leisure facilities that they can enjoy all year round.

The **internal audit** examines all aspects of the company. It covers the whole *value chain* described by Michael Porter.[6] It includes the primary activities that follow the flow of goods or services through the organization: inbound logistics, operations, outbound logistics, sales and marketing, and after-sales services. In addition, it extends to the support activities on which the primary activities depend: procurement, technology development, human resource management and the infrastructure of the firm. These go beyond traditional marketing activities, but marketing strategy depends on all of them. A key to the Italian Benetton's international success is a system that allows it to change styles and colours rapidly. Unlike traditional mass-clothing manufacturers, which have to order fabrics in colours and patterns over a year ahead of seasons, Benetton's design and manufacturing technology allows it to change within a season. Long before the idea of close supplier relationships was re-imported from Japan, Marks & Spencer and C & A made supplier relations and human resource management central strategies.

Reading financial statements is basic to understanding the state of a company and seeing how it is developing. The operating statement and the balance sheet are the two main financial statements used. The **balance sheet** shows the assets, liabilities and net worth of a company at a given time. The **operating statement** (also called profit-and-loss statement or income statement) is the more important of the two for marketing information. It shows company sales, cost of goods sold, and expenses during a specified time period. By comparing the operating statement from one time period to the next, the firm can spot favourable or

external audit
A detailed examination of the markets, competition, business and economic environment in which the organization operates.

internal audit
An evaluation of the firm's entire value chain.

balance sheet
A financial statement that shows assets, liabilities and net worth of a company at a given time.

operating statement
(profit-and-loss statement or income statement)
A financial statement that shows company sales, cost of goods sold and expenses during a given period of time.

unfavourable trends and take appropriate action. Marketing Highlight 3.2 describes these statements in more detail and explains their construction.

SWOT Analysis

SWOT analysis
A distillation of the findings of the internal and external audit which draws attention to the critical organizational strengths and weaknesses and the opportunities and threats facing the company.

SWOT analysis draws the critical strengths, weaknesses, opportunities and threats (SWOT) from the strategic audit. The audit contains a wealth of data of differing importance and reliability. SWOT analysis distils these data to show the critical items from the internal and external audit. The number of items is small for forceful communications, and they show where a business should focus its attention.

● *Opportunities and Threats*

Managers need to identify the main threats and opportunities that their company faces. The purpose of the analysis is to make the manager anticipate important developments that can have an impact on the firm. A large pet food division of a multinational company could list the following.

Opportunities:
● *Economic climate*. Because of improved economic conditions, pet ownership is increasing in almost all segments of the population.
● *Demographic changes*. (1) Increasing single parenthood, dual-income families and ageing will increase the trend towards convenient pet foods (from wet to dry); and (2) the aged population will grow and increasingly keep pets as company.
● *Market*. The pet food market will follow the human market in the concern for healthy eating and pre-prepared luxury foods.
● *Technology*. New forms of pet food that are low in fat and calories, yet highly nutritious and tasty, will soon emerge. These products will appeal strongly to many of today's pet food buyers, whose health concerns extend to their pets.

Threats:
● *Competitive activity*. A large competitor has just announced that it will introduce a new premium pet food line, backed by a huge advertising and sales promotion blitz.
● *Channel pressure*. Industry analysts predict that supermarket chain buyers will face more than 10,000 new grocery product introductions next year. The buyers accept only 38 per cent of these new products and give each one only five months to prove itself.
● *Demographic changes*. Increasing single parenthood and dual-income families (1) will encourage the trend towards pets that need little care (cats rather than dogs), and (2) will encourage the trend towards smaller pets who eat less.
● *Politics*. European Union legislation will force manufacturers to disclose the content of their pet food. This will adversely affect the attractiveness of some ingredients like kangaroo and horse meat.

Not all threats call for the same attention or concern – the manager should assess the likelihood of each threat and the potential damage each could cause.

The manager should then focus on the most probable and harmful threats and prepare plans in advance to meet them.

Opportunities occur when an environmental trend plays to a company's strength. The manager should assess each opportunity according to its potential attractiveness and the company's probability of success. Companies can rarely find ideal opportunities that exactly fit their objectives and resources. The development of opportunities involves risks. When evaluating opportunities, the manager must decide whether the expected returns justify these risks. A trend or development can be a threat or an opportunity depending on a company's strengths. The development of the steel-braced radial tyre was an opportunity for Michelin, which used its technological lead to gain market share. To the rest of the industry, the new technology was a threat because the tyre's longer life reduced total demand and the new technology made their plant obsolete.

● *Strengths and Weaknesses*

The strengths and weaknesses in the SWOT analysis do not list all features of a company, but only those relating to **critical success factors**. A list that is too long betrays a lack of focus and an inability to discriminate what is important. The strengths or weaknesses are *relative*, not absolute. It is nice to be good at something, but it can be a weakness if the competition is stronger. Mercedes is good at making reliable luxury cars with low depreciation, but this stopped being a strength when Honda's Acura and Toyota's Lexus beat Mercedes on all three fronts in the American market. The Japanese products were not cheap, but they were styled for the American market and came with all the extras that buyers of German luxury cars had to pay for. Finally, the strengths should be *based on fact*. In buying Skoda, VW has acquired a well-known brand name, but is the name a strength? A failure to understand true strengths can be dangerous. A well-known aircraft manufacturer for years promoted the quality of its after-sales service. Only after another company acquired it did it find out that its reputation was the worst in the industry.

critical success factors
The strengths and weaknesses that most critically affect an organization's success. These are measured relative to competition.

Land Rover compete in the competitive car market by concentrating on their strength in making credible cross-country vehicle.
Photography: Max Forsythe

A major pet food manufacturer could pitch the following strengths and weaknesses against the opportunities and threats.

Strengths:
- Market leader in the dry cat food market.
- Access to the group's leading world position in food technology.
- Market leader in luxury pet foods.
- The group's excellent worldwide grocery distribution.
- Pet food market leader in several big markets, including France, Italy, Spain and South America.

Weaknesses:
- Number three in the wet pet food market.
- Excessive product range with several low-volume brands.
- Most brand names are little known, and are cluttered following acquisitions.
- Relatively low advertising and promotions budget.
- Product range needs many manufacturing skills.
- Poor store presence in several large markets: Germany, UK, USA and Canada.
- Overall poor profits performance.

The pet food company shows how some parts of the SWOT balance. The strengths in dry and luxury pet foods match demographic trends, so this looks like an opportunity for growth. Access to food technology should also help the company face changing consumer tastes and legislation. The weaknesses suggest a need for more focus. Dropping some uneconomic lines in the mass wet pet food market, simplifying the brand structure and concentrating on fewer manufacturing processes could release resources for developing the dry and luxury markets. By using its access to worldwide grocery distribution, the company could become profitable and focused.

The Business Portfolio

business portfolio
The collection of businesses and products that make up the company.

The **business portfolio** is the collection of businesses and products that make up the company. It is a link between the overall strategy of a company and those of its parts. The best business portfolio is the one that fits the company's strengths and weaknesses to opportunities in the environment. The company must (1) analyze its *current* business portfolio and decide which businesses should receive more, less or no investment, and (2) develop growth strategies for adding *new* products or businesses to the portfolio.

Analysing the Current Business Portfolio

portfolio analysis
A tool by which management identifies and evaluates the various businesses that make up the company.

Portfolio analysis helps managers evaluate the businesses making up the company. The company will want to put strong resources into its more profitable businesses and phase down or drop its weaker ones. Recently, Sweden's Volvo has started disposing of its non-core businesses to strengthen its portfolio. It plans to sell its interests in consumer products (holdings in BCP), pharmaceuticals (28 per cent of Pharmacia), stock brokering, property and investment. The tighter portfolio will allow Volvo to concentrate on revitalizing its passenger car, truck and bus operations.

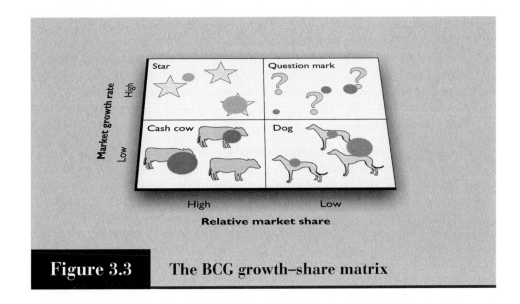

| Figure 3.3 | The BCG growth–share matrix |

Management's first step is to identify the key businesses making up the company. These are strategic business units. A **strategic business unit (SBU)** is a unit of the company that has a separate mission and objectives, and which can be planned independently from other company businesses. An SBU can be a company division, a product line within a division, or sometimes a single product or brand.

The next step in business portfolio analysis calls for management to assess the attractiveness of its various SBUs and decide how much support each deserves. In some companies, this occurs informally. Management looks at the company's collection of businesses or products and uses judgement to decide how much each SBU should contribute and receive. Other companies use formal portfolio-planning methods.

The purpose of strategic planning is to find ways in which the company can best use its strengths to take advantage of attractive opportunities in the environment. So most standard portfolio-analysis methods evaluate SBUs on two important dimensions: the attractiveness of the SBU's market or industry; and the strength of the SBU's position in that market or industry. The best-known portfolio-planning methods are from the Boston Consulting Group, a leading management consulting firm, and by General Electric and Shell.

THE BOSTON CONSULTING GROUP BOX. Using the Boston Consulting Group (BCG) approach, a company classifies all its SBUs according to the **growth–share matrix** shown in Figure 3.3. On the vertical axis, *market growth rate* provides a measure of market attractiveness. On the horizontal axis, *relative market share* serves as a measure of company strength in the market. By dividing the growth–share matrix as indicated, four types of SBU can be distinguished:

1. **Stars.** Stars are high-growth, high-share businesses or products. They often need heavy investment to finance their rapid growth. Eventually their growth will slow down, and they will turn into cash cows.

2. **Cash cows**. Cash cows are low-growth, high-share businesses or products. These established and successful SBUs need less investment to hold their market share. Thus they produce cash that the company uses to pay its bills and to support other SBUs that need investment.

strategic business unit (SBU)
A unit of the company that has a separate mission and objectives and that can be planned independently from other company businesses. An SBU can be a company division, a product line within a division, or sometimes a single product or brand.

growth–share matrix
A portfolio-planning method that evaluates a company's strategic business units (SBUs) in terms of their market growth rate and relative market share. SBUs are classified as stars, cash cows, question marks or dogs.

stars
High-growth, high-share businesses or products that often require heavy investment to finance their rapid growth.

cash cows

Low-growth, high-share businesses or products; established and successful units that generate cash that the company uses to pay its bills and support other business units that need investment.

question marks

Low-share business units in high-growth markets that require a lot of cash in order to hold their share or become stars.

dogs

Low-growth, low-share businesses and products that may generate enough cash to maintain themselves, but do not promise to be large sources of cash.

3. **Question marks.** Question marks are low-share business units in high-growth markets. They require cash to hold their share, let alone increase it. Management has to think hard about question marks – which ones they should build into stars and which ones they should phase out.

4. **Dogs.** Dogs are low-growth, low-share businesses and products. They may generate enough cash to maintain themselves, but do not promise to be large sources of cash.

The ten circles in the growth–share matrix represent a company's ten current SBUs. The company has two stars, two cash cows, three question marks and three dogs. The areas of the circles are proportional to the SBUs' sales value. This company is in fair shape, although not in good shape. It wants to invest in the more promising question marks to make them stars, and to maintain the stars so that they will become cash cows as their markets mature. Fortunately, it has two good-sized cash cows whose income helps finance the company's question marks, stars and dogs. The company should take some decisive action concerning its dogs and its question marks. The picture would be worse if the company had no stars, or had too many dogs, or had only one weak cash cow.

Once it has classified its SBUs, the company must determine what role each will play in the future. There are four alternative strategies for each SBU. The company can invest more in the business unit to *build* its share. It can invest just enough to *hold* the SBU's share at the current level. It can *harvest* the SBU, milking its short-term cash flow regardless of the long-term effect. Finally, the company can *divest* the SBU by selling it or phasing it out and using the resources elsewhere.

As time passes, SBUs change their positions in the growth–share matrix. Each SBU has a life cycle. Many SBUs start out as question marks and move into the star category if they succeed. They later become cash cows as market growth falls, then finally die off or turn into dogs towards the end of their life cycle. The company needs to add new products and units continuously, so that some of them will become stars and, eventually, cash cows that will help finance other SBUs.

strategic business-planning grid

A portfolio planning method that evaluates a company's strategic business units using indices of industry attractiveness and the company's strength in the industry.

THE GENERAL ELECTRIC GRID. General Electric introduced a comprehensive portfolio planning tool called a **strategic business-planning grid** (see Figure 3.4). It is similar to Shell's *directional policy matrix*. Like the BCG approach, it uses a matrix with two dimensions – one representing industry attractiveness (the vertical axis) and one representing company strength in the industry (the horizontal axis). The best businesses are those located in highly attractive industries where the company has high business strength.

The GE approach considers many factors besides market growth rate as part of *industry attractiveness*. It uses an industry attractiveness index made up of market size, market growth rate, industry profit margin, amount of competition, seasonality and cycle of demand, and industry cost structure. Each of these factors is rated and combined in an index of industry attractiveness. For our purposes, an industry's attractiveness is high, medium or low. As an example, the Kraft subsidiary of Philip Morris has identified numerous highly attractive industries – natural foods, speciality frozen foods, physical fitness products and others. It has withdrawn from less attractive industries, such as bulk oils and cardboard packaging. The Dutch chemical giant Akzo Nobel has identified speciality chemicals, coatings and pharmaceuticals as attractive. Its less attractive bulk chemical and fibre businesses are being sold.

For *business strength*, the GE approach again uses an index rather than a simple measure of relative market share. The business strength index includes factors such as the company's relative market share, price competitiveness,

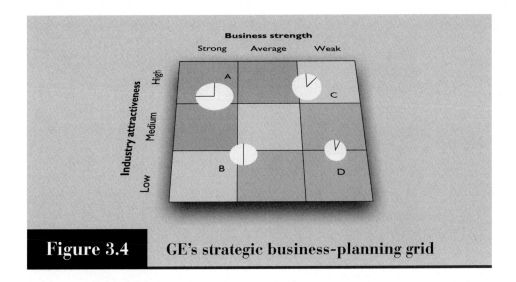

| Figure 3.4 | GE's strategic business-planning grid |

product quality, customer and market knowledge, sales effectiveness and geographic advantages. These factors are rated and combined in an index of business strengths described as strong, average or weak. Thus, Kraft has substantial business strength in food and related industries, but is relatively weak in the home appliances industry.

The grid has three zones. The green cells at the upper left include the strong SBUs in which the company should invest and grow. The beige diagonal cells contain SBUs that are medium in overall attractiveness. The company should maintain its level of investment in these SBUs. The three mauve cells at the lower right indicate SBUs that are low in overall attractiveness. The company should give serious thought to harvesting or divesting these SBUs.

The circles represent four company SBUs; the areas of the circles are proportional to the relative sizes of the industries in which these SBUs compete. The pie slices within the circles represent each SBU's market share. Thus circle A represents a company SBU with a 75 per cent market share in a good-sized, highly attractive industry in which the company has strong business strength. Circle B represents an SBU that has a 50 per cent market share, but the industry is not very attractive. Circles C and D represent two other company SBUs in industries where the company has small market shares and not much business strength. Altogether, the company should build A, maintain B and make some hard decisions on what to do with C and D.

Management would also plot the projected positions of the SBUs with and without changes in strategies. By comparing current and projected business grids, management can identify the primary strategic issues and opportunities it faces. One of the aims of portfolio analysis is to direct firms away from investing in markets that look attractive, but where they have no strength:

> In their rush away from the declining steel market, four of Japan's
> 'famous five' big steel makers (Nippon, NKK, Kawasaki, Sumitomo and
> Kobe) diversified into the microchip business. They had the misplaced
> belief that chips would be to the 1980s what steel had been to the 1950s
> and that they, naturally, had to be part of it. The market was attractive
> but it did not fit their strengths. So far, none have made money from
> chips. The misadventure also distracted them from attending to their
> core business. In 1987 they said they would reduce fixed costs by 30 per
> cent but their 'salary-men' stayed in place. By 1993, their costs were up
> by 3.6 per cent and their losses huge.

Back to the Basics

During the 1970s and early 1980s, strategic planners caught expansion fever. Big was beautiful and it seemed that everyone wanted to get bigger and grow faster by broadening their business portfolios. Companies milked their stodgy but profitable core businesses to get the cash needed to acquire glamorous businesses in more attractive industries. It did not seem to matter that many of the acquired businesses fitted poorly with old ones, or that they operated in markets unfamiliar to company management.

Thus many firms exploded into huge conglomerates, sometimes containing hundreds of unrelated products and businesses. Extreme cases involved French bank and Japanese electronics companies buying Hollywood film studios. Managing these 'smorgasbord' portfolios often proved difficult. Managers learned that it was tough to run businesses they knew little about. Many newly acquired businesses were bogged down under added layers of corporate management and increased administrative costs. Meanwhile, the profitable core businesses that had financed the acquisitions withered from lack of investment and management attention.

By the mid-1980s, as attempt after attempt at scattergun diversification foundered, acquisition fever gave way to a new philosophy – getting back to the basics. The new trend had many names: 'narrowing the focus', 'sticking to your knitting' and 'the urge to purge'. They all mean narrowing the company's market focus and returning to the idea of serving one or a few core industries that the firm knows. The company sheds businesses that do not fit its narrowed focus and rebuilds by concentrating resources on other businesses that do. The result is a smaller, but more focused company; a stronger firm serving fewer markets, but serving them much better.

Since the mid-1980s, companies in all industries have worked at getting back in focus and shedding unrelated operations. For example, during the 1970s Gulf & Western acquired businesses in dozens of diverse sectors: from auto

industrial equipment and cement to cigars and racetracks. Then, in 1983 and 1984, to regain focus and direction, the company purged itself of over 50 business units that made up nearly half of its $8 billion in sales. In 1989 the company changed its name to Paramount Communications, to reflect better its narrower focus on entertainment and communications. It now concentrates its operations on a leaner, tighter portfolio of entertainment and publishing units: Paramount Pictures, Simon & Schuster/Prentice Hall publishers, USA Cable Network, Pocket Books, Cinamerica Theatres and other related companies.

Food companies are building strength by going back to their bread-and-butter basics. Quaker Oats sold its speciality retailing businesses – Jos. A. Bank (clothing), Brookstone (tools) and Eyelab (optical). It used the proceeds to strengthen current food brands and to acquire the Golden Grain Macaroni Company (Rice-a-Roni and Noodle-Roni) and Gaines Foods (pet foods), whose products strongly complement Quaker's. Some food companies are still growing by acquisitions and mergers, but the new expansion fever differs notably from that of the last decade. The growth is not through broad diversification into attractive but unrelated new businesses. Instead, most are acquiring or merging with *related* companies, often competitors, in an attempt to build market power *within* their core businesses. Philip Morris has acquired General Foods and Kraft, and Nestlé has acquired Rowntree, Perrier, Carnation, Cereal Partners and others.

In the mid-1980s Lloyds Bank, along with many other banks, almost went bust in Latin America's debt crisis. Many hard-up banks went back to their shareholders to ask for more money and continued on the financial and international adventures. Expect some of that to be lost in south-east Asia's debt crisis. Lloyds behaved differently. The bank's chief executive, Sir Brian Pitman, 'was the first to realise that planting flags around the world was not always the best way to make money'. It sold its loss-making foreign subsidiaries, pulled out of investment banking, and wound down international lending to concentrate on selling financial services to consumers. Now known as Lloyds TSB, the bank is only the no. 33 in the world based on assets, but it is number the world's no. 1 in terms of market capitalization – ahead of Bank of Tokyo-Mitsubishi, HSBC, Citicorp, etc. Earning too much money is the bank's problem now!

These and other companies have concluded that fast-growing businesses in attractive industries are not good investments if they spread the company's resources too thinly, or if the company's managers cannot run them properly. They have learned that a company without market focus – one that tries to serve too many diverse markets – might end up serving few markets well.

SOURCES: See Thomas Moore, 'Old-line industry shapes up', *Fortune* (27 April 1987), pp. 23–32; Walter Kiechel III, 'Corporate strategy for the 1990s', *Fortune* (29 February 1988), pp. 34–42; 'G & W plans to expand in entertainment and publishing', press release, Paramount Communications (9 April 1990); Brian Bremner, 'The age of consolidation', *Business Week* (14 October 1991), pp. 86–94; Christopher Lorenz, 'Sugar daddy', *Financial Times* (20 April 1994), p. 19; Ian Verchère, 'Nestlé told to sell stake in L'Oréal', *The European* (22–8 April 1994), p. 17; 'The Lloyds money machine', *The Economist* (17 January 1998), pp. 81–2.

The 'famous five's' failure contrasts with Eramet, a focused French company who are the world's biggest producer of Ferro-nickel and high speed steels. They owe their number one position to their decision to invest their profits in a 'second leg' that would be a logical industrial and geographical diversification for them. They bought French Commentryene and Swedish Kloster Speedsteel. They quickly integrated them and, according to Yves Rambert, their chairman and chief executive, 'found that the French and the Swedes can work together'. The unified international marketing team is doing better than when the companies were separate. Eramet are now looking for a 'third industrial leg' that will have customers and technologies with which the group's management are familiar but does not compete for their present customers.[7]

● *Problems with Matrix Approaches*

The BCG, GE, Shell and other formal methods revolutionized strategic planning. However, such approaches have limitations. They can be difficult, time consuming and costly to implement. Management may find it difficult to define SBUs and measure market share and growth. In addition, these approaches focus on classifying *current* businesses, but provide little advice for *future* planning. Management must still rely on its judgement to set the business objectives for each SBU, to determine what resources to give to each and to work out which new businesses to add.

Formal planning approaches can also lead the company to place too much emphasis on market-share growth or growth through entry into attractive new markets. Using these approaches, many companies plunged into unrelated and new high-growth businesses that they did not know how to manage – with very bad results. At the same time, these companies were often too quick to abandon, sell or milk to death their healthy, mature businesses. As a result, many companies that diversified in the past are now narrowing their focus and getting back to the industries that they know best (see Marketing Highlight 3.3).

Despite these and other problems, and although many companies have dropped formal matrix methods in favour of customized approaches better suited to their situations, most companies remain firmly committed to strategic planning. Roughly 75 per cent of the *Fortune 500* companies practise some form of portfolio planning.[8]

Such analysis is no cure-all for finding the best strategy. Conversely, it can help management to understand the company's overall situation, to see how each business or product contributes, to assign resources to its businesses, and to orient the company for future success. When used properly, strategic planning is just one important aspect of overall strategic management, a way of thinking about how to manage a business.[9]

Developing Growth Strategies

The product/market expansion grid,[10] shown in Figure 3.5, is a useful device for identifying growth opportunities. This shows four routes to growth: market development, new markets, new products and diversification. We use the grid to explain how Mercedes-Benz, the luxury car division of German Daimler-Benz industrial group, hoped return to profits after its DM1.8bn loss in 1993.[11]

MARKET PENETRATION. The new C-class model (replacing the ageing 190) helped the company increase its sales by 23 per cent in 1994. Sales were up 40 per cent in western Europe (excluding Germany), 34 per cent in the United States and 30 per cent in Japan. In Germany, the 38 per cent growth gave a 2 per cent rise in market share.

MARKET DEVELOPMENT. Its original 190 launched Mercedes into the executive saloon market for the first time. With its A series, an 'even smaller car' produced at Rastatt, Mercedes will enter the family saloon market. German reunification gave the company an immediate sales boost. In eastern Europe and China, the brand's image and reputation for reliability and quality have made it *the* transport for the new rich.

DIVERSIFICATION. Diversification is an option taken by Mercedes' parent company Daimler-Benz. It has rapidly moved into aerospace by buying Dornier, Motoren Turbinen Union (MTU) and a 51 per cent stake in Messerschmitt Böelkow-Blohm (MBB). Its new Deutsche Aerospace (DASA) is now Germany's biggest aerospace and defence group. The motives behind the strategy were to offset stagnating vehicle sales and to use high technology from the acquisitions in cars and trucks. Like many other firms, Daimler-Benz is finding diversification a difficult route. Shortly after consolidating the acquisitions, the 'peace dividend' damaged the defence sector and the international airline industry was in recession. Observers now question the logic of the acquisitions and doubt whether even a company with Daimler's management and financial strength can handle such a radical diversification.

Marketing Within Strategic Planning

Planning Functional Strategies

The company's strategic plan establishes what kinds of business the company will be in and its objectives for each. Then, within each business unit, more detailed

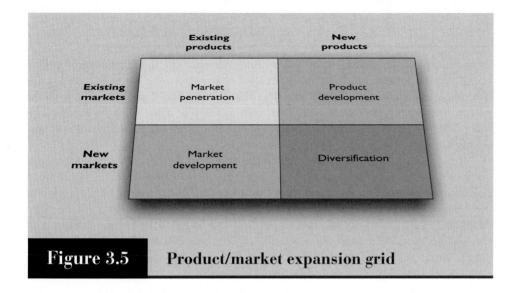

	Existing products	New products
Existing markets	Market penetration	Product development
New markets	Market development	Diversification

Figure 3.5 | **Product/market expansion grid**

planning takes place. The main functional departments in each unit – marketing, finance, accounting, buying, manufacturing, personnel and others – must work together to accomplish strategic objectives.

Each functional department deals with different publics to obtain resources such as cash, labour, raw materials, research ideas and manufacturing processes. For example, marketing brings in revenues by negotiating exchanges with consumers. Finance arranges exchanges with lenders and stockholders to obtain cash. Thus the marketing and finance departments must work together to obtain needed funds. Similarly, the personnel department supplies labour, and the buying department obtains materials needed for operations and manufacturing.

Marketing's Role in Strategic Planning

There is much overlap between overall company strategy and marketing strategy. Marketing looks at consumer needs and the company's ability to satisfy them; these factors guide the company mission and objectives. Most company strategic planning deals with marketing variables – market share, market development, growth – and it is sometimes hard to separate strategic planning from marketing planning. Some companies refer to their strategic planning as 'strategic marketing planning'.

Marketing plays a key role in the company's strategic planning in several ways. First, marketing provides a guiding *philosophy* – company strategy should revolve around serving the needs of important consumer groups. Second, marketing provides *inputs* to strategic planners by helping to identify attractive market opportunities and by assessing the firm's potential to take advantage of them. Finally, within individual business units, marketing designs *strategies* for reaching the unit's objectives.

Within each business unit, marketing management determines how to help achieve strategic objectives. Some marketing managers will find that their objective is not to build sales. Rather, it may be to hold existing sales with a smaller marketing budget, or even to reduce demand. Thus marketing management must manage demand to the level decided upon by the strategic planning prepared at headquarters. Marketing helps to assess each business unit's potential, set objectives for it and then achieve those objectives.

Marketing and the Other Business Functions

In some firms, marketing is just another function – all functions count in the company and none takes leadership. At the other extreme, some marketers claim that marketing is the *principal* function of the firm. They quote Drucker's statement: 'The aim of the business is to create customers.' They say it is marketing's job to define the company's mission, products and markets, and to direct the other functions in the task of serving customers.

More enlightened marketers prefer to put the *customer* at the centre of the company. These marketers argue that the firm cannot succeed without customers, so the crucial task is to attract and hold them. Customers are attracted by promises and held by satisfaction. Marketing defines the promise and ensures its delivery. However, because actual consumer satisfaction is affected by the performance of other departments, *all* functions should work together to sense, serve and satisfy customer needs. Marketing plays an integrative role in ensuring that all departments work together towards consumer satisfaction.

Conflict Between Departments

Each business function has a different view of which publics and activities are most important. Manufacturing focuses on suppliers and production; finance addresses stockholders and sound investment; marketing emphasizes consumers and products, pricing, promotion and distribution. Ideally, all the different functions should blend to achieve consumer satisfaction. In practice, departmental relations are full of conflicts and misunderstandings. The marketing department takes the consumer's point of view. But when marketing tries to develop customer satisfaction, it often causes other departments to do a poorer job *in their terms*. Marketing department actions can increase buying costs, disrupt production schedules, increase inventories and create budget headaches. Thus the other departments may resist bending their efforts to the will of the marketing department.

Despite the resistance, marketers must get all departments to 'think consumer' and to put the consumer at the centre of company activity. Customer satisfaction requires a total company effort to deliver superior value to target customers.

Creating value for buyers is much more than a 'marketing function'; rather, it is 'analogous to a symphony orchestra in which the contribution of each subgroup is tailored and integrated by a conductor – with a synergistic effect. A seller must draw upon and integrate effectively … its entire human and other capital resources … [Creating superior value for buyers] is the proper focus of the entire business and not merely of a single department in it.'[12]

ABB Asea Brown Boveri, formed in 1987 by the merger of Sweden's Asea and Switzerland's Brown Boveri, shows the benefits of customer focus. ABB launched a customer focus programme in 1990. It was initially a regional effort stressing time-based management to quicken response to customers by cutting total customer order to delivery time. The customer focus programme has since extended to all its operations. It encourages people in all its 5,000 plus profit centres to 'think customer', track customer satisfaction and to find ways to continually improve customer service.

The company keeps 'close to the customer' by extreme decentralization and a flat, team driven organization. Sune Karlsson, who

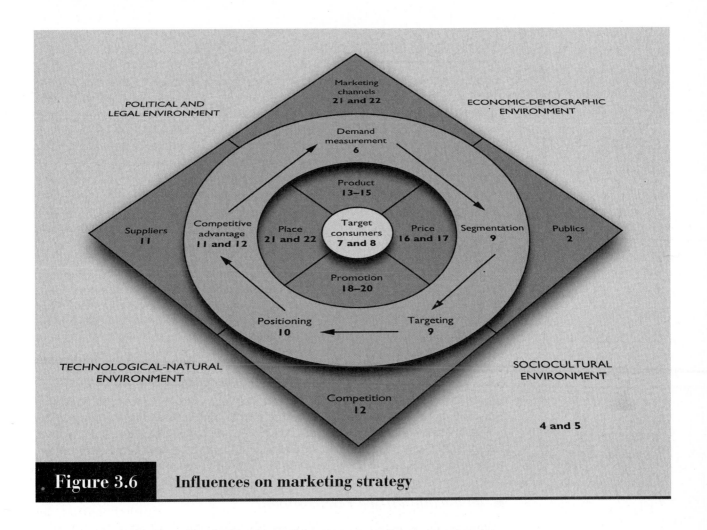

POLITICAL AND
LEGAL ENVIRONMENT

ECONOMIC-DEMOGRAPHIC
ENVIRONMENT

Marketing
channels
21 and 22

Demand
measurement
6

Product
13–15

Suppliers
11

Competitive
advantage
11 and 12

Place
21 and 22

Target
consumers
7 and 8

Price
16 and 17

Segmentation
9

Publics
2

Promotion
18–20

TECHNOLOGICAL-NATURAL
ENVIRONMENT

SOCIOCULTURAL
ENVIRONMENT

Positioning
10

Targeting
9

Competition
12

4 and 5

| **Figure 3.6** | **Influences on marketing strategy** |

is responsible for the customer focus programme, says: 'the people in our many small groups are close to the customer, are more sensitive to their needs, and are more able to respond to those needs'. The role of keeping the customer satisfied and happy is not just the role of marketing people. Employees work together to develop a system of functional plans and then use cross-border co-ordination to accomplish the company's overall objectives. Furthermore, Karlsson suggests, 'We have learned that the customer focus programme reduces the optimal size of an operation (that is, improves efficiency). It ensures that the customer is better served and brings us closer to the ultimate goal of partnering (that is, long-term relationships).'[13]

The Marketing Process

The strategic plan defines the company's overall mission and objectives. Within each business unit, marketing plays a role in helping to accomplish the overall strategic objectives. Marketing's role and activities in the organization are shown in Figure 3.6, which summarizes the **marketing process** and the forces influencing marketing strategy.

marketing process
The process of (1) analyzing marketing opportunities; (2) selecting target markets; (3) developing the marketing mix; and (4) managing the marketing effort.

Marketing Strategy

marketing strategy
The marketing logic by which the business unit hopes to achieve its marketing objectives.

Target consumers are at the centre of the **marketing strategy**. The company identifies the total market, divides it into smaller segments, selects the most promising segments and focuses on serving them. It designs a marketing mix using mechanisms under its control: product, price, place and promotion. The company engages in marketing analysis, planning, implementation and control to find the best marketing mix and to take action. The company uses these activities to enable it to watch and adapt to the marketing environment. We will now look briefly at each factor in the marketing process and say where it is developed elsewhere in this book.

● *Target Consumers*

To succeed in today's competitive marketplace, companies must be customer centred – winning customers from competitors by delivering greater value. However, before it can satisfy consumers, a company must first understand their needs and wants. So, sound marketing requires a careful analysis of consumers. An understanding of buyer behaviour, discussed in Chapters 7 and 8, guides this process. Companies know that they cannot satisfy all consumers in a given market – at least, not all consumers in the same way. There are too many kinds of consumer with too many kinds of need, and some companies are in a better position to serve certain segments of the market. As a consequence, each company must divide the total market, choose the best segments and design strategies for profitably serving chosen segments better than its competitors do. This process involves five steps: demand measurement and forecasting, market segmentation, market targeting, market positioning and competitive positioning.

● *The Competitive Environment*

Companies aim to serve their customers, but they must do so in an environment with many other influences. At the widest level is the *macroenvironment* of Political, Economic, Social and Technological (PEST) influences that all organizations face. Besides this companies also face a unique microenvironment, including suppliers, competitors, channels of distribution and publics – such as employees and the media – that are not necessarily customers. Chapters 4 and 5 explore these environments and their increasingly global dimensions.

● *Demand Measurement and Forecasting*

Suppose a company is looking at possible markets for a potential new product. First, the company needs to estimate the current and future size of the market and its segments. To estimate current market size, the company would identify all competing products, estimate the current sales of these products, and determine whether the market is large enough to support another product profitably. Chapter 6 explores ways of doing this and other types of marketing research and information system.

Equally important is future market growth. Companies want to enter markets that show strong growth prospects. Growth potential may depend on the growth rate of certain age, income and nationality groups that use the product. Growth may also relate to larger developments in the environment, such as economic conditions, the crime rate and lifestyle changes. For example, the future markets for quality children's toys and clothing relate to current birth rates, trends in consumer affluence and projected family lifestyles. Forecasting the effect of these environmental forces is difficult, but it is necessary in order to make decisions about the market. The company's marketing information specialists will probably use complex techniques to measure and forecast demand.

● *Market Segmentation*

If the demand forecast looks good, the company next decides how to enter the market. The market consists of many types of customers, products and needs. The marketer has to determine which segments offer the best opportunity for achieving company objectives. Consumers are grouped in various ways based on geographic factors (countries, regions, cities); demographic factors (sex, age, income, education); psychographic factors (social classes, lifestyles); and behavioural factors (purchase occasions, benefits sought, usage rates). The process of dividing a market into groups of buyers with different needs, characteristics or behaviour, who might require separate products or marketing mixes, is **market segmentation**.

Every market has market segments, but not all ways of segmenting a market are equally useful. For example, Panadol would gain little by distinguishing between male and female users of pain relievers if both respond the same way to marketing stimuli. A **market segment** consists of consumers who respond in a similar way to a given set of marketing stimuli. In the car market, for example, consumers who choose the biggest, most comfortable car regardless of price make up one market segment. Another market segment would be customers who care mainly about price and operating economy. It would be difficult to make one model of car that was the first choice of every consumer. Companies are wise to focus their efforts on meeting the distinct needs of one or more market segments.

market segmentation
Dividing a market into distinct groups of buyers with different needs, characteristics or behaviour, who might require separate products or marketing mixes.

market segment
A group of consumers who respond in a similar way to a given set of marketing stimuli.

● *Market Targeting*

After a company has defined market segments, it can enter one or many segments of a given market. **Market targeting** involves evaluating each market segment's attractiveness and selecting one or more segments to enter. A company should target segments in which it has a differential advantage over its competitors; where it can generate the greatest customer value and sustain it over time. A company with limited resources might decide to serve only one or a few special segments; this strategy limits sales, but can be very profitable. Alternatively, a company might choose to serve several related segments – perhaps those with different kinds of customer, but with the same basic wants. Or perhaps a large company might decide to offer a complete range of products to serve all market segments. The closely linked processes of market segmentation and targeting are both developed in Chapter 9.

Most companies enter a new market by serving a single segment, and if this proves successful, they add segments. Large companies eventually seek full market coverage. They want to be the 'General Motors' (GM) of their industry. America's GM says that it makes a car for every 'person, purse, and personality'. Similarly, Japan's Seiko is proud of its range of 2,500 watches designed to cover consumer segments across the world. The leading company normally has different products designed to meet the special needs of each segment.

market targeting
The process of evaluating each market segment's attractiveness and selecting one or more segments to enter.

● *Positioning*

After a company has decided which market segments to enter, it must decide what 'position' it wants to occupy in those segments. A **product's position** is the

product position
The way the product is defined by consumers on important attributes – the place the product occupies in consumers' minds relative to competing products.

Market positioning: Red Roof Inns positions on value – it doesn't 'add frills that only add to your bill.' In contrast, Four Seasons Hotels positions on luxury. For those who can afford it, Four Seasons offers endless amenities – such as a seamstress, a valet and a 'tireless individual who collects your shoes each night and returns them at dawn, polished to perfection'.

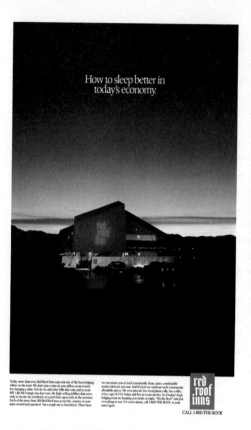

market positioning
Arranging for a product to occupy a clear, distinctive and desirable place relative to competing products in the minds of target consumers. Formulating competitive positioning for a product and a detailed marketing mix.

place the product occupies in consumers' minds. If a product were perceived to be exactly like another product on the market, consumers would have no reason to buy it.

Market positioning gives a product a clear, distinctive and desirable place in the minds of target consumers compared with competing products. Marketers plan positions that distinguish their products from competing brands and give them the greatest strategic advantage in their target markets. For example, Ford says, 'Everything we do is driven by you'. Renault builds cars that 'take your breath away'. Mitsubishi's are 'designed to be driven'. BMW is 'the ultimate driving machine'. Rolls-Royce cars are 'Strictly for the wealthy arrived individual', while the equally luxurious Bentley is 'The closest a car can come to having wings'. Such simple statements are the backbone of a product's marketing strategy.

In positioning its product, the company first identifies possible competitive advantages upon which to build the position. To gain competitive advantage, the company must offer greater value to chosen target segments, either by charging lower prices than competitors or by offering more benefits to justify higher prices. However, if the company positions the product as *offering* greater value, it must *deliver* greater value. Effective positioning begins with actually *differentiating* the company's marketing offer so that it gives consumers more value than is offered by the competition.

The company can position a product on only one important differentiating factor or on several. However, positioning on too many factors can result in consumer confusion or disbelief. Once the company has chosen·a desired position, it must take steps to deliver and communicate that position to target consumers. Chapter 10 focuses on positioning and tells how the company's entire marketing programme should support the chosen positioning strategy.

Marketing Strategies for Competitive Advantage

To be successful, the company must do a better job than its competitors of satisfying target consumers. Chapter 11 shows how this increasingly depends upon establishing relationships with customers and other participants in the value chain by providing them with quality, value and service. Recently there has been a major shift from marketing as a single transaction between supplier and buyer to establishing a longer-term relationship with customers through loyalty schemes and data-based marketing. These recognize that it is far more expensive to obtain customers than to retain them.

Providing excellent value and customer service is a necessary but not sufficient means of succeeding in the marketplace. Besides embracing the needs of consumers, marketing strategies must build an advantage over the competition. The company must consider its size and industry position, then decide how to position itself to gain the strongest possible competitive advantage. Chapter 12 explains how to do this.

The design of competitive marketing strategies begins with competitor analysis. The company constantly compares the value and customer satisfaction delivered by its products, prices, channels and promotion with those of its close competitors. In this way it can discern areas of potential advantage and disadvantage. The company must formally or informally monitor the competitive environment to answer these and other important questions: Who are our competitors? What are their objectives and strategies? What are their strengths and weaknesses? How will they react to different competitive strategies we might use?

Which competitive marketing strategy a company adopts depends on its industry position. A firm that dominates a market can adopt one or more of several **market leader** strategies. Well-known leaders include Chanel (fragrances), Coca-Cola (soft drinks), McDonald's (fast food), Komatsu (large construction equipment), Kodak (photographic film), Lego (construction toys) and Boeing (civil aircraft).

Market challengers are runner-up companies that aggressively attack competitors to get more market share. For example, Pepsi challenges Coke and Airbus challenges Boeing. The challenger might attack the market leader, other firms of its own size, or smaller local and regional competitors. Some runner-up firms will choose to follow rather than challenge the market leader. Firms using **market follower** strategies seek stable market shares and profit by following competitors' product offers, prices and marketing programmes.[14] Smaller firms in a market, or even larger firms that lack established positions, often adopt **market nicher** strategies. They specialize in serving market niches that large competitors overlook or ignore. Market nichers avoid direct confrontations with the big companies by specializing along market, customer, product or marketing-mix lines. Through clever niching, low-share firms in an industry can be as profitable as their large competitors.

Developing the Marketing Mix

Once the company has chosen its overall competitive marketing strategy, it is ready to begin planning the details of the marketing mix. The marketing mix is one of the dominant ideas in modern marketing. We define **marketing mix** as the set of controllable tactical marketing tools that the firm blends to produce the response it wants in the target market. The marketing mix consists of everything the firm can do to influence the demand for its product. The many possibilities gather into four groups of variables known as the 'four Ps': product, price, place

market leader
The firm in an industry with the largest market share; it usually leads other firms in price changes, new product introductions, distribution coverage and promotion spending.

market challenger
A runner-up firm in an industry that is fighting hard to increase its market share.

market follower
A runner-up firm in an industry that wants to hold its share without rocking the boat.

market nicher
A firm in an industry that serves small segments that the other firms overlook or ignore.

marketing mix
The set of controllable tactical marketing tools – product, price, place and promotion – that the firm blends to produce the response it wants in the target market.

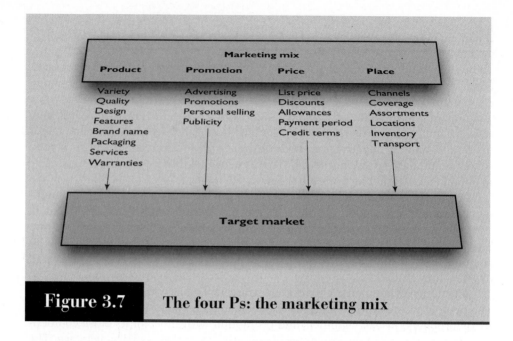

| **Figure 3.7** | **The four Ps: the marketing mix** |

product

Anything that can be offered to a market for attention, acquisition, use or consumption that might satisfy a want or need. It includes physical objects, services, persons, places, organizations and ideas.

price

The amount of money charged for a product or service, or the sum of the values that consumers exchange for the benefits of having or using the product or service.

place

All the company activities that make the product or service available to target customers.

promotion

Activities that communicate the product or service and its merits to target customers and persuade them to buy.

and promotion.[15] These are the subject of the second part of this book, Chapters 13–22. Figure 3.7 shows the particular marketing tools under each P.

Product means the totality of 'goods and services' that the company offers the target market. The Honda Civic 'product' is nuts, bolts, spark plugs, pistons, head-lights and many other parts. Honda offers several Civic styles and dozens of optional features. The car comes fully serviced, with a comprehensive warranty and financing that is as much a part of the product as the exhaust pipe. Increasingly, the most profitable part of the business for car companies is the loan that they offer to car buyers.

Price is what customers pay to get the product. Honda suggests retail prices that its dealers might charge for each car, but dealers rarely charge the full asking price. Instead, they negotiate the price with each customer. They offer discounts, trade-in allowances and credit terms to adjust for the current competitive situa-tion and to bring the price into line with the buyer's perception of the car's value.

Place includes company activities that make the product available to target consumers. Honda maintains a body of independently owned dealerships that sell the company's cars. They select dealers carefully and support them strongly. The main dealers keep a stock of Hondas, demonstrate them to potential buyers, nego-tiate prices, close sales, arrange finance, and service the cars after the sale.

Promotion means activities that communicate the merits of the product and persuade target customers to buy it. Honda spends millions on advertising each year to tell consumers about the company and its products. Dealership sales-people assist potential buyers and persuade them that a Honda is the car for them. Honda and its dealers offer special promotions – sales, cash rebates, low financing rates – as added purchase incentives.

An effective marketing programme blends the marketing mix elements into a co-ordinated programme designed to achieve the company's marketing objec-tives. The marketing mix constitutes the company's tactical tool kit for estab-lishing strong positioning in target markets. However, note that the four Ps represent the sellers' view of the marketing tools available for influencing buyers. From a consumer viewpoint, each marketing tool must deliver a customer benefit. One marketing expert suggests that companies should view the four Ps as the customer's four Cs:[16]

2. *Planning system*. Does the company prepare annual, long-term and strategic plans? Are they used?
3. *Marketing control system*. Are annual plan objectives being achieved? Does management periodically analyze the sales and profitability of products, markets, territories and channels?
4. *New-product development*. Is the company well organized to gather, generate and screen new-product ideas? Does it carry out adequate product and market testing? Has the company succeeded with new products?

PRODUCTIVITY AUDIT

1. *Profitability analysis*. How profitable are the company's different products, markets, territories and channels? Should the company enter, expand or withdraw from any business segments? What would be the consequences?
2. *Cost-effectiveness analysis*. Do any activities have excessive costs? How can costs be reduced?

MARKETING FUNCTION AUDIT

1. *Products*. Has the company developed sound product-line objectives? Should some products be phased out? Should some new products be added? Would some products benefit from quality, style or feature changes?
2. *Price*. What are the company's pricing objectives, policies, strategies and procedures? Are the company's prices in line with customers' perceived value? Are price promotions used properly?
3. *Distribution*. What are the distribution objectives and strategies? Does the company have adequate market coverage and service? Should existing channels be changed or new ones added?
4. *Advertising, sales promotion and publicity*. What are the company's promotion objectives? How is the budget determined? Is it sufficient? Are advertising messages and media well developed and received? Does the company have well-developed sales promotion and public relations programmes?
5. *Sales force*. What are the company's sales force objectives? Is the sales force large enough? Is it properly organized? Is it well trained, supervised and motivated? How is the sales force rated relative to those of competitors?

scheduling, personnel planning and marketing operations. Budgeting can be very difficult and budgeting methods range from simple 'rules of thumb' to complex computer models.[17]

Controls

The last section of the plan outlines the controls that will monitor progress. Typically, there are goals and budgets for each month or quarter. This practice allows higher management to review the results of each period and to spot businesses or products that are not meeting their goals. The managers of these businesses and products have to explain these problems and the corrective actions they will take.

Implementation

Planning good strategies is only a start towards successful marketing. A brilliant marketing strategy counts for little if the company fails to implement it properly.

Rethinking the role of the product manager: Campbell set up 'brand sales managers'.

marketing implementation
The process that turns marketing strategies and plans into marketing actions in order to accomplish strategic marketing objectives.

Marketing implementation is the process that turns marketing strategies and *plans* into marketing *actions* to accomplish strategic marketing objectives. Implementation involves day-to-day, month-to-month activities that effectively put the marketing plan to work. Whereas marketing planning addresses the *what* and *why* of marketing activities, implementation addresses the *who, where, when* and *how*.

Marketing Organization

The company must have people who can carry out marketing analysis, planning, implementation and control. If the company is very small, one person might do all the marketing work – research, selling, advertising, customer service and other activities. As the company expands, organizations emerge to plan and carry out marketing activities. In large companies there can be many specialists: brand managers, salespeople and sales managers, market researchers, advertising experts and other specialists.

Modern marketing activities occur in several forms. The most common form is the *functional organization*, in which functional specialists head different marketing activities – a sales manager, advertising manager, marketing research manager, customer service manager, new-product manager. A company that sells across the country or internationally often uses a *geographic organization*, in which its sales and marketing people run specific countries, regions and districts. A geographic organization allows salespeople to settle into a territory, get to know their customers, and work with a minimum of travel time and cost.

Companies with many, very different products or brands often create a *product management* or *brand management* organization. Using this approach, a manager develops and implements a complete strategy and marketing programme for a specific product or brand. Product management first appeared in Procter & Gamble in 1929. A new soap, Camay, was not doing well, and a young P & G executive was assigned to give his exclusive attention to developing and promoting this brand. He was successful, and the company soon added other product managers. Since then, many organizations, especially in the food, soap, toiletries and chemical industries, have introduced the brand management system, which is in widespread use today.

Recent dramatic changes in the marketing environment have caused many companies to rethink the role of the product manager. Today's consumers face an ever-growing set of brands and are now more deal-prone than brand-prone. As a result, companies are shifting away from national advertising in favour of pricing and other point-of-sale promotions. Brand managers have traditionally focused on long-term, brand-building strategies targeting a mass audience, but today's marketplace realities demand shorter-term, sales-building strategies designed for local markets.

A second significant force affecting brand management is the growing power of retailers. Larger, more powerful and better-informed retailers are now demanding and getting more trade promotions in exchange for their scarce shelf space. The increase in trade promotion spending leaves less resources for national advertising, the brand manager's primary marketing tool.

To cope with this change, Campbell Soups created *brand sales managers*. These combine product manager and sales roles charged with handling brands in the field, working with the trade, and designing more localized brand strategies. The managers spend more time in the field working with salespeople, learning what is happening in stores, and getting closer to the customer.

Other companies, including Colgate-Palmolive, Procter & Gamble, Kraft and Lever Bros, have adopted *category management*, which has brands grouped according to the sections or aisles in supermarkets or other stores. Under this system, brand managers report to a category manager who has total responsibility for a category. For example, at Procter & Gamble, the brand manager for Dawn liquid dishwashing detergent reports to a manager who is responsible for Dawn, Ivory, Joy and all other light-duty liquid detergents. The light-duty liquids manager, in turn, reports to a manager who is responsible for all of P & G's packaged soaps and detergents, including dishwashing detergents, and liquid and dry laundry detergents. This offers many advantages. First, the category managers have broader planning perspectives than brand managers do. Rather than focusing on specific brands, they shape the company's entire category offering. Second, it better matches the buying processes of retailers. Recently, retailers have begun making their individual buyers responsible for working with all suppliers of a specific product category. A category management system links up better with this new retailer 'category buying' system. The aim of a supplier is to become a *category leader* who works closely with the retailer to increase category sales rather than that of one brand. These category leaders have considerable power and responsibility. They can clearly directly influence the sales of their competitors' products but not if it damages retailers' profits.

Some companies, including Nabisco, have started combining category management with another idea: *brand teams* or *category teams*. Instead of having several brand managers, Nabisco has three teams covering biscuits – one each for adult rich, nutritional and children's biscuits. Headed by a category manager, each category team includes several marketing people – brand managers, a sales planning manager and a marketing information specialist handling brand strategy, advertising, and sales promotion. Each team also includes specialists from other company departments: a finance manager, a research and development specialist, and representatives from manufacturing, engineering and distribution.

Thus category managers act as a small business, with complete responsibility for the performance of the category and with a full complement of people to help them plan and implement category marketing strategies.

For companies that sell one product line to many different types of market that have different needs and preferences, a *market management organization* might be best. Many companies are organized along market lines. A market management organization is similar to the product management organization. Market managers are responsible for developing long-range and annual plans for the sales and profits in their markets. This system's main advantage is that the company is organized around the needs of specific customer segments.

Elida Gibbs, Unilever's personal care products division, has scrapped both brand manager and sales development roles. It had many strong brands, including Pears, Fabergé Brut, Signal and Timotei, but sought to improve its service to retailers and pay more attention to developing the brands. To do this it created two new roles: brand development managers and customer development managers. *Customer development managers* work closely with customers and have also taken over many of the old responsibilities of brand management. This provides an opportunity for better co-ordination of sales, operations and marketing campaigns. The change leaves *brand development managers* with more time to spend on the strategic development of brands and innovation. They have the authority to pull together technical and managerial resources to see projects through to their completion.

Elida Gibbs' reorganization goes beyond sales and marketing. Cross-functional teamwork is central to the approach and this extends to the shop floor. The company is already benefiting from the change. Customer development managers have increased the number of correctly completed orders from 72 per cent to 90 per cent. In addition, brand development managers developed Aquatonic – an aerosol deodorant – in six months, less than half the usual time.[18]

Marketing Control

marketing control
The process of measuring and evaluating the results of marketing strategies and plans, and taking corrective action to ensure that marketing objectives are attained.

operating control
Checking on-going performance against annual plans and taking corrective action.

strategic control
Checking whether the company's basic strategy matches its opportunities and strengths.

Because many surprises occur during the implementation of marketing plans, the marketing department must engage in constant marketing control. **Marketing control** is the process of measuring and evaluating the results of marketing strategies and plans and taking corrective action to ensure the achievement of marketing objectives. It involves the four steps shown in Figure 3.8. Management first sets specific marketing goals. It then measures its performance in the marketplace and evaluates the causes of any differences between expected and actual performance. Finally, management takes corrective action to close the gaps between its goals and its performance. This may require changing the action programmes or even changing the goals.

Operating control involves checking on-going performance against the annual plan and taking corrective action when necessary. Its purpose is to ensure that the company achieves the sales, profits and other goals set out in its annual plan. It also involves determining the profitability of different products, territories, markets and channels. **Strategic control** involves looking at whether the company's basic strategies match its opportunities and strengths. Marketing strategies and programmes can quickly become outdated and each company should periodically reassess its overall approach to the marketplace. Besides providing the background for marketing planning, a *marketing audit* can also be a positive tool for strategic control. Sometimes it is conducted by an objective and

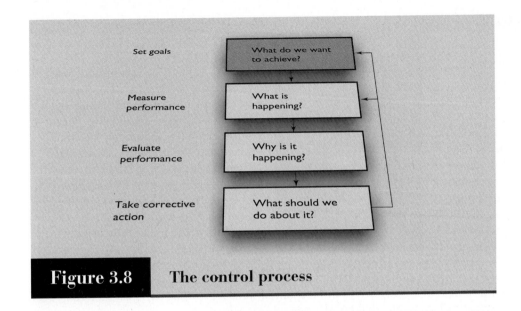

Set goals	What do we want to achieve?
Measure performance	What is happening?
Evaluate performance	Why is it happening?
Take corrective action	What should we do about it?

Figure 3.8   The control process

experienced outside party who is independent of the marketing department. Table 3.2 shows the kind of questions the marketing auditor might ask. The findings may come as a surprise – and sometimes as a shock – to management. Management then decides which actions make sense and how and when to implement them.

Implementing Marketing

Many managers think that 'doing things right' (implementation) is as important, or even more important, than 'doing the right things' (strategy):

> A surprisingly large number of very successful large companies don't have long-term strategic plans with an obsessive preoccupation on rivalry. They concentrate on operating details and doing things well. Hustle is their style and their strategy. They move fast and they get it right ... Countless companies in all industries, young or old, mature or booming, are finally learning the limits of strategy and concentrating on tactics and execution.[19]

Implementation is difficult – it is easier to think up good marketing strategies than it is to carry them out.

People at all levels of the marketing system must work together to implement marketing plans and strategies. Marketing implementation requires day-to-day decisions and actions by thousands of people both inside and outside the organization. Marketing managers make decisions about target segments, branding, packaging, pricing, promoting and distributing. They work with people elsewhere in the company to get support for their products and programmes. They talk to engineering about product design, with manufacturing about production and inventory levels, and with finance about funding and cash flows. They also work with outside people. They meet with advertising agencies to plan ad campaigns and with the media to obtain publicity support. The sales force urges retailers to advertise, say, Nestlé's products, provide ample shelf space and use company displays.

Successful implementation depends on several key elements. First, it requires an *action programme* that pulls all the people and activities together. The action

Marketing Highlight 3.4

Hewlett-Packard's structure evolves

In 1939, two engineers, Bill Hewlett and David Packard, started Hewlett-Packard in a garage. Bill and Dave did everything themselves, from designing and building their equipment to marketing it. As the firm grew out of the garage and began to offer more and different types of test equipment, Hewlett and Packard could no longer make all the necessary operating decisions themselves. They hired functional managers to run various company activities.

By the mid-1970s, Hewlett-Packard's 42 divisions employed more than 30,000 people. The company's structure evolved to support its heavy emphasis on innovation and autonomy. Each division operated as an autonomous unit and was responsible for its own strategic planning, product development, marketing programmes and implementation.

Peters and Waterman, in their book *In Search of Excellence*, cited HP's structure as an important reason for the company's continued excellence. They praised HP's non-restrictive structure and high degree of informal communication (its

Hewlett-Packard began in this garage in 1939. It now operates globally through a sophisticated complex of facilities and communications networks. Its structure and culture have changed with growth.

MBWA style – management by wandering around), which fostered autonomy by decentralizing decision-making responsibility and authority. The approach became known as the 'HP Way', a structure that encouraged innovation by abolishing rigid chains of command and putting managers and employees on a first-name basis.

But by the mid-1980s, although still profitable, Hewlett-Packard had begun to encounter problems in the fast-changing microcomputer and minicomputer markets. According to *Business Week*:

Hewlett-Packard's famed innovative culture and decentralization [had] spawned such enormously successful products as its 3000 minicomputer, the hand-held scientific calculator, and the ThinkJet non-impact printer. But when a new climate required its fiercely autonomous divisions to co-operate in product development and marketing, HP's passionate devotion to 'autonomy and entrepreneurship' that Peters and Waterman advocate became a hindrance.

Thus Hewlett-Packard moved to change its structure and culture in order to bring them in line with its changing situation. It established a system of committees to foster communication within and across its many and varied divisions and to co-ordinate product development, marketing, and other activities.

The new structure seemed to work well, for a while. However, the move towards centralization soon got out of hand:

The committees kept multiplying, like a virus. [Soon] everything was by committee ... no one could make a decision ... By the late 1980s, an unwieldy bureaucracy had bogged down the HP Way. A web of committees, originally designed to foster communication ... had pushed costs up and slowed down development.

Entering the 1990s, HP had no fewer than 38 in-house committees that made decisions on everything from technical specifications for new products to the best cities for staging product launches. This suffocating structure dramatically increased HP's decision-making and market-reaction time. For example, in one case, it took almost 100 people over seven weeks just to come up with a name for the company's New Wave Computing software.

In 1990, when one of HP's most important projects, a series of high-speed workstations, slipped a year behind schedule as a result of seemingly endless meetings about technical decisions, top management finally took action. It removed the project's 200 engineers from the formal management structure, so that they could continue work on the project free of the usual committee red tape. The workstation crisis convinced HP management that it must make similar changes throughout the company.

> [Top management] wiped out HP's committee structure and flattened the organisation. 'The results are incredible,' says [HP executive Bob] Frankenberg, who

now deals with three committees instead of 38. 'We are doing more business and getting product out quicker with fewer people.'

In less than a decade, Hewlett-Packard's structure has evolved from the decentralized and informal 'HP Way' to a centralized committee system and back again to a point in between. HP is not likely to find a single best structure that will satisfy all of its future needs. Rather, it must continue adapting its structure to suit the requirements of its ever-changing environment.

SOURCES: See Donald F. Harvey, *Business Policy and Strategic Management* (Columbus, OH: Merrill, 1982), pp. 269–70; Thomas J. Peters and Robert H. Waterman, *In Search of Excellence: Lessons from America's best-run companies* (New York: Harper & Row, 1982). Excerpts from 'Who's excellent now?', *Business Week* (5 November 1984), pp. 76–8; Barbara Buell, Robert D. Hof and Gary McWilliams, 'Hewlett-Packard rethinks itself', *Business Week* (1 April 1991), pp. 76–9; and Robert D. Hof, 'Suddenly, Hewlett-Packard is doing everything right', *Business Week* (23 March 1992), pp. 88–9.

programme shows what must be done, who will do it, and how decisions and actions will be co-ordinated. Second, the company's formal *organization structure* plays an important role in implementing marketing strategy. In their study of successful companies, Peters and Waterman found that these firms tended to have simple, flexible structures that allowed them to adapt quickly to changing conditions.[20] Their structures also tended to be more informal – Hewlett-Packard's MBWA (management by walking around), 3M's 'clubs' to create small-group interaction, and Nokia's youthful, egalitarian culture.[21] However, the structures used by these companies may not be right for other types of firm, and many of the study's excellent companies have had to change their structures as their strategies and situations have changed. For example, the same informal structure that made Hewlett-Packard so successful caused problems later. The company has since moved towards a more formal structure (see Marketing Highlight 3.4).

Another factor affecting successful implementation is the company's **decision-and-reward systems** – formal and informal operating procedures that guide planning, budgeting, compensation and other activities. For example, if a company compensates managers for short-run results, they will have little incentive to work towards long-run objectives. Companies recognizing this are broadening their incentive systems to include more than sales volume. For instance, Xerox rewards include customer satisfaction and Ferrero's the freshness of its chocolates in stores. Effective implementation also requires careful planning. At all levels, the company must fill its structure and systems with people who have the necessary skills, motivation and personal characteristics. In recent years,

decision-and-reward system
Formal and informal operating procedures that guide planning, targeting, compensation and other activities

more and more companies have recognized that long-run human resources planning can give the company a strong competitive advantage.

Finally, for successful implementation, the firm's marketing strategies must fit with its culture. *Company culture* is a system of values and beliefs shared by people in an organization. It is the company's collective identity and meaning. The culture informally guides the behaviour of people at all company levels. Marketing strategies that do not fit the company's style and culture will be difficult to implement. Because managerial style and culture are so hard to change, companies usually design strategies that fit their current cultures rather than trying to change their styles and cultures to fit new strategies.[22]

Thus successful marketing implementation depends on how well the company blends the five elements – action programmes, organization structure, decision-and-reward systems, human resources and company culture – into a cohesive programme that supports its strategies.

Summary

Strategic planning involves developing a strategy for long-run survival and growth. Marketing helps in strategic planning, and the overall strategic plan defines marketing's role in the company. Not all companies use formal planning or use it well, yet formal planning offers several benefits. Companies develop three kinds of plan: *annual plans*, *long-range plans* and *strategic plans*.

Strategic planning sets the stage for the rest of company planning. The strategic planning process consists of developing the company's mission, understanding a company's strengths and weaknesses, its environment, business portfolio, objectives and goals, and functional plans. Developing a sound *mission statement* is a challenging undertaking. The mission statement should be market-oriented, feasible, motivating and specific, if it is to direct the firm to its best opportunities.

Companies have plans at many levels: global, regional, national and so forth. The higher-level plans contain objectives and strategies that become part of subordinate plans. These *strategic imperatives* are objectives or defined practices. At each level a *strategic audit* reviews the company and its environment. A *SWOT analysis* summarizes the main elements of this audit into a statement of the company's strengths and weaknesses and the chief threats and opportunities that exist.

From here, strategic planning calls for analyzing the company's *business portfolio* and deciding which businesses should receive more or fewer resources. The company might use a formal portfolio-planning method like the *BCG growth–share matrix* or the *General Electric grid*. However, most companies are now designing more customized portfolio-planning approaches that better suit their unique situations.

This analysis and mission lead to strategic objectives and goals. Management must decide how to achieve growth and profits objectives. The *product/market expansion grid* shows four avenues for market growth: *market penetration*, *market development*, *product development* and *diversification*.

Once strategic objectives and strategies are defined, management must prepare a set of *functional plans* that co-ordinate the activities of the marketing, finance, manufacturing and other departments. Each of the company's *functional departments* provides inputs for strategic planning. Each department has a different idea about which objectives and activities are most important. The marketing department stresses the consumer's point of view. Marketing managers must understand the point of view of the company's other functions and work with other functional managers to develop a system of plans that will best accomplish the firm's overall strategic objectives.

To fulfil their role in the organization, marketers engage in the *marketing process*. Consumers are at the centre of the marketing process. The company divides the total market into smaller segments and selects the segments it can best serve. It then designs its *marketing mix* in order to differentiate its marketing offer and to position this offer in selected target segments. To find the best mix and put it into action, the company engages in marketing analysis, marketing planning, marketing implementation and marketing control.

Each business must prepare marketing plans for its products, brands and markets. The main components of a *marketing plan* are the executive summary, current marketing situation, threats and opportunities, objectives and issues, marketing strategies, action programmes, budgets and controls. To plan good strategies is often easier than to carry them out. To be successful, companies must implement the strategies effectively. *Implementation* is the process that turns marketing strategies into marketing actions. The process consists of five key elements:

1. The *action programme* identifies crucial tasks and decisions needed to implement the marketing plan, assigns them to specific people and establishes a timetable.

2. The *organization structure* defines tasks and assignments and co-ordinates the efforts of the company's people and units.

3. The company's *decision-and-reward systems* guide activities such as planning, information, budgeting, training, control and personnel evaluation and rewards. Well-designed action programmes, organization structures and decision-and-reward systems can encourage good implementation.

4. Successful implementation also requires careful *human resources planning*. The company must recruit, allocate, develop and maintain good people.

5. The firm's *company culture* can also make or break implementation. Company culture guides people in the company; good implementation relies on strong, clearly defined cultures that fit the chosen strategy.

Most of the responsibility for implementation goes to the company's marketing department. Modern marketing activities occur in a number of ways. The most common form is the *functional marketing organization*, in which marketing functions are directed by separate managers who report to the marketing director. The company might also use a *geographic organization*, in which its sales force or other functions specialize by geographic area. The company may also use the *product management organization*, in which products are assigned to product managers who work with functional specialists to develop and achieve their plans. Another form is the *market management organization*, in which main markets are assigned to market managers who work with functional specialists.

Marketing organizations carry out marketing control. *Operating control* involves monitoring results to secure the achievement of annual sales and profit goals. It also calls for determining the profitability of the firm's products, territories, market segments and channels. *Strategic control* makes sure that the company's marketing objectives, strategies and systems fit with the current and forecast marketing environment. It uses the *marketing audit* to determine marketing opportunities and problems, and to recommend short-run and long-run actions to improve overall marketing performance. The company uses these resources to watch and adapt to the marketing environment.

Key Terms

Annual plan 85
Balance sheet 93
Business portfolio 96
Cash cows 97
Critical success factors 95
Current marketing situation 11
Decision-and-reward systems 121
Dogs 98
External audit 93
Growth–share matrix 97
Internal audit 93
Long-range plan 85
Market challenger 109
Market follower 109
Market leader 109

Market nicher 109
Market positioning 108
Market segment 107
Market segmentation 107
Market targeting 107
Marketing audit 111
Marketing control 118
Marketing implementation 116
Marketing mix 109
Marketing process 105
Marketing strategy 106
Mission statement 88
Operating control 118
Operating statement 93
Place 110

Portfolio analysis 96
Price 110
Product 110
Product position 107
Promotion 110
Question marks 98
Stars 97
Strategic business-planning grid 98
Strategic business unit (SBU) 97
Strategic control 118
Strategic plan 85
Strategic planning
SWOT analysis 94

Discussing the Issues

1. What are the benefits of a long-range plan? Why should managers take time to develop a long-term plan that will be changed every year?

2. Many companies undertake a marketing audit to identify the firm's strengths and weaknesses relative to competitors, and in relation to the opportunities and threats in the external environment. Why is it important that such an analysis should address relative, not absolute, company strengths and weaknesses?

3. An electronics manufacturer obtains the semiconductors it uses in production from a company-owned subsidiary that also sells to other manufacturers. The subsidiary is smaller and less profitable than are the competing products. Its growth rate has been below the industry average during the past five years. Into what cell of the BCG growth–share matrix does this strategic business unit fall? What should the parent company do with this SBU?

4. A consumer electronics company finds that sales in its main product line – videocassette recorders – are beginning to stabilize. The market is reaching maturity. What growth strategies might the firm pursue for this product line? How might the strategic-focus tool help managers examine the growth opportunities for this line?

5. The General Electric strategic business-planning grid gives a broad overview that can be helpful in strategic decision making. For what types of decision would this grid be helpful? For what types of strategic decision would it be less useful?

6. Sony is the market leader in audio/hi-fi systems, offering a wide range of equipment at moderately high prices. Discuss how a competitor would use market-challenger, market-follower and market-nicher strategies to compete effectively with Sony.

Applying the Concepts

1. Think about the shopping area near where you live. Assume that you wish to start a business here and are looking for a promising opportunity for a restaurant, a clothing store or a music store.

   ● Is there an opportunity to open a distinctive and promising business? Describe your target market and how you will serve it differently than current businesses do.

   ● What sort of marketing mix would you use for your business?

2. Take a product or service organization you are familiar with (you may refer to your college or university).

   ● List the key external environmental opportunities or threats that face the organization.

- What do you think are the organization's main strengths and weaknesses?
- Suggest ways in which the organization might respond to the external forces.

- Recommend a possible marketing strategy which will ensure that the organization matches its internal capabilities with external opportunities.

References

1. See 'Dockers muscle in on Sweden with the world's biggest advertisement', *The European* (1–7 April 1994), p. 21; 'Levi's: the jeans giant slipped as the market shifted', *Business Week* (5 November 1984), pp. 79–80; Miriam Rozen, 'The 501 blues', *Madison Avenue* (November 1984), pp. 22–6; Marc Beauchamp, 'Tight fit', *Forbes* (11 August 1986); Joshua Hyatt, 'Levi Strauss learns a fitting lesson', *Inc.* (August 1985), p. 17; Brenton R. Schlender, 'How Levi Strauss did an LBO right', *Fortune* (7 May 1990), pp. 105–7; Maria Shao, 'For Levi's, a flattering fit overseas', *Business Week* (5 November 1990), pp. 76–7; 'A comfortable fit', *The Economist* (22 June 1991), pp. 67–8; Marcy Magiera and Pat Sloan, 'Levi's, Lee loosen up for baby boomers', *Advertising Age* (3 August 1992), p. 9; Marcy Magiera, 'Levi's Dockers looks for younger, upscale men with authentics', *Advertising Age* (18 January 1993), p. 4.

2. Malcolm MacDonald investigates the barriers to marketing planning in his article 'Ten barriers to marketing planning', *Journal of Marketing Management*, 5, 1 (1989), pp. 1–18.

3. To see how planning and entrepreneurship exist side by side and how the best-performing companies have balanced orientation towards marketing and technology, see Veronica Wong and John Saunders, 'Business orientation and corporate success', *Journal of Strategic Marketing*, 1, 1 (1993), pp. 20–40.

4. Michael E. Porter, *Competitive Advantage: Creating and sustaining competitive performance* (New York: Free Press, 1985).

5. For more on mission statements, see G. Hooley and Laura Nash, 'Mission statements – mirrors and windows', *Harvard Business Review* (March–April 1988), pp. 155–6; Fred R. David, 'How companies define their missions statements', *Long Range Planning*, 22, 1 (1989), pp. 90–7.

6. Michael Porter popularized his view of value chains through his book *Competitive Advantage*, op. cit.

7. Kenneth Goading, 'High speed steel group rolls towards flotation', *Financial Times* (24 June 1994), p. 27.

8. See Daniel H. Gray, 'Uses and misuses of strategic planning', *Harvard Business Review* (January–February 1986), pp. 89–96; Roger A. Kerin, Vijay Mahajan and P. Rajan Varadarajan, *Contemporary Perspectives on Strategic Planning* (Boston: Allyn & Bacon, 1990).

9. Richard G. Hamermesh, 'Making planning strategic', *Harvard Business Review* (July–August 1986), pp. 115–20.

10. H. Igor Ansoff, 'Strategies for diversification', *Harvard Business Review* (September–October 1957), pp. 113–24.

11. Information taken from: Guy de Jonquières, 'Pell-mell expansion has sparked controversy', *Financial Times* (11 June 1991), p. 8; Christopher Parkes, 'New car plant will be test for "lean production"', *Financial Times* (25 June 1992), p. 4.

12. John C. Narver and Stanley F. Slater, 'The effect of a marketing orientation on business profitability', *Journal of Marketing* (October 1990), pp. 20–35.

13. 'Quality '93: empowering people with technology', advertising supplement, *Fortune* (20 September 1993). For more reading, see Yoram Wind, 'Marketing and the other business functions', in Jagdish N. Sheth (ed.), *Research in Marketing*, vol. 5 (Greenwich, CT: JAI Press, 1981), pp. 237–56; Robert W. Ruekert and Orville C. Walker, Jr, 'Marketing's interaction with other functional units: a conceptual framework and empirical evidence', *Journal of Marketing* (January 1987), pp. 1–19.

14. For more on follower strategies, see Daniel W. Haines, Rajan Chandran and Arvind Parkhe, 'Winning by being first to market … or second?', *Journal of Consumer Marketing* (Winter 1989), pp. 63–9.

15. The four-P classification was first suggested by E. Jerome McCarthy, *Basic Marketing: A managerial approach* (Homewood, IL: Irwin, 1960). For more discussion of this classification scheme, see Walter van Waterschoot and Christophe Van den Bulte, 'The 4P classification of the marketing mix revisited', *Journal of Marketing* (October 1992), pp. 83–93.

16. Robert Lauterborn, 'New marketing litany: four Ps passé; C-words take over', *Advertising Age* (1 October 1990), p. 26.

17. For an interesting discussion of marketing budgeting methods and processes, see Nigel F. Piercy, 'The marketing budgeting process: marketing management implications', *Journal of Marketing* (October 1987), pp. 45–59.

18. See Robert Dewar and Don Schultz, 'The product manager: an idea whose time has gone', *Marketing Communications* (May 1989), pp. 28–35; Kevin T. Higgins, 'Category management: new tool changing life for manufacturers and retailers', *Marketing News* (25 September 1989), pp. 2, 19; Ira Teinowitz, 'Brand managers: 90s dinosaurs?', *Advertising Age* (19 December 1988); Betsey Spethman, 'Category management multiplies', *Advertising Age* (11 May 1992), p. 42; Guy de Jonquières, 'A clean break with tradition', *Financial Times* (12 July 1993), p. 12.

19. Amar Bhide, 'Hustle as strategy', *Harvard Business Review* (September–October 1986), p. 59.

20. See Thomas J. Peters and Robert H. Waterman, *In Search of Excellence: Lessons from America's best-run companies* (New York: Harper & Row, 1982). For an excellent summary of the study's findings on structure, see David A. Aaker, *Strategic Market Management*, 2nd edn (New York: Wiley, 1988), pp. 154–7.

21. Greg McIvor, 'Nokia becomes a world leader', *The European* (26 August–6 September 1994), p. 28.

22. For more on company cultures, see Rohit Deshpande and Frederick E. Webster, Jr, 'Organizational culture and marketing: defining the research agenda', *Journal of Marketing* (January 1989), pp. 3–15; Brian Dumaine, 'Creating a new company culture', *Fortune* (15 January 1990), pp. 127–31; John P. Kotter and James L. Heskett, *Corporate Culture and Performance* (New York: Free Press, 1992).

Case 3

Look Out Lipton, Here Comes Oolong!

Heating up an old product

Chinese Emperor Shen Nung was boiling water under a Camellia Sinensis tree in 2,737 BC. When some leaves fell into the pot, he found the resulting infusion pleasant. So, the legend has it, tea was born. From this accident flowed the Opium Wars, the annexation of Hong Kong and rituals that have made tea far more than just a drink in the great tea-drinking nations of China, Japan and Britain.

Thomas J. Lipton Company has been in the tea business ever since *Cutty Sark* and other tea clippers raced *Cape Horn* and *The Cape of Good Hope* to be the first to the European and American coffee houses with their crop from the Orient. By the 1990s the excitement had left the declining tea market. To enliven the old-fashioned product market leader, Unilever resorted to selling Lipton, along with its other leading brands, Brook Bond, PG Tips, Red Label and Taaza, using frantic sales promotions and comical characters. Then, the boring business heated up by cooling down.

Chalk up the change to those fickle consumers. Forget soft drinks. They were the rage of the 1980s, as the cola companies added 'diet everything' to their lines and experimented with all sorts of flavours. Forget sports drinks. They became the glamour drinks of the late 1980s and early 1990s as the soft-drink market levelled and the cola companies searched for growth opportunities. Forget those flavoured sparkling waters, like Oasis and Perrier. They had a wild ride in the early 1990s and became a health sensation. Forget coffee. After being battered by soft drinks, the venerable standby has risen as people have begun to turn away from alcoholic drinks and entrepreneurs have rediscovered the coffee house. However, today's hot drink is iced tea. Yes, iced tea. In fact, it's iced tea in a bottle or can, already prepared and ready to drink. No fuss, no boiling and no tea bags.

Iced tea is not new. We can trace iced tea's invention to the 1904 World's Fair in St Louis. Richard Blechynden, a promoter of Indian and Ceylon tea, found it impossible to peddle his hot tea in the stifling Missouri heat. In desperation he dumped some ice cubes into his tea and discovered that the spectators were willing to gulp anything cold. Iced tea in a can isn't new either. That's been around since the early 1970s, but it had never been more than a blip on the beverage market's radar screen.

Adding flavour

Flavour is what's new. In the USA, Snapple started the trend by building a regional cult following based on bottled iced teas that featured zany flavours like cranberry, peach and raspberry. Snapple's flavoured, hot-filled tea (the manufacturer bottles the tea while it is still warm from brewing) offered consumers a better-tasting tea. Before Snapple, Lipton and others offered iced teas in plain and lemon flavour. Young, trend-setting consumers bought

Snapple directly from ice cabinets in convenience stores and delicatessens and drank it straight from the bottle.

The flavoured teas hit a bull's-eye with consumers. They were willing to move away from traditional colas in search of new flavours. Consumers seemed to have a short attention span for new products and were willing to try new drinks. They were interested in so-called 'New Age' beverages – drinks that appealed to their desire for healthier, lighter refreshment. Consumers responded to the all natural, no-calorie, relaxing and refreshing claims that the new-age beverages made. Increasingly on the go, consumers also liked the convenience and availability of ready-to-drink teas.

Forming teams
Despite the small size of the iced tea market, the big players noticed the growth rate and jumped in. Coca-Cola made the first move by teaming up with Nestlé to form Coca-Cola Nestlé Refreshments, combining Coca-Cola's powerful distribution network with Nestlé's tea expertise and its Nestea brand. Pepsi-Cola followed by joining forces with Thomas J. Lipton Company. Barq's energized its Luzianne tea brand, A & W announced it would make and distribute Tetley tea, Cadbury uncovered little-known All Seasons to serve as its tea partner and Perrier joined forces with Celestial Seasonings.

Lipton was already no. 1 in the tea market, but like Coca-Cola, Pepsi's top management argued that the company's alliance with Lipton would leverage Pepsi's distribution strength with Lipton's leadership in tea to produce a can't-miss proposition. Lipton's president observed that the new partnership would make Lipton 'as widely available as Pepsi'.

The entrance of Pepsi, Coca-Cola and their competitors should invigorate the ready-to-drink tea market. One observer noted that the iced-tea market was still a small market despite growing 50 per cent between 1990 and 1991. And it was getting very overcrowded. Indeed, all this attention produced almost 200 new ready-to-drink teas during 1991 and 1992. The tea category leaped another 50 per cent in 1992 and the same again in 1993. The competitors generated this growth by dusting off tea's boring image and recasting it as a natural, better-for-you beverage. Further, scientific evidence emerged that tea inhibited certain types of cancer in laboratory mice and seemed to be linked to lower cholesterol rates. Lipton, Nestea and Snapple lured customers with new flavours and pointed out that lack of carbonation makes iced tea easier to drink rapidly and in quantity.

Although Coca-Cola/Nestlé's Nestea sales soared, Snapple's and Lipton's grew even faster. As a result, Nestea narrowed its promotion to target 18- to 29-year-olds with a promotional blitz consisting of sponsorships and sampling. It dispatched five 18-wheeler demonstration trucks, which it called its 'Cool Out Caravans' to sporting events, theme parks and beaches in 60 markets.

Pepsi continued its cola-style marketing for Lipton teas. Its radio ads argued that Snapple is 'mixed up from a powder', but Lipton is 'real brewed'. Pepsi also promoted Lipton in supermarkets by offering customers 'value packs' that contained one bottle each of three new drinks: Lipton Original, Ocean Spray Lemonade and AllSport sports drink. Pepsi also pursued sponsorship of a Rolling Stones concert tour, to which it would link a massive sampling programme.

Because of its efforts, Lipton's teas seemed ready to unseat Coca-Cola/ Nestlé, despite its early market entry, was falling behind in the iced-tea wars. Lipton was taking market share from both Snapple and Nestea. One observer noted that Pepsi had done a better job with Lipton and new-age beverages than the Coke system had. Perhaps as a result, Coca-Cola and Nestlé announced they were dissolving their relationship. Coca-Cola would take the primary responsibility for marketing ready-to-drink Nestea, while Nestlé would focus on ready-to-drink coffees. Analysts suggested that the new arrangement would give Coca-Cola more speed and flexibility because it would not have to deal with Nestlé on every decision.

Oolong enters from the East

Just as Lipton seems to be pulling ahead in the 'new tea' market, a threat looms from tea's homeland. Shin Shii Industrial Company, a little-known beverage company based in a dusty industrial city in southern Taiwan, has emerged as a giant-killer in the Taiwanese beverage market. In 1985 Shin Shii launched Kai Shii oolong tea, a canned ready-to-drink iced tea. Although iced tea was popular in other Pacific Rim countries like Japan, the Taiwanese had never heard of iced tea. They drank only fresh-brewed hot tea.

Beginning in 1991, Shin Shii and its advertising agency Metaphysical Punctuality Advertising Company used an offbeat multimillion dollar advertising campaign to propel Kai Shii from back shelves in mom-and-pop stores to prominent spots in rapidly growing convenience-store chains, grocery stores, hypermarkets and warehouse clubs. The ads proclaimed that Kai Shii was the choice of a 'new breed of people' in a 'new world' and featured 'neo-people' who spanned all age groups, even the tradition-bound older generation. The ads presented Kai Shii as a natural drink that fits with people's concerns for their health and the environment. Some ads made fun of inebriated businesspeople who drank foreign liquors, picturing them alongside fresh-faced Kai Shii tea drinkers.

In 1993 Kai Shii's advertising team travelled to China to film scenes of Chinese peasants clad in colourful traditional costumes. They put these scenes in Kai Shii ads that played on the emotions generated by Taiwan's growing ties with mainland China. The ads won a first-place award at the Cannes Film festival.

Through aggressive advertising, Kai Shii now dominates the nearly 100 brands in the Oolong sector of Taiwan's ready-to-drink tea market. Kai Shii doubled its share to 25 per cent of the overall market and 70 per cent of the Oolong tea segment.

Furthermore, consumer demand for ready-to-drink iced tea has cut sharply into sales of carbonated soft drinks. Soft-drink sales in Taiwan have plummeted by 16 per cent, while ready-to-drink sales have more than doubled. The sales trend hit Coke and Pepsi especially hard, and Pepsi said it would move to reduce costs.

Next, Kai Shii's ads went global, featuring young Chinese living in New York City and Europeans living in London and Paris. These ads were just the opening salvos as Shin Shii turned its sights on foreign markets. Its managers plan to use the skills they have honed in Taiwan to enter the US market.

In entering western markets, Shin Shii will face the challenge of introducing consumers to the smooth-tasting, amber-coloured oolong tea. Lipton and Pepsi will face the challenge of a new competitor that has already shown it can succeed in selling iced tea and in taking share from soft drinks. The local producers are not standing still. They now intend to use hot tea to displace colas and other soft drinks sold to people to consume 'on the hoof'. In late 1997 Unilever was adding to its Liptonice with a radical new way of selling hot tea. Having spent £10 million developing hot cans to be sold in convenience stores and petrol stations, it was ready to test market the product in Manchester, England. Brooks Bond's PG Tips will be sold in ring-pull tins kept at 56°C in a heated cabinet on shop counters. On sale alongside PG Tips, with or without sugar, will be Red Mountain coffee, sweetened or unsweetened, and Choky, the leading French hot chocolate brand. Watch out Oolong, Brook Bond's waiting!

Questions

1. What bases can companies use to segment the iced-tea market?

2. What potential market segments can you identify?

3. How would you go about forecasting demand in the iced-tea market and in any given segment?

4. Which type of market coverage strategy should Pepsi/Lipton adopt? Why? How should they position Lipton iced teas and Brook Bond canned teas?

5. If you were advising Shin Shii, what marketing strategy recommendations would you make concerning its entry into the market?

6. How should it position Kai Shii?

SOURCES: Sally D. Goll, 'Taiwan soft drink sales break for tea', *Wall Street Journal* (29 July 1994), p. A7B, used with permission of *Wall Street Journal*. See also: Laurie M. Grossman, 'Coca-Cola, Nestlé are ending venture in tea and coffee but plan other ties', *Wall Street Journal* (30 August 1994), p. B3; Laura Bird, 'Trouble is brewing for Snapple as rivals fight for iced tea sales', *Wall Street Journal* (9 June 1994), p. B4; Eric Sfiligoj, 'Ladies and gentlemen and beverages of all ages', *Beverages World* (April 1994), pp. 42–7; Gerry Khermouch, 'Nestea iced tea plans summer push', *Adweek* (21 March 1994), p. 13; Michael J. McCarthy, 'Competition heats up iced-tea industry', *Wall Street Journal* (15 June 1993), p. B1; Kevin Goldman, 'Snapple goes big time for new age drink', *Wall Street Journal* (20 April 1993), p. B6; Greg W. Prince, 'Tea for all', *Beverage World* (April 1992), pp. 24–32; Maggie Urry, 'Tea in a can is hot tip from Brook Bond,' *Financial Times* (13 December 1997), p. 4; Gary Mead, 'Brewing a healthier image for tea', *Financial Times*, 7 April 1997 (FT web archives); 'Twinings', http://www.cuttsark.org.uk/twining; 'Lipton', http://www.lipton.com; 'Tea Council', http://www.teacouncil.co..uk.

KitKat: Have a break …

Sylvie Laforet* and Andy Hirst**

Introduction

 Sonia Ng sat down to have a cup of tea with her friend, David Johnson, in the company's dimly lit canteen in York, in the north of England. She unwrapped the bright red paper band from a KitKat, then ran a finger down the foil between the two biscuits. She snapped the biscuits apart, handed one to David and sighed: 'This KitKat is not going to be like any I have eaten before.' As a new assistant brand manager, Sonia had to prepare the 1995 brand plan for KitKat. It was a great break for her as KitKat was Nestlé's top confectionery brand. Her first action was to gather what information she could about the brand, then talk to managers who knew about it.

Nestlé Rowntree

Rowntree launched KitKat in August 1935 as 'Chocolate Crisp'. Renamed twice – in 1937 as 'KitKat Chocolate Crisp' and in 1949 as 'KitKat' – by 1950 it was Rowntree's biggest brand and it has remained so ever since. The origin of KitKat's name is uncertain. Some believe the name came from the eighteenth-century political KitKat Club, itself named after one Christopher (or Kit) Cat, who kept a pie house where the club met. The name KitKat has favourable onomatopoeic qualities that help the association of the wafer biscuit with a dry, soft snapping or cracking, as of the biscuit being broken or bitten. Other Rowntree brands include Rowntree's Fruit Pastilles (launched 1881), Rowntree's Fruit Gums (1893), Black Magic (1933), Aero (1935), Dairy Box (1936), Smarties (1937), Polo (1948) and After Eight (1962).

Nestlé Rowntree is Nestlé's largest works and the United Kingdom's largest exporter of chocolate and sugar confectionery, selling to over 120 countries. The most important markets are Europe and the Middle East. Besides the United Kingdom, the European markets include France, Germany, Belgium, Holland,

* Birmingham University.   ** Loughborough University

Italy and Ireland. The chocolate biscuit countline (CBCL) market is not as large in the rest of Europe as it is in the United Kingdom. The proportions of KitKat volume sales are 67 per cent for the United Kingdom, 10.6 for Germany and 5.6 for France. And since the early 1990s Nestlé has developed its overseas markets by more than 50 per cent.

Strategic Objectives

Net operating profits, return on capital employed (ROCE) and market shares drive the company. Each product group has objectives. The company has a cascade system so that each brand has its objectives as well. Each has a brand plan – business plans for each brand. One of the strategic objectives of Nestlé is to increase sales across the European markets. Often the marketing managers are not always able to put in capital to supply across Europe. To do this Nestlé have had to adopt a penetration strategy, which means that the margins are lower and this has a depressing effect on the group's ROCE.

The company's long-term aims are to become the clear leader in the UK confectionery industry and to generate real growth in the profitability and productivity of its confectionery business. It also aims to increase the efficiency of its supply chain and so improve customer service.

Business Strategy

The company's strategy is to pursue the company's objectives rather than to defend its position against competitors. For example, some countlines are 'below threshold size'. The objective for these is to improve the performance up to the threshold level. Rod Flint, the director of J. Walter Thompson, which is responsible for Nestlé Rowntree's advertising, comments: 'Their objective is not always driven by the stock market. That gives Nestlé a long-term perspective. They are into world brand domination and they are highly global in their approach now, since they are also organizing their European marketing department.'

Basic principles drive the company's brand strategy. It believes in offering the consumer value for money. It also believes in developing long-term brands and aims to differentiate its products from one another within the brand portfolio, which the company thinks will offer a competitive advantage over those of its competitors. The company works to ensure that its brands maintain clear positions in order to prevent cannibalization. Up to now, the best way to achieve this has been stand-alone product brands, as opposed to umbrella brands. More recently, however, the cost of establishing new brands has increased very dramatically. The company is continually looking for ways to leverage the brand across the confectionery business and other product categories. Nestlé also wishes to improve its corporate image by associating its name more closely with successful brands. For example, KitKat has become Nestlé KitKat. Part of the company's brand policy is also to dedicate significant sums of money to advertising and promotions. This helps to build customer loyalty and block the entrance of new competitors. On average, 10 per cent of the sales value of the brand goes on advertising and promotions.

KitKat

When launched KitKat entered a market already dominated by Cadbury's Dairy Milk. From its beginning, KitKat was positioned as both a confectionery and a snack. It is now positioned half-way between a snack and an indulgence. In the consumers' eyes, however, KitKat is essentially a snack product and its 1957 slogan 'Have a break, have a KitKat' is widely known through long-running ads on TV and in other media.

The KitKat brand has two formats in the UK. The two-finger format is bought in a multipack (packs of eight or more) at large grocers by parents for their children. In contrast, the four-finger format is bought individually by 16–24-year-olds for their consumption (Exhibits 1.1 and 1.2). The two-finger format is part of the CBCL sector, which implies specific usage, non-personal and 'family' consumption, as well as in snack and lunch boxes for kids' consumption. The four-finger format is part of the general chocolate countline sector, which implies personal consumption, broad usage and the 'adults' and 'self-eats' categories. The

EXHIBIT 1.1 CBCL MULTIPACKS MARKET (£M)

YEAR	KITKAT 2-FINGER MULTIPACKS	PENGUIN MULTIPACKS	CLUB MULTIPACKS	CBCL MULTIPACKS AND MINIS
1990	91	50	40	449
1991	95	55	39	478
1992	101	58	39	508
1993	110	53	45	530
1994	112	48	47	535

SOURCES: BCCCA, AC Nielsen TN-AGB and despatches.

EXHIBIT 1.2 CBCL MANUFACTURER PERFORMANCE (1994)

	% SHARE	% CHANGE YEAR ON YEAR
Nestlé Rowntree	25.3	−2.6
United Biscuits	17.4	−15.7
Jacobs Bakery	12.0	−1.5
Mars Confectionery	3.3	−14.0
Burtons	7.1	−14.3
Thomas Tunnocks	3.8	−3.5
Fox's	7.8	51.8
Others	5.7	3.6
Cadbury	2.2	n/a
Private label	15.3	25.6
Total market		0.9

SOURCE: AGB Superpanel.

EXHIBIT 1.3 COUNTLINE MARKET (£M)

YEAR	KITKAT 4-FINGER	MARS	TIME OUT	COUNTLINES
1990	76	137	0	1,529
1991	87	138	0	1,677
1992	92	142	18	1,723
1993	93	148	20	1,787
1994	96	159	39	1,865

SOURCES: BCCCA, AC Nielsen and despatches.

four-finger format was the main volume format, but was overtaken by the two-finger format (Exhibit 1.3) as the grocery sector rose at the expense of the CTNs (confectioner/tobacconist/newsagent). About 18 per cent of KitKat two-finger's volume goes through cash-and-carry to CTN, compared with 80 per cent of the four-finger format.

Nestlé Rowntree divides the chocolate market into three categories: chocolate box assortments (a gift-oriented marketplace); the countline market (a 'self-eat' market) – a consumer-product category (i.e. KitKat four-finger); and CBCL – a sector that the company created. Thus Nestlé Rowntree has developed the KitKat business by marketing it as a countline product in its four-finger format, and by developing it as a CBCL in its two-finger format. This helped KitKat cover two sections in their stores, one selling confectionery and the other selling biscuits.

Another reason for promoting KitKat as a CBCL is the growing power of the multiple grocers (Exhibits 1.4 and 1.5). There is a shift from a less structured retail sector into multiple businesses that are sophisticated and powerful. The company produces different packs for the multiple grocers and the independent sector. This avoids direct price and value comparison by the consumer and, therefore, restricts the power of the multiple retailers in their negotiations to increase their profitability.

EXHIBIT 1.4 KITKAT VOLUME DISTRIBUTION

(A) DISTRIBUTION (%)

| YEAR | INDEPENDENT GROCERS COVERED | | INDEPENDENT CTNs COVERED | | |
	KITKAT 2-FINGER	PENGUIN	KITKAT 4-FINGER	MARS BAR	TIME OUT
1990	49	65	99	99	0
1991	50	50	99	99	3
1992	57	52	99	99	33
1993	64	64	99	99	95
1994	65	71	99	99	94

(B) KITKAT 2-FINGER SHARE OF CBCL FORWARD STOCKS (%)

| YEAR | MULTIPLE GROCERS | | MULTIPLE CTNs | | INDEPENDENT GROCERS | |
	KITKAT	PENGUIN	KITKAT	PENGUIN	KITKAT	PENGUIN
1990	20.3	12.9	45.2	3.8	12.8	15.9
1991	14.9	12.3	43.9	5.1	12.1	14.6
1992	11.9	10.3	43.4	6.5	15.0	14.3
1993	12.2	9.3	28.0	8.4	12.6	14.4
1994	12.6	9.9	38.5	5.5	13.4	15.8

(C) KITKAT 4-FINGER SHARE COUNTLINE OF FORWARD STOCKS (%)

YEAR	MULTIPLE GROCERS	MULTIPLE CTNs	INDEPENDENT CTNs	INDEPENDENT GROCERS
1990	5.4	4.2	4.7	5.8
1991	5.3	4.1	4.6	6.0
1992	4.4	3.7	4.8	5.4
1993	4.4	4.0	4.5	5.5
1994	6.0	3.6	4.4	5.1

SOURCE: AC Nielsen.

EXHIBIT 1.5 KITKAT SALES BY PACK AND SECTOR (TONNES)

	2-FINGER			4-FINGER		
YEAR	SINGLES	MULTIPACKS	OTHER	SINGLES	MULTIPACKS	OTHER
All customers						
1990	1,150	20,750	300	15,550	3,000	0
1991	1,200	20,800	200	16,950	3,700	50
1992	1,200	21,300	100	17,150	3,250	0
1993	800	21,900	0	16,300	3,300	0
1994	700	23,150	100	15,850	3,750	0
Multiple retail						
1990	50	18,750	100	1,800	2,750	0
1991	50	18,850	50	2,050	3,450	0
1992	50	19,300	50	2,100	3,100	0
1993	50	19,950	0	1,950	3,200	0
1994	50	21,200	50	1,900	3,600	0
Wholesale/ independent						
1990	1,100	2,000	200	13,750	250	0
1991	1,150	1,950	150	14,900	250	50
1992	1,150	2,000	50	15,050	150	0
1993	750	1,950	0	14,350	100	0
1994	650	1,950	50	13,950	150	0

SOURCES: Internal.

The market share for KitKat two-finger was 19.5 per cent of the CBCL market in 1994 – the no. 1 seller (Exhibit 1.6). KitKat's nearest competitors are Mars Bars and Twix, both Mars products. Twix was launched as a countline product, but is now marketed as single fingers in the multipack format in the CBCL category. KitKat two-finger's main CBCL competitors are United Biscuits and Jacobs; in the general chocolate countline category, KitKat four-finger's main competitors are Mars and Cadbury.

EXHIBIT 1.6 CBCL BRAND PERFORMANCE

BRAND	% SHARE (EXPENDITURE)	% CHANGE (YEAR ON YEAR)
KitKat 2-finger	19.5	2.5
Penguin	8.8	7.4
Club	9.0	–7.7
Twix	3.3	–13.6
Rocky	4.1	159.3
Blue Riband	2.7	–4.0
Breakaway	2.7	–7.9
Wagon Wheel	4.7	–15.3
Tunnocks CW	3.4	–2.1
Classic	2.4	–11.2
Trio	2.2	–5.3
Private label	15.3	25.6

SOURCE: AGB Superpanel.

The Market

The chocolate confectionery market is concentrated, stable and very competitive. The leading suppliers are Cadbury (28 per cent market share), Nestlé Rowntree (25), Mars (21) and Terry's Suchard (5). KitKat has the biggest advertising expenditure in the UK confectionery market. The £1.5 billion confectionery snack market, including countlines and chocolate blocks, is 38 per cent of the confectionery market. This market has grown by 20 per cent over the past five years, following the rise in popularity of snacking. Growth in both the countline market and the CBCL sector has now stabilized. As market leader, KitKat has retained a price premium and set prices for its competitors to follow. There is a risk to volume if the market does not follow. The market share for KitKat four-finger was 7 per cent within the general countline market. KitKat four-finger had lost some of its market share to Mars Bar (Exhibit 1.7). However, it still remains a weak no. 3, competing with two other Mars products, Twix and Snickers.

EXHIBIT 1.7 BRAND SHARES

	VALUE		VOLUME	
BRAND	% 1994	% POINTS CHANGE	% 1994	% POINTS CHANGE
KitKat 4-finger	6.7	–0.1	7.1	0
Mars Bar	13.9	0.8	19.0	1.1
Snickers	7.5	–0.3	9.2	–0.3
Twix	4.9	0	6.1	0
Twirl	3.3	–0.2	2.7	–0.3
Time Out	2.7	–0.3	2.2	–0.2
Drifter	1.3	0	1.4	0

SOURCE: Nielsen (countlines and filled blocks excluding CBCL multis).

New-product development, which fuelled countline growth, has seen a number of new entrants. Firstly, the CBCL market has seen the entrance of Fox's Rocky bar. Rocky has claimed 4.1 per cent of the market. The second major new-product development has been made by Cadbury. It launched the Fuse bar – a mixture of chocolate, fudge and raisins. It cost £7 million to create, sold 40 million bars in its first week and was becoming the second most popular chocolate bar in the UK.

Pressure will continue to be on the countline market as the population of 15–24-year-olds declines. The KitKat two-finger sales are biased towards the C1 and C2 socioeconomic and the 35–44 age groups. There is also a high penetration of very young consumers, particularly in the 12–15 age group. The four-finger format has a smarter image, inclines more towards 'chocolate occasions' consumption, and is consumed on the street. Consumption is heavily biased towards female buyers. The two-finger format ads aim at the 35–44 year olds through morning television. Children are not specifically targeted. The four-finger format ads target the 16–24–year-olds through TV and youth press. The ad strategy for this format is different from that of the two-finger. The company puts an emphasis on updating KitKat's brand image by making it appeal to the younger generation through advertising in trendy and young people's magazines and independent radio.

The promotions for the two-finger format are value- and grocery-trade-oriented (for example, 'one bar free' activity, or repeat purchase incentives). For the four-finger format, the promotions are different because of the different segments targeted (for example, 1p off). However, there is an annual pan-

promotion for KitKat as a whole that consists of big promotions, price and emphasis on brand awareness. There is a price differentiation between the two formats. KitKat four-finger is 'twin-priced' in parallel with Twix, and 2p below the Mars Bar. This is because KitKat is 'snacky' and not as hunger satisfying as the Mars Bar. If the company deviated from this pricing strategy, its volume share might drop. The two-finger format is not as price-sensitive as the four-finger. As a market leader within the CBCL category, it can more or less dictate price. Thus its competitor Penguin is priced 2p below KitKat two-finger. According to Nestlé brand managers, 'The objective for KitKat is to maintain customer loyalty by being innovative, and to remain *the* number one UK confectionery brand.' There is evidence of relative brand loyalty for KitKat. However, people who buy KitKat two-finger will also be likely to buy other brands, such as Classic, Club Orange, Penguin, Twix, Blue Riband and Gold. According to Brian Ford, the brand manager for the KitKat two-finger: 'Although Nestlé has tried to differentiate the two formats of KitKat in its segmentation and positioning strategies, the consumer sees no difference in the total brand.'

In light of the recent developments, KitKat has worked hard to maintain its position as the market leader. In the spring of 1996, the UK's favourite confectionery brand took on a new taste. Nestlé launched KitKat Orange, the first flavour variant in its 59-year history. However, the variant was launched as a limited edition and the product was released for only one month. The success of the product was so phenomenal that customers were writing letters to have the product re-released. On 31 January 1997 a Nestlé press release revealed that Nestlé was launching a limited edition Mint KitKat. This new variant was even more popular in trials than KitKat Orange.

Competition

Competition is likely to come from small brands, grocery retailers' own labels and other lines coming into the United Kingdom. There is also a cross-over between the chocolate countline and the CBCL sector. Cadbury has recently encroached into KitKat's 'Have a break' territory with Time Out – a bar aimed at the CBCL sector. Time Out aims to bridge the gap between chocolate snack bars, such as Twirl, and wafer-based snacks, such as KitKat. It will compete with KitKat and Twix and should take sales away from brands with a 'heavy sweet' product image, like Spira and Twix.

Competition from other European confectioners has intensified with the growth of discounters such as Aldi and Netto. This might lead to a price-cutting war in the multiple grocery sector, especially among Kwik Save, Lo-Cost and Asda. Aldi is a particular concern because it is importing bags of KitKat minis from Germany. Although Nestlé Rowntree sells many of its countlines as minis, it does not make or sell KitKat in that format. Besides losing it revenue, Aldi's KitKat minis cause other problems: first, large grocers, like Sainsbury and Tesco, now want supplies of minis like Aldi's; second, the biscuit and chocolate used to make the German KitKat are distinctly different from those used in Britain.

Outside the United Kingdom, the four-finger format sells more than the two-finger format. European retailers outside the United Kingdom also emphasize minis (Aldi only imports that form). Nestlé Rowntree does sell minis in the United Kingdom, but these are very low-volume products and appear only in variety packs with other Nestlé minis. The company does not see them as a threat to its existing brands as the volume of minis is relatively low in comparison.

The company is now producing to capacity. The problem is managing demand in the marketplace. 'We can't give them any more, so we use price to limit demand and to get maximum profit return on the amount we produce,' explains Ford. In his opinion, this is easier for the two-finger format because it is the market leader in the CBCL category, but is less easy in the four-finger case. 'It is not the market leader in the chocolate countline sector, therefore we cannot dictate price.'

Pan-European Marketing

To fit the regulations across Europe, some KitKats produced by Nestlé Rowntree have different chocolate to others. Although they taste different consumers cannot tell the difference. The management of so many internationally important brands limits Nestlé Rowntree's freedom of action outside the United Kingdom. The pricing relationships between, say, France, Germany and the United Kingdom need careful controlling. At the same time, the company needs to achieve its UK business objectives. The marketing of brands will be different because these brands are at different product life-cycle states in different markets. 'The United Kingdom is probably the most sophisticated confectionery market in Europe,' claims Robertson. 'Therefore, for example, the company's advertising style for KitKat is not directly transferable to Germany. The German consumer does not understand the British sense of humour,' explains Robertson. 'So, from the business perspective, there is a pulling together in Europe, while from the consumer perspective, there are still marked differences between different types of consumers, and that is the biggest problem.'

The packing used for KitKat in the United Kingdom is different from that used elsewhere. So KitKat exported to Germany does not have UK packaging and vice versa. Germany's KitKat is flow-wrapped, whereas the United Kingdom has a foil and band. This relatively expensive format appeared because of the early competition with Cadbury, whose market-leading milk chocolate bars had blue foil and a blue wrapper. To differentiate it from Cadbury, the KitKat pack is a silver foil with a visually strong red band wrapped end to end.

Standardization to less expensive flow wrap is resisted in the United Kingdom because of the ritualistic way that UK consumers eat KitKat. Often they eat KitKat socially over a cup of tea. When eating KitKat, many consumers first take off the red wrapper, then run a finger down the foil between two biscuits. With the top of the foil broken, the KitKat fingers are snapped off and then eaten one by one, just as KitKat's new assistant brand manager, Sonia Ng, did. Her job was to develop a brand plan for KitKat. For her it was a great break; but not an easy one.

SOURCES: Prepared with assistance from: the advertising agency J. Walter Thompson, London; Nestlé Rowntree, York; and Nestec, Vevey, Switzerland. Updated from the original by Sylvie Laforet: Kotler, Armstrong, Saunders and Wong, *Principles of Marketing: The European Edition* (London: Prentice Hall, 1996), pp. 115–26. Names, statistics and some details have been changed for commercial reasons.

Questions

1. What is the situation facing KitKat: the strengths and weaknesses of the brand and the opportunities and threats it faces?
2. Why are the KitKat two-fingers and four-fingers marketed differently? How do the customers for the KitKat four-finger differ from those for the KitKat two-finger? What are the differences in the way the company addresses the two target markets?

package was changed to concentrate use of the product in lower temperatures and on white fabrics. The company attempted to reassure consumers through advertisements that guaranteed the safety of its revamped product. But then the Dutch consumers' union confirmed the damaging effects of the upgraded Power.

In late 1994, Unilever management finally admitted: 'We made a mistake. We launched a product which had a defect which we had not detected. We were very enthusiastic about an exciting new product and did not look closely enough at the negatives. Somewhere between research and marketing something went wrong – under the normal pressure to be first to the market.'

Unilever obviously failed to anticipate how violently its arch rival would react. By the end of the year, new independent tests, including the UK Consumers' Association *Which?* investigation, confirmed everybody's suspicions – that Power, even the reformulated version with reduced manganese, was defective.

What are the Costs of the Power Fiasco to Unilever?

After spending more than £200 million on developing, manufacturing and marketing Power products, Unilever remains a poor second to P & G in the European detergent market. A heavy price was exacted on reputations – the company's and those of the Persil and Omo brands. Unilever's image as a shrewd marketer and innovator was undermined. The whole affair has exacerbated consumers' scepticism towards manufacturers; as one retailer said, 'the whole [detergents] sector is drowning in over-claiming and publicity which leaves consumers confused'.

The Lessons

Many soap war observers would conclude that, with Power products, Unilever had practised socially irresponsible marketing – and deservedly paid heavily for it. However, the case has much broader lessons for businesses. The marketing environment for goods and services is getting fiercer. Unilever had failed to appreciate how competition and other environmental forces impact on its organization.

QUESTIONS

1. What are the key actors and forces in the company's marketing environment that affect its ability to serve its target customers effectively?

2. Identify the most critical actors or forces that accounted for Persil/Omo Power's ultimate downfall.

3. Show how each of the actors/forces you have identified in question 2 directly (or indirectly) impacted on Unilever's final decision to revamp and relaunch the defective Omo/Persil Power.

4. Critically evaluate the motives of P & G.

5. What are the key lessons for management?

6. Could the problems have been anticipated and avoided? How?

Introduction

In Chapter 3 we examined the marketing strategy and planning process which helps marketing management develop and maintain successful transactions with its target customers. Companies succeed as long as they have matched their products or services to today's marketing environment. This chapter addresses the key forces in the firm's marketing environment and how they affect its ability to maintain satisfying relationships with target customers.

A company's **marketing environment** consists of the actors and forces outside marketing that affect marketing management's ability to develop and maintain successful transactions with its target customers. The marketing environment offers both opportunities and threats. Successful companies know the vital importance of using their marketing research and intelligence systems constantly to watch and adapt to the changing environment. Too many other companies, unfortunately, fail to think of change as opportunity. They ignore or resist critical changes until it is almost too late. Their strategies, structures, systems and culture grow increasingly out of date. Corporations as mighty as IBM and General Motors have faced crises because they ignored environmental changes for too long.

A company's marketers take the major responsibility of identifying significant changes in the environment. More than any other group in the company, marketers must be the trend trackers and opportunity seekers. Although every manager in an organization needs to observe the outside environment, marketers have two special aptitudes. They have disciplined methods – marketing intelligence and marketing research – for collecting information about the marketing environment. They also normally spend more time in the customer and competitor environment. By conducting systematic environmental scanning, marketers are able to revise and adapt marketing strategies to meet new challenges and opportunities in the marketplace.

The marketing environment consists of a microenvironment and a macroenvironment. The **microenvironment** consists of the forces close to the company that affect its ability to serve its customers – the company, suppliers, marketing channel firms, customer markets, competitors and publics. The **macroenvironment** consists of the larger societal forces that affect the whole microenvironment – demographic, economic, natural, technological, political and cultural forces. We look first at the company's microenvironment.

marketing environment
The actors and forces outside marketing that affect marketing management's ability to develop and maintain successful transactions with its target customers.

microenvironment
The forces close to the company that affect its ability to serve its customers – the company, market channel firms, customer markets, competitors and publics.

macroenvironment
The larger societal forces that affect the whole microenvironment – demographic, economic, natural, technological, political and cultural forces.

The Company's Microenvironment

Marketing management's job is to create attractive offers for target markets. However, marketing managers cannot simply focus on the target market's needs. Their success will also be affected by actors in the company's microenvironment. These actors include other company departments, suppliers, marketing intermediaries, customers, competitors and various publics (see Figure 4.1).

The Company

In designing marketing plans, marketing management should take other company groups, such as top management, finance, research and development (R & D), purchasing, manufacturing and accounting, into consideration. All these interrelated

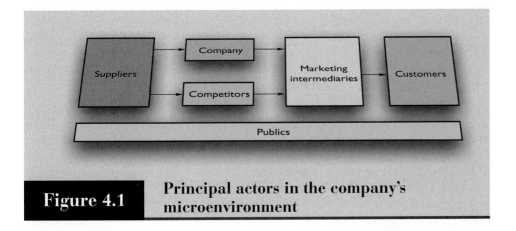

| **Figure 4.1** | **Principal actors in the company's microenvironment** |

groups form the internal environment (see Figure 4.2). Top management sets the company's mission, objectives, broad strategies and policies. Marketing managers must make decisions consistent with the plans made by top management, and marketing plans must be approved by top management before they can be implemented.

Marketing managers must also work closely with other company departments. Finance is concerned with finding and using funds to carry out the marketing plan. The R & D department focuses on the problems of designing safe and attractive products. Purchasing worries about getting supplies and materials, whereas manufacturing is responsible for producing the desired quality and quantity of products. Accounting has to measure revenues and costs to help marketing know how well it is achieving its objectives. Therefore, all of these departments have an impact on the marketing department's plans and actions. Under the marketing concept, all of these functions must 'think customer' and they should work together to provide superior customer value and satisfaction.

Suppliers

Suppliers are an important link in the company's overall customer 'value delivery system'. They provide the resources needed by the company to produce its goods and services. Supplier developments can seriously affect marketing. Marketing managers must watch supply availability – supply shortages or delays, labour strikes and other events can cost sales in the short run and damage customer satisfaction in the long run. Marketing managers must also monitor the price trends of their key inputs. Rising supply costs may force price increases that can harm the company's sales volume.

Marketing Intermediaries

Marketing intermediaries are firms that help the company to promote, sell and distribute its goods to final buyers. They include *resellers*, *physical distribution firms*, *marketing services agencies* and *financial intermediaries*. **Resellers** are distribution channel firms that help the company find customers or make sales to them. These include wholesalers and retailers which buy and resell merchandise. Selecting and working with resellers is not easy. No longer do manufacturers have many small, independent resellers from which to choose. They now face large and growing reseller organizations. These organizations frequently have enough power to dictate terms or even shut the manufacturer out of large markets.

suppliers
Firms and individuals that provide the resources needed by the company and its competitors to produce goods and services.

marketing intermediaries
Firms that help the company to promote, sell and distribute its goods to final buyers; they include physical distribution firms, marketing-service agencies and financial intermediaries.

resellers
The individuals and organizations that buy goods and services to resell at a profit

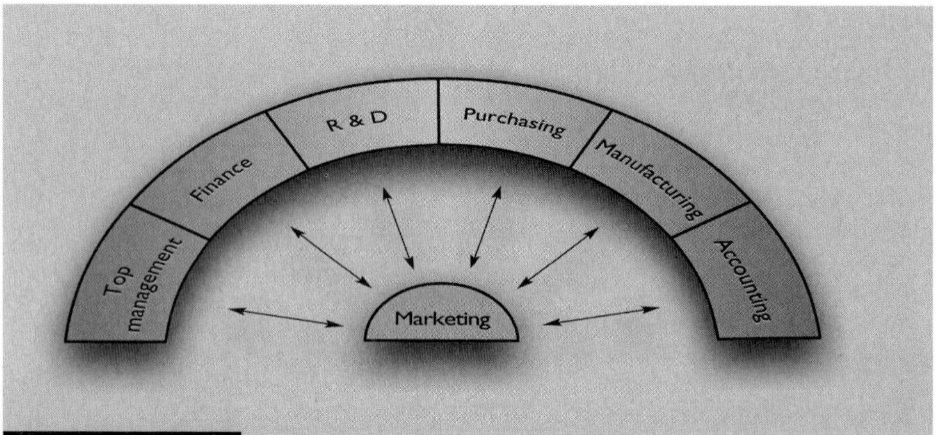

Figure 4.2   **The company's internal environment**

physical distribution firms
Warehouse, transportation and other firms that help a company to stock and move goods from their points of origin to their destinations.

marketing services agencies
Marketing research firms, advertising agencies, media firms, marketing consulting firms and other service providers that help a company to target and promote its products to the right markets.

financial intermediaries
Banks, credit companies, insurance companies and other businesses that help finance transactions or insure against the risks associated with the buying and selling of goods.

Physical distribution firms help the company to stock and move goods from their points of origin to their destinations. Working with warehouse and transportation firms, a company must determine the best ways to store and ship goods, balancing such factors as cost, delivery, speed and safety.

Marketing services agencies are the marketing research firms, advertising agencies, media firms and marketing consultancies that help the company target and promote its products to the right markets. When the company decides to use one of these agencies, it must choose carefully because the firms vary in creativity, quality, service and price. The company has to review the performance of these firms regularly and consider replacing those that no longer perform well.

Financial intermediaries include banks, credit companies, insurance companies and other businesses that help finance transactions or insure against the risks associated with the buying and selling of goods. Most firms and customers depend on financial intermediaries to finance their transactions. The company's marketing performance can be seriously affected by rising credit costs and limited credit. For example, small and medium-sized businesses in the United Kingdom have often found difficulty in obtaining finance for market and product development activities. Many such businesses blame this on the insupportive financial system in the UK. In marked contrast, the Japanese *kieretsu* system favours lower-cost financing for both large and small companies that form part of the informal network of banking, trading and commercial organizations within the *kieretsu*. Whether or not businesses enjoy the support of a favourable financial system, individual businesses must be aware of financial organizations' impact on marketing effectiveness. For this reason, the company has to develop strong relationships with the most important financial institutions.

Like suppliers, marketing intermediaries form an important component of the company's overall value delivery system. In its quest to create satisfying customer relationships, the company must do more than just optimize its own performance. It must partner effectively with suppliers and marketing intermediaries to optimize the performance of the entire system.

Customers

The company must study its customer markets closely. Figure 4.3 shows six types of customer market. *Consumer markets* consist of individuals and households

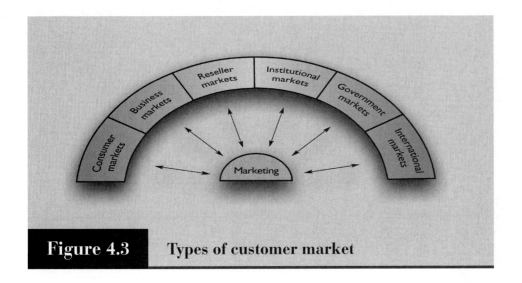

Figure 4.3 **Types of customer market**

that buy goods and services for personal consumption. *Business markets* buy goods and services for further processing or for use in their production process, whereas *reseller markets* buy goods and services to resell at a profit. *Institutional markets* are made up of schools, hospitals, nursing homes, prisons and other institutions that provide goods and services to people in their care. *Government markets* are made up of government agencies that buy goods and services in order to produce public services or transfer the goods and services to others who need them. Finally, *international markets* consist of buyers in other countries, including consumers, producers, resellers and governments. Each market type has special characteristics that call for careful study by the seller. At any point in time, the firm may deal with one or more customer markets: for example, Unilever has to communicate detergent brand benefits to consumers as well as maintaining a dialogue with retailers that stock and resell its branded products.

Competitors

The marketing concept states that, to be successful, a company must provide greater customer value and satisfaction than its competitors do. Thus, marketers must do more than simply adapt to the needs of target consumers. They must also gain strategic advantage by positioning their offerings strongly against competitors' offerings in the minds of consumers.

No single competitive marketing strategy is best for all companies. Each firm should consider its own size and industry position compared to those of its competitors. Large firms with dominant positions in an industry can use certain strategies that smaller firms cannot afford. But being large is not enough. There are winning strategies for large firms, but there are also losing ones. And small firms can develop strategies that give them better rates of return than large firms enjoy.

Publics

The company's marketing environment also includes various publics. A **public** is any group that has an actual or potential interest in or impact on an organization's ability to achieve its objectives. Figure 4.4 shows seven types of public:

public
Any group that has an actual or potential interest in or impact on an organization's ability to achieve its objectives.

Communicating with publics: Unilever magazine communicates news and information to employees.

The Kemira Group uses this ad to communicate to both national and international customers, public and institutional investors. Its 'super-league' feels great about working for the firm; its customers feel they are in safe hands.

1. *Financial publics.* Financial publics influence the company's ability to obtain funds. Banks, investment houses and stockholders are the principal financial publics.

2. *Media publics.* Media publics are those that carry news, features and editorial opinion. They include newspapers, magazines and radio and television stations.

3. *Government publics.* Management must take government developments into account. Marketers must often consult the company's lawyers on issues of product safety, truth-in-advertising and other matters.

4. *Citizen action publics.* A company's marketing decisions may be questioned by consumer organizations, environmental groups, minority groups and other pressure groups. Its public relations department can help it stay in touch with consumer and citizen groups.

5. *Local publics.* Every company has local publics, such as neighbourhood residents and community organizations. Large companies usually appoint a community-relations officer to deal with the community, attend meetings, answer questions and contribute to worthwhile causes.

6. *General public.* A company needs to be concerned about the general public's attitude towards its products and activities. The public's image of the company affects its buying. Thus, many large corporations invest huge sums of money to promote and build a healthy corporate image.

7. *Internal publics.* A company's internal publics include its workers, managers, volunteers and the board of directors. Large companies use newsletters and other means to inform and motivate their internal publics. When employees feel good about their company, this positive attitude spills over to their external publics.

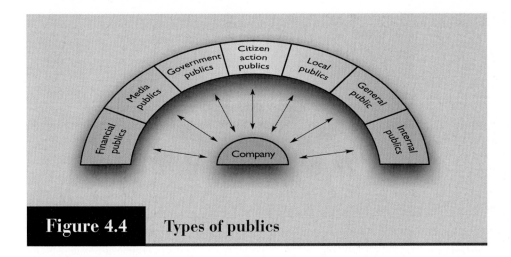

| **Figure 4.4** | **Types of publics** |

A company can prepare marketing plans for these publics as well as for its customer markets. Suppose the company wants a specific response from a particular public, such as goodwill, favourable word of mouth, or donations of time or money. The company would have to design an offer to this public that is attractive enough to produce the desired response.

Organizations today are under the watchful eyes of their various publics. As we saw in the case of Unilever's soap war with P & G, the company must explain its actions to a wider audience when things go wrong. Those that overlook the power of serious interest groups often learn painful lessons (see Marketing Highlight 4.1).

We have looked at the firm's immediate or microenvironment. Next we examine the larger macroenvironment.

The Company's Macroenvironment

The company and all the other actors operate in a larger macroenvironment of forces that shape opportunities and pose threats to the company. Figure 4.5 shows the six most influential forces in the company's macroenvironment. The remaining sections of this chapter examine these forces and show how they affect marketing plans.

Demographic Environment

Demography is the study of human populations in terms of size, density, location, age, gender, race, occupation and other statistics. The demographic environment is of considerable interest to marketers because it involves people, and people make up markets. Here, we discuss the most important demographic characteristics and trends in the largest world markets.

demography
The study of human populations in terms of size, density, location, age, sex, race, occupation and other statistics.

● *Population Size and Growth Trends*

In any geographic market, population size and growth trends can be used to gauge its broad potential for a wide range of goods and services. We often refer to the United States, Japan and Europe as the 'triad' markets. The European Union (EU),

Speaking for Herman the Bull

Nutricia, a Dutch producer of baby foods and powders and a leading investor in biotechnology research, entered into a joint venture with the Dutch subsidiary of US biotechnology firm GenPharm International, to carry out research which attempted to genetically engineer cows' milk. A human gene was inserted into the genetic material of a bull called Herman. The two companies hoped that the milk produced by Herman's female descendants would contain large amounts of lactoferrine, a substance normally found in human milk. The Dutch Society for the Protection of Animals (DSPA) subsequently launched an anti-Herman campaign. A first series of shock posters showed a starry-eyed cow with the question posed: 'Soon to be marketed with blonde hair and blue eyes?' A second depicted a woman's naked chest with two neat rows of udders. Campaigners threatened to call an all-out boycott of Nutricia products.

The Dutch government, which has introduced 'never unless' rules to regulate genetic manipulation of animals, exceptionally permitted the Nutricia project to go ahead as scientists argued that large-scale production of lactoferrine serves unique medical goals. The DSPA, however, stressed that the Nutricia project's motive was purely commercial – to manufacture the equivalent of mother's milk on an agribusiness scale at potential cost to animal welfare. A Nutricia spokesman said, 'When the project was presented to us four years ago, it didn't seem likely to cause controversy. There is great pressure on us to keep investing in technology. But in the current climate, if a similar offer came up, the company would probably prefer to decline it.'

The project had to be abandoned. Nutricia admitted a loss of some DFl 4 million and said it would handle such pioneering efforts more carefully in the future. Pressure groups in Holland declare that they have effectively scared investors from venturing into the most delicate and controversial field of modern biotechnology – the genetic modification of an animal, which the Nutricia case exemplified. According to a spokesman for NIABA, a group representing the Dutch food industry for biotechnology matters, food companies in the country would invest between two and three times more in such research if they did not fear damaging upheavals. He added, 'The animal rights and environmental pressure groups may not represent a very large section of opinion, but their blackmailing tactics have been known to work in the past. Any company that ignores their signals takes a very big chance.'

Dutch 'novel foods' laws now dictate that firms which want to market an entirely new

NIEUW
Moedermelk uit koeien!

STOP BIOTECHNOLOGIE BIJ DIEREN
Koeien met menselijke genen moeten moedermelk gaan geven. Genetische manipulatie wordt onze kinderen met de paplepel ingegoten. Help de Dierenbescherming deze waanzin te stoppen! Word lid of vraag meer informatie.

DE DIERENBESCHERMING: 070-3 423 423

The power of interest groups: the 'anti-Herman' campaign led by the Dutch Society for the Protection of Animals forced Nutricia and GenPharm International to abandon the controversial biotechnology research project.

product must first present their plans to the authorities and let them undergo a long series of safety tests. On top of national and European rules, some large companies in the Netherlands have adopted their own corporate policy statement to clarify their views on biotechnology development to avoid damaging controversy. In the light of the Nutricia affair, both investors and companies urge an update of ethical rules at European levels.

SOURCE: Adapted from Barbara Smit, 'Herman the Bull scares off Dutch research pioneers', *The European* (22–8 July 1994), p. 25.

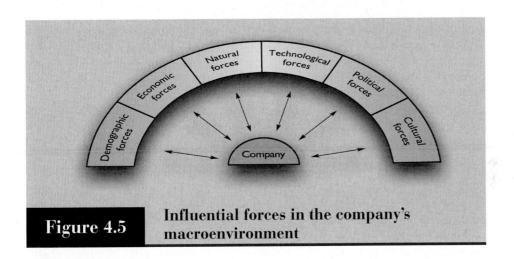

Figure 4.5 **Influential forces in the company's macroenvironment**

together with members of the European Free Trade Area (EFTA), has a population of around 370 million. With another 120 million from eastern Europe and 280 million from the former USSR, the overall European market will be significantly larger than the North America Free Trade Area – the United States, Canada and Mexico – with a population of 370 million and Japan with 128 million. Marketers also view China, with 1.2 billion people, as a potentially lucrative growth market.[2]

Population growth trends are important because they can offer marketers an indication of demand for certain goods and services. A 'baby boom' would suggest growing demand for infant foods, nursery appliances, maternity services, baby clothing, toys and so forth, in the short to medium term, with rising demand for family-size accommodation, larger cars, schools and educational services over the longer term. Differences in population growth patterns between country markets may also suggest different international marketing opportunities for firms.

● *Changing Age Structure of a Population*

The most noticeable demographic shift in Europe, the United States and affluent Asian countries is the changing age structure of the population. In all three groups, the national populations are getting older, and the trend is forecast to continue over the next 50 years. The ageing population structure reflects two influences. First, there is a long-term slowdown in birth rate, so there are fewer young people to pull the population's average age down. Western European countries, with the exception of Ireland, rank below the 2.1 children per woman (fertility) level found in the United States, and well below the 3.3 world average. Italy, reporting 1.3 children per woman, has the lowest fertility level in the world.

THE BRANDS **YOU** WANT AT PRICES YOU'LL **LOVE**

To serve the large and growing 'kid market', many retailers are opening separate children's chains. For example, Toys 'Я' US opened Kids 'Я' Us.

Fertility rates in Japan, Singapore, South Korea and Hong Kong have declined steadily over the last two decades, and all lie below America's 2.1 average. This 'birth-dearth' linked to smaller family sizes is due to people's desire to improve personal living standards, women's desire to work outside the home, and widely available and effective birth control practices.

Secondly, as longevity increases there are more elderly people (see Figure 4.6) to pull the average age of the population up. By 2031, 38 per cent of the UK population will be over 50 years old. Compare this with 32 per cent in 1991 and only 28 per cent in 1951. In Germany, the balance of people over 65 years of age to persons of working age (or the *dependency ratio*) is expected to exceed 1:1 by 2031. Put more colourfully by the historian and demographer Peter Laslett, 'Europe and the West are growing older and will never be young again.' The picture is repeated in developed Asian countries. The rapid ageing of the Japanese population is one of the government's biggest long-term worries.[3] Further, the demographic change of longer life is not confined to advanced countries. In Latin America and most of Asia, the share of over-60s is set to double between now and 2030, to 14 per cent. In China, it will increase from less than 10 per cent now to around 22 per cent in 2030.

Demographic shifts have important implications for marketing managers. Marketers thus track demographic trends and moves carefully (see Marketing Highlight 4.2).

● *The Changing Family*

The notion of an ideal family – mum, dad and two kids – has lately been losing some of its lustre. People are marrying later and having fewer children. The specific figures may vary among countries, but the general trend is towards fewer married couples with children. In fact, couples with no children under 18 now make up a high proportion of all families. These are worrying trends too for wealthy Asian countries like Singapore, Japan and Hong Kong.

Also, the number of working mothers is increasing. Marketers of goods ranging from cars, insurance and travel to financial services are increasingly directing their advertising to working women. As a result of the shift in the traditional roles and values of husbands and wives, with male partners assuming more domestic functions such as shopping and child care, more food and household appliance marketers are targeting this group of individuals.

Finally, the number of non-family households is increasing. Many young adults leave home and move into apartments. Other adults choose to remain single. Still others are divorced or widowed people living alone. By the year 2000, one-person/non-family and single-parent households – the fastest growing category of households – will represent a sizeable proportion of all households. In

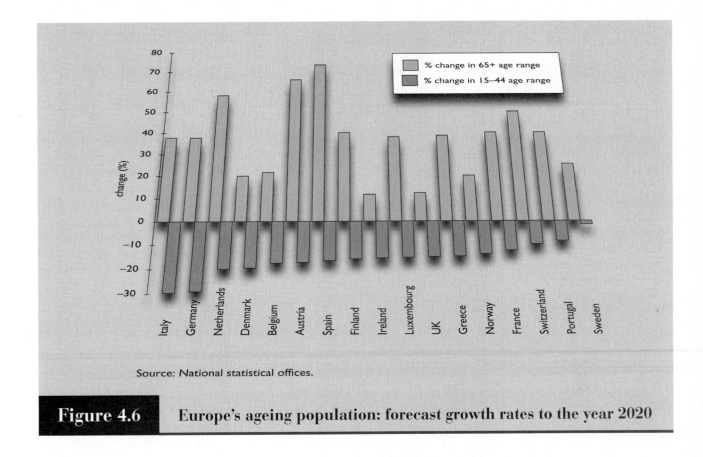

Source: National statistical offices.

| **Figure 4.6** | **Europe's ageing population: forecast growth rates to the year 2020** |

Sweden, for example, one-person households now account for over 40 per cent of all homes. Between 1981 and 1991, there has been an upward trend towards single-person households (see Figure 4.7). In the United States, figures are comparable, with estimates putting the number at 47 per cent by the year 2000. These groups have their own special needs. For example, they need smaller apartments, inexpensive and smaller appliances, furniture and furnishings, and food that is packaged in smaller sizes.[4]

● *Rising Number of Educated People*

As economies in eastern Europe and Asia develop, we may expect to see more money spent on education. The proportion of the population that is educated will rise and the population, as a whole, will become better educated. The rising number of educated people will increase the demand for quality products, books, magazines and travel.

In many developed and industrializing countries, the workforce is also becoming more white collar. The most growth comes in the following occupational categories: computers, engineering, science, medicine, social service, buying, selling, secretarial, construction, refrigeration, health service, personal service and protection.[5]

● *Increasing Diversity*

In the 1990s, efforts towards European integration have escalated. The EU now comprises 15 member states – France, Luxembourg, Italy, Germany, with East Germany on unification, Netherlands, Belgium, Denmark, Ireland, United Kingdom, Greece, Spain, Portugal, Sweden, Austria and Finland. The EU's enlargement

'Third Agers' and 'Generation Xers'

Two of today's most important demographic groups are the 'Third Agers' and 'Generation Xers'. For example, the Henley Centre, a UK forecasting organization, draws attention to the emerging Third Agers. They will be 50–75 years old and will have more free time and money and higher expectations than their predecessors. They are brought up to value aspirations and self-fulfilment. They are now in their forties, but will represent the first mass leisure class. Unlike preceding generations, whose upbringing gave them a more frugal outlook, Third Agers were socialized in the 1960s, the era of expanding individual choices and economic growth. One implication is the rise in 'grey power' in western Europe. 'Grey power' has already manifested itself in the USA, where the postwar baby boom occurred a decade earlier than in Europe. The baby boom created a huge bulge in America's age distribution. As the 75 million or so baby boomers age, so the US average age climbs and, along with it, 'grey power'. The 37 million members of the American Association of Retired People represents a powerful lobby – and important new markets for leisure and education. The Henley Centre study argues that such dynamic consumers, who have both the time and money, should already be the most sought-after target for the leisure industry. Time-use studies show that in the UK, for example, Third Agers already take part more widely in active leisure pursuits – long country walks, short-break holidays, visits to museums or historic buildings – than younger people. They are also 'catching' their juniors in terms of playing team sports, swimming and using sports centres, visiting cinemas and attending evening classes. Participation rates for the 45–59-year-olds have risen sharply since 1986.

Some marketers think that focusing on the boomers has caused companies to overlook other important segments, especially younger consumers. Focus is shifting in recent years to a new group, the generation born between 1965 and 1976 – the 'Generation Xers'. Increasing divorce rates and higher employment for mothers have made them the first generation of latchkey kids. Whereas the boomers of the 1960s created a sexual revolution, the Xers have lived in the age of AIDS. Having grown up during times of recession and corporate downsizing, they have developed a pessimistic economic outlook. As a result, the Xers are a more sceptical bunch, cynical of frivolous marketing pitches that promise easy success. They know better. The Xers buy lots of products, such as sweaters, boots, cosmetics, electronics, cars, fast food, beer, computers and

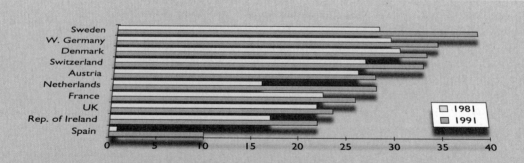

Figure 4.7   **The rise of the one-person household**

mountain bikes. However, their cynicism makes them more savvy shoppers. Their financial pressures make them value conscious and they like lower prices and a more functional look. The Generation Xers respond to honesty in advertising. They like irreverence and impudence and ads that mock the traditional advertising approach.

Generation Xers share new cultural concerns. They care about the environment and respond favourably to companies which have proven records of environmentally and socially responsible actions. Although they seek success, the Xers are less materialistic. They want better quality of life and are more interested in job satisfaction than in sacrificing personal happiness and growth for promotion. They prize experience, not acquisition.

Surveys on Asian youth culture highlight the emergence of the region's first 'children of plenty', its very own Generation X, teenagers and 20-somethings who have grown up knowing nothing but peace, dazzling economic growth and an ever-rising flood of consumer goods. Compared to their western counterparts, Asian Generation Xers stress the importance of family, jobs, marriage, saving for the future, respect for elders and other such traditional values. Broad generalizations are, of course, fraught with controversy, not least over the definition of what exactly constitutes 'values'. And in a region as vast as Asia there are naturally many local variations, even exceptions. 'But one by one as we research the

different topics, we find one thing in common ... the values they hold in areas like family,' says Jacky Pang of the Hong Kong Federation of Youth Groups. 'They may mimic American trends – music and fashion – but they aren't like American kids,' echoes Ben Tan, of advertising agency Leo Burnelt in Kuala Lumpur. 'We have been as surprised as anyone by the results of our research,' concludes Jacky Pang.

The Generation Xers, as a whole, will have a big impact on the workplace and marketplace in the future. They are poised to displace the lifestyles, culture and materialistic values of the baby boomers. By the year 2010, they will have overtaken the Third Agers as a primary market for almost every product category.

SOURCES: Jeff Giles, 'Generalizations X', *Newsweek* (6 June 1994), pp. 62–9; Nicholas Zill and John Robinson, 'The Generation X Difference', *American Demographics* (April 1995), pp. 24–9; 'Rock solid', *Far Eastern Economic Review* (5 December 1996), pp. 50–2; Dyan Machan, 'A more tolerant generation', *Forbes* (8 September 1997), pp. 46–7; Barbara Beck, 'The luxury of longer life, a survey of the economics of ageing', *The Economist* (27 January 1996), pp. 3–5; David Nicholson-Lord, 'Mass leisure class is on the way, say forecasters', *Independent* (18 April 1994), p. 4; see also *Leisure Futures*, vol. 1 (London: Henley Centre, 1994); James U. McNeal, 'Growing up in the market', *American Demographics* (October 1992), pp. 46–50; Diane Crispell and William H. Frey, 'American maturity', *American Demographics* (March 1993), pp. 31–42; Melinder Beck, 'The geezer boom', in 'The 21st century family', a special issue of *Newsweek* (Winter/Spring 1990), pp. 62–7.

programme is still high on politicians' agendas. Eastern and central European countries, including former Soviet bloc states, are seeking to participate in the EU, which, in the longer term, could become a reality.

The EU, in its present state, and in a potentially enlarged form, presents huge challenges for domestic and international marketers. We will discuss international marketing issues in more detail in Chapter 5. In general, marketers operating in the vastly expanded EU must recognize the great diversity across member states. Unification strives to achieve harmonization of rules and regulations, which will affect business practices across the Union. Many marketers believe the single European market will lead to convergence in consumer tastes. Global advertising agencies like Saatchi & Saatchi and Young and Rubicam were strong supporters of the idea of the 'Euroconsumer'. However, consumer needs, values, beliefs, habits and lifestyles differ across individual country markets, just as spending power and consumption patterns are likely to vary. Businesses will do well to identify national and regional differences, and to develop appropriate marketing strategies that take on board this diversity. Where there are European consumers who display similar cultural values and tastes for particular goods and services, then pan-European strategies may be more cost-effective. For example, the internationalism of snob items, such as Rolex watches or Cartier jewellery, which appeal to a small number of like-minded consumers, or high-fashion purchases like Swatch watches and Benetton clothes, which pander to the younger generation of dedicated fashion followers, lend themselves to pan-European marketing or advertising.

In most markets, however, firms have found that the 'one sight, one sound, one sell' dictum loses out to the more effective strategy of customization. Even Coca-Cola, arch exponent of globalism, tailors the marketing of its drinks to suit different markets. Kronenbourg, France's most popular beer, is sold to a mass market with the eternal images of France, like cafés, boules and Citroen 2CVs. In the United Kingdom, Kronenbourg is presented as a drink for 'yuppies'. Unilever customizes its advertisements for Impulse, a body spray. In the UK, the handsome young fellow who gets a whiff of Impulse from the woman nearby presents her with a bunch of flowers. In the Italian version, Romeo offers the woman a rose.

Whether the Euroconsumer is a myth or reality is widely debated today. Marketers must address a marketing basic: identify consumer needs and respond to them. Converging lifestyles, habits and tastes may often not mean converging needs. Europe remains a pot-pourri of cultures and systems, which present immense marketing opportunities for sellers. Although social and demographic factors and the marketing strategies of multinational consumer goods companies may combine to make lifestyles of different European (and rising wealthy Asian) nations more alike, diversity will feature just as much as convergence in the new world economy. Companies that overlook diversity in favour of pan-European or global strategies must carefully develop and execute their standardized approaches.[6] We discuss pan-European versus standardized marketing practices in greater depth in the next chapter.

Economic Environment

Economic environment
Factors that affect consumer buying power and spending patterns.

Markets require buying power as well as people. The **economic environment** consists of factors that affect consumer purchasing power and spending patterns. Marketers should be aware of the following predominant economic trends.

Income Distribution and Changes in Purchasing Power

Global upheavals in technology and communications over the 1990s brought about a shift in the balance of economic power from the West (mainly North American, Canadian and western European nations) towards the rapidly expanding economies of the Asian Pacific Rim. Many of the Asian 'tiger' economies, notably South Korea, Thailand, Malaysia, Indonesia and Singapore, were enjoying annual growth rates in excess of 7 per cent, compared to the 2–3 per cent found in western Europe and the USA. Official statistics suggest that, by 2010, purchasing power income per head in countries like Singapore and South Korea will exceed that of the United States. Economic growth projections suggest that Europe will drop down the economic rankings. Assuming annual growth in western Europe and the United States of 2.5 per cent, and 6 per cent in Asia as a whole, the share of world gross domestic product (GDP) taken by Asian developing countries, including China and India, could rise to 28 per cent in 2010 from 18 per cent in 1990. Western Europe's share will fall to 17 per cent from 22 per

gambling on substantial innovations. The high costs and risks of commercialization failure make firms take this cautious approach to their R & D investment. Most companies are content to put their money into copying competitors' products, making minor feature and style improvements, or offering simple extensions of current brands. Thus much research is in danger of being defensive rather than offensive.

● *Increased Regulation*

As products become more complex, people need to know that they are safe. Thus, government agencies investigate and ban potentially unsafe products. In the EU and America, complex regulations exist for testing new drugs. The US Federal Food and Drug Administration, for example, is notorious for its strict enforcement of drug testing and safety rules. Statutory and industry regulatory bodies exist to set safety standards for consumer products and penalize companies that fail to meet them. Such regulations have resulted in much higher research costs and in longer times between new-product ideas and their introductions. Marketers should be aware of these regulations when seeking and developing new products.

Marketers need to understand the changing technological environment and the ways that new technologies can serve customer and human needs. They need to work closely with R & D people to encourage more market-oriented research. They must also be alert to the possible negative aspects of any innovation that might harm users or arouse opposition.

Political Environment

Marketing decisions are strongly affected by developments in the political environment. The **political environment** consists of laws, government agencies and pressure groups that influence and limit various organizations and individuals in a given society.

political environment
Laws, government agencies and pressure groups that influence and limit various organizations and individuals in a given society.

● *Legislation Regulating Business*

Even the most liberal advocates of free-market economies agree that the system works best with at least some regulation. Well-conceived regulation can encourage competition and ensure fair markets for goods and services. Thus governments develop *public policy* to guide commerce – sets of laws and regulations that limit business for the good of society as a whole. Almost every marketing activity is subject to a wide range of laws and regulations.

Understanding the public policy implications of a particular marketing activity is not a simple matter. First, there are many laws created at different levels: for example, in the EU, business operators are subject to European Commission, individual member state and specific local regulations; in the USA, laws are created at the federal, state and local levels, and these regulations often overlap.

Second, the regulations are constantly changing – what was allowed last year may now be prohibited. In the single European market, deregulation and ongoing moves towards harmonization are expected to take time, creating a state of flux, which challenges and confuses both domestic and international marketers. They must therefore work hard to keep up with these changes in the regulations and their interpretations.

In many developed economies, legislation affecting business has increased steadily over the years. This legislation has been enacted for a number of reasons.

The first is to *protect companies* from each other. Although business executives may praise competition, they sometimes try to neutralize it when it threatens them. So laws are passed to define and prevent unfair competition. Anti-trust agencies and monopolies and mergers commissions exist to enforce these laws.

The second purpose of government regulation is to *protect consumers* from unfair business practices. Some firms, if left alone, would make shoddy products, tell lies in their advertising and deceive consumers through their packaging and pricing. Unfair business practices have been defined and are enforced by various agencies.

The third purpose of government regulation is to *protect the interests of society* against unrestrained business behaviour. Profitable business activity does not always create a better quality of life. Regulation arises to ensure that firms take responsibility for the social costs of their production or products.

New laws and their enforcement are likely to continue or increase. Business executives must watch these developments when planning their products and marketing programmes. Marketers need to know about the main laws protecting competition, consumers and society. International marketers should additionally be aware of regional, country and local laws that affect their international marketing activity.

● *Growth of Public Interest Groups*

The number and power of public interest groups have increased during the past two decades. In Chapter 2 we discussed a broad range of societal marketing issues. The pioneering efforts of Ralph Nader's Public Citizen group in the United States raised the importance of the role of public interest groups as watchdogs on consumer interests and lifted consumerism into a powerful social force. Consumerism has spilled over to countries in western Europe and other developed market economies such as Australia. Hundreds of other consumer interest groups, private and governmental, operate at all levels – regional, national, state/county and local levels. Other groups that marketers need to consider are those seeking to protect the environment and to advance the rights of various groups such as women, children, ethnic minorities, senior citizens and the handicapped. As we saw in the case of Nutricia's failed biotechnology project (see Marketing Highlight 4.1), companies cannot afford to ignore the views of powerful public interest groups.

● *Increased Emphasis on Ethics and Socially Responsible Actions*

Written regulations cannot possibly cover all potential marketing abuses, and existing laws are often difficult to enforce. However, beyond written laws and regulations, business is also governed by social codes and rules of professional ethics. Enlightened companies encourage their managers to look beyond what the regulatory system allows and simply to 'do the right thing'. These socially responsible firms actively seek out ways to protect the long-run interests of their consumers and the environment.

Increased concerns about the environment have created fresh interest in the issues of ethics and social responsibility. Almost every aspect of marketing involves such issues. Unfortunately, because these issues usually involve conflicting interests, well-meaning people can disagree honestly about the right course of action in a particular situation. Thus many industrial and professional trade associations have suggested codes of ethics, and many companies are now developing policies and guidelines to deal with complex social responsibility issues.

In Chapter 2, we discussed in greater depth public and social responsibility issues surrounding key marketing decisions, the legal issues that marketers should understand, and the common ethical and societal concerns that marketers face.

Cultural Environment

The **cultural environment** is made up of institutions and other forces that affect society's basic values, perceptions, preferences and behaviours. People grow up in a particular society that shapes their basic beliefs and values. They absorb a world-view that defines their relationships with others. The following cultural characteristics can affect marketing decision making. Marketers must be aware of these cultural influences and how they vary across societies within the markets served by the firm.

cultural environment
Institutions and other forces that affect society's basic values, perceptions, preferences and behaviours.

● *Persistence of Cultural Values*

People in a given society hold many beliefs and values. Their core beliefs and values have a high degree of persistence. For example, most of us believe in working, getting married, giving to charity and being honest. These beliefs shape more specific attitudes and behaviours found in everyday life. *Core* beliefs and values are passed on from parents to children and are reinforced by schools, religious groups, business and government.

Secondary beliefs and values are more open to change. Believing in marriage is a core belief; believing that people should get married early in life is a secondary belief. Marketers have some chance of changing secondary values, but little chance of changing core values. For example, family-planning marketers could argue more effectively that people should get married later than that they should not get married at all.

● *Shifts in Secondary Cultural Values*

Although core values are fairly persistent, cultural swings do take place. Consider the impact of popular music groups, movie personalities and other celebrities on young people's hair styling, clothing and sexual norms. Marketers want to predict cultural shifts in order to spot new opportunities or threats. Such information helps marketers cater to trends with appropriate products and communication appeals.

The principal cultural values of a society are expressed in people's views of themselves and others, as well as in their views of organizations, society, nature and the universe.

PEOPLE'S VIEWS OF THEMSELVES. People vary in their emphasis on serving themselves versus serving others. Some people seek personal pleasure, wanting fun, change and escape. Others seek self-realization through religion, recreation or the avid pursuit of careers or other life goals. People use products, brands and services as a means of self-expression and buy products and services that match their views of themselves.

In the last decade or so, personal ambition and materialism increased dramatically, with significant marketing implications. In a 'me-society', people buy their 'dream cars' and take their 'dream vacations'. They spend more time in outdoor health activities (jogging, tennis, etc.), in thought, and on arts and crafts. The leisure industry (camping, skiing, boating, arts and crafts, and sports) faces good growth prospects in a society where people seek self-fulfilment.

Marketing Highlight 4.4

Ronald McDonald Children's Charities: Playing a Role in Local Communities

Ronald McDonald Children's Charities (RMCC) was founded in 1984 in the United States. It was established in memory of Ray Kroc, founder of McDonald's Corporation. He believed that 'It is important to have an involvement in the life and spirit of a community and the people around you.' This belief lives on in the McDonald's system and is evident in a variety of community programmes practised by McDonald's the world over. In 1989, for example, RMCC was set up in the United Kingdom, and through the efforts of McDonald's Restaurants Limited, its staff, customers and suppliers, over £3 million has since been raised for a wide variety of charitable causes that help children.

RMCC grants have been awarded to programmes which help young people reach their full potential and make a real difference for children and their wellbeing. The 'Ronald McDonald House' is a cornerstone of RMCC. The first was built at Philadelphia in the United States in 1974, close to the Philadelphia Children's Hospital. When a child is taken seriously ill and has to spend some time in hospital, families are usually faced with the problem of where to stay to be close at hand. The Ronald McDonald House has a set number of beds for parents to stay overnight and a family accommodation block. This means that the family can be together again as a unit, while also providing a brief respite in a family environment.

There are now over 160 Ronald McDonald Houses in the United States, Canada, Australia,

Ronald McDonald House

a home from home
at
Alder Hey Children's Hospital

"It is important to have an involvement in the life and spirit of a community and the people around you."

Ray A Kroc
Founder
McDonald's Corporation

What is McDonald's Involvement?

As well as their generous £1 million donation, McDonald's has lent expertise in setting up the House along with legal, design and construction advice. McDonald's is totally committed to working with representatives of the hospital and parents through the Alder Hey Family House Trust Ltd, a registered charity, which is responsible for raising funds and running the House now it is open.

Paul Preston, McDonald's UK President, explains: "With diminishing public-sector resources, it is vital that private enterprise plays a role in developing concepts such as the Ronald McDonald House where, at long last, parents can live in home-like surroundings whilst their child undergoes treatment. Hopefully the days in which parents have to camp out in the hospital are numbered.

"Ronald McDonald House is the result of team effort; a caring partnership between McDonald's, the Hospital staff and the families of the children."

The Tree of Life

The "Tree of Life" which is on display at the house. A visible thank-you to those who support the Trust.

McDonald's plays its role in the life and spirit of the surrounding local communities

Japan and Europe. Each House is a 'home away from home' with the feel, aesthetics and comfort of family living. Families are able to prepare their own meals, relax and rest in privacy or enjoy the company of others living in when they so desire. The House is the result of a team effort between the hospital doctors and staff, the parents of the children and McDonald's. Each House is run by a separate charitable trust set up to oversee fund raising and to manage the house. The boards of these trusts are made up of parents, hospital representatives and senior management of McDonald's. The trusts initiate their own fund-raising events. Throughout the year, McDonald's own restaurant staff are involved in local events to raise money for RMCC, and collecting boxes for donations from customers are placed in every restaurant. McDonald's Restaurants Limited, its franchisees and also its suppliers all donate to RMCC. Other recipients of money raised by

RMCC include children's charities – such as hospitals, youth organizations, schools and many more worthy causes. ·

McDonald's restaurants not only display posters and collecting boxes for the RMCC programme, but also provide customers with information leaflets to disseminate information about their community involvement. These leaflets also sometimes contain requests for funds and/or volunteers who may be interested in helping in specific campaigns. This type of communication effort is also designed to raise customers' as well as other local and general publics' awareness of Ray Kroc's philosophy of 'giving something back to the communities that give so much to us [McDonald's Corporation]'.

SOURCE: 'Your questions answered', Ronald McDonald Children's Charities, London; The Public Relations Department, McDonald's Restaurants Limited, London.

PEOPLE'S VIEWS OF OTHERS. More recently, observers have noted a shift from a 'me-society' to a 'we-society', in which more people want to be with and serve others. Flashy spending and self-indulgence appear to be on the way out, whereas saving, family concerns and helping others are on the rise. A recent survey showed that more people are becoming involved in charity, volunteer work and social service activities.[16] This suggests a bright future for 'social support' products and services that improve direct communication between people, such as health clubs, family vacations and games. It also suggests a growing market for 'social substitutes' – things like VCRs and computers that allow people who are alone to feel that they are not.

PEOPLE'S VIEWS OF ORGANIZATIONS. People vary in their attitudes towards corporations, government agencies, trade unions, universities and other organizations. By and large, people are willing to work for big organizations and expect them, in turn, to carry out society's work. There has been a decline in organizational loyalty, however. People are giving a little less to their organizations and are trusting them less.

This trend suggests that organizations need to find new ways to win consumer confidence. They need to review their advertising communications to make sure their messages are honest. Also, they need to review their various activities to make sure that they are coming across as 'good corporate citizens'. More companies are linking themselves to worthwhile causes, measuring their images with important publics and using public relations to build more positive images (see Marketing Highlight 4.4).

PEOPLE'S VIEWS OF SOCIETY. People vary in their attitudes toward their society – from patriots who defend it, to reformers who want to change it, and

Environmental marketing: here Hewlett Packard attempts to market its high quality technology while promoting a good cause – the protection of endangered wildlife

The versatile HP LaserJet 4 Plus.
Saves money. Saves paper. Saves wildlife.

malcontents who want to leave it. People's orientation to their society influences their consumption patterns, levels of savings and attitudes toward the marketplace.

In the affluent and industrializing Asian nations, consumers aspire to achieve the high living standards and lifestyles of people in the more advanced western countries. The display of conspicuous consumption and fondness for expensive western brands – the common label for achievement and westernization – are highly acceptable behaviour. Consumer patriotism, for example, is not an issue, since locally made goods are often viewed as inferior or less desirable than foreign imported brands. By contrast, in the western developed countries, the late 1980s and early 1990s saw an increase in consumer patriotism. European consumers reckoned that sticking to locally produced goods would save and protect jobs. Many US companies also responded to American patriotism with 'made in America' themes and flag-waving promotions, such as Chevrolet is 'the heartbeat of America', Black & Decker's flag-like symbol on its tools, and the textile industry's 'Crafted with Pride in the USA' advertising campaign, which insisted that 'made in the USA' matters.[17]

PEOPLE'S VIEWS OF NATURE.   People vary in their attitudes towards the natural world. Some feel ruled by it, others feel in harmony with it and still others seek to master it. A long-term trend has been people's growing mastery over nature through technology and the belief that nature is bountiful. More recently, however, people have recognized that nature is finite and fragile – that it can be destroyed or spoiled by human activities.

Love of nature is leading to more camping, hiking, boating, fishing and other outdoor activities. Business has responded by offering more hiking gear, camping equipment, better insect repellents and other products for nature enthusiasts. Tour operators are offering more tours to wilderness areas. Food producers have found growing markets for 'natural' products like natural cereal, natural ice cream, organically farmed produce and a variety of health foods. Marketing communicators are using appealing natural backgrounds in advertising their products.

PEOPLE'S VIEWS OF THE UNIVERSE. Finally, people vary in their beliefs about the origin of the universe and their place in it. While the practice of religion remains strong in many parts of the world, religious conviction and practice have been dropping off through the years in certain countries, notably in the United States and Europe where, for example, church attendance has fallen gradually. As people lose their religious orientation, they seek goods and experiences with more immediate satisfactions. During the 1980s, people increasingly measured success in terms of career achievement, wealth and worldly possessions. Some futurists, however, have noted an emerging renewal of interest in religion, perhaps as part of a broader search for a new inner purpose. Starting in the 1990s, they believe, people are moving away from materialism and dog-eat-dog ambition to seek more permanent values and a more certain grasp of right and wrong. The 'new realists', found mainly in the developed western markets, reflect a move away from overt consumerism. However, in many markets such as India, China and south-east Asia, society's value systems place great importance on economic achievement and material possession. The values of these 'enthusiastic materialists' are also shared by the developing markets of Europe, such as Turkey, and some Latin American countries.[18]

Responding to the Marketing Environment

Many companies view the marketing environment as an 'uncontrollable' element to which they must adapt. They passively accept the marketing environment and do not try to change it. They analyze the environmental forces and design strategies that will help the company avoid the threats and take advantage of the opportunities the environment provides.

Other companies take an **environmental management perspective**.[19] Rather than simply watching and reacting, these firms take aggressive actions to affect the publics and forces in their marketing environment. Such companies hire lobbyists to influence legislation affecting their industries and stage media events to gain favourable press coverage. They run 'advertorials' (ads expressing editorial points of view) to shape public opinion. They take legal action and file complaints with regulators to keep competitors in line. They also form contractual agreements to control their distribution channels better.

Marketing management cannot always affect environmental forces. In many cases, it must settle for simply watching and reacting to the environment. For example, a company would have little success trying to influence geographic population shifts, the economic environment or important cultural values. But whenever possible, clever marketing managers will take a *proactive* rather than *reactive* approach to the marketing environment.

environmental management perspective
A management perspective in which the firm takes aggressive actions to affect the publics and forces in its marketing environment rather than simply watching it and reacting to it.

Summary

All companies operate within a *marketing environment*. This environment consists of all the actors and forces that affect the company's ability to transact effectively with its target market. The company's marketing environment can be divided into the microenvironment and the macroenvironment.

The *microenvironment* consists of five components. The first is the company's *internal environment* – its departmental and managerial structure, which affects marketing management's decision making. The second component is the marketing channel firms that co-operate to create value. These include the firm's suppliers and marketing intermediaries (middlemen, physical distribution firms, financial intermediaries, marketing services agencies). The third component refers to the five types of *market* in which the company can sell: the consumer, producer, reseller, government and international markets. The *competitors* facing the company make up the fourth component. The final component is the group of *publics* that have an actual or potential interest in or impact on the organization's ability to achieve its objectives. These constituencies include financial, media, government, citizen action, local, general and internal publics.

The company's *macroenvironment* consists of primary forces that shape opportunities and pose threats to the company. These forces include demographic, economic, natural, technological, political and cultural forces.

In many developed western and Asian countries, the *demographic environment* presents problems with the challenges of changing age and family structures, a population that is becoming better educated and increasing diversity. The *economic environment* shows changing patterns of real income and shifts in consumer spending patterns. The *natural environment* has pending shortages of certain raw materials, growing energy costs, higher pollution levels, more government intervention in natural resource management and higher levels of citizen concern and activism about these issues. The *technological environment* reveals rapid technological change, unlimited innovation opportunities, a need for high R & D budgets, concentration on minor improvements rather than big discoveries, and growing regulation of technological change. The *political environment* shows increasing business regulation, the rising importance of public interest groups and increased emphasis on ethics and socially responsible actions. The *cultural environment* suggests long-term trends towards a 'we-society', less organizational loyalty, increasing patriotism and conservatism, greater appreciation for nature and a search for more meaningful and enduring values.

Key Terms

Cultural environment 169
Demography 151
Economic environment 158
Engel's laws 162
Environmental management
    perspective 173
Financial intermediaries 148

Macroenvironment 146
Marketing environment 146
Marketing intermediaries 147
Marketing services agencies 148
Microenvironment 146
Natural environment 162
Physical distribution firms 148

Political environment 167
Public 149
Resellers 147
Suppliers 147
Technological environment
    165

Discussing the Issues

1. Select a sports and leisure footwear company. What microenvironmental trends will affect the success of the company in the decade ahead? What marketing plans would you make to respond to these trends?

regular intervals until 1985. Under South African law as it stood at the time, a company lost its right to the trademark it if languished unused on the books for five years, unless there was a good reason. Again, the judge did not believe that 'special circumstances' – pressure from anti-apartheid groups and sanctions – were the real reasons that McDonald's had left its trademark unused for so long: 'there is no explanation for the failure to commence business in South Africa,' he declared, 'other than the fact that South Africa simply did not rank on McDonald's list of priorities'.

These legal setbacks were temporary. McDonald's was allowed to press ahead with opening restaurants while it prepared its case for the Appeal Court. In 1996 the American burger chain won this second battle: the Appeal Court, in essence, applied a less strict test of what it meant to be well known in South Africa, and accepted the evidence in the two surveys because it thought that whites represented McDonald's *target* markets.

The case was a harbinger of the sort of trouble that McDonald's was to experience throughout South Africa. But, McDonald's had not given up so easily. The firm continued to invest in opening new outlets after that. At the end of 1997, it operated 35 restaurants in the country – a small-fry, though, compared to the 337 it runs in Brazil. It has scored well against local rivals in slick service and a studied appeal to children. However, there are still worries that McDonald's is treating its South African market as if it were uniform. It offers its standard worldwide menu – hamburgers of every imaginable size, with a few chicken products as alternatives. Some of its local managers have expressed how odd the choice is given that the majority of local black consumers tend to favour chicken, which is cheaper than red meat. White consumers, by contrast, tend to be beef-obsessed. They argue that 'politically correct' McDonald's seems unwilling to acknowledge, in the overt way that its local rivals do, the point that the split between beef hamburgers and chicken has as much to do with race as with products. McDonald's judged that the South African market was not different enough to merit product adaptation from the start. It would wait instead to see how well the standard McDonald's menu went down.

McDonald's experience in the market is a stark reminder of the challenges facing companies seeking to penetrate new country markets. Even the most powerful, established, global brands from developed countries can hit a number of unexpected barriers to entry into a foreign market. Importantly, the company cannot expect to trample all before it in developing or emerging country markets – particularly when local consumers can choose established local alternatives. If the owner of the world's leading brand encounters such troubles, companies with a less well-known trademark must think twice before venturing into foreign markets.[1]

When deciding to take advantage of an international marketing opportunity, firms should consider a number of questions.

QUESTIONS

You should attempt these questions only after completing your reading of this chapter. International marketing is more than simply taking what products or services are successful at home and exporting to a foreign market. It requires huge investment and long-term commitment to the target market, cultural sensitivity, and a willingness to adapt one's product and marketing strategies. Tailoring the firm's offering to suit target customer needs cannot be over-emphasized. Once the firm learns to do this, overseas markets can be lucrative and a recipe for success.

1. What are the attractions of international market expansion?
2. What might be the risks attached to expanding into a foreign or emerging market?
3. How can these risks be minimized?
4. Outline the key lessons we can draw from McDonald's experience in the South African market.
5. What criteria must the firm consider when deciding on which country market to enter?
6. What constitutes an effective marketing programme for the target country market?

Introduction

This chapter discusses the importance of global marketing and explains the key elements of the planning process: analyzing international market opportunities; deciding whether or not to go abroad; establishing market entry mode; allocating resources; developing the marketing plan; organizing for international marketing; implementing the marketing strategy; and evaluation and control.

Companies pay little attention to international trade when the home market is big and teeming with opportunities. The home market is also much safer. Managers do not need to learn other languages, deal with strange and changing currencies, face political and legal uncertainties or adapt their products to different customer needs and expectations. This has been the attitude of many western companies, which saw little need to sell in overseas markets because their domestic market alone seemed to offer attractive opportunities for growth.

Today, however, the business environment is changing and firms cannot afford to ignore international markets. The increasing dependency of nations around the world on each other's goods and services has raised awareness among companies of the need for a more international outlook in their approach to business. International markets are important because most firms are geared towards growth and so must seek new opportunities in foreign countries as their domestic markets mature. As international trade becomes more liberalized, firms are facing tougher foreign competition in the domestic market. They must develop the ability to fight off competitors on their own home ground, or to exploit business opportunities in foreign markets.

Furthermore, time and distance are shrinking rapidly with the advent of faster communication, transportation and financial flows. Products developed in one country are finding enthusiastic acceptance in other countries. Across western Europe and North America, names such as Toyota, Sony and Toshiba have become household words in the same way McDonald's, Toys 'Я' Us, Philips and IKEA are familiar names to most young consumers in Asian countries like Japan, Singapore and Hong Kong.

Thus, as global competition intensifies, local companies that never thought about foreign competitors suddenly find these competitors in their own back-yards. The firm that stays at home to play it safe not only misses the opportunity to enter other markets, but also risks losing its home market.

Consider, for example, Japanese victories over western producers in many sectors – motorcycles, cars, cameras, consumer electronics, machine tools, photocopiers. These markets used to be the stronghold of US, German and British companies in the 1970s, but are now dominated by Japanese manufacturers. The latter are not insulated from foreign competitors either. Increasing competition from lower-cost newly industrializing countries (NICs) in the Far East, notably South Korea and Taiwan, are posing a big threat to established Japanese firms in traditional industries like steel, chemicals and heavy machinery.

In the United States, American firms are fighting off aggressive assaults by international European companies: Bic's successful attacks on Gillette and Nestlé's gains in the coffee and confectionery markets are a reflection of the growing level of international competition in 'safe' home markets. In the European Union (EU), foreign firms' direct investment is on the increase and intra-Union flows of investment in all kinds of business sectors – cars, clothing, retailing, financial services – are particularly active. Many sophisticated and aggressive foreign companies also see the emerging eastern European economies as longer-term opportunities. So, more than ever, firms must learn how to enter foreign markets and increase their global competitiveness.

Although some companies would like to stem the tide of foreign imports through protectionism, this response would be only a temporary solution. Suppressing a free flow of foreign imports would lead to fewer choices for the consumer and higher prices for indigenously produced goods. In the long run, it would raise the cost of living and protect inefficient domestic firms. It also means that consumers' needs and wants would not be met effectively and efficiently. A better solution is to encourage more firms to learn to make the world their market.

The importance of internationalization is also reflected by the fact that most governments run an export promotion programme, which tries to persuade local companies to export. Denmark pays more than half the salary of marketing consultants who help small and medium-size Danish companies get into exports. Many countries go even further and subsidize their companies by granting preferential land and energy costs – they even supply cash outright so that their companies can charge lower prices than do their foreign competitors.

Today the pressure on firms operating in global industries is not just to export to other countries, but to strive to be a global firm. A **global industry** is one in which the strategic positions of competitors in given geographic or national markets are affected by their overall global positions. A **global firm**, therefore, is one that, by operating in more than one country, gains research and development, production, marketing and financial advantages in its costs and reputation that are not available to purely domestic competitors.[2] The global company sees the world as one market. It minimizes the importance of national boundaries, and raises capital, sources materials and components, and manufactures and markets its goods wherever it can do the best job. For example, Ford's 'world truck' sports a cab made in Europe and a chassis built in North America. It is assembled in Brazil and imported to the United States for sale. Thus global firms gain advantages by planning, operating and co-ordinating their activities on a worldwide basis. These gains are a key reason behind recent global restructuring programmes undertaken by leading German car producers, BMW and Mercedes-Benz. **Global marketing** is concerned with integrating or standardizing marketing actions across a number of geographic markets. This does not rule out forceful adaptation of the marketing mix to individual countries, but suggests that firms, where possible, ignore traditional market boundaries and capitalize on similarities between markets to build competitive advantage.

Because firms around the world are globalizing at a rapid rate, domestic firms in global industries must act quickly before the window closes on them. This does not mean that small and medium-size firms must operate in a dozen countries to

global industry
An industry in which the strategic positions of competitors in given geographic or national markets are affected by their overall global positions.

global firm
A firm that, by operating in more than one country, gains R & D, production, marketing and financial advantages in its costs and reputation that are not available to purely domestic competitors.

global marketing
Marketing that is concerned with integrating or standardizing marketing actions across different geographic markets.

succeed. These firms can practise global nichemanship. The world, however, is becoming smaller and every company operating in a global industry – whether large or small – must assess and establish its place in world markets.

Firms that confront international competitors in their existing markets must ask some basic questions: What market position should we try to establish in our country, in the geographic region (e.g. Europe, North America, Asia, Australasia) and globally? Who will our global competitors be and what are their strategies and resources? Where should we produce or source our products? What strategic alliances should we form with other firms around the world?

This chapter surveys the global marketplace and addresses the important decisions that firms have to make in international marketing planning. Each decision will be discussed in detail. First, however, let us take a look at the risks in doing business abroad.

Risks in International Marketing

Although the need for companies to go abroad is greater today than in the past, so are the risks. Managers must anticipate the risks and obstacles in doing business in foreign markets. Several complex problems confront companies that 'go global'.

High Foreign Country Debt

High debt, inflation and unemployment in several countries have resulted in highly unstable governments and currencies, which limit trade and expose firms to many risks. Debt-laden and/or currency-starved countries are often not able to pay despite their willingness to purchase. The inability of poorer countries, for example in eastern Europe, to pay by normal (cash) methods becomes a serious obstacle for supplying companies.

Exchange Rate Volatility

The level of a country's exchange rate affects the company's competitiveness in the foreign market. A weak pound will favour exports of British goods. A strong exchange rate intensifies the level of competition the firm faces at home. For European companies whose countries are members of the Exchange Rate Mechanism (ERM), much of the uncertainty is removed from fluctuating exchange rates. On the one hand, this is favourable for companies doing a great portion of their international business in the EU. On the other, however, the ERM does impose constraints on company decisions, such as productivity levels and government policy (e.g. in its flexibility to reduce interest rates).

Foreign Government Entry Requirements

Companies often face constraints imposed by the foreign or 'host' country government. Some of these market entry conditions relate to a variety of working practices including: degree of control (ownership) allowed; the hiring of local nationals; local content rules; the percentage of output exported; and the amount of profits that can be taken from the country. India, China, Mexico, Brazil and many African countries maintain formal, and often strict, entry conditions, while more advanced countries, such as Japan and the United States, impose strict 'quality' criteria.

Costs of Marketing Mix Adaptation

Although the international firm gains from economies of scale in production, these must be weighed against the higher costs of product modification, distribution and communication expenditures in overseas markets. For example, the complex, multilayered distribution system traditionally used in Japan, together with high Japanese product quality expectations and expensive media costs, is a considerable barrier to market entry for many foreign firms.

Other Problems

War, terrorism and corruption are other dangers that confront international businesses. The number of localized conflicts in eastern Europe is predicted to increase as a result of the resurgence in nationalism and ethnic rivalries in the post-cold war 'new world order'. Previous hostage-taking episodes in the Middle East and the widely publicized murders of western businessmen in Turkey, Shanghai (China) and Russia highlight a problem that international companies have long been aware of. The problem of widespread corruption in some countries, where officials often award contracts to the highest briber, not the lowest bidder, also presents a dilemma to many western businesspeople, particularly where anti-corruption principles are well laid down in their firm's own business charter. The firm must therefore establish clear guidelines for their staff who have to do business in countries where corruption is an increasing problem. These guidelines should help them decide whether or not to bid for business, in the first instance, and, if so, where and when to draw the line.

The difficulties associated with doing business in foreign markets, however, should not deter firms from engaging in international marketing. Rather, these risks and problems must be identified by managers and planned for. Like all marketing activities, the chance of success is far higher when obstacles are anticipated rather than reacted to.

The rest of this chapter is devoted to examining the important international marketing decisions that firms make. Figure 5.1 presents a framework for analysis, planning, implementation and control in relation to international marketing. The eight dimensions shown are useful for identifying the keys to foreign market success. Each dimension will be discussed in turn.

Analysis of International Market Opportunity

Deciding Whether or Not to Go Abroad

Doing international business successfully requires firms to take a market-led approach. A critical evaluation of why firms enter foreign markets shows that, in many cases, the practice of international business falls short of the market-led approach essential for long-term success. Firms must consider the factors that draw them into the international arena.

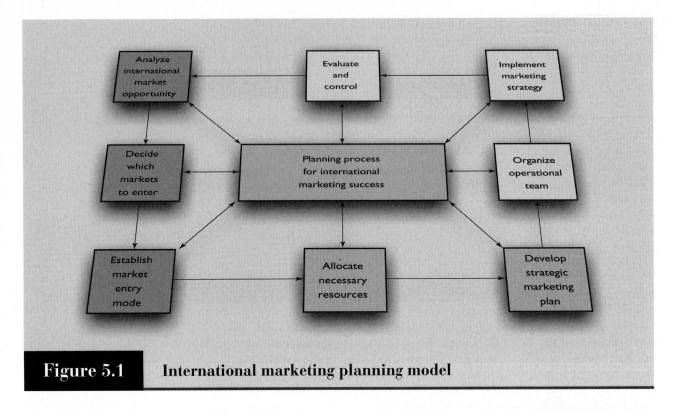

Figure 5.1 International marketing planning model

A surprisingly large proportion of sales to foreign markets are made in response to *chance orders* coming either from customers who are international players or from other sources such as foreign buyers attending a domestic exhibition. Such 'passive exporting' is not international marketing, although it contributes to international trade. It does not associate with the central principle of creating customer value and market targeting, there is little assessment of critical factors for competitive success, and it is unlikely to build a long-term market position.

Limited domestic growth and/or intense domestic competition is a key reason why firms enter foreign markets and was a prime motivator behind the Japanese companies' overseas expansion programme during the 1970s and 1980s. In practice, many firms quickly suspend foreign market activity when the domestic economy improves or when they fail to make money in the overseas operation. Firms driven to exporting because of domestic recession often fail to anticipate the wider external constraints to doing business in a foreign market and tend to take a short-term orientation to international marketing.[3]

Furthermore, companies that are struggling to survive at home are highly unlikely to successfully take on and beat sophisticated competitors in foreign markets. The domestic market must be secured first before going abroad and it should be maintained thereafter. Japan's top two car manufacturers, Toyota and Nissan, are arch rivals at home. They took this rivalry overseas and in the process have raised the level of competitive activity to new heights in North America and Europe, while striving to remain strong performers in their home base.

Geographic market diversification to reduce country-specific risk – that is, the risk of operating in only one country, due to different political-economic cycles – is a popular reason behind firms' international expansion drive. Firms must understand that market needs may be strikingly different, even for apparently similar products, and that different management skills and approaches are needed for different country markets. So, managers must weigh the costs and barriers to global diversification against the benefits of risk reduction.

Asia: a growing market. This Hongkong-Bank ad reinforces the region's potential, and illustrates how the bank can meet the needs of its international customers.

Firms spread the costs of production over more units if output is expanded for overseas markets. While *economies of scale* give firms a strong incentive to expand into foreign markets, the firm must also take on board additional administration, selling, distribution and marketing costs. A 'cost-led' approach or a 'selling orientation' in international marketing is unlikely to lead to long-term success. Without a marketing-led orientation, where customers' needs are identified and satisfied, and the firm's marketing mix adapted for the foreign market, the international business activity of the firm is unlikely to flourish.

In summary, firms enter overseas markets for profits and/or survival. But firms must not confuse exporting with international marketing. The latter is about taking a long-term perspective of foreign market potential and relentlessly adopting a market-led approach to identifying, anticipating and satisfying the needs of customers in target international markets. Before going abroad, the firm must weigh the risks and question its ability to operate globally. Can the company learn to understand the preferences and buying behaviour of customers in other country markets? Can it offer competitively attractive products? Will it be able to adapt to other countries' business cultures and to deal effectively with foreign nationals? Do the company's managers have the requisite international experience? Has management considered the impact of foreign regulations and political environments? International marketing is really about exploiting market opportunities based upon sound environment and specific market analyses.

Understanding the Global Environment

Before deciding whether or not to sell abroad, a company must thoroughly understand the international marketing environment. That environment has changed a

Many companies have made the world their market: opening the megastore in Milan (top left) and Virgin megastores in London, Los Angeles, Vienna and Tokyo.

great deal in the last two decades, creating both new opportunities and new problems. The world economy has globalized. First, world trade and investment have grown rapidly, with many attractive markets opening up in western and eastern Europe, Russia, China, the Pacific Rim and elsewhere. Official sources suggest that world trade in goods grew by 8 per cent in volume terms and FDI rose some 40 per cent over 1996 alone. In fact, during the 1990s, international trade has grown faster than world output.[4] There has been a growth of global brands in motor vehicles, food, clothing, electronics and many other categories. The number of global companies has grown dramatically. While the United States' dominant position in world trade has declined, other countries, such as Japan and Germany, have increased their economic power in world markets (see Marketing Highlight 5.1). The international financial system has become more complex and fragile. In some country markets, foreign companies face increasing trade barriers, erected to protect domestic markets against outside competition. There has also been increasing concern among members outside the European Union that 'Fortress Europe' presents greater barriers to penetrating the EU markets. Japanese car plants, for example, have been attracted to the United Kingdom by the thought that they can by-pass the EU's restrictions on imports of Japanese cars.

● *The International Trade System*

The company looking abroad must develop an understanding of the international trade system. When selling to another country, the firm faces various trade restrictions. The most common is the **tariff**, which is a tax levied by a foreign government against certain imported products. The tariff may be designed either to raise revenue or to protect domestic firms: for example, those producing motor vehicles in Malaysia and whisky and rice in Japan. The exporter also may face a **quota**, which sets limits on the amount of goods the importing country will accept

tariff
A tax levied by a government against certain imported products. Tariffs are designed to raise revenue or to protect domestic firms.

quota
A limit on the amount of goods that an importing country will accept in certain product categories; it is designed to conserve on foreign exchange and to protect local industry and employment.

in certain product categories. The purpose of the quota is to conserve foreign exchange and to protect local industry and employment. An **embargo** is the strongest form of quota, which totally bans some kinds of import.

Firms may face **exchange controls** that limit the amount of foreign exchange and the exchange rate against other currencies. The company may also face **non-tariff trade barriers**, such as biases against company bids or restrictive product standards that favour or go against product features.[5]

At the same time, certain forces help trade between nations. Examples are the General Agreement on Tariffs and Trade (replaced by the World Trade Organization in 1993) and various regional free trade agreements.

● *The General Agreement on Tariffs and Trade/ Word Trade Organization*

The General Agreement on Tariffs and Trade (GATT) is an international treaty designed to promote world trade by reducing tariffs and other international trade barriers. There have been eight rounds of GATT talks since its inception in 1948, in which member nations reassess trade barriers and set new rules for international trade. The first seven rounds of negotiations reduced average worldwide tariffs on manufactured goods from 45 per cent to around 4 per cent in industrial countries.

The most recent GATT round, the Uruguay round, ended in 1993. Although the benefits of the Uruguay round will not be felt for many years, the new accord should promote robust long-term global trade growth. It reduces the world's remaining manufactured goods tariffs by 30 per cent, which could boost global merchandise trade by up to 10 per cent, or $270 billion in current US dollars, by the year 2002.

The Uruguay round did much more than cut tariffs on goods. It heralded a big institutional change, creating the World Trade Organization (WTO) as a successor to GATT. WTO now boasts 132 members. It also introduced three big changes to world trade rules. First, it began to open up the most heavily protected industries: agriculture and textiles. Second, it vastly extended the scope of international trade rules to cover services as well as goods. New issues, such as the use of spurious technical barriers and health regulations to keep out imports and the protection of foreigners' 'intellectual property', such as patents and copyright, were addressed for the first time.

The third big change brought by the Uruguay round was the creation of a new system for settling disputes. In the past, countries could (and sometimes did) break GATT rules with impunity. Under the new system, decisions can be blocked only by a consensus of WTO members. Once found guilty of breaking the rules, and after appeal, countries are supposed to mend their ways. Under the WTO international trade issues continue to be addressed. As the new WTO builds up its credibility, more and more countries, including China, are wanting to join.[6]

● *Regional Free-Trade Zones*

In recent years, we have seen the growth of regional free-trade zones or economic communities – groups of nations organized to secure common goals in the regulation of international trade. One such community is the European Union, which aims to create a single European market by reducing physical, financial and technical barriers to trade among member nations.[7]

Other free-trade communities exist. In fact, almost every member of the WTO is also a member of one or more such communities. And, of the one

embargo
A ban on the import of a certain product.

exchange controls
Government limits on the amount of its country's foreign exchange with other countries and on its exchange rate against other currencies.

non-tariff trade barriers
Non-monetary barriers to foreign products, such as biases against a foreign company's bids or product standards that go against a foreign company's product features.

World-Class Marketing: The Japanese

Marketing Highlight 5.1

Few dispute that the Japanese have performed an economic miracle since the Second World War. In a very short time, they have achieved global market leadership in many industries: motor vehicles, watches, cameras, optical instruments, steel, shipbuilding, computers and consumer electronics. They have made strong inroads into tyres, chemicals, machine tools and financial services, and even designer clothes, cosmetics and food. Some credit the global success of Japanese companies to their unique business and management practices. Others point to the help they get from Japan's government, powerful trading companies and banks. Still others say Japan's success was based on low wage rates and unfair dumping policies.

In any case, one of the main keys to Japan's success is certainly its skilful use of marketing. The Japanese came to the United States to study marketing and went home understanding it better than many US companies do. They know how to select a market, enter it in the right way, build market share and protect that share against competitors. Having practised and seen how well it works in the US market, the Japanese came to Europe with the same game plan.

Selecting markets. The Japanese work hard to identify attractive global markets. First, they look for industries that require high skills and high labour intensity, but few natural resources. These include consumer electronics, cameras, watches, motorcycles and pharmaceuticals. Second, they prefer markets in which consumers around the world would be willing to buy the same product designs. Finally, they look for industries in which the market leaders are weak or complacent.

Entering markets. Japanese study teams spend several months evaluating a target market and searching for market niches that are not being satisfied. Sometimes they start with a low-priced, stripped-down version of a product, like cameras and radio receivers. At other times, they start with a product that is as good as the competition's but priced lower, such as radios and televisions, or with a product of higher quality or incorporating new features, as in the case of cars and photocopiers.

The Japanese line up good distribution channels in order to provide quick service. They also use effective advertising to bring their products to the consumers' attention. Their basic entry strategy is to build market share rather than early profits, and they are often willing to wait as long as a decade before realizing their profits.

Building market share. Once Japanese firms gain a market foothold, they begin to expand their market share. Money is poured into product improvements and new models so that they can offer more and better products than the competition does. They spot new opportunities through market segmentation, develop markets in new countries, and work to build a network of world markets and production locations.

Protecting market share. Once the Japanese achieve market leadership, they become defenders rather than attackers. Their defence strategy is continuous product development and refined market segmentation. Their philosophy is to make 'tiny improvements in a thousand places'.

Recently, some experts have questioned whether Japanese companies can sustain their push towards global marketing dominance. They suggest that the Japanese emphasis on the long-term market share over short-term profits and their ability to market high-quality products at low prices have come at the expense of their employees, stockholders and communities. They note that, compared to western firms, Japanese companies work their employees longer hours, pay their stockholders lower dividends, and contribute less to community and environmental causes. Other analysts, however, predict that Japan's marketing success is likely to continue.

In America and Europe, western firms that have survived the Japanese onslaught are fighting back by adding new product lines, pricing more aggressively, streamlining production, buying or making components abroad and forming strategic partnerships with foreign companies. With the help of a weakened Japanese economy, a soaring yen and strong political trade pressures, western companies are winning back market share in industries ranging from automobiles and earthmovers to semiconductors and computers. Many companies are also gaining ground in Japan.

US firms, for example, hold leading market shares: Coke leads in soft drinks (60 per cent share), Schick in razors (71 per cent), Polaroid in instant cameras (66 per cent), and McDonald's in fast food. Procter & Gamble markets the leading brand in several categories, ranging from disposable nappies and liquid laundry detergents to acne treatments.

A growing number of European companies have successfully penetrated the daunting Japanese market. Success, however, has not been limited to large companies like Glaxo or those with well-established marques. For example, Teknek Electronics, a small British company which makes a precision machine that cleans sheet materials in the printed circuit industry, successfully entered the Japanese market despite its chief competitor in the market being a Japanese machine. Solid State Logic, a relatively young British company that makes professional audio equipment, has made significant progress within 20 months of setting up its subsidiary in Japan. In the consumer market, Foseco, a speciality chemicals maker, sold its Sedex filters at a loss for one year in Japan while it set up local production to meet intense domestic price competition. It emerged from the trauma with 55 per cent of the Japanese market, and a reduction in production costs that enabled it to bring its own sales price down by 30 per cent. Foseco Japan now sells three times as many different types and sizes of Sedex filter as any Foseco company.

The success of western companies in Japan stems largely from the firms' willingness to meet the Japanese market on its own, highly competitive terms. The key ingredients for success are: not treating the Japanese market as any other market; a high-quality or latest technology product; a high level of commitment to – invariably meaning a high level of investment in – the market; an ability to respond efficiently to specific market segment needs; and an understanding of the specific business culture. For most consumer products, tying up with a local distributor or partner is critical. Understanding the complex distribution system with its layers of wholesalers, and having the patience to handle it, are crucial in Japan because it is difficult to get products on the shelves by directly approaching the retailer. A strong marketing plan, encompassing intensive and aggressive advertising, and close co-operation with wholesalers and retailers, is also essential, not only to reach and impress the consumer, but also to convince the wholesaler and the retail buyers that the firm is serious about its product.

In fact, very similar ingredients are found in western and Japanese overseas marketing success recipes. These all point to one outstanding dimension – superior marketing – as reflected in the firms' focus on market needs, sustained commitment to product and market development, and environmental, particularly cultural, sensitivity.

This suggests that the broad principles for success in international marketing are not country specific, but readily transferable to other national players.

SOURCES: See Peter Doyle, John Saunders and Veronica Wong, 'Competition in global markets: a case study of American and Japanese competition in the British market', *Journal of International Business Studies*, 23, 3 (1992), pp. 419–42; Michiyo Nakamoto, 'British companies reap benefits of Japanese markets', *Financial Times* (8 May 1991), p. 6; Michiyo Nakamoto, 'Use the system, win shelf space', *Financial Times* (16 February 1994), p. 19; Philip Kotler, Liam Fahey and Somkid Jatusripitak, *The New Competition* (Englewood Cliffs, NJ: Prentice Hall, 1985); Vernon R. Alden, 'Who says you can't crack Japanese markets?', *Harvard Business Review* (January–February 1987), pp. 52–6; Ford S. Worthy, 'Keys to Japanese success in Asia', *Fortune* (7 October 1991), pp. 157–60; 'Why Japan must change', *Fortune* (9 March 1992), pp. 66–7.

Income distribution: Even poorer countries may have small but wealthy segments. Although citizens of Budapest, Hungary have relatively low annual incomes, well-dressed shoppers flock to elegant stores like this one, stocked with luxury goods.

hundred or so free-trade arrangements listed by the WTO, over half have come into being in the 1990s (see Marketing Highlight 5.2).

● *Economic Environment*

The international marketer must study each country's economy. Two economic factors reflect the country's attractiveness as a market: the country's *industrial structure* and its *income distribution*.

The country's industrial structure shapes its product and service needs, income levels and employment levels. Four types of industrial structure should be considered:

1. *Subsistence economies.* In a subsistence economy, the vast majority of people engage in simple agriculture. They consume most of their output and barter the rest for simple goods and services. They offer few market opportunities.

2. *Raw-material-exporting economies.* These economies are rich in one or more natural resources, but poor in other ways. Much of their revenue comes from exporting these resources. Examples are Chile (tin and copper), Zaire (copper, cobalt and coffee) and Saudi Arabia (oil). These countries are good markets for large equipment, tools and supplies, and trucks. If there are many foreign residents and a wealthy upper class, they are also a market for luxury goods.

3. *Industrializing economies.* In an industrializing economy, manufacturing accounts for 10–20 per cent of the country's economy. Examples include China, the Philippines, India and Brazil. As manufacturing increases, the country needs more imports of raw textile materials, steel and heavy machinery, and fewer imports of finished textiles, paper products and motor vehicles. Industrialization typically creates a new rich class and a small but growing middle class, both demanding new types of imported goods. In China, for example, people with rising disposable income want to spend on items such as fashion, video recorders, CD players and instant coffee.

4. *Industrial economies*. Industrial economies are large exporters of manufactured goods and investment funds. They trade goods among themselves and also export them to other types of economy for raw materials and semi-finished goods. The varied manufacturing activities of these industrial nations and their large middle class make them rich markets for all sorts of goods. Asia's newly industrialized economies, such as Taiwan, Singapore, South Korea and Malaysia, fall into this category.

The second economic factor is the country's income distribution. The international marketer might find countries with one of five different income distribution patterns: (1) very low family incomes; (2) mostly low family incomes; (3) very low/very high family incomes; (4) low/medium/high family incomes; and (5) mostly medium family incomes.

However, even people in low-income countries may find ways to buy products that are important to them, or sheer population numbers can counter low average incomes. Also, in many cases, poorer countries may have small but wealthy segments of upper-income consumers:

> In the US the first satellite dishes sprang up in the poorest parts of Appalachia ... The poorest slums of Calcutta are home to 70,000 VCRs. In Mexico, homes with colour televisions outnumber those with running water. Remember also that low average-income figures may conceal a lively luxury market. In Warsaw (average income: $2,500) well-dressed shoppers flock to elegant boutiques stocked with Christian Dior perfume and Valentino shoes ... In China, where per capita income is less than $600, the Swiss company Rado is selling thousands of its $1,000 watches.[8]

Thus, international marketers face many challenges in understanding how the economic environment will affect decisions about which global markets to enter and how.

● *Political-Legal Environment*

Nations differ greatly in their political-legal environments. At least four political-legal factors should be considered in deciding whether to do business in a given country: attitudes towards international buying, political stability, monetary regulations and government bureaucracy. We will consider each of these in turn.

ATTITUDES TOWARDS INTERNATIONAL BUYING. Some nations are quite receptive to foreign firms, and others are quite hostile. Western firms have found newly industrialized countries in the Far East attractive overseas investment locations. In contrast, others like India are bothersome with their import quotas, currency restrictions and limits on the percentage of the management team that can be non-nationals.

Switzerland remains a difficult market for many imports as protectionism, mainly in the form of technical barriers, is rampant, and the cantonical governments remain reluctant to buy anything outside their borders.[9]

In Poland, Slovakia and the Czech Republic, after an initial infatuation with all things 'western', a backlash has started as national pride reasserts itself and consumers begin to resent the commercial advance from the West.[10]

POLITICAL STABILITY. Governments change hands, sometimes violently. Even without a change, a government may decide to respond to new popular feel-

Regional Free-Trading Groups: Blocking Up

Marketing Highlight 5.2

The growth of regional trade arrangements has excited keen controversy in recent years. More than 100 have been formed, 29 since 1992, and almost all the roughly 130 members of the World Trade Organization belong to one or more of them. Figure 1 shows the main regional trade groups.

More recently, the EU, 11 southern Mediterranean governments and the Palestine National Authority launched the 'Euro-Mediterranean partnership' zone, which creates a new trading bloc. Goods made in countries such as Morocco and Turkey will gain free access to the single European market.

By 2010 it is envisaged that the Mediterranean basin will be open for reciprocal free trade in most manufactured goods and services – creating a trading bloc to rival the North American Free Trade Agreement and the Asia-Pacific Economic Co-operation forum.

In Asia, the fashion for regionalism is in the ascendant. One example is the recent push for a free-trade area embracing the seven-member Association of South East Asian Nations. Another is the Asia Pacific Economic Co-operation forum, two thirds of whose 18 members are Asian.

By lowering barriers between national markets, such groupings can make life easier for exporters – provided they operate inside the club. If they are outsiders, however, they risk facing continued discrimination and – where regional trade arrangements overlap – confusion.

Enthusiasts say regional groupings promote free trade by acting as building blocks, which can eventually unite. But sceptics fear the more likely result will be to fragment the global economy into mutually exclusive, possible warring, blocs.

Regionalism is undoubtedly posing another type of challenge to the world trade system, in the form of proliferating rules and regulations. For instance, 22 of the 24 regional agreements being analyzed by the WTO contain their own anti-dumping provisions, 18 have provisions relating to subsidies, 19 deal with competition policy and 12 have their own disputes settlement procedures. Some experts fear this trend could undermine the WTO's rules-based system by encouraging the spread of regional regulations that conflict with it. It is hard to be sure just how serious a risk this is, because of the weakness of procedures for vetting whether regional groups are compatible with WTO rules.

These problems are finally starting to be addressed. A formal WTO committee is examining regional trade arrangements. However, developing firm and workable disciplines, which command support from all WTO members, will take many years. Much work is still needed to clarify countries' often differing interpretations of the GATT/WTO rules on regional trade agreements and to define more precisely areas of incompatibility. Furthermore, the new committee seeks to set up effective procedures for reaching decisions and for reviewing regularly the operation of existing regional arrangements. Where these are found inconsistent with WTO rules, some mechanism will be needed to ensure they fall back in line.

SOURCES: Paul Magnusson, '"Free trade": They can hardly wait', *Business Week* (14 September 1992), pp. 24–5; Andrew Hilton, 'Mythology, markets, and the emerging Europe', *Harvard Business Review* (November–December 1992), pp. 50–4; Larry Armstrong, 'NAFTA isn't out, but it sure is down', *Business Week* (22 March 1993), pp. 30–1; Guy de Jonquières, 'Building blocks or warring blocs?', *Financial Times*, FT Exporter, 11 (Spring 1996), p. 3; Jon Marks, 'New kids on the Eurotrading bloc', *Financial Times, FT Exporter*, 11 (Spring 1996), p. 7.

ings. The foreign company's property may be taken, its currency holdings may be blocked, or import quotas or new duties may be set. International marketers may find it profitable to do business in an unstable country, but the unsteady situation will affect how they handle business and financial matters.

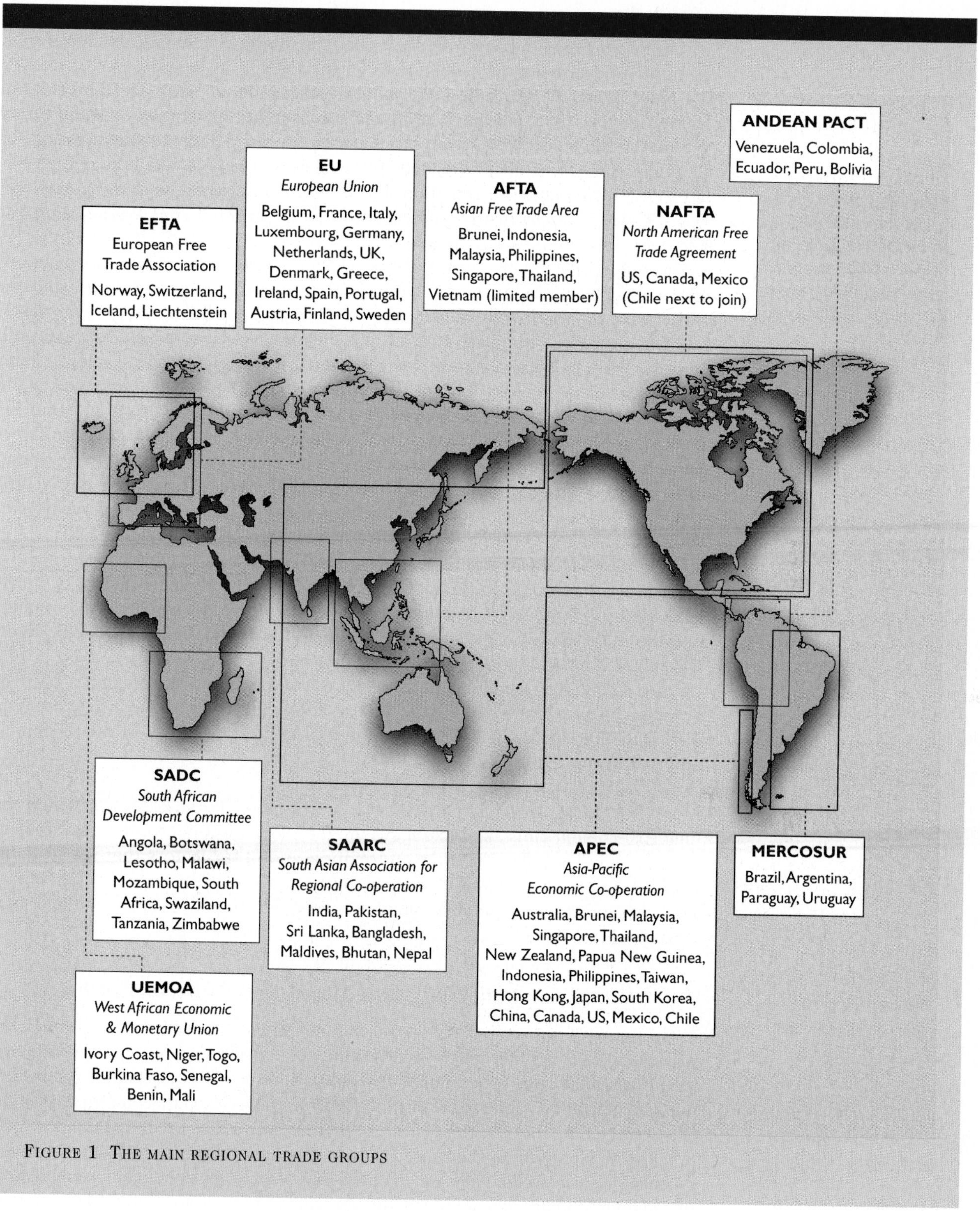

EFTA
European Free
Trade Association

Norway, Switzerland,
Iceland, Liechtenstein

EU
European Union

Belgium, France, Italy,
Luxembourg, Germany,
Netherlands, UK,
Denmark, Greece,
Ireland, Spain, Portugal,
Austria, Finland, Sweden

AFTA
Asian Free Trade Area

Brunei, Indonesia,
Malaysia, Philippines,
Singapore, Thailand,
Vietnam (limited member)

NAFTA
*North American Free
Trade Agreement*

US, Canada, Mexico
(Chile next to join)

ANDEAN PACT
Venezuela, Colombia,
Ecuador, Peru, Bolivia

SADC
*South African
Development Committee*

Angola, Botswana,
Lesotho, Malawi,
Mozambique, South
Africa, Swaziland,
Tanzania, Zimbabwe

SAARC
*South Asian Association for
Regional Co-operation*

India, Pakistan,
Sri Lanka, Bangladesh,
Maldives, Bhutan, Nepal

APEC
*Asia-Pacific
Economic Co-operation*

Australia, Brunei, Malaysia,
Singapore, Thailand,
New Zealand, Papua New Guinea,
Indonesia, Philippines, Taiwan,
Hong Kong, Japan, South Korea,
China, Canada, US, Mexico, Chile

MERCOSUR
Brazil, Argentina,
Paraguay, Uruguay

UEMOA
*West African Economic
& Monetary Union*

Ivory Coast, Niger, Togo,
Burkina Faso, Senegal,
Benin, Mali

FIGURE 1 THE MAIN REGIONAL TRADE GROUPS

MONETARY REGULATIONS   Sellers want to take their profits in a currency
of value to them. Ideally, the buyer can pay in the seller's currency or in other
world currencies. Short of this, sellers might accept a blocked currency – one
whose removal from the country is restricted by the buyer's government – if they

can buy other goods in that country that they need themselves or can sell else-where for a needed currency. Besides currency limits, a changing exchange rate, as mentioned earlier, creates high risks for the seller.

Most international trade involves cash transactions. Many Third World and former Eastern bloc nations do not have access to hard currency or credit terms to pay for their purchases from other countries. So western companies, rather than lose the opportunity of a good deal, will accept payment in kind, which has led to a growing practice called **countertrade**. Countertrade is nothing new and was the way of doing business before money was invented. Today it accounts for about 25 per cent of all world trade.

countertrade
International trade involving the direct or indirect exchange of goods for other goods instead of cash. Forms include barter compensation (buyback) and counterpurchase.

Countertrade takes several forms. *Barter* involves the direct exchange of goods or services. For example, British coal mining equipment has been 'sold' for Indonesian plywood; Volkswagen cars were swapped for Bulgarian dried apricots; and Boeing 747s, fitted with Rolls-Royce engines, were exchanged for Saudi oil. Another form is *compensation* (or *buyback*), whereby the seller sells a plant, equipment or technology to another country and agrees to take payment in the resulting products. Thus, Goodyear provided China with materials and training for a printing plant in exchange for finished labels. Another form is *counter-purchase*. Here the seller receives full payment in cash, but agrees to spend some portion of the money in the other country within a stated time period. For example, Pepsi sells it syrup to Russia for roubles, and agrees to buy Russian vodka for reselling in the United States.

Countertrade deals can be very complex. For example, Daimler-Benz recently agreed to sell 30 trucks to Romania in exchange for 150 Romanian jeeps, which it then sold to Ecuador for bananas, which were in turn sold to a German super-market chain for German currency. Through this roundabout process, Daimler-Benz finally obtained payment in German money.[11]

For some firms the bartering system has worked. However, companies must be aware of the complexities and/or the limits: Rank Xerox, trying to sell high technology to Russia, not surprisingly drew the line at accepting payment in racing camels and goat horns!

GOVERNMENT BUREAUCRACY.   A fourth factor is the extent to which the host government runs an efficient system for helping foreign companies: efficient customs handling, good market information and other factors that aid in doing business. A common shock to western businesspeople is how quickly barriers to trade disappear if a suitable payment (bribe) is made to some official (see Marketing Highlight 5.3).

● *Cultural Environment and Building Cultural Empathy*

Each country has its own traditions, norms and taboos. The seller must examine the way consumers in different countries think about and use certain products before planning a marketing programme. The cultural barriers in target country markets must be identified. **Culture** is defined simply as *the learned distinctive way of life of a society*. The dimensions of culture include: the social organization of society (e.g. the class system in the United Kingdom, the caste system in India, the heavy reliance on social welfare in Sweden or the lack of it in Japan); religion (ranging from the Islamic fundamentalism of Iran to the secular approaches of western countries such as the United Kingdom); customs and rituals; values and attitudes towards domestic and international life; education provision and literacy levels; political system; aesthetic systems (e.g. folklore, music, arts, literature); and language.

culture
The set of basic values, perceptions, wants and behaviours learned by a member of society from family and other important institutions.

Culture permeates the lifestyles of customer targets and is manifested through the behavioural patterns of these customers. Culture and people's general behaviour influence the customer's actions in the marketplace, which, in turn, impact upon the firm's marketing decisions. There are often surprises. For example, the average Frenchman uses almost twice as many cosmetics and beauty aids as does his wife. The Germans and the French eat more packaged,

To Bribe or Not?

Marketing Highlight 5.3

In Germany, the tax office gives tacit approval to backhanders: bribes are tax-deductible. The exact extent of the corruption is not known, but experts reckon that in the German public sector contracts alone, the volume is at least DM20 billion a year. Such corruption is rarely exposed to the public, of course, but in Germany it is by all accounts a widespread and profitable affair. It starts out at local council level and goes on up the chain.

There have been a few sensational cases in the past 20 years. The Flick affair revealed in the 1980s the substantial payments an industrialist made to Germany's main political parties. In another case, Eduard Swick, a Bavarian businessman, was alleged to have paid leading members of the Bavarian government, including the late president Franz Josef Strauss, in return for help in his battle with tax collectors. Outside government circles, the most spectacular corruption case has been the Herzklappen affair, whereby doctors were alleged to have colluded with manufacturers in overcharging health insurers for heart valves.

In Germany, a company can offset any bribes it makes as a necessary business expense. All the finance authorities ask for is the name of the recipient of the bribe. The information is not used specifically to track down the corrupt official – who, by taking the bribe, is actually breaking the law – but simply to ensure that he or she declares the money received on his or her tax return.

Unlike domestic corruption, the bribery of people in a foreign country is not an offence in Germany. Moreover, German companies are not alone in adopting this practice. Only in the United States, which passed the Foreign Corrupt Practices Act in 1977, are such payments illegal. Not surprisingly, the US Department of Trade complains of unfair competition when confronted

with these modes of working by European companies, especially in developing countries.

Naturally, there are German parliamentary members who want to see changes. Ingomar Hanchler, a Social Democratic member of parliament, argued that corruption damages free competition and subverts the market economy while also encouraging monopolies, which can pay most. But there are those who disagree, saying that bribery is a necessary vehicle for business. Outlawing it would damage German firms in the international market and threaten jobs. The federation of German industry, the BDI, also challenges the view that bribes should be considered corrupt, maintaining that unusual payments are not bribes at all, but an essential expense and marketing cost.

What would a keen British businessperson hoping to invest in a deprived east German town do to get fast entry into this market? Well, one such British businessman hoping to invest in the town of Potsdam, near Berlin, did the unthinkable (by German standards!):

The British businessman was confronted with an unusual offer from a local politician. Pay DM25,000 consultancy fee to a law company, the politician told him, and your case will be dealt with quickly and to your satisfaction. Needless to say, the British executive knew the official had connections with the law firm in question and what the money was for and where it was going. He chose not to pay the 'consultancy fee'. In refusing, he was probably an exception. He also did not get to invest in the town of Potsdam.

SOURCE: Frederick Stüdemann, 'A land where bribes are tax-deductible', *The European* (17–23 June 1994), p. 3.

branded spaghetti than do Italians. Italian children like to eat chocolate bars between slices of bread as a snack. Women in Tanzania will not give their children eggs for fear of making them bald or impotent. A good example of cultural differences is the case of a Scandinavian company wishing to sell baby clothes in Belgium. It discovered its clothes were virtually unsaleable because, in most regions, clothes for baby girls are trimmed with blue and those for baby boys with pink.

Business norms and behaviour also vary from country to country. The unwary business executive needs to be briefed on these factors before conducting business in another country. Mistakes due to lack of understanding of foreign business behaviour affect business relations greatly. Here are some examples of different global business behaviour:

- In face-to-face communications, Japanese business executives rarely say 'no' to the western business executive. Thus westerners tend to be frustrated and may not know where they stand. Where westerners come to the point quickly, Japanese business executives may find this behaviour offensive.

- In France, wholesalers don't want to promote a product. They ask their retailers what they want and deliver it. If a foreign company builds its strategy around the French wholesaler's co-operation in promotions, it is likely to fail.

- When British executives exchange business cards, each usually gives the other's card a cursory glance and stuffs it in a pocket for later reference. In Japan, however, executives dutifully study each other's cards during a greeting, carefully noting company affiliation and rank. They hand their card to the most important person first.

- In the United Kingdom and the United States, business meals are common. In Germany, these are strictly social. Foreigners are rarely invited to dinner and such an invitation suggests a very advanced association. The opposite applies in Italy where entertaining is an essential part of business life (guests should offer to pay but, in the end, should defer to their Italian host). In France, watch out. There are two kinds of business lunch – one for building up relations, without expecting anything in return, and the other to discuss a deal in the making or to celebrate a deal afterwards. Deals, however, should be concluded in the office, never over a lunch table.

- Shaking hands on meeting and on parting is common in Germany, Belgium, France and Italy. Ignoring this custom, especially in France, causes offence. In France, it is advisable to shake hands with everyone in a crowded room.

The key to success for the international marketer lies in assiduously researching and coming to terms with a country's culture. The firm must build *cultural empathy* and overcome the cultural differences with a view to establishing long-term market position. Cultural empathy is achieved in a number of ways:

- *Acquire in-company knowledge and experience.* This is a slow and arduous approach, but it does provide a lasting means for understanding foreign culture.

- *Continuous market research.* The firm should undertake market research for general background information as well as commission more specific research for individual projects.

- *Visit foreign country and customers.* This is invaluable for developing first-hand knowledge of customers and markets. Such activities also build goodwill, clearly show the firm's commitment to the markets served and yield valuable feedback to the company's home base.

● *Hire local personnel*. Local personnel may be employed to speed up information gathering. This has been the approach used by many Japanese multinational firms in overseas markets. Sound local market knowledge helps to develop marketing strategies that are better geared to local requirements and conditions.

● *Use distributors/agents*. Firms may gain inside information from local distributors or agents who are familiar with the marketplace. Baskin Robbin's, an American ice-cream maker, relied on its sales agent, a subsidiary of the military-run China Satellite Launch and Tracking Control Group, for its knowledge of how to work the Chinese bureaucracy in order to bring its US-made ice cream through customs.[12]

● *Joint ventures and strategic alliances*. Firms accelerate the process of building cultural sensitivity through a joint venture or alliance with a host country company. The Japanese market, as mentioned earlier, is noted for its complex distribution system. To succeed foreign firms are advised to form strategic partnerships with local Japanese firms and to get to grips with the 'chosen people' problem.[13] The typical Japanese businessman, like many of his western counterparts, regards his own culture as the world's most nearly perfect. Thus, when foreigners are on Japanese turf, they would do well to learn, respect and observe as many local customs as possible.

● *Build language skills*. Language is an essential part of a country's culture. It is important to distinguish between the cultural and technical aspects of language. The technical characteristics are easily learnt and readily available in translation dictionaries and language courses. The cultural empathy derives from a deep understanding of the language and its use in both the verbal and non-verbal forms.[14] A lack of cultural understanding of language leads to errors in translation which can be, at best, embarrassing to both parties and, at worst, offensive to the host client/customer (see Marketing Highlight 5.4).

Deciding which Markets to Enter

Defining International Marketing Objectives and Policies

The company should define its international *marketing objectives* and *policies*. First, it should decide what *volume* of foreign sales it wants. Most companies start small when they go abroad. Some plan to stay small, seeing foreign sales as a small part of their business. Other companies have bigger plans, seeing foreign business as equal to or even more important than their domestic business. Second, the company must choose *how many* countries it wants to market in. Generally, it makes better sense to operate in fewer countries with deeper penetration in each. Third, the company must decide on the *types* of country to enter. A country's attractiveness depends on the product, geographical factors, income and population, political climate and other factors. The seller may prefer certain country groups or parts of the world.

Marketing Highlight 5.4

Mind Your Language

Here are some examples of careless translations which make an international marketer look downright foolish to foreign customers:

● A delicate pair of characters in the Chinese-language version of Microsoft's flagship Windows 95 operating system threatened to scramble the company's long-term plans for China. Things looked bad for Microsoft when Beijing offices discovered the phrase 'communist bandits' embedded in the Windows 95 Chinese-character selection system – which, to make matters even more dicey, was designed in Taiwan. Reports began to circulate that Chinese Public Security Officers were visiting computer users in Beijing demanding that they turn in their disks, and that authorities were considering a total ban on Windows 95. The reports tuned out to be false. Microsoft had moved quickly to head off a potential disaster, sending a group of top officials to Beijing for a hasty series of meetings. The two sides agreed temporarily to halt sales of Windows 95 in China, and Microsoft promised to send corrective diskettes to all licensed users that will scratch 'communist bandits' and other offending phrases from the system. Such fleet footwork is part of Microsoft's new conciliatory approach on the mainland. It's a big change from the situation three years ago, when Beijing nearly barred the company from its markets for selling Taiwan-designed programmes that differed from Beijing's standards. In that nearly disastrous episode, Microsoft ultimately acquiesced after a series of angry exchanges.

● When Coca-Cola first entered China, it provided shopkeepers with point-of-sale signs printed in English. This error was exacerbated when the shopkeepers translated the signs into their own calligraphy as 'Bite the wax tadpole'. Today the characters on Chinese Coke bottles translate as 'happiness in the mouth', which is an improvement on the 'Coke adds life' theme in the Japanese market, which translates into 'Coke brings your ancestors back from the dead'.

● Rolls-Royce avoided the name Silver Mist in German markets, where Mist means 'manure'. Sunbeam, an electrical appliances manufacturer, entered the German market with its Mist-Stick hair-curling iron. Not surprisingly, the Germans had little use for a 'manure wand'.

Careless blunders are soon discovered and amended. They may result in little more than embarrassment for the marketer. Countless other, more subtle errors, however, may go undetected and damage the brand's performance in less obvious ways. Consequently, the international company must carefully screen its brand names and advertising messages to avoid those that might harm sales, make the product look silly or, worse, offend consumers in specific markets.

SOURCE: Matt Forney, Dimon Fluendy and Emily Thornton, 'A matter of wording', *Far Eastern Economic Review* (10 October 1996), pp. 72–3.

After listing possible international markets, the company must screen and rank each one on several factors, including market size, market growth, cost of doing business, competitive advantage and risk level. The goal is to determine the potential of each market, using indicators like those shown in Table 5.1 All aspects of the product concept should be considered in relation to these indicators. The key determinant is whether or not the product is accepted in the proposed country markets and the investment is profitable. Then the marketer

And despite its flaws, the ordinance does seem to be moving the country rapidly towards its goal of waste reduction. For example, during the first three years under the new system, total household waste production fell by more than 10 per cent, while recycling quantities increased by 90 per cent. Germany collects, sorts and recycles 60 per cent of its post-consumer plastic-packaging waste, well ahead of the 35 per cent target. Producers and retailers are now working together to help solve environmental problems.

France and Austria have passed similar legislation, and France has begun using the green dot, although with a different collection system. In Germany, new ordinances are on the horizon,

including ones for mandating producer take-back of cars and electronic equipment. The EU is now working on a directive that would set minimum standards for recycling in all of its member states. 'It may take another year or two, but the train is running,' assures one German ministry official. 'The idea of product responsibility is spreading around the world.'

SOURCE: Adapted from Marilyn Stern, 'Is this the ultimate in recycling?' *Across the Board* (May 1993), pp. 28–31. See also Peter Sibbald, 'Manufacturing for reuse,' *Fortune*, (6 February 1995), pp. 102–12; 'Plastics waste: Germany beats recycling targets,' *Chemical Week* (5 June 1996), p. 22.

Table 6.1   **UK socioeconomic classification scheme**

CLASS NAME	SOCIAL STATUS	OCCUPATION OF HEAD OF HOUSEHOLD	% OF POPULATION
A	Upper middle	Higher managerial, administrative or professional	3
B	Middle	Intermediate managerial, administrative or professional	14
C1	Lower middle	Supervisors or clerical, junior managerial, administrative or professional	27
C2	Skilled working	Skilled manual workers	25
D	Working	Semi-skilled and unskilled manual workers	19
E	Those at lowest levels	State pensioners or widows, casual or lower-grade workers of subsistence	12

SOURCE: Office of Population Censuses and Surveys.

---

people, Anna Flores' buying behaviour will be influenced by her subculture identification. It will affect her food preferences, clothing choices, recreation activities and career goals. Subcultures attach different meanings to picture taking and this could affect both Anna's interest in cameras and the brand she buys.

● *Social Class*

Almost every society has some form of social class structure. **Social classes** are society's relatively permanent and ordered divisions whose members share similar values, interests and behaviours. The British scale with six social classes is widely used, although all big countries have their own system (see Table 6.1). In these

social classes
Relatively permanent and ordered divisions in a society whose members share similar values, interests and behaviours.

Using Reference Groups to Sell: Home-Party and Office-Party Selling

Marketing Highlight 6.2

Many companies capitalize on reference-group influence to sell their products. Home-party and office-party selling involves throwing sales parties in homes or workplaces and inviting friends and neighbours or co-workers to see products demonstrated. Companies such as Mary Kay Cosmetics, Avon and Tupperware are masters at this form of selling.

Mary Kay Cosmetics provides a good example of home-party selling. A Mary Kay beauty consultant (of which there are 170,000) asks different women to host small beauty shows in their homes. Each hostess invites her friends and neighbours for a few hours of refreshments and informal socializing. Within this congenial atmosphere, the Mary Kay representative gives a two-hour beauty plan and free make-up lessons to the guests, hoping that many of them will buy some of the demonstrated cosmetics. The hostess receives a commission on sales plus a discount on personal purchases. Usually, about 60 per cent of the guests buy something, partly because of the influence of the hostess and the other women attending the party.

In recent years, changing demographics have adversely affected home-party selling. Increasingly, women are working, which leaves fewer women with the time for shopping and fewer women at home to host or attend home sales parties. To overcome this problem, most party-plan sellers have followed their customers into the workplace with office-party selling. For example, Avon now trains its 400,000 salespeople to sell through office parties during coffee and lunch breaks and after hours. The company once sold only door to door, but currently picks up a quarter of its sales from buyers at businesses. The well-known home Tupperware party has also invaded the office, as Tupperware 'rush-hour parties' held at the end of the workday in offices. At these parties, office workers meet in comfortable, familiar surroundings, look through Tupperware catalogues, watch product demonstrations and discuss Tupperware products with their friends and associates. Tupperware's 85,000 sales representatives now make about 20 per cent of their sales outside the home.

Home-party and office-party selling is now being used to market everything from cosmetics, kitchenware and lingerie to exercise instruction and hand-made suits. Such selling requires a sharp understanding of reference groups and how people influence each other in the buying process.

SOURCES: See Shannon Thurman, 'Mary Kay still in the pink', *Advertising Age* (4 January 1988), p. 32; Len Strazewski, 'Tupperware locks in a new strategy', *Advertising Age* (8 February 1988), p. 30; Kate Ballen, 'Get ready for shopping at work', *Fortune* (15 February 1988), pp. 95–8; Vic Sussman, 'I was the only virgin at the party', *Sales and Marketing Management* (September 1989), pp. 64–72.

social class is not determined by a single factor, such as income, but is measured as a combination of occupation, income, education, wealth and other variables.

Not only do class systems differ in various parts of the world: the relative sizes of the classes vary with the relative prosperity of countries. The 'diamond'-shaped classification (few people at the top and bottom with most in the middle) in Table 6.1 is typical of developed countries, although the Japanese and Scandinavian scales are flatter. In less developed countries, such as in Latin America and Africa, the structure is 'pyramid' shaped with a concentration of poor people at the base. As countries develop, their class structure moves towards the diamond shape, although there is evidence that the gap between the richest and poorest in the English-speaking countries is now widening.

Some class systems have a greater influence on buying behaviour than others. In most western countries 'lower' classes may exhibit upward mobility, showing buying behaviour similar to that of the 'upper' classes. But in other cultures, where a caste system gives people a distinctive role, buying behaviour is more firmly linked to social class. Upper classes in almost all societies are often more similar to each other than they are to the rest of their own society. When selecting products and services, including food, clothing, household items and personal-care products, they make choices that are less culture-bound than those of the lower classes. Generally, the lower social classes are more culture-bound, although young people of all classes are less so.[8]

Anna Flores' social class may affect her camera-buying decision. If she comes from a higher social class background, her family probably owned an expensive camera and she might have dabbled in photography.

Social Factors

A consumer's behaviour is also influenced by social factors, such as the consumer's small groups, family, and social roles and status. Because these social factors can strongly affect consumer responses, companies must take them into account when designing their marketing strategies.

● *Groups*

Groups influence a person's behaviour. Groups that have a direct influence and to which a person belongs are called **membership groups**. Some are *primary groups* with whom there is regular but informal interaction – such as family, friends, neighbours and fellow workers. Some are *secondary groups*, which are more formal and have less regular interaction. These include organizations like religious groups, professional associations and trade unions.

Reference groups are groups that serve as direct (face-to-face) or indirect points of comparison or reference in forming a person's attitudes or behaviour. Reference groups to which they do not belong often influence people. For example, an **aspirational group** is one to which the individual wishes to belong, as when a teenage football player hopes to play some day for Manchester United. He identifies with them, although there is no face-to-face contact between him and the team.

Marketers try to identify the reference groups of their target markets. Reference groups influence a person in at least three ways. They expose the person to new behaviours and lifestyles. They influence the person's attitudes and self-concept because he or she wants to 'fit in'. They also create pressures to conform that may affect the person's product and brand choices (see Marketing Highlight 6.2).

The importance of group influence varies across products and brands, but it tends to be strongest for conspicuous purchases.[9] A product or brand can be conspicuous for one of two reasons. First, it may be noticeable because the buyer is one of few people who owns it – luxuries, such as a vintage Wurlitzer juke box or a Rolex, are more conspicuous than necessities because fewer people own the luxuries. Second, a product such as Carlsberg ICE beer or Perrier can be conspicuous because the buyer consumes it in public where others can see it. Figure 6.3 shows how group influence might affect product and brand choices for four types of product – public luxuries, private luxuries, public necessities and private necessities.

A person considering the purchase of a public luxury, such as a yacht, will generally be influenced strongly by others. Many people will notice the yacht

membership groups
Groups that have a direct influence on a person's behaviour and to which a person belongs.

reference groups
Groups that have a direct (face-to-face) or indirect influence on the person's attitudes or behaviour.

aspirational group
A group to which an individual wishes to belong.

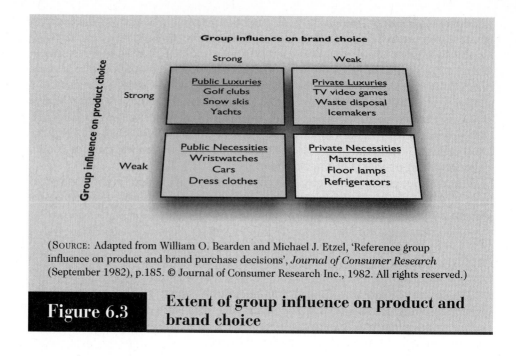

Figure 6.3   **Extent of group influence on product and brand choice**

because few people own one. If interested, they will notice the brand because the boat is used in public. Thus both the product and the brand will be conspicuous and the opinions of others can strongly influence decisions about whether to own a boat and what brand to buy. At the other extreme, group influences do not much affect decisions about private necessities because other people will notice neither the product nor the brand.

● *Family*

Family members can strongly influence buyer behaviour. We can distinguish between two families in the buyer's life. The buyer's parents make up the *family of orientation*. Parents provide a person with an orientation towards religion, politics and economics, and a sense of personal ambition, self-worth and love. Even if the buyer no longer interacts very much with his or her parents, the latter can still significantly influence the buyer's behaviour. In countries where parents continue to live with their children, their influence can be crucial.

The *family of procreation* – the buyer's spouse and children – have a more direct influence on everyday buying behaviour. This family is the most important consumer buying organization in society and it has been researched extensively. Marketers are interested in the roles and relative influence of the husband, wife and children on the purchase of a large variety of products and services.

Husband–wife involvement varies widely by product category and by stage in the buying process. Buying roles change with evolving consumer lifestyles. Almost everywhere in the world, the wife is traditionally the main purchasing agent for the family, especially in the areas of food, household products and clothing. But with over 60 per cent or more women holding jobs outside the home in developed countries and the willingness of some husbands to do more of the family's purchasing, all this is changing. For example, in the United States women now buy about 45 per cent of all cars and men account for about 40 per cent of expenditure on food shopping.[10] Such roles vary widely among different countries and social classes. As always, marketers must research specific patterns in their target markets.

Flora is bought by women (buyer) who care about their men (user).

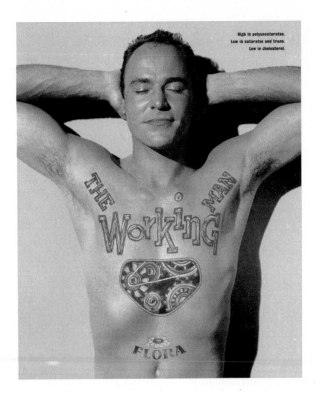

In the case of expensive products and services, husbands and wives more often make joint decisions. Anna Flores' husband may play an *influencer role* in her camera-buying decision. He may have an opinion about her buying a camera and about the kind of camera to buy. At the same time, she will be the primary decider, purchaser and user.[11]

CONSUMERS' BUYING ROLES. Group members can influence purchases in many ways. For example, men normally choose their own newspaper and women choose their own tights. For other products, however, the **decision-making unit** is more complicated with people playing one or more roles:

- **Initiator**. The person who first suggests or thinks of the idea of buying a particular product or service. This could be a parent of friends who would like to see a visual record of Anna's holiday.

- **Influencer**. A person whose view or advice influences the buying decision, perhaps a friend who is a camera enthusiast or a salesperson.

- **Decider**. The person who ultimately makes a buying decision or any part of it – whether to buy, what to buy, how to buy or where to buy.

- **Buyer**. The person who makes an actual purchase. Once the buying decision is made, someone else could make the purchase for the decider.

- **User**. The person who consumes or uses a product or service. Once bought, other members of her family could use Anna's camera.

Roles and Status

A person belongs to many groups – family, clubs, organizations. The person's position in each group can be defined in terms of both *role* and *status*. With her parents, Anna Flores plays the role of daughter; in her family, she plays the role of

decision-making unit (DMU)
All the individuals who participate in, and influence, the consumer buying-decision process.

initiator
The person who first suggests or thinks of the idea of buying a particular product or service.

influencer
A person whose views or advice carries some weight in making a final buying decision; they often help define specifications and also provide information for evaluating alternatives.

decider
The person who ultimately makes a buying decision or any part of it - whether to buy, what to buy, how to buy, or where to buy.

buyer
The person who makes an actual purchase.

user
The person who consumes or uses a

Table 6.2	**Family life-cycle stages**

YOUNG	MIDDLE-AGED	OLDER
Single	Single	Older married
Married without children	Married without children	Older unmarried
Married with children	Married with children	
Infant children	Young children	
Young children	Adolescent children	
Adolescent children	Married without dependent	
Divorced with children	children	
	Divorced without children	
	Divorced with children	
	Young children	
	Adolescent children	
	Divorced without	
	dependent children	

SOURCES: Adapted from Patrick E. Murphy and William A. Staples, 'A modernized family life cycle', *Journal of Consumer Research* (June 1979), p. 16; © Journal of Consumer Research, Inc., 1979. See also Janet Wagner and Sherman Hanna, 'The effectiveness of family life cycle variables in consumer expenditure research', *Journal of Consumer Research* (December 1983), pp. 281–91.

role
The activities a person is expected to perform according to the people around him or her.

status
The general esteem given to a role by society.

wife; in her company, she plays the role of brand manager. A **role** consists of the activities that people are expected to perform according to the persons around them. Each of Anna's roles will influence some of her buying behaviour.

Each role carries a **status** reflecting the general esteem given to it by society. People often choose products that show their status in society. For example, the role of brand manager has more status in our society than the role of daughter. As a brand manager, Anna will buy the kind of clothing that reflects her role and status.

Personal Factors

A buyer's decisions are also influenced by personal characteristics such as the buyer's age and life-cycle stage, occupation, economic situation, lifestyle, and personality and self-concept.

● *Age and Life-Cycle Stage*

People change the goods and services they buy over their lifetimes. Tastes in food, clothes, furniture and recreation are often age related. Buying is also shaped by the **family life cycle** – the stages through which families might pass as they mature over time. Table 6.2 lists the stages of the family life cycle. Marketers often define their target markets in terms of life-cycle stage and develop appropriate products and marketing plans for each stage.

family life cycle
The stages through which families might pass as they mature over time.

Psychological life-cycle stages have also been identified.[12] Adults experience certain passages or transformations as they go through life. Thus Anna Flores may

Eastpak use a strong image to communicate that it is a product to have.

move from being a satisfied brand manager and wife to being an unsatisfied person searching for a new way to fulfil herself. In fact, such a change may have stimulated her strong interest in photography. The main stimuli to people taking photographs are holidays, ceremonies marking the progression through the life cycle (weddings, graduations and so on) and having children to take photographs of. Marketers must pay attention to the changing buying interests that might be associated with these adult passages.

● *Occupation*

A person's occupation affects the goods and services bought. Blue-collar workers tend to buy more work clothes, whereas white-collar workers buy more suits and ties. Marketers try to identify the occupational groups that have an above-average interest in their products and services. A company can even specialize in making products needed by a given occupational group. Thus computer software companies will design different products for brand managers, accountants, engineers, lawyers and doctors.

● *Economic Circumstances*

A person's economic situation will affect product choice. Anna Flores can consider buying an expensive Olympus autofocus superzoom camera if she has enough disposable income, savings or borrowing power. Marketers of income-sensitive goods closely watch trends in personal income, savings and interest

	Table 6.3	**Lifestyle dimensions**

ACTIVITIES	INTERESTS	OPINIONS	DEMOGRAPHICS
Work	Family	Themselves	Age
Hobbies	Home	Social issues	Education
Social events	Job	Politics	Income
Vacation	Community	Business	Occupation
Entertainment	Recreation	Economics	Family size
Club membership	Fashion	Education	Dwelling
Community	Food	Products	Geography
Shopping	Media	Future	City size
Sports	Achievements	Culture	Stage in life cycle

SOURCE: Joseph T. Plummer, 'The concept and application of lifestyle segmentation', *Journal of Marketing* (January 1974), p. 34.

rates. If economic indicators point to a recession, marketers can take steps to redesign, reposition and reprice their products.

● *Lifestyle*

lifestyle
A person's pattern of living as expressed in his or her activities, interests and opinions.

psychographics
The technique of measuring lifestyles and developing lifestyle classifications; it involves measuring the chief AIO dimensions (activities, interests, opinions).

People coming from the same subculture, social class and occupation may have quite different lifestyles. **Lifestyle** is a person's pattern of living as expressed in his or her activities, interests and opinions. Lifestyle captures something more than the person's social class or personality. It profiles a person's whole pattern of acting and interacting in the world.

The technique of measuring lifestyles is known as **psychographics**. It involves measuring the primary dimensions shown in Table 6.3. The first three are known as the *AIO dimensions* (activities, interests, opinions). Several research firms have developed lifestyle classifications. The most widely used is the SRI *Values and Lifestyles (VALS)* typology. The original VALS typology classifies consumers into nine lifestyle groups according to whether they were inner directed (for example, 'experientials'); outer directed ('achievers', 'belongers'); or need driven ('survivors'). Using this VALS classification, a bank found that the businessmen they were targeting consisted mainly of 'achievers' who were strongly competitive individualists.[13] The bank designed highly successful ads showing men taking part in solo sports such as sailing, jogging and water skiing.[14]

Everyday-Life Research by SINUS GmbH, a German company, identifies 'social milieus' covering France, Germany, Italy and the UK. This study describes the structure of society with five social classes and value orientations:

- Basic orientation: traditional – *to preserve*.
- Basic orientation: materialist – *to have*.
- Changing values: hedonism – *to indulge*.
- Changing values: postmaterialism – *to be*.
- Changing values: postmodernism – *to have, to be and to indulge*.

Table 6.4	Typology of social milieus

MILIEU	GERMANY	FRANCE	ITALY	UK	DESCRIPTION
Upper conservative	Konservatives-gehobenes	Les Héritiers	Neoconservatori	Upper class	Traditional upper-middle-class conservatives
Traditional mainstream	Floresbürgerliches	Les conservateurs installés	Piccola borghesia	Traditional middle class	*Petit bourgeois* group mainly oriented to preserving the status quo
Traditional working class	Traditionsloses Arbeitermilieu	Les laborieux traditionnels	Cultura operaia	Traditional working class	Traditional blue-collar worker
Modern mainstream	Aufstiegsorien-tiertes	Les nouveaux ambitieux	Rampanti, plus crisaldi	Social climbers, plus progressive working class	Social climber and achievement-oriented white- and blue-collar workers
Trendsetter	Technokratisch-liberales	Les managers moderns	Borghesia illuminata	Progressive middle class	Technocratic-liberals with a postmaterial orientation
Avant-garde	Hedonistisches	Les post-modernistes	Edonisti	'Thatcher's children'	Mainly young pleasure seekers
Sociocritical	Alternatives	Les néo-moralistes	Critica sociale	Socially centred	Pursuing an alternative lifestyle
Under-privileged	Traditionsloses Arbeitermilieu	Les oubliés, plus les rebelles hédonistes	Sotto-proletariato urbano	Poor	Uprooted blue-collar workers and destitute

It distinguishes two types of value: traditional values, emphasizing hard work, thrift, religion, honesty, good manners and obedience; and material values concerned with possession and a need for security. From these, SINUS developed a typology of social milieus (see Table 6.4): groups of people who share a common set of values and beliefs about work, private relationships, leisure activities and aesthetics, and a common perception of future plans, wishes and dreams. The size and exact nature of these milieus vary between the countries studied, but there are broad international comparisons.

Knowing the social milieu of a person can provide information about his or her everyday life, such as work likes and dislikes, which helps in product development and advertising. The study finds that the upmarket segments share a similar structure in all four countries; and it identifies trend-setting milieus in each country, containing heavy consumers with comparable attitudinal and sociodemographic characteristics. Important values shared by all these consumers include: tolerance, open-mindedness, an outward-looking approach; career and success, education and culture, a high standard of living, hedonistic luxury consumption, individualism and Europe.

The Anticipating Change in Europe (ACE) study, by the RISC research agency of Paris, investigated social changes in 12 European countries, the United

States, Canada and Japan. The objective was to try to understand how social changes influence market trends. RISC describes people using sociodemographic characteristics, sociocultural profile, activities (sports, leisure, culture), behaviour towards the media (press, radio, television), political inclinations and mood. Using these dimensions, RISC developed six Eurotypes:

1. *The traditionalist* (18 per cent of the European population) is influenced by the culture, socioeconomic history and unique situation of his or her country, with a profile reflecting deep-rooted attitudes specific to that country. Consequently, this is the least homogeneous group across countries.

2. *The homebody* (14 per cent) is driven by a strong attachment to his or her roots and childhood environment. Less preoccupied with economic security than the traditionalist, the homebody needs to feel in touch with the social environment. The homebody seeks warm relationships and has difficulty coping with violence in society.

3. *The rationalist* (23 per cent) has an ability to cope with unforeseeable and complex situations, and a readiness to take risks and start new endeavours. Personal fulfilment is more about self-expression than financial reward. The rationalist believes science and technology will help resolve the challenges facing humanity.

4. *The pleasurist* (17 per cent) emphasizes sensual and emotional experiences, preferring non-hierarchically structured groups built around self-reliance and self-regulation and not around leaders or formal decision-making processes.

5. *The striver* (15 per cent) holds the attitudes, beliefs and values that underlie the dynamics of social change. The striver believes in autonomous behaviour and wants to shape his or her life and to exploit mental, physical, sensual and emotional possibilities to the full.

6. *The trendsetter* (13 per cent) favours non-hierarchical social structures and enjoys spontaneity rather than formal procedures. Trendsetters see no need to prove their abilities. Even more individualistic than strivers, they exemplify the flexible response to a rapidly changing environment.

These studies do suggest that there are European lifestyles although, as with social class, there is greater similarity between wealthy Europeans than between poor ones. For this reason, luxury brands and their advertising are often more standardized internationally than other products.[15]

Lifestyle classifications need not be universal – they can vary significantly from country to country. McCann-Erickson, for example, found the following British lifestyles: *Avant Guardians* (interested in change); *Pontificators* (traditionalists, very British); *Chameleons* (follow the crowd); and *Sleepwalkers* (contented under-achievers). Contrast this with Survey Research Malaysia's seven categories from their developing country: *Upper Echelons* (driven by status and desire to stand out in society); *Not Quite Theres* (ambition for self and family); *Rebel Hangouts* (want to look off mainstream); *Sleepwalkers* (want to get through the day); *Inconspicuous* (want to blend in); *Kampung Trendsetters* (ambitious, city-influenced village dwellers); and *Rural Traditionalists* (abide by traditional rules).[16] Finally, advertising agency D'Arcy, Masius, Benton & Bowles identified five categories of Russian consumer: *Kuptsi* (merchants), *Cossacks*, *Students*, *Business Executives* and *Russian Souls*. Cossacks are characterized as ambitious, independent and status seeking, Russian Souls as passive, fearful of choices and hopeful. Thus, a typical Cossack might drive a BMW, smoke Dunhill cigarettes and drink Remy Martin liquor, whereas a Russian Soul would drive a Lada, smoke Marlboros and drink Smirnoff Vodka.[17]

The lifestyle concept, when used carefully, can help the marketer understand changing consumer values and how they affect buying behaviour. Anna Flores, for example, can choose to live the role of a capable homemaker, a career woman or a free spirit – or all three. She plays several roles, and the way she blends them expresses her lifestyle. If she ever became a professional photographer, this would change her lifestyle, in turn changing what and how she buys.

● *Personality and Self-Concept*

Each person's distinct personality influences his or her buying behaviour. **Personality** refers to the unique psychological characteristics that lead to relatively consistent and lasting responses to one's own environment. Personality is usually described in terms of traits such as self-confidence, dominance, sociability, autonomy, defensiveness, adaptability and aggressiveness.[18] Personality can be useful in analyzing consumer behaviour for certain product or brand choices. For example, coffee makers have discovered that heavy coffee drinkers tend to be high on sociability. Thus Nescafé ads show people coming together over a cup of coffee.

Many marketers use a concept related to personality – a person's **self-concept** (also called *self-image*). The basic self-concept premise is that people's possessions contribute to and reflect their identities: that is, 'we are what we have'. Thus, in order to understand consumer behaviour, the marketer must first understand the relationship between consumer self-concept and possessions. For example, people buy books to support their self-images:

> People have the mistaken notion that the thing you do with books is read them. Wrong … People buy books for what the purchase says about them – their taste, their cultivation, their trendiness. Their aim … is to connect themselves, or those to whom they give the books as gifts, with all the other refined owners of Edgar Allen Poe collections or sensitive owners of Virginia Woolf collections. … [The result is that] you can sell books as consumer products, with seductive displays, flashy posters, an emphasis on the glamour of the book, and the fashionableness of the bestseller and the trendy author.[19]

Anna Flores may see herself as outgoing, fun and active. Therefore, she will favour a camera that projects the same qualities. In that case the Polaroid Vision autofocus SLR could attract her. 'The fun develops instantly.'[20]

Really, it is not that simple. What if Anna's *actual self-concept* (how she views herself) differs from her *ideal self-concept* (how she would like to view herself) and from her *others self-concept* (how she thinks others sees her)? Which self will she try to satisfy when she buys a camera? Because this is unclear, self-concept theory has met with mixed success in predicting consumer responses to brand images.

Psychological Factors

A person's buying choices are further influenced by four important psychological factors: motivation, perception, learning, and beliefs and attitudes.

● *Motivation*

We know that Anna Flores became interested in buying a camera. Why? What is she *really* seeking? What *needs* is she trying to satisfy?

personality
A person's distinguishing psychological characteristics that lead to relatively consistent and lasting responses to his or her own environment.

self-concept
Self-image, or the complex mental pictures that people have of themselves.

'Touchy-Feely' Research into Consumer Motivations

The term *motivation research* refers to qualitative research designed to probe consumers' hidden, subconscious motivations. Because consumers often don't know or can't describe just why they act as they do, motivation researchers use a wide variety of non-directive and projective techniques to uncover underlying emotions and attitudes towards brands and buying situations. The techniques range from sentence completion, word association and inkblot or cartoon interpretation tests, to having consumers describe typical brand users or form daydreams and fantasies about brands or buying situations. Some of these techniques verge on the bizarre. One writer offers the following tongue-in-cheek summary of a motivation research session:

> Good morning, ladies and gentlemen. We've called you here today for a little consumer research. Now, lie down on the couch, toss your inhibitions out the window and let's try a little free association. First, think about brands as if they were your *friends* … think of your shampoo as an animal. Go on, don't be shy. Would it be a panda or a lion? A snake or a woolly worm? For our final exercise, let's all sit up and pull out our magic markers. Draw a picture of a typical cake-mix user. Would she wear an apron or a negligee? A business suit or a can-can dress?

Other researchers use *transaction analysis* (TA), based originally on psychoanalytic theory, to study the relationship between the consumer and the brand. In this the consumer and the brand role player assume the 'ego states' of a parent, adult (equal) or child. Data are obtained from recording a dialogue between the consumer and a brand:

> Smoker to ideal cigarette: 'I can taste you; your tobacco is good … I like you. Smart

box … You taste nice … not harsh.' Ideal cigarette to smoker: 'If I can make you relaxed and happy, that's what I am here for. I always try to please my customers.'

Such projective techniques seem dotty, but more and more marketers are turning to these touchy-feely, motivation research approaches to help them probe consumer psyches and develop better marketing strategies.

Many advertising agencies employ teams of psychologists, anthropologists and other social scientists to carry out their motivation research. Says the research director of one large agency: 'We believe people make choices on a basic primitive level … we use the probe to get down to the unconscious.' This agency routinely conducts one-on-one, therapy-like interviews to delve into the inner workings of consumers. Another agency asks consumers to describe their favourite brands as animals or cars (say, Saab versus BMW) in order to assess the prestige associated with various brands. Still another agency has consumers draw figures or make clay models of typical brands or brand users:

> In one instance, the agency asked 50 interviewees to sketch likely buyers of two different brands of cake mixes. Consistently, the group portrayed Pillsbury customers as apron-clad, grandmotherly types, while they pictured Duncan Hines purchasers as svelte, contemporary women.

In a similar study, American Express had people sketch likely users of its gold card versus its green

Motivation research: when asked to sketch figures of typical cake-mix users, subjects portrayed Pillsbury customers as grandmotherly types and Duncan Hines buyers as svelte and contemporary.

card. Respondents depicted gold card holders as active, broad-shouldered men; green card holders were perceived as 'couch potatoes' lounging in front of television sets. Based on these results, the company positioned its gold card as a symbol of responsibility for people capable of controlling their lives and finances.

Some motivation research studies employ more basic techniques, such as simply mingling with consumers to find out what makes them tick:

Saatchi & Saatchi, the London based ad agency, recently hired anthropologist Joe Lowe to spend a week in Texas sidling up to wearers of Wranglers blue jeans at rodeos and barbecues. His findings reinforced what the jeans company suspected: buyers associated Wranglers with cowboys. The company responded by running ads with plenty of Western touches. For a consumer-goods manufacturer, Lowe went to health clubs where he observed patrons applying deodorant. And for shampoo maker Helene Curtis, he spent three days in salons before coming to a somewhat predictable conclusion – going to the beauty shop makes women feel good.

Some marketers dismiss such motivation research as mumbo-jumbo. And these approaches do present some problems: they use small samples and researcher interpretations of results are often highly subjective, sometimes leading to rather exotic explanations of otherwise ordinary buying behaviour. However, others believe strongly that these approaches can provide interesting nuggets of insight into the relationships between consumers and the brands they buy. To marketers who use them, motivation research techniques provide a flexible and varied means of gaining insights into deeply held and often mysterious motivations behind consumer buying behaviour.

Sources: Excerpts from M. Blackthorn and M. Holmes, 'The use of transactional analysis in the development of a new brand's personality', ESOMAR Seminar on New Product Development, 1983; G. De Groot, 'Deep, dangerous or just plain dotty?', ESOMAR Seminar on Qualitative Methods of Research, Amsterdam, 1986; Annetta Miller and Dody Tsiantar, 'Psyching out consumers', *Newsweek* (27 February 1989), pp. 46–7; see also Sidney J. Levy, 'Dreams, fairy tales, animals and cars', *Psychology and Marketing* (Summer 1985), pp. 67–81; Peter Sampson, 'Qualitative research and motivational research', in Robert Worcester (ed.), *Consumer Marketing Research Handbook* (London: McGraw-Hill, 1986), pp. 29–55; Ronald Alsop, 'Advertisers put consumers on the couch', *Wall Street Journal* (13 May 1988), p. 21; Rebecca Piirto, 'Measuring minds in the 1990s', *American Demographics* (December 1990), pp. 31–5, and 'Words that sell', *American Demographics* (January 1992), p. 6.

A person has many needs at any given time. Some are *biological*, arising from states of tension such as hunger, thirst or discomfort. Others are *psychological*, arising from the need for recognition, esteem or belonging. Most of these needs will not be strong enough to motivate the person to act at a given point in time. A need becomes a *motive* when it is aroused to a sufficient level of intensity. A **motive** (or *drive*) is a need that is sufficiently pressing to direct the person to seek satisfaction. Psychologists have developed theories of human motivation. Two of the most popular – the theories of Sigmund Freud and Abraham Maslow – have quite different meanings for consumer analysis and marketing.

FREUD'S THEORY OF MOTIVATION. Freud assumes that people are largely unconscious of the real psychological forces shaping their behaviour. He sees the person as growing up and repressing many urges. These urges are never eliminated or under perfect control; they emerge in dreams, in slips of the tongue, in neurotic and obsessive behaviour or ultimately in psychoses.

Thus Freud suggests that a person does not fully understand his or her motivation. If Anna Flores wants to purchase an expensive camera, she may describe her motive as wanting a hobby or career. At a deeper level, she may be purchasing the camera to impress others with her creative talent. At a still deeper level, she may be buying the camera to feel young and independent again.

Motivation researchers collect in-depth information from small samples of consumers to uncover the deeper motives for their product choices. They use non-directive depth interviews and various 'projective techniques' to throw the ego off guard – techniques such as word association, sentence completion, picture interpretation and role playing.

Motivation researchers have reached some interesting and sometimes odd conclusions about what may be in the buyer's mind regarding certain purchases. For example, one classic study concluded that consumers resist prunes because they are wrinkled looking and remind people of sickness and old age. Despite its sometimes unusual conclusions, motivation research remains a useful tool for marketers seeking a deeper understanding of consumer behaviour (see Marketing Highlight 6.3).[21]

MASLOW'S THEORY OF MOTIVATION.   Abraham Maslow sought to explain why people are driven by particular needs at particular times.[22] Why does one person spend much time and energy on personal safety and another on gaining the esteem of others? Maslow's answer is that human needs are arranged in a hierarchy, from the most pressing to the least pressing. Maslow's hierarchy of needs is shown in Figure 6.4. In order of importance, they are (1) *physiological* needs, (2) *safety* needs, (3) *social* needs, (4) *esteem* needs and (5) *self-actualization* needs. A person tries to satisfy the most important need first. When that important need is satisfied, it will stop being a motivator and the person will then try to satisfy the next most important need. For example, a starving man (need 1) will not take an interest in the latest happenings in the art world (need 5), or in how he is seen or esteemed by others (need 3 or 4), or even in whether he is breathing clean air (need 2). But as each important need is satisfied, the next most important need will come into play:

> The wine market shows how the different levels of the need hierarchy can be at play at the same time. Buyers of premium wines are seeking self-esteem and self-actualisation. They may achieve this by showing their knowledge by buying 1986 Châteaux Ausone from a specialist wine merchant. Wine buying makes many other people anxious, particularly if it is a gift. They buy the product to fill a social need but are unable to gauge quality. To be safe they buy from a reputable store (Marks and Spencer) or a brand legitimised by advertising (Le Piat d'Or).[23]

Maslow's hierarchy is not universal for all cultures. As the heroes of Hollywood movies amply show, Anglo-Saxon culture values self-actualization and individuality above all else, but that is not universally so. In Japan and German-speaking countries, people are most highly motivated by a need for personal security and conformity, while in France, Spain, Portugal and other Latin and Asian countries, people are most motivated by the need for security and belonging.[24]

What light does Maslow's theory throw on Anna Flores' interest in buying a camera? We can guess that Anna has satisfied her physiological, safety and social needs; they do not motivate her interest in cameras. Her camera interest might come from a strong need for more esteem from others. Or it might come from a need for self-actualization – she might want to be a creative person and express herself through photography.

● *Perception*

A motivated person is ready to act. How the person acts is influenced by his or her perception of the situation. Two people with the same motivation and in the same

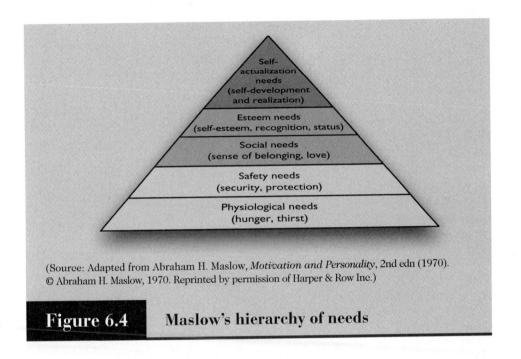

(Source: Adapted from Abraham H. Maslow, *Motivation and Personality*, 2nd edn (1970). © Abraham H. Maslow, 1970. Reprinted by permission of Harper & Row Inc.)

Figure 6.4 **Maslow's hierarchy of needs**

situation may act quite differently because they perceive the situation differently. Anna Flores might consider a fast-talking camera salesperson loud and false. Another camera buyer might consider the same salesperson intelligent and helpful.

Why do people perceive the same situation differently? All of us learn by the flow of information through our five senses: sight, hearing, smell, touch and taste. However, each of us receives, organizes and interprets this sensory information in an individual way. Thus **perception** is the process by which people select, organize and interpret information to form a meaningful picture of the world.

People can form different perceptions of the same stimulus because of three perceptual processes: selective attention, selective distortion and selective retention.

SELECTIVE ATTENTION. People are exposed to a great number of stimuli every day. For example, the average person may be exposed to more than 1,500 ads a day. It is impossible for a person to pay attention to all these stimuli and some studies show people remembering only three or four.[25] **Selective attention** – the tendency for people to screen out most of the information to which they are exposed – means that marketers have to work especially hard to attract the consumer's attention. Their message will be lost on most people who are not in the market for the product. Moreover, even people who are in the market may not notice the message unless it stands out from the surrounding sea of other ads.

SELECTIVE DISTORTION. Even noted stimuli do not always come across in the intended way. Each person fits incoming information into an existing mind-set. **Selective distortion** describes the tendency of people to adapt information to personal meanings. Anna Flores may hear the salesperson mention some good and bad points about a competing camera brand. Because she already has a strong leaning towards Nikon, Olympus or Polaroid, she is likely to distort those points in order to conclude that one camera is better than the others. People tend to interpret information in a way that will support what they already believe. Selective distortion means that marketers must try to understand the mind-sets of consumers and how these will affect interpretations of advertising and sales information:

perception
The process by which people select, organize and interpret information to form a meaningful picture of the world.

selective attention
The tendency of people to screen out most of the information to which they are exposed.

selective distortion
The tendency of people to adapt information to personal meanings.

Selected attention: the average person is exposed to more than 1500 ads per day – in magazines and newspapers, on radio and TV, and all around them.

Cathay Pacific, the Hong Kong-based airline, found out that although Caucasians saw Cathay as an Asian airline, Asians perceived the airline as being well managed and safe, but not Asian. Seeing their future in Asia where 80 per cent of their passengers came from, Cathay wants to change their view. Peter Sutch, Cathay's chairman, explains their new livery: 'We wanted something Asian in appearance: we wanted a quality look with an Asian flavour.' The airline now offers a wide range of Asian meals and communicates in many Asian languages. In-flight information is now in Japanese, Korean, Mandarin and Cantonese as well as English.[26]

SELECTIVE RETENTION. People will also forget much of what they learn. They tend to retain information that supports their attitudes and beliefs. Because of **selective retention**, Anna is likely to remember good points made about the Nikon and forget good points made about competing cameras. She may remember Nikon's good points because she 'rehearses' them more whenever she thinks about choosing a camera.

selective retention
The tendency of people to retain only part of the information to which they are exposed, usually information that supports their attitudes or beliefs.

Because of selective exposure, distortion and retention, marketers have to work hard to get their messages through. This fact explains why marketers use so much drama and repetition in sending messages to their market. Although some consumers are worried that they will be affected by marketing messages without even knowing it, most marketers worry about whether their offers will be perceived at all.[27]

● *Learning*

learning
Changes in an individual's behaviour arising from experience.

When people act, they learn. **Learning** describes changes in an individual's behaviour arising from experience. Learning theorists say that most human behaviour is learned. Learning occurs through the interplay of *drives*, *stimuli*, *cues*, *responses* and *reinforcement*.

We saw that Anna Flores has a drive for self-actualization. A *drive* is a strong internal stimulus that calls for action. Her drive becomes a motive when it is directed towards a particular *stimulus object* – in this case, a camera. Anna's response to the idea of buying a camera is conditioned by the surrounding cues. *Cues* are minor stimuli that determine when, where and how the person responds. Seeing cameras in a shop window, hearing a special sale price, and her husband's support are all cues that can influence Anna's *response* to her interest in buying a camera.

Suppose Anna buys the Nikon. If the experience is rewarding, she will probably use the camera more and more. Her response to cameras will be *reinforced*. Then the next time she shops for a camera, binoculars or some similar product, the probability is greater that she will buy a Nikon product. We say that she *generalizes* her response to similar stimuli.

The reverse of generalization is *discrimination*. When Anna examines binoculars made by Olympus, she sees that they are lighter and more compact than Nikon's binoculars. Discrimination means that she has learned to recognize differences in sets of products and can adjust her response accordingly.

The practical significance of learning theory for marketers is that they can build up demand for a product by associating it with strong drives, using motivating cues and providing positive reinforcement. A new company can enter the market by appealing to the same drives that competitors appeal to and by providing similar cues, because buyers are more likely to transfer loyalty to similar brands than to dissimilar ones (generalization). Or a new company may design its brand to appeal to a different set of drives and offer strong cue inducements to switch brands (discrimination).

● *Beliefs and Attitudes*

Through doing and learning, people acquire their beliefs and attitudes. These, in turn, influence their buying behaviour. A **belief** is a descriptive thought that a person has about something. Anna Flores may believe that a Nikon camera takes great pictures, stands up well under hard use and is good value. These beliefs may be based on real knowledge, opinion or faith, and may or may not carry an emotional charge. For example, Anna Flores' belief that a Nikon camera is heavy may or may not matter to her decision.

Marketers are interested in the beliefs that people formulate about specific products and services, because these beliefs make up product and brand images that affect buying behaviour. If some of the beliefs are wrong and prevent purchase, the marketer will want to launch a campaign to correct them.

People have attitudes regarding religion, politics, clothes, music, food and almost everything else. An **attitude** describes a person's relatively consistent evaluations, feelings and tendencies towards an object or idea. Attitudes put people into a frame of mind of liking or disliking things, of moving towards or away from them. Thus Anna Flores may hold such attitudes as 'Buy the best', 'The Japanese make the best products in the world' and 'Creativity and self-expression are among the most important things in life'. If so, the Nikon camera would fit well into Anna's existing attitudes.

Attitudes are difficult to change. A person's attitudes fit into a pattern and to change one attitude may require difficult adjustments in many others. Thus a company should usually try to fit its products into existing attitudes rather than try to change attitudes. Of course, there are exceptions in which the great cost of trying to change attitudes may pay off. For example:

> In the late 1950s, Honda entered the US motorcycle market facing a major decision. It could either sell its motorcycles to the small but already established motorcycle market or try to increase the size of this market by attracting new types of consumer. Increasing the size of the

belief
A descriptive thought that a person holds about something.

attitude
A person's consistently favourable or unfavourable evaluations, feelings and tendencies towards an object or idea.

Attitudes are hard to change, but it can be done. Honda's classic 'You meet the nicest people on a Honda' campaign changed people's attitudes about who rides motorcycles.

market would be more difficult and expensive because many people had negative attitudes toward motorcycles. They associated motorcycles with black leather jackets, switchblades and outlaws. Despite these adverse attitudes, Honda took the second course of action. It launched a major campaign to position motorcycles as good clean fun. Its theme 'You meet the nicest people on a Honda' worked well and many people adopted a new attitude toward motorcycles. In the 1990s, however, Honda faces a similar problem. With the ageing of the baby boomers, the market has once again shifted toward only hard-core motorcycling enthusiasts. So Honda has again set out to change consumer attitudes. Its 'Come Ride With Us' campaign aims to re-establish the wholesomeness of motorcycling and to position it as fun and exciting for everyone.[28]

Consumer Decision Process

The consumer's choice results from the complex interplay of cultural, social, personal and psychological factors. Although the marketer cannot influence many of these factors, they can be useful in identifying interested buyers and in shaping products and appeals to serve their needs better. Marketers have to be extremely careful in analyzing consumer behaviour. Consumers often turn down what appears to be a winning offer. Polaroid found this out when it lost millions on its Polarvision instant home movie system; Ford when it launched the Edsel; RCA on its Selecta-Vision and Philips on its LaserVision video-disc player; Sony with DAT tapes; and Bristol with its trio of the Brabazon, Britannia and Concorde airliners. So far we have looked at the cultural, social, personal and psychological

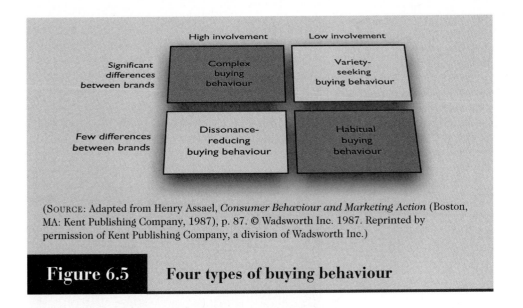

(SOURCE: Adapted from Henry Assael, *Consumer Behaviour and Marketing Action* (Boston, MA: Kent Publishing Company, 1987), p. 87. © Wadsworth Inc. 1987. Reprinted by permission of Kent Publishing Company, a division of Wadsworth Inc.)

Figure 6.5 | **Four types of buying behaviour**

influences that affect buyers. Now we look at how consumers make buying decisions: first, the types of decision that consumers face; then the main steps in the buyer decision process; and finally, the processes by which consumers learn about and buy new products.

Types of Buying Decision Behaviour

Consumer decision making varies with the type of buying decision. Consumer buying behaviour differs greatly for a tube of toothpaste, a tennis racket, an expensive camera and a new car. More complex decisions usually involve more buying participants and more buyer deliberation. Figure 6.5 shows types of consumer buying behaviour based on the degree of buyer involvement and the degree of differences among brands.[29]

Complex Buying Behaviour

Consumers undertake **complex buying behaviour** when they are highly involved in a purchase and perceive significant differences among brands, or when the product is expensive, risky, purchased infrequently and highly self-expressive. Typically, the consumer has much to learn about the product category. For example, a personal computer buyer may not know what attributes to consider. Many product features carry no real meaning: an 'Intel 200MHz Pentium II Pro', 'SVGA display', '16Mb Sync DRAM, 256 Kb Cache' or even a '16X Max CD-ROM with 33.6 BPS fax/data (upgradeable to 56K)'.

This buyer will pass through a learning process, first developing beliefs about the product, then developing attitudes, and then making a thoughtful purchase choice. Marketers of high-involvement products must understand the information-gathering and evaluation behaviour of high-involvement consumers. They need to help buyers learn about product-class attributes and their relative importance and about what the company's brand offers on the important attributes. Marketers need to differentiate their brand's features, perhaps by describing the

complex buying behaviour
Consumer buying behaviour in situations characterized by high consumer involvement in a purchase and significant perceived differences among brands.

Marketers can convert low-involvement products into higher-involvement ones by linking them to involving situations. Here Nestlé creates involvement with soap-opera-like ads featuring the romantic relationship between two neighbours, Tony and Sharon.

brand's benefits using print media with long copy. They must motivate store sales-people and the buyer's acquaintances to influence the final brand choice. Recognizing this problem, Dixons, the electrical retailers, is setting up the Link chain of stores dedicated to helping baffled buyers on to the information super-highway and multimedia.[30]

Dissonance-Reducing Buying Behaviour

dissonance-reducing buying behaviour
Consumer buying behaviour in situations characterized by high involvement but few perceived differences among brands.

Dissonance-reducing buying behaviour occurs when consumers are highly involved with an expensive, infrequent or risky purchase, but see little difference among brands. For example, consumers buying carpeting may face a high-involvement decision because carpeting is expensive and self-expressive. Yet buyers may consider most carpet brands in a given price range to be the same. In this case, because perceived brand differences are not large, buyers may shop around to learn what is available, but buy relatively quickly. They may respond primarily to a good price or to purchase convenience. After the purchase, consumers might experience post-purchase dissonance (after-sales discomfort) when they notice certain disadvantages of the purchased carpet brand or hear favourable things about brands not purchased. To counter such dissonance, the marketer's after-sale communications should provide evidence and support to help consumers feel good both before and after their brand choices.[31]

Habitual Buying Behaviour

habitual buying behaviour
Consumer buying behaviour in situations characterized by low consumer involvement and few significant perceived brand differences.

Habitual buying behaviour occurs under conditions of low consumer involvement and little significant brand difference. For example, take salt. Consumers have little involvement in this product category – they simply go to the store and reach for a brand. If they keep reaching for the same brand, it is out of habit rather than strong brand loyalty. Consumers appear to have low involvement with most low-cost, frequently purchased products.

Consumers do not search extensively for information about the brands, evaluate brand characteristics and make weighty decisions about which brands to buy.

Instead, they passively receive information as they watch television or read magazines. Ad repetition creates *brand familiarity* rather than *brand conviction*. Consumers do not form strong attitudes towards a brand; they select the brand because it is familiar and may not evaluate the choice even after purchase.

Because buyers are not highly committed to any brands, marketers of low-involvement products with few brand differences often use price and sales promotions to stimulate product trial. Gaining distribution and attention at the point of sale is critical. In advertising for a low-involvement product, ad copy should stress only a few key points. Visual symbols and imagery are important because they can be remembered easily and associated with the brand. Ad campaigns should include high repetition of short-duration messages. Television is usually more effective than print media because it is a low-involvement medium suitable for passive learning. Advertising planning should be based on classical conditioning theory, in which buyers learn to identify a certain product, by a symbol repeatedly attached to it.

Products can be linked to some involving personal situation. Nestlé did this in a recent series of ads for Gold Blend coffee, each consisting of a new soap-opera-like episode featuring the evolving romantic relationship between neighbours, Sharon and Tony. Nestlé's success in doing this contrasts with the tea market in the United Kingdom where, although it is the national drink, sales promotions dominate sales.

Variety-Seeking Buying Behaviour

Consumers undertake **variety-seeking buying behaviour** in situations characterized by low consumer involvement, but significant perceived brand differences. In such cases, consumers often do a lot of brand switching. For example, when purchasing biscuits, a consumer may hold some beliefs, choose a biscuit without much evaluation, then evaluate that brand during consumption. But the next time, the consumer might pick another brand out of boredom or simply to try something different. Brand switching occurs for the sake of variety rather than because of dissatisfaction.

In such product categories, the marketing strategy may differ for the market leader and minor brands. The market leader will try to encourage habitual buying behaviour by dominating shelf space, avoiding out-of-stock conditions and running frequent reminder advertising. Challenger firms will encourage variety seeking by offering lower prices, deals, coupons, free samples and advertising that presents reasons for trying something new.

variety-seeking buying behaviour
Consumer buying behaviour in situations characterized by low consumer involvement, but significant perceived brand differences.

The Buyer Decision Process

Most large companies research consumer buying decisions in great detail to answer questions about what consumers buy, where they buy, how and how much they buy, when they buy and why they buy. Marketers can study consumer purchases to find answers to questions about what they buy, where and how much. But learning about the *whys* of consumer buying behaviour and the buying decision process is not so easy – the answers are often locked within the consumer's head.

We will examine the stages that buyers pass through to reach a buying decision. We will use the model in Figure 6.6, which shows the consumer as passing through five stages: *need recognition, information search, evaluation of alternatives, purchase decision* and *postpurchase behaviour*. Clearly the buying process starts long before actual purchase and continues long after. This encourages

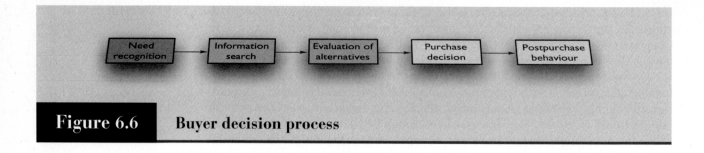

| Figure 6.6 | **Buyer decision process** |

the marketer to focus on the entire buying process rather than just the purchase decision.

This model implies that consumers pass through all five stages with every purchase. But in more routine purchases, consumers often skip or reverse some of these stages. A woman buying her regular brand of toothpaste would recognize the need and go right to the purchase decision, skipping information search and evaluation. However, we use the model in Figure 6.6 because it shows all the considerations that arise when a consumer faces a new and complex purchase situation.

To illustrate this model, we return to Anna Flores and try to understand how she became interested in buying a camera and the stages she went through to make the final choice.

Need Recognition

need recognition
The first stage of the buyer decision process in which the consumer recognizes a problem or need.

The buying process starts with **need recognition** – the buyer recognizing a problem or need. The buyer senses a difference between his or her *actual* state and some *desired* state. The need can be triggered by *internal stimuli* when one of the person's normal needs – hunger, thirst, sex – rises to a level high enough to become a drive. From previous experience, the person has learned how to cope with this drive and is motivated towards objects that he or she knows will satisfy it.

A need can also be triggered by *external stimuli*. Anna passes a bakery and the smell of freshly baked bread stimulates her hunger; she admires a neighbour's new car; or she watches a television commercial for a Caribbean vacation. At this stage, the marketer needs to determine the factors and situations that usually trigger consumer need recognition. The marketer should research consumers to find out what kinds of need or problem arise, what brought them about and how they led the consumer to this particular product. Anna might answer that she felt she needed a camera after friends showed her the photographs they took on holiday. By gathering such information, the marketer can identify the stimuli that most often trigger interest in the product and can develop marketing programmes that involve these stimuli.

information search
The stage of the buyer decision process in which the consumer is aroused to search for more information; the consumer may simply have heightened attention or may go into active information search.

Information Search

An aroused consumer may or may not search for more information. If the consumer's drive is strong and a satisfying product is near at hand, the consumer is likely to buy it then. If not, the consumer may simply store the need in memory or undertake an **information search** related to the need.

At one level, the consumer may simply enter *heightened attention*. Here Anna becomes more receptive to information about cameras. She pays attention to camera ads, cameras used by friends and camera conversations. Or Anna may go into *active information search*, in which she looks for reading material, phones friends and gathers information in other ways. The amount of searching she does will depend upon the strength of her drive, the amount of information she starts with, the ease of obtaining more information, the value she places on additional information and the satisfaction she gets from searching. Normally the amount of consumer search activity increases as the consumer moves from decisions that involve limited problem solving to those that involve extensive problem solving.

The consumer can obtain information from any of several sources:

- *Personal sources*: family, friends, neighbours, acquaintances.
- *Commercial sources*: advertising, salespeople, dealers, packaging, displays.
- *Public sources*: mass media, consumer-rating organizations.
- *Experiential sources*: handling, examining, using the product.

The relative influence of these information sources varies with the product and the buyer. Generally, the consumer receives the most information about a product from commercial sources – those controlled by the marketer. The most effective sources, however, tend to be personal. Personal sources appear to be even more important in influencing the purchase of services.[32] Commercial sources normally *inform* the buyer, but personal sources *legitimize* or *evaluate* products for the buyer. For example, doctors normally learn of new drugs from commercial sources, but turn to other doctors for evaluative information.

As more information is obtained, the consumer's awareness and knowledge of the available brands and features increases. In her information search, Anna learned about the many camera brands available. The information also helped her drop certain brands from consideration. A company must design its marketing mix to make prospects aware of and knowledgeable about its brand. If it fails to do this, the company has lost its opportunity to sell to the customer. The company must also learn which other brands customers consider so that it knows its competition and can plan its own appeals.

The marketer should identify consumers' sources of information and the importance of each source. Consumers should be asked how they first heard about the brand, what information they received and the importance they place on different information sources.

Evaluation of Alternatives

We have seen how the consumer uses information to arrive at a set of final brand choices. How does the consumer choose among the alternative brands? The marketer needs to know about **alternative evaluation** – that is, how the consumer processes information to arrive at brand choices. Unfortunately, consumers do not use a simple and single evaluation process in all buying situations. Instead, several evaluation processes are at work.

Certain basic concepts help explain consumer evaluation processes. First, we assume that each consumer is trying to satisfy some need and is looking for certain *benefits* that can be acquired by buying a product or service. Further, each consumer sees a product as a bundle of *product attributes* with varying capacities for delivering these benefits and satisfying the need. For cameras,

alternative evaluation
The stage of the buyer decision process in which the consumer uses information to evaluate alternative brands in the choice set.

product attributes might include picture quality, ease of use, camera size, price and other features. Consumers will vary as to which of these attributes they consider relevant and will pay the most attention to those attributes connected with their needs.

Second, the consumer will attach different *degrees of importance* to each attribute. A distinction can be drawn between the importance of an attribute and its salience. *Salient attributes* are those that come to a consumer's mind when he or she is asked to think of a product's characteristics. But these are not necessarily the most important attributes to the consumer. Some of them may be salient because the consumer has just seen an advertisement mentioning them or has had a problem with them, making these attributes 'top-of-the-mind'. There may also be other attributes that the consumer forgot, but whose importance would be recognized if they were mentioned. Marketers should be more concerned with attribute importance than attribute salience.

Third, the consumer is likely to develop a set of *brand beliefs* about where each brand stands on each attribute. The set of beliefs held about a particular brand is known as the **brand image**. The consumer's beliefs may vary from true attributes based on his or her experience and the effect of selective perception, selective distortion and selective retention.

brand image
The set of beliefs that consumers hold about a particular brand.

Fourth, the consumer is assumed to have a *utility function* for each attribute. The utility function shows how the consumer expects total product satisfaction to vary with different levels of different attributes. For example, Anna may expect her satisfaction from a camera to increase with better picture quality; to peak with a medium-weight camera as opposed to a very light or very heavy one; to be a compact 35 mm camera rather than a single lens reflex camera with interchangeable lenses. If we combine the attribute levels at which her utilities are highest, they make up Anna's ideal camera. The camera would also be her preferred camera if it were available and affordable.

Fifth, the consumer arrives at attitudes towards the different brands through some *evaluation procedure*. Consumers have been found to use one or more of several evaluation procedures, depending on the consumer and the buying decision.

In Anna's camera-buying situation, suppose she has narrowed her choice set to four cameras: Nikon AF400, Olympus Superzoom 110, Pentax Espio Jr. and Ricoh RW1. In addition, let us say she is interested primarily in four attributes – picture quality, ease of use, camera size and price. Table 6.5 shows how she believes each brand rates on each attribute.[33] Anna believes the Nikon will give her picture quality of 8 on a 10-point scale; is easy to use, 8; is of medium size, 9; and is very inexpensive, 10. Similarly, she has beliefs about how the other cameras rate on these attributes. The marketer would like to be able to predict which camera Anna will buy.

Clearly, if one camera rated best on all the attributes, we could predict that Anna would choose it. But the brands vary in appeal. Some buyers will base their buying decision on only one attribute and their choices are easy to predict. If Anna wants low price above everything, she should buy the Nikon, whereas if she wants the camera that is easiest to use, she could buy either the Olympus or the Pentax.

Most buyers consider several attributes, but assign different importance to each. If we knew the importance weights that Anna assigns to the four attributes, we could predict her camera choice more reliably. Suppose Anna assigns 40 per cent of the importance to the camera's picture quality, 30 per cent to ease of use, 20 per cent to its size and 10 per cent to its price. To find Anna's perceived value for each camera, we can multiply her importance weights by her beliefs about each camera. This gives us the following perceived values:

| Table 6.5 | A consumer's brand beliefs about cameras |

| | ATTRIBUTE | | | |
CAMERA	PICTURE QUALITY	EASE OF USE	CAMERA SIZE	PRICE
Nikon	8	8	9	10
Olympus	8	10	7	4
Pentax	8	10	9	6
Ricoh	6	8	9	8

Nikon	$= 0.4(8) + 0.3(8) + 0.2(9) + 0.1(10) = 8.4$
Olympus	$= 0.4(8) + 0.3(10) + 0.2(7) + 0.1(4) = 8.0$
Pentax	$= 0.4(8) + 0.3(10) + 0.2(9) + 0.1(6) = 8.6$
Ricoh	$= 0.4(6) + 0.3(8) + 0.2(9) + 0.1(8) = 7.4$

We would predict that Anna will favour the Pentax.

This model is called the *expectancy value model* of consumer choice.[34] This is one of several possible models describing how consumers go about evaluating alternatives. Consumers might evaluate a set of alternatives in other ways. For example, Anna might decide that she should consider only cameras that satisfy a set of minimum attribute levels. She might decide a camera must have a super-zoom lens. In this case, we would predict that she would choose Olympus because it is the only one that satisfies that requirement. This is called the *conjunctive model* of consumer choice. Or she might decide that she would settle for a camera that had a picture quality greater than 7 *or* ease of use greater than 9. In this case, the Nikon, Olympus or the Pentax would do, since they all meet at least one of the requirements. This is called the *disjunctive model* of consumer choice.

How consumers go about evaluating purchase alternatives depends on the individual consumer and the specific buying situation. In some cases, consumers use careful calculations and logical thinking. At other times, the same consumers do little or no evaluating; instead they buy on impulse and rely on intuition. Sometimes consumers make buying decisions on their own; sometimes they turn to friends, consumer guides or salespeople for buying advice.

Marketers should study buyers to find out how they actually evaluate brand alternatives. If they know what evaluative processes go on, marketers can take steps to influence the buyer's decision. Suppose Anna is now inclined to buy a Pentax camera because of its ease of use and lightness. What strategies might another camera maker, say Olympus, use to influence people like Anna? There are several. Olympus could modify its camera to produce a version that has fewer features, but is lighter and cheaper. It could try to change buyers' beliefs about how its camera rates on key attributes, especially if consumers currently under-estimate the camera's qualities. It could try to change buyers' beliefs about Pentax and other competitors. Finally, it could try to change the list of attributes that buyers consider or the importance attached to these attributes. For example, it might advertise that all good cameras need a superzoom lens to get the picture quality that active people like Anna want.

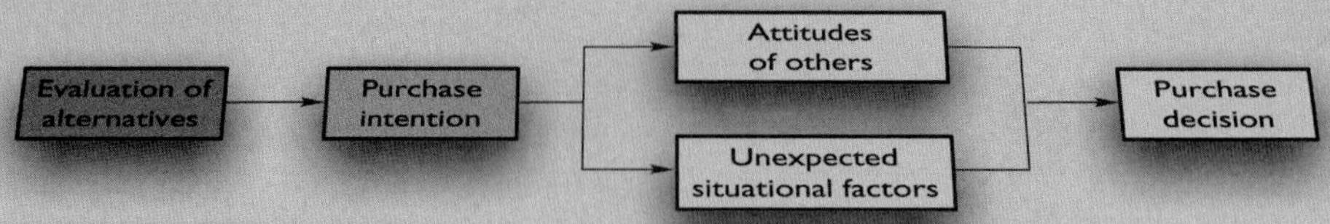

Figure 6.7   **Steps between evaluation of alternatives and a purchase decision**

Purchase Decision

purchase decision
The stage of the buyer decision process in which the consumer actually buys the product.

In the evaluation stage, the consumer ranks brands and forms purchase intentions. Generally, the consumer's **purchase decision** will be to buy the most preferred brand, but two factors, shown in Figure 6.7, can come between the purchase *intention* and the purchase *decision*. The first factor is the *attitudes of others*. For example, if Anna Flores' husband feels strongly that Anna should buy the lowest-priced camera, then the chance of Anna buying a more expensive camera is reduced. He may like the specification of the Pentax, but be offended by its name being Espio Jr (junior). How much another person's attitudes will affect Anna's choices depends both on the strength of the other person's attitudes towards her buying decision and on Anna's motivation to comply with that person's wishes.

Purchase intention is also influenced by *unexpected situational factors*. The consumer may form a purchase intention based on factors such as expected family income, expected price and expected benefits from the product. When the consumer is about to act, unexpected situational factors may arise to change the purchase intention. Anna may lose her job, some other purchase may become more urgent or a friend may report being disappointed in her preferred camera. Thus preferences and even purchase intentions do not always result in actual purchase choice. They may direct purchase behaviour, but may not fully determine the outcome.

A consumer's decision to change, postpone or avoid a purchase decision is influenced heavily by *perceived risk*. Many purchases involve some risk taking.[35] Anxiety results when consumers cannot be certain about the purchase outcome. The amount of perceived risk varies with the amount of money at stake, the amount of purchase uncertainty and the amount of consumer self-confidence. A consumer takes certain actions to reduce risk, such as avoiding purchase decisions, gathering more information and looking for national brand names and products with warranties. The marketer must understand the factors that provoke feelings of risk in consumers and must provide information and support that will reduce the perceived risk.

Postpurchase Behaviour

postpurchase behaviour
The stage of the buyer decision process in which consumers take further action after purchase based on their satisfaction or dissatisfaction.

The marketer's job does not end when the product is bought. After purchasing the product, the consumer will be satisfied or dissatisfied and will engage in **postpurchase behaviour** of interest to the marketer. What determines whether the buyer is satisfied or dissatisfied with a purchase? The answer lies in the relationship between the *consumer's expectations* and the product's *perceived performance*. If the product falls short of expectations, the consumer is disappointed; if it meets expectations, the consumer is satisfied; if it exceeds expectations, the consumer is delighted.

Consumers base their expectations on messages they receive from sellers, friends and other information sources. If the seller exaggerates the product's performance, consumer expectations will not be met – a situation that leads to dissatisfaction. The larger the gap between expectations and performance, the greater the consumer's dissatisfaction. This fact suggests that the seller should make product claims that represent faithfully the product's performance so that buyers are satisfied.

Motoring organizations regularly give pessimistic quotes about how long they will take to reach a customer whose car breaks down. If they say they will be 30 minutes and get there in 20, the customer is impressed. If, however, they get there in 20 minutes after promising 10, the customer is not so happy.

Almost all large purchases result in **cognitive dissonance** or discomfort caused by postpurchase conflict. Consumers are satisfied with the benefits of the chosen brand and glad to avoid the drawbacks of the brands not purchased. On the other hand, every purchase involves compromise. Consumers feel uneasy about acquiring the drawbacks of the chosen brand and about losing the benefits of the brands not purchased. Thus consumers feel at least some postpurchase dissonance for every purchase.[36]

cognitive dissonance
Buyer discomfort caused by postpurchase conflict.

Why is it so important to satisfy the customer? Such satisfaction is important because a company's sales come from two basic groups – *new customers* and *repeat customers*. It usually costs more to attract new customers than to retain current ones. Keeping current customers is therefore often more critical than attracting new ones, and the best way to do this is to make current customers happy. A satisfied customer buys a product again, talks favourably to others about the product, pays less attention to competing brands and advertising, and buys other products from the company. Many marketers go beyond merely *meeting* the expectations of customers – they aim to *delight* the customer. A delighted customer is even more likely to purchase again and to talk favourably about the product and company.

A dissatisfied consumer responds differently. Whereas, on average, a satisfied customer tells three people about a good product experience, a dissatisfied customer gripes to 11 people. In fact, one study showed that 13 per cent of the people who had a problem with an organization complained about that company to more than 20 people.[37] Clearly, bad word of mouth travels farther and faster than good word of mouth and can quickly damage consumer attitudes about a company and its products.

Therefore, a company would be wise to measure customer satisfaction regularly. It cannot simply rely on dissatisfied customers to volunteer their complaints when they are dissatisfied. In fact, 96 per cent of unhappy customers never tell the company about their problem. Companies should set up suggestion systems to *encourage* customers to complain. In this way, the company can learn how well it is doing and how it can improve. The 3M Company claims that over two-thirds of its new-product ideas come from listening to customer complaints. But listening is not enough – the company must also respond constructively to the complaints it receives.

Thus, in general, dissatisfied consumers may try to reduce their dissonance by taking any of several actions. In the case of Anna – a Pentax purchaser – she may return the camera, or look at Pentax ads that tell of the camera's benefits, or talk with friends who will tell her how much they like her new camera. She may even avoid reading about cameras in case she finds a better deal than she got.

Beyond seeking out and responding to complaints, marketers can take additional steps to reduce consumer postpurchase dissatisfaction and to help customers feel good about their purchases. For example, Toyota writes or phones new car owners with congratulations on having selected a fine car. It places ads showing satisfied owners talking about their new cars ('I love what you do for me, Toyota!'). Toyota also obtains customer suggestions for improvements and lists the locations of available services.

Understanding the consumer's needs and buying process is the foundation of successful marketing. By understanding how buyers go through need recognition, information search, evaluation of alternatives, the purchase decision and post-purchase behaviour, the marketer can pick up many clues as to how to meet the buyer's needs. By understanding the various participants in the buying process and the strongest influences on their buying behaviour, the marketer can develop an effective programme to support an attractive offer to the target market.

The Buyer Decision Process for New Products

We have looked at the stages that buyers go through in trying to satisfy a need. Buyers may pass quickly or slowly through these stages and some of the stages may even be reversed. Much depends on the nature of the buyer, the product and the buying situation.

We now look at how buyers approach the purchase of new products. A **new product** is a good, service or idea that is perceived by some potential customers as new. It may have been around for a while, but our interest is in how consumers learn about products for the first time and make decisions on whether to adopt them. We define the **adoption process** as 'the mental process through which an individual passes from first learning about an innovation to final adoption',[38] and **adoption** as the decision by an individual to become a regular user of the product.

new product
A good, service or idea that is perceived by some potential customers as new.

adoption process
The mental process through which an individual passes from first hearing about an innovation to final adoption.

adoption
The decision by an individual to become a regular user of the product.

Stages in the Adoption Process

Consumers go through five stages in the process of adopting a new product:

1. *Awareness*. The consumer becomes aware of the new product, but lacks information about it.
2. *Interest*. The consumer seeks information about the new product.
3. *Evaluation*. The consumer considers whether trying the new product makes sense.
4. *Trial*. The consumer tries the new product on a small scale to improve his or her estimate of its value.
5. *Adoption*. The consumer decides to make full and regular use of the new product.

This model suggests that the new-product marketer should think about how to help consumers move through these stages. A manufacturer of large-screen televisions may discover that many consumers in the interest stage do not move to the trial stage because of uncertainty and the large investment. If these same consumers would be willing to use a large-screen television on a trial basis for a small fee, the manufacturer should consider offering a trial-use plan with an option to buy.

Clothes store Wallis use shock tactics to get attention and to appeal to their younger customers who are clearly not men.

Individual Differences in Innovativeness

People differ greatly in their readiness to try new products. In each product area, there are 'consumption pioneers' and early adopters. Other individuals adopt new products much later. This has led to a classification of people into the adopter categories shown in Figure 6.8.

After a slow start, an increasing number of people adopt the new product. The number of adopters reaches a peak and then drops off as fewer non-adopters remain. Innovators are defined as the first 2.5 per cent of the buyers to adopt a new idea (those beyond two standard deviations from mean adoption time); the early adopters are the next 13.5 per cent (between one and two standard deviations); and so forth.

The five adopter groups have differing values. *Innovators* are adventurous: they try new ideas at some risk. *Early adopters* are guided by respect: they are opinion leaders in their community and adopt new ideas early but carefully. The *early majority* is deliberate: although they are rarely leaders, they adopt new ideas before the average person. The *late majority* is sceptical: they adopt an innovation only after most people have tried it. Finally, *laggards* are tradition bound: they are suspicious of changes and adopt the innovation only when it has become something of a tradition itself.

This adopter classification suggests that an innovating firm should research the characteristics of innovators and early adopters and should direct marketing efforts to them. For example, home computer innovators have been found to be middle-aged and higher in income and education than non-innovators and they tend to be opinion leaders. They also tend to be more rational, more introverted and less social. In general, innovators tend to be relatively younger, better educated and higher in income than later adopters and non-adopters. They are more receptive to unfamiliar things, rely more on their own values and judgement, and are more willing to take risks. They are less brand loyal and more likely to take advantage of special promotions such as discounts, coupons and samples.[39]

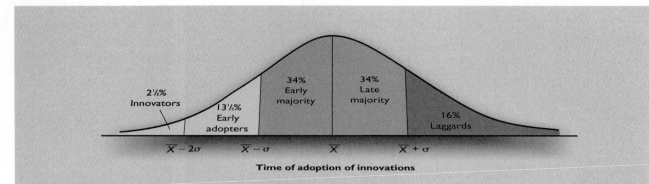

(SOURCE: Redrawn from Everett M. Rogers, *Diffusion of Innovations*, 3rd edn (New York: Macmillan, 1983), p. 247. Adapted with permission of Macmillan Publishing Company Inc. © 1962, 1971, 1983 by the Free Press.)

Figure 6.8 **Adopter categorization on the basis of relative time of adoption of innovations**

opinion leaders
People within a reference group who, because of special skills, knowledge, personality or other characteristics, exert influence on others.

Manufacturers of products and brands subject to strong group influence must find out how to reach the opinion leaders in the relevant reference groups. **Opinion leaders** are people within a reference group who, because of special skills, knowledge, personality or other characteristics, exert influence on others. Opinion leaders are found in all strata of society and one person may be an opinion leader in certain product areas and an opinion follower in others. Marketers try to identify the personal characteristics of opinion leaders for the products, determine what media they use and direct messages at them. In some cases, marketers try to identify opinion leaders for their products and direct marketing efforts towards them. This often occurs in the music industry, where clubs and radio DJs are influential. In other cases, advertisements can simulate opinion leadership, showing informal discussions between people and thereby reducing the need for consumers to seek advice from others. For example, in a recent ad for Herrera for Men cologne, two women discuss the question, 'Did you ever notice how good he smells?' The reason? 'He wears the most wonderful cologne.'[40]

If Anna Flores buys a camera, both the product and the brand will be visible to others whom she respects. Her decision to buy the camera and her brand choice may therefore be influenced strongly by opinion leaders, such as friends who belong to a photography club.

Role of Personal Influence

personal influence
The effect of statements made by one person on another's attitude or probability of purchase.

Personal influence plays a distinctive role in the adoption of new products. **Personal influence** describes the effect of statements made by one person on another's attitude or probability of purchase. Consumers consult each other for opinions about new products and brands, and the advice of others can strongly influence buying behaviour.

Personal influence is more important in some situations and for some individuals than for others. Personal influence is more important in the evaluation stage of the adoption process than in the other stages; it has more influence on later adopters than on early adopters; and it is more important in risky buying situations than in safe situations.

Influence of Product Characteristics on Rate of Adoption

The characteristics of the new product affect its rate of adoption. Some products catch on almost overnight (Virtual Pets), whereas others take a long time to gain acceptance (Digital TV). Five characteristics are especially important in influencing an innovation's rate of adoption. For example, consider the characteristics of the MiniDisc in relation to the rate of adoption:

● *Relative advantage*: the degree to which the innovation appears superior to existing products. The greater the perceived relative advantage of using a MiniDisc over a cassette – say, it does not tangle or lose quality – the sooner MiniDiscs will be adopted.

● *Compatibility*: the degree to which the innovation fits the values and experiences of potential consumers. MiniDiscs, for example, are highly compatible with an active lifestyle.

● *Complexity*: the degree to which the innovation is difficult to understand or use. CDs have already introduced customers to the benefits of digital recordings, so the idea no longer seems complex.

● *Divisibility*: the degree to which the innovation may be tried on a limited basis. MiniDiscs have a problem here. They require a big investment if people are to replace their in-home, in-car and on-street music systems. And what if the technology changes again?

● *Communicability*: the degree to which the results of using the innovation can be observed or described to others. The benefits of MiniDiscs are easy to demonstrate on a hi-fi system, but are the differences big enough to show in a car or Walkman?

Other characteristics influence the rate of adoption, such as initial and ongoing costs, risk and uncertainty, social approval and the efforts of opinion leaders. The new-product marketer has to research all these factors when developing the new product and its marketing programme.

Consumer Behaviour Across International Borders

Understanding consumer behaviour is difficult enough for companies marketing in a single country. For companies operating in many countries, however, understanding and serving the needs of consumers is daunting. Although consumers in different countries may have some things in common, their values, attitudes, and behaviours often vary greatly. International marketers must understand such differences and adjust their products and marketing programmes accordingly.

Sometimes the differences are obvious. For example, in the UK, where most people eat cereal regularly for breakfast, Kellogg focuses its marketing on persuading consumers to select a Kellogg's brand rather than a competitor's brand. In France, however, where most people prefer croissants and coffee or no breakfast at all, Kellogg's advertising simply attempts to convince people that they should eat cereal for breakfast. Its packaging includes step-by-step instructions on how to prepare cereal. In India, where many consumers eat heavy, fried breakfasts and 22 per cent of consumers skip the meal altogether, Kellogg's advertising attempts to convince buyers to switch to a lighter, more nutritious breakfast diet.[41]

Often, differences across international markets are subtler. They may result from physical differences in consumers and their environments. For example, Remington makes smaller electric shavers to fit the smaller hands of Japanese consumers; and battery-powered shavers for the British market, where some bathrooms have no electrical outlets. Other differences result from varying customs. Consider the following examples:

● Shaking your head from side to side means 'no' in most countries but 'yes' in Bulgaria and Sri Lanka.

● In South America, southern Europe and many Arab countries, touching another person is a sign of warmth and friendship. In the Orient, it is considered an invasion of privacy.

● In Norway or Malaysia, it's rude to leave something on your plate when eating; in Egypt, it's rude *not* to leave something on your plate.

● A door-to-door salesperson might find it tough going in Italy, where it is improper for a man to call on a woman if she is home alone.[42]

Failing to understand such differences in customs and behaviours from one country to another can spell disaster for a marketer's international products and programmes.

Marketers must decide on the degree to which they will adapt their products and marketing programmes to meet the unique cultures and needs of consumers in various markets. On the one hand, they want to standardize their offerings in order to simplify operations and take advantage of cost economies. On the other hand, adapting marketing efforts within each country results in products and programmes that better satisfy the needs of local consumers. The question of whether to adapt or standardize the marketing mix across international markets has created a lively debate in recent years.

Summary

Markets have to be understood before marketing strategies can be developed. The consumer market buys goods and services for personal consumption. Consumers vary tremendously in age, income, education, tastes and other factors. Marketers must understand how consumers transform marketing and other inputs into buying responses. *Consumer behaviour* is influenced by the buyer's characteristics and by the buyer's decision process. *Buyer characteristics* include four main factors: cultural, social, personal and psychological.

Culture is the most basic determinant of a person's wants and behaviour. It includes the basic values, perceptions, preferences and behaviours that a person learns from family and other key institutions. Marketers try to track cultural shifts that might suggest new ways to serve customers. *Social classes* are subcultures whose members have similar social prestige based on occupation, income, education, wealth and other variables. People with different cultural, subculture and social class characteristics have different product and brand preferences.

Social factors also influence a buyer's behaviour. A person's *reference groups* – family, friends, social organizations, professional associations – strongly affect product and brand choices. The person's position within each group can be defined in terms of *role and status*. A buyer chooses products and brands that reflect his or her role and status.

The buyer's age, life-cycle stage, occupation, economic circumstances, lifestyle, personality and other *personal characteristics* and *psychological factors* influence his or her buying decisions. Young consumers have different needs and wants from older consumers; the needs of young married couples differ from those of retired people; consumers with higher incomes buy differently from those who have less to spend.

Before planning its marketing strategy, a company needs to understand its consumers and the decision processes they go through. The number of buying participants and the amount of buying effort increase with the complexity of the buying situation. There are three types of *buying decision behaviour: routine response behaviour, limited problem solving* and *extensive problem solving*.

In buying something, the buyer goes through a decision process consisting of *need recognition, information search, evaluation of alternatives, purchase decision* and *postpurchase behaviour*. The marketer's job is to understand the buyers' behaviour at each stage and the influences that are operating. This allows the marketer to develop a significant and effective marketing programme for the target market. With regard to new products, consumers respond at different rates, depending on the consumer's characteristics and the product's characteristics. Manufacturers try to bring their new products to the attention of potential early adopters, particularly those with opinion leader characteristics.

A person's buying behaviour is the result of the complex interplay of all these cultural, social, personal and psychological factors. Although marketers cannot control many of these factors, they are useful in identifying and understanding the consumers that marketers are trying to influence.

Key Terms

Adoption 260
Adoption process 260
Alternative evaluation 255
Aspirational group 235
Attitude 249
Belief 249
Brand image 256
Buyer 237
Cognitive dissonance 259
Complex buying behaviour 251
Consumer buying behaviour 229
Consumer market 229
Culture 230
Decider 237
Decision-making unit 237
Dissonance-reducing buying behaviour 252

Family life cycle 238
Habitual buying behaviour 252
Influencer 237
Information search 254
Initiator 237
Learning 248
Lifestyle 240
Membership groups 235
Motive 245
Need recognition 254
New product 260
Opinion leaders 262
Perception 247
Personal influence 262
Personality 243
Postpurchase behaviour 258
Psychographics 240

Purchase decision 258
Reference groups 235
Role 238
Selective attention 247
Selective distortion 247
Selective retention 248
Self-concept 243
Social classes 233
Status 238
Subculture 231
User 237
Variety-seeking buying behaviour 253

Discussing the Issues

1. Thinking about the purchase of an audio hi-fi system, indicate the extent to which cultural, social, personal and psychological factors affect how a buyer evaluates hi-fi products and chooses a brand.

2. Describe and contrast any differences in the buying behaviour of consumers for the following products: Blur's new album; a notebook computer; a pair of jogging shoes; and a breakfast cereal.

3. Why might a detailed understanding of the model of the consumer buying decision process help marketers develop more effective marketing strategies to capture and retain customers? How universal is the model? How useful is it?

4. In designing the advertising for a soft drink, which would you find more helpful: information about consumer demographics or about consumer lifestyles? Give examples of how you would use each type of information.

5. Take, for example, a new method of contraception, which is being 'sold' to young males. It is a controversial, albeit innovative concept. Your firm is the pioneer in launching this device. What are the main factors your firm must research when developing a marketing programme for this product?

6. It has been said that consumers' buying behaviour is shaped more by perception than by reality. Do you agree with this comment? Why or why not?

Applying the Concepts

1. Different types of product can fulfil different functional and psychological needs.

   ● List five luxury products or services that are very interesting or important to you. Some possibilities are cars, clothing, sports equipment, cosmetics, golf club membership. List five other necessities that you use which have little interest to you, such as pens, laundry detergent or petrol.

   ● Make a list of words that describe how you feel about each of the products/services listed. Are there differences between the types of word you used for luxuries and necessities? What does this tell you about the different psychological needs these products fulfil?

2. Different groups may have different types of effect on consumers.

   ● Consider an item you bought which is typical of what your peers (a key reference group) buy, such as a compact disc, a mountain bike or a brand of athletic shoes. Were you conscious that your friends owned something similar when you made the purchase? Did this make you want the item more or less? Why or why not?

   ● Now, think of brands that you currently use which your parents also use. Examples may include soap, shaving cream or margarine. Did you think through these purchases as carefully as those influenced by your peers or were these purchases simply the result of following old habits?

References

1. *World Bank Atlas* (1994); *Microsoft Bookshelf* (1998).
2. Several models of the consumer buying process have been developed by marketing scholars. The most prominent models are those of John A. Howard and Jagdish N. Sheth, *The Theory of Buyer Behaviour* (New York: Wiley, 1969); Francesco M. Nicosia, *Consumer Decision Processes* (Englewood Cliffs, NJ: Prentice Hall, 1966); James F. Engel, Roger D. Blackwell and Paul W. Miniard, *Consumer Behaviour*, 5th edn (New York: Holt, Rinehart & Winston, 1986); James R. Bettman, *An Information Processing Theory of Consumer Choice* (Reading, MA: Addison-Wesley, 1979). For a summary, see Leon G. Schiffman and Leslie Lazar Kanuk, *Consumer Behaviour*, 4th edn (Englewood Cliffs, NJ: Prentice Hall, 1991), ch. 20.
3. For an insight into this problem see Rik Pieters, 'A control view on the behaviour of consumers: turning the triangle', *European Journal of Marketing*, 27, 8 (1993), pp. 17–27.
4. For this and other examples of the effects of culture in international marketing, see Philip R. Cateora, *International Marketing*, 8th edn (Homewood, IL: Irwin, 1993), ch. 4; Sak Onkvisit and John J. Shaw, *International Marketing:*

Analysis and strategy, 3rd edn (Upper Saddle River, NJ: Prentice Hall, 1997), ch. 6.
5. Richard Tomkin, 'Quaker buys "new age" drinks', *Financial Times* (3 November 1994), p. 25; Sara McConnell, 'Banks put their future on the line', *The Times* (9 October 1994), p. 29; Ralph Atkins, 'Families choose direct insurers', *Financial Times* (8–9 October 1994), p. 5.
6. For more on marketing to Hispanics, blacks, mature consumers and Asians, see Gary L. Berman, 'The Hispanic market: getting down to cases', *Sales and Marketing Management* (October 1991), pp. 65–74; Christy Fisher, 'Poll: Hispanics stick to brands', *Advertising Age* (15 February 1993), p. 6; Melissa Campanelli, 'The African-American market: community, growth and change', *Sales and Marketing Management* (May 1991), pp. 75–81; Eugene Morris, 'The difference in black and white', *American Demographics* (January 1993), pp. 44–9; Melissa Campanelli, 'The senior market: rewriting the demographics and definitions', *Sales and Marketing Management* (February 1991), pp. 63–70; Joseph M. Winski, 'The mature market: marketers mature in depicting seniors', *Advertising*

Age (16 November 1992), p. S1; Tibbett L. Speer, 'Older consumers follow different rules', *American Demographics* (February 1993), pp. 21–2; Maria Shao, 'Suddenly, Asian-Americans are a marketer's dream', *Business Week* (17 June 1991), pp. 54–5; Carol J. Fouke, 'Asian-American market more important than ever', *Marketing News* (14 October 1991), p. 10.

7. Richard P. Coleman, 'The continuing significance of social class to marketing', *Journal of Consumer Research* (December 1983), pp. 265–80; Laura Mazur, 'Golden oldies', *Marketing Business* (February 1993), pp. 10–13; David Nicholson-Lord, 'Mass leisure class is on the way, say forecasters', *Independent* (18 April 1994), p. 4.

8. For a broad discussion of international social class, see Edward W. Cundiff and Marye Tharp Higler, *Marketing in the International Environment* (Hemel Hempstead: Prentice Hall, 1988); Ernest Dichter, 'The world customer', *Harvard Business Review* (July–August 1962), pp. 113–23, and 'Rich man, poor man', *The Economist* (24 July 1993), p. 73; 'Slicing the cake' and 'For richer, for poorer', *The Economist* (5 November 1994), pp. 13–14 and 19–21 respectively.

9. William O. Bearden and Michael J. Etzel, 'Reference group influence on product and brand purchase decisions', *Journal of Consumer Research* (September 1982), p. 185.

10. Debra Goldman, 'Spotlight men', *Adweek* (13 August 1990), pp. M1–M6; Dennis Rodkin, 'A manly sport: building loyalty', *Advertising Age* (15 April 1991), pp. S1, S12; Nancy Ten Kate, 'Who buys the pants in the family?', *American Demographics* (January 1992), p. 12; Laura Zinn, 'Real men buy paper towels, too', *Business Week* (9 November 1992), pp. 75–6; 'The war between the sexes', *The Economist* (5 March 1994), pp. 96–7.

11. For more on family decision making, see Schiffman and Kanuk, *Consumer Behaviour*, op. cit., ch. 12; Rosann L. Spiro, 'Persuasion in family decision making', *Journal of Consumer Research* (March 1983), pp. 393–402; Michael B. Menasco and David J. Curry, 'Utility and choice: an empirical study of husband/wife decision making', *Journal of Consumer Research* (June 1989), pp. 87–97; Eileen Fisher and Stephen J. Arnold, 'More than a labor of love: gender roles and Christmas gift shopping', *Journal of Consumer Research* (December 1990), pp. 333–45.

12. See Lawrence Lepisto, 'A life span perspective of consumer behavior', in Elizabeth Hirshman and Morris Holbrook, *Advances in Consumer Research*, vol. 12 (Provo, UT: Association for Consumer Research, 1985), p. 47.

13. Kim Foltz, 'Wizards of Marketing', *Newsweek* (22 July 1985), p. 44.

14. For more on VALS and on psychographics in general, see William D. Wells, 'Psychographics: a critical review', *Journal of Marketing Research* (May 1975), pp. 196–213; Arnold Mitchell, *The Nine American Lifestyles* (New York: Macmillan, 1983); Rebecca Piirto, 'Measuring minds in the 1990s', *American Demographics* (December 1990), pp. 35–9; 'VALS the second time', *American Demographics* (July 1991), p. 6. For more reading on the pros and cons of using VALS and other lifestyle approaches, see Lynn R. Kahle, Sharon E. Beatty and Pamela Homer, 'Alternative measurement approaches to consumer values: the list of values (LOV) and values and life styles (VALS)', *Journal of Consumer Research* (December 1986), pp. 405–9; Mark Landler, 'The bloodbath in market research', *Business Week* (11 February 1991), pp. 72–4.

15. Taken from RISC SA, *ACE* (Lyon: RISC SA, 1989); CCA, *CCA*

Euro-styles (Paris: CCA, 1989); Norbert Homma and Jorg Uelzhoffer, 'The internationalisation of everyday-life and milieus', ESOMAR Conference on America, Japan and EC'92: The Prospects for Marketing, Advertising and Research, Venice, 18–20 June 1990; Marieke de Mooij, *Advertising Worldwide: Concepts, theories and practice of international and global advertising* (Hemel Hempstead: Prentice Hall, 1994).

16. Based on details in Marieke de Mooij, *Advertising Worldwide* (Hemel Hempstead: Prentice Hall, 1994), who obtained his information from Eugine Wong of Survey Research Malaysia.

17. Stuart Elliot, 'Sampling Tastes of a Changing Russia', *The New York Times*, 1 April 1992, pp. D1, D19.

18. See Harold H. Kassarjian and Mary Jane Sheffet, 'Personality in consumer behaviour: an update', in Harold H. Kassarjian and Thomas S. Robertson (eds), *Perspectives in Consumer Behaviour* (Glenview, IL: Scott Foresman, 1981), pp. 160–80; Joseph T. Plummer, 'How personality can make a difference', *Marketing News* (March–April 1984), pp. 17–20.

19. Myron Magnet, 'Let's go for growth', *Fortune*, 7 March 1994, p. 70.

20. See M. Joseph Sirgy, 'Self-concept in consumer behaviour: a critical review', *Journal of Consumer Research* (December 1982), pp. 287–300; Russel W. Belk, 'Possessions and the extended self', *Journal of Consumer Research* (September 1988), pp. 139–59.

21. See Annetta Miller and Dody Tsiantar, 'Psyching out consumers', *Newsweek* (27 February 1989), pp. 46–7; Rebecca Piirto, 'Words that sell', *American Demographics* (January 1992), p. 6.

22. Abraham H. Maslow, *Motivation and Personality*, 2nd edn (New York: Harper & Row, 1970), pp. 80–106.

23. Robert L. Gluckman, 'A consumer approach to branded wines', *European Journal of Marketing*, **24**, 4 (1990), pp. 27–46.

24. Geert Hofstede, *Cultural Consequences* (London: Sage, 1984).

25. John Fiske, *Understanding Popular Culture* (London: Routledge, 1989).

26. Simon Holberton, 'Cathay Pacific puts its future in Hong Kong', *Financial Times* (3 November 1994), p. 32.

27. For a discussion of subliminal perception, see Timothy Moore, 'What you see is what you get', *Journal of Marketing* (Spring 1982); Walter Weir, 'Another look at subliminal "facts"', *Advertising Age* (15 October 1984), p. 46.

28. See 'Honda hopes to win new riders by emphasizing "fun" of cycles', *Marketing News* (28 August 1989), p. 6.

29. Henry Assael, *Consumer Behaviour and Marketing Action* (Boston, MA: Kent Publishing, 1987), ch. 4. An earlier classification of three types of consumer buying behaviour – routine response behaviour, limited problem solving and extensive problem solving – can be found in John A. Howard and Jagdish Sheth, *The Theory of Consumer Behaviour* (New York: Wiley, 1969), pp. 27–8. Gordon R. Foxall proposes a more sophisticated Behavioural Perspective Model (BPM) in 'A behavioural perspective on purchasing and consumption' and 'Consumer behaviour as an evolutionary process', *European Journal of Marketing*, **27**, 8 (1993), pp. 7–16 and 46–57 respectively; see also John A. Howard, *Consumer Behaviour in Marketing Strategy* (Englewood Cliffs, NJ: Prentice Hall, 1989).

30. Tom Stevenson, 'Dixons opens shops for baffled buyers', *Independent* (17 October 1994), p. 28.

31. V. W. Mitchell and Pari Boustani, 'A preliminary investigation into pre- and post-purchase risk perception and reduction',

European Journal of Marketing, **28**, 1 (1990), pp. 56–71.

32. Keith B. Murray, 'A test of services marketing theory: consumer information acquisition theory', *Journal of Marketing* (January 1991), pp. 10–25.

33. The ratings are based on those given in 'Product test: compact cameras', *Which?* (November 1994), pp. 21–6.

34. This was developed by Martin Fishbein. See Martin Fishbein and Icek Ajzen, *Belief, Attitude, Intention, and Behaviour* (Reading, MA: Addison-Wesley, 1975). For a critical review of this model, see Paul W. Miniard and Joel B. Cohen, 'An examination of the Fishbein–Ajzen behavioral intentions model's concepts and measures', *Journal of Experimental Social Psychology* (May 1981), pp. 309–99.

35. Raymond A. Bauer, 'Consumer behaviour as risk taking', in Donald F. Cox (ed.), *Risk Taking and Information Handling in Consumer Behaviour* (Boston, MA: Division of Research, Harvard Business School, 1967); John W. Vann, 'A multi-distributional conceptual framework for the study of perceived risk', in Thomas C. Kinnear (ed.), *Advances in Consumer Research*, vol. 11 (Provo, UT: Association for Consumer Research, 1983), pp. 442–6; Robert B. Settle and Pamela L. Alreck, 'Reducing buyers' sense of risk', *Marketing Communications* (January 1989), pp. 19–24.

36. See Leon Festinger, *A Theory of Cognitive Dissonance* (Stanford, CA: Stanford University Press, 1957); Schiffman and Kanuk, *Consumer Behaviour*, op. cit., pp. 304–5.

37. See Karl Albrect and Ron Zemke, *Service America!* (Homewood, IL: Dow-Jones Irwin, 1985), pp. 6–7; Frank Rose, 'Now quality means service too', *Fortune* (22 April 1991), pp. 97–108.

38. The following discussion draws heavily from Everett M. Rogers, *Diffusion of Innovations*, 3rd edn (New York: Free Press, 1983); see also Hubert Gatignon and Thomas S. Robertson, 'A propositional inventory for new diffusion research', *Journal of Consumer Research* (March 1985), pp. 849–67.

39. See Schiffman and Kanuk, *Consumer Behaviour*, op. cit., ch. 18.

40. For these and other examples, see ibid.

41. Mir Maqbool Alam Khan, 'Kellogg reports brisk cereal sales in India', *Advertising Age*, 14 November 1994, p. 60.

42. For these and other examples, see William J. Stanton, Michael J. Etzel and Bruce J. Walker, *Fundamentals of Marketing* (New York: McGraw-Hill, 1991), p. 536.

Case 6

Bic Versus Gillette: The Disposable Wars

ABOUT HALF OF ALL WESTERN men get up each morning, confront their stubble in the bathroom mirror and reach for a cheap disposable plastic razor. Schick, Bic, Gillette, Wilkinson or whatever, most men think that one brand does as well as the next. Also, the razor makers seem always to have them on sale, so you can scoop up a dozen of them for next to nothing.

The Gillette Company does not like this sort of thinking. Of course, women also use Gillette's razors, but Gillette worries about the growing number of men who use disposables. The company makes about three times more money per unit on cartridge refills for its Atra and Trac II razor systems than it does on its Good News! disposables. However, since the first disposables appeared in 1975, their sales have grown faster than those of system razors. By 1988 disposables accounted for 40 per cent of shaving-product money sales and more than 50 per cent of unit sales.

Gillette: The Defender

Gillette dominates the world wet-shave industry with a 61 per cent share. Schick is second with a 16.2 per cent share, Bic has 9.3 per cent and others, including Wilkinson, account for most of the rest of the market. In 1988 Gillette's blades and razors produced 32 per cent of its $3.5 billion sales and 61 per cent of its $268 million net income.

Gillette earned its dominant position in the market through large investments in research and development and through careful consumer research. Every day, about 10,000 men carefully record the results of their shaves for Gillette. Five hundred of these men shave in special in-plant cubicles under carefully controlled and monitored conditions, including observation through two-way mirrors and video cameras. Shavers record the precise number of nicks and cuts. In certain cases, researchers even collect sheared whiskers to weigh and measure. As a result, Gillette scientists know that an average man's beard grows 0.04 cm a day (14 cm per year) and contains 15,500 hairs. During an average lifetime, a man will spend 140 days scraping 8.4 metres of whiskers from his face. Gillette even uses electron microscopes to study blade surfaces and miniature cameras to analyze the actual shaving process.

Armed with its knowledge of shavers and shaving, Gillette prides itself in staying ahead of the competition. As soon as competitors adjust to one shaving system, Gillette introduces another advance. In 1971 Gillette introduced the Trac II, the first razor system featuring two parallel blades mounted in a cartridge. In 1977, following $8 million in R & D expenditure, the company introduced Atra, a twin-blade cartridge that swivels during shaving to follow the face's contours. In 1985 Gillette launched the Atra Plus, which added a lubricating strip to the Atra cartridge to make shaving even smoother.

Although the company's founder, King Gillette, considered developing a disposable product early in the company's life, Gillette's marketing strategy has focused on developing products that use refill blades on a permanent handle. Gillette works to give its blades, and especially its handles, an aura of class and superior performance. By promoting new captive systems, in which blade cartridges fit only a certain razor handle, Gillette raises price and profit margins with each new technological leap. Atra cartridges do not fit the Trac II handle, so men had to buy a new handle to allow them to use the Atra blades when Gillette introduced that system.

Gillette has never bothered with the low end of the market – cheap, private-label blades. Status-seeking men, it believes, will always buy a classy product. Most men see shaving as a serious business and their appearance as a matter of some importance. Therefore, most men will not skimp and settle for an ordinary shave when, for a little more money, they can feel confident that Gillette's products give them the best shave.

Bic: The Challenge

The rapid rise of the disposable razor has challenged Gillette's view of men's shaving philosophy. Bic first introduced the disposable shaver in 1975 in Europe and then a year later in Canada. Realizing that the United States would be next, Gillette introduced the first disposable razor to the US market in 1976 – the blue plastic Good News! which used a Trac II blade. Despite its defensive reaction, Gillette predicted that men would use the disposable only for trips and in the changing room when they had forgotten their real razor. Disposables would never capture more than 7 per cent of the market, Gillette asserted.

Marcel Bich, Bic's French founder, is devoted to disposability. Bich made his money by developing the familiar ballpoint pen. He pursues a strategy of turning status products into commodities. Often a product has status because it is difficult to make and must sell at a high price. However, if a manufacturer develops ways to mass produce the product at low cost with little loss of functional quality, its status and allure disappear. Consumers will then not feel embarrassed to buy and be seen using the new, cheaper version of the product. Bich brands his products, strips them of their glamour, distributes them widely and sells them cheaply. His marketing strategy is simple: maximum service; minimum price.

Bic attacks the shaving business in a very different manner from Gillette. It does not have anyone exploring the fringe of shaving technology; it does not even own an electron microscope; and it does not know or care how many hairs the average man's beard contains. The company maintains only a small shave-testing panel consisting of about 100 people. The Bic shaver has only one blade mounted on a short, hollow handle. Nevertheless, the Bic disposable razor presents Gillette with its most serious challenge since the company's early days. In 1988 Bic's shaving products achieved $52 million in sales with a net income of $9.4 million and held a 22.4 per cent share of the disposable market.

Early Battles

In their pursuits of disposability, Gillette and Bic have clashed before on other product fronts. First, in the 1950s, they fought for market share in the writing pen market. Gillette's Paper Mate products, however, were no match for Bic's mass-market advertising and promotion skills. The two firms met again in the 1970s in the disposable cigarette lighter arena, where they again made commodities of what had once been prestigious and sometimes expensive items. Although Gillette did better in disposable lighters than it had in pens, Bic's lighter captured the dominant market share.

In the most recent skirmish, however, Gillette's Good News! brand is winning with a 58 per cent market share in the disposable razor market. For Gillette, the victory is bittersweet. Good News! sells for a lot less than any of Gillette's older products. The key to commodity competition is price. To stay competitive with the Bic razor and with other disposables, Gillette has to sell Good News! for much less than the retail price of an Atra or Trac II cartridge. As many Trac II and Atra users have concluded, why pay more for a twin-blade refill cartridge from Gillette when the same blade mounted on a plastic handle costs half as much? Good News! not only produces less revenue per blade sold, it also costs more because Gillette has to supply the handle as well as the cartridge. Each time Good News! gains a market share point, Gillette loses millions of dollars in sales and profits from its Atra and Trac II products.

The Psychology of Shaving

The battle between Bic and Gillette represents more than a simple contest over what kinds of razor people want to use. It symbolizes a clash over one of the most enduring daily rituals. Before King Gillette invented the safety razor, men found shaving a tedious, difficult, time-consuming and often bloody task that they endured at most twice a week. Only the rich could afford to have a barber shave them daily.

Gillette patented the safety razor in 1904, but it was not until World War I that the product gained wide consumer acceptance. Gillette had the brilliant idea of having the military give a free Gillette razor to every soldier. In this manner, millions of men just entering the shaving age were introduced to the daily, self-shaving habit.

The morning shaving ritual continues to occupy a very special place in most men's lives – it affirms their masculinity. The first shave remains a rite of passage into manhood. A survey by New York psychologists reported that, although men complain about the bother of shaving, 97 per cent would not want to use a cream that would permanently rid them of all facial hair. Gillette once introduced a new razor that came in versions for heavy, medium and light beards. Almost no one bought the light version because few men wanted to acknowledge publicly their modest beard production. Although shaving may require less skill and involve less danger than it once did, many men still want the razors they use to reflect their belief that shaving is a serious business. A typical man regards his razor as an important personal tool, a kind of extension of self, like an expensive pen, cigarette lighter, attaché case or set of golf clubs.

Gillette's Fight Back

For more than 80 years Gillette's perception of the men's shaving market and the psychology of shaving has been perfect. Its products hold a substantial 61 per cent share and its technology and marketing philosophy have held sway over the entire industry. Gillette has worked successfully to maintain the razor's masculine look, weight and feel as well as its status as an item of personal identification. Now, however, millions of men are scraping their faces each day with small, nondescript, passionless pieces of plastic – an act that seems to be the ultimate denial of the shaving ritual. Good News! is bad news for Gillette. Gillette must find a way to dispose of the disposables.

QUESTIONS

1. Who is involved in a man's decision to buy a disposable razor and what roles do various participants play?

2. Do these participants and roles differ for the decision to buy a system razor?

3. What types of buying-decision behaviour do men exhibit when purchasing razors?

4. Examine a man's decision process for buying a wet-shave razor. How have Gillette and Bic pursued different strategies concerning this process?

5. What explains Bic's differing success in competing against Gillette in the disposable pen, lighter and shaver market? Why do you think Bic perfume failed?

6. What marketing strategy should Gillette adopt to encourage men to switch from disposables to system razors? How would buyer decision processes towards new products affect your recommendations?

SOURCE: Portions adapted from 'The Gillette Company', in Subhash C. Jain, *Marketing Strategy and Policy*, 3rd edn (Cincinnati, OH: Southwestern, 1990). Used with permission.

7

Business Markets
and Business
Buyer Behaviour

CHAPTER OBJECTIVES

After reading this chapter, you should be able to:

● Explain how business markets differ from consumer markets.

● Identify the main factors that influence business buyer behaviour.

● List and define the steps in the business buying decision process.

● Explain how institutional and government buyers make their buying decisions.

Preview Case

Selling Business Jets: The Ultimate Executive Toy

TINY ROWLAND AGREED TO RETIRE from the board of Lonrho after a long and bitter struggle against German property owner Dieter Bock. On that day he lost more than the job he had held for 33 years; he also lost access to Lonrho's Gulfstream executive jet. Tiny Rowland often used the jet to visit Lonrho's 500 companies or many international contacts, especially in Africa, but it was a £2 million a year item that many of Lonrho's shareholders resented.

The shareholders' views on Lonrho's business jet were akin to those held by many people. As Brian Barents, president of Learjet explained: 'The business jet has gone from being the sign of a dynamic, fast-moving,

entrepreneurial corporation to one of corporate privilege and excess.' The business jet market was hitting hard times. Businesses were looking at their costs and there seemed to be fewer and fewer charismatic and powerful people like Tiny Rowland or King Fahd of Saudi Arabia who were willing and able to buy a jet. Shareholders had reason to be sceptical about the cost-effectiveness of the jets. Unlike commercial airlines that spend most of their time flying, business jets spend most of their time on the ground. In Europe they fly on average for only about six hours a week.

'There is simply not enough viable business for seven or eight competing manufacturers,' complained one business jet marketing executive. 'There is bound to be more consolidation, since there is probably room for only three or four manufacturers.' Business jets' low utilization means that they last a long time and ownership is limited. The United States is by far the biggest market with 4,000 business jets operating; France has 490, Germany 360 and the United Kingdom 260. Japan is a very wealthy market, but government restrictions have kept private ownership down to 90.

Recognizing potential buyers is simple – the organizations that can afford to own and operate a business jet are easily identified. The difficult problem is reaching key decision makers for jet purchases, understanding their complex motivations and decision processes, analyzing what factors will be important in their decisions, and designing marketing approaches.

There are *rational* motives and *subjective* factors in buyers' decisions. A company buying a business jet will evaluate the aircraft on quality and performance, prices, operating costs and service. At times, these may appear to be the only things that drive the buying decision. But having a superior product isn't enough to land the sale: marketers must also consider the more subtle *human factors* that affect the choice of a jet. According to Gulfstream, a leading American supplier of business jets:

> The purchase process may be initiated by the chief executive officer (CEO), a board member wishing to increase efficiency or security, the company's chief pilot, or through vendor efforts like advertising or a sales visit. The CEO will be central in deciding whether to buy the jet, but he or she will be heavily influenced by the company's pilot, financial officer and perhaps by the board itself.

Each party in the buying process has subtle roles and needs. The salesperson who, for example, tries to impress both the CEO with depreciation schedules and the chief pilot with minimum runway statistics will almost certainly not sell a plane if he or she overlooks the psychological and emotional components of the buying decision. 'For the chief executive', observes one salesperson, 'you need all the numbers for support, but if you can't find the kid inside the CEO and excite him or her with the raw beauty of the new plane, you'll never sell the equipment. If you sell the excitement, you sell the jet.'

The chief pilot, as an equipment expert, often has veto power over purchase decisions and may be able to stop the purchase of a certain brand of jet by simply expressing a negative opinion about, say, the plane's bad weather capabilities. In this sense, the pilot not only influences the decision but also serves as an information 'gatekeeper' by advising management on the equipment to select. Though the corporate legal staff will handle the purchase agreement and the purchasing department will acquire the jet, these parties may have little to say about whether or how the plane will be obtained and which type will be selected. The users of the jet – middle and upper management of the buying company, important customers and others – may have at least an indirect role in choosing the equipment.

The involvement of many people in the purchase decision creates a group dynamic that the selling company must factor into its sales planning. Who makes up the buying group? How will the parties interact? Who will dominate and who submit? What priorities do the individuals have?

Two European companies think they have an answer to competing in this competitive and increasingly cost-conscious business aircraft market. France's Aérospatiale's Socata subsidiary, with Mooney of the United States, have spent FFr500 million developing the TBM700, a single-engined turbo-prop aircraft. It is smaller and slower than conventional twin-engined business jets, but much less expensive to buy and run. Aérospatiale, which claims that the TBM700 has some of the capabilities and comfort of the larger executive jets, hopes to sell 600 of them.

The other market entrant is JetCo. It does not make aircraft, but offers a 'fractional ownership' scheme that claims to offer all the benefits of private ownership at a fraction of the cost. 'As little as $7,000' per month buys a share in one of JetCo's fleet of Hawker 800 or Beechjet 400A 860-plus kilometres per hour jets, or Beechcraft Super King Air B200 twin-turboprop aircraft. Michael Riegal, managing director of JetCo, explains the financial advantages of JetShare: 'A corporate jet is an extremely expensive asset with annual operating cost of between $800,000 and $1 million if you include fixed and variable cost as well as depreciation.' As an alternative JetShare offers one-quarter ownership of a corporate jet, with an entitlement to 150 flying hours, for $287,500 per year. When in use, JetCo puts a temporary company logo on the front of the jet and will even personalize 'cushion covers and things – items that are easily changeable'.

Not all business jet makers are taking the frugal route. Canada's Bombardier is developing the Global Express (Gex) BD-700 business jet, capable of carrying eight passengers and four crew non-stop on sectors such as San Francisco–Tokyo, London–Tokyo and Paris–Buenos Aires. Gex is faster than other business jets: cruising at Mach 0.88 (that is, 88 per cent of the speed of sound), it will knock an hour off their times on shorter routes like Johannesburg–Moscow or Berlin–Los Angeles. Gex was launched at the end of 1993 with a development cost of C$1.4 billion, and within a year the company had orders and options for 40 aircraft worth C$1.5 billion. Wow, some toy![1]

QUESTIONS

1. What are the reasons for businesses buying executive jets?
2. Is it correct to say that, unlike people in consumer markets, business buyers are rational?
3. Who are the critical people to influence when selling executive jets?
4. What features of the product are most likely to interest people involved in the decision to purchase an executive jet?
5. Since it is unlikely that people will respond to an advertisement by buying an executive jet, why are they advertised?
6. Develop the economic argument for a business jet that is likely to be acceptable to a firm's shareholders.

Introduction

In some ways, selling corporate jets to business buyers is like selling cars and kitchen appliances to families. Business jet makers ask the same questions as consumer marketers: Who are the buyers and what are their needs? How do buyers make their buying decisions and what factors influence these decisions? What marketing programme will be most effective? But the answers to these questions are usually different in the case of the business buyer. Thus the jet makers face many of the same challenges as consumer marketers – and some additional ones.

In one way or another, most large companies sell to other organizations. Many companies, such as Asea Brown Boveri, Norsk Hydro, Du Pont and countless others, sell *most* of their products to other businesses. Even large consumer-products companies, which make products used by final consumers, must first sell their products to other businesses. For example, Allied Domecq makes many consumer products – La Ina sherry, Presidente brandy, Tetley tea and others. To sell these products to consumers, Allied Domecq must first sell them to wholesalers and retailers that serve the consumer market. Allied Domecq also sells food ingredients directly to other businesses through its Margetts Food and DCA Food Industries subsidiaries.

The **business market** consists of all the organizations that buy goods and services to use in the production of other products and services that are sold, rented or supplied to others. It also includes retailing and wholesaling firms that acquire goods for the purpose of reselling or renting them to others at a profit. The **business buying process** is the decision-making process by which business buyers establish the need for purchased products and services, and identify, evaluate and choose among alternative brands and suppliers.[2] Companies that sell to other business organizations must do their best to understand business markets and business buyer behaviour.

business market
All the organizations that buy goods and services to use in the production of other products and services, and identify, evaluate and choose among alternative brands and suppliers

business buying process
The decision-making process by which business buyers establish the need for purchased products and services, and identify, evaluate and choose among alternative brands and suppliers.

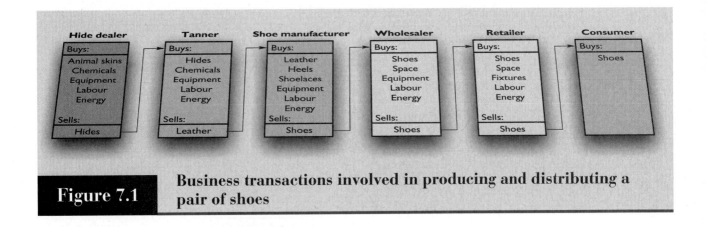

| **Figure 7.1** | **Business transactions involved in producing and distributing a pair of shoes** |

Business Markets

The business market is *huge*: most businesses just sell to other businesses, and sales to businesses far outstrip those to consumers. The reason for this is the number of times that parts of a consumer product are bought, processed and resold before reaching the final consumer. For example, Figure 7.1 shows the large number of business transactions needed to produce and sell a simple pair of shoes. Hide dealers sell to tanners, who sell leather to shoe manufacturers, who sell shoes to wholesalers, who in turn sell shoes to retailers, who finally sell the shoes to consumers. Each party in the chain also buys many other related goods and services. This example shows why there is more business buying than consumer buying – many sets of *business* purchases were made for only one set of *consumer* purchases.

Characteristics of Business Markets

In some ways, business markets are similar to consumer markets. Both involve people who assume buying roles and make purchase decisions to satisfy needs. However, business markets differ in many ways from consumer markets.[3] The main differences are in market structure and demand, the nature of the buying unit, and the types of decision and the decision process involved.

● *Market Structure and Demand*

The business marketer normally deals with *far fewer but far larger buyers* than the consumer marketer does. For example, when Michelin sells replacement tyres to final consumers, its potential market includes the owners of cars currently in use. But Michelin's fate in the business market depends on getting orders from a few large car makers. These sales of original equipment are doubly important, since many people replace their tyres with the brand already on the car. Even in large business markets, a few buyers normally account for most of the purchasing.

Business markets are also more *geographically concentrated*: international financial services in London, petrochemicals and synthetic fibers around Rotterdam and Amsterdam, and the movie industry in Hollywood. Further, business demand is **derived demand** – it ultimately derives from the demand for consumer goods. Mercedes buys steel because consumers buy cars. If consumer

derived demand
Business demand that ultimately comes from (derives from) the demand for consumer goods.

Courtaulds Fibres sells Tencel to the people who sell fabrics, to the people who sell garments, to the retailers who sell them to consumers. Advertising Tencel to consumers pulls the fibre through the chain.

demand for cars drops, so will the demand for steel and all the other products used to make cars. Therefore, business marketers sometimes promote their products directly to final consumers to increase business demand (see Marketing Highlight 7.1).[4]

> In late 1997 Ron Woodard, the boss of Boeing Commercial Airplane Group, was half-jokingly asking airlines to decrease their orders to ease Boeing's over-stretched production. In January 1998 he got more than he asked for. Following the economic troubles in south-east Asia and the resultant decline in local air travel, airlines all over the region were renegotiating orders. Philippine Airlines said it planned to cancel four 747-400 jets, Malaysian Airlines System wants to delay the delivery of 20 aircraft up to five years, Garuda Indonesia left Boeing stranded with jets it ordered but could not afford and stopped lease payments on six new Airbus A330s. More trouble is on the way as Korean Air's value drops to less than three of its fleet of 45 747s.[5]

inelastic demand
Total demand for a product that is not much affected by price changes, especially in the short run.

Many business markets have **inelastic demand**: that is, total demand for many business products is not affected much by price changes, especially in the short run. A drop in the price of leather will not cause shoe manufacturers to buy much more leather unless it results in lower shoe prices, which, in turn, will increase consumer demand for shoes.

Finally, business markets have more *fluctuating demand*. The demand for many business goods and services tends to change more – and more quickly – than the demand for consumer goods and services does. A small percentage increase in consumer demand can cause large increases in business demand. Sometimes a rise of only 10 per cent in consumer demand can cause as much as a 200 per cent rise in business demand during the next period.

● *Nature of the Buying Unit*

Compared with consumer purchases, a business purchase usually involves *more buyers* and a *more professional purchasing effort*. Often, business buying is done by trained purchasing agents, who spend their working lives learning how to buy well. The more complex the purchase, the more likely that several people will participate in the decision-making process. Buying committees made up of technical experts and top management are common in the buying of primary goods. Therefore, business marketers must have well-trained salespeople to deal with well-trained buyers.

● *Types of Decision and the Decision Process*

Business buyers usually face *more complex* buying decisions than do consumer buyers. Purchases often involve large sums of money, complex technical and economic considerations, and interactions among many people at many levels of the buyer's organization. Because the purchases are more complex, business buyers may take longer to make their decisions. For example, the purchase of a large computer system might take many months or more than a year to complete and could involve millions of pounds, thousands of technical details and dozens of people ranging from top management to lower-level users.

The business buying process tends to be *more formalized* than the consumer buying process. Large business purchases usually call for detailed product specifications, written purchase orders, careful supplier searches and formal approval. The buying firm might even prepare policy manuals that detail the purchase process.

Finally, in the business buying process, buyer and seller are often much *more dependent* on each other. Consumer marketers are usually at a distance from their customers. In contrast, business marketers may roll up their sleeves and work closely with their customers during all stages of the buying process – from helping customers define problems, to finding solutions, to supporting after-sales operations. For instance, 60 per cent of the money needed to develop Bombardier's Gax business jet came from suppliers, and risk-sharing partners including engine suppliers BMW/Rolls-Royce. They customize their offerings to meet individual customer needs. In the short run, orders go to suppliers that meet buyers' immediate product and service needs. However, business marketers must also build close *long-run* relationships with customers. In the long run, business marketers keep a customer's orders by meeting current needs *and* thinking ahead to meet the customer's future needs.

Volkswagen is breaking new ground at its Skoda factory by having suppliers' operations directly inside the car plant. Lucas, Johnson Controls and Pelzer are producing rear axles, seats and carpets in the Czech factory. This is one step ahead of Japanese manufacturers, which often have suppliers near by.[6]

● *Other Characteristics of Business Markets*

DIRECT PURCHASING. Business buyers often buy directly from producers rather than through intermediaries, especially for items that are technically complex or expensive. For example, in the United States, Ryder buys thousands of trucks each year in all shapes and sizes. It rents some of these trucks to move-it-yourself customers (yellow Ryder trucks), leases some to other companies for their truck fleets and uses the rest in its own freight-hauling business. When Ryder buys GMC trucks, it purchases them directly from General Motors rather than from independent GM truck dealers. Similarly, airlines buy aircraft directly from Boeing, European Airbus or McDonnell Douglas, Kroger buys packaged

Marketing Highlight 7.1

Wintel (Not) Inside, Please

The 'Wintel-twosome', Intel and Microsoft's Windows, are in trouble. In mid-1991, Intel launched its two-year, $100 million 'Intel Inside' advertising campaign to sell personal computer buyers on the virtues of its microprocessors, the tiny chips that serve as the brains of microcomputers. In 1994 that was followed by an $80 million campaign to persuade consumers and businesses to buy PCs based on its latest Pentium microprocessor. So what, you say? Lots of companies run big consumer ad campaigns. However, although such a campaign might be business as usual for companies like Nestlé, Shell and Unilever that market products directly to final consumers, it is anything but usual for Intel.

Computer buyers can't purchase a microprocessor chip directly – in fact, most will never even see one. Demand for microprocessors is *derived demand* – it ultimately comes from demand for products that *contain* microprocessors. Consumers simply buy the computer and take whatever brand of chip the computer manufacturer chose to include as a component. Traditionally, chip companies like Intel market only to the manufacturers that buy chips directly. In contrast, the innovative 'Intel Inside' campaign appeals directly to computer buyers – its customers' customers. If Intel can create brand preference among buyers for *its* chips, this in turn will make Intel chips more attractive to computer manufacturers. According to industry observers: 'Intel is treating the (PC) industry merely as a distribution arm, seeing the PC user as its ultimate consumer.'

Intel invented the first microprocessor in 1971 and for 20 years has held a near-monopoly, dominating the chip market for desktop computers. Its sales and profits have soared accordingly. In the decade since IBM introduced its first PCs based on Intel's 8088 microprocessor, Intel sales have jumped fivefold to more than $5 billion and its earnings have grown even faster. Its popular 286, 386, 486 and Pentium chips power most of the microcomputers in use today.

However, a rush of imitators – Advanced Micro Devices (AMD), Chips & Technologies, Cyrix and others – have begun to crack Intel's monopoly, marketing new and improved clones of Intel chips.

Intel has responded fiercely to the cloners, slashing prices, spending heavily to develop new products and advertising to differentiate its products. It has cut prices on its new processors faster than for any new chip in its history. Moreover, Intel invested hugely in R & D to get new products to the market more quickly. The Pentium II microprocessor is a veritable one-chip mainframe. The Pentium contains 3 million transistors and will process 100 million instructions per second (MIPS), as compared to only 0.5 million transistors and five MIPS for the 386 chip. New software ensures that computer users need 'Pentium power'. Standard Microsoft Windows 95 and Office 98 are increasingly sluggish without Pentium-like processors, so users are often forced to trade up.

Still, the clone makers are likely to continue nipping at Intel's heels, and advertising provides another means by which Intel can differentiate its 'originals' from competitors' imitations. The 'Intel Inside' campaign advances on two fronts. First, in its brand-awareness ads, Intel attempts to convince microcomputer buyers that Intel microprocessors really are better. The ads carry the message 'It's amazing what you can do with a Pentium processor'. After spending little on advertising for many years, other hi-tech firms are now spending a small fortune on building brands.

It remains to be seen whether the 'Intel Inside' campaign can convince buyers to care about what chip comes in their computers. But as long as microprocessors remain anonymous little lumps hidden inside a user's computer, Intel remains at the mercy of the clone makers. In contrast, if Intel can convince buyers that its chips are superior, it will achieve even more power in the market.

The reaction of IBM and Compaq, the leading PC supplier in the United States and Europe, suggests that Intel may be being too successful. For years Intel and Compaq collaborated in bringing Intel microprocessor-based PCs to markets, but the two firms are hardly on speaking terms now. Eckhard Pfeffer, Compaq president and chief executive, has accused Intel of undermining Compaq's marketing effort. 'What upsets us generally is that a component supplier should try to influence the end user. The end user market is not their business. They are interfering,' says Andreas Barth, head of Compaq's European operations. Not surprisingly, Compaq's latest PCs for the consumer market will have an AMD microprocessor inside.

IBM is also annoyed about the rapid obsolescence of the Intel products it buys. 'Customers are telling us to slow down the pace of technology,' says IBM's Chairman, Lou Gerstner. 'How powerful a computer do you really need on a desk?' To challenge Intel's dominance, IBM is linking with Nexgen and Cyrix to give credibility to its clones.

The world is also turning against Bill Gates' Microsoft, the other half of the increasingly hated 'Wintel twosome'. In the USA and Europe the firm's anti-competitive behaviour is under scrutiny, particularly Microsoft's bundling of its Web browser with its dominant Windows operating system.

Will Intel and Microsoft successfully assure their dominance of the microprocessor and software markets, or have they forgotten the golden rule: the customer is always right? Will their dominance melt like that of the earlier hi-tech darling: IBM?

SOURCES: Quotes from Kate Bertrand, 'Advertising a chip you'll never see', *Business Marketing* (February 1992), p. 19; and Richard Brandt, 'Intel: way out in front, but the footsteps are getting larger', *Business Week* (29 April 1991), pp. 88–9. See also Robert D. Hof, 'Inside Intel', *Business Week* (1 June 1992), pp. 86–94; Bertrand, 'Chip wars', *Business Marketing* (February 1992), pp. 16–18; Alan Deutschman, 'If they're gaining on you, innovate', *Fortune* (2 November 1992), pp. 56–61; Richard Brandt, 'Intel: what a tease – and what a strategy', *Business Week* (22 February 1993), p. 40; Louise Kehoe and Alan Cane, 'Chips down for PC partner', *Financial Times* (20 September 1994), p. 21; Louise Kehoe and Geoff Wheelwright, 'Breaking windows', *Financial Times* (4 October 1994), p. 16; 'High-tech brands: soap powder, with added logic', *The Economist* (6 December 1997); 'Beleaguered Microsoft: why Bill Gates should worry', *The Economist* (20 December 1997); 'Persecuting Bill', *The Economist* (20 December 1997); Louise Kehoe, 'Hard case for software', *Financial Times* (22 January 1988), p. 27.

goods directly from Procter & Gamble, and universities buy mainframe computers directly from IBM, Bull and so on.

RECIPROCITY. Business buyers often practise *reciprocity*, selecting suppliers that also buy from them. For example, a paper company might buy needed chemicals from a chemical company that in turn buys the company's paper.

> Shaken by European Airbus's success in the airliner market, market leader Boeing has started a worldwide review of its purchasing policies. They intend to match aircraft parts contracts to countries that buy Boeings. With an apparent eye on the Canadian government's purchase of search-and-rescue helicopters and Canadian Airlines International's 737 replacements, Boeing warned: 'Our Canadian business placement must understandably be market based, as it is elsewhere.[7]

LEASING. Business buyers are increasingly leasing equipment instead of buying it outright. Everything from printing presses to power plants, business jets to hay balers, and office copiers to off-shore drilling rigs. The biggest buyer of airliners in the world is not a large airline but GPA, a company based in Ireland which buys airliners to resell or lease. The lessee can gain a number of advantages, such as having more available capital, getting the seller's latest products, receiving

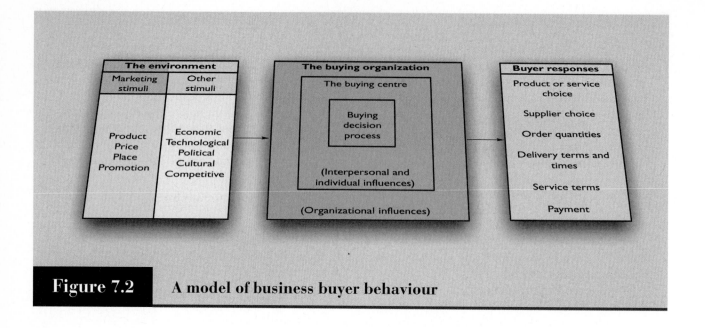

The environment		The buying organization	Buyer responses
Marketing stimuli	**Other stimuli**	**The buying centre**	Product or service choice
Product Price Place Promotion	Economic Technological Political Cultural Competitive	Buying decision process (Interpersonal and individual influences) (Organizational influences)	Supplier choice Order quantities Delivery terms and times Service terms Payment

Figure 7.2   **A model of business buyer behaviour**

better servicing and gaining some tax advantages. The lessor often ends up with a larger net income and the chance to sell to customers that might not have been able to afford outright purchase.

A Model of Business Buyer Behaviour

At the most basic level, marketers want to know how business buyers will respond to various marketing stimuli. Figure 7.2 shows a model of business buyer behaviour. In this model, marketing and other stimuli affect the buying organization and produce certain buyer responses. As with consumer buying, the marketing stimuli for business buying consist of the four Ps: product, price, place and promotion. Other stimuli include influential forces in the environment: economic, technological, political, cultural and competitive. These stimuli enter the organization and are turned into buyer responses: product or service choice; supplier choice; order quantities; and delivery, service and payment terms. In order to design good marketing-mix strategies, the marketer must understand what happens within the organization to turn stimuli into purchase responses.

Within the organization, buying activity consists of two main parts: the buying centre, made up of all the people involved in the buying decision, and the buying decision process. Figure 7.2 shows that the buying centre and the buying decision process are influenced by internal organizational, interpersonal and individual factors as well as by external environmental factors.

Business Buyer Behaviour

The model in Figure 7.2 suggests four questions about business buyer behaviour: What buying decisions do business buyers make? Who participates in the buying process? What are the strongest influences on buyers? How do business buyers make their buying decisions?

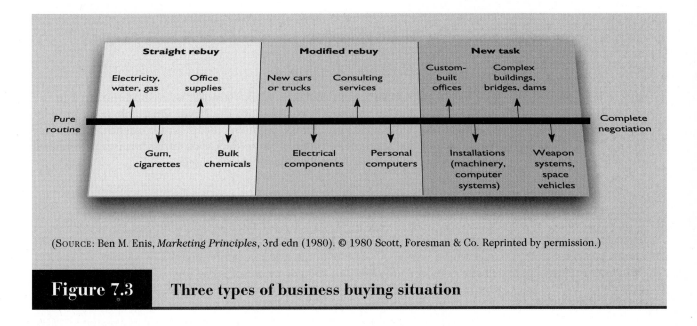

(SOURCE: Ben M. Enis, *Marketing Principles*, 3rd edn (1980). © 1980 Scott, Foresman & Co. Reprinted by permission.)

| **Figure 7.3** | **Three types of business buying situation** |

What Buying Decisions Do Business Buyers Make?

The business buyer faces a whole set of decisions in making a purchase. The number of decisions depends on the type of buying situation.

● *Main Types of Buying Situation*

There are three main types of buying situation.[8] At one extreme is the *straight rebuy*, which is a fairly routine decision. At the other extreme is the *new task*, which may call for thorough research. In the middle is the *modified rebuy*, which requires some research. (For examples, see Figure 7.3.)

STRAIGHT REBUY. In a **straight rebuy**, the buyer reorders something without any modifications. It is usually handled on a routine basis by the purchasing department. Based on past buying satisfaction, the buyer simply chooses from the various suppliers on its list. 'In' suppliers try to maintain product and service quality. They often propose automatic reordering systems so that the purchase agent will save reordering time. The 'out' suppliers try to offer something new or exploit dissatisfaction so that the buyer will consider them. 'Out' suppliers try to get their foot in the door with a small order and then enlarge their purchase share over time.

MODIFIED REBUY. In a **modified rebuy**, the buyer wants to modify product specifications, prices, terms or suppliers. The modified rebuy usually involves more decision participants than the straight rebuy. The 'in' suppliers may become nervous and feel pressured to put their best foot forward to protect an account. 'Out' suppliers may see the modified rebuy situation as an opportunity to make a better offer and gain new business.

NEW TASK. A company buying a product or service for the first time faces a **new task** situation. In such cases, the greater the cost or risk, the larger will be the number of decision participants and the greater their efforts to collect information. The new-task situation is the marketer's greatest opportunity and challenge.

straight rebuy
A business buying situation in which the buyer routinely reorders something without any modifications.

modified rebuy
A business buying situation in which the buyer wants to modify product specifications, prices, terms or suppliers.

new task
A business buying situation in which the buyer purchases a product or service for the first time.

The marketer not only tries to reach as many key buying influences as possible, but also provides help and information.

● Specific Buying Decisions

The buyer makes the fewest decisions in the straight rebuy and the most in the new-task decision. In the new-task situation, the buyer must decide on product specifications, suppliers, price limits, payment terms, order quantities, delivery times and service terms. The order of these decisions varies with each situation and different decision participants influence each choice.

● Systems Buying and Selling

systems buying
Buying a packaged solution to a problem and without all the separate decisions involved.

Many business buyers prefer to buy a packaged solution to a problem from a single seller. Called **systems buying**, this practice began with government buying of powerful weapons and communication systems. Instead of buying and putting all the components together, the government asked for bids from suppliers that would supply the components *and* assemble the package or system.

Sellers have increasingly recognized that buyers like this method and have adopted systems selling as a marketing tool.[9] Systems selling is a two-step process. First, the supplier sells a group of interlocking products: for example, the supplier sells not only glue, but also applicators and dryers. Second, the supplier sells a system of production, inventory control, distribution and other services to meet the buyer's need for a smooth-running operation.

Systems selling is a key business marketing strategy for winning and holding accounts. The contract often goes to the firm that provides the most complete system meeting the customer's needs. Consider the following:

> The Indonesian government requested bids to build a cement factory near Jakarta. An American firm's proposal included choosing the site, designing the cement factory, hiring the construction crews, assembling the materials and equipment and turning the finished factory over to the Indonesian government. A Japanese firm's proposal included all of these services, plus hiring and training workers to run the factory, exporting the cement through their trading companies and using the cement to build some needed roads and new office buildings in Jakarta. Although the Japanese firm's proposal cost more, it won the contract. Clearly the Japanese viewed the problem not as one of just building a cement factory (the narrow view of systems selling) but of running it in a way that would contribute to the country's economy. They took the broadest view of the customers' needs. This is true systems selling.

Who Participates in the Business Buying Process?

buying centre
All the individuals and units that participate in the business buying-decision process.

users
Members of the organization who will use the product or service; users often initiate the buying proposal and help define product specifications.

Who buys the goods and services needed by business oganizations? The decision-making unit of a buying organization is called its **buying centre**, defined as all the individuals and units that participate in the business decision-making process.[10]

The buying centre includes all members of the organization who play any of five roles in the purchase decision process.[11]

1. **Users.** Members of the organization who will use the product or service. In many cases, users initiate the buying proposal and help define product specifications.

Businesses are the dominant 'buyers' of business travel and luxury hotels but most promotions aim to attract 'users'.

2. **Influencers**. People who affect the buying decision. They often help define specifications and also provide information for evaluating alternatives. Technical personnel are particularly important influencers.

3. **Buyers**. People with formal authority to select the supplier and arrange terms of purchase. Buyers may help shape product specifications, but they play their most important role in selecting vendors and in negotiating. In more complex purchases, buyers might include high-level officers participating in the negotiations.

4. **Deciders**. People who have formal or informal power to select or approve the final suppliers. In routine buying, the buyers are often the deciders or at least the approvers.

5. **Gatekeepers**. People who control the flow of information to others. For example, purchasing agents often have authority to prevent salespersons from seeing users or deciders. Other gatekeepers include technical personnel and even personal secretaries.

The buying centre is not a fixed and formally identified unit within the buying organization. It is a set of buying roles assumed by different people for different purchases. Within the organization, the size and make-up of the buying centre will vary for different products and for different buying situations. For some routine purchases, one person – say, a purchasing agent – may assume all the buying centre roles and serve as the only person involved in the buying decision. For more complex purchases, the buying centre may include 20 or 30 people from different levels and departments in the organization. One study of business buying showed that the typical business equipment purchase involved seven people from three management levels representing four different departments.

influencers
People in an organizations buying centre who affect the buying decision; they often help define specifications and also provide information for evaluating alternatives

buyers
People in an organization's buying centre with formal authority to select the supplier and arrange terms of purchase.

deciders
People in the organization's buying centre who have formal or informal powers to select or approve the final suppliers.

gatekeepers
People in the organization's buying centre who control the flow of information to others.

The buying-centre concept presents a significant marketing challenge. The business marketer must learn who participates in the decision, each participant's relative influence and what evaluation criteria each decision participant uses. Consider the following example:

> Baxter sells disposable surgical gowns to hospitals. It tries to identify the hospital personnel involved in this buying decision. They turn out to be the purchasing manager, the operating room administrator and the surgeons. Each participant plays a different role. The vice-president of purchasing analyzes whether the hospital should buy disposable gowns or reusable gowns. If analysis favours disposable gowns, then the operating room administrator compares competing products and prices and makes a choice. This administrator considers the gown's absorbency, antiseptic quality, design and cost, and normally buys the brand that meets requirements at the lowest cost. Finally, surgeons affect the decision later by reporting their satisfaction or dissatisfaction with the brand.

The buying centre usually includes some obvious participants who are involved formally in the buying decision. For example, the decision to buy a corporate jet will probably involve the company's chief pilot, a purchasing agent, some legal staff, a member of top management and others formally charged with the buying decision. It may also involve less obvious, informal participants, some of whom may actually make or strongly affect the buying decision. Sometimes, even the people in the buying centre are not aware of all the buying participants. For example, the decision about which corporate jet to buy may actually be made by a corporate board member who has an interest in flying and knows a lot about aircraft. This board member may work behind the scenes to sway the decision. Many business buying decisions result from the complex interactions of ever-changing buying-centre participants.

What are the Main Influences on Business Buyers?

Business buyers are subject to many influences when they make their buying decisions. Some marketers assume that the strongest influences are economic. They think buyers will favour the supplier that offers the lowest price or the best product or the most service. They concentrate on offering strong economic benefits to buyers. However, business buyers actually respond to both economic and personal factors:

> It has not been fashionable lately to talk about relationships in business. We're told that it has to be devoid of emotion. We must be cold, calculating and impersonal. Don't you believe it! Relationships make the world go round. Business people are human and social as well as interested in economics and investments and salespeople need to appeal to both sides. Purchasers may claim to be motivated by intellect alone, but the professional salesperson knows that they run on both reason and emotion.[12]

When suppliers' offers are very similar, business buyers have little basis for strictly rational choice. Because they can meet organizational goals with any supplier, buyers can allow personal factors to play a larger role in their decisions. However, when competing products differ greatly, business buyers are more accountable for their choice and tend to pay more attention to economic factors.

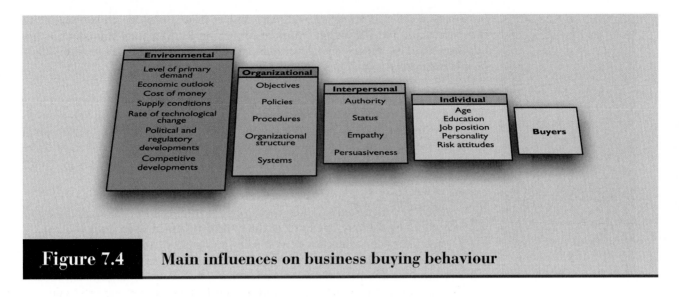

| **Figure 7.4** | **Main influences on business buying behaviour** |

Figure 7.4 lists various groups of influences on business buyers – environmental, organization, interpersonal and individual.[13]

● *Environmental Factors*

Business buyers are influenced heavily by factors in the current and expected *economic environment*, such as the level of primary demand, the economic outlook and the cost of money. As economic uncertainty rises, business buyers cut back on new investments and attempt to reduce their inventories.

An increasingly important environmental factor is shortages in key materials. Many companies are now more willing to buy and hold larger inventories of scarce materials to ensure adequate supply. Business buyers are also affected by technological, political and competitive developments in the environment. Culture and customs can strongly influence business buyer reactions to the marketer's behaviour and strategies, especially in the international marketing environment (see Marketing Highlight 7.2). The business marketer must watch these factors, determine how they will affect the buyer, and try to turn these challenges into opportunities.

● *Organizational Factors*

Each buying organization has its own objectives, policies, procedures, structure and systems, which must be understood by the business marketer. Questions such as these arise: How many people are involved in the buying decision? Who are they? What are their evaluative criteria? What are the company's policies and limits on its buyers? In addition, the business marketer should be aware of the following organizational trends in the purchasing area.

UPGRADED PURCHASING. Buying departments have often occupied a low position in the management hierarchy, even though they often manage more than half of the company's costs. In some industries, such as telecommunications, manufacturers buy in items approaching 80 per cent of total cost. With good reason many companies are upgrading their purchasing activities. Some companies have combined several functions – such as purchasing, inventory control, production scheduling and traffic – into a high-level function called *strategic materials management*. Buying departments in many multinational companies have responsibility for buying materials and services around the world. Many companies are offering higher compensation in order to attract top talent in the buying area. This means that business marketers must also upgrade their sales-people to match the quality of today's business buyers.[14]

CENTRALIZED PURCHASING. In companies consisting of many divisions with differing needs, much of the purchasing is carried out at the division level. Recently, however, some large companies have tried to centralize purchasing. Headquarters identifies materials purchased by several divisions and buys them centrally. Centralized purchasing gives the companies more purchasing clout, which can produce substantial savings.

> PepsiCo aims to save $100m a year, out of total costs of $2bn, by combining the buying power of their separate businesses. Paul Steele, their European vice-president of sales and marketing: 'When we went through the list it was surprising. For example, Pizza Hut buys an enormous quantity of cardboard for the boxes; Pepsi-Cola buys cardboard for soft drink trays. We're looking at whether we can leverage the sale.' They will try the same with buying flour, salt, spices, cooking oil and TV advertising air-time. 'The businesses developed very separately. We didn't have the scale to do this before, but it has suddenly become a very exciting proposition.'[15]

For the business marketer, this development means dealing with fewer, higher-level buyers. Instead of using regional sales forces to sell a large buyer's separate plants, the seller may use a *national account sales force* to service the buyer. For example, at Xerox, over 250 national account managers each handle one to five large national accounts with many scattered locations. The national account managers co-ordinate the efforts of an entire Xerox team – specialists, analysts, salespeople for individual products – to sell and service important national customers.[16] National account selling is challenging and demands both a high-level sales force and sophisticated marketing effort.

LONG-TERM CONTRACTS. Business buyers are increasingly seeking long-term contracts with suppliers. For example, GM wants to buy from fewer suppliers which are willing to locate close to its plants and produce high-quality components. Business marketers are also beginning to offer *electronic order interchange* systems to their customers. When using such systems, the seller places terminals hooked to the seller's computers in customers' offices. Then the customer can order needed items instantly by entering orders directly into the computer. The orders are transmitted automatically to the supplier. Many hospitals order directly from Baxter using order-taking terminals in their stockrooms. And many booksellers order from Follett's in this way.

Although buyers are seeking closer relations with suppliers, businesses do not always have each other's interests at heart. In all relationships there is a tension between the comfort of loyalty and the freedom to shop around. Economic and technological changes can make long-term business-to-business relationships inherently unstable.[17] The result is serial monogamy as firms switch between medium-term relationships.

EXTRANET EXCHANGES. The European Commission was worried that *electronic order interchanges* would reduce competition by tying together buyers and suppliers through expensive IT systems. New Internet developments are now limiting the threat. Using extranet exchanges, buyers post their detailed require-

Discussing the Issues

1. Identify the ways in which the fashion clothing market differs from the military uniform market.

2. Which of the main types of buying situation are represented by the following individual circumstances?

   ● BMW's purchase of computers that go in cars and adjust engine performance to changing driving conditions.

   ● Volkswagen's purchase of spark plugs for its line of Jettas.

   ● Honda's purchase of light bulbs for a new Legend model.

3. How would a marketer of office equipment identify the buying centre for a law firm's purchase of dictation equipment for each of its partners?

4. Discuss the principal environmental factors that would affect the purchase of radar speed detectors by national and local police forces.

5. Industrial products companies have advertised products to the general public that consumers are not able to buy. How does this strategy help a company sell products to resellers?

6. Assume you are selling a fleet of fork-lift trucks to be used by a large distribution and warehousing firm. The drivers of the fork-lift trucks need the latest technology that provides comfort, makes driving easy and improves manoeuvrability. This means more expensive trucks that are more profitable for you. The fleet buyer, however, wants to buy established (not necessarily latest) technology that gives the highest productivity. Who might be in the buying centre? How might you meet the varying needs of these participants?

Applying the Concepts

1. Take your college/university as an example of a business customer for books and other educational materials. Imagine that you are a representative from a publisher who intends to establish sales to the college/university. How might you use the model of business buyer behaviour to help you develop a strategy for marketing effectively to this customer? How useful is the model? What (if any) are the limitations? Are there different levels of customers in this situation (e.g. the library as a buying centre; course team members who agree on the textbooks to recommend for student adoption and library stocks;

   the individual tutor who chooses recommended textbooks and requests the library to stock; or the college/university bookshop)? How might you deal with these different levels of customer?

2. Make a list of the key factors that a local government institution or agency might consider when deciding to purchase new coffee-making machines for users in its offices. Remembering how government buyers make their buying decisions, suggest a scenario that you, as a potential supplier, would use to sell to this institutional buyer.

References

1. Excerpts from 'Major sales: who really does the buying', by Thomas V. Bonoma (May–June 1982). Copyright © 1982 by the President and Fellows of Harvard College; all rights reserved. See also Scott Ticer, 'Why Gulfstream's rivals are gazing up in envy', *Business Week* (16 February 1987), pp. 66–7; David Boggis, 'Consolidation is the key to economy and progress', *Financial Times* (2 September 1992), p. XIII; Chuck Hawkins, 'Can a new bird get Gulfstream flying?', *Business Week* (15 February 1993), pp. 114–16; Roland Rudd and Robert Peston, 'Tiny Rowland faces his day of reckoning', *Financial Times* (31 August 1994), p. 17; Paul Betts, 'Weighed down by high-flying image', *Financial Times*

(28 September 1994), p. 24; Robert Peston, 'Rowland to quit Lonrho board', *Financial Times* (4 November 1994), p. 1; Penny Hughes, 'The $600 million gamble', *BusinessAge* (November 1994), p. 30B; Ian Verchère, 'Long-haul luxury from bombardier', *The European* (4–10 November 1994), p. 30.

2. This definition is adapted from Frederick E. Webster, Jr and Yoram Wind, *Organizational Buying Behavior* (Englewood Cliffs, NJ: Prentice Hall, 1972), p. 2.

3. For discussions of similarities and differences in consumer and business marketing, see Edward F. Fern and James R. Brown, 'The industrial/consumer marketing dichotomy: a

case of insufficient justification', *Journal of Marketing* (Fall 1984), pp. 68–77; Ron J. Kornakovich, 'Consumer methods work for business marketing: yes; no', *Marketing News* (21 November 1988), pp. 4, 13–14.

4.   See William S. Bishop, John L. Graham and Michael H. Jones, 'Volatility of derived demand in industrial markets and its management implications', *Journal of Marketing* (Spring 1984), pp. 68–77.

5.   'That sinking feeling', *The Economist* (17 January 1998), pp. 71–2; Sheila McNutty, 'Malaysia seeks Boeing delay', *Financial Times* (19 January 1988); John Ridding and Michael Skainker, 'Aircraft makers' confidence dented', *Financial Times* (20 January 1998); Alkman Grantisas, 'Scant Shelter,' *Far Eastern Economic Review* (22 January 1998), pp. 54–5.

6.   See James C. Anderson and James A. Narus, 'Value-based segmentation, targeting and relationship-building in business markets', ISBM Report No.12 – 1989, The Institute for the Study of Business Markets, Pennsylvania State University, University Park, PA, 1989; Lawrence A. Crosby, Kenneth R. Evans and Deborah Cowles, 'Relationship quality and services selling: an interpersonal influence perspective', *Journal of Marketing* (July 1990), pp. 68–81; Barry J. Farber and Joyce Wycoff, 'Relationships: six steps to success', *Sales and Marketing Management* (April 1992), pp. 50–8; Kevin Done, 'Harmony under the bonnet', *Financial Times* (8 November 1994), p. 17.

7.   Bernard Simon and Paul Betts, 'Boeing may tie component deals to aircraft sales', *Financial Times* (8 November 1994), p. 1.

8.   Patrick J. Robinson, Charles W. Faris and Yoram Wind, *Industrial Buying Behavior and Creative Marketing* (Boston: Allyn & Bacon, 1967). See also Erin Anderson, Weyien Chu and Barton Weitz, 'Industrial purchasing: an empirical exploration of the buyclass framework', *Journal of Marketing* (July 1987), pp. 71–86.

9.   For more on systems selling, see Robert R. Reeder, Edward G. Brierty and Betty H. Reeder, *Industrial Marketing: Analysis, planning and control* (Englewood Cliffs, NJ: Prentice Hall, 1991), pp. 264–7.

10. Webster and Wind, *Organizational Buying Behavior*, op.cit., p. 6. For more reading on buying centres, see Bonoma, 'Major sales', op. cit.; and Donald W. Jackson, Jr, Janet E. Keith and Richard K. Burdick, 'Purchasing agents' perceptions of industrial buying center influence: a situational approach', *Journal of Marketing* (Fall 1984), pp. 75–83.

11. Webster and Wind, *Organizational Buying Behavior*, op.cit., pp. 78–80.

12. Clifton J. Reichard, 'Industrial selling: beyond price and persistence', *Harvard Business Review* (Marrch–April 1985), p. 128.

13. Webster and Wind, *Organizational Buying Behavior*, op.cit., pp. 33–7.

14. Peter W. Turnbull, 'Organisational buying behaviour', in Michael J. Baker (ed.), *The Marketing Book* (London: Heinemann, 1994), pp. 147–64.

15. Diane Summers, 'Living life to the max', *Financial Times* (29 September 1994), p. 15.

16. Thayer C. Taylor, 'Xerox's sales force learns a new game', *Sales and Marketing Management* (1 July 1985), pp. 48–51.

17. Keith Blois, 'Are business-to-business relationships inherently unstable?', *Journal of Marketing Management*, 13, 5 (1997), pp. 367–79.

18. 'To byte the hand that feeds', The Economist (17 January 1998), pp. 75–6.

19. Michiyo Nakamoto, 'Building networks', *Financial Times* (13 November 1992), p. 8; Richard Gourlay, 'From fat to lean enterprises', *Financial Times* (8 November 1994), p. 11; Carlos Cordon, 'Doing justice to just in time', *Financial Times* (9 November 1994), p. 14.

20. Bonoma, 'Major sales', op.cit., p. 114. See also Ajay Kohli, 'Determinants of influence in organizational buying: a contingency approach', *Journal of Marketing* (July 1989), pp. 50–65.

21. Malcom Brown, 'Signed, sealed, delivered', *Marketing Business* (June 1992), pp. 30–2.

22. Robinson, Faris and Wind, *Industrial Buying Behavior*, op.cit., p. 14.

23. See 'What buyers really want', *Sales and Marketing Management* (October 1989), p. 30.

24. Donald R. Lehmann and John O'Shaughnessy, 'Decision criteria used in buying different categories of products', *Journal of Purchasing and Materials Management* (Spring 1982), pp. 9–14.

25. General H. Norman Schwartzkopf, *It Doesnít Take a Hero* (London: Bantam, 1992); General Sir Peter de la Billiere, *Storm Command* (London: HarperCollins, 1992); Andrew Bolgar, 'Diversifying out of lumpiness', *Financial Times* (2 November 1994), p. 26.

Case 7

Troll-AEG

Javier Sarda, Franscesc Parès and Lluìs G. Renart*

J. FELIU DE LA PEÑA, SA (JFP) is a Spanish manufacturer of electric lamps[1] known for its modern Troll products. In the late afternoon of 21 January 1992 Miguel Tey Feliu de la Peña, JFP's managing director, was reflecting on the reciprocal commercial distribution contracts to be signed the next day with the managers of AEG's Technical Lighting Business Area (AEG Aktiengesellschaft Fachbereich Lichttechnik, or AEG-LT) from Germany.

The first JFP 'mirror' contract granted AEG a non-exclusive right to distribute its products in Germany. The second granted JFP and its subsidiary Troll-France a non-exclusive right to distribute AEG products in Spain and France. Miguel Tey did not doubt that the contracts needed signing, but reflected on several questions:

> First, when I review the decisions that have been taken up to this point in time, I wonder if we are doing the right thing in entering into this type of agreement or whether it would have been better to continue following our own fully autonomous growth path, as we have done until now. At the same time, I wonder whether AEG is the best partner for us. Also, when I reread the two contracts, I wonder if something is missing or should not be there, or whether any of the sections should be reworded.
>
> Second, if we accept everything done until now and do sign the contracts, then there are two major questions with regard to our immediate future that must be answered: What must we decide and do to ensure that this new reciprocal relationship between Troll and AEG works, and works well? And finally, how will all this end up? In other words, where will our company be three, five or ten years from now? Will these agreements still be in full force?

No doubt because of the obvious difference in size between JFP and AEG, someone had recently said, only half jokingly: 'In no time at all, we'll all be wearing AEG T-shirts.'

J. Feliu de la Peòa, SA (JFP)

Mr Julio Feliu de la Peña, grandfather of the brothers Xavier and Miguel Tey Feliu de la Peña, started manufacturing 'classic' design lamps in 1929, in Barcelona. In 1974 Miguel and Xavier became owners of JFP, which then operated from ground floor premises very close to the centre of Barcelona. In the same year Nordart Industria, SA offered them the possibility of selling its products marketed under the Troll brand. It was a new lighting system made up by spot projectors, power tracks and adapters (the adapter being the part

* IESE, University of Navarra, Barcelona-Madrid

linking the spot projector to the power-carrying track). Miguel saw that the product had a well-presented, modern design, and he offered to buy Nordart's entire output if given exclusive sales rights for Spain. Nordart Industria, SA was a small factory without any sales force that was badly stung when a distributor had copied its product and left it in the lurch. Joaquim Masò, the company's owner, accepted the appointment of JFP as its sole agent after establishing that JFP would operate with a gross margin of 30 per cent.

By 1977, their Troll sales had increased to Pta130 million. Miguel realized that 'the future was Troll'. In 1978 Joaquim Masó and the Tey brothers agreed to merge both companies. During the next decade, the company's sales grew at slightly more than 50 per cent per annum. The workforce increased from 25 to 100 employees and the company became market leader in Spain in this type of accent lighting elements. JFP's success is attributable to the changes in the distribution channel and the continuous improvement and redesign of its products. JFP ceased selling through traditional (normally classic design) lamp retailers and pioneered the sale of spotlights and down-lights through electrical goods wholesalers-stockists.

Miguel Tey considered that this change of distribution policy had been only partly successful. He soon realized his limited negotiating power with these wholesalers. To counteract this, Miguel sought an alliance with non-competing companies whose products sold through the same electrical goods stores. He managed to persuade the general managers of a wire company, a transformer company and a cable fastener company to join in an alliance. A network of self-employed representatives sold the products of all four manufacturers. All four manufacturers placed their products on consignment in the representative's warehouse. The representative would then sell and deliver the goods, sending the delivery note to each manufacturer. In Spain, this kind of wholesaler-stockist sells mostly to contractors specializing in electrical installations, either in new buildings or in building refurbishing jobs. Most of their sales were 'counter' sales, made on the spot to contractors who came to their outlet with a list of their immediate needs and would take the goods with them. In exchange for these functions, the representative received a commission agreed upon separately with each one of the four manufacturing companies. Thirteen joint 'branches' covered practically the entire Spanish market.

> And all that with just paying a commission – that is, a variable cost – and with a minimum investment in stock in all thirteen warehouses. An important point to remember is that thanks to our pioneering role in selling accent lighting elements in Spain, JFP's margins were very high. Our sale price to the electrical goods store was between 2.5 and 3 times our manufacturing cost!

In time JFP became the unofficial leader of the network as the representatives mainly followed Miguel Tey's lead. JFP's young general manager had managed to win them over through a combination of an extremely cordial personal relationship, an excellent service from his company, a product range with skyrocketing sales and a 10 per cent commission. The other three companies paid them 5 per cent commission or less.

Range Changes

Design changes helped JFP's success. Originally each lamp model and variants, of which there were about 50, came in 16 colours and consisted of several parts that were specific to each model. In total, there were about 3,200 different stock-keeping units (skus). Miguel reduced the colour range from 16 to 4 (white, black, gold and stainless steel) and redesigned the lamps. This innovation made the four basic parts of the lighting systems manufactured fully interchangeable, which allowed the number of skus to be cut down to less than 200. This produced a dramatic increase in turnover for warehouses in the logistics chain for JFP and its immediate customers.

Miguel also implemented significant changes in the design process of its lighting elements. By 1985 Miguel had decided that he needed to create an aesthetic consistency and identifying style in his lighting element designs and started to commission original designs from two freelance industrial designers. He wanted his lighting elements to be immediately recognizable.

The combination of pioneering accent lighting in Spain (with downlights, spots and tracks), the network of 'branches' made up of the 13 independent representatives, a well-designed product range and ample margins turned the company into one of the most profitable in Spain in this industry. Forecast sales for 1989 were about Pta1.5 billion, with net income of about Pta400 million and a market share between 25 and 30 per cent of indoor accent lighting elements.

Recruitment of Javier Rocasalbas

Faced with a strong increase in demand, the company no longer had sufficient capacity to supply all the orders. Furthermore, Miguel was in serious danger of being overwhelmed by the increasing complexity of the company's management. Consequently, in 1988 he decided to recruit Javier Rocasalbas as general manager. Miguel became managing director and his brother Xavier became president. Javier Rocasalbas was 40 years old. He had graduated as an industrial engineer, but his early work experience was in engineering production. Before joining JFP, he had worked in a plastics factory where, for the first time, his duties went beyond the technical.

Rocasalbas realized that, although the products were aesthetically excellent, their technical quality was poor. The electromechanical aspects had been neglected to a considerable extent, which led to difficulties when attempting to assemble the lamps on an industrial scale. In 1989 he increased the design team by recruiting Carlos Galán, an industrial engineer and electromechanical designer, as its manager. A designer specialized in mechanical functions and a draughtsman was also recruited to the team.

By the end of 1991, the design and quality department had between 12 and 14 people responsible for product performance, compliance with electrical safety standards, and aesthetic quality of the products as individual items and as parts of the entire collection. The company changed from a design process in which the cost price was known only at the end, to one where a cost price was set before starting the design work.

The 'star' products in 1988 were the fixed, low-voltage built-in downlight in black or white and the swivelling ball-spot. They were relatively simple products to design, manufacture, assemble and install at the point of use. They were standard products of average quality, usually bought by electricians or electrical contractors for easy installation in private homes, shops, offices and so forth. The 'branches' – the 13 sales representatives with their own warehouse – sold indiscriminately and massively, without distinguishing between different types of customer. JFP published a single price list, which carried a 45 per cent discount for all customers.

Tensions in the Range

From 1988, competition in Spain became much fiercer. A large number of lamp manufacturers appeared, flooding the market with lighting elements that had designs very similar to Troll's. Some even used Troll products to take the photographs for some competitor's catalogue. By the end of 1991, between 25 and 30 Spanish lamp manufacturers offered virtually identical, standard accent lighting elements. The resulting price war severely eroded sales margins from about 30 per cent in 1988 to about 15 per cent in 1991.

Miguel's response was to decide that if Troll products sold well in Spain, they should also be successful in France, which had accounted for almost Pta4 million of the company's exports. Always impulsive and quick off the mark, Miguel went to Lyon, bought an old building near the high-speed train (TGV) station and recruited Josep Sitjà as general manager of Troll-France. A Catalan by birth, he had worked until that time as an electrical contractor in Marseilles.

By 1988 JFP was exporting Pta46 million worth of products to France, but part of this export figure included the start-up stock of finished product shipped to Lyon. The standard products also had serious difficulties in the French market. The quality was not right, the price was not right and they were not certified as conforming to the French standards. However, aesthetically they were very well accepted and that could become the decisive factor differentiating Troll lamps.

It was very difficult to achieve a significant level of sales in France without offering an integral, complete and coherent product range. The Troll range was solely interior accent lighting elements: that is, tracks and spots, down-lights and suspended fluorescent lights self-connected by jacks. The company had no built-in fluorescent panels (used mainly in offices), industrial lights (for lighting factories) or any type of lighting elements for installation and use outdoors, to light public highways, parks and gardens, tunnels, sports facilities and so on.

Miguel and Javier's reaction to this setback was a firm resolve to gain a presence in the European market, and to do this by changing their product range, slowly phasing out their standard products and starting to design, manufacture and sell technical architectural lighting elements. Rocasalbas explains:

> We considered that the more sophisticated features of the new generation of lighting elements we wanted to design and launch onto the market would be more difficult for our direct competitors, most of which were small companies, to imitate. We were up against companies which were limited not only by their technical skills but also by their financial possibilities, as an 'architectural' lighting element of this type may mean investing about Pta20 million in design, tooling, moulds, etc.
>
> It was rather an intuitive change; I don't think we really knew what we were letting ourselves in for. Or, at least, at that time, we were not aware that the change in focus of the product range would also necessarily involve a drastic change in the type of final customer, in distribution channels, and in the marketing resources to be used to promote our products.

When they launched the first new-generation lighting elements on the market, the electrical goods wholesaler-stockholders neither bought nor distributed technical architectural lighting products. These were too sophisticated, designed for specific applications and slow-selling, and their installation required a prior analysis to ensure their match with specific lighting needs, circumstances or environments.

The Prescribers
Technical architectural lighting was promoted by persuading the prescribers to use them. Within the field of technical lighting, a prescriber could be an

architect, an interior decorator, a shop window designer, an engineer or technician specializing in lighting, an engineering firm, and so on. When faced with a lighting requirement (a hotel, a stadium, a modern shop, a hospital, etc.), the prescriber studied the lighting needs (light intensity, colorimetry, possible combinations within the surroundings, etc.) and decided the type, quantity, characteristics and location of each lighting point to be installed in order to obtain the desired decorative and lighting results. In the case of new buildings, it was vital to incline the prescriber in favour of a certain light brand and model while the architectural design was still on the drawing-board. Rocasalbas explains:

> The prescriber was a new factor to be reckoned with during the sales process carried out by JFP ... Until then, we had not taken any steps to influence their decisions because, given the relative simplicity of our products, it was simply not necessary ... We realized that the image they had of us – if they had any at all – would be something like that of SEAT, when it was manufacturing the '600', while now we had decided to make Mercedes-Benz! ... Perhaps at that time we might have given other strategic responses to our competitors, such as trying to cut them short by lowering prices or creating a second 'fighting' brand name but the fact is we consciously didn't. This does not mean, however, that we did not fight hard to defend our position in the standard product market, as we were fully aware that the bulk of our sales were precisely composed – and, at the close of 1991, they still are – of these standard products.

Meanwhile the Madrid and Barcelona representatives had secretly come to an agreement in 1988 to propose a change in their role. They wanted to be fully independent and exclusive distributors in their geographical area, buying set quantities and reselling the product on their own account, thus earning a margin instead of a commission. The proposal had a mixed reception from the four manufacturers in the alliance. The transformer manufacturer accepted the proposed change, but the cable manufacturer not only rejected the proposal but also cancelled the agency agreement with them.

Rocasalbas turned down the proposal but continued to work with them, trying to get them to start promoting to prescribers while continuing to sell the standard lighting elements. To help them they took on four middle-aged, well-groomed women (two in Madrid and two in Barcelona). These women would start to contact prescribers, introducing them to the company and telling them that JFP was entering the technical architectural lighting market. Said Rocasalbas:

> We were not yet out 'project hunting'. But we soon realized that 'good grooming' was not enough. We had to be able to solve the prescribers' problem or at least to be able to provide them with all the necessary means for them to solve it themselves. This included providing prescribers with all the necessary technical data and free product samples, and having a showroom where they could handle the lights and test lighting effects.
>
> The selling process was very complex because the final decision on the light brand and model to be installed depends not only on the prescriber but also on the contractor installing the entire electrical and lighting system and, in the final analysis, on the building's owner, as the person footing the bill.

JFP managed slowly to penetrate the technical architectural lighting market, selling by promoting and carrying out projects for the prescriber. However, in 1990, this market only accounted for about 5 per cent of JFP's total sales, and marketing and sales costs had increased substantially.

To speed up the change process, in 1991 JFP decided to terminate their relationship with the Barcelona and Madrid representatives and open a sales office with showroom. Its Barcelona branch – responsible for promotion and sales through Catalonia – had two sales teams. One team of three full-time employed salesmen covered the electrical goods wholesaler-stockists, while the other focused on speciality retailers, mainly selling them the more 'standard' product range. By the end of 1991, the other Barcelona-Catalonia sales team targeted the prescription market. It had three salaried salesmen who visited prospective customers and another person who drew up the design projects. The first team was much more profitable than the second as, at the end of 1991, sales of standard products continued to account for about 80 per cent of the company's total sales.

There was a possibility that, in the future, JFP would open similar fully owned branches in other large Spanish cities. The decision would depend on two factors: first, the degree of sales and financial success achieved by the two JFP branches already operating (Barcelona and Madrid);and second, the current 'old' representatives' attitude and behaviour. They had to show their willingness and effectiveness in promoting the new generation of architectural technical lighting products.

At the end of 1991, Javier Rocasalbas commented:

> Perhaps I'm wrong, but I think that even the minimally observant person had realized that lighting in houses and apartments, offices, shops, public areas, etc., had become increasingly sophisticated. Indeed, lighting was becoming an increasingly important part of the building's or premises' aesthetics. The challenge for us, then, is to *give* Troll lamps the technical capacity to contribute lighting solutions, on the one hand, and to be able to integrate themselves aesthetically with their surroundings, on the other hand. But we also have to explain this to prescribers, without forgetting to 'close the loop', that is, acting actively and positively on the contractor and on the building's owner or his purchasing manager. Any one of these people, at any particular time, can act for or against a type, brand or model of lamp. It is crucial to identify new projects at an early stage, in order to mature the final decision in our favour. This selling and 'maturing' process can take several months, with a significant investment in time. And even with all that, we only manage to get one out of every ten projects we bid for! To put it another way, when we 'mature' a project, we are not selling 'lighting elements'. We are selling 'a particular lighting solution'.

In 1991 the company had spent a total of about Pta100 million in advertising expenses, brochures and product catalogues, and attending trade fairs. This amount includes the cost of similar expenses by Troll-France, SA.

Internationalization

In mid-1990 Philippe Martinez became Troll-France, SA's new general manager. He was of Spanish descent, but was very knowledgeable about the French lighting market. He quickly established a team of six salaried sales reps selling only Troll products. They had two tasks: to 'sell in' to the wholesaler-stockists and to promote to prescribers. As in Spain, they never sold directly to contractors or to end customers.

By the end of 1991, JFP re-evaluated its French venture. Troll-France had used Pta250 million start-up funds and between 1988 and 1991 had had Pta120 million. 'From a strictly economic point of view, the economic effort undertaken in France was highly questionable,' commented Miguel Tey. 'But,' he continued, 'if we had not taken the good (even if expensive) decision to go out of Spain at the time the Spanish economy was buoyant, we would find ourselves in a difficult position today, when the Spanish market is stagnant.'

The Contacts and Negotiations with AEG

Dr Kappler of AEG made contact with JFP in April 1990. AEG belongs to the Daimler-Benz Group. AEG-LT specialized in manufacturing lighting elements, particularly fluorescent strip lighting. Its product range included almost all categories of technical lighting for indoors or outdoors, the only exception being accent lighting. Its sales were Pta23 billion in 1990, two-thirds indoor-lighting elements and the remainder outdoor lighting.

From the start, Dr Kappler's proposal was crystal-clear, in that he was offering JFP a double contract for reciprocal distribution. AEG-LT did not have a range of technical decorative indoor accent lighting elements. Its present customers in Germany were asking for this type of lighting element, but they did not want to develop this new line themselves as the investment required would be too large. They preferred an agreement with a company like JFP that had already developed such a product line. The German company's managers had been watching the development of JFP since 1987, mainly at the international trade fairs, and considered that the company was following a line that could be interesting for them.

Initially, JFP's management, especially Miguel, was very wary of starting discussions. The early contacts were fairly informal: visits to each other's factory, lunches together, and so on. However, they picked up pace and consolidated significantly when Dr Kappler transferred to another area and Dr Herbert Willmy became the business area's new president. Until then, Dr Willmy had been the area's marketing and sales director. 'Willmy is overwhelmingly straightforward and clear. He is a person who immediately wins you over with his humanity and honesty,' reports Rocasalbas.

The negotiator for AEG was Willmy in person. The negotiators for JFP were Miguel Tey and Javier Rocasalbas, who explains: 'The negotiation was very much based on the human relationship between both parties and was by no means plain sailing because Miguel had difficulties in following the English.'

Apparently AEG-LT's managers were attracted by JFP's advanced and original design, good in-house and subcontract industrial production capacity, and good range of indoor accent lighting elements – all in an effectively managed and economically sound company. Rocasalbas commented:

> I think that they were aware that there was only 'an embryo' AEG distributor in Spain and France. However, even so, we were perhaps the best distributor available to them.
>
> Sometimes, the negotiations were even fun. For example, sometimes we were wary and even expressed fears that, should we sign an agreement with AEG-LT, somehow we would be putting ourselves in their power and that 'if they sneezed, we could catch a double pneumonia'. On these occasions, in order to get the negotiations out of

the rut, Willmy suggested that we do a kind of role-playing, challenging us to put ourselves in his place, as if Miguel and I were the managers of the AEG-LT business area, and try to identify decisions or actions that could harm JFP. As soon as we said something, each time Willmy would come up with the defensive or protective countermeasure that JFP could take, thus effectively knocking down all our objections. Willmy caught on very quickly to JFP's way of operating and doing business.

The possibility of obtaining a high-volume and almost instantaneous distribution of Troll lighting elements in Germany, through AEG-LT's sales network of about 70 sales engineers attracted JFP. Also, the link with the Daimler-Benz Group, and through them Deutsche Bank, could lead to 'captive' or induced sales. The other companies in the Group presumably gave purchasing priority to AEG-LT. They also hoped that their association with AEG-LT would be a decisive factor in helping them rapidly to obtain the 'VDE' certifications in Germany for their lighting elements. In addition, wherever AEG had subsidiaries in Europe, JFP could sell through them its accent lighting elements. However, if JFP managers considered that some or any of AEG's subsidiaries were not adequate for this task, they could freely choose any other distributor or marketing channel.

JFP also saw big advantages in distributing AEG-LT's products in Spain and France:

Obviously, the AEG brand, and its German origin, count for a lot. We realised that AEG-LT's products would be positioned in the high-quality, high-price segment in Spain, so perhaps we might not achieve high sales volumes or high margins for JFP as importers-distributors. However, it was clear to us that the 'partnership' with AEG-LT would give prestige to JFP in Spain and would help us consolidate the image of the Troll products and our image as a company. This would help us to gain easier access to prescribers.

Also, it would obviously help us complete the product range we could offer in France and Spain. Now, we would be able to quote virtually all the lighting elements needed for an entire new building or for a complete architectural project. In other words, we would have a complete product range, and we could suggest a solution for any technical lighting need, in the broadest sense.

Rocasalbas expected that distributing AEG-LT lighting elements in Spain and France would not require any more salespeople, but would need higher stocks and more warehouse space. Negotiating the agreement had not been without its problems and there had even been moments when it seemed that negotiations would break down. One of them concerned setting each company's sales targets and purchase commitments for the other company's products. Another difficulty appeared when Miguel Tey said that he would not stop supplying Troll lamps to Ulrich Settler, an electrical contractor with a retail store in Stuttgart. He had been JFP's importer-distributor since 1989 and had bought about DM1 million worth in 1991. Miguel did not want to lose this sales volume and thought it would be wise to keep Settler on, just in case the agreement with AEG did not happen or did not work out properly.

Reflections before the Signing

Everything seemed taken care of, but there were still a number of points that worried Miguel. On one hand, there was the 'big guy will eat the little guy' complex. He felt that if AEG's purchases were to attain very high volumes, the Germans would have too much power over the Catalans and would end up taking them over. Was this a real danger? How could he prevent it? Another point was that he did not know to what extent he should commit himself to this alliance. Should it be a purely commercial alliance or should it include other aspects? How could they get maximum benefit from the alliance? What other synergies were there that might be yet untapped? He also wondered what he should do with Settler, the German distributor, and whether AEG had any kind of 'hidden agenda'.

It was late afternoon on 21 January 1991 when Miguel got up, went to his desk and started to read, once again, the contracts that had to be signed the next day. It seemed to him that for both companies, the 'Spain sells to Germany' flow or relationship was much more important than the 'Germany sells to Spain and France' relationship. Miguel estimated the weighting of the former as 90 and that of the latter at perhaps only 10.

QUESTIONS

1. What are the chief strengths and weaknesses of the Catalan company? How and why did they change over time?

2. What were the vital strategic shifts of JFP and what stimulated them?

3. What are the roles in the buying centre for lamps towards the end of the case? How does JFP seek to influence people in the buying process?

4. How does the market vary across Europe? What mistakes were made in Spain and France?

5. What is JFP looking for in its joint ventures?

6. Would you recommend the company to sign the deal with AEG-LT?

8

Market Information and Marketing Research

CHAPTER OBJECTIVES

After reading this chapter, you should be able to:

- Explain the importance of information to the company.
- Define the marketing information system and discuss its parts.
- Describe the four steps in the marketing research process.
- Compare the advantages and disadvantages of various methods of collecting information.
- Discuss the main methods for estimating current market demand.
- Explain specific techniques that companies use to forecast future demand.

Preview Case

Qantas: Taking Off in Tomorrow's Market

QANTAS, AUSTRALIA'S INTERNATIONAL AIRLINE, WAS experiencing a demand bonanza. Its market area in the Pacific Basin contained some of the fastest-growing economies in the world – including Australia, China, Japan and the newly industrializing countries of Hong Kong, Malaysia, Singapore, South Korea, Taiwan and Thailand. The area's growth in air travel far exceeded world averages. Industry forecasts suggest that Pacific Basin air travel would grow

at 10–14 per cent per year through 1998. By the year 2000 the area will have a 40 per cent share of all international air passenger traffic.

Such explosive growth presents a huge opportunity for Qantas and the other airlines serving the Pacific Basin. However, it also presents some serious headaches. To take *advantage* of the growing demand, Qantas must first *forecast* it accurately and prepare to *meet* it. Air-travel demand has many dimensions. Qantas must forecast how many and what kinds of people will be travelling, where they will want to go and when. It must project total demand as well as demand in each specific market it intends to serve. And Qantas must estimate what share of this total demand it can capture under alternative marketing strategies and in various competitive circumstances. Moreover, it must forecast demand not just for next year, but also for the next two years, five years and even further into the future.

Forecasting air-travel demand is no easy task. A host of factors affect how often people will travel and where they will go. To make accurate demand forecasts, Qantas must first anticipate changes in the factors that influence demand: worldwide and country-by-country economic conditions, demographic characteristics, population growth, political developments, technological advances, competitive activity and many other factors. Qantas has little control over many of these factors.

Demand can shift quickly and dramatically. For example, relative economic growth and political stability in Japan, Australia and the other Pacific Basin countries have caused a virtual explosion of demand for air travel there. Ever-increasing numbers of tourists from around the world are visiting these areas. In Australia, for instance, foreign tourism more than doubled between 1984 and 1988, and could triple between 1988 and the year 2000. Also, people from the Pacific Basin countries are themselves travelling more. For example, almost 12 million Japanese took holidays abroad in 1996, a 10 per cent increase over the previous year. Pampered business travellers bolstered the profitability of airlines in the region, but most new travellers are non-business people. By the turn of the century fewer than one in five passengers worldwide will be flying for business reasons – and many of those will be sitting in the economy section. Forecasting demand in the face of such drastic shifts can be difficult. There was also talk about southern Asia's boom going to bust. China's regaining Hong Kong had gone smoothly, but there were warning signals that the economies of some of the newly industrialized countries in the region were over heating. What if the bubble bursts?

To make things even more complicated, Qantas must forecast more than just demand. The airline must also anticipate the many factors that can affect its ability to meet that demand. For example, what airport facilities will be available and how will this affect Qantas? Will there be enough skilled labour to staff and maintain its aircraft? In the Pacific Basin, as demand has skyrocketed, the support system has not. A shortage of runways and airport terminal space already limits the number of flights Qantas can schedule. As a result, Qantas may decide to buy fewer but larger planes. Fewer planes would require fewer crews, and larger planes could hold more passengers at one time, which might make flights more profitable.

Competition in the region is hotting up too. Efficient non-Asian carriers, such as American Airlines, British Airways, United and Virgin, are attacking the region's markets and slashing fares in the process. Meanwhile, new local competitors, such as Taiwan's EVA Airways and Malaysia's Air Asia, are cutting into the market. Singapore Airlines and Cathay Pacific are two of the world's most profitable airlines and are fighting to hold on to their strong positions in the market. Singapore Airlines already has 62 aircraft including 42 Boeing 747 jumbos. It plans to buy at least 50 more jets – all 747s or large wide-body Airbuses.

Qantas bases many important decisions on its forecasts. Perhaps the most important decision involves aircraft purchases. To meet burgeoning demand, Qantas knows that it will need more planes. But how many more planes? At about A$200 million for each new Boeing 747-400, ordering even a few too many planes can be very costly. On the other hand, if Qantas buys too few planes, it has few short-run solutions. It usually takes about two years to get delivery of a new plane. If Qantas overestimates demand by even a few percentage points, it will have costly overcapacity. If it underestimates demand, it could miss out on profit opportunities and disappoint customers who prefer to fly Qantas, resulting in long-term losses of sales and goodwill. Airlines have got these numbers badly wrong in the past, resulting in thousands of redundant jets parked in the deserts of the United States.

Besides rapid growth, Qantas needs to know about the changing nature of demand in the region. The declining proportion of business passengers means airlines are fighting harder for them, by offering not just cheaper fares but also extra service. In Europe, where the battle for the business traveller is well developed, Lufthansa has completed a huge study to find out what its business traveller wants. More leg and elbow room said most travellers, but others want separate check-ins and passport controls. Fine, but all these options cost money, so what is the best set of benefits to offer and are the needs to be standardized across the region? There are even more unknowns about the needs of the hugely growing non-business market. What do these new flyers want and what is the best way to look after them economically?

Ultimately, for Qantas, the forecasting problem is more than a matter of temporary gains or losses of customer satisfaction and sales – it's a matter of survival. Thus Qantas has a lot flying on the accuracy of its forecasts.[1]

QUESTIONS

1. Why is market forecasting so important to airlines like Cathay Pacific and Qantas?

2. Is it realistic for Qantas to conduct a single forecast for passenger traffic in the region, or should it base its projections on several separate forecasts? If so, what separate forecasts should be conducted?

3. Does the past steady growth of the economies in the region mean it is reasonable to project similar levels of growth for the next decade?

4. Are Lufthansa's findings from its study likely to apply in south-east Asia? What is likely to make customer research in southern Asia more complicated than in Europe?

5. What techniques should Qantas use to forecast overall demand over the next ten years? How should it estimate what customers' tastes are likely to be over the next decade?

6. If Qantas's conclusion is that the market is uncertain, how should it proceed in acquiring new airliners?

Introduction

To carry out marketing analysis, planning, implementation and control, managers need information. Like Qantas, they need information about market demand, customers, competitors, dealers and other forces in the marketplace. One marketing executive put it this way: 'To manage a business well is to manage its future; and to manage the future is to manage information.[2] Increasingly, marketers are viewing information as not just an input for making better decisions, but also a marketing asset that gives competitive advantage of strategic importance.[3]

During the twentieth century, most companies have been small and have known their customers at first hand. Managers picked up marketing information by being around people, observing them and asking questions. However, many factors have increased the need for more and better information. As companies become national or international in scope, they need more information on larger, more distant markets. As incomes increase and buyers become more selective, sellers need better information about how buyers respond to different products and appeals. As sellers use more complex marketing approaches and face more competition, they need information on the effectiveness of their marketing tools. Finally, in today's rapidly changing environments, managers need up-to-date information to make timely decisions.

The supply of information has also increased greatly. John Neisbitt suggests that the world is undergoing a 'mega-shift' from an industrial to an information-based economy.[4] He found that more than 65 per cent of the US workforce now work at producing or processing information, compared to only 17 per cent in 1950. Using improved computer systems and other technologies, companies can now provide information in great quantities. Many of today's managers sometimes receive too much information. For example, one study found that with companies offering all the information now available through supermarket scanners, a brand manager gets one million to one *billion* new numbers each week.[5] As Neisbitt points out: 'Running out of information is not a problem, but drowning in it is.'[6]

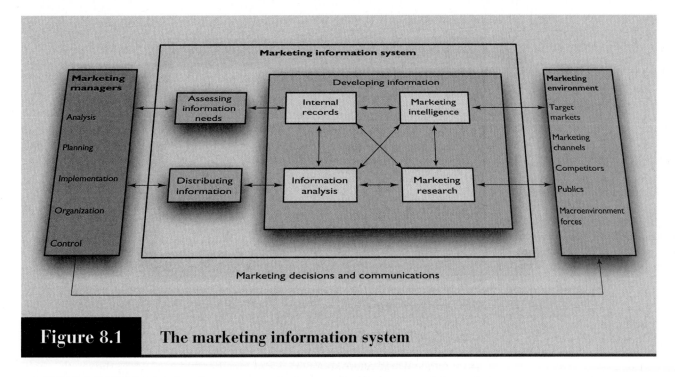

Figure 8.1   The marketing information system

Marketers frequently complain that they lack enough information of the *right* kind or have too much of the *wrong* kind. Regarding the spread of information throughout the company, they say that it takes great effort to locate even simple facts. Subordinates may withhold information that they believe will reflect badly on their performance. Often, important information arrives too late to be useful, or on-time information is not accurate. Companies have greater capacity to provide managers with information, but have often not made good use of it. Many companies are now studying their managers' information needs and designing information systems to meet those needs.

The Marketing Information System

A **marketing information system (MIS)** consists of people, equipment and procedures to gather, sort, analyze, evaluate and distribute needed, timely and accurate information to marketing decision makers. Figure 8.1 illustrates the marketing information system concept. The MIS begins and ends with marketing managers. First, it interacts with these managers to assess their information needs. Next, it develops the needed information from internal company records, marketing intelligence activities and the marketing research process. Information analysis processes the information to make it more useful. Finally, the MIS distributes information to managers in the right form at the right time to help them in marketing planning, implementation and control.

marketing information system (MIS)
People, equipment and procedures to gather, sort, analyze, evaluate and distribute needed, timely and accurate information to marketing decision makers.

Developing Information

The information needed by marketing managers comes from *internal company records*, *marketing intelligence* and *marketing research*. The information analysis system then processes this information to make it more useful for managers.

Internal Records

internal records information
Information gathered from sources within the company to evaluate marketing performances and to detect marketing problems and opportunities.

Most marketing managers use internal records and reports regularly, especially for making day-to-day planning, implementation and control decisions. **Internal records information** consists of information gathered from sources within the company to evaluate marketing performance and to detect marketing problems and opportunities. The company's accounting department prepares financial statements and keeps detailed records of sales, orders, costs and cash flows. Manufacturing reports on production schedules, shipments and inventories. The sales force reports on reseller reactions and competitor activities. The customer service department provides information on customer satisfaction or service problems. Research studies done for one department may provide useful information for several others. Managers can use information gathered from these and other sources within the company to evaluate performance and to detect problems and opportunities.

Here are examples of how companies use internal records information in making better marketing decisions:[7]

> *Office World* offers shoppers a free membership card when they make their first purchase at their store. The card entitles shoppers to discounts on selected items, but also provides valuable information to the chain. Since Office World encourages customers to use their card with each purchase, it can track what customers buy, where and when. Using this information, it can track the effectiveness of promotions, trace customers who have defected to other stores and keep in touch with them if they relocate.
>
> *Istel* is a cross-fertilization scheme set up by AT & T in Europe. The system helps retailers share information about customers. Under the programme customers join the Istel club, which gives them discounts when buying a range of products from member stores. AT & T estimates that its card will save the average customer £180 a year. The retailers then use the information to build databases and to target incentives to valuable customers. 'The grocer may like to know who is a high spender in the scheme but is not shopping with them,' says Ruth Kemp of Istel. 'Then they can offer incentives to use their store.'

Information from internal records is usually quicker and cheaper to get than information from other sources, but it also presents some problems. Because internal information was for other purposes, it may be incomplete or in the wrong form for making marketing decisions. For example, accounting department sales and cost data used for preparing financial statements need adapting for use in evaluating product, sales force or channel performance. In addition, the many different areas of a large company produce great amounts of information, and keeping track of it all is difficult. The marketing information system must gather, organize, process and index this mountain of information so that managers can find it easily and get it quickly.

marketing intelligence
Everyday information about developments in the marketing environment that helps managers prepare and adjust marketing plans.

Marketing Intelligence

Marketing intelligence is everyday information about developments in the marketing environment that helps managers prepare and adjust marketing plans.

The marketing intelligence system determines the intelligence needed, collects it by searching the environment and delivers it to marketing managers who need it.

Marketing intelligence comes from many sources. Much intelligence is from the company's personnel – executives, engineers and scientists, purchasing agents and the sales force. But company people are often busy and fail to pass on important information. The company must 'sell' its people on their importance as intelligence gatherers, train them to spot new developments and urge them to report intelligence back to the company.

The company must also persuade suppliers, resellers and customers to pass along important intelligence. Some information on competitors comes from what they say about themselves in annual reports, speeches, press releases and advertisements. The company can also learn about competitors from what others say about them in business publications and at trade shows. Or the company can watch what competitors do – buying and analyzing competitors' products, monitoring their sales and checking for new patents.

Companies also buy intelligence information from outside suppliers. Dun & Bradstreet is the world's largest research company with branches in 40 countries and a turnover of $1.26 billion. Its largest subsidiary is Nielsen, which sells data on brand shares, retail prices and percentages of stores stocking different brands. Its Info*Act Workstation offers companies the chance to analyze data from three sources on the PCs: Retail Index, which monitors consumer sales and in-store conditions; Key Account Scantrack, a weekly analysis of sales, price elasticity and promotional effectiveness; and Homescan, a new consumer panel. Alliances between marketing research companies allow access to pan-European research. Other big international research companies are WPP; Taylor Nelson, which owns AGB; GfK; MAI, which owns NOP; and Infratest. The globalization of markets has led both large and small firms to form alliances in order to gain better international coverage and wider services. Taylor Nelson's AGB has joined with Information Resources Inc. of the United States to strengthen their position as international suppliers of retail audit and scanner data.[8] The services of these and other agencies now provide over 500 accessible computer databases:

> Doing business in Germany? Check out CompuServe's German Company Library of financial and product information on over 48,000 German-owned firms. Want biographical sketches of key executives? Punch up Dun & Bradstreet Financial Profiles and Company Reports. Demographic data? Today's Associated Press news wire reports? A list of active trademarks? It's all available from on-line databases.[9]

Marketing intelligence can work not only for, but also against a company. Companies must sometimes take steps to protect themselves from the snooping of competitors. For example, Kellogg's had treated the public to tours of its plants since 1906, but recently closed its newly upgraded plant to outsiders to prevent competitors from getting intelligence on its high-tech equipment. In Japan corporate intelligence is part of the industrial culture. Everyone from assembly-line workers to top executives considers it their duty to filter intelligence about the competition back to management. Western companies are less active, although most of America's Fortune 500 now have in-house corporate intelligence units. Businesses are becoming increasingly aware of the need both to gather information and to protect what they have. In its Bangkok offices one European organization has a huge poster outside its lavatory saying: 'Wash and hush up! You never know who's listening! Keep our secrets secret.'[10]

Some companies set up an office to collect and circulate marketing intelligence. The staff scan relevant publications, summarize important news and send news bulletins to marketing managers. They develop a file of intelligence information and help managers evaluate new information. These services greatly improve the quality of information available to marketing managers. The methods used to gather competitive information range from the ridiculous to the illegal. Managers routinely shred documents because wastepaper baskets can be an information source. Other firms have uncovered more sinister devices such as Spycatcher's TPR recording system that 'automatically interrogates telephones and faxes. Also a range of tiny microphones.' These and other methods appear in Marketing Highlight 8.1.[11]

Marketing Research

Managers cannot always wait for information to arrive in bits and pieces from the marketing intelligence system. They often require formal studies of specific situations. For example, Apple Computer wants to know how many and what kinds of people or companies will buy its new ultralight personal computer. Or a Dutch pet product firm needs to know the potential market for slimming tablets for dogs. What percentage of dogs are overweight, do their owners worry about it, and will they give the pill to their podgy pooches?[12] In these situations, the marketing intelligence system will not provide the detailed information needed. Because managers normally do not have the skills or time to obtain the information on their own, they need formal marketing research.

marketing research
The function that links the consumer, customer and public to the marketer through information – information used to identify and define marketing opportunities and problems; to generate, refine and evaluate marketing actions; to monitor marketing performance; and to improve understanding of the marketing process.

Marketing research is the function linking the consumer, customer and public to the marketer through information – information used: to identify and define marketing opportunities and problems; to generate, refine and evaluate marketing actions; to monitor marketing performance; and to improve understanding of the marketing process.[13] Marketing researchers specify the information needed to address marketing issues, design the method for collecting information, manage and implement the data collection process, analyze the results and communicate the findings and their implications.

Marketing researchers engage in a wide variety of activities, ranging from analyses of market potential and market shares to studies of customer satisfaction and purchase intentions. Every marketer needs research. A company can conduct marketing research in its research department or have some or all of it done outside. Although most large companies have their own marketing research departments, they often use outside firms to do special research tasks or special studies. A company with no research department will have to buy the services of research firms.

Many people think of marketing research as a lengthy, formal process carried out by large marketing companies. But many small businesses and non-profit organizations also use marketing research. Almost any organization can find informal, low-cost alternatives to the formal and complex marketing research techniques used by research experts in large firms.

The Marketing Research Process

The marketing research process (see Figure 8.2) consists of four steps: defining the problem and research objectives; developing the research plan; implementing the research plan; and interpreting and reporting the findings.

● *Defining the Problem and Research Objectives*

The marketing manager and the researcher must work closely together to define the problem carefully and must agree on the research objectives. The manager

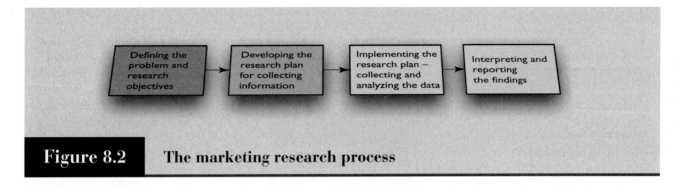

Figure 8.2 | **The marketing research process**

understands the decision for which information is needed; the researcher understands marketing research and how to obtain the information.

Managers must know enough about marketing research to help in the planning and in the interpretation of research results. If they know little about marketing research, they may obtain the wrong information, accept wrong conclusions, or ask for information that costs too much. Experienced marketing researchers who understand the manager's problem also need involvement at this stage. The researcher must be able to help the manager define the problem and to suggest ways that research can help the manager make better decisions.

Defining the problem and research objectives is often the hardest step in the research process. The manager may know that something is wrong, without knowing the specific causes. For example, managers of a discount retail store chain hastily decided that poor advertising caused falling sales, so they ordered research to test the company's advertising. It puzzled the managers when the research showed that current advertising was reaching the right people with the right message. It turned out that the chain stores were not delivering what the advertising promised. Careful problem definition would have avoided the cost and delay of doing advertising research. It would have suggested research on the real problem of consumer reactions to the products, service and prices offered in the chain's stores.

After the problem has been defined carefully, the manager and researcher must set the research objectives. A marketing research project might have one of three types of objective. The objective of **exploratory research** is to gather preliminary information that will help define the problem and suggest hypotheses. The objective of **descriptive research** is to describe things such as the market potential for a product or the demographics and attitudes of consumers who buy the product. The objective of **causal research** is to test hypotheses about cause-and-effect relationships. For example, would a 10 per cent cut in CD prices increase sales sufficiently to offset the lost margin? Managers often start with exploratory research and later follow with descriptive or causal research.

The statement of the problem and research objectives guides the entire research process. The manager and researcher should put the statement in writing to be certain that they agree on the purpose and expected results of the research.

• *Developing the Research Plan*

The second step of the marketing research process calls for determining the information needed, developing a plan for gathering it efficiently and presenting the plan to marketing management. The plan outlines sources of existing data and explains the specific research approaches, contact methods, sampling plans and instruments that researchers will use to gather new data.

exploratory research
Marketing research to gather preliminary information that will help better to define problems and suggest hypotheses.

descriptive research
Marketing research to better describe marketing problems, situations or markets, such as the market potential for a product or the demographics and attitudes of consumers.

causal research
Marketing research to test hypotheses about cause-and-effect relationships.

Snooping on Competitors

Marketing Highlight 8.1

European firms lag behind their Japanese and American competitors in gathering competitive intelligence. In Japanese companies it is a long-established practice, for, as Mitsui's corporate motto says: 'Information is the life blood of the company.' In the United States, competitive intelligence gathering has grown dramatically as more and more companies need to know what their competitors are doing. Such well-known companies as Ford, Motorola, Kodak, Gillette, Avon, Kraft, Mitsubishi and the 'Big Six' accounting firms are known to be busy snooping on their competitors. TMA, FCI and Kirk Tyson International specialize in this sort of business. The techniques they use to collect intelligence fall into four main groups.

Getting Information from Published Materials and Public Documents

Keeping track of seemingly meaningless published information can provide competitor intelligence. For instance, the types of people sought in help-wanted ads can indicate something about a competitor's new strategies and products. Government agencies are another good source. For example, according to *Fortune*:

> Although it is often illegal for a company to photograph a competitor's plant from the air ... Aerial photos often are on file with geological survey or environmental protection agencies. These are public documents, available for a nominal fee.

> According to Leonard Fuld, founder of FCI: 'in some countries the government is a rare font of information ... France has the Minitel, in the US we have an opus of information databases and networks.'

Getting Information by Observing Competitors or Analyzing Physical Evidence

Companies can get to know competitors better by buying their products or examining other physical evidence. An increasingly important form of competitive intelligence is benchmarking, taking apart competitors' products and imitating or improving upon their best features. Benchmarking has helped JCB keep ahead in earth-moving equipment. The company takes apart its international competitors' products, dissecting and examining them in detail. JCB also probed the manufacturing operations, the types of machine tools used, their speeds, manning levels, labour costs, quality control and testing procedures, and raw material. It built up a profile of all its main competitors' operations and performance ratios against which to benchmark. In this way, the company knew the extent to which competitors could vary their prices, what their strengths and weaknesses were, and how JCB could exploit these data to its advantage.

Beyond looking at competitors' products, companies can examine many other types of physical evidence:

> In the absence of better information on market share and the volume of product competitors are shipping, companies have measured the rust on rails of railroad sidings to their competitors' plant or have counted the tractor-trailers leaving loading bays.

Some companies even rifle their competitors' rubbish:

> Once it has left the competitors' premises, refuse is legally considered abandoned property. While some companies now shred the paper coming out of their design labs, they often neglect to do this for all most revealing refuse from the marketing or public relations departments.

Avon hired private detectives to paw through Mary Kay Cosmetics' rubbish skips. Although an outraged Mary Kay sued to get its rubbish back, Avon claimed that it had done nothing illegal. The skips had been located in a public car park and Avon had videotapes to prove it.

Getting Information from People who Do Business with Competitors

Key customers can keep the company informed about competitors and their products:

> For example, a while back Gillette told a large account the date on which it planned to begin selling its new Good News disposable razor. The distributor promptly called Bic and told it about the impending product launch. Bic put on a crash programme and was able to start selling its razor shortly after Gillette did.

Intelligence can also be gathered by infiltrating customers' business operations:

> Companies may provide their engineers free of charge to customers … The close, cooperative relationship that the engineers on loan cultivate with the customers' design staff often enables them to learn what new products competitors are pitching.

Getting Information from Recruits and Competitors' Employees

Companies can obtain intelligence through job interviews or from conversations with competitors' employees.

> When they interview people for jobs, some companies pay special attention to those who have worked for competitors, even temporarily.
>
> Companies send engineers to conferences and trade shows to question competitors' technical people.
>
> Companies sometimes advertise and hold interviews for jobs that don't exist in order to entice competitors' employees to spill the beans.

In the United States one of the most common ploys is to telephone competitors' employees and ask direct and indirect questions. 'The rule of thumb,' says Jonathan Lax, founder of TMA, 'is to target employees a level below where you think you should start, because that person often knows just as much as his or her senior, and they are not as frequently asked or wary.' Secretaries, receptionists and switchboard operators regularly give away information inadvertently.

One European company is now being accused of beating the Americans at their own game. When Spanish-born José Ignacio Lopez de Arriotua defected from General Motors to Volkswagen to be its new purchasing and production chief, he took seven GM executives with him.

Why Europe is Different

Niame Fine, founder of Protec Data, believes there are two main differences between US and European companies. Language and cultural blocks limit cross-border intelligence gathering. Approaching competitors' employees is a subtle business and people are often put on their guard if approached by someone from a different country. She also says Europeans have greater loyalty than their job-hopping American counterparts.

Although most of these techniques are legal and some are considered to be shrewdly competitive, many involve questionable ethics. The company should take advantage of publicly available information, but avoid practices that might be considered illegal or unethical. A company does not have to break the law or accepted codes of ethics to get good intelligence. So far European businesses 'do as they would be done by' and linger at the ethical end of the spectrum of competitive intelligence. Will they be able to stay there?

SOURCES: Excerpts from Steven Flax, 'How to snoop on your competitors', *Fortune* (14 May 1984), pp. 29–33; Brian Dumaine, 'Corporate spies snoop to conquer', *Fortune* (7 November 1988), pp. 68–76; Jeremy Main, 'How to steal the best ideas around', *Fortune* (19 October 1992), pp. 102–6. Copyright © 1984, 1988 and 1992, Time Inc. All rights reserved. Also see Wendy Zellner and Bruce Hager, 'Dumpster raids? That's not very ladylike, Avon', *Business Week* (1 April 1991), p. 32; Michele Galen, 'These guys aren't spooks, they're "competitive analysts"', *Business Week* (14 October 1991), p. 97; Richard S. Teitalbaum, 'The new race for intelligence', *Fortune* (2 November 1992), pp. 104–8; 'Mr Lopez's many parts', *The Economist* (23 May 1993), p. 89; Tony McBurnie and David Clutterbuck, *The Marketing Edge* (London: Penguin, 1988); Kate Button, 'Spies like us', *Marketing Business* (March 1994), pp. 7–9.

DETERMINING INFORMATION NEEDS. Research objectives need translating into specific information needs.

> Bolswessanen, the Dutch food and drinks company, decides to conduct research to find out how consumers would react to a new breakfast cereal aimed at the adult market. Across Europe young health-conscious people are abandoning croissants in France, rolls in Belgium and lonely espresso in Italy. Since Nestlé and General Mills set up Cereal Partners Worldwide as a joint venture, they have been very active in the market and the project has started to develop. The European breakfast cereal market has been growing fast, but own labels dominate the adult sector.[14] Can Bolswessanen successfully compete with Kellogg's, the market leader, and the aggressive new competitor, Cereal Partners Worldwide? The company's research might call for the following specific information:
>
> - The demographic, economic and lifestyle characteristics of current breakfast cereal users. (How do social and demographic trends affect the breakfast cereal market?)
> - Consumer-usage patterns for cereals: how much do they eat, where and when? (Will all the family eat the cereal or does each family member have their favourite?)
> - Retailer reactions to the new product. (Failure to get retailer support could hurt its sales.)
> - Consumer attitudes towards the new product. (Will consumers switch from own brands and is the product attractive enough to compete with Kellogg's?)
> - Forecasts of sales of the new product. (Will the new packaging increase Bolswessanen's profits?)
>
> Bolswessanen's managers will need this and many other types of information to decide whether to introduce the new product.

GATHERING SECONDARY INFORMATION. To meet the manager's information needs, the researcher can gather secondary data, primary data or both. **Secondary data** is information that already exists somewhere, having been collected for another purpose. **Primary data** consist of information collected for the specific purpose at hand.

Researchers usually start by gathering secondary data. Table 8.1 shows the many secondary data sources, including *internal* and *external* sources.[15] Secondary data are usually quicker and cheaper to obtain than primary data. For example, a visit to the library might provide all the information Bolswessanen needs on cereal usage, at almost no cost. A study to collect primary information might take weeks or months and cost a lot. Also, secondary sources can sometimes provide data that an individual company cannot collect on its own – information that either is not directly available or would be too expensive to collect. For example, it would be too expensive for Bolswessanen to conduct a continuing retail store audit to find out about the market shares, prices and displays of competitors' brands. But it can buy Neilsen's Scantrack service.

Secondary data also have problems. The needed information may not exist – researchers can rarely obtain all the data they need from secondary sources. For example, Bolswessanen will not find existing information about consumer reactions to a new product that it has not yet placed on the market. Even when data are found, they might not be very usable. The researcher must evaluate

---

secondary data
Information that already exists somewhere, having been collected for another purpose.

primary data
Information collected for the specific purpose at hand.

Table 8.1	Sources of secondary data

Internal sources

Internal sources include company profit and loss statements, balance sheets, sales figures, sales call reports, invoices, inventory records and prior research reports.

Government publications

Statistical Abstract, usually updated annually, provides summary data on demographic, economic, social and other aspects of the economy and society.

Industrial Outlook provides projections of industrial activity by industry and includes data on production, sales, shipments, employment, etc.

Marketing Information Guide provides a monthly annotated bibliography of marketing information. Other government publications include the *Annual Survey of Manufacturers*; *Business Statistics*; *Census of Manufacturers*; *Census of Population*; *Census of Retail Trade, Wholesale Trade*, and *Selected Service Industries*; *Census of Transportation*; *Federal Reserve Bulletin*; *Monthly Labor Review*; *Survey of Current Business*; and *Vital Statistics Report*.

Periodicals and books

Business Periodicals Index, a monthly, lists business articles appearing in a wide variety of business publications.

Standard & Poor's Industry Surveys provide updated statistics and analyses of industries.

Moody's Manuals provide financial data and names of executives in big companies.

Encyclopaedia of Associations provides information on every large trade and professional association in the United States.

Marketing journals include the *Journal of Marketing, Journal of Marketing Research, Journal of Consumer Research* and *International Journal of Research in Marketing*.

Useful trade magazines include *Advertising Age, Chain Store Age, Progressive Grocer, Sales and Marketing Management, Stores, Marketing Week* and *Campaign*.

Useful general business magazines include *Business Week, Fortune, Forbes, The Economist* and *Harvard Business Review*.

Commercial data

Here are just a few of the dozens of commercial research houses selling data to subscribers:

A.C. Nielsen Company provides supermarket scanner data on sales, market share and retail prices (Scantrack), data on household purchasing (Scantrack National Electronic Household Panel), data on television audiences (Nielsen National Television Index) and others.

IMS International provides reports on the movement of pharmaceuticals, hospital laboratory supplies, animal health products and personal care products.

Information Resources, Inc. provides supermarket scanner data for tracking grocery product movement (InfoScan) and single-source data collection (BehaviorScan).

MRB Group (Simmons Market Research Bureau) provides annual reports covering television markets, sporting goods and proprietary drugs. The reports give lifestyle and geodemographic data by sex, income, age and brand preferences (selective markets and media reaching them).

NFO Research provides data for the beverage industry (SIPS), for mail order businesses (MOMS), and for carpet and rug industries (CARS). It also provides a mail panel for concept and product testing, attitude and usage studies, and tracking and segmentation (Analycor).

International data

Here are only a few of the many sources providing international information:

United Nations publications include the *Statistical Yearbook*, a comprehensive source of international data for socioeconomic indicators; *Demographic Yearbook*, a collection of demographics data and vital statistics for 220 countries; and the *International Trade Statistics Yearbook*, which provides information on foreign trade for specific countries and commodities.

Europa Yearbook provides surveys on history, politics, population, economy and natural resources for most countries of the world, along with information on the chief international organizations.

Political Risk Yearbook contains information on political situations in foreign countries, with reference to US investment. It predicts the political climate in each country.

Foreign Economic Trends and Their Implications for the United States provides reports on recent business, economic and political developments in specific countries.

International Marketing Data and Statistics provides marketing statistics by country, including data on consumer product markets for countries outside the United States and Europe.

Other sources include *Country Studies*, *OECD Economic Surveys*, *Economic Survey of Europe*, *Asian Economic Handbook* and *International Financial Statistics*.

secondary information carefully to make certain it is *relevant* (fits research project needs), *accurate* (reliably collected and reported), *current* (sufficiently up to date for current decisions) and *impartial* (objectively collected and reported).

Secondary data provide a good starting point for research and often help to define problems and research objectives. In most cases, however, secondary sources cannot provide all the needed information and the company must collect primary data.

PLANNING PRIMARY DATA COLLECTION. Good decisions require good data. Just as researchers must carefully evaluate the quality of secondary information they obtain, they must also take great care in collecting primary data to ensure that they provide marketing decision makers with relevant, accurate, current and unbiased information. This could be **qualitative research** that measures a small sample of customers' views, or **quantitative research** that provides statistics from a large sample of consumers. Table 8.2 shows that designing a plan for primary data collection calls for a number of decisions on research approaches, contact methods, sampling plan and research instruments.

RESEARCH APPROACHES. **Observational research** is the gathering of primary data by observing relevant people, actions and situations. For example:

- A food-products manufacturer sends researchers into supermarkets to find out the prices of competing brands or how much shelf space and display support retailers give its brands.
- A bank evaluates possible new branch locations by checking traffic patterns, neighbourhood conditions and the locations of competing branches.
- A maker of personal-care products pretests its ads by showing them to people and measuring eye movements, pulse rates and other physical reactions.
- A department store chain sends observers who pose as customers into its stores to check on store conditions and customer service.
- A museum checks the popularity of various exhibits by noting the amount of floor wear around them.

Several companies sell information collected through *mechanical observation*. For example, Nielsen and AGB attach 'people meters' to television sets in selected homes to record who watches which programmes. They provide summaries

qualitative research
Exploratory research used to uncover consumers' motivations, attitudes and behaviour. Focus-group interviewing, elicitation interviews and repertory grid techniques are typical methods used in this type of research.

quantitative research
Research which involves data collection by mail or personal interviews from a sufficient volume of customers to allow statistical analysis.

observational research
The gathering of primary data by observing relevant people, actions and situations.

| Table 8.2 | Planning primary data collection | | |

RESEARCH APPROACHES	CONTACT METHODS	SAMPLING PLAN	RESEARCH INSTRUMENTS
Observation	Mail	Sampling unit	Questionnaire
Survey	Telephone	Sample size	Mechanical instruments
Experiment	Personal	Sampling procedure	

of the size and demographic make-up of audiences for different television programmes. The television networks use these ratings to judge programme popularity and to set charges for advertising time. Advertisers use the ratings when selecting programmes for their commercials. *Checkout scanners* in retail stores also provide mechanical observation data. These laser scanners record consumer purchases in detail. Consumer products companies and retailers use scanner information to assess and improve product sales and store performance.[16] Some marketing research firms now offer **single-source data systems** that electronically monitor both consumers' purchases and consumers' exposure to various marketing activities to evaluate better the link between the two.[17]

Observational research can obtain information that people are unwilling or unable to provide. In some cases, observation is the only way to obtain the needed information. In contrast, some things are simply not observable, such as feelings, attitudes and motives, or private behaviour. Long-term or infrequent behaviour is also difficult to observe. Because of these limitations, researchers often use observation along with other data collection methods.

Survey research is the approach best suited for gathering *descriptive* information. A company that wants to know about people's knowledge, attitudes, preferences or buying behaviour can often find out by asking them directly. Survey research is structured or unstructured. *Structured* surveys use formal lists of questions asked of all respondents in the same way. *Unstructured* surveys let the interviewer probe respondents and guide the interview according to their answers.

Survey research may be direct or indirect. In the *direct* approach, the researcher asks direct questions about behaviour or thoughts: for example, 'Why don't you buy clothes at C & A?' In contrast, the researcher might use the *indirect* approach by asking, 'What kinds of people buy clothes at C & A?' From the response to this indirect question, the researcher may be able to discover why the consumer avoids C & A clothing and why it attracts others. It may suggest reasons the consumer is not conscious of.

Survey research is the most widely used method for primary data collection and it is often the only method used in a research study. The principal advantage of survey research is its flexibility. It can obtain many different kinds of information in many different marketing situations. Depending on the survey design, it may also provide information more quickly and at lower cost than observational or experimental research.

However, survey research also presents some problems. Sometimes people are unable to answer survey questions because they do not remember, or never thought about, what they did and why they did it. Or people may be unwilling to respond to unknown interviewers or about things they consider private.

single-source data systems
Electronic monitoring systems that link consumers' exposure to television advertising and promotion (measured using television metres) with what they buy in stores (measured using store checkout scanners).

survey research
The gathering of primary data by asking people questions about their knowledge, attitudes, preferences and buying behaviour.

Table 8.3	Strengths and weaknesses of the four contact methods

	MAIL	TELEPHONE	PERSONAL	INTERNET
1. Flexibility	Poor	Good	Excellent	Fair
2. Quantity of data that can be collected	Good	Fair	Excellent	Good
3. Control of interviewer effects	Excellent	Fair	Poor	Excellent
4. Control of sample	Fair	Excellent	Fair	Fair
5. Speed of data collection	Poor	Excellent	Good	Excellent
6. Response rate	Poor	Good	Good	Poor
7. Cost	Good	Fair	Poor	Excellent
8. Sample frame	Good	Excellent	Fair	Poor

SOURCE: Adapted with permission of Macmillan Publishing Company from *Marketing Research: Measurement and Method*, 6th edn, by Donald S. Tull and Del I. Hawkins. Copyright © 1993 by Macmillan Publishing Company.

Respondents may answer survey questions even when they do not know the answer, simply in order to appear smarter or more informed than they are. Or they may try to help the interviewer by giving pleasing answers. Finally, busy people may not take the time, or they might resent the intrusion into their privacy. Careful survey design can help to minimize these problems.

experimental research
The gathering of primary data by selecting matched groups of subjects, giving them different treatments, controlling related factors and checking for differences in group responses.

Experimental research gathers *causal* information. Experiments involve selecting matched groups of subjects, giving them different treatments, controlling unrelated factors and checking for differences in group responses. Thus experimental research tries to explain cause-and-effect relationships. Observation and surveys can collect information in experimental research.

Before extending their product range to include fragrances, researchers at Virgin Megastores might use experiments to answer questions such as the following:

● How much will the fragrances increase Virgin's sales?

● How will the fragrances affect the sales of other menu items?

● Which advertising approach would have the greatest effect on sales of their fragrances?

● How would different prices affect the sales of the product?

● How will the product affect the stores' overall image?

For example, to test the effects of two prices, Virgin could set up a simple experiment. It could introduce fragrances at one price in one city and at another price in another city. If the cities are similar and if all other marketing efforts for the fragrances are the same, then differences in the price charged could explain the sales in the two cities. More complex experimental designs could include other variables and other locations.

CONTACT METHODS. Mail, telephone, personal interviews and the Internet, a recent development, can collect data. Table 8.3 shows the strengths and weaknesses of each of these contact methods.

Postal questionnaires have many advantages. They can collect large amounts of information at a low cost per respondent. Respondents may give more honest answers to more personal questions on a postal questionnaire than to an unknown interviewer in person or over the phone, since there is no interviewer to bias the respondent's answers.

However, postal questionnaires also have disadvantages. They are not very flexible: they require simple and clearly worded questions; all respondents answer the same questions in a fixed order; and the researcher cannot adapt the questionnaire based on earlier answers. Mail surveys usually take longer to complete and the response rate – the number of people returning completed questionnaires – is often very low. Finally, the researcher often has little control over the postal questionnaire sample. Even with a good mailing list, it is often hard to control *who* at the mailing address fills out the questionnaire.[18]

Telephone interviewing is the best method for gathering information quickly and it provides greater flexibility than postal questionnaires. Interviewers can explain questions that are not understood. Depending on the respondent's answers, they can skip some questions or probe further on others. Telephone interviewing also allows greater sample control. Interviewers can ask to speak to respondents with the desired characteristics, or even by name. Response rates tend to be higher than with postal questionnaires.[19]

However, telephone interviewing also has drawbacks. The cost per respondent is higher than with postal questionnaires and people may not want to discuss personal questions with an interviewer. Using interviewers increases flexibility, but also introduces interviewer bias. The way interviewers talk, small differences in how they ask questions and other differences may affect respondents' answers. Finally, different interviewers may interpret and record responses differently, and under time pressure some interviewers might even cheat by recording answers without asking questions.

Personal interviewing takes two forms – individual and group interviewing. *Individual interviewing* involves talking with people in their homes or offices, in the street, or in shopping malls. The interviewer must gain their co-operation and the time involved can range from a few minutes to several hours. Sometimes people get a small payment in return for their time.

Group interviewing consists of inviting six to ten people to gather for a few hours with a trained moderator to talk about a product, service or organization. The moderator needs objectivity, knowledge of the subject and industry, and some understanding of group and consumer behaviour. The participants are normally paid a small sum for attending. The meeting is usually in a pleasant place and refreshments are served to foster an informal setting. The moderator starts with broad questions before moving to more specific issues, and encourages easy-going discussion, hoping that group interactions will bring out actual feelings and thoughts. At the same time, the moderator 'focuses' the discussion – hence the name **focus-group** interviewing. The comments are recorded by written notes or on videotapes for study later. Focus-group interviewing has become one of the key marketing research tools for gaining insight into consumer thoughts and feelings.[20]

focus group
A small sample of typical consumers under the direction of a group leader who elicits their reaction to a stimulus such as an ad or product concept.

Personal interviewing is quite flexible and can collect large amounts of information. Trained interviewers can hold a respondent's attention for a long time and can explain difficult questions. They can guide interviews, explore issues and probe as the situation requires. Personal interviews can utilize any type of questionnaire. Interviewers can show subjects actual products, advertisements or packages, and observe reactions and behaviour. In most cases, personal interviews can be conducted fairly quickly.

The main drawbacks of personal interviewing are costs and sampling problems. Personal interviews may cost three to four times as much as telephone interviews. Group interview studies usually employ small sample sizes to keep time and costs down, and it may be hard to generalize from the results. Because interviewers have more freedom in personal interviews, the problem of interviewer bias is greater.

Which contact method is best depends on what information the researcher wants and on the number and types of respondents needed. Advances in computers and communications have had an impact on methods of obtaining information. For example, most research firms now do Computer Assisted Telephone Interviewing (CATI). Professional interviewers call respondents, often using phone numbers drawn at random. When the respondent answers, the interviewer reads a set of questions from a video screen and types the respondent's answers directly into the computer. Although this procedure requires a large investment in computer equipment and interviewer training, it eliminates data editing and coding, reduces errors and saves time. Other research firms set up terminals in shopping centres – respondents sit down at a terminal, read questions from a screen and type their answers into the computer.[21]

Internet data collection is still in its infancy. But as the use of the World Wide Web and online services widens, online research is becoming a quick, easy and inexpensive method.[22] Online researchers recognize that Web surfers are not representative of the population. Online users tend to be better educated, more affluent and younger than the average consumer, and a higher proportion are male. These are important consumers to companies offering products and services online. They are also some of the hardest to reach when conducting a research study. Online surveys and chat sessions (or online focus groups) often prove effective in reaching elusive groups, such as teen, single, affluent and well-educated audiences.

When appropriate, online research offers marketers two distinct advantages over traditional surveys and focus groups: speed and cost-effectiveness. Online researchers can field quantitative studies and fill response quotas in only a matter of days. Online focus groups require some advance scheduling, but results are practically instantaneous. Research on the Internet is also relatively inexpensive. Participants can dial in for a focus group from anywhere in the world, eliminating travel, lodging and facility costs, making online chats cheaper than traditional focus groups. And for surveys, the Internet eliminates most of the postage, phone, labour and printing costs associated with other survey approaches. Moreover, sample size has little influence on costs. There is little difference between 10 and 10,000 on the Web. There is also no difference in the speed and cost of conducting an international survey rather than a domestic one.

However, using the Internet to conduct marketing research does have some drawbacks. The method shares a problem with postal surveys: knowing who's in the sample. Trying to draw conclusions from a 'self-selected' sample of online users, those who clicked through to a questionnaire or accidentally landed in a chat room, can be troublesome. Online research is not right for every company or product. For example, mass marketers who need to survey a representative cross-section of the population will find online research methodologies less useful, since most low-income consumers do not have online access.

Eye contact and body language are two direct, personal interactions of traditional focus-group research that are lost online. And while researchers can offer seasoned moderators, the Internet format – running, typed commentary and online 'emoticons' (punctuation marks that express emotion, such as :-) to signify happiness or :-o for surprise) – greatly restrict respondent expressiveness. Similarly, technology limits researchers' capability to show visual cues to research subjects. But just as it hinders the two-way assessment of visual cues, Web research can actually permit some participants the anonymity necessary to elicit an unguarded response.

| Table 8.4 | Data collection methods: quantitative and qualitative (% of expenditure for 1991) |

	POSTAL SURVEY (%)	TELEPHONE (%)	FACE-TO-FACE (%)	GROUP DISCUSSIONS (%)	IN-DEPTH INTERVIEWS (%)
Belgium	7	15	57	10	8
Denmark	16	24	31	6	21
Finland	19	38	37	n.a.	n.a.
France	n.a.	n.a.	n.a.	n.a.	n.a.
Germany	5	18	56	6	10
Greece	_a	3	82b	10	3
Ireland	1	2	72	23	3
Italy	4	27	44	10	10
Luxembourg	–	10	65	5	–
Netherlands	31	18	34	4	9
Norway	10	20	50	10	5
Portugal	12	9	65	7	3
Spain	3	16	63	13	3
Sweden	23	39	23	4	5
Switzerland	8	27	46	n.a.	n.a.
Turkey	6	4	60	15	5
United Kingdom	8	15	67	10	–

NOTES: [a] Less than 0.5 per cent; [b] including panel turnover.

SOURCE: *Report of ESOMAR Working Party on 1991 Market Statistics* (1992).

To overcome such sample and response problems, NPD and many other firms that offer online services construct panels of qualified Web regulars to respond to surveys and participate in online focus groups. NPD's panel consists of 15,000 consumers recruited online and verified by telephone; Greenfield Online picks users from its own database, then calls them periodically to verify that they are who they say they are. Another online research firm, Research Connections, recruits in advance by telephone, taking time to help new users connect to the Internet, if necessary.

Some researchers are wildly optimistic about the prospects for marketing research on the Internet; others are more cautious. One expert predicts that in the next few years, 50 per cent of all research will be done on the Internet, although others are more sceptical.

There is no one best contact method to use. The one chosen depends on the information needs, cost, speed and other issues. Table 8.4 shows the traditional data collection methods used across Europe. Rational reasons may account for only part of the variation shown. Face-to-face interviews account for half the number, but these figures are particularly high in southern Europe and the United Kingdom. The low penetration of telephones in some of these countries may be an influence, but it may also reflect cultures who like socializing. Ireland's high use of group discussions may show that land's love of conversation. The Scandinavians' use of telephone interviews is partly explained by their being large countries with small populations. Their mobile phone use also shows their telephone orientation:

10 per cent are mobile phone users compared with 6 per cent in the United States and about 3 per cent in Germany and Japan.[23] In some countries, postal surveys do not work because of low literacy, but another reason is the unwillingness of people to respond. Research agencies and managers also have preferred methods, so they will also exert some personal influence on the choice of method. The relatively low use of the Internet in Europe means that Internet data collection in Europe will lag behind the United States. In addition, the large differences in penetration of the Internet across Europe mean that its use will not be uniform.

Increasing consumer resentment has become a major problem for the research industry. This resentment has led to lower survey response rates in recent years – one study found that 38 per cent of consumers now refuse to be interviewed in an average survey, up dramatically from a decade ago. Another study found that 59 per cent of consumers had refused to give information to a company because they thought it was not really needed or too personal, up from 42 per cent just five years earlier.[24] The research industry is considering several options for responding to this problem. One is to educate consumers about the benefits of marketing research and to distinguish it from telephone selling and database building. Another option is to provide a freephone number that people can call to verify that a survey is legitimate. The industry has also considered adopting broad standards, such as Europe's International Code of Marketing and Social Research Practice. This code outlines researchers' responsibilities to respondents and to the general public. For example, it says that researchers should make their names and addresses available to participants, and it bans companies from representing activities like database compilation or sales and promotional pitches as research.

SAMPLING PLANS.   Marketing researchers usually draw conclusions about large groups of consumers by studying a small sample of the total consumer population. A **sample** is a segment of the population selected to represent the population as a whole. Ideally, the sample should be representative, so that the researcher can make accurate estimates of the thoughts and behaviours of the larger population.

Designing the sample calls for three decisions. First, *who* is to be surveyed (what *sampling unit*)? The answer to this question is not always obvious. For example, to study the decision-making process for a family car purchase, should the researcher interview the husband, wife, other family members or all of these? The responses obtained from different family members vary, so the researcher must determine the information needed and from whom.[25]

Second, *how many* people are to be surveyed (what *sample size*)? Large samples give more reliable results than small samples. However, it is not necessary to sample the entire target market or even a large portion to get reliable results. If well chosen, samples of less than 1 per cent of a population can often give good reliability.

Third, *how* are the people in the sample *to be chosen* (what *sampling procedure*)? Table 8.5 describes different kinds of sample. Using *probability samples*, each population member has a known chance of being included in the sample, and researchers can calculate confidence limits for sampling error. But when probability sampling costs too much or takes too long, marketing researchers often take *non-probability samples*, even though their sampling error is not measurable. These varied ways of drawing samples have different costs and time limitations, as well as different accuracy and statistical properties. Which method is best depends on the needs of the research project.

RESEARCH INSTRUMENTS.   In collecting primary data, marketing researchers have a choice of two main research instruments: the *questionnaire* and *mechanical devices*.

sample
A segment of the population selected for marketing research to represent the population as a whole.

Table 8.5	**Types of sampling**

Probability sample	
Simple random sample	Every member of the population has a known and equal chance of selection.
Stratified random sample	The population is divided into mutually exclusive groups (such as age groups), and random samples are drawn from each group.
Cluster (area) sample	The population is divided into mutually exclusive groups (such as blocks), and the researcher draws a sample of the groups to interview.
Non-probability sample	
Convenience sample	The researcher selects the easiest population members from which to obtain information.
Judgement sample	The researcher uses his or her judgement to select population members who are good prospects for accurate information.
Quota sample	The researcher finds and interviews a prescribed number of people in each of several categories.

The *questionnaire* is by far the most common instrument. Broadly speaking, a questionnaire consists of a set of questions presented to a respondent for his or her answers. The questionnaire is very flexible – there are many ways to ask questions. Questionnaires need to be developed carefully and tested before their large-scale use. A carelessly prepared questionnaire usually contains several errors (see Table 8.6).

In preparing a questionnaire, the marketing researcher must decide what questions to ask, the form of the questions, the wording of the questions and the ordering of the questions. Questionnaires frequently leave out questions that need answering, but include questions that cannot be answered, will not be answered, or need not be answered. Each question should be checked to see that it contributes to the research objectives.

The *form* of the question can influence the response. Marketing researchers distinguish between closed-end and open-end questions. **Closed-end questions** include all the possible answers, and subjects make choices among them. Part A of Table 8.7 shows the most common forms of closed-end questions as they might appear in an SAS survey of airline users. **Open-end questions** allow respondents to answer in their own words. The most common forms are shown in part B of Table 8.7. Open-end questions often reveal more than closed-end questions because respondents are not limited in their answers. Open-end questions are especially useful in exploratory research in which the researcher is trying to find out *what* people think, but not measuring *how many* people think in a certain way. Closed-end questions, on the other hand, provide answers that are easier to interpret and tabulate.

Researchers should also use care in the *wording* of questions. They should use simple, direct, unbiased wording. The questions should be pretested before use. The *ordering* of questions is also important. The first question should create interest if possible. Ask difficult or personal questions last, so that respondents do not become defensive. The questions should be in a logical order.

closed-end questions
Questions that include all the possible answers and allow subjects to make choices among them.

open-end questions
Questions that allow respondents to answer in their own words.

Table 8.6	A 'questionable questionnaire'

Suppose that an adventure holiday director had prepared the following questionnaire to use in interviewing the parents of prospective campers. How would you assess each question?

1. What is your income to the nearest hundred pounds?
   People don't usually know their income to the nearest hundred pounds nor do they want to reveal their income that closely. Moreover, a researcher should never open a questionnaire with such a personal question.
2. Are you a strong or a weak supporter of overnight camping for your children?
   What do 'strong' and 'weak' mean?
3. Do your children behave themselves well on adventure holidays?
   Yes ( ) No ( )
   'Behave' is a relative term. Furthermore, are 'yes' and 'no' the best response options for this question? Besides, will people want to answer this? Why ask the question in the first place?
4. How many adventure holiday operators mailed literature to you last April? This April?
   Who can remember this?
5. What are the most salient and determinant attributes in your evaluation of adventure holidays?
   What are 'salient' and 'determinant' attributes? Don't use big words on me!
6. Do you think it is right to deprive your child of the opportunity to grow into a mature person through the experience of adventure holidays?
   A loaded question. Given the bias, how can any parent answer 'yes'?

Although questionnaires are the most common research instrument, *mechanical instruments* are also used. We discussed two mechanical instruments – people meters and supermarket scanners – earlier in the chapter. Another group of mechanical devices measures subjects' physical responses. For example, a galvanometer (lie detector) measures the strength of interest or emotions aroused by a subject's exposure to different stimuli: for instance, an ad or picture. The galvanometer detects the minute degree of sweating that accompanies emotional arousal. The tachistoscope flashes an ad to a subject at an exposure range from less than one-hundredth of a second to several seconds. After each exposure, the respondents describe everything they recall. Eye cameras study respondents' eye movements to determine at what points their eyes focus first and how long they linger on a given item.[26]

● *Presenting the Research Plan*

At this stage, the marketing researcher should summarize the plan in a *written proposal*. A written proposal is especially important when the research project is large and complex, or when an outside firm carries it out. The proposal should cover the management problems addressed and the research objectives, the information obtained, the sources of secondary information or methods for collecting primary data, and the way the results will help management decision making. The proposal should also include research costs. A written research plan or proposal makes sure that the marketing manager and researchers have considered all the important aspects of the research and that they agree on why and how to do the research.

• *Implementing the Research Plan*

The researcher next puts the marketing research plan into action. This involves collecting, processing and analyzing the information. Data collection can be by the company's marketing research staff or, more usually, by outside firms. The company keeps more control over the collection process and data quality by using its staff. However, outside firms that specialize in data collection can often do the job more quickly and at lower cost.

The data collection phase of the marketing research process is generally the most expensive and the most subject to error. The researcher should watch field-work closely to make sure that the plan is implemented correctly and to guard against problems with contacting respondents, with respondents who refuse to co-operate or who give biased or dishonest answers, and with interviewers who make mistakes or take short cuts.

Researchers must process and analyze the collected data to isolate important information and findings. They need to check data from questionnaires for accuracy and completeness, and code it for computer analysis. The researchers then tabulate the results and compute averages and other statistical measures.

• *Interpreting and Reporting the Findings*

The researcher must now interpret the findings, draw conclusions and report them to management. The researcher should not try to overwhelm managers with numbers and fancy statistical techniques. Rather, the researcher should present important findings that are useful in the important decisions faced by management.

However, interpretation should not be by the researchers alone. They are often experts in research design and statistics, but the marketing manager knows more about the problem and the decisions needed. In many cases, findings can be interpreted in different ways and discussions between researchers and managers will help point to the best interpretations. The manager will also want to check that the research project was conducted properly and that all the necessary analysis was completed. Or, after seeing the findings, the manager may have additional questions that can be answered from the data. Finally, the manager is the one who must ultimately decide what action the research suggests. The researchers may even make the data directly available to marketing managers so that they can perform new analyses and test new relationships on their own.

Interpretation is an important phase of the marketing process. The best research is meaningless if the manager blindly accepts wrong interpretations from the researcher. Similarly, managers may have biased interpretations – they tend to accept research results that show what they expected and to reject those that they did not expect or hope for. Thus managers and researchers must work together closely when interpreting research results and both share responsibility for the research process and resulting decisions.[27]

Demand Estimation

When a company finds an attractive market, it must estimate that market's current size and future potential carefully. The company can lose a considerable amount of profit by overestimating or underestimating the market.

Demand is measured and forecast on many levels. Figure 8.3 shows 90 types of demand measurement! Demand might be measured for six different *product levels* (product item, product form, product line, company sales, industry sales

Table 8.7	Types of question

A. CLOSED-END QUESTIONS

NAME	DESCRIPTION
Dichotomous	A question offering two answer choices.
Multiple choice	A question offering three or more choices.
Likert scale	A statement with which the respondent shows the amount of agreement or disagreement.
Semantic differential	A scale is inscribed between two bipolar words, and the respondent selects the point that represents the direction and intensity of his or her feelings.
Importance scale	A scale that rates the importance of some attribute from 'not at all important' to 'extremely important'.
Rating scale	A scale that rates some attribute from 'poor' to 'excellent'.
Intention-to-buy scale	A scale that describes the respondent's intentions to buy.

B. OPEN-END QUESTIONS

NAME	DESCRIPTION
Completely unstructured Word association	A question that respondents can answer in an almost unlimited number of ways. Words are presented, one at a time, and respondents mention the first word that comes to mind.
Sentence completion Story completion	Incomplete sentences are presented, one at a time, and respondents complete the sentence. An incomplete story is presented, and respondents are asked to complete it. in me the following thoughts and feelings.' *Now complete the story*.
Picture completion	A picture of two characters is presented, with one making a statement. Respondents are asked to identify with the other and fill in the empty balloon.
Thematic Apperception Tests (TAT)	A picture is presented, and respondents are asked to make up a story about what they think is happening or may happen in the picture.

'In arranging this trip, did you personally phone SAS?'   Yes ☐   No ☐

'With whom are you travelling on this flight?'

No one	☐	Children only	☐
Spouse	☐	Business associates/friends/relatives	☐
Spouse and children	☐	An organized tour group	☐

'Small airlines generally give better service than large ones.'

Strongly disagree	Disagree	Neither agree nor disagree	Agree	Strongly agree
1 ☐	2 ☐	3 ☐	4 ☐	5 ☐

SAS Airlines

Large	×__ : ___ : ___ : ___ : ___ : ___ :	Small
Experienced	___ : ___ : ___ : ___ : _×_ : ___ :	Inexperienced
Modern	___ : ___ : ___ : _×_ : ___ : ___ :	Old-fashioned

'Airline food service to me is'

Extremely important	Very important	Somewhat important	Not very important	Not at all important
1 ____	2 ____	3 ____	4 ____	5 ____

'SAS's food service is'

Excellent	Very good	Good	Fair	Poor
1 ____	2 ____	3 ____	4 ____	5 ____

'If in-flight telephone service were available on a long flight, I would'

Definitely buy	Probably buy	Not certain	Probably not buy	Definitely not buy
1 ____	2 ____	3 ____	4 ____	5 ____

'What is your opinion of SAS?' _____

'What is the first word that comes to your mind when you hear the following?'

Airline _____

Delta _____

Travel _____

'When I choose an airline, the most important consideration in my decision is _____.'

'I flew SAS a few days ago. I noticed that the exterior and interior of the plane had very bright colours. This aroused

Fill in the empty balloon.

WELL HERE'S THE FOOD.

Make up a story about what you see.

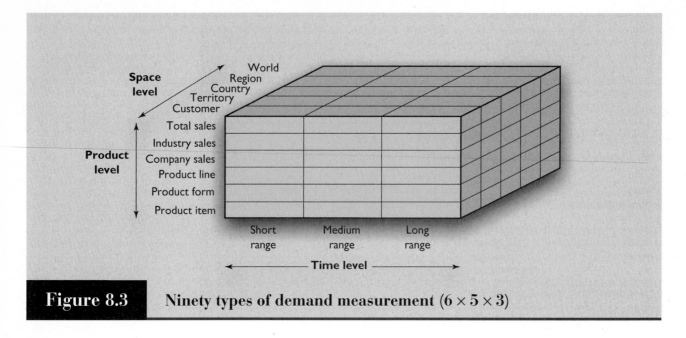

| Figure 8.3 | **Ninety types of demand measurement (6 × 5 × 3)** |

and total sales); five different *space levels* (customer, territory, country, region, world); and three different *time levels* (short range, medium range and long range).

Each demand measure serves a specific purpose. A company might forecast short-run total demand for a product as a basis for ordering raw materials, planning production and borrowing cash. Or it might forecast long-run regional demand for a big product line as a basis for designing a market expansion strategy.

Defining the Market

Market demand measurement calls for a clear understanding of the market involved. The term *market* has acquired many meanings over the years. In its original meaning, a market is a physical place where buyers and sellers gather to exchange goods and services. Medieval towns had market squares where sellers brought their goods and buyers shopped for goods. Markets still dominate retailing in the Third World and remain in many towns, but most of today's buying and selling occurs in shopping areas.

To an economist, a market describes all the buyers and sellers who transact over some good or service. Thus the soft-drink market consists of sellers such as Coca-Cola, Pepsi-Cola, Tango and Lilt and all the consumers who buy soft drinks. The economist's interest is the structure, conduct and performance of each market.

To a marketer, a **market** is the set of all actual and potential buyers of a product or service. A market is the set of buyers and an **industry** is the set of sellers. The size of a market hinges on the number of buyers who might exist for a particular market offer. Potential buyers for something have three characteristics: *interest*, *income* and *access*.

Consider the consumer market for Finnish Tunturi exercise cycles. To assess its market, Tunturi must first estimate the number of consumers who have a potential interest in owning an exercise bike. To do this, the company could

market
The set of all actual and potential buyers of a product or service.

industry
A group of firms which offer a product or class of products that are close substitutes for each other. The set of all sellers of a product or service.

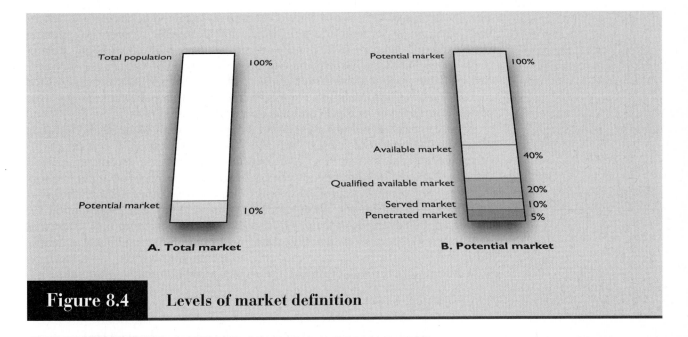

Figure 8.4   **Levels of market definition**

contact a random sample of consumers and ask the following question: 'Do you have an interest in buying and owning an exercise bike?' If one person out of ten says yes, Tunturi can assume that 10 per cent of the total number of consumers would constitute the potential market for exercise bikes. The **potential market** is the set of consumers who profess some level of interest in a particular product or service.

Consumer interest alone is not enough to define the exercise bike market. Potential consumers must have enough income to afford the product. They must be able to answer yes to the following question: 'Would you pay Fmk1,000 for an exercise bike?' The higher the price, the lower the number of people who can answer yes to this question. Thus market size depends on both interest and income.

Access barriers further reduce exercise bike market size. If Tunturi has no distributors for its products in some areas, potential consumers in those areas are not available as customers. The **available market** is the set of consumers who have interest, income and access to a particular product or service.

Tunturi might restrict sales to certain groups. Excessive repetitive exercise can damage young children, so sale of exercise bikes to anyone under 12 years of age may be discouraged. The remaining adults make up the **qualified available market** – the set of consumers who have interest, income, access and qualifications for the product or service.

Tunturi now has the choice of going after the whole qualified available market or concentrating on selected segments. Tunturi's **served market** is the part of the qualified available market it decides to pursue. For example, Tunturi may decide to concentrate its marketing and distribution efforts in northern Europe, where the winter nights are cold and long. This becomes its served market.

Tunturi and its competitors will end up selling a certain number of exercise bikes in their served market. The **penetrated market** is the set of consumers who have already bought exercise bikes.

Figure 8.4 brings all these market ideas together using hypothetical numbers. The bar on the left of the figure shows the ratio of the potential market – all interested persons – to the total population. Here the potential market is 10 per cent. The bar on the right shows several possible breakdowns of the potential market.

potential market
The set of consumers who profess some level of interest in a particular product or service.

available market
The set of consumers who have interest, income and access to a particular product or service.

qualified available market
The set of consumers who have interest, income, access and qualifications for a particular product or service.

served market (target market)
The part of the qualified available market that the company decides to pursue.

penetrated market
The set of consumers who have already bought a particular product or service.

The available market – those who have interest, income and access – is 40 per cent of the potential market. The qualified available market – those who can meet the legal requirements – is 50 per cent of the available market (or 20 per cent of the potential market). Tunturi concentrates its efforts on 50 per cent of the qualified available market – the served market, which is 10 per cent of the potential market. Finally, Tunturi and its competitors have already penetrated 50 per cent of the served market (or 5 per cent of the potential market).

These market definitions are a useful tool for marketing planning. If Tunturi is unsatisfied with current sales, it can take a number of actions. It can expand to other available markets in Europe or elsewhere. It can lower its price to expand the size of the potential market. It can try to attract a larger percentage of buyers from its served market through stronger promotion or distribution efforts to current target consumers. Or it can try to expand the potential market by increasing its advertising to convert non-interested consumers into interested consumers. Concern over heart diseases means that many middle-aged people who have avoided exercise for years are being encouraged to do more. Perhaps Tunturi can work through the health industry to attract these.

Measuring Current Market Demand

Marketers need to estimate three aspects of current market demand: total market demand; area market demand; and actual sales and market shares.

Estimating Total Market Demand

total market demand
The total volume of a product or service that would be bought by a defined consumer group in a defined geographic area in a defined time period in a defined marketing environment under a defined level and mix of industry marketing effort.

The **total market demand** for a product or service is the total volume that would be bought by a defined consumer group in a defined geographic area in a defined time period in a defined marketing environment under a defined level and mix of industry marketing effort.

Total market demand is not a fixed number, but a function of the stated conditions. One of these conditions, for example, is the level and mix of industry marketing effort. Another is the state of the environment. Part A of Figure 8.5 shows the relationship between total market demand and these conditions. The horizontal axis shows different possible levels of industry marketing expenditure in a given period. The vertical axis shows the resulting demand level. The curve represents the estimated level of market demand for varying levels of industry marketing expenditure. Some base sales (called the *market minimum*) would take place without any marketing expenditure. Greater marketing expenditures would yield higher levels of demand, first at an increasing rate and then at a decreasing rate. Marketing expenditures above a certain level would not cause much more demand, suggesting an upper limit to market demand called the *market potential*. The industry market forecast shows the level of market demand corresponding to the planned level of industry marketing expenditure in the given environment.[28]

The distance between the market minimum and the market potential shows the overall sensitivity of demand to marketing efforts. We can think of two extreme types of market: the *expandable* and the *non-expandable*. An expandable market, such as the market for compact disc players, is one whose size depends upon the level of industry marketing expenditures. For Figure 8.5A, in an expandable market, the distance between Q_0 and Q_1 would be fairly large. In a

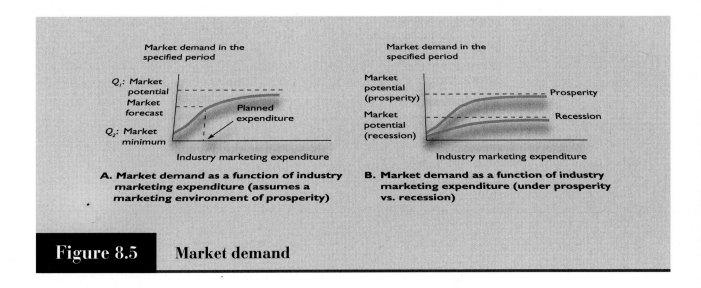

Market demand in the specified period

Q_1: Market potential
Market forecast

Planned expenditure

Q_2: Market minimum

Industry marketing expenditure

A. Market demand as a function of industry marketing expenditure (assumes a marketing environment of prosperity)

Market demand in the specified period

Market potential (prosperity) — Prosperity

Market potential (recession) — Recession

Industry marketing expenditure

B. Market demand as a function of industry marketing expenditure (under prosperity vs. recession)

| **Figure 8.5** | **Market demand** |

non-expandable market, such as that for opera, marketing expenditures generate little demand; the distance between Q_0 and Q_1 would be fairly small. Organizations selling in a non-expandable market can take **primary demand** – total demand for all brands of a given product or service – as given. They concentrate their marketing resources on building **selective demand** – demand for *their* brand of the product or service.

primary demand
The level of total demand for all brands of a given product or service – for example, the total demand for motor cycles.

Given a different marketing environment, we must estimate a new market demand curve. For example, the market for exercise bikes is stronger during prosperity than during recession. Figure 8.5B shows the relationship of market demand to the environment. A given level of marketing expenditure will always result in more demand during prosperity than it would during a recession. The main point is that marketers should carefully define the situation for which they are estimating market demand.

selective demand
The demand for a given brand of a product or service.

Companies have developed various practical methods for estimating total market demand. We will illustrate two here. Suppose Dutch-owned Polygram wants to estimate the total annual sales of recorded compact discs. A common way to estimate total market demand is as follows:

$$Q = n \times q \times p$$

where

Q = total market demand;
n = number of buyers in the market;
q = quantity purchased by an average buyer per year; and
p = price of an average unit.

Thus, if there are 10 million buyers of CDs each year and the average buyer buys six discs a year and the average price is DFl 40, then the total market demand for cassette tapes is DFl 2,400 million (= 10,000,000 × 6 × DFl 40).

A variation on the preceding equation is the *chain ratio method*. Using this method, the analyst multiplies a base number by a chain of adjusting percentages. For example, the United Kingdom has no national service, so the British Army needs to attract 20,000 new male recruits each year. There is a problem here, since the Army is already under strength and the population of 16 to 19-year-olds is declining. The marketing question is whether this is a reasonable target in relation to the market potential. The Army estimates market potential using the following method:

Estimating total market demand for a new product like RCA's Digital Satellite System presents a difficult challenge.

Total number of male secondary-school leavers	1,200,000
Percentage who are militarily qualified (no physical, emotional, or mental handicaps)	× 0.50
Percentage of those qualified who are potentially interested in military service	× 0.05
Percentage of those qualified and interested in military service who consider the Army the preferred service	× 0.60

This chain of numbers shows a market potential of 18,000 recruits. Since this is less than the target number of recruits sought, the Army needs to do a better job of marketing itself. They responded by doing motivational research that showed existing advertising did not attract the target age group, although a military career did give them what they wanted. A new campaign therefore aimed to increase the attractiveness of a military career to both men and women.[29]

Estimating Area and Market Demand

Companies face the problem of selecting the best sales territories and allocating their marketing budget optimally among these territories. Therefore they need to estimate the market potential of different cities, regions and even nations (see Marketing Highlight 8.2). Two main methods are available: the market-build-up method, used primarily by business-goods firms; and the market-factor index method, used primarily by consumer-goods firms.

The **market-build-up method** identifies all the potential buyers in each market and estimates their potential purchases. Suppose a manufacturer of mining instruments developed an instrument for assessing the actual proportion of gold content in gold-bearing ores. The portable instrument tests gold ore in the field. By using it, miners would not waste their time digging deposits of ore containing too little gold to be commercially profitable. It sees each mine as buying one or more instruments, depending on the mine's size. The company wants to determine the market potential for this instrument in each gold-mining country and whether to hire a salesperson to cover it.

To estimate the market potential in each country, the manufacturer first finds out the number of gold-mining operations in each country, their locations, the

market-build-up method
A method used mainly by business products firms to estimate the market potential of a city, region or country based on determining all the potential buyers in the market and estimating their potential purchases.

KFC Gets Japan Finger Lickin'

Everyone is familiar with complaints about the bilateral trade deficits of the European Union (EU) and United States with Japan. Many reasons are suggested for why the Japanese market is 'impenetrable': because it is a closed market, the non-tariff barriers, the stranglehold of the *keiretsu kigyi* (banking groups), the archaic tied distribution system of mama and papa stores, or just because the Japanese are 'workaholics' who live in 'little more than rabbit hutches'. If these claims are true, the fast-food market must be particularly hard to crack in a country that cooks creatures alive in Cruel Grill and Hell Tufo cuisine.

But not so – KFC (previously known as Kentucky Fried Chicken) is now the second largest fast-food chain in Japan. It is also the market leader in China, South Korea, Malaysia, Thailand and Indonesia, and it is second only to McDonald's in Singapore. KFC's 1,470 Asian outlets average $1.2 million per store, about 60 per cent more than its US average. In Tiananmen Square, KFC operates its busiest outlet, a 701-seat restaurant serving 2.5 million customers a year. No wonder KFC plans to double its number of Asian outlets during the next five years.

Why is KFC so successful in Asia? First, many of the large Asian cities have a growing concentration of young middle-class urban workers with rising incomes. Fast-food outlets represent a step up from buying food at hawkers' stalls, and Asians are willing to pay more for sitting in an American-style restaurant. Second, Asian women have been entering the labour force in large numbers, leaving them with less time for cooking meals at home. Third, chicken is more familiar to the Asian palate than pizza, and more available than beef. Further, chicken faces none of the religious strictures that beef faces in India or that pork faces in Muslim countries. KFC serves its standard chicken, mashed potatoes and coleslaw throughout Asia, but has offered a few adaptations, such as Hot Wings, a spicier chicken, in Thailand, and fried fish and chicken curry in Japan.

As *Le Monde* recognized years ago: 'To continue to complain about the bilateral deficit with Japan as the result of Japanese protectionism only serves to obscure the problem, not resolve it.' All markets have entry barriers and Japan's are more discouragement to enter than real costs. Japan is the largest market that the United States and Europe have never been close to. It has a strong culture that is so different from the West's that we have to try very hard to grasp it. The trade barriers are often an excuse for European and US failures to penetrate the Japanese market. Often those who complain most loudly about the barriers are businesspeople who have never tried or who have tried once and failed. The Japanese rarely give up after only one attempt.

KFC has tried and won. So has Nestlé, and KitKat is now Japan's second-best-selling confectionery. Clearly companies can succeed if they view the world as their market and take the time to learn. They must find those areas that promise the greatest potential sales and profit growth, whether in their neighbourhood, state or nation, or even in Japan.

SOURCES: Andrew Tanzer, 'Hot wings take off', *Forbes* (18 January 1993), p. 74; George Staunton, 'Tokyo: aller au fond des choses', *Le Monde* (12 December 1977), p. 7; Endymion Wilkinson, *Japan Versus the West: Image and reality* (London: Penguin, 1990); Leonard Koren, *283 Useful Ideas from Japan* (San Francisco, CA: Chronicle, 1988); Sheridan M. Tatsumo, *Created in Japan: From imitation to world-class innovators* (London: Harper & Row, 1990).

number of employees, annual sales and net worth. This will be harder in some countries than others, since some have poor records and others, like China, are secretive about gold mining. Using these data, the company can estimate the market potential of each country based on the number of mines that are big enough and wealthy enough to buy the instrument.

market-factor index method
A method used mainly by consumer products firms to estimate the market potential for consumer products.

The **market-factor index method** estimates the market potential for consumer goods. Consider the following example. An American manufacturer of men's dress shirts wishes to evaluate its sales performance with market potential in the Indianapolis region. It estimates total national potential for dress shirts at $2 billion per year. The company's current nationwide sales are $140 million – about a 7 per cent share of the total potential market. Its sales in the Indianapolis metropolitan area are $1,100,000. It wants to know whether its share of the Indianapolis market is higher or lower than its national 7 per cent market share. To find this out, the company first needs to calculate market potential in the Indianapolis area.

The company calculates this by multiplying together population and the area's income per capita by the average share of income spent on shirts. The product then compares with that for the whole country. Using this calculation, the shirt manufacturer finds that Indianapolis accounts for 0.51 per cent of the nation's total potential demand for dress shirts. Since the total national potential is $2 billion each year, total potential in Indianapolis equals $10,200,000 (= $2 billion × 0.0051). Thus the company's sales in Indianapolis of $1,100,000 amount to a 10.8 per cent share (= $1,100,000/$10,200,000) of area market potential. Comparing this with the 7 per cent national share, the company appears to be doing better in Indianapolis than in other parts of the country.

Estimating Actual Sales and Market Shares

Besides estimating total and area demand, a company will want to know the actual industry sales in its market. Thus it must identify its competitors and estimate their sales.

The industry's trade association will often collect and publish total industry sales, although not listing individual company sales separately. In this way, each company can evaluate its performance against the industry as a whole. Suppose the company's sales are increasing at a rate of 5 per cent a year and industry sales are increasing at 10 per cent. This company is losing its relative standing in the industry.

Another way to estimate sales is to buy reports from marketing research firms that audit total sales and brand sales. For example, Nielsen, AGB and other marketing research firms use scanner data to audit the retail sales of various product categories in supermarkets and pharmacies, and sell this information to interested companies. A company can obtain data on total product category sales as well as brand sales. It can compare its performance with that of the total industry or any particular competitor to see whether it is gaining or losing in its relative standing.[30]

forecasting
The art of estimating future demand by anticipating what buyers are likely to do under a given set of conditions.

Forecasting Future Demand

Having looked at ways to estimate current demand, we now examine ways to forecast future market demand. **Forecasting** is the art of estimating future demand by

Table 8.8	**Common sales forecasting techniques**

BASED ON:	METHODS
What people say	Surveys of buyers' intentions
	Composite sales force opinions
	Expert opinion
What people do	Test markets
What people have done	Time-series analysis
	Leading indicators
	Statistical demand analysis

anticipating what buyers are likely to do under a given set of conditions. Very few products or services lend themselves to easy forecasting. Those that do generally involve a product with steady sales, or sales growth in a stable competitive situation. But most markets do not have stable total and company demand, so good forecasting becomes a key factor in company success. Poor forecasting can lead to excessively large inventories, costly price mark-downs, or lost sales due to being out of stock. The more unstable the demand, the more the company needs accurate forecasts and elaborate forecasting procedures.

Companies commonly use a three-stage procedure to arrive at a sales forecast. First they make an *environmental forecast*, followed by an *industry forecast*, followed by a *company sales forecast*. The environmental forecast calls for projecting inflation, unemployment, interest rates, consumer spending and saving, business investment, government expenditures, net exports and other environmental events important to the company. The result is a forecast of gross national product, which is used along with other indicators to forecast industry sales. Then the company prepares its sales forecast assuming a certain share of industry sales.

Companies use several specific techniques to forecast their sales. Table 8.8 lists some of these techniques.[31] All forecasts build on one of three information bases: what people say, what people do, or what people have done. The first basis – *what people say* – involves surveying the opinions of buyers or those close to them, such as salespeople or outside experts. It includes three methods: surveys of buyer intentions, composites of sales force opinions and expert opinion. Building a forecast on *what people do* involves another method, that of putting the product into a test market to assess buyer response. The final basis – *what people have done* – involves analyzing records of past buying behaviour or using time-series analysis or statistical demand analysis.

Survey of Buyers' Intentions

One way to forecast what buyers will do is to ask them directly. This suggests that the forecaster should survey buyers. Surveys are especially valuable if the buyers have clearly formed intentions, will carry them out and can describe them to interviewers.

Several research organizations conduct periodic surveys of consumer buying intentions. These organizations ask questions like the following:

<small>DO YOU INTEND TO BUY A CAR WITHIN THE NEXT SIX MONTHS?</small>

0.0	0.1	0.2	0.3	0.4	0.5	0.6	0.7	0.8	0.9	1.0
No chance		Slight chance		Fair chance		Good chance		Strong chance		For certain

This is a *purchase probability scale*. In addition, the various surveys ask about the consumer's present and future personal finances and their expectations about the economy. Consumer durable goods companies subscribe to these indices to help them anticipate significant shifts in consumer buying intentions, so that they can adjust their production and marketing plans accordingly. For *business buying*, various agencies carry out intention surveys about plant, equipment and materials purchases. These measures need adjusting when conducted across nations and cultures. Overestimation of intention to buy is higher in southern Europe than it is in northern Europe and the United States. In Asia, the Japanese tend to make fewer overstatements than the Chinese.[32]

Composite of Sales Force Opinions

When buyer interviewing is impractical, the company may base its sales forecasts on information provided by the sales force. The company typically asks its salespeople to estimate sales by product for their individual territories. It then adds up the individual estimates to arrive at an overall sales forecast.

Few companies use their sales force's estimates without some adjustments. Salespeople are biased observers. They may be naturally pessimistic or optimistic, or they may go to one extreme or another because of recent sales setbacks or successes. Furthermore, they are often unaware of larger economic developments and do not always know how their company's marketing plans will affect future sales in their territories. They may understate demand so that the company will set a low sales quota. They may not have the time to prepare careful estimates or may not consider it worthwhile.

Accepting these biases, a number of benefits can be gained by involving the sales force in forecasting. Salespeople may have better insights into developing trends than any other group. After participating in the forecasting process, the salespeople may have greater confidence in their quotas and more incentive to achieve them. Also, such grass-roots' forecasting provides estimates broken down by product, territory, customer and salesperson.[33]

Expert Opinion

Companies can also obtain forecasts by turning to experts. Experts include dealers, distributors, suppliers, marketing consultants and trade associations. Thus motor vehicle companies survey their dealers periodically for their forecasts of short-term demand. Dealer estimates, however, are subject to the same strengths and weaknesses as sales force estimates.

Many companies buy economic and industry forecasts. These forecasting specialists are in a better position than the company to prepare economic forecasts because they have more data available and more forecasting expertise.

Occasionally companies will invite a special group of experts to prepare a forecast. They may exchange views and come up with a group estimate (group

Information Analysis

Information gathered by the company's marketing information systems often requires more analysis, and sometimes managers may need more help in applying it to marketing problems and decisions. This help may include advanced statistical analysis to learn more about both the relationships within a set of data and their statistical reliability (Chapters 9 and 10 show these factors used in segmentation and positioning research). Such analysis allows managers to go beyond means and standard deviations in the data. In an examination of consumer non-durable goods in the Netherlands, regression analysis gave a model that forecast a brand's market share (B_t) based upon predicted marketing activity:[36]

$$B_t = -7.85 - 1.45P_t + 0.08A_{t-1} + 1.23D_t$$

where

P_t = relative price of brand;
A_{t-1} = advertising share in the previous period; and
D_t = effective store distribution.

This, and models like it, can help answer marketing questions such as:

- What are the chief variables affecting my sales and how important is each one?
- If I raised my price 10 per cent and increased my advertising expenditures 20 per cent, what would happen to sales?
- How much should I spend on advertising?
- What are the best predictors of which consumers are likely to buy my brand versus my competitor's brand?
- What are the best variables for segmenting my market and how many segments exist?

Information analysis might also involve a collection of mathematical models that will help marketers make better decisions. Each model represents some real system, process or outcome. These models can help answer the questions of *what if?* and *which is best?* During the past 20 years, marketing scientists have developed numerous models to help marketing managers make better marketing-mix decisions, design sales territories and sales-call plans, select sites for retail outlets, develop optimal advertising mixes and forecast new-product sales.[37]

Distributing Information

Information has no value until managers use it to make better marketing decisions. The information gathered needs distributing to the right marketing managers at the right time. Most companies have centralized marketing information systems that provide managers with regular performance reports, intelligence updates and reports on the results of studies. Managers need these routine reports for making regular planning, implementation and control decisions. But marketing managers may also need non-routine information for special situations and on-the-spot decisions. For example, a sales manager having trouble with a large customer may want a summary of the account's sales and profitability over the past year. Or a retail store manager who has run out of a best-selling product

European Research

Marketing Highlight 8.4

Neither Europe nor even the European Union can be researched as one market. The market is getting closer to fulfilment, but some difficulties remain. The market research industry structure is fairly standard across the EU and most services are available everywhere. However, many large agencies including Control Data Corporation, IRI, GfK and Video Research, cover only a few countries.[1] Frequently, if conducting international studies, agencies have to use the facilities provided by local research companies. To serve multinational clients better, many large and small firms are now forming alliances in order to ease cross-border research. Co-operative ventures have allowed medium-sized companies to build a reputation for international research. For example, Research Services and its associates conduct both the European Businessman's Readership Survey and the Asian Businessman's Readership Survey. Euroline is a one-stop-shop telephone interviewing consortium set up by agencies in France, Germany, Italy, Spain and the United Kingdom. This will allow one questionnaire to be written, transmitted to other countries, translated, then hopefully checked carefully.

There is a huge disparity of incomes and consumption within the EU: Denmark, Germany and Luxembourg have a gross domestic product per capita more than four times that of Portugal and three times that of Greece. New members from eastern Europe will make the gap even wider. Differences in wealth account for only a small part of the variation in consumption and consumer behaviour. Some differences, like eating habits, are clearly rooted in the different languages, cultural traditions and cuisine of the EU, but there are also big differences in the consumption of modern industrial goods. In Spain, the penetration of consumer durables shows they are in the early stages of a slowly unwinding product life cycle, whereas the same products are maturing elsewhere. For example, in Spain penetration of home computers (11 per cent), CD players (9 per cent) and microwave ovens (9 per cent) contrasts with the penetration of home computers in Belgium (29 per cent), CD players in the Netherlands (60 per cent) and microwave ovens in the United Kingdom (60 per cent).

Competition and distribution also vary. Many European markets have locally dominant companies and competitive structures that are unique to them. The big multinationals now operate in most markets, but their strength in each market varies. The structure of retailing within the EU varies massively. The greatest contrast is between the United Kingdom, dominated by a few large retailers, and Italy where mama and papa stores dominate. Europe has many large chains, such as Germany's Tengelmann, France's Leclerc, Britain's J. Sainsbury and Dutch Ahold, but most

TABLE 1 THE EUROPEAN UNION 1998: IN THE CLUB, IN THE QUEUE AND IN THE DISTANCE

STATUS	POPULATION (MILLION)	COUNTRIES
EU	372.5	Austria, Belgium, Denmark, Finland, France, Germany, Greece, Holland, Ireland, Italy, Luxembourg, Portugal, Spain, Sweden and United Kingdom
Fast-track applicants	63.1	Cyprus, Czech Republic, Estonia, Hungary, Poland Slovenia
Pre-accession partnership applicants	42.7	Bulgaria, Latvia, Lithuania, Romania and Slovakia
Other applicants	60.8	Turkey

1. Research and development
2. Partnering
3. Product development cycle

II. Specific questions to be addressed
   A. What problems do equipment manufacturers and retailers face in making and selling home appliances? How can ACT help solve those problems?
   B. Who are the decision makers in the electronics buying process? Who has the power between the retailer and the equipment manufacturer?
   C. Are there any unidentified issues from ACT's, the manufacturers' or the retailers' perspectives?
   D. How rapidly will manufacturers adopt electronic controls for their appliances, by category of appliances?
   E. How sensitive are manufacturers to the price of electronic controls versus standard electromechanical controls?
   F. What are the manufacturers' impressions of suppliers' strengths and weaknesses?
   G. What features and issues other than price drive the use of electronic controls?
   H. How can manufacturers use electronic controls to add value to mid-level appliances?
   I. How can a supplier be a better partner to manufacturers?
   J. What can a supplier do to speed up manufacturers' product development efforts?

III. Who should be interviewed?
   A. Manufacturers
      1. Functional areas
         a. Purchasing
         b. Marketing
         c. Engineering
      2. Specific companies
         a. Whirlpool
         b. Frigidaire
         c. General Electric
         d. Maytag
         e. Raytheon
   B. Retailers
      1. Functional areas
         a. Buyers
         b. Store-level management
         c. Floor sales personnel
      2. Specific companies
         a. Sears
         b. Montgomery Ward
         c. Highland
         d. Wal-Mart
   C. Other
      1. Association of Home Appliance Manufacturers

EXHIBIT 8.3 VERSION 1 – ACT MARKETING RESEARCH QUESTIONNAIRE

Introduction

ACT is conducting a survey of decision makers and industry experts in the electronic appliance controls industry. We would appreciate your help in answering our questions. Your responses will be reported anonymously, if they are reported at all. Your responses will be used to help ACT determine how to serve the appliance industry better.

Questions

1. A. What are your opinions on the level of electronic control usage, expressed in percentages, in the following appliance categories for 1991 and 1996?

B. What are your opinions on the average cost per electronic control by appliance category in 1991 and 1996?

Category	Percentage of units using electronic controls in:		Average cost per control unit in:	
	1991	1996	1991	1996
Cookers, electric	____	____	____	____
Cookers, gas	____	____	____	____
Dishwashers	____	____	____	____
Dryers, electric	____	____	____	____
Dryers, gas	____	____	____	____
Microwaves	____	____	____	____
Refrigerators	____	____	____	____
Washers	____	____	____	____
Room air conditioners	____	____	____	____

2. For each of the following categories, what price must a supplier charge for an electronic control unit such that a manufacturer would be indifferent as to using electronic or electromechanical controls, taking into account the differences in functions and features?

Category	Price per electronic unit
Cookers, electric	_____
Cookers, gas	_____
Dishwashers	_____
Dryers, electric	_____
Dryers, gas	_____
Microwaves	_____
Refrigerators	_____
Washers	_____
Room air conditioners	_____

3. What features, functions and attributes do electronic controls need to have if they are to be used more often in appliances?

4. What impact will the forthcoming Department of Energy regulations have on the appliance industry?

5. What can an electronic controls company do to be a better supplier?

QUESTIONS

1. Based on information in the case and in Exhibits 2 and 3, just what *is* Leyshon trying to learn through marketing research? What additional trends and information might he want to monitor as part of his ongoing marketing information system?

2. What sources of marketing intelligence can ACT use to gather information on the industry and its competition?

3. What decisions has ACT made about its research approach, contact method and sampling plan?

4. Evaluate ACT's proposed questionnaire (Exhibit 3). Does it address the issues raised in Exhibit 2? What changes would you recommend?

5. Based on the marketing research process discussed in the text, what is ACT's marketing research objective, and what problem is the company addressing?

6. Evaluate ACT's marketing research process (Exhibit 1).

Ballygowan Springs into New Age Kisqua

*Brenda Cullen**

Introduction

IN JANUARY 1991 GEOFF READ, managing director of Ballygowan Spring Water Company, had to make a decision that could alter the whole direction of the company. Since August 1988 the management team had shaped a strategy to launch a drink to develop upon the success of Ballygowan Spring Water. The objective was to provide Ballygowan with a product to enter the soft-drinks market and so remove the weakness of being a one-product company. After identifying the market for 'new age' products, and carrying out research at each stage in the product development process, the results of a final test market were disappointing. Ballygowan had to consider whether to withdraw the product, to redesign and reposition the new range, or to go ahead and launch as originally planned.

Geoff Read founded Ballygowan in 1981 and by 1991 the company exported to 15 countries and held 77 per cent of the 12.5 million litre water market in Ireland and had developed an extensive range of bottled spring water products. Tipperary was no. 2 in the market with 13.5 per cent market share. Since 1987 Perrier's share had dropped from 13 to 4 per cent.

Between 1987 and 1989 the company grew to be a medium-sized enterprise geared for expansion and growth. A joint investment with Anheuser Busch provided a very modern production facility covering 30,000 square metres with a capacity of 600 bottles per minute. Ballygowan's success came from being an innovator in the market for water-based products, and also from astute management of the Ballygowan brand franchise. Management now saw the need to exploit the assets of the company more profitably. In particular, the plant was not at full capacity and the company's strong distribution network and experienced management were not being fully utilized.

● *Bottled Water Market*

By the end of 1985 the bottled water market in Ireland was I£1.2 million (2.8 million litres) with about 10 per cent of adults drinking mineral water regularly.

* University College Dublin, Ireland.

By 1990 it had grown to I£12.5 million (12.5 million litres), 5.5 per cent of the Irish soft-drinks market. The bottled water market was 'one of the fastest growing sectors in the food trade in both Ireland and the UK'. Reasons for this were a reduction in the quality of tap water and changing attitudes towards health and fitness, which led to an increase in the demand for drinks perceived as natural, alcohol free and with fewer calories. Furthermore, *increasingly* stringent drink-driving legislation was leading to an increase in the consumption of bottled water. A Euromonitor survey in 1989 showed that the Irish consumed far less bottled water per person than other countries (Ireland: 3 litres; United Kingdom: 5.5; Italy: 80; Germany: 76; France: 68; and the United States: 30).

The market potential for spring water in Ireland was small considering the number of competitor brands on the market. While some niche brands had high prices, low prices were becoming common because of aggressive high-street pricing, own-label products and cheap imports. With a proliferation of products and the threat of commoditization, it was becoming difficult to develop new niches in the market.

● *Ballygowan Spring Water*

Ballygowan's success came from the sparkling and non-sparkling waters – Ballygowan Sparkling Irish Spring Water and Ballygowan Natural Irish Spring Water. A later addition to the range was Ballygowan Light, and in 1988 Ballygowan successfully launched a range of flavoured spring waters. By 1990 the company's turnover was I£10 million, a figure it hoped to double within the next two years. An important part of this strategy was the launch of soft drinks – a market where the company saw significant volume potential.

The management wanted to launch a new drink to bring Ballygowan further into the mainstream soft-drinks market. It would enhance the company's reputation for innovation, market leadership, excellence and product quality. The product would be purer, juicier, fruitier and healthier than any other soft drink on the market. The brand should be consistent with developing consumer behaviour, particularly attitudes and behaviours towards healthy diets and lifestyles.

The Irish carbonated soft-drinks market in 1990 was about 235 million litres, including approximately 40 million litres of adult soft drinks, up from 179 million litres in 1987. Soft-drink consumers were the target market for the proposed new product. They were likely to be more adult than young and would prefer to drink 7-Up (38 per cent) or Club Orange (25 per cent) to Coke or Pepsi (24 per cent). The profile of this consumer was 'a sophisticated, self-righteous and reasonably health-conscious adult', 18–30 years old, who wants and will pay for drinks that look good, taste good and portray a certain image.

● *Product Development Process*

A product development process identified product development, brand development and business planning stages. In December 1988, Ballygowan employed a marketing consultancy firm, Dimension, to help in the first two stages. The consultancy's brief was as follows:

- Identify and brief three companies to develop prototype products based on pure juices and Ballygowan Spring Water with natural flavours and sweeteners, carbonated, containing preservatives, but not pasteurized.
- Develop formulations for up to six flavours.
- Develop name, branding, positioning, communication and marketing strategies.

- Target the branded soft-drink sector – Coke, 7-Up, Club, Lilt, and so on.
- Develop a brand with a premium but accessible imagery, and superior product quality, but priced competitively with major brands.
- The brand should have no overt Ballygowan endorsement.
- It should be packed in 1.5 litre plastic bottles, 330 ml cans and 250 ml glasses.
- Primary focus to be the Irish market, but with export potential.

● *Product Sourcing*

The first task was to find a company that could manufacture the pure fruit juice to mix with Ballygowan Spring Water. Criteria for the selection of a company were degree of technological sophistication, ability to produce a range of flavours, expertise in producing fruit juices and flavours, product quality, hygiene standards and speed of response. Three short-listed companies were briefed. Visits to each company appraised their production processes and capabilities.

The three companies each made laboratory-scale products, which were tested using a structured questionnaire assessing aroma, appearance, taste and overall opinion on each of the test products. All tests were 'blind', and the products were compared with successful brands already on the market as 'controls'. The range of flavours screened included orange, lemon, apple, passion fruit, grapefruit, peach, pineapple, blackberry and blackcurrant. The aim was to achieve product ratings competitive with the 'controls' (see Exhibit 2.1).

EXHIBIT 2.1 TASTE TEST

PRODUCT	AROMA[a]	APPEARANCE[a]	TASTE[a]	OVERALL SCORE	LIKELIHOOD OF PURCHASE[b]
Club Orange	6.9	7.5	7.3	7.4	3.5
Dohler Orange	5.9	5.6	6.1	6.1	2.6
Dohler Orange and Peach	7.4	7.2	7.1	7.5	3.3
Dohler Orange and Passion Fruit	6.6	6.3	7.0	7.0	3.2
Dohler Orange and Lemon	6.4	6.4	6.9	7.2	3.2
Club Lemon	6.7	6.5	7.2	7.4	3.5
Dohler Lemon	6.5	6.9	6.9	7.4	3.2
Dohler Grapefruit and Pineapple	5.8	6.2	5.5	6.1	2.5

NOTES: [a] Average scores on nine-point scale, in which 9 = most favourable and 1 = least favourable; [b] on a scale of 1 to 5.

SOURCE: Dimension, March 1989.

After the analysis of each batch, the three companies were rebriefed, shown the taste test results and told the changes required. After repeating the process six times, a German company, which responded particularly well to the product brief and to the taste tests, was appointed as the supplier. Both companies then agreed plant and equipment specifications.

• *Product Formulations*

Six products were produced for a quantitative market research survey conducted in May 1989 by Behaviour & Attitudes, a market research agency in Dublin. A questionnaire, developed from Dimension's earlier one, focused on aroma, appearance and flavour. The flavours tested were 10 per cent orange juice, 15 per cent orange and peach juice, 15 per cent orange and passion fruit juice, 10 per cent orange and lemon juice, 10 per cent lemon juice, and 15 per cent grapefruit and pineapple juice, with Club Orange and Club Lemon as 'controls'. Each of 200 respondents taste-tested two Ballygowan samples and one of the 'controls', to give 75 assessments of each Ballygowan product.

The results convinced the Ballygowan team to focus on orange, orange and peach, orange and passion fruit, and orange and lemon. Lemon, and grapefruit and pineapple, could extend the range later (see Exhibit 2.2). Since the results of the orange formulation were not satisfactory, a second round of quantitative market research would take place with performance isolated from packaging and advertising effects.

EXHIBIT 2.2 SUMMARY RATINGS

	ORANGE PEACH (15% JUICE)	ORANGE LEMON (10% JUICE)	CLUB ORANGE	ORANGE (10% JUICE)	ORANGE PASSION FRUIT (15% JUICE)	LEMON (10% JUICE)	CLUB LEMON	GRAPEFRUIT AND PINEAPPLE (15% JUICE)
Aroma								
Attractiveness	5	3	4	2	3	4	4	2
Naturalness	5	2	2	2	4	3	3	2
Overall	5	3	3	2	3	4	4	2
Appearance								
Attractiveness	4	2	5	1	3	5	2	3
Naturalness	5	3	4	1	3	5	3	3
Overall	5	3	5	2	3	5	4	2
Flavour								
Good taste	4	3	5	1	3	4	5	1
Real fruit flavour	5	3	3	1	4	5	3	1
Sweetness (right)	5	3	3	3	3	5	5	3
Refreshment	5	3	5	1	3	5	5	1
Overall taste	5	3	4	1	4	4	4	1
Overall rating	5	4	4	1	3	4	5	1

Key: 5 Well above average
      4 Above average
      3 Average
      2 Below average
      1 Well below average

SOURCE: Behaviour & Attitudes, Market Research Survey, May 1989.

Some questions remained. Should the products be pasteurized, and should essence or preservatives be used? Each of these options had complications. Pasteurization meant that it would not be possible to use plastic bottles and there were also shelf-life implications. However, with pasteurization, the product ingredients are '100 per cent natural'. Using essence would overcome shelf-life difficulties, but would not be consistent with the brand propositions. Finally, preservatives were in most soft drinks on the market, but the management felt that they could compromise Ballygowan's image of purity and naturalness.

● *Product Concept and Brand Name Development*

The development of the product concept and branding began with brainstorming sessions by Dimension. Ballygowan's specification for the name was that it should be relevant, attractive, distinctive, memorable and registerable, and should have the attributes of a global brand name. Out of the hundreds of names generated, Juisca, Juzze, Artesia, Kisqua, Prima and Viva became prototype brand names. Five positioning options also helped explore the attitudes and motivations of soft-drink consumers:

1. *Health drink.* A pure, natural and healthy drink for mainstream soft-drink consumers who care about what they consume.
2. *Sophisticated.* A high-status drink of superior quality for discerning consumers.
3. *Healthy lifestyle.* For those who unselfconsciously lead and aspire to a healthy but full lifestyle in terms of diet, exercise and a relaxed but full life.
4. *Youthful peer groups.* The Pepsi/Club generation.
5. *Generic.* Refreshment, cooling, youthful and Coke sociability values.

Behaviour & Attitudes designed and conducted four focus groups representing market segments with different relationships to soft drinks (see Exhibit 2.3). The focus groups aimed to:

● Investigate the response to five prototype brand names.

● Explore reaction to seven prototype pack designs.

● Consider pack designs and bottling formats.

● Give direction to brand positioning.

EXHIBIT 2.3 FOCUS GROUPS

The four groups were:

1. Young teenage girls	Middle class	
2. Young men	18–24	C1 C2
3. Women	22–32	C2 with children
4. Women	22–32	B1 B2 with children

Target markets:

Primary	Secondary
Health/body conscious	Soft-drink consumers
A B C1	
Late teens/twenties	
Young and early teens	
Teenage adults	

SOURCE: Behaviour & Attitudes, Market Research, August 1989.

Discussions with each group followed a similar pattern. Initially respondents freely discussed their use and purchase of soft drinks. This naturally led to conversations about different brands. Next, the groups were told about the new idea for a soft drink and shown a board illustrating the new product concept. Following their responses to the concept, the groups were told that there were alternative prototype brand names and packaging designs. These were presented one by one, with the order of presentation being rotated between different groups. Proposed brand names and pack designs were presented separately.

Later, discussion group members were asked to help market the new brand; 'mood boards' were presented and associated with the different brand names and pack designs. Finally, copy statements, presented on boards representing different positioning options, were discussed.

EXHIBIT 2.4 GENERAL CONSUMER ATTITUDES TO SOFT DRINKS

YOUNG MEN	YOUNG GIRLS	YOUNG MARRIED WOMEN
• Perceived as the province of children and teenagers • Believe they are not emotionally involved in the market • Yet they are regular consumers – for thirst/refreshment • Therefore taste and refreshment are their criteria for judging soft drinks • Coca-Cola is the preferred brand • They associate 7-Up with contemporary youth, and refreshment • Will be difficult to impress – little emotional interest in soft drinks	• Very involved with brands as badges of both individuality and groups • Very conscious of style and fashion • Very high level of health consciousness • Brands reflect social valuations and status – Ballygowan, Perrier and 7-Up are stylish, sophisticated and healthy • Are high-volume users of soft drinks	• Regular purchasers for themselves and their families • Soft drinks are an essential household purchase item • Oriented towards health and exercise, reflected in their attitude to food and drink brands • Disposed towards natural products and low-calorie products • 'Natural' products identified as contemporary and fashionable • Working class want brands to be accessible; middle class focus on style

In September 1989, Behaviour & Attitudes debriefed Ballygowan about the research. First, it presented consumer attitudes to soft drinks generally (see Exhibit 2.4). The research indicated that teenage boys, teenage girls and young married women had different attitudes and motivations to soft drinks. Secondly, it examined consumer attitudes to soft-drink brands (see Exhibit 2.5) and consumer reaction to the five prototype brands (see Exhibit 2.6). Behaviour & Attitudes made the following points about reactions to the product concept:

1. The ingredients make it more sophisticated than mainstream soft drinks.
2. It was not seen as a totally novel idea. Consumers were aware of Nashs, Citrus Spring and Britvic.

3. The pleasant product and the endorsement of Ballygowan aroused a high predisposition to try it.

4. Price parity with Coke and 7-Up raised consumers' disposition to try the product.

EXHIBIT 2.5 CONSUMER ATTITUDES TO SOFT-DRINK BRANDS

Coke
- Perceived as the archetypal soft drink.
- Strong consistent branding, massive advertising support.
- Two problems: perceived by some as harsh, causing tooth decay, overly masculine personality.

Club Orange
- The archetypal orange soft drink.
- Its appeal is primarily based on its product characteristics – real orange taste with lots of orange in it.
- Advertising not consistent with the brand.

Lilt
- Has no clear product focus – a mix of different things.
- Dissonance between advertising and product knowledge.

7-Up
- Very coherent brand, with well-rounded persona.
- Very popular and the most contemporary soft drink.
- 'The soft drink for the 1990s.'
- Healthy perception – clean and clear.
- Appeals to male and female.
- Not limited to teenagers: helped by its mixer usage; helped by its healthy image.
- Strong perception of being refreshed.

Club Lemon
- Valued for its product characteristics of taste and refreshment.
- Very loyal consumers – almost a cult.

Lucozade
- Strong healthy drink imagery.
- Regarded as a soft drink by young men.
- Well out of its old hospital/sick bed positioning.
- Reparative quality for handling hangovers.

EXHIBIT 2.6 CONSUMER REACTIONS TO FIVE PROTOTYPE BRANDS

PROTOTYPE BRAND	REACTION TO NAME	REACTION TO DESIGN
Artesia	• Distinctive but difficult to come to terms with. • Far too up-market/exclusive. • Not appropriate to the product concept. • Will not appeal to a mass market. • More relevant to wine.	• Very up-market, albeit very beautiful. • Very 'designery', 'yuppie' and exclusive. • Very aspirational. • Very distinctive, but so sophisticated as to exclude the large majority.
Prima	• Very favourably received by working class – very easy to empathize with. • Straightforward, direct and impactful for the working class. • Targeted at mass market – no pretensions.	• Appealed only to a small minority, and contemporary. • Otherwise perceived as oriented to very young children. • Very dissonant with product concept.

PROTOTYPE BRAND	REACTION TO NAME	REACTION TO DESIGN
	• But: rejected by middle class. • Just another name, pedestrian. • Little depth of imagery. • Association with Pennys gives it a down-market image. • No distinctiveness.	
Viva	• Strong appeal to teenage girls – they associated it with beauty, fashion and style. • International – but clichéd and pedestrian. • Strong negative Spanish association: cheap. • Spanish orange drink; 'Viva España'; Costa del Sol. • Lively, bright, extrovert and exuberant. • Dynamic and modern brand.	• Lacked novelty, not stylish, not sophisticated. • Cheap. • Dissonant with the Ballygowan heritage. • Looked Spanish – negative imagery. • Blue colour not liked.
Juzze	• Significant pronunciation difficulties. • Superficial and artificial. • Yet youthful, contemporary and up to date. • International. • Correlated with the product concept, except for a phoniness in its spelling. • Associated with zest, zing and vitality. • Suggested pure fruit juice.	• In mainstream of soft-drinks market. • Very OK, but no surprise or aspirational qualities. • Lacks excitement or fun, too logical. • Consistently compared with Squeez and Britvic – but concentrated – is not pure orange juice. • Might position it against Britvic rather than Club.
Kisqua	• Pronunciation initially difficult, but quickly overcome. • Very definite and individualistic name. • Novel and unique brand name. • Drew favourable emotional relationships. • International and cosmopolitan – potential to be a 'world brand'. • Elegant and sophisticated. • High quality and accessible.	• The best representative of the new product. • Much more depth than other concept alternatives. • Good impact, will generate trial easily. • Stylish yet solidly in the mainstream of soft drinks – but a bit too straightforward? • Very good typography.

A series of meetings between Dimension and the Ballygowan management team considered brand positioning and target market strategies. They chose Kisqua as the brand name. It was stylish, novel, distinctive, memorable, appropriate and warm, and had the attributes of a world brand name. Ballygowan Spring Water's name would endorse Kisqua. Ballygowan also applied for registration of Artesia in case the company should wish to launch an up-market spring water.

• Marketing Mix

The Ballygowan company next needed to know the impact of the brand name, label design, price, positioning and advertising options on Kisqua's branding strategy. A further question was the reason for people's preference for Kisqua or Club Orange. In October 1989 Behaviour & Attitudes researched these key areas. It used a central location to approach a quota sample of 200 respondents. The respondents were in two equal subgroups: one group to taste-test Club Orange and Kisqua blind, and the other group with both products branded. The results in percentages were:

	Blind	Branded
Prefer Club a lot	59	39
Prefer Club a little	16	19
Prefer Kisqua a lot	19	0
Prefer Kisqua a little	6	6
No preferences	6	3

Ballygowan believed that by working on Kisqua's colour and sweetness it could significantly improve its appeal to the market, and also develop much higher ratings by fine-tuning Kisqua's advertising strategy. Response to Kisqua's name was positive: 71 per cent liked the name Kisqua compared to 20 per cent who did not. When assessing Kisqua's label, 36 per cent of respondents considered it above average, 36 per cent average and 26 per cent below average.

Two advertising concepts were presented. 'Kisqua – what could be more natural' received better than average scores from 38 per cent of respondents, while 45 per cent rated it average. Projective tests associated Kisqua with sports-minded and health-conscious people and with people who really care about quality and who may be described as trendsetters. The target market was confirmed as soft-drink consumers in social classes A, B, C1 and C2, 15–30 years old and of either sex. Following the research, Dimension made the appropriate adjustment to the advertising concept.

Pack design was a very important aspect of this project. Ballygowan had proprietorial rights to the distinctive bottle designs used for its spring water range. However, it believed that Kisqua should be differentiated from Ballygowan's other products and that the branding and bottle design of Kisqua should help distinguish it within the soft-drinks market. The pack design assumed that Kisqua would compete directly with Club Orange.

• Business Plan

Initially the business plan had Kisqua available in three pack sizes: 1.5 litre plastic, 250 ml glass and 330 ml cans. Distribution would be through the existing Ballygowan network of grocery, wholesalers (grocery and bottlers), cash-and-carry and independent outlets.

Three pricing options were considered: a low-pricing strategy that would put Kisqua into the market with prices comparable to Coke and 7-Up, a medium-pricing strategy, and a high-pricing strategy positioning Kisqua as a premium brand. Early projections gave strategies yielding the following percentage market shares in 1990:

	Plastic	Cans	Overall[a]
Low-price strategy	4.2	3.1	3.0
Medium-price strategy	3.3	2.2	2.1
High-price strategy	2.1	1.5	1.6

[a] Includes plastic bottles, cans and glass bottles.

The marketing department projected that these volumes would increase by 33 per cent during the second year and by 16 per cent during the third year. After three years and assuming a medium pricing strategy, Kisqua's market share would be approximately 3 per cent of Ireland's soft-drinks market. This compared with Club Orange's 10 per cent market share in 1990. With a capital investment of I£1.5 million and I£120,000 for additional technical staff, generous trade margins and all other relevant costs, the profits projections gave a reasonable return on investment and room to discount to supermarkets to compete with Coke and 7-Up if necessary.

● *Test Market*

From August to October 1990 Ballygowan test marketed Kisqua as a pasteurized drink in 250 ml glass bottles. The test was conducted in the Dublin area using Ballygowan's main independent distributor serving 250 CTNs (combined confectioner, tobacconist and newsagents), delicatessens and petrol stations. The results were discouraging. Most of the negative reaction centred on the pack and retailers not knowing where to position the range in their store. Ballygowan's management now faced a difficult decision. Should they withdraw Kisqua altogether, redesign and reposition it, or go ahead as originally planned? They knew that if they were to delay and relaunch, the payback on the expensive research and development would be put back considerably.

QUESTIONS

1. What types of market research method did Ballygowan use?

2. What sorts of information were Ballygowan's management hoping to get from the different methods they used? Is quantitative marketing research intrinsically more reliable than qualitative research?

3. Relate the market research to the stages in the product development process and explain how they contributed to Ballygowan's understanding of the strategy for launching Kisqua.

4. Were the methods appropriately used and what alternatives would you suggest? Why could in-depth marketing research lead to wrong strategic choices?

5. What explains Ballygowan's poor showing in the market? Did Ballygowan do too much, or too little, market research?

6. Where should Ballygowan's management go from here? What extra research should they do, if any? Should they go ahead with the existing marketing strategy, reposition the product, start again or give up?

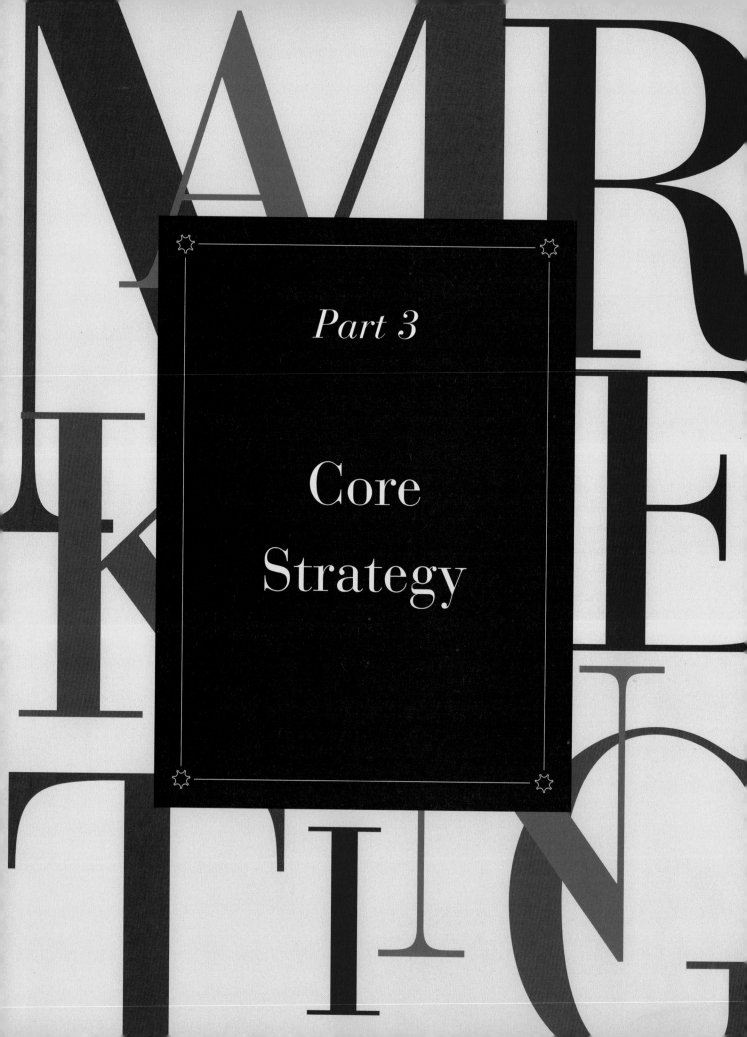

Part 3

Core

Strategy

> *'The meek shall inherit the earth, but they'll not increase market share.'*
> WILLIAM G. MCGOWAN

Part Introduction

PART THREE OF *PRINCIPLES OF MARKETING* covers core strategy, the centre of the marketing process.

Within core strategy, marketing knowledge is made into the strategies that guide marketing action. Businesses mostly succeed by concentrating on a group of customers they can serve better than anyone else. Chapter 9 explains how markets can be broken down into customer segments and how to choose the ones to target. Chapter 10 then looks at ways to address the target segments by creating mental associations that attract customers to the product or services.

A Levi ad once claimed that 'quality never goes out of style'. That has become a byword for much of modern marketing, as marketers try to escape from making single transactions with customers to establishing relationships that both enjoy. Chapter 11 returns to marketing's central belief in customer satisfaction to see how quality, value and service can help.

Increasingly, it is not enough for marketers to look at customers; they must also look at what their competitors are doing and respond to them. Chapter 12 shows that success in marketing does not mean direct confrontation with competitors. It is often best to find new ways to please customers that build upon a business's unique strengths.

CHAPTER 9
Market Segmentation and Targeting

CHAPTER 10
Positioning

CHAPTER 11
Building Customer Relationships: Customer Satisfaction, Quality, Value and Service

CHAPTER 12
Creating Competitive Advantages

PART OVERVIEW CASE:
Cadbury's TimeOut: Choc Around the Clock

9

Market Segmentation and Targeting
Satisfying Human Needs

CHAPTER OBJECTIVES

After reading this chapter, you should be able to:

- Define market segmentation and market targeting.
- List and discuss the primary bases for segmenting consumer and business markets.
- Explain how companies identify attractive market segments and choose a market-coverage strategy.

Preview Case

Procter & Gamble: How Many is Too Many?

PROCTER & GAMBLE IS THE market leader in the United States and the European detergent markets. In the United States it markets nine brands of laundry detergent (Tide, Cheer, Gain, Dash, Bold 3, Dreft, Ivory Snow, Oxydol and Era). The cultural and competitive diversity in Europe means that even more brands, such as Ariel, are used to serve that market. Why so many?

Besides its many detergents Procter & Gamble sells eight brands of hand soap (Zest, Coast, Ivory, Safeguard, Camay, Oil of Ulay, Kirk's and Lava); six shampoos (Prell, Head & Shoulders, Ivory, Pert, Pantene and Vidal Sassoon); four brands each of liquid dish-washing detergents (Joy, Ivory, Dawn and Liquid Cascade), toothpaste (Crest, Gleam, Complete and Denquel), coffee

(Folger's, High Point, Butternut and Maryland Club) and toilet tissue (Charmin, White Cloud, Banner and Summit); three brands of floor cleaner (Spic & Span, Top Job and Mr Clean); and two brands each of deodorant (Secret and Sure), cooking oil (Crisco and Puritan), fabric softener (Downy and Bounce) and disposable nappies (Pampers and Luvs). Moreover, many of the brands are offered in several sizes and formulations (for example, you can buy large or small packages of powdered or liquid Tide in any of three forms – regular, unscented or with bleach).

These P & G brands compete with one another on the same supermarket shelves. Why would P & G introduce several brands in one category instead of concentrating its resources on a single leading brand? The answer lies in different people wanting different *mixes of benefits* from the products they buy. Take laundry detergents as an example. People use laundry detergents to get their clothes clean. They also want other things from their detergents – such as economy, bleaching powder, fabric softening, fresh smell, strength or mildness and suds. We all want *some* of every one of these benefits from our detergent, but we may have different *priorities* for each benefit. To some people, cleaning and bleaching power are most important; to others, fabric softening matters most; still others want a mild, fresh-scented detergent. Thus there are groups – or segments – of laundry detergent buyers and each segment seeks a special combination of benefits.

Procter & Gamble has identified at least nine important laundry detergent segments, along with numerous subsegments, and has developed a different brand designed to meet the special needs of each. The nine P & G brands aim at different segments:

1. *Tide* is 'so powerful, it cleans down to the fibre'. It's the all-purpose family detergent for extra-tough laundry jobs. 'Tide's in, dirt's out.' *Tide with Bleach* is 'so powerful, it whitens down to the fibre'.

2. *Cheer* with Colour Guard gives 'outstanding cleaning *and* colour protection. So your family's clothes look clean, bright and more like new.' Cheer is also formulated for use in hot, warm or cold water – it's 'all tempera-Cheer'. *Cheer Free* is 'dermatologist tested ... contains no irritating perfume or dye'.

3. *Oxydol* contains bleach. It 'makes your white clothes really white and your coloured clothes really bright. So don't reach for the bleach – grab a box of Ox!'

4. *Gain*, originally P & G's 'enzyme' detergent, was repositioned as the detergent that gives you clean, fresh-smelling clothes – it 'freshens like sunshine'.

5. *Bold* is the detergent with fabric softener. It 'cleans, softens and controls static'. Bold liquid adds 'the fresh fabric softener scent'.

6. *Ivory Snow* is 'Ninety-nine and forty-four one hundredths percentages pure'. It's the 'mild, gentle soap for diapers and baby clothes'.

7. *Dreft* is also formulated for baby's nappies and clothes. It contains borax, 'nature's natural sweetener' for 'a clean you can trust'.

8. *Dash* is P & G's value entry. It 'attacks tough dirt', but 'Dash does it for a great low price'.

9. *Era Plus* has 'built-in stain removers'. It 'gets tough stains out and does a great job on your whole wash too'.

By segmenting the market and having several detergent brands, P & G has an attractive offering for customers in all important preference groups. All its brands combined hold a market share much greater than any single brand could obtain.

Questions

1. Why does P & G spread its marketing effort across so many brands rather than concentrating on one?

2. When a company like P & G has so many brands, many of them often do not make money. That being the case, why do you think it keeps the loss-making brands?

3. If you were in competition with P & G, would you match it brand for brand, concentrate on fewer segments or try to find new ones?

4. Why do competitors in the same market segment the market differently?

5. Many people without babies use Dreft. Why do you think that is the case and would you encourage such 'off target' consumption?

6. Suggest alternative segments for P & G to enter and suggest how the brands for that segment should be promoted.

Introduction

Organizations that sell to consumer and business markets recognize that they cannot appeal to all buyers in those markets, or at least not to all buyers in the same way. Buyers are too numerous, too widely scattered and too varied in their needs and buying practices. Companies vary widely in their abilities to serve different segments of the market. Rather than trying to compete in an entire market, sometimes against superior competitors, each company must identify the parts of the market that it can serve best. Segmentation is thus a compromise between mass marketing, which assumes everyone can be treated the same, and the assumption that each person needs a dedicated marketing effort.

Few companies now use mass marketing. Instead, they practise **target marketing** – identifying market segments, selecting one or more of them, and developing products and marketing mixes tailored to each. In this way, sellers can develop the right product for each target market and adjust their prices, distribution channels and advertising to reach the target market efficiently. Instead of scattering their marketing efforts (the 'shotgun' approach), they can focus on the buyers who have greater purchase interest (the 'rifle' approach).

Figure 9.1 shows the major steps in target marketing. **Market segmentation** means dividing a market into distinct groups of buyers with different needs, characteristics or behaviours, who might require separate products or marketing mixes. The company identifies different ways to segment the market and develops profiles of the resulting market segments. **Market targeting** involves evaluating each market segment's attractiveness and selecting one or more of the market segments to enter. **Market positioning** is setting the competitive positioning for the product and creating a detailed marketing mix. We discuss each of these steps in turn.

target marketing
Directing a company's effort towards serving one or more groups of customers sharing common needs or characteristics.

market segmentation
Dividing a market into distinct groups of buyers with different needs, characteristics or behaviour, who might require separate products or marketing mixes.

market targeting
The process of evaluating each market segment's attractiveness and selecting one or more segments to enter.

market positioning
Arranging for a product to occupy a clear, distinctive and desirable place relative to competing products in the minds of target consumers. Formulating competitive positioning for a product and a detailed marketing mix.

Market Segmentation

Markets consist of buyers, and buyers differ in one or more ways. They may differ in their wants, resources, locations, buying attitudes and buying practices. Through market segmentation, companies divide large, heterogeneous markets into smaller segments that can be reached more efficiently with products and services that match their unique needs. In this section, we discuss seven important segmentation topics: levels of market segmentation, segmenting consumer markets, segmenting business markets, segmenting international markets, multivariate segmentation, developing market segments and requirements for effective segmentation.

Levels of Market Segmentation

Because buyers have unique needs and wants, each buyer is potentially a separate market. Ideally, then, a seller might design a separate marketing programme for each buyer. However, although some companies attempt to serve buyers individually, many others face larger numbers of smaller buyers and do not find complete segmentation worthwhile. Instead, they look for broader classes of buyers who differ in their product needs or buying responses. Thus, market segmentation can

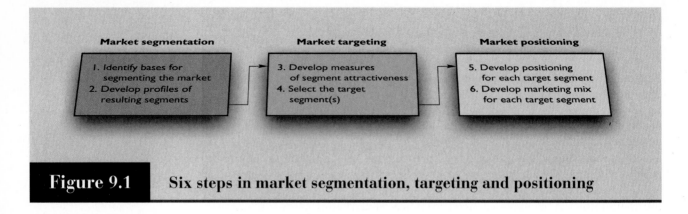

| **Figure 9.1** | **Six steps in market segmentation, targeting and positioning** |

be carried out at many different levels. Companies can practise no segmentation (mass marketing), complete segmentation (micromarketing) or something in between (segment marketing or niche marketing).

● *Mass Marketing*

mass marketing
Using almost the same product, promotion and distribution for all consumers.

Companies have not always practised target marketing. In fact, for most of the twentieth century, major consumer-products companies held fast to **mass marketing** – mass producing, mass distributing and mass promoting about the same product in about the same way to all consumers. Henry Ford epitomized this marketing strategy when he offered the Model T Ford to all buyers; they could have the car 'in any colour as long as it is black'. That cost Ford the world market leadership that it has never regained.

The traditional argument for mass marketing is that it creates the largest potential market, which leads to the lowest costs, which in turn can translate into either lower prices or higher margins. However, many factors now make mass marketing more difficult. For example, the world's mass markets have slowly splintered into a profusion of smaller segments – the baby boomer segment here, the generation Xers there; here the Asian market, there the black market; here working women, there single parents; people living close to the Arctic circle, those living on the Mediterranean. It is very hard to create a single product or programme that appeals to all of these diverse groups. The proliferation of advertising media and distribution channels has also made it difficult to practise 'one size fits all' marketing:

> [Consumers] have more ways to shop: at out of town malls, specialty shops, and superstores; through mail-order catalogs, home shopping networks, and virtual stores on the Internet. And they are bombarded with messages pitched through a growing number of channels: broadcast and narrow-cast television, radio, online computer networks, the Internet, telephone services such as fax and telemarketing, and niche magazines and other print media.[1]

No wonder some have claimed that mass marketing is dying. Not surprisingly, many companies are retreating from mass marketing and turning to segmented marketing.

● *Segmenting Markets*

segment marketing
Adapting a company's offerings so they more closely match the needs of one or more segments.

A company that practises **segment marketing** recognizes that buyers differ in their needs, perceptions and buying behaviours. The company tries to isolate broad segments that make up a market and adapts its offers to match more closely the needs of one or more segments. Thus, BMW has designed specific models for different income and age groups. In fact, it sells models for segments with varied *combinations* of age and income: for instance, the short wheelbase 3 for young urban drivers. Hilton markets to a variety of segments – business travellers, families and others – with packages adapted to their varying needs.

Segment marketing offers several benefits over mass marketing. The company can market more efficiently, targeting its products or services, channels and communications programmes towards only consumers that it can serve best. The company can also market more effectively by fine-tuning its products, prices and programmes to the needs of carefully defined segments. And the company may face fewer competitors if fewer competitors are focusing on this market segment.

● *Niche Marketing*

Market segments are normally large identifiable groups within a market – for example, luxury car buyers, performance car buyers, utility car buyers and economy car buyers. **Niche marketing** focuses on subgroups within these segments. A *niche* is a more narrowly defined group, usually identified by dividing a segment into subsegments or by defining a group with a distinctive set of traits who may seek a special combination of benefits. For example, the utility vehicles segment might include light trucks and off-the-road vehicles. And the off-the-road vehicles subsegment might be further divided into the utilitarian segment (Land Rover), light sports utility vehicles (Suzuki) and luxury sports utility vehicles (Range Rover and Lexus) niches.

> **niche marketing**
> *Adapting a company's offerings to more closely match the needs of one or more subsegments where there is often little competition.*

Whereas segments are fairly large and normally attract several competitors, niches are smaller and normally attract only one or a few competitors. Niche marketers presumably understand their niches' needs so well that their customers willingly pay a price premium. For example, Ferrari gets a high price for its cars because its loyal buyers feel that no other automobile comes close to offering the product-service-membership benefits that Ferrari does.

Niching offers smaller companies an opportunity to compete by focusing their limited resources on serving niches that may be unimportant to or overlooked by larger competitors. For example, Mark Warner succeeds by selling to distinct holiday niches: all-inclusive family water sports holidays in southern Europe to northern Europeans, and no-kids holidays for older people who want some peace and quiet. However, large companies also practise niche marketing. For example, American Express offers not only its traditional green cards but also gold cards, corporate cards and even platinum cards aimed at a niche consisting of the top-spending 1 per cent of its 36 million cardholders.[2] And Nike makes athletic gear for basketball, running and soccer, but also for smaller niches such as biking and street hockey.

In many markets today, niches are the norm. As an advertising agency executive observed: 'There will be no market for products that everybody likes a little, only for products that somebody likes a lot.'[3] Other experts assert that companies will have to 'niche or be niched'.[4]

● *Micromarketing*

Segment and niche marketers tailor their offers and marketing programmes to meet the needs of various market segments. At the same time, however, they do not customize their offers to each individual customer. Thus, segment marketing and niche marketing fall between the extremes of mass marketing and

Markets of One: Customizing the Marketing Offer

Marketing Highlight 9.1

Several technologies have converged in recent years to allow companies in a wide range of industries to treat large numbers of customers as unique 'markets of one'. Advances in computer-design, database, interactive-communication and manufacturing technologies have given birth to 'mass customization', the process through which firms interact one-to-one with masses of customers to design products and services tailor-made to individual needs. Here are some examples:

Check into any Ritz-Carleton hotel around the world, and you'll be amazed at how well the hotel's employees manage to anticipate your slightest need. Without ever asking, they seem to know that you want a non-smoking room with a king-size bed, a non-allergenic pillow, and breakfast with decaffeinated coffee in your room. How does the Ritz-Carleton work this magic? Starting with a fervent dedication to satisfying the unique needs of each of its thousands of guests, the hotel employs a system that combines information technology and flexible operations to customize the hotel experience. At the heart of the system is a huge customer database, which contains information about guests gathered through the observations of hotel employees. Each day, hotel staffers – from those at the front desk to those in maintenance and housekeeping – discretely record the unique habits, likes and dislikes of each guest on small 'guest preference pads'. These observations are then transferred to a corporate-wide 'guest history database'. Every morning, a 'guest historian' at each hotel reviews the files of all new arrivals who have previously stayed at a Ritz-Carleton and prepares a list of suggested extra touches that might delight each guest.

Guests have responded strongly to such markets-of-one service. Since inaugurating the guest-history system in 1992, the Ritz-Carleton has boosted guest retention by 23 per cent. An amazing 95 per cent of departing guests report that their stay has been a truly memorable experience.

At Andersen Windows, customers now help design their own windows, whether they're complex, lofty Gothic windows or centimetres-high miniatures. Previously, as the number of different products offered by Andersen grew from 28,000 in 1985 to 86,000 in 1991, the company's customers – mainly homeowners and building contractors – faced a mind-numbing array of standard window choices, displayed in rows of hefty catalogues. Designing a complicated custom treatment – such as an arched window – required advanced design skills and a working knowledge of trigonometry. Preparing a price quote for windows could take several hours, and the quote itself could run as long as 15 pages. One alarming result of this complexity was a rising error rate. By 1991, 20 per cent of deliveries of Andersen windows contained at least one discrepancy. Andersen responded by supplying its distributors and retailers with what is essentially an interactive, computerized catalogue system called Windows of Knowledge. An industry analyst describes the system: 'Using this tool, a salesperson can help customers [select from 50,000 possible window components] and add, change and strip away features until they've designed a window they're pleased with. It's akin to playing with building blocks. The computer automatically checks the window specs for structural soundness and then generates a price quote. ...The retailer's computer transmits each order to [the factory] where it's assigned a unique "licence plate number", which can be tracked ... using bar-code technology from the assembly line through to the warehouse.'

Such 'batch-of-one' manufacturing has greatly increased the customer's product selection while at the same time reducing errors. By 1996 Andersen offered 188,000 different products, yet fewer than one in 200 truckloads contained an order problem. Moreover, by making almost everything to order, Andersen has greatly reduced its inventory requirements. Distributors are delighted with the Windows of Knowledge system. Says one retailer, 'It's a terrific tool. It does things that would drive me crazy when I used to have to do them by hand.' But the real winners are Andersen's, the homeowners and contractors, who get just the windows they want with a minimum of hassle. All this has made Andersen a real markets-of-one advocate. Sums up one executive, 'We're on a journey toward purer and purer mass customization.'

SOURCES: B. Joseph Pine II, Don Peppers and Martha Rogers, 'Do you want to keep your customers forever?', *Harvard Business Review* (March–April 1995), pp. 103–14; Christopher W. Hart, 'Made to order,' *Marketing Management* (Summer 1996), pp. 11–22; Justin Martin, 'Are you as good as you think you are?', *Fortune* (30 September 1996); James H. Gilmore and B. Joseph Pine II, 'The four faces of mass customization,' *Harvard Business Review* (January–February 1997), pp. 91–101; Kim Cleland, 'Peapod, Shoppers Express vie for online grocery business,' *Advertising Age* (9 June 1997), p. 40.

micromarketing. **Micromarketing** is the practice of tailoring products and marketing programmes to suit the tastes of specific individuals and locations. Micromarketing includes *local marketing* and *individual marketing*.

LOCAL MARKETING. Local marketing involves tailoring brands and promotions to the needs and wants of local customer groups – cities, neighbourhoods and even specific stores. Thus, retailers such as Akia and C & A customize each store's merchandise and promotions to match its specific clientele. Kraft helps supermarket chains identify the specific cheese assortments and shelf positioning that will optimize cheese sales in low-income, middle-income and high-income stores, and in different ethnic communities.

Local marketing has some drawbacks. It can drive up manufacturing and marketing costs by reducing economies of scale. It can also create logistical problems as companies try to meet the varied requirements of different regional and local markets. And a brand's overall image may be diluted if the product and message vary in different localities. Still, as companies face increasingly fragmented markets, and as new supporting technologies develop, the advantages of local marketing often outweigh the drawbacks. Local marketing helps a company to market more effectively in the face of pronounced regional and local differences in community demographics and lifestyles. It also meets the needs of the company's 'first-line customers' – retailers – who prefer more fine-tuned product assortments for their neighbourhoods.

INDIVIDUAL MARKETING. In the extreme, micromarketing becomes **individual marketing** tailoring products and marketing programmes to the needs and preferences of individual customers. Individual marketing has also been labelled 'markets-of-one marketing', 'customized marketing' and 'one-to-one marketing' (see Marketing Highlight 9.1).[5] The prevalence of mass marketing has obscured the fact that for centuries consumers were served as individuals: the tailor custom-made the suit, the cobbler designed shoes for the individual, the cabinet maker made furniture to order. Today, however, new technologies are permitting many companies to return to customized marketing. More powerful

micromarketing
A form of target marketing in which companies tailor their marketing programmes to the needs and wants of narrowly defined geographic, demographic, psychographic or behavioural segments.

individual marketing
Tailoring products and marketing programmes to the needs and preferences of individual customers.

mass customization
Preparing individually designed products and communications on a large scale.

computers, detailed databases, robotic production, and immediate and interactive communication media such as e-mail, fax and the Internet – all have combined to foster 'mass customization'.[6] **Mass customization** is the ability to prepare on a mass basis individually designed products and communications to meet each customer's requirements.

Consumer marketers are now providing custom-made products in areas ranging from hotel stays and furniture to clothing and bicycles. For example, Suited for Sun, a swimwear manufacturer, uses a computer/camera system in retail stores to design custom-tailored swimsuits for women. The customer puts on an 'off the rack' garment, and the system's digital camera captures her image on the computer screen. The shop assistant applies a stylus to the screen to create a garment with perfect fit. The customer can select from more than 150 patterns and styles, which are re-imaged over her body on the computer screen until she finds the one that she likes best. The system then transmits the measurements to the factory, and the one-of-a-kind bathing suit is mailed to the delighted customer in a matter of days.

Another example is the National Industrial Bicycle Company in Japan, which uses flexible manufacturing to turn out large numbers of bikes specially fitted to the needs of individual buyers. Customers visit their local bike shop where the shopkeeper measures them on a special frame and faxes the specifications to the factory. At the factory, the measurements are punched into a computer, which creates blueprints in three minutes that would take a draftsman 60 times that long. The computer then guides robots and workers through the production process. The factory is ready to produce any of 18 million variations on 18 bicycle models in 199 colour patterns and about as many sizes as there are people. The price is steep – between Y65,000 and Y400,000 – but within two weeks the buyer is riding a custom-made, one-of-a-kind machine.

Business-to-business marketers are also finding new ways to customize their offerings. For example, Motorola salespeople now use a hand-held computer to custom-design pagers following a business customer's wishes. The design data are transmitted to the Motorola factory, and production starts within 17 minutes. The customized pagers are ready for shipment within two hours.

The move towards individual marketing mirrors the trend in consumer *self-marketing*. Increasingly, individual customers are taking more responsibility for determining which products and brands to buy. Consider two business buyers with two different purchasing styles. The first sees several salespeople, each trying to persuade him to buy their product. The second sees no salespeople but rather logs on to the Internet; searches for information on and evaluations of available products; interacts electronically with various suppliers, users and product analysts; and then makes up her own mind about the best offer. The second purchasing agent has taken more responsibility for the buying process, and the marketer has had less influence over her buying decision.

As the trend towards more interactive dialogue and less advertising monologue continues, self-marketing will grow in importance. As more buyers look up consumer reports, join Internet product-discussion forums, and place orders via phone or online, marketers will have to influence the buying process in new ways. They will need to involve customers more in all phases of the product-development and buying process, increasing opportunities for buyers to practise self-marketing.

According to the chief designer for Mazda, 'Customers will want to express their individuality with the products they buy.' The opportunities offered by these technologies promise to turn marketing from 'a broadcast medium to a dialog medium', where the customer participates actively in the design of the product and offer.[7]

Segmenting Consumer Markets

There is no single way to segment a market. A marketer has to try different segmentation variables, alone and in combination, to find the best way to view the market structure. Table 9.1 outlines the major variables used in segmenting consumer markets. Here we look at the major *geographic*, *demographic*, *psychographic* and *behavioural variables*.

● *Geographic Segmentation*

Geographic segmentation calls for dividing the market into different geographical units, such as nations, states, regions, counties, cities or neighbourhoods. A company may decide to operate in one or a few geographical areas, or to operate in all areas but pay attention to geographical differences in needs and wants.

International lifestyles are emerging, but there are counterforces that continue to shape markets. Cross-cultural research has defined five 'mentality fields' for cars in Europe.[8] These show how much language demarcates common cultures and ways of life:

1. The north (Scandinavia).
2. The north-west (the United Kingdom, Iceland and parts of Norway, Belgium and Holland).
3. The centre (German mentality field extending to Switzerland and parts of eastern Europe).
4. The west (the French-speaking area, including parts of Switzerland and Belgium).
5. The south (the Mediterranean, covering Spanish, Portuguese, Italian and Greek languages).

geographic segmentation
Dividing a market into different geographical units such as nations, states, regions, counties, cities or neighbourhoods.

Intermarket separation: teens show surprising similarity no matter where in the world they live. For instance, this young woman could live almost anywhere. Thus, many companies target teenagers with worldwide marketing campaigns.

Table 9.1	Market segmentation variables for consumer markets

VARIABLE	TYPICAL BREAKDOWNS
Geographic	
Region	In the USA these are Pacific, Mountain, West North Central, West South Central, East North Central, East South Central, South Atlantic, Middle Atlantic, New England. Each country has its own variation on this.
County size	A, B, C, D.
City size	Under 5,000; 5,000–20,000; 20,000–50,000; 50,000–100,000; 100,000–250,000; 250,000–500,000; 500,000–1,000,000; 1,000,000–4,000,000; 4,000,000 and over.
Density	Urban, suburban, rural.
Climate	Northern, Southern.
Demographic	
Age	Under 6, 6–11, 12–19, 20–34, 35–49, 50–64, 65+.
Gender	Male, female.
Family size	1–2, 3–4, 5+.
Family life cycle	Young, single; young, married, no children; young, married, youngest child under 6; young, married, youngest child 6 or over; older, married with children; older, married, no children under 18; older, single; other.
Income	Under $10,000; $10,000–15,000; $15,000–20,000; $20,000–30,000; $30,000–50,000; $50,000–75,000; $75,000 and over.
Occupation	Professional and technical; managers, officials and proprietors; clerical, sales; craftsmen, foremen; operatives; farmers; retired; students; homemakers; unemployed.
Education	Grade school or less; some high school; high school graduate; some college; college graduate.
Religion	Catholic, Protestant, Jewish, other.
Race	White, Black, Asian, Hispanic, other.
Nationality	American, British, French, German, Scandinavian, Italian, Latin American, Middle Eastern, Japanese, other.
Psychographic	
Social class	Lower lowers, upper lowers, working class, middle class, upper middles, lower uppers, upper uppers.
Lifestyle	Achievers, believers, strivers.
Personality	Compulsive, gregarious, authoritarian, ambitious.
Behavioural	
Purchase occasion	Regular occasion, special occasion.
Benefits sought	Quality, service, economy.
User status	Non-user, ex-user, potential user, first-time user, regular user.
Usage rate	Light user, medium user, heavy user.
Loyalty status	None, medium, strong, absolute.
Readiness state	Unaware, aware, informed, interested, desirous, intending to buy.
Attitude towards product	Enthusiastic, positive, indifferent, negative, hostile.

Self-expression is important to car buyers in all the geographical regions, but the similarity ends there. The western group seek quality and practicality, the south want value for money, while the north-western group see their car in very personal terms. The differences influence the cars they buy and how they are equipped. Although all developed nations worry about the environment, they do so in different ways. In Italy, France and the UK, motorists do not see their car as a source of pollution, while in Germany, demand for environmentally friendly cars is growing fast.

> Pargasa, the large Swiss investment group, concentrates on francophone Europe. It has ten core holdings including French Paribas, Swiss Orior and Belgium's Petrofina, but these and other holdings are all concentrated in France and the French-speaking parts of Belgium and Switzerland. According to Aimery Langois-Meurinne, the group's chief executive, it would like to extend its core holdings to much more than ten. Geographically it is pulling in its wings from the United Kingdom and the United States, but it wants to expand closer to home. 'We are trying to understand Germany and German-speaking Switzerland,' he says, 'but we are starting from a low base.'[9]

Climatic differences lead to different lifestyles and eating habits. In countries with warm climates, social life takes place outdoors and furniture is less important than in Nordic countries. Not noticing the different sizes of kitchens has caused many marketing mistakes. Philips started making profits in the Japanese market only after it made small coffee-makers to fit the cramped conditions there. In Spain, Coca-Cola withdrew its two-litre bottle after finding it did not fit local refrigerators.[10]

Many companies today have regional marketing programmes within national boundaries – localizing their products, advertising, promotion and sales efforts to fit the needs of individual regions, cities and even neighbourhoods. Others are seeking to cultivate yet untapped territory. For example, IKEA expanded globally using its large blue-and-yellow stores and dedicated out-of-town sites. IKEA was part of a marked 1980s trend towards out-of-town shopping. Its stores attracted customers from great distances, so that countries were served by a handful of stores. IKEA changed its strategy when acquiring the Habitat furniture chain from Storehouse in the early 1990s. The small stores gave it access to passing trade and new customer segments who are less willing to travel. The Habitat chain also serves small towns. In making this significant shift, IKEA is also following the European trend towards town-centre malls. Having seen American urban decay, European politicians are resisting out-of-town developments.[11]

● *Demographic Segmentation*

demographic segmentation
Dividing the market into groups based on demographic variables such as age, sex, family size, family life cycle, income, occupation, education, religion, race and nationality.

Demographic segmentation consists of dividing the market into groups based on variables such as age, gender, family size, family life cycle, income, occupation, education, religion, race and nationality. Demographic factors are the most popular bases for segmenting customer groups. One reason is that consumer needs, wants and usage rates often vary closely with demographic variables. Another is that demographic variables are easier to measure than most other types of variable. Even when market segments are first defined using other bases – such as personality or behaviour – their demographics need knowing to assess the size of the target market and to reach it efficiently.

life-cycle segmentation
Offering products or marketing approaches that recognize the consumer's changing needs at different stages of their life.

AGE. Consumer needs and wants change with age. Some companies use age and **life-cycle segmentation**, offering different products or using different marketing approaches for different age and life-cycle groups. For example, Life Stage vitamins come in four versions, each designed for the special needs of specific age segments: chewable Children's Formula for children from 4 to 12 years old; Teen's Formula for teenagers; and two adult versions (Men's Formula and Women's Formula). Johnson & Johnson developed Affinity Shampoo to help women over 40 overcome age-related hair changes. McDonald's targets children, teens, adults and senior citizens with different ads and media. Its ads to teens feature dance-beat music, adventure and fast-paced cutting from scene to scene; ads to senior citizens are softer and more sentimental.

> LEGO's range shows the limits of age-based segmentation. For babies there are Duplo rattles (0 to 3 months), then there are round-edged activity toys made of two or three pieces (3 to 18 months). All these have the familiar LEGO lugs so that they will fit on to LEGO products. Next come Duplo construction kits or toys (2 to 5 years). Duplo bricks look like LEGO bricks, but are twice the size so that young children can manipulate but not swallow them. Duplo kits start simple, but there are more complex ones – like train sets or zoo sets – that are suitable for children with increasing sophistication. By the age of 3, children have developed the manipulative skills that allow them to progress to LEGO Basic. This is targeted at 3 to 12-year-olds. The progression is made easy by the small LEGO bricks fitting to Duplo ones.
>
> Age-based segmentation works until children are 5 years old when fewer and fewer girls buy LEGO and boys' interests diversify. In comes LEGO Pirates (6–12 years), Space Police (6–12), Railways (6–12), Technic (7–12), Model Team (9–12) and so on. To counter girls' decline in interest, LEGO launched Fabuland, a heavily merchandised product backed by Ladybird books and videos. It failed, leaving Legoland with an incongruous Fabuland monorail and play area. Pastel-coloured Fantia is another attempt to attract girls.
>
> LEGO's product for the new millennium is Mindstorm, intelligent LEGO bricks. The result of a ten-year, DKr100 million project with Massachusetts Institute of Technology, the bricks are programmed via an infrared transmitter connected to a Pentium-powered PC. According to LEGO's Tormod Askildsen: 'It can be used to make all kinds of devices', such as an intruder alarm set up to empty ping pong balls on an unsuspecting parent visiting a child's room. LEGO has great faith in Mindstorm's ability to enliven stagnant toy sales and woo children away from the virtual world of computer games. It also claims that the intelligent bricks appeals to girls as much as boys.[12]

LIFE-CYCLE STAGE. Life-cycle stage is important in recreation markets. In the holiday market, for instance, Club 18–30 aims at young singles seeking the four Ss: sun, sand, sea and sex. This boisterous segment does not mix well with the families that the Club Mediterranean caters for. Children's activities and all-day child care are an important part of the latter's provision. Saga Holidays caters for older people. Its prices are kept low by travelling off-peak. Saga also provides insurance for older people and aims to set up and run radio stations for them. Given the ageing population in Europe and other developed economies, Saga looks set to grow.[13]

In the United Kingdom housing market, Barratts was the first to identify two life-cycle stage segments. It provided Solo apartments as starter homes for young people. These had full furnishing and household equipment included in the basic

By segmenting by age LEGO products grow with the children.

price. These extras would not have appealed to Barratts' other target market, older people with 'empty nests' trading down to a small, single-floor home.

GENDER.   **Gender segmentation** is usual in clothing, hairdressing, cosmetics and magazines. Recently, marketers have noticed other opportunities for gender segmentation. For example, both men and women use most deodorant brands. Procter & Gamble, however, developed Secret as the brand specially formulated for a woman's chemistry, and then packaged and advertised the product to re-inforce the female image. In contrast, Gillette's association with shaving makes its deodorant male oriented.

The car industry has also begun to use gender segmentation extensively. Women are a growing part of the car market. 'Selling to women should be no different than selling to men,' notes one analyst. 'But there are subtleties that make a difference.'[14] Women have different frames, less upper-body strength and greater safety concerns. To address these issues, car makers are redesigning their cars with bonnets and boots that are easier to open, seats that are easier to adjust and seat belts that fit women better. They have also increased their emphasis on safety, highlighting features such as air bags and remote door locks. In their advertising, some manufacturers target women directly. Indeed, much TV adver-tising of small cars is now aimed at women, pioneered by Volkswagen: an angry, smartly dressed woman leaves a town house – she throws away a ring, discards a fur coat but, after hesitating, keeps the keys to the Volkswagen Golf. Volkswagen now devotes 30 per cent of its television advertising budget to advertisements for women.

Large advertising spreads are designed especially for women consumers in such magazines as *Cosmopolitan* and *Vogue*. Other companies avoid direct appeals, fearing that it will offend women. It sometimes comes across as conde-scending. Some companies, such as Toyota and GM, try to include a realistic balance of men and women in their ads without specific reference to gender. Sometimes the medium changes, but the message does not. Alongside the tra-ditionally feminine ads for fragrances and fashion in one issue of *Vogue* are product ads for the BMW 850Csi, Audi S2, Toyota MR2, etc., showing no people. Rover's ad for its Metro Manhattan differentiates: 'For the woman who has every-thing'. Ford's ad for its Maverick 4 × 4 is interesting: it shows two pictures with a man driving and a woman by his side.

INCOME.   **Income segmentation** is often used for products and services such as cars, boats, clothing, cosmetics and travel. Many companies target affluent consumers with luxury goods and convenience services. The brands behind the

gender segmentation
Dividing a market into different groups based on sex.

income segmentation
Dividing a market into different income groups.

Caffrey's Irish Ale attracts discerning young males.

Photography: Jonathan Glynn-Smith.

French LVMH group's initials betray its focus on affluent consumers: Louis Vuitton luggage, Moët & Chandon champagne and Hennessy cognac. The group's links with the UK's Guinness, which owns Johnnie Walker Red and Black Labels as well as Guinness, mean it has an interest in five out of Europe's top ten brands. Not surprisingly, LVMH is growing fast and appears recession-proof. The company's brands are growing and it is seeking other luxury brands. Besides its *haute couture* activities, LVMH owns Parfums Christian Dior, has taken control of Guerain, the French fragrance house, and is stalking Van Clef & Aprels, the Paris-based jeweller.[15]

However, not all companies grow by retaining their focus on the top-income segment. Foreign and long-haul travel was once for the wealthy, but the travel market is now a mass industry. P & O aims to do the same with cruises. Once the preserve of the rich and retired, P & O Cruises are entering the mass market. With the help of its German-built *Oriana*, it intends to bring prices down. For example, in 1995 a 12-day Mediterranean cruise on P & O's *Canberra* for two adults and two children cost £2,877, cheaper by £640 than the 1994 price. The mass-market tour operator Airtours is also entering the cruise market and aiming even further down market. It will sail the Mediterranean and the Canary Islands with a ship bought from Closter Cruise of Norway. P & O's marketing director welcomes Airtours' market entry: 'What Airtours are good at is talking to a slightly younger, more down-market group of customers. They will put cruising in people's minds.' Airtours' managing director pledged to 'revolutionize the market … You've seen nothing yet. This is a different end of the market to where cruising has been before.'[16]

Established retailers, following the wheel of retailing and developing more sophisticated stores with added values, have allowed new entrants to succeed by targeting less affluent market segments. In the United Kingdom grocery market, Kwik Save did this with a lean organization, economically located stores and a no-frills operation that kept prices to the minimum. The more up-market positioning of other United Kingdom grocers has also allowed Germany's cost-cutting Aldi into the market.

Geodemographics

Geodemographics is an increasingly used segmentation method. Originally developed by the CACI Market Analysis Group as ACORN (A Classification Of Residential Neighbourhoods), it uses 40 variables from population census data to group residential areas. Marketing Highlight 9.2 shows ACORN in use.

geodemographics
The study of the relationship between geographical location and demographics.

Marketing Highlight 9.2

ACORN and Related Classificatory Systems

As a direct challenge to the socio-economic classification system, the ACORN (A Classification Of Residential Neighbourhoods) system was developed by the CACI Market Analysis Group.[1] The system is based on population census data and classifies residential neighbourhoods into 54 types within 17 groups and 6 main categories. The groupings were derived through a clustering of responses to census data required by law on a regular basis. The groupings reflect neighbourhoods with similar characteristics. (Table 1 shows how the main categories break down into increasingly small subgroups and types.)

Early uses of ACORN were by local authorities to isolate areas of inner-city deprivation (the idea came from a sociologist working for local authorities), but it was soon seen to have direct marketing relevance, particularly because the database enabled postcodes to be ascribed to each ACORN type. Hence its use particularly in direct mail marketing.

The introduction of CACI's ACORN geodemographic database represented one of the biggest steps forward in segmentation and targeting techniques. Although the measure is crude, the great strength of the service depends on CACI's own research linking the neighbourhood groups to demographics and buyer behaviour, together with the ability to target households. The system, therefore, provides a direct link between off-the-peg segmentation and individuals, unlike earlier methods which only provided indirect means of contacting the demographic or personality segments identified.

Like the other a priori techniques, the limitations of CACI's approach are the variability within neighbourhoods and the similarity between their buying behaviour for many product classes. English[2] provides an example of this where five enumeration districts (individual neighbourhood groups of 150 households) are ranked according to geodemographic techniques. Of the five, two were identified as being prime mailing prospects. However, when individual characteristics were investigated, the five groups were found to contain 31, 14, 10, 10 and 7 prospects respectively: the enumeration districts had been ranked according to the correct number of prospects, but neighbourhood classifications alone appeared to be a poor method of targeting. With only 31 prime target customers being in the most favoured enumeration district, 119 out of 150 households would have been wrongly targeted.

IKEA's Catalogue Targeting[3]

Many companies now use geodemographic segmentation to help their decision making. IKEA, the Swedish furniture retailer, used it to analyze its customer base. The store provides a vast range of stylish and original furniture, fittings and fabrics at affordable prices. The IKEA concept is a simple and effective one that has worked throughout the world. The company retails from large out-of-town stores and sells furniture in easy-to-assemble kit format, passing on the cost savings it gains from this to the customer.

A key element in IKEA's success is its catalogue: produced once a year, it features a broad selection of products, showing the depth and breadth of the range available in the stores. The company's local catalogue distribution around each of its stores represents a large promotional investment. Geodemographic analysis of its store catchment areas helps IKEA define its local

TABLE 1 A CLASSIFICATION OF RESIDENTIAL NEIGHBOURHOODS (ACORN)

UK ACORN CATEGORIES

CATEGORY	NAME	%
A	Thriving	19.8
B	Expanding	11.6
C	Rising	7.5
D	Settling	24.1
E	Aspiring	13.7
F	Striving	22.8

UK ACORN CATEGORY A GROUPS

GROUP	NAME	%
1	Wealthy achievers, suburban areas	15.1
2	Affluent greys, rural communities	2.3
3	Prosperous pensioners, retirement areas	2.3

UK ACORN GROUP 1 TYPES

TYPE	NAME	%
1.1	Wealthy suburbs, large detached houses	2.6
1.2	Villages with wealthy commuters	3.2
1.3	Mature affluent home-owning areas	2.7
1.4	Affluent suburbs, older families	3.7
1.5	Mature, well-off suburbs	3.0

SOURCE: CACI Market Analysis Group.

distribution plans for the catalogue and to evaluate how effective the previous distribution had been. To do this, IKEA analyzed its customer data to see where customers were coming from, and also their level of expenditure before and after the distribution. This helped IKEA predict likely return on its investment in the next catalogue distribution. The analysis also looked at the size of purchase, the frequency of purchase and the distance its customers live from each store. Using this information combined with its ACORN classification types has allowed IKEA to improve understanding of the relationship between each of these elements. In addition to determining the postcode sectors that offer best potential for catalogue distribution, this information will help IKEA across its marketing mix to assess other promotional opportunities.

Targeting Sottini's Customers[4]

Ideal Standard is a leading manufacturer of bathrooms. Its range covers a wide selection of prices and styles, from cost-effective suites for first-time buyers through to the top of the range for those who want the very best that money can buy. The company used geodemographics to understand more about customers' perception of the luxury Sottini range. The company knew that a very distinctive type of customer bought the Sottini range: it wanted more detailed information about these customer types so that it could target dealerships more accurately and provide local dealer support for the Sottini product.

Sottini is sold through a network of independent retail outlets. As such, the company had only limited information on its end customers, collected from responses to advertisements. CACI was able to take this information and substantiate it with data from the Target Group Index survey of people with high levels of spend on bathroom suites and home enhancement. CACI profiled these data using the ACORN consumer classification. This analysis generated a strong profile that showed that the Sottini range was bought primarily by wealthy achievers in suburbs and better-off retirement areas. A typical Sottini customer would have a large disposable income – with their mortgage paid off and cash to spend – and would live in an affluent area.

The information helped find large concentrations of Sottini's target market and define the optimum catchment area for the Sottini dealers. Comparing the customer profiles with the catchment areas of dealers showed where to concentrate marketing support.

As a second phase to this project, Ideal Standard is looking at individual dealers. Within each dealer's catchment, specific postal areas of highest customer potential can be identified. The dealers can then use this information for direct marketing campaigns or door-to-door leaflet distributions to raise awareness of the Sottini product and inform people about their local Sottini dealership.

Kelvin Baldwin, Commercial Executive at Ideal Standard, states: the 'analysis helped us to evaluate potential for the Sottini brand across the country. We are now assessing how we can use this information at individual dealership level to aid us in dealer-support activities for our Sottini products, such as identifying new customers and locating new areas for the introduction of the Sottini product.'

To be fair, like other means of off-the-peg segmentation discussed, geodemographics are powerful when related to products linked directly to characteristics of the neighbourhood districts: for instance, the demand for double glazing or gardening equipment. Even in the case described above, targeting the best enumeration districts increases the probability of hitting a target customer from less than 10 per cent to over 20 per cent, but misses are still more common than hits.

References

1. *ACORN User Guide* (London: CACI Information Services, 1993).
2. J. English, 'Selecting and analysing your customer/market through efficient profile modelling and prospecting', Institute of International Research Conference on Customer Segmentation and Lifestyle Marketing, London, 11–12 December 1989.
3. Mark Mulcahey, 'CACI's customer analysis helping IKEA define their target markets', *Marketing Systems*, 9, 1 (1994), p. 11.
4. Julie Randall, 'CACI working with Ideal Standard to identify their optimum dealership areas', *Marketing Systems*, 9, 1 (1994), p. 12.

Geodemographics is developing fast. Databases are now available in all the large economies. ACORN has been joined by PIN (Pinpoint Identified Neighbourhoods), Mosaic and Super Profile. In the Netherlands, the Post Office and Dutch *Reader's Digest* have produced Omnidata based on telephone subscribers, and, in Sweden, Postaid is run by a subsidiary of the Post Office. Both these systems are voluntary, and are sold to consumers as a way of avoiding junk mail. The power of basic geodemographic databases is being increased by linking them to consumer panel databases. This allows trends to be tracked: for example, over a four-year period, 28 per cent more people living in 'less well-off public housing' took package holidays.[17] CCN Marketing has since extended this process to cover the EU using its EuroMOSAIC (Table 9.2).

● *Psychographic Segmentation*

Psychographic segmentation divides buyers into groups based on social class, lifestyle or personality characteristics. People in the same demographic group can have very different psychographic make-ups.

psychographic segmentation
Dividing a market into different groups based on social class, lifestyle or personality characteristics.

SOCIAL CLASS. In Chapter 6, we described social classes and showed how they affect preferences in cars, clothes, home furnishings, leisure activities, reading habits and retailers. Many companies design products or services for specific social classes, building in features that appeal to them. In the UK, Butlin's

Table 9.2	CCN EuroMOSAIC Households Across Europe

CATEGORY	NAME	BELGIUM	GERMANY	IRELAND	ITALY	NETHERLANDS	NORWAY	SPAIN	SWEDEN	UK
		%	%	%	%	%	%	%	%	%
E01	Elite suburbs	8	16	6	4	5	18	1	8	12
E02	Service (sector) communities	22	20	29	12	14	7	17	18	16
E03	Luxury flats	9	7	2	5	8	8	7	3	5
E04	Low-income inner city	5	9	10	8	11	10	1	8	9
E05	High-rise social housing	...	3	...	8	11	4	1	7	5
E06	Industrial communities	12	13	5	19	14	10	18	12	19
E07	Dynamic families	17	8	10	13	14	15	5	9	14
E08	Lower-income families	9	4	12	8	6	7	7	7	8
E09	Rural/ agricultural	14	14	21	17	13	17	23	19	6
E10	Vacation/ retirement	4	6	4	5	4	3	19	9	6

holiday camps cater for working-class families. They cater for the whole family, but prominent attractions are variety shows, bingo, slot machines, discos, dancing and organized entertainment. The camps are very busy and the emphasis is upon fun. Much of the accommodation is basic, regimented, crowded and self-catering. The almost industrial atmosphere contrasts with Center Parc's woodlands, where in these middle-class establishments, the layout and attractions are unregimented, and the emphasis is on sporting activities and relaxation.

LIFESTYLE.   As discussed in Chapter 7, people's interest in goods is affected by their lifestyles. Reciprocally, the goods they buy express their lifestyles. Marketers are increasingly segmenting their markets by consumer lifestyles. For example, General Foods used lifestyle analysis in its successful repositioning of Sanka decaffeinated coffee. For years Sanka's staid, older image limited the product's market. To turn this situation around, General Foods launched an advertising campaign that positioned Sanka as an ideal drink for today's healthy, active lifestyles. The campaign targeted achievers of all ages, using a classic achiever appeal that Sanka 'Lets you be your best'. Advertising showed people in adventurous lifestyles, such as kayaking through rapids.[18]

Lifestyle segments are either off-the-shelf methods from agencies or customized methods for individual companies. Many companies opt for off-the-shelf methods because of their familiarity and the high cost and complexity of developing their own. The ad agency Young and Rubican's Cross-Cultural Consumer Characterization (4Cs) is a typical off-the-shelf method. It has three main segments:

1. *The Constrained.* People whose expenditure is limited by income. It includes the *resigned poor* who have accepted their poverty and the more ambitious *struggling poor*.
2. *The Middle Majority.* This segment contains *mainstreams* – the largest group of all – *aspirers* and *succeeders*.
3. *The Innovators.* A segment consisting of *transitionals* and *reformers*.

The *succeeders* are a successful group of people who like to feel in control. By showing travellers – having lost their traveller's cheques and had them quickly returned – in complete control of the situation, American Express advertising would appeal to this segment. They would be equally attracted to the ability to customize their Mercedes-Benz car. In contrast, *mainstreams* need security. They will buy well-known, safe major brands and avoid risk. In the UK, the Conservative Party under Margaret Thatcher is believed to have won elections by appealing to this segment's fear of change. Highly educated *reformers* would have none of that. They would trust their own judgement and try new ideas. These people are at the forefront of many new trends, such as ecologically friendly products and new tourist destinations.

Lifestyle segments can be superimposed on other segmentation methods. For instance, Third Age Research recognizes the different lifestyles of older people. It identifies *explorers* who like to take up new activities, the *organizers*, the *apathetic*, the *comfortable*, the *fearful*, the *poor me*, the *social lion* and the *status quo*.

Based on a study of over 2,000 respondents and 30,000 'snacking occasions' Nestlé developed its own lifestyle segments of the snacking market. Two major segments it identified were the very different *depressive chocolate lovers* and *energetic males*. The *depressive chocolate lovers* are predominantly young women who buy fast food and eat chocolate. They eat chocolate at anytime, but particularly when depressed, to unwind or when bored in the evening at home. For these people taste is important, so they buy expensive products, like boxed chocolates, for themselves. Terry's Chocolate Orange, All Gold, Cadbury's Milk Flake and Black Magic appeal to them. In contrast, *energetic males* are young and disproportionately C2 in social class. They live at a fast pace, work hard, eat fast food and are reckless shoppers. Work tires them, but they exercise regularly and like lively places. They also eat chocolate in a hurry in the evening, at lunch or at mid-morning or afternoon breaks. Boxed chocolates are not for them, but they get their energy fix from countlines like KitKat, Lion and Snickers.

Being multidimensional, lifestyle segments provide a rich picture of consumers. The *depressive chocolate lovers* and *energetic males* may be the same age and social class, but the lifestyle segments start to tell us about the people and what appeals to them. An ad for the *energetic males* needs to be lively, social and fast – the product grabbed firmly and eaten. Hofmeister used such a campaign showing George the Bear on a night out with the lads to revitalize the sales and image of its lager. In contrast, Cadbury's adverts show a quiet, solitary woman anticipating and indulging herself with a Milk Flake.[19]

Lifestyle segmentation: Duck Head targets a casual student lifestyle, claiming, 'You can't get them old until you get them new.'

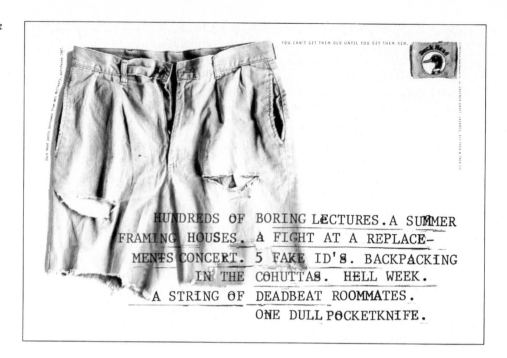

PERSONALITY. Marketers have also used personality variables to segment markets, giving their products personalities that correspond to consumer personalities. Successful market segmentation strategies based on personality work for products such as cosmetics, cigarettes, insurance and alcohol.[20] Honda's marketing campaign for its motor scooters provides another good example of personality segmentation:

> Honda *appears* to target its Spree, Elite and Aero motor scooters at the hip and trendy 16- to 22-year-old age group, but the company's ads aim at a much broader personality group. One ad, for example, shows a delighted child bouncing up and down on his bed while the announcer says, 'You've been trying to get there all your life.' The ad reminds viewers of the euphoric feelings they got when they broke away from authority and did things their parents told them not to do. And it suggests that they can feel that way again by riding a Honda scooter. So even though Honda seems to be targeting young consumers, the ads appeal to trendsetters and independent personalities in all age groups. In fact, over half of Honda's scooter sales are to young professionals and older buyers – 15 per cent are purchased by the over-50 group. Thus, Honda is appealing to the rebellious, independent kid in all of us.[21]

● *Behavioural Segmentation*

behavioural segmentation
Dividing a market into groups based on consumer knowledge, attitude, use or response to a product.

occasion segmentation
Dividing the market into groups according to occasions when buyers get the idea to buy, actually make their purchase, or use the purchased item.

Behavioural segmentation divides buyers into groups based on their knowledge, attitudes, uses or responses to a product. Many marketers believe that behaviour variables are the best starting point for building market segments.

OCCASIONS. Buyers can be grouped according to occasions when they get the idea to buy, make their purchase or use the purchased item. **Occasion segmentation** can help firms build up product usage. For example, most people drink orange juice at breakfast, but orange growers have promoted drinking orange juice as a cool and refreshing drink at other times of the day. Mother's Day

and Father's Day are promoted to increase the sale of confectionery, flowers, cards and other gifts. The turkey farmer Bernard Matthews fought the seasonality in the turkey market. In some European countries the American bird was as synonymous with Christmas as Santa Claus. He had a problem. In most families, Christmas dinner was the only meal big enough to justify buying such a big bird. His answer was to repackage the meat as turkey steaks, sausages and burgers, and promote them for year-round use. His reformulated turkey is so successful that he is now reformulating New Zealand lamb.

Kodak uses occasion segmentation in designing and marketing its single-use cameras, consisting of a roll of film with an inexpensive case and lens sold in a single, sealed unit. The customer simply snaps off the roll of pictures and returns the film, camera and all, to be processed. By mixing lenses, film speeds and accessories, Kodak has developed special versions of the camera for just about any picture-taking occasion, from underwater photography to taking baby pictures:

> Standing on the edge of the Grand Canyon? [Single-use cameras] can take panoramic, wide-angle shots. Snorkelling? Focus on that flounder with a [different single-use camera]. Sports fans are another target: Kodak now markets a telephoto version with ultra fast … film for the stadium set. … Planners are looking at a model equipped with a short focal-length lens and fast film requiring less light … they figure parents would like … to take snapshots of their babies without the disturbing flash. … In one Japanese catalogue aimed at young women, Kodak sells a package of five pastel-coloured cameras … including a version with a fish-eye lens to create a rosy, romantic glow.[22]

Polaroid shows different uses for its instant camera. Originally promoted as capturing happy family events, the product is now shown in other uses – to photograph a damaged car, an antique seen in a shop or a possible house purchase.

BENEFITS SOUGHT. A powerful form of segmentation is to group buyers according to the different *benefits* that they seek from the product **Benefit**

| Table 9.3 | Benefit segmentation of the toothpaste market |

BENEFIT SEGMENTS	DEMOGRAPHICS	BEHAVIOUR	PSYCHOGRAPHICS	FAVOURED BRANDS
Economy (low price)	Men	Heavy users	High autonomy, value oriented	Brands on sale
Medicinal (decay prevention)	Large families	Heavy users	Hypochondriacal, conservative	Crest
Cosmetic (bright teeth)	Teens, young adults	Smokers	High sociability, active	Aqua-Fresh, Ultra Brite
Taste (good tasting)	Children	Spearmint lovers	High self-involvement, hedonistic	Colgate, Aim

SOURCES: Adapted from Russell J. Haley, 'Benefit segmentation: a decision-oriented research tool', *Journal of Marketing* (July 1968), pp. 30–5; see also Haley, 'Benefit segmentation: backwards and forwards', *Journal of Advertising Research* (February–March 1984), pp. 19–25; and Haley, 'Benefit segmentation – 20 years later', *Journal of Consumer Marketing*, **1** (1984), pp. 5–14.

benefit segmentation
Dividing the market into groups according to the different benefits that consumers seek from the product.

segmentation requires finding the main benefits people look for in the product class, the kinds of people who look for each benefit and the major brands that deliver each benefit. One of the best examples of benefit segmentation was for the toothpaste market (see Table 9.3). Research found four benefit segments: economic, medicinal, cosmetic and taste. Each benefit group had special demographic, behavioural and psychographic characteristics. For example, the people seeking to prevent decay tended to have large families, were heavy toothpaste users and were conservative. Each segment also favoured certain brands. Most current brands appeal to one of these segments. For example, Crest tartar control toothpaste stresses protection and appeals to the family segment; Aim looks and tastes good and appeals to children.

Colgate-Palmolive used benefit segmentation to reposition its Irish Spring soap. Research showed three deodorant soap benefit segments: men who prefer lightly scented deodorant soap; women who want a mildly scented, gentle soap; and a mixed, mostly male segment that wanted a strongly scented, refreshing soap. The original Irish Spring did well with the last segment, but Colgate wanted to target the larger middle segment. Thus it reformulated the soap and changed its advertising to give the product more of a family appeal.[23]

In short, companies can use benefit segmentation to clarify why people should buy their product, define the brand's chief attributes and clarify how it contrasts with competing brands. They can also search for new benefits and launch brands that deliver them.

USER STATUS. Some markets segment into non-users, ex-users, potential users, first-time users and regular users of a product. Potential users and regular users may require different kinds of marketing appeal. For example, one study found that blood donors are low in self-esteem, low risk takers and more highly concerned about their health; non-donors tend to be the opposite on all three

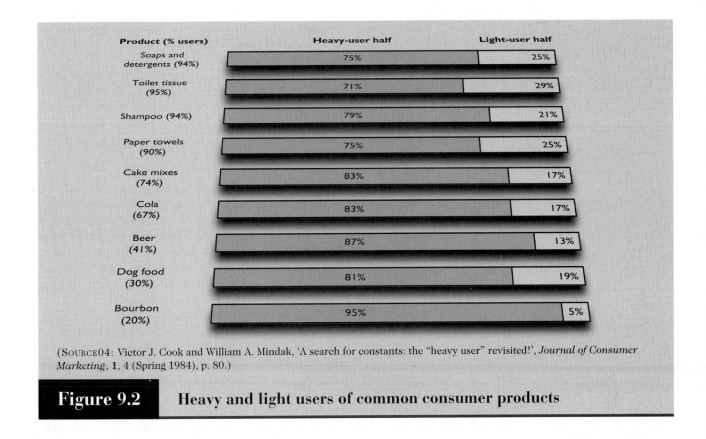

(SOURCE04: Victor J. Cook and William A. Mindak, 'A search for constants: the "heavy user" revisited!', *Journal of Consumer Marketing*, **1**, 4 (Spring 1984), p. 80.)

Figure 9.2   **Heavy and light users of common consumer products**

dimensions. This suggests that social agencies should use different marketing approaches for keeping current donors and attracting new ones.

A company's market position will also influence its focus. Market share leaders will aim to attract potential users, whereas smaller firms will focus on attracting current users away from the market leader. Golden Wonder concentrated on regular users to give it a dominant market share with its Pot Noodle and Pot Rice. It was first on the market with its dehydrated snack meals in pots, but new entrants took sales from it. It gained 80 per cent market share by making its brand more appealing to existing users. Kellogg's took a different approach with its Bran Flakes breakfast cereal. Rather than keeping to the original health conscious users, it aimed at non-users by promoting the superior flavour of the product.[24]

USAGE RATE.   Some markets also segment into light, medium and heavy-user groups. Heavy users are often a small percentage of the market, but account for a high percentage of total buying. Figure 9.2 shows usage rates for some popular consumer products. Product users were divided into two halves, a light-user and a heavy-user half, according to their buying rates for the specific products. Using beer as an example, the figure shows that 41 per cent of the households studied buy beer. However, the heavy users accounted for 87 per cent of the beer consumed – almost seven times as much as the light users. Clearly, a beer company would prefer to attract one heavy user to its brand rather than several light users.

Airlines' frequent flyer programmes are aimed at heavy users who, because they are business travellers, also buy expensive tickets. British Airways Executive Club blue card members get free AirMiles each time they travel and other priority benefits when booking and checking in. As usage mounts, Club members are upgraded to silver and gold cards, each giving extra benefits and services. Almost all airlines offer similar incentives, but since benefits mount with usage, it pays the frequent flyer to be loyal. Some operators share their schemes to provide wider benefits to the regular traveller. American Express's Membership Miles scheme integrates Air France's Frequence Plus, Austrian Swissair's Qualiflyer, Virgin's Freeway and Continental Airline's OnePass together with a string of hotel chains and car rental firms. Continental's scheme is already bundled with others, so with it comes Air Canada, BWIA International Airways, Malaysian Airlines and Cathay Pacific.

LOYALTY STATUS.   Many firms are now trying to segment their markets by loyalty, and are using loyalty schemes to do it. They assume that some consumers are completely loyal – they buy one brand all the time. Others are somewhat loyal – they are loyal to two or three brands of a given product, or favour one brand while sometimes buying others. Still other buyers show no loyalty to any brand. They either want something different each time they buy or always buy a brand on sale. In most cases, marketers split buyers into groups according to their loyalty to their product or service, then focus on the profitable loyal customers.

Loyalty schemes go beyond the continuity programmes, like Esso Tiger Cards, that have been used for decades. They seek to build a relationship between the buyer and the brand. In Australia members of Unilever's Omomatic Club – for people with front-loading washing machines – get newsletters, brochures, samples and gift catalogues. 'Front loaders' are rare in Australia, so the club keeps Unilever in touch with a micromarket that its Omomatic detergent is made for. Nestlé's Casa Buitoni Club is for people interested in an Italian lifestyle and cooking. The pasta market is fragmented and penetrated by retailers' own brands, so the club aims to build loyalty and Buitoni's brand heritage of focusing on enthusiasts. The Swatch's Club was formed after Swatch studied the market for cult objects. Members are helped to build up their Swatch collection and offered special editions.

The effectiveness of loyalty schemes and segmentation by loyalty is limited by how people buy. Loyal customers are few and very hard to find in most markets. Most customers are promiscuous and polygamous in their relationship with brands. Those with favoured brands will promiscuously try alternatives occasionally, and most customers choose from a repertoire of favourites. But even the polygamous brand users change their repertoires and make opportunistic purchases. There is also a limit to the attention customers devote to some brands, plus the low cost of switching from one brand to another. In many markets, attempts to build brand loyalty will, like most sales promotions, last only as long as the campaign. There is also a danger of loyalty being displaced from the brand to the loyalty scheme – the air miles acquired becoming more important than the airline flown.[25]

buyer-readiness stages
The stages that consumers normally pass through on their way to purchase, including awareness, knowledge, liking, preference, conviction and purchase.

BUYER-READINESS STAGE.   A market consists of people in different **buyer-readiness stages** of readiness to buy a product. Some people are unaware of the product; some are aware; some are informed; some are interested; some want the product; and some intend to buy. The relative numbers at each stage make a big difference in designing the marketing programme. Car dealers use their databases to increase customer care and to estimate when customers are ready to buy. Guarantees lock customers into having the first few services from a dealer, but after that, the dealer can estimate when services are needed. Close to the due date the customer is sent a reminder or rung to arrange for a service. Some time later the dealer can estimate that the customer is getting ready to buy a new car and can then send out details of new models or deals. Indiscriminate mailing that does not take into account the buyer-readiness stage can damage relationships. By sending unwanted brochures the dealer becomes a source of junk mail. Even worse, recent customers' satisfaction reduces if they are told about a better deal or replacement model soon after their purchase.

ATTITUDE TOWARDS PRODUCT.   People in a market can be enthusiastic, positive, indifferent, negative or hostile about a product. Door-to-door workers in a political campaign use a given voter's attitude to determine how much time to spend with that voter. They thank enthusiastic voters and remind them to vote; they spend little or no time trying to change the attitudes of negative and hostile voters. They reinforce those who are positive and try to win the votes of those who are indifferent. In such marketing situations, attitudes can be effective segmentation variables.

The world charity Oxfam needs to keep donations up and costs down. Segmentation helps it do this. It values all donors, but treat segments differently. A lot of its income is from *committed givers* who donate regularly, but want low involvement with the charity. They get *Oxfam News*, special appeals and gift catalogues. *Oxfam Project Partners* want and get much more contact with Oxfam. These are further segmented by their choice of project, on which they get regular feedback. Through this scheme, Oxfam, like Action Aid, develops a relationship between the giver and the final recipient. *Leading donors* receive special customer care and information about how their money was spent. Many donors can give little time to Oxfam, but other groups enjoy working in the charity's shops or are enthusiastic *lottery ticket vendors*.[26]

Segmenting Business Markets

Consumer and business marketers use many of the same variables to segment their markets. Business buyers segment geographically or by benefits sought, user status, usage rate, loyalty status, readiness state and attitudes. Yet business marketers also use some additional variables which, as Table 9.4 shows, include business customer *demographics* (industry, company size); *operating characteristics*; *buying approaches*; *situational factors*; and *personal characteristics*.[27]

The table lists important questions that business marketers should ask in determining which customers they want to serve. By going after segments instead of the whole market, companies have a much better chance to deliver value to consumers and to receive maximum rewards for close attention to consumer needs. Thus Pirelli and other tyre companies should decide which *industries* they want to serve. Manufacturers buying tyres vary in their needs. Makers of luxury and high-performance cars want higher-grade tyres than makers of economy models. In addition, the tyres needed by aircraft manufacturers must meet much higher safety standards than tyres needed by farm tractor manufacturers.

Within the chosen industry, a company can further segment by *customer size* or *geographic location*. The company might set up separate systems for dealing with larger or multiple-location customers. For example, Steelcase, a big producer of office furniture, first segments customers into ten industries, including banking, insurance and electronics. Next, company salespeople work with independent Steelcase dealers to handle smaller, local or regional Steelcase customers in each segment. Many national, multiple-location customers, such as Shell or Philips, have special needs that may reach beyond the scope of individual dealers. So Steelcase uses national accounts managers to help its dealer networks handle its national accounts.

Within a given target industry and customer size, the company can segment by *purchase approaches and criteria*. For example, government, university and

Table 9.4   Primary segmentation variables for business markets

Demographics

Industry. Which industries that buy this product should we focus on?

Company size. What size companies should we focus on?

Location. What geographical areas should we focus on?

Operating variables

Technology. What customer technologies should we focus on?

User/non-user status. Should we focus on heavy, medium or light users, or non-users?

Customer capabilities. Should we focus on customers needing many services or few services?

Purchasing approaches

Purchasing function organizations. Should we focus on companies with highly centralized or decentralized purchasing organizations?

Power structure. Should we focus on companies that are engineering dominated, financially dominated or marketing dominated?

Nature of existing relationships. Should we focus on companies with which we already have strong relationships or simply go after the most desirable companies?

General purchase policies. Should we focus on companies that prefer leasing? Service contracts? Systems purchases? Sealed bidding?

Purchasing criteria. Should we focus on companies that are seeking quality? Service? Price?

Situational factors

Urgency. Should we focus on companies that need quick delivery or service?

Specific application. Should we focus on certain applications of our product rather than all applications?

Size of order. Should we focus on large or small orders?

Personal characteristics

Buyer–seller similarity. Should we focus on companies whose people and values are similar to ours?

Attitudes towards risk. Should we focus on risk-taking or risk-avoiding customers?

Loyalty. Should we focus on companies that show high loyalty to their suppliers?

SOURCES: Adapted from Thomas V. Bonoma and Benson P. Shapiro, *Segmenting the Industrial Market* (Lexington, MA: Lexington Books, 1983); see also John Berrigan and Carl Finkbeiner, *Segmentation Marketing: New methods for capturing business* (New York: Harper Business, 1992).

industrial laboratories typically differ in their purchase criteria for scientific instruments. Government labs need low prices (because they have difficulty in getting funds to buy instruments) and service contracts (because they can easily get money to maintain instruments). University labs want equipment that needs little regular service because they do not have service people on their payrolls. Industrial labs need highly reliable equipment because they cannot afford downtime.

Table 9.4 focuses on business buyer *characteristics*. However, as in consumer segmentation, many marketers believe that *buying behaviour* and *benefits* provide the best basis for segmenting business markets. For example, a recent study of the customers of Signode Corporation's industrial packaging division revealed four segments, each seeking a different mix of price and service benefits:

1. *Programmed buyers*. These buyers view Signode's products as not very important to their operations. They buy the products as a routine purchase,

usually pay full price and accept below-average service. Clearly this is a highly profitable segment for Signode.

2. *Relationship buyers*. These buyers regard Signode's packaging products as moderately important and are knowledgeable about competitors' offerings. They prefer to buy from Signode as long as its price is reasonably competitive. They receive a small discount and a modest amount of service. This segment is Signode's second most profitable.

3. *Transaction buyers*. These buyers see Signode's products as very important to their operations. They are price and service sensitive. They receive about a 10 per cent discount and above-average service. They are knowledgeable about competitors' offerings and are ready to switch for a better price, even if it means losing some service.

4. *Bargain hunters*. These buyers see Signode's products as very important and demand the deepest discount and the highest service. They know the alternative suppliers, bargain hard and are ready to switch at the slightest dissatisfaction. Signode needs these buyers for volume purposes, but they are not very profitable.[28]

This segmentation scheme has helped Signode to do a better job of designing marketing strategies that take into account each segment's unique reactions to varying levels of price and service.[29]

Segmenting International Markets

Few companies have either the resources or the will to operate in all, or even most, of the more than 170 countries that dot the globe. Although some large companies, such as Unilever or Sony, sell products in more than 100 countries, most international firms focus on a smaller set. Operating in many countries presents new challenges.[30] The different countries of the world, even those that are close together, can vary dramatically in their economic, cultural and political make-up. Thus, just as they do within their domestic markets, international firms need to group their world markets into segments with distinct buying needs and behaviours.

Companies can segment international markets using one or a combination of several variables. They can segment by *geographic location*, grouping countries by regions such as western Europe, the Pacific Rim, the Middle East or Africa. Countries in many regions have already organized geographically into market groups or 'free trade zones', such as the European Union, the Association of South-East Asian Nations and the North American Free Trade Association. These associations reduce trade barriers between member countries, creating larger and more homogeneous markets.

Geographic segmentation assumes that nations close to one another will have many common traits and behaviours. Although this is often the case, there are many exceptions. For example, although the United States and Canada have much in common, both differ culturally and economically from neighbouring Mexico. Even within a region, consumers can differ widely:

> Many marketers think everything between the Rio Grande and Tierra del Fuego at the southern tip of South America is the same, including the 400 million inhabitants. They are wrong. The Dominican Republic is no more like Argentina than Sicily is like Sweden. Many Latin Americans do not speak Spanish, including 140 million Portuguese-speaking Brazilians and the millions in other countries who speak a variety of Indian dialects.[31]

Some world markets segment on *economic factors*. For example, countries might group by population income levels or by their overall level of economic development. Some countries, such as the so-called Group of Eight – the United States, the United Kingdom, France, Germany, Japan, Canada, Italy and Russia – have established highly industrialized economies. Other countries have newly industrialized or developing economies (Singapore, Malaysia, Taiwan, South Korea, Brazil, Mexico and now China). Still others are less developed (India, sub-Saharan Africa). A company's economic structure shapes its population's product and service needs and, therefore, the marketing opportunities it offers.

Political and legal factors such as the type and stability of government, receptivity towards foreign firms, monetary regulations and the amount of bureaucracy can segment countries. These factors can play a crucial role in a company's choice of which countries to enter and how. *Cultural factors* can also segment markets. International markets can group according to common languages, religions, values and attitudes, customs and behavioural patterns.

Segmenting international markets by geographic, economic, political, cultural and other factors assumes that segments should consist of clusters and countries. However, many companies use a different approach, called *inter-market segmentation*. Using this approach, they form segments of consumers who have similar needs and buying behaviour even though they are from different countries.[32] For example, BMW, Mercedes-Benz, Saab and Volvo target the world's well-to-do, regardless of their country. Similarly, an agricultural chemicals manufacturer might focus on small farmers in a variety of developing countries:

> These [small farmers], whether from Pakistan or Indonesia or Kenya or Mexico, appear to represent common needs and behaviour. Most of them till the land using bullock carts and have little cash to buy agricultural inputs. They lack the education ... to appreciate fully the value of using fertiliser and depend on government help for such things as seeds, pesticides and fertiliser. They acquire farming needs from local suppliers and count on word-of-mouth to learn and accept new things and ideas. Thus, even though these farmers are continents apart and even though they speak different languages and have different cultural backgrounds, they may represent a homogeneous market segment.[33]

Multivariate Segmentation

Most of the time companies integrate ways of segmenting markets. We have already mentioned how Lego segments by age until children develop different interests, and how Third Age Research first focuses on older people, then forms lifestyle segments. There are several ways of combining segments.

● *Simple Multivariate Segmentation*

Many companies segment markets by combining two or more demographic variables. Consider the market for deodorant soaps. Many different kinds of consumer use the top-selling deodorant soap brands, but gender and age are the most useful variables in distinguishing the users of one brand from those of another. In the United States, men and women differ in their deodorant soap preferences. Top men's brands include Dial, Safeguard and Irish Spring – these brands account for over 30 per cent of the men's soap market. Women, in contrast, prefer Dial, Zest and Coast, which account for 23 per cent of the women's soap market.

Applying the Concepts

1. Thinking about the participants in this course, segment them into different groups (allocate a mnemonic to each group if you wish). What is your chief segmentation variable? Select several products or services and assess if you could effectively market them to these segments. How effective was your segmentation effort in the first instance?

2. By looking at advertising and at the products themselves, we can often see what target segments marketers hope to reach. Find advertisements of several products. Can you gauge what target markets the ads are aimed at? Do you think the products have distinctive target markets? Are some more clearly defined than others?

References

1. Regis McKenna, 'Real-time marketing', *Harvard Business Review* (July–August 1995), p. 87.
2. Edward Baig, 'Platinum cards: move over AmEx', *Business Week* (19 August 1996), p. 84.
3. Laurel Cutler, quoted in 'Stars of the 1980s cast their light', *Fortune* (3 July 1989), p. 76.
4. Robert E. Linneman and John L. Stanton, Jr, *Making Niche Marketing Work: How to grow bigger by acting smaller* (New York: McGraw-Hill, 1991).
5. See Don Peppers and Martha Rogers, *The One-to-One Future: Building relationships one customer at a time* (New York: Currency/Doubleday, 1993).
6. See B. Joseph Pine II, *Mass Customization* (Boston, MA: Harvard Business School Press, 1993); B. Joseph Pine II, Don Peppers and Martha Rogers, 'Do you want to keep your customers forever?', *Harvard Business Review* (March–April 1995), pp. 103–14; Christopher W. Hart, 'Made to order', *Marketing Management* (Summer 1996), pp. 11–22; James H. Gilmore and B. Joseph Pine II, 'The four faces of customization', *Harvard Business Review* (January–February 1997), pp. 91–101.
7. McKenna, 'Real-time marketing', op. cit., p. 87.
8. Jocken Pläcking, *Marketing-Kommunikation im Autobilmarkt Europa* (Stuttgart: Motor-Presse, 1990).
9. Ian Rogers, 'Pergesa emerges from the gloom under a new guise', *Financial Times* (3 August 1994), p. 21.
10. Marieke De Mooij, *Advertising Worldwide: Concepts, theories and practical multinational and global advertising*, 2nd edn (London: Prentice Hall, 1994).
11. 'High street renaissance', *The Economist* (16 October 1993), pp. 35–6.
12. David Blackwell, 'Intelligent as a brick', *Financial Times* (27 January 1998), p. 18.
13. 'Can Europe compete? Ageing Europe', *Financial Times* (8 March 1994), p. 14.
14. See Frieda Curtindale, 'Marketing cars to women', *American Demographics* (November 1988), pp. 29–31; Betsy Sharkey, 'The many faces of Eve', *Adweek* (25 June 1990), pp. 44–9. The quote is from 'Automakers learn better roads to women's market', *Marketing News* (12 October 1992), p. 2.
15. Alice Rawsthorn, 'LVMH see strong profits growth', *Financial Times* (18–19 June 1994), p. 11; 'LVMH and Guinness: rearranging their affairs', *EuroBusiness* (February 1994), p. 6; David Short, 'Nescafé still strongest brew on top shelf',

The European (22–8 July 1994), p. 22; Ian Harding, 'Takeovers fail to slake Arnault's thirst for a fight', *The European* (5–11 August 1994), p. 32.
16. Michael Skapinker, 'Cruise industry charts mass-market course', *Financial Times* (10 June 1994), p. 11.
17. Graham J. Hooley and John Saunders, *Competitive Positioning* (London: Prentice Hall, 1993); David Tonks, 'Market segmentation', in Michael J. Thomas (ed.), *Marketing Handbook* (Aldershot: Gower, 1989), pp. 573–87.
18. Bickley Townsend, 'Psychographic glitter and gold', *American Demographics* (November 1985), p. 22.
19. Peter Field and Adam Morgan, 'Hofmeister: a study of advertising and brand imagery in the lager market', in Charles Channon (ed.), *20 Advertising Histories* (London: Cassell, 1989), pp. 16–29.
20. For a detailed discussion of personality and buyer behaviour, see Leon G. Schiffman and Leslie Lazar Kanuk, *Consumer Behavior*, 4th edn (Englewood Cliffs, NJ: Prentice Hall, 1991), ch. 4.
21. See Laurie Freeman and Cleveland Horton, 'Spree: Honda's scooters ride the cutting edge', *Advertising Age* (5 September 1985), pp. 3, 35.
22. Mark Maremont, 'The hottest thing since the flashbulb', *Business Week* (7 September 1992).
23. See Schiffman and Kanuk, *Consumer Behavior*, op. cit., p. 48.
24. Jeremy Elliott, 'Breaking the bran barrier – Kellogg's Bran Flakes', in Channon (ed.), *20 Advertising Histories*, op. cit., pp. 1–15; Terry Bullen, 'Golden Wonder: a potted success', in ibid., pp. 178–98.
25. For a comprehensive discussion of loyalty schemes, see Mark Uncles, 'Do you or your customers need a loyalty scheme?', *Journal of Targeting, Measurement and Analysis for Marketing*, **2**, 4 (1994), pp. 335–50; see also F.F. Reichheld, 'Loyalty-based management', *Harvard Business Review* (March–April 1993), pp. 64–73; Andrew S.C. Ehrenberg, 'Locking them in forever', *Admap*, **28**, 11 (1992), p. 14.
26. Martin Howard, 'The practicalities of developing better analysis and segmentation techniques for fine focusing and improving targeting', Institute for International Research, Conference on Advanced Customer Profiling, Segmentation and Analysis, London, 10 February 1994.
27. See Thomas V. Bonoma and Benson P. Shapiro, *Segmenting the Industrial Market* (Lexington, MA: Lexington Books,

1983). For examples of segmenting business markets, see Kate Bertrand, 'Market segmentation: divide and conquer', *Business Marketing* (October 1989), pp. 48–54.

28. V. Kasturi Rangan, Rowland T. Moriarty and Gordon S. Swartz, 'Segmenting customers in mature industrial markets', *Journal of Marketing* (October 1992), pp. 72–82.

29. For another interesting approach to segmenting the business market, see John Berrigan and Carl Finkbeiner, *Segmentation Marketing: New methods for capturing business* (New York: Harper Business, 1992).

30. P.G. Walters, 'Global market segmentation and challenges', *Journal of Marketing Management*, **13**, 1–3 (1997), pp. 163–80.

31. Marlene L. Rossman, 'Understanding five nations of Latin America', *Marketing News* (11 October 1985), p. 10; as quoted in Subhash C. Jain, *International Marketing Management*, 3rd edn (Boston, MA: PWS–Kent Publishing, 1990), p. 366.

32. For more on intermarket segmentation, see Jain, *International Marketing Management*, op. cit., pp. 369–70.

33. Ibid., pp. 370–1.

34. Thomas Exter, 'Deodorant demographics', *American Demographics* (December 1987), p. 39.

35. Taken from Jens Maier and John Saunders, 'The implementation of segmentation in sales management', *Journal of Personal Selling and Sales Management*, **10**, 1 (1990), pp. 39–48.

36. Gert-Olof Boström and Timothy L. Wilson, 'Market segmentation in professional services – case of CAD adoption amongst architectural firms', European Marketing Academy Proceedings, Barcelona, Spain, 25–8 May 1993, pp. 249–60.

37. Mark Jemkins and Malcolm MacDonald, 'Market segmentation: organisational archetypes and research

agendas', *European Journal of Marketing*, **31**, 1 (1997), pp. 17–32; Francisco J. Sarabia, 'Model for market segments: evaluation and selection', *European Journal of Marketing*, **30**, 1 (1996), pp. 58–74; Erwin Danneels, 'Market segmentation: normative model versus business reality: an explanatory study of the apparel market in Belgium', *European Journal of Marketing*, **30**, 12 (1996), pp. 39–49.

38. See Joe Schwartz, 'Southpaw strategy', *American Demographics* (June 1988), p. 61; and 'Few companies tailor products for lefties', *Wall Street Journal* (2 August 1989), p. 2.

39. For an example of how customer profitability can be used to determine target segments in the Scandinavian banking industry, see K. Storbacka, 'Segmentation based on customer profitability – retrospective analysis of retail banking customer bases', *Journal of Marketing Management*, **13**, 5 (1997), pp. 479–93.

40. See Michael Porter, *Competitive Advantage* (New York: Free Press, 1985), pp. 4–8, 234–6.

41. The methods are introduced in S.J.Q. Robinson, R.E. Hitchins and D.P. Wade, 'The directional policy matrix: tool for strategic planning', *Long Range Planning*, **11**, 3 (1978), pp. 8–15; Yoram Wind and Vejay Mahajan, 'Designing product and business portfolios', *Harvard Business Review* (January–February 1981), pp. 155–65. They are reviewed in Robin Wensley, 'Strategic marketing: boxes, betas or basics', *Journal of Marketing*, **45**, 3 (Summer 1981), pp. 173–82.

42. Angelika Dreher, Angelika Ritter and Hans Mühlbacher, 'Systematic positioning: a new approach and its application', European Marketing Academy Proceedings, Aarhus, Denmark, 26–9 May 1992, pp. 313–29.

43. Rein Rijkens, *European Advertising Strategies* (London: Cassell, 1992), pp. 121–32.

Case 9

Coffee-Mate

Andy Hirst and John Saunders*

THE COFFEE CREAMER MARKET GREW consistently, following its introduction in the United Kingdom in the early 1970s, to approximately £25 million in 1995. In volume terms, however, the creamer market is small, with a household penetration of 18 per cent. Coffee-Mate has dominated the market since its launch as a result of a strong brand and consistent advertising. Despite the growth of private labels in the late 1980s, Coffee-Mate's increased advertising spending (from £400,000 to £1.5 million) has enabled it to squeeze both private label and other brands (Exhibits 9.1 and 9.2).

* The Business School, Loughborough University.

EXHIBIT 9.1 MEDIA ADVERTISING ON MILK (£000s)

Cadbury	616
Carnation Coffee-Mate	1,482
Carnation Evaporated	398
Carnation Light Skimmed	166
DCNI	173
Fresh 'n' Low	157
Kerrygold Light Skimmed	211
MMB Cans	286
NDC	10,427
NDC Milk Race	1,664
Nestlé TipTop	1,443
SMCP	703
Others	211

Source: MEAL.

EXHIBIT 9.2 VOLUME BRAND SHARES (%)

BRAND	SHARE
Coffee-Mate – total:	55.5
Standard	41.0
Lite	14.5
Compliment	2.6
Kenco	3.0
Compleat	1.4
Own label	37.3
All others	0.3

Competition in the Coffee Creamer Market

The coffee creamer market is distinct from the instant dry milk market, which includes brands such as Marvel, St Ivel Five Pints and Pint Size, which, although worth £43 million, has seen a 25 per cent decline since 1988. Dried or powdered milk had been associated with slimming (e.g. Marvel adopted this positioning). The availability of low-fat, skimmed and semi-skimmed milks has had a substantial impact upon sales in this sector. Dried/instant milk, used for its convenience and low cost, has shown a 6 per cent decline in value sales in real terms consequent upon the increased availability of skimmed milk. Dried or powdered milk is not a direct substitute for coffee creamers because of its poor mixing qualities. It is used as a whitener in tea or coffee only in emergency situations in which the household has run out or run low on supplies of milk.

The dynamics of the coffee creamer market appear to be undergoing a change in parallel with consumers' developing tastes for skimmed and semi-skimmed milk in their coffee. Milk is the most popular whitener for coffee. Although cream is thought to be the best whitener, it represents an aspirational flavour goal only for some. Most consumers perceive cream as a reserved, ritualistic practice, whose taste, while appropriate for an occasion, is not to be replicated on a daily basis.

Powdered or dried milk is a distress product, used only in emergency situations. As such, the brands are bought, but the product is only tolerated. Creamers are regarded more as an indulgence and treat by users, although non-users did not see creamers as anything like a substitute for cream and were generally highly negative and suspicious of the product (consumers' and non-users' perceptions of the product category will be described in a later section).

Coffee-Mate is a blend of dried glucose and vegetable fat, but cannot be legally defined as non-dairy, since it also contains milk derivatives. Recent improvements to the product include the relaunch of Coffee-Mate 100 g and 200 g in straight-sided glass jars with paper labels, and a 'Nidoll-contoured' jar with shrink-wrapped label. Packs of 500 g and 1 kg are available in cartons with an inner bag. At the end of 1990, Coffee-Mate Lite, a low-fat alternative to Coffee-Mate, was introduced. Cannibalization of volume has been minimal. The volume generated by Lite has been a key feature in the development of the brand, which has experienced a 10 per cent growth in sales volume in the first three years following Lite's launch.

Coffee-Mate Consumer

The demographic profile of Coffee-Mate and Lite buyers is summarized in Exhibit 9.3. The average Coffee-Mate consumer buys 1.5 kg annually. AGB Superpanel data suggest that buyers of Coffee-Mate tend to use all brands and types of coffee. The market is characterized by its low interest level, since most buyers do not see it as a weekly shopping item. The main reason given by respondents for not purchasing Coffee-Mate is preference for milk in their coffee: as many as one-third of non-users gave this as their reason for rejecting the product. An equally high proportion of the non-users simply have no reason to purchase, because they don't drink coffee, drink it black, or simply have no need to use the creamer. Reasons given spontaneously for lapsed usage were very similar to the main ones articulated by non-users: 50 per cent of respondents stated that they preferred milk in coffee, while around 21 per cent said that they don't drink coffee, drink it black or don't think to buy creamers (Exhibit 9.4).

EXHIBIT 9.3 COFFEE CREAMER BUYERS: DEMOGRAPHIC PROFILE

PRODUCT	PROFILE
Coffee creamers	No *strong* demographic bias. Slightly skewed towards 45–64-year-olds, 2-person households and households without children.
Coffee-Mate – std	Slight bias towards C2, DE and 45+ households as heavier buyers; 2–3-person households and households with children.
Coffee-Mate Lite	Slightly biased towards 45–64-year-olds, full-time working housewives, and households without children.

EXHIBIT 9.4 REASONS FOR LAPSING AND REJECTION (NUMBER OF RESPONDENTS)

SPONTANEOUS RESPONSE	LAPSING	REJECTION
Don't drink coffee	11	22
Drink black coffee	5	6
Prefer milk	50	33
Prefer skimmed milk	5	3
Don't like them	10	18
Leaves coffee too hot	2	1

No need to use them	5	5
Don't think to buy them	1	4
Doesn't mix	4	1
Prefer pure things	4	3
Fattening	2	2
Too rich/creamy	1	2
Other	5	3
Don't know	4	9
Total sample	409	664

Because Coffee-Mate and Coffee-Mate Lite are 'consumed' with coffee, popularity and demand will also be affected by the annual coffee consumption in the United Kingdom, which has been static at under 3 kg per head since 1985, compared with over 5 kg in Italy, France and Germany, and well below countries like Finland and the Netherlands with 11–13 kg. Exhibit 9.5 shows the trend in coffee consumption in the UK. The National Food Survey (EIU Retail Business 1992) suggests that the higher a household's income, the more it spends on coffee (Exhibit 9.6). Childless households are the most intense coffee drinkers (Exhibit 9.7).

EXHIBIT 9.5 COFFEE CONSUMPTION (CUPS/PERSON/DAY)

YEAR	1970	1981	1990	1995
Any coffee	1.22	1.54	1.57	1.48
Instant coffee	1.07	1.39	1.39	1.34
Ground coffee	0.01	0.13	0.14	0.12
Special coffee	–	–	–	0.10
Food beverage	0.09	0.06	0.06	0.04
Choc/cocoa	0.10	0.07	0.07	0.07

SOURCE: National Food Survey.

EXHIBIT 9.6 CONSUMPTION BY INCOME GROUP (PER PERSON/WEEK)

WEEKLY INCOME (£)	CONSUMPTION (g)	EXPENDITURE (p)
645+	2.60	25.20
475–644	1.79	19.30
250–474	1.76	20.03
125–249	1.54	18.20
0–124	1.62	17.24
125+ (no earners)	3.08	32.19
0–125 (no earners)	1.65	19.41
OAPs	1.76	18.64

SOURCE: National Food Survey.

For both users and non-users, consumers' perceptions, attitudes towards and motivations behind usage of whiteners and creamers vary. Overall, consumers display a relatively clear understanding of the whitener market, which they tend to define under two headings: *dried* or *powdered milks*, and *whiteners*.

EXHIBIT 9.7 CONSUMPTION BY HOUSEHOLD SIZE (PER PERSON/WEEK)

NUMBER OF ADULTS	CHILDREN	CONSUMPTION (g)	EXPENDITURE (p)
1	0	2.32	27.24
1	1+	1.18	14.82
2	0	2.32	25.34
2	1	1.68	17.97
2	2	1.34	14.55
2	3	1.26	14.63
2	4+	1.12	11.38
3	0	1.93	22.95
3+	1–2	1.43	15.51
3+	3+	0.92	12.22
4+	0	2.07	25.42

SOURCE: National Food Survey.

Perceptually, the dried- or powdered-milk product is more prominent. The product's great versatility and its heritage ('milk') are responsible for this. Consumers regard dried milk as a substitute product, the alternative to turn to in an emergency when the real thing, milk, has run out or is running low. There was also an association with slimming, with brands such as Marvel adopting precisely this positioning. The advent of skimmed milk has, however, made the role in this respect redundant. A few older respondents who used powdered milk in cooking and baking nonetheless reported beneficial results, such as lighter cakes.

The prevailing image of powdered milk as a distress or convenience product means that the *brand* is *bought*, but the *product* is *tolerated*: 'You tend to buy powdered milk thinking that you will need it when you run out, and occasionally you do.' 'Powdered milk is useful if you run out of real milk. You can make it up and use it just like the real thing, but it doesn't taste too good. You have to be a bit desperate to want to use it.'

Other negatives are attached to dry milk. Respondents considered it to be an inconvenient product to prepare. Frequently the product's performance is perceived as disappointing. Consumers here spoke of the product's poor mixing qualities: it is 'lumpy', resulting in 'bits' floating on the top of their coffee. The product also tended to 'congeal' when spooned into tea or coffee. When made up and poured the product's poor taste qualities were also apparent: 'We have had it in our cornflakes when we've run out, but quite honestly, it tastes so disgusting that in the future I don't think I'd bother.' 'It's all right for baking, but if you want to use it like real milk, it's not really advisable.'

A stigma is attached to dried milk because of its poor performance and taste delivery. The image of dried milk was consistent across both users and non-users. Negative perceptions of the product do, however, impact on consumers' perceptions of coffee creamers or whiteners, acting to constrain or to taint perceptions, especially among non-users.

Whiteners/Coffee Creamers

Coffee creamers have a more polarized image across users and non-users. First, *loyal or confirmed creamer users* regard creamer as almost a treat. It is looked upon as an indulgence, solely for their pleasure. These hedonistic and indulgent properties are sometimes enhanced by the brand (e.g. Coffee-Mate) being perceived as having relaxing or comforting benefits: 'Creamers are a little bit of an indulgence. They make coffee taste so much better. They add something to it which improves the taste.' 'First thing in the morning I tend to have coffee with semi-skimmed milk, but towards 11 o'clock I want something which is more relaxing, more substantial, so I have coffee with Coffee-Mate. It seems to be comforting.'

Creamers' taste benefits are undoubtedly a motivating force behind usage. Loyal users enjoy and appreciate the thicker, creamier taste. Creamers are considered to supplement the taste of coffee, to complement and improve its flavour. Where Coffee-Mate is concerned, the perceptions are extremely positive. Users enjoy its sweet delivery, stating that they need not add sugar to it. Coffee-Mate fans feel that it does produce a creamy cup of coffee whether or not it is added to instant or freshly brewed 'real' coffee: 'Coffee without Coffee-Mate, just made with milk, tastes like it's got something missing.' 'Coffee-Mate kind of lifts the flavour. It makes a richer, better-tasting cup of coffee, whether it be an instant or a real one.'

Secondly, *non-users'* perceptions of coffee creamers are tainted by their generally negative attitudes towards dried milk. Creamers are something you have by for an emergency. You don't really want to use them – they're only there if there's no other choice: 'If someone gave me a cup of coffee with creamer in it, I would think they were doing it because they had run out of milk. I wouldn't have thought it was because they like the taste of it. Surely nobody could like the taste.'

Thus, in marked contrast to the users, where the creamy taste of Coffee-Mate is a totally apposite adjective, non-users criticized its sweetness. Non-users describe creamers as changing the taste of coffee, masking its pure taste rather than enhancing it. They also criticized its high sugar content, given that it is a glucose-based product. These consumers feel that Coffee-Mate delivers a flavour that is unacceptably sweet. They are not impressed with the product and perceive it to be a poor synthetic alternative to cream: 'You can always tell when someone's used creamers, it just tastes powdery. It doesn't taste like cream, it has a taste all of its own.' 'Whiteners taste nothing like cream. They taste powdery. You always know when they're there.'

The polarized perceptions of users and non-users are therefore summarized as follows:

> **Taste reactions of users:** Creamy, rich, comforting, sweet and relaxing. 'Coffee without Coffee-Mate tastes as if it's lacking something.'
> **Taste reactions of non-users:** Clawy, heavy and sweet. 'You lose the flavour of the coffee.'

Thirdly, *lapsed users* still see creamers as a bit of an indulgence and a treat. However, they feel an element of guilt in using the product, and often it has been this anxiety that has caused them to drift away from it: 'I like coffee creamers – I like the taste. But I stopped using them because I felt I was putting on too much weight and I needed to cut down. I just think there is too much in there, it's just glucose syrup and vegetable fat.' 'My husband had to go on a low-cholesterol diet and I figured that there was just too much fat in the coffee creamers. We've become accustomed now to drinking it black, or with very little skimmed milk.'

Looking ahead, health concerns are having an impact upon milk consumption, particularly the use of skimmed milk and other low-fat varieties. This change has been prompted by consumers' concern over health in general, and their level of fat intake in particular. Some consumers found it difficult to wean themselves and their families off milk, initially, and then semi-skimmed milk, in favour of the fully skimmed variety. However, many are persistent in adopting an overall preventative health maintenance regime as well as controlling their weight. So, while a few respondents retained the notion that a cup of real coffee made with cream was still the ideal, many others considered their ideal to be coffee drunk with just a dash of milk or black. Unfortunately, Coffee-Mate is perceived to be too close to cream in its taste and textural delivery, and is in danger of being rendered redundant since its creamy association is increasingly deemed undesirable. Coffee-Mate Lite may, however, redeem the situation by offering the same benefits of creamy and rich taste without causing injury to health and weight.

Consumer Analyses
TGI User Surveys covering instant/ground coffee and powdered milk/coffee creamer markets yielded five potential consumer groups for Coffee-Mate, some of which are potentially more attractive than others. These clusters warrant further evaluation.

Cluster 1: 'Sharon and Tracy' – Experimentalists
(Sample Proportion: 15.4 per cent)
They like to enjoy themselves and try new things. They enjoy spending money happily and seem to be very materialistic and status conscious. They go out frequently and are uninterested in political or environmental issues. They are products of the Thatcher years.

Although they are heavy users of instant coffee, they are low-level users of ground coffee. They claim to use Nescafé granules and Maxwell House powder most often. They are below-average users of the category and average users of Coffee-Mate, but heavy users of cream.

They are younger (15–44 years) with a mid- to down-market bias (C2D) and children. They are of middle income (£15,000 up to £30,000), but live in council property, in fading industrial areas and underprivileged areas. They tend to be found in the north of the country (e.g. Scotland, Yorkshire, the north-east).

They read many of the tabloids (e.g. *The Sun, Daily Star, Today, News of the World*) and the 'mums' magazines such as *Bella, Chat* and *Woman*. They are heavy users of ITV (not Channel 4), TV AM and satellite, and heavy listeners to independent radio. They cannot resist buying magazines, and read papers for entertainment rather than for news.

They spend average to high amounts on the main grocery shop, and shop at Asda and M & S (all those exciting new foods). They love shopping for anything, be it food, clothes, kitchen gadgets or whatever. They like to keep up with fashion and believe they are stylish, and feel it is important to try to keep looking young. They will try anything new. They will respond to seeing new things in advertising or in the store.

They are very gregarious and socialize often (heavy users of pubs, wine bars and restaurants). They like to enjoy life and not worry about the future. They holiday abroad (eat, lie and drink in the sun) and like to treat themselves. A fairly hedonistic bunch, they tend to spend money without thinking, spend more with their credit card, and are no good at saving their money. They feel that it is important for people to think they are doing well. They buy cars for their looks and believe that brands are better than own labels.

At present they are not really using Coffee-Mate as much as one would have expected.

Cluster 2: 'Eileen and Mary' – Cost Constrained, Older, Conservative (Sample Proportion: 23.6 per cent)

Very price aware, they budget when shopping and look for lowest prices. They are very traditional in their habits (don't like foreign food or foreign holidays). They seem to worry about food (food is not safe nowadays), feel safe using products recommended by experts, think fast food is junk, and think it is worth paying more for organic fruit and vegetables and environmentally friendly products), but don't do much about it, perhaps because they can't afford to. They seem to be looking back.

They are light users of instant coffee compared with the population as a whole, but when they do use instant coffee they claim to use Maxwell House granules and powder most often. They are average users of the category and buy Marvel and St Ivel. They are not really users of Coffee-Mate and never use cream. Older (55+) and down-market (C2DE). They are not working or are retired in 1 or 2-person households; hence fewer of this type have children at home. They live in multiethnic areas, council areas and underprivileged areas on a low household income (£5,000–11,000).

They read the tabloid press and *Bella* and *Chat*. They are also heavy users of ITV, Channel 4 and TV AM, and listen to independent radio.

Not surprisingly, their expenditure on the main grocery shop is low and they tend to shop daily at places such as Kwik Save and the Co-op. They enjoy shopping, but always look for the lowest prices, decide what they want before they go shopping and budget for every penny. They frequently enter competitions, find saving difficult, save for items they want, and like to pay cash.

They are by nature very conservative. They like routine, dislike untidiness, would buy British if they could, have a roast on Sundays and prefer brands to own label. They believe job security is more important than money, would rather have a boring job than no job, and prefer to do rather than take responsibility. Due to both their age and financial constraints, they socialize rarely. Most of this group never entertain friends to a meal, and never go to a pub, a wine bar or a restaurant.

Cluster 3: 'Sarah and Anna' – Affluent, Young Foodies (Sample Proportion: 24.4 per cent)

Unencumbered by children and well off, they love both travelling and food (many claim to be vegetarian). They do not have to budget and can afford to treat themselves to perfume and foreign holidays, preferably more than once a year. They are not interested in additional channels on satellite TV and tend to be light users of all media.

They are heavy users of coffee and ground coffee. They buy decaffeinated, Gold Blend, Alta Rica, Cap Colombie, Sainsbury, M & S and Tesco. They are above average users of the category, claim to buy Coffee-Mate and Marvel most often, and also use cream.

Aged 35–54, predominantly ABC1, they earn above-average incomes and tend to be working full time. They live in areas of affluent minorities, young married suburbs and metro singles, in 1 or 2-person households. They are more likely to be found in London, the south and the south-west.

They read the quality press including the *Guardian*, the *Independent*, *The Times*, the *Financial Times* and the *Daily Telegraph*. They also read the *Mail* and the *Express* and all the equivalent Sunday papers including the

Observer. They are light users of independent radio, but they do listen to the radio in the car.

They have a high expenditure on their main grocery shop (£71+) but shop infrequently at, of course, Sainsbury, Tesco and Safeway. They really enjoy cooking and food, read recipes in magazines and like to try out new foods. Their tastes will be varied as they also enjoy travelling abroad on holiday, where they avoid the package trips and like to do as much as possible.

They entertain frequently and invite friends for meals. They also use pubs and wine bars, though not as much as 'Sharon and Tracy', and they are heavy users of restaurants.

They are health conscious (well, they can afford to be) and claim to include fibre in their diet, eat wholemeal bread, have less fat in their diet and eat fewer sweets and cakes. They are prepared to pay more for food without additives and for environmentally friendly products. They also claim to exercise.

They can afford to treat themselves and prefer to buy one good thing rather than many cheap ones. They also like to keep up with technology and want to stand out from the crowd. In their fortunate position they enjoy life and don't worry about the future.

They also claim never to buy any product tested on animals, buy unleaded petrol, use recycling banks and disapprove of aerosols more than the population at large. They make use of credit cards, especially for business, like to be well insured and consult professional advisers.

Cluster 4: 'Dawn and Lisa – Cost Constrained, Young Families (Sample Proportion: 13.9 per cent)

Rather like 'Eileen and Mary', this group is severely constrained by their low incomes. But unlike the previous group, they are often younger and often working part time or are unemployed or students, although they may have children. They are also not remotely concerned about health or the environment. Many left school before the age of 16.

They are heavy users of instant coffee, but do not use ground coffee. They buy Nescafé granules and Maxwell House powder. They are below average users of the category and never use cream.

This group is biased towards the 15–34 age group and is down-market (C2DE) with low incomes (£5,000–11,000). They are to be found in council estates, fading industrial areas and underprivileged areas in the east, northeast and London. They have young families and there is a slight bias to larger families than in other groups.

They read the tabloid press, *Bella* and *Chat*, and they are heavy viewers of ITV, TV AM and satellite, and heavy listeners to independent radio.

Their expenditure on the main grocery shop is low and they shop daily or once a week at Kwik Save. They always look for the lowest price, watch what they spend, budget for every penny and look out for special offers. They want to save, but find it difficult.

As a result of their difficult financial circumstances, they rarely use wine bars, pubs or restaurants. They claim to enjoy going to the pub, but cannot afford to these days. Similarly, when they can afford a holiday, they prefer to holiday in the United Kingdom.

They have little time or money to worry about the environment or health issues, and claim that health food is bought by fanatics. They believe that frozen food is as nutritious as fresh foods. They tend to buy own label, presumably because it is cheaper rather than because they believe own-label goods are better than branded goods.

EXHIBIT 9.8 PROPOSED TV AD

A TV CAMPAIGN AIMS TO BOOST SALES. THE FOLLOWING AD IS PROPOSED.

VISION	SOUND
Jane and John, an affluent thirty-something couple, are entertaining two other similar couples.	Soft soul music playing throughout.
They are ending their meal by drinking coffee out of fine china cups and eating After Eights.	John (to one of the other guests): 'Do you want another cup?' Guest 1: 'Yes, please.' Guest 2: 'Me, too! With cream!'
Jane looks alarmed at John. John glances at the empty cream jug. Jane rushes into kitchen and frantically looks for cream (there is none) and milk (all gone). Jane pauses, smiles, then gets out the Coffee-Mate. Jane pours the coffee and adds the Coffee-Mate. Jane returns with coffee. Guest sips the coffee containing Coffee-Mate.	Jane (thinking quickly): 'I'll make it!'
John smiles quizzically (and admiringly) at Jane. Jane leans back in her chair, smiling knowingly.	Guest 1: 'Lovely, even better than the last one!' Guest 2: 'Yes, how do you do it?' Voice: 'Coffee-Mate, never be without it!'

**Cluster 5: 'Dorothy and Amy' – Affluent
(Sample Proportion: 22.7 per cent)**
This group does not have to be price conscious. They are older, sometimes retired or working part time, and are well off. Often they own their house outright. They are, however, fairly traditional. They are not interested in holidaying abroad, they are not health conscious and they are not media aware.

They are the people most likely to be buying Coffee-Mate. They buy instant coffee to the same degree as the rest of the population and are light users of ground coffee. But they use the category as well as cream.

Dorothy and Amy are older (55+) and are upmarket (AB and C1). They still have a reasonable household income despite being retired (£25,000+) and their children have left home. They are clearly a group who have disposable income as many own their homes, and they are not worried about budgeting. They are to be found in affluent minorities, older suburbs and young married suburbs in the north-east, Scotland, Wales and the west.

They are readers of quality press and light viewers of ITV. They rarely watch Channel 4 and never listen to independent radio. They are not media aware, claiming to watch little TV and not to notice posters, and do not expect ads to entertain. They are not interested in satellite TV or more channels.

Their expenditure on the main grocery shop is above average, although they shop infrequently at places such as Safeway, Budgens and the Co-op.

They do not enjoy shopping as much as other groups and they are not price conscious at all, but are prudent with money (consider themselves good at saving). They do not want to try new things, are not keen to keep up with the latest fashion, and are not concerned with their appearance. They prefer to buy British if possible, and will pay extra for quality goods, but are not really indulgent.

This is a group whose attitudes tend to lag the other groups. They get a great deal of pleasure from gardening and others often ask their advice on the matter. As a group they are happy with their standard of living. They do not often go to pubs, wine bars or restaurants, but they do have people in for meals.

QUESTIONS

1. What are the main benefits of Coffee-Mate and what is limiting its sales?

2. How would the promotion of Coffee-Mate change with the benefits promoted and the competition targeted?

3. Should Coffee-Mate be mass marketed, aimed at one segment or aimed at multiple segments?

4. How would the different alternatives alter the marketing mix used to market Coffee-Mate? Why launch Coffee-Mate Lite?

5. Evaluate the segments from TGI's user survey for target attractiveness and their fit to Coffee-Mate's strengths. Which of the segments would you target and why?

6. Look at Exhibit 9.8. Evaluate the proposed ad for target market and benefits promoted. Will the ad help propel Coffee-Mate's further growth? Create an alternative ad for your chosen target market.

SOURCES: Economist Intelligence Unit, *Retail Business*, no. 418 (December 1992); British Market Research Bureaux, *Instant Powdered Milk and Coffee Creamers* (1992); company sources.

10

Positioning

CHAPTER OBJECTIVES

After reading this chapter, you should be able to:

- Define differentiation and market positioning.
- Explain why companies seek to differentiate their markets and use positioning strategies.
- List and discuss the principal ways in which companies can differentiate their products.
- Explain how companies can position their products for maximum competitive advantage in the marketplace.

Preview Case

Castrol: Liquid Engineering

The Enthusiast

ANTONI CAREFULLY MEASURED FOUR LITRES of Syntec into his greatest love, his new Van Dieman Formula Ford single-seater racing car. Tomorrow he was racing her for the first time at Silverstone and wanted to do well. Racing the Formula Fords was exciting, but his real dream was to race for Ferrari. That is why he had left his home in Barcelona to work for a specialist engineering firm in rural England.

Leaving Spain was hard, but he was now near where he needed to be: at the heart of the world's motor sports industry. It still seemed odd to him that a sport as international as motor racing was so localized, but the evidence was all around. More than three-quarters of the world's purpose-built single-seater cars – including 10,000 Formula Fords – came from small firms like Reynard, Ralt and Van Dieman. Many of the Grand Prix teams were also close by – McLaren, Williams, Lotus, Tyrell, Lola, March, Arrow and, best of

*Castrol's positioning varies
from market to market.
In this case they aim a
specialist oil at motor
sports enthusiasts.*

all, Benetton. Local engineers also did much of the design work on the new Ferraris. Local firms even dominated the United States 'Indy' car championships. Few of the 450,000 people watching the Indianapolis 500 race knew that almost all the cars and engines originated in rural England. Antoni got his Syntec oil from an American friend, and fellow motor enthusiast, living nearby. He was glad of the gift, since the synthetic motor oil cost four times as much as regular lubricants. In motor racing every little helps and the oil could make the difference between winning and losing. Even if he had not been given the oil, he would have bought some.

Syntec

Syntec is Burmah Castrol's 'flagship' product. Targeted at enthusiasts and technically advanced users of motor oil, the product appeared on the United States market with a $20 million budget. Despite its high price, Syntec sells well and broke even in 1994. It will never have a high market share, but the 'flagship' product allows Castrol to create gradations in the market at intermediate prices.

Syntec fits Castrol's strategy of having a high price and high marketing expenditure. Sponsorship of rallying, Grand Prix racing and the Indy car series in the United States positions Castrol as a quality, high-performance product used by the experts. Its TV advertising shows Castrol GTX as 'liquid engineering' and so encourages motorists to cosset their engines by using a premium-priced product. In the United States the campaign has helped Castrol increase its share of the DIY market from 5 to 15 per cent in ten years. Sales are now just behind Pennzoil, the market leader.

The 'Have Somes' and 'Near Haves'

Castrol has operations in 50 countries and sells to another 100. Some of its greatest successes are in developing countries, where economic development fuels growth. The company's positioning in the developing world is not the same as in developed countries. According to Ian Pringle, Castrol's Asia director, 'have somes' are the key to its marketing in Asia. They are the real middle class of Asia who want to buy cars, houses and consumer durables. They treasure and care for their possessions. The segment is growing fast. For instance, in India the domestically produced Maruti-Suzuki 800 cc car is *the* status symbol of the rapidly growing middle class. By a combination of political patronage and Japanese technology, the company has 71 per cent of the Indian car market, which grew by 30 per cent in 1993. Castrol estimates that in 1994 Asia had 55–60 million of these 'have somes', but that there would be 300 million by the end of the century.

Castrol's marketing also covers the Asian 'near haves', who are likely to buy a motor cycle as their first vehicle. According to Mr Pringle, these groups are important because of the way that rapid economic development leads to consumers 'leapfrogging' intermediate technologies: for example, people progressing from having no telephone direct to a cellular phone, or from no radio to hi-fi system with a compact disc player. These changes happen quickly and, Mr Pringle believes, some brand loyalty persists when 'near haves' become 'have somes'. That is why Castrol has made the motorcycle market central to its marketing strategy in Vietnam and Thailand. In Thailand, Castrol concentrated on building distribution and its image among motorcyclists despite government controls restricting profits in the 1970s. Then, when the motorcycle population leapt from 1 million to 5 million in the late 1980s, it was able to hold on to its leading position.

World Coverage

Appropriate targeting and positioning of Castrol lubricants ensures that the company makes profits in markets as different as Vietnam's 'near haves' and the US enthusiasts. By positioning product to fit the market's stage of development, Castrol is profitable in both mature and developing markets. In 1993 the United States and Germany were the two most profitable markets, but India was the third and Thailand the sixth.

Burmah Castrol: Lubricants Division, 1993

Region	Turnover (£m)	Operating profits (£m)
Europe	679.4	95.9
North America	502.5	50.7
Asia	242.2	40.0
Southern hemisphere	201.3	15.8

Mr Tim Stevenson, Castrol's chief executive, says that the company has 'proved wrong the sceptics who for years have been arguing that Castrol is a mature business, liable to be snuffed out by the major oil dinosaurs'. He has good reason to boast. Excluding the 1990 Gulf crisis year, Castrol's profits have maintained a 14 per cent compound annual growth rate since 1985. While the world lubricant market has been almost flat over the last ten years, Castrol has increased its sales by 6 per cent per year on average – some maturity; some snuffing out.[1]

QUESTIONS

1. How does Castrol's positioning differ across the globe?

2. How can Castrol's involvement in motor sports help it in markets where few people will ever have a chance to see the sport live, never mind participate in it?

3. Why do you think Burmah Oil concentrates on engine oils rather than the huge market for motor fuel?

4. What strengths has Castrol cultivated in order to allow it to compete?

5. What personalities could be used to help strengthen people's perception of Castrol?

6. Do people buy the expensive Castrol brands for *emotional* reasons or because of their unique performance characteristics?

Introduction

core strategy
It has two parts: the identification of a group of customers for whom the firm has a differential advantage; and then positioning itself in that market.

Core strategy is at the hub of marketing strategy. It is where the strengths of a company meet market opportunities. It has two parts: first, the identification of a group of customers for whom the firm has a differential advantage; and second, positioning itself in the customer's mind. Castrol did that. While the big oil companies saw the lubricant market as mature, Castrol identified target markets and built strengths in them. Its motor racing experience, knowledge of high-performance oils and brand name were competitive advantages in the motor enthusiast market. In the United States, its support of Grand Prix and Indy car racing helped position Castrol Syntec as a high-performance product. In developing countries, its early investments in distribution gave Castrol a differential advantage in the emergent markets. There, too, Castrol's association with Grand Prix racing gives the products an exotic international appeal. This chapter first examines how firms can differentiate themselves and then the positioning alternatives.

Differentiation

competitive advantage
An advantage over competitors gained by offering consumers greater value, either through lower prices or by providing more benefits that justify higher prices.

Consumers typically choose products and services that give them the greatest value. Thus the key to winning and keeping customers is to understand their needs and buying processes better than competitors do, and to deliver more value. To the extent that a company can position itself as providing superior value to selected target markets, either by offering lower prices than competitors do or by providing more benefits to justify higher prices, it gains **competitive advantage**.[2] Solid positions are not built upon empty promises. If a company positions its product as *offering* the best quality and service, it must then *deliver* the promised quality and service. Positioning therefore begins with *differentiating* the company's marketing offer, so that it will give consumers more value than competitors' offers do (see Marketing Highlight 10.1). It is not just a matter of being different; success comes from being different in a way that customers want. Arby's, the fast-food chain, explains how it competes by being different: 'Being

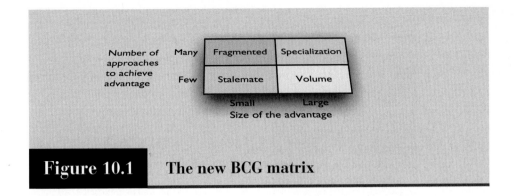

| **Figure 10.1** | **The new BCG matrix** |

different makes you more interesting. Of course it's not always good to be different (you don't want to be the only one standing up in an electrical storm). But in most cases being different is good. Great tasting, lean Roast Beef and 3 fantastic ways. And *no* dull, boring burger!'

Not every company can find many opportunities for differentiating its offer and gaining competitive advantage.[3] In some industries it is harder than others. The Boston Consulting Group explains four types of industry based on the number of competitive advantages and the size of those advantages (see Figure 10.1). The four industry types are:

1. **Volume industries**, where there are a few large advantages to be had. The airline industry is one of these. A company can strive for low costs or differentiate by service quality, but can win 'big' on both bases. In these industries, profitability is correlated with company size and market share. As a result, most minor airlines lose money while the main players try to form global alliances to build share. In this case almost all the industry leaders, like United Airlines, Hoechst, Hitachi, Unilever and Glaxo Wellcome are large, low-cost operators providing a high-quality service.[4]

2. **Stalemate industries** produce commodities where there are few potential advantages and each is small. Many old industries like steel and bulk chemicals fall into this category. In these industries it is hard to differentiate products or have significantly lower costs. European firms in these sectors often lose money, since they are unable to compete with products from economies with low-cost labour. Even size and modern plant cannot counter high labour costs.

3. **Fragmented industries** offer many opportunities to differentiate, but each opportunity is small. Many service industries are fragmented. Restaurants are an extreme example: Hard Rock Café has a global reputation and long queues, but its overall share of the market is small. Even market leaders, like McDonald's and KFC, have a small share of the market relative to leaders in other industries. In fragmented industries, profitability is not closely related to size. For many years, global Pizza Hut was not profitable, while every large town has restaurateur millionaires who own few eating places. At the same time, many small restaurants fail each year.

4. **Specialized industries** offer companies many opportunities to differentiate in a way that gives a high pay-off. Pharmaceuticals is a specialized industry. A disproportionately large proportion of the world's most successful companies come from the sector where firms like Novartis, Glaxo Wellcome and Roche are market leaders for particular treatment. Less conspicuous specialized industries are those for scientific instruments and publishing.

volume industry
An industry characterized by few opportunities to create competitive advantages, but each advantage is huge and gives a high pay-off.

stalemate industry
An industry that produces commodities and is characterized by a few opportunities to create competitive advantages, with each advantage being small.

fragmented industry
An industry characterized by many opportunities to create competitive advantages, but each advantage is small.

specialized industry
An industry where there are many opportunities for firms to create competitive advantages that are huge or give a high pay-off.

Nintendo: More than Just Fun and Games

Marketing Highlight 10.1

In the early 1980s, no home could be without a video game console and a dozen cartridges. By 1983 Atari, Coleco, Mattel and a dozen other companies offered some version of a video game system and industry sales topped $3.2 billion. Then, by 1985, home video game sales had plummeted to $100 million. Game consoles gathered dust and cartridges, originally priced as high as $35 each, sold for $5. Industry leader Atari, a subsidiary of Warner Communications, was hardest hit. Warner fired Atari's president, sacked 4,500 employees, and sold the subsidiary at a fraction of its 1983 worth. Industry experts blamed the death of the video game industry on fickle consumer tastes. Video games, they asserted, were just another fad.

However, one company, Nintendo, a 100-year-old toy company from Kyoto, Japan, did not agree. In late 1985, on top of ruins of the video game business, the company introduced its Nintendo Entertainment System (NES). Just one year later, Nintendo had sold over 1 million NES units. By 1991 Nintendo and its licensees were reaping annual sales of $4 billion in a now revitalized $5 billion video game industry. Nintendo had captured 80 per cent share of the market, and more than one out of every five United States households, slightly fewer in the EU, and 40 per cent of Japanese households had a Nintendo system hooked up to one of its television sets.

How did Nintendo manage to revive a dying industry? First, it recognized that video game customers were not so much fickle as bored. The company sent researchers to visit video arcades to find out why alienated home video game fans still spent hours happily pumping arcade machines. The researchers found that Nintendo's Donkey Kong and similar games were still mainstays of the arcades, even though home versions were failing. The reason? The arcade games offered better quality, full animation and challenging plots. Home video games, on the other hand, offered only crude quality and simple plots.

Despite their exotic names and introductory hype, each new home game was boringly identical to all the others, featuring slow characters that moved through ugly animated scenes to the beat of monotonous, synthesized tones. The video kids of the early 1980s had outgrown the first-generation home video games.

Nintendo saw the fall of the video game industry as an opportunity. It set out to differentiate itself by offering superior quality – by giving home video game customers a full measure of quality entertainment value for their money. Nintendo designed a basic game system that sold for under $100 yet boasted near arcade-quality graphics. Equally important, it developed innovative and high-quality 'Game Paks' to accompany the system. New games constantly appear and mature titles are weeded out to keep the selection fresh and interesting. The games contain consistently high-quality graphics, and game plots vary and challenge the user. Colourful, cartoon-like characters move fluidly about cleverly animated screens. Amidst a chorus of bongs, whistles and bleeps, players can punch out the current heavyweight boxing champ or wrestle Hulk Hogan, play ice hockey or golf, or solve word and board games. The most popular games, however, involved complex sword-and-sorcery conflicts, or the series of Super Mario Brothers fantasy worlds, where young heroes battle to save endangered princesses or fight the evil ruler, Wart, for peace in the World of Dreams.

By differentiating itself through superior products and service, and by building strong relationships with its customers, Nintendo built a seemingly invincible quality position in the video game market. But it soon came under attack. New competitors such as Sony and Sega exploited the opportunities created as Nintendo junkies became bored and sought the next new video thrill. Sony beat Nintendo at its own game – product superiority – when it hit the market with its PlayStation machine, an advanced new system that offered even richer graphics, more lifelike sound and more complex plots. Nintendo countered with the Nintendo 64 and a fresh blast of promotion, but the competition has intensified and, while Nintendos were being discounted, the PlayStation was the Christmas hit toy of 1997.

Meanwhile the computer games world is attacked for being 'violent, destructive, xenophobic, racist and sexist'. Sega Europe has also been attacked for marketing gruesome games such as Mortal Kombat and 'MDK' (Murder Death Kill). The industry has been criticized for cultivating a generation of 'Video Kids' for whom 30 seconds without scoring is boring; moral zombies hooked on worlds where the rules are shot or be shot, consume or be consumed, fight or lose. In Japan, where many of the games come from, consumers are more broad-minded than in most western countries. Nintendo needs to extend its customer range beyond the terminally fickle teenage males. Sega sponsored roadshows with teen magazines, and put girls in its TV ads after complaints from schoolchildren on its 'advisory board' about sexism in advertising. Sega Europe created a new toy division to target 'housewives with children, instead of 14-year-old boys'. The first product will be Pico, an electronic learning aid for kids that has taken a 'significant' share of the Japanese high-tech toys market. The $8 million European launch included TV, press and posters with a full below-the-line campaign. Next will be an 'electronic learning aid that thinks it's a toy' for three- to seven-year-olds.

All to no avail. While Nintendo and Sega chased the new markets, Sony's PlayStation blasted the 1997 Christmas market with the 'arcade feel' of Ridge Racer and Crash Bindicoot and 'scary, tension building' Doom. Also a new company appeared with a little gadget that attracted masses of new customers. Tamagotchi's virtual pets rose and fell like the fad they were. Although the sophistication and range of Giga Pups and Nano Pets grew and prices declined, virtual pet owners proved as capricious as other computer game players. Euromonitor forecasts that the world market for video games will fall by 30 per cent by the year 2000. Other pundits suggest that few people will buy a game machine when all houses have a Pentium II wired to the World Wide Web. Could all computer games machine makers now be heading for Henry's Virtual Pet Cemetery? Will 2000 be doom for the Tomb Raiders?

SOURCES: See Rebecca Fannin, 'Zap?', *Marketing and Media Decisions* (November 1989), pp. 35–40; Raymond Roel, 'The power of Nintendo', *Direct Marketing* (September 1989), pp. 24–9; Stewart Wolpin, 'How Nintendo revived a dying industry', *Marketing Communications* (May 1989), pp. 36–40; Kate Fitzgerald, 'Nintendo, Sega slash price of videogames', *Advertising Age* (8 June 1992), p. 44; Richard Brandt, 'Clash of the Titans', *Business Week* (7 September 1992), p. 34; Mark Jones and Margaret Bennett, 'Game over?', *Marketing Business* (December–January 1993–4), pp. 8–11; Ros Snowden, 'New Sega arm targets mothers', *Marketing Week* (7 October 1994), p. 9; 'Dip into the future, faras cyborg eye can see: and wince', *The Economist* (3 January 1997), pp. 81–3; 'Computing: that's entertainment', *Which?* (December 1997); Henry's Virtual Pet Cemetery (/hmal.home.mindsring.com).

Figure 10.2 shows the returns to be had from differentiation. It shows results taken from the Profit Implications of Marketing Strategy (PIMS) study of American and European firms.[5] This study shows that firms with the lowest return on investment (ROI) operate in commodity markets where there is no differentiation on quality or anything else, such as the coal industry. Where there is room for differentiation, losers have inferior quality (Aeroflot) and more returns than winners (KLM). The most highly performing group of companies are 'power companies', which have superior quality in differentiable markets (BMW, Bertelsmann and Nokia). These are ahead of nichers (local airlines), which score lower on quality and ROI than the 'power companies'. According to PIMS, the 'power companies' often have a high market share, since quality, share and ROI are interrelated.

Differentiation may be harder in some industries than others, but creative firms have shown that any market can be differentiated.[6] Few people see the brick market as exciting, but one brick company found a way of getting a competitive

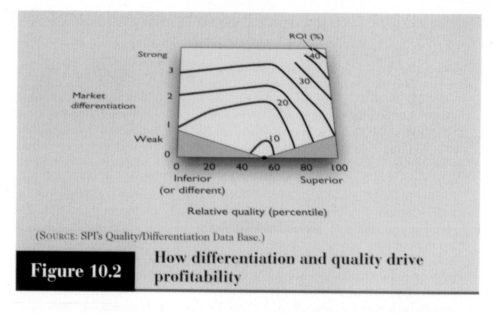

(SOURCE: SPI's Quality/Differentiation Data Base.)

Figure 10.2 **How differentiation and quality drive profitability**

advantage. Bricks used to be delivered to building sites in a truck that tipped them on to the ground. In the process many bricks got broken or lost. Workers on the site also had to spend time stacking the bricks. The brick company's idea was to put the bricks on pallets that were lifted off the truck by a small integral crane. The idea was so successful that soon all bricks came that way. The firm's next idea was to carry a small off-the-road fork-lift truck with the bricks, so that it could deliver them to the exact spot where the site manager wanted them.

Oil is a *stalemate industry*, but Shell remains the leading petroleum retailer by understanding that fuel is a distress purchase that people do not enjoy. They succeed by making their petrol stations easy to use and paying attention to all the other reasons people stop on a journey: to find their way, get a snack, make a phone call or go to a clean toilet.

Differential advantages can be transient. Some companies find many major advantages that are easily copied by competitors and are, therefore, highly perishable. This is particularly true in financial services, where successful ideas are quickly followed by competitors. The Bank of Scotland's Direct Line insurance company succeeded by offering an economic and high-quality personal insurance service through television advertising and telephone selling. It was so successful that established insurers had to follow. Zurich Insurance intends to attack the conservative German and Italian insurance markets in the same way.[7]

The solution for companies facing the erosion of their advantage is to keep identifying new potential advantages and to introduce them one by one to keep competitors off balance. These companies do not expect to gain a single substantial permanent advantage. Instead, they hope to manage a series of advantages that will increase their share over time. This is how market leaders like Microsoft, Intel, Sony and Gillette have held their position for so long. The true competitive advantage of these firms is their market knowledge, technological expertise, creativity and entrepreneurship, which give them the ability to develop products quickly.

Differentiating Markets

In what specific ways can a company differentiate its offer from those of competitors? A company or market offer can be differentiated along the lines of product, services, personnel or image.

In the vastly competitive fashion market Damart differentiates itself on comfort and thermal performance.

Product Differentiation

A company can differentiate its physical product. At one extreme, some companies offer highly standardized products that allow little variation: chicken, steel and aspirin. Yet even here, some meaningful differentiation is possible. For example, Perdue claims that its branded chickens are better – fresher and more tender – and gets a 10 per cent price premium based on this differentiation.

Other companies offer products that can be highly differentiated, such as cars, commercial buildings and furniture. Here the company faces an abundance of design parameters.[8] It can offer a variety of standard or optional *features* not provided by competitors. Thus Volvo provides new and better safety features, while Lufthansa offers wider seats to business-class flyers. In the United Kingdom, Whitbread has targeted its chain of Brewers Fayre pubs at families. Besides the usual food and drink, most Brewers Fayres have a toddlers' area, a play zone for bigger children and a 'Charlie Chalk Fun Factory – a large self-contained area full of games, toys and adventure equipment'.

Companies can also differentiate their products on *performance*. Whirlpool designs its dishwasher to run more quietly; Unilever formulates Radion to remove odours as well as dirt from washing. *Style* and *design* can also be important differentiating factors. Thus many car buyers pay a premium for Jaguar cars because of their extraordinary look, even though Jaguar has sometimes had a poor reliability record. Similarly, companies can differentiate their products on such attributes as *consistency*, *durability*, *reliability* or *repairability*.

Services Differentiation

In addition to differentiating its physical product, the firm can also differentiate the services that accompany the product. Some companies gain competitive advantage through speedy, reliable or careful *delivery*. Harrods, the luxury retailer, delivers to its customers using replica vintage vans – a service particularly popular at Christmas. At the other end of the scale, Domino's Pizza promises delivery in less than 30 minutes or reduces the price.

Installation can also differentiate one company from another. IBM, for example, is known for its quality installation service. It delivers all pieces of purchased equipment to the site at one time, rather than sending individual components to sit and wait for others to arrive. And when asked to move IBM equipment and install it in another location, IBM often moves competitors' equipment as well. Companies can further distinguish themselves through their *repair services*. Many a car buyer would gladly pay a little more and travel a little further to buy a car from a dealer that provides top-notch repair service.

Some companies differentiate their offers by providing a *customer training* service. For instance, General Electric not only sells and installs expensive X-ray equipment in hospitals, but also trains the hospital employees who will use the equipment. Other companies offer free or paid *consulting services* – data, information systems and advice services that buyers need. For example, reinsurance company M & G provides information and advice to its customers. It also provides specialist help in developing new products.

Companies can find many other ways to add value through differentiated services. In fact, they can choose from a virtually unlimited number of specific services and benefits through which to differentiate themselves from the competition. Milliken & Company provides one of the best examples of a company that has gained competitive advantage through superior service:

> Milliken sells shop towels to industrial launderers who rent them to factories. These towels are physically similar to competitors' towels. Yet Milliken charges a higher price for its towels and enjoys the leading market share. How can it charge more for essentially a commodity? The answer is that Milliken continuously 'decommoditizes' this product through continuous service enhancement for its launderer customers. Milliken trains its customers' salespeople; supplies prospect leads and sales promotional material to them; supplies on-line computer order entry and freight optimization systems; carries on marketing research for customers; sponsors quality improvement workshops; and lends its salespeople to work with customers on Customer Action Teams. Launderers are more than willing to buy Milliken shop towels and pay a price premium because the extra services improve their profitability.[9]

Speed of service is a competitive advantage used by many firms. Fast food is now common on the world's high streets and malls, along with services like one-hour photo processing and Vision Express's one-hour service for spectacles. These services provide a direct benefit to customers by giving rapid gratification and allowing services to be completed within one shopping trip. Speed also helps sell more expensive goods. Abbey National found that its success in providing large mortgages depended upon how fast it could confirm that it would give a person a home loan. It responded by allowing local managers to make loan decisions rather than processing applications centrally. In the car market Toyota's two-day policy means that it can supply a well-equipped Lexus within two days, while many other luxury car makers expect prospects to wait several weeks for custom-built cars.

The success of courier services like TNT and DHL shows that many people are willing to pay extra for a quick, secure service. A study of the importance of service responsiveness to users of small business-computer-based systems shows how speed is valued:

Lindbergh'. When asked, 'Who was the second person to do it?', they draw a blank. That is why companies fight for the no. 1 position. In reality, the first people to fly the Atlantic were Alcock and Brown, but Charles Lindbergh won the publicity battle.

Ries and Trout point out that the 'size' position can be held by only one brand. What counts is to achieve a no. 1 position along some valued attribute, not necessarily 'size'. Thus 7-Up is the no. 1 'Uncola', Porsche is the no. 1 small sports car and Foster's is Australia's top-selling lager. In the United States, Heineken is 'the' imported beer because it was the first heavily promoted imported beer. The marketer should identify an important attribute or benefit that can convincingly be won by the brand. In that way brands hook the mind in spite of the incessant advertising bombardment reaching consumers.

According to Ries and Trout, there are three positioning alternatives:

1. The first strategy they suggest is to strengthen a brand's *current position* in the mind of consumers. Thus Avis took its second position in the car rental business and made a strong point about it: 'We're number two. We try harder.' This was believable to the consumer. 7-Up capitalized on *not* being a cola soft drink by advertising itself as the Uncola.

2. Their second strategy is to search for a new *unoccupied position* that is valued by enough consumers and grab it: 'Cherchez le creneau', 'Look for the hole'. Find a hole in the market and fill it, they say. Vidal Sassoon's Wash & Go was based on recognizing that the fashion for exercise meant that people washed their hair frequently, quickly and away from home. By combining a shampoo and hair conditioner in one the company was able to fill a latent market need. Similarly, after recognizing that many housewives wanted a strong washing powder to treat smelly clothes, Unilever successfully launched Radion.

> Across Europe new 'newspapers' have filled a down-market gap left by the traditional press. In Britain the *Sunday Sport* started as a weekly paper reporting on sensationalist stories – 'Double decker bus found in iceberg' – sport and sex, but has now grown into a daily paper. In France the new *Infos du Monde* reached sales of 240,000 a week after just two months. 'Our readers don't want "dirty" news', says *Infos*. It instead seeks the bizarre in ordinary life; fairground freaks are popular – 'Four-legged woman from Cannes looks for love'. Another sensationalist publication is the German-owned *Voici*, a glossy scandal sheet full of show-biz personalities. *Infos* has sent some of its staff to the United States to learn from their *Weekly World News*, a magazine specializing in blood, sex and gore. Some newspaper vendors are embarrassed about the newspapers and the established press sees the new publications as distasteful. They also worry about the disturbing misinformation they monger. But, as a Gare du Nord news kiosk seller says: 'If people lead such dull and boring lives that their day is brightened by reading about a man with an axe stuck in his head, what's wrong with that?'[12]

3. Their third strategy is to *deposition* or *reposition* the competition. Most US buyers of dinnerware thought that Lenox china and Royal Doulton both came from England. Royal Doulton countered with ads showing that Lenox china is from New Jersey, but theirs came from England. In a similar vein, Stolichnaya vodka attacked Smirnoff and Wolfschmidt vodka by pointing out that these brands were made locally, but 'Stolichnaya is different. Similarly, it is Russian.' Guinness, the world's leading brown ale, has strong Irish associations. However, the focus on individuality in its Rutger Hauer 'Pure Genius' campaign has allowed Murphy's and Beamish to attack Guinness's

Iomega disks depositions its generic competitor: floppy disks.

Irish heritage. A final example is Kaliber no-alcohol beer, drunk by people who want a good time or, as Billy Connolly says in its ads posted next to those for Wonderbra, 'Hello girls!'

Ries and Trout essentially deal with the psychology of positioning – or repositioning – a current brand in the consumer's mind. They acknowledge that the positioning strategy might call for changes in the product's name, price and packaging, but these are 'cosmetic changes done for the purpose of securing a worthwhile position – in the prospect's mind'.

Perceptual Mapping

perceptual maps
A product positioning tool that uses multidimensional scaling of consumers' perceptions and preferences to portray the psychological distance between products and segments.

Perceptual maps are a valuable aid to product positioning. These maps use *multidimensional scaling* of perceptions and preferences that portray psychological distance between products and segments, using many dimensions. They contrast with conventional maps that use two dimensions to show the physical distance between objects. Physical and psychological maps of the same items can be quite different. Disneyland in California and Disney's Magic Kingdom in Florida are thousands of kilometres apart physically, but psychologically close together.

In their simplest form, perceptual maps use two dimensions. For example, Figure 10.3 shows the average *value for money* and *accessibility* rating of European holiday destinations.[13] The perceptual map shows that France, Germany and the Netherlands, which are physically close together, are also psychologically close holiday destinations using these two criteria. In contrast,

Spain and the United Kingdom are psychologically close together, but are physically distant. France is Europe's most popular holiday destination and this map partly shows why: it offers the best value for money among the accessible nations. The lack of destinations in the high *value for money* and easy *access* quadrant suggests a *cherchez le creneau* positioning opportunity for new destinations. Hungary and the Czech Republic could fill the hole in the market.

Of course, holidaymakers have a more complicated view of destinations than the two-dimensional map suggests. And if the map had other dimensions, it would change: for instance, adding weather would certainly separate Spain and the United Kingdom. Multidimensional scaling produces maps that show many dimensions at the same time (Figure 10.4). To read these maps, trace back the individual dimensions one at a time. For example, the perception is that Switzerland has *good facilities*; Germany and Sweden quite good ones; Denmark, the Netherlands and Norway average ones; and the United Kingdom, Spain and Ireland *poor facilities*. Finland has an extreme position on the map. Prospective travellers see its people as *friendly and hospitable*, while the country is a *unique and different* place with *wild areas*, *beautiful scenery* and *peace and quiet*. More negatively, travellers do not perceive Finland as *accessible*, or as a place for *entertainment*, or as a *cultural experience*.

The perceptual map shows how holidaymakers segment, as well as the possible destinations. A, the largest segment, wants cheap, sunshine holidays and liked Spain. Segment C, who represented 15 per cent of the sample population,

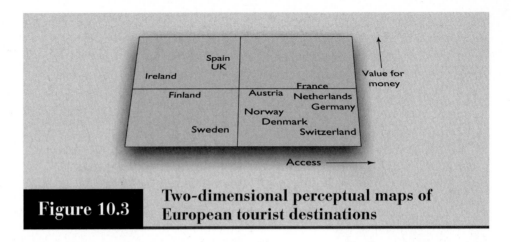

| Figure 10.3 | **Two-dimensional perceptual maps of European tourist destinations** |

are a natural target market for Finland. They want peaceful, quiet holidays in places with beautiful scenery. Norway is already successful at marketing these 'back to nature' ideals as 'natural tourism'.[14] The target group mainly consists of high-income couples or families with one child who organize their holidays themselves. They are mainly Dutch, German or Scandinavian, but half have never visited Finland. To attract this segment the Finnish Tourist Board does not need massively to reposition Finland as a holiday destination. It needs to promote the country as the segment sees it, while reducing the perception that it is an *inaccessible* place. Promoting luxury car ferries that allow travellers to start their holiday with a relaxing cruise across the Baltic Sea would be one way of doing this. Strangely, Barbados has a similar positioning problem to Finland as a holiday destination. Europeans perceive the Caribbean island as a millionaire's playground that is a long way away. In response, Barbados tries to reposition itself by promoting 'Barbados. It's closer than you think ... A sunshine holiday there can cost as little as one of Europe's premier resorts.' (Marketing Highlight 10.2 gives more advice on how to develop perceptual maps.)

Positioning Strategies

Marketers can follow several positioning strategies. These strategies use associations to change consumers' perception of products.

Product attributes position many technical products. The positioning of Ericsson's EH237 mobile phone is its *low weight* and number of *features*, while much of BMW's advertising promotes individual *technical items* like fresh air filters. In the exclusive watch market Breitling, Baume & Mercier and Audemars Piguet's positioning are on their mechanical movements. Some of their designs leave the mechanisms exposed and one ad argues 'Since 1735 there has never been a quartz Blancpain. And there never will be.'

The *benefits* they offer or the needs they fill position many products – Crest toothpaste reduces cavities. Aim tastes good and Macleans Sensitive relieves the pain of sensitive teeth. In the confectionery industry, Italian Baci and Ferrero Rocher are gifts, while Mars and Snickers bars satisfy hunger.

Huhtamaki is Finland's largest industrial company but LEAF, its confectionery division, is only ten in size worldwide. It developed competitive advantage in 'functional chewing and bubble gums'. Its

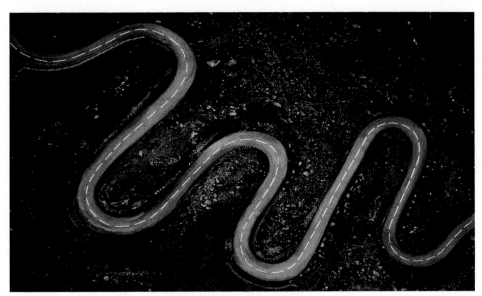

Tear along the dotted line.

With the quattro four wheel drive system, which monitors each wheel to deliver power and grip when needed, you can hold the road firmly, and open up.
(Within speed limits, of course.)

AUDI ⊙⊙⊙⊙
Vorsprung durch Technik

Audi ad positions the product explaining their car's performance and it being of German origin.

want to compete head-on with Nike anymore. They'll do their thing and we'll do ours,' said Reebok's Paul Fireman. 'Getting stars to endorse products has been a priority for the past three years, and hasn't given us much of a payback.' Reebok will concentrate on older consumers, who are less susceptible to fashion and star endorsements. It will back away from Nike's dominant position in basketball and cross training shoes to focus on its traditional strengths in running and walking. 'We're the tortoise, not the hare,' explained Fireman.[19]

Origin positions product by association with its place of manufacture. Much of Perrier's success depended on the sophistication its French origin gave to it. Similarly, Audi's 'Vorsprung durch Technik' positioned its cars as German. Drinks are often positioned using origin. Foster's and Castlemaine XXXX lagers' positioning uses their Australian heritage, plus masculine humour to reinforce their character. The strategy also works at a local level. Boddingtons was a local Manchester beer that was not in the United Kingdom's top ten sellers. Then, in 1992 it was relaunched with a campaign using Manchester people and a setting that played upon the creamy froth on the product. Plays on ice cream, face cream, smooth, rich cream helped to make the product the top take-home beer.

Other brands can help position products. Clinique's advertising for its 'skin supplies for men' prominently features a Rolex watch. Where firms have traditionally crafted products, such as Wilkinson's Sword or Holland & Holland shotguns, these lend glamour to more recent products – in these instances, shaving products and men's clothing respectively. After Volkswagen bought the Czech Skoda company, it used the Volkswagen name to transfer some of its strong reputation to Skoda. 'Volkswagen were so impressed, they bought the company' ran one press ad. The responsible ad agency, GGK, explains: 'The Volkswagen connection hit the spot. People immediately latched on to it. It allowed susceptible people [who might be persuaded to buy a Skoda] a route into the brand.' Dealers reported 50 per cent sales increases.[20]

The Ruhr's advertising positions it against the competition at the heart of Europe.

Competitors provide two positioning alternatives. A product can be positioned directly *against a competitor*. For example, in ads for their personal computers, Compaq and Tandy have directly compared their products with IBM personal computers. The direct-selling computer company dan compares its performance with all other suppliers: '1st in repurchase intention, 1st in repair satisfaction', and so on. In its famous 'We're number two, so we try harder' campaign, Avis successfully positioned itself against the larger Hertz. A product may also be positioned *away from competitors* – 7-Up became the no. 3 soft drink when it was positioned as the 'Uncola', the fresh and thirst-quenching alternative to Coke and Pepsi. River Island Expeditions positions its holidays, its adventures for travellers, away from package holidays and the tourists who go on them. It says: 'The traveller is active; he goes strenuously in search of people, of adventure, of experience. The tourist is passive; expects interesting things to happen to him. He goes "sight-seeing"' (Daniel J. Boorstin, 1962).

Product class membership is the final means of positioning. For example, Van Den Bergh's I Can't Believe It's Not Butter is clearly positioned against butter, while other yellow fats are promoted as cooking oils. Camay hand soap is positioned with bath oils rather than with soap. Marketers often use a *combination* of these positioning strategies. Johnson & Johnson's Affinity shampoo is positioned as a hair conditioner for women over 40 (product class *and* user). And in its Christmas campaigns, Martell cognac and Glenlivet malt whisky both neglect the lucrative 18- to 35-year olds to concentrate on the over-35s (*usage situation* and *user*).

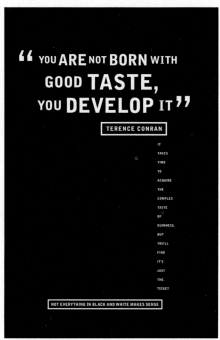

" YOU **ARE** NOT **BORN** WITH **GOOD TASTE,** YOU **DEVELOP** IT "

TERENCE CONRAN

IT
TAKES
TIME
TO
ACQUIRE
THE
COMPLEX
TASTE
OF
GUINNESS,
BUT
YOU'LL
FIND
IT'S
JUST
THE
TICKET

NOT EVERYTHING IN BLACK AND WHITE MAKES SENSE

Guinness' stark advertising emphasizes its unique position in the marketplace.

Choosing and Implementing a Positioning Strategy

Some firms find it easy to choose their positioning strategy. For example, a firm well known for quality in certain segments will go for this position in a new segment if there are enough buyers seeking quality. In many cases, two or more firms will go after the same position: for instance, British Airways and Lufthansa in the European business market. Then, each will have to find other ways to set itself apart, such as Lufthansa's promise of reliability and wider seats, and BA's spacious cabins and executive lounges. Each firm must differentiate its offer by building a unique bundle of competitive advantages that appeal to a substantial group within the segment.

Having identified a set of possible competitive advantages upon which to build a position, the next stages are to select the right competitive advantages and effectively communicate the chosen position to the market (see Marketing Highlight 10.3).

Selecting the Right Competitive Advantages

Suppose a company is fortunate enough to have several potential competitive advantages. It must now choose the ones upon which it will build its positioning strategy. It must decide *how many* differences to promote and *which ones*.

● *How Many Differences to Promote?*

Many marketers think that companies should aggressively promote only one benefit to the target market. Ad man Rosser Reeves, for example, said a company

Battling for Position in the Fast Lane

Marketing Highlight 10.3

In the late 1980s, Europe dominated the world luxury car market. Germany reigned with Mercedes, BMW and Audi followed by Sweden's Saab and Volvo. Rover's re-entry into the crowded luxury car market contained a clue to the future. Realizing that it did not have the scale to design and build a range of cars by itself, Rover made a deal with Honda. For Rover it was to be the 800, a replacement for its SD1; for Honda, the Legend. Both firms intended to sell them in the North American market. Rover got there first in 1986. The car was good value and fitted well with the United Kingdom's reputation for traditional luxury products. The Rover 800 sold in the United States as the Stirling, with no Rover badge, to avoid association with the SD1's unsuccessful career in the United States. Although voted *International Car of the Year* when it was launched in 1977, the SD1 had quickly acquired a reputation for poor quality and unreliability. In 1987 initial sales of the Stirling were good, reaching 14,000. Then, by 1988, they had dropped to less than 9,000. Again unreliability killed Rover in the United States market. Quality problems plagued the Stirling. It was not ready for any market, let alone the American market.

Honda's aims for the Legend were higher than Rover's. The Honda Accord was already America's top-selling car. It had an excellent reputation for economy, reliability and comfort, and was no. 1 in the US compact car market. Honda, however, had its sights on the US luxury market dominated by the Europeans. The market was growing fast, and margins were high. To attack the luxury end Honda had to straddle the US car market. The Accord was smaller and less expensive than regular American cars. In contrast, the European luxury cars now targeted were exclusive and priced above regular cars. Honda realized that to succeed it had to position the Accord and Legend differently, and that is what it did. The Legend was already bigger and more expensive than the Accord, but that was not enough. Honda decided not to extend the Honda brand name, but to launch the Legend as an Acura, a new luxury brand. It also established a new Acura distribution chain and set up a special hot-line service for Acura suppliers and users. However, unlike Mercedes and BMW, Honda intended to sell its cars fully equipped to luxury standards – cruise control, air conditioning, the lot. With the cars being made in Japan, it would have taken too long to have them 'made to measure' and shipped.

Honda had decided to take on Europe's leading car manufacturers in the world's largest car market – and with a new product, in a segment it did not know, using a new brand name and new dealerships, and pricing higher than it had ever done before. Honda's declared aim was to give the discerning Acura driver 'total customer satisfaction'.

Honda's Legend did much better than Rover's Stirling in the United States market. In its first year 70,770 Acuras were sold, 80 per cent more than Mercedes, which had been the class leader up to that point. The Acura also had one of the best reliability records in the United States market and one of the highest residual values. However, Acura supremacy in the United States did not last long: Toyota soon followed with its luxury Lexus range.

America's economic recession and their loss of market share to the Japanese hit European luxury car makers. Some responded with violent repositioning to help attract new customers. Mercedes tried to adjust its staid, reliable, quality reputation and so address customers' views that 'I can't afford one at the moment' and 'I'm not old enough yet'. One Mercedes ad asked: 'Has our reputation for the highest quality also given us a reputation for the highest price?' and then explained how inexpensive it was. Mercedes wanted to be sporty too. One ad headlined 'What do 27 of the 34 Grand Prix drivers drive on their day off?' Mercedes' concern about perceived expense continues. It advertises its S-class using quotes from *Autocar & Motor*, which says it is the best car in the world: 'Sit in an S-class, regardless of engine size, and you know you've arrived.' But the ad continues: '"A genuine bargain": as *What Car?* so neatly puts it.' The ad's headlines betray Mercedes' positioning dilemma: 'It wouldn't be the best car in the world if nobody could afford it.'

Volvo is also repositioning its products. In 1990 its position was clear when it ran an ad with five pictures of toddlers with the headline: 'Are they as safe around town as they are around the house?' It goes on: 'If you'd like your children to be as safe as houses on the road …'. Shortly after, Volvo's TV ads were showing a horse galloping through a dark wood. The car had become so exciting to drive that it was almost alive – a position close to BMW's 'The Ultimate Driving Machine'.

Saab's repositioning is no less dramatic. In the late 1980s Saab's Carlsson series ads had the car juxtaposed with the Saab Viggen jet fighters: 'For Saab Viggen, getting behind the controls is proof of incredible mental and physical stamina, years of intensive training and an ally or two at the Royal Swedish Air Force.' Their strapline was 'Saab: The Aircraft Manufacturer'. The aggressive masculinity of the product and the strapline have now gone. The Saab is a thoughtfully designed car. Designers appear in the ads and one of them is a woman, 'Aina Nilsson, chief interior designer of the Saab 900'.

The 1990 European launch positioned Lexus as one of the great marques. Names like Rolls-Royce, Mercedes, BMW and Jaguar littered the copy. They ignored Japanese cars such as the Acura Legend and Nissan Infiniti. The car impressed the press, so later ads incorporated their favourable comments: 'Imagine a big saloon that is faster than a BMW 735i, quieter than a Jaguar Sovereign and as meticulously engineered as a Mercedes. The Lexus LS400 is all of these and more.' The launches of other Japanese models have used positioning strategies similar to that used by Toyota for Lexus. Nissan's new coupé used a quotation from *Autocar & Motor* as a headline: 'Brilliant new 200SX, Ferrari looks, Porsche pace'. Underneath the Nissan logo they also promote: 'Nissan UK Ltd, Worthing, Sussex'. Mazda's MX-5 Miata is also in the mood of more exotic antiques and must have Rover sobbing. It was designed in the United Kingdom, but when it was being road tested in California, the drivers were plagued by people demanding to know where they could get one. The car's launch used 1960s imagery and profuse references to Austin Healey, MG and Triumph. Like Nissan's nostalgia cars, the MX-5 is a 'back to basics' car whose performance is not outstanding but, as *What Car?* says, it has 'Sixties looks with Nineties fun and finesses … Over to you MG'.

SOURCES: Timothy Jacobs, *The World's Worst Cars* (London: Bison, 1991); Nick Georgano, *Cars of the Seventies and Eighties* (Gothenburg: Crescent, 1990); Peter Nunn, 'Class barriers fall', *Financial Times* (18 September 1994), p. XI; Neil Weinberg, 'Domestic luxury car sales accelerate', *Financial Times* (25 June 1994), p. VI; Michiyo Nakamoto, 'A taste of their own medicine', *Financial Times* (30 June 1994), p. 11.

should develop a **unique selling proposition (USP)** for each brand and stick to it. Each brand should pick an attribute and tout itself as 'no. 1' on that attribute. Buyers tend to remember 'no. 1' better, especially in an overcommunicated society. Thus Crest toothpaste consistently promotes its anti-cavity protection, and Mercedes promotes its great automotive engineering. What are some of the 'no. 1' positions to promote? The most significant ones are 'best quality', 'best service', 'lowest price', 'best value' and 'most advanced technology'. A company that hammers away at one of these positions and consistently achieves it will probably become best known and remembered for it.

The difficulty of keeping functional superiority has made firms focus on having a unique **emotional selling proposition (ESP)** instead of a USP. The product may be similar to competitors', but it has unique associations for consumers. Leading names like Rolls-Royce, Ferrari and Rolex have done this. Other cars outperform Ferrari on the road and track, but 'the red car with the

unique selling proposition (USP) *The unique product benefit that a firm aggressively promotes in a consistent manner to its target market. The benefit usually reflects functional superiority: best quality, best services, lowest price, most advanced technology.*

I Can't Believe It's Not Butter uses dual positioning: it is 'light' but it tastes like 'butter'.

emotional selling proposition (ESP)
A non-functional attribute that has unique associations for consumers.

underpositioning
A positioning error referring to failure to position a company, its product or brand.

overpositioning
A positioning error referring to too narrow a picture of the company, its product or a brand being communicated to target customers.

prancing horse' is the world's no. 1 sports car. Many Formula One racing drivers still dream of racing a Ferrari, even when the team is not winning.

Other marketers think that companies should position themselves on more than one differentiating factor. This may be necessary if two or more firms are claiming to be best on the same attribute. Steelcase, an office furniture systems company, differentiates itself from competitors on two benefits: best on-time delivery and best installation support. Volvo positions its automobiles as 'safest' and 'most durable'. Fortunately, these two benefits are compatible – a very safe car would also be very durable.

Today, in a time when the mass market is fragmenting into many small segments, companies are trying to broaden their positioning strategies to appeal to more segments. For example, Beecham promotes its Aquafresh toothpaste as offering three benefits: 'anti-cavity protection', 'better breath' and 'whiter teeth'. Clearly, many people want all three benefits, and the challenge is to convince them that the brand delivers all three. Beecham's solution was to create toothpaste that squeezed out of the tube in three colours, thus visually confirming the three benefits. In doing this, Beecham attracted three segments instead of one.

However, as companies increase the number of claims for their brands, they risk disbelief and a loss of clear positioning. Usually, a company needs to avoid three serious positioning errors. The first is **underpositioning** – that is, failing to position the company at all. Some companies discover that buyers have only a vague idea of the brand, or that they do not really know anything special about it. This has occurred with dark spirits – whisky and brandy – where young drinkers have drifted away from them. United Distillers and Hiram Walker aim to reverse this trend with their Bells and Teacher's brands by targeting 25- to 35-year-old men. There is much focus on extending the use of both brands as a mixer. This is an anathema to many whisky drinkers, but United Distillers has successfully promoted it as a mixer in both Spain and Greece.[21] The second positioning error is **overpositioning** – that is, giving buyers too narrow a picture of the company.

When Positions Collide

Some positions, just like some segments, do not mix. In an attempt to understand classical concert goers, London's South Bank Centre commissioned CRAM International to analyze its audience. The resulting segments include *classical purists, mainstream stalwarts, new modernists* and *good time novices*. The problem for the South Bank Centre is that the segments don't only differ in their musical tastes, but they also dislike each other.

Marketers can sometimes use this alienation profitably. When the marketers of 'ever so nice' Smarties children's confectionery recognized that growing 'pest power' meant that they had to attract children rather than parents, they did it with a vengeance. Not only did Smarties TV advertising become exciting for children, but the company also tapped into playground cults. The first was 'cool dood' sunglasses, then came the 'gruesome greenies' pouch and the 'zapper', a pocket-sized machine that made noises guaranteed to annoy parents and teachers. Ironically, from the same stable comes the Milky Bar Kid – a squeaky clean nice boy dressed in white whom many parents love but who is far from appealing to streetwise kids. The Milky Bar Kid works because it is aimed at parents who buy white chocolate Milky Bar products for their very young children.

Sometimes trying to appeal directly to the tastes of children can backfire. Healthy children's cereal Weetabix had to withdraw a campaign showing its cereal bars dressed as skin-heads who came too close to looking like football hooligans. Lego faced a similar backlash when it promoted its educational toys using an unsavoury Lego character driving a Lego car recklessly. Some parents thought it looked too much like joy riding.

This alienation positioning has been used by a succession of pop musicians. Often their positioning is by behaviour. It is hard to imagine that part of the appeal of the classic 1960s rock bands The Who and the Rolling Stones was their noisy music as well as their wrecking of their instruments and hotel rooms. Even the Beatles were 'mop heads' until the Stones out-alienated them. They followed in the tradition set by such objectionable creatures as Elvis Presley and Cliff Richard. Each generation discovers alienation positions, although few went so far as punk bands such as the Sex Pistols.

Sometimes the excitement, youth and energy makes these outsiders attractive to people trying to position themselves. In the 'swinging sixties', the then British prime minister, Harold Wilson, held parties at 10 Downing Street where he could be photographed alongside pop personalities. Probably the saddest case of this pop positioning was Richard Nixon being photographed with Elvis as part of an anti-drugs campaign. Pop positioning was too good a trick for Britain's new Labour to miss. Soon after gaining power, Tony Blair was photographed with Oasis's Noel Gallagher at a 10 Downing Street pop party. It became one pop position too far at the 1998 Brit music industry awards. While the music industry was helping pop position new Labour, anarchist pop group Chumbawamba exploited alienation positioning by pouring a bucket of water over John Prescott, deputy prime minister. It is dangerous when positions collide.

SOURCES: David Murray, 'What the audience really wants', *Financial Times* (29 December 1997), p. 7; Alice Rawsthorn, 'Ministers may launch fashion policy collection', *Financial Times* (17 February 1998), p. 12.

Thus a consumer might think that the Steuben glass company makes only fine art glass costing $1,000 and up, when it also makes affordable fine glass starting at around $50.

Finally, companies must avoid **confused positioning** – that is, leaving buyers with a confused image of the company. For example, Burger King has struggled

confused positioning
A positioning error that leaves consumers with a confused image of the company, its product or a brand.

implausible positioning
Making claims that stretch the perception of the buyers too far to be believed.

without success for years to establish a profitable and consistent position. Since 1986, it has undertaken five separate advertising campaigns, with themes ranging from 'Herb the nerd doesn't eat here' and 'This is a Burger King town', to 'The right food for the right times' and 'Sometimes you've got to break the rules'. This barrage of positioning statements has left consumers confused and Burger King with poor sales and profits.[22]

Implausible positioning occurs when the positioning strategy stretches the perception of the buyers too far. Toyota recognized this when it created the Lexus brand rather than try to stretch its highly respected name into the luxury car market. With the help of Volkswagon, Skoda is very successful in eastern Europe, but it will be many years before many people will accept the product as an alternative to an Audi or Ford. Some market positions, while attracting one group of customers, can alienate others and so backfire, as Marketing Highlight 10.4 tells.

● *Which Differences to Promote?*

Not all brand differences are meaningful or worthwhile. Not every difference makes a good differentiator. Each difference has the potential to create company costs as well as customer benefits. Therefore, the company must carefully select the ways in which it will distinguish itself from competitors. A difference is worth establishing insofar as it satisfies the following criteria:

● *Important.* The difference delivers a highly valued benefit to target buyers.

● *Distinctive.* Competitors do not offer the difference, or the company can offer it in a more distinctive way.

● *Superior.* The difference is superior to other ways that customers might obtain the same benefit.

● *Communicable.* The difference is communicable and visible to buyers.

● *Pre-emptive.* Competitors cannot easily copy the difference.

● *Affordable.* Buyers can afford to pay for the difference.

● *Profitable.* The company can introduce the difference profitably.

Many companies have introduced differentiations that failed one or more of these tests. The Westin Stamford hotel in Singapore advertises that it is the world's tallest hotel, a distinction that is not important to many tourists – the fact scared many. AT & T's original picturevision phones failed, partly because the public did not think that seeing the other person was worth the phone's high cost. Philips Laservision failed too. Although the laser disks gave excellent picture quality, there were few disks available and the machines could not record. These drawbacks meant that consumers saw Laservision as offering no advantage over videotape machines.

Some competitive advantages are too slight, too costly to develop, or too inconsistent with the company's profile. Suppose that a company is designing its positioning strategy and has narrowed its list of possible competitive advantages to four. The company needs a framework for selecting the one advantage that makes the most sense to develop. Table 10.2 shows a systematic way of evaluating several potential competitive advantages and choosing the right one.

In the table, the company compares its standing on four attributes – technology, cost, quality and service – to the standing of its chief competitor. Let's assume that both companies stand at 8 on technology (1 = low score, 10 = high score), which means that they both have good technology. The company ques-

Table 10.2	Finding competitive advantage

COMPETITIVE ADVANTAGE	COMPANY STANDING (1–10)	COMPETITOR STANDING (1–10)	IMPORTANCE OF IMPROVING STANDING (H-M-L)	AFFORDABILITY AND SPEED (H-M-L)	COMPETITOR'S ABILITY TO IMPROVE STANDING (H-M-L)	RECOMMENDED ACTION
Technology	8	8	L	L	M	Hold
Cost	6	8	H	M	M	Watch
Quality	8	6	L	L	H	Watch
Service	4	3	H	H	L	Invest

tions whether it can gain much by improving its technology further, especially given the high cost of new technology. The competitor has a better standing on cost (8 instead of 6), and this can hurt the company if the market gets more price sensitive. The company offers higher quality than its competitor (8 instead of 6). Finally, both companies offer below-average service (4 and 3).

At first glance, it appears that the company should go after cost or service to improve its market appeal over the competitor. However, it must consider other factors. First, how important are improvements in each of these attributes to the target customers? The fourth column shows that both cost and service improvements would be highly important to customers. Next, can the company afford to make the improvements? If so, how fast can it complete them? The fifth column shows that the company could improve service quickly and affordably. But if the firm decided to do this, would the competitor be able to improve its service also? The sixth column shows that the competitor's ability to improve service is low, perhaps because the competitor does not believe in service or has limited funds. The final column then shows the appropriate actions to take on each attribute. It makes the most sense for the company to invest in improving its service. Service is important to customers; the company can afford to improve its service and can do it fast, and the competitor will probably not be able to catch up.

Communicating and Delivering the Chosen Position

Once it has chosen a position, the company must take strong steps to deliver and communicate the desired position to target consumers. All the company's marketing-mix efforts must support the positioning strategy. Positioning the company calls for concrete action – it is not just talk. If the company decides to build a position on better quality and service, it must first *deliver* that position. Designing the marketing mix – product, price, place and promotion – involves working out the tactical details of the positioning strategy. Thus a firm that seizes upon a 'high-quality position' knows that it must produce high-quality products, charge a high price, distribute through high-quality dealers and advertise in high-quality media. It must hire and train more service people, find retailers that have a good reputation for service, and develop sales and advertising messages that broadcast its superior service. This is the only way to build a consistent and believable high-quality, high-service position.

Calvin Klein Cosmetics has noticed a shift in the fragrance market. Shiseido launched a classic fragrance by Jean-Paul Gaultier, *enfant terrible* of French fashion, that broke industry rules with its punky advertising and packaging – a bottle in the shape of a woman's torso encased in an aluminium can. L'Oréal responded with Eden, a new Cacharel fragrance for ecologically concerned consumers.

Calvin Klein's response is *cK one*, a 'shared fragrance for young consumers who, he believes, are ready to buy a scent created for both sexes'. The designer's other fragrances, Obsession, Eternity and Escape, are for women only. The positioning of *cK one* is radical and covers the whole marketing mix. The range will include youth-oriented products, such as massage oil. The bottles and display material are by Fabien Baron, designer of advertising campaigns for other Calvin Klein products as well as Valentino, Burberry's and Giorgio Armani. He also collaborated with Madonna in the production of her *Sex* book. He says Calvin's response to the bottle was 'Boom! Yeah! Right on.' It is a frosted glass flask with aluminium top and recycled paper packaging.

The rest of the marketing mix that backs *cK one* is radical positioning. Prices are low – about 70 per cent of Obsession's – and it will sell in novel distribution outlets, notably Tower Records. To ensure that the multi-million dollar launch is a success, Calvin Klein's corporation will send 12,000 gorgeous members of both sexes to stores to splash it on shoppers.[23]

Companies often find it easier to come up with a good positioning strategy than to implement it. Establishing a position or changing one usually takes a long time. In contrast, positions that have taken years to build can quickly disappear. Once a company has built the desired position, it must take care to maintain the position through consistent performance and communication. It must closely monitor and adapt the position over time to match changes in consumer needs and competitors' strategies. This is how world leading brands Coca-Cola, Nescafé, Snickers, BMW, Rolex, Estée Lauder, Johnnie Walker and Chanel have remained pre-eminent for so long. The company should avoid abrupt changes that might confuse consumers. Coca-Cola forgot this when it introduced its disastrous new Coke, Marlboro's price cuts made the brand fall from being the most highly valued brand to out of the top ten, and Unilever's hasty introduction of the Persil/Omo Power benefited Procter & Gamble. Violent changes rarely succeed – a product's position should evolve as it adapts to the changing market environment.

Summary

The *core strategy* of a company shows how it will address the markets it has targeted. By *differentiation* it develops the strengths of the company, so that they meet the target markets' needs; then, by market positioning, it manages the way consumers view the company and its products.

Differentiation helps a firm compete profitably. It gives it a *competitive advantage*. If a firm does not differentiate, it will be like 'all the rest' and be forced to compete on price. Differentiation is harder in some industries than others, but it is rare that a creative marketer cannot differentiate a market in some way. There are four main ways to differentiate: *product differentiation, service differentiation, personnel differentiation* and *image differentiation*. The ease of following new technological innovations means that the product is becoming an increasingly difficult way to differentiate. Now service and image are the main ways people distinguish between products. As systems and methods become more common, personnel differentiation becomes more important. The firm is its people and they are usually what the customer is most sensitive to.

A firm's functional strengths give it its competitive advantage. Market positioning is about managing customers' view of the company and its products. It is about perception. *Perceptual maps* are a way of revealing how customers see markets. They show which products customers see as alike and those that are not. They can also show segments and the dimensions that customers use to split up the market.

There are several positioning strategies for shifting and holding customers' perceptions. Positioning works by associating products with product attributes or other stimuli. Successful firms usually maintain a clear differential advantage and do not make violent changes to their market positions.

Key Terms

Competitive advantage 434	Implausible positioning 460	Stalemate industry 435
Confused positioning 459	Overpositioning 458	Underpositioning 458
Core strategy 434	Perceptual maps 446	Unique selling proposition
Emotional selling proposition (ESP) 457	Product position 443	(USP) 457
Fragmented industry 435	Specialized industry 435	Volume industry 435

Discussing the Issues

1. In marketing products and services, 'being different is good', so the pros say. Why should firms differentiate their product or service offerings? What are the specific ways in which a producer of goods or services differentiates its offer from those of competitors? Discuss, using specific examples.

2. What roles do product attributes and perceptions of attributes play in positioning a product? Can an attribute held by several competing brands be used in a successful positioning strategy?

3. A company is looking to deposition or reposition the competition. What does this mean? How might the company go about depositioning its rivals in the marketplace?

4. Think of well-known beer or lager brands. How well are these positioned in relation to one another? Do manufacturers clarify or confuse the positioning themes? Are the differences they promote meaningful or worthwhile?

5. Perceptual mapping is a valuable aid to product positioning. What are its benefits and limitations?

6. Is positioning helpful to not-for-profit organizations? If so, how should a charity select and implement a positioning strategy? If not, why?

Applying the Concepts

1. By looking at advertising and at products themselves, we can often see how marketers are attempting to position their products and what target market they hope to reach.

   ● Define the positionings of and target markets for Coca-Cola, Pepsi Cola, Red Bull, Tango and 7-Up.

   ● Define the positionings of and target markets for KitKat, Lion Bar, Snickers, Aero, Mars Bars and Twix.

   ● Do you think that the soft drinks and confectionery industries achieve distinctive positionings and target markets? Are some more clearly defined than others?

2. It is possible to market people as well as products or services. When marketing a person, we can *position* that individual for a particular target market. Describe briefly how you could position yourself for the following target markets: (a) for a potential employer; (b) for a potential boyfriend or girlfriend; (c) for your boyfriend or girlfriend's mother and father. Do you position yourself differently for the different target markets? How do the positionings differ? Why do the positionings differ?

References

1. Based on John Griffiths, 'The pace hots up', *Financial Times* (26 January 1990), p. I; Andrew Bolger, 'Growth by successful targeting', *Financial Times* (21 June 1994), p. 12; Shiraz Sidhva, 'Carmakers drive deep into India', *Financial Times* (20 July 1994), p. 28; David Done, 'Benetton Grand Prix team changes gear', *Financial Times* (24 August 1994), p. 2; Meg Carter, 'Wheels of fortune', *Marketing Week* (26 August 1994), pp. 28–30; Anil Bhoyrul, 'Devil take the hindmost', *Business Age*, 4, 49 (1994), pp. 20–3; John Griffiths, 'Steering into a commanding lead', *Financial Times* (15 January 1998), p. 25.

2. For a discussion of the concepts of differentiation and competitive advantage, and methods for assessing them, see Michael Porter, *Competitive Advantage* (New York: Free Press, 1985), ch. 2; George S. Day and Robin Wensley, 'Assessing advantage: a framework for diagnosing competitive superiority', *Journal of Marketing* (April 1988), pp. 1–20; Philip Kotler, *Marketing Management*, 7th edn (Englewood Cliffs, NJ: Prentice Hall, 1991), ch. 11; Grahan Hooley and John Saunders, *Competitive Positioning: The key to market success* (Hemel Hempstead: Prentice Hall, 1993).

3. For an interesting discussion of finding ways to differentiate marketing offers, see Ian C. MacMillan and Rita Gunther McGrath, 'Discovering new points of differentiation', *Harvard Business Review* (July–August 1997, pp. 133–45.

4. *Financial Times Survey*, 'Global business outlook' (13 January 1998).

5. For a review of this and other results, see Robert D. Buzzell and Bradley T. Gale, *The PIMS Principle: Linking strategy to performance* (New York: Free Press, 1987).

6. Theodore Levitt, 'Making success through differentiation – of anything', *Harvard Business Review* (January–February 1980).

7. 'Western Europe's insurance tangle', *The Economist* (18 June 1994), pp. 115–16.

8. See David A. Garvin, 'Competing on the eight dimensions of quality', *Harvard Business Review* (November–December 1987), pp. 101–9.

9. See Tom Peters, *Thriving on Chaos* (New York: Knopf, 1987), pp. 56–7.

10. For details of this and other examples, see George Stalker and Thomas M. Hout, *Competing Against Time* (London: Collier Macmillan, 1990).

11. Positioning was introduced in the seminal work by Al Ries and Jack Trout, *Positioning: The battle for your mind* (New York: McGraw-Hill, 1981); see also Al Ries and Jack Trout, *Marketing Warfare* (New York: McGraw-Hill, 1986). Al Ries develops his ideas in 'The mind is the ultimate battlefield', *Journal of Business Strategy* (July–August 1988), pp. 4–7.

12. Julie Street, 'Success crowns crash course in sensationalism', *The European – élan* (10–16 June 1994), p. 5.

13. These figures and others relating to European tourist destinations are based on a study by A. Haahti, Helsinki School of Economics, R.R. van den Heuvel, Groningen University and G. J. Hooley of Aston University. The results are disguised for the purpose of confidentiality. A case study called 'Finnish Tourist Board' by Graham Hooley appears in Peter Doyle and Norman Hart (eds), *Case Studies in International Marketing* (London: Heinemann, 1982), pp. 61–86.

14. Leiv Gunner Lie, 'Norway cashes in on the magic of the mountains', *The European* (10–16 June 1994), p. 20.

15. David Short, 'Red Bull set to lock horns with multinationals', *The European* (19–25 August 1994).

16. Susan Jacquet, 'Ethics and responsibility', *Swiss Quality Timing*, 6 (Spring 1994), pp. 40–1.

17. Birna Helgadottir, 'Time has come to realise your dreams', *The European – élan* (16–22 September 1994), p. 6.

18. Mike Baldwin, 'Nice car, shame about the driver', *Today* (20 September 1994), p. 7.

19. Victoria Griffith, 'Reebok backs off in sponsorship battle', *Financial Times* (15 January 1998), p. 36.

20. Diane Summers, 'Skoda's sales drive is no joke', *Financial Times* (12 May 1994), p. 11; Stephen Bayley, 'Freedom and its discontents', *The European Magazine* (6–12 March 1997), pp. 14–17.

21. Ros Snowden, 'Spirit of adventure', *Marketing Week* (15 August 1994), pp. 32–5.

22. Mark Landler and Gail DeGeorge, 'Tempers are sizzling over Burger King's new ads', *Business Week* (12 February 1990), p. 33; Philip Stelly, Jr, 'Burger King rule breaker', *Adweek* (9 November 1990), pp. 24, 26.

23. Alice Rawsthorn, 'A nose for innovation', *Financial Times* (4 August 1994), p. 11; Bronwyn Cosgrove, 'Fabulous Fabien's pure object of desire', *The European – élan* (23–9 September 1994), pp. 14–15.

Case 10

Schott: Positioning for Success

SCHOTT, THE GERMAN MANUFACTURER OF glass for industrial and consumer products, had a problem deciding how to position its innovative product, Ceran, in the American market. The product, a glass-ceramic material made to cover the cooking surface of electric ranges, seemed to have everything going for it. It was completely non-porous (and thus stain resistant), easy to clean and long-lasting. Best of all, when one burner was lit, the heat didn't spread; it stayed confined to the circle directly above the burner. And after ten years, hobs made of Ceran still looked and performed like new.

Schott anticipated some difficulty in igniting demand for Ceran in US markets. First it would have to win over American cooker manufacturers, which would then have to promote Ceran to middle markets – dealers, designers, architects and builders. These middle-market customers would, in turn, need to influence final consumers. Thus, Schott's US subsidiary set out to sell Ceran aggressively to its target of 14 North American appliance manufacturers. The subsidiary positioned Ceran on its impressive technical and engineering attributes – showing cross-sections of stoves and using plenty of high-tech talk – then waited optimistically for the orders to roll in. The appliance companies listened politely to the rep's pitch, ordered sample quantities – 25 or so of each available colour – and then ... nothing. Absolutely nothing.

Research by Schott's advertising agency revealed two problems. First, Schott had failed to position Ceran at all among the manufacturers' customers. The material was still virtually unknown, not only among final consumers but also among dealers, designers, architects and builders. Second, the company was attempting to position the product on the wrong benefits. When selecting a hob to buy, customers seemed to care less about the sophisticated engineering that went into it and more about its appearance and cleanability. Their biggest questions were 'How does it look?' and 'How easy is it to use?'

Based on these findings, Schott repositioned Ceran, shifting emphasis towards the material's inherent beauty and design versatility. And it launched an extensive promotion campaign to communicate the new position to middle-market and final buyers. Advertising had themes like 'Formalware for your kitchen', which presented the black hob as streamlined and elegant as a tuxedo. As a follow-up, to persuade designers to add Ceran to their palette of materials, Schott positioned Ceran as 'More than a rangetop, a means of expression'. To reinforce this beauty and design positioning, ads featured visuals, including a geometric grid of a hob with one glowing red burner.

In addition to advertising, Schott's agency launched a massive public relations effort that resulted in substantial coverage in home improvement publications. It also produced a video news release featuring Ceran that was picked up by 150 local TV stations nation-wide. To reinforce a weak link in the selling chain – appliance salespeople who were poorly equipped to answer customer questions about Ceran – the agency created a video that the salespeople could show customers on the TVs in their own appliance stores.

The now properly and strongly positioned Ceran is selling well. All 14 North American appliance makers are buying production quantities of Ceran and using it in their hobs. All offer not one, but several smooth-top models. Schott is the major smooth-top supplier in the United States, and smooth tops now account for more than 15 per cent of the electric stove market. And at a recent Kitchen & Bath Show, 69 per cent of all range models on display had smooth tops. Schott recently introduced Ceran-topped portable units as an interesting design alternative to traditional hot plates. Also positioned on aesthetics and ease of cleaning, the tabletop units are rapidly gaining popularity in both residential and commercial markets. To keep up with increasing demand, Schott has built a US plant just to produce Ceran for the North American market.

QUESTIONS

1. Compare the positioning strategies used by Schott in the case.

2. Why did one succeed and the other fail?

3. Could country of origin be used to help position the product?

4. What types of product could be successfully positioned as German, French, Italian, Swedish, Dutch, etc.?

5. What associations could Schott have used to communicate its successful positioning? What personalities?

6. To what extent does successful positioning depend upon the tangible features of a product being marketed?

SOURCES: Adapted from Nancy Arnott, 'Heating up sales: formalware for your kitchen', *Sales and Marketing Management* (June 1994), pp. 77–8. See also Richard J. Babyak, 'Tabletop cooking', *Appliance Manufacturer* (February 1997), pp. 65–7.

11

Building Customer Relationships: Customer Satisfaction, Quality, Value and Service

CHAPTER OBJECTIVES

After reading this chapter, you should be able to:

● Define *customer value* and discuss its importance in creating customer satisfaction and company profitability.

● Discuss the concepts of *value chains* and *value delivery* systems and explain how companies go about producing and delivering customer value.

● Explain the importance of retaining current customers as well as attracting new ones.

● Discuss customer relationship marketing and the main steps in establishing a customer relationship programme.

● Define quality and explain the importance of total quality marketing in building value-laden, profitable relationships with customers.

Preview Case

Rubbermaid: Want to Buy an Expensive Rubber Dustpan?

THE BEST-SELLING CAR IN the world is not a VW, Toyota or Chevy, but the Little Tikes Cozy Coupé – a leg-powered, Flintstones-like car for toddlers. It

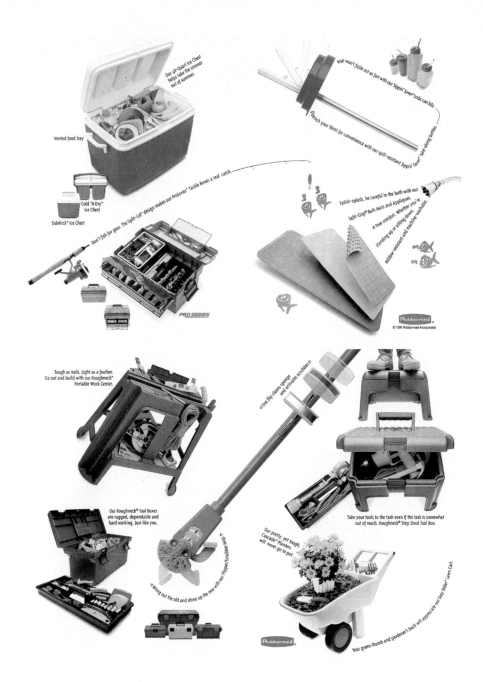

is one of the thousands of products made by one of the world's most successful companies, Rubbermaid. The company's rise started in 1934 when the then Wooster Rubber Company made a little-noticed addition to its line of balloons: a rubber dustpan. It sold the new dustpan door to door for twice what competitors were charging for their metal versions. But this dustpan was special: it was well designed, long lasting and very high in quality, and it was good value. The Wooster Rubber Company became Rubbermaid and that lowly dustpan turned out to be a real winner. Since then, the same concepts that led to the development of the rubber dustpan have transformed Rubbermaid from a sleepy, small-town rubber-products company into a dynamic market leader.

Today, Rubbermaid thoroughly dominates its fragmented industry, without serious competition. It produces a dazzling array of more than

5,000 products, ranging from food containers, pedal bins and home organizers to toy cars, mailboxes and plastic bird feeders. It sells $2.2 billion worth of rubber and plastic household goods, toys, outdoor furniture and office products each year. Rubbermaid's rise has been spectacular. In the past decade or so, its sales have quadrupled and profits have grown sixfold. It has achieved 54 consecutive years of profits, 57 consecutive quarters of sales and earnings growth, and 15 per cent average earnings per share since 1985. *Fortune* magazine has rated Rubbermaid among the top seven most admired US corporations for ten years running.

Rubbermaid's success results from a simple but effective competitive marketing strategy: to offer consistently the best value to customers. First, the company carefully studies and listens to consumers. It uses demographic and lifestyle analysis to spot consumer trends and conducts focus groups, interviews and in-home product tests to learn about consumer problems and needs, likes and dislikes. Then it gives consumers what they want – a continuous flow of useful, innovative and high-quality products.

Rubbermaid has forged a strong market position. To most consumers, the Rubbermaid name has become the gold standard of good value and quality. Customers know that Rubbermaid products are well designed and well made, and they willingly pay premium prices to own them. Rubbermaid management jealously protects this reputation. The company has an obsession with quality. Under its strict quality-control programme, no product with so much as a scratch ever leaves the factory floor. It's said that former Rubbermaid CEO Stanley Gault, who guided the company through its spectacular growth during the 1980s, used to visit retail stores several times a week to see how the company's products were displayed and to check on quality and workmanship. If he found a problem, he bought up the merchandise on the spot, brought it back to headquarters and severely lectured responsible company executives. Throughout the company, he was known to get livid about product defects.

Rubbermaid thrives on finding new ways to serve customers. Innovation and new-product development have become a kind of religion in the company. Rubbermaid introduces around 400 a year. Its goal is to generate at least 33 per cent of its total sales from products less than five years old, a goal that it usually meets or exceeds. The company even bases part of its executive compensation on new products' share of sales. Despite the hectic pace of new introductions, Rubbermaid has met with astonishing success. In a fiercely competitive industry where 90 per cent of all new products typically fail, Rubbermaid boasts an amazing 90 per cent *success* rate for its new products.

To speed up the flow of new products, Rubbermaid assigns small teams – made up of experts from marketing, design, manufacturing and finance – to each of its 50 or so product categories. These teams identify new product ideas and usher them through design, development and introduction. The teams tackle the new-product development challenge with enthusiasm. For example, the manager of Rubbermaid's bath accessories, decorative coverings and home organizational products notes that her 'bath team' lives and breathes soap dishes, vanity wastebaskets and shower caddies. Team members go to trade shows, scour magazines, scan supermarket shelves and travel the globe searching for new-product ideas. 'We are like sponges,' she says.

Rubbermaid's versions of ordinary products usually offer simple but elegant improvements. For example, its simple yet stylish new Sidekick 'litter-free' lunch box features plastic containers that hold a sandwich, a drink and another item, eliminating the need for plastic wrapping, milk cartons, cans and other potential litter. The Sidekick is priced 20 per cent higher than competing products. Still, the colourful new lunch box has become all the rage among parents worried about America's garbage glut and among schoolchildren who have had environmental messages pounded into them at school. Rubbermaid's share of the lunch box market is expected to continue to exhibit strong growth and the company plans to introduce new Sidekick versions.

In addition to developing new products from scratch, Rubbermaid has been very successful at buying up and building small, undervalued companies. For example, in 1984 it added Little Tikes, a small producer of plastic toys, to its portfolio of businesses. In 1991, with the acquisition of Eldon Industries, it established its Office Products Group, which makes desktop accessories, office containers and organizers, modular furniture and other products for home and commercial offices. Such smart strategic planning moves have paid off. Little Tikes is now the company's second largest unit – it introduced over 50 new toys last year and currently contributes about 25 per cent of total sales. Rubbermaid is also gearing up to expand its dominance into global markets. By the year 2000, it plans to generate 30 per cent of sales from outside the United States, compared to the current 15 per cent.

Rubbermaid has also built strong relationships with its 'other customers' – retailers which operate the more than 120,000 outlets in the United States alone that sell Rubbermaid products. Retailers appreciate the company's consistent high quality, larger margins, outstanding service and strong consumer appeal. In fact, Rubbermaid recently received 'Vendor of the Year' honours from the mass-merchandising industry. It has built alliances aggressively with fast-growing discount stores that account for the bulk of household goods sales. It created 'Rubbermaid boutiques', which are whole sections within stores that stock only Rubbermaid products. For example, Twin Valu stores set up ten 24-foot-long shelves with Rubbermaid products, displacing between 20 and 490 feet of competing products. As a result, most of Rubbermaid's competitors have trouble simply getting shelf space.

Thus Rubbermaid has done all of the things that an outstanding marketing company must do to establish and retain its leadership. As one industry analyst notes: '[Rubbermaid has] the ability to execute strategy flawlessly. There's something about Rubbermaid that's magical, that is so difficult for competitors to replicate.' Rubbermaid has positioned itself strongly and gained competitive advantage by providing the best value to consumers. It has set the pace for its industry and kept competitors at bay through continuous innovation. Finally, it has developed a constant stream of useful, high-quality products in a constant quest to deliver ever more value to consumers. In fact, some observers wonder if Rubbermaid can maintain its current torrid pace. How many more new products and approaches, they ask, can the company find? 'It's a little like in 1900, when there was legislation to close the patent office,' answers a Rubbermaid executive. 'The country was convinced that everything that could be invented already was. [But when it comes to fresh and saleable new ways to serve our customers], we're never going to run out of ideas.'[1]

QUESTIONS

1. What is the basis of Rubbermaid's success?
2. Why are people willing to pay a premium price for the sort of commodity products that Rubbermaid sells?

3. What accounts for Rubbermaid's extraordinary rate of new-product innovation and new-product success?

4. Why do you think the company aims to achieve such a large number of new products each year?

5. Why do companies like Rubbermaid and Arm & Hammer stick so closely to using such limiting raw materials in their products?

6. It is hard to beat Rubbermaid in its own market, but can its lessons be replicated in other countries with other products?

Introduction

Today's companies face tough competition and things will only get harder. In previous chapters, we argued that to succeed in today's fiercely competitive markets, companies have to move from a *product and selling philosophy* to a *customer and marketing philosophy*. This chapter tells in more detail how companies can win customers and outperform competitors. The answer lies in the marketing concept – in doing a better job of *meeting and satisfying customer needs*.

In sellers' markets – those characterized by shortages and near-monopolies – companies do not make special efforts to please customers. In eastern Europe, for example, millions of would-be consumers used to stand sullenly in line for hours only to receive poorly made clothes, toiletries, appliances and other products at high prices. Producers and retailers showed little concern for customer satisfaction with goods and services. Sellers paid relatively little heed to marketing theory and practice.

In buyers' markets, in contrast, customers can choose from a wide array of goods and services. In these markets, if sellers fail to deliver acceptable product and service quality, they will quickly lose customers to competitors. Also, what is acceptable today may not be acceptable to tomorrow's ever-more-demanding consumers. Consumers are becoming more educated and demanding, and their quality expectations have been raised by the practices of superior manufacturers and retailers. The decline of many traditional western industries in recent years – cars, cameras, machine tools, consumer electronics – offers dramatic evidence that firms offering only average quality lose their consumer franchises when attacked by superior competitors.

Satisfying Customer Needs

To succeed or simply to survive, companies need a new philosophy. To win in today's marketplace, companies must be **customer-centred** – they must deliver superior value to their target customers. They must become adept in *building customer relationships*, not just *building products*. They must be skilful in *market engineering*, not just *product engineering*. New chief executive of GEC Industries, George Simpson's views were honed at Rover where the corporate culture had to shift to the notion that customers need to like the cars they

customer-centred company
A company that focuses on customer developments in designing its marketing strategies and on delivering superior value to its target customers.

buy. There was, he says, 'a bit of a tendency to have technology for technology's sake'.[2]

Too many companies think that obtaining customers is the job of the marketing or sales department. But winning companies have come to realize that marketing cannot do this job alone. Although marketing plays a leading role, it is only a partner in attracting and keeping customers. The world's best marketing department cannot successfully sell poorly made products that fail to meet consumer needs. The marketing department can be effective only in companies in which all departments and employees have teamed up to form a competitively superior *customer value-delivery system*.

Consider McDonald's. People do not swarm to the world's 11,000 McDonald's restaurants only because they love the chain's hamburgers. Many other restaurants make better-tasting hamburgers. Consumers flock to the McDonald's *system*, not just to its food products. Throughout the world, McDonald's finely tuned system delivers a high standard of what the company calls QSCV – Quality, Service, Cleanliness and Value. The system consists of many components, both internal and external. McDonald's is effective only to the extent that it successfully partners its employees, franchisees, suppliers and others in jointly delivering exceptionally high customer value.

This chapter discusses the philosophy of customer-value-creating marketing and the customer-focused firm. It addresses several important questions: What is customer value and customer satisfaction? How do leading companies organize to create and deliver high value and satisfaction? How can companies keep current customers as well as get new ones? How can companies practise total quality marketing?

Defining Customer Value and Satisfaction

More than 35 years ago, Peter Drucker observed that a company's first task is 'to create customers'. However, creating customers can be a difficult task. Today's customers face a vast array of product and brand choices, prices and suppliers. The company must answer a key question: How do customers make their choices?

The answer is that customers choose the marketing offer that gives them the most value. Customers are value-maximizers, within the bounds of search costs and limited knowledge, mobility and income. They form expectations of value and act upon them. Then they compare the actual value they receive in consuming the product to the value expected, and this affects their satisfaction and repurchase behaviour. We will now examine the concepts of customer value and customer satisfaction more carefully.

Customer Value

customer delivered value
The difference between total customer value and total customer cost of a marketing offer – 'profit' to the customer.

Consumers buy from the firm that they believe offers the highest **customer delivered value** – the difference between *total customer value* and *total customer cost* (see Figure 11.1). For example, suppose that an Irish farmer wants to buy a tractor. He can either buy the equipment from his usual supplier, Massey-Ferguson, or a cheaper east European product. The salespeople for the two companies carefully describe their respective offers to the farmer.

Triumph communicates specific benefits that target consumers.

The farmer evaluates the two competing tractors and judges that Massey-Ferguson's tractor provides higher reliability, durability and performance. The customer also decides that Massey-Ferguson has better accompanying services – delivery, training and maintenance – and views Massey-Ferguson personnel as more knowledgeable and responsive. Finally, the customer places higher value on Massey-Ferguson's reputation. The farmer adds all the values from these four sources – *product*, *services*, *personnel* and *image* – and decides that Massey-Ferguson offers more **total customer value** than does the east European tractor.

Does the farmer buy the Massey-Ferguson tractor? Not necessarily. The firm will also examine the **total customer cost** of buying the Massey-Ferguson tractor versus the east European tractor product. First, the buying firm will compare the prices it must pay for each of the competitors' products. The Massey-Ferguson tractor costs a lot more than the east European tractor does, so the higher price might offset the higher total customer value. Moreover, total customer cost consists of more than just monetary costs. As Adam Smith observed more than two centuries ago: 'The real price of anything is the toil and trouble of acquiring it.' Total customer cost also includes the buyer's anticipated time, energy and psychic costs. The farmer will evaluate these costs along with monetary costs to form a complete estimate of his costs.

The farmer compares total customer value to total customer cost and determines the total delivered value associated with Massey-Ferguson's tractor. In the same way, he assesses the total delivered value for the east European tractor. The farmer then will buy from the competitor that offers the highest delivered value.

How can Massey-Ferguson use this concept of buyer decision making to help it succeed in selling its tractor to this buyer? Massey-Ferguson can improve its offer in three ways. First, it can increase total customer value by improving product, services, personnel or image benefits. Second, it can reduce the buyer's non-monetary costs by lessening the buyer's time, energy and psychic costs. Third, it can reduce the buyer's monetary costs by lowering its price, providing easier terms of sale or, in the longer term, lowering its tractor's operating or maintenance costs.

total customer value
The total of all of the product, services, personnel and image values that a buyer receives from a marketing offer.

total customer cost
The total of all the monetary, time, energy and psychic costs associated with a marketing offer.

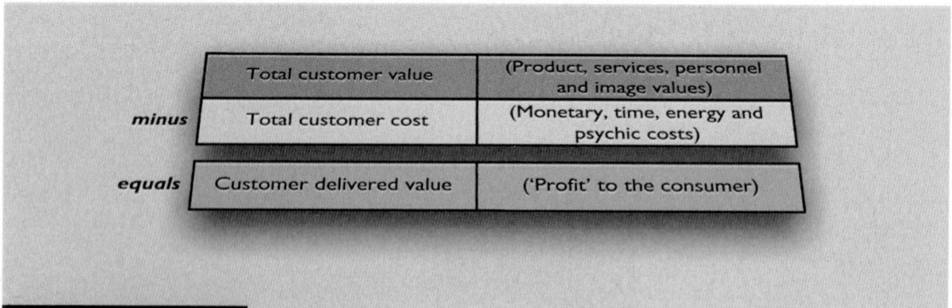

	Total customer value	(Product, services, personnel and image values)
minus	Total customer cost	(Monetary, time, energy and psychic costs)
equals	Customer delivered value	('Profit' to the consumer)

Figure 11.1 **Customer delivered value**

Suppose Massey-Ferguson carries out a *customer value assessment* and concludes that buyers see Massey-Ferguson's offer as worth I£20,000. Further suppose that it costs Massey-Ferguson I£14,000 to produce the tractor. This means that Massey-Ferguson's offer potentially generates I£6,000 (I£20,000 − I£14,000) of *total added value*. Massey-Ferguson needs to price its tractor between I£14,000 and I£20,000. If it charges less than I£14,000, it won't cover its costs. If it charges more than I£20,000, the price will exceed the total customer value. The price Massey-Ferguson charges will determine how much of the total added value will be delivered to the buyer and how much will flow to Massey-Ferguson. For example, if Massey-Ferguson charges I£16,000, it will grant I£4,000 of total added value to the customer and keep I£2,000 for itself as profit. If Massey-Ferguson charges I£19,000, it will grant only I£1,000 of total added value to the customer and keep I£5,000 for itself as profit. Naturally, the lower Massey-Ferguson's price, the higher the delivered value of its offer will be and, therefore, the higher the customer's incentive to purchase from Massey-Ferguson. Delivered value should be viewed as 'profit to the customer'. Given that Massey-Ferguson wants to win the sale, it must offer more delivered value than the east European tractor does.[3]

Some marketers might rightly argue that this concept of how buyers choose among product alternatives is too rational. They might cite examples in which buyers did not choose the offer with an objectively measured highest delivered value. Consider the following situation:

> The Massey-Ferguson salesperson convinces the farmer that, considering the benefits relative to the purchase price, Massey-Ferguson's tractor offers a higher delivered value. The salesperson also points out that the east European tractor uses more fuel and requires more frequent repairs. Still, the farmer decides to buy the east European tractor.

How can we explain this appearance of non-value-maximizing behaviour? There are many possible explanations. For example, perhaps the farmer has a long-term friendship with the east European tractor salesperson. Or the farmer might have a policy of buying at the lowest price. Or perhaps the farmer is short of cash, and therefore chooses the cheaper east European tractor, even though the Massey-Ferguson machine will perform better and be less expensive to operate in the long run.

Clearly, buyers operate under various constraints and sometimes make choices that give more weight to their personal benefit than to company benefit. However, the customer delivered value framework applies to many situations and yields rich insights. The framework suggests that sellers must first assess the total

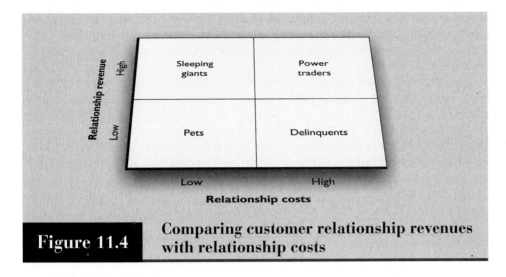

| Figure 11.4 | Comparing customer relationship revenues with relationship costs |

install and learn, that save the customer a lot of money, and that promise to improve through time.

The appropriateness of transaction versus relationship marketing depends on the type of industry and the wishes of the particular customer. Some customers value a high-service supplier and will stay with that supplier for a long time. Other customers want to cut their costs and will switch suppliers readily to obtain lower costs. In the latter case, the company can still try to keep the customer by agreeing to reduce the price, providing that the customer is willing to accept fewer services. For example, the customer may forgo free delivery, design assistance, training or some other extra. However, the seller should probably treat this type of customer on a transaction basis rather than on a relationship-building basis. As long as the company cuts its own costs by as much as or more than its price reduction, the transaction-oriented customer will still be profitable.

Thus relationship marketing is not the best approach in all situations. For it to be worthwhile, relationship revenue needs to exceed relationship costs. Figure 11.4 suggests that some customers are very profitable *sleeping giants*, which generate significant revenue and are profitable but relatively undemanding. Much of the relationship marketing activity is taken up by the *power traders*, which provide significant revenue but are demanding. These are as profitable as the *pets*, which provide little revenue but have appropriately small relationship costs. Transaction marketing is probably adequate for these. The most difficult group is the *delinquents*, which provide little revenue but are demanding. What can a company do about these? One option is to shift the *delinquents'* customers to products that are likely to be less difficult to operate or less complicated. Vodaphone's *Pay as you Talk* phone service does this by providing contracts to less well-off customers who prepay for the phone's use. Banks' high charges on unnegotiated overdrafts are a way of doing this. If these actions cause the unprofitable customer to defect, so be it. In fact, the company might benefit by *encouraging* these unprofitable customers to switch to competition.[19]

The Ultimate Test: Customer Profitability

Ultimately, marketing is the art of attracting and keeping *profitable customers*. Yet, companies often discover that between 20 and 40 per cent of their customers are unprofitable. Further, many companies report that their most profitable customers are not their largest customers, but their mid-size customers. The largest customers demand greater service and receive the deepest discounts, thereby reducing the company's profit level. The smallest customers pay full price and receive less service, but the costs of transacting with small customers reduce their profitability. In many cases, mid-size customers that pay close to full price and receive good service are the most profitable. This helps to explain why many large firms that once targeted only large customers are now invading the middle market.

A company should not try to pursue and satisfy every customer. For example, if business customers of Courtyard (Marriott's less expensive motel) start asking for Marriott-level business services, Courtyard should say no. Providing such service would only confuse the respective positionings of the Marriott and Courtyard systems. Similarly, airlines differentiate between tourist- and business-class flyers, and Visa offers more services to gold-card users.

> Some organizations ... try to do anything and everything customers suggest. ... Yet, while customers often make many good suggestions, they also suggest many courses of action that are unactionable or unprofitable. Randomly following these suggestions is fundamentally different from market-focus – making a disciplined choice of which customers to serve and which specific combination of benefits and price to deliver to them (and which to deny them).[20]

What makes a customer profitable? We define a *profitable customer* as a person, household or company whose revenues over time exceed, by an acceptable amount, the company's costs of attracting, selling and servicing that customer. Note that the definition emphasizes lifetime revenues and costs, not profit from a single transaction. Here are some dramatic illustrations of **customer lifetime value**:

customer lifetime value
The amount by which revenues from a given customer over time will exceed the company's costs of attracting, selling and servicing that customer.

> Stew Leonard, who operates a highly profitable single-store supermarket, says that he sees $50,000 flying out of his store every time he sees a sulking customer. Why? Because his average customer spends about $100 a week, shops 50 weeks a year and remains in the area for about 10 years. If this customer has an unhappy experience and switches to another supermarket, Stew Leonard has lost $50,000 in revenue. The loss can be much greater if the disappointed customer shares the bad experience with other customers and causes them to defect.

> Tom Peters, noted author of several books on managerial excellence, runs a business that spends $1,500 a month on Federal Express service. His company spends this amount 12 months a year and expects to remain in business for at least another 10 years. Therefore, he expects to spend more than $180,000 on future Federal Express service. If Federal Express makes a 10 per cent profit margin, Peters' lifetime business will contribute $18,000 to Federal Express's profits. Federal Express risks all of this profit if Peters receives poor service from a Federal Express driver or if a competitor offers better service.

Few companies actively measure individual customer value and profitability. For example, banks claim that this is hard to do because customers use different banking services and transactions are logged in different departments. However, banks that have managed to link customer transactions and measure customer profitability have been appalled by how many unprofitable customers they find. Some banks report losing money on over 45 per cent of their retail customers. It

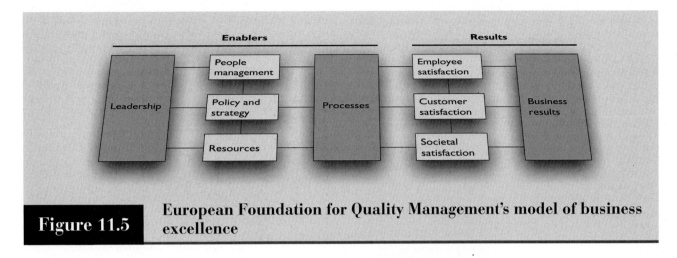

| **Figure 11.5** | **European Foundation for Quality Management's model of business excellence** |

is not surprising that many banks now charge fees for services that they once supplied free.

Implementing Total Quality Marketing

Customer satisfaction and company profitability are linked closely to product and service quality. Higher levels of quality result in greater customer satisfaction, while at the same time supporting higher prices and often lower costs. Therefore, *quality improvement programmes* normally increase profitability. The Profit Impact of Marketing Strategies studies show similarly high correlations between relative product quality and profitability for Europe and the United States (see Figure 11.6).[21]

The task of improving product and service quality should be a company's top priority. Much of the striking global successes of Japanese companies resulted from their building exceptional quality into their products. Most customers will no longer tolerate poor or average quality. Companies today have no choice but to adopt total quality management if they want to stay in the race, let alone be profitable. According to GE's chairman, John F. Welch, Jr: 'Quality is our best assurance of customer allegiance, our strongest defence against foreign competition and the only path to sustained growth and earnings.'[22]

Quality has been variously defined as 'fitness for use', 'conformance to requirements' and 'freedom from variation'.[23] The American Society for Quality Control defines **quality** as the totality of features and characteristics of a product or service that bear on its ability to satisfy stated or implied needs. This is clearly a customer-centred definition of quality. It suggests that a company has delivered quality whenever its product and service meets or exceeds customers' needs, requirements and expectations. A company that satisfies most of its customers' needs most of the time is a quality company.

It is important to distinguish between performance quality and conformance quality. *Performance quality* refers to the *level* at which a product performs its functions. Compare two German cars: Volkswagen, Europe's leading volume car maker, and Mercedes, Europe's leading luxury car maker. A Mercedes provides higher performance quality than a VW: it has a smoother ride, handles better and lasts longer. It is more expensive and sells to a market with higher means and requirements. *Conformance quality* refers to freedom from defects and the

quality
The totality of features and characteristics of a product or service that bear on its ability to satisfy stated or implied needs.

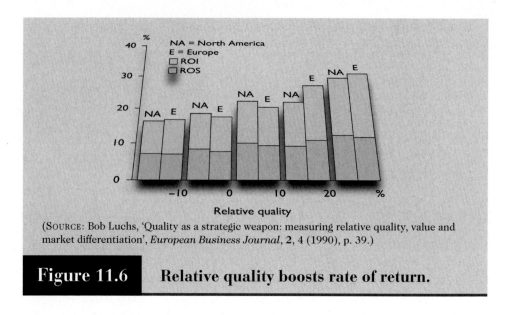

(SOURCE: Bob Luchs, 'Quality as a strategic weapon: measuring relative quality, value and market differentiation', *European Business Journal*, **2**, 4 (1990), p. 39.)

Figure 11.6 Relative quality boosts rate of return.

consistency with which a product delivers a specified level of performance. Both a Mercedes and a VW could offer equivalent conformance quality to their respective markets, since each consistently delivers what its market expects. A DM50,000 car that meets all of its requirements is a quality car; so is a DM15,000 car that meets all of its requirements. However, if the Mercedes handles badly or if the VW gives poor fuel efficiency, then both cars have failed to deliver quality, and customer satisfaction suffers accordingly.

The European Foundation for Quality Management's excellence model, in Figure 11.5, is used widely across Europe. Marketing shares with other functions the responsibility for striving for the highest quality of a company, product or service. Marketing's commitment to the whole process needs to be particularly strong because of the central role of customer satisfaction to both marketing and **total quality management (TQM)**. Within a quality-centre company, marketing management has two types of responsibility. First, marketing management participates in formulating the *strategies and policies* that direct *resources* and strive for quality excellence. Secondly, marketing has to deliver marketing quality alongside product quality. It must perform each marketing activity to consistently high standards: marketing research, sales training, advertising, customer services and others. Much damage can be done to customer satisfaction with an excellent product if it is oversold or is 'supported' by advertising that builds unrealistic expectations.

Within quality programmes, marketing has several distinct roles. Firstly, marketing has responsibility for correctly identifying customers' needs and wants, and for communicating them correctly to aid product design and to schedule production. Second, marketing has to ensure that customers' orders are filled correctly and on time, and must check to see that customers receive proper instruction, training and technical assistance in the use of their product. Thirdly, marketers must stay in touch with customers after the sale, to make sure that they remain satisfied. Finally, marketers must gather and convey customers' ideas for product and service improvement back to the company.

TQM has played an important role in educating businesses that quality is more than products and services being well produced, but is about what marketing has been saying all the time: *customer satisfaction*. At the same time, TQM extends marketing's view to realize that the acquisition, retention and satisfaction of good employees is central to the acquisition, retention and satisfaction of customers.[24]

total quality management (TQM)
Programmes designed to continuously improve the quality of product, service and marketing processes.

Total quality is the key to creating customer value and satisfaction. Total quality is everyone's job, just as marketing is everyone's job:

> Marketers who don't learn the language of quality improvement, manufacturing and operations will become as obsolete as buggy whips. The days of functional marketing are gone. We can no longer afford to think of ourselves as market researchers, advertising people, direct marketers, marketing strategists – we have to think of ourselves as customer satisfiers – customer advocates focused on whole processes.[25]

With TQM's commonality with marketing's aims, it is ironic that one study found that marketing people were responsible for more customer complaints than any other department (35 per cent). Marketing mistakes included cases in which the sales force ordered special product features for customers, but failed to notify manufacturing of the changes; in which incorrect order processing resulted in the wrong product being made and shipped; and in which customer complaints were not properly handled.[26]

The implication here is that marketers must spend time and effort not only to improve external marketing, but also to improve internal marketing. Marketers must be the customer's watchdog or guardian, complaining loudly for the customer when the product or the service is not right. Marketers must constantly uphold the standard of 'giving the customer the best solution'. Marketing Highlight 11.4 presents some important conclusions about total quality marketing strategy.

Pursuing a Total Quality Marketing Strategy

Marketing Highlight 11.4

Design to Distribution (D2D), winner of the 1994 European Quality Award, attributes its improved performance to total quality management (TQM). 'Quality management satisfies customers, reduces costs and motivates people,' says Alistair Kelly, D2D's managing director. TQM helped D2D, a contract electronics manufacturer, increase labour productivity by 300 per cent and save £2 million a year by 'getting things right first time'.

Not long ago, many companies were complacent about product and service quality. Then they awoke to the realization that the Japanese were gaining market domination by offering products of superior design and quality. The first to be hurt were makers of overexpensive shabby goods, but even top manufacturers have now learned that what was the best is no longer good enough.

Leica, now owned by the Swiss Anova company, invented the 35 mm camera and still makes cameras renowned for their beautifully engineered bodies with lenses giving razor-sharp pictures. At DM4,000 their M6 is still a great status symbol, but now nearly all professional photographers use Japanese-made Canon, Nikon, Minolta or the like. Leica now has a technology co-operation agreement with Minolta that has helped it produce the Leica Mini, which sells for about DM400.

The Japanese took early to TQM. In 1947 General Douglas MacArthur invited W. Edwards Deming to Japan to help assess their postwar industrial needs. Deming was no ordinary management consultant; he was the man who invented quality. To the Japanese he was a prophet whom they invited back many times to lecture on quality and statistical theory. Meanwhile the United States and Europe ignored him. In 1951 the Japanese created the Deming Prize, an award that symbolized Japanese industry's commitment to Deming's quality ideals. Honda, Nissan, Toyota, Nippondenso, Tanabe Seiyaku and Matsushita all won that prize more than 30 years ago. Consumers around the world flocked to buy high-quality Japanese products, leaving many American and European firms trying to catch up.

TQM recognizes the following premises:

1. *Quality is in the eyes of the customer.* Quality must begin with customer needs and end with customer perceptions. As Motorola's vice-president of quality suggests: 'Quality has to do something for the customer … Beauty is in the eye of the beholder. If [a product] does not work the way that the user needs it to work, the defect is as big to the user as if it doesn't work the way the designer planned it. Our definition of a defect is, "if the customer doesn't like it, it's a defect".' Thus the fundamental aim of today's quality movement has now become 'total customer satisfaction'. Quality improvements are meaningful only when perceived by customers. British Telecom's first quality programme launched in the late 1980s became bogged down in its quality processes and bureaucracy. It failed to focus its efforts on customers.

2. *Quality must reflect not just in the company's products, but in every company activity.* 'Quality is a way of life,' declares Jan Timmer, president of Philips Electronics. 'Total quality is not a passing business fad but embedded in the permanent principles of human philosophy,' says Louis Schweitzer, président directeur général of Renault.

3. *Quality requires total employee commitment.* Quality comes only from companies whose employees commit to quality and who have the motivation and training to deliver it. Successful companies remove the barriers between departments. Their employees work as a team to carry out core business processes and to create desired outcomes. Employees work to satisfy their internal customers as well as external customers.

4. *Quality requires high-quality partners.* Quality comes only from companies whose value chain partners also deliver quality. Therefore, a quality-driven company must find and align itself with high-quality suppliers and distributors. 'Unless suppliers are in tune with quality demands of their customers, they will not be able to meet their demands,' says Clive Capp of Howard UK.

5. *A quality programme cannot save a poor product.* The Pontiac Fiero launched a quality programme, but because the car didn't have a performance engine to support its performance image, the quality programme did not save the car. A quality drive cannot compensate for product deficiencies.

6. *Quality can always improve.* The best companies believe in the Japanese idea of *kaizen*: continuous improvement of everything by everyone. The best way to improve quality is to benchmark the company's performance against the 'best-of-class' competitors or the best performers in other industries, striving to equal or even surpass them. For example, Alcoa measured the best-of-class competitors and then set a goal of closing the gap by 80 per cent within two years.

7. *Quality improvement sometimes requires quantum leaps.* Although the company should strive for continuous quality improvement, it must at times seek a quantum quality improvement. Companies can sometimes obtain small improvements by working harder. But large improvements call for fresh solutions and for working smarter. For example, John Young of Hewlett-Packard did not ask for a 10 per cent reduction in defects, he asked for a tenfold reduction and got it.

8. *Quality does not cost more.* Philip Crosby argues that 'quality is free'. Managers once argued that achieving more quality would cost more and slow down production. But improving quality involves learning ways to 'do things right the first time'. Quality is not *inspected* in – it is *designed* in. Doing things right the first time reduces the costs of salvage, repair and redesign, not to mention losses in customer goodwill. Motorola claims that its quality drive has saved $700 million in manufacturing costs during the last five years.

9. *Quality is necessary but may not be sufficient.* Improving a company's quality is necessary to meet the needs of more demanding buyers. At

the same time, higher quality may not ensure a winning advantage, especially as all competitors increase their quality to approximately the same extent. For example, Singapore Airlines enjoyed a reputation as the world's best airline. However, competing airlines have attracted larger shares of passengers recently by narrowing the perceived gap between their service quality and Singapore's service quality.

10. *Quality needs long-term commitment.* It is not a quick fix. A 'blitz approach' can lead to disaster, says quality consultant John Oakland. 'You raise employees' expectations but they are invariably not given the means of doing things differently ... People talk the language of quality, but the capability of the organization doesn't live up to the language; it's still using lousy systems and materials.'

In recent years, some European and US firms have struggled to close the quality gap between them and the Japanese. About ten years ago Motorola, Texas Instruments and Harley Davidson took up TQM. Rank Xerox, one of the earliest European adherents, started some years later. Many started their TQM programmes to compete on a global and domestic basis against the Japanese. Europe's acceptance of TQM remains well behind that of the United States and Japan. A survey by the Brussels-based European Foundation for Quality Management (EFQM) found that only 30 per cent of European companies claim to have adopted TQM compared with 55 per cent in the United States and 53 per cent in Asia.

The European Commission worries about this quality shortfall and its failure to reach some European countries, such as Germany, where it has made little impact. 'In Germany where quality has always been established, TQM is not as easily accepted as in many other countries,' says Geert de Raad, EFQM's general secretary. Such complacency is dangerous. An IBM–London Business School study shows that only 1 in 50 manufacturers in four European countries were world class, although three-quarters believed that they could compete with their best international rivals. The United Kingdom had the most 'punchbags' – weak on both practice and performance – while Finland had no world-class manufacturers at all. Germany had most (2.9 per cent) world-class manufacturers, but also large numbers that wrongly thought they were. Many had not realized that total quality and customer service are no longer a source of sustainable advantage, but merely a qualification for competing.

SOURCES: Quotes from Lois Therrien, 'Motorola and NEC: going for glory', *Business Week*, special issue on quality (1991), pp. 60–1; and Simon Holberton, 'An idea whose time has not only come but will prevail', *Financial Times* (20 March 1991), p. 10. See also David A. Garvin, 'Competing on eight dimensions of quality', *Harvard Business Review* (November–December 1987), p. 109; Robert Jacobson and David A. Aaker, 'The strategic role of product quality', *Journal of Marketing* (October 1987), pp. 31–44; Frank Rose, 'Now quality means service too', *Fortune* (22 April 1992), pp. 97–108; Frederick Stüdemann, 'Leica develops a sharper focus', *The European* (30 September–6 October 1994), p. 32; Tom Lloyd, 'How Mr Quality made his mark', *The European* (11–17 February 1994), p. 20; 'The cracks in quality', *The Economist* (18 April 1992), pp. 85–6; Vanessa Houlder, 'Satisfaction guaranteed' and 'Two steps forward, one step back', *Financial Times* (23 October 1994), p. 10; Jessica Berry, 'Scathing survey blames inertia for poor manufacturing performance', *The European* (25 November–1 December 1994), p. 28; Christopher Lorenz, '"World-class" delusion of multinationals', *Financial Times* (2 December 1994), p. 11; IBM, *Made in Europe* (London: IBM UK, 1994).

Summary

Today's customers face a growing range of choices in the products and services they can buy. They base their choices on their perceptions of *quality*, *value* and *service*. Companies need to understand the determinants of *customer value* and *satisfaction*. *Customer delivered value* is the difference between *total customer value* and *total customer cost*. Customers will normally choose the offer that maximizes their delivered value.

Customer satisfaction is the outcome felt by buyers who have experienced a company performance that has fulfilled expectations. Customers are satisfied when their expectations are met and delighted when their expectations are exceeded. Satisfied customers remain loyal longer, buy more, are less price sensitive and talk favourably about the company.

To create customer satisfaction, companies must manage their own *value chains* and the entire *value delivery system* in a customer-centred way. The company's goal is not only to get customers, but, even more importantly, to retain customers. *Customer relationship marketing* provides the key to retaining customers and involves building financial and social benefits as well as structural ties to customers. Companies must decide the level at which they want to build relationships with different market segments and individual customers, from such levels as basic, reactive, accountable and proactive to full partnership. Which is best depends on a customer's lifetime value relative to the costs required to attract and retain that customer.

Total quality management has become a leading approach to providing customer satisfaction and company profitability. Companies must understand how their customers perceive quality and how much quality they expect. Companies must then do a better job of meeting consumer quality expectations than their competitors do. Delivering quality requires total management and employee commitment as well as measurement and reward systems. Marketers play an especially critical role in their company's drive towards higher quality.

Key Terms

Customer-centred company 471
Customer delivered value 472
Customer lifetime value 490
Customer value delivery system 481

Quality 491
Relationship marketing 483
Total customer cost 473
Total customer value 473

Total quality management (TQM) 492
Value chain 480

Discussing the Issues

1. Describe a situation in which you became a 'lost customer'. Did you drop the purchase because of poor product quality, poor service quality or both? What should the firm do to 'recapture' lost customers?

2. Recall a purchase experience in which the sales assistant or sales representative went beyond the normal effort and 'gave his/her all' to produce the utmost in quality. What impact did the noticeable effort have on the purchase outcome? (Did you buy the product as a result? If it was a frequently purchased product, did you repeatedly buy the product from the same outlet or company?) Give reasons for your answer.

3. Total quality management is an important approach to providing customer satisfaction and company profits.

How might total quality be managed for the following product and service offerings: (a) a packaged food product; (b) a restaurant meal; (c) a new car; (d) a family holiday; (e) a university education?

4. Who should define quality standards: research and development, design, engineering, operations/production or marketing? Give reasons for your choice.

5. Thinking of a service provided by a not-for-profit organization, propose some meaningful ways to measure quality that could be used in efforts to improve the service.

6. Just-in-time inventory management makes suppliers responsible for delivering parts in exact quantities at

happened to Germany's Klöckner-Werke, a high-cost, undersized steel and engineering group. The moral? Do not play in the murky middle of the road.

SOURCES: 'Is there room for Volkswagen?', *The Economist* (28 August 1993), p. 55; *The Financial Times – FT500* (10 February 1993); and portions adapted from Kathleen Deveny, 'Middle-price brands come under siege', *Wall Street Journal* (2 April 1990), pp. B1, B7.

and competing products obsolete. It is open to new ideas, relentlessly pursues new solutions, and works to reduce cycle times so that it can get new products to market quickly. It serves customers who want state-of-the-art products and services, regardless of the costs in terms of price or inconvenience. Examples include Nokia, Tefal and Nike.

Some companies successfully pursue more than one value discipline at the same time. For example, Federal Express excels at both operational excellence and customer intimacy in the US. However, such companies are rare – few firms can be the best at more than one of these disciplines. By trying to be *good at all* of the value disciplines, a company usually ends up being *best at none*.

Treacy and Wiersema have found that leading companies focus on and excel at a single value discipline, while meeting industry standards on the other two. They design their entire value delivery system to support single-mindedly the chosen discipline. For example, Benetton knows that customer intimacy and product leadership are important. Compared with other clothes shops, it offers good customer service and an excellent product assortment. Still, it offers less customer service and less depth in its product assortment than some other retailers do. Instead, it focuses obsessively on operational excellence – on reducing costs and streamlining its order-to-delivery process in order to make it convenient for customers to buy just the right products at the lowest prices.

Classifying competitive strategies as value disciplines is appealing. It defines marketing strategy in terms of the single-minded pursuit of delivering superior value to customers. It recognizes that management must align every aspect of the company with the chosen value discipline – from its culture, to its organization structure, to its operating and management systems and processes.

Competitive Moves

Businesses maintain their position in the marketplace by making *competitive moves* to attack competitors or defend themselves against competitive threats. These moves change with the role that firms play in the target market – that of leading, challenging, following or niching. Suppose that an industry contains the firms shown in Figure 12.3. Some 40 per cent of the market is in the hands of the **market leader**, the firm with the largest market share. Another 30 per cent is in the hands of a **market challenger**, a runner-up that is fighting hard to increase its market share. Another 20 per cent is in the hands of a **market follower**, another runner-up that wants to hold its share without rocking the boat. The remaining 10 per cent is in the hands of **market nichers**, firms that serve small segments not being pursued by other firms.

We now look at specific marketing strategies that are available to market leaders, challengers, followers and nichers. In the sections that follow, you should remember that the classifications of competitive positions often apply not to a

market leader
The firm in an industry with the largest market share; it usually leads other firms in price changes, new product introductions, distribution coverage and promotion spending.

market challenger
A runner-up firm in an industry that is fighting hard to increase its market share.

market follower
A runner-up firm in an industry that wants to hold its share without rocking the boat.

market nicher
A firm in an industry that serves small segments that the other firms overlook or ignore.

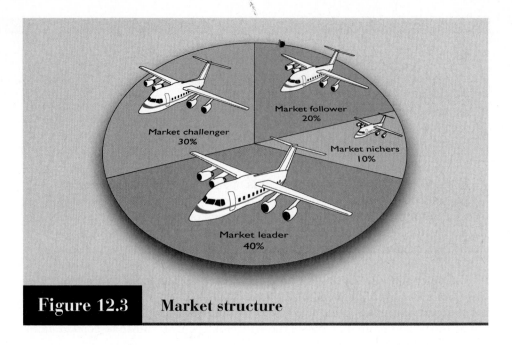

| **Figure 12.3** | **Market structure** |

whole company, but only to its position in a specific industry. For example, large and diversified companies such as P & G, Unilever, Nestlé, Procordia or Société Générale de Belgique – or their individual businesses, divisions or products – might be leaders in some markets and nichers in others. For example, Procter & Gamble leads in dishwashing and laundry detergents, disposable nappies and shampoo, but it is a challenger to Unilever in hand soaps. Companies' competitive strengths also vary geographically. Buying Alpo from Grand Metropolitan in 1994 made Nestlé the challenger in the US pet-foods market behind Ralston Purina's 18 per cent share. However, in the submarket for US canned cat food, Nestlé has a commanding 39 per cent share. By contrast, in the fragmented European pet-foods market, Nestlé Friskies languishes in fourth place behind Mars' Pedigree (47 per cent), Dalgety and Quaker. However, even with that low base, Nestlé's Go Cat is Europe's top-selling dry cat food.[13]

Market-Leader Strategies

Most industries contain an acknowledged market leader. The leader has the largest market share and usually leads the other firms in price changes, new product introductions, distribution coverage and promotion spending. The leader may or may not be admired, but other firms concede its dominance. The leader is a focal point for competitors, a company to challenge, imitate or avoid. Some of the best-known market leaders are Boeing (airliners), Nestlé (food), Microsoft (software), L'Oréal (cosmetics), Royal Dutch/Shell (oil), McDonald's (fast food) and De Beer (diamonds).

A leading firm's life is not easy. It must maintain a constant watch. Other firms keep challenging its strengths or trying to take advantage of its weaknesses. The market leader can easily miss a turn in the market and plunge into second or third place. A product innovation may come along and hurt the leader – as when Tylenol's non-aspirin painkiller took the lead from Bayer Aspirin or when P & G's Tide, the first synthetic laundry detergent, beat Unilever's leading brands. Sometimes leading firms grow fat and slow, losing out against new and more energetic rivals – Xerox's share of the world copier market fell from over 80 per cent to

The London International Group defend their leading position focusing on the growth markets they dominate.

less than 35 per cent in just five years when Fuji and Canon challenged it with cheaper and more reliable copiers.

Leading firms want to remain no. 1. This calls for action on four fronts. First, the firm must find ways to expand total demand. Second, the firm can try to expand its market share further, even if market size remains constant. Third, a company can retain its strength by reducing its costs. Fourthly, the firm must protect its current market share through good defensive and offensive actions (Figure 12.4).

● *Expanding the Total Market*

The leading firm normally gains the most when the total market expands. If people take more pictures, then as the market leader, Kodak stands to gain the most. If Kodak can persuade more people to take pictures, or to take pictures on more occasions, or to take more pictures on each occasion, it will benefit greatly. Generally, the market leader should look for new users, new uses and more usage of its products.

NEW USERS. Every product class can attract buyers who are still unaware of the product, or who are resisting it because of its price or its lack of certain features. A seller can usually find new users in many places. For example, L'Oréal might find new fragrance users in its current markets by convincing women who do not use expensive fragrance to try it. Or it might find users in new demographic segments: for instance, men's fragrances are currently a small but fast-growing market. Or it might expand into new geographic segments, perhaps by selling its fragrances to the new wealthy in eastern Europe.

Johnson's Baby Shampoo provides a classic example of developing new users. When the baby boom had passed and the birth rate slowed down, the company grew concerned about future sales growth. J & J's marketers noticed that other

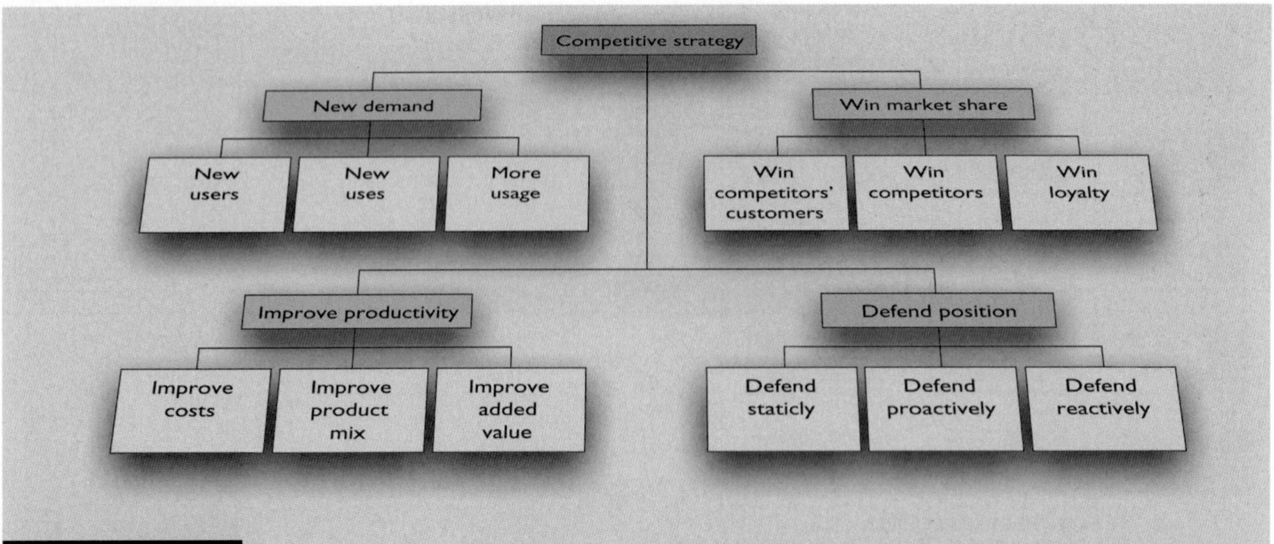

Figure 12.4 **Market leader strategies**

family members sometimes used the baby shampoo for their own hair. Management developed an advertising campaign aimed at adults. In a short time, Johnson's Baby Shampoo became a leading brand in the total shampoo market.

NEW USES. The marketer can expand markets by discovering and promoting new uses for the product. DuPont's nylon is an example of new-use expansion. Every time nylon became a mature product, some new use appeared. Nylon was first used as a fibre for parachutes; then for women's stockings; later as a leading material in shirts and blouses; and still later in vehicle tyres, upholstery and carpeting. Another example of new-use expansion is Arm & Hammer baking soda. Its sales had flattened after 125 years. Then the company discovered that consumers were using baking soda as a refrigerator deodorizer. It launched a heavy advertising and publicity campaign focusing on this use and persuaded consumers to place an open box of baking soda in their refrigerators and to replace it every few months.

MORE USAGE. A third market expansion strategy is to persuade people to use the product more often or to use more per occasion. Campbell encourages people to consume more of its soup by running ads using it as an ingredient in recipes in women's magazines. P & G advises users that its Head & Shoulders shampoo is more effective with two applications instead of one per hair wash.

The Michelin Tyre Company found a creative way to increase usage per occasion. It wanted French car owners to drive more miles per year, resulting in more tyre replacement. Michelin began rating French restaurants on a three-star system and publishing them in its Red Guides. It reported that many of the best restaurants were in the south of France, leading many Parisians to take weekend drives south. Michelin also publishes its Green Guide containing maps and graded sights to encourage additional travel.

● *Expanding Market Share*

Market leaders can also grow by increasing their market shares further. In many markets, small market-share increases mean very large sales increases. For

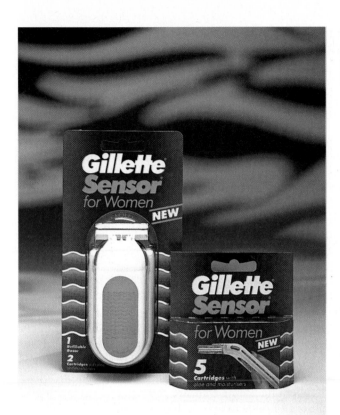

Gillette is building on its strength in the market place by moving into the women's market.

example, in the coffee market, a 1 per cent increase in market share is worth $48 million; in soft drinks, $440 million! No wonder normal competition turns into marketing warfare in such markets. Many studies have found that profitability rises with increasing market share.[14] Businesses with very large relative market shares averaged substantially higher returns on investment. Because of these findings, many companies have sought expanded market shares to improve profitability. General Electric, for example, declared that it wants to be at least no. 1 or 2 in each of its markets or else get out. GE shed its computer, air-conditioning, small appliances and television businesses because it could not achieve a top-dog position in these industries. Nestlé intends to hold its position as the world's leading food company, although France's Danone also has designs on that spot. Both have been acquiring businesses, Nestlé buying Perrier and Rowntree among others, while Danone own Jacobs, Kronenbourg, Amora, Lee & Perrins and HP sauce.[15] There are three main ways by which these firms can further increase their leading position.

WIN CUSTOMERS. Winning competitors' customers is rarely easy. Sales promotions and price reductions can produce increased share quickly, but such gains are made at the expense of profitability and disappear once the promotion ends. Exceptions to this are price fights stimulated by market leaders with more resources than competitors. The financial strength of Rupert Murdoch's global media empire has allowed him to gain share in newspaper and satellite TV markets by pricing very aggressively over an extended period. More often market share gains are achieved by long-term investment in quality, innovation or brand building. For instance, Mercedes C class model (replacing the ageing 190) helped the company increase its sales by 23 per cent. Sales were up 40 per cent in western Europe (excluding Germany), 34 per cent in the United States and 30 per cent in

Japan. In Germany the 38 per cent growth gave a 2 per cent rise in market share. The company hopes to repeat that success with the much smaller A class.

WIN COMPETITORS.   Leading mature companies often find it easier to buy competitors rather than win their customers. Sometimes this can launch the company into new sectors, as did BMW's purchase of the Rover Group with its small cars and cross-country vehicles, or the £23 billion merger of GrandMet and Guinness to form Diageo, the world's largest alcoholic drinks company. More often it is a dash for firms to achieve scale by acquiring businesses similar to themselves. This is occurring among European insurers as Zurich bids for BAT Industries' insurance arm, Allianz AG and Credit Suisse battle it out over Assurance Générale de France, while Générale de France itself fights for Warms, and Prudential bids for Scottish Amicable.[16]

WIN LOYALTY.   Loyalty schemes have grown hugely in recent years. At their best these are attempts to build customer relationships based on the long-run customer satisfaction discussed in Chapter 11. In the UK grocery market Tesco challenged and overtook Sainsbury's as the market leader by introducing a hugely popular loyalty scheme while Sainsbury's was resisting the trend. Too often these schemes are sales promotions where the customer's loyalty is to the scheme, not the company using it. To have any lasting effects they must establish customer relationships that go beyond collecting points that are redeemable against a gift. Such schemes are easy to follow and once everyone has one, they impose a cost with little benefit.

Gaining increased market share will improve a company's profitability automatically. Much depends on its strategy for gaining increased market share. We see many high-share companies with low profitability and many low-share companies with high profitability. The cost of buying higher market share may far exceed the returns. Higher shares tend to produce higher profits only when unit costs fall with increased market share, or when the company's premium price covers the cost of supplying higher-quality goods.

In addition, many industries contain one or a few highly profitable large firms, several profitable and more focused firms, and a large number of medium-sized firms with poorer profit performance:

> The large firms ... tend to address the entire market, achieving cost advantages and high market share by realizing economies of scale. The small competitors reap high profits by focusing on some narrower segment of the business and by developing specialized approaches to production, marketing and distribution for that segment. Ironically, the medium-sized competitors ... often show the poorest profit performance. Trapped in a strategic 'No Man's Land', they are too large to reap the benefits of more focused competition, yet too small to benefit from the economies of scale that their larger competitors enjoy.[17]

Thus it appears that profitability increases as a business gains share relative to competitors in its *served market*. For example, BMW holds only a small share of the total car market, but it earns high profits because it is a high-share company in its luxury car segment. It achieved this high share in its served market because it does other things right, such as producing high quality, giving good service and holding down its costs.

● *Improving Productivity*

Market productivity means squeezing more profits out of the same volume of sales. The size advantage of market leaders can give them lower costs than the competition. Size itself is not sufficient to achieve low costs because this could be achieved by owning unrelated activities that impose extra costs, as Marketing Highlight 12.3 explains. The lowest costs often occur when a market leader, such as McDonald's, keeps its business simple. The buying and selling of subsidiary businesses often reflects businesses trying to gain strength by simplifying their activities. This explains the sales of Orangina, a soft-drinks business, to Coca-Cola for Ffr5 billion by the French drinks company Pernod Ricard. By this transaction Coca-Cola gains in efficiency and scale by having more soft drinks to sell globally. With the proceeds from the sale, Pernod Ricard aims to add more wines and spirits brands to its existing range, which includes Wild Turkey, Dubonnet, Havana Club and Jacob's Creek.[18]

IMPROVE COSTS. To remain competitive, market leaders fight continually to reduce costs. After facing difficulties in the early 1990s Mercedes used all the classical means of cutting costs:

● *Reduce capital cost.* Firms reduce their capital cost by doing less or doing things quickly. Just-in-time (JIT) methods mean firms have less capital tied up in raw materials, work in progress on the shop floor and finished goods. By accelerating its product development Mercedes will increase its market responsiveness and accumulated development costs. It will also reduce capital costs by doing less itself. Component manufacturers will provide more preassembled parts and a joint venture with a Romanian company will make car-interior parts.

● *Reduce fixed costs.* Mercedes acknowledges that Japan's manufacturers have an average 35 per cent cost advantage over their German competitors. Japan's lower capital cost and longer working hours explain only 10 per cent of the difference. Mercedes responded by cutting 18,000 jobs in 1993 to save DM5 billion. Forced redundancies are almost unknown in Germany, so the deduction is made by the 'social measures' of the non-replacement of people, early retirement and retraining.

● *Reduce variable cost.* The company is sticking to its unconventional production methods where 10–15 'group workers' operate round cradles holding body shells. Meanwhile its new car plant at Rastatt will pioneer methods of 'lean production', logistics, total quality and workforce management. Other plants will adopt the proven methods. Car design will also change. It will be quicker, and future cars will be designed to a target price, rather than making the best car and then pricing it. The lessons will be passed on to Mercedes' suppliers. In future they will work closer to Mercedes' research and development. The aim is to reduce the number of parts fitted at the works. The company is also changing its 'Made in Germany' policy, to produce where labour costs are lower. In 1996 it launched a US-made sports utility vehicle.

CHANGE PRODUCT MIX. The aim here is to sell more high-margin vehicles. Mercedes' current range does not cover luxury off-road vehicles, people movers or small sports cars – all growth areas commanding premium prices. Moving into these markets will reduce Mercedes' dependence on its 'lower-priced' models. While other tour operators were faced with discounting wars, Airtours profits rose by 29 per cent in 1997 thanks to its product mix moving away from the United

Kingdom's low-cost package holidays to concentrate on less price-sensitive customers in Canada, California and Scandinavian countries.

ADD VALUE.   Mercedes makes and sells cars, but its customers want prestige and transport. Mercedes can add value by offering long-term service contracts, leasing deals or other financial packages that make buying easier and less risky for customers. In the past Mercedes sold basic models that are poorly equipped by modern standards. Customers then paid extra to have a car custom made for them with the features they wanted. The 'Made in Germany' label that has served the company for so long is no longer enough to command a premium price. The aim is to maintain a price premium by the brand's strength and superior quality across a broad range of products. This contrasts with the Japanese, whose well-equipped luxury Lexus (Toyota), Acura (Honda) and Infiniti (Nissan) brands have tightly targeted small ranges.

● *Defending its Position*

While trying to expand total market size, the leading firm must also constantly protect its current business against competitor attacks. Shell must constantly guard against BP, Exxon and Elf Aquitane; Gillette against Bic; Kodak against Fuji; Boeing against Airbus; Nestlé against BSN.

What can the market leader do to protect its position? First, it must prevent or fix weaknesses that provide opportunities for competitors. It needs to keep its costs down and its prices in line with the value that the customers see in the brand. The leader should 'plug holes' so that competitors do not jump in. The best defence is a good offence and the best response is *continuous innovation*. The leader refuses to be content with the way things are and leads the industry in new products, customer services, distribution effectiveness and cost cutting. It keeps increasing its competitive effectiveness and value to customers. It takes the offensive, sets the pace and exploits competitors' weaknesses.

Increased competition in recent years has sparked management's interest in models of military warfare. Leader companies can protect their market positions with competitive strategies patterned after successful military defence strategies. Figure 12.5 shows six defence strategies that a market leader can use.[19]

POSITION DEFENCE.   The most basic defence is a position defence in which a company holds on to its position by building fortifications around its markets. Simply defending one's current position or products rarely works. Henry Ford tried it with his Model T and brought an enviably healthy Ford Motor Company to the brink of financial ruin. Even lasting brands such as Coca-Cola and Nescafé cannot supply all future growth and profitability for their companies. These brands must be improved and adapted to changing conditions and new brands developed. Coca-Cola today, in spite of being the world leader in soft drinks, is aggressively extending its beverage lines and has diversified into desalinization equipment and plastics.

FLANKING DEFENCE.   When trying to hold its overall position, the market leader should watch its weaker flanks closely. Smart competitors will normally attack the company's weaknesses. Thus the Japanese successfully entered the US small car market because local car makers left a gaping hole in that submarket. Using a flanking defence, the company carefully checks its flanks and protects the more vulnerable ones. In this way Nestlé's Nescafé and Gold Blend have the support of flanking brands Blend 37, Alta Rica and Cap Colombie. By acquiring Rover,

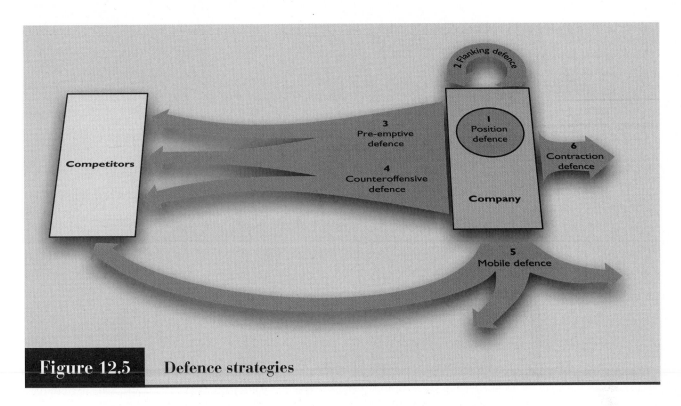

Figure 12.5 **Defence strategies**

BMW obtained access to small cars and cross-country vehicles and so defended its flanks in two growing sectors of the luxury car market where it was not active.

PRE-EMPTIVE DEFENCE. The leader can be proactive and launch a pre-emptive defence, striking competitors before they can move against the company. A pre-emptive defence assumes that an ounce of prevention is worth a pound of cure. Thus, when threatened in the mid-1980s by the impending entry of Japanese manufacturers into the US market, Cummins Engine slashed its prices by almost a third to save its no. 1 position in the $2 billion heavy-duty truck engine market. Today, Cummins claims a commanding 50 per cent market share in North America and not a single US-built tractor-trailer truck contains a Japanese engine.[20]

COUNTEROFFENSIVE DEFENCE. When attacked, despite its flanking or pre-emptive efforts, a market leader may have to be reactive and launch a counter-offensive defence. When Fuji attacked Kodak in the film market, Kodak counterattacked by dramatically increasing its promotion and introducing several innovative new film products. Mars' attack on the ice-cream market, using its brand extensions of Mars Bars, Snickers, Bounty and so on, created a new product class of ice-confectionery. Unilever's Walls ice-cream division, which is market leader in parts of Europe, had difficulty countering this because it had no confectionery brands to use in that way. It overcame the problem by developing brand extensions of Cadbury's products, a competitor of Mars, which has no ice-cream interests. In other parts of Europe, Nestlé is leader in the ice-cream market. With its strength in both confectionery and ice cream, it was able to launch brand extensions to match Mars.

Sometimes companies hold off for a while before countering. This may seem a dangerous game of 'wait and see', but there are often good reasons for not jumping in immediately. By waiting the company can understand more fully the competitor's attack and perhaps find a gap through which to launch a successful counteroffensive.

Airlines in the Star Alliance defend their position in the marketplace with their global network.

MOBILE DEFENCE. In a mobile defence a company is proactive in aggressively defending a current market position. The leader stretches to new markets that can serve as future bases for defence and attack. Through *market broadening*, the company shifts its focus from the current product to the broader underlying consumer need. For example, Armstrong Cork redefined its focus from 'floor covering' to 'decorative room covering' (including walls and ceilings) and expanded into related businesses balanced for growth and defence. *Market diversification* into unrelated industries is the other alternative for generating 'strategic depth'. When the tobacco companies like British American Tobacco (BAT) and Philip Morris faced growing curbs on cigarette smoking, they moved quickly into new consumer products industries. Philip Morris bought up General Foods and Kraft to become the world's largest consumer packaged goods company and BAT Industries is now one of Europe's largest firms.

CONTRACTION DEFENCE. Large companies sometimes find they can no longer defend all of their positions, since their resources are spread too thin and competitors are nibbling away on several fronts. So they react with a contracting defence (or strategic withdrawal). The company gives up weaker positions and concentrates its resources on stronger ones. During the 1970s, many companies diversified wildly and spread themselves too thin. In the slow-growth 1980s, ITT, Paribas, Suez, ENI, Gulf & Western, Quaker, Storehouse and dozens of other companies pruned their portfolios to concentrate resources on products and businesses in their core industries. These companies now serve fewer markets, but serve them much better.

The British motorcycle industry showed an extreme case of a contracting defence. Norton, Triumph, BSA, etc. once dominated the world motorcycle market. First challenged by the small bikes made by Honda, Yamaha and others, they contracted into making medium-sized (250 cc) to super-bikes. When the Japanese made 250 cc machines, the British market retreated from entry-level machines to concentrate on larger ones. Eventually only Triumph and Norton super-bikes remained as small, out-of-date specialist manufacturers facing the Japanese giants, and they did not last long. A successful contracting defence must be a retreat into a position of strength.

Market-Challenger Strategies

Firms that are second, third or lower in an industry are sometimes quite large, such as Colgate, Fiat, Toyota, Roche, Sandoz, HSBC (Hong Kong and Shanghai Banking Corp.), Carlsberg and PepsiCo. These runner-up firms can adopt one of two competitive strategies: they can attack the leader and other competitors in an aggressive bid for more market share (market challengers); or they can play along with competitors and not rock the boat (market followers). We now look at competitive strategies for market challengers.

● *Defining the Strategic Objective and the Competitor*

A market challenger must first define its strategic objective. Most market challengers seek to increase their profitability by increasing their market shares. The strategic objective chosen depends on who the competitor is. In most cases, the company can choose which competitors it will challenge.

The challenger can attack the market leader – a high-risk but potentially high-gain strategy that makes good sense if the leader is not serving the market well. To succeed with such an attack, a company must have some sustainable competitive advantage over the leader – a cost advantage leading to lower prices or the ability to provide better value at a premium price. In the construction

Airbus challenges the market leader, Boeing, by providing an ever-increasing range of aircraft.

Reebok confront their major competitor with a unique cushioning system.
Photography: Buggy G. Riphead

equipment industry, Komatsu successfully challenged Caterpillar by offering the same quality at much lower prices. Glaxo became Europe's leading drug company by aggressively marketing Zantac, its anti-ulcer drug.[21]

The challenger can avoid the leader and instead attack firms its size, or smaller local and regional firms. Many of these firms are underfinanced and will not be serving their customers well. Several of the large beer companies grew to their present size not by attacking large competitors, but by gobbling up small local or regional competitors.

Thus the challenger's strategic objective depends on which competitor it chooses to attack. If the company goes after the market leader, its objective may be to wrest a certain market share. Bic knows that it cannot topple Gillette in the razor market – it simply wants a larger share. Or the challenger's goal might be to take over market leadership. Compaq entered the personal computer market late, as a challenger, but quickly became the market leader. If the company goes after a small local company, its objective may be to put that company out of business. The important point remains: the company must choose its opponents carefully and have a clearly defined and attainable objective.

● *Choosing an Attack Strategy*

How can the market challenger best attack the chosen competitor and achieve its strategic objectives? Figure 12.6 shows five possible attack strategies.

FRONTAL ATTACK. In a full frontal attack, the challenger matches the competitor's product, advertising, price and distribution efforts. It attacks the competitor's strengths rather than its weaknesses. The outcome depends on who has the greater strength and endurance. Even great size and strength may not be enough to challenge a firmly entrenched and resourceful competitor successfully.

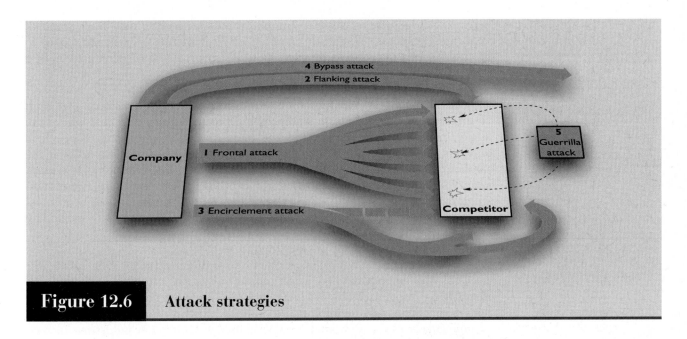

| **Figure 12.6** | **Attack strategies** |

Unilever has twice the world-wide sales of P & G and five times the sales of Colgate-Palmolive, but its American subsidiary trails P & G by a wide margin in the United States. Unilever launched a full frontal assault against P & G in the detergent market while Unilever's Wisk was already the leading liquid detergent. In quick succession, it added a barrage of new products – Sunlight dishwashing detergent, Snuggle fabric softener, Surf laundry powder – and backed them with aggressive promotion and distribution efforts. P & G spent heavily to defend its brands and held on to most of its business. It counterattacked with Liquid Tide, which came from nowhere in just 17 months to run neck-and-neck with Wisk. Unilever did gain market share, but most of it came from smaller competitors.[22]

If the market challenger has fewer resources than the competitor, a frontal attack makes little sense.

FLANKING ATTACK.   Rather than attacking head on, the challenger can launch a flanking attack. The competitor often concentrates its resources to protect its strongest positions, but it usually has some weaker flanks. By attacking these weak spots, the challenger can concentrate its strength against the competitor's weakness. Flank attacks make good sense when the company has fewer resources than the competitor.

When Airbus Industries started making airliners it was up against Boeing, a company that dominates the industry. Lockheed and McDonnell Douglas had once challenged Boeing as plane makers, but Lockheed had withdrawn from the industry and McDonnell Douglas was reduced to making derivatives of its old aircraft. Airbus's first move was to develop the A300 with range and payload performance different from Boeing's established 727, 737 and 747 range.

Another flanking strategy is to find gaps that are not being filled by the industry's products, fill them and develop them into strong segments. European and Japanese car makers do not try to compete with American car makers by producing large, flashy, gas-guzzling contraptions. Instead they recognized an unserved consumer segment that wanted small, fuel-efficient cars and moved to fill this hole. To their satisfaction and Detroit's surprise, the segment grew to be a large part of the market.

ENCIRCLEMENT ATTACK.   An encirclement attack involves attacking from all directions, so that the competitor must protect its front, sides and rear at the same time. The encirclement strategy makes sense when the challenger has superior resources and believes that it can break the competitor's hold on the market quickly. An example is Seiko's attack on the watch market. For several years, Seiko has been gaining distribution in every big watch outlet and over-whelming competitors with its variety of constantly changing models. In most markets Seiko offers about 400 models, but its marketing strength is backed by the 2,300 models it makes and sells worldwide.

BYPASS ATTACK.   A bypass attack is an indirect strategy. The challenger bypasses the competitor and targets easier markets. The bypass can involve diversifying into unrelated products, moving into new geographic markets or leapfrogging into new technologies to replace existing products. Technological leapfrogging is a bypass strategy used often in high-technology industries. Instead of copying the competitor's product and mounting a costly frontal attack, the challenger patiently develops the next technology. When satisfied with its superiority, it launches an attack where it has an advantage. Thus Minolta toppled Canon from the lead in the 35-mm SLR camera market when it introduced its technologically advanced auto-focusing Maxxum camera. Canon's market share dropped towards 20 per cent, while Minolta's zoomed passed 30 per cent. It took Canon three years to introduce a matching technology.[23]

GUERRILLA ATTACK.   A guerrilla attack is another option available to market challengers, especially smaller or poorly financed ones:

> When entrepreneur Freddie Laker frontally attacked the established airlines (then BOAC and TWA) by offering cheap transatlantic flights, they fought back and bankrupted him. Now TWA has all but disappeared and British Airways is facing Virgin Atlantic run by a much wilier entrepreneur, Richard Branson. He makes guerrilla attacks on his much larger competitors. In these attacks the agile challenger typically makes small, periodic attacks to harass and demoralize the competitor, hoping eventually to establish permanent footholds. It might use selective price cuts, novel products, executive raids, intense promotional outbursts or assorted legal actions. Virgin has been successful so far and taken 22 per cent of the London to New York market. It is also expanding quickly using franchising, an approach new to the airline industry.[24]

Normally, guerrilla actions are by smaller firms against larger ones. The smaller firms need to be aware, however, that continuous guerrilla campaigns can be expensive and must eventually be followed by a stronger attack if the challenger wishes to 'beat' the competitor.

Market-Follower Strategies

Not all runner-up companies will challenge the market leader. The effort to draw away the leader's customers is never taken lightly by the leader. If the challenger's

Case 12

BMW: Putting the 'Brrrrum' Back in Brum

THE 63-YEAR-OLD WIDOW scorns expensive jewellery, drinks mineral water and tea, gives no parties and rarely attends them. Outside her family she has few friends and, like many other middle-class German women, she takes her car when she goes shopping. However, unlike most shoppers, her car is a BMW 525. She also has a Mercedes 500 and a chauffeur-driven 12-cylinder 7 series BMW. She is Mrs Joanna Brauhn, one of Europe's richest people, whose DM7 billion business interests stretch from baby food to batteries. She also owns Bayerische Motorenwerke (Bavarian Motor Works), better known as BMW.

After a decade of success, BMW faced problems in the early 1990s. Between 1992 and 1993 European car sales dropped 16 per cent and BMW did worse than average. Its archrival, Mercedes, and the Japanese car makers had also lost, but not as badly as BMW. Only one of the world's car makers had gained over that period – Rover's sales grew by 9 per cent in 1993.

Under Attack

BMW was squeezed on several fronts. Recessions in Europe, Japan and the United States brought car sales down in all the world's major markets. Like Audi, Mercedes and Porsche, BMW's sales were also hit by Japan's aggressive and successful attack on the US luxury car market. In less than a year after launch, Honda's Acura range became America's top-selling luxury car, knocking Mercedes off the top spot. Toyota soon followed with its Lexus, a car that quickly became the benchmark for luxury and quality. As Japan's luxury car sales grew in the United States, German sales declined: BMW's US sales fell from 97,000 in 1986 to 57,000 in 1991. BMW could not follow two leading trends in the car market – the shift towards smaller cars, and to large off-the-road vehicles. In Europe, the number of wealthy working women was increasing rapidly and these were opting to buy fashionable super-minis or small sporty cars, not BMW's executive saloons. In addition, senior executives who had once bought 5 or 7 series BMWs increasingly opted for Range Rovers, Toyota Land Cruisers or other bulky giants. Volvo was similarly hit as wealthy parents opted for an off-the-road vehicle rather than a Volvo estate to transport their children.

Honda

Honda caused BMW particular problems. Japan's third largest car maker, behind Toyota and Nissan, Honda positioned itself close to BMW. Even before the launch of Acura, Honda had an excellent reputation for quality, reliability and being sporty. Honda cars also came well equipped and had many advanced features. BMW, like Mercedes, could have sophisticated accessories, such as microscopic air filters and parking aids, but these were rarely fitted to cars unless customers paid extra for them. Even radios are optional extras on most BMWs. Unlike BMW, Honda also made small sports cars and the Civic, an attractive small family car. One motoring correspondent said: 'If Mercedes ever made a small car, it would be like the Civic.'

In the early 1990s, Europe's 13 million cars a year industry had 2 million cars a year excess capacity, and too many manufacturers making too many models. This did not stop Toyota, Nissan and Honda building further new factories, mostly in England. By doing this the Japanese avoided their own country's high labour costs, gained access to the United Kingdom's flexible and inexpensive workforce, and avoided the European Union's Japanese car import quotas. The strategy proved successful. The workers quickly learned to produce cars of Japanese quality. Japanese management practices (just-in-time, total quality, continuous improvement, etc.) blended easily with the British tradition of improvization. In its Sunderland plant, well away from the traditional car-making area round Coventry and Birmingham (Brum), Nissan achieved production rates equal to those in Japan – 80 cars per worker per year. This compares with a European average of 45 cars per worker per year achieved only after productivity gains in the early 1990s.

Being smaller than Toyota and Nissan, Honda initially chose a joint venture with the UK's Rover as an inexpensive way of entering the European market. Honda took a 20 per cent stake in Rover, the other 80 per cent being owned by British Aerospace (BAe). In exchange BAe took a 20 per cent share of Honda (UK). Exhibit 12.1 shows the extent of the deal.

Exhibit 12.1 The Honda–Rover deal

Agreement	Content
Equity holding	Honda owns 20 per cent of Rover Cars. Rover owns 20 per cent of Honda (UK).
Licensing	Honda car designs for Rover 200, 400, 600 and 800. Honda component designs, such as gearbox for 2-litre Rover engine. Honda supplies production equipment and technology to Rover for its 200, 400 and 600 series cars.
Component supplies	Each sells the other about £400 million worth of car parts and components a year: for example, Honda sells 1.6, 2.0, 2.3 and 2.7-litre engines to Rover; Honda sells Rover fascias for 600 series; and Rover sells body panels for UK-made Honda Accords.
Vehicle sales	Rover makes Honda Concertos in Birmingham and supplies Land Rover Discoveries for sale as Honda Crossroads in Japan.

Rover, by any other Name

The Rover group in 1990 was the product of governments, not enterprise. The company has its origins in the early days of the motor industry, the first Rover being a bicycle made by the Starley company in 1884. In 1938 Lord Nuffield combined the Riley, Wolseley, Morris and MG companies. Austin and Vanden Plas joined them in 1952 to form the British Motor Corporation (BMC). Then, with the addition of Jaguar and Daimler in 1966, the group became British Motor Holdings (BMH).

Successive Labour governments encouraged these and further mergers. Prime Minister Harold Wilson explained that the policy was 'to encourage the UK's chief strategic industry to become more internationally competitive'. The idea was to merge companies, and then to select the best managers to run them. The clear failure of the earlier mergers did not deter the government, which in 1968 encouraged the formation of British Leyland (BL) by combining BMH with Rover, Triumph and Leyland. Leyland's Donald Stokes took over the group, which made over 1 million cars a year, had 40 per cent of the UK car market, 30 factories, 13 brands and dozens of models.

Donald Stokes, whose reputation came from selling buses and trucks worldwide, was out of his depth running this hugely complex and under-invested company. Under his directorship BL deteriorated. It faced increasing competition from European rivals and started losing its traditional overseas markets. The company became synonymous with low quality, strikes and trade unions resistant to the reform of working practices. In 1973 the oil supply crisis sent the company reeling. Even the successful truck and bus division struggled after being starved of cash to subsidize the loss-making car business. Finally, in 1975, the Labour government nationalized BL and brought in Michael Edwards, a South African, as chief executive. He persuaded first the Labour government, and then the Conservative government that succeeded it, to give BL money to revamp its range. To help do this, he established the company's first links with Honda. BL continued losing money, but Michael Edwards succeeded – where Donald Stokes had failed – in breaking the power of the trade unions. Under the premiership of Margaret Thatcher he threatened the unions with the ultimate sanction – closing the company.

While state-owned, BL absorbed £2 billion in government aid and accumulated a further £2.6 billion losses – £200 worth of aid for each person in the United Kingdom. Margaret Thatcher refused to give BL any more. The sale of Jaguar provided some funds, but by 1986 Margaret Thatcher had lost patience and called in Graham Day, a Canadian, to sort out the company. He had earlier 'rationalized' British Shipbuilding. Taking BMW as a model, Graham Day shifted the product range up-market and, with the help of Honda, rationalized products and introduced new work practices. In cut after cut, some of the great names of the car industry disappeared: Vanden Plas, Riley, Austin-Healey, Wolseley, Triumph, Morris and Austin. BL was sliced and sold off: trucks went to Daf of the Netherlands; buses went eventually to Sweden's Volvo; the spares operation, Unipart, went to a group of financial institutions; and finally Rover, the renamed rump of the company, went to BAe. Both Ford and GM tried to buy parts of Rover, particularly the famous Land Rover division. However, fearing the political backlash, the sales fell through. Now Thatcher's government could boast that the deal kept Rover 'British' by putting it safely in the hands of the UK's biggest engineering group – an aeroplane maker.

Rover: Going Japanese

The link with Honda saved Rover from extinction. It provided product and manufacturing knowledge that Rover lacked. Rover gained first-hand experience of Japan's world-beating manufacturing ways and drank deeply from the pool of experience. Licensing Honda's car designs allowed Rover's 2,000 engineering and development staff to concentrate upon their own new K-series engine and off-the-road vehicle design.

One of the most valuable lessons Rover learned from Honda was how to break down barriers between departments to ease production and product development. It was taught how to bring product to market more quickly and with fewer mistakes in product development. Product development was done at production plants rather than at a centralized location. For the new Rover 600, the project leader was based at Cowley, where the car would be made. He chose a team from around the company who worked out of one room while shaping the car. In this way Rover developed its small-capacity multivalve K-series engine from scratch. Its 4- and 6-cylinder developments could power almost any of Rover's future cars.

Land Rover had made civilian and military off-road vehicles for years, but changed direction in 1970 with its Range Rover – a luxury vehicle with polished wood trim and the capability to cross fields, streams, deserts and jungles. Designed for the United Kingdom's wealthy country-living classes, the 'Hollywood Jeep' appeared wherever there was money. The Range Rover defined a new product class. It became a fashion statement – the only vehicle to have been exhibited in the Louvre in Paris as a work of art. People who never got their shoes or car dirty liked the Range Rover's classic design and the way it allowed its drivers to stare over and look down on other road users. Other car makers followed Rover's lead and helped Europe's off-the-road sports/utility vehicle market grow from 50,000 in 1980 to 300,000 in 1990. Rover's new-found product development skills allowed it to defend Land Rover's strong position at the top of the market. Its all-new Rover Discovery model went into production in a record-breaking 21 months. Launched in 1989, it helped Land Rover's sales to grow from 46,700 in 1988 to 73,527 in 1993, during a period in which other car makers suffered declining sales. Priced between £17,500 and £26,800 the Discovery was not cheap, but it allowed Land Rover to move its new-generation, 200 kph, £31,950 to £43,950 Range Rover up-market to compete with top-of-the-range BMW, Mercedes, Jaguar and Lexus.

Honda saved Rover – but at a price. The sumo held the recovering Rover in a constricting embrace. Honda protected Rover, but stopped the car business making profits. Rover had to pay Honda handsomely for the floor-plans and engines it needed for its larger models. It also paid a royalty to Honda for each jointly developed car Rover sold. The technology agreement barred Rover from selling Honda-based models in markets that Honda wanted for itself, such as the United States. Rover needed a better deal with Honda, but its weak position and Honda's intractability left BAe in a jam. 'We were involved in some kind of Japanese poker game,' said Richard Evans, chief executive of BAe.

Enter BMW

The play of Richard Evans' last poker card sent Honda reeling. On 29 January 1994, BAe sold its 80 per cent stake in Rover to BMW. With one bold move BMW's share of the European car market doubled to 6.4 per cent, it became market leader in the off-the-road market, and it gained a range of small cars, a low-cost manufacturing base and access to Honda's production know-how. Simultaneously, it wrecked Honda's European strategy.

The speed of Honda's undoing left its managers in Tokyo bewildered and resentful. 'Now our partner has been acquired by our competitor we must start to reassess our entire operation in Europe,' said Kiyoshi Ikemi, councillor to Honda's president, Nobuhiko Kawamoto. 'Mr Kawamoto has made it quite clear that he has no intention of collaborating with BMW in the UK. We did not want to collaborate with Rover through BMW. Such collaboration was not called for – we had nothing to gain from it.' According to industry observers, the collapse of Honda's European alliance could not have

Exhibit 12.2 Ranges

Type	Honda	Rover	BMW	Rolls-Royce
Basic		Mini		
Super Mini		Metro		
Small family	Civic	200[a]		
Saloon	Concerto	400[a]		
		Maestro		
Large family Saloon		Montego	300	
Executive	Accord	600[a]	500	
Luxury	Legend	800[a]	700	
Exotic			800	All
Sports		MG	Z3	
Off-the-road		Defender Discovery Freelander Range Rover		

Note: [a] Based on Honda.

happened at a worse time for the company. Management attention was on the very depressed Japanese market and the United States, where Honda were losing share to the revitalized American car makers. Honda had offered to buy a 47.5 per cent share in Rover, but, explained Mr Kawamoto, 'We did not want to make Rover Japanese. We wanted to increase Rover's Roverness. We wanted it to be more British – that was the way the collaboration would work best.'

BMW's campaign on Honda's seemingly impregnable position had started in September 1993. It had identified Rover as a target that would extend its car range and achieve economies of scale in distribution, component sourcing and R & D. BMW's initial offer to BAe was repulsed because of Rover's relationship with Honda. Despite the rebuff, BMW continued scrutinizing Rover. Wolfgang Reitzle, BMW's R & D director, quietly visited Rover's plants and, back in Germany, test drove the entire fleet (see Exhibit 12.2). Hagan Lüderitz, BMW's director of corporate planning, says BMW delivered a letter to Honda's Mr Kawamoto, stating its interest in Rover. He got no response. Mr Kawamoto's councillor, Mr Ikemi, denies any direct approach, saying Honda only had indirect hints of BMW's interest. 'We weren't informed properly until Friday last week [the day before the BMW deal],' he protested.

After the deal, the mood among BMW's management was different to Honda's. Mr Volker Doppelfeld, BMW's finance director, explained that they had taken the shortest and cheapest route to fulfil their long-term aim of expanding BMW's core car business into new market segments. The long route would have meant a step-by-step move from BMW's up-market saloon base. In the event, the DM2,000 million paid for Rover is what BMW would normally spend on developing a single new model. Included in the price, he explained, were 17 brands, including Land Rover and Range Rover, which came equipped with 'the most interesting, the best, and the longest heritage in off-the-road vehicles'. Since the takeover the Mini has been relaunched as an up-market small car, the MG has been reborn, sales of the Freelander – Land Rover's baby off-the-road – have soared to 40 per cent above expectations and BMW has announced its biggest ever foreign investment to make its workhorse Defender in Brazil. BMW has also signed a deal with another British company, Rolls-Royce. After beating off competition from Mercedes, BMW will supply V8 and V12 engines for Rolls-Royce and Bentley cars. Soon Mrs Joanna Brauhn will have an even bigger choice of cars when she goes for a spin.

Questions

1. Why did combining a large number of car makers to form British Leyland not help the United Kingdom's 'chief strategic industry'?

2. Given Rover's much wider range, why was it not as successful as BMW, which had a much smaller range of vehicles to sell?

3. Attacking the US luxury car market forced Honda, Toyota and Nissan to move from making cars equivalent to American inexpensive 'compacts' to large expensive luxury Acura, Infiniti and Lexus models. Why do you think they attacked these segments rather than the mass market for 'regular'-sized cars in the United States?

4. Why did the Japanese attack the luxury car market in the United States rather than taking the battle to Europe?

5. What enabled Land Rover to hold its position in the market even though the Rover group could not? Why did Rover manage to increase sales when the rest of the world's car industry was in decline?

6. If BAe wanted to get rid of Rover, and Honda did not want it, what good is it to BMW? What do you think explains Honda's reaction to the supposed contact with BMW? Would you recommend Honda to pull the plug on its deal with Rover?

SOURCES: Simon Davies, 'BAe flies away from Rover with a sack full of cash', *Financial Times* (1 February 1994), p. 1; Christopher Parkes, 'A quick route into new market segments', *Financial Times* (1 February 1994), p. 22; Paul Abrahams and John Griffiths, 'Honda's European strategy wrecked', *Financial Times* (1 February 1994), p. 22; Kenneth Gooding, 'Rich British ancestry fails to provide independent future', *Financial Times* (1 February 1994), p. 23; 'Europe's car makers: then there were seven', *The Economist* (5 February 1994), pp. 19–24; Andrew Lorenz and Matthew Lynn, 'BMW drives in', *Sunday Times: Business Focus* (6 February 1994), pp. 2–3; Peter Miller, 'One careful lady owner', *Sunday Times: News Review* (6 February 1994), p. 1; B. John Griffiths, 'Capable of producing from the ground up', *Financial Times* (22 February 1994), p. 24; Tony Lewin, 'Rebirth of the Range Rover', *The European* (30 September–6 October 1994), p. 23; 'Ecstasy meets Mercedes', *The Economist* (17 December 1994), p. 72; John Griffiths, 'Rolls-Royce keep hold of the steering wheel', *Financial Times* (20 December 1994), p. 8; Richard Wolffe, 'Demand creates 400 jobs at Land Rover', *Financial Times* (27 January 1998), p. 8.

Cadbury's TimeOut:
Choc Around the Clock

Damien McLoughlin * *and Benoit Heilbrunn* **

Introduction

Cadbury's TimeOut is the most successful product ever developed and launched by Cadbury in Ireland. The development was by the management of Cadbury Ireland, at their plant in Coolock, Dublin. The product's success came from a combination of technological advance, strong domestic and international market orientation, and original positioning strategy at the time of launch.

Cadbury started manufacturing in Ireland in the 1930s, at a time when the protectionist policies of the Irish government effectively forbade the importation of chocolate to Ireland. Ireland and the United Kingdom's entry to the EEC in 1973 made them an open market for confectionery. The effect on the industry in Ireland was that several indigenous firms such as Lemons (hard-boiled sweets) and Urnies (chocolates) disappeared from the marketplace. The implication for Cadbury Ireland was the need to reshape its manufacturing so that it was positioned to benefit from economies of scale internationally rather than simply domestically.

Cadbury Ireland as a Partner in Cadbury-Schweppes International
Within the Cadbury-Schweppes group, Cadbury Ireland identified its particular strengths and competences, and set out to develop in these areas. The company identified three technologies in which it felt that it had, or could develop, global expertise. These three areas were:

1. *Extrusion.* This involves putting one form of confectionery inside another: for example, Cadbury's Eclairs wrapped chocolate in caramel; the Moro bar is a centre of chocolate paste with biscuit encased in caramel and covered in chocolate.

2. *Flake chocolate manufacture.* Cadbury's Flake is a light, crumbly, melt-in-the-mouth product positioned in the indulgence section of the confectionery market. The Flake brand is very well established and its advertising is legendary. The brand has been leveraged to include confectionery, catering

* Marketing Group, DCUBS, Dublin City University, Dublin, Ireland.
** Department of Marketing, Graduate School of Business, UCD, Blackrock, Co. Dublin, Ireland.

and ice-cream usage. However, the Flake recipe and process provide unique product properties, which were the key for future development.

3. *Wafer making and baking.* Wafer is an important part of a number of strong-selling products in Ireland, in particular the 'pink Snack brand'. Cadbury Ireland is the only Cadbury-Schweppes affiliate in the northern hemisphere to manufacture the wafer product.

Building on Core Competences at Cadbury Ireland

From the mid-1970s Cadbury Ireland developed centres of excellence around these core competences. The strong product development process in Cadbury Ireland produced products such as Cadbury's Chomp, Moro, TimeOut and Twirl. Twirl is a two-finger casual chocolate snack based on flake technology. These developments led to a doubling of Cadbury Ireland's throughput and allowed it to develop its brand successfully on both the domestic and international markets.

The Perspective of Cadbury Ireland on the Marketplace

Cadbury sees itself as a 'range house'. This describes a company that provides the consumer with a complete range of options in every segment of the market. In addition, all Cadbury products bear the distinctive Cadbury logo. The core product of the Cadbury group is Dairy Milk chocolate, which is used in its products and which is also marketed under the Dairy Milk brand name. This chocolate, which uses fresh Irish milk, has been the basis of success in a great number of segments. Cadbury defines segments on the basis of how customers buy rather than on how a product is made. For example, it identifies products as serving impulse markets, take-home markets or gift usage. This has allowed Cadbury Ireland management to identify a significant consumption pattern whereby the take-home segment is increasing its share of the confectionery market. This trend is driven by supermarket purchases of chocolate. In addition, they had noticed a certain overlap in the marketplace where brands that were traditionally seen as bars – for example, Twix and KitKat – were extending their franchise into the biscuit market. The main snack brands in Ireland (see Exhibit 3.1) are as follows:

- *KitKat.* KitKat was first sold in Ireland in 1937. It has become one of the most popular brands on the market with in the region of I£11 million sales in 1992. KitKat had initiated the move into the biscuit market with the memorable advert debating 'it's a biscuit … it's a bar'. This ad showed the product being used in different ways and suggested that it had multiple uses. Nestlé-Rowntree, the owners of the brand, maintained this position by heavy advertising and maintaining the price of the product at a below market par level. Usually 2–4p below its main competitors, KitKat is also available in bar and snack-size formats.

- *Twix.* Owned by the Mars corporation, Twix was launched in Ireland in 1968. The effort was made to develop a position for the product in the snack market with the advertising slogan, 'Whenever there's a snack gap, Twix fits.' Its packaging format, in a flow wrapper, however, also allowed it to fit into the bar/impulse market segment. The success of Twix has been attributed to its good value-for-money position and the heavy advertising support that it has traditionally received. Total brand sales in 1992 were estimated to be in the region of I£6–7 million. Twix was among the first products to be sold in the snack and fun-size formats.

- *Jacob's Club Milk.* The oldest brand on the market, Jacob's Club Milk has been sold in Ireland since the 1900s. It is sold singly and in family six-pack formats. The Club Milk acts as a flagship for a range of different-flavoured, chocolate-covered Club biscuits. For example, the Club bar is available in Club Orange and Club Mint formats. The position of Club Milk in the snack market is firmly achieved with the advertising message, 'If you're going to have a cuppa, have a Club.'

● *Cadbury's Snack.* Since its launch in the 1960s, the Cadbury's Snack brand has grown to lead the chocolate snack market. This domination is achieved through grocery sales, but also includes the important catering market. The Snack comes in three formats, differentiated by the colour of the packaging. The 'yellow' snack comprises a chocolate-covered shortcake biscuit. The 'purple' snack is a sandwich-filled biscuit heavily covered with thick milk chocolate. The third option is the 'pink' snack, which comprises three fingers of chocolate-covered wafer. Cadbury's Snack is sold in a variety of formats incorporating single bar, multipacks and treat size. Its combined sales from grocery, newsagent and catering outlets were in excess of I£11 million in 1992.

EXHIBIT 3.1 THE MAIN SNACK BRANDS IN IRELAND, 1992

	MANUFACTURER	LAUNCHED	SALES (I£M)
KitKat	Nestlé-Rowntree	1937	11.0
Twix	Mars	1968	6.5
Jacobs Club Milk	Jacobs	1900s	5.0
Cadbury's Snack	Cadbury	1960s	11.0

The Snack Market

The snack is a particularly prominent product market in the United Kingdom and Ireland. It is essentially a lifestyle market linked to a destructured approach to food. Snack products are most successful in those countries in which eating habits are not centred on two or three main meals. In these countries the consumption of food may be scattered around various occasions during the day. Thus the 11 a.m. and 4 p.m. snack breaks are usual practice in Irish and English lifestyles. These breaks generally consist of a cup of tea/coffee together with fruit, a chocolate bar or a cake. Internationally, this snack habit is linked to the grazing phenomenon, which is representative of the slow but steady change in cultural habits concerning eating (destruction of family meals and less time devoted to meals) and accounts for the growth of the snack market in other European countries. That the Irish are accomplished 'snackers' is evidenced by their large confectionery market with annual sales in 1992 of over I£240 million (see Exhibit 3.2).

EXHIBIT 3.2 THE CONFECTIONERY MARKET IN IRELAND

	1988	1989	1990	1991	1992
Estimated market value at RSP (I£m)	210	216	228	245	242
Annual growth rate (%)	–	3.0	5.0	3.0	2.9

SOURCE: Nestlé-Rowntree.

Break-Time in Ireland

Ireland is also a great tea-drinking nation. A survey carried out by Nielsen in 1993 in Ireland showed that 20 of the top 100 grocery brands are liquid consumables.

However, leading tea brands in Ireland are positioned on value for money rather than taste. This means that tea might be viewed as a depersonalized drink. Therefore there is considerable need for a beverage complement with strong personality in order to personalize break-times.

In trying to meet this need, Cadbury was faced with what was a mature marketplace. Irish consumption of confectionery is the highest in Europe (see Exhibit 3.3). Chocolate consumption alone is 8.3 kg per annum per capita. This figure is matched only by their British neighbours.

The Concept of TimeOut

Based on these trends in the marketplace and Cadbury's core technological competences, the management of Cadbury Ireland saw the opportunity to bring confectionery values to the biscuit market and biscuit values to the confectionery market. In this sense TimeOut set out specifically to target the bridge-brand position and satisfy all uses from mainstream confectionery luxury to straight beverage accompaniment, but with values firmly rooted in the break market.

It also had to compete with existing competitors in this market, particularly KitKat and Twix, both brands that had also targeted the bridge-brand position for the future. TimeOut therefore 'institutionalized' the coexistence of three elements: the need for a break during the day; tea or coffee as a liquid consumable; and the need for a snack to accompany that drink. This can be paraphrased as 'Wherever you are, whatever you are doing, when it's that time (i.e. your time for a break) it's TimeOut time.'

The Positioning Mix for the Launch of TimeOut

Product

TimeOut stems from a technological advance at Cadbury Ireland that allowed it to layer flake on to wafer. The competitive advantage of this product lies in the unique blend of flake sandwiched between two wafers and covered in dairy milk chocolate. In product terms, TimeOut bridges both the snack and bar markets as the Flake ingredient was sufficiently biscuity to be a suitable accompaniment to a beverage break. On the one hand its biscuit constituency made it an ideal snack, while its Flake content made it a suitable bar of chocolate in its own right.

The Branding Ingredients: Brand Name, Logo and Identity Colours

Many names were proposed for the new product, including 'Switch' and 'Ultra'. However, it was discovered that using a name indicating the timing and situation in which the bar should be consumed greatly enhanced the consumer's understanding of what the product was designed for. The TimeOut name was proposed and accepted as it more clearly communicated the desired position as *the snack* accompaniment. These brand-name objectives were supported by the use of a

EXHIBIT 3.3 EU CONSUMPTION OF CONFECTIONERY (KG PER CAPITA)

	IRELAND	UK	GREECE	BELGIUM	DENMARK	GERMANY	FRANCE	NETHER-LANDS	ITALY	SPAIN	PORTUGAL	EU AVERAGE
Chocolate	8.3	8.3	2.4	7.0	7.2	5.9	5.2	6.0	1.3	2.3	0.5	4.8
Biscuits	17.9	13.0	17.9	5.2	5.5	3.1	6.5	2.8	5.9	5.2	4.6	6.6
Ice cream	8.0	7.1	5.3	9.8	9.1	7.8	4.7	4.5	6.1	3.8	1.8	6.0
Total	34.2	28.4	25.6	22.0	21.8	16.8	16.4	13.3	13.3	11.3	6.9	17.4

SOURCE: *Irish Consumer Market Handbook: A guidebook for marketing managers*, ed. M. V. Lambkin (Dublin: Marketing Society of Ireland, 1993), adapted from *European Marketing Data and Statistics*, 27th edn (London: Euromonitor, 1992).

clock (suggesting that any time is suitable for TimeOut) and a mug (which reinforced the beverage break accompaniment role).

The new brand needed a strong visual identity system to reinforce the other positioning elements. Hence the use of bold primary colours on the packaging to attract attention and create competitive distinction. The two main colours used were blue, considered the main identity colour, and red, which is used to write the brand name. The brand name is surrounded by yellow; this blue/red/yellow association is the colour scheme most easily associated with light biscuit bars. Blue also has a symbolic connotation and is considered as a peaceful and restful colour. The choice of colour is interesting because the market is dominated by darker brand colours such as black/brown (Mars) and gold (Twix).

Pricing

Consumer knowledge of price in the snack market, given its habitual nature, is high. However, the standard-size chocolate bars are only slightly differentiated in terms of price. Given the power of retailers, the producer often has little discretion in the determination of price. TimeOut was launched at a price of 28p, while a standard bar was priced at 30p.

Packaging Configuration

Packaging was particularly important in positioning TimeOut as a bridge brand. Most brands establish themselves in standard format initially and then expand to different formats. TimeOut, however, was required to meet the needs of a number of groups and so came in a variety of formats from the start:

- *Standard.* The standard product to be sold in newsagents, workplace restaurants and coffee shops. The format is two full-size fingers in a flow wrapper. In newsagents or supermarkets, TimeOut is placed with other Cadbury brands.

- *5-pack.* The five-pack format was five TimeOut fingers in a convenience pack to allow the product to be bought in bulk from supermarkets. It is positioned with the multipacks for other confectionery products.

- *Breakpack.* The breakpack consisted of six shorter twin-finger packs individually wrapped. This is also sold in supermarkets and is intended for the home snack market. In supermarkets the breakpack would be put on shelf space with the biscuit range.

- *Treat-size.* The treat-size format is intended to meet the demands of the children's treat/party market. The treat-size format was 14 full-size, individually wrapped TimeOut fingers. These are mainly distributed through supermarkets. The shelf position for the treat size is with the treat and fun-size formats of other confectionery products.

Advertising and Promotion

At its initial launch in early 1992 TimeOut was supported by a complete range of advertising and promotion. Heavy TV and radio advertising emphasized the 'TimeOut at any time' theme. Promotions included balloon releases at several centres around the country, a variety of street activities involving a national radio station and using branded characters, and participation at the annual St Patrick's Day parade in Dublin. Free samples were generously distributed at street activities and during in-store promotions. TimeOut has also made effective and large-scale use of poster advertising.

TimeOut used both family brand promotions and brand alliance promotions in its initial positioning. An example of the family brand promotions was one with

Lyons tea, the largest selling brand of tea in Ireland. The promotion gave customers a free bar of TimeOut with every standard box of tea. This achieved two goals. First, given the market share of Lyons, it facilitated trial of the product. Secondly, it was an opportunity to nail down the position of TimeOut as a beverage accompaniment. The overall promotional message was one of a new, friendly, modern, fun and young, beverage-break accompaniment that was suitable for use at any time.

The Success of TimeOut

Six to eight months after the launch of TimeOut, a national trade magazine completed a brand evaluation (*Checkout*, July–August 1993). Primary research completed by an independent research company highlighted some extraordinary results.

User Profile

The user profile of the brand demonstrated a widespread acceptance. The vast majority of adults and all children had used the brand at some stage since its introduction (see Exhibit 3.4). Women, a prime market for chocolate consumption, represented over 60 per cent of TimeOut consumers. Users were drawn from all areas of Ireland, but were particularly strong in urban areas. This user profile was assisted by a high conversion ratio for both adults and children (see Exhibit 3.5).

EXHIBIT 3.4 BRAND ACCEPTANCE AMONG ADULTS AND CHILDREN (%)

	ADULTS (15 YEARS +)	CHILDREN (11–14 YEARS)
Ever used	68	97
Used once/twice	23	13
Occasional user	22	41
Regular user	14	43

SOURCE: Lansdowne Market Research.

EXHIBIT 3.5 CADBURY'S TIMEOUT CONVERSION RATIO (%)

	ADULTS (15 YEARS +)	CHILDREN (11–14 YEARS)
Aware	86	100
Awareness to trial	69	97
Trial to repeat user	61	87
Lost consumers	7	1

SOURCE: Lansdowne Market Research.

Attitudes Towards the Brand

As might be expected, given the high levels of trial achieved for the brand, consumer attitudes towards the brand were very positive (see Exhibit 3.6). This is particularly evidenced by the positive appeal that the brand had for both adults and children. Among the target group of 11–25-year-olds there was virtually no criticism of the brand. This sort of consumer support should allow TimeOut to build on its initial success even after its large-scale media support is reduced.

EXHIBIT 3.6 CADBURY'S TIMEOUT BRAND APPEAL (%)

	ADULTS (15 YEARS +)	CHILDREN (11–14 YEARS)
Positive	66	86
Neutral	27	14
Negative	7	1

QUESTIONS

1. What criteria did Cadbury Ireland use in developing TimeOut?
2. What role did they play in the positioning strategy of TimeOut?
3. What are the risks of the 'bridge-brand' position?
4. Which marketing-mix variables were most important in positioning TimeOut?
5. How did the positioning and marketing strategies of its main competitor influence TimeOut's positioning?
6. What are the cultural factors that account for the success of TimeOut? Could TimeOut be successful in other European countries?

Part 4

Product

Part Introduction

IN PART FOUR WE LOOK at the first component in the marketing mix – the product.

Designing good products that customers want to buy is a challenging task. Customers do not buy mere products. They seek product benefits and are often willing to pay more for a brand that genuinely solves their problems. Chapter 13 explores how marketers can satisfy customer needs by adding value to the basic product; it also shows the complexity arising in product, branding and packaging decisions, and how various forces in the environment pose tough challenges for marketers heading towards the twenty-first century.

Markets do not stand still. Companies must adapt their current offerings or create new ones in response to changing customer needs, or to take advantage of new marketing and technological opportunities. Chapter 14 looks at how to develop and commercialize new products. Importantly, after launch, marketing managers must carefully manage the new product over its lifetime to get the best out of their new-product effort.

While Chapters 13 and 14 deal with products, Chapter 15 looks more specifically at intangible products or services. It examines the unique characteristics of services and how organizations adapt their approach when marketing them.

CHAPTER 13
Brands, Products, Packaging and Services

CHAPTER 14
Product Development and Life-Cycle Strategies

CHAPTER 15
Marketing Services

PART OVERVIEW CASE:
Mattel: Getting it Right is No Child's Play

Brands, Products, Packaging and Services

CHAPTER OBJECTIVES

After reading this chapter, you should be able to:

- Define the term *product* including the core, actual and *augmented* product.
- Explain the main classifications of consumer and industrial products.
- Outline the range of individual product decisions that marketers make.
- Explain the purpose of branding and identify the chief branding decisions.
- Explain the decisions that companies make when developing product lines and mixes.
- List the considerations that marketers face in making international product decisions.

Preview Case

Revlon

REVLON SELLS COSMETICS, TOILETRIES AND fragrances to consumers around the world. Revlon is the no. 1 firm in the popular-price segment of the fragrance market. In one sense, Revlon's perfumes are no more than careful mixtures of oils and chemicals that have nice scents. But Revlon knows that when it sells perfume, it sells much more than fragrant fluids – it sells what the fragrances can do for the women who use them.

Perfume is actually shipped from the fragrance houses in big, ugly drums. Although a £100-an-ounce perfume may cost no more than £7 to produce, to perfume consumers the product is much more than a few pounds' worth of ingredients and a pleasing smell.

Many things beyond the ingredients and scent add to a perfume's allure. In fact, the scent may be the last element developed. Revlon first researches women's feelings about themselves and their relationships with others. It then develops and tests new perfume concepts that match women's changing values, desires and lifestyles. When Revlon finds a promising new concept, it creates and names a scent to fit the idea. Revlon's research in the early 1970s showed that women were feeling more competitive with men and that they were striving to find individual identities. For this woman of the 1970s, Revlon created Charlie, the first of the 'lifestyle' perfumes. Thousands of women adopted Charlie as a bold statement of independence, and it quickly became the world's best-selling perfume.

In the late 1970s, Revlon research showed a shift in women's attitudes: 'women had made the equality point, which Charlie addressed. Now women were hungering for an expression of femininity.' They now wanted perfumes that were subtle rather than shocking. Thus Revlon subtly shifted Charlie's position. The perfume still made its 'independent lifestyle' statement, but with an added tinge of 'femininity and romance'. Revlon also launched a perfume for the woman of the 1980s, Jontue, which was positioned on a theme of romance.

Revlon continues to refine Charlie's position, now targeting the woman of the 1990s who is 'able to do it all, but smart enough to know what she wants to do'. After almost 20 years, aided by continuous but subtle repositioning, Charlie remains the best-selling mass-market perfume.

A perfume's *name* is an important product attribute. Revlon uses such brand names as Charlie, Fleurs de Jontue, Ciara, Scoundrel, Guess and Unforgettable to create images that support each perfume's positioning. Competitors offer perfumes with such names as Obsession, Passion, Uninhibited, Opium, Joy, White Linen and Eternity. These names suggest that the perfumes will do something more than just make you smell better. Oscar de la Renta's Ruffles perfume *began* as a name, one chosen because it created images of whimsy, youth, glamour and femininity – all well suited to the target market of young, stylish women. Only later was a scent selected to go with the product's name and positioning.

Revlon must also carefully *package* its perfumes. To consumers, the bottle and package are the most tangible symbols of the perfume and its image. Bottles must feel comfortable, be easy to handle and look impressive when displayed in stores. Most important, they must support the perfume's concept and image.

So when a woman buys perfume, she buys much, much more than simply fragrant fluids. The perfume's image, its promises, its scent, its name and package, the company that makes it and the stores that sell it all become a part of the *total* perfume *product*. When Revlon sells perfume, it sells more than the tangible product. It sells lifestyle, self-expression and exclusivity; achievement, success and status; femininity, romance, passion and fantasy; memories, hopes and dreams.[1]

QUESTIONS

1. What is the core product that Revlon sells?
2. What is the tangible product that the company sells?
3. What is the augmented product?
4. A perfume's name is a central product attribute. How should Revlon go about deciding and selecting an appropriate brand name for its perfumes?
5. What are the key branding decisions that Revlon marketing managers have to make?
6. Revlon markets its perfumes worldwide. What major considerations does the firm face in determining global product decisions?

Introduction

Clearly, perfume is more than just perfume when Revlon sells it. Revlon's great success in the rough-and-tumble fragrance world comes from developing an innovative product concept. An effective product concept is the first step in marketing-mix planning.

This chapter begins with a deceptively simple question: *What is a product?* After answering this question, we look at ways to classify products in consumer and business markets and look for links between types of product and types of marketing strategy. Next, we see that each product requires several decisions that go beyond product design. These decisions involve *branding*, *packaging*, *labelling* and *product-support services*. We move from decisions about individual products to decisions about building *product lines* and *product mixes*. Finally, we address some complex considerations in international product decisions.

What is a Product?

A pair of Adidas trainers, a Volvo truck, a Nokia mobile telephone, a Vidal Sassoon haircut, an Oasis concert, a EuroDisney vacation, advice from a solicitor and tax preparation services are all products. We define a **product** as anything that is offered to a market for attention, acquisition, use or consumption and that might satisfy a want or need. Products include more than just tangible goods. Broadly defined, products include physical objects, services, persons, places, organizations, ideas or mixes of these entities.

Services are products that consist of activities, benefits or satisfactions that are offered for sale, such as haircuts, tax preparation and home repairs. Services are essentially intangible and do not result in the ownership of anything. (Because of the importance of services in the world economy, we will look at them more closely in Chapter 15.)

Product planners need to think about the product on three levels. The most basic level is the **core product**, which addresses the question: *What is the buyer really buying?* As Figure 13.1 illustrates, the core product stands at the centre of the total product. It consists of the problem-solving services or core benefits that consumers seek when they buy a product. A woman buying lipstick buys more than lip colour. Charles Revson of Revlon saw this early: 'In the factory, we make cosmetics; in the store, we sell hope.' Theodore Levitt has pointed out that buyers 'do not buy quarter-inch drills; they buy quarter-inch holes'. Thus when designing products, marketers must first define the core of *benefits* that the product will provide to consumers.

The product planner must next build an **actual product** around the core product. Actual products may have as many as five characteristics: a *quality level*, *features*, *styling*, a *brand name* and *packaging*. For example, Sony's Handycam camcorder is an actual product. Its name, parts, styling, features, packaging and other attributes have all been combined carefully to deliver the core benefit – a convenient, high-quality way to capture important moments.

Finally, the product planner must build an **augmented product** around the core and actual products by offering additional consumer services and benefits. Sony must offer more than a camcorder. It must provide consumers with a complete solution to their picture-taking problems. Thus when consumers buy a Sony Handycam, Sony and its dealers might also give buyers a warranty on parts and workmanship, free lessons on how to use the camcorder, quick repair services when needed and a freephone number to call if they have problems or questions. To the consumer, all of these augmentations become an important part of the total product.

Therefore, a product is more than a simple set of tangible features. Consumers tend to see products as complex *bundles of benefits* that satisfy their

product
Anything that can be offered to a market for attention, acquisition, use or consumption that might satisfy a want or need. It includes physical objects, services, persons, places, organizations and ideas.

services
Activities, benefits or satisfactions that are offered for sale.

core product
The problem-solving services or core benefits that consumers are really buying when they obtain a product.

actual product
A product's parts, quality level, features, design, brand name, packaging and other attributes that combine to deliver core product benefits.

augmented product
Additional consumer services and benefits built around the core and actual products.

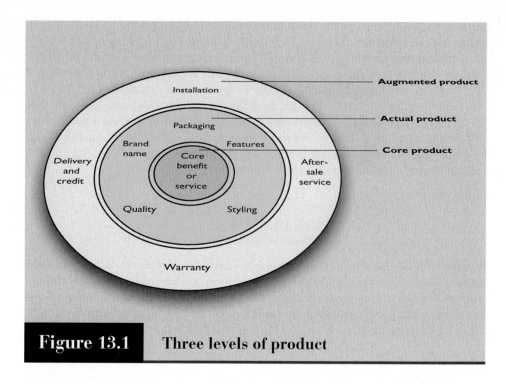

Figure 13.1   **Three levels of product**

needs. When developing products, marketers must first identify the *core* consumer needs that the product will satisfy, then design the *actual* product and finally find ways to *augment* it in order to create the bundle of benefits that will best satisfy consumers.

Today, most competition takes place at the product augmentation level. Successful companies add benefits to their offers that will not only *satisfy*, but also *delight* the customer. For instance, hotel guests find chocolates on the pillow or a bowl of fruit or a VCR with optional videotapes. The company is saying 'we want to treat you in a special way'. However, each augmentation costs the company money, and the marketer has to ask whether customers will pay enough to cover the extra cost. Moreover, augmented benefits soon become *expected* benefits: hotel guests now expect cable television, trays of toiletries and other amenities in their rooms. This means that competitors must search for still more features and benefits to differentiate their offers.

Product Classifications

non-durable product
A consumer product that is normally consumed in one or a few uses.

durable product
A consumer product that is usually used over an extended period of time and that normally survives many uses.

Before we examine individual product decisions, let us explain several product-classification schemes. Products can be classified according to their durability and tangibility. **Non-durable products** are goods that are normally consumed quickly and used on one or a few usage occasions, such as beer, soap and food products. **Durable products** are products used over an extended period of time and normally survive for many years. Examples are refrigerators, cars and furniture. *Services* are activities, benefits and satisfactions offered for sale which are essentially intangible and do not result in the ownership of anything. Examples include haircuts, holiday packages and banking services. Marketers have also divided products and services into two broad classes based on the types of customer that use them – consumer products and industrial products.

producers can do little to prevent the loss of sales to less expensive suppliers – consumers are loyal to the brands, not to the producers. In the past, Japanese and South Korean companies, however, have not made this mistake. They have spent heavily to build up brand names such as Sony, Panasonic, JVC, Hyundai, Goldstar and Samsung for their products. Even when these companies can no longer afford to manufacture their products in their homelands, their brand names continue to command customer loyalty.[8]

Powerful brand names have *consumer franchise* – that is, they command strong consumer loyalty. This means that a sufficient number of customers demand these brands and refuse substitutes, even if the substitutes are offered at somewhat lower prices. Companies that develop brands with a strong consumer franchise are insulated from competitors' promotional strategies. Thus it makes sense for a supplier to invest heavily to create strong national or even global recognition and preference for its brand name.

● *What is a Brand?*

Perhaps the most distinctive skill of professional marketers is their ability to create, maintain, protect, reinforce and enhance brands. A **brand** is a name, term, sign, symbol, design or a combination of these, which is used to identify the goods or services of one seller or group of sellers and to differentiate them from those of competitors.[9] Thus a brand identifies the maker or supplier of a product. Take a product such as a cola drink – any manufacturer can produce a cola drink, but only the Coca-Cola Company can produce Coke.

Branding is not a new phenomenon. In the last hundred years, however, its use has developed considerably. Legal systems recognize that brands are also property in a very real sense. Currently, over 160 countries have trademark laws allowing owners of brands to claim title in their brand names and logos through trademark registration. But brands, unlike other forms of intellectual property, such as patents and copyrights, do not have expiration dates and their owners have exclusive rights to use their brand name for an unlimited period of time.

A brand conveys a specific set of features, benefits and services to buyers. It is a mark, a tangible emblem, which says something about the product. The best brands, for example, often convey a warranty of quality. A brand can deliver up to four levels of meaning:

brand
A name, term, sign, symbol or design, or a combination of these, intended to identify the goods or services of one seller or group of sellers and to differentiate them from those of competitors.

1. *Attributes.* A brand first brings to mind certain product attributes. For example, Mercedes suggests such attributes as 'well engineered', 'well built', 'durable', 'high prestige', 'fast', 'expensive' and 'high resale value'. The company may use one or more of these attributes in its advertising for the car. For years, Mercedes advertised 'Engineered like no other car in the world'. This provided a positioning platform for other attributes of the car.

2. *Benefits.* Customers do not buy attributes, they buy benefits. Therefore, attributes must be translated into functional and emotional benefits. For example, the attribute 'durable' could translate into the functional benefit, 'I won't have to buy a new car every few years.' The attribute 'expensive' might translate into the emotional benefit, 'The car makes me feel important and admired.' The attribute 'well built' might translate into the functional and emotional benefit, 'I am safe in the event of an accident.'

3. *Values.* A brand also says something about the buyers' values. Thus Mercedes buyers value high performance, safety and prestige. A brand marketer must identify the specific groups of car buyers whose values coincide with the delivered benefit package.

4. *Personality.* A brand also projects a personality. Motivation researchers sometimes ask, 'If this brand were a person, what kind of person would it be?' Consumers might visualize a Mercedes automobile as being a wealthy, middle-aged business executive. The brand will attract people whose actual or desired self-images match the brand's image.[10]

All this suggests that a brand is a complex symbol. If a company treats a brand only as a name, it misses the point of branding. The challenge of branding is to develop a deep set of meanings or associations for the brand.

Given the four levels of a brand's meaning, marketers must decide the levels at which they will build the brand's identity. It would be a mistake to promote only the brand's attributes. Remember, buyers are interested not so much in brand attributes as in brand benefits. Moreover, competitors can easily copy attributes. Or the current attributes may later become less valuable to consumers, hurting a brand that is tied too strongly to specific attributes.

Even promoting the brand on one or more of its benefits can be risky. Suppose Mercedes touts its main benefit as 'high performance'. If several competing brands emerge with as high or higher performance, or if car buyers begin placing less importance on performance as compared to other benefits, Mercedes will need the freedom to move into a new benefit positioning.

The most lasting and sustainable meanings of a brand are its core values and personality. They define the brand's essence. Thus Mercedes stands for 'high achievers and success'. The company must build its brand strategy around creating and protecting this brand personality. Although Mercedes has recently yielded to market pressures by introducing lower-price models, this might prove risky. Marketing less expensive models might dilute the personality that Mercedes has built up over the decades.

● *Brand Equity*

Brands vary in the amount of power and value they have in the marketplace. Some brands are largely unknown to most buyers. Other brands have a high degree of consumer *brand awareness*. Still others enjoy *brand preference* – buyers select them over the others. Finally, some brands command a high degree of *brand loyalty*. A top executive at H.J. Heinz proposes this test of brand loyalty: 'My acid test … is whether a [consumer], intending to buy Heinz Ketchup in a store but finding it out of stock, will walk out of the store to buy it elsewhere or switch to an alternative product.'

brand equity
The value of a brand, based on the extent to which it has high brand loyalty, name awareness, perceived quality, strong brand associations, and other assets such as patents, trademarks and channel relationships.

A powerful brand has high **brand equity**. Brands have higher brand equity to the extent that they have higher brand loyalty, name awareness, perceived quality, strong brand associations and other assets such as patents, trademarks and channel relationships.[11] A brand with strong brand equity is a valuable asset. In fact, it can even be bought or sold for a price. Many companies base their growth strategies on acquiring and building rich *brand portfolios*. For example, Grand Metropolitan acquired various Pillsbury brands, including Green Giant vegetables, Häagen-Dazs ice cream and Burger King restaurants. Switzerland's Nestlé bought Rowntree (UK), Carnation (US), Stouffer (US), Buitoni-Perugina (Italy) and Perrier (France), making it the world's largest food company controlling many desirable 'brands'.

Measuring the actual equity of a brand name is difficult.[12] Because it is so hard to measure, companies usually do not list brand equity on their balance sheets. Still, they pay handsomely for it. For example, Nestlé paid £2.5 billion to buy Rowntree, six times its reported asset value. And when Grand Metropolitan bought Heublein, it added $800 million to its assets to reflect the value of Smirnoff

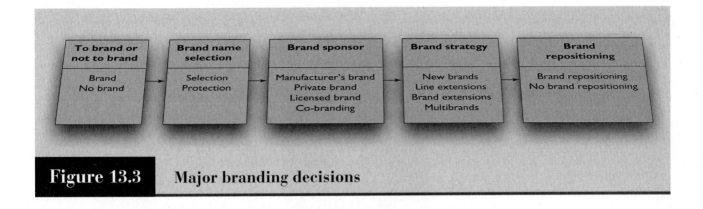

To brand or not to brand	Brand name selection	Brand sponsor	Brand strategy	Brand repositioning
Brand No brand	Selection Protection	Manufacturer's brand Private brand Licensed brand Co-branding	New brands Line extensions Brand extensions Multibrands	Brand repositioning No brand repositioning

Figure 13.3 **Major branding decisions**

and other names. According to one estimate, the brand equity of Marlboro is $31 billion, Coca-Cola $24 billion and Kodak $13 billion.[13]

The world's top brands include such superpowers as McDonald's, Coca-Cola, Campbell, Disney, Kodak, Sony and Mercedes-Benz (see Marketing Highlight 13.2). High brand equity provides a company with many competitive advantages. Because a powerful brand enjoys a high level of consumer brand awareness and loyalty, the company will incur lower marketing costs relative to revenues. Because consumers expect stores to carry the brand, the company has more leverage in bargaining with retailers. And because the brand name carries high credibility, the company can more easily launch brand extensions. Above all, a powerful brand offers the company some defence against fierce price competition.

Marketers need to manage their brands carefully in order to preserve brand equity. They must develop strategies that effectively maintain or improve brand awareness, perceived brand quality and usefulness, and positive brand associations over time. This requires continuous R & D investment to provide a constant flow of improved and innovative products to satisfy customers' changing needs, skilful advertising and excellent trade and consumer service. Some companies, such as Colgate-Palmolive and Canada Dry, appoint 'brand equity managers' to guard their brands' images, associations and quality. They work to prevent brand managers from overpromoting brands in order to produce short-term profits at the expense of long-term brand equity.

Some analysts see brands as *the* most enduring asset of a company, outlasting the company's specific products and facilities. Yet, behind every powerful brand stands a set of loyal customers. Therefore, the basic asset underlying brand equity is *customer equity*. This suggests that marketing strategy should focus on extending *loyal customer lifetime value*, with brand management serving as an essential marketing tool.

Branding poses challenging decisions to the marketer. Figure 13.3 shows the key branding decisions. We will examine each of these in turn.

• *To Brand or not to Brand*

The company must first decide whether it should put a brand name on its product. Branding has become so strong that today hardly anything goes unbranded. Salt is packaged in branded containers, common nuts and bolts are packaged with a distributor's label, and automotive parts – spark plugs, tyres, filters – bear brand names that differ from those of the car makers. Even fruit and vegetables are branded – Sunkist oranges, Del Monte pineapples and Chiquita bananas.

The World's Top Ten Brands

Marketing Highlight 13.2

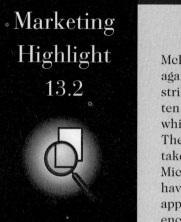

Companies around the world invest large amounts of money each year to create awareness and preference for their top brands. Powerful brand names command strong consumer loyalty and provide competitive advantage in the marketplace.

What are the world's most powerful brands? Interbrand, a consultancy that specializes in branding, released a new piece of research in 1996, naming McDonald's as the world's leading brand. Interbrand drew up an initial list of some 1,200 brands by polling staff in its 12 offices, spread across Europe, America, Asia, Australia and South Africa. This long list of brands was then trimmed down arbitrarily to 500 global brands and the survivors graded according to four criteria to give a final score. The criteria were: brand weight (or the brand's market share within its category), which accounted for 35 per cent of the final total; breadth (how wide a slice of the world in terms of age, gender, religion and nationality the brand appeals to) was another 30 per cent; depth (the loyalty of its customers) was 20 per cent; and length (how far the brand has stretched or is likely to stretch beyond its original category) was 15 per cent.

Under Interbrand's system, McDonald's scored 856 points against 849 for Coke. The most striking absence from the new top ten (see Table 1) was Kellogg's, which fell from second to 17th. The cereal maker has been overtaken by high-tech arrivals such as Microsoft, and by old brands that have done more to extend their appeal. Whereas Kellogg's influence is confined to the breakfast table, names such as Disney and Levi's are no longer just confined to the cinema and jeans. Disney also gained from being the only brand in an otherwise unbranded industry; nobody asks you to go and see a 'Paramount film' or talks about 'Warner' characters.

Given the obvious power of brands, some argue that they should be included alongside other assets in their owners' balance sheets. Various accounting standards boards (including the United Kingdom's) are looking at this issue. At present, most balance sheets concentrate on historic-cost assets, rather than trying to guess the future value of intangible assets, such as brands. Interbrand is one of several firms that tries to calculate the value of brands by estimating each product's expected net cash flow and discounting it at a rate that reflects how secure Interbrand guesses the brand's future is.

The suspicion remains that putting brands on a balance sheet would simply be an excuse for excessively *creative accounting*. Brands may be deep, but some argue that valuing them is not necessarily meaningful. Although there is still disagreement among business analysts and academics about how to measure brand power, few marketers doubt the value of a powerful brand. As one brand consultant states, almost anywhere in the world, 'When you mention Kodak, I'm pretty sure everyone sees that yellow box.'

TABLE 1 TOP TEN GLOBAL BRANDS

	1996	1990
1	McDonald's	Coca-Cola
2	Coca-Cola	Kellogg's
3	Disney	McDonald's
4	Kodak	Kodak
5	Sony	Marlboro
6	Gillette	IBM
7	Mercedes-Benz	American Express
8	Levi's	Sony
9	Microsoft	Mercedes-Benz
10	Marlboro	Nescafé

SOURCE: Interbrand, 1996.

SOURCES: 'Assessing brands: broad, deep, long and heavy", *The Economist* (16 November 1996), pp. 112–13; Jon Rees, 'McDonald's heads top brands list', *Marketing Week* (15 November 1996), p. 10; Interbrand, *World's Greatest Brands* (New York: Wiley, 1996).

Some products, however, carry no brands. 'Generic' products are unbranded, plainly packaged, less expensive versions of common products ranging from such items as spaghetti to paper towels and canned peaches. They often bear only black-stencilled labels and offer prices as much as 40 per cent lower than those of main brands. The lower price is made possible by lower-quality ingredients, lower-cost packaging and lower advertising costs.

Despite the limited popularity of generics, the issue of whether or not to brand is very much alive today. This situation highlights some key questions: Why have branding in the first place? Who benefits? How do they benefit? At what cost?

Branding helps buyers in many ways:

● Brand names tell the buyer something about product quality. Buyers who always buy the same brand know that they will get the same quality each time they buy.

● Brand names also increase the shopper's efficiency. Imagine a buyer going into a supermarket and finding thousands of generic products.

● Brand names help call consumers' attention to new products that might benefit them. The brand name becomes the basis upon which a whole story can be built about the new product's special qualities.

Branding also gives the supplier several advantages:

● The brand name makes it easier for the supplier to process orders and track down problems.

● The supplier's brand name and trademark provide legal protection for unique production features that otherwise might be copied by competitors.

● Branding enables the supplier to attract a loyal and profitable set of customers.

● Branding helps the supplier to segment markets. For example, Cadbury can offer Dairy Milk, Milk Tray, Roses, Flake, Fruit and Nut and many other brands, not just one general confectionery product for all consumers.

Branding also adds value to consumers and society:

● Those who favour branding suggest that it leads to higher and more consistent product quality.

● Branding also increases innovation by giving producers an incentive to look for new features that can be protected against imitating competitors. Thus, branding results in more product variety and choice for consumers.

● Branding helps shoppers because it provides much more information about products and where to find them.

● *Brand Name Selection*

Selecting the right name is a crucial part of the marketing process. The brand name should be carefully chosen. A good name can add greatly to a product's success. Most large marketing companies have developed a formal, brand-name selection process. Finding the best brand name is a difficult task. It begins with a careful review of the product and its benefits, the target market and proposed marketing strategies.

Finding a name for a product designed for worldwide markets is not easy. Companies must avoid the pitfalls inherent in injudicious product naming.

Desirable qualities for a brand name include the following:

1. It should suggest something about the product's benefits and qualities. Examples: Oasis (a still fruit drink), Kleenex (tissue paper), Frisp (a light savoury snack).

2. It should be easy to pronounce, recognize and remember. Short names help. Examples: Dove (soap), Yale (security products), Hula Hoops (potato crisps shaped like the name). But longer ones are sometimes effective. Examples: 'Love My Carpet' carpet cleaner, 'I Can't Believe It's Not Butter' margarine, Better Business Bureau.

3. The brand name should be distinctive. Examples: Shell, Kodak, Virgin.

4. The name should translate easily (and meaningfully) into foreign languages. For example, in Chinese Ferrari is pronounced as 'fa li li', the Chinese symbols for which mean 'magic, weapon, pull, power', which flatter the brand. But accountancy firm Price Waterhouse was reported to have been translated as 'expensive water closet'.

5. It should be capable of registration and legal protection. A brand name cannot be registered if it infringes on existing brand names. Also, brand names that are merely descriptive or suggestive may be unprotectable. For example, the Miller Brewing Company registered the name Lite for its low-calorie beer and invested millions in establishing the name with consumers. But the courts later ruled that the terms *lite* and *light* are generic or common descriptive terms applied to beer and that Miller could not use the Lite name exclusively.[14]

Once chosen, the brand name must be registered with the appropriate Trade Marks Register, giving owners intellectual property rights and preventing competitors from using the same or similar name. Many firms try to build a brand name that will eventually become identified with the product category. Brand names such as Hoover, Kleenex, Levi's, Scotch Tape, Formica and Fiberglas have succeeded in this way. However, their very success may threaten the company's

states what the package should *be* or *do* for the product. Should the main functions of the package be to offer product protection, introduce a new dispensing method, communicate certain qualities about the product, the brand or the company, or something else? Decisions, then, must be made on package design that cover specific elements of the package, such as size, shape, materials, colour, text and brand mark. These various elements must work together to support the product's position and marketing strategy. The package must be consistent with the product's advertising, pricing and distribution.

After selecting and introducing the package, the company should check it regularly in the face of changing consumer preferences and advances in technology. In the past, a package design might last for 15 years before it needed changes. However, in today's rapidly changing environment, most companies must recheck their packaging every two or three years.[22]

Keeping a package up to date usually requires only minor but regular changes – changes so subtle that they may go unnoticed by most consumers. But some packaging changes involve complex decisions, drastic action and high cost. Whether the changes are minor or major, marketers must weigh the costs of change against the risks, on the one hand, and, on the other, the impact on consumer perceptions of the value added by the new packaging and the extent of fulfilling marketing objectives. For example, in 1996 Pepsi spent $500 million on revamping the Pepsi packaging – it changed the colour from red to blue – but survey results revealed that this had done little to arouse attention or dent rival Coca-Cola's supremacy. Only half of all fizzy-drink buyers had noticed the change and only 18 per cent who had noticed the change thought that it made the packaging more attractive.[23] In making packaging decisions, the company also must heed growing environmental concerns about packaging and make decisions that serve society's interests as well as immediate customer and company objectives. However, determining just what serves the best interests of consumers and society can sometimes be tricky (see Marketing Highlight 13.4).

Labelling Decisions

Labels may range from simple tags attached to products to complex graphics that are part of the package. They perform several functions. At the very least, the label *identifies* the product or brand, such as the name 'Sunkist' stamped on oranges. The label might also *grade* the product, or *describe* several things about the product – who made it, where it was made, when it was made, its contents, how it is to be used and how to use it safely. Finally, the label might *promote* the product through attractive graphics.

There has been a long history of legal concerns about labels. Labels can mislead customers, fail to describe important ingredients or fail to include needed safety warnings. As a result, many countries have laws to regulate labelling. Sellers must ensure that their labels contain all the required information and comply with national or international (e.g. USA, EU) requirements.

Product-Support Services Decisions

Customer service is another element of product strategy. A company's offer to the marketplace usually includes some services, which can be a minor or a major part of the total offer. In fact, the offer can range from a pure good on the one hand to a pure service on the other. In Chapter 15, we will discuss services as products in themselves. Here, we address **product-support services** – services that augment

product-support services
Services that augment actual products.

Eyeful Power: Packaging Toys is not Kids' Stuff

Marketing Highlight 13.4

Designing effective packaging for toys is getting increasingly difficult as this is an area that manufacturers claim is strewn with clichés and restrictions. Why is this so?

Take a typical toy shop. In it, often hundreds to thousands (in the case of Toys 'R' Us) of items are stacked from floor to ceiling and all rely upon eye-catching packaging to attract little consumers', and their parents', attention. Being noticed among all this is akin to trying to whistle a jingle while a Nirvana record plays.

In the battle to gain attention, toy manufacturers have literally to 'turn up the visual volume' to the extent that packaging in the norm becomes violently loud. This loud visual display is exemplified by banks of pink, pale blue and frills (reminiscent of an evening with Dame Edna) with Barbie, Sindy, My Little Pony and their 'me-toos' and accessories reaching out to small girls. These are counter-matched by the fluorescent yellows, oranges, blacks and blues of ever larger, uglier and more deadly looking toy weapons, vehicles, Crash Dummies and Biker Mice from Mars – all seeking to attract the boys. Political correctness has no place here! Toy packaging aimed at children aged five years and older is apparently violently garish (and unashamedly sexist).

Interestingly, only in the pre-school and more educational categories does some tranquillity (in terms of colours) reign, maybe because

these are targeted at parents who are doing the choosing.

The old-timer Matchbox is abandoning its old, dated blue-grid packs and introducing the 'obligatory' fluorescents. Bright orange and yellow are found across its full product mix of 340 different lines. Matchbox has had to jettison its familiar old blue look and move in pace with everything else on the shelves.

Packaging design, however, seems to look different and dull when it comes to educational toys for 8-year-olds and older children. Here manufacturers avoid sledgehammer colours and brash presentation on packaging because these toys are generally aimed at both sexes.

Manufacturers seem to face a general problem in finding a balance between worthiness and aspiration. For example, the 'Fun With ...' range is, by most parents' standards, a worthy toy because of the educational benefits offered to kids. But it comes in exceptionally dull packaging that seems to contradict the aspirational value of the toy (the pack features two children using the product, but even they do not seem to be having much fun).

Manufacturers can get it right sometimes. Hornby's The Eliminator (a big-gun toy) and Duplo's range are presented in packaging that effectively communicates the benefits of their individual products.

Hornby's packaging for The Eliminator, sporting sci-fi style with lots of exaggerated perspec-

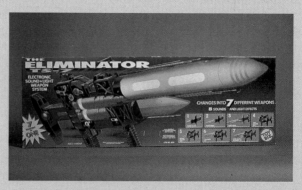

Toy packaging: loud and violent colours reign when it comes to packaging toys for boys.

tive, is dramatic and exciting. It clearly conveys the toy's fantasy value. The box size – almost as big as the child – is also important. The colours are loud, but still manage to stand out from the general clutter of colour on-shelf. Uses and benefits are also clearly explained on the front of the box, just as an adult would expect these to be displayed on a drill's packaging.

Duplo's packaging has been designed to appeal to under-5s, although parents are the main buyers for this age group. Duplo has strong brand identification, which helps, given that this is a very important element for mums and dads. The packaging's visual character is supposed to amplify the product inside. The happy, smiling child showing off the end result of play reinforces the worthiness of the toy (and fulfils mum's and

dad's aspirations for the child!). The pack's exciting physical presence also has an edge – you can tell it is Duplo from a mile off.

Packaging design for toys is not just getting 'eyeful power'. Manufacturers say that it is easy to get it wrong, difficult to strike a balance between aspirations and worthiness, and difficult to be really innovative. Manufacturers must, nonetheless, pay attention to target consumers (who uses the toy, who does the choosing, etc.) and design appropriate packaging that will effectively do the job of attracting and communicating with its target audience. Only then will it stand out from the crowd – on-shelf and in sales!

SOURCE: Rod Springett, 'Eyeful power', *Marketing Week* (29 April 1994), pp. 48–9.

actual products. More and more companies are using product-support services as a vital tool in gaining competitive advantage.

Good customer service makes sound business sense. It costs less to keep the goodwill of existing customers than it does to attract new customers or woo back lost customers. Firms that provide high-quality service usually outperform their less service-oriented competitors. A study comparing the performance of businesses that had high and low customer ratings of service quality found that the high-service businesses managed to charge more, grow faster and make more profits.[24] Clearly, marketers need to think about their service strategies.

● *Deciding on the Service Mix*

A company should design its product and support services to meet the needs of target customers. Customers vary in the value they assign to different services. Some consumers want credit and financing services, fast and reliable delivery, or quick installation. Others put more weight on technical information and advice, training in product use, or after-sale service and repair. Thus the first step in deciding which product-support services to offer is to determine both the services that target consumer value and the relative importance of these services.

Determining customers' service needs involves more than simply monitoring complaints that come in over freephone lines or on comment cards. The company should periodically survey its customers to get ratings of current services as well as ideas for new ones.

Products can often be designed to reduce the amount of servicing required. Thus companies need to co-ordinate their product-design and service-mix decisions. For example, the Canon home copier uses a disposable toner cartridge that greatly reduces the need for service calls. Kodak and 3M design products that can be 'plugged in' to a central diagnostic facility that performs tests, locates troubles and fixes equipment over telephone lines. A key to successful service strategy, therefore, is to design products that rarely break down and are easily fixable with little service expense.

● *Delivering Product-Support Services*

Finally, companies must decide how they want to deliver product-support services to customers. For example, consider the many ways an electrical appliance manufacturer might offer repair services on its main appliances. It could hire and train its own service people and locate them across the country. It could arrange with distributors and dealers to provide the repair services, or it could leave it to independent companies to provide these services.

● *The Customer Service Department*

Given the importance of customer service as a marketing tool, many companies have set up strong customer service departments to handle complaints and adjustments, credit service, maintenance service, technical service and consumer information. Many others have set up hot lines to handle consumer complaints and requests for information. By keeping records on the types of request and complaint, the customer service department can press for needed changes in product design, quality control, high-pressure selling and so on. An active customer service department co-ordinates all the company's services, creates consumer satisfaction and loyalty, and helps the company to further set itself apart from competitors.

Product Line Decisions

product line
A group of products that are closely related because they function in a similar manner, are sold to the same customer groups, are marketed through the same types of outlet, or fall within given price ranges.

We have looked at product strategy decisions such as branding, packaging, labelling and services for individual products. But product strategy also calls for building a product line. A **product line** is a group of products that are closely related because they function in a similar manner, are sold to the same customer groups, are marketed through the same types of outlet, or fall within given price ranges. For example, Volvo produces several lines of cars, Philips produces several lines of hi-fi systems and Nike produces several lines of athletic shoes. In formulating product line strategies, marketers face a number of tough decisions.

Product Line-Length Decisions

Product line managers have to decide on product line length. Product line length is influenced by company objectives. Companies that want to be positioned as full-line companies, or that are seeking high market share and market growth, usually carry longer lines. Companies that are keen on high short-term profitability generally carry shorter lines consisting of selected items.

Over time, product line managers tend to add new products either to use up excess manufacturing capacity, or because the sales force and distributors are calling for a more complete product line to satisfy their customers, or because the firm needs to add items to the product line to increase sales and profits.

However, as the manager adds items, several costs rise: design and engineering costs, inventory carrying costs, manufacturing changeover costs, order-processing costs, transportation costs, and promotional costs to introduce new items. Consequently, the company must plan product line growth carefully. It can systematically increase the length of its product line in two ways: by *stretching* its line and by *filling* its line. Every company's product line covers a certain range of

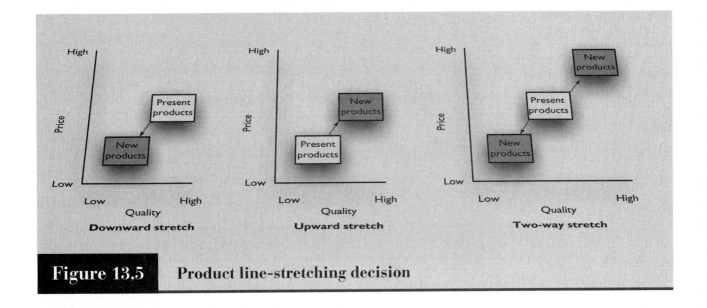

| **Figure 13.5** | **Product line-stretching decision** |

the products offered by the industry as a whole. For example, BMW cars are located in the medium-high price range of the car market. Nissan focuses on the low-to-medium price range. **Product line stretching** occurs when a company lengthens its product line beyond its current range. Figure 13.5 shows that the company can stretch its line downwards, upwards or both ways.

product line stretching
Increasing the product line by lengthening it beyond its current range.

• *Downward Stretch*

Downward stretching occurs when a company that is located at the upper end of the market later stretches its lines downwards. The firm may have first entered the upper end to establish a quality image and intended to roll downwards later. It may be responding to an attack on the upper end by invading the low end. Or a company may add a low-end product to plug a market hole that otherwise would attract a new competitor. It may find faster growth taking place at the low end.

Xerox, for example, expanded into the small copier segment for all of these reasons. Although Xerox has long dominated the medium and large copier segments, by the late 1980s, the small copier segment was growing at a much faster rate. Canon, Sharp and other Japanese competitors had entered the low-end segment, where they quickly dominated. Moreover, these competitors used their success at the low end as a base for competing with Xerox in the mid-size copier segment. Thus, to meet shifts in the market demand and to blunt competitor thrusts, Xerox introduced a line of small copiers. Similarly, Compaq and IBM had to add less expensive personal computer lines to fend off competition from low-priced 'clones' and to take advantage of faster market growth in the lower end of the computer market.

In stretching downwards, the company faces some risks. The low-end item might provoke competitors to counteract by moving into the higher end. The company's dealers may not be willing or able to handle the lower-end products. Or the move may confuse the customer. Parker Pen introduced a cheap disposable ball point, called Itala, in 1976, in an attempt to take on the Japanese in the low end of the market. Parker had always been positioned at the top end of the market as a high-quality, high-price product (it cost more, but delivered more). The foray into the disposable pen sector was a classic brand-confusing error. According to Mr Jacques Margry, Parker's chairman: 'By going down-market we confused the

With the Compact, BMW 'downward stretched' its product line to meet competitors head-on in the 'small-size high-volume' car sector.

customer; the consumer no longer knew what Parker stood for. We were all over the place, dissipating the advertising.'[25]

A more serious problem with downward stretching is that the new low-end item might eat away at the sales of or *cannibalize* the company's higher-end items, leaving the company worse off. Consider the following:

> General Electric's Medical Systems Division is the market leader in CAT scanners, expensive diagnostic machines used in hospitals. GE learned that a Japanese competitor was planning to attack its market. GE executives guessed that the new Japanese model would be smaller, more electronically advanced and less expensive. GE's best defence would be to introduce a similar lower-priced machine before the Japanese model entered the market. But some GE executives expressed concerns that this lower-priced version would hurt the sales and higher profit margins on their large CAT scanner. One manager finally settled the issue by saying: 'Aren't we better off to cannibalize ourselves than to let the Japanese do it?'

● *Upward Stretch*

Companies at the lower end of the market may want to enter the higher end. They may be attracted by a faster growth rate or higher margins at the higher end, or they may simply want to position themselves as full-line manufacturers. Sometimes, companies move up-market in order to add prestige to their current products, as when America's Chrysler purchased Lamborghini, the maker of exotic, hand-crafted sports cars.

An upward stretch decision can be risky. The higher-end competitors not only are well entrenched, but also may strike back by entering the lower end of the market. Prospective customers may not believe that the newcomer can produce quality products. Finally, the company's salespeople and distributors may lack the talent and training to serve the higher end of the market.

● *Two-Way Stretch*

Companies in the middle range of the market may decide to stretch their lines in both directions. Sony did this to hold off copycat competitors of its Walkman line of personal tape players. Sony introduced its first Walkman in the middle of the market. As imitative competitors moved in with lower-priced models, Sony stretched downwards. At the same time, in order to add lustre to its lower-priced models and to attract more affluent consumers keen to trade up to a better model, Sony stretched the Walkman line upwards. It sells more than 100 models, ranging from a plain playback-only version for £20 to a high-tech, high-quality £350 version that both plays and records. Using this two-way stretch strategy, Sony came to dominate the global personal tape player market.

● *Product Line-Filling Decisions*

Rather than stretching into lower- or higher-end segments, the firm can lengthen its product line by adding more items within the present range of the line. There are several reasons for **product line filling**: reaching for extra profits, trying to satisfy dealers, trying to use excess capacity, trying to be the leading full-line company, and trying to plug holes to keep out competitors. Thus Sony filled its line by adding solar-powered and waterproof Walkmans and an ultralight model that attaches to a sweatband for joggers, cyclists, tennis players and other exercisers.

> **product line filling**
> *Increasing the product line by adding more items within the present range of the line.*

However, line filling is overdone if it results in cannibalization and customer confusion. The company should, therefore, ensure that new items are *noticeably different* from existing ones.

● *Product Line-Modernization Decisions*

In some cases, product line length is adequate but performance may be improved by modernizing or revamping the products. For example, a company's machine tools may have a 1950s look and lose out to better-styled competitors' lines.

The firm can overhaul the line piecemeal or all at once. A piecemeal approach allows the company to test customers' and dealers' response to the new styles before changing the whole line. It also causes less drain on the company's cash flow. A big disadvantage of piecemeal modernization is that it allows competitors to see changes and start redesigning their own lines.

Product-Mix Decisions

Some companies may offer, not one, but several lines of products which form a **product mix** or *product assortment*. For example, a cosmetics firm may have four main product lines in its product mix: cosmetics, jewellery, fashions and household items. Each product line may consist of a range of items or sublines. Take cosmetics. This could be broken down into several sublines – lipstick, powder, nail varnish, eye-shadows and so on. Each subline may have many individual items. For example, eye-shadows contain a string of items, ranging from different colours to alternative application modes (e.g. pencil, roll-on, powder).

> **product mix (product assortment)**
> *The set of all product lines and items that a particular seller offers for sale to buyers.*

A company's product mix has four important dimensions: width, length, depth and consistency. Table 13.2 illustrates these concepts with selected Procter & Gamble consumer products.

The *width* of the product mix refers to the number of different product lines the company carries – 6 in the case of Procter & Gamble. (In fact, P & G produces many more lines, including mouthwashes, paper towels, disposable nappies, pain relievers and cosmetics.)

Table 13.2	**Product mix width and product line length shown for selected Procter & Gamble products**

	PRODUCT MIX WIDTH				
DETERGENTS	TOOTHPASTE	BAR SOAP	DEODORANTS	FRUIT JUICES	LOTIONS
Ivory Snow	Gleem	Ivory	Secret	Citrus Hill	Wondra
Dreft	Crest	Camay	Sure	Sunny Delight	Noxema
Tide	Complete	Lava		Winter Hill	Oil of Ulay
Joy	Denquel	Kirk's		Texsun	Camay
Cheer		Zest		Lincoln	Raintree
Oxydol		Safeguard		Speas Farm	Tropic Tan
Dash		Coast			Bain de Soleil
Cascade		Oil of Ulay			
Ivory Liquid					
Gain					
Dawn					
Era					
Bold 3					
Liquid Tide					
Solo					

(Product line length — left margin label)

The *length* of P & G's product mix refers to the total number of items the company carries, which is 42. We can also compute the average length of a line at P & G by dividing the total length (here, 42) by the number of lines (here, 6). So, the average P & G product line consists of 7 brands.

The *depth* or number of versions offered of each brand or product in the line can also be counted. Thus, if Crest comes in three sizes and two formulations (paste and gel), Crest has a depth of 6.

The *consistency* of the product mix refers to how closely related the various product lines are in end use, production requirements, distribution channels or some other way. P & G's product lines are consistent insofar as they are consumer goods that go through the same distribution channels. The lines are less consistent insofar as they perform different functions for buyers.

These product-mix dimensions provide the handles for defining the company's product strategy. The company can increase its business in four ways:

1. It can add new product lines, thus widening its product mix. In this way, its new lines build on the company's reputation in its other lines.

2. The company can lengthen its existing product lines to become a more full-line company.

3. It can add more product versions of each product and thus deepen its product mix.

4. The company can pursue more product line consistency, or less, depending on whether it wants to have a strong reputation in a single field or in several fields.

International Product Decisions

We now turn to some of the key issues that marketers consider in making international product decisions. International marketers face special product and packaging challenges. As discussed in Chapter 5, they must decide what products to introduce in which countries, and how much of the product to standardize or adapt for world markets. Companies must usually respond to national differences by adapting their product offerings. Something as simple as an electrical outlet can create big product problems:

> Those who have travelled to Europe know the frustration of electrical plugs, different voltages, and other annoyances of international travel. … Philips, the electrical appliance manufacturer, has to produce 12 kinds of irons to serve just its European market. The problem is that Europe still lacks a universal [electrical] standard. The ends of irons bristle with different plugs for different countries. Some have three prongs, others two; prongs protrude straight or angled, round or rectangular, fat, thin, and sometimes sheathed. There are circular plug faces, squares, pentagons, and hexagons. Some are perforated and some are notched. One French plug has a niche like a keyhole; British plugs carry fuses.[26]

Packaging also presents new challenges for international marketers. Packaging issues can be subtle. For example, names, labels and colours may not translate easily from one country to another. Consumers in different countries also vary in their packaging preferences. Europeans like efficient, functional, recyclable boxes with understated designs. In contrast, the Japanese often use packages as gifts. Thus in Japan, Lever Brothers packages its Lux soap in stylish gift boxes. Packaging may even have to be tailored to meet the physical characteristics of consumers in various parts of the world. For instance, soft drinks are sold in smaller cans in Japan to fit the smaller Japanese hand better.

Companies may have to adapt their packaging to meet specific regulations regarding package design or label contents. For instance, some countries ban the use of any foreign language on labels; other countries require that labels be printed in two or more languages. Labelling laws vary greatly from country to country. The international firm would do well to study these and modify its product packaging and labels to conform with local requirements.

In summary, whether domestic or international, product strategy calls for complex decisions on product mix, product line, branding, packaging and service strategy. These decisions must be made not only with a full understanding of consumer wants and competitors' strategies, but also with considerable sensitivity to the regulatory environment affecting both product and packaging.

Summary

The concept of a *product* is complex and includes three levels: the *core product*, the *actual product* and the *augmented product*. Marketers must develop a product strategy that calls for co-ordinated decisions on product items, product lines and the product mix.

The *core product* is the essential benefit that the customer is really buying. The *actual product* includes the features, styling, quality, brand name and packaging of the product offered for sale. The *augmented product* is the actual product plus the various services offered with it, such as warranty, installation, maintenance and free delivery.

There are three basic types of *product classification*. *Durable goods* are used over an extended period of time. *Non-durable goods* are consumed more quickly, usually in a single use or on a few usage occasions. *Services* are activities or benefits offered for sale which are basically intangible and do not result in ownership of anything. Each of these products can be bought by either consumer or industrial customers. *Consumer goods* are sold to the final end-user for personal consumption. *Industrial goods* are bought by individuals or organizations as goods that will receive further processing, or for use in conducting a business.

Marketers make *individual product decisions* for each product, including *product attribute decisions*, *brand*, *packaging*, *labelling* and *product-support services* decisions. *Product attributes* deliver benefits through tangible aspects of the product, including quality, features and design. A *brand* is a way to identify and differentiate goods or services through use of a name or distinctive design element, resulting in long-term value known as *brand equity*. Branding poses challenging decisions to the marketer, ranging from deciding whether to brand or not, selecting a brand name and deciding the brand sponsor to determining the brand strategy and brand repositioning opportunities. The product *package* and *labelling* are also important elements in the product decision mix, as they both carry brand equity through appearance and affect product performance with functionality.

The level of *product-support services* provided can also have a major effect on the appeal of the product to a potential purchaser. They add value for customers and are effective weapons against competitors. The company must determine the most important services to offer and the best ways to deliver them. The *service mix* should be co-ordinated by a customer service department that handles complaints and adjustments, credit, maintenance, technical service and customer information. *Customer service* should be used as a marketing tool to create customer satisfaction and competitive advantage.

Product strategy goes a step beyond individual product decisions, requiring that offerings be built into a logical portfolio through *product line decisions*. A product line is a group of products that are closely related because of similar function, customers, channels of distribution or pricing. A key dimension of the product line is the number of items it contains, referred to as the *product line length*. Profits are optimal when the line is of proper length. The product line length can be increased by *stretching upwards* to a higher-priced segment, or by *stretching both ways*. Profits can sometimes be increased by *product line filling*, adding more items within the present range of the line. Managers also keep their products current through *product line modernization*.

Organizations manage multiple product lines through *product-mix decisions*. A company's product mix has four basic dimensions: *width*, *length*, *depth* and *consistency*. The *width* of a product mix refers to the number of different types of product line that a company offers. Product-mix *length* is the total number of items that the company carries. *Depth* pertains to the number of versions, such as colours or flavours, offered for each product in a line. *Consistency* is a measure of how closely related different product lines are to one another. Consistency can be judged based on end use, channels of distribution or production methods.

Marketers face complex considerations in *international product decisions* including: a decision about what products to introduce in what countries; whether to *standardize* the product and packaging; and whether to *adapt* it to local conditions.

Overall, developing products and brands is a complex and demanding task. There are no firm rules that can assure success in these decisions. Market-oriented firms use the product as a means of creating a differential advantage. A sound product strategy always takes customers' needs and wants into consideration. For long-term success, marketing decision makers must evaluate the many issues in making product decisions and maintain consistency with broad company objectives.

Key Terms

Actual product 561
Augmented product 561
Brand 571
Brand equity 572
Brand extension 581
Capital items 566
Co-branding 577
Company and individual brand strategy 582
Consumer product 563
Convenience product 563
Core product 561
Corporate brand strategy 582
Corporate licensing 580

Durable product 562
Industrial product 565
Licensed brand 577
Line extension 580
Manufacturer's brand (or national brand) 577
Materials and parts 565
Multibrand strategy 582
Non-durable product 562
Packaging 583
Packaging concept 584
Private brand (middleman, distributor or store brand) 577
Product 561

Product line 588
Product line filling 591
Product line stretching 588
Product mix (or product assortment) 591
Product quality 566
Product-support services 585
Range branding strategy 582
Services 561
Shopping product 564
Speciality product 564
Supplies and services 566
Unsought product 564

Discussing the Issues

1. What are the core, tangible and augmented products of the educational experience that universities offer?

2. How would you classify the product offered by restaurants: as durable goods or as services? Why?

3. In recent years, many European and US car makers have tried to reposition many of their brands. Thinking about examples of such repositioning efforts, describe whether a brand has moved to a high-quality end of the market or moved down-market. How easy is it for car makers to reposition their brands? What else could they do to change consumers' perceptions of their cars?

4. Why are many people willing to pay more for branded products than for unbranded products? What does this say about the value of branding?

5. Coca-Cola started with one type of cola drink. Now we find Coke in nearly a dozen varieties. Why do consumer-goods manufacturers extend their brands? What issues do these brand extensions raise for manufacturers, retailers and consumers?

6. Compare brand extension by the brand owner with licensing a brand name for use by another company. What are the opportunities and risks of each approach?

Applying the Concepts

1. Go to your local supermarket/major grocery retail outlet. Select a product category ranging from food, beverages and household detergents to toiletries and paper products (e.g. baked beans, soft drinks, dishwashing or laundry detergents, household disinfectants, toilet tissues). Identify the branded

labels. Do you see any own-label products? Are there any differences between the branded and the retailer's private label? If so, why do you think these differences exist? If the answer is no, how do you think brand manufacturers could differentiate their brands from those of the retailers?

2. Refer to the world's top ten brands (Marketing Highlight 13.2). Select any one of the brands listed,

preferably one with which you are familiar. Considering the product, identify the roles that quality, design, packaging and product-support services play in projecting brand values and differentiating the brand from competitors' offerings. Can you also indicate the importance of the core, tangible and augmented product in building the brand's strength and identity?

References

1. See 'What lies behind the sweet smell of success', *Business Week* (27 February 1984), pp. 139–43; S.J. Diamond, 'Perfume equals part mystery, part marketing', *Los Angeles Times* (22 April 1988), sect. 4, p. 1; Pat Sloan, 'Revlon leads new fragrance charge', *Advertising Age* (16 July 1990), p. 14; Joanne Lipman, 'Big "outsert" really puts Revlon in vogue', *Wall Street Journal* (17 September 1992), p. B6.

2. For more information on product classifications, see Patrick E. Murphy and Ben M. Enis, 'Classifying products strategically', *Journal of Marketing* (July 1986), pp. 24–42.

3. Otis Port, 'The quality imperative: questing for the best', *Business Week*, special issue on quality (1991), p. 7.

4. David A. Garvin, 'Competing on eight dimensions of quality', *Harvard Business Review* (November–December 1987), p. 109. See also Robert Jacobson and David A. Aaker, 'The strategic role of product quality', *Journal of Marketing* (October 1987), pp. 31–44; Frank Rose, 'Now quality means service too', *Fortune* (22 April 1992), pp. 97–108.

5. Gunilla Kines, 'A walk on the safe side', *The European Magazine* (24–30 April 1997), p. 12; Maria Werner, 'IKEA's design for thrifty, stylish living', *The European Magazine* (24–30 April 1997), p. 15.

6. Susan Lambert, *Form Follows Function* (London: Victoria and Albert Museum, 1993), p. 57.

7. For more on design, see Christopher Lorenz, *The Design Dimension* (Oxford: Blackwell, 1990); see also Philip Kotler, 'Design: a powerful but neglected strategic tool', *Journal of Business Strategy* (Fall 1984), pp. 16–21; Stephen Potter, Robin Roy, Claire H. Capon, Margaret Bruce, Vivien Walsh and Janny Lewis, *The Benefits and Costs of Investment in Design: Using professional design expertise in product, engineering and graphics projects* (Manchester: Open University/UMIST, September 1991).

8. Pete Engardio, 'Quick, name five Taiwanese PC makers', *Business Week* (18 May 1992), pp. 128–9.

9. See Peter D. Bennett, *Dictionary of Marketing Terms* (Chicago, IL: American Marketing Association, 1988).

10. Jean-Noel Kapferer, *Strategic Brand Management: New approaches to creating and evaluating brand equity* (London: Kogan Page, 1992), pp. 38 ff.

11. David A. Aaker, *Managing Brand Equity* (New York: Free Press, 1991).

12. See T.P. Barwise, C.J. Higson, J.A. Likierman and P.R. Marsh, *Accounting for Brands* (London: Institute of Chartered Accountants in England and Wales, 1990); Peter H. Farquhar, Julia Y. Han and Yuji Ijiri, 'Brands on the balance sheet', *Marketing Management* (Winter 1992), pp. 16–22; Kevin

Lane Keller, 'Conceptualising, measuring, and managing customer-based brand equity', *Journal of Marketing* (January 1993), pp. 1–22.

13. Keith J. Kelly, 'Coca-Cola shows that top-brand fizz', *Advertising Age* (11 July 1994), p. 3.

14. Thomas M.S. Hemnes, 'How can you find a safe trademark?', *Harvard Business Review* (March–April 1995), p. 44.

15. For a discussion of legal issues surrounding the use of brand names, see Dorothy Cohen, 'Trademark strategy', *Journal of Marketing* (January 1986), pp. 61–74; 'Trademark woes: help is coming', *Sales and Marketing Management* (January 1988), p. 84; Jack Alexander, 'What's in a name? Too much, said the FCC', *Sales and Marketing Management* (January 1989), pp. 75–8.

16. Terry Lefton, 'Warner Brothers' not very looney path to licensing gold', *Brandweek* (14 February 1994), pp. 36–7.

17. Al Ries and Jack Trout, *Positioning: The battle for your mind* (New York: McGraw-Hill, 1981).

18. For more on line extensions, see Kevin Lane Keller and David A. Aaker, 'The effects of sequential introduction of line extensions', *Journal of Marketing* (February 1992), pp. 35–50; Srinivas K. Reddy, Susan L. Holak and Subodh Bhat, 'To extend or not to extend: success determinants of line extensions', *Journal of Marketing Research* (May 1994), pp. 243–62.

19. Daniel C. Smith and C. Whan Park, 'The effects of brand extensions on market share and advertising efficiency', *Journal of Marketing Research* (August 1992), pp. 296–313. For more on the use of brand extensions and consumer attitudes towards them, see David A. Aaker and Kevin L. Keller, 'Consumer evaluations of brand extensions', *Journal of Marketing* (January 1990), pp. 27–41; Julie Liesse, 'Brand extensions take centre stage', *Advertising Age* (8 March 1993), p. 12.

20. 'Brand stretching can be fun and dangerous', *The Economist* (5 May 1990), pp. 105–6, 110; Hugh Aldersey-Williams, 'Elastic band', *Marketing Week* (29 April 1994), pp. 43–5, 47.

21. See David A. Aaker and Kevin L. Keller, 'Consumer evaluations of brand extensions', *Journal of Marketing* (January 1990), pp. 27–41; Susan Broniarczyk and Joseph Alba, 'The importance of brand in brand extension', *Journal of Marketing Research* (May 1994), pp. 214–28.

22. See Alicia Swasy, 'Sales lost their vim? Try repackaging', *Wall Street Journal* (11 October 1989), p. B1.

23. 'Spotlight: Pepsi revamp lacks sparkle', *Marketing Week* (12 July 1996), pp. 26–7; Alan Mitchell, 'Pepsi still losing the cola wars', *Marketing Week* (12 April 1996), pp. 26–7.

24. Bro Uttal, 'Companies that serve you best', *Fortune* (7 December 1987), pp. 98–116; see also William H. Davidow, 'Customer service: the ultimate marketing weapon', *Business Marketing* (October 1989), pp. 56–64; Barry Farber and Joyce Wycoff, 'Customer service: evolution and revolution', *Sales and Marketing Management* (May 1991), pp. 44–51.

25. Gary Mead, 'Parker prepares to write a new chapter', *Financial Times* (10 February 1992), p. 13.

26. Philip Cateora, *International Marketing*, 7th edn (Homewood, IL: Irwin, 1990), p. 260.

Case 13

Colgate: One Squeeze Too Many?

YOU PROBABLY KNOW ABOUT COLGATE toothpaste – perhaps you have even used it. But what would you think of Colgate aspirin or Colgate antacid? Would you buy Colgate laxatives or Colgate dandruff shampoo?

That is exactly what Colgate-Palmolive would like to know. Colgate wants to investigate the possibility of entering the over-the-counter (OTC) drugs market. Can it use its Colgate brand name, developed in the oral-care products market, in the OTC healthcare market?

Why does the OTC market interest Colgate? The first reason is market size. The worldwide OTC market annually accounts for about $30 billion sales. The US OTC market is $12 billion and Europe's is $8 billion. It is the largest non-food consumer products industry, and it is growing at over 6 per cent annually.

Several trends are fuelling this rapid growth. Consumers are more sophisticated than they were and they increasingly seek self-medication rather than seeing a doctor. Companies are also switching many previously prescription-only drugs to OTC drugs. The companies can do this when they can show, based on extensive clinical tests, that the drug is safe for consumers to use without monitoring by a doctor. Moreover, OTC drugs tend to have very long product life cycles. Medical researchers are also discovering new drugs or new uses or benefits of existing drugs. For example, researchers have found that the psyllium fibre used in some OTC natural laxatives is effective in controlling cholesterol.

Beyond the size and growth of the market, Colgate also knows that the OTC market can be extremely profitable. Analysts estimate that the average cost of goods sold for an OTC drug is only 29 per cent, leaving a gross margin of 71 per cent. Advertising and sales promotions are the largest expenditure categories for these products, accounting for an average of 42 per cent of sales. OTC drugs produce on average 11 per cent after-tax profit.

Because of the OTC market's attractiveness, Colgate conducted studies to learn the strength of its brand name with consumers. Colgate believes in the following equation: brand awareness + brand image = brand equity. Its studies found that Colgate was no. 1 in brand awareness, no. 2 in brand image and no. 2 in brand equity among OTC consumers, even though it did not sell OTC products. The Tylenol brand name earned the no. 1 spot in both brand image and brand equity.

Thus Colgate's research shows that the OTC market is very large, is growing rapidly and is very profitable, and that Colgate has a strong brand equity position with OTC consumers. Most companies would find such a situation very attractive.

Colgate realizes that entering the OTC market will not be easy. First, its research suggests that the typical OTC product does not reach the break-even point for four years and does not recover development costs until the seventh year. OTC firms must therefore be correct in their product development decisions or they risk losing a great deal of money.

Second, OTC drugs require a high level of advertising and promotion expenditures: 25 per cent of sales on year-round media alone. A firm must have substantial financial resources to enter this market.

Third, because of the market's attractiveness, entering firms face stiff competition. The market has many competitors and is the least concentrated of any large consumer market. In Europe, no company has more than 3.5 per cent of the market and the top 15 companies account for only 25 per cent market share. Established companies like Bayer, Rhône-Poulenc Rorer, Sanofi, Boots, Boehringer Ingelheim and Warner-Lambert have strong sales forces and marketing organizations. They are strong financially and are willing to take competitors to court if they perceive any violations of laws or regulations. These firms also have strong research and development organizations that spin out new products. As governments squeeze state drug budgets, ethical drug companies have been aggressively working their way into the OTC market. Among notable acquisitions are Hoffmann-La Roche's of Nicholas Laboratories and SmithKline Beecham's purchase of Stirling Winthrop from Kodak, while Merck, America's leading drug company, has teamed up with Johnson & Johnson in the OTC market. Market leaders have also bought interests in drug distribution, such as SmithKline Beecham's acquisition of Diversified Pharmaceuticals Services, US pharmacy benefits managers.

Fourth, because of the high and rising level of fixed costs, such as the costs of advertising and R & D, many smaller firms are leaving the industry or being acquired by larger firms. Many of the world's leading ethical drug companies' industry observers estimate that an OTC firm must have at least several hundred million dollars in sales. It needs this to cover fixed costs and to have the power to match big retailers. So the OTC firms are growing larger and larger, and they are willing to fight aggressively for market share.

Given all these barriers to entry, you might wonder why Colgate would want to pursue OTC products, even if the industry is growing and profitable. Colgate has adopted a strategy that aims to make it the best global consumer products company. It believes that oral-care and OTC products are very similar. Both rely on their ingredients for effectiveness, are highly regulated and use similar marketing channels.

Colgate set up its Colgate Health Care Laboratories to explore product and market development opportunities in the OTC market. In 1987 and 1988 Colgate carried out a test market for a line of OTC products developed by its Health Care Laboratories. It test marketed a wide line of OTC products, from a nasal decongestant to a natural fibre laxative, under the brand name Ektra. The predominantly white packages featured the Ektra name with the Colgate name in smaller letters below it.

Following the test market results, Colgate quietly established another test market to test a line of ten OTC healthcare products, all using the Colgate name as the brand name. The line includes Colgate aspirin-free pain reliever to compete against Tylenol, Colgate ibuprofen (versus Advil),

Colgate cold tablets (v. Contact), Colgate night-time cold medicine (v. Nyquil), Colgate antacid (v. Rolaids), Colgate natural laxative (v. Metamucil) and Colgate dandruff shampoo (v. Head and Shoulders).

Industry observers realize that the new line represents a significant departure from Colgate's traditional, high-visibility household goods and oral-care products. Responding to enquiries, Colgate chairman Reuben Marks suggests that: 'The Colgate name is already strong in oral hygiene, now we want to learn whether it can represent health care across the board. We need to expand into more profitable categories.'

Colgate will not talk specifically about its new line. Pharmacists, however, say that Colgate has blitzed the town with coupons and ads. Representatives have given away free tubes of toothpaste with purchases of the new Colgate products and have handed out coupons worth virtually the full price of the new products. One store owner noted: 'They're spending major money out there.'

If all that promotion was not enough, the manager of one store points out that Colgate has priced its line well below competing brands – as much as 20 per cent below in some cases. The same manager reports that the new products' sales are strong, but also adds: 'With all the promotion they've done, they should be. They're cheaper, and they've got Colgate's name on them.'

Yet even if Colgate's test proves a resounding success, marketing consultants say expanding the new line could prove dangerous and, ultimately, more expensive than Colgate can imagine. 'If you put the Colgate brand name on a bunch of different products, if you do it willy-nilly at the lowest end, you're going to dilute what it stands for – and if you stand for nothing, you're worthless,' observes Clive Chajet, chairman of Lipincott and Margolies, a firm that handles corporate identity projects.

Mr Chajet suggests that Colgate might also end up alienating customers by slapping its name on so many products. If consumers are 'dissatisfied with one product, they might be dissatisfied with everything across the board. I wouldn't risk it,' he says. What would have happened to Johnson & Johnson during the Tylenol poison scare, he asks, if the Tylenol name appeared on everything from baby shampoo to birth control pills?

Colgate's test is one of the bolder forays into line extensions by consumer products companies. Companies saddled with 'mature' brands – brands that cannot grow much more – often try to use those brands' solid gold name to make a new fortune, generally with a related product. Thus Procter & Gamble's Ivory soap came up with a shampoo and conditioner. Mars bars were turned into ice-confectionery. Persil extended into washing-up liquids.

Unlike those products, however, Colgate's new line moves far afield from its familiar turf. Although its new line is selling well, sales might not stay so strong without budget prices and a barrage of advertising and promotion. 'People are looking at it right now as a generic-style product,' observes one store manager. 'People are really price conscious, and as long as the price is cheaper, along with a name that you can trust, people are going to buy that over others.'

Al Ries, chairman of Trout & Ries marketing consultants, questions whether any line extensions make sense – not only for Colgate, but also for other strong brand names. He says the reason Colgate has been able to break into the OTC drugs market is that other drugs have expanded and lost their niches. Tylenol and Alka-Seltzer both now make cold medicines, for example, and 'that allows an opportunity for the outsiders, the Colgates, to come in and say there's no perception that anybody is any different. The consumer will look for any acceptable brand name.'

Mr Ries argues that Colgate and the traditional OTC medicine companies are turning their products into generic drugs instead of brands. They are losing 'the power of a narrow focus,' he says. 'It reflects stupidity on the part of the traditional over-the-counter marketers. ... If the traditional medicines maintained their narrow focus, they wouldn't leave room for an outsider such as Colgate.'

If Colgate is too successful, meanwhile, it also risks cannibalizing its flagship product. Consultants note that almost all successful line extensions, and many not-so-successful ones, hurt the product from which they took their name. They cite Miller High Life, whose share of the US beer market has dwindled since the introduction of Miller Lite. 'If Colgate made themselves to mean over-the-counter medicine, nobody would want to buy Colgate toothpaste,' contends Mr Ries.

Mr Chajet agrees. Colgate could 'save tens of millions of dollars by not having to introduce a new brand name' for its new products, he says. But in doing so, it might also 'kill the goose that laid the golden egg'. Other marketing consultants believe that Colgate may be able to break into the market, but that it will take much time and money. 'They just don't bring a lot to the OTC party,' one consultant indicates.

Although chairman Marks admits that Colgate will continue to try to build share in its traditional cleanser and detergent markets, the company seems to consider personal care a stronger area. Leveraging a name into new categories can be tricky, requiring patience from sceptical retailers and fickle consumers. 'It isn't so much a question of where you can put the brand name,' says one marketing consultant. 'It's what products the consumer will let you put the brand name on.'

QUESTIONS

1. What core product is Colgate selling when it sells toothpaste or the other products in its new line?

2. How would you classify these new products?

3. What implications does this classification have for marketing the new line?

4. What brand decisions has Colgate made? What kinds of product line decision? Are these decisions consistent?

5. If you were the marketing manager for the extended Colgate line, how would you package the new products?

6. What risks do you see in these packaging decisions?

SOURCES: Adapted from Joanne Lipman, 'Colgate tests putting its name on over-the-counter drug line', *Wall Street Journal* (19 July 1989). Used with permission. See also Dan Koeppel, 'Now playing in Peoria: Colgate generics', *Adweek's Marketing Week* (18 September 1989), p. 5; Sean Brierley, 'Drug dependence', *Marketing Week* (14 November 1994), pp. 32–5; Clive Cookson, 'Roche deal puts fizz in the drug races', *Financial Times* (4 June 1991), p. 19; Paul Abrahams, 'A dose of OTC medicine for growth strategy', *Financial Times* (30 August 1994), p. 19; 'Hoffmann-La Roche: staying calm', *The Economist* (28 September 1991), p. 120; Colgate Health Care Laboratories also co-operated in the development of this case.

14

Product Development and Life-Cycle Strategies

CHAPTER OBJECTIVES

After reading this chapter, you should be able to:

- Explain how companies find and develop new-product ideas.
- List and define the steps in the new-product development process.
- Describe the stages of the product life cycle.
- Explain how marketing strategy changes during a product's life cycle.

Preview Case

Aerostructures Hamble

MARKETS DO NOT STAND STILL. When customer needs and technology change, companies, big or small, must create new products and invest in new technology to keep abreast of such changes in the marketplace.

Aerostructures Hamble, a Hampshire (UK)-based aircraft components manufacturer, is one company that has survived many changes in its industry. Through its emphasis upon customer-oriented innovation and lean management techniques to speed up product development, it has maintained outstanding performance in a highly competitive aircraft components industry.

The company started in 1936, making the Midge and Gnat aircraft. Hawker Siddeley took it over in 1963. The aircraft-manufacturing side of Hawker Siddeley was nationalized as part of the British Aircraft Corporation, which was privatized in 1979. It became Aerostructures Hamble in 1989 when British Aerospace decided to make it more accountable as a profit centre. In 1990 Andy Barr, chief executive, joined from Rover Group and led a £46.7 million management buyout.

With a small team of ten senior managers, including Mr Barr and an operations director, Mr Wyman, who had also come from Rover, new management techniques were introduced – notably Japanese techniques devised by car manufacturers.

In the 1930s, the slipway of Aerostructures Hamble was used to launch seaplanes. In the 1990s, it is being used to dispatch cargo doors of transport planes. Its transformation from aircraft to aircraft component manufacturer is not the surprising element in Aerostructure's strategy, which reflects the many changes undergone by the British aerospace industry. What is noteworthy is the speed of execution of the order and its on-time delivery – something, Mr Wyman claims, that is totally alien to the aircraft industry.

The company stresses the need to introduce the 'right product' first time, like the Japanese car makers do. It is hard work, but all functions in the firm must be involved in innovation.

The company has invested heavily in new plant equipment, including riveting machinery, a large press, machine tools and a world-class aluminium finishing plant. It also sets tight parameters for component manufacture, using computer technology and techniques such as statistical process control, which ensure that a part will fit and comes out right first time.

In order to get things right first time, the firm approaches each new project through a multidisciplinary team with a manager who becomes the main contact with the customer. People are seconded from other parts of the firm. The manager sticks with the team from the initial bid through to completion of the project. While some of the team members might change, there is a consistent thread running right through the project, from initial conception to final delivery. The goal is to achieve a 'seamless' process as Mr Wyman suggests, which is in marked contrast with the old method of passing a project from one department to another.

Quality is given heavy emphasis, and quality control techniques, including suggestion schemes in which over 50 per cent of the staff have taken part, have borne fruitful results.

Other parts of its operations have been reworked or reorganized to allow the company to utilize just-in-time delivery of components to specific parts of its factory. It has introduced 'kitting', through which parts are dispatched to a customer in a carefully laid out package. This simple innovation enables any part missing to be immediately visible and has revolutionized the traceability of orders and saved hours of dispute.

The company's reliance on its former owner, British Aerospace, which accounted for 93 per cent of its business in 1990, fell to 78 per cent in 1993 and is expected to fall further in the late 1990s. It has successfully secured new orders and acquired an impressive blue-chip customer base, including Boeing, McDonnell Douglas, Vought and Raytheon.

The company claims that its methods are new in the aircraft components industry. While the new techniques ensure that it creates new products which are a perfect fit with customer requirements, management are well aware that it gets tougher as they go on – customer and market needs are continually evolving, and products and methods must follow suit.[1]

QUESTIONS

1. How do firms identify and develop new-product opportunities?
2. What are the steps involved in developing and commercializing new products?
3. Is new-product development a risky business, and how might firms such as Aerostructures Hamble minimize these risks?
4. What role does marketing play in new-product development?
5. Why should the firm invest continually in new-product development?
6. As the new product ages, how should the firm adapt its marketing strategies in the face of changing tastes, technologies and competition?

Introduction

In the face of changing customer needs, technologies and competition, product innovation or the development of new products has become vital to a company's survival. Introducing new products, however, is not sufficient. The firm must also know how to manage the new product as it goes through its life cycle: that is, from its birth, through growth and maturity, to eventual demise as newer products come along that better serve consumer needs.

This product life cycle presents two principal challenges. First, because all products eventually decline, the firm must find new products to replace ageing ones (the problem of *new-product development*). Second, the firm must understand how its products age and adapt its marketing strategies as products pass through life-cycle stages (the problem of *product life-cycle strategies*). We therefore look initially at the problem of finding and developing new products, and then at the challenge of managing them successfully over their life cycles.

Innovation and New-Product Development

Given the rapid changes in taste, technology and competition, a company cannot rely solely on its existing products to sustain growth or to maintain profitability. The firm can hope to maintain market and profit performance only by continuous product innovation. Product innovation encompasses a variety of product development activities – product improvement, development of entirely new ones, and extensions that increase the range or number of lines of product the firm can offer. Product innovations are not to be confused with **inventions**. The latter are a new technology or product which may or may not deliver benefits to customers. An **innovation** is defined as *an idea, product or piece of technology that has been developed and marketed to customers who perceive it as novel or new*. We may call it a process of identifying, creating and delivering new-product values or benefits that were not offered before in the marketplace. In this chapter we look specifically at new products as opposed to value creation through marketing actions (such as product/brand repositioning, segmentation of current markets).

We also need to distinguish between obtaining new products through *acquisition* – by buying a whole company, a patent or a licence to produce someone

invention
A new technology or product that may or may not deliver benefits to customers.

innovation
An idea, product or technology that has been developed and marketed to customers who perceive it as novel or new. It is a process of identifying, creating and delivering new-product service values that did not exist before in the marketplace.

new-product development
The development of original products, product improvements, product modifications and new brands through the firm's own R & D efforts.

else's product – and through **new-product development** in the company's own research and development department. As the costs of developing and introducing major new products have climbed, many large companies have decided to acquire existing brands rather than to create new ones. Other firms have saved money by copying competitors' brands or by reviving old brands. These routes can contribute to a firm's growth and have both advantages and limitations. In this chapter, we are mainly concerned with how businesses create and market new products. By new products we mean original products, product improvements, product modifications and new brands that the firm develops through its own research and development efforts.

Risks and Returns in Innovation

Innovation can be very risky for a number of reasons:

1. New-product development is an expensive affair – it cost Tate & Lyle around £150 million to develop a new sugar substitute; pharmaceutical firms spend an average of £100–50 million to develop a new drug; while developing a super-jumbo project could cost billions.

2. New-product development takes time. Although companies can dramatically shorten their development time, in many industries, such as pharmaceuticals, biotechnology, aerospace and food, new-product development cycles can be as long as 10–15 years. The uncertainty and unpredictability of market environments further raise the risks of commercialization. Boots had to withdraw Manoplex, a heart drug, less than a year after its launch in the United Kingdom, after a trial on 3,000 patients in the United States and Scandinavia suggested an adverse effect on patient survival. The pharmaceuticals division lost about £200 million on the drug, which cost nearly £100 million to develop over a period of 12 years, and about £20 million was spent on promoting and marketing it.[2]

3. Unexpected delays in development are also a problem. History is littered with grand pioneering engineering projects which have failed to satisfy the original expectations of bankers, investors and politicians. The Seikan rail tunnel, connecting the island of Hokkaido to mainland Japan, was completed 14 years late and billions of pounds over budget; the £10 billion cost of the Channel tunnel, which opened on 6 May 1994, a year later than originally planned, is more than double the £4.8 billion forecast in 1987.

4. The new-product success record is not encouraging either. New products continue to fail at a disturbing rate. One recent study estimated that new consumer packaged goods (consisting mostly of line extensions) fail at a rate of 80 per cent. The same high failure rate appears to afflict new financial products and services, such as credit cards, insurance plans and brokerage services. Another study found that about 33 per cent of new industrial products fail at launch.[3]

Despite the risks, firms that learn to innovate well become less vulnerable to attacks by new entrants which discover new ways of delivering added values, benefits and solutions to customers' problems.

Why Do New Products Fail?

Concorde aircraft (an Anglo-French project), PCjr personal computer (IBM), Betamax video cassette recorder (Sony), EuroDisneyland (Walt Disney/ EuroDisney

The Net Worker.

www.nokia.com

The Nokia 9000 Communicator.
A phone, fax, Web browser, E-Mail terminal,
SMS message device and personal organiser in one.

NOKIA
CONNECTING PEOPLE

Nokia and the arrows symbol are registered trademarks.

With this all-in-one pocket phone, fax, diary and E-Mail terminal, Nokia creates value that has never existed before.

Group), the C5 (Clive Sinclair's electric car) all have one thing in common – they all failed to meet target returns on investment, and therefore joined the ranks of new-product failure.

Why do so many new products fail? There are several reasons. Although an idea may be good, the market size may have been overestimated. Perhaps the actual product was not designed as well as it should have been. It may be a 'me too' product which is no better than products that are already established in the marketplace. Or maybe it was incorrectly positioned in the market, priced too high, or advertised and promoted poorly. A high-level executive might push a favourite idea despite poor marketing research findings. Sometimes the costs of product development are higher than budgeted and sometimes competitors fight back harder than expected.

What Governs New-Product Success?

Because so many new products fail, companies are anxious to learn how to improve their odds of new-product success. One way is to identify successful new products and find out what they have in common. One study of new-product successes found that the no. 1 success factor is a *unique superior product*, one with higher quality, new features and higher value in use. Another key success factor is a *well-defined product concept* prior to development, in which the company carefully defines and assesses the target market, the product requirements and the benefits before proceeding. New products that *meet market needs* more closely than existing products invariably do well. Other success factors included *technological and marketing synergy, quality of execution in all stages* and *market attractiveness*.⁴ Thus to create successful new products, a company must understand its consumers, markets and competitors, and develop products that deliver superior value to customers.

Successful new-product development may be even more difficult in the future. Keen competition has led to increasing market fragmentation – companies must now aim at smaller market segments rather than the mass market, and this means smaller sales and profits for each product. New products must meet growing social and government constraints, such as consumer safety and environmental standards. The costs of finding, developing and launching new products will increase steadily due to rising manufacturing, media and distribution costs. Many companies cannot afford or cannot raise the funds needed for new-product development. Instead, they emphasize product modification and imitation rather than true innovation. Even when a new product is successful, rivals are so quick to copy it that the new product is typically fated to have only a short life.

So, companies face a problem – they must develop new products, but the odds weigh heavily against success. The solution lies in strong *new-product planning* and in setting up a systematic *new-product development process* for finding and growing new products. Top management is ultimately accountable for the new-product success record. It must take the lead, rather than simply ask lower-level staff or the new-product manager to come up with great ideas. It must define the business domains and product categories that the company wants to focus on. Many or most new-product ideas are likely to be unsuitable for development. Management must encourage the search for a large pool of ideas from which potential winners emerge. To facilitate the selection process, it must establish specific criteria for new-product idea acceptance, based on the specific *strategic role* the product is expected to play. The product's role might be to help the company maintain its industry position as an innovator, to defend a market-share position, or to get a foothold in a future new market. Or the new product might help the company to take advantage of its special strengths or exploit technology in a new way.

Another crucial decision facing top management is how much to budget for new-product development. New-product outcomes are so uncertain that it is difficult to use normal investment criteria for budgeting. Some companies solve this problem by encouraging and financing as many projects as possible, hoping to achieve a few winners. Other companies set their R & D budgets by applying a conventional percentage-to-sales figure or by spending what the competition spends. Still other companies decide how many successful new products they need and work backwards to estimate the required R & D investment.

Another important factor in new-product development work is to set up effective organizational structures for nurturing innovation and handling new products. Successful new-product development requires a company-wide effort. Successful innovative companies make a consistent commitment of resources to new-product development, design and new-product strategy that is linked to their strategic planning process, and set up formal and sophisticated organizational arrangements for managing the new-product development process (see Marketing Highlight 14.1). Let us now take a look at the major steps in the new-product development process.

New-Product Development Process

The new-product development process for finding and growing new products consists of nine main steps (see Figure 14.1).

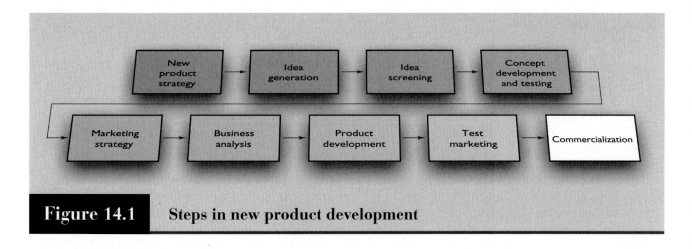

Figure 14.1 **Steps in new product development**

New-Product Strategy

Effective product innovation is guided by a well-defined *new-product strategy*. The new-product strategy achieves four main goals: first, it gives direction to the new-product team and *focuses team effort*; second, it helps to *integrate* functional or departmental efforts; third, where understood by the new-product team, it allows tasks to be *delegated* to team members, who can be left to operate independently; and fourth, the very act of producing and getting managers to agree on a strategy requires *proactive*, not reactive, management, which increases the likelihood of a more thorough search for innovation opportunities. For example, Bausch & Lomb, the contact lens and lens-care products maker, was on the verge of losing its market position in the late 1980s because its managers had concentrated for too long on product improvement. It almost missed new product opportunities like extended-wear contact lenses. Fortunately, managers reviewed their new-product strategy and spotted many more opportunities for innovation, which they eventually capitalized on.[5]

Successful innovative companies are placing more emphasis upon the use of definitive strategy statements or a **product innovation charter (PIC)**. The PIC draws managers' attention to the reasons or *rationale* behind the firm's search for innovation opportunities, the *product/market* and *technology* to focus on, the miscellaneous *goals* or *objectives* (market share, cash flow, profitability, etc.) to be achieved, and *guidelines* on the nature or level of innovativeness that will sell the new product.[6] The charter spells out the priority that managers should place on developing breakthrough products, changing existing ones and imitating competitors' products.

product innovation charter (PIC)
A new-product strategy statement formalizing management's reasons or rationale behind the firm's search for innovation opportunities, the product/market and technology to focus upon, and the goals and objectives to be achieved.

idea generation
The systematic search for new-product ideas.

Idea Generation

The PIC should then direct the search for new-product ideas. **Idea generation** should be systematic rather than haphazard. Otherwise, although the company will find many ideas, most will not be good ones for its type of business. A company typically has to generate many ideas in order to find a few good ones. A recent survey of product managers found that of 100 proposed new product ideas, 39 begin the product development process, 17 survive the development process, 8 actually reach the marketplace and only 1 eventually reaches its business objectives.[7]

To obtain a flow of new-product ideas, the company can tap many sources. Chief sources of new-product ideas include internal sources, customers, competitors, distributors and suppliers.

3M: Championing Innovation

The 3M Company markets more than 60,000 products. These products range from sandpaper, adhesives and floppy disks to contact lenses, laser optical disks, aerosol inhalers, heart-lung machines, translucent braces and futuristic synthetic ligaments; from coatings that sleeken boat hulls to hundreds of sticky tapes – Scotch Tape, masking tape, superbonding tape and even refastening disposable nappy tape. 3M views innovation as its path to growth, and new products as its lifeblood. Up till 1992, the company's longstanding goal was to derive 25 per cent of annual sales from products which had been on the market for less than five years. In the light of increasing competition in recent years, the company has, accordingly, raised its sights. Today an astonishing 30 per cent of each year's sales come from products introduced within the previous four years. Its legendary emphasis on innovation has consistently made 3M one of the world's most admired companies.

3M's impressive record is due to several factors. The company works hard to create an environment that supports innovation. It invests nearly 7 per cent of annual group sales in research and development – twice as much as the average company. Its Innovation Task Force seeks out and destroys corporate bureaucracy that might interfere with new-product progress. Hired consultants help 3M find ways to make employees more inventive.

3M's culture is innovative. Its management encourages everyone to look for new products. The company's renowned '15 per cent rule' allows all employees to spend up to 15 per cent of their time 'bootlegging' – that is, working on projects of personal interest whether or not those projects directly benefit the company. When a promising idea comes along, 3M forms a venture team made up of the researcher who developed the idea and volunteers from manufacturing, sales, marketing and legal. Developing cross-functional teams is the touchstone of 3M's efforts to facilitate the flow of technology around the company. The team nurtures the product and protects it from company bureaucracy. Team members stay with the product until it succeeds or fails and then return to their previous jobs. Some teams have tried three or four times before finally making a success of an idea. Each year, 3M hands out Golden Step Awards to venture teams whose new products earned more than $2 million in US sales, or $4 million in worldwide sales, within three years of introduction.

3M's management culture encourages the cross-fertilization of ideas between its 40 or more business units. Much of this is done through informal networking such as employee-run technical forums or getting technicians to go out and meet customers. Cross-fertilization is also reinforced by official bodies, such as audit teams, whose main function is

Championing innovation: 3M's innovation track record is hard to beat.

to go round laboratory groups and assess the commercial potential of their new-product programmes. Often they come across developments in one lab that can be helpful to another.

The company knows that it must try thousands of new-product ideas to hit one big jackpot. One well-worn slogan at 3M is 'You have to kiss a lot of frogs to find a prince.' This often means making mistakes, but 3M accepts blunders and dead ends as a normal part of creativity and innovation. Its philosophy seems to be 'If you aren't making mistakes, you probably aren't doing anything.' In line with its tolerance of failure, 3M's employees are allowed to perform their work in their own way and be allowed to make mistakes – what we call worker 'empowerment' today. As it turns out, 'blunders' have turned into some of 3M's most successful products. There is the familiar story about the chemist who accidentally spilled a new chemical on her tennis shoes. Some days later, she noticed that the spots hit by the chemical had not become dirty. Eureka! The chemical eventually became Scotchgard fabric protector.

And then there's the one about 3M scientist Spencer Silver who started out to develop a superstrong adhesive; instead he came up with one that didn't stick very well at all. He sent the apparently useless substance on to other 3M researchers to see if they could find something to do with it. Nothing happened for several years. Then Arthur Fry, another 3M scientist, had a problem – and an idea. As a choir member in a local church, Mr Fry was having trouble marking places in his hymnal – the little scraps of paper he used kept falling out. He tried dabbing some of Mr Silver's weak glue on one of the scraps. It stuck nicely and later peeled off without damaging the hymnal. Thus were born 3M's ubiquitous Post-it notes, a product that now has sales of almost $100 million a year!

3M recognizes that to maintain its formidable reputation for innovation, management must keep alive its traditional innovative culture. It must be willing to engage in self-criticism and benchmarking against other companies to ensure that it continues to create products that become winners in the marketplace. Staff must keep close to customers and be given the freedom to 'bootleg', and communication channels around the company must remain open, with cross-functional teamwork upheld to ensure inventiveness is maximized, not stifled. Reward systems must recognize group efforts, given that getting inventions and new ideas to market invariably requires extremely complex corporate teamwork. 3M acknowledges that there is no room for complacency if it wants to remain a corporate superstar.

SOURCES: Martin Dickson, 'Back to the future', *Financial Times* (30 May 1994), p. 7; '3M, 60,000 and counting', *The Economist* (30 November 1991), pp. 86–9; Russel Mitchell, 'Master of innovation: how 3M keeps its new products coming', *Business Week* (10 April 1989), pp. 58–64; Joyce Anne Oliver, '3M vet enjoys taking risks, knocking down barriers', *Marketing News* (15 April 1991), p. 13; Kevin Kelly, '3M running scared? Forget about it', *Business Week* (16 September 1991), pp. 59–62.

● *Internal Sources*

Many new-product ideas come from internal sources within the company. The company can find new ideas through formal research and development. It can pick the brains of its scientists, engineers, designers and manufacturing people. Or company executives can brainstorm new-product ideas. The company's salespeople are another good source of ideas because they are in daily contact with customers. Formal or informal suggestion schemes can also be used to tap staff's ideas. Toyota claims that employees submit two million ideas annually – about 35 suggestions per employee – and that more than 85 per cent of these ideas are implemented.

● *Customers*

Almost 28 per cent of all new-product ideas come from watching and listening to customers. The company can conduct surveys to learn about consumer needs and wants. It can analyze customer questions and complaints to find new products that better solve consumer problems. Company engineers or salespeople can meet with customers to get suggestions. General Electric's Video Products Division, Sony, Toyota and many other effective innovators are known to have their design engineers talk with final consumers to get ideas for new products. Many new ideas come from simply observing consumers.[8]

> Honda's highly acclaimed City model was conceived in this manner. Honda sent designers and engineers from the City project team to Europe to 'look around' for the best product concept for the City. Based on the British Mini-Cooper, developed decades earlier, the Honda team designed a 'short and tall' car which countered the prevailing wisdom that cars should be long and low.
>
> Observing the growing market potential in Third World countries, Boeing sent a team of engineers to those countries to study the idiosyncrasies of Third World aviation. The engineers found that many runways were too short for jet planes. Boeing redesigned the wings on its 737, added lower-pressure tyres to prevent bouncing on short landings, and redesigned the engines for quicker takeoff. As a result, the Boeing 737 became the best-selling commercial jet in history.

Customers, however, may not always know their future needs and wants. If Philips had questioned consumers in 1975 about what new technology they wanted, they would never have said a personal stereo – the idea would not have occurred to them. This is one of the reasons why Finnish mobile communications company Nokia employs a team of seven people around the world whose job is to think ten years ahead and dream up ideas. They have to anticipate future needs before the consumer has even become aware of them. They must also predict the innovations of their rivals, so that the company can be one step ahead. Every so often, the ideas team hold focus groups for ordinary users and ask them what they want from their phones when they are on the move. The users are offered a handful of new ideas and their reactions are videoed. The team always pay attention to the quirky suggestions because there is often a lot of truth in them. The company also consults anthropologists to help unravel consumers' reactions, and these generate leads which give the team something to build on. It was anticipating needs before they exist that brought about Nokia's revolutionary 9000 Communicator, which is the world's first all-in-one mobile communications device – a fax, phone, digital diary, calculator and palm-top computer all rolled into one. In time, Nokia claims that the handset will become a mobile office and multimedia communications device the size of a business card![9]

Consumers often create new products on their own, and companies can benefit by finding these products and putting them on the market. Pillsbury gets promising new recipes through its annual Bake-Off. One of Pillsbury's four cake-mix lines and several variations of another came directly from Bake-Off winners' recipes. About one-third of all the software IBM leases for its computers is developed by outside users.[10]

● *Competitors*

About 30 per cent of new-product ideas come from analyzing competitors' products. The company can watch competitors' ads and other communications to get clues about their new products. Companies buy competing products, take them apart to see how they work, analyze their sales, and decide whether the company should bring out a new product of its own. For example, when designing its highly successful Taurus, Ford tore down more than 50 competing models, layer by layer, looking for things to copy or improve upon. It copied the Audi's accelerator-pedal 'feel', the Toyota Supra fuel gauge, the BMW 528e tyre and jack storage system and 400 other such outstanding features.[11]

● *Distributors, Suppliers and Others*

Resellers are close to the market and can pass along information about consumer problems and new-product possibilities. Suppliers can tell the company about new concepts, techniques and materials that can be used to develop new products. Other idea sources include trade magazines, shows and seminars; government agencies; new-product consultants; advertising agencies; marketing research firms; university, commercial laboratories and science parks; and inventors.

Idea Screening

The purpose of idea generation is to create a large number of ideas. The purpose of the succeeding stages is to *reduce* that number to a manageable few which deserve further attention. The first idea-reducing stage is **idea screening**. The purpose of screening is to spot good ideas and drop poor ones as soon as possible. As product development costs rise greatly in later stages, it is important for the company to go ahead only with those product ideas that will turn into profitable products.

idea screening
Screening new-product ideas in order to spot good ideas and drop poor ones as soon as possible.

Most companies require their executives to write up new-product ideas on a standard form that can be reviewed by a new-product committee. The write-up describes the product, the target market and the competition, and makes some rough estimates of market size, product price, development time and costs, manufacturing costs and rate of return. The committee then evaluates the idea against a set of general criteria. At Kao Company of Japan, for example, the committee asks questions such as these: Is the product truly useful to consumers and society? Is this product good for our particular company? Does it mesh well with the company's objectives and strategies? Do we have the people, skills and resources to make it succeed? Is its cost performance superior to competitive products? Is it easy to advertise and distribute?

Surviving ideas can be screened further using a simple rating process, such as the one shown in Table 14.1. The first column lists factors required for the successful launching of the product in the marketplace. In the next column, management rates these factors on their relative importance. Thus management believes that marketing skills and experience are very important (0.20) and purchasing and supplies competence is of minor importance (0.05).

Next, on a scale of 0.0 to 1.0, management rates how well the new-product idea fits the company's profile on each factor. Here management feels that the product idea fits very well with the company's marketing skills and experience (0.9), but not too well with its purchasing and supplies capabilities (0.5). Finally, management multiplies the importance of each success factor by the rating of fit to obtain an overall rating of the company's ability to launch the product successfully. Thus, if marketing is an important success factor and if this product fits the company's marketing skills, this will increase the overall rating of the product idea. In the example, the product idea scored 0.74, which places it at the high end of the 'fair idea' level.

Table 14.1	Product idea rating process

NEW-PRODUCT SUCCESS FACTORS	(A) RELATIVE IMPORTANCE	FIT BETWEEN PRODUCT IDEA AND COMPANY CAPABILITIES (B)											IDEA RATING (A × B)
		0.0	0.1	0.2	0.3	0.4	0.5	0.6	0.7	0.8	0.9	1.0	
Company strategy and objectives	0.20									X			0.160
Marketing skills and experience	0.20										X		0.180
Financial resources	0.15								X				0.105
Channels of distribution	0.15									X			0.120
Production capabilities	0.10									X			0.080
Research and development	0.10								X				0.070
Purchasing and supplies	0.05						X						0.025
Total	1.00												0.740[a]

NOTE: [a]Rating scale: 0.00–0.40, poor; 0.50–0.75, fair; 0.76–1.00, good. Minimum acceptance level: 0.70.

The checklist promotes a more systematic product idea evaluation and basis for discussion. However, it is *not* designed to make the decision for management.

Concept Development and Testing

Attractive ideas must now be developed into product concepts. It is important to distinguish between a *product idea*, a *product concept* and a *product image*. A **product idea** is an idea for a possible product that the company can see itself offering to the market. A **product concept** is a detailed version of the idea stated in meaningful consumer terms. A **product image** is the way consumers perceive an actual or potential product.

● *Concept Development*

Suppose a car manufacturer figures out how to design an electric car that can go as fast as 90 km per hour and as far as 170 km before needing to be recharged. The manufacturer estimates that the electric car's operating costs will be about half those of a regular car.

This is a product idea. Customers, however, do not buy a product idea; they buy a product *concept*. The marketer's task is to develop this idea into some alternative product concepts, find out how attractive each concept is to customers, and choose the best one.

The marketer might create the following product concepts for the electric car.

● *Concept 1.* A moderately priced subcompact designed as a second family car to be used around town. The car is ideal for running errands and visiting friends.

product idea
An idea for a possible product that the company can see itself offering to the market.

product concept
A detailed version of the new-product idea stated in meaningful consumer terms.

product image
The way consumers perceive an actual or potential product.

- *Concept 2.* A medium-cost sporty compact appealing to young people.
- *Concept 3.* An inexpensive subcompact 'green' car appealing to environmentally conscious people who want practical transportation and low pollution.

To increase the likelihood of concept acceptance, some firms involve the customer (or potential customer) in concept development – as in the case of Aerostructures Hamble, the aircraft components manufacturer, which invites customers to its design reviews in the early stages of the new-product process.

● *Concept Testing*

Concept testing calls for testing new-product concepts with a group of target consumers. The concepts may be presented to consumers symbolically or physically. Here, in words, is *Concept 3*:

> An efficient, fun-to-drive, fuel-cell-powered electric subcompact car that seats four. This high-tech wonder runs on hydrogen created from methanol fuel, providing practical and reliable transportation with almost no pollution. It goes up to 110 km per hour and, unlike battery-powered electric cars, never needs recharging. It's priced, fully equipped, at £12,000.

concept testing
Testing new product concepts with a group of target consumers to find out if the concepts have strong consumer appeal.

For some concept tests, a word or picture description might be sufficient. However, a more concrete and physical presentation of the concept will increase the reliability of the concept test. Today, marketers are finding innovative ways to make product concepts more real to consumer subjects. For example, some are using virtual reality to test product concepts. Virtual reality programmes use computers and sensory devices (such as goggles or gloves) to simulate reality. For example, a designer of kitchen cabinets can use a virtual reality programme to help a customer 'see' how his or her kitchen would look and work if remodelled with the company's products. Virtual reality is still in its infancy, but its applications are increasing daily.

After being exposed to the concept, consumers may then be asked to react to it by answering the questions in Table 14.2. The answers will help the company decide which concept has the strongest appeal. For example, the last question asks about the consumer's intention to buy. Suppose 10 per cent of the consumers said they 'definitely' would buy and another 5 per cent said 'probably'. The company could project these figures to the population size of this target group to estimate sales volume. Concept testing offers a rough estimate of potential sales, but managers must view this with caution. The estimate is uncertain largely because consumers do not always carry out stated intentions.[12] Drivers, for example, might like the idea of the electric car that is kind to the environment, but might not want to pay for one! It is, nonetheless, important to carry out such tests with product concepts so as to gauge customers' response as well as to identify aspects of the concept that are particularly liked or disliked by potential buyers. Feedback might suggest ways to refine the concept, thereby increasing its appeal to customers.

Marketing Strategy Development

Suppose Toyota finds that Concept 3 for the fuel-cell-powered electric car tests best. The next step is to develop a **marketing strategy** for introducing this car to the market.

marketing strategy
The marketing logic by which the business unit hopes to achieve its marketing objectives.

marketing strategy statement

A statement of the planned strategy for a new product that outlines the intended target market, the planned product positioning, and the sales, market share and profit goals for the first few years.

The **marketing strategy statement** consists of three parts. The first part describes the target market, the planned product positioning, and the sales, market share and profit goals for the first few years. Thus:

> The target market is younger, well-educated, moderate-to-high income individuals, couples or small families seeking practical, environmentally responsible transportation. The car will be positioned as more economical to operate, more fun to drive and less polluting than today's internal combustion engine cars, and as less restricting than battery-powered electric cars which must be recharged regularly. The company will aim to sell 100,000 cars in the first year, at a loss of not more than £10 million. In the second year, the company will aim for sales of 120,000 cars and a profit of £18 million.

The second part of the marketing strategy statement outlines the product's planned price, distribution and marketing budget for the first year.

> The fuel-cell-powered electric car will be offered in three colours and will have optional air-conditioning and power-drive features. It will sell at a retail price of £12,000 – with 15 per cent off the list price to dealers. Dealers who sell more than 10 cars per month will get an additional discount of 5 per cent on each car sold that month. An advertising budget of £10 million will be split fifty-fifty between national and local advertising. Advertising will emphasize the car's fun and low emissions. During the first year, £70,000 will be spent on marketing research to find out who is buying the car and to determine their satisfaction levels.

The third part of the marketing strategy statement describes the planned long-run sales, profit goals and marketing mix strategy:

> The company intends to capture a 3 per cent long-run share of the total car market and realize an after-tax return on investment of 15 per cent. To achieve this, product quality will start high and be improved over time. Price will be raised in the second and third years if competition permits. The total advertising budget will be raised each year by about 10 per cent. Marketing research will be reduced to £40,000 per year after the first year.

Business Analysis

business analysis

A review of the sales, costs and profit projections for a new product to find out whether these factors satisfy the company's objectives.

Once management has decided on its product concept and marketing strategy, it can evaluate the business attractiveness of the proposal. **Business analysis** involves a review of the sales, costs and profit projections for a new product to find out whether they satisfy the company's objectives. If they do, the product can move to the product development stage.

To estimate sales, the company should look at the sales history of similar products and should survey market opinion. The firm should estimate minimum and maximum sales to assess the range of risk. After preparing the sales forecast, management can estimate the expected costs and profits for the product, including marketing, R & D, manufacturing, accounting and finance costs. The company then uses the sales and costs figures to analyze the new product's financial attractiveness.

Table 14.2	Questions for electric car concept test

1. Do you understand the concept of an electric car?
2. Do you believe the claims about the electric car's performance?
3. What are the main benefits of the electric car compared with a conventional car?
4. What improvements in the car's features would you suggest?
5. For what uses would you prefer an electric car to a conventional car?
6. What would be a reasonable price to charge for the electric car?
7. Who would be involved in your decision to buy such a car? Who would drive it?
8. Would you buy such a car? (Definitely, probably, probably not, definitely not)

Product Development

So far, the product concept may have existed only as a word description, a drawing or perhaps a crude mock-up. If the product concept passes the business test, it moves into **product development**. Here, R & D or engineering develops the product concept into a physical product. The product development step, however, now calls for a large jump in investment. It will show whether the product idea can be turned into a workable product.

The R & D department will develop one or more physical versions of the product concept. R & D hopes to design a prototype that will satisfy and excite consumers and that can be produced quickly and at budgeted costs. Developing a successful prototype can take days, weeks, months or even years. The prototype must have the required functional features and also convey the intended psychological characteristics. The fuel-cell electric car, for example, should strike consumers as being well built and safe. Management must learn what makes consumers decide that a car is well built. To some consumers, this means that the car has 'solid-sounding' doors. To others, it means that the car is able to withstand heavy impact in crash tests.

When the prototypes are ready, they must be tested. Functional tests are then conducted under laboratory and field conditions to make sure that the product performs safely and effectively. The new car must start easily; it must be comfortable; it must be able to go around corners without overturning. Consumer tests are conducted, in which consumers test-drive the car and rate its attributes. For some products, prototyping and product development may involve both the key intermediaries that supply the product or service and the final consumer or end-user. Consider the following example:

> In the 1980s, Philips Consumer Electronics, Sony and Matsushita joined forces to develop a common format for consumer-based multimedia systems using compact discs. CD-interactive or CD-i was the result.
>
> The CD-i player plugs into a TV set and the user interface is a remote control device. The initial use of CD-i is for playing games and watching movies, but other applications such as home shopping are potentially very probable.
>
> Philips, however, recognizes that, as with any new technology, the potential for home shopping must be demonstrated. First, home shopping companies are unlikely to replace their current paper-based shopping

product development
Developing the product concept into a physical product in order to ensure that the product idea can be turned into a workable product.

catalogues with CDs without knowing if the multimedia home-shopping system works.

Philips launched the HOMESTEAD (Home Shopping by Television and Discs) ESPRIT project in June 1992, which involved several user organizations – Freemans, one of the largest home-shopping catalogue companies in the UK, Page & Moy, a major holiday provider, Barclays Bank and Little Big One, a Belgian audio-visual company.

Barclays and Little Big One each received a 'multimedia toolkit' developed earlier by Philips. The toolkit was designed to be versatile and to allow the user company to assemble CD-based multimedia catalogues for itself and its partners. The customer test results were exceedingly encouraging: for example, Freeman's clothes catalogue showed its clothes and accessories in full-motion video and allowed consumers either to browse through the catalogue or to go straight to the section that interested them. The Page & Moy catalogue helped users plan their cruise holidays, which were brought to life on the TV screen. The package takes the user on a tour of the ships from five different cruise companies, while also providing all the itinerary and booking details.

Philips then started an extensive consumer trial in the middle of 1994, the largest of its type ever undertaken – 5,500 homes were issued with the Freeman, Page & Moy and Barclays catalogues and a questionnaire designed to obtain consumers' response. Some 300 homes had never used CD-i and were vital for providing information on how the new product might be promoted to non-users of CD-i.[13] Tests such as these can be expensive, but the feedback from potential customers is invaluable in helping the firm to prepare for the next steps in the new product programme.

When designing products, the company should look beyond simply creating products that satisfy consumer needs and wants. Too often, companies design their new products without enough concern for how the designs will be produced. The designs are then passed along to manufacturing, where engineers must try to find the best ways to produce the product. Companies may minimize production problems by adopting an approach towards product development called *design for manufacturability and assembly* (DFMA). Using this approach, companies work to fashion products that are *both* satisfying *and* easy to manufacture. This often results not only in lower costs, but also in higher-quality and more reliable products. For example, using DFMA analysis, Texas Instruments redesigned an infrared gun-sighting mechanism that it supplies to the Pentagon. The redesigned product required 75 fewer parts, 78 per cent fewer assembly steps and 85 per cent less assembly time. The new design did more than reduce production time and costs; it also worked better than the previous, more complex version. Thus DFMA can be a potent weapon in helping companies to get products to market sooner and to offer higher quality at lower prices.[14]

Test Marketing

test marketing
The stage of new-product development where the product and marketing programme are tested in more realistic market settings.

If the product passes functional and consumer tests, the next step is **test marketing**, the stage at which the product and marketing programme are introduced into more realistic market settings.

Test marketing gives the marketer experience with marketing the product before going to the great expense of full introduction. It lets the company test the product and its entire marketing programme – positioning strategy, advertising,

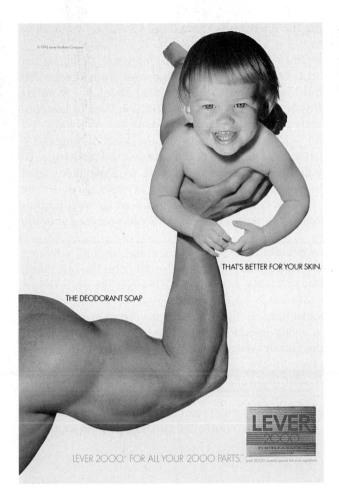

THAT'S BETTER FOR YOUR SKIN.

THE DEODORANT SOAP

LEVER 2000

LEVER 2000® FOR ALL YOUR 2000 PARTS.™

Lever USA spent two years testing its highly-successful Lever 2000 bar soap before introducing it internationally.

distribution, pricing, branding and packaging, and budget levels – in real market situations. The company uses test marketing to learn how consumers and dealers will react to handling, using and repurchasing the product. The results can be used to make better sales and profit forecasts. Thus a good test market can provide a wealth of information about the potential success of the product and marketing programme.

The amount of test marketing needed varies with each new product. Test marketing costs can be enormous and test marketing takes time that may allow competitors to gain advantages. When the costs of developing and introducing the product are low or when management is already confident that the new product will succeed, the company may do little or no test marketing. Companies often do not test market simple line extensions, minor modifications of current products or copies of successful competitors' products. However, when the new-product introduction requires a large investment, or when management is not sure of the product or marketing programme, the company may do a lot of test marketing. For example, Lever USA spent two years testing its highly successful Lever 2000 bar soap in Atlanta before introducing it internationally.

In principle, the idea of test marketing also applies to new service products. For example, an airline company preparing to introduce a secure, cost-saving system of electronic ticketing may try out the new service first on domestic routes before rolling out the service to international flights. Or, it might offer the ticketless system on its busiest routes and restrict the test to its most frequent travellers. The system's effectiveness and customers' acceptance and reactions can then be gauged prior to making the decision to extend the service to cover all of its domestic or global networks.

Consider another example. In July 1995, Mondex International, a consortium of 17 international banks and telecommunication companies from the United Kingdom, Asia, Australasia and North America, pilot tested Mondex – a 'smart card' that acts as a replica of cash – in Swindon, some 100 km west of London, with some 10,000 people, mainly participating NatWest Bank and Midland Bank customers. A second test site – Exeter University, in the west of England – was later added to assess students' and staff's use of the card as a university identification card, library and building security card as well as a payment card for everything from meals to laundry. Mondex officials say the card will be launched nationwide in the UK in 1998. Meanwhile, tests are under way in other consortia members' home countries to assess the international acceptance of the card.[15]

Whether or not a company decides to test-market, and the amount of testing it does, depends on the cost and risk of introducing the product on the one hand, and on the testing costs and time pressures on the other. Although the costs of test marketing can be high, they are often small when compared to the costs of making a major mistake. For example, as illustrated in the 'chapter preview' in Chapter 4, Unilever learned a costly lesson when it decided to skip formal test marketing for its new European laundry detergent, Power, and forged ahead with its £200 million, Europe-wide launch. The company spent another £70 million on the withdrawal of the defective, clothing-annihilating Power detergent a year after its introduction.

When using test marketing, consumer-products companies usually choose one of three approaches – standard test markets, controlled test markets or simulated test markets.

● *Standard Test Markets*

Using standard test markets, the company finds a small number of representative test cities, conducts a full marketing campaign in these cities and uses store audits, consumer and distributor surveys, and other measures to gauge product performance. It then uses the results to forecast national sales and profits, to discover potential product problems and to fine-tune the marketing programme.

Standard market tests have some drawbacks. They can be costly (the average standard test market costs around £2 million and can go much higher) and they may take a long time – some last as long as three years. If the testing proves to be unnecessary, the company will have lost many months of sales and profits. Moreover, competitors can monitor test market results or even interfere with them by cutting their prices in test locations, increasing their promotion or even buying up the product being tested. Finally, test markets give competitors a look at the company's new product well before it is introduced nationally. Thus, competitors may have time to develop defensive strategies and may even beat the company's product to the market. For example, prior to its launch in the United Kingdom, Carnation Coffee-Mate, a coffee-whitener, was test marketed over a period of six years. This gave rival firm Cadbury ample warning and the opportunity to develop and introduce its own product – Marvel – to compete head on with Coffee-Mate.

Despite these disadvantages, standard test markets are still the most widely used approach for major market testing. However, many companies today are shifting towards quicker and cheaper controlled and simulated test marketing methods.

● *Controlled Test Markets*

Several research firms keep controlled panels of stores which have agreed to carry new products for a fee. The company with the new product specifies the number of stores and geographical locations it wants. The research firm delivers the product to the participating stores and controls shelf location, amount of shelf space, displays and point-of-purchase promotions, and pricing according to specified plans. Sales results are tracked to determine the impact of these factors on demand.

Controlled test-marketing systems are particularly well developed in the United States. Systems like Nielsen's Scantrack and Information Resources Inc.'s (IRI) BehaviorScan track individual behaviour from the television set to the checkout counter. IRI, for example, keeps panels of shoppers in carefully selected cities. It uses microcomputers to measure TV viewing in each panel household and can send special commercials to panel member television sets. Panel consumers buy from co-operating stores and show identification cards when making purchases. Detailed electronic-scanner information on each consumer's purchases is fed into a central computer, where it is combined with the consumer's demographic and TV viewing information and reported daily. Thus BehaviorScan can provide store-by-store, week-by-week reports on the sales of new products being tested. And because the scanners record the specific purchases of individual consumers, the system can also provide information on repeat purchases and the ways that different types of consumer are reacting to the new product, its advertising and various other elements of the marketing programme.[16]

Controlled test markets take less time than standard test markets (six months to a year). However, some companies are concerned that the limited number of small cities and panel consumers used by the research services may not be representative of their products' markets or target consumers. And, as in standard test markets, controlled test markets allow competitors to get a look at the company's new product.

● *Simulated Test Markets*

Companies also can test new products in a simulated shopping environment. The company or research firm shows, to a sample of consumers, ads and promotions for a variety of products, including the new product being tested. It gives consumers a small amount of money and invites them to a real or laboratory store, where they may keep the money or use it to buy items. The researchers note how many consumers buy the new product and competing brands. This simulation provides a measure of trial and the commercial's effectiveness against competing commercials. The researchers then ask consumers the reasons for their purchase or non-purchase. Some weeks later, they interview the consumer by phone to determine product attitudes, usage, satisfaction and repurchase intentions. Using sophisticated computer models, the researchers then project national sales from results of the simulated test market. Recently, some marketers have begun to use interesting new high-tech approaches to simulated test market research, such as virtual reality and the Internet (see Marketing Highlight 14.2).

Simulated test markets overcome some of the disadvantages of standard and controlled test markets. They usually cost much less, can be run in eight weeks and keep the new product out of competitors' view. Yet, because of their small samples and simulated shopping environments, many marketers do not think that simulated test markets are as accurate or reliable as larger, real-world tests. Still, simulated test markets are used widely, often as 'pretest' markets. Because

Marketing Highlight 14.2

Virtual Reality Test Marketing: The Future Is Now

It's a steamy summer Saturday afternoon. Imagine that you're stopping off at the local supermarket to pick up some icy bottles of your favourite sports drink before heading to the tennis courts. You park the car, cross the car park and walk through the shop's automatic doors. You head for aisle 5, passing several displays along the way, and locate your usual sports-drink brand. You pick it up, check the price and take it to the checkout counter. Sounds like a pretty typical shopping experience, doesn't it? But in this case, the entire experience took place on your computer screen, not at the supermarket.

You've just experienced virtual reality – the wave of the future for test-marketing and concept-testing research – courtesy of Gadd International Research. Gadd has developed a research tool called Simul-Shop, a CD-ROM virtual-reality approach that recreates shopping situations in which researchers can test consumers' reactions to such factors as product positioning, store layouts and package designs. For example, suppose a cereal marketer wants to test reactions to a new package design and store-shelf positioning. Using Simul-Shop on a standard desktop PC, test shoppers begin their shopping spree with a screen showing the outside of a grocery store. They click to enter the virtual store and are guided to the appropriate store section. Once there, they can scan the shelf, pick up various cereal packages, rotate them, study the labels – even look around to see what is on the shelf behind them. About the only thing they can't do is open the box and taste the cereal. The virtual shopping trip includes full sound and video, along with a guide who directs users through the experience and answers their questions.

Virtual reality testing can take any of several forms. For example, Alternative Realities Corporation (ARC) has created a virtual reality amphitheatre called the VisionDome. The Dome offers 360 by 160 degrees of film projection, allowing as many as 40 people at one time to participate in a virtual reality experience. The VisionDome is like an IMAX theatre, but with one big difference – it's interactive. According to an ARC executive, when conducting research on a car, 'we can go into a VisionDome, see that car in three dimensions, look at it from every angle, take it out for a test drive and allow the customer to configure that car exactly the way he wants it'. Caterpillar sees enormous potential for the Dome. 'We can put one of our tractors in a VisionDome and actually have a customer sit in it and test it under whatever conditions they would use it for,' says a Caterpillar design engineer. 'The ability to immerse people in the product makes it a phenomenal [research and sales] tool.'

Virtual reality as a research tool offers several advantages. It's relatively inexpensive. For example, a firm can conduct a Simul-Shop study for only about ecu 20,000, including initial programming and the actual research on 75–100 people. This makes such research accessible to firms that can't afford full market-testing campaigns or the expense of creating actual mock-ups for each different product colour, shape or size. Another advantage is flexibility. A virtual reality store can display an almost infinite variety of products, sizes, styles and flavours in response to consumers' desires and needs. Research can be conducted in almost any simulated surroundings, ranging from food store interiors and new car showrooms to farms, fields or the open road. The technique's interactivity allows marketers and consumers to work together via computer on designs of new products and marketing programmes.

Finally, virtual reality has great potential for international research, which has often been difficult for marketers to conduct. With virtual reality, researchers can use a single standardized approach to evaluate products and programmes worldwide. For example, a multinational company conducting virtual-shopping studies in North and South America, Europe, Asia and Australia can create virtual stores in each country and region using the appropriate local products, shelf layouts and currencies. Once the stores are on-line, a product concept can be quickly tested across locations. Research results, revealing which markets offer the greatest opportunity for a successful launch, can be communicated to headquarters electronically.

Virtual reality research has its limitations. Simulated shopping situations never quite match the real thing. It is not clear how true test participants' responses are in a simulated experience. So what's ahead for virtual reality in marketing? Some pioneers are extremely enthusiastic about the technology – not just as a research tool, but as a place where even real buying and selling can occur. They predict that the virtual store may become a major channel for personal and direct interactions with consumers – interactions that encompass not only research, but sales and service as well. They see great potential for conducting this type of research over the Internet, and virtual stores have become a reality on the Web. As one observer notes, 'This is what I read about in science fiction books when I was growing up. It's the thing of the future.' For many marketers, that future is already a virtual reality.

SOURCES: Quotes and extracts from Raymond R. Burke, 'Virtual shopping: breakthrough in marketing research', *Harvard Business Review* (March–April 1996), pp. 120–31; Tom Dellacave, Jr, 'Curing market research headaches', *Sales and Marketing Management* (July 1996), pp. 84–5; Brian Silverman, 'Get 'em while they're hot', *Sales and Marketing Management* (February 1997), pp. 47–8, 52.

they are fast and inexpensive, they can be run to assess quickly a new product or its marketing programme. If the pretest results are strongly positive, the product might be introduced without further testing. If the results are very poor, the product might be dropped or substantially redesigned and retested. If the results are promising but indefinite, the product and marketing programme can be tested further in controlled or standard test markets.[17]

● *Test Marketing New Industrial Products*

Business marketers use different methods for test marketing their new products, such as: product-use tests; trade shows; distributor/dealer display rooms; and standard or controlled test markets.

PRODUCT-USE TESTS. Here the business marketer selects a small group of potential customers who agree to use the new product for a limited time. The manufacturer's technical people watch how these customers use the product. From this test the manufacturer learns about customer training and servicing requirements. After the test, the marketer asks the customer about purchase intent and other reactions. For some products, product-use tests may involve both the business customer and final or end-user.

TRADE SHOWS. These shows draw a large number of buyers who view new products in a few concentrated days. The manufacturer sees how buyers react to various product features and terms, and can assess buyer interest and purchase intentions.

DISTRIBUTOR AND DEALER DISPLAY ROOMS. Here the new industrial product may stand next to other company products and possibly competitors' products. This method yields preference and pricing information in the normal selling atmosphere of the product.

STANDARD OR CONTROLLED TEST MARKETS. These are used to measure the potential of new industrial products. The business marketer produces a limited supply of the product and gives it to the sales force to sell in a limited number of geographical areas. The company gives the product full advertising, sales promotion and other marketing support. Such test markets let the company test the product and its marketing programme in real market situations.

Commercialization

commercialization
Introducing a new product into the market.

Test marketing gives management the information needed to make a final decision about whether to launch the new product. If the company goes ahead with **commercialization** – that is, introducing the new product into the market – it will face high costs. The company will have to build or rent a manufacturing facility. It must have sufficient funds to gear up production to meet demand. Failure to do so can leave an opening in the market for competitors to step in. For example, London-based electronics company Psion's new Series 5 palmtop organizers, launched in 1997, were so popular that the firm could not meet demand initially, due to problems at one of its component suppliers. The backlog of orders was taking some four months to clear. Potentially, that left a gap in the hand-held computer market for American and Japanese rivals, which built similar machines based on an operating system designed by US software giant Microsoft.

Companies may have to spend millions of pounds for advertising and sales promotion in the first year of launch. For example, Spillers spent £3 million for its launch of GoodLife Breakfast dog meal. Gillette spent £8 million in the UK launch of its new shaving system, the Sensor Excel. Unilever spent nearly £200 million to promote Omo and Persil Power across Europe, in addition to the £100 million already invested in three new factories to produce its revolutionary laundry powder.

The company launching a new product must make four decisions.

● *When?*

The first decision is introduction timing – whether the time is right to introduce the new product. If it will eat into the sales of the company's other products, its introduction may be delayed. If it can be improved further, or if the economy is down, the company may wait until the following year to launch it.[18]

● *Where?*

The company must decide where to launch the new product. Should it be in a single location, or region, several regions, the national market or the international market? Few companies have the confidence, capital and capacity to launch new products into full national or international distribution. They will develop a planned market rollout over time. In particular, small companies may enter attractive cities or regions one at a time. Larger companies may quickly introduce new products into several regions or into the national market.

Companies with international distribution systems may introduce new products through global rollouts. Colgate-Palmolive used a 'lead-country' strategy for its Palmolive Options shampoo and conditioner: it was first introduced in Australia, the Philippines, Hong Kong and Mexico, then rapidly rolled out into Europe, Asia, Latin America and Africa. However, international firms are increasingly introducing their new products in swift global assaults. Procter & Gamble did this with the Pampers Phases line of disposable nappies. In the past, P & G typically introduced a new product in the US market. If it was successful, overseas competitors would copy the product in their home markets before P & G could expand distribution globally. With Pampers Phases, however, the company introduced the new product into global markets within one month of introducing it in the United States. It planned to have the product on the shelf in 90 countries within just 12 months of introduction. Such rapid worldwide expansion solidified the brand's market position before foreign competitors could react. P & G has since mounted worldwide introductions of several other new products.[19]

● *To Whom?*

Within the roll-out markets, the company must target its distribution and promotion to customer groups who represent the best prospects. These prime prospects should have been profiled by the firm in earlier research and test marketing. For instance, Psion's Series 5 palmtop organizer, with a price tag of £500, is targeted at high income executives. When *The European* newspaper launched a multimedia version of the paper, it was initially targeted at professionals, who were sent an electronic version of the paper via telephone to personal computers at work. Generally, firms must fine-tune their targeting efforts, starting with the innovators, then looking especially for early adopters, heavy users and opinion leaders. Opinion leaders are particularly important as their endorsement of the new product has a powerful impact upon adoption by other buyers in the marketplace.

● *How?*

The company also must develop an *action plan* for introducing the new product into the selected markets. It must spend the marketing budget on the marketing mix and various other activities. For example, in August 1995, Microsoft introduced its Windows 95 operating system for personal computers in a fanfare of publicity. Observers estimated that the company spent some $1 billion, one of the biggest ever blitzes in advertising. The company paid up to $600,000 to fund 1.5 million copies of the software for *The Times* newspaper in London on the day of the product's launch. The soundtrack to the campaign was the Rolling Stones song, 'Start me up', for which the company had to pay $8 million. The first European markets to get Windows 95 were Benelux, France, Ireland and the United Kingdom, followed immediately by Denmark, Finland, Germany, Norway, Portugal, Spain and Sweden, and then Greece. Distributors the world over wanted to be the first to sell a copy of the software. Thousands queued late at night outside stores for the first copies. The world's first buyer was a business student in New Zealand, 12 hours ahead of the European launch![20]

Speeding Up New-Product Development

Many companies organize their new-product development process into an orderly sequence of steps, starting with idea generation and ending with commercialization. Under this **sequential product development** approach, one company department works individually to complete its stage of the process before passing the new product along to the next department and stage. This orderly, step-by-step process can help bring control to complex and risky projects. But it also can be dangerously slow. In today's fast-changing, highly competitive markets, such slow-but-sure product development can result in product failures, lost sales and profits, and crumbling market positions. 'Speed to market' and reducing new-product development 'cycle time' have become pressing concerns to companies in all industries. One study, for example, found that a six-month delay in introducing a new product cut its lifetime profits by one-third. By contrast,

sequential product development
A new-product development approach in which one company department works individually to complete its stage of the process before passing the new product along to the next department and stage.

Simultaneous Product Development: Speeding New Products to Market

Philips, the giant Dutch consumer electronics company, marketed the first practical video cassette recorder in 1972, gaining a three-year lead on its Japanese competitors. But in the seven years that it took Philips to develop its second generation of VCR models, Japanese manufacturers had launched at least three generations of new products. A victim of its own creaky product development process, Philips never recovered from the Japanese onslaught. Today, the company is an also-ran with only 2 per cent market share; it still loses money on VCRs. The Philips story is typical – during the past few decades, dozens of large companies have fallen victim to competitors with faster, more flexible new-product development programmes.

Companies have traditionally used a sequential product development approach in which new products are developed in an orderly series of steps. In a kind of relay race, each company department completes its phase of the development process before passing the new product on. The sequential process has its merits – it helps bring order to risky and complex new-product development projects. But the approach also can be fatally slow.

To speed up their product development cycles, many companies are now adopting a faster, more agile, team-oriented approach called 'simultaneous product development'. Instead of passing the new product from department to department, the company assembles a team of people from various departments that stays with the new product from start to finish. Such teams usually include representatives from the marketing, finance, design, manufacturing and legal departments, and even supplier companies. Simultaneous development is more like a rugby match than a relay race – team members pass the new product back and forth as they move down field towards the common goal of a speedy and successful new-product launch.

Top management gives the product development team general strategic direction, but on a clear-cut product idea or work plan. It challenges the team with stiff and seemingly contradictory goals – 'turn out carefully planned and superior new products, but do it quickly' – and then gives the team whatever freedom and resources it needs to meet the challenge. The team becomes a driving force that pushes the product forward. In the sequential process, a bottleneck at one phase can seriously slow or even halt the entire project. In the simultaneous approach, if one functional area hits snags, it works to resolve them while the team moves on.

In the car industry, companies have discovered the benefits of simultaneous product development. The approach is called 'simultaneous engineering' at Toyota and GM, the 'team concept' at Ford, and 'process-driven design' at Chrysler. Using simultaneous product development, Ford slashed development time from 60 months to less than 40. It squeezed 14 weeks from its cycle by simply getting the engineering and finance departments to review designs at the same time instead of sequentially. It claims that such actions have helped cut average engineering costs for a project by 35 per cent. In an industry that has typically taken five or six years to turn out a new model, Mazda now brags about two-to-three-year product development cycles – a feat that would be impossible without simultaneous development.

However, the simultaneous approach has some limitations. Superfast product development can be riskier and more costly than the slower, more orderly sequential approach. And it often creates increased organizational tension and confusion. But in rapidly changing industries, facing increasingly shorter product life cycles, the rewards of fast and flexible product development far exceed the risks. Companies that get new and improved products to the market faster than competitors gain a dramatic competitive edge. They can respond more quickly to emerging consumer tastes and charge higher prices for more advanced designs. As one motor industry executive states, 'What we want to do is get the new car approached, built, and in the consumer's hands in the shortest time possible ... Whoever gets there first gets all the marbles.'

SOURCES: Hirotake Takeuchi and Ikujiro Nonaka, 'The new product development game', *Harvard Business Review* (January–February 1986), pp. 137–46; Bro Uttal, 'Speeding new ideas to market', *Fortune* (2 March 1987), pp. 62–5; John Bussey and Douglas R. Sease, 'Speeding up: manufacturers strive to slice time needed to develop new products', *Wall Street Journal* (23 February 1988), pp. 1, 24; Craig A. Chambers, 'Transforming new product development', *Research-Technology Management* (November–December 1996), pp. 32–8; Srikant Datar, Jordan C. Clark, Sundre Kekre, Surendra Rajiv and Kannan Srinivasan, 'Advantages of time-based new product development in a fast-cycle industry', *Journal of Marketing Research* (February 1997), pp. 36–49.

spending 10 per cent over the development budget will reduce profits by only 2 per cent.[21]

Today, in order to get their new products to market more quickly, many companies are dropping the sequential product development method in favour of the faster, more flexible **simultaneous product development** approach. Under the new approach, company departments work closely together, overlapping the steps in the product development process to save time and increase effectiveness (see Marketing Highlight 14.3).

simultaneous product development
An approach to developing new products in which various company departments work closely together, overlapping the steps in the product development process to save time and increase effectiveness.

Organization for Innovation

Table 14.3 illustrates the most common form of organization for new-product development: product managers, new-product managers, new-product committees/departments and venture teams.

The organizational format used in a new-product development project can influence the time taken to complete the project. As suggested in Marketing Highlight 14.3, multidisciplinary teams and a concurrent approach to handling new-product process activities have been the main driving force behind fast-paced innovation.

But successful new-product development is not just about having a special organizational *structure* for new-product development. An innovative organization must have, at its helm, *top management* that gives priority to new products, which are seen as the life blood of the company. Their *vision* for innovation is clearly communicated to, and its *value shared* by, staff at all levels of the organization. A clear *strategy* as guiding force, backed by top management support, ensures that teams consistently perform. Top management not only believes wholeheartedly in, but also devotes sufficient resources to new-product development. A strongly innovative organization is also committed to its people (*staff*), investing continually in helping them to acquire and maintain the necessary *skills* for innovation. The organization must also embrace the *product champions* who, against all the odds, strive to take projects to completion. They, in turn, rely on the *executive champion*, whose authority is invaluable in fighting off the political battles that interfere with new-product progress. Furthermore, information and communication *systems* are designed to facilitate learning and to ensure that information flows quickly to critical individuals responsible for making or implementing new-product development decisions. Real innovation is a risky activity, so firms must foster an *entrepreneurial culture* and *climate* for

Table 14.3	Ways companies organize for new-product development

Product managers

Many companies assign responsibility for new-product ideas to their product managers. Because these managers are close to the market and competition, they are ideally situated to find and develop new-product opportunities. In practice, however, this system has several faults. Product managers are usually so busy managing their product lines that they give little thought to new products other than brand modifications or extensions. They also lack the specific skills and knowledge needed to evaluate and develop new products.

New-product managers

Some companies have new-product managers who report to group product managers. This position 'professionalizes' the new-product function. On the other hand, new-product managers tend to think in terms of product modifications and line extensions limited to their current product and markets.

New-product committees

Most companies have a high-level management committee charged with reviewing and approving new-product proposals. It usually consists of representatives from marketing, manufacturing, finance, engineering and other departments. Its function is not developing or co-ordinating new products so much as reviewing and approving new-product plans.

New-product departments

Large companies often establish a new-product department headed by a manager who has substantial authority and access to top management. The department's chief responsibilities include generating and screening new ideas, working with the R & D department, and carrying out field testing and commercialization.

New-product venture teams

A more free-standing approach involves assigning major new-product development work to venture teams. A venture team is a group brought together from various operating departments and charged with developing a specific product or business. Team members are relieved of their other duties, and given a budget and a time frame. In some cases, this team stays with the product long after it is successfully introduced.

innovation, with planning, control and reward systems encouraging risk-taking as opposed to its avoidance. Last, but, not least, to innovate effectively, firms must build customer-focused, functionally integrated organizations. In successful innovative firms, new-product development is seldom left to chance. There may be an element of luck underpinning successful commercialization of innovations. Luck, unfortunately, is not easy to replicate. The lessons of strategic new-product planning and implementation, however, are.[22]

We have looked at the problem of finding and developing new products. Next, let us examine the problem of managing them over their life cycle.

Product Life-Cycle Strategies

After launching the new product, management wants the product to enjoy a long and healthy life. Although it does not expect the product to sell for ever, the

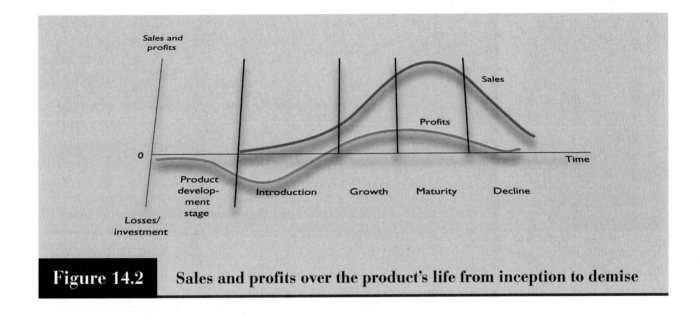

| **Figure 14.2** | **Sales and profits over the product's life from inception to demise** |

company wants to earn a decent profit to cover all the effort and risk that went into launching it. Management is aware that each product will have a life cycle, although the exact shape and length is not known in advance.

Figure 14.2 shows a typical **product life cycle (PLC)**, the course that a product's sales and profits take over its lifetime. The .product life cycle has five distinct stages:

1. *Product development* begins when the company finds and develops a new-product idea. During product development, sales are zero and the company's investment costs mount.

2. *Introduction* is a period of slow sales growth as the product is being introduced in the market. Profits are non-existent in this stage because of the heavy expenses of product introduction.

3. *Growth* is a period of rapid market acceptance and increasing profits.

4. *Maturity* is a period of slowdown in sales growth because the product has achieved acceptance by most potential buyers. Profits level off or decline because of increased marketing outlays to defend the product against competition.

5. *Decline* is the period when sales fall off and profits drop.

Not all products follow this S-shaped product life cycle. Some products are introduced and die quickly; others stay in the mature stage for a long, long time. Some enter the decline stage and are then cycled back into the growth stage through strong promotion or repositioning.

The PLC concept can describe a product class (petrol-engined cars), a product form (coupé) or a brand (the BMW 325is). The PLC concept applies differently in each case. Product classes have the longest life cycles. The sales of many product classes stay in the mature stage for a long time. Product forms, in contrast, tend to have the standard PLC shape. Product forms such as 'cream deodorants', the 'dial telephone' and 'phonograph records' passed through a regular history of introductions, rapid growth, maturity and decline. A specific brand's life cycle can change quickly because of changing competitive attacks and responses. For example, although teeth-cleaning products (product class) and

product life cycle (PLC)
The course of a product's sales and profits over its lifetime. It involves five distinct stages: product development, introduction, growth, maturity and decline.

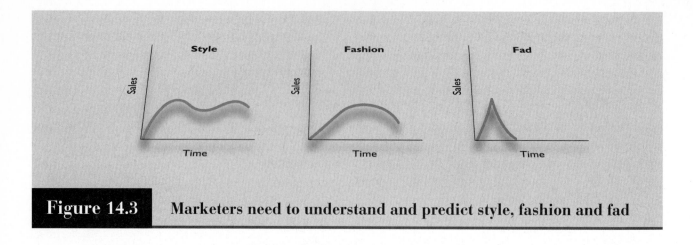

| Figure 14.3 | Marketers need to understand and predict style, fashion and fad |

style
A basic and distinctive mode of expression.

fashion
A currently accepted or popular style in a given field.

fads
Fashions that enter quickly, are adopted with great zeal, peak early and decline very fast.

toothpaste (product form) have enjoyed fairly long life cycles, the life cycles of specific brands have tended to be much shorter.

The PLC concept can also be applied to what are known as styles, fashions and fads. Their special life cycles are shown in Figure 14.3. A **style** is a basic and distinctive mode of expression. For example, styles appear in British homes (Edwardian, Victorian, Georgian); clothing (formal, casual); and art (realistic, surrealistic, abstract). Once a style is invented, it may last for generations, coming in and out of vogue. A style has a cycle showing several periods of renewed interest.

A **fashion** is a currently accepted or popular style in a given field. For example, the 'preppie look' in the clothing of the late 1970s and 1980s gave way to the 'loose and layered' look of the 1990s. Fashions pass through many stages. First, a small number of consumers typically take an interest in something new that sets them apart. Then other consumers take an interest out of a desire to copy the fashion leaders. Next, the fashion becomes popular and is adopted by the mass market. Finally, the fashion fades away as consumers start moving towards other fashions that are beginning to catch their eye. Thus fashions tend to grow slowly, remain popular for a while, then decline slowly.

Fads are fashions that enter quickly, are adopted with great zeal, peak early and decline very fast. They last only a short time and tend to attract only a limited following. Fads often have a novel or quirky nature, as when people start buying Rubik's cubes, 'pet rocks' or yo-yos. Fads appeal to people who are looking for excitement, a way to set themselves apart or something to talk about to others. Fads do not survive for long because they normally do not satisfy a strong or lasting need or satisfy it well.[23]

The PLC concept can be applied by marketers as a useful framework for describing how products and markets work. But using the PLC concept for forecasting product performance or for developing marketing strategies presents some practical problems.[24] For example, managers may have trouble identifying which stage of the PLC the product is in, pinpointing when the product moves into the next stage and determining the factors that affect the product's movement through the stages. In practice, it is difficult to forecast the sales level at each PLC stage, the length of each stage and the shape of the PLC curve.

Using the PLC concept to develop marketing strategy can also be difficult because strategy is both a cause and a result of the product's life cycle. The product's current PLC position suggests the best marketing strategies, and the resulting marketing strategies affect product performance in later life-cycle stages. Yet when used carefully, the PLC concept can help in developing good marketing strategies for different stages in the product life cycle.

We looked at the product development stage of the product life cycle in the first part of the chapter. Now let us look at strategies for each of the other life-cycle stages.

Introduction Stage

The **introduction stage** starts when the new product is first launched. Introduction takes time, and sales growth is apt to be slow. Well-known products such as instant coffee, personal computers and mobile telephones lingered for many years before they entered a stage of rapid growth.

In this stage, as compared to other stages, profits are negative or low because of the low sales and high distribution and promotion expenses. Much money is needed to attract distributors and build their inventories. Promotion spending is relatively high to inform consumers of the new product and get them to try it. Because the market is not generally ready for product refinements at this stage, the company and its few competitors produce basic versions of the product. These firms focus their selling on those buyers who are the readiest to buy – usually the higher-income groups. For radical product technologies, such as the video cassette recorder (VCR), electronic calculators and mobile telecommunications, business or professional users were the earliest targets.

A company might adopt one of several marketing strategies for introducing a new product. It can set a high or low level for each marketing variable, such as price, promotion, distribution and product quality. Considering only price and promotion, for example, management might *skim* the market *slowly* by launching the new product with a high price and low promotion spending. The high price helps recover as much gross profit per unit as possible, while the low promotion spending keeps marketing spending down. Such a strategy makes sense when the market is limited in size, when most consumers in the market know about the product and are willing to pay a high price (these consumers are typically called the 'innovators'), and when there is little immediate potential competition. If, however, most consumers in the limited market are unaware and know little about the innovation, and require educating and convincing, a high level of promotion spending is required. A high-price, high-promotion strategy also helps the firm to *skim rapidly* the price-insensitive end of the market in the early stages of the new product's launch.

On the other hand, a company might introduce its new product with a low price and heavy promotion spending (a *rapid penetration* strategy). This strategy promises to bring the fastest market penetration and the largest market share, and it makes sense when the market is large, potential buyers are price sensitive and unaware of the product, there is strong potential competition, and the company's unit manufacturing costs fall with the scale of production and accumulated manufacturing experience. A low-price, but low promotion spend (or *slow penetration* strategy) may be chosen instead if buyers are price conscious, but the firm wants to keep its launch costs down because of resource constraints.

A company, especially the *market pioneer*, must choose a launch strategy consistent with its intended product positioning. It should realize that the initial strategy is just the first step in a grander marketing plan for the product's entire life cycle. If the pioneer chooses its launch strategy to make a 'killing', it will be sacrificing long-run revenue for the sake of short-run gain. As the pioneer moves through later stages of the life cycle, it will have continuously to formulate new pricing, promotion and other marketing strategies. It has the best chance of building and retaining market leadership if it plays its cards correctly from the start.

introduction stage
The product life-cycle stage when the new product is first distributed and made available for purchase.

Growth Stage

growth stage
The product life-cycle stage at which a product's sales start climbing quickly.

If the new product meets market needs or stimulates previously untapped needs, it will enter a **growth stage**, in which sales will start climbing quickly. The early adopters will continue to buy, and later buyers will start following their lead, especially if they hear favourable word of mouth. Attracted by the opportunities for profit, new competitors will enter the market. They will introduce new product features, improve on the pioneer's product and expand the market for the product. The increase in competitors leads to an increase in the number of distribution outlets, and sales jump just to build reseller inventories. Prices remain where they are or fall only slightly. Companies keep their promotion spending at the same or a slightly higher level. Educating the market remains a goal, but now the company must also meet the competition.

Profits increase during the growth stage, as promotion costs are spread over a large volume and as unit-manufacturing costs fall. The firm uses several strategies to sustain rapid market growth as long as possible. It improves product quality and adds new product features and models. It enters new market segments and tries to grow sales further by selling through new distribution channels. It shifts some advertising from building product awareness to building product conviction and purchase, and it lowers prices at the right time to attract more buyers.

In the growth stage, the firm faces a trade-off between high market share and high current profit. By spending a lot of money on product improvement, promotion and distribution, the company can capture a dominant position. In doing so, however, it gives up maximum current profit, which it hopes to make up in the next stage.

Maturity Stage

maturity stage
The stage in the product life cycle where sales growth slows or levels off.

At some point, a product's sales growth will slow down and the product will enter a **maturity stage**. This maturity stage normally lasts longer than the previous stages, and it poses strong challenges to marketing management. Most products are in the maturity stage of the life cycle, and, therefore, most of marketing management deals with the mature product.

The slowdown in sales growth results in many producers with many products to sell. In turn, this overcapacity leads to greater competition. Competitors begin to cut prices, increase their advertising and sale promotions, and increase their R & D budgets to find better versions of the product. These steps lead to a drop in profit. Often some of the weaker competitors start to lag behind and soon drop out of the industry, which eventually contains only well-established competitors.

Although many products in the mature stage appear to remain unchanged for long periods, most successful ones stay alive through continually evolving to meet changing consumer needs. Product managers should do more than simply ride along with or defend their mature products – a good offensive is the best defence. They should stretch their imagination and look for new ways to innovate in the market (market development), or to modify the product (product development) and the marketing mix (marketing innovation).

● *Market Development*

Here, the company tries to increase the consumption of the current product. It looks for new users or market segments which the company is not currently serving, as when Johnson & Johnson targeted the adult market with its baby

two people and their shopping through dense city traffic. It would be a super-environmentally efficient car, with a fuel consumption rate half that of today's average family car. The performance would be equal to a basic Ford Escort, but it would have a range of 550 km on a tank of petrol. According to Hayek, to be successful on a global scale today, a wrist watch – and by extension, a microcar – 'must also be a *provocation*'. The Swatchmobile will be 'an effort to change people's habits because it is only a two-seater'.

Although he was an engineer, he does not design Swatches; nor will he design Swatchmobiles. He saw marketing energy and style as his strength. Swatches were designed by an in-house team of Swiss engineers led by Jacques Müller. He aimed to employ dozens of designers and artists as well as engineers to work on the Swatchmobile. 'Expect it to be offered in any colour – and any combination of colours – you want, *including* black,' says Hayek.

Please, Not Another European Car Maker

Some saw Hayek's ideas as foolhardy. There was already overcapacity in the world car market. The European industry was in deep recession and had high labour costs – Japan's were Sfr26 per hour compared with Germany's Sfr40. In addition, further traffic growth was seen by some as an impossibility on the world's overcrowded roads. Bankers and other potential backers were openly critical of the venture. It was one step too far at the wrong time and in the wrong market.

SMH wanted a partner for its new venture. It partnered with Europe's market leader in small cars, Volkswagen, with the idea of making a Sfr10,000 Swatch-VW in China. Then, in 1993, VW pulled out. It was short of money and doubted the Swatchmobile's economic viability. It also questioned Hayek's philosophy for the microcar – like the successful Swatch watch, cheap cars can also become fashion items. It opted instead for the Chico, a more conventional car than Hayek envisaged. It will also bring back the Beetle. In 1999 production of the 'back to the future' design based on VW's Concept 1 prototype will start in Mexico.

The meeting between Chirac and Hayek stimulated speculation about a French suitor for SMH. Was there the prospect of an exciting alliance combining French style, Swiss engineering excellence and Hayek's marketing hype? A deal with Matra-Hachette, Renault or Peugeot-Citroën, perhaps? Chirac left the meeting smiling but saying nothing. Hayek told reporters that the partner would certainly not be GM, but that they would have to wait until the Geneva Motor Show to find out more.

A Swatchmomerc?

The news finally broke at the Stuttgart Motor Show in 1994, where the prototype Swatch Eco-Sprinter coupé and Eco-Speedster convertible were revealed. They were expected to cost between Sfr15,000 and Sfr21,000. Now the partner was Mercedes-Benz, the German executive and luxury car maker. The board of its parent company, Daimler-Benz, had given permission for the car division to set up with SMH a joint-venture company, called Micro-Compact-Car (MCC), which had 'promising possibilities for the development, manufacture and marketing of automobiles geared particularly to city use'. MCC aimed to unveil the car at the 1996 Olympic Games in Atlanta, United States, for which Swatch Timing, Swatch's sister company, was handling the official timing, with sale in Europe planned for late 1997–8. The company planned to have an initial production of 100,000–150,000 cars a year and to reach full capacity of 200,000 cars by 1999.

The deal fitted Mercedes' growth plans and 'Made in Germany' policy. To lower its high labour costs and counter the recession, the company had cut its workforce for the first time. It was radically transforming its new model development programme. Cars were now being designed to a cost target, rather than designing the best cars possible and then pricing them. Mercedes also intended to change itself from a luxury car maker into a full-range producer by broadening its product range to cover four-wheel-drive sports/recreational vehicles, people carriers and small cars. The plan to build 200,000 small family cars a year in Germany had recently been announced. Its Vision A-93 concept car had been shown at several motor shows. It was smaller than the VW Golf or Ford Escort, but much larger than the Swatchmobile.

Some industry observers were not impressed by the joint venture. Was it one diversification too far for both Mercedes and Swatch? How could the flamboyant Hayek work with Mercedes' technocrats? Would the Swatch and Mercedes brand names fit together?

MORI's survey for the 1994 *Lex Report on Marketing* sheds another light on the changing market. The study showed that 85 per cent of drivers still saw their car as an essential part of their lives. The younger generation agreed: 80 per cent of 13- to 16-year-olds said that cars were indispensable. People still wanted cars, but the report showed a sea change in attitudes. Security and environmental friendliness were top of the new car-buyer's agenda, especially for women and the young. Top speed had dropped to tenth place in the priority. Few drivers were happy about their car's safety standards. Most wanted air bags, anti-locking brakes and catalytic converters in their next car, and wanted to trade up to get them. A similar survey in Japan showed similar attitude shifts. The report heralded the 'light green' consumers, who rely on their car but care about its environmental impact. However, European Commission pressure on the motor industry has been escalating, and car manufacturers were expected to reduce emissions from the current fleet average of 7 litres per 100 km to 5 litres per 100 km by 2005.

Smart or Not So Smart Car?

Despite the odds of failure, Hayek and Mercedes believed more than ever in the microcar and development got unde rway. According to Hayek, 'What we want to do is change people's habits ... You have to approach the product (cars, like watches) in a different way.' The Smart Car, as the Swatchmobile came to be called, hit serious trouble just as it was about to be launched at the Frankfurt Motor Show in September 1997. It looked like Smart Car sceptics were about to be proved right. Hayek bowed to pressure from shareholders, announcing that he would not participate in a Sfr200 million capital injection into the Smart joint venture, cutting SMH's stake from 49 per cent to 19 per cent. Daimler-Benz increased its exposure to the venture in raising its investment from DM300 million to DM500 million. The task of realizing Hayek's dream had fallen to Mercedes, which was setting up a special network of dealers and arranging leasing finance to attract customers. MCC still believed that it could sell 200,000 cars a year and make a profit in five or six years. The first model to be produced at a factory in Hambach in Lorraine, France, will be a three-cylinder petrol engine with fuel consumption of 4 litres per 100 km and a top speed of 130 kmh. A later diesel model will cut this to 3 litres per 100 km. Industry analysts remained unconvinced. Although the two-seater was aimed at the growing segment of the mainly sluggish car market, its chances of succeeding against four-seater microcars

equipment. However, marketing principles can also be applied to organizations that offer services, such as Lufthansa.

QUESTIONS

1. For a traveller flying with Lufthansa, what exactly constitutes the 'service offering'?

2. Identify the tangible and intangible aspects of the service.

3. What are the main aspects of the service that distinguish it from physical products?

4. What criteria might customers consider when selecting an airline for business travel?

5. For physical products, the buyer can touch, see or feel and compare alternative offers before deciding which brand to purchase. Taking into account the relative intangibility of airline services, how might an airline customer determine the choice of carrier?

6. How would the marketing of a service offering differ from that of physical products? Identify the main ways in which the service provider would adapt its marketing strategies to create a competitive advantage.

Introduction

One of the chief trends in our modern economy in the past two decades has been the dramatic growth of services. In the major European countries, America and Japan, more people are employed in services than in all other sectors of the economy put together. Both public and private sector services in these countries account for between 60 and 70 per cent of national output. In international trade, services make up nearly a quarter of the value of total world exports.[2] Service jobs include not only those in service industries – hotels, airlines, banks, telecommunications and others – but also service jobs in product-based industries, such as corporate lawyers, medical staff and sales trainers. Consumer services are marketed to individuals and households, while industrial services are those offered to business and other organizations.

The increase in demand for consumer and industrial services has been attributed to a number of factors. First, rising affluence has increased consumers' desire to contract out mundane tasks such as cleaning, cooking and other domestic activities, giving rise to a burgeoning convenience industry. Second, rising incomes and more leisure time have created greater demand for a whole array of leisure services and sporting activities. Third, higher consumption of sophisticated technologies in the home (e.g. home computers, multimedia entertainment equipment, security systems) has triggered the need for specialist services to install and maintain them. In the case of business clients, more complex markets and technologies mean that companies are in greater need of the expertise and knowledge of service organizations, such as market research agencies, marketing and technical consultants. Furthermore, the rising pressure on firms to reduce fixed costs means that many are buying in services rather than incur the overheads involved in performing specialized tasks in-house. The need to remain flexible has also led to firms hiring services that provide use without ownership. Finally, an increasing number of firms are keen to focus on their core competences. They are beginning to contract out non-core activities, such as warehousing and transportation, thus stimulating the growth of specialist business service organizations. All these developments have, in turn, led to a growing interest in the special problems of marketing services.

Service industries vary greatly. In most countries, the *government sector* offers services: for example, legal, employment, health care, military, police, fire and postal services, education and regulatory agencies. The *private non-profit* sector offers services such as museums, charities, churches, colleges, foundations and hospitals. A large part of the *business sector* includes profit-oriented service suppliers like airlines, banks, hotels, insurance companies, consulting firms, medical and law practices, entertainment companies, advertising and research agencies, and retailers.

As a whole, selling services presents some special problems calling for special marketing solutions. Let us now examine the nature and special characteristics of service organizations.

Nature and Characteristics of a Service

Defining Services

service
Any activity or benefit that one party can offer to another which is essentially intangible and does not result in the ownership of anything.

A **service** is any activity or benefit that one party can offer to another which is essentially intangible and does not result in the ownership of anything. Activities such as renting a hotel room, depositing money in a bank, travelling on an aeroplane, visiting a doctor, getting a haircut, having a car repaired, watching a professional sport, seeing a movie, having clothes cleaned at a dry cleaner and getting advice from a solicitor all involve buying a service. Note, however, that many manufacturers also supply a range of services alongside their products, such as distribution and delivery, equipment repair and maintenance, training programmes, technical consultation and advice. Furthermore, many service providers also supply physical products along with their basic service. For example, airlines offer food, drinks and newspapers as part of their transportation services. As such, there is rarely such a thing as a pure service or pure good. In trying to distinguish between goods and services, it may be more appropriate to consider the notion of a goods–service continuum, with offerings ranging from tangible-dominant to intangible-dominant (see Figure 15.1).

Firms can create a differential advantage by moving along the continuum, seeking to alter the balance of tangible and intangible elements associated with their offering. For example, a manufacturer of kitchen units can enhance its offer by supplying a professional design and advisory service for customers.

Types of Service

There are many types of service organization. We can distinguish them in a number of ways. One distinction is the nature of ownership – that is, whether they are private (e.g. warehousing and distribution firms, banks) or public (e.g. police, state-run hospitals) sector organizations. Another is the type of market – consumer (e.g. household insurance policy provider, retailer) or industrial (e.g.

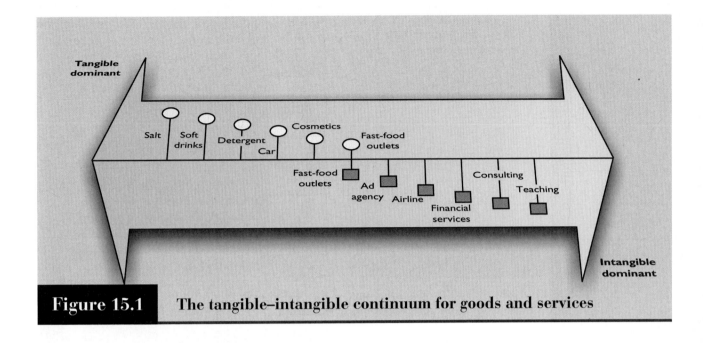

| **Figure 15.1** | **The tangible–intangible continuum for goods and services** |

computer bureaux). Services can also involve high customer contact, where the service is directed at people, as in the case of hairdressing and healthcare. Or there is low customer contact, as in dry cleaning and automated car-washes, where the services are directed at objects. Services can be people-based (e.g. consultancies, education) or equipment-bound (e.g. vending machines, bank cash dispensers). People-based services can be further distinguished according to whether they rely on highly professional staff, such as legal advisers and medical practitioners, or unskilled labour, such as porters and caretakers. The wide variety of service offerings means that service providers must address the problems specific to their particular service when seeking to create and maintain a competitive advantage. Despite this heterogeneity across sectors, there are a number of characteristics that are unique to services.

Service Characteristics

A company must consider five main service characteristics when designing marketing programmes: *intangibility, inseparability, variability, perishability* and *lack of ownership*. We will look at each of these characteristics in the following sections.[3]

● *Intangibility*

Service intangibility means that services cannot be readily displayed, so they cannot be seen, tasted, felt, heard or smelled before they are bought. A buyer can examine in detail before purchase the colour, features and performance of an audio hi-fi system that he or she wishes to buy. In contrast, a person getting a hair-cut cannot see the result before purchase, just as an airline passenger has nothing but a ticket and the promise of safe delivery to a chosen destination.

Because service offerings lack tangible characteristics that the buyer can evaluate before purchase, uncertainty is increased. To reduce uncertainty, buyers look for 'signals' of service quality. They draw conclusions about quality from the

service intangibility
A major characteristic of services – they cannot be seen, tasted, felt, heard or smelled before they are bought.

Gold's tangibilizes its service by advertising the Gym's equipment line.

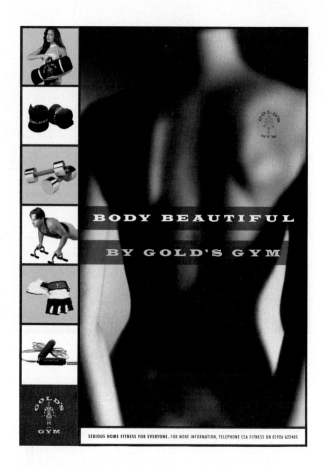

place, people, equipment, communication material and price that they can see. Therefore, the service provider's task is to make the service tangible in one or more ways. Whereas product marketers try to add intangibles (e.g. fast delivery, extended warranty, after-sales service) to their tangible offers, service marketers try to add tangible cues suggesting high quality to their intangible offers.[4]

Consider a bank that wants to convey the idea that its service is quick and efficient. It must make this positioning strategy tangible in every aspect of customer contact. The bank's physical setting must suggest quick and efficient service: its exterior and interior should have clean lines; internal traffic flow should be planned carefully; and waiting lines should seem short. The bank's staff should be busy and properly dressed. The equipment – computers, copying machines, desks – should look modern. The bank's ads and other communications should suggest efficiency, with clean and simple designs and carefully chosen words and photos that communicate the bank's positioning. The bank should choose a name and symbol for its service that suggest speed and efficiency. Because service intangibility increases purchase risk, buyers tend to be more influenced by word of mouth, which gives credibility to the service, than by advertising messages paid for by the service provider. As such, the service marketer (the bank in this case) should stimulate word-of-mouth communication by targeting opinion leaders who could be motivated to try its services, and satisfied customers who could be encouraged to recommend its service(s) to peers and friends. Its pricing for various services should be kept simple and clear. Similarly, in the case of Lufthansa and other airlines, marketing managers must identify ways to 'make tangible' their service, such as highly efficient ground staff and provision of excellent in-flight comforts.

● *Inseparability*

Physical goods are produced, then stored, later sold and still later consumed. In contrast, services are first sold, then produced and consumed at the same time and in the same place. **Service inseparability** means that services cannot be separated from their providers, whether the providers are people or machines. If a person provides the service, then the person is a part of the service. A rock concert is an example. The pop group or band is the service. It cannot deliver the service without consumers (the audience) being present. A teacher cannot deliver a service if there are no students attending class. Because the customer is also present as the service is produced, *provider–customer interaction* is a special feature of services marketing. Both the provider and the client affect the service outcome. How a legal adviser relates to his client, for example, influences the client's judgement of the overall service delivered. The extent to which a teacher is able to develop a rapport with her students will influence the quality of their learning experience. Thus, it is important for service staff to be trained to interact well with clients.

A second feature of the inseparability of services is that other customers are also present or involved. The concert audience, students in the class, other passengers in a train, customers in a restaurant, all are present while an individual consumer is consuming the service. Their behaviour can determine the satisfaction that the service delivers to the individual customers. For example, an unruly crowd in the restaurant would spoil the atmosphere for other customers dining there and reduce satisfaction. The implication for management would be to ensure at all times that customers involved in the service do not interfere with each other's satisfaction.

Because of the simultaneity of service production and consumption, service providers face particular difficulty when demand rises. A goods manufacturer can make more, or mass produce and stock up in anticipation of growth in demand. This is not possible for service operators like restaurants or a law firm. Service organizations have therefore to pay careful attention to managing growth, given the constraints. A high price is used to ration the limited supply of the preferred provider's service. Several other strategies exist for handling the problem of demand growth. First, the service provider can learn to work with larger groups, so that more customers are serviced simultaneously. For example, bigger sites or premises are used by retailers to accommodate larger numbers of customers, and a pop concert will cater for a larger audience if held in an open-air sports arena than in an enclosed concert hall. Second, the service provider can learn to work faster. Productivity can be improved by training staff to do tasks and utilize time more efficiently. Finally, a service organization can train more service providers.

● *Variability*

As services involve people in production and consumption, there is considerable potential for variability. **Service variability** means that the quality of services depends on who provides them, as well as when, where and how they are provided. As such, service quality is difficult to control. For example, some hotels have reputations for providing better service than others. Within a given hotel, one registration-desk employee may be cheerful and efficient, whereas another, standing just a few metres away, may be unpleasant and slow. Even the quality of a single employee's service varies according to his or her energy and frame of mind at the time of each customer contact. For example, two services offered by the same solicitor may not be identical in performance.

service inseparability
A major characteristic of services – they are produced and consumed at the same time and cannot be separated from their providers, whether the providers are people or machines.

service variability
A major characteristic of services – their quality may vary greatly, depending on who provides them and when, where and how.

Services are perishable: empty seats at slack times cannot be stored for later use during peak periods.

Service firms can take several steps towards quality control.[5] First, they can select and train their personnel carefully. Airlines, banks and hotels, for example, invest large sums of money in training their employees to give good service. Business-class customers flying SIA should find friendly and helpful personnel servicing them, whatever the time, duration and destination of their travel. Second, they can motivate staff by providing employee incentives that emphasize quality, such as employee-of-the-month awards or bonuses based on customer feedback. Third, they can make service employees more visible and accountable to consumers – car dealerships can let customers talk directly with the mechanics working on their cars. A firm can check customer satisfaction regularly through suggestion and complaint systems, customer surveys and comparison shopping. When poor service is found, it is corrected. Fourth, service firms can increase the consistency of employee performance by substituting equipment for staff (e.g. vending machines, automatic cash dispensers), and through heavy enforcement of standardized as well as detailed job procedures (e.g. Walt Disney's theme parks, McDonald's and Club Med).

● *Perishability*

service perishability
A major characteristic of services – they cannot be stored for later sale or use.

Service perishability means that services cannot be stored for later sale or use. In some countries, dentists and general practitioners charge patients for missed appointments because the service value existed only at that point and disappeared when the patient did not show up. The perishability of services is not a problem when demand is steady. However, when demand fluctuates, service firms often have difficult problems. For example, public transportation companies have to own much more equipment because of rush-hour demand than they would if demand were even throughout the day.

Service firms can use several strategies for producing a better match between demand and supply. On the demand side, differential pricing – that is, charging different prices at different times – will shift some demand from peak periods to off-peak periods. Examples are cheaper early-evening movie prices, low-season holidays and reduced weekend train fares. Airline companies offer heavily discounted 'stand-by' tickets to fill unbooked seats. Or non-peak demand can be increased, as in the case of business hotels developing minivacation weekends for

Most of the industrialized nations want their banks, insurance companies, construction firms and other service providers to be allowed to move people, capital and technology around the globe unimpeded. Instead they face a bewildering complex of national regulations, most of them designed to guarantee jobs for local competitors. A Turkish law, for example, forbids international accounting firms to bring capital into the country to set up offices and requires them to use the names of local partners, rather than prestigious international ones, in their marketing. To audit the books of a multinational company's branch in Buenos Aires, an accountant must have the equivalent of a high school education in Argentinian geography and history ... India is perhaps the most [difficult] big economy in the world [to enter] these days ... New Delhi prevents international insurance companies from selling property and casualty policies to the country's swelling business community or life insurance to its huge middle class.[17]

Clearly, service organizations face plenty of difficulties when seeking to enter foreign markets. The most recent round of the General Agreement on Tariffs and Trade (GATT), the Uruguay round, which ended in 1993 (see Chapter 5), began to address some of these problems by extending international trade rules to cover services in addition to manufactured goods. New service agreements should ease the barriers that limit such trade. Thus, despite the difficulties in international service marketing, the trend towards growth of global service companies will continue, especially in banking, telecommunications and professional services. Today, service firms are no longer simply following their manufacturing customers. Instead, many are taking the lead in international expansion.

Summary

Marketing has been broadened in recent years to cover services.

As developed countries move increasingly towards a *service economy*, marketers need to know more about marketing services. *Services* are activities or benefits that one party can offer to another which are essentially intangible and *do not result in* the *ownership* of anything. Services are *intangible, inseparable, variable* and *perishable*. Each characteristic poses problems and requires strategies. Marketers have to find ways to make the service more tangible; to increase the productivity of providers who are inseparable from their products; to standardize the quality in the face of variability; and to improve demand movements and supply capacities in the face of service perishability.

Service industries have typically lagged behind manufacturing firms in adopting and using marketing concepts, but this situation is now changing. Services marketing strategy calls not only for external marketing, but also for *internal marketing* to motivate employees and *interactive marketing* to create service delivery skills among service providers. To succeed, service marketers must create *competitive differentiation*, offer high service *quality* and find ways to increase *service productivity*.

Key Terms

Interactive marketing 654
Internal marketing 654
Service 646

Service inseparability 649
Service intangibility 647
Service perishability 650

Service variability 649

Discussing the Issues

1. Why is demand for services growing? How would marketers gain a competitive advantage by satisfying the growing demand for increased services?

2. How can a theatre deal with the intangibility, inseparability, variability and perishability of the service it provides? Give examples.

3. A fast-food restaurant serves its hamburgers 'fresh off the grill'. This ensures high quality, but creates leftover hamburgers if the staff overestimates demand. The restaurant solves this perishability problem by using the leftover meat in other dishes such as meat pies and spaghetti sauce. How do airlines solve the perishability of unsold seats? Give additional examples of perishability and how service firms address it.

4. Services marketing calls for external, internal and interactive marketing. Select examples of firms that provide services to other business organizations (e.g. an advertising agency, a transportation firm or a management consultancy). Explain how these other types of marketing can help such service firms create and maintain a competitive advantage.

5. Marketing is defined as satisfying needs and wants through exchange processes. What exchanges occur in marketing non-profit organizations, such as a museum, the Red Cross or other charities?

6. Referring to examples of non-profit (both public and private) service organizations, discuss how their effectiveness and efficiency might be increased by applying marketing principles.

Applying the Concepts

1. Select an educational institution you are familiar with (it could be the one at which you are currently studying for a qualification). Take the concept of the marketing mix as a framework to guide your evaluation of the organization. Start with the product (i.e. the service offering), then work through pricing, promotion, place and the other three *P*s – people, physical environment and process. Show how attention to all seven *P*s can affect the effectiveness and efficiency of the institution you have selected.

2. Perishability is very important in the airline industry: unsold seats are gone for ever, and too many unsold seats mean large losses. With computerized ticketing, airlines can easily use pricing to deal with perishability and variations in demand.

   ● Call a travel agent or use an online service that is accessible to check airline fares. Get prices on the same route for 60 days in advance, two weeks, one week and today. Is there a clear pattern to the fares?

   ● When a store is overstocked on ripe fruit, it may lower the price to sell out quickly. What are airlines doing to their prices as the seats get close to 'perishing'? Why? What would you recommend as a pricing strategy to increase total revenues?

6. Is the European theme park market already oversubscribed? Will Tibigarden succeed despite the failure of EuroDisney and the other theme parks in France?

SOURCES: Toni Burns, 'Riding the theme park roller coaster', *Financial Times* (14 February 1994), p. 15; Alice Rawsthorn, 'Only a month to make the refinancing fly', *Financial Times* (1 March 1994), p. 23; 'EuroDisney: waiting for Dumbo', *The Economist* (1 May 1993), p. 86; 'EuroDisney's plight worsens', *The European* (4–10 February 1994), p. 1; John Ridding, 'EuroDisney suffers huge loss', *Financial Times* (11 November 1993), p. 1; Mickael Skapinher and John Ridding, 'Unlucky or unwise', *Financial Times* (13–14 November 1993), p. 4; Alice Rawsthorn, 'Poisoned apple within the magic kingdom', *Financial Times* (25 November 1993), p. 6; 'Meltdown at the cultural Chernobyl', *The Economist* (5 February 1994), pp. 69–70; 'A profitable theme', *The Economist* (1 May 1993), p. 86.

Mattel: Getting it Right is No Child's Play

THE MATTEL TOY DESIGNER HELD everyone's interest as he prepared to push the green launch button. The assembled Hot Wheels brand managers and Mattel top executives marvelled as a tiny plastic car, called Top Speed, leaped off the launcher, zipped through a plastic accelerator tube and whizzed around the race track's curves and loops. The managers were impressed, especially given that Mattel's designers had developed the new car models at Mattel's toy-design centre in El Segundo, California, in only five months. However, they knew that many challenges remained. They wondered if the new toy would be the market hit they needed, or whether it would turn out to be just another of the nightmares that were all too common in the toy industry.

Nightmares

It's every parent's nightmare. Suddenly the kids start asking for something called Mighty Morphin Power Rangers for Christmas. First, they have to explain to their parents what a Mighty Morphin is, while giving them that 'don't-grown-ups-know-anything' look. Then the parents start looking for the toys casually on shopping trips. No luck. Then, Mum takes a day off from work to do some serious looking. Still, no luck. Over the weekend, Dad sneaks off to a major mall in another town or city while Mum calls out-of-town relatives to ask them to look. Again, they come up empty handed. It's panic time! Christmas is only two weeks away and all the kids are talking about is Mighty Morphin Power Rangers. How can Mum and Dad explain that Santa has run out of Power Rangers?

It's also every toy retailer's nightmare. Buyers travel to the region's annual Toy Fair, a trade show where toy manufacturers present their products. Thousands of retail toy buyers attend the show to place orders for the following Christmas season. As they wander down the aisles, they see the usual assortment of brand extensions for the perennial favourites, like Barbie, G.I. Joe and Hot Wheels. However, they also see 5,000–6,000 new toys each year, 80 per cent of which won't be around next year. The trick is to pick those that will be big hits.

So, a buyer places a small order for something new called Mighty Morphin Power Rangers. The manufacturer, Bandai America, claims that the toys will be popular after the September start of a television show about the Rangers. Later in the year, the toys begin to sell, even before the television show debuts. The buyer is not sure what to make of it and decides to wait until two weeks into the show to see how the new product moves. The delay proves costly. By the time the buyer places a new order in early October, every other retailer has seen the same trend and has also reordered. Bandai is able to ship only 600,000 Power Rangers despite orders for 12 *million*! During the next two months, angry parents flood the buyer's store wanting to know how they will explain to their children that Santa ran out of Power Rangers.

This process is no picnic for toy manufacturers either. The annual Toy Show is a make-or-break event. Sometime well before the February show, manufacturers have to decide which toys to present, which toys will be popular *two* Christmases away. Then they have to hope that they can manufacture enough toys between February and late summer to meet demand. To make matters worse, the major retailers like Toys 'Я' Us and major department stores have moved to a just-in-time philosophy to replenish inventory. Instead of placing one big order for toys, they place small orders initially, then reorder based on demand. They want to replace toys on their shelves just as they sell out. This strategy improves cash flow and avoids storerooms full of dud toys. But the just-in-time plan has a significant disadvantage for both retailers and manufacturers. If a surprise hit appears, neither can gear up fast enough to respond.

The Toy Industry

The toy industry is risky. If companies bet right, they make a lot of money. If not, they lose a lot of money. Toys are also big business. The Toy Manufacturers' Association estimated that the European toy market produced sales of ecu22 billion in 1996. The US toy market is even larger at over ecu23 billion. US manufacturers invent, engineer and market about two-thirds of all the toys in the world.

Analysts attribute toy industry growth to three factors. First, although birth rates in developed countries are declining, parents tend to buy more toys and more expensive toys for their children. Second, the increased number of divorced or separated parents often means the children have many adult relatives to give them toys. Also, many women are waiting later to have children, meaning they and their families may have higher disposable incomes.

Mattel's Top Speed

Mattel is one of the key players in the toy industry. With annual sales of $3 billion, it owns the 38-year-old Barbie and 28-year-old Hot Wheels brands. Barbie alone accounts for 35 per cent of Mattel's sales. Barbie's success, however, has created problems. In the mid-1990s, Mattel needed to lessen its dependence on the Barbie line. It also wanted to reverse a string of recent failures in its boys' division, including the Masters of the Universe and Demolition Man action figures.

As a result, Mattel prepared to launch its new line of Top Speed racers, the first Hot Wheels made from lightweight plastic rather than die-cast metal. The lighter-weight cars could zip around faster. The translucent plastic also allowed Mattel to give the 6 cm cars iridescent body colours that it believed would appeal to 7 to 10-year-old boys.

Further, Top Speed cars, unlike traditional Hot Wheels models, did not resemble real cars. They had a futuristic design, more like Indianapolis-style racing cars. The cars featured detailed engines; a floating front axle to improve performance on the track; stylish moulded mag wheels; and a front-mounted launching hook. Special rubber bands contained in a launcher powered the lightweight cars, allowing them to be hurled along tracks and through clear plastic tubes at amazing speeds. Mattel planned to offer Top Speed cars in six different models, each with its own exciting name: Cryo Pump, Road Vac, Corkscrew, Shock Rod, Sting Shot and Back Burner.

Mattel planned to package the cars in pairs, including a tube and launcher, with each pair selling for about $5 at retail. This price compared favourably with a $2 per car retail price for traditional Hot Wheels models. Kids could also buy

NI stressed the newspaper would not remain at 30p indefinitely – a move that would cost the newspaper £14 million per year in lost revenue. 'It is felt that the premium quality that the *Independent* achieves will, in the longer term, warrant a premium cover price,' said its editorial.[1]

QUESTIONS

1. What was the impact of the price war on the sales volume (number of newspapers sold) and sales value (monetary value of the newspapers sold) of the competing newspapers?
2. What did *The Times* hope to gain from starting such a costly price war?
3. Why did the other competitors follow the price lead of *The Times*?
4. When does it pay for a company start charging prices below industry rates?
5. What industries do you think are prone to price competition?
6. Should governments intervene to prevent aggressive price competition?

Introduction

All products and services have a price just as they have a value. Many non-profit and all profit-making organizations must also set prices, be they the predatory price of *The Times*, the price of access to see the island where Lady Diana lies, or the price of World Cup tickets for those who cannot get them officially. *Pricing* is controversial and goes by many names:

> Price is all around us. You pay *rent* for your apartment, *tuition* for your education and a *fee* to your physician or dentist. The airline, railway, taxi and bus companies charge you a *fare*; the local utilities call their price a *rate*; and the local bank charges you *interest* for the money you borrow … The guest lecturer charges an *honorarium* to tell you about a government official who took a *bribe* to help a shady character steal *dues* collected by a trade association. Clubs or societies to which you belong may make a special *assessment* to pay unusual expenses. Your regular lawyer may ask for a *retainer* to cover her services. The 'price' of an executive is a *salary*, the price of a salesperson may be a *commission* and the price of a worker is a *wage*. Finally, although economists would disagree, many of us feel that *income taxes* are the price we pay for the privilege of making money.[2]

In the narrowest sense, **price** is the amount of money charged for a product or service. More broadly, price is the sum of all the values that consumers exchange for the benefits of having or using the product or service.

How are prices set? Historically, prices were usually set by buyers and sellers bargaining with each other. Sellers would ask for a higher price than they expected to get and buyers would offer less than they expected to pay. Through bargaining, they would arrive at an acceptable price. Individual buyers paid different prices for the same products, depending on their needs and bargaining skills.

price
The amount of money charged for a product or service, or the sum of the values that consumers exchange for the benefits of having or using the product or service.

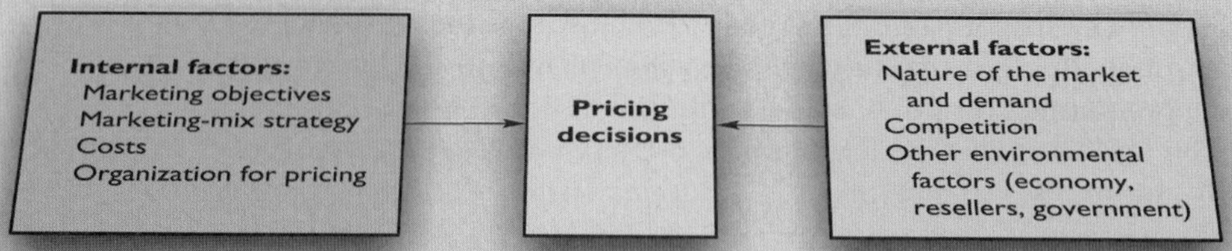

Figure 16.1 **Factors affecting price decisions**

Today, most sellers set *one* price for *all* buyers. Large-scale retailing led to the idea at the end of the nineteenth century. F.W. Woolworth and other retailers advertised a 'strictly one-price policy' because they carried so many items and had so many employees.

Historically, price has been the most significant factor affecting buyer choice. This is still true in poorer nations, among poorer groups and with commodity products. However, non-price factors have become more important in buyer-choice behaviour in recent decades.

Price is the only element in the marketing mix that produces revenue; all other elements represent costs. Price is also one of the most flexible elements of the marketing mix. Unlike product features and channel commitments, price can be changed quickly. At the same time, pricing and price competition is the no. 1 problem facing many marketing executives. Yet many companies do not handle pricing well. The most common mistakes are: pricing that is too cost-oriented; prices that are not revised often enough to reflect market changes; pricing that does not take the rest of the marketing mix into account; and prices that are not varied enough for different products, market segments and purchase occasions.

In this and the next chapter, we focus on the problem of setting prices. This chapter looks at the factors that marketers must consider when setting prices and at general pricing approaches. In the next chapter, we examine pricing strategies for new-product pricing, product mix pricing, price changes and price adjustments for buyer and situational factors.

Factors to Consider when Setting Prices

A company's pricing decisions are affected both by internal company factors and by external environmental factors (see Figure 16.1).[3]

Internal Factors Affecting Pricing Decisions

Internal factors affecting pricing include the company's marketing objectives, marketing-mix strategy, costs and organization.

● *Marketing Objectives*

Before setting price, the company must decide on its strategy for the product. If the company has selected its target market and positioning carefully, then its marketing-mix strategy, including price, will be fairly straightforward. For example, if Toyota decides to produce its Lexus cars to compete with European luxury cars in the high-income segment, this suggests charging a high price. Travel Lodge positions itself as motels that provide economical rooms for budget-minded travellers; this position requires charging a low price. Thus pricing strategy is largely determined by past decisions on market positioning.

At the same time, the company may seek additional objectives. The clearer a firm is about its objectives, the easier it is to set price. Examples of common objectives are *survival*, *current profit maximization*, *market-share maximization* and *product-quality leadership*.

Companies set *survival* as their fundamental objective if they are troubled by too much capacity, heavy competition or changing consumer wants. In Europe and Japan steel-makers sell steel at a loss as demand declines. To keep a plant going, a company may set a low price, hoping to increase demand. In this case, profits are less important than survival. As long as their prices cover variable costs and some fixed costs, they can stay in business. However, survival is only a short-term objective. In the long run, the firm must learn how to add value or face extinction.[4]

Many companies use *current profit maximization* as their pricing goal. They estimate what demand and costs will be at different prices and choose the price that will produce the maximum current profit, cash flow or return on investment. In all cases, the company wants current financial results rather than long-run performance. Other companies want to obtain *market-share leadership*. They believe that the company with the largest market share will enjoy the lowest costs and highest long-run profit. To become the market-share leader, these firms set prices as low as possible.

A variation of this objective is to pursue a specific *market-share gain*. Say the company wants to increase its market share from 10 per cent to 15 per cent in one year. It will search for the price and marketing programme that will achieve this goal.

> Digital television transmission is set to make the current analogue television as outdated as 16mm cine film or vinyl albums. It produces cinema quality pictures while cramming hundreds of channels through the wave bands needed for a dozen analogue transmissions. Seeing the mould-breaking potential of digital TV satellite television company, BSkyB and terrestrial BDB are set to battle for market leadership of digital television transmission. BSkyB's consortium of BT, HSBC and Matsushita aims to subsidize its TV set-top converters by ecu1 billion, retailing them at ecu300, although they will cost at least twice that to manufacture.

A company might decide that it wants to achieve *product-quality leadership*. This normally calls for charging a high price to cover such quality and the high cost of R & D:

> For example, Jaguar's limited edition XJ220 sold for £400,000 each, but had wealthy customers queuing to buy one. Less exotically, Pitney Bowes pursues a product-quality leadership strategy for its fax equipment. While Sharp, Canon and other competitors fight over the low-price fax machine market with machines selling at around $500, Pitney Bowes targets large corporations with machines selling at about $5,000. As a result, it captures some 45 per cent of the large-corporation fax niche.[5]

A company might also use price to attain other more specific objectives. It can set prices low to prevent competition from entering the market or set prices at competitors' levels to stabilize the market:

> In 1994 grocery market leaders Sainsbury and Tesco used 'Essentials' and 'Everyday super value range' campaigns to counter the attack of discounters Aldi and Netto on the UK market. Originally projected to take 20 per cent of the grocery market by the year 2000, forecasters later predicted the discounters would take only 12 per cent.[6]

Prices can be set to keep the loyalty and support of resellers or to avoid government intervention. Prices can be reduced temporarily to create excitement for a product or to draw more customers into a retail store. One product may be priced to help the sales of other products in the company's line. Thus pricing may play an important role in helping to accomplish the company's objectives at many levels.

Non-profit and public organizations may adopt a number of other pricing objectives. A university aims for *partial cost recovery*, knowing that it must rely on private gifts and public grants to cover the remaining costs. A non-profit hospital may aim for *full cost recovery* in its pricing. A non-profit theatre company may price its productions to fill the maximum number of theatre seats. A social service agency may set a *social price* geared to the varying income situations of different clients.

● *Marketing-Mix Strategy*

Price is only one of the marketing-mix tools that a company uses to achieve its marketing objectives. Price decisions must be co-ordinated with product design, distribution and promotion decisions to form a consistent and effective marketing programme. Decisions made for other marketing-mix variables may affect pricing decisions. For example, producers using many resellers that are expected to support and promote their products may have to build larger reseller margins into their prices. The decision to position the product on high performance quality will mean that the seller must charge a higher price to cover higher costs. The perfume houses argue that their high margins, expensive advertising and exclusive distribution are essential to the brands and in the public interest.[7]

Companies often make their pricing decisions first and then base other marketing-mix decisions on the prices they want to charge. Here, price is a crucial product-positioning factor that defines the product's market, competition and design. The intended price determines what product features can be offered and what production costs can be incurred.

Many firms support such price-positioning strategies with a technique called **target costing**, a potent strategic weapon. Target costing reverses the usual process of first designing a new product, determining its cost and then asking 'Can we sell it for that?' Instead, it starts with a target cost and works back:

target costing

A technique to support pricing decision, which starts with deciding a target cost for a new product and works back to designing the product.

> Compaq Computer Corporation calls this process 'design to price'. After being battered for years by lower-priced rivals, Compaq used this approach to create its highly successful, lower-priced Prolinea personal computer line. Starting with a price target set by marketing and with profit-margin goals from management, the Prolinea design team determined what costs *had* to be in order to charge the target price. From this crucial calculation all else followed. To achieve target costs, the design team negotiated doggedly with all the company departments

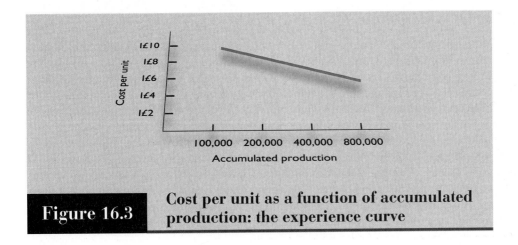

| **Figure 16.3** | **Cost per unit as a function of accumulated production: the experience curve** |

economies of scale. As a result, average cost tends to fall with accumulated production experience. This is shown in Figure 16.3.[11] Thus the average cost of producing the first 100,000 clocks is I£10 per clock. When the company has produced the first 200,000 clocks, the average cost has fallen to I£9. After its accumulated production experience doubles again to 400,000, the average cost is I£7. This drop in the average cost with accumulated production experience is called the **experience curve** (or **learning curve**).

If a downward-sloping experience curve exists, this is highly significant for the company. Not only will the company's unit production cost fall; it will fall faster if the company makes and sells more during a given time period. But the market has to stand ready to buy the higher output. And to take advantage of the experience curve, Roberts must get a large market share early in the product's life cycle. This suggests the following pricing strategy. Roberts should price its clocks low; its sales will then increase and its costs will decrease through gaining more experience, and then it can lower its prices further.

Some companies have built successful strategies around the experience curve. For example, during the 1980s, Bausch & Lomb consolidated its position in the soft contact lens market by using computerized lens design and steadily expanding its one Soflens plant. As a result, its market share climbed steadily to 65 per cent. Yet a single-minded focus on reducing costs and exploiting the experience curve will not always work. Experience curves became somewhat of a fad during the 1970s and, like many fads, the strategy was sometimes misused. Experience-curve pricing carries some serious risks. The aggressive pricing might give the product a cheap image. The strategy also assumes that competitors are weak and not willing to fight it out by meeting the company's price cuts.

> An 'experience curve war' broke out between the Japanese makers of DRAM (dynamic random-access memory) chips, the semiconductor memory devices used in computers. Hitachi, Toshiba, NEC and Mitsubishi reduced the price of their 4-megabyte DRAMs from ¥12,000 to ¥2,500 within a year of its launch, at the same time spending heavily to develop the next generation's 16-megabyte DRAM. Within two years 1-megabyte DRAM sold for ¥1,600, probably too low to recoup the cost of the production lines needed to make them.[12]

Finally, while the company is building volume under one technology, a competitor may find a lower-cost technology that lets it start at lower prices than the market leader, who still operates on the old experience curve.

experience curve (learning curve)
The drop in the average per-unit production cost that comes with accumulated production experience.

● *Organizational Considerations*

Management must decide who within the organization should set prices. Companies handle pricing in a variety of ways. In small companies, prices are often set by top management rather than by the marketing or sales departments. In large companies, pricing is typically handled by divisional or product line managers. In industrial markets, salespeople may be allowed to negotiate with customers within certain price ranges. Even so, top management sets the pricing objectives and policies, and it often approves the prices proposed by lower-level management or salespeople. In industries in which pricing is a key factor (aerospace, railways, oil companies), companies will often have a pricing department to set the best prices or help others in setting them. This department reports to the marketing department or top management. Others who have an influence on pricing include sales managers, production managers, finance managers and accountants.

External Factors Affecting Pricing Decisions

External factors that affect pricing decisions include the nature of the market and demand, competition and other environmental elements.

● *The Market and Demand*

Whereas costs set the lower limit of prices, the market and demand set the upper limit. Both consumer and industrial buyers balance the price of a product or service against the benefits of owning it. Thus, before setting prices, the marketer must understand the relationship between price and demand for its product.

In this section, we explain how the price–demand relationship varies for different types of market and how buyer perceptions of price affect the pricing decision. We then discuss methods for measuring the price–demand relationship.

PRICING IN DIFFERENT TYPES OF MARKET. The seller's pricing freedom varies with different types of market. Economists recognize four types of market, each presenting a different pricing challenge.

pure competition
A market in which many buyers and sellers trade in a uniform commodity – no single buyer or seller has much effect on the going market price.

Under **pure competition**, the market consists of many buyers and sellers trading in a uniform commodity such as wheat, copper or financial securities. No single buyer or seller has much effect on the going market price. A seller cannot charge more than the going price because buyers can obtain as much as they need at the going price. Nor would sellers charge less than the market price because they can sell all they want at this price. If price and profits rise, new sellers can easily enter the market. In a purely competitive market, marketing research, product development, pricing, advertising and sales promotion play little or no role. Thus sellers in these markets do not spend much time on marketing strategy.

monopolistic competition
A market in which many buyers and sellers trade over a range of prices rather than a single market price.

Under **monopolistic competition**, the market consists of many buyers and sellers that trade over a range of prices rather than a single market price. A range of prices occurs because sellers can differentiate their offers to buyers. Either the physical product can be varied in quality, features or style, or the accompanying services can be varied. Buyers see differences in sellers' products and will pay different prices for them. Sellers try to develop differentiated offers for different customer segments and, in addition to price, freely use branding, advertising and personal selling to set their offers apart. For example, Danone's Lea and Perrins and several other bottled sauces compete with dozens of national and international varieties differentiated by price and non-price factors. Because there are many competitors, each firm is less affected by competitors' marketing strategies than in oligopolistic markets.

Monopolistic competition: in the industrial market, Stanley sets its hinges apart from dozens of other brands using both price and nonprice factors.

NINE OUT OF TEN INMATES PREFER OUR COMPETITOR'S HINGE.

In prisons and hospitals there's no contest between our new Stanley LifeSpan™ Institutional Hinge and the competition's.

First, our hinge is wrought steel, not cast. Instead of two ball bearings, Stanley uses two stainless steel plus two Stanite™ bearings to handle vertical *and* lateral loads. There's no visible change in the configuration of our hinge when it's electrified. Plus, it's guaranteed for the life of the building.

The only thing their hinge has in common with ours is an invisible pin line. But rather than being cast, ours is electron-beam welded then hospital tip ground, making it virtually impossible to hammer out the pin.

Now you can understand why inmates think it's a crime for prisons to use our hinges.

For more information including a brochure, samples, specifications and a demonstration of our new LifeSpan™ Hinge, contact your Stanley Hardware representative, or Dave Loughran

at Stanley Hardware, 195 Lake Street, New Britain, CT 06050 (203) 225-5111.

STANLEY HARDWARE

Under **oligopolistic competition**, the market consists of a few sellers that are highly sensitive to each other's pricing and marketing strategies. The product can be uniform (steel, aluminium) or non-uniform (cars, computers). There are few sellers because it is difficult for new sellers to enter the market. Each seller is alert to competitors' strategies and moves. If a steel company slashes its price by 10 per cent, buyers will quickly switch to this supplier. The other steel makers must respond by lowering their prices or increasing their services. An oligopolist is never sure that it will gain anything permanent through a price cut. In contrast, if an oligopolist raises its price, its competitors might not follow this lead. The oligopolist would then have to retract its price increase or risk losing customers to competitors.[13]

In a **pure monopoly**, the market consists of one seller. The seller may be a government monopoly (a Postal Service), a private regulated monopoly (a power company) or a private non-regulated monopoly (Microsoft with DOS and Windows). Pricing is handled differently in each case. A government monopoly can pursue a variety of pricing objectives. It might set a price below cost because the product is important to buyers who cannot afford to pay full cost. Or the price might be set either to cover costs or to produce good revenue. It can even be set quite high to slow down consumption. In a regulated monopoly, the government permits the company to set rates that will yield a 'fair return', one that will let the company maintain and expand its operations as needed. Non-regulated monopolies are free to price at what the market will bear. However, they do not always charge the full price for a number of reasons: for example, a desire not to attract competition, a desire to penetrate the market faster with a low price, or a fear of government regulation.

CONSUMER PERCEPTIONS OF PRICE AND VALUE. In the end, the consumer will decide whether a product's price is right. When setting prices, the

oligopolistic competition
A market in which there are a few sellers that are highly sensitive to each other's pricing and marketing strategies.

pure monopoly
A market in which there is a single seller – it may be a government monopoly, a private regulated monopoly or a private non-regulated monopoly.

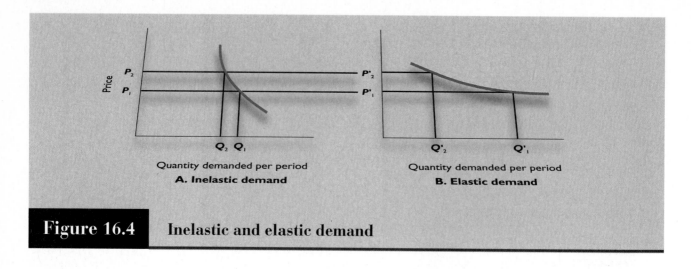

Figure 16.4   **Inelastic and elastic demand**

company must consider consumer perceptions of price and how these perceptions affect consumers' buying decisions. Pricing decisions, like other marketing-mix decisions, must be buyer-oriented.

When consumers buy a product, they exchange something of value (the price) to get something of value (the benefits of having or using the product). Effective, buyer-oriented pricing involves understanding how much value consumers place on the benefits they receive from the product and setting a price that fits this value. These benefits can be actual or perceived. For example, calculating the cost of ingredients in a meal at a fancy restaurant is relatively easy. But assigning a value to other satisfactions such as taste, environment, relaxation, conversation and status is very hard. And these values will vary both for different consumers and for different situations.

> Functional confectionery , such as Clorets or Fisherman's Friends, offers tangible problem solutions that customers value. These products may cost little more to make than conventional sugar-based confectionery, such as Polo Mints or Rowntree's Fruit Pastilles, but customers value their physical performance. Makers of these products do not rely on consumers' perception of their brand's value, but convey the products on the pack and by promotions. For instance, the flavour, strength and packaging of Hall's Mentho-Lyptus is fine tuned for local markets but remains true to its core benefit: throat soothing.

Thus the company will often find it hard to measure the values that customers will attach to its product. But consumers do use these values to evaluate a product's price. If customers perceive that the price is greater than the product's value, they will not buy the product. If consumers perceive that the price is below the product's value, they will buy it, but the seller loses profit opportunities (see Marketing Highlight 16.2).

Marketers must therefore try to understand the consumer's reasons for buying the product and set the price according to consumer perceptions of the product's value. Because consumers vary in the values they assign to different product features, marketers often vary their pricing strategies for different segments. They offer different sets of product features at different prices. For example, Philips offers DFl 550 small 41-cm portable TV models for consumers who want basic sets and DFl 2,500 68-cm 100-Hz Nicam stereo models loaded with features for consumers who want the extras.

The MX-5's Popularity Drives Its Prices

Marketing Highlight 16.2

How much would you pay for a curvaceous new two-seat convertible that has the reliability of modern engineering yet the look, feel and sound of such classic roadsters as the 1959 Triumph TR3, the 1958 MGA, the 1962 Lotus Elan or the Austin-Healey 3000? The car was the Mazda MX-5. It is a Japanese car designed in Europe for the US market. When being road tested in California, the car was such an instant hit that passing drivers kept making it pull over to ask where they could buy one. Not only did consumers rave about its looks, but car critics passionately praised its performance. According to *Car and Driver*, if the MX-5 'were any more talented or tempting, driving one would be illegal'. Judging on design, performance, durability and reliability, entertainment and value, *Road and Track* named it one of the five best cars in the world. Included in the rankings along with the MX-5 were the Porsche 911 Carrera, the Corvette ZR-1, the Mercedes-Benz 300E and the $140,000 Ferrari Testarossa. Not bad company for a car with a base sticker price of only $13,800 and designed 'just to be fun'. Besides its good looks, performance and price, the MX-5 rocketed to success because it had no substitutes. Its closest competitors were the Honda CRX Si and the Toyota MR2, but they lacked its singular looks and neither came as a convertible. Thus the MX-5 drove rivals to despair and customers into a covetous swoon.

Mazda had a hard time with the question of how to price its classy little car. The Japanese importer carefully controlled costs to keep the MX-5's base price below $15,000. But it seems that consumers cared little about the MX-5's costs, or about its intended price. When the MX-5 made its debut, sales soared – and so did its prices. The first few thousand MX-5s to arrive at Mazda dealerships sold out instantly. To make things even more interesting, Mazda planned to ship only 20,000 MX-5s (in three colours – red, white and blue) to its 844 dealers in 1989, and only 40,000 more in 1990. Thus demand exceeded the limited supply by a reported ratio of ten to one.

The MX-5 was in such demand that dealers increased the price way beyond that advertised on the sticker and still had barely enough cars to sell. Because of the car's popularity, customers were more than willing to pay the higher price. As one dealer noted: 'People are offering more than what we're asking just to get [the car].' On average, dealers across the United States marked up prices by $4,000; in California, they added as much as $8,000. Some enterprising owners even offered to sell their MX-5s for prices ranging up to $45,000. Ads appeared daily in the *Los Angeles Times* from owners in Kansas, Nebraska or Michigan proffering their MX-5s for $32,000 plus delivery fees.

Thus although many companies focus on costs as a key to setting prices, consumers rarely know of or care about the seller's costs. What really counts is what consumers are willing to pay for the benefits of owning the product. To some consumers, the sharp little MX-5 added up to much more than the sum of its mechanical parts. To them, it delivered the same pleasures and prestige as cars selling at much higher prices. Therefore, even at above-sticker prices, most buyers got a good deal. Mazda on the other hand, may have left some money on the table. Aside from its good looks, performance and price, the Mazda MX-5 rocketed to success because it had no substitutes.

SOURCES: Rebecca Fannin, 'Mazda's sporting chance', *Marketing and Media Decisions* (October 1989), pp. 24–30; S.C. Gwynne, 'Romancing the roadster', *Time* (24 July 1989), p. 39; 'The roadster returns', *Consumer Reports* (April 1990), pp. 232–4; Larry Armstrong, 'After the Miata, Mazda isn't just idling', *Business Week* (2 September 1991), p. 35.

ANALYZING THE PRICE-DEMAND RELATIONSHIP. Each price the company might charge will lead to a different level of demand. The relation between the price charged and the resulting demand level is shown in the demand curve in Figure 16.4A. The demand curve shows the number of units that the market will buy in a given time period at different prices that might be charged. In the normal case, demand and price are inversely related: that is, the higher the price, the lower the demand. Thus the company would sell less if it raised its price from P_1 to P_2. In short, consumers with limited budgets will probably buy less of something if its price is too high.

In the case of prestige goods, the demand curve sometimes slopes upwards. For example, one perfume company found that to be the case by raising its price on a more desirable perfume. However, if the company charges too high a price, the level of demand will be lower. The demand curve for theatre tickets can show similarly strange patterns. For mid-range tickets, demand goes up as prices go down, but below a critical point demand declines with price as people assume the seats are no good. Also, demand for 'the best seats in the house' sometimes increases with price.[14]

Most companies try to measure their demand curves by estimating demand at different prices. The type of market makes a difference. In a monopoly, the demand curve shows the total market demand resulting from different prices. If the company faces competition, its demand at different prices will depend on whether competitors' prices stay constant or change with the company's own prices. Here, we will assume that competitors' prices remain constant. Later in this chapter, we will discuss what happens when competitors' prices change.

In measuring the price–demand relationship, the market researcher must not allow other factors affecting demand to vary. For example, if Philips increased its advertising at the same time that it lowered its television prices, we would not know how much of the increased demand was due to the lower prices and how much was due to the increased advertising. The same problem arises if a holiday weekend occurs when the lower price is set – more gift giving over some holidays causes people to buy more portable televisions. Economists show the impact of non-price factors on demand through shifts in the demand curve rather than movements along it.

price elasticity
A measure of the sensitivity of demand to changes in price.

PRICE ELASTICITY OF DEMAND. Marketers also need to know **price elasticity** – how responsive demand will be to a change in price. Consider the two demand curves in Figure 16.4. In Figure 16.4A, a price increase from P_1 to P_2 leads to a relatively small drop in demand from Q_1 to Q_2. In Figure 16.4B, however, a similar price increase leads to a large drop in demand from Q'_1 to Q'_2. If demand hardly changes with a small change in price, we say the demand is *inelastic*. If demand changes greatly, we say the demand is *elastic*. The price elasticity of demand is given by the following formula:

$$\text{Price elasticity of demand} = \frac{\%\text{ change in quantity demanded}}{\%\text{ change in price}}$$

Suppose demand falls by 10 per cent when a seller raises its price by 2 per cent. Price elasticity of demand is therefore –5 (the minus sign confirms the inverse relation between price and demand) and demand is elastic. If demand falls by 2 per cent with a 2 per cent increase in price, then elasticity is –1. In this case, the seller's total revenue stays the same: that is, the seller sells fewer items, but at a higher price that preserves the same total revenue. If demand falls by 1 per cent when the price is increased by 2 per cent, then elasticity is –1/2 and

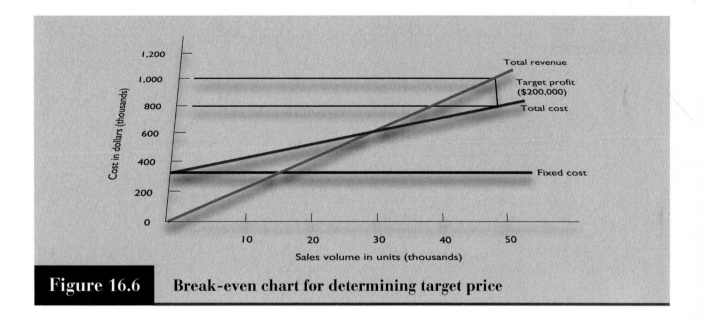

Figure 16.6 **Break-even chart for determining target price**

● *Break-Even Analysis and Target Profit Pricing*

Another cost-oriented pricing approach is **break-even pricing** or a variation called **target profit pricing**. The firm tries to determine the price at which it will break even or make the target profit it is seeking. Target pricing is used by General Motors, which prices its cars to achieve a 15–20 per cent profit on its investment. This pricing method is also used by public utilities, which are constrained to make a fair return on their investment. Target pricing uses the concept of a *break-even chart*. A break-even chart shows the total cost and total revenue expected at different sales volume levels. Figure 16.6 shows a break-even chart for the toaster manufacturer discussed here. Fixed costs are $300,000 regardless of sales volume. Variable costs are added to fixed costs to form total costs, which rise with volume. The total revenue curve starts at zero and rises with each unit sold. The slope of the total revenue curve reflects the price of $20 per unit.

The total revenue and total cost curves cross at 30,000 units. This is the *break-even volume*. At $20, the company must sell at least 30,000 units to break even: that is, for total revenue to cover total cost. Break-even volume can be calculated using the following formula:

$$\text{Break-even volume} = \frac{\text{fixed cost}}{(\text{price} - \text{variable cost})} = \frac{\$300,000}{(\$20 - \$10)} = 30,000$$

If the company wants to make a target profit, it must sell more than 30,000 units at $20 each. Suppose the toaster manufacturer has invested $1,000,000 in the business and wants to set a price to earn a 20 per cent return or $200,000. In that case, it must sell at least 50,000 units at $20 each. If the company charges a higher price, it will not need to sell as many toasters to achieve its target return. But the market may not buy even this lower volume at the higher price. Much depends on the price elasticity and competitors' prices.

The manufacturer should consider different prices and estimate break-even volumes, probable demand and profits for each. This is done in Table 16.2. The table shows that as price increases, break-even volume drops (column 2). But as price increases, demand for the toasters also falls off (column 3). At the $14 price,

break-even pricing (target profit pricing)
Setting price to break even on the costs of making and marketing a product; or setting price to make a target profit.

target profit pricing
See Break-even pricing.

Table 16.2	Breakeven volume and profits at different prices

(1) Price ($)	(2) Unit demand needed to break even	(3) Expected unit demand at given price	(4) Total revenues ($) (1) × (3)	(5) Total costs ($)*	(6) Profit (4) – (5)
14	75,000	71,000	994,000	1,100,000	–106,000
16	50,000	67,000	1,072,000	970,000	102,000
18	37,500	60,000	1,080,000	900,000	180,000
20	30,000	42,000	840,000	720,000	120,000
22	25,000	23,000	506,000	530,000	–24,000

NOTE:* Assumes fixed costs of $300,000 and constant unit variable costs of $10.

because the manufacturer clears only $4 per toaster ($14 less $10 in variable costs), it must sell a very high volume to break even. Even though the low price attracts many buyers, demand still falls below the high break-even point and the manufacturer loses money. At the other extreme, with a $22 price the manufacturer clears $12 per toaster and must sell only 25,000 units to break even. But at this high price, consumers buy too few toasters and profits are negative. The table shows that a price of $18 yields the highest profits. Note that none of the prices produces the manufacturer's target profit of $200,000. To achieve this target return, the manufacturer will have to search for ways to lower fixed or variable costs, thus lowering the break-even volume.

Value-Based Pricing

value-based pricing
Setting price based on buyers' perceptions of product values rather than on cost.

An increasing number of companies are basing their prices on the product's perceived value. **Value-based pricing** uses buyers' perceptions of value, not the seller's cost, as the key to pricing. Value-based pricing means that the marketer cannot design a product and marketing programme and then set the price. Price is considered along with the other marketing-mix variables *before* the marketing programme is set.

Figure 16.7 compares cost-based pricing with value-based pricing. Cost-based pricing is product driven. The company designs what it considers to be a good product, totals the costs of making the product and sets a price that covers costs plus a target profit. Marketing must then convince buyers that the product's value at that price justifies its purchase. If the price turns out to be too high, the company must settle for lower mark-ups or lower sales, both resulting in disappointing profits.

Value-based pricing reverses this process. The company sets its target price based on customer perceptions of the product value. The targeted value and price then drive decisions about product design and what costs can be incurred. As a result, pricing begins with analyzing consumer needs and value perceptions and a price is set to match consumers' perceived value:

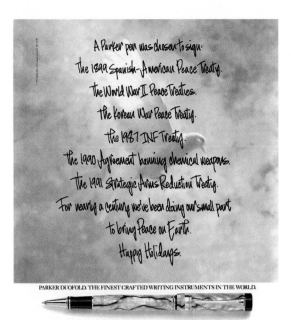

The finest crafted writing instruments in the world.

Perceived value: a less expensive pen might write as well, but some consumers will pay much more the intangibles. This Parker model runs at $185. Others are priced as high as $3,500.

Consider Thorn selling its 10W 2D energy-saving electric light bulbs to a hotel manager. The SL18 costs far more to make than a conventional 60-watt tungsten light bulb, so a higher price has to be justified. Value pricing helps by looking at the hotel manager's total cost of ownership rather than the price of electric light bulbs. The life-cycle costs of the manager using a tungsten bulb for the 1,000 hours that they last includes the price of the bulb (60p), the labour cost of replacing it (50p) and electricity (£4.80). The life-cycle cost of the tungsten bulb is therefore £5.90. The Thorn 10W 2D bulb uses a sixth of the electricity of a conventional bulb and lasts eight times longer. Its life-cycle cost must therefore be compared with the cost of owning eight tungsten bulbs: 8 x £5.90 = £47.20. To work out the value of the Thorn bulb, its cost of ownership is also considered: changing the bulb 50p and electricity £6.40 (one-sixth the electricity costs of eight tungsten bulbs). The maximum value-based price of the Thorn bulb to the hotel manager is therefore:

Maximum value-based price = competitor's cost of ownership – own operating costs
= £47.20 – (£6.40 + 50p)
= £40.30

Using this evidence, Thorn can argue that it is worth the hotel manager paying a lot more than 60p to buy the energy-saving bulb. It is unrealistic to think that the manager would pay the full £40.30, but based on these figures, the actual price of £10.00 for the Thorn energy-saving bulb looks very reasonable. At first sight it seems hard to justify replacing a 60p tungsten bulb with a £10.00 energy-saving one, but value-based pricing shows the hotel manager is saving £30.00 by doing so. The value-based pricing using life-cycle costs can be used to justify paying a premium price on products: from low energy-condensation boilers as domestic boilers to low maintenance jet fighters.[18]

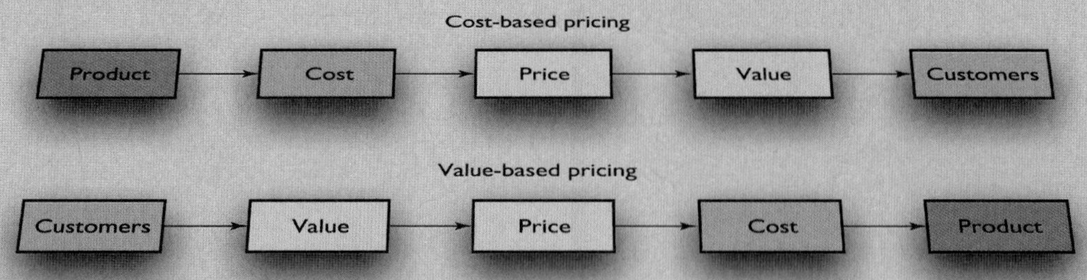

(SOURCE: Thomas T. Nagle and Reed K. Holden, *The Strategy and Tactics of Pricing*, 2nd edn (Englewood Cliffs, NJ: Prentice Hall, 1995), p. 5.)

Figure 16.7 **Cost-based versus value-based pricing**

A company using perceived-value pricing must find out what value buyers assign to different competitive offers. However, measuring perceived value can be difficult. Sometimes consumers are asked how much they would pay for a basic product and for each benefit added to the offer. Or a company might conduct experiments to test the perceived value of different product offers. If the seller charges more than the buyers' perceived value, the company's sales will suffer. Many companies overprice their products and their products sell poorly. Other companies underprice. Underpriced products sell very well, but they produce less revenue than they would if prices were raised to the perceived-value levels.

Competition-Based Pricing

Consumers will base their judgements of a product's value on the prices that competitors charge for similar products. Here, we discuss two forms of competition-based pricing: *going-rate pricing* and *sealed-bid pricing*.

● *Going-Rate Pricing*

going-rate pricing
Setting price based largely on following competitors' prices rather than on company costs or demand.

In **going-rate pricing**, the firm bases its price largely on *competitors'* prices, with less attention paid to its *own* costs or to demand. The firm might charge the same as, more, or less than its chief competitors. In oligopolistic industries that sell a commodity such as steel, paper or fertilizer, firms normally charge the same price. The smaller firms follow the leader: they change their prices when the market leader's prices change, rather than when their own demand or costs change. Some firms may charge a bit more or less, but they hold the amount of difference constant. Thus, minor petrol retailers usually charge slightly less than the big oil companies, without letting the difference increase or decrease.

> Going-rate pricing applies to complex products as well as commodities. Fierce competition between aerospace producers cut world aircraft prices by a fifth between 1996 and 1998. Manfred Bischoff, chief executive of Daimler-Benz's Dasa, cites Boeing as the chief culprit. 'There is a crumbling of prices in certain markets,' he says. 'The price is dictated by Boeing. We are followers in this case.'[19]

Eurostar consider their competition when setting prices aimed at the business traveller.

Although it gives firms little control of their revenue, going-rate pricing can be quite popular. When demand elasticity is hard to measure, firms feel that the going price represents the collective wisdom of the industry concerning the price that will yield a fair return. They also feel that holding to the going price will prevent harmful price wars.

● *Sealed-Bid Pricing*

Competition-based pricing is also used when firms *bid* for jobs. Using **sealed-bid pricing**, a firm bases its price on how it thinks competitors will price, rather than on its own costs or on the demand. The firm wants to win a contract and winning the contract requires pricing less than other firms.

Yet the firm cannot set its price below a certain level. It cannot price below cost without harming its position. In contrast, the higher the company sets its price above its costs, the lower its chance of getting the contract.

The net effect of the two opposite pulls can be described in terms of the *expected profit* of the particular bid (see Table 16.3). Suppose a bid of $9,500 would yield a high chance (say, 0.81) of getting the contract, but only a low profit (say, $100). The expected profit with this bid is therefore $81. If the firm bid $11,000, its profit would be $1,600, but its chance of getting the contract might be reduced to 0.01. The expected profit would be only $16. Thus the company might bid the price that would maximize the expected profit. According to Table 16.3, the best bid would be $10,000, for which the expected profit is $216.

sealed-bid pricing
Setting price based on how the firm thinks competitors will price rather than on its own costs or demand – used when a company bids for jobs.

| Table 16.3 | Effects of different bids on expected profit | | |

COMPANY'S BID ($)	(1) COMPANY'S PROFIT ($)	(2) PROBABILITY OF WINNING WITH THIS BID (ASSUMED)	(3) EXPECTED PROFIT (1) × (2)
9,500	100	0.81	81
10,000	600	0.36	216
10,500	1,100	0.09	99
11,000	1,600	0.01	16

Using expected profit as a basis for setting price makes sense for the large firm that makes many bids. In playing the odds, the firm will make maximum profits in the long run. But a firm that bids only occasionally or needs a particular contract badly will not find the expected-profit approach useful. The approach, for example, does not distinguish between a $100,000 profit with a 0.10 probability and a $12,500 profit with a 0.80 probability. Yet the firm that wants to keep production going would prefer the second contract to the first.

Summary

Despite the increased role of non-price factors in the modern marketing process, *price* remains an important element in the marketing mix. Many internal and external factors influence the company's pricing decisions. *Internal factors* include the firm's *marketing objectives*, *marketing-mix strategy*, *costs* and *organization for pricing*.

The pricing strategy is largely determined by the company's *target market and positioning objectives*. Common pricing objectives include survival, current profit maximization, market-share leadership and product-quality leadership.

Price is only one of the marketing-mix tools that the company uses to accomplish its objectives, and pricing decisions affect and are affected by product design, distribution and promotion decisions. Price decisions must be carefully co-ordinated with the other marketing-mix decisions when designing the marketing programme.

Costs set the floor for the company's price – the price must cover all the costs of making and selling the product, plus a fair rate of return. Management must decide who within the organization is responsible for setting price. In large companies, some pricing authority may be delegated to lower-level managers and salespeople, but top management usually sets pricing policies and approves proposed prices. Production, finance and accounting managers also influence pricing.

External factors that influence pricing decisions include the nature of the market and demand; competitors' prices and offers; and factors such as the economy, reseller needs and government actions. The seller's pricing freedom varies with different types of market. Pricing is especially challenging in markets characterized by monopolistic competition oligopoly.

In the end, the consumer decides whether the company has set the right price. The consumer weighs the price against the perceived values of using the product – if the price exceeds the sum of the values, consumers will not buy the product. Consumers differ in the values they assign to different product features and marketers often vary their pricing strategies for different price segments. When assessing the market and demand, the company estimates the demand curve, which shows the probable quantity purchased per period at alternative price levels. The more *inelastic* the demand, the higher the company can set its price. *Demand* and *consumer value perceptions* set the ceiling for prices.

Consumers compare a product's price to the prices of *competitors'* products. A company must learn the price and qualities of competitors' offers and use them as a starting point for its own pricing.

The company can select one or a combination of three general pricing approaches: the *cost-based approach* (cost-plus pricing, break-even analysis and target profit pricing); the *value-based approach* (value-based pricing); and the *competition-based approach* (going-rate or sealed-bid pricing).

Key Terms

Break-even pricing (target profit pricing) 701
Cost-plus pricing 699
Demand curve
Experience curve (learning curve) 689
Fixed costs 685
Going-rate pricing 704

Mark-up/mark-down 699
Monopolistic competition 690
Net profit 695
Oligopolistic competition 691
Price 681
Price elasticity 694
Pure competition 690

Pure monopoly 691
Sealed-bid pricing 705
Target costing 684
Total costs 688
Value-based pricing 702
Variable costs 685

Discussing the Issues

1. Certain 'inexpensive' products that waste energy, provide few savings per package or require frequent maintenance may cost much more to own and use than products selling for a higher price. How would marketers use this information on 'true cost' to gain a competitive edge in pricing and promoting their products?

2. Companies must consider both the internal company factors and external environmental influences that impact on their pricing decisions. Consider a relatively new entrant in the world car industry – Malaysia's Proton Saga – which has sought a low-cost, value-for-money positioning in the volume sector. Its low price supports this positioning. What type of pricing approach is the manufacturer pursuing? How appropriate is this pricing approach, taking into consideration the key factors that the company should evaluate when pricing its products? Explain your answer.

3. Sales of a brand of malt whisky increased when prices were raised by 20 per cent over a two-year period. What does this tell you about the demand curve and the elasticity of demand for this whisky? What does this suggest about using perceived-value pricing in marketing alcoholic drinks?

4. Genentech, a high-technology pharmaceutical company, developed a clot-dissolving drug called TPA that would halt a heart attack in progress. TPA saves lives, minimizes hospital stays and reduces damage to the heart itself. It was initially priced at $2,200 per dose. What pricing approach does Genentech appear to have been using? Is demand for this drug likely to be elastic with price? Why or why not?

5. In the early years of global market expansion, Japanese car and camera makers took advantage of the experience or learning curve when pricing their products to penetrate overseas markets. What does this suggest about their pricing approach? How

successful do you think this approach has been for the Japanese companies that have taken advantage of the learning curve?

6. Select a personal care product or cosmetic item that you regularly use. Notice the price of the item. What are the main benefits you are looking for in using this product? Does the price communicate the total benefits sought? Does the product's price suggest good value? Do you think the manufacturer or retailer is overcharging or undercharging consumers for this product? Why or why not? What pricing approach do you think is most appropriate for setting the price for this product?

Applying the Concepts

1. Do a pricing survey of several petrol stations in your town in different locations. If possible, check prices at the following: stations at a service area on a main road/motorway, stations on a local street in or near the town, a station not near any other stations, and (where appropriate) a station that is tied to a supermarket. Write down the brand of petrol, prices of regular and premium grades, type of location, distance to the nearest competitor and the competitor's prices.

   ■ Is there a pattern to the pricing of petrol at various forecourts?

   ■ Are these stations using cost-based, buyer-based or going-rate pricing?

2. You are faced with setting the price for an automatic car wash. Your annual fixed costs are £50,000 and variable costs are £0.50 per vehicle washed. You think customers would be willing to pay £2.50 to have their car washed. What would be the break-even volume at that price? What opportunities are there for pricing high? What might be the most significant constraints on your pricing decision?

References

1. Allan Ruddock and Ivan Fallon, 'Blood begins to flow in the battle for the *Independent*', *Sunday Times* (6 February 1994), pp. 3, 6; 'Newspapers: indirubber', *The Economist* (29 January 1994), pp. 33–4; 'Cheaper *Times* here to stay', *The European* (10–16 June 1994), p. 22; Andreas Whittam Smith, 'An ugly struggle for dominance of the newspaper market', *Independent* (24 June 1994), p. 1; Roger Cowe, Tony May and Andrew Culf, '*Telegraph* in shares inquiry', *Guardian* (24 June 1994), p. 1; Tony Jackson, 'Ruthless killers or paper tigers', *Financial Times* (2–3 July 1994), p. 9; 'Scale of Indie's cut surprises ad industry', *Marketing Week* (5 August 1994), p. 14; Raymond Snoddy, 'Undaunted by hit to newspaper profits', *Financial Times* (26 August 1994), p. 15.

2. See David J. Schwartz, *Marketing Today: A basic approach*, 3rd edn (New York: Harcourt Brace Jovanovich, 1981), pp. 270–3.

3. For an excellent discussion of factors affecting pricing decisions, see Thomas T. Nagle and Reed K. Holden, *The Strategy and Tactics of Pricing*, 2nd edn (Englewood Cliffs, NJ: Prentice Hall, 1995), ch. 1.

4. Michiyo Makamoto, 'Weak Japanese recovery hits results at steelmakers', *Financial Times* (14 November 1994), p. 21; Andrew Baxter, 'Sweet and sour flow from British Steel', *Financial Times* (14 November 1994), p. 19.

5. Norton Paley, 'Fancy footwork', *Sales and Marketing Management* (July 1994), pp. 41–2.

6. Helen Slingsby, 'Discounters lose at their own game', *Marketing Week* (23 September 1994), pp. 21–2; Neil Buckley, 'Sainsbury launch price war campaign', *Financial Times* (10 October 1994), p. 8.

7. 'A funny smell from the scent counter', *Independent* (12 November 1993), p. 17.

8. Christopher Farrell, 'Stuck! How companies cope when they can't raise prices', *Business Week* (15 November 1993), pp. 146–55; see also John Y. Lee, 'Use target costing to improve your bottom line', *CPA Journal* (January 1994), pp. 68–71; 'The Texas computer massacre', *The Economist* (2 July 1994), pp. 65–6; Robin Cooper and W. Bruce Chew, 'Control tomorrow's costs through today's designs', *Harvard Business Review* (January–February, 1996), pp. 88–98.

9. Brian Dumaine, 'Closing the innovation gap', *Fortune* (2 December 1991), pp. 56–62.

10. Alice Rawsthorn, 'Discord over online music royalties', *Financial Times* (21 January 1998), p. 4.

11. Here accumulated production is drawn on a semi-log scale, so that equal distances represent the same percentage increase in output.

12. 'Japan's chip makers: falling off the learning curve', *The Economist* (23 February 1991), pp. 84–5.

13. For a view of how managers perceive these price response curves, see A. Diamantopoulos and Brian P. Mathews, 'Managerial perceptions of the demand curve: evidence from multiproduct firms', *European Journal of Marketing*, **27**, 9 (1993), pp. 5–18.

14. Paul A. Huntington, 'Perception of product quality in a static state utility model', *European Journal of Marketing*, **24**, 3 (1990), pp. 57–71.

15. Nagle and Holden, *Strategy and Tactics of Pricing*, op. cit., ch. 4.

16. Tim Burt, 'Yorkshire Chemicals ahead 19%', *Financial Times* (3 August 1994), p. 20.

17. For an operable example of this, see Kai Kristenson and Hans Jorn Juhl, 'Pricing and correspondence to market conditions: some Danish evidence', *European Journal of Marketing*, **24**, 5 (1989), pp. 50–5.

18. Values taken from 'Energy-saving light bulbs', *Which?* (May 1993), pp. 8–10.

19. Graham Bowley, 'Aircraft prices down a fifth, says Dasa', *Financial Times* (21 January 1998), p. 27.

Case 16

Proton MPi: Malaysian Styling, Japanese Engineering and European Pricing

Richard Lynch*

Doreen and Shem felt criminal as they sidled into the second-hand car dealer's showroom. For years they had bought a new Rover every four years, but this time, after carefully reading the *Which? Guide to New and Used Cars*, they were thinking of buying a second-hand car for the first time. Shem loved the smell and feel of a new car, and he could afford one, but the numbers just did not add up. As Doreen and he looked round the dealer's, he caught himself humming an old Bruce Springsteen song: 'Now mister, the day the lottery I win, I ain't ever gonna ride in no used car again.' 'Well,' thought Shem, 'I haven't won the lottery. So here we are.'

Just then he felt a glow. He noticed Doreen looking at the new cars also sold by the dealer. Quite a nice-looking car, but with an unfamiliar name. A Proton MPi and from a far-away place too – Malaysia! Still the price looked reasonable and the label said Japanese engineering. 'Maybe we needn't buy a used car after all,' suggested Doreen. 'Maybe not,' replied Shem. 'We could also look at a Skoda,' he said, swallowing hard. 'They're not expensive and now they're made by VW or something.' The Proton salesperson overheard them. 'Lovely cars, aren't they?' he said. 'We can give you a good deal too.'

It was late 1994 and Proton, the Malaysian maker of economical small cars, had an opportunity. Proton cars were manufactured in Malaysia using Japanese car engineering and some car parts. They were then shipped to the United Kingdom for sale. Proton had a chance to seize an increased share of the market in the United Kingdom, its biggest export market. Sales of new cars to private buyers were plunging. Not because of lack of money or lack of consumer confidence, but because of discontent with high prices, fast depreciation and the knowledge that the price of cars in the UK was higher than in the United States and some neighbouring European countries. Evidence suggested that private buyers, like Doreen and Shem, who once bought new cars, were now buying two- or three-year-old, second-hand ones

* Richard Lynch is managing director of Aldersgate Consultancy Ltd. This case is largely based, with permission, on 'European car pricing' from his book *Cases in European Marketing* (London: Kogan Page, 1993).

instead. The buyers found that the second-hand cars were problem-free and a bargain after two or three years of depreciation. Statistics from the Society of Motor Manufacturers and Traders showed that sales of all new cars rose 8.5 per cent in the first ten months of 1994 compared with the same period in 1993, but private sales were only up 2.2 per cent.

The private car buyers were, at last, getting their own back on the fleet buyers whom they had subsidized for years. Car makers' fleet-first policy in the United Kingdom meant that the average price of a medium-sized family car was £2,000 higher than it would otherwise be. In the United Kingdom, fleet buyers include car-hire companies and cars bought as additional re-muneration for professional employees. As a result the fleet buyers, accounting for 60 per cent of the market, were very influential and powerful buyers. Director of the National Franchised Dealers Association, Alan Pulham, explained why the private buyer had to pay so much:

- Dealers need to fund the discounts, free servicing and other inducements that are usually given to fleet buyers who have bargaining power. Private buyers, with little bargaining power, rarely get these perks but subsidize the fleet buyer by paying close to the list price.
- Cars in the United Kingdom are usually equipped to a high specification because that is what the fleet buyers want. The equipment was more than the private buyer often wanted or could afford, but that is what there was.

This price discrimination gave Proton a market opportunity. Although the United Kingdom had few British-owned car companies, fleet buyers followed a made-in-Britain policy (Ford, Rover or GM) or, increasingly, made in the European Union. They also bought from the big dealers repre-senting the market leaders. Proton was neither, so its price to private buyers did not have to subsidize fleet sales. Proton had a choice. It could cut prices to gain market share or charge moderate prices but keep the comfortable margins that the current prices gave them.

Background

According to the UK Monopolies and Mergers Commission's 1992 study of small cars in Europe, there are considerable variations in price between EU countries. These cannot be explained by currency differences, tax vari-ations or extra equipment supplied on some models. They originate with the manufacturers themselves and their ability to maintain higher prices in some EU countries, principally the United Kingdom.

On larger cars in Europe and taking into account the same factors, the study found that there was no significant difference in price levels between the countries. With the coming of the single European market, should Proton and the other car manufacturers set the same prices across the EU? Should there be a pan-European pricing policy?

In 1990 the EU car market was larger than that in the United States. Sales in the EU were 12.4 million cars in 1990, with the United Kingdom entering a period of decline, but Germany, and to a lesser degree other EU countries, still showing significant growth. Exhibit 16.1 estimates annual registrations for countries. Then, in late 1992, the EU market produced its first real drop in volume.

For many years, some European car companies, such as American-owned Ford, have manufactured cars on a pan-European basis. For example, its small car, named the 'Fiesta', combined parts produced in the United Kingdom,

EXHIBIT 16.1 CAR OWNERSHIP ACROSS THE EUROPEAN UNION

	TYPICAL ANNUAL CAR REGISTRATIONS (MILLIONS)	GDP PER HEAD IN 1992 ($000)	CARS PER 1,000 OF POPULATION IN 1992	% OF SENIOR MANAGERS WITH COMPANY CARS 1991
Germany	2.9	15	469	80
Italy	2.3	9	457	75
France	2.4	11	420	53
United Kingdom	2.0	9	387	95
Belgium/ Luxembourg	0.5	10	401	n.a.
Netherlands	0.4	10	374	85
Denmark	0.1	12	309	n.a.
Spain	1.1	5	419	50
Ireland	0.1	7	242	n.a.
Portugal	0.3	3	163	n.a.
Greece	0.2	3	178	n.a.

SOURCES: *Panorama of EU Industry* (New York: World Bank, 1991/2), pp. 13–21; various OECD Statistics, Paris; and Aldersgate Consultancy estimates.

Germany and Spain in the finished model. Other companies essentially produced one model in one location. For example, Germany's Volkswagen always produced its medium-sized Polo at Wolfsburg, Germany. The cars were then shipped across the EU.

The EU car market is not truly pan-European in the sense that any model can be readily sold in any other country. There are detailed car and legal regulations in each EU country – yellow headlights in France and car emission standards in Germany, for instance – that effectively stopped this happening. However, it was for precisely this reason that the Single Market Act 1986 was enacted: over time, it was envisaged that, apart from some obvious differences such as the British and Irish driving on the left, car market standards would become the same. At this time, if not before, prices could also surely become the same across Europe.

Car Prices across Europe

As champions of the European car customer, the Bureau Européenne des Unions des Consommateurs (BEUC) has been campaigning for many years to bring down car prices in the expensive countries in Europe. BEUC is made up of the national consumer associations of most EU member countries. It produces surveys of car prices such as that shown in Exhibit 16.2. From that survey there would appear to be large differences between prices in different countries. BEUC reported that average new car prices varied by 70 per cent between the lowest and highest countries net of tax. The difference including taxes was as much as 128 per cent. Since EU rules lay down that the maximum difference should only be 18 per cent, some concern was expressed. It should be noted that the EU rules specifically exclude those countries with exceptionally high national taxes, such as Denmark and Greece. The price differences stimulated parallel imports, despite the process being complicated and risky. Two hundred thousand cars had been bought by UK residents between 1980 and 1985 from outside the United Kingdom, mainly from Belgium. The car manufacturers complained that this undermined their profitability.

EXHIBIT 16.2 NEW CAR PRICES ACROSS EUROPE (ECU)

CAR	DENMARK	GERMANY	FRANCE	UNITED KINGDOM
BMW 316i	8,926	10,919	11,071	13,218
Citroën CX 22TRS	8,982	13,012	12,361	14,282˙
Fiat Tipo 1400	5,416	7,359	7,081	9,143
Ford Orion 1400	–	8,197	7,837	10,799
Renault 19	6,390	9,543[a]	9,493	11,310

[a]With catalytic converter.
NOTE: All prices per model, per country, net of taxes at June 1989.
SOURCE: BEUC.

According to BEUC, the main reason for these price differences was that the manufacturers were taking advantage of a system of exclusive dealerships in EU countries. These meant that manufacturers could stop shipping cars to any dealer who sold the cars to anyone resident in a country different from the dealer's own. The manufacturers argued a number of other essential reasons for the differences in price between EU countries: different tax systems, exchange rate variations, different car specifications, different dealer discounts. They said it was not a question of 'what the market would bear'.

In 1984 the European Commission agreed a Block Exemption Regulation to exempt the passenger car industry from the Treaty of Rome rules on competition. It allowed the motor trade to operate a system of exclusive distributor franchises so that the manufacturer controlled the market supply in an area. The reason the Commission gave for allowing the exemption was that motor vehicles are complex products and require a high level of after-sales service, which would be best served by allowing dealers to have exclusive rights in a geographical area.

With the exemption coming up for review in 1994 and the single European market becoming more established, the manufacturers had to decide whether to seek a continuation of this policy. They said they would like to keep the special arrangement and, to the chagrin of many consumer movements, the European Commission agreed.

Reasons for Differing Car Prices Across Europe

The real question is whether the reasons for the differences across Europe were sufficient to justify the absence of a pan-European pricing policy. The evidence comes under four headings: customers, tax variations, dealer arrangements and other areas.

Customers

As Exhibit 16.1 shows, car ownership across the EU follows wealth to a limited extent. It is distorted by the availability of public service transport, the level of car sales taxes and the likelihood of obtaining a car as part of a work pay and remuneration package. The provision of company cars has distorted car prices. Company fleet buyers purchase in large quantities, and they are therefore able to get price discounts not available to private buyers. To maintain their profits, car companies charge private buyers high prices.

Tax Variations

Exhibit 16.3 shows substantial variations across the EU in the tax on cars. When car manufacturers complained about price comparisons made by the consumer groups, their responses often concerned this area.

EXHIBIT 16.3 VAT AND ADDITIONAL SALES TAXES ON NEW CARS IN 1992

COUNTRY	VAT	CAR TAX
Belgium	25% up to 3,000 cc 33% above	None
Denmark	22%	105% up to Dkr19,750 180% on the rest
France	22%	None
Germany	14%	None
Greece	6%	Between 45% and 400%, depending upon engine size
Italy	19% up to 2,000 cc, 38% above	None
Luxembourg	12%	None
Portugal	17%	Esc95–1,700 per cc on an increasing scale
Ireland	21%	21.7% up to 2,016 cc 24.7% above
Spain	33%	None
United Kingdom	17.5%	10%

SOURCE: Monopolies and Mergers study, UK, 1992.

Dealer Arrangements

Across Europe, car manufacturers have agreements with dealers in a geographical area for the sale of their product ranges. There are a number of restrictions placed on the dealers, which:

● Limit the dealer's ability to advertise outside its franchise area.
● Stop the dealer from acquiring or holding dealerships outside the existing area from other suppliers.
● Prevent the dealer acquiring or holding other dealerships except on a distinct and separate site.
● Restrict the ability of the dealer to sell other products, such as second-hand cars or car parts from other manufacturers.
● Limit the dealer to selling a maximum quantity of cars in a given period and a maximum percentage of the total cars from the manufacturer in one year.

While these restrictions limit dealer freedom, the car manufacturers say that they do make it more likely that car service levels are of the highest quality. Moreover, European car companies are engaged in a fiercely competitive battle in each EU country, so that the EU has accepted that these dealer restrictions are acceptable in terms of the EU Block Exemption Regulation.

Data have been published on the number of dealers that each of the main EU car manufacturers has in each country. In general terms in 1991, manufacturers tended to have rather more dealers in the main country of manufacture, e.g. Renault in France, Rover in the United Kingdom. The Japanese car companies had rather fewer dealers, but this would be consistent with their overall share of the European car market at around 9 per cent in 1989. The US multinationals, Ford and General Motors (trading as Opel in

EXHIBIT 16.4 WAGE COSTS IN SOME CAR-PRODUCING
COUNTRIES

	DEUTSCHMARKS PER HOUR 1991	TYPICAL PRODUCERS
Germany	45	Volkswagen and BMW
United States	35	GM and Ford
Japan	34	Toyota and Nissan
Italy	32	Fiat
Spain	29	SEAT (Volkswagen/Audi group)
France	29	Renault
United Kingdom	29	Rover
Malaysia	15	Proton

SOURCES: German Auto Industry Association and Aldersgate Consultancy Ltd estimates.

Germany and Vauxhall in the United Kingdom), were well represented in numbers of dealerships across Europe, reflecting their market share of 21 per cent. However, the *number* of dealers provides no indication of their *quality* in terms of location, size, trained staff, workshop facilities and so forth. Proton dealers were almost exclusively confined to the United Kingdom.

Other Areas

As will be generally true in all pricing decisions, the costs of car production need to be reflected in the prices: there would be no point in pricing below marginal costs. In fact, such a pricing policy is illegal in some EU countries. While European car manufacturers do not publish detailed comparative cost data for competitive reasons, outline data on wage costs by country are summarized in Exhibit 16.4.

Other areas that would need to be considered include the extra items added to some cars as standard, such as electric windows, in-car stereo systems and fuel injection. European car manufacturers have commented that this is the area that has made UK cars more expensive.

Reasons for National Price Differences

To assist understanding of how prices are constructed and explain why some national prices are higher than others, the European car manufacturer General Motors commissioned a study of comparative prices in 1991 (see Exhibit 16.5). The detailed study shows that significant price differences exist for what is basically the same car.

Proton's Pricing

Given a system which meant that the price of Doreen and Shem's car would subsidize fleet purchases, it seemed sensible for them to think about buying a 'second-hand new car'. In that way the private buyer benefits from fleet buyers absorbing the heavy depreciation in the first few years of a car's life. Will the car manufacturers ever recapture the private-buyer market again? Car industry expert Garel Rhys thinks not until 'prices of new cars in Europe … come down in real terms to American levels'. He continues, 'That's when the fur will fly. There are simply too many car makers in Europe and they can't all survive.'

As a low-cost supplier of cars to the EU without a vested interest in fleet buyers and expensive dealerships, Proton could start the 'fur flying'. Should it, or should it not cut prices to gain market share? What would happen if it

EXHIBIT 16.5 COMPARATIVE CAR PRICES, 1991 ($)

	UK ASTRA GL 1.4 5-DOOR NON-CATALYTIC	GERMANY KADETT GL 1.4 5-DOOR CATALYTIC	FRANCE KADETT GL 1.4 5-DOOR NON-CATALYTIC
List price inc. tax	8,749	7,407	7,764
List excluding tax	7,023	6,497	7,764
Equipment adjustments (EA)	–	482	257
EA list price excluding tax	7,023	6,979	6,468
Discounts dealer (%)	13.7	7.1	2.8
On-road costs	350	152	314
On-road price ex tax	5,411	6,636	6,601
Financing support	672	160	–
On-the-road with finance	5,739	6,578	6,601

SOURCE: GM Vauxhall 1991 survey.

did? Would the European manufacturers fight back, or would the European Commission step in to limit Proton's access to the market? Charging a lower price would help Doreen and Shem, and many other private customers, but would it, in the long run, help Proton? Maybe Proton would do better to accept the high margins that the European car industry forces upon them.

QUESTIONS

1. Is Shem justified in his concern about being charged too much for new cars in the United Kingdom?

2. What explains the big difference between EU and US car prices? Does the price demand function vary from country to country in Europe and is that in the United States completely different?

3. How should Proton price its cars? Should it keep its list prices high, reduce them or give big discounts to buyers?

4. Why might giving discounts be better than lowering the list price?

5. What is likely to happen if Proton cuts its prices to gain market share?

6. Clearly there is currently no pan-European price, but should that ever exist across the EU? Should the car companies continue with what are essentially national policies?

SOURCES: Song extract from Bruce Springsteen, 'Used cars', on *Nebraska* (CBS 25100, 1982); other sources are Monopolies and Mergers Commission, *New Motor Cars* (London: HMSO, 1992); Y. Doz, *Strategic Management in Multinational Companies* (Oxford: Pergamon, 1986); John Griffith, 'Bad dreams return to the motor trade', *Financial Times* (10 May 1992), p. ii; John Griffith, 'Market distorted by use of company cars as perks,' *Financial Times* (6 February 1992), p. 6; European Commission, *Panorama of EC Industry 1991/92* (Luxembourg: OPECE, 1991), pp. 30–8; D. Fisher, 'Time to become lean and mean', *Financial Times* (23 June 1992), p. 18; John Griffiths, 'Price is wrong for some motorists', *Financial Times* (26–7 November 1994), p. 9.

17

Pricing Strategies

CHAPTER OBJECTIVES

After reading this chapter, you should be able to:

● Understand new-product pricing strategies and know when to use them.

● Explain how pricing decisions are influenced by the product mix.

● Appreciate price adjustment strategies and how to make price changes.

● Differentiate between geographical pricing strategies and know their implications.

Preview Case

Mobile Phones: Even More Mobile Customers

VODAFONE AND CELLNET, THE UNITED Kingdom's leading mobile phone suppliers, are losing market share to new digital competitors, One-2-One and Orange. Between July and September 1994, 227,000 subscribers joined Vodafone, but more significantly, 104,000 left. The pricing policy explains why Vodafone and Cellnet gain and lose so many customers. Vodafone pumps about £300 subsidy into the sale of each phone and connection, and then makes a huge profit on the phone's use. Often the mobile phone and its connection charge come free with a large purchase, such as a car or photocopier. Then, depending on the deal, subscribers pay between 15p and 50p per minute for what costs the cellular company 1.5p per minute off-peak and 0.5p for local calls. The margins helped Vodafone in 1997 to post pretax profits of £363 million on a turnover of £850 million. Gerry Whent, Vodafone's chief executive, describes the market: 'Every month people are leaving us for a variety of reasons. They've died, changed jobs, just decided to hand the phone back, or whatever. A lot of people we take on are attracted to the idea of using a mobile phone, until they see the bill. If they only use it once a day, it's only a matter of time before they give it back.' He continues, 'This problem is not exclusive to us. I'd argue that Cellnet is losing just as many subscribers over the year. The important thing is that we are both taking in new ones.'

Li Ka-shing, Asian billionaire boss of Orange's parent company Hutchinson Whampoa, sees things differently. As Vodafone subscribers scrutinize their bills at renewal time, they are tempted to switch to the cheaper and technically more advanced Orange or One-2-One services. As Hans Snook, Orange's UK manager, says, 'Vodafone has rested on its laurels far too long. Now it's paying the price.' About 70 per cent of Orange's subscribers are switchers, not first-time buyers.

Hans Snook had better be right. By the end of 1995 Hutchinson spent £1 billion on developing the UK market – 'the price for four brand new skyscrapers' in Li Ka-shing's Hong Kong home town. The investment is in the latest DCS 1800 digital technology that gives the same voice quality as conventional telephones. Digital is also intrinsically cheaper than Vodafone and Cellnet's older analogue systems and gives access to more features. The investment so far has bought Orange a total of 980 Nokia base stations and aerials costing £75,000 each across the United Kingdom, covering 50 per cent of the population. To get to its target 90 per cent coverage, Orange will need 2,000 stations. The fruity brand name is already a success. Launched using a huge teaser campaign, customers are already asking people to 'Call me back on Orange' or saying 'Can I give you my Orange phone number?' One month after launch the company already had 65 per cent unprompted name recognition.

Orange's pricing strategy is different from that of the analogue suppliers. Its phones are not cheap, costing between £150 and £300 each, and it doesn't give them away to get new customers. Instead Orange has introduced package calls to the market. Orange customers buy between £15 and £100 worth of calls a month. The cost per call is about half that of the traditional networks.

Mercury's One-2-One has taken a less aggressive approach to the cellular market. It did not strive to go national, but concentrated on giving a cheap service to Londoners living within the M25 orbital motorway. That means that it can offer a package to users in its catchment area for much less than Orange. One-2-One gives unlimited free local calls, too. Will its good value for the 'not very mobile' phone user work? So far it has, and it has also tempted about 10,000 new subscribers a month, about half of them coming from Vodafone. As a second careful step Mercury has just extended One-2-One to the West Midlands, the United Kingdom's second largest conurbation, covering Birmingham and Coventry.

Orange and One-2-One became a hit with consumers after 25 December 1994 became the Christmas of the mobile phone, with many being given as gifts. The new growth markets switched from executives to travellers worried about being out alone at night. By 1999 forecasters expect Orange to outsell Vodafone to domestic consumers and One-2-One to be close to Cellnet in the same market. One-2-One has placed itself firmly in the gift market by offering unlimited free phone calls on Christmas Day. Will anyone get through? Whatever happens, the signs are that the days of the 43 per cent profit margin for the cellular operators are coming to an end.[1]

QUESTIONS

1. Explain the different pricing of the mobile phone competitors.

2. Why don't the mobile phone companies used cost-based pricing, where customers just pay for their phone, the connection cost and the direct cost of them using the phone?

3. How is the emergence of the mobile phone as a gift or a security device likely to change its pricing?

4. What other mobile phone segments could emerge and how should products be priced for them?

5. How would you expect the marketing and pricing of mobile phones to change as the product life cycle evolves?

6. Is the 'churning' of customers a sign of poor marketing, overmarketing or just healthy competition?

Introduction

In this chapter, we will look at the complex dynamics of pricing. A company does not set a single price, but rather a *pricing structure* that covers different items in its line. This pricing structure changes over time as products move through their life cycles. The company adjusts product prices to reflect changes in costs and demand, and to account for variations in buyers and situations. As the competitive environment changes, the company considers when to initiate price changes and when to respond to them. And as the cellular phone example demonstrates forcefully, pricing decisions are subject to an incredibly complex array of environmental and competitive forces.

This chapter examines the dynamic pricing strategies available to management. In turn, we look at *new-product pricing strategies* for products in the introductory stage of the product life cycle, *product-mix pricing strategies* for related products in the product mix, *price-adjustment strategies* that account for customer differences and changing situations, and *strategies for initiating and responding to price changes.*[2]

New-Product Pricing Strategies

Pricing strategies usually change as the product passes through its life cycle. The introductory stage is especially challenging. We can distinguish between pricing a product that imitates existing products and pricing an innovative product that is patent protected.

A company that plans to develop an imitative new product faces a product-positioning problem. It must decide where to position the product versus competing products in terms of quality and price. Figure 17.1 shows four possible positioning strategies. First, the company might decide to use a *premium pricing* strategy – producing a high-quality product and charging the highest price. At the other extreme, it might decide on an *economy pricing* strategy – producing a

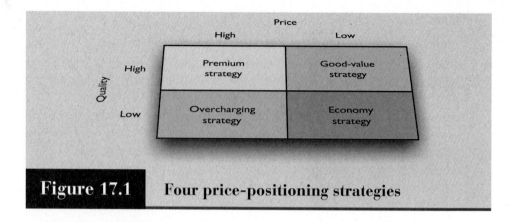

Figure 17.1 **Four price-positioning strategies**

lower-quality product, but charging a low price. These strategies can coexist in the same market as long as the market consists of at least two groups of buyers, those who seek quality and those who seek price. Thus, Tag-Heuer offers very high-quality sports watches at high prices, whereas Casio offers digital watches at almost throwaway prices.[3]

The *good-value* strategy represents a way to attack the premium pricer. The United Kingdom's leading grocery chain always uses the **strapline**: 'Good food costs less at Sainsbury's'. If this is really true and quality-sensitive buyers believe the good-value pricer, they will sensibly shop at Sainsbury's and save money – unless the premium product offers more status or snob appeal. Using an *over-charging* strategy, the company overprices the product in relation to its quality. In the long run, however, customers are likely to feel 'taken'. They will stop buying the product and will complain to others about it. Thus this strategy should be avoided.[4]

Companies bringing out an innovative, patent-protected product face the challenge of setting prices for the first time. They can choose between two strategies: *market-skimming* pricing and *market-penetration pricing*.

Market-Skimming Pricing

Many companies that invent new products initially set high prices to 'skim' revenues layer by layer from the market. Intel is a prime user of this strategy, called **market-skimming pricing**. When Intel first introduces a new computer chip, it charges the highest price it can, given the benefits of the new chip over competing chips. It sets a price that makes it *just* worthwhile for some segments of the market to adopt computers containing the chip. As initial sales slow down and as competitors threaten to introduce similar chips, Intel lowers the price to draw in the next price-sensitive layer of customers.[5]

Maaväl was launched in Sweden at Skr12, more than twice the price of ordinary yoghurt. Developed by Scotia and a consortium of 1,300 Swedish farmers, Maaväl contains Olibra, a 'nutriceutical' made of a patent combination of palm oil extract, oat oil and water. It encourages the small intestine to release chemicals that tell the brain that enough has been eaten, giving a 'prolonged feeling of fullness'. The high price indicates the product's uniqueness and special properties, and allows quicker recovery of development costs. Similar value-added foods have proved profitable. Finland's Rasio has seen its share price increase tenfold since it launched Benecol, a cholesterol-lowering margarine.[6]

strapline
A slogan often used in conjunction with a brand's name, advertising and other promotions.

Market-skimming pricing
Setting a high price for a new product to skim maximum revenues layer by layer from the segments willing to pay the high price; the company makes fewer but more profitable sales.

SHE COULD BE ARABELLA,
DESDEMONA, MARGUERITE
OR MANON LESCAUT.

BUT YOU'D ALWAYS
RECOGNIZE THE FACE.

Dame Kiri Te Kanawa is indeed a woman of many parts. However, her career both onstage and as a recording artist is characterized by a constant quest for perfection. No wonder then that one of her most treasured possessions is her Rolex Lady Datejust. For the rigorous standards of precision required to bring together its many parts are commensurate with those that Dame Kiri applies to the discipline of her own performance. Whoever she may be.

 ROLEX

Lady Datejust
Officially Certified Swiss Chronometer

For the name and location of an Official Rolex Jeweler near you, please call 1-800-36ROLEX. Rolex, ®, Oyster Perpetual and Lady Datejust are trademarks.

YOU MAY BE TOO OLD FOR A BLANKIE,
BUT YOU CAN STILL HAVE A NIGHT-LIGHT.

Sure, this watch is rugged and manly. But, then again, with its handy Indiglo night-light it's also the perfect complement to your favorite jammies. There's even **INDIGLO** a compass so you'll never get lost. For retailers call 1-800-367-8463. **BY TIMEX**

TIMEX. IT TAKES A LICKING AND KEEPS ON TICKING.

Rolex pursues a premium pricing strategy, selling very high quality watches at a high price. In contrast Timex uses a value-pricing strategy, offering good quality watches at more affordable prices.

Market-Penetration Pricing

Rather than setting a high initial price to skim off small but profitable market segments, some companies use **market-penetration pricing**. They set a low initial price in order to *penetrate* the market quickly and deeply – to attract a large number of buyers quickly and win a large market share. The high sales volume results in falling costs, allowing the company to cut its price even further. For example, Dell and Dan used penetration pricing to sell high-quality computer products through lower-cost mail-order channels. Their sales soared when IBM, Compaq, Apple and other competitors selling through retail stores could not match their prices. The Bank of Scotland and Winterthur of Switzerland used their Direct Line, Privilege and Churchill subsidiaries to grab profits and share in the motor insurance market by selling direct to consumers at market-penetrating prices. The high volume results in lower costs that, in turn, allow the discounters to keep prices low.[7]

Several conditions favour setting a low price. First, the market must be highly price sensitive, so that a low price produces more market growth. Second, production and distribution costs must fall as sales volume increases. Finally, the low price must help keep out the competition – otherwise the price advantage may be only temporary. For example, Dell faced difficult times when IBM and Compaq established their own direct distribution channels.

market-penetration pricing
Setting a low price for a new product in order to attract large numbers of buyers and a large market share.

Home Depot practices market-penetration pricing. It charges 'guaranteed low prices, day-in . . . day-out' to attract high volume, which in turn results in lower costs and still lower prices.

Product-Mix Pricing Strategies

The strategy for setting a product's price often has to be changed when the product is part of a product mix. In this case, the firm looks for a set of prices that maximizes the profits on the total product mix. Pricing is difficult because the various products have related demand and costs, and face different degrees of competition. We now take a closer look at five *product-mix pricing* situations, summarized in Table 17.1.

Product Line Pricing

product line pricing
Setting the price steps between various products in a product line based on cost differences between the products, customer evaluations of different features, and competitors' prices.

Companies usually develop product lines rather than single products. For example, Merloni's sells Indesit, Ariston and Scholte with price and status ascending in that order. There are full ranges of Indesit to Ariston appliances, from washing machines to freezers, covering the first two price bands, while Scholte sells expensive built-in kitchen equipment. Kodak offers not just one type of film, but an assortment including regular Kodak film, higher-priced Kodak Royal Gold film for special occasions, and a lower-priced, seasonal film called Funtime that competes with store brands. Each of these brands is available in a variety of sizes and film speeds. In **product line pricing**, management must decide on the price steps to set between the various products in a line.

The price steps should take into account cost differences between the products in the line, customer evaluations of their different features and competitors' prices. If the price difference between two successive products is small, buyers will usually buy the more advanced product. This will increase company profits if the cost difference is smaller than the price difference. If the price difference is large, however, customers will generally buy the less advanced products.

| Table 17.1 | **Product-mix pricing strategies** | | | |

PRODUCT LINE PRICING	OPTIONAL-PRODUCT PRICING	CAPTIVE-PRODUCT PRICING	BY-PRODUCT PRICING	PRODUCT-BUNDLE PRICING
Setting price steps between product line items	Pricing optional or accessory products sold with the main product	Pricing products that must be used with the main product	Pricing low-value by-products to get rid of them	Pricing bundles of products sold together

In many industries, sellers use well-established *price points* for the products in their line. Thus record stores might carry CDs at four price levels: budget, mid-line, full-line and superstar. The customer will probably associate low to high-quality recordings with the four price points. Even if the four prices are raised a little, people will normally buy CDs at their own preferred price points. The seller's task is to establish perceived quality differences that support the price differences.[8]

Optional-Product Pricing

Many companies use **optional-product pricing** – offering to sell optional or accessory products along with their main product. For example, a car buyer may choose to order power windows, cruise control and a radio with a CD player. Pricing these options is a sticky problem. Car companies have to decide which items to include in the base price and which to offer as options. BMW's basic cars come famously underequipped. Typically the 318i is about DM40,000, but the customer then has to pay extra for a radio (prices vary), electric windows (DM700), sun roof (DM1,800) and security system (DM1,100). The basic model is stripped of so many comforts and conveniences that most buyers reject it. They pay for extras or buy a better-equipped version. More recently, however, American and European car makers have been forced to follow the example of the Japanese car makers and include in the basic price many useful items previously sold only as options. The advertised price now often represents a well-equipped car.

optional-product pricing
The pricing of optional or accessory products along with a main product.

Captive-Product Pricing

Companies that make products that must be used along with a main product are using **captive-product pricing**. Examples of captive products are razors, camera film and computer software. Producers of the main products (razors, cameras and computers) often price them low and set high mark-ups on the supplies. Thus Polaroid prices its cameras low because it makes its money on the film it sells. And Gillette sells low-priced razors, but makes money on the replacement blades.

captive-product pricing
Setting a price for products that must be used along with a main product, such as blades for a razor and film for a camera.

Camera makers that do not sell film have to price their main products higher in order to make the same overall profit.

The strategy used by the cellular operators is called **two-part pricing**. The price of the service is broken into a *fixed fee* plus a *variable usage rate*. Thus a telephone company charges a monthly rate – the fixed fee – plus charges for calls beyond some minimum number – the variable usage rate. Amusement parks charge admission plus fees for food, midway attractions and rides over a minimum. The service firm must decide how much to charge for the basic service and how much for the variable usage. The fixed amount should be low enough to induce usage of the service, and profit can be made on the variable fees.

two-part pricing
A strategy for pricing services in which price is broken into a fixed fee plus a variable usage rate.

By-Product Pricing

In producing processed meats, petroleum products, chemicals and other products, there are often **by-products**. If the by-products have no value and if getting rid of them is costly, this will affect the pricing of the main product. Using **by-product pricing**, the manufacturer will seek a market for these by-products and should accept any price that covers more than the cost of storing and delivering them. This practice allows the seller to reduce the main product's price to make it more competitive. By-products can even turn out to be profitable. For example, many lumber mills have begun to sell bark chips and sawdust profitably as decorative mulch for home and commercial landscaping.

by-products
Items produced as a result of the main factory process, such as waste and reject items.

by-product pricing
Setting a price for by-products in order to make the main product's price more competitive.

Sometimes companies don't realize how valuable their by-products are. For example, most Zoos don't realize that one of their by-products – their occupants' manure – can be an excellent source of additional revenue. But the Zoo-Doo Compost Company has helped many zoos understand the costs and opportunities involved with these by-products. Zoo-Doo licenses its name to zoos and receives royalties on manure sales. 'Many zoos don't even know how much manure they are producing or the cost of disposing of it,' explains president and founder Pierce Ledbetter. Zoos are often so pleased with any savings they can find on disposal that they don't think to move into active by-product sales. However, sales of the fragrant by-product can be substantial. So far novelty sales have been the largest, with tiny containers of Zoo Doo (and even 'Love, Love Me Doo' valentines) available in 160 zoo stores and 700 additional retail outlets. For the long-term market, Zoo-Doo looks to organic gardeners who buy 15 to 70 pounds of manure at a time. Zoo Doo is already planning a 'Dung of the Month' club to reach these lucrative by-product markets.[9]

Product-Bundle Pricing

Using **product-bundle pricing**, sellers often combine several of their products and offer the bundle at a reduced price. Thus theatres and sports teams sell season tickets at less than the cost of single tickets; hotels sell specially priced packages that include room, meals and entertainment; computer makers include attractive software packages with their personal computers. Price bundling can promote the sales of products that consumers might not otherwise buy, but the combined price must be low enough to get them to buy the bundle.[10]

In other cases, *product-bundle pricing* is used to sell more than the customer really wants. Obtaining a ticket to an exclusive sports event is difficult, but World Cup football finals tickets are available to people willing to buy them bundled with a supersonic Concorde flight.

product-bundle pricing
Combining several products and offering the bundle at a reduced price.

Table 17.2	Price adjustment strategies

DISCOUNT AND ALLOWANCE PRICING	SEGMENTED PRICING	PSYCHOLOGICAL PRICING	VALUE PRICING	PROMOTIONAL PRICING	GEOGRAPHICAL PRICING	INTERNATIONAL PRICING
Reducing prices to reward customer responses such as paying early or promoting the product	Adjusting prices to allow for differences in customers products, and locations	Adjusting prices for psychological effect	Adjusting prices to offer the right combination of quality and service at a fair price	Temporarily reducing prices to increase short-run sales	Adjusting prices to account for the geographic location of customers	Adjusting prices in international markets

Price-Adjustment Strategies

Companies usually adjust their basic prices to account for various customer differences and changing situations. Table 17.2 summarizes seven price-adjustment strategies: *discount and allowance pricing, segmented pricing, psychological pricing, promotional pricing, value pricing, geographical pricing* and *international pricing*.

Discount and Allowance Pricing

Most companies adjust their basic price to reward customers for certain responses, such as early payment of bills, volume purchases and off-season buying. These price adjustments – called *discounts* and *allowances* – can take many forms.

A **cash discount** is a price reduction to buyers who pay their bills promptly. A typical example is '2/10, net 30', which means that although payment is due within 30 days, the buyer can deduct 2 per cent if the bill is paid within 10 days. The discount must be granted to all buyers meeting these terms. Such discounts are customary in many industries and help to improve the sellers' cash situation and reduce bad debts and credit-collection costs.

A **quantity discount** is a price reduction to buyers who buy large volumes. A typical example might be '$10 per unit for less than 100 units, $9 per unit for 100 or more units'. Wine merchants often give 'twelve for the price of eleven' and Makro, the trade warehouse, automatically gives discounts on any product bought in bulk. Discounts provide an incentive to the customer to buy more from one given seller, rather than from many different sources.

cash discount
A price reduction to buyers who pay their bills promptly.

quantity discount
A price reduction to buyers who buy large volumes.

Promotional pricing: companies often reduce their prices temporarily to produce sales.

quantity premium
A surcharge paid by buyers who purchase high volumes of a product.

functional discount (trade discount)
A price reduction offered by the seller to trade channel members that perform certain functions, such as selling, storing and record keeping.

seasonal discount
A price reduction to buyers who buy merchandise or services out of season.

trade-in allowance
A price reduction given for turning in an old item when buying a new one.

promotional allowance
A payment or price reduction to reward dealers for particapting in advertising and sales-support programmes.

A **quantity premium** is sometimes charged to people buying higher volumes. In Japan it often costs more per item to buy a twelve-pack of beer or sushi than smaller quantities because the larger packs are more giftable and therefore less price sensitive. Quantity surcharges can also occur when the product being bought is in short supply or in sets – for example, several seats together at a 'sold-out' rock concert or sports event – and some small restaurants charge a premium to large groups. Similarly, in buying antiques, it costs more to buy six complete place settings of cutlery than a single item. In this case the price will continue to increase with volume, eight place settings costing more than six, and twelve place settings costing more than eight. Quantity premiums are more common than people imagine, and that is why they work. Consumers expect prices to decrease with volume and so do not check unit prices. This allows retailers to slip in high-margin items. Quantity surcharge increases with the variety and complexity of pack sizes and, in some markets, over 30 per cent of ranges include some quantity surcharging.[11]

A **trade discount** (also called a **functional discount**) is offered by the seller to trade channel members that perform certain functions, such as selling, storing and record keeping. Manufacturers may offer different functional discounts to different trade channels because of the varying services they perform, but manufacturers must offer the same functional discounts within each trade channel.

A **seasonal discount** is a price discount to buyers who buy merchandise or services out of season. For example, lawn and garden equipment manufacturers will offer seasonal discounts to retailers during the autumn and winter to encourage early ordering in anticipation of the heavy spring and summer selling seasons. Hotels, motels and airlines will offer seasonal discounts in their slower selling periods. Seasonal discounts allow the seller to keep production steady during the entire year.

Allowances are another type of reduction from the list price. For example, **trade-in allowances** are price reductions given for turning in an old item when buying a new one. Trade-in allowances are most common in the car industry, but are also given for other durable goods. **Promotional allowances** are payments or price reductions to reward dealers for participating in advertising and sales-support programmes.

Segmented Pricing

Companies will often adjust their basic prices to allow for differences in customers, products and locations. In **segmented pricing**, the company sells a product or service at two or more prices, even though the difference in prices is not based on differences in costs. Segmented pricing takes several forms:

- *Customer-segment pricing.* Different customers pay different prices for the same product or service. Museums, for example, will charge a lower admission for young people, the unwaged, students and senior citizens. In many parts of the world, tourists pay more to see museums, shows and national monuments than do locals.

- *Product-form pricing.* Different versions of the product are priced differently, but not according to differences in their costs. For instance, the Dutch company Skil prices its 6434H electric drill at DFl200, which is DFl125 more than the price of its 6400H. The 6434H is more powerful and has more features, yet this extra power and features cost only a few more guilders to build in.

- *Location pricing.* Different locations are priced differently, even though the cost of offering each location is the same. For instance, theatres vary their seat prices because of audience preferences for certain locations and EU universities charge higher tuition fees for non-EU students.

- *Time pricing.* Prices vary by the season, the month, the day and even the hour. Public utilities vary their prices to commercial users by time of day and weekend versus weekday. The telephone company offers lower 'off-peak' charges and resorts give seasonal discounts.

segmented pricing
Pricing that allows for differences in customers, products and locations. The differences in prices are not based on differences in costs.

For segmented pricing to be an effective strategy, certain conditions must exist. The market must be segmentable and the segments must show different degrees of demand. Members of the segment paying the lower price should not be able to turn around and resell the product to the segment paying the higher price. Competitors should not be able to undersell the firm in the segment being charged the higher price. Nor should the costs of segmenting and watching the market exceed the extra revenue obtained from the price difference. The practice should not lead to customer resentment and ill will. Finally, the segmented pricing must be legal.

Psychological Pricing

Price says something about the product. For example, many consumers use price to judge quality. A $100 bottle of perfume may contain only $3 worth of scent, but some people are willing to pay the $100 because this price indicates something special.

In using **psychological pricing**, sellers consider the psychology of prices and not simply the economics. For example, one study of the relationship between price and quality perception of cars found that consumers perceive higher-priced cars as having higher quality.[12] By the same token, higher-quality cars are perceived as even higher priced than they actually are. When consumers can judge the quality of a product by examining it or by calling on past experience with it, they use price less to judge quality. When consumers cannot judge quality because they lack the information or skill, price becomes an important quality signal (see Marketing Highlight 17.1).

psychological pricing
A pricing approach that considers the psychology of prices and not simply the economics; the price is used to say something about the product.

Expense marks diamonds desirable and very giftable.

reference prices
Prices that buyers carry in their minds and refer to when they look at a given product.

Another aspect of psychological pricing is **reference prices** – prices that buyers carry in their minds and refer to when looking at a given product. The reference price might be formed by noting current prices, remembering past prices or assessing the buying situation. Sellers can influence or use these consumers' reference prices when setting price. For example, a company could display its product next to more expensive ones in order to imply that it belongs in the same class. Department stores often sell women's clothing in separate departments differentiated by price: clothing found in the more expensive department is assumed to be of better quality. Companies also can influence consumers' reference prices by stating high manufacturer's suggested prices, by indicating that the product was originally priced much higher or by pointing to a competitor's higher price.

Even small differences in price can suggest product differences. Consider a stereo priced at £400 compared to one priced at £399.95. The actual price difference is only 5p, but the psychological difference can be much greater. For example, some consumers will see the £399.95 as a price in the £300 range rather than the £400 range. Whereas the £399.95 is more likely to be seen as a bargain price, the £400 price suggests more quality. Complicated numbers, such as £347.41, also look less appealing than rounded ones, such as £350. Some psychologists argue that each digit has symbolic and visual qualities that should be considered in pricing. Thus, 8 is round and even and creates a soothing effect, whereas 7 is angular and creates a jarring effect.[13]

Promotional Pricing

promotional pricing
Temporarily pricing products below the list price, and sometimes even below cost, to increase short-run sales.

With **promotional pricing**, companies will temporarily price their products below list price and sometimes even below cost. Promotional pricing takes several forms. Supermarkets and department stores will price a few products as *loss*

How Price Signals Product Quality

Marketing Highlight 17.1

Heublein produces Smirnoff, America's leading brand of vodka. Some years ago another brand, Wolfschmidt, attacked Smirnoff. Wolfschmidt claimed to have the same quality as Smirnoff, but priced at $1 less per bottle. Concerned that customers might switch to Wolfschmidt, Heublein considered several possible counterstrategies. It could lower Smirnoff's price by $1 to hold on to market share; it could hold Smirnoff's price but increase advertising and promotion expenditures; or it could hold Smirnoff's price and let its market share fall. All three strategies would lead to lower profits, and it seemed that Heublein faced a no-win situation.

At this point, however, Heublein's marketers thought of a fourth strategy – and it was brilliant. Heublein *raised* the price of Smirnoff by $1! The company then introduced a new brand, Relska, to compete with Wolfschmidt. Moreover, it introduced yet another brand, Popov, priced even *lower* than Wolfschmidt. This product line-pricing strategy positioned Smirnoff as the élite brand and Wolfschmidt as an ordinary brand. Heublein's clever strategy produced a large increase in its overall profits.

The irony is that Heublein's three brands are much the same in taste and manufacturing costs. Heublein knew that a product's price signals its quality. Using price as a signal, Heublein sells roughly the same product at three different quality positions.

leaders to attract customers to the store in the hope that they will buy other items at normal mark-ups. Sellers will also use *special-event pricing* in certain seasons to draw in more customers. Thus linens are promotionally priced every January to attract weary Christmas shoppers back into the stores. Manufacturers will sometimes offer *cash rebates* to consumers who buy the product from dealers within a specified time; the manufacturer sends the rebate directly to the customer. Rebates have recently been popular with car makers and producers of durable goods and small appliances. Some manufacturers offer *low-interest financing, longer warranties* or *free maintenance* to reduce the consumer's 'price'. This practice has recently become a favourite of the car industry. Or, the seller may simply offer *discounts* from normal prices to increase sales and reduce inventories.

Value Pricing

During the slow-growth 1990s, many companies have adjusted their prices to bring them into line with economic conditions and with the resulting fundamental shift in consumer attitudes towards quality and value. More and more, marketers have adopted **value-pricing** strategies – offering just the right combination of quality and good service at a fair price. In many cases, this has involved the introduction of less expensive versions of established, brand name products. Thus Campbell introduced its Great Starts Budget frozen-food line, Holiday Inn opened several Holiday Express budget hotels, Revlon's Charles of the Ritz offered the Express Bar collection of affordable cosmetics, and McDonald's offered 'value menus'. In other cases, value pricing has involved redesigning existing brands in order to offer more quality for a given price or the same quality for less (see Marketing Highlight 17.2).

value pricing
Offering just the right combination of quality and good service at a fair price.

Value Pricing: Offering More for Less

Marketing Highlight 17.2

Marketers have a new buzzword: V-A-L-U-E. Once marketers pitched luxury, prestige, extravagance – even expensiveness – for everything from ice cream to cars. But after the recession began, they started redesigning, repackaging, repositioning and remarketing products to emphasize value. Now, value pricing – offering more for a lot less, by underscoring a product's quality while at the same time featuring its price – has gone from a groundswell to a tidal wave.

Value pricing can mean many things to marketers. To some, it means price cutting. To others, it means special deals, such as providing more of a product at the same price. And to still others, it means a new image – one that convinces consumers they're receiving a good deal. No matter how it's defined, however, value pricing has become a prime strategy for wooing consumers. The up-market tactics have virtually disappeared.

Marketers are finding that the flat economy and changing consumer demographics have created a new class of sophisticated, bargain-hunting shoppers who are careful of where and how they shop. Whereas it used to be fashionable to flaunt affluence and spend conspicuously, now it's fashionable to say you got a good deal. To convince consumers they're getting more for their money, companies from fast-food chains to stock brokerages and car makers have revamped their marketing pitches:

● 'Everyday low prices' is the central philosophy of 'category killers', such as Toys 'Я' Us and IKEA. These often sell from low-cost out-of-town 'sheds' offering a huge range and good value. Economies of scale and buying power help these traders keep costs down, but they also get customers to do more. Buy a bike from Toys 'Я' Us or furniture from IKEA and you will have to assemble it yourself. IKEA also does not deliver, so it keeps costs down by having a simple operation where customers work as warehouse, distribution and assembly staff.

● Marks & Spencer uses a similar 'Outstanding value' campaign across its European stores. It froze prices on 75 per cent of its items, and reduced the price of the remainder. It then continued to pass on its own efficiency gains and suppliers' price cuts to the customer. The suppliers rose to the challenge, cut their prices and gained a significant increase in sales volume during a recession. Marks & Spencer's profits also rose.

● Across Europe discount airlines such as EasyJet, Virgin Express and other entrants are taking an increased market share. The main barrier they are now facing is access to airports dominated by high-priced domestic carriers.

● Most office supplies are now bought direct from warehouses such as Office World, 'The No. 1 Office Supplies Discount Superstore' or by direct mail from 'Price Busters' such as Viking Direct. Software Warehouse has a price pledge: 'If you can find it cheaper – CALL US! We will beat ANY advertised price.' The low-cost, high-service approach to selling pioneered by Dell is rapidly becoming the favoured way to buy PCs.

● Makers of luxury goods are losing control of their premium prices and exclusive distribution. Chanel, Yves Saint Laurent and Christian Dior fragrances are discounted along with other goods by discounters such as Superdrug and grocery stores. Littlewoods, a big high-street chain, has struck 25 per cent off dozens of famous brands. Specialist discounters What Everyone Wants and Eau Zone are also entering the fray. Selfridges, the exclusive department store, claims that it 'would never do anything as down-market as discounting', but even the snootiest retailers may find that they have to respond to the discounters.

Value pricing involves more than just cutting prices. It means finding the delicate balance between quality and price that gives target consumers the value they seek. To consumers, 'value' is not the same as 'cheap'. Value pricing requires price cutting coupled with finding ways to maintain or even improve the quality while still making a profit. Consumers who once enjoyed high-quality brand-name products now want the same high quality, but at much lower prices. Thus value pricing often involves redesigning products and production processes to lower costs, while preserving profit margins at lower prices.

Although the trend towards value pricing began with the recession, its roots run much deeper. The trend reflects marketers' reactions to a fundamental change in consumer attitudes, resulting from the ageing of the baby boomers and their increased financial pressures. Today's 'squeezed consumers' – saddled with debt and facing increased expenses for child rearing, home buying and pending retirement – will continue to demand more value long after the economy improves. Even before the economy soured, buyers were beginning to rethink the price–quality equation. Thus value pricing is

likely to remain a crucial strategy. Winning over tomorrow's increasingly shrewd consumers will require finding ever-new ways to offer them more for less.

SOURCES: Portions adapted from 'Scenting trouble', *The Economist* (2 November, 1991), p. 38; Gary Strauss, 'Marketers plea: let's make a deal', *USA Today* (29 September 1992), pp. B1–B2. See also Joseph B. White, '"Value pricing" is hot as shrewd consumers seek low-cost quality', *Wall Street Journal* (12 March 1991), pp. A1, A9; Faye Rice, 'What intelligent consumers want', *Fortune* (28 December 1992), pp. 56–60; Bill Kelley, 'The new consumer revealed', *Sales and Marketing Management* (May 1993), pp. 46–52; Bradford W. Morgan, 'It's the myth of the "value consumer"', *Brandweek* (28 February 1994), p. 17; Neil Buckley, 'Potential cost of selling cheap every day', *Financial Times* (24 March 1994), p. 17; The Lex Column, 'Sinking into the trough: Kingfisher', *Financial Times* (24 March 1994), p. 22; David Blackwell, 'M & S sees sales in Europe rise 20%', *Financial Times* (9 November 1994), p. 25; Alan Mitchell, 'Going a bundle on marketing', *Marketing Week* (2 December 1994), pp. 30–1; Doug Cameron, Lois Jones and Nick Moss, 'Jet jam', *The European* (26 January 1998), pp. 8–13; Michael Skapinker, 'EasyJet bids to secure base in the Netherlands', *Financial Times* (13 January 1998), p. 22.

In many business-to-business marketing situations, the pricing challenge is to find ways to adjust the value of the company's marketing offer in order to escape price competition and to justify higher prices and margins. This is especially true for suppliers of commodity products, which are characterized by little differentiation and intense price competition. In such cases, many companies adopt *value-added* strategies. Rather than cutting prices to match competitors, they attach value-added services to differentiate their offers and thus support higher margins.

When General Electric expanded a no-frost refrigerator, it needed more shipping boxes fast. The Irish packaging supplier Smurfit Corporation assigned a co-ordinator to juggle production from three of its plants – and sometimes even divert products intended for other customers – to keep GE's Decatur plant humming. This kind of value-added hustling helped Smurfit win the GE appliance unit's 'Distinguished Supplier Award'. It has also sheltered Smurfit from the struggle of competing only on price. 'Today, it's not just getting the best price but getting the best value – and there are a lot of pieces to value,' says a vice president for procurement at Emerson Electric Company, a major Smurfit customer that has cut its supplier count by 65 per cent.[14]

Geographical Pricing

A company must also decide how to price its products to customers located in different parts of the country or the world. Should the company risk losing the business of more distant customers by charging them higher prices to cover the higher shipping costs? Or should the company charge all customers the same prices regardless of location? We will look at five **geographical pricing** strategies for the following hypothetical situation:

> The Tromsø a.s. is a Norwegian paper products company selling to customers all over Europe. The cost of freight is high and affects the companies from whom customers buy their paper. Tromsø wants to establish a geographical pricing policy. It is trying to determine how to price a Nkr1,000 order to three specific customers: Customer A (Oslo); Customer B (Amsterdam) and Customer C (Barcelona).

One option is for Tromsø to ask each customer to pay the shipping cost from the factory to the customer's location. All three customers would pay the same factory price of Nkr1,000, with Customer A paying, say, Nkr100 for shipping; Customer B, Nkr150; and Customer C, Nkr250. Called **FOB-origin pricing**, this practice means that the goods are placed *free on board* (hence, *FOB*) a carrier. At that point the title and responsibility pass to the customer, which pays the freight from the factory to the destination.

Because each customer picks up its own cost, supporters of FOB pricing feel that this is the fairest way to assess freight charges. The disadvantage, however, is that Tromsø will be a high-cost firm to distant customers. If Tromsø's main competitor happens to be in Spain, this competitor will no doubt outsell Tromsø in Spain. In fact, the competitor would outsell Tromsø in most of southern Europe, whereas Tromsø would dominate the north.

Uniform delivered pricing is the exact opposite of FOB pricing. Here, the company charges the same price plus freight to all customers, regardless of their location. The freight charge is set at the average freight cost. Suppose this is Nkr150. Uniform delivered pricing therefore results in a higher charge to the Oslo customer (which pays Nkr150 freight instead of Nkr100) and a lower charge to the Barcelona customer (who pays Nkr150 instead of Nkr250). On the one hand, the Oslo customer would prefer to buy paper from another local paper company that uses FOB-origin pricing. On the other hand, Tromsø has a better chance of winning over the Spanish customer. Other advantages of uniform delivered pricing are that it is fairly easy to administer and it lets the firm advertise its price nationally.

Zone pricing falls between FOB-origin pricing and uniform delivered pricing. The company sets up two or more zones. All customers within a given zone pay a single total price; the more distant the zone, the higher the price. For example, Tromsø might set up a Scandinavian zone and charge Nkr100 freight to all customers in this zone, a northern Europe zone in which it charges Nkr150 and a southern Europe zone in which it charges Nkr250. In this way, the customers within a given price zone receive no price advantage from the company. For example, customers in Oslo and Copenhagen pay the same total price to Tromsø. The complaint, however, is that the Oslo customer is paying part of the Copenhagen customer's freight cost. In addition, even though they may be within a few miles of each other, a customer just barely on the south side of the line dividing north and south pays much more than one that is just barely on the north side of the line.

Using **basing-point pricing**, the seller selects a given city as a 'basing point' and charges all customers the freight cost from that city to the customer location, regardless of the city from which the goods actually are shipped. For example, Tromsø might set Oslo as the basing point and charge all customers Nkr100 plus the freight from Oslo to their locations. This means that a Copenhagen customer

geographical pricing
Pricing based on where customers are located.

FOB-origin pricing
A geographic pricing strategy in which goods are placed free on board a carrier; the customer pays the freight from the factory to the destination.

uniform delivered pricing
A geographic pricing strategy in which the company charges the same price plus freight to all customers, regardless of their location.

zone pricing
A geographic pricing strategy in which the company sets up two or more zones. All customers within a zone pay the same total price; the more distant the zone, the higher the price.

basing-point pricing
A geographic pricing strategy in which the seller designates some city as a basing point and charges all customers the freight cost from that city to the customer location, regardless of the city from which the goods are actually shipped.

pays the freight cost from Oslo to Copenhagen, even though the goods may be shipped from Tromsø. Using a basing-point location other than the factory raises the total price for customers near the factory and lowers the total price for customers far from the factory.

If all sellers used the same basing-point city, delivered prices would be the same for all customers and price competition would be eliminated. Industries such as sugar, cement, steel and cars used basing-point pricing for years, but this method has become less popular today. Some companies set up multiple basing points to create more flexibility: they quote freight charges from the basing-point city nearest to the customer.

Finally, the seller that is anxious to do business with a certain customer or geographical area might use **freight-absorption pricing**. Using this strategy, the seller absorbs all or part of the actual freight charges in order to get the desired business. The seller might reason that if it can get more business, its average costs will fall and more than compensate for its extra freight cost. Freight-absorption pricing is used for market penetration and to hold on to increasingly competitive markets.

freight-absorption pricing
A geographic pricing strategy in which the company absorbs all or part of the actual freight charges in order to get the business.

International Pricing

Companies that market their products internationally must decide what prices to charge in the different countries in which they operate. In some cases, a company can set a uniform worldwide price. For example, Airbus sells its jetliners at about the same price everywhere, whether in the United States, Europe or a Third World country. However, most companies adjust their prices to reflect local market conditions and cost considerations.

The price that a company should charge in a specific country depends on many factors, including economic conditions, competitive situations, laws and regulations, and development of the wholesaling and retailing system. Consumer perceptions and preferences may also vary from country to country, calling for

International price escalation: a pair of Levi's selling for $30 in the United States goes for over $60 in a Levi's boutique in Korea and other Pacific Rim countries.

different prices. Or the company may have different marketing objectives in various world markets, which require changes in pricing strategy. For example, Sony might introduce a new product into mature markets in highly developed countries with the goal of quickly gaining mass-market share – this would call for a penetration pricing strategy. In contrast, it might enter a less developed market by targeting smaller, less price-sensitive segments – in this case, market-skimming pricing makes sense.

Costs play an important role in setting international prices. Travellers abroad are often surprised to find that goods which are relatively inexpensive at home may carry outrageously higher price tags in other countries. A pair of Levi's selling for $30 in the United States goes for about $63 in Tokyo and $88 in Paris. A McDonald's Big Mac selling for a modest $2.25 in the United States costs $5.75 in Moscow. Pink Floyd's 'Dark Side of the Moon' CD sells for $14.99 in the United States, but costs about $22 in the EU. Conversely, a Gucci handbag going for only $60 in Milan, Italy, fetches $240 in the United States. In some cases, such price escalation may result from differences in selling strategies or market conditions. In most instances, however, it is simply a result of the higher costs of selling in foreign markets – the additional costs of modifying the product, higher shipping and insurance costs, import tariffs and taxes, costs associated with exchange-rate fluctuations and higher channel and physical distribution costs.

For example, Campbell found that its distribution costs in the United Kingdom were 30 per cent higher than in the United States. US retailers typically purchase soup in large quantities – 48-can cases of a single soup by the dozens, hundred or carloads. In contrast, English grocers purchase soup in small quantities – typically in 24-can cases of *assorted* soups. Each case must be hand-packed for shipment. To handle these small orders, Campbell had to add a costly extra wholesale level to its European channel. The smaller orders also mean that English retailers order two or three times as often as their US counterparts, bumping up billing and order costs. These and other factors caused Campbell to charge much higher prices for its soups in the UK.[15]

Thus international pricing presents some special problems and complexities. We discussed international pricing issues in more detail in Chapter 5.

Price Changes

After developing their price structures and strategies, companies often face situations in which they must initiate price changes or respond to price changes by competitors.

Initiating Price Changes

In some cases, the company may find it desirable to initiate either a price cut or a price increase. In both cases, it must anticipate possible buyer and competitor reactions.

● *Initiating Price Cuts*

Several situations may lead a firm to consider cutting its price. One such circumstance is excess capacity. In this case, the firm needs more business and cannot get it through increased sales effort, product improvement or other measures. It may drop its follow-the-leader pricing – charging about the same price as its leading competitor – and aggressively cut prices to boost sales. But as the airline, construction equipment and other industries have learned in recent years, cutting prices in an industry loaded with excess capacity may lead to price wars as competitors try to hold on to market share.

Another situation leading to price changes is falling market share in the face of strong price competition. Several American industries – cars, consumer electronics, cameras, watches and steel, for example – lost market share to Japanese competitors whose high-quality products carried lower prices than did their American counterparts. In response, American companies resorted to more aggressive pricing action. General Motors, for example, cut its subcompact car prices by 10 per cent on the West Coast, where Japanese competition was strongest.[16]

A company may also cut prices in a drive to dominate the market through lower costs. Either the company starts with lower costs than its competitors or it cuts prices in the hope of gaining market share that will further cut costs through larger volume. Bausch & Lomb used an aggressive low-cost, low-price strategy to become an early leader in the competitive soft contact-lens market.

● *Initiating Price Increases*

In contrast, many companies have had to *raise* prices in recent years. They do this knowing that the price increases may be resented by customers, dealers and even their own sales force. Yet a successful price increase can greatly increase profits. For example, if the company's profit margin is 3 per cent of sales, a 1 per cent price increase will increase profits by 33 per cent if sales volume is unaffected.

A considerable factor in price increases is cost inflation. Rising costs squeeze profit margins and lead companies to regular rounds of price increases. Companies often raise their prices by more than the cost increase in anticipation of further inflation. Another factor leading to price increases is overdemand: when a company cannot supply all its customers' needs, it can raise its prices, ration products to customers or both.

Companies can increase their prices in a number of ways to keep up with rising costs. Prices can be raised almost invisibly by dropping discounts and adding higher-priced units to the line. Or prices can be pushed up openly. In passing price increases on to customers, the company should avoid the image of price gouging. The price increases should be supported with a company communication programme telling customers why prices are being increased. The company sales force should help customers find ways to economize.

Where possible, the company should consider ways to meet higher costs or demand without raising prices. For example, it can shrink the product instead of raising the price, as confectionery manufacturers do. Or it can substitute less expensive ingredients or remove certain product features, packaging or services. Or it can 'unbundle' its products and services, removing and separately pricing elements that were formerly part of the offer. IBM, for example, now offers training and consulting as separately priced services.

● *Buyer Reactions to Price Changes*

Whether the price is raised or lowered, the action will affect buyers, competitors, distributors and suppliers, and may interest government as well. Customers do not always interpret prices in a straightforward way. They may view a price *cut* in several ways. For example, what would you think if Sony were suddenly to cut its

Buyer reactions to price changes. What would you think if the price of Joy was suddenly cut in half?

VCR prices in half? You might think that these VCRs are about to be replaced by newer models or that they have some fault and are not selling well. You might think that Sony is in financial trouble and may not stay in the business long enough to supply future parts. You might believe that quality has been reduced. Or you might think that the price will come down even further and that it will pay to wait and see.

Similarly, a price *increase*, which would normally lower sales, may have some positive meanings for buyers. What would you think if Sony *raised* the price of its latest VCR model? On the one hand, you might think that the item is very 'hot' and may be unobtainable unless you buy it soon. Or you might think that the recorder is unusually good value. On the other hand, you might think that Sony is greedy and charging what the traffic will bear.

● *Competitor Reactions to Price Changes*

A firm considering a price change has to worry about the reactions of its competitors as well as its customers. Competitors are most likely to react when the number of

Fighting brands: When challenged on price by store brands and other low-priced entrants, Procter & Gamble turned a number of its brands into fighting brands, including Luvs disposable diapers.

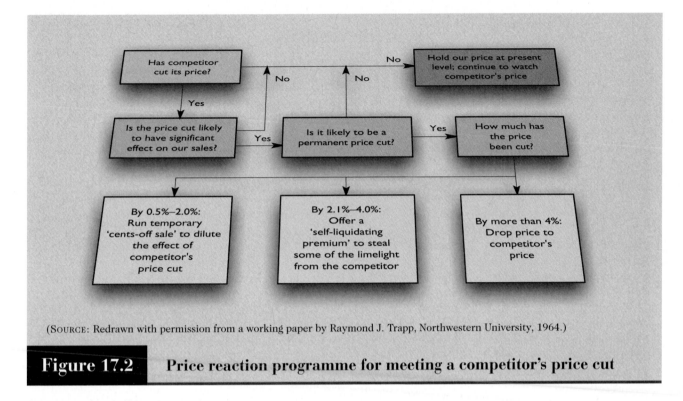

(SOURCE: Redrawn with permission from a working paper by Raymond J. Trapp, Northwestern University, 1964.)

Figure 17.2 **Price reaction programme for meeting a competitor's price cut**

firms involved is small, when the product is uniform and when the buyers are well informed.

How can the firm figure out the likely reactions of its competitors? If the firm faces one large competitor and if the competitor tends to react in a set way to price changes, that reaction can be easily anticipated. But if the competitor treats each price change as a fresh challenge and reacts according to its self-interest, the company will have to figure out just what makes up the competitor's self-interest at the time.

The problem is complex because, like the customer, the competitor can interpret a company price cut in many ways. It might think the company is trying to grab a larger market share, that the company is doing poorly and trying to boost its sales or that the company wants the whole industry to cut prices to increase total demand.

When there are several competitors, the company must guess each competitor's likely reaction. If all competitors behave alike, this amounts to analyzing only a typical competitor. In contrast, if the competitors do not behave alike – perhaps because of differences in size, market shares or policies – then separate analyses are necessary. However, if some competitors will match the price change, there is good reason to expect that the rest will also match it.

Responding to Price Changes

Here we reverse the question and ask how a firm should respond to a price change by a competitor. The firm needs to consider several questions: Why did the competitor change the price? Was it to make more market share, to use excess capacity, to meet changing cost conditions or to lead an industry-wide price change? Is the price change temporary or permanent? What will happen to the company's market share and profits if it does not respond? Are other companies

Excuse Me, But Do You Accept Money?

Marketing Highlight 17.3

Cash is out of fashion. Increasingly people pay, for even small transactions, by credit card, debit card or, in many parts of Europe, prepaid smart cards. People are as uninterested in seeing their money as they are the petrol they buy for their car – with a credit card, of course. Money, and the constraints it imposes, will disappear. Because of financial liberalization, the spending of both households and companies is becoming less determined by immediate income or money in the bank than by their expected wealth. Even the resistance of ultra conservative Germany and Marks & Spencer is crumbling; they will liberalize the use of credit and debit cards soon.

People and companies are increasingly turning to trading their skills and produce without using money. Want a plumbing job done? Fred will do it if you will mow his lawn for a week and baby-sit one night. What if the plumber does not want anything you can provide? In that case, clubs exist to trade credits. The plumber does the job for you, but he can use his credits to get goods or services from someone else and you have to work off your debt. These networks are growing so fast that governments are starting to worry about them. They exist outside the tax system, so people pay no VAT or income tax. Maybe that is why people like them so much.

London's Capital Barter Corporation (CBC) orchestrates third-party deals for a pool of 150 companies that offer their services for trade credits rather than cash. CBC's deals range from a £15 restaurant meal to a £15,000 stock of computers. The most popular items are airline tickets, photocopiers and computers. Barter is not just for small deals between small firms – in the United States, Lufthansa, Playtex and US Networks have all had deals worth $2 million or more.

CBC and other barter companies, including The Bartering Company, Business Barter Exchange and Eurotrade, debit and credit their members' accounts in 'trade pounds'. Each member has a credit limit depending upon the size of the company and the tradability of its products. But why barter rather than get money instead? The marketing manager of Konica Business machines explains: 'A lot of companies, when they find out how much a fax machine is in trade pounds, say they can get a better deal by getting a discount in cash. But if they think how much it would cost to generate that cash, they would find it cheaper to do the deal in barter.' The value of bartering is best when the incremental cost of serving an extra client is low, explains the chief executive of the International Reciprocal Trade Association. Letting a room on barter, for example, costs the hotel only the price of laundry and cleaning, since all the other costs are fixed. But the buying power it earns in trade pounds is equal to the full retail value of the room.

The Internet now has its own money. Customers 'net-surfing' through online 'shops' in electronic 'shopping malls' usually buy information, but increasingly they buy music, books and clothes from 'e-catalogues'. How do they pay? Punching in credit card numbers is one way, but hackers make this method insecure. Lee Stern, a Californian entrepreneur, thinks he has the answer with his First Virtual Holdings bank, 'The world's first truly electronic bank'. In this, both buyers and sellers must have accounts with the First Virtual. To buy through the Internet, the buyers give the sellers their account numbers and the goods are shipped. Periodically, the seller reports sales to First Virtual, which uses e-mail to ask the buyer for confirmation. That being done, the buyer's credit card is automatically debited.

The Dutch firm DigiCash is close to having a system that is simpler than the virtual banks. Its e-money works like a prepaid smart card. The problem it has had to solve is, again, security: how to make sure the e-money is spent only once. DigiCash checks the card's electronic signature with the card's supplier for each transaction in order to make sure the transaction is valid. Governments worry about e-money. The 'virtual economy' is already the size of the Netherlands' and who can guess how big it will be within a decade?

With digital cash zipping across the Internet's 'cyberspace', how can tax inspectors keep tabs on it? E-cash pushes the idea of money to the limit. It has no intrinsic value and hardly a trace of physical existence. Internet is pushing to the limits the question: what makes money worth what it is worth? Two Irish economists, Browne and Fell, see money disappearing altogether. They argue that e-money will replace cash, bonds will replace the money market, and a standard of value will be established in which prices are divorced from the means of payment. Values, they say, will ultimately be measured with a unit of account defined for a basket of goods. Maybe the Mars Bar will become the ultimate unit of currency because it contains a very representative balance of commodities and manufacture.

SOURCES: Neil Buckley, 'M & S close to accepting debit card payments', *Financial Times* (29 August 1994), p. 6; Motoka Rich, 'Abracadabra! It's the barter magicians', *Financial Times* (1–2 October 1994), p. 4; Michael Lindemann, 'Germany flexible at last on credit cards', *Financial Times* (11 November 1994), p. 3; Samuel Britten, 'Post-money world on our doorstep', *Financial Times* (17 November 1994), p. 20; and 'Electric money: so much for the cashless society', *The Economist* (26 November 1994).

going to respond? What are the competitor's and other firms' responses to each possible reaction likely to be?

Besides these issues, the company must make a broader analysis. It has to consider its own product's stage in the life cycle, its importance in the company's product mix, the intentions and resources of the competitor and the possible consumer reactions to price changes. The company cannot always make an extended analysis of its alternatives at the time of a price change, however. The competitor may have spent much time preparing this decision, but the company may have to react within hours or days. About the only way to cut down reaction time is to plan ahead for both possible price changes and possible responses by the competitor.

Figure 17.2 shows the ways that a company might assess and respond to a competitor's price cut. Once the company has determined that the competitor has cut its price and that this price reduction is likely to harm company sales and profits, it might simply decide to hold its current price and profit margin. The company might believe that it will not lose too much market share or that it would lose too much profit if it reduced its own price. It might decide that it should wait and respond when it has more information on the effects of the competitor's price change. For now, it might be willing to hold on to good customers, while giving up the poorer ones to the competitor. The argument against this holding strategy, however, is that the competitor may get stronger and more confident as its sales increase and the company might wait too long to act.

If the company decides that effective action can and should be taken, it might make any of the four responses:

1. *Reduce price.* The leader might drop its price to the competitor's price. It may decide that the market is price sensitive and that it would lose too much market share to the lower-priced competitor. Or it might worry that recapturing lost market share later would be too hard. Cutting price will reduce the company's profits in the short run. Some companies might also reduce their product quality, services and marketing communications to retain profit margins, but this ultimately will hurt long-run market share. The company should try to maintain its quality as it cuts prices.

2. *Raise perceived quality.* The company might maintain its price but strengthen the perceived value of its offer. It could improve its communications, stressing the relative quality of its product over that of the lower-price competitor. The firm may find it cheaper to maintain price and spend money to improve its perceived quality than to cut price and operate at a lower margin.

3. *Improve quality and increase price.* The company might increase quality and raise its price, moving its brand into a higher price position. The higher quality justifies the higher price, which in turn preserves the company's higher margins. Or the company can hold price on the current product and introduce a new brand at a higher price position.

4. *Launch low-price 'fighting brand'.* One of the best responses is to add lower-price items to the line or to create a separate lower-price brand. This is necessary if the particular market segment being lost is price sensitive and will not respond to arguments of higher quality. Thus, when attacked on price by Fuji, Kodak introduced low-priced Funtime film. When challenged on price by store brands and other low-priced entrants, Nestlé turned a number of its brands into fighting brands, including Fussell's condensed milk. In response to price pressures, Miller cut the price of its High Life brand by 20 per cent in most markets and sales jumped 9 per cent in less than a year.[17]

Pricing strategies and tactics form an important element of a company's marketing mix. In setting prices, companies must carefully consider a great many internal and external factors before choosing a price that will give them the greatest competitive advantage in selected target markets. However, companies are not usually free to charge whatever prices they wish. Several laws restrict pricing practices and a number of ethical considerations affect pricing decisions. Pricing strategies and tactics also depend upon the way that we pay for things. Increasingly what we spend does not depend on how much money we have on us or how much we earned that week. These days our money is rarely something we see or feel; it is the electronic transmission of data between files. Also, as currency is becoming an increasingly small part of our lives, barter is coming back in international and interpersonal dealing. Marketing Highlight 17.3 tells more about how money is changing.

Summary

Pricing is a dynamic process. Companies design a *pricing structure* that covers all their products. They change this structure over time and adjust it to account for different customers and situations.

Pricing strategies usually change as a product passes through its life cycle. The company can decide on one of several price–quality strategies for introducing an imitative product. In pricing innovative new products, it can follow a *skimming policy* by initially setting high prices to 'skim' the maximum amount of revenue from various segments of the market. Or it can use *penetration pricing* by setting a low initial price to win a large market share.

When the product is part of a product mix, the firm searches for a set of prices that will maximize the profits from the total mix. The company decides on *price steps* for items in its product line and on the pricing of *optional products*, *captive products*, *by-products* and *product bundles*.

Companies apply a variety of *price-adjustment strategies* to account for differences in consumer segments and situations. One is *discount and allowance pricing*, whereby the company establishes cash discounts, quantity discounts, functional discounts, seasonal discounts and allowances. A second is *segmented pricing*, whereby the company sets different prices for different customers, product forms, places or times. A third is *psychological pricing*, whereby the company adjusts the price to communicate better a product's intended position. A fourth is *promotional pricing*, whereby the company decides on loss-leader pricing, special-event pricing and psychological discounting. A fifth is *value pricing*, whereby the company offers just the right combination of quality and good service at a fair price. A sixth is *geographical pricing*, whereby the company decides how to price to distant customers, choosing from such alternatives as FOB pricing, uniform delivered pricing, zone pricing, basing-point pricing and freight-absorption pricing. A seventh is *international pricing*, whereby the company adjusts its price to meet different conditions and expectations in different world markets.

When a firm considers initiating a *price change*, it must consider customers' and competitors' reactions. Customers' reactions are influenced by the meaning that customers see in the price change. Competitors' reactions flow from a set reaction policy or a fresh analysis of each situation. The firm initiating the price change must also anticipate the probable reactions of suppliers, intermediaries and government.

The firm that faces a price change initiated by a competitor must try to understand the competitor's intent as well as the likely duration and impact of the change. If a swift reaction is desirable, the firm should preplan its reactions to different possible price actions by competitors. When facing a competitor's price change, the company might sit tight, reduce its own price, raise perceived quality, improve quality and raise price, or launch a fighting brand.

Key Terms

Basing-point pricing 732
By-product pricing 724
By-products 724
Captive-product pricing 723
Cash discount 725
FOB-origin pricing 732
Freight-absorption pricing 733
Functional discount (trade discount) 726
Geographical pricing 732

Market-penetration pricing 721
Market-skimming pricing 720
Optional-product pricing 723
Product-bundle pricing 724
Product line pricing 722
Promotional allowance 726
Promotional pricing 728
Psychological pricing 727
Quantity discount 725
Quantity premium 726

Reference prices 728
Seasonal discount 726
Segmented pricing 727
Strapline 720
Trade-in allowance 726
Two-part pricing 724
Uniform delivered pricing 732
Value pricing 729
Zone pricing 732

Discussing the Issues

1. Describe which strategy – market skimming or market penetration – is appropriate for the following products: (a) Procter & Gamble's new Ariel Future laundry detergent; (b) Reebok's latest, 'new-tech' aerobics shoes; (c) an American Diner that has recently opened a restaurant right opposite McDonald's in the city's shopping centre. Why are these the right strategies for these companies?

2. American Express offers three tiers of 'product' to customers – a green card, a gold card and a platinum card. The membership fee (price) rises from £100 for the green card to £200 for the gold and £300 for the platinum. What pricing strategy is adopted by AmEx? Do you think this type of strategy is effective? Why or why not?

3. A leading brand of room spray is priced at £2.50 for a 150 ml bottle. A close competitor launched a similar product priced at £1.99 for 300 ml and quickly became the no. 1 brand. Discuss the psychological aspects of this pricing. What sort of company image do you think the competitor possesses to allow the use of this superb-value strategy? Would a similar strategy work for the leading no. 1 brand? Why or why not?

4. The formula for household chlorine bleaching agents is virtually identical for all brands. One brand, Clorox, charges a premium price for this same product, yet remains an unchallenged market leader in some national markets. What does this imply about the value of a brand name? Are there ethical issues involved in this type of pricing?

5. Manufacturers of clothing, confectionery, crockery and other consumer products are often faced with 'by-products' – such as reject goods that are not quite perfect and fail to meet the high standards of retailers and consumers. There is, however, a market for such 'rejects'. What strategy should be used for pricing these products?

6. A Bodum coffee percolator sells for under £20 in a department store in London. The same device is priced at £80 in Tang's, a local department store in Singapore. What do you think accounts for the discrepancy in price? Can you list other products or services that would reflect a similar international pricing pattern?

Applying the Concepts

1. Go to your local supermarket or a grocery store you regularly shop at. Take a few product categories. Observe the sizes and prices within product categories. Are the package sizes (weight or number of units contained) comparable across brands? Find instances where a manufacturer seems to have made a smaller package in order to charge (a) a lower price and (b) a higher price. Are there any instances where (a) a higher price is charged for larger packages and (b) a discount is given on larger packages? Why do you think manufacturers adopt these pricing strategies? Do they appear effective? Under what circumstances are they effective?

2. You are probably familiar with the seasonal sales that take place at certain times of the year. Examples are the 'summer sales', 'Christmas sales' and 'New Year sales'. Why do retailers run these sales each year? Would it be more effective for a retailer to differentiate from others by offering discounts outside, rather than during, the conventional seasonal sales periods? Why or why not? In general, how effective are discount and allowance pricing strategies?

References

1. Tom Rubython, 'A roll of the orange dice', *BusinessAge* (July 1994), pp. 56–8; Anil Bhoyrul, 'Boom to gloom', *BusinessAge* (November 1994), pp. 4B–6B; Alan Cane, 'Santa receives a call for rapid growth', *Financial Times* (22 November 1994), p. 28; Alison Smith, 'Talk is cheap as handsets appear', *Financial Times* (24 November 1997), p. 15.

2. For a comprehensive discussion of pricing strategies, see Thomas T. Nagle and Reed K. Holen, *The Strategy and Tactics of Pricing*, 2nd edn (Englewood Cliffs, NJ: Prentice Hall, 1995).

3. John Parry, 'Times are changing for Tag-Heuer', *The European* (11–17 November 1994), p. 32; Ian Fraser, 'Don't crack under the pressure', *European Business* (June 1994), pp. 66–8.

4. Bridget Williams, *The Best Butter in the World: A history of Sainsbury's* (London: Ebury, 1994).

5. David Kirkpatrick, 'Intel goes for broke', *Fortune* (16 May 1994), pp. 62–8; Andy Reinhardt, 'Pentium: the next

generation', *Business Week* (12 May 1997), pp. 42–3; David Kirkpatrick, 'Intel's amazing profit machine', *Fortune* (17 February 1996), pp. 60–72.

6. Daniel Green, 'Yogurt may yield fat profit', *Financial Times* (9 January 1998), p. 16; Anna-Maija Tanttu, 'Spreading the benefits of science', *The European Magazine* (17 April 1997), pp. 10–11.

7. Ralph Atkins, 'A certain lack of drive', *Financial Times* (25 November 1994), p. 18.

8. Gregory Viscusi, 'Merloni makes a clean break for eastern markets', *The European* (25 November 1994), p. 21; 'Britain's music business: the sound barrier', *The Economist* (15 May 1993), p. 103.

9. Susan Krafft, 'Love, Love Me Doo', *American Demographics* (June 1994), pp. 15–16.

10. Nagle and Holden, op cit., pp. 225–8; Manjit S. Yadav and Kent B. Monroe, 'How buyers perceive savings in a bundle price: an examination of a bundle's transaction value',

Journal of Marketing Research (August 1993), pp. 350–8.

11. S.M. Widrick, 'Measurement of incidence of quantity surcharge among selected grocery products', *Journal of Consumer Affairs* (Summer 1979); Yiorgos Zotos and Steven Lysonski, 'An exploration of the quantity surcharge concept in Greece', *European Journal of Marketing*, **27**, 10 (1993), pp. 5–18.

12. Gary M. Erickson and Johnny K. Johansson, 'The role of price in multi-attribute product evaluations', *Journal of Consumer Research* (September 1985), pp. 195–9.

13. For more reading on reference prices and psychological pricing, see Nagle and Holden, op. cit., p. 12; K.N. Rajendran and Gerard J. Tellis, 'Contextual and temporal components of reference price', *Journal of Marketing* (January 1994), pp. 22–34; Richard A. Briesch, Lakshman Krishnamurthi, Tridib Mazumdar and S. P. Raj, 'A comparative analysis of reference price models', *Journal of Consumer Research* (September 1997), pp. 202–14; John Huston and Nipoli Kamdar, '$9.99: can 'just-below pricing be reconciled with rationality?', *Eastern Economic Journal* (Spring 1996), pp. 137–45; Robert M. Schindler and Patrick N. Kirby, 'Patterns of right-most digits used in advertised prices: implications for nine-ending effects', *Journal of Consumer Research* (September 1997), pp. 192–201.

14. Jim Morgan, 'Value added: from cliché to the real thing', *Purchasing* (3 April 1997), pp. 59–61; James E. Ellis, 'There's even a science to selling boxes', *Business Week* (3 August 1992), pp. 51–2; Erika Rasmusson, 'The pitfalls of price cutting', *Sales and Marketing Management* (May 1997), p. 17.

15. Philip R. Cateora, *International Marketing*, 7th edn (Homewood, IL: Irwin, 1990), p. 540; see also S. Tamer Cavusgil, 'Pricing for global markets', *Columbia Journal of World Business* (Winter 1996), pp. 66–78.

16. For more on price cutting and its consequences, see Kathleen Madigan, 'The latest mad plunge of the price slashers', *Business Week* (11 May 1992), p. 36; Bill Saporito, 'Why the price wars never end', *Fortune* (23 March 1992), pp. 68–78; Erika Rasmusson, 'The pitfalls of price cutting', *Sales and Marketing Management* (May 1997), p. 17; David R. Henderson, 'What are price wars good for? *Absolutely nothing*', *Fortune* (12 May 1997), p. 156.

17. Jonathon Berry and Zachary Schiller, 'Attack of the fighting brands', *Business Week* (2 May 1994), p. 125.

Case 17

Amaizer: It Tastes Awful, but We're Working on It

AMAIZER IS A NEW SAVOURY snack made from maize. Its method of manufacture is similar to cornflakes breakfast cereal, but it is to be sold as a savoury snack. Amaizers look like potato crisps, but are more golden and regular in shape. Raw materials and manufacturing costs are higher than for potato chips, but they are healthier – in their basic form, they contain the same calories, but are low in saturates and cholesterol.

Amaizer is sweeter than potato crisps, but it can be flavoured. Unfortunately, consumer trials showed that the Amaizer versions of popular crisp flavours – salt and vinegar, cheese and onion, etc. – 'taste awful'. Research and development was still working on the taste of these flavours. Meanwhile, the aim was to launch the product with four flavours that consumers did like: regular, sweet and sour, honey roasted ham and '1,000 Islands' dressing.

Although originally designed to use spare breakfast cereal capacity, the developed product needed dedicated plant. This produces Amaizer for a direct cost of £1,500 per tonne, excluding the cost of capital. With potato snacks selling for £3,000 per tonne, the brand manager was confident about the product's profitability.

The brand manager's confidence crashed, however, when sales, finance and market research each came up with recommended prices. The finance officer demanded that the price be set to cover the usual 100 per cent overhead charge plus a 20 per cent margin. His suggested price of £3,600 per tonne gave a very satisfactory £180,000 profit for the targeted 300 tonne annual sales.

Unfortunately, the finance officer's view conflicted with the sales manager's, who wanted the price to be £100 per tonne below potato crisps. The sales manager claimed that only with a price advantage could they achieve the target sales against the established competition. The sales manager added that a low initial price would also compensate traders for the extra shelf space Amaizer used. Amaizer was bulkier than potato crisps and therefore needed about 20 per cent extra shelf space.

The marketing researcher's contribution to the pricing debate confused the brand manager even more. Rather than giving a price, the researcher gave a string of prices and sales and, to the annoyance of the finance officer, some financial information:

Price (£000)	2.5	3.0	3.5	4.0	4.5
Sales (tonnes)	400	350	280	200	100

The researcher also estimated £300,000 annual fixed operating cost for the product and capital investment that depended upon the annual volumes produced.

Annual sales (tonnes)	400	350	280	200	100
Capital investment (£000)	2,250	2,000	1,650	1,200	600

'I assume you know that our average cost of capital is 15 per cent,' commented the finance officer.

'All very impressive,' said the brand manager, 'but what price should we charge?'

'That all depends on what you want to achieve,' replied the researcher.

QUESTIONS

1. Evaluate the pricing suggestions of the sales, finance and market research officers.

2. What criteria should be used to select the best price?

3. What prices give the highest gross margins, return on investment, capital cost covered (C^3), economic value added (EVA), net contribution, sales value and sales volume (Marketing Highlight 16.3 shows how to calculate these)?

4. Based on the EVA results, what price would you choose and why? What do you notice about the room to manoeuvre around the optimum prices?

5. Assuming a price of £3,500 per tonne, what would be the best advertising strategy, given the following advertising response?

Advertising (£000)	25	50	100	200	400
Sales (tonnes)	180	210	280	360	420
Capital investment (£000)	1,100	1,250	1,650	2,050	2,300

6. How does the optimum advertising level influenced by the price?

SOURCES: Adapted from in-company information. Names and figures have been changed for commercial reasons.

Stena Sealink versus Le Shuttle, Eurostar and the Rest

The Channel Tunnel: about as welcome to cross-channel ferry operators as Henry Ford was to carriage makers.

In July 1994 Stena Sealink, the Swedish ferry company, was waiting for the outcome of a battle caused by the opening of the Channel Tunnel between Folkestone and Calais. Although the tunnel carried only four Eurostar trains a day in each direction between London and Paris, cross-channel ferry prices had already dropped to 20 per cent of 1993 levels. On some routes the competition was particularly intensive and it had given rise to the court battle between France's Brittany Ferries and the United Kingdom's P & O. At the heart of the case was P & O's Ffr49 three-day return fare for passengers originating in France on the 'long route' between Cherbourg and Le Havre in France and Portsmouth in England.

To qualify for the reduced fare, passengers had to collect three coupons from *Ouest-France*, a regional newspaper covering the main catchment area for the Cherbourg–Portsmouth service. Brittany applied for an immediate injunction against P & O's 'loss-leading' prices at the Tribunal de Commerce in Rennes. Since Brittany Ferries' owners are 4,000 French farmers and regional councils, they have considerable influence in that part of France. Brittany Ferries' main accusation was: 'predatory pricing, which we believe breaks French law if it is proved to be intentionally aimed at eliminating rivals'. It complained that the massive price cut to 75 per cent of normal tariffs throughout the peak summer season made profits impossible. P & O asked the court to find itself unable to rule, since it was impossible to stipulate fares when some sailings carried 1,600 passengers and others as few as 10. Industry experts say companies can gain by packing ferries with cheap-rate passengers, who swell profits by spending on food, drink and souvenirs during the voyage.

Stena Sealink entered the fray at the end of the summer season when promotional fares in the United Kingdom dropped to £1. The Central Committee of French Ship Owners (CCFSO) and their sailors' union demanded that the EU should impose minimum fares on cross-channel routes. They also wanted to bar all non-EU citizens from working on the ferries and claimed that, for safety reasons, all crew members must speak French. 'We believe it our duty to offer the keenest possible fare and that is what we do,' argued P & O in defence of its low fares. 'We thrive on competition which benefits the consumer and we would oppose any move to disrupt that.' Stena Sealink added: 'It would be ridiculous to increase prices in such a competitive industry.' The CCFSO responded to these comments: 'It is not our intention to be protectionist. Protection is where you erect customs or other barriers to trade. It is not protectionist to seek to save the jobs of French seafarers.' Brittany Ferries had other problems, too. In 1993 it lost Ffr90 million on a turnover of Ffr500 million, and had borrowings of Ffr1,400 million.

Competition by Sea

Stena Sealink has 30 per cent of the cross-channel market of 30 million annual passengers. P & O is market leader with a 42 per cent share, and Brittany Ferries is no. 3 with 9 per cent. Other contenders are Sally Line, owned by the Finnish Effjohn Oy group, and the United Kingdom's Hoverspeed, each with about 7 per cent of the market. Hoverspeed is unlike the other operators in that it uses fast car-carrying hovercraft and Seacats rather than boats. A further 40 million passengers cross the channel by air each year.

Short routes dominate the cross-channel market. Of the 24 million passengers travelling between the United Kingdom and France, 16 million take the intensively competitive Dover–Calais route. Of these, 9 million go by P & O, 6 million by Stena Sealink and 1 million by Hoverspeed. Although conspicuous for their consumer pricing and advertising, Sally Lines and Brittany Ferries are minor contenders on the short routes most threatened by the Channel Tunnel. Not only are fares down by an average of 20 per cent, but the quality of the ships and the frequency of the service they offer is also up. Both P & O and Stena Sealink have five vessels on the route.

The short route is critical to both the big operators. In 1993 P & O made £77 million operating profits on sales of £615 million, while Stena Sealink made £24 million profits on £380 million sales. However, P & O depended upon duty and tax-free sales for one-third of its profits. The market will decline. Eurotunnel aimed for half of a 40 million sea-going cross-channel passenger market by 1996. In the opinion of London-based brokers, NatWest Markets: 'The route can work with six vessels between them operating a service every 45 minutes.' The competition has already claimed one victim. Olau Lines, subsidiary of the German TT Line, stopped trading in May 1994. As the Channel Tunnel's threat increases and competition on the short routes intensifies, Stena Sealink and P & O are looking to the less competitive long routes. Hence P & O's quick purchase of Olau's luxury ferries to compete against Brittany Ferries between Portsmouth and Le Havre.

The Channel Tunnel will not affect all ferry traffic equally. Travellers between England and western France and Spain can avoid London and the congested south-east of England by taking a ferry from the south coast to Brittany or Spain. Similarly, travellers to or from the Midlands or north of England have a choice of ferries from the east coast to north European destinations. A problem with these routes is time. Ferries are slow and the journeys take between several hours to over a day, depending on the route. That means less regular services, provisions of cabins, bigger ships and, of course, higher costs. Nevertheless, Le Havre has spent £27 million building a new terminal to cope with increased demand and Dieppe has been given £6 million of regional funds to help pay for a new ferry terminal.

Ferry operators also hope to keep a high share of the commercial trade on the short routes. Along with the 4 million cars that cross the channel each year are 170,000 coaches and 1.3 million commercial vehicles. A survey among 102 senior transport executives found 62 per cent of transport companies believed that their drivers would prefer to stick with the ferries, while 84 per cent thought that the ferries would offer better facilities than the tunnel. 'We've managed perfectly well without a tunnel; I don't see it making a big difference except for the novelty value,' said one transport executive. Scania, the heavy-truck company which commissioned the survey, commented: 'Eurotunnel has predicted it will carry more than 8 million tonnes of freight in its first full year of operation and it aims to take a significant share of the ferries' freight business. Our survey shows they may be in for a big surprise.'

The removal of customs between European countries has created a new business for the ferry companies. The British are pouring across the channel to buy alcoholic drinks in France, where excise duties are much lower than in the United Kingdom. France levies £1.57 less than the United Kingdom on a bottle of champagne; 99p less on a bottle of still wine; and 25p less on a pint of beer. Since pretax prices are also low in France, total savings can be up to £60 on a case of champagne or £10 on six litres of some beers. The Wine and Spirits Federation reckons that 9 per cent of domestic sales of wine and 15 per cent of beer drunk in British homes are personal imports that avoid UK taxes. Some of the imports are from holiday-makers 'stocking-up' on their way through France or from legitimate day-trippers whose main aim is to get the tax-free booze. They can import up to a year's supply of alcohol for personal consumption. The ferry companies benefited from the doubling of the day-tripper market in 1994. However, Whitbread, the brewers, estimates that 30 per cent of the cross-channel booze trade, and the fastest growing part, was by organized bootleggers. They can make a profit of £324 per journey and can make up to four trips a day. After each trip they unload their vans on to trucks at Dover for distribution in the north of England. The British government and the Brewers and Licensed Retailers Association are unhappy about this trade, but not the ferry companies.

Competition Under and Over the Sea

The Channel Tunnel poses two commercial challenges to Stena Sealink: Eurostar and Le Shuttle. Eurostar is a passenger rail service, initially operating on the main London–Brussels and London–Paris routes, and Le Shuttle transports cars, commercial vehicles, their drivers and passengers between Folkestone and Calais. Eurostar's pricing is targeting the business passenger between the European capitals, which are on Europe's busiest air routes. Eurostar's £195 first-class fare between London and Paris savagely undercuts British Airways' and Air France's £318 business class fare. However, both prices are well above the £79 first-class passenger rail fare for using British Rail, Stena Sealink and SNCF to get between the centres of London and Paris. In contrast, the cheapest Eurostar fare (£95) is more expensive than both the cheapest air fares (£85) and the lowest price for rail-sea-rail (£62).

Eurostar aims to capture 60 per cent of the London–Paris and London–Brussels traffic, but British Airways see Eurostar as just another player in an already competitive market. The airline expects a dent in its business, but only in the London area. Many of its daily flights to Paris depart from elsewhere in the United Kingdom. Similarly, British Midland, a regional airline, is confident. It concedes that Eurostar will have the benefit of novelty, but does not think it will halt the airline's progress – it achieved a 27 per cent increase in year-on-year demand for its European services in the last quarter of 1994. British Midland believes that the inner-city location of the train terminals will count against Eurostar. Sabina, Belgium's national airline, is similarly dismissive: 'The tunnel is not a major worry. Parking facilities are poor at both Waterloo and Gare du Midi in Brussels, which will be an off-putting factor for businesspeople using the train. We're confident we can stay on top.' Nevertheless, Sabina has entered the fray by joining with Avis to give businesspeople flying to Brussels from Gatwick or Manchester a free day's car hire. British Airways also admits that its £75 million relaunch of its Club Europe service for business travellers was in direct response to the tunnel. Eurostar has started small, but plans services from Birmingham, Edinburgh, Glasgow and Manchester. By 1996 European Night Trains, whose sleeper will have *en suite* bathrooms, will run from London to Amsterdam, Dortmund and Frankfurt.

Stena Sealink's initial skirmish with Le Shuttle has given Stena confidence. The cross-channel freight and passenger businesses are very price sensitive. When Le Shuttle first started carrying trucks it did well, but then lost much of the business once initial price offers had finished. Le Shuttle's prices for the launch of its full service in June 1995 were also thought too high compared with those of ferries. Many in the industry believe that an attractive price would boost customers. Christopher Garnett, commercial director of Eurotunnel, disagrees: 'Our research shows that there is no requirement to undercut the ferries. People get worried when you talk about premium pricing, but we have scope to add value and we will still be competitive.' Wendy Wong, Smith New Court analyst, explains the conflict: 'Eurotunnel has to be careful with any price-cutting – it has some anxious [and very long suffering] shareholders to consider.'

Fast, Luxurious or Inexpensive

Consultants Healey & Baker think the days of ferries and short-hop air travel are numbered. They report that: 'it is now generally accepted that for distances over 300 km, rail is more economical than road'. Rail will compete with air for passengers' journeys within Europe and with road for freight. The importance of higher-speed travel having been realized, there has been wide-scale development of high-speed networks and rail terminals throughout Europe. Brave new ventures with high-speed trains have confounded critics. Spain's high-speed train, the AVE, almost broke even on its first full year of service. The train runs 471 km between Madrid and Seville using trains similar to France's Train à Grande Vitesse (TGV) and built by the same Anglo-French engineering group, GEC-Alsthom. The AVE slashed the rail time for the journey from 5 hours 55 minutes to 2 hours 40 and mirrors the TGV's results:

● The high-speed train captures most of the market. Before the AVE 51 per cent of travellers on the route went by car and only 20 per cent by rail. The figures are now 39 per cent by car and 44 per cent by AVE.

● Air travel is hard hit by high-speed trains. Iberia's share of the traffic on the route dropped from 18 to 7 per cent because of AVE.

● High-speed trains generate new customers. Twenty-four per cent of AVE users had never before travelled between Madrid and Seville. Originally the TGV between Paris and Lyon was projected to carry 6 million passengers a year; in 1993 21 million people travelled the route.

Eurostar achieves similar drastic cuts in travel time. Eurostar's journey time between London and Paris is 3 hours and between London and Brussels 3 hours and 15 minutes – times that will fall even further with the completion of Belgian and British high-speed links. Le Shuttle will take only 35 minutes and at peak times there will be four trains an hour. It will also be unaffected by weather and high seas. In competition P & O operates 25 sailings a day between Dover and Calais and a 'proven motorway-to-motorway time of 105 minutes'. It intends to speed up too, and has ordered a new high-speed Seacat for its Folkestone–Boulogne route.

The threat of the Channel Tunnel has stimulated other forms of competition besides price cutting and speed. Targeting the frequent traveller, Sally Line has extended its nautical miles, frequent traveller programme. P & O's advertising promotes the pleasure of the sea crossing: 'Why sail across the channel when you can cruise across?' A substantial investment programme aims to give P & O 'the best appointed ships on the channel'. Borrowing a lesson from the airlines, sailings have a new Club Class. This provides comfortable lounges, guaranteed seating and free coffee and newspapers. Perhaps the ultimate attraction is peace and freedom from Euro-schoolchildren. The company also intends to give its passengers a lot more reason to spend money on board. P & O claims that revenue from duty-free shops and other retail services already keeps fares down by an average of 25 per cent. Shipboard shoppers are a captive market with time on their hands. The whole 'cruise' experience contrasts with the service that Le Shuttle offers. 'People want style and comfort, not the commodity-like impersonal service of Le Shuttle,' says P & O's passenger marketing and sales director, Brian Langford. Le Shuttle's advantage is speed, but 'the time advantage will be wiped out', says Langford, 'when people need to take a break after enduring the "spartan" 30-minute tunnel journey'. Also, 'Le Shuttle will be charging a premium for speed', claims another P & O spokesman, 'so it's unlikely they can match our fares.' P & O's five-day return rates for a car and driver start at £57.

In many ways Eurotunnel's views concur with P & O's: 'You must remember,' says Christopher Garnett, 'we're in the business of transport, not leisure.' Unlike truck drivers, who may leave their cabs for a quick meal in a separate carriage, car passengers must remain with their vehicles. There is nothing to see while in the tunnel and little for the passengers to do. 'Le Shuttle is a means to an end for most users and we will market it to those consumers simply as a way of reaching their chosen destination,' says Garnett. 'But we can build our business by giving customers reasons to travel. We could, for example, use direct marketing to communicate with people we know enjoy practising sports in the north of France and persuade them to visit the area because of the ease of using the tunnel.' Wunderman Cato Johnson is handling the direct marketing and David Butter, its executive vice-president (Europe), predicts that Eurostar will be 'the leading brand in European travel'. He says Le Shuttle will 'change the way people relate to the Channel and remove it as an obstacle to travel'.

Breaking All the Rules

A year after the full operation of the Channel Tunnel began, it was hard to square the competition with financial reality. With 35 per cent market share of the short route, the tunnel was still not attracting enough traffic to staunch its overwhelming losses. In an attempt to compete with one overexpensive venture, the ferry operators were competing to spend even greater amounts themselves by operating bigger, faster ferries and planning to bring in even bigger and more luxurious boats. The competition has stimulated more passengers with 35 million crossings in 1997 compared with 22 million a decade earlier. The biggest increase is in French and other mainland European visitors crossing *la manche*, who now make up 30 per cent of the traffic. For many travellers the duty-free shopping is a great incentive for the journey. Fares are so low that they can often be saved in the duty-free shop. Lewis Carroll, author of *Alice's Adventures in Wonderland*, could not have invented a market more bizarre – ferry companies spending fortunes to compete with a huge loss-making competitor which will never go away, all supported by allowing people to buy health-damaging drugs duty free!

Stena's Dilemma

Stena Sealink had faced many sea squalls in the channel, but nothing like the competitive squall it was facing now. Was the cross-channel ferry market going to collapse? If so, how could Stena justify the investment that was necessary for it to compete effectively? Should it cut prices to match P & O's bargain basement prices or invest in refurbishing ships to provide a luxury service? Could it cross-subsidize its price by getting passengers to spend more while on board, or should it concentrate on running a basic efficient service like Le Shuttle? Should it invest in new terminals to help it serve the long channel crossings? One option was to invest in radically new ships. There was a chance to leapfrog the competition by buying huge high-speed, high-tech catamarans costing £130 million each. Being the size of a football stadium, the vessels would be the biggest ferries in the world and cruise at 40 knots. They could carry commercial vehicles, trailers, coaches and cars plus 1,500 passengers each. They would have considerable room for seating, bars, restaurants, cafeterias and duty-free shops, and, because of the unique hull construction, be stable in all weathers. Should Stena, like P & O, invest in new terminals with even larger duty-free areas? And what will happen when duty-free ends on 30 June 1999?

Maybe the competition from the Channel Tunnel would reduce. After saying it had got its forecasts wrong, London & Continental Railway, the people who run the rail link between London and the tunnel asked for an extra £1.2 billion subsidy over the next ten years on top of the £1.8 billion already agreed. At 5 million passengers a year, their request was for £100 per passenger over the period. The government refused and threatened to nationalize the rail link, including Eurostar, within 30 days.

QUESTIONS

1. Explain P & O's heavy discounting and Eurostar's pricing strategy.
2. Is Brittany Ferries right in saying the fares make profits impossible?
3. Should Stena Sealink follow P & O's price cutting? What else could it do?
4. Is P & O's discounting consistent with its luxury 'cruise' positioning?
5. What prevents Le Shuttle driving the ferries out by cutting prices? Does Le Shuttle's speed advantage make its victory over the ferries inevitable?
6. Can Stena Sealink get away with charging more than P & O at any time, any place, any way? What strategy should Stena Sealink follow? Should it follow all P & O's moves, follow some, do something completely different or, like Olau Line, get out?

SOURCES: 'Rough waters for P & O', *Marketing Business* (June 1990), p. 4; Charles Batchelor, 'Freight companies to shun the tunnel', *Financial Times* (7 March 1994), p. 7; Tom Burns, 'Madrid–Seville fast rail link heads for profit', *Financial Times* (15 March 1994), p. 2; 'Cross-channel booze: glug glug', *The Economist* (23 April 1994), pp. 30–1; Julie Read, 'Cut-price ferry fare sparks all-out war', *The European* (1–7 July 1994), p. 1; Chris Butler, 'Ferries chart new course for survival', *The European* (1–7 July 1994), p. 19; Claire Murphy, 'A severe case of tunnel vision', *Marketing Week* (2 September 1994), pp. 21–2; Ian Fletcher, 'French sailors move to stop £1 ferry bargain', *Today* (20 September 1994), pp. 1–2; 'Tunnel vision', *EuroBusiness* (October 1994), p. 18; Charles Batchelor, 'Watch out, the drive ahead could be rough', *Financial Times* (3 October 1994), p. 14; Clive Branson, 'The importance of being well connected', *The European* (21–7 October 1994), p. 25; Roderick Oram, 'A stiff one for drink lobby', *Financial Times* (22–3 October 1994), p. 6; Tony Patey, 'Battle of the Channel that breaks every rule', *The European* (20 June 1996) p. 21; Jon Rees, 'That sinking feeling', *Marketing Week* (8 March 1996), pp. 38–9; Jon Rees, 'Ferry operators plan sea-change', *Marketing Week* (26 July 1996), pp. 24–5; Charis Gresser, 'Channel rail link in disarray', *Financial Times* (29 January 1998), p. 1.

Part 6

Promotion

Part Introduction

IN PART SIX WE COVER THE third element of the marketing mix – promotion. We show how organizations communicate and reach their various target markets.

Being able to design and develop a product or service that has all the features that attract customers is one thing. Getting the message across to them, and ultimately capturing or retaining a customer is quite a different matter; consequently, marketers must learn how to communicate effectively with their customers. Chapter 18 shows how to do this and gives an overview of the types of marketing communication or the promotion mix. There is no one best communication tool or approach to use; rather, marketers must employ a combination of tools and co-ordinate their strategies for each.

Chapter 19 addresses three mass communication tools – advertising, sales promotion and public relations efforts. We see how they help to achieve different types of response from consumers. Furthermore, we explore the opportunities and the barriers facing marketers seeking to communicate to customers worldwide.

Moving on from the discussion of indirect, non-personal forms of communication, Chapter 20 examines the role of direct, personal communications – that is, the use of a sales force to reach the firm's customers. Increasingly, the sales force is seen by firms as a source of value creation, not just as order takers. Through them, customer relationships can be forged and sustained. As a result, new forms of sales organization, such as key account management, have arisen to allow firms to maximize the returns from investment in personal selling.

CHAPTER 18
*Integrated Marketing
Communication Strategy*

CHAPTER 19
*Mass Communications:
Advertising, Sales Promotion
and Public Relations*

CHAPTER 20
*Personal Selling and Sales
Management*

PART OVERVIEW CASE
*Bang & Olufsen:
Different by Design*

Integrated Marketing Communication Strategy

CHAPTER OBJECTIVES

After reading this chapter, you should be able to:

- Name and define the four tools of the promotion mix.
- Outline the steps in developing effective marketing communications.
- Explain the methods for setting the promotion budget and factors that affect the design of the promotion mix.
- Identify the major factors that are changing today's marketing communications environment.
- Discuss the process and advantages of integrated marketing communications.

Preview Case

British Home Stores

BRITISH HOME STORES (BHS), THE retailer which is part of the United Kingdom's Storehouse Group, recently embarked on a campaign to revamp its staid image. BHS has long been noted for its good quality and value-for-money range of clothing, household furnishings and appliances, and food. This long-established institution has been a big player in British high streets. The problem, however, is that in the face of increasing high-street competition and retailing innovations in the 1990s, the stores no longer came across as 'exciting' to consumers. A marketing executive at BHS put the problem this way: 'Not enough people get up in the morning and think "I must go to BHS". Shoppers just drift into the store from the high street. Unlike Marks & Spencer, the BHS brand is "too neutral". There appeared to be a big gap between consumers' perception of what the BHS brand offered and the reality – good quality and well-priced products, besides the convenience of its high-street location. When you go in the store it is actually better than you expected!'

To remedy the situation, BHS spent three to four years developing a new image and culture – a young, energetic organization – and defining the store's 'value propositions'. (These moves were all part of the restructuring and recovery of the Storehouse Group itself.) The BHS brand is promoted on three platforms: fashion-moderate products, which are up-to-date but mainstream, not at the cutting edge of fashion; consistent and appropriate quality; and low prices that are attractive to mothers on tight budgets, who are by far the largest group among BHS's customers.

The company undertook a vast brand-building exercise. The retailer's goal was to communicate its revamped positioning to its target market and to attract shoppers to the store.

BHS uses several promotion tools to communicate its new message to its customers. A chief component of its communication programme is TV advertising. The ads are adapted to show each season's clothes and can be extended to other BHS lines (e.g. lighting). In-store 'events', such as beach parties, are staged to display the season's fashions. These are organized in stores around the country to gain local publicity and as a general promotional tool.

The BHS logo has also been revamped. The new logo is a 'more feminine, more fluid' version of the one it replaces and seeks to communicate the feeling of 'excitement and energy' that is to be associated with the brand. To support the repositioning of the BHS brand, the company had to refurbish its stores and replace the old fascias in order to reflect its new image. Not only do the insides of stores display the new logo, but carrier bags and labels also carry it. Moreover, store interiors have been revamped with a new look that communicates the brand's new and fresher image. In-store design shows off merchandise to greater effect and 'allows it to breathe'.

BHS uses advertising to raise consumers' awareness of the BHS brand. The ad campaign is also about elevating the brand in the minds of people to whom it might be neutral. The public relations and sales promotions exercises, like the in-store events, are used to draw consumers into the stores in order for them to see what the store really has to offer. The company also uses other elements in the marketing mix – product quality, the way merchandise is presented in the store, its logo and low price – to communicate its total offering to its target market. BHS has to co-ordinate all these aspects to get the most out of its promotional programme.[1]

QUESTIONS

1. Identify the different forms of communication that BHS uses to reach its target customers.

2. What are the key objectives of these communications tools?

3. Why does BHS use a combination of approaches to communicate with its target customers?

4. How effective do you think is BHS's communications mix?

5. What should BHS do to ensure that all aspects of its communication programme are well co-ordinated?

6. Thinking about the major changes that are occurring in the communications environment (e.g. advances in computer/information technology, growth in direct marketing), how might the retailer exploit recent developments to create effective communications strategies?

promotion mix
The specific mix of advertising, personal selling, sales promotion and public relations that a company uses to pursue its advertising and marketing objectives.

advertising
Any paid form of non-personal presentation and promotion of ideas, goods or services by an identified sponsor.

personal selling
Oral presentation in a conversation with one or more prospective purchasers for the purpose of making sales.

sales promotion
Short-term incentives to encourage purchase or sales of a product or service.

public relations
Building good relations with the company's various publics by obtaining favourable publicity, building up a good 'corporate image', and handling or heading off unfavourable rumours, stories and events. Major PR tools include press relations, product publicity, corporate communications, lobbying and counselling.

Introduction

The questions posed above relate to some of the key issues that marketers must address when designing a marketing communications strategy. Modern marketing calls for more than just developing a good product, pricing it attractively, and making it available to target customers. Companies must also *communicate* with their customers, and what they communicate should not be left to chance.

To communicate well, companies often hire advertising agencies to develop effective ads, sales promotion specialists to design sales-incentive programmes, direct-marketing specialists to develop databases and interact with customers and prospects by mail and telephone, and public relations firms to develop corporate images. They train their salespeople to be friendly, helpful and persuasive. For most companies, the question is not *whether* to communicate, but *how much to spend* and *in what ways*.

A modern company manages a complex marketing communications system (see Figure 18.1). The company communicates with its intermediaries, consumers and various publics. Its intermediaries communicate with their consumers and publics. Consumers have word-of-mouth communication with each other and with other publics. Meanwhile, each group provides feedback to every other group.

A company's total marketing communications mix – called its **promotion mix** – consists of the specific blend of advertising, personal selling, sales promotion and public relations tools that the company uses to pursue its advertising and marketing objectives. Let us define the four main promotion tools:

● **Advertising.** Any paid form of non-personal presentation and promotion of ideas, goods or services by an identified sponsor.

● **Personal selling.** Oral presentation in a conversation with one or more prospective purchasers for the purpose of making sales and building customer relationships.

● **Sales promotion.** Short-term incentives to encourage the purchase or sale of a product or service.

● **Public relations.** Building good relations with the company's various publics by obtaining favourable publicity, building up a good 'corporate image', and handling or heading off unfavourable rumours, stories and events.[2]

In recent years, direct communications with carefully targeted individual consumers to obtain an immediate response are gaining importance as a communication tool. Unlike a salesperson confronting a customer face to face, arguably the most direct sort of marketing, the new direct approaches, typically

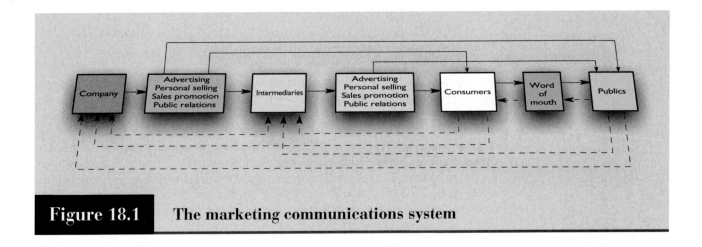

Figure 18.1 | **The marketing communications system**

called **direct marketing**, involve the use of mail, telephone, fax, e-mail and other *non-personal* tools to communicate *directly* with specific consumers or to solicit a direct response. Because of its rising importance, modern marketers have frequently referred to it as the fifth element of the communications mix. However, direct marketing techniques are not just communication devices, they are also *sales channels* in their own right. For example, many companies use direct channels to sell their products. A wide range of products and services, including computers, software, financial services, clothing and household appliances can be purchased by phone, mail and even the Internet.

Within these categories are specific tools. For example, advertising includes print, radio and television broadcast, outdoor and other forms. Personal selling includes sales presentations, fairs and trade shows, and incentive programmes. Sales promotion includes activities such as point-of-purchase displays, premiums, discounts, coupons, competitions, speciality advertising and demonstrations. Direct marketing includes catalogues, telemarketing, fax, the Internet and more. Thanks to technological breakthroughs, people can now communicate through traditional media, such as newspapers, radio, telephone and television, as well as through newer types of media (e.g. fax machines, cellular phones, pagers and computers). The new technologies have encouraged more companies to move from mass communication to more targeted communication and one-to-one dialogue.

At the same time, communication goes beyond these specific promotion tools. The product's design, its price, the shape and colour of its package, and the stores that sell it – *all* communicate something to buyers. Thus, although the promotion mix is the company's primary communication activity, the entire marketing mix – promotion *and* product, price and place – must be co-ordinated for greatest communication impact.

In this chapter, we begin by examining three questions. First, *how does the communication process work?* Second, *what are the main steps in developing effective marketing communication?* Third, *how should the promotion budget and mix be determined?* We then look at recent dramatic changes in marketing communications that have resulted from shifting marketing strategies and advances in computers and information technologies. Finally, we outline the legal, ethical and social responsibility issues in marketing communications. In Chapter 19, we will look at *mass-communication tools* – that is, advertising, sales promotion and public relations. Chapter 20 examines the sales force as a communication and promotion tool. Given the 'hybrid' role of direct marketing, we will review developments in *direct and online marketing* and address the implications for the firm's communications as well as distribution strategies in Chapter 22.

direct marketing
Marketing through various advertising media that interact directly with consumers, generally calling for the consumer to make a direct response.

A View of the Communication Process

Too often, marketing communications focus on overcoming immediate awareness, image or preference problems in the target market. This approach to communication has limitations: It is too short term and costly, and most messages of this nature fall on deaf ears. Today, marketers are moving towards viewing communications as *the management of the customer buying process over time* – that is, from pre-selling through selling, to consuming and post-consumption stages. Because customers differ, the firm's communications programmes need to be developed for specific segments, niches and even individuals. Importantly, given the new interactive communications technologies, companies must ask not only 'How can we reach our customers?', but also 'How can we find ways to let our customers reach us?'

Thus, the communication process should start with an audit of all the potential interactions that target customers may have with the product and company. For example, someone buying a new computer may talk to others, see television commercials, read articles and advertisements in newspapers and magazines, and try out computers in the store. The marketer needs to assess the influence that each of these communications experiences will have at different stages of the buying process. This understanding will help marketers to allocate their communication budget more effectively and efficiently.

To communicate effectively, marketers need to understand how communication works. Communication involves the nine elements shown in Figure 18.2. Two of these elements are the major parties in a communication – the *sender* and the *receiver*. Another two are the essential communication tools – the *message* and the *media*. Four more are primary communication functions – *encoding*, *decoding*, *response* and *feedback*. The latest element is *noise* in the system. We will explain each of these elements using an ad for Hewlett Packard colour copiers.

- *Sender.* The *party sending the message* to another party – in this case, Hewlett Packard..
- *Encoding.* The process of *putting the intended message or thought into symbolic form* – Hewlett Packard's advertising agency assembles words and illustrations into an advertisement that will convey the intended message.
- *Message.* The *set of words, pictures or symbols* that the sender transmits – the actual HP copier ad.
- *Media.* The *communication channels* through which the message moves from sender to receiver – in this case, the specific magazines that Hewlett Packard selects.
- *Decoding.* The process by which the receiver *assigns meaning to the symbols* encoded by the sender – a consumer reads the HP copier ad and interprets the words and illustrations it contains.
- *Receiver.* The *party receiving the message* sent by another party – the home office or business customer who reads the HP copier ad.
- *Response.* The reactions of the receiver after being exposed to the message – any of hundreds of possible responses, such as the customer is more aware of the attributes of HP copiers, actually buys an HP copier or does nothing.
- *Feedback.* The part of the *receiver's response communicated back to the sender* – Hewlett Packard's research shows that consumers like and remember the ad, or consumers write or call HP praising or criticizing the ad or HP's products.

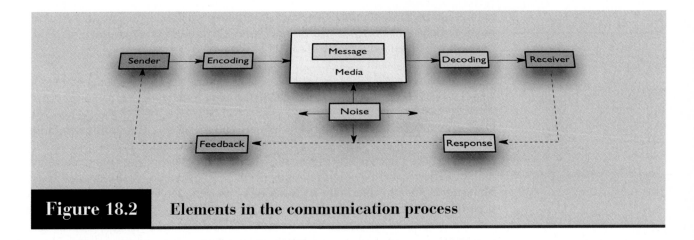

Figure 18.2 **Elements in the communication process**

● *Noise.* The *unplanned static or distortion* during the communication process, which results in the receiver getting a different message than the one the sender sent – for example, the customer is distracted while reading the magazine and misses the HP copier ad or its key points.

For a message to be effective, the sender's encoding process must mesh with the receiver's decoding process. Thus, the best messages consist of words and other symbols that are familiar to the receiver. The more the sender's field of experience overlaps with that of the receiver, the more effective the message is likely to be. Marketing communicators may not always *share* their consumers' field of experience. For example, an advertising copywriter from one social stratum might create an ad for consumers from another stratum – say, blue-collar workers or wealthy business executives. However, to communicate effectively, the marketing communicator must understand the consumer's field of experience.

This model points out the key factors in good communication. Senders need to know what audiences they want to reach and what responses they want. They must be good at encoding messages that take into account how the target audience decodes them. They must send messages through media that reach target audiences and they must develop feedback channels so that they can assess the audience's response to the message.

Steps in Developing Effective Communication

We now examine the steps in developing an effective integrated communications and promotion programme. The marketing communicator must do the following: identify the target audience; determine the communication objectives; design a message; choose the media through which to send the message; and collect feedback to measure the promotion's results. Let us address each of these steps in turn.

Identifying the Target Audience

A marketing communicator starts with a clear target audience in mind. The audience may be potential buyers or current users, those who make the buying decision or those who influence it. The audience may be individuals, groups, special publics or the general public. The target audience will heavily affect the communicator's decisions on *what* will be said, *how* it will be said, *when* it will be said, *where* it will be said and *who* will say it.

Determining the Communication Objectives

Once the target audience has been defined, the marketing communicator must decide what response is sought. Of course, in many cases, the final response is *purchase*. But purchase is the result of a long process of consumer decision making. The marketing communicator needs to know where the target audience now stands and to what state it needs to be moved. To do this he or she must determine whether or not the customer is ready to buy.

The target audience may be in any of six **buyer-readiness stages** – the stages that consumers normally pass through on their way to making a purchase. These stages are *awareness, knowledge, liking, preference, conviction* and *purchase* (see Figure 18.3). They can be described as a *hierarchy of consumer response stages*. The purpose of marketing communication is to move the customer along these stages and ultimately to achieve final purchase.

buyer-readiness stages
The stages that consumers normally pass through on their way to purchase, including awareness, knowledge, liking, preference, conviction and purchase.

● *Awareness*

The communicator must first know how aware the target audience is of the product or organization. The audience may be totally unaware of it, know only its name or know one or a few things about it. If most of the target audience is unaware, the communicator tries to build awareness, perhaps starting with just name recognition. This process can begin with simple messages that repeat the company or product name. For example, when Nissan introduced its Infiniti automobile line, it began with an extensive 'teaser' advertising campaign to create name familiarity. Initial ads for the Infiniti created curiosity and awareness by showing the car's name, but not the car.

● *Knowledge*

The target audience might be aware of the existence of the company or of the product, but not know much more. Nissan may want its target audience to know more about the Infiniti. The company needs to learn how many people in its target audience have little, some or much knowledge about the Infiniti. To create product knowledge Infiniti ads must inform potential buyers of the car's high quality and other innovative features.

● *Liking*

Assuming target audience members *know* the product, how do they *feel* about it? Once potential buyers knew about the Infiniti, Nissan's marketers would want to move them along to the next stage – to develop favourable feelings about the Infiniti. If the audience looks unfavourably on the Infiniti, the communicator has to find out why, and then resolve the problems identified before developing a communications campaign to generate favourable feelings.

● *Preference*

The target audience might *like* the product, but not *prefer* it to others. In this case, the communicator must try to build consumer preference by promoting the

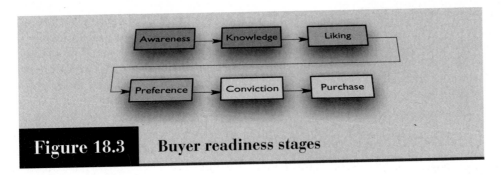

Figure 18.3   **Buyer readiness stages**

product's quality, value and other beneficial features. The communicator can check on the campaign's success by measuring the audience's preferences again after the campaign. If Nissan finds that many potential customers like the Infiniti, but prefer other car brands, it will have to identify those areas where its offerings are not as good as competing deals and where they are better. It must then promote its advantages to build preference among prospective clients, while redressing its weaknesses.

● *Conviction*

A target audience might *prefer* the product, but not develop a *conviction* about buying it. Thus some customers may prefer the Infiniti to other car brands, but may not be absolutely sure that it is what they should buy. The communicator's job is to build conviction that the product is the best one for the potential buyer. Infiniti used a combination of the promotion-mix tools to create preference and conviction. Advertising extolled the Infiniti's advantages over rival brands. Press releases and public relations activities stressed the car's innovative features and performance. Dealer salespeople told buyers about options, value for the price and after-sales service.

● *Purchase*

Finally, some members of the target audience might have *conviction*, but not quite get around to making the *purchase*. Potential Infiniti buyers might have decided to wait for more information or for the economy to improve. The communicator must lead these consumers to take the final step. Actions might include offering special promotional prices, rebates or premiums. Salespeople might call or write to selected customers, inviting them to visit the dealership for a special showing or test drive.

In discussing buyer readiness stages, we have assumed that buyers pass through *cognitive* (awareness, knowledge); *affective* (liking, preference, conviction); and *behavioural* (purchase) stages, in that order. This 'learn–feel–do' sequence is appropriate when buyers have high involvement with a product category and perceive brands in the category to be highly differentiated, as is the case when they purchase a product such as a car. But consumers often follow other sequences. For example, they might follow a 'do–feel–learn' sequence for high-involvement products with little perceived differentiation, such as a central heating system. Still a third sequence is the 'learn–do–feel' sequence, where consumers have low involvement and perceive little differentiation, as is the case when they buy a product such as salt.

  Furthermore, marketing communications alone cannot create positive feelings and purchases for the product. So, for example, the Infiniti must provide superior value to potential buyers. In fact, outstanding marketing communications can actually speed the demise of a poor product. The more quickly potential buyers learn about the poor product, the faster they become aware of its faults. Thus, good marketing communications calls for 'good deeds followed by good words'. Nonetheless, by understanding consumers' buying stages and their appropriate sequence, the marketer can do a better job of planning communications.

Designing a Message

Having defined the desired audience response, the communicator turns to developing an effective message. Ideally, the message should get *Attention*, hold *Interest*, arouse *Desire* and obtain *Action* (a framework known as the AIDA model). In practice, few messages take the consumer all the way from awareness to purchase, but the AIDA framework suggests the desirable qualities of a good message.

In putting the message together, the marketing communicator must decide what to say (*message content*) and how to say it (*message structure and format*).

● *Message Content*

rational appeals
Message appeals that relate to the audience's self-interest and show that the product will produce the claimed benefits; examples are appeals of product quality, economy, value or performance.

The communicator has to figure out an appeal or theme that will produce the desired response. There are three types of appeal: rational, emotional and moral. **Rational appeals** relate to the audience's self-interest. They emphasize the functional benefits – better performance, higher quality, outstanding economy or value – of the product. Thus, in its ads, Mercedes offers automobiles that are 'engineered like no other car in the world', stressing engineering design, performance and safety. One Volvo ad gives 'a whole stack of reasons' for buying the car – it has a rigid passenger safety cage, front and rear absorbing crumple zones, a catalytic converter that always works at peak efficiency, and many more reasons stressing design, safety and economy. When pitching computer systems to business users, IBM salespeople talk about quality, performance, reliability and improved productivity. Rational appeals are particularly appropriate in industrial buying situations and for the purchase of expensive consumer durable products.

emotional appeals
Message appeals that attempt to stir up negative or positive emotions that will motivate purchase; examples are fear, guilt, shame, love, humour, pride and joy appeals.

Emotional appeals attempt to stir up either negative or positive emotions that can motivate purchase. These include fear, guilt and shame appeals that get people to do things they should (brush their teeth, buy new tyres) or to stop doing things they shouldn't (smoke, drink too much, eat fatty foods). For example, a recent Crest ad invoked mild fear when it claimed, 'There are some things you just can't afford to gamble with' (cavities). So did Michelin tyre ads that featured cute babies and suggested 'Because so much is riding on your tyres'.[3] Communicators of industrial goods can also use emotional appeals, as in the case of Alcatel, which played on managers' fear of investing in technology that could become obsolete rapidly. Its ad says: 'Before you invest in the latest technology make sure it has a future.'

Advertisers also use positive emotional appeals such as love, humour, pride, promise of success and joy. Thus some ad themes, such as British Telecom's 'Make someone happy with a phone call', stir a bundle of strong emotions. Ad campaigns for Häagen-Dazs in the United Kingdom equated ice cream with pleasure (foreplay, to be more precise). 'It is the *intense* flavour of the finest ingredients combined with *fresh* cream that is essentially Häagen-Dazs', followed by the strapline: 'Now it's on everybody's lips'. The firm claimed that the ad was a success. During the three months it advertised in newspapers and their supplements, brand awareness doubled while sales in big outlets rose by a third. Over the year, the campaign had boosted sales by 59 per cent.[4]

Before you invest in the latest technology, make sure it has a future.

Remember the furry radio? Back in the Fifties, no self-respecting Doris Day fan would have been without one. The very latest innovations are always the most exciting. But have you noticed that they're sometimes the least enduring? So, when it comes to investing in your business, you want to be certain that the communications technology you choose will be as relevant in 20 years' time as it is today. Which is why we developed the Alcatel 4000 Series, a range of advanced ATM compatible communications systems. Because they evolve with your business, they can be easily upgraded to incorporate new services, as and when you need them. If you'd like further information on business systems with a future, call (33.1) 47.69.48.82 or fax (33.1) 47.69.47.75. **Alcatel. Your reliable partner in communications systems.**

Alcatel Business Systems, Information Service, 54, avenue Jean-Jaurès, 92707 Colombes, France

ALCATEL

This Alcatel ad is a good example of the use of 'fear appeal'. It stresses the upgradability of its innovations, arresting potential buyers' fear of technological obsolescence.

Moral appeals are directed to the audience's sense of what is 'right' and 'proper'. They are often used to urge people to support social causes such as a cleaner environment, better race relations, equal rights for women and aid to the disadvantaged. An example of a moral appeal is a Financial Times and Salomon Brothers ad drawing attention to a family festival and fun run in aid of the Imperial Cancer Research Fund and the Queen Elizabeth's Foundation for Disabled People. The ad informs viewers of the date and time of a fun/entertainment event. Runners taking part in a three-mile competitive run and a one-mile fun run each donate a sum of money to the charities. The ad stresses that the two charities count on the generosity of sponsors to continue their vital work – in the United Kingdom alone, about 2.6 million people are severely disabled; cancer is a disease which affects one in three people and kills one in four. If readers want more information and an entry form, they are invited to complete the reply coupon at the end of the ad or to telephone the event hot line. The advertisement also uses an emotional appeal – concern and sympathy for sufferers – to convey its cause to the target audience.

moral appeals
Message appeals that are directed to the audience's sense of what is right and proper.

● *Message Structure*

The communicator must decide *how* to say it. This requires the communicator to handle three message-structure issues. The first is whether to draw a conclusion or to leave it to the audience. Early research showed that drawing a conclusion was usually more effective where the target audience is less likely to be motivated or may be incapable of arriving at the appropriate conclusion. More recent research, however, suggests that in many cases where the targets are likely to be interested in the product, the advertiser is better off asking questions to stimulate involvement and motivate customers to think about the brand, and then letting them come to their own conclusions.

The second message structure issue is whether to present a one-sided argument (mentioning only the product's strengths), or a two-sided argument (touting the product's strengths while also admitting its shortcomings). Usually, a one-sided argument is more effective in sales presentations – except when audiences are highly educated or likely to hear opposing claims or are negatively disposed.

Here, not-for-profit organizations, such as the United Nations High Commission for Refugees (UNHCR) and companies like The Body Shop use moral and emotional appeals to reach their target audience.

The third message-structure issue is whether to present the strongest arguments first or last. Presenting them first gets strong attention, but may lead to an anti-climactic ending.[5]

● *Message Format*

The communicator also needs a strong *format* for the message. In a print ad, the communicator has to decide on the headline, copy, illustration and colour. To attract attention, advertisers can use: novelty and contrast; eye-catching pictures and headlines; distinctive formats; message size and position; and colour, shape and movement. If the message is to be carried over the radio, the communicator has to choose words, sounds and voices. The 'sound' of an announcer promoting a used car should be different from one promoting quality furniture.

If the message is to be transmitted on television or conveyed in person, then all these elements plus body language have to be planned. Presenters plan their facial expressions, gestures, dress, posture and even hairstyle. If the message is carried on the product or its package, the communicator has to watch texture, scent, colour, size and shape. For example, colour plays an important communication role in food preferences.

When consumers sampled four cups of coffee that had been placed next to brown, blue, red and yellow containers (all the coffee was identical, but the consumers did not know this), 75 per cent felt that the coffee next to the brown container tasted too strong; nearly 85 per cent judged the coffee next to the red container to be the richest; nearly everyone felt that the coffee next to the blue container was mild; and the coffee next to the yellow container was seen as weak.

Thus, if a coffee company wants to communicate that its coffee is rich, it should probably use a red container along with label copy boasting the coffee's rich taste.

Even when an individual is exposed to a message, he or she may pay no attention to the message because it is either boring or irrelevant. The communicator increases the chances of the message attracting the attention of the target audience by taking into consideration the following factors:

- The message must have a practical value to the target audience because individuals are in the market for the product (for example, advertising pension schemes to undergraduates is a waste of time as they are likely to find such policies irrelevant to them for the time being).
- The message must interest the target group.
- The message must communicate new information about the product or brand. Consumers pay more attention to new messages.
- The message must reinforce or help to justify the buyer's recent purchase decisions – if you have recently bought a personal computer, it is likely that you will notice or your attention will be quickly drawn to ads for the PC (the phenomenon is called cognitive dissonance reduction).
- The presentation of the message must be impactful. As explained above, this objective can be achieved by paying attention to message formats and stressing creativity in the way the copy, artwork/illustrations and physical layout or presentation are delivered.

While advertisers' basic aim is to get their ads noticed, they must be sensitive to, and comply with, codes of practice operated by the industry watchdogs or country regulators. Messages should be designed to create maximum impact but, at the same time, not cause public offence and irritation (see Marketing Highlight 18.1).

● *Selecting the Message Source*

Studies show that the message's impact on the target audience is also affected by how the audience views the communicator. The credibility and attractiveness of the **message source** – the company, the brand name, the spokesperson for the brand or the actor in the ad who endorses the product – must therefore be considered.

Messages delivered by highly credible sources are more persuasive. Pharmaceutical firms want doctors to tell about their products' benefits because doctors rank high on expertise in their field, so they have high credibility. Many food companies promote to doctors, dentists and other healthcare experts to motivate these professionals to recommend their products to patients. For example, Sensodyne Toothpaste has, for years, promoted the product in dental surgeries, and ads use endorsements by dental practitioners to persuade target users to adopt the brand. However, the expert loses credibility if the audience believes the person is being paid to make product claims. To remain credible, the

message source
The company, the brand name, the salesperson of the brand, or the actor in the ad who endorses the product.

Communications: The Fine Line Between Attraction and Irritation

Marketing Highlight 18.1

Very few advertisers set out deliberately to trick, mislead, insult or offend the public. Those that do, face a backlash from consumers and other parties, or find themselves debarred at source from the means to publicize their messages further because the media reject the ads that conflict with a country's codes of advertising practices.

Teasers: Good Campaigns Get the Punters Talking, a Bad One Attracts Complaints

Advertisers acknowledge that getting viewers to solve a puzzle in an advertisement is fair game in advertising. However, campaigns can backfire. Britvic Soft Drinks aired a 'Still Tango' ad which appealed to consumers to report any sightings of an apparently unlicensed product in the ad. Almost 30,000 consumers responded, only to be told that it was all a joke – they'd been 'Tango'd'! Sixty-three of those 'Tango'd' were so annoyed that they complained to the Independent Television Commission (ITC), which accused Britvic and its agency of undermining the credibility and authority of the medium – TV – and misleading consumers. People felt used, expressing irritation with the company for playing a prank on them. Britvic's teaser grabbed the audience's attention, but it ended up getting the wrong kind of publicity!

A campaign of a different kind caused uproar in Spain. An agency in Madrid sent out love letters to 50,000 young mothers in a direct-marketing campaign for Fiat's Cinquento car. A second batch of letters was then sent revealing the Cinquento as the secret admirer. Rather than this being seen as an amusing piece of junk mail, it caused a storm of protest. The agency claimed the reaction was mainly positive. The Spanish Women's Institute denounced the campaign. Some women were so troubled they were scared to leave the house.

There is a fine dividing line between attracting and irritating consumers. For most of the time, people are prepared to enjoy a light-hearted

puzzle. A little intrigue adds interest. But the intrigue can only be stretched so far.

Bad Taste Ads?

Established brands using shock tactics can also do as much damage, although observers argue that it is really a question of what is socially intolerable and a matter of taste. Recently, charities and pressure groups have inspired a considerable amount of criticism.

An RSPCA (Royal Society for the Prevention of Cruelty to Animals) campaign drew attention to the plight of horses exported for consumption by using a harrowing image of a dead pony hanging from a hook. The advertising watchdog, the ASA, upheld complaints against the ad, not because it had any wish to frustrate the RSPCA's efforts to enlighten the public, but because the visual image used was deemed misleading and grossly offensive. The advertisement did not successfully reflect either the argument advanced in the text or the way live horses were actually herded for transportation.

A British Rail (BR) newspaper advertisement featuring 12 yellow condoms arranged in a circle against a blue background was severely criticized for being 'grossly irresponsible in its encouragement of promiscuity', and for 'denigrating the European Union flag', after the ASA received 164 complaints. The ad was intended to boost BR's Young Person's European rail card sales. Its cap-

UNITED COLORS OF BENETTON.

Benetton has backed away from its confrontational pitch after almost universal criticism.

tion was 'Inter-Rail. You've got the rest of your life to be good' and supported the European Commission's 'Europe Against AIDS' initiative. BR denied that the ad encouraged promiscuity. Rather it was consistent with research evidence – that a significant proportion of 18–25-year-olds had sexual encounters without a condom while on holiday. BR was urged to avoid further advertisements in that style!

More noteworthy is the controversy that has dogged Italian clothing designer and manufacturer Benetton's 'United Colors' ads throughout the late 1980s and mid-1990s. In 1989 public opinion in the United States forced it to withdraw those showing a black woman breastfeeding a white child. In 1991 a blood-smeared newborn baby ad received more than 800 complaints to the UK's ASA, criticizing Benetton for provoking public distress and outrage, and displaying a conspicuous disregard for the sensitivities of the public. Benetton agreed to withdraw the advertisement. Magazine publishers and poster contractors supported the ASA in its ruling against Benetton by refusing space to the advertiser. Other Benetton ads – a black child depicting a devil contrasting with a white cherub, an AIDS victim, a baby's bottom stamped 'HIV positive', the Queen of England as a black woman, the bloodied uniform of a dead Bosnian soldier, a nun kissing a priest, a black stallion mounting a white mare – consistently created furore. Benetton argues that the campaigns were not about pushing sales. Nor were they intended to insult or hurt. Rather they were designed to capture people's interest, promote tolerance and provoke reflection.

There is little doubt that Benetton's shocking ads succeeded in creating worldwide publicity and kept its name on everybody's lips. But was it good or bad publicity? Over the years, its campaigns have been rejected in a number of coun-

tries. For example, in 1995 some ads were banned in Germany following protests from the firm's retailers, and three of Belgium's largest billboard operators refused to carry the 'black horse on white horse' poster in August 1996.

More recently, Benetton has been changing its style, dropping its 'shock' posters in favour of more subtle ways of communicating its business philosophy to target audiences. The company is opening up shops all over the world. But its new shops are no ordinary outlets. One in Milan, for example, is staffed by penniless north African immigrants. And there is a common thread – shops in the Bosnian capital of Sarajevo, in Siberia, Albania, Estonia, Ukraine, Libya, Cameroon and Croatia. Benetton's publicity strategy is 'to make consumers think', says the controversial Oliviero Toscani, Benetton's freelance photographer and advertising guru. Benetton's new-image shops do just that. The one in Milan was a response to European Union moves to restrict immigration to Europe. Benetton's message remains the same as in its 'shock' ads. But now, these shops give Benetton another channel to make challenging gestures. The big question is: Will this help to sell lots and lots of clothes?

SOURCES: 'Brands that backfired badly', *The European* (25–31 March, 1994), p. 22; Claire Murphy, 'When the teasers become unbearable', *Marketing Week* (15 July, 1994), p. 21; Diane Summers, 'BR's condom-flag advert is labelled "irresponsible"', *Financial Times* (5 October 1994), p. 9; Sarah Cunningham, 'Benetton to drop its shock tactics', *The European* (8–14 July 1994), p. 23; 'As you sow, so shall you reap' and 'Benetton cover story', *Marketing Week* (3 February 1995), pp. 5 and 21 respectively; Francine Cunningham, 'Mounting pressure', *The European* (15–21 August 1996), p. 15; Stephanie Bentley, 'Benetton risks fresh outrage', *Marketing Week* (13 September 1996), p. 9.

source must be perceived by the target audience as being an expert where the product is concerned and trustworthy: that is, objective and honest in his or her opinion of the benefits claimed for the product.

Marketers also use celebrities to speak for their products. For example, when the pan-European television station MTV launched its UK-only music channel VH-1 in September 1994, it chose a cast of UK celebrities who would appeal to its target audience of 'older' viewers. Ads featured, among others, fashion designer Bruce Oldfield, England rugby captain Will Carling and Anglo-Norwegian television presenter Mariella Frostrup.[6]

Other notable examples are Michael Jackson, who was the star in Pepsi-Cola's ad, and O.J. Simpson for the car rental firm Hertz. Celebrities are effective when they personify a key product attribute, but there can be a backlash, as in the case of both Jackson and Simpson, when they are caught up in unsavoury publicity, which tarnishes their credibility and esteem with the audience.

Attractiveness is associated with the prestige of the source, his or her similarity with the receiver, or the physical or personal attractiveness of the source. It is also likely that the more attractive the source, the more he or she will be liked by the audience. It is therefore not surprising that many advertisers use well-known film stars, fashion models and top sports people to endorse their products.

Choosing Media

The communicator must now select *channels of communication*. There are two broad types of communication channel: *personal* and *non-personal*.

● *Personal Communication Channels*

personal communication channels
Channels through which two or more people communicate directly with each other, including face to face, person to audience, over the telephone, or through the mail.

In **personal communication channels**, two or more people communicate directly with each other. They might communicate face to face, over the telephone, through the mail or even through an Internet 'chat'. Personal communication channels are effective because they allow for personal addressing and feedback.

Some personal communication channels are controlled directly by the communicator, as in the case of company salespeople who contact buyers in the target market. Other personal communications about the product may reach buyers through channels not directly controlled by the company. These might include independent experts – consumer advocates, consumer buying guides and others – making statements to target buyers. Or, they might be neighbours, friends, family members and associates talking to target buyers. This last channel, known as **word-of-mouth influence**, has considerable effect in many product areas.

word-of-mouth influence
Personal communication about a product between target buyers and neighbours, friends, family members and associates.

Here, Anglo-Norwegian television presenter, Mariella Frostrup, takes part in VH-1's launch campaign to promote the new music channel in Britain.

Personal influence carries great weight for products that are expensive, risky or highly visible. For example, buyers of cars and major appliances often go beyond mass-media sources to seek the opinions of knowledgeable people.

Companies can take several steps to put personal communication channels to work for them:

● They can devote extra effort to selling their products to well-known people or companies, which may, in turn, influence others to buy.

● They can create *opinion leaders* – people whose opinions are sought by others – by supplying certain people with the product on attractive terms. For example, companies can work through community members, such as local radio personalities and leaders of local organizations.

● They can use influential people in their advertisements or develop advertising that has high 'conversation value'.

● Finally, the firm can work to manage word-of-mouth communications by finding out what consumers are saying to others, by taking appropriate actions to satisfy consumers and correct problems, and by helping consumers seek information about the firm and its products.[7]

● *Non-Personal Communication Channels*

Non-personal communication channels are media that carry messages without personal contact or feedback. They include major media, atmospheres and events. Important **media** consist of print media (newspapers, magazines, direct mail); broadcast media (radio, television); and display media (billboards, signs, posters). **Atmospheres** are designed environments that create or reinforce the buyer's leanings towards buying a product. Thus lawyers' offices and banks are designed to communicate confidence and other factors that might be valued by their clients. **Events** are occurrences staged to communicate messages to target audiences. For example, public relations departments arrange press conferences, grand openings, shows and exhibits, public tours and other events to communicate with specific audiences.

Non-personal communication affects buyers directly. In addition, using mass media often affects buyers indirectly by causing more personal communication. Communications first flow from television, magazines and other mass media to opinion leaders and then from these opinion leaders to others. Thus opinion leaders step between the mass media and their audiences and carry messages to people who are less exposed to media. This suggests that mass communicators affect attitudes and behaviour through a *two-step flow-of-communication process*.[8]

The two-step flow concept challenges the notion that people's buying is affected by a 'trickle-down' of opinions and information from higher social classes. Because people mostly interact with others in their own social class, they pick up their fashion and other ideas from people *like themselves*, who are opinion leaders. The two-step flow concept also suggests that mass communicators should aim their messages directly at opinion leaders, letting them carry the message to others. Pharmaceutical firms direct their new drugs promotions at the most influential doctors and medical experts first – the 'thought leaders' in the profession; if they are persuaded, their opinions have an impact upon the new product's acceptance by others in the field. Thus opinion leaders extend the influence of the mass media. Or, they may alter the message or not carry the message, thus acting as gatekeepers.

non-personal communication channels
Media that carry messages without personal contact or feedback, including media, atmospheres and events.

media
Non-personal communications channels including print media (newspapers, magazines, direct mail); broadcast media (radio, television); and display media (billboards, signs, posters).

atmospheres
Designed environments that create or reinforce the buyer's leanings towards consumption of a product.

events
Occurrences staged to communicate messages to target audiences; examples are news conferences and grand openings.

Collecting Feedback

After sending the message, the communicator must research its effect on the target audience. This involves asking the target audience members whether they remember the message, how many times they saw it, what points they recall, how they felt about the message, and their past and present attitudes towards the product and company. The communicator would also like to measure behaviour resulting in the message – how many people bought a product, talked to others about it or visited the store.

Figure 18.4 shows an example of feedback measurement for two hypothetical brands. Looking at Brand A, we find that 80 per cent of the total market is aware of it, that 60 per cent of those aware of it have tried it, but that only 20 per cent of those who tried it were satisfied. These results suggest that although the communication programme is creating *awareness*, the product fails to give consumers the *satisfaction* they expect. Therefore, the company should try to improve the product while staying with the successful communication programme. In contrast, only 40 per cent of the total market is aware of Brand B, only 30 per cent of those aware of Brand B have tried it, but 80 per cent of those who have tried it are satisfied. In this case, the communication programme needs to be stronger to take advantage of the brand's power to obtain satisfaction.

Setting the Total Promotion Budget and Mix

We have looked at the steps in planning and sending communications to a target audience. But how does the company decide on the total *promotion budget* and its division among the major promotional tools to create the *promotion mix*? We now look at these questions.

Setting the Total Promotion Budget

One of the hardest marketing decisions facing a company is how much to spend on promotion. John Wanamaker, an American department store magnate, once said: 'I know that half of my advertising is wasted, but I don't know which half. I spent $2 million for advertising, and I don't know if that is half enough or twice too much.' It is not surprising, therefore, that industries and companies vary widely in how much they spend on promotion. Promotion spending may be 20–30 per cent of sales in the cosmetics industry and only 5–10 per cent in the industrial machinery industry. Within a given industry, both low and high spenders can be found.

How does a company decide on its promotion budget? There are four common methods used to set the total budget for advertising: the affordable method, the percentage-of-sales method, the competitive-parity method and the objective-and-task method.[9]

affordable method
Setting the promotion budget at the level management thinks the company can afford.

● *Affordable Method*

A common 'rule-of-thumb' used by many companies is the **affordable method**: they set the promotion budget at the level they think the company can afford. They start with total revenues, deduct operating expenses and capital outlays, and then devote some portion of the remaining funds to advertising.

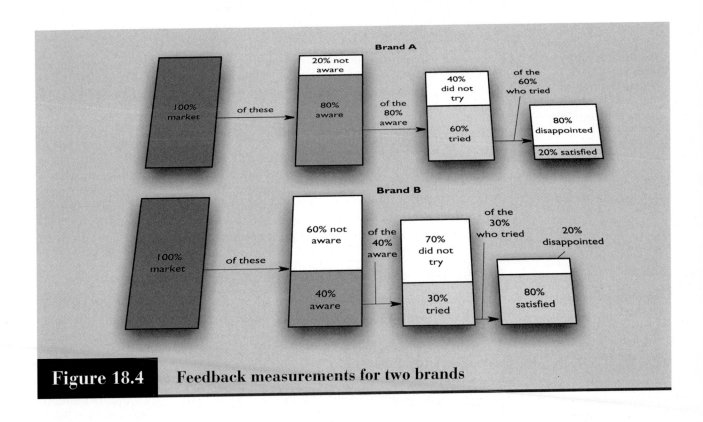

Figure 18.4   **Feedback measurements for two brands**

Unfortunately, this method of setting budgets completely ignores the effect of promotion on sales. It tends to place advertising last among spending priorities, even in situations where advertising is critical to the firm's success. It leads to an uncertain annual promotion budget, which makes long-range market planning difficult. Although the affordable method can result in overspending on advertising, it more often results in underspending.

● *Percentage-of-Sales Method*

In the **percentage-of-sales method**, marketers set their promotion budget at a certain percentage of current or forecast sales. Or they budget a percentage of the sales price. Automotive companies usually budget a fixed percentage for promotion based on the planned car price. Fast-moving consumer goods companies usually set it at some percentage of current or anticipated sales.

The percentage-of-sales method has advantages. It is simple to use and helps managers think about the relationship between promotion spending, selling price and profit per unit. The method supposedly creates competitive stability because competing firms tend to spend about the same percentage of their sales on promotion.

Despite these claimed advantages, however, there is little to justify the method. It wrongly views sales as the *cause* of promotion rather than as the *result*.[10] The budget is based on availability of funds rather than on opportunities. It may prevent the increased spending sometimes needed to turn around falling sales. It fails to consider whether a higher or lower level of spending would be more profitable. Because the budget varies with year-to-year sales, long-range planning is difficult. Finally, the method does not provide any basis for choosing a *specific* percentage, except what has been done in the past or what competitors are doing.

percentage-of-sales method
Setting the promotion budget at a certain percentage of current or forecast sales or as a percentage of the sales price.

● *Competitive-Parity Method*

competitive-parity method
Setting the promotion budget to match competitors' outlays.

Other companies use the **competitive-parity method**, setting their promotion budgets to match competitors' outlays. They watch competitors' advertising or get industry promotion-spending estimates from publications or trade associations, and then set their budgets based on the industry average.

Two arguments support this method. First, competitors' budgets represent the collective wisdom of the industry. Second, spending what competitors spend helps prevent promotion wars. Unfortunately, neither argument is valid. There are no grounds for believing that the competition has a better idea of what a company should be spending on promotion than does the company itself. Companies differ greatly, in terms of market opportunities and profit margins, and each has its own special promotion needs. Finally, there is no evidence that budgets based on competitive parity prevent promotion wars.

● *Objective-and-Task Method*

objective-and-task method
Developing the promotion budget by (1) defining specific objectives; (2) determining the tasks that must be performed to achieve these objectives; and (3) estimating the costs of performing these tasks. The sum of these costs is the proposed promotion budget.

The most logical budget-setting method is the **objective-and-task method**, whereby the company sets its promotion budget based on what it wants to accomplish with promotion. The method entails: (1) defining specific objectives; (2) determining the tasks needed to achieve these objectives; and (3) estimating the costs of performing these tasks. The sum of these costs is the proposed promotion budget.

The objective-and-task method forces management to spell out its assumptions about the relationship between amount spent and promotion results. But it is also the most difficult method to use. Managers have to set sales and profit targets and then work back to what tasks must be performed to achieve desired goals. Often it is hard to figure out which specific tasks will achieve specific objectives. For example, suppose Sony wants 95 per cent awareness for its latest camcorder model during the six-month introductory period. What specific advertising messages and media schedules would Sony need in order to attain this objective? How much would these messages and media schedules cost? Sony management must consider such questions, even though they are hard to answer. By comparing the campaign cost with expected profit gains, the financial viability of the promotions campaign can be determined.

The main advantage of this method is that it forces managers to define their communication objectives, to determine the extent to which each objective will be met using selected promotion tools and the financial implications of alternative communication programmes.

Setting the Promotion Mix

The company must divide the total promotion budget among the main promotion tools – advertising, personal selling, sales promotion and public relations. It may also have to decide just how much of its promotions will involve direct marketing. It must blend the promotion tools carefully into a co-ordinated *promotion mix*. Companies within the same industry differ greatly in how they design their promotion mixes. For example, Avon spends most of its promotion funds on personal selling and catalogue marketing, whereas Revlon spends heavily on consumer advertising. Electrolux sells most of its vacuum cleaners door to door, whereas Hoover relies more on advertising and promotion to retailers.

Companies are always looking for ways to improve promotion by replacing one promotion tool with another that will do the same job more economically.

Many companies have replaced a portion of their field sales activities with telephone sales and direct mail. Other companies have increased their sales promotion spending in relation to advertising to gain quicker sales.

Designing the promotion mix is even more complex when one tool must be used to promote another. Thus when British Airways decides to offer air miles for flying with the company (a sales promotion), it has to run ads to inform the public. When Lever Brothers uses a consumer advertising and sales promotion campaign to back a new washing powder, it has to set aside money to promote this campaign to the resellers to win their support.

Many factors influence the marketer's choice of promotion tools. We now look at these factors.

● *The Nature of Each Promotion Tool*

Marketers have to understand the unique characteristics and the costs of each promotion tool in deciding the promotion mix. Let us examine each of the major tools.

ADVERTISING. The many forms of advertising make it hard to generalize about its unique qualities. However, several qualities can be noted:

- Advertising can reach masses of geographically dispersed buyers at a low cost per exposure.
- Because of advertising's public nature, consumers tend to view advertised products as standard and legitimate – buyers know that purchasing the product will be understood and accepted publicly.
- Advertising enables the seller to repeat a message many times, and it lets the buyer receive and compare the messages of various competitors.
- Large-scale advertising by a seller says something positive about the seller's size, popularity and success.
- Advertising is also very expensive, allowing the company to dramatize its products through the artful use of print, sound and colour.
- On the one hand, advertising can be used to build up a long-term image for a product (such as Coca-Cola ads). On the other hand, advertising can trigger quick sales (as when a department store advertises a weekend sale).
- Advertising can reach masses of geographically spread-out buyers at a low cost per exposure.

Advertising also has some shortcomings:

- Although it reaches many people quickly, advertising is impersonal and cannot be as persuasive as company salespeople.
- Advertising is only able to carry on a one-way communication with the audience, and the audience does not feel that it has to pay attention or respond.
- In addition, advertising can be very costly. Although some advertising forms, such as newspaper and radio advertising, can be done on smaller budgets, other forms, such as network TV advertising, require very large budgets.

PERSONAL SELLING. Personal selling is the most effective tool at certain stages of the buying process, particularly in building up buyers' preferences, convictions and actions. Compared to advertising, personal selling has several unique qualities:

Promotions for Children: Can Childish Things Build Sales and Brand Loyalty?

Marketing Highlight 18.2

Many consumer-goods companies consciously target their sales promotions at kids. They argue that it is great for building sales and loyalty. Manufacturers also agree that children are not easy targets. They are fickle, so it is crucial for the firm to 'strike the right note', while avoiding venturing too far into the delicate area of 'pester power'. Parents are all too familiar with pester power – the child's demand for the latest craze, be it a food or toy, that has been hyped on television. Observers argue that, in the long run, it is the fun promotions that are educational and offer *real value* to target consumers which will build brand loyalty.

Creating Brand Loyalty

One of the most successful kids' crazes in recent years has been dinosaurs – Dino stickers, Dino cups, Dino cards, Dino games, Dino crisps, Dino biscuits – all stalked supermarket shelves. (Remember Ninja Turtles? Well, the story is very much the same, although parents were spared Ninja Turtle crisps and biscuits!) The Spielberg blockbuster *Jurassic Park* was partly responsible, but manufacturers and merchandisers have also deliberately focused upon kids' interest in the dinosaur itself – they learn about dinosaurs at school, how they lived and the mystery of their extinction. McDonald's, the restaurant chain, was one of the many big names which signed up for a themed promotion, where kids could collect all six of its *Jurassic Park* cups. McDonald's argues that 'children are very finicky and anything that is of the moment will interest them, ... this means you will have to be on top of the trends'. McDonald's, however, is a consistent investor in promotions, as reflected in its long-standing 'Happy Meals' offer for children. The challenge lies in maintaining the appeal of the offers, which calls for creativity in value creation.

Sometimes, authorities can get in the way of booms. In Israel, consumers were urged to boy-cott food companies mounting such promotions because dinosaurs were ruled as not kosher. Moreover, they died 65 million years ago, so the rabbinical authorities decreed that they could never have existed as the world was created only 5,753 years ago.

It is difficult to decide whether the children themselves create the trends or simply follow them. Nevertheless, most promoters agree that promotions linked to current crazes have a superior chance of success, so long as they follow trends discriminatingly and ensure that they do not conflict with the product.

Backing Up Promotions

Jacob's, a biscuit manufacturer, joined the dinosaur boom and successfully launched dinosaur biscuits throughout Europe. The biscuits were promoted on television and in cinemas, and the company also sponsored a dinosaur exhibition at London's Alexandra Park. Extensive back-up is often required to build awareness for the promotion as well as to maintain the momentum over its duration.

In the United Kingdom, Rayner Burgess invested in a mix of promotional tools for Crusha, its milk drink – PR, sales promotions and competitions in women's magazines and youth press, and samplings at the Milk Marketing Board and National Dairy Council roadshows around the country.

What Appeals to Children?

T-shirts seem to be a big hit. Crusha offered T-shirts that changed design when worn, which reported a redemption of 250 per cent higher than any previous offer it promoted. Parents liked the product as it encouraged kids to drink milk. The promotion also added genuine value to the product – kids do not just want instant appeal with no substance. Walkers (crisps) offered Looney Tunes T-shirts, which also worked because they were made relevant and desirable by picking up one of the most popular characters within the Looney Tunes portfolio, the Tasmanian Devil, and positioning it as the Big Taz T. The T-shirt itself was promoted on design and quality. Even the colour was carefully chosen – kids prefer coloured T-shirts to white.

Experts suggest that other items like stickers and models retain popularity. If these also leak into the current crazes, they have a good chance of success. Although kids still prefer traditional items, practitioners draw attention to two main considerations when planning sales promotions for children. First, children are usually more comfortable with modern technology than their parents are, so the promoter must avoid patronizing them. Secondly, children enjoy the challenge of being required to make some effort (e.g. participate in competitions, or patiently collect tokens). Parents, on the other hand, may find it hard to summon the energy for such tasks, but can find the motivation if the effort is worth it (e.g. educational, enthuses the child) and offers genuine value. Thus, childish things can build sales and loyalty but it's not child's play.

SOURCE: Louella Miles, 'Childish things', *Marketing Business* (December–January 1993), pp. 36–8.

- It involves personal interaction between two or more people, so each person can observe the other's needs and characteristics and make quick adjustments.
- Personal selling also allows all kinds of relationships to spring up, ranging from a matter-of-fact selling relationship to a deep personal friendship. The effective salesperson keeps the customer's interests at heart in order to build a long-term relationship.
- Finally, with personal selling the buyer usually feels a greater need to listen and respond, even if the response is a polite 'no thank you'.

These unique qualities come at a cost, however. A sales force requires a longer-term commitment than does advertising – advertising can be turned on and off, but sales force size is harder to change. Personal selling is also the company's most expensive promotion tool, costing industrial companies an average of almost £200 per sales call.

SALES PROMOTION.   Sales promotion includes a wide assortment of tools – coupons, contests, price reductions, premium offers, free goods and others – all of which have many unique qualities:

- They attract consumer attention and provide information that may lead to a purchase.
- They offer strong incentives to purchase by providing inducements or contributions that give additional value to consumers.
- Moreover, sales promotions invite and reward quick response. Whereas advertising says 'buy our product', sales promotion offers incentives to consumers to 'buy it now'.

Companies use sales promotion tools to create a stronger and quicker response. Sales promotion can be used to dramatize product offers and to boost sagging sales. Sales promotion effects are usually short-lived, however, and are not effective in building long-run brand preference. To work, manufacturers must carefully plan the sales promotion campaign and offer target customers genuine value. Only then will they enhance perceived brand image, build sales and maintain customer loyalty (see Marketing Highlight 18.2).

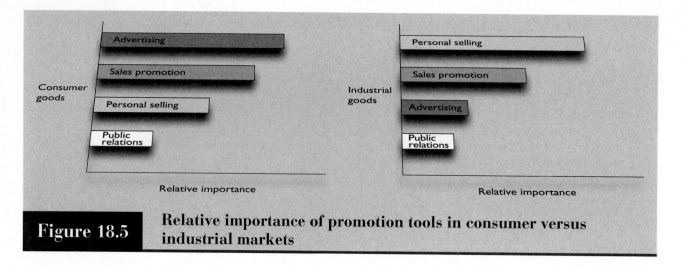

Figure 18.5 Relative importance of promotion tools in consumer versus industrial markets

PUBLIC RELATIONS. Public relations or PR offers several unique qualities. It is all those activities that the organization does to communicate with target audiences which are not directly paid for.

● PR is very believable: news stories, features and events seem more real and convincing to readers than ads do.

● Public relations can reach many prospects who avoid salespeople and advertisements, since the message gets to the buyers as 'news' rather than as a sales-directed communication.

● And, like advertising, PR can dramatize a company or product. The Body Shop is one of the few international companies that have used public relations as a more effective alternative to mass TV advertising.

Marketers tend to underuse public relations or to use it as an afterthought. Yet a well-thought-out public relations campaign used with other promotion-mix elements can be very effective and economical.

DIRECT MARKETING. Although there are many forms of direct marketing – direct mail, telemarketing, electronic marketing, online marketing and others – they all share four distinctive characteristics.

● Direct marketing is non-public as the message is normally addressed to a specific person.

● Direct marketing is immediate and customized, so messages can be prepared quickly and tailored to appeal to specific customers.

● Direct marketing is interactive: it allows a dialogue between the communicator and the consumer, and messages can be altered depending on the consumer's response.

Thus, direct marketing is well suited to highly targeted marketing efforts and to building one-to-one relationships.

● Factors in Setting the Promotion Mix

Companies consider many factors when developing their promotion mixes: namely, the type of product/market, the use of a push or pull strategy, the buyer-readiness stage and the product life-cycle stage.

"I don't know who you are.
I don't know your company.
I don't know your company's product.
I don't know what your company stands for.
I don't know your company's customers.
I don't know your company's record.
I don't know your company's reputation.
Now–what was it you wanted to sell me?"

MORAL: Sales start **before** your salesman calls–with business publication advertising.

McGRAW-HILL MAGAZINES
BUSINESS•PROFESSIONAL•TECHNICAL

Advertising can play a dramatic role in industrial marketing, as shown in this classic McGraw-Hill ad.

TYPE OF PRODUCT/MARKET.   The importance of different promotional tools varies between consumer and business markets (see Figure 18.5). Consumer-goods companies usually put more of their funds into advertising, followed by sales promotion, personal selling and then public relations. Advertising is relatively more important in consumer markets because there are a larger number of buyers, purchases tend to be routine, and emotions play a more important role in the purchase-decision process. In contrast, industrial-goods companies put most of their funds into personal selling, followed by sales promotion, advertising and public relations. In general, personal selling is used more heavily with expensive and risky goods, and in markets with fewer and larger sellers.

Although advertising is less important than sales calls in business markets, it still plays an important role. Advertising can build product awareness and knowledge, develop sales leads and reassure buyers. Similarly, personal selling can add a lot to consumer goods marketing efforts. It is simply not the case that 'salespeople put products on shelves and advertising takes them off'. Well-trained consumer-goods salespeople can sign up more dealers to carry a particular brand, convince them to give more shelf space and urge them to use special displays and promotions.

PUSH VERSUS PULL STRATEGY.   The promotional mix is influenced by whether the company chooses a *push* or *pull* strategy. Figure 18.6 contrasts the two strategies. A **push strategy** involves 'pushing' the product through distribution channels to final consumers. The firm directs its marketing activities (primarily personal selling and trade promotion) towards channel members to induce them to carry the product and to promote it to final consumers. Using a **pull strategy**, the producer directs its marketing activities (primarily advertising and

push strategy
A promotion strategy that calls for using the sales force and trade promotion to push the product through channels. The producer promotes the product to wholesalers, the wholesalers promote to retailers, and the retailers promote to consumers.

pull strategy
A promotion strategy that calls for spending a lot on advertising and consumer promotion to build up consumer demand. If the strategy is successful, consumers will ask their retailers for the product, the retailers will ask the wholesalers, and the wholesalers will ask the producers.

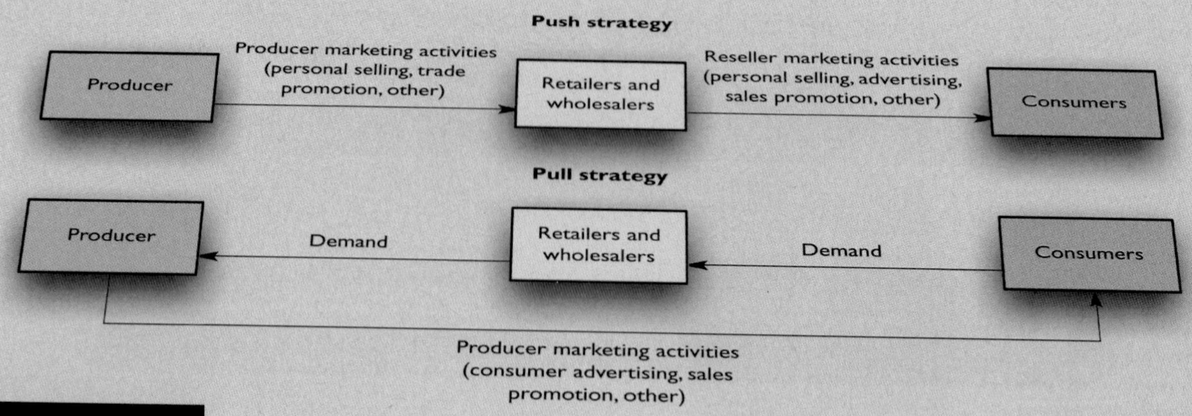

Push strategy

Producer → Producer marketing activities (personal selling, trade promotion, other) → Retailers and wholesalers → Reseller marketing activities (personal selling, advertising, sales promotion, other) → Consumers

Pull strategy

Producer ← Demand ← Retailers and wholesalers ← Demand ← Consumers

Producer marketing activities (consumer advertising, sales promotion, other)

Figure 18.6   **Push versus pull promotion strategy**

consumer promotion) towards final consumers to induce them to buy the product. If the pull strategy is effective, consumers will then demand the product from channel members, which will in turn demand it from producers. Thus under a pull strategy, consumer demand 'pulls' the product through the channels.

Some small industrial-goods companies use only push strategies; some direct-marketing companies use only pull. However, most large companies use some combination of both. For example, Lever Brothers uses mass-media advertising to pull consumers to its products and a large sales force and trade promotions to push its products through the channels.

In recent years, consumer-goods companies have been decreasing the pull portions of their promotion mixes in favour of more push. There are a number of reasons behind this shift in promotion strategy. One is that mass-media campaigns have become more expensive and many companies in Europe, the United States and Japan have cut back due to recessionary pressures over the early 1990s. Many firms have also found advertising less effective in recent years. Companies are increasing their segmentation efforts and tailoring their marketing programmes more narrowly, making national advertising less suitable than local-ized retailer promotions. In these days of heavy brand extensions and me-too products, many companies are finding it difficult to feature meaningful product differentiations in advertising. Instead, they differentiate their brands through price reductions, premium offers, coupons and other promotions aimed at the trade.

The growing strength of retailers is also a key factor speeding the shift from pull to push. Big retail chains in Europe and the United States have greater access to product sales and profit information. They have the power to demand and get what they want from suppliers. And what they want is margin improvements – that is, more push. Mass advertising bypasses them on its way to the consumers, but push promotion benefits them directly. Consumer promotions give retailers an immediate sales boost and cash from trade allowances pads retailer profits. So, manufacturers are compelled to use push promotions just to obtain good shelf space and advertising support from their retailers.

However, reckless use of push promotion leads to fierce price competition and a continual spiral of price slashing and margin erosion, leaving less money to invest in the product R & D, packaging and advertising that is required to improve and maintain long-run consumer preference and loyalty. Robbing the advertising budget to pay for more sales promotion could mortgage a brand's long-term future for short-term gains. While push strategies will remain important, particularly in packaged-goods marketing, companies that find the best mix between the two – consistent advertising to build long-run brand value and consumer preference and sales promotion to create short-run trade support and consumer excitement – are most likely to win the battle for loyal and satisfied customers.[11]

BUYER-READINESS STAGE. The effects of the promotional tools vary for the different buyer-readiness stages. Advertising, along with public relations, plays the leading role in the awareness and knowledge stages, more important than that played by 'cold calls' from salespeople. Customer liking, preference and conviction are more affected by personal selling, which is closely followed by advertising. Finally, closing the sale is mostly done with sales calls and sales promotion. Clearly, advertising and public relations are the most cost effective at the early stages of the buyer decision process, while personal selling, given its high costs, should focus on the later stages of the customer buying process.

PRODUCT LIFE-CYCLE STAGE. The effects of different promotion tools also vary with stages of the product life cycle. In the introduction stage, advertising and public relations are good for producing high awareness, and sales promotion is useful in getting early trial. Personal selling efforts must be geared to persuading the trade to carry the product. In the growth stage, advertising and public relations continue to be powerful influences, whereas sales promotion can be reduced because fewer incentives are needed. In the mature stage, sales promotion again becomes important relative to advertising. Buyers know the brands and advertising is needed only to remind them of the product. In the decline stage, advertising is kept at a reminder level, public relations is dropped and salespeople give the product only a little attention. Sales promotion, however, might continue at a high level in order to stimulate trade and prop up sales to customers.

The Changing Face of Marketing Communications

During the past few decades, companies around the world have perfected the art of mass marketing – selling highly standardized products to masses of customers. In the process, they have developed effective mass-media advertising techniques to support their mass-marketing strategies. These companies routinely invest huge sums of money in the mass media, reaching tens of millions of customers with a single ad. However, as we move into the twenty-first century, marketing managers are facing some new marketing communications realities.

The Changing Communications Environment

Two major factors are changing the face of today's marketing communications. First, as mass markets have fragmented, marketers are shifting away from mass marketing. More and more, they are developing focused marketing programmes designed to build closer relationships with customers in more narrowly defined micromarkets. Second, vast improvements in computer and information technology are speeding the movement towards segmented marketing. Today's information technology helps marketers to keep closer track of customer needs – more information is available about customers at the individual and household levels than ever before. New technologies also provide new communications avenues for reaching smaller customer segments with more tailored messages.

The shift from mass marketing to segmented marketing has had a dramatic impact on marketing communications. Just as mass marketing gave rise to a new generation of mass-media communications, so the shift towards one-to-one marketing is spawning a new generation of more specialized and highly targeted communications efforts.[12]

Given this new communications environment, marketers must rethink the roles of various media and promotion-mix tools. Mass-media advertising has long dominated the promotion mixes of consumer-product companies. However, although television, magazines and other mass media remain very important, their dominance is declining. Market fragmentation has resulted in media fragmentation – in an explosion of more focused media that better match today's targeting strategies. For example, back in the 1970s and 1980s, in many developed countries, the three or four major TV networks attracted a majority of the nation's viewing audience. By the mid-1990s, that number had dropped significantly as cable television and satellite broadcasting systems offered advertisers dozens or even hundreds of alternative channels that reach smaller, specialized audiences.[13] Similarly, there has been a proliferation of special-interest magazines in recent decades, reaching more focused audiences. Beyond these media channels, companies are making increased use of new, highly targeted media, ranging from video screens on supermarket shopping trolleys to CD-ROM catalogues, online computer services and Web sites on the Internet.

More generally, advertising appears to be giving way to other elements of the promotion mix. In the glory days of mass marketing, consumer-product companies, such as Heinz, P & G and Mars, spent the lion's share of their promotion budgets on mass-media communications. Today, media advertising captures a much reduced proportion of the total promotion spend.[14] The rest goes to various sales promotion activities, which can be focused more effectively on individual consumer and trade segments. In all, companies are doing less *broadcasting* and more *narrowcasting*, relying on a richer variety of focused communication tools which allow them to reach their many and diverse target markets.

Integrated Marketing Communications

The recent shift from mass marketing to targeted marketing, and the corresponding use of a richer mixture of communication channels and promotion tools, poses a problem for marketers. Consumers are being exposed to a greater variety of marketing communications from and about the company from a broader array of sources. However, customers do not distinguish between message sources in the way marketers do. In the consumer's mind, advertising messages from different media such as television, magazines or online sources blur into one. Messages delivered via different promotional approaches – such as advertising, personal selling, sales promotion, public relations or direct marketing – all become part of a single overall message about the company. Conflicting messages from these different sources can result in confused company images and brand positions.

All too often, companies fail to integrate their various communications channels. The result is a hodgepodge of communications to consumers. Mass advertisements say one thing, a price promotion sends a different signal, a product label creates still another message, company sales literature says something altogether different and the company's Web site seems out of sync with everything else.

19

Mass Communications: Advertising, Sales Promotion and Public Relations

CHAPTER OBJECTIVES

After reading this chapter, you should be able to:

- Define the roles of advertising, sales promotion and public relations in the promotion mix.
- Describe the main decisions involved in developing an advertising programme.
- Explain how sales promotion campaigns are developed and implemented.
- Explain how companies use public relations to communicate with their publics.

Preview Case

Promotions Medley!

'MARS CONFECTIONERY LAUNCHES A £140 MILLION European advertising campaign in a bid to maximize its appeal to Europe's male teenage market.'

'Sony doubles its pan-European advertising spend to back its new video games system, Playstation, with press and TV campaigns that will feature comic testimonies of people who have had their lives changed by playing Playstation.'

'The UK's third largest charity, the Royal National Lifeboat Institution (RNLI), spends £1.5 million on direct marketing and will consider direct response television following a successful trial campaign – in which more than £55 million in voluntary income was received.'

'IBM will use generic advertising for its personal computers. To start off with, corporate advertising will emphasize IBM as a brand rather than a series of products. IBM also will run a £12 million pan-European advertising campaign for its new operating system.'

'Spanish designer Paco Rabanne launches XS pour Elle, a women's version of its XS men's fragrance. TV advertisements break simultaneously in France, the UK and Belgium.'

'Ready Brek, an instant hot oat cereal from Weetabix, teams up with Disney Home Video for an in-pack promotion. Children collect a set of eight moving picture cards based on original illustrations from the Disney film, *Snow White and the Seven Dwarfs*. The cards become available before the video of the film goes on sale. Children can also send away for a 12-page booklet in which to mount cards for £1.50 and one completed order form. Over the period of the in-pack promotion campaign, Ready Brek packs also offer "10 per cent extra free". A national TV ad campaign focuses on the *Snow White* promotion and a full publicity programme is implemented to raise awareness of the video release.'

'Richard Branson's everywhere – the beard, the smile, the stories about this irrepressibly optimistic businessman leaping out of every newspaper, television and radio station, the publication of the man's second biography in five years. Virgin is his brand and that is going places too – Virgin launches into vodka, Virgin takes on Coca-Cola, Virgin gets FM frequency in London ... Radio 1 listeners vote Virgin's Branson the man they would most like to rewrite the ten commandments.' Branson shows how a well-lubricated PR (public relations) machine can work wonders for the company's leader and its brands.

These accounts are just a few examples reflecting the array of non-personal mass communication tools that organizations use to create awareness for their products or services, to secure greater support for their brands, to build or strengthen company image or to generate sales.[1]

Questions

1. Identify the range of mass-marketing techniques that marketers use to reach target customers.

2. What are their specific roles?

3. What are the major decisions involved in developing a mass-marketing campaign?

4. What is an integrated communications strategy and how might firms benefit from pursuing such a strategy?

5. What are the advantages and limitations of pan-European campaigns?

6. Consider the barriers to effective implementation of Europe-wide promotions and discuss the implications for international marketing managers.

Introduction

The questions in the preview case get us to think about the alternative mass-marketing options open to marketers seeking to communicate with their target customers and to evoke desired responses. In this chapter, we address the major non-personal forms of communication and promotion. Personal selling is discussed in Chapter 20, whereas direct marketing and online approaches are examined in Chapter 22.

Companies must do more than offer good products or services. They must inform consumers about product or service benefits and carefully position these in consumers' minds. To do this, they must skilfully use the mass-promotion tools of *advertising*, *sales promotion* and *public relations*. We take a closer look at each of these tools in this chapter.

Advertising

We define **advertising** as any paid form of non-personal presentation and promotion of ideas, goods or services through mass media such as newspapers, magazines, television or radio by an identified sponsor. Advertising is used by many organizations to communicate specific messages about themselves, their products and services, or their modes of behaviour to a predefined target audience, in order to stimulate a response from the audience. The response may be perceptual in nature: for example, the consumer develops specific views or opinions about the product or brand, or these feelings are altered by the ad. The response could be behavioural: for instance, the consumer buys the product or increases the amount that he or she buys. Advertisers that sponsor advertisements include not only business firms, but also non-profit and social institutions such as charities, museums and religious organizations that promote causes to various target publics. Advertising is a good way to inform and persuade, whether the purpose is to build brand preference for Nokia mobile phones worldwide, or to motivate a nation's young consumers to drink more milk, or to encourage smokers to give up the habit.

In the European Union, advertisers run up an annual advertising bill of more than ecu45.4 billion. As recession in Europe lifts, and national economies revive, advertising spend in most EU countries has been forecast to rise towards the end of the 1990s. However, advertisers will remain cautious in terms of how best to use their advertising budget in order to achieve desired communication goals.[2]

advertising
Any paid form of non-personal presentation and promotion of ideas, goods or services by an identified sponsor.

Important Decisions in Advertising

Marketing management must make five important decisions when developing an advertising programme (see Figure 19.1).

Setting Objectives

The first step in developing an advertising programme is to set *advertising objectives*. These objectives should be based on decisions about the target market,

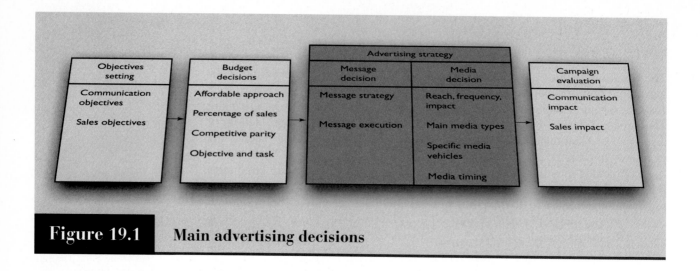

| **Figure 19.1** | **Main advertising decisions** |

positioning and marketing mix, which define the job that advertising must achieve in the total marketing programme.

advertising objective
A specific communication task to be accomplished with a specific target audience during a specific period of time.

An **advertising objective** is a specific communication task to be accomplished with a specific target audience during a specific period of time.[3] Advertising objectives can be classified by purpose: that is, whether their aim is to inform, persuade or remind. Table 19.1 lists examples of each of these objectives.

Informative advertising is used heavily when introducing a new product category. In this case, the objective is to build primary demand. Thus producers of compact disc players first informed consumers of the sound and convenience benefits of CDs. **Persuasive advertising** becomes more important as competition increases. Here, the company's objective is to build selective demand. For example, when compact disc players became established and accepted, Sony began trying to persuade consumers that its brand offered the best quality for their money.

informative advertising
Advertising used to inform consumers about a new product or feature and to build primary demand.

persuasive advertising
Advertising used to build selective demand for a brand by persuading consumers that it offers the best quality for their money.

Some persuasive advertising has become **comparison advertising**, in which a company directly or indirectly compares its brand with one or more other brands:

comparison advertising (knocking copy)
Advertising that compares one brand directly or indirectly to one or more other brands.

Among the most frequent users of comparison advertising or *knocking copy* is the car industry. In the UK, Korean car maker Hyundai sought to raise awareness of its cars with a series of light-hearted efforts: 'Even a kettle has a longer guarantee than Rover'. Another example was the war of words between two yellow-fat manufacturers. Van den Berghs, part of Unilever, provoked a battle with a campaign for its low-fat spread, Delight, that made taste comparisons with St Ivel Gold, produced by Unigate, and parodied some of its ad lines. St Ivel retaliated with an ad for its Gold brand that targeted Flora, another Van Den Berghs product, and turned one of Flora's catchlines, 'For your blooming generation', into 'For your ballooning generation'. The argument was that Flora contained twice as much fat as Gold. This led to a telling-off from the UK's Advertising Standards Authority (ASA) on grounds that, as Flora was a different type of spread (a full-fat margarine), St Ivel was not comparing like with like. The ASA finally urged both advertisers to refrain from using the approach.[4]

There are potential dangers in using comparison advertising, especially when comparisons are unfair and escalate into denigration of a rival's brand. The

Table 19.1	**Possible advertising objectives**

To inform
- Telling the market about a new product.
- Suggesting new uses for a product.
- Informing the market of a price change.
- Explaining how the product works.

- Describing available services.
- Correcting false impressions.
- Reducing buyers' fears.
- Building a company image.

To persuade
- Building brand preference.
- Encouraging switching to your brand.
- Changing buyer perceptions of product attributes.

- Persuading buyers to purchase now.
- Persuading buyers to receive a sales call.

To remind
- Reminding buyers that the product may be needed in the near future.
- Reminding buyers where to buy the product.

- Keeping the product in buyers' minds during off seasons.
- Maintaining top-of-mind product awareness.

approach is legal in both the United States and United Kingdom, but in some other European countries it is banned. Belgium and Germany regard it as tantamount to unfair competition. For example, a relatively innocuous Carlsberg commercial with the tagline 'Probably the best lager in the world' could not be run in those countries because it implicitly identified with products offered by rivals. Similarly, the car-hire company Avis's 'We try harder' ad would not be allowed in Germany because, although nobody is named, Hertz, the no. 1, is presumed to be the only real competitor. Efforts to produce a European directive to harmonize rules on comparative advertising across the EU have been relatively unsuccessful to date. Until such a directive is issued, however, advertisers in the region must remain sensitive to individual nations' codes of practice and legislation. This style of communication will probably always exist in one form or another, as most advertising is essentially comparative – after all, the aim of the advertiser is to persuade the consumer to respond to one product offering rather than another.[5]

Reminder advertising is important for mature products as it keeps consumers thinking about the product. Expensive Coca-Cola ads on television are often designed to remind people about Coca-Cola, not merely to inform or persuade them.

reminder advertising
Advertising used to keep consumers thinking about a product.

Advertisers might also seek to assure existing customers that they have made the right choice. For example, car firms might use reinforcement advertising that depicts satisfied owners enjoying some special feature of their new car.

The choice of advertising objective is based on a good understanding of the current marketing situation. If the product is new and the company is not the market leader, but the brand is superior to the leading brand, then the advertising objective is to inform and convince the market of the brand's superiority. On the other hand, if the market is mature and brand usage is declining, the advertising objective would probably be to stimulate sales by persuading customers to increase frequency of usage, or by encouraging competitors' customers to switch.

Comparative advertising: this ad reflects the 'war of words' between St Ivel (Gold) and Van den Berghs (Flora).

Setting the Advertising Budget

After determining its advertising objectives, the company next sets its *advertising budget* for each product. The role of advertising is to create demand for a product. The company wants to spend the amount needed to achieve the sales goal. Four commonly used methods for setting the advertising budget were discussed in Chapter 18. Here we describe some specific factors that should be considered when setting the advertising budget:

● *Stage in the product life cycle.* New products typically need large advertising budgets to build awareness and to gain consumer trial. Mature brands usually require lower budgets as a ratio to sales.

● *Market share.* High-market-share brands usually need more advertising spending as a percentage of sales than do low-share brands. Building the market or taking share from competitors requires larger advertising spending than does simply maintaining current share.

● *Competition and clutter.* In a market with many competitors and high advertising spending, a brand must advertise more heavily to be heard above the noise in the market.

● *Advertising frequency.* When many repetitions are needed to present the brand's message to consumers, the advertising budget must be larger.

● *Product differentiation.* A brand that closely resembles other brands in its product class (coffee, laundry detergents, chewing gum, beer, soft drinks) requires heavy advertising to set it apart. When the product differs greatly from competitors, advertising can be used to point out the differences to consumers.[6]

Table 19.4	Advantages and limitations of media forms

MEDIUM	ADVANTAGES	LIMITATIONS
Newspapers	Flexibility; timeliness; local market coverage; broad acceptance; high believability.	Short life; poor reproduction quality; small pass-along audience.
Television	Combines sight, sound and motion; appealing to the senses; high attention; high reach.	High absolute cost; high clutter; fleeting exposure; less audience selectivity.
Radio	Mass use; high geographic and demographic selectivity; low cost.	Audio presentation only; lower attention than TV; fleeting exposure.
Magazines	High geographic and demographic selectivity; credibility and prestige; high-quality reproduction; long life; good pass-along readership.	Long ad purchase lead time; some waste circulation; no guarantee of position.
Outdoor	Flexibility; high repeat exposure; low cost; low competition.	No audience selectivity; creative limitations.

media planner ultimately decides which vehicles give the best reach, frequency and impact for the money.

Media planners have to compute the cost per thousand persons reached by a vehicle. For example, if a full-page, four-colour advertisement in *The Economist* costs £30,000 and its readership is 3 million people, the cost of reaching each group of 1,000 persons is about £10. The same advertisement in *Business Week* may cost only £20,000 but reach only 1 million persons, giving a cost per thousand of about £20. The media planner would rank each magazine by cost per thousand and favour those magazines with the lower cost per thousand for reaching target consumers. Additionally, the media planner considers the cost of producing ads for different media. Whereas newspaper ads may cost very little to produce, flashy television ads may cost millions. Media costs vary across different countries, so care must be taken not to generalize the figures.

Thus the media planner must balance media cost measures against several media impact factors. First, the planner should balance costs against the media vehicle's *audience quality*. For a mobile telephone ad, business magazines would have a high-exposure value; magazines aimed at new parents or woodwork enthusiasts would have a low-exposure value. Second, the media planner should consider *audience attention*. Readers of *Vogue*, for example, typically pay more attention to ads than do *Business Week* readers. Third, the planner should assess the vehicle's *editorial quality*. For example, the *Financial Times* and *Wall Street Journal Europe* are more credible and prestigious than the *News of the World*.

DECIDING ON MEDIA TIMING. Another decision that must be made concerns timing: how to schedule the advertising over the course of a year. Suppose sales of a product peak in December and drop in March. The firm can vary its advertising to follow the seasonal pattern, to oppose the seasonal pattern, or to be the same all year. Most firms do some seasonal advertising. Some do *only*

continuity
Scheduling ads evenly within a given period.

pulsing
Scheduling ads unevenly, in bursts, over a certain time period.

seasonal advertising: for example, many department stores advertise – usually their seasonal sales – in specific periods in the year, such as Christmas, Easter and summer. Finally, the advertiser has to choose the pattern of the ads. **Continuity** means scheduling ads evenly within a given period **Pulsing** means scheduling ads unevenly over a given time period. Thus 52 ads could either be scheduled at one per week during the year or pulsed in several bursts. The idea is to advertise heavily for a short period to build awareness that carries over to the next advertising period. Those who favour pulsing feel that it can be used to achieve the same impact as a steady schedule, but at a much lower cost. However, some media planners believe that although pulsing achieves minimal awareness, it sacrifices depth of advertising communications.

Advertising Evaluation

copy testing
Measuring the communication effect of an advertisement before or after it is printed or broadcast.

The advertising programme should regularly evaluate both the communication impact and the sales effects of advertising. Measuring the communication effect of an ad or **copy testing** tells whether the ad is communicating well. Copy testing can be done before or after an ad is printed or broadcast. There are three principal methods of *pretesting* in advertising. The first is through *direct rating*, where the advertiser exposes a consumer panel to alternative ads and asks them to rate the ads. These direct ratings indicate how well the ads gain attention and how they affect consumers. Although this is an imperfect measure of an ad's actual impact, a high rating indicates a potentially more effective ad. In *portfolio tests*, consumers view or listen to a portfolio of advertisements, taking as much time as they need. They are then asked to recall all the ads and their content, aided or unaided by the interviewer. Their recall level indicates the ability of an ad to stand out and for its message to be understood and remembered. *Laboratory tests* use equipment to measure consumers' physiological reactions to an ad, such as their heartbeat, blood pressure, pupil dilation and perspiration. These tests measure an ad's attention-getting power, but reveal very little about the overall impact on brand awareness, attitudes and brand preference of a completed advertising campaign.

There are two popular methods of *post-testing* ads. Using *recall tests*, the advertiser asks people who have been exposed to magazines or television programmes to recall everything they can about the advertisers and products they saw. Recall scores indicate the ad's power to be noticed and retained. In *recognition tests*, the researcher asks readers of a given issue of, say, a magazine to point out what they recognize as having seen before. Recognition scores can be used to assess the ad's impact in different market segments and to compare the company's ads with competitors' ads.

To identify the extent to which the campaign increased brand awareness, or affected brand comprehension, brand beliefs and preference or intentions to buy, the advertiser must, in the first instance, measure these levels before a campaign. It then draws a random sample of consumers after the campaign to assess the communication effects. If a company intended to increase brand awareness from 20 to 50 per cent, but succeeded only in increasing it to 30 per cent, then something is wrong: it is not spending enough, its ads are poor, its message is ill-targeted, or some other factor is missing.

Figure 19.2 shows the levels of communication effect that advertisers are likely to monitor and measure with respect to a campaign:

● The change in brand awareness is determined by the number of customers who were previously *unaware* of the brand and the number who *notice* the advertisement and are now *aware* of the brand, or by the difference in the number of customers who are aware that the brand exists before and after the campaign. If there has been little increase or even a decline in brand awareness, the advertiser has to determine whether the reason is the poor impact achieved by the communications campaign or that customers *forget* because of poor recall or inadequate advertising investment.

● The nature of consumers' attitudes towards a brand can be ascertained before and after a campaign. An informative ad allows consumers to *learn* more about product/brand benefits. If the message is poorly targeted, or conveys an undesirable or unbelievable message, consumers are *antipathetic* towards the brand. They do not develop any liking for the product. Advertisers may have to redesign the copy to generate greater interest among customers or improve message content in order to enhance the level of comprehension of brand benefits among target customers.

● Consumers who are *sympathetic* towards advertised brand benefits would manifest their favourable response in the form of stated brand preference. Similarly, before-and-after (the campaign) studies would enable changes in consumer brand preference to be determined. Reasons for brand *rejection* should be identified so that communication weaknesses can be redressed.

● An advertising campaign may be used to turn preference among customers into more definite *intention* to buy. Again, this response can be measured and changes in the level of buying intent may be determined.

● It is usually difficult to measure the sales effect of a campaign. Questions such as 'What sales are caused by an ad that increases brand awareness by 20 per cent and brand preference by 10 per cent?' are not easy to answer. Sales or *trial* are affected by many factors besides advertising, such as product features, price and availability. One way to measure the sales effect of advertising is to compare past sales with past advertising expenditures. Another way is through experiments. For example, to test the effects of different advertising levels, Pizza Hut could vary the amount it spends on advertising in different market areas and measure the differences in resulting sales levels. It could spend the normal amount in one market area, half the normal amount in another area, and twice the normal amount in a third area. If the three market areas are similar, and if all other marketing efforts in the area are the same, then the differences in sales in the three cities could be related to advertising level. More complex experiments could be designed to include other variables, such as differences in the ads or media used.

● If the customer is *satisfied* with the brand he or she has bought, this will lead to *repeat* purchase on another buying occasion. The extent to which advertising or a specific 'reminder' campaign affects repeat purchase is difficult to measure because of the difficulty of separating out the immediate and long-term effects of advertising. 'Before-and-after' type studies and controlled experiments can be used, nonetheless, to detect changes in purchase and usage frequency. Again, advertisers should obtain consumer feedback to increase their understanding of the impact of communications on repeat purchase. Advertising may not be blamed for non-repeat sales due to the nature of product consumption: for example, consumers get *bored* with the same product and want variety. In this case, advertising is not powerful enough to arrest that desire. Few of us would relish the thought of surviving on an uninterrupted diet of Heinz beans, Heinz soup and Heinz sausages all year round!

Organizing for Advertising

Different organizations handle advertising in different ways. In small and medium-sized companies, advertising might be handled by someone in the sales or marketing department. Large companies might set up advertising departments whose job it is to set the advertising budget, work with the ad agency and handle dealer displays and other advertising not done by the agency. Most companies, small or large, tend to use outside advertising agencies because they offer several advantages:

● Agencies have specialists who can perform specialist functions (e.g. research, creative work) better than a company's own staff.

● Agencies bring an outside point of view to solving a company's problems, together with years of experience from working with different clients and situations.

● Agencies have more buying power in media than the firm. They are also paid partly from media discount, which would cost the firm less.

There are disadvantages in relinquishing the advertising function to an outside agency: loss of total control of the advertising process, a reduction in flexibility, conflicts arising when the agency dictates working practices, and client inability to exercise control or co-ordination. Despite the potential problems, however, most firms find that they benefit from employing the specialized expertise of agencies.

How does an advertising agency work? Advertising agencies were started in the mid-to-late 1800s by salespeople and brokers who worked for the media and received commission for selling advertising space to companies. As time passed, the salespeople began to help customers prepare their ads. Eventually they formed agencies and grew closer to the advertisers than to the media.

Some ad agencies are huge – Leo Burnett has annual billings (the value of advertising placed for clients) of more than $2.6 billion. In recent years, many agencies launched a series of mergers and takeovers to build global marketing companies. The largest of these 'agency mega-groups', WPP Group, includes several large agencies – Ogilvy & Mather, J. Walter Thompson, Fallon McElligot and others – with combined billings approaching $25 billion.

Most large agencies have staff and resources to handle all phases of an ad campaign for their clients, from creating a marketing plan to developing campaigns and preparing, placing and evaluating ads. Agencies usually have four departments: creative, which develops and produces ads; media, which selects media and places ads; research, which studies audience characteristics and wants; and business, which handles the agency's business activities. Each account is supervised by an account executive and people in each department are usually assigned to work on one or more accounts.

Ad agencies have traditionally been paid through commission and fees. Higher commissions are paid to the well-recognized agencies for their ability to place more advertisements in media. However, both avertisers and agencies are becoming more and more unhappy with the commission system. Larger advertisers complain that they have to pay more for the same services received by smaller ones simply because they place more advertising. Advertisers also believe that the commission system drives agencies away from low-cost media and short advertising campaigns. Agencies are unhappy because they perform extra services for an account without getting more pay. As a result the trend is now

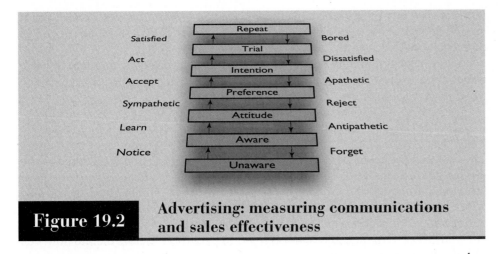

| **Figure 19.2** | **Advertising: measuring communications and sales effectiveness** |

towards paying a straight fee or a combination commission and fee. Some are tying agency compensation to the performance of the agency's ad campaigns.

There is another trend affecting the agency business. Many agencies are seeking growth by diversifying into related marketing services. These diversified agencies offer a one-stop shop – a complete list of integrated marketing and promotion services under one roof, including advertising, sales promotion, direct marketing and marketing research. Some have added marketing consulting, television production and sales training units in an effort to become full 'marketing partners' to their clients. Some companies favour buying marketing services from a consolidated one-stop-shop. Reckitt & Colman, a British maker of soaps and household polishes, Burger King, the restaurant chain, S.C. Johnson & Son, which makes household products, and German pharmaceuticals firm Bayer AG have relied on a single agency rather than many. These companies argue that there are a number of benefits to be gained from using one agency: it increases their clout with the agency; it is more efficient to deal with one 'contractor' than with many; it greatly simplifies the advertising for their products, including gaining the convenience of having to negotiate fees once only; it ensures that their marketing will be consistent worldwide; and a big international broad-line agency can help carry good ideas into many country markets quickly.

However, many agencies are finding that advertisers do not want much more from them than traditional media advertising services plus direct marketing, sales promotion and sometimes public relations. Client companies may want to keep a few agencies on call in a state of perpetual competition. Some, like Coca-Cola, seek creative variety, so they scatter the work to many different small and large agencies. Others such as Procter & Gamble, Unilever and Nestlé tended to keep a 'club' of three to six agencies on call to cover one agency's weak spots by drawing on the ideas of another with more talent in a particular market or service. Thus, many agencies have recently dropped unrelated activities in order to focus more on traditional services or their core expertise. Some have even started their own 'creative boutiques' – smaller and more independent agencies that can develop creative campaigns for clients free of large-agency bureaucracy.[17]

International Advertising

We have discussed advertising decisions in general. International advertisers face many complexities not encountered by domestic advertisers. We define international or worldwide advertising as: *advertising that promotes a cause, or an organization and the sale of its goods or services in more than one country and in different parts of the world.*[18]

When developing advertising for international markets, a number of basic issues must be considered.

Standardization or Differentiation

The first issue concerns the degree to which advertising should be adapted to the unique characteristics of various country markets. Some large advertisers have attempted to support their global brands with highly standardized worldwide advertising. The chances of success for standardized advertising depend on how culture-bound a product or service is, the buying behaviour of consumers, the competition, and national laws and regulations. All these factors dictate how well the advertising concepts cross borders.

Standardization produces many benefits, such as lower advertising costs, greater co-ordination of global advertising efforts and a more consistent world-wide company or product image. However, standardization also has drawbacks. Most importantly, it ignores the fact that country markets, not just across the continents, but also within supposedly 'harmonized' trading communities, such as the European Union, differ greatly in their cultures, demographics and economic conditions. Pan-European advertising, for example, is complicated because of the EU's cultural diversity as reflected in the differences in circum-stances, language, traditions, music, beliefs, values and lifestyles among member nations. Ironically, the English have more in common with the Australians, who live on the opposite side of the globe, than with the Germans or the French, their closer neighbours. Cultural differences also exist across Asian countries (Japanese and Indonesian consumers are as alike as the Germans and Italians), as they do among emerging European markets. For example, the three Baltic states – Estonia, Latvia and Lithuania – are far from being a common market, with each displaying different languages, currencies and consumer habits.

Although advertising messages might be standardized, their executions cannot be, as culture invariably dominates communications.[19] Indeed, a recent survey in Europe among 210 pan-European brand managers showed that a majority (57 per cent) believe it is difficult to standardize advertising execution.[20] Most international advertisers must therefore think globally, but act locally. They develop global advertising *strategies* that bring efficiency and consistency to their worldwide advertising efforts. Then they adapt their advertising *programmes* to make them more responsive to consumer needs and expectations within local markets. In many cases, even when a standard message is used, execution styles are adapted to reflect local moods and consumer expectations.

For example, one Kellogg's Frosted Flakes ad campaign is almost identical worldwide, with only minor adjustments for local cultural differences.[21] The advertising uses a tennis theme that has worldwide appeal and features teenage actors with generic good looks – neither too northern European nor too Latin American. Of course, Kellogg's translates the commercials into different languages. In the English version, for example, Tony growls 'They're Gr-r-reat!', whereas in the German version it's 'Gr-r-rossartig!' Other adaptations are more subtle. In the American ad, after winning the match, Tony leaps over the net in celebration. In other versions, he simply 'high fives' his young partner. The reason: Europeans do not jump over the net after winning at tennis.

In contrast, Parker Pen Company changes its advertising substantially from country to country:

Print ads in Germany simply show the Parker Pen held in a hand that is writing a headline – 'This is how you write with precision.' In the UK, where it is the brand leader, [ads emphasize] the exotic processes used to make pens, such as gently polishing the gold nibs with walnut chips ... In America, the ad campaign's theme is status and image. The headlines are ... 'Here's how you tell who's boss', and 'There are times when it has to be Parker.' The company considers the different themes necessary because of different product images and ... customer motives in each market.[22]

Successful standardized advertising is most likely to work for capital goods or business-to-business marketing, where targets are more homogeneous in their needs and buy the product for the same reasons. For example, whether it be a European, Asian or American construction company, the purchase of bulldozers is governed by similar economic rationality (for example, productivity, lifetime cost of running the equipment, parts delivery). Consumer-goods advertising is less amenable to cross-cultural standardization. However, considerable similarities are found in segments, such as the world's rich to whom lifestyle goods and brands like Cartier, Montblanc, Mercedes and Hugo Boss appeal. Similarly, youth culture across the globe may be targeted with a common message. Brands such as Nike, Pepsi and Jeep are advertised in much the same way globally; Jeep has created a worldwide brand image of ruggedness and reliability; Nike urges Americans, Africans, Asians and Europeans alike to 'Just do it'; Pepsi uses a standard appeal to target the world's youth.

Several basic conditions favour a standardized approach:

- Product or brand values offered to consumers and as conveyed by the advertisement are similar in every target country.

- Target customers in each country have similar expectations regarding the product and they do not differ in the way they evaluate the product. For example, business airline passengers' expectations of airline services are virtually the same in all countries.

- The target groups in each country are homogeneous, so that similar media can be used to reach them.

- The advertised product is in the same stage of its life cycle in every country market. Different messages and executions are needed for the product that is newly launched into one market and one that is already in its growth stage in another.

- The brand is a true 'megabrand' with a strong position in each market as well as the advertising budget necessary to support it in each market.

- The advertising idea must be transportable (universal, functional appeals, fantasies and symbols, fashions, movies/television, international celebrities and current events travel better than cultural values such as idiosyncratic lifestyles, habits and sports and leisure activities, local accents and language, and endorsements by local celebrities).

- The different countries can support the same advertising style of execution, or the company's preferred style can be accommodated in each country. Many European countries find the display of emotions in American ads ludicrous, and whereas lifestyle and glamour work well in the United States, innovative, modern and attention-getting styles are better received in France. Humour, subtlety, understatement and irony are favoured in the United Kingdom; while in Germany, rational, descriptive and informative executions will not go wrong.

● If countries can be clustered on the basis of showing similar economic, cultural, legal and media characteristics, standardized advertising becomes more feasible.[23]

There is no simple answer for companies as to whether a standardized or differentiated approach would work best for their brand. They must therefore identify both the differences and similarities among target audiences in different national or regional markets, and determine opportunities for standardization or differentiation.

Centralization or Decentralization

Global advertisers are concerned with the degree to which advertising decision making and implementation should be centralized or decentralized. This decision is directly linked to the decision about whether to follow a standardized or differentiated advertising approach. Five key factors influence the choice between centralization and decentralization of the responsibility for international advertising decisions and implementation:

1. *Corporate and marketing objectives.* A company whose global marketing objectives dominate over domestic objectives is likely to centralize advertising and communications decisions. Where it emphasizes short-term profit and local objectives, decentralized decision making is favoured.

2. *Product uniformity.* The more similar the product or service marketed across different countries, the greater the feasibility of a uniform approach, which allows for centralized management of advertising.

3. *Product appeal.* Underpinning the product's appeal are the reasons why customers use the product. The reasons for consumption may differ among different cultures, whatever the demographic or psychographic characteristics of consumers. French women drink mineral water to stay slim; German women drink it to keep healthy. Golf club membership is a status purchase in Singapore; in the United Kingdom it is a moderate leisure activity, without the same label of exclusivity attached. Where underlying appeals vary significantly, decentralized decision making makes better sense.

4. *Cultural sensitivities.* Where a product's usage and appeal are culture-bound in terms of the local attitudes towards consumption, habits and preferences, as in the case of drinks and food products, more decentralization is necessary.

5. *Legal constraints.* Individual country rules and regulations affect advertising decisions and their implementation. Decentralization of responsibility, with the aim of tapping local wisdom and knowledge, is necessary where strict country regulations apply. In the European Union, until real 'harmonization' exists, cross-border advertisers must remain alert to subtle differences in nations' rules and codes of practice in order to avoid costly mistakes.

There has been a tendency for international organizations, especially in Europe, to centralize their marketing activities, resulting in more attempts to centralize the advertising function. In many product categories, including cars, durable goods, electronics products, cosmetics and alcoholic beverages, European multinationals have adopted single-agency networks across Europe. Retailers, media companies and food and drinks manufacturers, however, remain less positive about centralization as they have to respond to cultural differences and legislation.[24]

The modes used by firms vary. Some organizations exert tight control from the centre and executionary changes for local culture and conditions are closely monitored, as in the case of Unilever's Lever Europe. Some corporations, like Nestlé, grant local management some degree of freedom to develop advertising within broad strategic guidelines, but with central directives on agencies and media buying groups. Yet others, such as Heinz, have tended to give local management total autonomy in both strategy determination and local implementation of product and advertising strategies.

Worldwide Advertising Media

The international media comprise an extensive mix:

- *Newspapers.* Faster and more efficient circulation is possible with new technologies, such as satellite printing, which allows advertising copy to be sent by satellite to the printers. Many international newspapers (e.g. *International Herald Tribune, Financial Times, Asahi Shimbun, Wall Street/Asian Wall Street Journal*) are printed simultaneously in more than one country. In general there have been enormous developments in local and global press, and more newspapers have gone global to reach specific audiences.

- *Magazines.* There are some national and international journals which carry ads that target regional, international or global customers (e.g. *Fortune, Newsweek, Time, The Economist*). Women's magazines, such as *Cosmopolitan, Elle, Vogue* and *Harper's Bazaar*, are printed in different editions for readers in different target countries/regions. And there are other international magazines such as *Reader's Digest* and men's magazines like *Playboy* and *Penthouse*.

- *Professional and technical magazines.* In Europe alone, there are more than 15,000 titles, and the number is rising yearly.

- *Cinema.* This is a relatively popular medium for reaching younger viewers, such as teenagers. In developing and less developed nations, cinema remains important.

- *Television.* There are few country markets where television is not available or where advertising is not carried via that medium. Satellite and cable opportunities have expanded enormously and accelerated the use of TV for international advertising. A few stations – notably, CNN, NBC Super Channel and Eurosport – are well-recognized international media channels. Other international TV channels include Dow Jones's European Business News, BBC Worldwide, Bloomberg Information's TV Europe and NBC's CNBC.

- *Outdoor advertising and transport advertising.* This medium is used throughout the world. In the western developed markets, advertisers are expanding their repertoire of outside media (e.g. park benches, trucks, taxis, bus stop shelters). This medium is used as an alternative in cases where the product category cannot be advertised on TV, as in the case of tobacco and alcoholic products. In some countries, such as India and the People's Republic of China, outdoor advertising has become more important.

- *Interactive communication media.* Interactive systems, such as videotext and pay-TV, are gaining importance as cable TV continues to develop. France's Minitel, for example, offers over 3,000 different services to subscribers.

- *Radio.* As a medium for international advertising, radio is constrained by availability in the sense that most commercial radio is regional. Radio Luxembourg, the international European station, transmits ads in several languages and reaches the whole of Europe.

- *Place-based media.* This is a worldwide development and advertisers are increasingly deploying the medium to reach audiences wherever they happen to be – at work, the fitness centre, the supermarket, airports and in the aeroplane. The programming and advertising can be produced internationally.

- *Trade fairs and exhibitions.* These can be costly, but are useful media for international communications.

- *Sponsorship.* Sponsorship of sports or art events, like the Olympic Games and the soccer World Cup, offers vast audience reach. However, such global audiences are rare and the effectiveness of the initiatives is not easy to measure.

- *Other media.* Point-of-sale materials are not easy to reproduce internationally. Invariably, they have to be adapted to local conditions, specifically the language, regulations and distribution outlets. Direct mail is used in many countries, but it is primarily a local technique. As postal services vary from country to country, including within the EU, the medium has yet to be applied internationally. Nonetheless, credit card companies that have an international customer database can exploit this medium for worldwide communications. Online media such as the Internet are gaining recognition and organizations are increasingly investing in this channel given its potential to reach a global audience (Chapter 22 discusses online marketing in greater detail).

There have been important trends in media development worldwide. Most notable are developments in TV and telecommunications. A second force is deregulation, which results in the proliferation of commercial TV and satellite broadcasting. In deregulated central Europe and in Asia, as state control over media relaxes, opportunities open up for advertising. Another development in the 1990s is the emergence of megabrands as a result of merger activities. Such megabrands can concentrate media buying, which in turn influences media development. Furthermore, as more companies seek a pan-European or global approach to media buying, only large media groups with a broad European or international base, owning a network of media companies worldwide – such as Berlusconi, Bertelsmann, Time-Warner and Murdoch – are in a position to negotiate at this level and have their own grip on media developments.[25]

Media Planning, Buying and Costs

International media planning is more complicated than local media planning as the media situation differs from country to country. To plan effectively, international advertisers require high-quality, reliable cross-country media and audience research data. In some countries, there is inadequate media research. Moreover, research techniques and measurement standards vary greatly across countries, making cross-country comparisons of media research data almost impossible. Research into international media is still relatively expensive. Unless reliable intercountry comparisons can be made, international advertisers will find it difficult to evaluate and quantify international media effectiveness. In the EU, the European Association of Advertising Agencies is working on the harmoniza-

advantageous to use sales promotion because they cannot afford to match the large advertising budgets of the market leaders. Nor can they obtain shelf space without offering trade allowances or stimulate consumer trial without offering consumer incentives.[32]

Despite the dangers, many consumer packaged-goods companies have had to use sales promotion more than they would like. Recently, however, traditional brand leaders like Kellogg's, Kraft and Procter & Gamble have been putting more emphasis on 'pull' promotion and increasing their advertising budgets. They blame the heavy use of sales promotion for decreased brand loyalty, increased consumer price sensitivity, a focus on short-run marketing planning and an erosion of brand-quality image.

Some marketers dispute this criticism, arguing that the heavy use of sales promotion is a symptom of these problems, not a cause. They point to more basic causes, such as slower population growth, more educated consumers, industry overcapacity, the decreasing effectiveness of advertising, the growth of reseller power and business's emphasis on short-run profits. These marketers assert that sales promotions benefit manufacturers by letting them adjust to short-term changes in supply and demand and to differences in customer segments. Sales promotions encourage consumers to try new products instead of always staying with their current ones. They lead to more varied retail formats, such as the everyday-low-price store or the promotional-pricing store, which give consumers more choice. Finally, sales promotions lead to greater consumer awareness of prices, and consumers themselves enjoy the satisfaction of taking advantage of price specials.[33]

Sales promotions are usually used together with advertising or personal selling. Consumer promotions are normally advertised and can add excitement and pulling power to ads. Trade and sales force promotions support the firm's personal selling process. In using sales promotion, a company must set objectives, select the right tools, develop the best programme, pretest and implement that programme, and evaluate the results. We will examine each of these issues in turn.

Setting Sales Promotion Objectives

Sales promotion objectives vary widely. Let us take *consumer promotions* first. Sellers may use consumer promotions to: (1) increase short-term sales; (2) help build long-term market share; (3) entice consumers to try a new product; (4) lure consumers away from competitors' products; (5) encourage consumers to 'load up' on a mature product; or (6) hold and reward loyal customers.

Objectives for *trade promotions* include: (1) motivating retailers to carry new items and more inventory; (2) inducing them to advertise the product and give it more shelf space; and (3) persuading them to buy ahead.

For the *sales force*, objectives may be to: (1) prompt more sales force support for current or new products; or (2) stimulate salespeople to sign up new accounts.

Objectives should be measurable. Rather than stating that the promotion aims to increase sales, the objective should be specific about the level of increase, who the main targets are and whether increased sales are expected to come from new trialists or from current consumers who are loading up or bringing forward their purchase.

In general, sales promotions should be **consumer relationship building**. Rather than creating only short-term sales volume or temporary brand switching, they should help to reinforce the product's position and build long-term relationships with customers. Increasingly, marketers are avoiding the 'quick fix', price-

consumer relationship-building promotions *Sales promotions that promote the product's positioning and include a selling message along with the deal.*

led promotions in favour of promotions designed to build brand equity. For example, in France, Nestlé set up roadside Relais Bébé centres, where travellers can stop to feed and change their babies. At each centre, Nestlé hostesses provide free disposable nappies, changing tables, high chairs and free samples of Nestlé baby food. Each summer, 64 hostesses welcome 120,000 baby visits and dispense 6,000,000 samples of baby food. This ongoing promotion provides real value to parents and an ideal opportunity to build relationships with customers. Nestlé also provides a freephone number for free baby nutrition counselling.[34]

Even price promotions can be designed to build customer relationships. Examples include all the 'frequency marketing programmes' and 'clubs' that have mushroomed in recent years. If properly designed, every sales promotion tool has consumer relationship-building potential.

Selecting Sales Promotion Tools

Many tools can be used to accomplish sales promotion objectives. The promotion planner should consider the type of market, the sales promotion objectives, the competition and the cost-effectiveness of each tool. Descriptions of the main consumer and trade promotion tools follow.

● *Consumer Promotion Tools*

The main consumer promotion tools include samples, coupons, cash refunds, price packs, premiums, advertising specialities, patronage rewards, point-of-purchase displays and demonstrations, and contests, sweepstakes and games.

samples
Offers to consumers of a trial amount of a product.

Samples are offers of a trial amount of a product. Some samples are free; for others, the company charges a small amount to offset its cost. The sample might be delivered door to door, sent by mail, handed out in a store, attached to another product or featured in an ad. Sampling is the most effective, but most expensive, way to introduce a new product.

coupons
Certificates that give buyers a saving when they purchase a product.

Coupons are certificates that give buyers a saving when they purchase specified products. Coupons can be mailed, included with other products or placed in ads in newspapers and magazines. They can stimulate sales of a mature brand or promote early trial of a new brand. Today, marketers are increasingly distributing coupons through shelf dispensers at the point of sale, by electronic point-of-sale printers or through 'paperless coupon systems' that dispense personalized discounts to targeted buyers at the checkout counter in stores. Some companies are now offering coupons on their Web sites or through online coupon services.

cash refund offers (rebates)
Offers to refund part of the purchase price of a product to consumers who send a 'proof of purchase' to the manufacturer.

Cash refund offers (or **rebates**) are like coupons except that the price reduction occurs after the purchase rather than at the retail outlet. The consumer sends a 'proof of purchase' to the manufacturer, which then refunds part of the purchase price by mail.

price packs
Reduced prices that are marked by the producer directly on the label or package.

Price packs or reduced prices offer consumers savings off the regular price of a product. The reduced prices are marked by the producer directly on the label or package. Price packs can be single packages sold at a reduced price (such as two for the price of one) or two related products banded together (such as a toothbrush and toothpaste). Price packs are very effective, even more so than coupons, in stimulating short-term sales.

premiums
Goods offered either free or at low cost as an incentive to buy a product.

Premiums are goods offered either free or at low cost as an incentive to buy a product. A premium may come inside the package (in-pack) or outside the package (on-pack) or through the mail. If reusable, the package itself may serve as a premium, such as a decorative biscuit container. Premiums are sometimes mailed to consumers who have sent in a proof of purchase, such as a box top. A

| Table 19.6 | Sales promotions in European countries: what is permitted and what is not |

	UK	IRL	SPA	GER	F	DEN	BEL	NL	POL	ITA	GRE	LUX	AUS	FIN	NOR	SWE	SWI	RUS	HUN	CZ
On-pack price cut	Y	Y	Y	Y	Y	Y	Y	Y	Y	Y	Y	Y	Y	Y	Y	Y	Y	Y	Y	Y
Branded offers	Y	Y	Y	?	Y	?	N	Y	Y	Y	Y	N	?	?	?	?	N	Y	Y	Y
In-pack premiums	Y	Y	Y	?	?	?	Y	?	Y	Y	Y	N	?	Y	N	?	N	Y	Y	Y
Multi-buy offers	Y	Y	Y	?	Y	?	?	Y	Y	Y	Y	N	?	?	Y	?	N	?	Y	Y
Extra product	Y	Y	Y	?	Y	Y	?	?	Y	Y	Y	Y	?	Y	?	?	?	Y	Y	Y
Free product	Y	Y	Y	Y	Y	Y	?	Y	Y	Y	Y	Y	Y	Y	Y	Y	Y	Y	Y	Y
Re-use pack	Y	Y	Y	Y	Y	Y	Y	Y	Y	Y	Y	Y	?	Y	Y	Y	Y	Y	Y	Y
Free mail-ins	Y	Y	Y	N	Y	?	Y	Y	Y	Y	Y	?	N	Y	Y	N	N	Y	Y	Y
With-purchase	Y	Y	Y	?	Y	?	?	?	Y	Y	Y	N	?	Y	?	?	N	Y	Y	Y
X-product offers	Y	Y	Y	?	Y	?	N	?	Y	Y	Y	N	?	Y	N	?	N	Y	Y	Y
Collector devices	Y	Y	Y	?	?	?	?	?	Y	Y	Y	N	N	?	N	N	N	Y	Y	Y
Competitions	Y	Y	Y	?	?	?	Y	?	Y	Y	Y	?	?	Y	?	Y	Y	Y	Y	Y
Self-liquidators	Y	Y	Y	Y	Y	Y	Y	?	Y	Y	Y	N	Y	Y	Y	Y	N	Y	Y	Y
Free draws	Y	Y	Y	N	Y	N	N	N	Y	Y	Y	N	N	Y	N	N	N	Y	?	Y
Share-outs	Y	Y	Y	N	?	N	N	N	Y	?	Y	N	N	?	?	N	N	Y	Y	Y
Sweep/lottery	?	?	?	?	?	N	?	?	?	?	?	N	?	Y	N	N	N	Y	?	?
Cash-off vouchers	Y	Y	Y	N	Y	?	Y	Y	Y	?	Y	?	?	?	N	?	Y	N	Y	Y
Cash off purchase	Y	Y	Y	N	Y	N	Y	Y	Y	?	Y	N	N	?	N	N	N	Y	Y	Y
Cash back	Y	Y	Y	?	Y	Y	Y	Y	Y	N	Y	N	?	?	?	Y	N	Y	Y	Y
In-store demos	Y	Y	Y	Y	Y	Y	Y	Y	Y	Y	Y	Y	Y	Y	Y	Y	Y	Y	?	Y

NOTES: Y permitted, N not permitted, ? maybe permitted with certain conditions.

SOURCE: IMP.

self-liquidating premium is a premium sold below its normal retail price to consumers who request it.

Advertising specialities are useful articles imprinted with an advertiser's name and given as gifts to consumers. Typical items include pens, calendars, key rings, matches, shopping bags, T-shirts, caps and coffee mugs. Such items can be very effective. In a recent study, 63 per cent of all consumers surveyed were either carrying or wearing an ad speciality item. More than three-quarters of those who had an item could recall the advertiser's name or message before showing the item to the interviewer.[35]

Patronage rewards are cash or other awards offered for the regular use of a certain company's products or services. For example, airlines offer 'frequent flyer plans', awarding points for miles travelled that can be turned in for free airline trips. Some international hotels like Holiday Inn and Marriott Hotels have an 'honoured guest' plan that awards points to users of their hotels.

Point-of-purchase (POP) promotions include displays and demonstrations that take place at the point of purchase or sale. Unfortunately, many retailers do not like to handle the hundreds of displays, signs and posters they receive from manufacturers each year. Manufacturers have responded by offering better POP materials, tying them in with television or print messages, and offering to set them up.

Competitions, sweepstakes, lotteries and games give consumers the chance to win something, such as cash, trips or goods, by luck or through extra effort. A

advertising specialities
Useful articles imprinted with an advertiser's name, given as gifts to consumers.

patronage rewards
Cash or other awards for the regular use of a certain company's products or services.

point-of-purchase (POP) promotions
Displays and demonstrations that take place at the point of purchase or sale.

Marketing Highlight 19.2

Sales Promotions: Creating Successful Europe-Wide Campaigns

Sales promotion tactics as marketing tools are difficult enough to gauge in domestic markets, let alone outside them. Like advertising, using a single theme, through one medium, to target a single audience across different countries is tempting, but rarely successful.

Experts from the European Federation of Sales Promotion argue that the mechanics of promotional campaigns can translate well across national borders, on the basis that the most powerful word which is understood across cultures is 'free'. Giving away items free with a purchase tends to work well in most countries. Samples, where permitted, also work well, especially if they are attached to something bought or given away. Pan-European sampling campaigns were run for Procter & Gamble's new Wash & Go and Johnson & Johnson's pH 5.5 shampoo: the colours, on-card samples and branding were consistent in each market. Only the language on the packaging was changed. Minipack Sampling Solutions, the company that ran the campaigns, stressed that the principle behind pan-European sampling campaigns is to look for cross-country convergences, not differences, and to leverage these similarities.

Pan-European sampling: Johnson & Johnson's pH5.5 sampling campaign worked on the basis of common packaging, with the language being changed for each different market.

Where there are cross-country segments that are looking for recognition and reward, then, according to David Butter, Wunderman Cato Johnson Europe's vice president, promotions that give customers the chance to win competitions and draws are very powerful.

There are a number of barriers that marketers should understand. One is the differing *legislation* across individual countries. For example, it is very liberal in Italy, Spain and Portugal, where gifts-with-purchase, prizes-with-purchase and on-pack promotions are commonplace. In Germany, laws dating back to the 1930s mean that a free or very cheap premium is illegal, as is sampling if the product is not new. France is moderately liberal in allowing premiums so long as they do not exceed 7 per cent of the value of products up to and including Ffr500 or go above Ffr350. In the Netherlands, premiums must not exceed 4 per cent of the value of the main purchase, while in Belgium the ceiling is 5 per cent.

Another hurdle to overcome is *national safety standards*. In Germany, safety standards are particularly tight, requiring a higher testing procedure than in the United Kingdom. In France, the firm's logo must be incorporated into promotional products.

The concept of the single European market is slowly making its impact on EC law. The latest ruling is that companies should not be disadvantaged due to individual national laws. Countries with restrictive legislation are compelled to open up to those which do not have the same restrictions. Thus German laws have been relaxed as a result. For example, the French cosmetics firm Yves Rocher produced catalogues full of special offers that were available in Germany but illegal. The European Court found in favour of Yves Rocher. Germany's *Rabattgesetz*, which forbids the offer of certain types of discount, has been amended. Discounting has since been permitted in Germany. Clearly, when organizations intend to run a promotion in a number of European countries, they should check on the legality of it across those markets.

If it is becoming easier to get round national laws in Europe, it is not so easy to overcome *cultural differences*, *prejudices* and *suspicions*. If a German buyer is offered a discounted product, he or she usually thinks that there is something wrong with it or it is deficient in some way. Any price reduction must therefore reassure the customer and offer a good rationalization for the discount. Cultural differences also affect the type of merchandise used in the promotion. Household items, especially electrical goods, are very popular in Germany. Beach towels, sunglasses and T-shirts are more popular in Spain and Portugal, while in France, it is pens, lighters and watches. In Italy, brand association is important – if the merchandise features a designer name, a recognized brand name or a football club, the chances are that it will be well received.

Media costs vary significantly. Marketers must take care not to put money-off vouchers in publications that are worth less than the voucher, since dishonest shopkeepers will simply keep the newspaper or cut the coupons out. *Fraud* is a problem too. In poorer countries, if an incentive is worth cheating for, people will cheat.

To achieve successful European promotional campaigns, managers have to carry out accurate research. Achieving economies of scale with global brands and consistent campaigns may be attractive, but insufficient. Successful Europe-wide promotions are invariably built around local and national criteria as opposed to being pan-European or global. Other experts, however, argue that firms can mix the two in the face of *mass customization* in many markets, where the mass is the *core idea or strategy*, which is customized to suit different markets. For example, Schweppes tonic devised a core theme based on the game Trivial Pursuit, which they called *Schquiz*. In France, tonic is a soft drink, while in the United Kingdom it is a mixer, in Spain a refreshment and in Germany a 'sophisticated' drink. The main difference in image across the different countries was the relative strength of the brand. In Spain it is a much stronger brand, which is popular among older consumers. A TV phone-in was used for Schquiz because of this and the fact that TV is a stronger medium. In France, the smaller market for Schweppes tonic meant a smaller media spend for the brand and a radio phone-in was used instead.

Experts stress that effective European promotional campaigns work best if marketers begin by clarifying and defining their objectives and then decide on the best means, within the limitations of budgets and resources, to meet these objectives on a country-by-country basis. It is also advisable to employ the knowledge of local experts, who understand the sales promotion business and their own consumers, in order to avoid costly errors or embarrassment. Procter & Gamble distributed thousands of its Wash & Go shampoo and conditioner to Russian households, only to find that people were breaking into letter boxes and selling the stolen samples on market stalls!

More recently, the European Federation of Sales Promotion (EFSP), comprising groups representing the sales promotion industries in the Netherlands, Ireland, the UK, Spain, Italy, France, Denmark, Germany and Belgium, has been working towards a common framework governing sales promotions introduced across Europe. This will prove to be a difficult challenge, as members seek to 'harmonize' rules and regulations for Europe-wide practices, without denying altogether individual country practitioners' freedom to promote.

SOURCES: Sean Brierley, 'Harmony in discount', *Marketing Week* (14 October 1994), pp. 61–2; David Waller, 'Charged up over competition law', *Financial Times* (23 June 1994), p. 16; Martin Croft, 'War of independence', *Marketing Week* (3 March 1995), pp. 47–51.

competition calls for consumers to submit an entry – a jingle, guess, suggestion – to be judged by a panel that will select the best entries. A *sweepstake* calls for consumers to submit their names for a draw. For a *lottery*, consumers buy tickets which enter their names into a draw. A *game* presents consumers with something, such as bingo numbers or missing letters, every time they buy, which may or may not help them win a prize.

• *Sales Promotions in Europe*

The sales promotion industry is significantly more developed in the United States than in Europe, where the United Kingdom leads other EU member states. In the UK, sales promotion activities are relatively free from legal constraints, with self-policing, in alignment with the industry's code of practice, being the norm. Supermarket retailing in the United Kingdom is dominated by a few key players and decisions regarding acceptance of manufacturers' sales promotion activities are centralized. Cost-effectiveness is increased as the sales promotion handling house is able to use the retailing groups' own administrative processes. Cultural differences also affect consumers' acceptance of different sales promotion techniques. Furthermore, the legal position of sales promotion techniques in different EU countries varies (see Table 19.6). In general, greater freedom is found in the United Kingdom, Ireland and Spain. Legal controls are stricter in the Benelux countries, Germany and, notably so, in Norway. Outside the EU, countries like Poland, Hungary, Russia and the Czech Republic have relatively liberal policies on promotions and incentives, whereas Switzerland appears to be the most restrictive.[36]

The European market for sales promotion remains fragmented for the time being and, until true harmonization is achieved, marketers must retain a sensitivity to national constraints and adapt strategies to fit individual country markets (see Marketing Highlight 19.2).

• *Trade Promotion Tools*

Trade promotion can persuade retailers or wholesalers to carry a brand, give it shelf space, promote it in advertising and push it to consumers. Shelf space is so scarce these days that manufacturers often have to offer price discounts, allowances, buy-back guarantees or free goods to retailers and wholesalers to get on the shelf and, once there, to stay on it.

discount

A straight reduction in price on purchases during a stated period of time.

allowance

Promotional money paid by manufacturers to retailers in return for an agreement to feature the manufacturer's product in some way.

Manufacturers use several trade promotion tools. Many of the tools used for consumer promotions – contests, premiums, displays – can also be used as trade promotions. Alternatively, the manufacturer may offer a straight **discount** off the list price on each case purchased during a stated period of time (also called a *price-off*, *off-invoice* or *off-list*). The offer encourages dealers to buy in quantity or to carry a new item. Dealers can use the discount for immediate profit, for advertising or for price reductions to their customers.

Manufacturers may also offer an **allowance** (usually so much off per case) in return for the retailer's agreement to feature the manufacturer's products in some way. An *advertising allowance* compensates retailers for advertising the product. A *display allowance* compensates them for using special displays.

Manufacturers may offer *free goods*, which are extra cases of merchandise, to intermediaries that buy a certain quantity or that feature a certain flavour or size. They may offer *push incentives* – cash or gifts to dealers or their sales force to 'push' the manufacturer's goods. Manufacturers may give retailers free *speciality advertising items* that carry the company's name, such as pens, pencils, calendars, paperweights, matchbooks, memo pads and ashtrays.

• *Business Promotion Tools*

Companies also promote to industrial customers. These business promotions are used to generate business leads, stimulate purchases, reward customers and motivate salespeople. Business promotion includes many of the same tools used for consumer or trade promotions. Here, we focus on two of the main business promotion tools – conventions and trade shows, and sales contests.

CONVENTIONS AND TRADE SHOWS. Many companies and trade associations organize conventions and trade shows to promote their products. Firms selling to the industry show their products at the trade show. Vendors receive many benefits, such as opportunities to find new sales leads, contact customers, introduce new products, meet new customers, sell more to present customers and educate customers with publications and audiovisual materials.

Trade shows also help companies reach many prospects not reached through their sales forces. Business managers face several decisions, including which trade shows to participate in, how much to spend on each trade show, how to build dramatic exhibits that attract attention, and how to follow up on sales leads effectively.[37]

SALES CONTESTS. A *sales contest* is a contest for salespeople or dealers to urge their sales force to increase their efforts over a given period. Called 'incentive programmes', these contests motivate and recognize good company performers, who may receive trips, cash prizes or other gifts. Sales contests work best when they are tied to measurable and achievable sales objectives (such as finding new accounts, reviving old accounts or increasing account profitability) and when employees believe they have an equal chance of winning. Otherwise, employees who do not think the contest's goals are reasonable or equitable will not take up the challenge.

Developing the Sales Promotion Programme

The marketer must decide on the *creative idea* and the *mechanics* of the promotion. The creative idea concerns adding some kind of value to the product. It is often difficult to generate an innovative idea which sets a sales promotion apart, since it is easy for competitors to copy price reductions, free products or gifts, and in-store demonstrations. The marketer must ensure the promotion genuinely offers extra value and incentives to targets, that it is not misleading, and that the firm has the ability to honour redemptions. If not, the campaign could backfire, exposing the firm to bad publicity which might damage its reputation and brand image (see Marketing Highlight 19.3).

Some of the large consumer packaged-goods firms have a sales promotion manager who studies past promotions and uses past experience to decide on incentive levels to adopt. Many firms also use marketing companies and agencies to assist them in designing and implementing the sales promotion campaign.

The marketer must also set *conditions for participation*. Incentives might be offered to everyone or only to select groups. For example, competitions may not be offered to families of company personnel or to people under a certain age. Conditions, such as the proof of purchase or closing date of the offer, must be clearly stated.

The marketer must then decide how to *promote and distribute the promotion* programme itself. A money-off coupon could be given out in a package, at the store, by mail or in an advertisement. Each distribution method involves a different level of reach and cost. Increasingly, marketers are blending several media into a total campaign concept. They must also decide on the choice of media used to announce the sales promotion programme:

Consider a food company which plans to launch a campaign to promote a new health snack product. The peak purchasing period for health snacks is usually after the winter, particularly Christmas, indulgence period and before summer. It schedules TV and magazine advertising to coincide

Hoover: Have Promotions, Will Travel

Marketing Highlight 19.3

In the summer of 1992, Hoover launched a promotion offering consumers two free return flights to Europe or America if they bought any of its vacuum cleaners, washing machines or other household appliances worth more than £100.

The campaign put the Hoover name on everybody's lips – but for the wrong reason. What happened? The promotion was a ploy dreamed up to tempt people to buy a new appliance. It seemed to have the advantage of raising cash on extra sales, at a time when the UK market for household appliances was depressed, with costs that did not have to be incurred until later, in the form of heavily discounted air tickets, when the appliance market would have improved. Hoover's mistake was to expect many consumers to be attracted by the promise of free flights, but to be deterred from redeeming their air tickets by the offer's small print, which lays down conditions about available dates for flights and choice of hotel accommodation, including one-application-per-household restrictions. Unfortunately, the company had miscalculated, although, according to a company lawyer for Hoover European Appliance Group, no fewer than three sales promotions agencies were involved in originating and costing the promotion. Each of them was sufficiently confident to accept the risk on take-up rates. As it happened, most consumers bought cheap vacuum cleaners that cost as little as £120. The cheapest pair of return air tickets to New York cost about £500. The firm was inundated with as many as 200,000 applications for free flights within the first ten months of the campaign. The company had only issued about 6,000 tickets within that same period. The travel agents hired by Hoover were also alleged to be unfairly dissuading consumers from taking up the offer. Angry customers were, nonetheless, adamant and many were still waiting for their tickets. Although Hoover had put aside some money to cover the air fares, it was nothing like enough. When the three agencies failed to fulfil their obligations, they left Hoover to honour their commitments. The parent company, Maytag, had to come to the rescue by paying out $30 million, which helped to fund fully the redemption of the free flights offer for those with a valid claim and the diligence to pursue it. The fiasco had cost the company £48 million (the initial promotional budget was £1.5 million). In the United Kingdom and Ireland, Hoover's name became a sick joke to millions of consumers.

However, this is not the end of the affair. Hundreds of disgruntled consumers have sought compensation since. Hoover does not release an up-to-date total of cases, but sources report that the company has lost one in five of the cases heard in small claims courts. In some cases where the company was found guilty of abusing the rules, complainants have been awarded over £450 in damages. Five years on, in 1997, Hoover returned to court to defend itself over new allegations of misconduct. Of the 600,000 people who expected a holiday from the promotion (some 300,000 vouchers were issued), 220,000 made it to the United States, leaving 380,000 disappointed customers.

Which party is to be blamed? Hoover's management or the promotions agencies it used? Both parties displayed errors in judgement. While the experts severely miscalculated, management at Hoover cannot put the blame entirely on them. It is the firm's responsibility to ask: How should it justify its spending on the sales promotion? What return on its promotional investment was it seeking? What would the take-up rates be and are they realistic? What would it cost the company given the size or attractiveness of the incentive?

It follows that the marketer must cost the sales promotion and carefully evaluate take-up rates when deciding the *size of the incentive*. A certain minimum incentive is necessary if the promotion is to succeed; a larger incentive will produce more sales response. It is important to strike a balance between an incentive of sufficient substance to induce consumers to experiment and to tempt lapsed users to buy, and too generous an incentive, triggering an extreme rate of redemption, that could financially cripple the firm.

A Hoover spokesperson insists that the company has publicly admitted it made a mistake. Technically, the promotion was legal. It did not breach the British Code of Sales Promotion Practice, since the small print spelled out the hurdles involved. But it played on consumers' lack of knowledge. And when the company faced difficulties, it did not act until the promotion got serious media attention. Subsequently, redemp-

tion rates soared as customers with a valid claim became determined to get their flights. After the fiasco, the company has learnt its lessons. But, as court cases open the floodgates to more claims, Hoover is busy sucking up the mess!

SOURCES: 'Hoover: it sucks', *The Economist* (3 April 1993), p. 88; 'Hoover flights offer: the facts', *Marketing Week* (21 October 1994), p. 36; David Reed, 'Holiday programme', *Marketing Week* (5 July 1996), pp. 39–42; Natalie Cheary, 'Hoover fails to shake off free flights horror', *Marketing Week* (1 May 1997), p. 22.

---

with this period. Some of the magazine advertising is used to announce a competition and free health booklet. It also plans a trade promotion to sustain retailer awareness and to ensure they stock up for demand. Sales force incentives are also planned to bolster the effects of the trade promotion.

The *duration of the promotion* is also important. If the sales promotion period is too short, many prospects (who may not be buying during that time) will miss it. If the promotion runs for too long, the deal will lose some of its 'act now' force.

The marketer also must decide on the *response mechanism*: that is, the redemption vehicle to be used by the customer who takes part in the promotion. The easier it is for the customer to respond to an offer, the higher the response rate. Immediate gratification – for example, a price reduction, or a free gift attached to the product on offer – often yields a higher response. If the incentive requires further action to be taken by the consumer – for instance, to make another purchase or to collect the required number of tokens in promotion packs and then post these off to claim a gift or free product – the redemption rate can be reduced.

Finally, the marketer must determine *the sales promotion budget*, which can be developed in one of two ways. The marketer may choose the promotions and estimate their total cost. However, the more common way is to use a percentage of the total budget for sales promotion. One study found three serious problems in the way companies budget for sales promotion. First, they do not consider cost effectiveness. Second, instead of spending to achieve objectives, they simply extend the previous year's spending, take a percentage of expected sales or use the 'affordable approach'. Finally, advertising and sales promotion budgets are too often prepared separately.[38]

Pretesting and Implementing

Whenever possible, sales promotion tools should be *pretested* to find out if they are appropriate and of the right incentive size. Consumer sales promotions can be pretested quickly and inexpensively. For example, consumers can be asked to rate or rank different possible promotions, or promotions can be tried on a limited basis in selected geographic areas.

Companies should prepare implementation plans for each promotion, covering lead time and sell-off time. *Lead time* is the time necessary to prepare the programme before launching it. *Sell-off time* begins with the launch and ends when the promotion ends.

Evaluating the Results

Evaluation is also very important. Many companies fail to evaluate their sales promotion programmes, while others evaluate them only superficially. Manufacturers can use one of many evaluation methods. The most common method is to compare sales before, during and after a promotion. Suppose a company has a 6 per cent market share before the promotion, which jumps to 10 per cent during the promotion, falls to 5 per cent right after and rises to 7 per cent later on. The promotion seems to have attracted new triers and more buying from current customers. After the promotion, sales fell as consumers used up their inventories. The long-run rise to 7 per cent means that the company gained some new users. If the brand's share had returned to the old level, then the promotion would have changed only the *timing* of demand rather than the *total* demand.

Consumer research would also show the kinds of people who responded to the promotion and what they did after it ended. *Surveys* can provide information on how many consumers recall the promotion, what they thought of it, how many took advantage of it and how it affected their buying. Sales promotions can also be evaluated through *experiments* that vary factors such as incentive value, timing, duration and distribution method.

Clearly, sales promotion plays an important role in the total promotion mix. To use it well, the marketer must define the sales promotion objectives, select the best tools, design the sales promotion programme, pretest and implement the programme, and evaluate the results.

public relations
Building good relations with the company's various publics by obtaining favourable publicity, building up a good 'corporate image', and handling or heading off unfavourable rumours, stories and events. Major PR tools include press relations, product publicity, corporate communications, lobbying and counselling.

publicity
Activities to promote a company or its products by planting news about it in media not paid for by the sponsor.

Public Relations

Another important mass-promotion technique is **public relations**. This concerns building good relations with the company's various publics by obtaining favourable publicity, building up a good 'corporate image' and handling or heading off unfavourable rumours, stories and events. The old name for marketing public relations was **publicity**, which was seen simply as activities to promote a company or its products by planting news about it in media not paid for by the sponsor. Public relations (PR) is a much broader concept that includes publicity as well as many other activities. Public relations departments use many different tools:

● *Press relations or press agency.* Creating and placing newsworthy information in the news media to attract attention to a person, product or service.

● *Product publicity.* Publicizing specific products.

● *Public affairs.* Building and maintaining local, national and international relations.

● *Lobbying.* Building and maintaining relations with legislators and government officials to influence legislation and regulation.

● *Investor relations.* Maintaining relationships with shareholders and others in the financial community.

● *Development.* Public relations with donors or members of non-profit organizations to gain financial or volunteer support.

Public relations is used to promote products, people, places, ideas, activities, organizations and even nations. Trade associations have used public relations to rebuild interest in declining commodities such as eggs, apples, milk and potatoes. Even nations have used public relations to attract more tourists, foreign investment and international support. Companies can use PR to manage their way out of crisis, as in the case of Johnson & Johnson's masterly use of public relations to save Tylenol from extinction after its product-tampering scare.

Public relations can have a strong impact on public awareness at a much lower cost than advertising. The company does not pay for the space or time in the media. Rather, it pays for a staff to develop and circulate information and to manage events. If the company develops an interesting story, it could be picked up by several different media, having the same effect as advertising that would cost a lot more money. And it would have more credibility than advertising.

Despite its potential strengths, public relations, like sales promotions, is often described as a marketing stepchild because of its limited and scattered use. The public relations department is usually located at corporate headquarters. Its staff is so busy dealing with various publics – stockholders, employees, legislators, city officials – that public relations programmes to support product marketing objectives may be ignored. Moreover, marketing managers and public relations practitioners do not always talk the same language. Many public relations practitioners see their job as simply communicating. In contrast, marketing managers tend to be much more interested in how advertising and public relations affect sales and profits.

This situation is changing, however. Many companies now want their public relations departments to manage all their activities with a view to marketing the company and improving the bottom line. Some companies are setting up special units to support corporate and product promotion and image making directly.

Many companies hire marketing public relations firms to handle their PR programmes or to assist the company public relations team. Major corporations and multinational firms are also placing greater emphasis on analyzing and measuring the effectiveness of their PR activities to provide a basis for forward planning of communication strategies.

Important Public Relations Tools

There are a number of PR tools. One essential tool is *news*. PR professionals find or create favourable news about the company and its products or people. Sometimes news stories occur naturally. At other times, the PR person can suggest events or activities that would create news.

Speeches also create product and company publicity. Increasingly, company executives must field questions from the media or give talks at trade associations or sales meetings. These events can either build or hurt the company's image.

Another common PR tool is *special events*, ranging from news conferences, press tours, grand openings and firework displays to laser shows, hot-air balloon releases, multimedia presentations and star-studded spectaculars designed to reach and interest target publics. Richard Branson, the chief executive of Virgin Group, offers a good example of a practitioner who has perfected the art of deploying both speeches and special events for self- and corporate promotion.

Public relations people also prepare *written materials* to reach and influence their target markets. These materials include annual reports, brochures, articles and company newsletters and magazines.

Audiovisual materials, such as films, slide-and-sound programmes and video and audio cassettes, are being used increasingly as communication tools.

Corporate-identity materials also help create a corporate identity that the public immediately recognizes. Logos, stationery, brochures, signs, business forms, business cards, buildings, uniforms and even company cars and trucks make effective marketing tools when they are attractive, distinctive and memorable.

Companies might improve public goodwill by contributing money and time to *public service activities*: campaigns to raise funds for worthy causes – for example, to fight illiteracy, support the work of a charity, or assist the aged and handicapped – help to raise public recognition.

Sponsorship is any vehicle through which corporations gain public relations exposure. In Europe, the sponsorship industry is growing, with many firms committing huge sums of money around the world to the sponsorship of sport and the arts because it makes good sense as a marketing tool (see Marketing Highlight 19.4).

A company's *Web site* can also be a good public relations vehicle. Consumers and members of other publics can visit the site for information and entertainment.

Main Public Relations Decisions

In considering when and how to use product public relations, management should set PR objectives; choose the PR messages and vehicles; implement the PR plan; and evaluate the results.

● *Setting Public Relations Objectives*

The first task is to set *objectives* for public relations. These are usually defined in relation to the types of news story to be communicated, the communication

34. 'Nestlé banks on databases', *Advertising Age* (25 October 1993), p.16.

35. See J. Thomas Russell and Ronald Lane, *Kleppner's Advertising Procedure*, 13th edn (Englewood Cliffs, NJ: Prentice Hall, 1996), pp. 453–6; 'Power to the key ring and T-shirt', *Sales and Marketing Management* (December 1989), p. 14.

36. A more extensive discussion of the legal position of sales promotion methods across EU states and developments towards EU harmonization is found in: *European Promotional Legislation Guide*, 3rd edn (London: Institute of Sales Promotion, 1992); *European Code of Sales Promotion Practice* (London: Institute of Sales Promotion, March 1991); R. Lawson, 'Key problems in Europe: can you implement a pan-European promotion?', Incorporated Society of British Advertisers' Conference on 'Controlling Sales Promotion: Getting it Right is a Joint Responsibility', London, July 1991.

37. Richard Szathmary, 'Trade shows', *Sales and Marketing Management* (May 1992), pp. 83–4. Srinath Gopalakrishna, Gary L. Lilien, Jerome D. Williams and Ian Sequeira, 'Do trade shows pay off?', *Journal of Marketing* (July 1995), pp. 75–83.

38. Roger A. Strang, 'Sales promotion, fast growth, faulty management', *Harvard Business Review* (July–August 1976), p. 119.

39. Jo-Anne Walker, 'News analysis', *Marketing Week* (24 November 1996), p. 39.

Case 19

Diesel Jeans & Workwear: 'We're All Different, But Aren't We All Different in the Same Way?'[1]

Malin Nilsson, Anki Sjöström, Anneli Zell and Thomas Helgesson*

DURING THE OIL CRISIS IN 1978, the idea of a trademark called Diesel came to Renzo Rosso, the son of an Italian farmer. To him Diesel represented something that everybody needs and always will need. He kept this in mind until 1985, when the real Diesel story began. In that year he decided to produce and sell clothes that he himself liked to wear; clothes that represented his lifestyle. His wild and masculine 'Renzo Rosso style' is what Diesel Jeans & Workwear is all about. It is a way of living …

Get Your Blue Jeans On

Blue jeans are the most successful clothes ever invented and the world's largest clothing companies depend on them. Why has this 'all American' workwear become the global uniform? Sociologist John Fiske tries to explain. He once asked a class to write down what jeans meant to each of them. He got back a set of staggeringly uniform results. Jeans were American, informal, classless, unisex and appropriate in town or country. Wearing them was a sign of freedom from constraints on behaviour and of class membership. *Free* was the word most commonly used, usually expressing 'freedom to be oneself'. By wearing jeans, Fiske's class were expressing their 'freedom to be themselves', yet 118 out of 125 students were 'being themselves' by wearing the same clothes, jeans. With everyone wearing the same clothes, people who are *really free* go one step further to

* Halmstad University, Sweden.

express themselves. Rockers wore greasy ones, mods smart ones, hippies old ones, skinheads new ones, punks damaged ones, indies torn ones and grunge shabby ones – but they all wore jeans.

Fashion Bubbles Up

Jeans are no longer as uniform, or cheap, as they used to be. The generic jeans, foundation of the Levi Strauss and Wrangler empires, mean classless, country, communal, unisex, work, traditional, unchanging and American. But not so designer jeans. These reached their zenith when Pakistan-born Shami Ahmed exhibited his Manchester-made, diamond-studded, Joe Bloggs jeans costing £150,000 a pair. In contrast to generic jeans, designer jeans mean up-market, city, socially distinctive, (usually) feminine, leisure, contemporary, transient and not American. So transient and non-American are Joe Bloggs jeans that the range changes twelve times a year and West Indian cricketer Brian Lara promotes their 375 and 501 range. The ranges are named after Lara's record-breaking batting scores, although Levi's is not happy about the Joe Bloggs 501 name.

Jeans are now not only high fashion, but the foundation for many new fashions. Jeans are the uniform of the street culture, and leading designers, such as Versace, Westwood, Gaultier and Lagerfield, concede that there is now a very strong 'bubble up' effect where the streets lead fashion. Top jeans companies 'bubble up' in the same way as street fashions do. Shami Ahmed and Renzo Rosso are typical of the clothing entrepreneurs who are leading the way in Europe's dynamic and varied fashion market, and foremost among these businesses is Rosso's Diesel Jeans & Workwear, a European firm that aims to overtake Levi's and become the world's no. 1 jeans company.

Diesel's Concept

To work for Rosso, you have to understand the Diesel concept. You have to love Diesel and devote your life to the company. This company spirit imbues the whole organization and is presumably the reason for Diesel's success. For example, Diesel is probably the only company where all employees, even the management team, wear Diesel clothes.

Rosso has managed to create a multinational concern out of Diesel. The turnover is approximately L8,000,000 million and rising. The profit margin of between 10 and 15 per cent is almost all reinvested in the company. This makes Diesel very strong financially. Today, Diesel is no. 2 in Europe after the American jeans-giant Levi's. Its goal is to become no. 1.

Diesel is today represented in 69 countries worldwide. Of Diesel's 3,000 employees, 150 work at its headquarters at Moldava, Italy. Small family-owned companies in northern Italy carry out about 70 per cent of production, and the rest is spread around low-cost countries such as Hong Kong, Thailand and Korea.

The Diesel collection contains jeans, jackets, sweaters, shoes, underwear and belts for both men and women. These account for 60 per cent of Diesel's products. The remainder includes sportswear, kids' wear and perfume for men. Diesel's products are sold through hand-picked agents, licensees and subsidiaries. Franchising is not popular as there is a risk of losing control of the company profile. Education and training of the international network is intensive. The resellers have a lot to live up to. They have to understand the Diesel concept and sell clothes that go well with Diesel.

Diesel has only two shops of its own, one in Berlin and the other in Stockholm. New stores in Paris, Rome and New York will open soon. There were strategic reasons for opening the first two flagship stores in Stockholm and Berlin. Germany is Diesel's largest market: 25 per cent of production is sold there. Sweden is seen as receptive to new fashions and useful for test marketing. Also, Diesel's vice-president and head of international marketing, Johan Lindeberg, is Swedish. Together with local advertising agency Paradiset, he directs all Diesel's marketing activities from his Swedish headquarters.

Diesel's Advertising

Lindeberg and Paradiset claim that much of their marketing success derives from their lack of respect for marketing strategies and their trend-setting advertising. Adverts are sent by courier-post from Paradiset to distributors in other countries which decide the local marketing arrangements them-selves. Local distributors spend 5 per cent of their turnover on national marketing, while Diesel spends 7 per cent of its total turnover on inter-nationals such as MTV and Sky Sport.

Paradiset has two ideas in mind when creating an advert: The ad should be conspicuous and also contain an ironic message. Diesel's advertising is targeted at modern intelligent people. Diesel often makes fun of current myths, as, for example, in its 'How to ...' campaign. In this campaign, one advert showed the cranium of a girl sucking on a cigarette. The text read, 'How to smoke 145 a day' and 'Man, who needs two lungs anyway?' This message caused much controversy in the United States, where Diesel was criticized for encouraging young people to smoke.

Rosso has his own way of running a company. He follows his own path, ignoring conventional marketing approaches – and it certainly works! Diesel has great growth potential. Rosso believes that, in the long run, a good orga-nization structure is much more important than good advertising. According to Rosso, a strong company is one 'with strong collaborators'. This requires work that employees enjoy and, above all, work that they find interesting. 'When you trust your own and your collaborators' intuitions, feelings and judgements, and not only text-book theories,' says Rosso, 'then you have reached the Diesel feeling.' Since Rosso owns 100 per cent of Diesel, he has his hands free to do whatever he wants. To buy other companies or to be listed on the stock exchange is not 'the Renzo Rosso style' and neither would he leave Moldava. The company's vision is expressed in its slogan: you need Diesel 'for successful living'.

QUESTIONS

1. How does the advertising for generic and designer jeans differ? Can one brand and advertising campaign straddle both markets?

2. Explain Joe Bloggs' choice of Lara and the £150,000 jeans as a way of promoting the brand. Are twelve ranges a year really necessary?

3. What is the controversial style of Diesel's advertising trying to achieve? Do you think it is effective? Ethical? Appropriate for all markets?

4. How does the centralized nature of Diesel's advertising fit the entrepreneurial style of the company? How can the advertising be linked in with the rest of the marketing mix in the many markets and distributors that Diesel serves?

5. What explains Rosso's choice of Sweden, rather than Italy, as the base for his international marketing activity? Why choose an agency and location outside the London and New York heartlands of modern global advertising?

6. Can 'the Renzo Rosso style' be separated from the brand identity and the advertising used? How well does 'the Renzo Rosso style' fit the needs of the jeans market and why?

[1] The quotation is copy from a 1970s Levi's ad.

SOURCES: John Fiske, *Understanding Popular Culture* (London: Routledge, 1990); Hunter Davies, 'Not any old Joe Bloggs', *Independent* (15 November 1994), p. 23; Stephanie Theobald, 'European street style', *The European – élan* (11–17 November1994), pp. 13–16.

Personal Selling and Sales Management

Preview Case

IBM Restructures the Sales Force

IN EARLY 1993, IBM'S BOARD of directors decided that the time was right for dramatic action. The once-proud company had seen its sales fall from almost $69 billion in 1990 to $64 billion in 1992. In the same period, profits had plunged from $5.9 billion to a loss of $4.96 billion. In April, the board hired Louis V. Gerstner, Jr, a former McKinsey Company consultant and R.J. Reynolds CEO, to serve as its new chairman and chief executive officer and to turn the company round.

In July 1993, Gerstner announced his first major strategic decision. He identified the IBM sales force as a key source of the company's problems. Many observers had expected that he would restructure the sales force, which was too large and unwieldy, and had become too slow to change to meet customers' needs. However, Gerstner surprised everyone by announcing that he would postpone the decision as to what to do about IBM's sales force. In an internal memo to his 13 top managers, he concluded that the company's current marketing organization does not always permit them to serve their customers in the most efficient and effective way. However, he noted: 'I don't want to undertake a major reorganization of IBM at this time', arguing that radical reform would pose unacceptable risks to customer loyalty. Rather he would try to make IBM's current sales and marketing systems work better.

How did IBM, one of the world's largest and most successful companies, get into such a fix? In the 1994 IBM Annual Report, Gerstner wrote that IBM's problems resulted from the company's failure to keep pace with rapid industry change. IBM had been too bureaucratic and too preoccupied with its own view of the world. The company was too slow to take new products to market and missed the higher profit margins that are typical of the computer industry early in its product life cycle.

Although bureaucracy and slowness were significant problems, IBM's customers and industry observers identified IBM's preoccupation with its own view of the world as the real problem. They argued that the company had stopped listening to its customers. It peddled mainframe computers to customers who wanted midrange systems and personal computers. It pushed products when its customers wanted solutions. One former sales-person noted that 'We were so well trained, we could sell anything, good or bad. Under quota pressures, we sold systems that our customers didn't need, didn't want and couldn't afford.'

IBM had designed its sales compensation system to encourage and reward selling mainframe systems. 'You could sell a PC and get a pat on the back. Sell a midrange system and get a lot of dollars. But when you sold a mainframe, you would walk on water. You were a hero,' observed another former salesperson. The salespeople always insisted that the customers buy all of their products from IBM and became indignant when a customer used another vendor. Salespeople were also inflexible, making 'one-size-fits-all' presentations using canned, 'off-the-shelf' marketing programmes. One customer added, 'They wouldn't tailor their programmes to what you needed. It was "This is our canned package. We know this works, Trust us."'

Despite the problems, Gerstner's decision not to make strategic changes to the 40,000-person sales force meant that he would continue to implement changes that former CEO John Akers had begun. Beginning in 1991, Akers restructured the sales force using a geographic focus. Senior managers acted as account executives for the top IBM clients in their regions, managing the full breadth of client relationships, including understanding the customer's company and its industry. The account executives could call on a pool of regional product specialists and service representatives to satisfy customer needs. They reported to branch managers, who reported to 'trading area managers', who ultimately reported to regional managers. In foreign countries, a country manager had full control over that country's sales force.

Akers' approach continued IBM's traditional focus on presenting 'one face to the customer'. The account executive structure allowed the customer to deal with one IBM interface rather than dealing with sales-people from each of IBM's product and services areas. Gerstner's reluctance to make sweeping changes probably resulted from a meeting where the firm's top 200 customers told him that they did not want to be confused by 20 different IBM salespeople calling on them. However, it was also hard for any IBM salesperson to be familiar with the wide range of products and services that the company offered.

Nevertheless, IBM had already begun to tinker with its sales approach. In response to increasing competition, declining sales and changing corporate buying habits, the company had already developed 'fighter pilots'. These were 'specialist' salespeople who tried to increase sales by pushing neglected products. Some product lines, such as the personal computers and printer divisions, were also allowed to develop their own sales forces. Aker also allowed some experimentation with salespeople who specialized in certain industries.

As for the sales force compensation plan, which was adjusted each January, the company had modified the plan to promote sales of certain products or increase market share in targeted areas. It was not unusual for a branch manager to have 240 separate measurements because different product groups would set quotas to encourage salespeople to sell their offerings. Until 1993, only 6 per cent of a salesperson's salary above the basic salary (the bulk of a person's pay) reflected the profitability of his or her sales. In 1993 the company increased the portion based on profitability to 20 per cent.

Why did Gerstner decide to forgo any major sales force changes? One consultant noted that Gerstner wanted to wait until the dust settled from cutbacks that had reduced IBM's employment from 344,000 to 256,000 between 1991 and 1993. Many industry observers argued that the decision reflected his desire to continue to study the problem. Microsoft chairman Bill Gates suggested that, although IBM was known for its unified sales force, 'I think it's inevitable that they'll get rid of it.'[1]

The question was: What sales force strategy should IBM use to revive sagging sales and profits while satisfying customer and employee requirements?

QUESTIONS

1. Why does IBM rely on a sales force to sell its products and services?

2. Outline the IBM sales force's objectives, strategy, structure and compensation.

3. What problems do you see in IBM's sales force objectives, strategy, structure and compensation?

4. What objectives would you set for IBM's sales force?

5. What strategy, structure and compensation plan would you establish to accomplish these objectives? Identify the trade-offs involved in each of these decisions.

6. Given your recommendations, how would you recruit, train, supervise, motivate and evaluate IBM's sales force?

Introduction

The above questions reflect the critical issues that IBM's management must face and resolve in order to build and maintain an effective sales force. Indeed, the decisions called for are relevant not only for IBM, but also for any firm that uses a sales force to help it market its goods and services. This chapter looks at the role and nature of personal selling and examines the key issues in managing the sales force.

Robert Louis Stevenson once noted that 'everyone lives by selling something'. We are all familiar with the sales forces used by business organizations to sell products and services to customers around the world. Sales forces are found in non-profit as well as profit organizations. Churches use membership committees to attract new members. Hospitals and museums use fund raisers to contact donors and raise money. In this chapter, we examine the role of personal selling in the organization, sales force management decisions and the basic principles of personal selling.

The Role of Personal Selling

Selling is one of the oldest professions in the world. The people who do the selling go by many names: *salespeople, sales representatives, account executives, sales consultants, sales engineers, field representatives, agents, district managers* and *marketing representatives*, to name a few.

The Nature of Personal Selling

People hold many stereotypes of salespeople. 'Salesman' may bring to mind the image of Arthur Miller's pitiable Willy Loman in *Death of a Salesman* or Meredith Willson's cigar-smoking, back-slapping, joke-telling Harold Hill in *The Music Man*. Both examples depict salespeople as loners travelling their territories trying to foist their wares on unsuspecting or unwilling buyers.

However, modern salespeople are a far cry from these unfortunate stereotypes. Today, most salespeople are well-educated, well-trained professionals who work to build and maintain long-term relationships with customers. They build relationships by listening to their customers, assessing customer needs and organizing the company's efforts to solve customer problems. Consider the case of IBM, which shows that it takes more than a friendly smile and a firm handshake to sell expensive computer systems. It also takes more than convincing sales presentations to win customers' trust in the company's products and services. Customers these days expect their suppliers to take an interest in their company, to understand their problems and to work closely with them to find solutions to these problems.

salesperson
An individual acting for a company by performing one or more of the following activities: prospecting, communicating, servicing and information gathering.

The term **salesperson** covers a wide range of positions. At one extreme, a salesperson might be largely an *order taker*, such as a department store salesperson standing behind the counter. At the other extreme are the *order getters*, salespeople whose job demands the creative selling of products and services ranging from appliances, industrial equipment or aeroplanes to insurance, advertising or consulting services. Other salespeople engage in *missionary selling*, whereby they are not expected or permitted to take an order, but only build goodwill or educate buyers. An example is a salesperson for a pharmaceutical company who calls on doctors to educate them about the company's drug products and to urge them to prescribe these products to their patients. Or there are salespeople whose position is to supply technical knowledge to the buyer, as in engineering salespeople who act as consultants to client companies. In this chapter, we focus on the more creative types of selling and on the process of building and managing an effective sales force.

The term 'salesperson' covers a wide range of jobs, from shop assistant to sales staff involved in consulting with client companies.

The Role of the Sales Force

Personal selling is the interpersonal arm of the promotion mix. Advertising consists of one-way, non-personal communication with target consumer groups. In contrast, personal selling involves two-way personal communication between salespeople and individual customers – whether face-to-face, by telephone, through videoconferences or by other means. As such, personal selling can be more effective than advertising in more complex selling situations. Salespeople can probe customers to learn more about their problems. They can adjust the marketing offer to fit the special needs of each customer and can negotiate terms of sale. They can build long-term personal relationships with key decision makers.

The role of personal selling varies from company to company. Some firms have no salespeople at all – for example, organizations that sell only through mail-order catalogues or through manufacturers' representatives, sales agents or brokers. In most cases, however, the sales force plays a major role. In companies that sell business products, such as ABB or Du Pont, the salespeople may be the only contact. To these customers, the sales force *is* the company. In consumer product companies, such as Nike or Unilever, that sell through intermediaries, final consumers rarely meet salespeople or even know about them. Still, the sales force plays an important behind-the-scenes role. It works with wholesalers and retailers to gain their support and to help them to be more effective in selling the company's products.

The sales force acts as the critical link between a company and its customers. In many cases, salespeople serve both masters – the seller and the buyer. First, they *represent the company to customers*. They find and develop new customers and communicate information about the company's products and services. They sell products by approaching customers, presenting their products, answering objections, negotiating prices and terms, and closing sales. In addition, they provide services to customers, carry out market research and intelligence work, and fill out call reports.

At the same time, salespeople *represent customers to the company*, acting inside the firm as a 'champion' of customers' interests. Salespeople relay customer concerns about company products and actions back to those who can handle them. They learn about customer needs and work with others in the

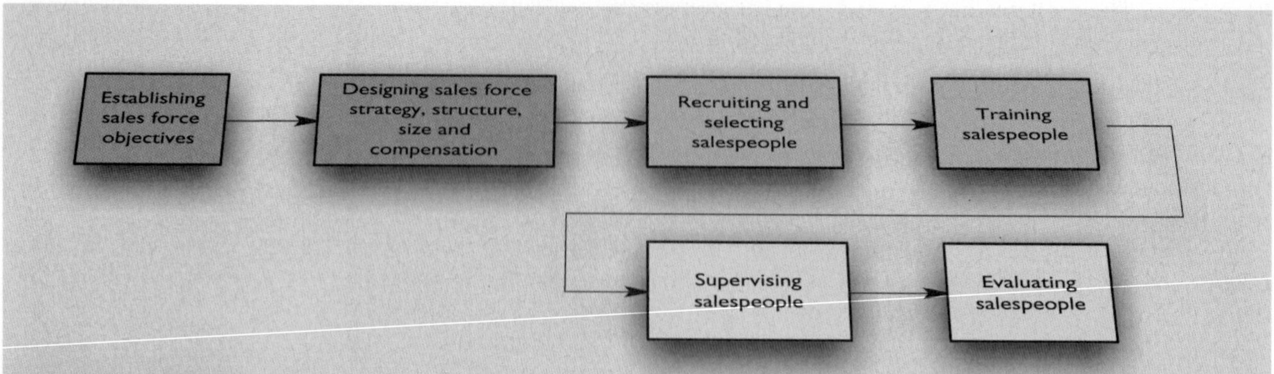

Figure 20.1 **Primary steps in sales force management**

company to develop greater customer value. Thus, the salesperson often act as an *'account manager'* who manages the relationship between the seller and buyer.

As companies move towards a stronger market orientation, their sales forces are becoming more market focused and customer oriented. The old view was that salespeople should worry about sales and the company should worry about profit. The current view holds that salespeople should be concerned with more than just producing sales — they also must know how to produce customer satisfaction and profit. Today, organizations expect salespeople to look at sales data, measure market potential, gather market intelligence and develop marketing strategies and plans. They should know how to orchestrate the firm's efforts towards delivering customer value and satisfaction. A market-oriented rather than a sales-oriented sales force will be more effective in the long run. Beyond winning new customers and making sales, it will help the company to create long-term, profitable relationships with customers. As such, the company's sales team can be a central force in an organization's relationship marketing programme. The topic concerning relationship marketing is discussed in greater detail in Chapter 11.

Managing the Sales Force

sales force management
The analysis, planning, implementation and control of sales force activities. It includes setting sales force objectives; designing sales force strategy; and recruiting, selecting, training, supervising and evaluating the firm's salespeople.

We define **sales force management** as the analysis, planning, implementation and control of sales force activities. It includes setting sales force objectives, designing sales force strategy and recruiting, selecting, training, supervising and evaluating the firm's salespeople. The primary sales force management decisions are shown in Figure 20.1. Let us take a look at each of these decisions next.

Setting Sales Force Objectives

Companies set different objectives for their sales forces. Salespeople usually perform one or more of the following tasks:

● *Prospecting.* They find and develop new customers.
● *Communicating.* They communicate information about the company's products and services.

- *Selling.* They sell products by approaching customers, presenting their products, answering objections and closing sales.
- *Servicing.* In addition, salespeople provide services to customers (e.g. consulting on problems, providing technical assistance, arranging finance).
- *Information gathering.* Salespeople carry out market research and intelligence work, and fill out sales call reports.

Some companies are very specific about their sales force objectives and activities. For example, a company may advise its salespeople to spend 80 per cent of their time with current customers and 20 per cent with prospects, and 85 per cent of their time on current products and 15 per cent on new products. The company believes that if such norms are not set, salespeople tend to spend almost of all of their time selling current products to current accounts and neglect new products and new prospects.

Designing Sales Force Strategy and Structure

Marketing managers face several sales force strategy and design questions. How should salespeople and their tasks be structured? How big should the sales force be? Should salespeople sell alone or work in teams with other people in the company? Should they sell in the field or by telephone? How should salespeople be compensated? And how should performance be rewarded where selling tasks are shared across members within the sales team? We will address these issues below.

● *Sales Force Strategy*

Every company competes with other firms to get orders from customers. Thus it must base its strategy on an understanding of the customer buying process. A company can use one or more of several sales approaches to contact customers. An individual salesperson can talk to a prospect or customer in person or over the phone, or make a sales presentation to a buying group. Similarly, a sales *team* (such as a company executive, a salesperson and a sales engineer) can make a sales presentation to a buying group. In *conference selling*, a salesperson brings resource people from the company to meet with one or more buyers to discuss problems and opportunities. In *seminar selling*, a company team conducts an educational seminar about state-of-the-art developments for a customer's technical people.

Often, the salesperson has to act as an account manager who arranges contacts between people in the buying and selling companies. Because salespeople need help from others in the company, selling calls for teamwork. Others who might assist salespeople include top management, especially when big sales are at stake; technical people who provide technical information to customers; customer service representatives who provide installation, maintenance and other services to customers; and office staff, such as sales analysts, order processors and secretaries.

Once the company decides on a desirable selling approach, it can use either a direct or a contractual sales force. A *direct (or company) sales force* consists of full- or part-time employees who work exclusively for the company. This sales force includes *inside salespeople*, who conduct business from their offices via telephone or visits from prospective buyers, and *field salespeople*, who travel to call on customers. A *contractual sales force* consists of manufacturers' reps, sales agents or brokers who are paid a commission based on their sales.

● *Sales Force Structure*

Sales force strategy influences the structure of the sales force. The sales force structure decision is simple if the company sells only one product line to one industry with customers in many locations. In that case the company would use a *territorial sales force structure*. If the company sells many products to many types of customer, it might need either a *product sales force structure* or *a customer sales force structure*, or a combination of the two.

territorial sales force structure
A sales force organization that assigns each salesperson to an exclusive geographic territory in which that salesperson carries the company's full line.

TERRITORIAL SALES FORCE STRUCTURE. In the **territorial sales force structure**, each salesperson is assigned to an exclusive territory in which to sell the company's full line of products or services. This sales force structure is the simplest sales organization and has many advantages. First, it clearly defines the salesperson's job, and because only one salesperson works the territory, he or she gets all the credit or the blame for territory sales. Second, the territorial structure increases the salesperson's desire to build local business ties that, in turn, improve the salesperson's selling effectiveness. Finally, because each salesperson travels within a small geographic area, travel expenses are relatively small.

product sales force structure
A sales force organization under which salespeople specialize in selling only a portion of the company's products or lines.

PRODUCT SALES FORCE STRUCTURE. Salespeople must know their products. The task is not easy if the company's products are numerous, unrelated and technically complex. To overcome this problem, many companies adopt a **product sales force structure**, in which the sales force sells along product lines. For example, Kodak uses different sales forces for its film products than for its industrial products. The film products sales force deals with simple products that are distributed intensively, whereas the industrial products sales force deals with complex products that require technical understanding.

The product structure can lead to problems, however, if a given customer buys many of the company's products. For example, a hospital supply company has several product divisions, each with a separate sales force. Several salespeople might end up calling on the same hospital on the same day. This means that they travel over the same routes and wait to see the same customer's purchasing agents. These extra costs must be weighed against the benefits of better product knowledge and attention to individual products.

customer sales force structure
A sales force organization under which salespeople specialize in selling only to certain customers or industries.

CUSTOMER SALES FORCE STRUCTURE. More and more companies are using a **customer sales force structure**, whereby they organize the sales force along customer or industry lines. Separate sales forces may be set up for different industries, for serving current customers versus finding new ones, and for large accounts versus regular accounts. For example, a company selling photocopiers could divide its customers into four main groups, each served by a different sales force. The top group consists of large national accounts with multiple and scattered locations, which would be handled by *national account managers*. Next are large accounts that, although not national in scope, may have several locations within a region and are handled by *senior account managers*. Customers with lower annual sales potential could be served by *account representatives* and all other customers could be handled by *marketing representatives*.

Organizing its sales force around customers can help a company to become more customer focused. For example, giant ABB, the Swiss-based industrial equipment maker, changed from a product-based to a customer-based sales force. The new structure resulted in a stronger customer orientation and improved service to clients:

David Donaldson sold boilers for ABB ... After 30 years, Donaldson sure knew boilers, but he didn't know much about the broad range of other products offered by ABB's US Power Plant division. Customers were frustrated because as many as a dozen ABB salespeople called on them at different times to peddle their products. Sometimes representatives even passed each other in customers' lobbies without realizing that they were working for the same company. ABB's bosses decided that this was a poor way to run a sales force. So, David Donaldson and 27 other power plant salespeople began new jobs. [Donaldson] now also sells turbines, generators, and three other product lines. He handles six major accounts ... instead of a [mixed batch] of 35. His charge: Know the customer intimately and sell him the products that help him operate productively. Says Donaldson: 'My job is to make it easy for my customer to do business with us ... I show him where to go in ABB whenever he has a problem.' The president of ABB's power plant businesses [adds]: 'If you want to be a customer-driven company, you have to design the sales organization around individual buyers rather than around your products.'[2]

COMPLEX SALES FORCE STRUCTURES.   When a company sells a wide variety of products to many types of customer over a broad geographical area, it often combines several types of sales force structure. Salespeople can be specialized by territory and product, by territory and market, by product and market, or by territory, product and market. A salesperson might then report to one or more line and staff managers. No single structure is best for all companies and situations. Each organization should select a structure that best serves the needs of its customers and fits its overall marketing strategy.

● *Sales Force Size*

Once the company has set its strategy and structure, it is ready to consider *sales force size*. Salespeople constitute one of the company's most productive – and most expensive – assets. Therefore, increasing their number will increase both sales and costs.

Many companies use some form of **workload approach** to set sales force size. The company groups accounts according to size, account status or other factors related to the amount of effort required to maintain them. It then determines the number of salespeople needed to call on them the desired number of times. The logic is as follows. Suppose we have 1,000 Type-A accounts and 2,000 Type-B accounts. Type-A accounts require 36 calls a year and Type-B accounts require 12 calls a year. In this case, the sales force's *workload*, as defined by the number of calls it must make per year, is 60,000 calls $[(1,000 \times 36) + (2,000 \times 12) = 36,000 + 24,000 = 60,000)]$. Suppose our average salesperson can make 1,000 calls a year. The company thus needs 60 salespeople (60,000/1,000).

● *Other Sales Force Strategy and Structure Issues*

Sales management also have to decide who will be involved in the selling effort and how various sales and sales support people will work together.

OUTSIDE AND INSIDE SALES FORCES.   The company may have an **outside sales force** (or field sales force), an **inside sales force** or both. Outside salespeople travel to call on customers, whereas inside salespeople conduct business from their offices via telephone or visits from prospective buyers.

To reduce time demands on their outside sales forces, many firms have increased the size of their inside sales team, which includes technical support

workload approach
An approach to setting sales force size, whereby the company groups accounts into different size classes and then determines how many salespeople are needed to call on them the desired number of times.

outside sales force
Outside salespeople (or field sales force) who travel to call on customers.

inside sales force
Salespeople who service the company's customers and prospect from their offices via telephone or visits from prospective customers.

people, sales assistants and telemarketers. Technical support people provide technical information and answers to customers' questions. Sales assistants provide clerical back-up for outside salespeople. They call ahead and confirm appointments, conduct credit checks, follow up on deliveries and answer customers' queries when salespeople cannot be reached. Telemarketers use the phone to find new leads and qualify prospects for the field sales force or to sell and service accounts directly.

The inside sales force frees salespeople to spend more time selling to major accounts and finding major new prospects. Depending on the complexity of the product and customer, a telemarketer can make 20–30 decision-maker contacts a day, compared to the average of four that an outside salesperson can make. For many types of product and selling situation, **telemarketing** can be as effective as a personal sales call, but much less expensive. For example, whereas a typical personal sales call can cost well over £200, a routine industrial telemarketing call costs between £5 and £20 depending on the complexity of the call. For example, chemicals company Du Pont uses experienced former field salespeople as telemarketing reps to help sell the company's complex chemical products. The telemarketers handle technical questions from customers, smooth out product and distribution problems, and alert field sales representatives to 'hot' prospects. According to Du Pont management, the inside–outside approach pays off, with some 80 per cent of the leads passed on to the field force converted into sales.[3]

TEAM SELLING. The days when a single salesperson handles a large and important account are vanishing. Today, as products become more complex, and as customers grow larger and more demanding, one person simply cannot handle all of a large customer's needs any more. Instead, most companies are now using **team selling** to service large complex accounts. Sales teams might include people from sales, marketing, engineering, finance, technical support and even upper management. For example, P & G assigns teams consisting of salespeople, marketing managers, technical service people and logistics and information systems specialists to work closely with large retail customers. In this case salespeople become 'orchestrators' who help co-ordinate a whole-company effort to build profitable relationships with key customers.[4]

Companies recognize that just asking their people for teamwork does not produce it. They have to revise their compensation and recognition systems to give credit for work on shared accounts. They must also set up better goals and measures for sales force performance. While honouring the importance of individual initiative, training programmes must also emphasize the value of teamwork.

KEY ACCOUNT MANAGEMENT. Continuing relationships with large customers dominate the activities of many sales organizations. For makers of consumer goods the relationship is with major retailers such as Tengelmann, Carrefour, Tesco or Ahold. As we saw in Chapter 3, the importance of these has changed the way marketing as a whole is being organized. *Account managers* often orchestrate the relationship with a single retailer, although some will manage several smaller retailers or a class of independent outlet. Any major retailer will probably always be carrying major manufacturers' brands, so the account manager's role is one of increasing the profitability of sales through the channel. In this arrangement a great deal of sales promotions effort and advertising is customized for retailers that want exclusive lines or restrict the sort of promotions that they accept.

The situation is very similar in industrial sales organizations when a supplier has to sell components, raw materials, supplier or capital equipment in the concentrated markets described in Chapter 8. Even when a prospect is not a

telemarketing
Using the telephone to sell directly to consumers.

team selling
Using teams of people from sales, marketing, production, finance, technical support, and even upper management to service large, complex accounts.

reasons. If left alone, many salespeople will spend most of their time with current customers, which are better-known quantities. Moreover, whereas a prospect may never deliver any business, salespeople can depend on current accounts for some business. Therefore, unless salespeople are rewarded for opening new accounts, they may avoid new-account development.

USING SALES TIME EFFICIENTLY.   Salespeople need to know how to use their time efficiently. One tool is the *annual call schedule* that shows which customers and prospects to call on in which months and which activities to carry out. Activities include taking part in trade shows, attending sales meetings and carrying out marketing research. Another tool is *time-and-duty analysis*. In addition to time spent selling, the salesperson spends time travelling, waiting, eating, taking breaks and doing administrative chores (see Marketing Highlight 20.1). Because of the tiny portion of the day most sales staff actually spend selling or negotiating and talking face-to-face with potential customers, companies must look for ways to save time. This can be done by getting salespeople to use phones instead of travelling, simplifying record-keeping forms, finding better call and routing plans, and supplying more and better customer information.

Advances in information and computer technology, such as laptop computers, telecommunications, personal selling software, videodisc players and automatic dialers, have encouraged many firms to adopt *sales force automation systems*, computerized sales operations for more efficient order-entry transactions, improved customer service and better salesperson decision-making support. Many sales forces have truly gone 'electronic'. A recent study of 100 large companies found that 48 per cent are 'actively pursuing' sales force automation; another 34 per cent are planning or considering it.[10] Salespeople use computers to profile customers and prospects, analyze and forecast sales, manage accounts, schedule sales calls, enter orders, check inventories and order status, prepare sales and expense reports, process correspondence and carry out many other activities. Sales force automation not only lowers sales force calls and improves productivity; it also improves the quality of sales management decisions. Here are some examples of companies that have introduced computer and other sophisticated technologies successfully into their sales force operations:

The Anglo-Dutch Shell Chemical Company developed a laptop computer package consisting of several applications. Although many salespeople initially resisted the computer – they couldn't type, or they didn't have time to learn the software, or whatever – some applications had great appeal. Salespeople responded first to the *automatic expense statement* programme, which made it easier for them to record expenses and get reimbursed quickly. Soon, they discovered the *sales inquiry function*, which gave them immediate access to the latest account information, including phone numbers, addresses, recent developments and prices. They no longer had to wait for the clerical staff to give them out-of-date information. Before long, salespeople were using the entire package. *Electronic mail* allowed them quickly to receive and send messages to others. Various *corporate forms*, such as territory work plans and sales call reports, could be filled out faster and sent electronically. Other useful applications included an *appointment calendar*, a 'to-do list' function, a *spreadsheet programme*, and a *graphics package* that helped salespeople prepare charts and graphs for customer presentations. Today, even salespeople who initially resisted the computer package wonder how they ever got along without it.[11]

So You Want to be a Professional Salesperson?

Marketing Highlight 20.1

Salespeople are often said to be unloved, foot-in-the-door creatures, whose superiors motivate them mainly in the form of alternate bouts of public humiliation and recognition. Not surprisingly, many people commonly regard selling as a very low form of life. The frequent portrayal of salespeople as sweet-talking, hard-selling pedlars does not boost their self-perception either. Stereotyping salespeople in this way is, of course, an unfair representation of company staff who are under constant pressure to create and keep a customer. Furthermore, salespeople are expected to perform many other tasks, most of which are arguably related to creating and maintaining sales for the company.

What do salespeople in fact do with their time? Given the many tasks that they are expected to perform, how many are truly professional in what they do? Do salespeople use their time well?

A recent international survey, conducted by Kinnaird Communications Group, a consultancy based in Glasgow, Scotland, sought to examine these questions. It covered about 1,000 salesmen and women operating in the United Kingdom, France, Italy and Germany, and was based on sales records and talking to chief executives, supervisors and customers. The consultancy's findings were also supplemented by observations over many years among clients' sales forces.

The study reported that only 5 per cent of field sales staff surveyed 'possess the natural selling skills that make them stand out as professionals'. The survey claimed that 35 per cent of salespeople 'just manage to pay their way', while 'an astounding 60 per cent [are] just there for the beer'. The study claimed that many of the sales reps 'drifted into the profession, attracted by the freedom, car and expense account'.

In terms of how salespeople spend their time, Kinnaird found that out of the average salesperson's day, 42 per cent of the time is spent in the car, while 26 per cent is spent at home, planning,

having lunch, telephoning, writing reports and parking the car (see Table 1). Less than one-third of the time is spent on customers' premises, and all of that time – except for about 6 per cent – is spent on fruitless 'cold' calls, waiting in reception, interruptions and, in the case of the poorest salespeople, inadequate forward planning and an excess of 'small talk'. Although 20 per cent of time is spent in face-to-face contact (including 'small talk': 7.5 per cent; customer interruptions, phone, colleagues and so forth: 7.5 per cent; and actual selling negotiation: 5 per cent), the survey found that much of this invaluable activity was spent talking to individuals with no influence on the purchasing decision.

TABLE 1 A DAY IN THE LIFE OF A TYPICAL SALESPERSON

ACTIVITY	% OF TOTAL TIME
Selling or negotiation	5.0
Home planning	5.0
'Cold canvass' calls – leaving card, no interview	6.0
Waiting in reception	6.0
'Small talk'	7.5
Customer interruptions, phone, colleagues, etc.	7.5
Walking, parking, taking notes, telephoning, etc.	8.0
Lunch	13.0
Car travel	42.0

NOTE: Based on a nine-hour day.
SOURCE: Kinnaird, 1994.

Kinnaird points out that what sets the upper 5 per cent sales élite apart from the rest is charisma in a sales situation. Arguably, charisma is elusive. However, there are other prime qualities to be found in a successful salesperson: a sense of humour; good planning and preparation skills; the ability to take initiatives (nearly all of the time, since sales reps are on their own); a belief in their company and their products or services (if they don't, why should their customers?); a trust in their colleagues (that is, those in marketing, accounting and distribution); and a belief in themselves. Other observers add to that list physical energy, tenacity and resilience in the face of rejection.

There are always going to be 'natural' salespeople, but for the rest, training is absolutely essential for developing sales professionalism and to overcome some of the deficiencies in personal skills. Another area that must be emphasized continually is management's commitment to pro-viding marketing and advertising support for the sales force. Salespeople are front-line troops. They are the valuable bridge between the business and its customers, they act as information and intelligence satellites, and they can make or break the sale. Where selling is a key activity, businesses must learn to utilize this valuable marketing tool, the salesperson. The unloved ranks of salespeople must be loved again.

SOURCE: Adapted from Diane Summers, 'Unloved and incompetent', *Financial Times* (25 August 1994), p. 9.

Computers have also changed the way commercial insurance company Sun Alliance International (SAI) uses information to support sales staff and to forge long-term relationships with customers and intermediaries. SAI deploys a PC-based sales system called ADAM – Agency Development and Management – among its 170-strong sales force, including 26 home workers known as 'on the road sales staff' (OTRs). Over 80 per cent of its business is generated by a network of agents, supported by a sales force of 140 across the UK. Their job is to build relationships with brokers and other intermediaries (some 4,000 agencies). According to SAI, paper-based systems were sketchy: salespeople's natural instinct is not to complete records; frequently the paperwork is incomplete or their reports do not tell the whole story. ADAM is developed from the view of field-based sales staff who need to share data with office-based colleagues. Customer information is accessible by anyone – all view the same record, which is synchronized in an overnight update. Arguably, the beauty of a distributed database is that you can share the information across a wide range of people. Gone are the days of relying on a dusty set of papers in someone's car 100 miles away. Steve Ginn, an SAI sales development manager, stresses that 'One of the fundamentals of selling is an understanding of customers' needs. Once we know the customer sectors, we can work more closely in partnership with brokers and the customer sees a far more professional approach.' He has been using his Toshiba laptop to access a menu, which shows a task organizer, in-tray, electronic mail and standard user reports and inquiries. The system offers him a far more structured way to analyze information on current sales campaigns and see instantly how long it is since he contacted clients. He can also append notes to the agency records for his account 'caretakers', something paper-based card systems could not do. One salesperson whose performance once gave concern has become an OTR and an enthusiastic and highly effective ADAM user. According to a senior marketing executive, and supporter of the system at SAI, 'you have got to open people's eyes to what the technology can do for them', but 'you can't do it overnight. The company trained total novices on the keyboard, and worked to put at rest the fears of those expelled from the cosy support of their office. The vast majority of staff, now they have seen it in action, see myriad advantages. ADAM converts task response into *customer care*, and that is what the technology can help us do.'[12]

Many companies award trips as incentives for outstanding sales performance.

Perhaps the fastest-growing sales force technology tool is the Internet. As more and more organizations and individuals embrace Internet technology, salespeople are beginning to use the Internet regularly in their daily selling activities. The most common uses include gathering competitive information, monitoring customer Web sites and researching industries and specific customers. While the inclusion of this technology in the salesperson's selling armoury is still in its infancy, as more and more companies provide their salespeople with Web access, experts expect explosive growth in sales force Internet usage in the coming decade.[13]

● *Motivating Salespeople*

Some salespeople will do their best without any special urging from management. To them, selling may be the most fascinating job in the world. But selling can also be frustrating. Salespeople usually work alone, and they must sometimes travel away from home. They may face aggressive, competing salespeople and difficult customers. They sometimes lack the authority to do what is needed to win a sale and may thus lose large orders that they have worked hard to obtain. Therefore, salespeople often need special encouragement to do their best. Management can boost sales force morale and performance through its organizational climate, sales quota and positive incentives.

ORGANIZATIONAL CLIMATE. Organizational climate reflects the feeling that salespeople have about their opportunities, value and rewards for a good performance within the company. Some companies treat salespeople as if they are not very important. Other companies treat their salespeople as their prime movers and allow virtually unlimited opportunity for income and promotion. Not surprisingly, a company's attitude towards its salespeople affects their behaviour. If they are held in low esteem, there is high turnover and poor performance. If they are held in high esteem, there is less turnover and higher performance.

Treatment from the salesperson's immediate superior is especially important. A good sales manager keeps close to his or her sales force. They are in touch with salespeople through letters and phone calls, visits in the field and evaluation sessions in the home office. At different times, the sales manager acts as the salesperson's boss, companion, coach and confessor. Most importantly, sales management must be able to convince salespeople that they can sell more by working harder and being trained to work smarter, and that the rewards – be they financial in nature or higher-order rewards for better performance, such as liking, peer recognition and respect, and a sense of accomplishment – are worth the extra effort.

SALES QUOTAS.   Many companies set **sales quotas** for their salespeople. Sales quotas are standards stating the amount they should sell and how sales should be divided among the company's products. Compensation is often related to how well salespeople meet their quotas.

Sales quotas are set at the time that the annual marketing plan is developed. The company first decides on a sales forecast that is reasonably achievable. Based on this forecast, management plans production, workforce size and financial needs. It then sets sales quotas for its regions and territories. Generally, sales quotas are set higher than the sales forecast to encourage sales managers and salespeople to give their best effort. If they fail to make their quotas, the company may still make its sales forecast.

sales quotas
Standards set for salespeople, stating the amount they should sell and how sales should be divided among the company's products.

POSITIVE INCENTIVES.   Companies also use several incentives to increase sales force effort. *Sales meetings* provide social occasions, breaks from routine, chances to meet and talk with 'company brass', and opportunities to air feelings and to identify with a larger group. Companies also sponsor *sales contests* to spur the sales force to make a selling effort above what would normally be expected. Other incentives include honours, merchandise and cash awards, trips and profit-sharing plans.

Evaluating Salespeople

So far we have described how management communicates what salespeople should be doing and motivates them to do it. This process requires good feedback, which means getting regular information from salespeople to evaluate their performance.

● *Sources of Information*

Management gets information about its salespeople in several ways. The most important source is the *sales report*. Additional information comes from personal observation, customers' letters and complaints, customer surveys and talks with other salespeople.

Sales reports are divided into plans for future activities and write-ups of completed activities. The best example of the first is the *work plan* that salespeople submit a week or month in advance. The plan describes intended calls and routing. From this report, the sales force plans and schedules activities. It also informs management of the salespeople's whereabouts and provides a basis for comparing plans and performance. Salespeople can then be evaluated on their ability to 'plan their work and work their plan'. Sometimes, managers contact individual salespeople to suggest improvements in work plans.

Companies also require their salespeople to draft *annual territory marketing plans*, in which they outline their plans for building new accounts and increasing sales from existing accounts. Formats vary greatly, in the sense that some ask for general ideas on territory development, while others ask for detailed sales and profit estimates. Sales managers study these territory plans, make suggestions and use the plans to develop sales quotas.

Salespeople write up their completed activities on *call reports*. Call reports keep sales managers informed of the salesperson's activities, show what is happening with each customer's account and provide information that might be useful in later calls. Salespeople also turn in *expense reports* for which they are partly or wholly repaid. Some companies also ask for reports on new business, lost business and local business and economic conditions.

These reports supply the raw data from which sales management can evaluate sales force performance. For example, are salespeople making too few calls per day? Are they spending too much time per call? Are they spending too much money on entertainment? Are they closing enough orders per hundred calls? Are they finding enough new customers and holding on to enough old customers?

● *Formal Evaluation of Performance*

Using sales force reports and other information, sales management formally evaluates members of the sales force. Formal evaluation produces four benefits. First, management must develop and communicate clear standards for judging performance. Second, management must gather well-rounded information about each salesperson. Third, salespeople receive constructive feedback that helps them to improve future performance. Finally, salespeople are motivated to perform because they know that they will have to sit down one morning with the sales manager and explain their performance.

COMPARING SALESPEOPLE'S PERFORMANCE. One type of evaluation compares and ranks the sales performance of different salespeople. Such comparisons can be misleading, however. Salespeople may perform differently because of differences in territory potential, workload, level of competition, company promotion effort and other factors. Furthermore, sales are not usually the best indicator of achievement. Management should be more interested in how much each salesperson contributes to net profits, a factor that requires analysis of each salesperson's sales mix and expenses.

COMPARING CURRENT SALES WITH PAST SALES. A second type of evaluation is to compare a salesperson's current performance with past performance. Such a comparison should directly indicate the person's progress. Table 20.2 provides an example.

The sales manager can learn many things about Chris Bennett from this table. Bennett's total sales increased every year (line 3). This does not necessarily mean that Bennett is doing a better job. The product breakdown shows that Bennett has been able to push the sales of product B further than those of product A (lines 1 and 2). According to the quotas for the two products (lines 4 and 5), the success in increasing product B sales may be at the expense of product A sales. According to gross profits (lines 6 and 7), the company earns twice as much gross profit (as a ratio to sales) on A as it does on B. Bennett may be pushing the higher-volume, lower-margin product at the expense of the more profitable product. Although Bennett increased total sales by £1,100 between 1996 and 1997 (line 3), the gross profits on these total sales actually decreased by £580 (line 8).

Sales expense (line 9) shows a steady increase, although total expense as a percentage of total sales seems to be under control (line 10). The upward trend in Bennett's total expenses, in money terms, does not seem to be explained by any increase in the number of calls (line 11), although it may be related to his success

| Table 20.2 | Evaluating salespeople's performance |

TERRITORY: MIDLAND	SALESPERSON: CHRIS BENNETT 1994	1995	1996	1997
1. Net sales product A	£251,300	£253,200	£270,000	£263,100
2. Net sales product B	£423,200	£439,200	£553,900	£561,900
3. Net sales total	£674,500	£692,400	£823,900	£825,000
4. Percentage of quota product A	95.6	92.0	88.0	84.7
5. Percentage of quota product B	120.4	122.3	134.9	130.8
6. Gross profits product A	£50,260	£50,640	£54,000	£52,620
7. Gross profits product B	£42,320	£43,920	£53,390	£56,190
8. Gross profits total	£92,580	£94,560	£109,390	£108,810
9. Sales expense	£10,200	£11,100	£11,600	£13,200
10. Sales expense to total sales (%)	1.5	1.6	1.4	1.6
11. Number of calls	1,675	1,700	1,680	1,660
12. Cost per call	£6.09	£6.53	£6.90	£7.95
13. Average number of customers	320	324	328	334
14. Number of new customers	13	14	15	20
15. Number of lost customers	8	10	11	14
16. Average sales per customer	£2,108	£2,137	£2,512	£2,470
17. Average gross profit per customer	£289	£292	£334	£326

in acquiring new customers (line 14). However, there is a possibility that in prospecting for new customers, Bennett is neglecting present customers, as indicated by an upward trend in the annual number of lost customers (line 15).

The last two lines on the table show the level and trend in Bennett's sales and gross profits per customer. These figures become more meaningful when they are compared with overall company averages. If Chris Bennett's average gross profit per customer is lower than the company's averages, Chris may be concentrating on the wrong customers or may not be spending enough time with each customer. Looking back at the annual number of calls (line 11), Bennett may be making fewer calls than the average salesperson. If distances in the territory are not much different, this may mean he is not putting in a full workday, he is poor at planning his routing or minimizing his waiting time, or he spends too much time with certain accounts.

QUALITATIVE EVALUATION OF SALESPEOPLE. A *qualitative evaluation* usually looks at a salesperson's knowledge of the company, products, customers, competitors, territory and tasks. Personal traits like manner, appearance, speech and temperament can be rated. The sales manager can also review any problems in motivation or compliance. Each company must decide what would be most useful to know. It should communicate these criteria to salespeople, so that they understand how their performance is evaluated and can make an effort to improve it.

We have looked at the key issues surrounding sales force management. Next we will address the principles of personal selling.

Principles of Personal Selling

We now turn from designing and managing a sales force to the actual personal selling process. Personal selling is an ancient art that has spawned a large literature and many principles. Effective salespeople operate on more than just instinct – they are highly trained in methods of territory analysis and customer management.

The Personal Selling Process

Companies spend a huge amount of money on seminars, books, cassettes and other materials to teach salespeople the 'art' of selling. Millions of books on selling are purchased every year, with tantalizing titles such as *How to Sell Anything to Anybody, How I Raised Myself from Failure to Success in Selling, The Four-Minute Sell, The Best Seller, The Power of Enthusiastic Selling, Where Do You Go from No. 1?* and *Winning Through Intimidation.* One of the most enduring books on selling is Dale Carnegie's *How to Win Friends and Influence People*, which is marketed all over the world.

Effective companies take a *customer-oriented approach* to personal selling. They train salespeople to identify customer needs and to find solutions. This approach assumes that customer needs provide sales opportunities, that customers appreciate good suggestions and that customers will be loyal to salespeople who have their long-term interests at heart – salespeople who do their homework, uncover customer needs and present convincing arguments of mutual benefits for both organizations. By contrast, those companies that use a *sales-oriented approach* rely on high-pressure selling techniques. They assume that the customers will not buy except under pressure, that they are influenced by a slick presentation and that they will not be sorry after signing the order (and that, even if they are, it no longer matters). The problem-solver salesperson fits better with the marketing concept than does the hard-sell salesperson. Buyers today want solutions, not smiles; results, not razzle-dazzle. They want salespeople who listen to their concerns, understand their needs and respond with the right products and services. A recent study showed that the qualities that purchasing agents dislike most in salespeople include being pushy, late and unprepared or disorganized. The qualities they value most include empathy, honesty, dependability, thoroughness and follow-through.[14]

Steps in the Selling Process

selling process
The steps that the salesperson follows when selling, which include prospecting and qualifying, preapproach, approach, presentation and demonstration, handling objections, closing and follow-up.

Most training programmes view the **selling process** as consisting of several steps that the salesperson must master (see Figure 20.2). These steps focus on the goal of getting new customers and obtaining orders from them. However, many salespeople spend much of their time maintaining existing accounts and building long-term customer relationships. More discussion of the relationship aspect of the personal selling process will be found in the final section of this chapter. For a fuller discussion of key account management and its importance in sustaining customer relationships, see Chapter 11.

prospecting
The step in the selling process in which the salesperson identifies qualified potential customers.

● *Prospecting and Qualifying*

The first step in the selling process is **prospecting** – identifying qualified potential customers. The salesperson must approach many prospects to get just a few sales.

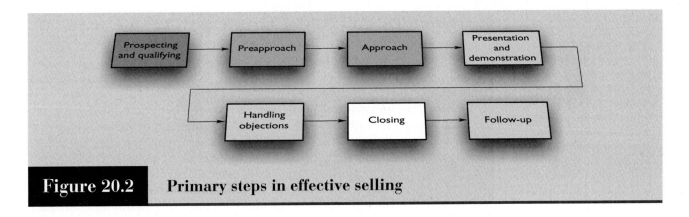

Figure 20.2 **Primary steps in effective selling**

Although the company supplies some leads, salespeople need skill in finding their own. They can ask current customers for the names of prospects. They can build referral sources, such as suppliers, dealers, non-competing salespeople and bankers. They can join organizations to which prospects belong, or can engage in speaking and writing activities that will draw attention. They can search for names in newsletters or directories and use the telephone and post to track down leads. Or they can drop in unannounced on various offices (a practice known as 'cold calling'). Cold calling, however, may not always be appropriate, as in the case of German or Japanese organizations, where third-party introduction is the norm.

Salespeople need to know how to *qualify* leads: that is, how to identify the good ones and screen out the poor ones. Prospects can be qualified by looking at their financial ability, volume of business, special needs, location and possibilities for sales growth.

● *Preapproach*

Before calling on a prospect, the salesperson should learn as much as possible about the organization (what it needs, who is involved in the buying) and its buyers (their characteristics and buying styles). This step is known as the **pre-approach**. The salesperson can consult standard business directories or information sources (e.g. *Moody's, Standard & Poor's, Dun & Bradstreet*), acquaintances and others to learn about the company. The salesperson should set *call objectives*, which may be to qualify the prospect, to gather information or to make an immediate sale. Another task is to decide on the best approach, which might be a personal visit, a phone call or a letter. The best timing should be considered carefully because many prospects are busiest at certain times. Finally, the salesperson should give thought to an overall sales strategy for the account.

preapproach
The step in the selling process in which the salesperson learns as much as possible about a prospective customer before making a sales call.

● *Approach*

During the **approach** step, the salesperson should know how to meet and greet the buyer, and get the relationship off to a good start. The salesperson's appearance, his or her opening lines and the follow-up remarks have a great deal of impact on relationship building in this early phase of the sales process. The opening lines should be positive: 'Mr Johnson, I am Chris Henderson from the Alltech Company. My company and I appreciate your willingness to see me. I will do my best to make this visit profitable and worthwhile for you and your company.' This opening might be followed by some key questions to learn more about the customer's needs, or the showing of a display or sample to attract the buyer's attention and curiosity.

approach
The step in the selling process in which the salesperson meets and greets the buyer to get the relationship off to a good start.

● *Presentation and Demonstration*

presentation
The step in the selling process in which the salesperson tells the product 'story' to the buyer, showing how the product will make or save money for the buyer.

The **presentation** is that step in the selling process where the salesperson tells the product 'story' to the buyer, showing how the product will make or save money. The salesperson describes the product features, but concentrates on presenting *customer benefits*.

Companies may use three styles of sales presentation: the canned approach; the formula approach; or the need-satisfaction approach. The *canned approach* is the oldest type and consists of a memorized or scripted talk covering the seller's main points. This approach has limited usefulness in industrial selling, but scripted presentations can be effective in some telephone-selling situations. A properly prepared and rehearsed script should sound natural and move the salesperson smoothly through the presentation. With electronic scripting, computers can lead the salesperson through a sequence of selling messages tailored on the spot to the prospect's responses.

Using the *formula approach*, the salesperson first identifies the buyer's needs, attitudes and buying style. The salesperson then moves into a formula presentation that shows how the product will satisfy that buyer's needs. Although not canned, the presentation follows a general plan.

The *need-satisfaction approach* starts with a search for the customer's needs by getting the customer to do most of the talking. This approach calls for good listening and problem-solving skills. One marketing director describes the approach this way:

> [High-performing salespeople] make it a point to understand customer needs and goals before they pull anything out of their product bag … Such salespeople spend the time needed to get an in-depth knowledge of the customer's business, asking questions that will lead to solutions our systems can address.[15]

Sales presentations can be improved with demonstration aids, such as booklets, flip charts, slides, videotapes or videodiscs, and product samples. If buyers can see or handle the product, they will better remember its features and benefits.

● *Handling Objections*

handling objections
The step in the selling process in which the salesperson seeks out, clarifies and overcomes customer objections to buying.

Customers almost always have objections during the presentation or when asked to place an order. The problem can be either logical or psychological, and objections are often unspoken. In **handling objections**, the salesperson should use a positive approach, seek out hidden objections, ask the buyer to clarify any objections, take objections as opportunities to provide more information, and turn the objections into reasons for buying. Every salesperson should be trained in the skills of handling objections.

● *Closing*

closing
The step in the selling process in which the salesperson asks the customer for an order.

After handling the prospect's objections, the salesperson now tries to close the sale. Some salespeople do not get around to **closing** or do not handle it well. They may lack confidence, feel guilty about asking for the order or fail to recognize the right moment to close the sale. Salespeople should know how to spot closing signals from the buyer, including physical actions, comments and questions. For example, the customer might sit forward and nod approvingly or ask about prices and credit terms. Salespeople can use one of several closing techniques. They can ask for the order, review points of agreement, offer to help write up the order, ask

Selling to the United States, Japan and China: Some Guidelines for European Businesses

Personal selling is the least easily controlled part of international marketing. Businesspeople selling abroad must adopt selling styles and strategies in accordance with the rules of social and business etiquette of the country in which they are doing business.

Here, we look at the sales process and examine the ways in which business behaviour varies across the three large economies – Japan, China and the United States.

SALES PROCESS ELEMENTS	UNITED STATES	CHINA	JAPAN
Preapproach – the entrée	Direct contact usually acceptable at junior level; cold-calling is common; salesperson telephones contact in the company.	Indirect, slow process; best to write to foreign trade corporations in Beijing or their branch offices, which act as intermediaries between their end-users and foreign firms; introductions via third parties/intermediaries (e.g. overseas offices, agents/distributors in Hong Kong, Macau, Chinese embassies and liaison offices abroad); contact made at senior level.	Write to contact, but expect slow response; third-party introduction is preferable; develop contacts via Japanese companies' representatives in own country; use acquaintances, embassies to facilitate introduction; contact made at senior level; cold-calling is inadvisable.
Opening – the approach	Brisk; get down to business quickly; a confident, positive and business-like approach works well; breakfast meetings are common; business cards are exchanged with little ritual.	Assiduous preparation for talks; establish trust and friendship first; business cards are rarely distributed; contacts keep their status vague.	Assiduous preparation is the norm; introduction is a ritual, as is the exchange of business calling cards (*meishi*), which must be presented with both hands, and to contacts in order of descending status; bowing is common, but understand the ritual, which, again, is dictated by the seniority of individuals (handshakes will do when meeting Japanese businesspeople who are used to dealing with westerners); avoid using first names – the family name should be used to introduce oneself.

Presentation and demonstrations – the negotiations	Professional presentations are expected; tactical and straightforward styles are common; persuasion by logic is acceptable negotiating style; meetings involve a lot of talking, with details put down in writing later on.	Less formal; tends to be unstructured; can be exhaustive; expect lengthy decision making; important to exercise patience, courtesy and self-control; they find being shamed intolerable, blame, even more so; a lot of technical information is expected; a discount on the final offer is expected, so always insert a cushion in one's quotation from the start.	Negotiations tend to be formal; ensure a high-ranking official in the company initially meets with an equal in the Japanese firm; expect the process to be lengthy because the Japanese negotiators must reach a consensus before making a commitment; expect long periods of silence (this means they are thinking and waiting for others to digest the information, but it could be that you have embarrassed them); probe (get details to help formulate a proposal that fits their needs); push (try all angles to get across issues that concern them); when desired results are not reached, they do not show emotions, but 'panic in silence', so try to salvage your position without causing embarrassment/shame or dishonour; beware, they try to 'save face' and avoid conceding by postponing the negotiation for further study.
Objections	Objections from audience are usually direct; the well-prepared salesperson is expected openly to counterdefend objections.	Objections are indirect (Confucian philosophy stresses need for harmony); difficult points have to be smoothed using compromise.	Objections are often indirect; open resistance is rare; beware, do not assume yes or *hai* in Japanese means agreement as it can also mean 'I see', 'I'll think about it' or 'I understand'; learn to read the objections – hesitancy in speech, facial expressions, unwillingness to be more specific, or silence are all signs of negative response.
Closing	Sales negotiator often asks for an order directly; deft footwork to persuade clients is acceptable.	The persuasive approach could cause great embarrassment, so avoid deft footwork; they emphasize good faith over legal safeguards in the business relationship; learn to read	Again, tactical close and hefty persuasion are alien to this group; like the Chinese, the Japanese emphasize friendship, loyalty and trust – a successful close occurs when the prospects feel the two parties

		non-verbal signals and act as the situation arises.	have reached this state of mutual understanding.
Extra-business activities	Breakfast and lunch meetings are common; business entertaining is moderate (managers see it as time wasting and, if lavish, a bit dubious); there is minimal celebration after the close.	Lavish entertainment is not the norm; the giving of gifts is not all that important, but, if offered, they are not seen as a bribe.	Entertainment is the foundation of Japanese business; it never takes place in the executive's home and is done invariably in the evening rather than at lunch; present giving is an established part of business etiquette – so, come prepared, and, when the Japanese counterpart offers gifts, it is rude to refuse them.

SOURCES: Sergey Frank, 'Global negotiating', *Sales and Marketing Management* (May 1992), pp. 64–9; John Saunders and Hon-Chung Ton, 'Selling to Japan', *Journal of Sales Management*, 1 (1984), pp. 9–15; John Saunders and Hon-Chung Tong, 'Selling to the People's Republic of China', *Journal of Sales Management*, 1, 2 (1984), pp. 16–20; J.C. Morgan and J.J. Morgan, *Cracking the Japanese Market* (New York: Free Press, 1991); F. Reinstein, 'Selling to Japan: we did it their way', *Export Today*, 3, 3 (1987), pp. 19–24.

whether the buyer wants this model or that one, or point out to the buyer that he or she will lose out if the order is not placed now. The salesperson may offer the buyer special reasons to close, such as a lower price or an extra quantity at no charge.

● *Follow-Up*

The last step in the selling process – **follow-up** – is necessary if the salesperson wants to ensure customer satisfaction and repeat business. Right after closing, the salesperson should complete any details on delivery time, purchase terms and other matters. The salesperson should then schedule a follow-up call when the initial order is received to make sure there is proper installation, instruction and servicing. This visit would reveal any problems, assure the buyer of the sales-person's interest and reduce any buyer concerns that might have arisen since the sale.

follow-up
The last step in the selling process, in which the salesperson follows up after the sale to ensure customer satisfaction and repeat business.

● *International Selling*

The typical sales process can be applied in international selling. However, inter-cultural trade always requires special efforts in tailoring sales and negotiation approaches (see Marketing Highlight 20.2).

Relationship Marketing

The principles of personal selling as described are *transaction oriented*, in that their aim is to help salespeople close a specific sale with a customer. But in many cases, the company is not seeking simply a sale: it has targeted a major customer that it would like to win and keep. The company would like to show the customer

Corporate Hospitality: Drawing the Line on Freebies

Marketing Highlight 20.3

Corporate entertaining or hospitality is an expected part of business life. But when does an all-expenses-paid golfing trip, a free weekend in Paris or a case of finest Moet and Chandon stop being part of corporate life and begin to look like sleaze?

Freebies, such as a calendar or a fountain pen carrying the supplier's logo, are usually accepted by clients without a second thought. A nice dinner to keep in touch with a valued customer rarely raises an eyebrow, but is a free trip for a client and an accompanying partner to somewhere warm improper inducement, or merely a relaxing opportunity to build relations?

What should businesspeople do when faced with freeloading opportunities? In the absence of clear corporate or standard guidelines, how would managers decide if a gift, meal or trip is acceptable or sleazy?

Some experts offer the following simple guidelines:

1. The first test is the *'means test'*. It draws the line at entertainment 'way beyond the level the person would normally be able to afford themselves'. It also depends on the level of superiority or importance of the individual. A steak in a wine bar at lunchtime is not beyond the means of most ordinary managers. However, if you want to talk business with the chief executive officer of a big company, you may have to meet him in more expensive surroundings.

2. The second test is the *'wow test'*. When you open an envelope containing an invitation, you may say 'how nice' (or you may groan and say 'I suppose I had better be there!'). However, if you find yourself saying 'Wow!', then you had better think twice.

3. The third test is the *reciprocity test*. It is worthwhile occasionally to check that entertaining is reciprocal – suppliers buy you lunch, but you also buy them lunch

back sometimes. That way, the relationship does not become too oppressive.

Corporate hospitality can be costly. At top sporting events – such as the football cup final at Wembley, or a day at Epsom for the horse racing – the cost could be astronomical. It costs something upwards of £1,500 per head to entertain at the Wimbledon men's tennis finals, but businesspeople will pay that if they have big international customers coming into the city to talk over deals that are worth millions of pounds. And don't ask what a meal for four in a Tokyo geisha club would amount to …

Is corporate entertaining necessary? Even though hospitality events are felt to be part of work, very little work is actually discussed. Some managers argue that such events serve other purposes. The idea is to get the contact out for a good time. They feel good about you, and the next time you or your sales representatives call, they will receive you ahead of the competition. Furthermore, a night at the theatre or opera, with a ticket for an accompanying partner, is quite useful when overseas visitors need to be entertained in the evening. Weekend outings for clients and potential customers allow the company to buy a little of a contact's private time to talk about business. In some business cultures (e.g. Japan, Malaysia, Thailand and most countries in the Far East), offering and accepting hospitality is part of work. Contacts or customers often expect it. It is a way of cultivating friendship. Money sometimes counts as a 'gift', which may be offered to help a business contact or to express appreciation of friendship.

Some western cultures frown upon others where special favours to family members or 'baksheesh' is a way of corporate life. Funnily enough, Americans and Japanese often frown on British standards. The Japanese are surprisingly quiet on the hospitality scene in the United Kingdom. They may visit clubs in their own time (after office hours), but are often horrified by the notion of taking a working day off to go to a sporting event. The Americans would think it 'barmy' to spend thousands of pounds at Wimbledon. An

MD of a big US corporation might entertain a senior partner at the ball game, but they would buy each other a hot dog and sit in public seats. How near you are to the Royal Enclosure at a race horse meeting and all those other layers of importance is very British,' according to Mr David Willis, a director of the UK's National Sporting Club.

Some companies actively discourage all employees from accepting hospitality. Some have no qualms about offering or receiving freebies. For those that have a problem on the morality or ethics side of all this, the experts have this to say: look at whether a mention of the hospitality arrangement – meal, trip or gift – in the press would cause embarrassment; try the 'means' test; do the *wow* test.

SOURCE: Anil Bhoyrul, 'A man for all seasons', *BusinessAge Magazine*, **4**, 49 (1994), pp. 104–6; Diane Summers, 'Hitching a ride on the corporate gravy train', *Financial Times* (24 October 1994), p. 7.

that it has the capabilities to serve the customer over the long haul, in a mutually profitable relationship.

More companies today are moving away from transaction marketing, with its emphasis on making a sale. Instead, they are practising **relationship marketing**, which emphasizes maintaining profitable long-term relationships with customers by creating superior customer value and satisfaction. They realize that, when operating in maturing markets and facing stiffer competition, it costs a lot more to wrest new customers from competitors than to keep current ones.

relationship marketing
The process of creating, maintaining and enhancing strong, value-laden relationships with customers and other stakeholders.

Today's customers are large and often global. They prefer suppliers that can sell and deliver a co-ordinated set of products and services to many locations. They favour suppliers which can quickly solve problems that arise in different parts of the nation or world, and who can work closely with customer teams to improve products and processes. For these customers, the sale is only the beginning of the relationship.

Unfortunately, many companies are not set up for these developments. They often sell their products through separate sales forces that do not work easily together. Their national account managers may be turned down when requesting help from a district salesperson. Their technical people may not be willing to lend time to educate a customer. Their engineering, design and manufacturing people may have the attitude that 'it's our job to make good products and the salesperson's to sell them to customers'. However, the more successful companies recognize that winning and keeping accounts requires more than making good products and directing the sales force to close lots of sales. It requires a carefully co-ordinated, whole-company effort to create value-laden, satisfying relationships with important customers.

Relationship marketing is based on the premise that important accounts need focused and continuous attention. Studies have shown that the best salespeople are those who are highly motivated and good closers, but more than this, they are customer-problem solvers and relationship builders. Salespeople working with key customers must do more than call when they think a customer might be ready to place an order. They must also monitor each key account, know its problems and be ready to serve in a number of ways. They must call or visit frequently, work with the customer to help solve the customer's problems and improve its business, and take an interest in customers as people. Taking care of customers by offering them gifts, free entertainment or corporate hospitality may be questioned by outsiders who equate such activities with bribery. Companies must therefore set guidelines for their managers and employees on where to draw the line (see Marketing Highlight 20.3).

Recognition of the importance of relationship marketing has increased rapidly in the past few years. Companies are finding that they earn a higher return from resources invested in retaining customers than from money spent to attract new ones. They realize the benefits of cross-selling opportunities with current customers. More and more, companies are forming strategic partnerships, making skilled relationship marketing essential.

Summary

Most companies use salespeople, and many companies assign them the key role in the marketing mix. The high cost of the sales force calls for an effective *sales management process* consisting of six steps: setting *sales force objectives*; designing *sales force strategy, structure, size* and *compensation*; *recruiting and selecting*; *training*; *supervising*; and *evaluating*.

As an element of the marketing mix, the sales force is very effective in achieving certain marketing objectives and carrying out such activities as prospecting, communicating, selling, servicing and information gathering. A market-oriented sales force works to produce *customer satisfaction* and *company profit*. To accomplish these goals, the sales force needs skills in marketing analysis and planning in addition to the traditional selling skills.

In designing a sales force, sales management must address issues such as: what type of sales force structure will work best (territorial, product, customer or complex structured); how large the sales force should be; who should be involved in the selling effort and how its various sales and sales-support people will work together (inside or outside and team selling). Sales management must also decide how the sales force should be compensated in terms of salary, commissions, bonuses, expenses and fringe benefits.

To hold down the high costs of hiring the wrong people, salespeople must be *recruited* and *selected* carefully. In recruiting salespeople, a company may look to job duties and the characteristics of its most successful salespeople to suggest the traits it wants in its sales force. *Training* programmes familiarize new salespeople not only with the art of selling, but with the company's history, its products and policies, and the characteristics of its market and competitors. All salespeople need *supervision*, and many need continuous encouragement in view of the many decisions they have to make and the many frustrations they invariably face. Periodically, the company must *evaluate* their performance to help them do a better job. Salespeople evaluation relies on information regularly gathered through sales reports, personal observations, customers' letters and complaints, customer surveys and conversations with other salespeople.

The art of selling involves a seven-step *selling process: prospecting and qualifying, preapproach, approach, presentation and demonstration, handling objections, closing* and *follow-up*. These steps help marketers close a specific sale and, as such, tend to be *transaction-oriented*. However, a seller's dealings with customers should be guided by the larger concept of *relationship marketing*. The company's sales force should help to orchestrate a whole-company effort to develop profitable long-term relationships with key customers based on superior customer value and satisfaction.

Key Terms

Approach 865
Closing 866
Customer sales force structure 850
Follow-up 869
Handling objections 866
Inside sales force 851
Outside sales force 851

Preapproach 865
Presentation 866
Product sales force structure 850
Prospecting 864
Relationship marketing 871
Sales force management 848
Sales quotas 861

Salesperson 846
Selling process 864
Team selling 852
Telemarketing 852
Territorial sales force structure 850
Workload approach 851

Discussing the Issues

1. The job of a salesperson can be exceedingly tough – it is challenging and varied, and the sales rep is under constant pressure to close and maintain sales. Describe the tasks performed by salespeople. Given the diversity of tasks and activities that management expect of salespeople, are there ways of ensuring that the sales force's time is spent more productively?

2. Who do so many sales force compensation plans combine salary with bonus or commission? What are the advantages and disadvantages of using bonuses as incentives, as opposed to using commissions?

3. 'Salespeople are born, not made.' Do you agree with this statement? Explain why or why not. What role does training play in helping someone develop selling skills?

4. There has been an increasing trend towards the use of computers to help sales managers analyze, plan and co-ordinate sales force activities. Discuss the effects of computer-based and related information technologies on the role of the sales force.

5. In many companies, talented salespeople are frequently promoted to top marketing or management positions. What are the pros and cons of rewarding top salespeople in this way?

6. Salespeople doing business abroad must not only acquire an understanding of prospects' needs and requirements, but also develop a great deal of sensitivity to foreign customs, traditions and business etiquette. What are the key considerations that the sales manager and his or her representatives must take on board when selling to businesspeople in the Far East? You may discuss the question in relation to components of the selling process and how selling behaviour must be adapted to accommodate local business traditions.

Applying the Concepts

1. Go to a retailer, such as a car dealership, a travel agency, a home appliance dealer or another outlet where salespeople are working on a commission basis.

   ● Rate the salesperson who dealt with you. Was his or her approach, presentation and demonstration effective?

   ● How did you respond to the sales pitch? Did you enjoy the experience or find it hard to endure? Why did you respond in this way?

2. Visit a retail outlet that specializes in complex products, such as audio and video equipment, computers and software, or mobile telephones. Get a salesperson in the shop to explain the product to you and ask specific questions. Based on your experience of the sales situation:

   ● Was the salesperson knowledgeable, helpful and able to answer your queries? Was he or she believable?

   ● To what extent did the expertise of the salesperson help to 'add value' to the product in question?

   ● If the product were available through mail order, would you rather buy it through that channel at a lower price, or from the salesperson you dealt with?

References

1. Laurie Hays, 'IBM's Gerstner holds back from sales force shake-up', *Wall Street Journal* (7 July 1993), p. B1; used with permission of Wall Street Journal. See also Geoffrey Brewer, 'Abort, retry, fail?', *Sales and Marketing Management* (October 1993), pp. 80–6; IBM Corporation 1993 *Annual Report*.

2. Patricia Sellers, 'How to remake your salesforce', *Fortune* (4 May 1992), pp. 96–103; see also Melissa Campanelli, 'Reshuffling the deck', *Sales and Marketing Management* (June 1994), pp. 83–9; for a discussion of empirical results concerning sales force management control systems, sales territory design and sales organization effectiveness, see Emin Babakus, David W. Cravens, Ken Grant, Thomas N. Ingram and Raymond W. LaForge, 'Investigating the relationships among sales, management control, sales territory design, salesperson performance, and sales organisation effectiveness', *International Journal of Research in Marketing* 13, 2 (October 1996), pp. 345–60.

3. See Martin Everett, 'Selling by telephone', *Sales and Marketing Management* (28 June 1993), pp. 75–9; Simon Rines, 'Forcing change', *Marketing Week* (8 March 1996), Special supplement on sales forces.

4. See Frank V. Cespedes, Stephen X. Doyle and Robert J. Freedman, 'Teamwork for today's selling', *Harvard Business Review* (March–April 1989), pp. 44–54, 58; Richard C. Whiteley, 'Orchestrating service', *Sales and Marketing Management* (April 1994), pp. 29–30.

5. For an innovative, thoughtful and thorough discussion of key account management, see Malcolm McDonald, *Key Account Management*, Butterworth-Heinemann, Oxford, 1998.

6. Geoffrey Brewer, 'Brain power', *Sales and Marketing Management* (May 1997), pp. 39–48; Don Peppers and Martha Rogers, 'The money trap', *Sales and Marketing Management* (May 1997), pp. 58–60.

7. Bill Kelley, 'How to manage a superstar', *Sales and Marketing Management* (November 1988), pp. 32–4; Geoffrey Brewer, 'Mind reading: what drives top salespeople to greatness?', *Sales and Marketing Management* (May 1994), pp. 82–8; Barry J. Farber, 'Success stories for salespeople', *Sales and Marketing Management* (May 1995), pp. 30–1.

8. See Robert G. Head, 'Systemizing salesperson selection', *Sales and Marketing Management* (February 1992), pp. 65–8; 'To test or not to test', *Sales and Marketing Management* (May 1994), p. 86.

9. See Bill Kelley, 'How much help does a salesperson need?', *Sales and Marketing Management* (May 1989), pp. 32–5.

10. Thayer C. Taylor, 'SFA: the newest orthodoxy', *Sales and Marketing Management* (February 1993), pp. 26–8; see also Rowland T. Moriarty and Gordon S. Swartz, 'Automation to boost sales and marketing', *Harvard Business Review* (January–February 1989), pp. 100–8; Thayer C. Taylor, 'Back from the future', *Sales and Marketing Management* (May 1992), pp. 47–60, and 'Getting in step with the computer age', *Sales and Marketing Management* (March 1993), pp. 52–60.

11. See 'Computer-based sales support: Shell Chemical's system' (New York: The Conference Board, Management Briefing), *Marketing* (April–May 1989), pp. 4–5.

12. Claire Gooding, 'Salesforce put on the record', *Financial Times* (28 July 1994), p. 14.

13. 'Nearly 20 per cent of salespeople are now online', www.dartnellcorp.com (May 1997).

14. Rosemary P. Ramsey and Ravipreet S. Sohi, 'Listening to your customers: the impact of perceived salesperson listening behavior on relationship outcomes', *Journal of the Academy of Marketing Science* (Spring 1997), pp. 127–37.

15. Thayer C. Taylor, 'Anatomy of a star salesperson', *Sales and Marketing Management* (May 1986), pp. 49–51; see also Stephen B. Castleberry and C. David Shepherd, 'Effective interpersonal listening and personal selling', *Journal of Personal Selling and Sales Management* (Winter 1993), pp. 35–49; John F. Yarbrough, 'Toughing it out', *Sales and Marketing Management* (May 1996), pp. 81–4.

Case 20

Britcraft Jetprop: Whose Sale is it Anyhow?[1]

ON 14 APRIL 1992, BOB LOMAS, sales administration manager at Britcraft Civil Aviation (BCA), received a telephone call from Wing Commander Weir, the air attaché for the United Kingdom in a European nation. The wing commander had found out that the national air force (NAF) of the European nation (hereafter Country) was looking for an aircraft to replace its ageing freight/transport aircraft for intra-European operations. It required equipment to fit between the large Lockheed Hercules that the air force had already decided to buy and lighter, utility/transport aircraft. The air attaché thought the Britcraft Jetprop was a suitable candidate.

Britcraft Aviation

Britcraft Aviation is the largest subsidiary owned by Britcraft Group Ltd, a British company with global engineering interests. Before being bought by Britcraft, the BCA was a differently named independent company founded by an aviation pioneer. It had designed and produced many famous military aircraft in the past. Military and executive aircraft were sold by the Britcraft Aviation (BMA) and Britcraft Executive Aviation (BEA), which were not based at the same site as the civil division. The Jetprop was BCA's top-selling aircraft, but the company was also a big subcontractor to Airbus Industries and Boeing.

Production of the Jetprop started a few years after that of a similar aircraft made by Fokker, a Dutch company that was Britcraft's main competitor. The Britcraft and Fokker aircraft were similar in many ways and used variants of the same engine. After intensive engineering and market research the Jetprop was designed as a regional airliner, particularly for developing countries. Unlike the Fokker, the Jetprop was a low-winged aircraft. Besides giving an unobstructed passenger area, Britcraft also claimed this gave its aircraft aerodynamic, structural and maintenance advantages. A primary design objective was for an aircraft that incurred low maintenance costs and that allowed high utilization by its operators. To achieve this, all components used on auxiliary services were selected for proven reliability, long overhaul life and ease of provisioning. Several important components were from aircraft already in service.

The aircraft was fully fail-safe. If there should be a failure of any part of the structure, sufficient members were available to allow redirection of loads. This gave a robust aircraft, where any failure due to fatigue developed sufficiently slowly for it to be detected during routine inspection before it became dangerous. To operate in the Third World, the Jetprop needed short take-off and landing (STOL) performance from semi-prepared runways. Eventually the Jetprop became well known for its outstanding performance out of hot and high air strips. The company's sales literature explains:

> The Jetprop represents no great technological 'breakthrough'. It is instead a classical example of the application of 'state of the art' technology in achieving highly satisfactory performance, reliability and comfort.

The original design objectives remained the main selling features of the aircraft.

By 1992 the Jetprop was one of the United Kingdom's most successful commercial aircraft (see Exhibit 20.1), but several new products were now on the market, including a Japanese aircraft very similar to the Jetprop, although significantly larger. Britcraft worked closely with the Japanese during the project stage of this aircraft, hoping to be awarded a large share of the work associated with this venture, but this never occurred. Less competitive, and aimed at the military market, were Russian and Canadian turboprop aircraft and pure jet aircraft from the Netherlands and Germany.

EXHIBIT 20.1 COMMERCIAL SUCCESS OF THE JETPROP AIRCRAFT, 1992

CONTINENT	NUMBER OF JETPROPS SOLD
Africa	11
America: North and South	62 (4)[a]
Asia	26
Australasia	11
Europe	25 (20)[b]
Oceania	6

[a] Figure in parentheses indicates total sales to United States and Canada.
[b] Figure in parentheses indicates sales to UK operators.

Sales Organization

The BCA's sales organization was responsible for selling the Jetprop. It covered civil and military sales, since several air forces had bought 30 Jetprops. A small number became VIP transports for heads of state. Each year markets were analyzed and a list was made of the most likely sales prospects for the coming 12 months. Area sales managers then received 'designated areas' comprising a number of prospective customers. These were usually grouped geographically, although there were exceptions due to special relationships that a salesperson had developed in the past. With time, new prospects were added to the designated areas, and the areas also had to be changed to balance the workload that developed.

Doug Watts was the area sales manager eventually responsible for the NAF prospect. Until then, his designated area included the air forces of Malaysia, Thailand, Zaire and Germany. Like several other area sales managers, he had joined Britcraft after a distinguished career in the UK's Royal Air Force (RAF). Immediately before joining the company in 1990 he was Group Captain, Air Plans RAF Germany. Three of the area sales managers had no RAF experience, but had previously worked in one or more of the company's technical departments. One had been in the Sales Engineering Department for a number of years before being promoted to the Sales Department. In the company the Sales Department had a very high status, occupying a series of offices on the ground floor at the front of the Jetprop factory.

The sales engineers were all technically qualified, a number having post-graduate degrees. Most had become sales engineers directly after completing a technical apprenticeship with the company, although some came from other technical departments. They were responsible for providing technical support to the Sales Department, but also did considerable routine work associated with the sales effort. Although the sales engineers were not working directly for the area sales managers, the work of each sales engineer usually related to one part of the world, requiring frequent contact with one or two people in the Sales Department. The Sales Engineering Department was close to the Sales Department and could be reached by a corridor that led from the 'front corridor' to the Sales Department in a corner of the design office occupied by the sales engineers.

Ian Crawford, the marketing director of all Britcraft, worked at Britcraft's HQ in London. He was responsible for marketing for the whole of Britcraft Aviation in the United Kingdom and overseas. He also managed Britcraft Aviation's regional executives – senior executives strategically based to cover all the world's markets.

The Opening Phase

After receiving the telephone call from Wing Commander Weir, Bob Lomas circulated news of the prospect, while Doug Watts took overall responsibility for it. Although BCA had agents in the Country, these had either not heard of the NAF requirement or failed to tell the company about it. Since the agents seemed dormant, BCA made direct contact with the national authorities in the Country. Following a visit to Herr Hans Schijlter, the defence secretary, Bob Lomas was asked to send copies of the standard Jetprop military brochure directly to the Ministry of Defence for the minister. A few days later, Lieutenant Colonel Schemann, junior defence secretary, wrote thanking Bob Lomas. The next contact made was with Lieutenant General Baron von Forster, defence attaché to the Country's embassy in London, whom Bob Lomas had met at the Hanover Air Show. The general confirmed the NAF's interest in new equipment and asked for details of the Jetprop to pass on the authorities.

On 6 July, Air Commodore Netherton informed John Upton of Britcraft that the NAF probably had a requirement for a state VIP aircraft. The air commodore had lived in the capital of the Country for eight years since retiring from the RAF, where he had been responsible for the Queen's Flight. After completing his military career he had become a founder member of Eilluft AG, a group that dominated civil aircraft maintenance and light aircraft operations in the Country. Britcraft had later used him as an *ad hoc* agent for the prospective sale of fighter aircraft. Having become an accredited agent for BMA, he was proposed as an agent in the Country for BCA.

Besides the Jetprop, Britcraft made another aircraft sold for VIP purposes. This was the Britcraft Executive Jet, a small, twin-jet aircraft manufactured and marketed by BEA. The sales organizations of both BEA and BCA were told of the sales opportunity.

In response, Geoff Lancaster, deputy sales manager of Britcraft Civil Aviation, sent copies of the Jetprop brochure to Air Commodore Netherton requesting that they be passed on to the prospective customer. As the air commodore was not familiar with the Jetprop, a letter enclosed with the brochures outlined some of the selling points that he could use:

> Although the JETPROP does not have the glamour of a fast jet
> aircraft, it has many other advantages which make it perhaps the
> most suitable choice for a State Aircraft … the size of the
> accommodation coupled with reasonably low purchase price. Most
> VIP layouts consist of a large rear state room with seats for four or
> five persons. These would be of the fully reclining and swivelling
> type. The forward part of the cabin would accommodate anything
> up to 20 attendants. The large size of the Jetprop also allows full
> galley and toilet facilities to be placed if need be both forward and
> aft in the aircraft, so that the VIP party could have complete privacy
> … uses short airfields … credit terms are available.

The letter also mentioned that the Country's minister of defence had recently flown in a Jetprop of the Queen's Flight and was favourably impressed.

On 10 July, Air Commodore Netherton met the officer in charge of the Operations Requirements Branch of the NAF, who confirmed that there was a study into the replacement of several types of transport aircraft. Simultaneously, Wing Commander Weir contacted Ron Hill, the executive director of marketing for BCA, saying that it was imperative that the company made direct contact with the Long Term Planning Department of the NAF about its requirement. Major Graff was the best contact, although Colonel Beauers and Lieutenant Colonel Horten were suitable alternatives if he was not available. Since Doug Watts was out of the country, Brian Cowley, the Jetprop sales manager, arranged a meeting. An exploratory meeting on 26 July preceded another on 7 August when Ron Hill would meet the senior personnel responsible for aircraft procurement.

Work in Iran prevented Ron Hill from attending the meeting, so Steve Williams, his executive assistant, took his place. The discussions – between Steve Williams, Air Commodore Netherton, Major Graff and Lieutenant Colonel Horten went well. Lieutenant Colonel Horten, the second in command of the Planning Department, outlined the need for the NAF completely to re-equip its tactical and transport squadrons before 1996. Large Lockheed Hercules had already been ordered, but the NAF was still looking for a small, more flexible aircraft. Major Graff, the officer in command of re-equipment evaluations, explained that he had already completed preliminary analysis of suitable replacements, which had included the Jetprop. Fokker had already demonstrated its aircraft, which many in the NAF favoured because a large part of the airframe was constructed in the Country. The final requirement would be for two or three general transport aircraft plus possibly one for the paratroop training school at NAF-Graz. A Short Skyvan had already given a demonstration as a paradrop aircraft and the Canadians wanted to demonstrate their aircraft.

The Jetprop's demonstration to the NAF would be on 20 October. Major Graff asked for further evidence to support the Jetprop. The advantages of the Jetprop over the Fokker aircraft were highlighted, which were lack of bonding and spot welding, no pneumatics, fail-safe design, progressive maintenance and rough-airfield performance. Also, since Hercules were already ordered, it would be advantageous if there was commonality of avionics.

During the visit they met briefly with Colonel Beauers, the officer commanding the Long Range Planning Department. Air Commodore Netherton had known him well for a number of years, but found that Colonel Beauers was soon to move to NATO HQ and would be replaced by an officer whom he did not know. After the meeting the air commodore expressed the hope that, provided the presentation in October went well and the NAF wanted the aircraft, the political people would agree to the purchase. He added that the sale of the paradrop aircraft seemed likely to depend upon support from Colonel Smit, the commanding officer of NAF-Graz, while the main issue, he thought, would be the aircraft's ability to operate safely, fully loaded for a parachute-training mission, from the NAF-Graz airstrip, which was grass and only 650 metres long.

Following the visit, Ernie Wise, a senior sales engineer, managed the technical selling effort. Through the Sales Department customer specifications engineer, the Production Planning Department was asked for a delivery schedule and the Estimating Department was requested to cost the aircraft. Other technical departments also became involved in supplying cost and performance evaluations. Eventually it would fall to the Contracts Department to negotiate a price for the package of aircraft, spares, guarantees, and after-sales services required.

Glynn Wills, a sales engineer who worked closely with Ernie Wise in the specification and requisitioning of artwork for the demonstration, became particularly involved with the avionics requirements. Several requests for detailed information were received from Major Graff, including details of the take-off and landing performance of the Jetprop at NAF-Graz. Since it was marginal, Air Commodore Netherton concluded that the only course was to convince the airfield's commanding officer to extend the runway.

Before the scheduled demonstration, the UK's biennial Farnborough Air Show took place. Invitations to attend went to a number of the NAF personnel, several of whom visited the show where they were entertained by Britcraft. The guests were: Lt. Col. Horten (chief of Plans and Studies), Lt. Col. Wabber (chief of Pilot Training), Major Bayer and Major Graff (Plans and Studies). The meeting progressed well, providing a useful prelude to the full demonstration. Then nine NAF officers visited BCA for the demonstration of the Jetprop in October, including officers from NAF Planning, Plans and Studies, Avionics, Technical Section, Supply/Spares and HQ Transport.

During the visit, technical specialists looked after most of the NAF officers, while the Long Range Planning Department people discussed contractual details. Prices presented for the aircraft in three configurations were £900,000 for the basic version, £950,000 for the basic version with strengthened floor for cargo operations, and £1,125,000 for the basic version with strengthened floor and large freight door. The cost of avionics, spares and other equipment that allowed the aircraft to perform a wide variety of roles would be additional.

On the whole, the demonstration and presentation went very well, although Major von Betterei, 'from whom it was difficult even to wring a smile', was evidently 'Fokker oriented'. Air Commodore Netherton and he had been able to talk separately with the senior officer present, with whom they had a 'long and useful discussion about compensation'.

The Second Phase

Compensation or offset is an increasingly common part of large international sales. It usually involves a provision being made for the vendor or the vendor's country to buy goods from the customer's country. The size of the offset varies considerably, ranging from a fraction of the contracted price to, on rare occasions, more than the contracted price. The discussion with Colonel Zvinek, of NAF Planning, Plans and Studies, during the demonstration marked the first occasion when offset appeared accompanying the NAF's procurement of transport aircraft.

BCA conducted investigations to determine the importance of offset arrangements to the Country's national government. News from BEA suggested that offset was critical. BEA had been attempting to sell two executive jet aircraft to the NAF: 'sales of the Britcraft Executive Jet failed mainly due to offset being ignored.' Two French aircraft were bought instead by the NAF as VIP transports with very high offset. This had been easy for the French to arrange as the aircraft were partly built in the Country. While continuing internal studies into offset, BMA warned BCA not to use any of the compensation it had already earmarked for a possible sale of military trainer aircraft.

To clarify the offset situation, Air Commodore Netherton visited Herr Maximilian, an under-secretary in the Ministry of Economic Affairs, who was responsible for advising the Country's ministerial committee on such matters. Herr Maximilian said offset had recently been between 60 and 70 per cent of the value of a contract and had been completed by the delivery date of the last aircraft. He felt that ideally the work should relate directly to the major project being considered, but should not involve the manufacture of main subassemblies such as wings, air frames or engines. He concluded by saying that negotiations were the responsibility of the vendor alone, who should not increase prices as a result of the required activities.

Soon after his visit to Herr Maximilian, the air commodore had obtained some encouraging information about the prospective sale. The NAF had given the replacement top priority with a schedule for action defined as follows:

March 1993   Finalized requirement.
Mid-1993   Signing of letter of intent.
Late 1993   Signing of contract and deposit payment.
1994   Delivery and full payment.

Colonel Zvinek, who had originally been doubtful about the Jetprop, had been converted since the demonstration, together with all the other important NAF officers concerned. Also, since the government had already earmarked funds for the procurement of three aircraft, all that was necessary was to assemble an acceptable offset.

Some time passed with little further progress being made with the sale. It became evident that, although the NAF staff officers favoured the Jetprop, Fokker was offering a very substantial offset. One reason for Fokker's ability to do this was its shareholding in Baden GmbH, which itself owned Nationale Flugzeugwerke AG (NFW), the Country's largest airframe manufacturer. Since NFW already manufactured Fokker parts, it was easy for it to show an advantageous offset capability.

Early in 1993, Kevin Murphy, the contracts manager for Britcraft Civil Aviation, sent a firm proposal to Colonel Zvinek. Simultaneously, members of the Sales Engineering Department were attempting to persuade the NAF to accept performance and weight information that showed Jetprop in a better light. The original figures requested by the NAF to allow direct comparison with the Fokker aircraft did not favour the Jetprop. The conditions for the 'paper comparison' were Fokker's and, not surprisingly, those conditions favoured Fokker's aircraft.

Some days later an urgent fax came from Roger Woods of Britcraft, who had met Colonel Horten at a cocktail party in the capital. He said that Fokker's exceptional offset looked like losing Britcraft the deal. Panic abated, however, when Air Commodore Netherton talked to Colonel Horten and confirmed that the offset was 'not big business'. Further, Messrs Jones and Bedwell of BMA, who were in the Country at that time negotiating a large offset deal with the Ministry of Economic Affairs, found that 'offset would not really be involved on such a small order'.

Major Graff and Air Commodore Netherton visited BCA on 11 April 1993, to discuss the contract. Major Graff said there was a feeling that the Jetprop was inferior to the Fokker on several technical grounds. Also the price of £1,393,000, being asked for an aircraft with a large cargo door and the required equipment, compared unfavourably with the Fokker offer. In addition, when adding the price of spares to the aircraft cost, the total was more than the amount budgeted. Negotiations centred on reducing the number of roles the aircraft had to perform, so reducing the amount of optional equipment supplied. By eliminating paradropping, supply dropping and aero-medical capabilities, the price reduced to a more acceptable £1,323,000. A new formal offer went to the Country before the end of April. This included details of an increased 'all up weight' for the aircraft, which would allow it to carry an extra 1,000 kg of fuel, thereby increasing performance over longer flights.

At the Paris Air Show on 13 June, Doug Watts again met Major Graff. They talked over two issues. First, the NAF desired to change the specifications of the aircraft to such an extent that a new quotation would be necessary. Secondly, Major Graff emphasized the importance of offset. Since by this time Steve Williams had left Britcraft, Geoff Lancaster took over negotiations. Wing Commander Weir, the air attaché in the capital, was contacted and questioned about the sale. He said he would probably be able to help in arranging some offset deal, but added that diplomatic circles generally felt that it was 'Britain's turn' to obtain a contract.

On 16 July Geoff Lancaster, Major Graff and Air Commodore Netherton visited Herr Maximilian at the Ministry of Economic Affairs to discuss alternative offset arrangements that the company could provide. There were four suggestions:

1. Bought-out equipment for the Jetprop could be purchased from the Country's firms.
2. Basic aircraft could be flown to the Country to be finished and new avionics fitted by a NAF contractor.
3. Britcraft's vendors could subcontract work into the Country.
4. The Country's industry could build a future batch of Jetprops.

Herr Maximilian's response to the suggestion was not enthusiastic. His main point was that offset must not relate directly to the main contract in question; nor should it involve the NAF or the government. He explained how critical offset arrangements were to the Country's aerospace industry, which designed and marketed few aircraft and was almost totally dependent upon outside work. To underline his government's concern, he quoted the offset associated with the recent sale of two Boeing aircraft to the Country's national airline. Boeing had agreed to place £3,000,000 of work with the Country's industry in the first year and £15,000,000 over the next ten years. The figures suggested that the offset was far more than the price of the two aircraft.

After leaving the ministry, Geoff Lancaster told Major Graff the consequence of further delay in placing a firm order. The three aircraft set aside for the NAF would go to other customers and eventually be supplied from a later batch of aircraft. Since each batch was costed separately, the price per aircraft could increase to almost £1,000,000. The longer the delay, the less likely it would become that Britcraft could supply at the original price. Furthermore, as several customers were on the verge of signing contracts for Jetprops, there was even greater need for a quick decision. Major Graff worried about the delay, but said there was little he could do. His recommendations for purchase would go on to General Petsch, at which stage they would constitute the official NAF requirements. They would then go to the air force adviser, and from him to the defence secretary, Hans Schijlter, who would examine the report closely but would not consider offset. The documents would then be passed to the minister of defence. He, together with the Prime Minister and the minister for economic affairs, would make the final decision. Before Geoff Lancaster left the Country it was agreed to arrange for a group of NAF officers to visit Schiller Aviation, an independent airline which had recently bought some Jetprops.

When the visit to Schiller took place, as the visitors' chief concern was the operation and maintenance of the aircraft, Chris Dyer helped. As an assistant customer liaison manager for Britcraft, he had been working closely with Schiller Aviation during the early stages of its Jetprop operation. Air Commodore Netherton escorted the group on the visit and later reported that the airline was 'very complimentary' about the aircraft and Britcraft support.

The Offset

In an attempt to arrange the necessary offset, several channels were investigated. One of the main problems facing Britcraft was the large part of a completed Jetprop aircraft being accounted for by very specialized bought-out equipment. There was little chance of this equipment being bought from anyone other than the normal vendor. The largest bought-out items were the engines. One source for the offset was for the aero-engine supplier to place work with Baden GmbH, which had been undertaking subcontract work for a number of years. Although there was a chance that the aero-engine supplier would help, since it supplied the same engines to Fokker, the offset would not give Britcraft any advantage over the competing supplier.

A team of Britcraft design and production engineers investigated what work could be 'put out' to subcontractors in the Country. They identified three types:

1. Design work on the Britcraft Quiet Jet, a small jet transport aircraft still at the project stage.

2. Machining of components required in small quantities, but which were difficult and heavy.

3. Sheet-metal work construction.

Negotiations with Nationale Flugzeugwerke (NFW), aimed at its doing about £1,000,000 of work, were started. However, although several exchanges of personnel, specifications and estimates took place, there was little progress towards a satisfactory agreement.

Meanwhile, Geoff Lancaster contacted Coles & Turf Ltd, a London-based company which had previously helped the company with offset. Coles & Turf offered to buy £4,500,000 worth of the Country's goods for a commission of 10 per cent. Within days the company again contacted Britcraft saying it had £1,500,000 worth of lard that was available for use as part of an offset. Meanwhile, Britcraft felt that the commission rate requested left no room for them to make a profit on the contract, so it wrote to Coles & Turf explaining this and stating that it needed £1,500,000 of offset rather than £4,500,000. Coles & Turf's response was to suggest that 10 per cent commission on £1,500,000 would leave plenty of room for Britcraft to make a profit and it subsequently offered alternative products for offset. Finally Roden AG, a subsidiary of The Roden Company Ltd, was contacted by Britcraft. After initial talks, packages of parts and drawings went to the company so that it could estimate prices for manufacture and assembly.

The situation became critical on 9 October when Air Commodore Netherton requested an urgent meeting with Geoff Lancaster at the NFA HQ. It seemed possible to sign 'a letter of intent' by 1 November, with the final contract signed by 1 April 1994. To achieve this, however, a global level for the total offset had to be presented, with details of it to be broken down. Negotiations with NFW, Coles & Turf, and Roden intensified as the deadline approached.

On 16 October there came a blow to the NAF deal. A Brazilian operator signed a contract for six aircraft. This meant that the NAF aircraft would be from the more expensive batch 15 rather than the original batch 14. The aircraft would be of slightly different configurations, and would cost more. The new price estimated for an aircraft with strengthened floor and large freight door was £1,470,000. The NAF reluctantly accepted the price increase and signed a letter of intent. Roden AG agreed to accept £450,000 worth of specified subcontract work. With this deal, it looked as though future activities would be mainly the responsibility of the Contracts Department. The pressure was off!

As April approached, a team at Britcraft was preparing to make a trip to the Country for final negotiations and contract signing. Then, a day before they were due to leave, Dick Drake, the commercial director, received a fax from the Country's authorities. It read:

> Department of Economic Affairs urgently expect more precision about your commitment and also a sensible increase of work for national industry. It is quite obvious that the 10 per cent offset is absolutely unsatisfactory. A reply is expected by 29 April.

A copy of the message went to Air Commodore Netherton, to which Dick Drake added:

> It is virtually certain that it will be necessary for me to reply on Friday that we regret we are unable to increase our commitment and the only other offset is that which they already know about from the aero-engine supplier. However, before replying, I would like to know whether Weir still believes it is Britain's turn.

QUESTIONS

1. Trace the stages in the buying process and how the Country's interests changed from one stage to the next. Why were the Country's interests changing and was Britcraft keeping pace with the changes?

2. How well did the strengths of the Jetprop match the needs of the NAF?

3. Identify the players in the buying centre and gauge their role and influence. How well did Britcraft manage the complexity of the buying centre and their diverse needs?

4. Discriminate between the sales roles of the people in Britcraft.

5. Did Britcraft's structure help or hinder its sales campaign? How could it be changed for the better?

6. What were Britcraft's main failings and strengths? Do you think it will win the sale or is it too out of touch with the needs of the NAF and the Country's government? What could it do at this late stage? Is it still 'Britain's turn'?

[1] This case is based on in-company records and documents. For this reason the identity of the buyer and the seller and the names of the people in the case have been disguised.

Bang & Olufsen: Different by Design

Anton Hartmann-Olesen[*]

 In 1983 Bang & Olufsen, a small Danish manufacturer of stylish consumer electronics products, had to make a double-or-quits decision. Should it try to penetrate the German market further or get out altogether? If it was to stay in, how was it to gain the market share it needed?

The company's German operation, based in Hamburg, had so far been unable to make much impression on the huge German market. Over the last five years, sales had grown by less than 3 per cent and the financial results were poor. The only way to motivate the dealer base had been a series of expensive special offers: 'this week's special offer', 'buy 10 and pay for 8', or 'buy now and we will offer you terms of payment of 120 days, better than anyone else in the market'.

Relationships with Bang & Olufsen's 450 dealers were difficult. Bang & Olufsen's turnover in the individual shops was so small that it did not matter to the dealer. Also, since turnover on the German market accounted for only 3 per cent of Bang & Olufsen's turnover in the Danish parent company, the German market was not significant to Bang & Olufsen either. Several other markets looked more attractive than Germany. The United States, Canada and Japan showed high growth and, due to the high value of the dollar, they also looked very profitable. The question often came up: 'Should Bang & Olufsen concentrate on selling in the most profitable markets and close the German subsidiary? Alternatively, should it re-establish and reposition the brand following a new marketing strategy?'

Until 1983 the company had had little experience of selling outside Denmark. The sales organization looked very professional with sales subsidiaries in the United States, Japan and every country in Europe. However, there were problems beneath the surface. Almost all subsidiaries were acquired as bankrupt agents. These agents could no longer handle the changed distribution systems. Everywhere in Europe there was a shift from specialized, selective radio and TV dealer-network to the very competitive and hard-selling mass distributors. Bang & Olufsen had traditionally used a push strategy that focused on getting retailers to stock Bang & Olufsen's products. Once displayed, the consumers would buy Bang & Olufsen's distinctively designed consumer electronics.

* Herning, Denmark.

The international sales organization was large but ill-defined. There was no common communication strategy, no distribution development strategy, no common approach to training and no corporate image strategy. As a result, each country developed its own strategy and they became a series of independent 'kingdoms'.

Under New Management

In early 1984 a new management team started analyzing the situation. The new managing director faced several problems, and one of the most serious problems was on Bang & Olufsen's doorstep. Germany is one of the world's largest markets for consumer electronics and, like Denmark, part of the EU. Bang & Olufsen Germany had to be healthy. But, first of all:

● *An overall target market* had to be defined. Until then each of the subsidiary 'kingdoms' had defined a target group that depended on local preferences and circumstances.

● *A new marketing strategy* needed formulating. The old push orientation was failing and could not resolve Bang & Olufsen's poor position in the market.

● *A new dealer base* was needed to increase the quality and profitability of the operation.

● *A new organization* had to meet the demands from the new marketing strategy. A move from Hamburg to Munich would signal that Bang & Olufsen Germany was part of the most dynamic, business and growth-oriented section of the country.

The 7 CIC

The changes followed from Bang & Olufsen's 7 CIC (Corporate Identity Components) that defined the *corporate culture* and the *product strategy*:

1. *Authenticity.* It is the company's aim to make products that guarantee faithful reproduction of programme material.
2. *Autovisuality.* The company's products must provide immediate understanding of their capabilities and manner of operation.
3. *Credibility.* We must constantly strive towards establishing confidence in the company, its actions, dealings and products.
4. *Domesticity.* The products are for use by people in the home. They must be problem-free and easy to operate – even though technically advanced. Technology is for the benefit of people – not the reverse.
5. *Essentiality.* The products must be concept bearing. Design must focus on the essentials of the concept.
6. *Individuality.* Bang & Olufsen has elected to be an alternative to the mass-producing giants of the trade.
7. *Inventiveness.* Product development and other tasks must be inventive. New approaches to solving practical tasks should characterize the company and its products.

The Consumer Target

So far, in the whole global Bang & Olufsen operation there was no single definition of the target group, but where such definitions did exist they used traditional demographic criteria: age, sex, income, education or geographic location. Experience had proved them to be no longer valid, if they ever had been. Bang &

Olufsen saw the 1990s consumers turning away from indiscriminate consumption. They instead chose a lifestyle and arranged their possessions to fit it with great care. The pan-European sociocultural ACE research identifies different groups of these people. The research divides the European population into ten homogeneous groups. The groups are of equal size, but differ sociologically and culturally.

A diamond-shaped model represents the ten segments (see Exhibit 6.1). This diagram indicates that:

- People close to the top of the diamond are vital and open-minded. They influence society and society influences them.
- People in the bottom groups focus on a secure and stable life. They are passive and will often resist change.
- The groups on the left have strong ethical anchors in life. They feel responsible for themselves and society.
- The groups on the right are constantly trying to bring pleasure and new experience into their lives.

EXHIBIT 6.1 PAN-EUROPEAN CONSUMER GROUPS

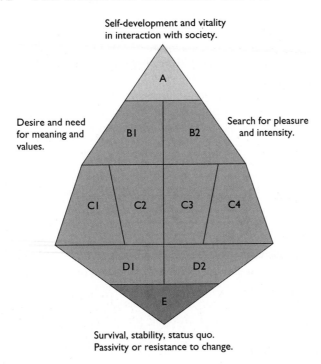

SOURCE: ACE Research.

Bang & Olufsen has selected the northern groups A, B1 and B2 as its primary target groups. They were selected because:

> Their attitudes and interests are in harmony with Bang & Olufsen's philosophy. They influence public opinion compared to other groups, they are more frequent buyers of and more likely to pay high prices for audio and video products.

Characteristically the groups are curious, open-minded and have a strong desire to learn new things. They are always changing.

The targeted groups A, B1 and B2 account for 30 per cent of Europe's total population, but only some 17 per cent in West Germany (as it then was). In contrast A, B1 and B2s make up 35 per cent of France's population and 37 per cent in Italy. This suggests that German consumers, on average, are more conservative than the French and Italians. For Germans, adjustment to change is the responsibility of institutions rather than individuals.

A New Promotions Strategy

The limitations of the push strategy used by Bang & Olufsen Germany showed in the low consumer awareness (10 per cent) and preference (2 per cent) for Bang & Olufsen products by Germans in 1984. Comparable figures in Denmark were 98 per cent awareness and 48 per cent preference. The situation had to improve and could only improve. A switch from a push to a pull strategy was needed to redress the balance between consumer demand and the availability of the products. The advertising strategy was built upon four ideas:

1. *Quality of advertising medium* has great influence on the attention and the effect of the advertising message.

2. *Activation of the main target group* by the careful choice of media (exclusive special magazines concerning *living*, *design*, *lifestyle* and so on) creates multiple purchase incentives without cannibalizing the Bang & Olufsen main target group.

3. *Target group analysis and purchase motives.* Main income and education levels decide the interest in the product and bear on the purchase decision.

4. *Increase in awareness of Bang & Olufsen.* Through advertising in high-profile *general-interest magazines*, the company would achieve a clear increase in the Bang & Olufsen awareness to an above-average level.

Marketing expenses increased from 3 to 10 per cent to support the new promotional effort – a change partly funded by cutting dealer margin from 38 to 33 per cent. 'We approach our main target group directly,' said Bernd D. Ehrengart, President of Bang & Olufsen Germany.

A New Dealer Base

In 1984 the dealer base was 450 *individual* dealers, each with a different agreement with Bang & Olufsen. Their rewards were based on their historical relationship with Bang & Olufsen's sales subsidiary rather than on the turnover and profits they generated. Their individuality was also expressed in the marketing strategy, the service performance and the price policy they offered. The sales strategy focused on transactions rather than on customer relations, a difference then unrecognized by Bang & Olufsen and the dealers.

A new strategy came under the banner: 'Mit dem Partner im Handel' (relationship marketing). The aim was to have a dealer network whose sales processes matched the quality of Bang & Olufsen's products. Dealers should project a 'perception of high quality' and 'heighten loyalty towards Bang & Olufsen'. Each geographical sales area would have a 'long-term potential coverage plan', and each area's plan would be tracked by the national sales office, which aimed to increase quality and loyalty within the distribution network. Dedicated Bang & Olufsen displays would increase the average turnover per dealer and the share of Bang & Olufsen turnover per dealer. Each dealer would have a partnership agreement with Bang & Olufsen covering: presentation, minimum range of products, exterior identification, service/installation provision, promotional activity policies, training and minimum turnover.

Bang & Olufsen's message to its chosen dealers was:

● Bang & Olufsen makes you an up-market store.

● Bang & Olufsen offers unique high technology on a full range of exclusive products.

● Bang & Olufsen caters for customers who want qualified guidance.

● Bang & Olufsen conducts its marketing in co-operation with its specialized dealers.

A New Organization

In 1984 Bang & Olufsen Germany had 25 staff. These worked mainly on the internal administration of stock keeping, servicing, book keeping and recording orders. The average sales per employee were Dkr452,000. The new marketing strategy required the staff to be more externally oriented, with a focus on communication, technical and sales training, distribution development, service and working in the field implementing the new marketing strategy. More staff were needed, but increased sales per employee would more than cover their cost.

QUESTIONS

1. Distinguish between the old push and the new pull policies followed by Bang & Olufsen. Why do you think the push strategy was not working? Is it likely that the pull strategy will increase sales significantly without making Bang & Olufsen's products more attractive to German consumers?

2. How is the new pull strategy being funded? In what way is the new strategy attractive or not attractive to distributors?

3. What compensates the retailers for having a lower margin and investing more in Bang & Olufsen's stock and display area?

4. How does the target market influence Bang & Olufsen's promotional strategy? Since there are so few of the target customers in Germany, would it pay Bang & Olufsen to target other groups in that market?

5. Would you 'double or quit' the German market? Why was Bang & Olufsen more attracted to the United States and other markets than to Germany, and was it right in being so?

6. What is the rationale behind Bang & Olufsen's new marketing and distribution strategy for Europe? Does it seem likely that the European market segments into ten equally sized groups that are similar across all European countries? Do you think Bang & Olufsen's strategy will work in Germany?

Part 7

Place

Part Introduction

The final part of this text includes two chapters covering the fourth element of the marketing mix – place. It will help you to understand the decisions and actions that companies take in order to bring products and services to customers. It also considers how new information and communication technologies are transforming distribution and retailing functions.

How products and services are delivered to customers for final usage or consumption can make a difference to how customers perceive the quality and value of the overall offering. Speed of delivery, guaranteed supply and availability, convenience to shoppers and so forth can enhance buyer–seller relationships and increase customer satisfaction. Consequently, firms are increasingly paying greater attention to how they manage their distribution channels to deliver goods and services that customers want at the right time, right place and right price. Chapter 21 shows what channel organizations and their functions are, and how firms can build more cost-effective routes to serving and satisfying their target markets.

The last decade has seen a revolution taking place in the field of communications and telecommunications technology, which has had a significant impact on marketing activities. Telephones, televisions and computers are becoming important channels for selling products and services; these media are increasingly used not just for communicating messages to customers, but for interacting with and doing business with customers. Chapter 22 explores the ways in which direct, non face-to-face forms of marketing can help organizations reach specific target markets quickly. Technologies such as TV Web boxes and the Internet are creating new challenges and opportunities in electronic commerce for firms. More and more companies are setting up 'stores' on the computer and virtual shopping is now a reality. In this final chapter we see how organizations conduct online marketing, and we speculate on future directions for this emerging channel for marketing.

CHAPTER 21
Managing Marketing Channels

CHAPTER 22
Direct and Online Marketing

PART OVERVIEW CASE:
*Freixenet Cava:
Bubbles Down a New Way*

Managing Marketing Channels

Preview Case

Economos

ECONOMOS, AN AUSTRIAN COMPANY, MAKES seals. These are rubber or plastic rings that are fitted at joints in fluid pipes to prevent leakage. It is difficult for anyone, even engineers, to get excited about seals. Economos, however, can. The company, founded by Helmut Mayerhofer, has achieved tremendous success in this $4 billion annual worldwide market through an impressive series of innovations in materials and production technologies and distribution methods. Economos has shaken up the world seal industry, and distribution advances have been a cornerstone of its marketing strategy.

There are thousands of seal types and sizes. Customers expect their distributors to keep stocks available of most of them. Seal makers like Economos also expect their distributors to buy large stocks. In this business, it is also apparent that the firm's own production technologies and the injection moulding process it uses encourages it to manufacture large batches of the product. The traditional production methods, however, mitigated against fast response to customers that ordered a small quantity of an item not in stock. Economos was considering how to overcome the inflexibility which, in a way, confined the company to the use of third-party distributors that are put under pressure to keep large inventories.

In the mid-1980s, Helmut Mayerhofer and his associates started to examine the possibility of developing compounds that could be machined on a numerically controlled lathe. When a customer ordered a small quantity of an item that was not in stock, the firm could simply take a rough block of synthetic rubber or polyurethane and turn out the required number of pieces. At that time, few of the existing polyurethane substances could be machined. Those that could were not sufficiently flexible to make suitable seals. Economos approached the Department of Material Science and Material Testing of the Mining University of Leoben in Styria in 1988, whose assistance resulted in the development of a formula that produced machinable polyurethane suitable for seals. A plastics machine maker that Economos was working with developed a process for extruding the material into rough seal moulds, resembling lengths of pipe, in industrial quantities. The company also came up with a third innovation – a lathe, cutting tools and software for machining the rough stock into precisely dimensioned seals. This enabled the firm to produce a finished product that had highly consistent elastic properties and was free of bubbles. As a result of the speed and automation of the company's lathe, it could now machine a seal in about one minute, slice it off the rough stock and immediately machine another from the remaining stock. Economos could use its system to produce normal as well as occasional seals.

It is clear that once such a system is enforced, Economos could create a competitive advantage in fast, flexible, manufacturing that could be translated into higher service levels for its customers: that is, any size of seal could be delivered to them in small or large quantities and, most importantly, quickly.

Since production could be done in immediate response to orders, Economos decided to set up as close to customers as possible. Its distributors would no longer need to carry large inventories, which meant lower prices and higher margins for their customers. Machinery makers could also contemplate abandoning the stocking and supplying of replacement seals. More recently, Economos has set up, together with local partners, seal service centres worldwide. It supplies the rough blocks of materials and the lathes to the local entrepreneur, who, under a franchise agreement, machines and supplies seals in response to manufacturers' orders. To date, there are 250 such service centres operating with the brand name Seal-Jet. The company's managing director, Ernst Stocker, estimates that its combined annual sales are about Sch1,424 million. Economos' own revenues of over Sch420 million have come from selling not only seals, but also, increasingly, machines and materials.

The Austrian group is set to adapt its strategy to obtain greater control over its seal service businesses in overseas markets. Through investment in technological innovation, the company has transformed the way it delivers value to its distributors and customers, while creating extra revenues for the firm. Through the transformation of its distribution method, Economos has been able to improve its delivery service in particular, thus lowering costs and improving margins for its customers. A seal is a seal is a seal – maybe for most people, but for Economos it is serious business in which the integration of production (in this case) and marketing channel strategies have created a significant source of competitive advantage, and a win-win situation for the company, its customers and distributors alike.[1]

QUESTIONS

1. In the case of Economos, who are the main players in the distribution channel for seals? Identify the supply chain.

2. What are the channel service needs of (a) Economos; (b) Economos' customers?

3. How would you describe the channel approach used by Economos (a) up to the mid-1980s; (b) following the introducion of the series of technological innovations that streamlined its production-delivery system?

4. Why is it important for the company to work closely with channel partners at different levels in the supply chain?

5. What are the changes in the channel environment that companies such as Economos and its distributors must be aware of?

6. How might these changes impact on Economos' business? Suggest a channel strategy that would enable the company to sustain a competitive advantage in the global seal market.

Introduction

The case of Economos shows how a firm can use technological innovations to achieve greater distribution effectiveness (including international expansion) and efficiency, and to enhance customer service delivery. Increasingly, many firms, operating in all types of product sectors, are utilizing technical advances in areas such as information gathering and processing, communications and logistical processes, and methods to improve distribution channel performance. In this chapter, we will take a closer look at an important, albeit often neglected, component of the marketing mix – place – and focus on decisions and activities relating to distribution channels and logistics management.

Marketing channel decisions are among the most important decisions that management faces. They determine how well target customers gain access to the firm's product or service and whether the distribution channel system is cost-effective for the organization concerned. A company's channel decisions directly affect every other marketing decision. The company's pricing depends on whether it uses mass merchandisers or high-quality speciality stores. The firm's sales force and advertising decisions depend on how much persuasion, training and motivation the dealers or resellers need. Whether a company develops or acquires certain new products may depend on how well those products fit the abilities of its channel members.

Companies often pay too little attention to their distribution channels. Managers who see channel functions merely as the physical transportation, storage and distribution of finished goods to the end-user fail to utilize the channel of distribution as a competitive weapon. As we saw in the case of Economos, like the rest of its competitors in the seal-making industry, the firm had relied on the use of a rigid distribution channel system. Constraints in materials and production technologies were generally accepted to rule out speed and flexibility in small-order delivery. However, by forceful investment in technological innovations, Economos overcame these barriers and found a means of creating superior channel advantage – closeness to customers, flexibility, no order-size restriction, faster customer-order response time, international reach, lower costs, higher margins and rewards for its distributors and entrepreneurial franchises. It had used a more imaginative distribution system to *gain* a competitive advantage.

Distribution channel decisions often involve long-term commitments to other firms. For example, companies can easily change their advertising, pricing or promotion programmes. They can scrap old products and introduce new ones as market tastes demand. But when they set up distribution channels through contacts with franchises, independent dealers or large retailers, they cannot readily replace these channels with company-owned stores if conditions change. Therefore, management must design its channels carefully, with an eye on tomorrow's likely selling environment as well as today's. In the case of Economos, the use of franchises has enabled it to expand its distribution network outside Austria, but these intermediaries must be properly managed if they are successfully to maintain sales, the Seal-Jet brand name and market position. Economos has to revise its channel strategy to maintain cost-effective service delivery to customers.

Single market reforms in the European Union have forced many companies to review their entire distribution strategy. The use of third-party as opposed to in-house distribution in the grocery retailing sector, for example, is on the increase, and current operators in Europe must look for new ways to differentiate their services by taking advantage of the trend.[2]

This chapter examines the following questions concerning marketing channels:

● What is the nature of marketing channels?

● How do channel firms organize to do the work of the channel?

● What problems do companies face in designing and managing their channels?

● What role does physical distribution play in attracting and satisfying customers?

● What are the changes taking place among channel institutions?

The Nature of Distribution Channels

distribution channel (marketing channel)
A set of interdependent organizations involved in the process of making a product or service available for use or consumption by the consumer or industrial user.

Most producers use third parties or intermediaries to bring their products to market. They try to forge a **distribution channel** – a set of interdependent organizations involved in the process of making a product or service available for use or consumption by the consumer or business user.[3] The channel of distribution is therefore all those organizations through which a product must pass between its point of production and consumption.[4]

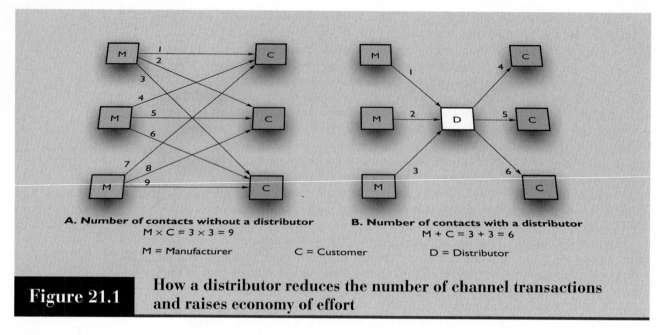

A. Number of contacts without a distributor
M × C = 3 × 3 = 9

B. Number of contacts with a distributor
M + C = 3 + 3 = 6

M = Manufacturer   C = Customer   D = Distributor

| **Figure 21.1** | **How a distributor reduces the number of channel transactions and raises economy of effort** |

Why are Marketing Intermediaries Used?

Why do producers give some of the selling job to intermediaries? After all, doing so means giving up some control over how and to whom the products are sold. The use of intermediaries results from their greater efficiency in making goods available to target markets. Through their contacts, experience, specialization and scale of operation, intermediaries usually offer the firm more than it can achieve on its own.

Figure 21.1 shows how using intermediaries can provide economies. Part A shows three manufacturers, each using direct marketing to reach three customers. This system requires nine different contacts. Part B shows the three manufacturers working through one distributor, which contacts the three customers. This system requires only six contacts. In this way, intermediaries reduce the amount of work that must be done by both producers and consumers.

From the economic system's point of view, the role of marketing intermediaries is to convert the assortments of products made by producers into the assortments wanted by consumers. Producers make narrow assortments of products in large quantities, but consumers want broad assortments of products in small quantities. In the distribution channels, intermediaries buy the large quantities of many producers and break them down into the smaller quantities and broader assortments wanted by consumers. As such, intermediaries play an important role in matching supply and demand.

Marketing Channel Functions

A distribution channel moves goods from producers to consumers. It fills the main time, place and possession gaps that separate goods and services from those who would use them. Members of the marketing channel perform many key functions. Some help to complete transactions:

● *Information.* Gathering and distributing marketing research and intelligence information about actors and forces in the marketing environment needed for planning and facilitating exchange.

- *Promotion.* Developing and spreading persuasive communications about an offer.
- *Contact.* Finding and communicating with prospective buyers.
- *Matching.* Shaping and fitting the offer to the buyer's needs, including such activities as manufacturing, grading, assembling and packaging.
- *Negotiation.* Reaching an agreement on price and other terms of the offer, so that ownership or possession can be transferred.

Others help to fulfil the completed transactions:

- *Physical distribution.* Transporting and storing goods.
- *Financing.* Acquiring and using funds to cover the costs of the channel work.
- *Risk taking.* Assuming the risks of carrying out the channel work.

The question is not *whether* these functions need to be performed, but rather *who* is to perform them. The producer can eliminate or substitute institutions in the channel system, but the functions cannot be eliminated. When channel members are eliminated, their functions are moved either forwards or backwards in the channel, only to be assumed by other members. In short, the producers can do without intermediaries, but they cannot eliminate their functions.

All these functions use up scarce resources and can often be performed better through specialization. To the extent that the manufacturer performs these functions, its costs go up and its prices have to be higher. At the same time, when some of these functions are shifted to intermediaries, the producer's costs and prices may be lower, but the intermediaries must charge more to cover the costs of their work. In dividing the work of the channel, the various functions should be assigned to the channel members that can perform them most efficiently and effectively to provide satisfactory assortments of goods to target consumers.

Number of Channel Levels

Distribution channels can be described by the number of channel levels involved. Each layer of marketing intermediaries that performs some work in bringing the product and its ownership closer to the final buyer is a **channel level**. Because the producer and the final consumer both perform some work, they are part of every channel. The *number of intermediary levels* indicates the *length* of a channel. Figure 21.2A shows several consumer distribution channels of different lengths.

Channel 1, called a **direct-marketing channel**, has no intermediary levels. It consists of a manufacturer selling directly to consumers. For example, Dell Computer sells personal computers by mail-order rather than through dealers or retailers, and Tupperware uses home parties to sell its kitchen products. Direct sales of consumer goods in some European countries have enjoyed record growth in recent years, and this is one sector of the retail economy, for example, that has survived the recession. (In Chapter 22, we examine the methods organizations use to market directly to consumers.)

The remaining channels in Figure 21.2A are *indirect*-marketing channels. Channel 2 contains one intermediary level. In consumer markets, this level is typically a retailer. For example, the makers of televisions, cameras, furniture, major appliances and many other products sell their goods directly to large retailers, which then sell the goods to final consumers. Channel 3 contains two intermediary levels, a wholesaler and retailer. This channel is often used by

channel level
A layer of intermediaries that performs some work in bringing the product and its ownership closer to the final buyer.

direct-marketing channel
A marketing channel that has no intermediary levels.

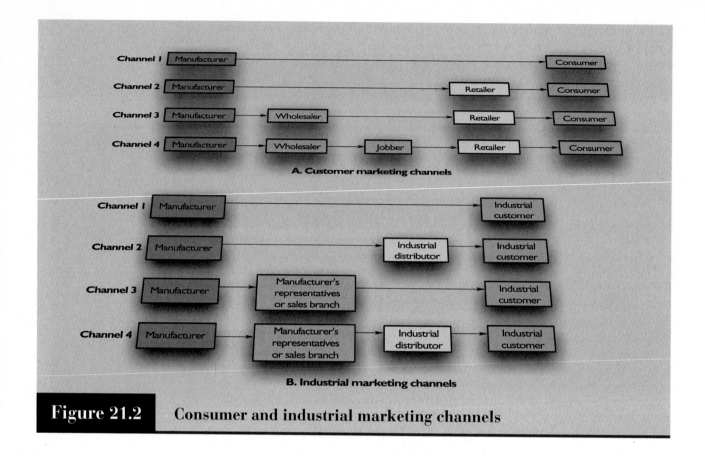

Figure 21.2 **Consumer and industrial marketing channels**

manufacturers of food, drugs, hardware and other products. Channel 4 contains three intermediary levels. In the meat-packing industry, for example, jobbers usually come between wholesalers and retailers. The jobber buys from wholesalers and sells to smaller retailers, which generally are not served by larger wholesalers. Distribution channels with even more levels are sometimes found, but less often. From the producer's point of view, a greater number of levels means less control and greater channel complexity.

Figure 21.2B shows some common industrial or business distribution channels. The business marketer can use its own sales force to sell directly to business customers. It can also sell to industrial distributors, which in turn sell to business customers. It can sell through manufacturers' representatives or its own sales branches to business customers, or it can use these representatives and branches to sell through industrial distributors. Thus business markets commonly include multilevel distribution channels.

In summary, channel institutions play an important role in making products or services available to customers. Between them, channel members ensure the transfer of several entities: the *physical product, ownership, money* or *payment, information* and *promotion*. These transfers can make even channels with only one or a few levels very complex. The types of intermediary channel will be discussed in greater detail in a later section.

Channels in the Service Sector

The concept of distribution channels is not limited to the distribution of tangible products. Producers of services and ideas also have to decide how they make their

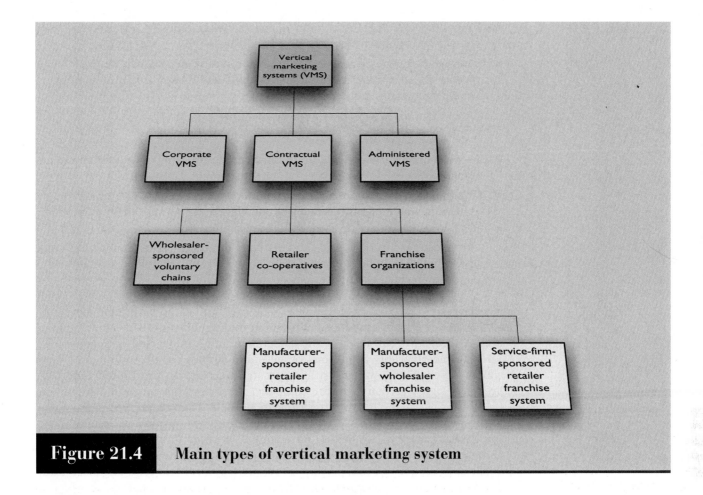

| Figure 21.4 | **Main types of vertical marketing system** |

of the profits. Franchising has been a fast-growing retailing form in recent years. Almost every kind of business has been franchised – from hotels and fast-food restaurants to dental and garden maintenance services, from wedding consultants and domestic services to funeral homes and fitness centres.

Franchising offers a number of benefits to both the franchisor and franchisee. The main advantages for the franchisor are as follows:

- The franchisor secures fast distribution for its products and services, but does not incur the full costs of setting up and running its own operations. Franchising also enables the franchisor to expand a successful business more rapidly than by using its own capital.
- The franchisor gets very highly motivated management as the franchisees are working for themselves rather than a salary.
- The contractual relationship ensures that franchisees operate to and maintain franchisors' standards.

The main advantages for franchisees are as follows:

- They are buying into a proven system if selling an established brand name (e.g. McDonald's, Shell, Interflora).
- They can start a business with limited capital and benefit from the experience of the franchisor. This way they reduce the costs and risks of starting a new business.

- Franchisees also get the benefits of centralized purchasing power – since the franchisors will buy in bulk for the franchisees.
- They get instant expertise in operational issues such as advertising, promotions, accounts and legal matters, and can rely on franchisors' help should things go wrong.

Franchise systems have several disadvantages:

- Franchisors invariably have to forfeit some control when operating through franchisees.
- The franchisees may not all perform exactly to franchisors' operating standards, and inconsistencies in service levels can tarnish the brand name.
- Franchisees may not always have a good deal, in that they have to work extremely hard to meet sales and financial targets to make the business pay, and although they have already paid their initial fee, they have to meet continuing management services or royalty payments.

There are three forms of franchise. The first form is the *manufacturer-sponsored retailer franchise system*, as found in the car industry. BMW, for example, licenses dealers to sell its cars; the dealers are independent businesspeople who agree to meet various conditions of sales and service. Shell, the oil company, adopts a franchising system on many of its forecourts in the United Kingdom. French designer garden furniture company, Jardin en Plus, has relied greatly on franchising to expand into other European markets. The second type of franchise is the *manufacturer-sponsored wholesaler franchise system*, as found in the soft-drinks industry. Coca-Cola, for example, licenses bottlers (wholesalers) in various markets, which buy Coca-Cola syrup concentrate and then carbonate, bottle and sell the finished product to retailers in local markets. The third franchise form is the *service-firm-sponsored retailer franchise system*, in which a service firm licenses a system of retailers to bring its service to consumers. Examples are found in: the fashion business (Benetton, Stefanel, The Body Shop); the car rental business (Hertz, Avis, Europcar); the fast-food service business (McDonald's, Burger King); the home furnishing business (IKEA and Marks & Spencer used franchising to expand into foreign markets); and the hotel business (Holiday Inn, Ramada Inn, Balladins).

The fact that most consumers cannot tell the difference between contractual and corporate VMSs shows how successfully the contractual organizations compete with corporate chains.

administered VMS
A vertical marketing system that co-ordinates successive stages of production and distribution, not through common ownership or contractual ties, but through the size and power of one of the parties.

ADMINISTERED VMS. An **administered VMS** co-ordinates successive stages of production and distribution, not through common ownership or contractual ties, but through the size and power of one of the parties. Manufacturers of a top brand can obtain strong trade co-operation and support from resellers. For example, in the fast-moving consumer-goods market, companies like Unilever and Procter & Gamble can command unusual co-operation from resellers regarding displays, shelf space, promotions and price policies. In the consumer electronics sector, Sony can obtain a great deal of trade support from retail stores for its top-selling brands. Similarly, large retailers like IKEA, Marks & Spencer and Toys 'Я' Us can exert strong influence on the manufacturers that supply the products they sell. Consider IKEA.

In just over four decades, IKEA, the privately owned Swedish furniture retailer, grew from a single store in Sweden's backwoods to become one of the most successful international retailers in the world. It now has more than 100 outlets in 28 countries across the globe, taking over Skr39 billion a year in sales. Smart targeting, careful attention to customer needs and rock-bottom prices have made IKEA the world's largest home furnishings company. Its success formula was based on reinventing the furniture-retailing business. Traditionally, selling furniture was a fragmented affair, shared between department stores and small family-owned shops. All sold expensive products and delivered up to two or three months after a customer's order. IKEA trims costs to a minimum while still offering service. It does this by using a global sourcing network stretching to about 2,300 suppliers in 67 countries. IKEA relies on long-term relationships with key suppliers that can supply high quality at low prices. In return these suppliers get technical advice and leased equipment from the company. IKEA's designers also work closely with suppliers to reduce product costs from the outset. Other savings come from IKEA displaying its vast product range in cheap out-of-town stores. It sells most of its furniture as knocked-down kits for customers to take home and assemble themselves. The firm enjoys huge economies of scale from operating such huge stores, and from enormous production runs made possible by selling the same furniture all around the world. This enables IKEA to compete on quality while undercutting rival manufacturers by up to 30 per cent on price. IKEA's success also means success for its suppliers. But they must operate to IKEA's terms and enable the global firm to fulfil its promise of quality merchandise at low cost to customers worldwide.[6]

• *Horizontal Marketing Systems*

Another channel development is the **horizontal marketing system**, in which two or more companies at one level join together to follow a new marketing opportunity. By combining their capital, production capabilities or marketing resources, companies can accomplish more than any one company working alone. Companies might join forces with competitors or non-competitors.[7] They might work with each other on a temporary or permanent basis, or they may even create a separate company:

> Nestlé and Coca-Cola formed a joint venture to market ready-to-drink coffee and tea worldwide. Coke provided worldwide experience in marketing and distributing beverages, and Nestlé contributed two established brand names – Nescafé and Nestea.
>
> Such channel arrangements work well globally. Because of its excellent coverage of international markets, Nestlé sells General Mills' Cheerios brand in markets outside North America. Seiko Watch's distribution partner in Japan, K. Hattori, markets Schick's razors and, as a result, Schick has the leading market share in Japan, despite Gillette's overall strength in many other markets.[8]

Other examples include **retailer co-operatives**, which are made up of independent retailers that band together to own wholesale operations jointly, or to conduct joint merchandising and promotions. The Swiss Migros, with its dozen or so co-operatives, and the UK's Co-operative Societies have tried to exploit group buying and promotion economies through setting up such horizontal marketing arrangements.

horizontal marketing systems
A channel arrangement in which two or more companies at one level join together to follow a new marketing opportunity.

retailer co-operatives
Contractual vertical marketing systems in which retailers organize a new, jointly-owned business to carry on wholesaling and possibly production.

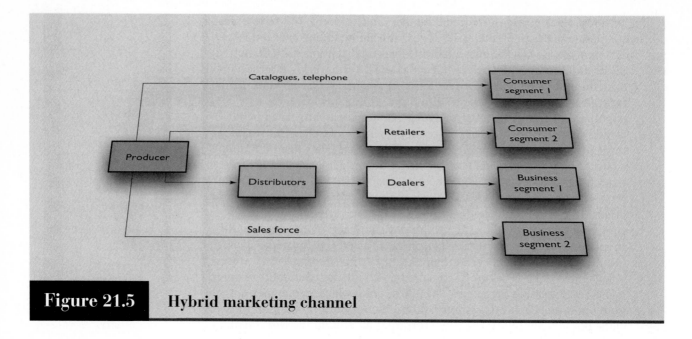

| Figure 21.5 | **Hybrid marketing channel** |

The number of horizontal marketing systems has increased dramatically in recent years, so businesses must develop flexibility and management capabilities to enable them to capitalize on the growing opportunities presented by such marketing channel systems.

● *Hybrid Marketing Systems*

In the past, many companies used a single channel to sell to a single market or market segment. Today, with the proliferation of customer segments and channel possibilities, more and more companies have adopted *multichannel distribution systems* – often called **hybrid marketing channels**. Such multichannel marketing occurs when a single firm sets up two or more marketing channels to reach one or more customer segments.

hybrid marketing channels
Multichannel distribution, as when a single firms sets up two or more marketing channels to reach one or more customer segments. A variety of direct and indirect approaches are used to deliver the firm's goods to its customers.

Figure 21.5 shows a hybrid channel system. In the figure, the producer sells directly to consumer segment 1 using direct-mail catalogues and telemarketing, and reaches consumer segment 2 through retailers. It sells indirectly to business segment 1 through distributors and dealers, and to business segment 2 through its own sales force.

Sony maintains a wide distribution coverage by adopting a hybrid marketing system. In the UK, Sony sells its consumer products through exclusive retail outlets such as the Sony Centres, through mass merchandisers like electrical chains and catalogue shops (e.g. Comet, Dixons and Argos), and by using direct marketing channels, such as mail-order catalogues operated by direct marketers Grattan, Freemans and Kays.

Hybrid channels offer many advantages to companies facing large and complex markets. With each new channel, the company expands its sales and market coverage, and gains opportunities to tailor its products and services to the specific needs of diverse customer segments. But such hybrid channel systems are harder to control, and they generate conflict as more channels compete for customers and sales. For example, when IBM began selling personal computers directly to customers at low prices through catalogues and telemarketing, many of its dealers cried 'unfair competition' and threatened to drop the IBM line or give it less emphasis. The key to managing hybrid channel systems successfully is minimizing interchannel member conflict, while maximizing consumer demand through superior product quality and design and extensive communications to reinforce brand values and identity. In some cases, the multichannel marketer brings all of its channels under its own ownership and control to minimize external channel conflict, although the marketer might face greater internal conflict over how much financial support each channel deserves.

Channel Design Decisions

We now look at several channel decisions facing manufacturers. In designing marketing channels, manufacturers struggle between what is ideal and what is practical. A new firm usually starts by selling in a limited market area – a few manufacturers' sales agents, a few wholesalers, some existing retailers, a few trucking companies and a few warehouses. Deciding on the *best* channels might not be a problem: the problem might simply be how to convince one or a few good intermediaries to handle the line.

If the new firm is successful, it might branch out to new markets. Again, the manufacturer will tend to work through the existing intermediaries, although this strategy might mean using hybrid marketing channels. In smaller markets, the firm might sell directly to retailers; in larger markets, it might sell through distributors. In one part of the country, it might grant exclusive franchises because that is the way merchants normally work; in another, it might sell through all outlets willing to handle the merchandise. In one country it might use international sales agents; in another, it might partner a local firm.

Thus channel systems often evolve to meet market opportunities and conditions. However, for maximum effectiveness, channel analysis and decision making should be more purposeful. Designing a channel system calls for:

- Analyzing customer service needs.
- Defining the channel objectives and constraints.
- Identifying the major channel alternatives.
- Evaluating those alternatives.

Analyzing Customer Service Needs

Like most marketing decisions, designing a channel begins with the customer. Marketing channels are viewed as *customer value delivery systems* in which each channel member adds value for the customer. Thus designing the distribution channel starts with finding out what *values* consumers in various target segments want from the channel.[9] Do customers want to buy from nearby locations or are they willing to travel to more centralized locations? Would they rather buy in person or over the phone or through the mail? Do they want immediate delivery or are they willing to wait? Do they value breadth of assortment or do they prefer specialization? Do customers want many add-on services (delivery, credit, repairs, installation) or will they obtain these elsewhere? The more decentralized the channel, the faster the delivery and the greater the assortment provided. Additionally, the more add-on services supplied, the greater the channel's service level.

Generally, customer service is determined by the interaction of all these factors that affect the process of making the product or service available to the customer. Companies that recognize these needs must then build channel strategies that will serve them better than the competition. Consider the distribution channel service needs of business computer-system buyers:

> The delivery of service might include such things as demonstration of the product before the sale or provision of long-term warranties and flexible financing. After the sale, there might be training programmes for using the equipment and a programme to install and repair it. Customers might appreciate 'loaners' while their equipment is being repaired or receiving technical advice over a telephone hot line.

For the individual buyer, purchasing a personal computer for the first time, channel service must be more sensitive to the consumer's relative ignorance of, 'shyness' with and discomfort about PC technology. The novice computer user needs advice not only on what PC (the hardware) to buy, but also on the range of software to do the tasks he or she requires. This group of buyers also needs help on how to set up the equipment, load the software and learn to use the 'new toy'.

Providing the fastest delivery, the greatest assortment and the most comprehensive services may not be possible or practical. As in the case of servicing the PC buyer, providing a high level of personal service, in addition to warranties, maintenance and after-sales support, does not come cheap. A morning's training on a new graphics package can cost up to several hundred pounds. The company and its channel members may not have the resources or skills needed to provide all the desired services. Also, providing higher levels of service results not only in higher costs for the channel, but also in higher prices for consumers. The company must balance consumer service needs against the feasibility and costs of meeting these needs as well as customer price preferences. Customers frequently make trade-offs between service quality and other purchase dimensions, such as price. The success of off-price and discount retailers, such as Germany's Aldi and Lidl, the British Kwik Save and Superdrug and the Dutch Makro, shows that consumers are often willing to accept lower service levels if this means lower prices. Makro, for example, has expanded outside its key European markets and boasts a successful operation in the Thai market. In Japan, where consumers are noted for their obsession with and preparedness to pay for quality, no-frills discount houses, too, are gaining in popularity.

Moreover, the success of one company depends not just on its own actions, but on how well its entire channel competes with the channels of other companies. This idea is based on the notion that the unit of competition is not the individual company or organization in the channel, but the entire channel system or supply chain.[10] For example, Marks & Spencer imposes rigorous quality control on its suppliers, which it relies on to maintain its own quality reputation in food retailing. Similarly, Toyota is just one link in a customer value delivery system that includes thousands of dealers worldwide. Even if Toyota makes the best cars in the world, it will lose out to Ford, General Motors, BMW and Nissan if these competitors have superior dealer networks. Equally, the best Toyota dealer in the world cannot do well if Toyota supplies inferior cars. And Toyota cannot supply superior quality and reliable cars if its suppliers fail to maintain their own quality standards for parts and components that go into Toyota cars. The company has to design an integrated marketing channel system that will deliver superior value to its customers.

Defining the Channel Objectives and Constraints

Channel objectives should be stated in terms of the desired service level of target customers. Usually, a company can identify several segments wanting different levels of channel service. The company should decide which segments to serve and the best channels to use in each case. In each segment, the company wants to minimize the total channel cost of supplying customers, while also meeting their service requirements.

The company's channel objectives are also influenced by the nature of its products, company policies, marketing intermediaries, competitors and the environment. *Product characteristics* greatly affect channel design. For example, perishable products require more direct marketing to avoid delays and too much handling. Bulky products, such as building materials and soft drinks, require channels that minimize shipping distance and the amount of handling.

Company characteristics also play an important role. For example, the company's size and financial situation determine which marketing functions it can handle itself and which it must give to intermediaries. Furthermore, a company marketing strategy based on speedy customer delivery affects the functions that the company wants its intermediaries to perform, the number of its outlets and the choice of its transportation methods.

The *characteristics of intermediaries* also influence channel design. The company must find intermediaries that are willing and able to perform the needed tasks. In general, intermediaries differ in their abilities to handle promotion, customer contact, storage and credit. For example, manufacturers' representatives who are hired by several different firms can contact customers at a low cost per customer because several clients share the total cost. However, the selling effort behind the product is less intense than if the company's own sales force did the selling.

When designing its channels, a company must also consider its *competitors' channels*. In some cases, a company may want to compete in or near outlets that carry competitors' products. Thus companies may want their brands to be displayed next to competing brands: in town or city centres, Burger King wants to locate near McDonald's; Pizzaland wants to be sited near Pizza Hut; Sony, Panasonic and Philips audio-video systems all compete for floor space in similar retail outlets; Nestlé and Mars confectionery brands want to be positioned side by side, and aggressively compete for shelf space, in the same grocery outlets.

In other cases, producers may avoid the channels used by competitors. Avon, for example, decided not to compete with other cosmetics makers for scarce positions in retail stores and, instead, set up a profitable door-to-door selling operation in the home and overseas markets.

Finally, *environmental factors*, such as economic conditions and legal constraints, affect channel design decisions. For example, in a depressed economy, producers want to distribute their goods in the most economical way, using shorter channels and dropping unneeded services that add to the final price of the goods. Legal regulations prevent channel arrangements that may lessen competition substantially or create a monopoly. In countries where governments are actively encouraging free competition, such regulatory restrictions have helped to keep competitive channels open, as in the case of telecommunications in the United Kingdom, where companies such as Cable & Wireless, Ionica and the privatized BT exist in parallel to supply telephone services.

An effective channel strategy is based on creating a differential advantage which allows the firm to compete successfully in its target markets. Consequently, the channel or channels selected must have the knowledge and experience not only to serve these segments effectively, but also to support and sustain the manufacturer's competitive advantage. The European construction machinery maker JCB recognized that its early problems in the French market were due to the inadequacies of its distribution outlet. It used manufacturers' agents to sell its equipment in France. These agents sold the products, but were not capable of providing the service facilities essential for competitive success in the market. JCB subsequently set up a company-owned full-service distribution network which was sufficiently competent to communicate the company's product advantages and provide the value-added services expected by customers.

Identifying Major Alternatives

Having defined its channel objectives, the firm then identifies its major channel alternatives in terms of the *types* and *number* of intermediaries to use and the *responsibilities* of each channel member.

● *Types of Alternative Channel*

A number of options exist:

Direct marketing
Marketing through various advertising media that interact directly with consumers, generally calling for the consumer to make a direct response.

Broker
A wholesaler who does not take title to goods and whose function is to bring buyers and sellers together and assist in negotiation.

Agent
A wholesaler who represents buyers or sellers on a relatively permanent basis, performs only a few functions, and does not take title to goods.

Intermediaries
Distribution channel firms that help the company find customers or make sales to them, including wholesalers and retailers that buy and resell goods.

wholesaler
A firm engaged primarily in selling goods and services to those buying for resale or business use.

full-service wholesalers
Wholesalers that provide a full set of services such as carrying stock, using a sales force, offering credit, making deliveries and providing management assistance.

- *Direct marketing.* A number of **direct marketing** approaches can be used, ranging from direct-response selling via advertisements in print media, on radio or television, by mail order and catalogues to telephone and Internet selling. These methods are discussed further in Chapter 22.

- *Sales force.* The company can sell directly through its own *sales force* or deploy another firm's sales force, as Glaxo did with its best-selling anti-ulcer drug, Zantac. Alternatively, a contract sales force might be used. This method of selling to customers is discussed in Chapter 20.

- *Intermediaries.* These are independent organizations that will carry out a number of activities. *Merchants*, which include wholesalers and retailers, buy, take title to and resell the firm's goods, whereas **brokers** and **agents** do not buy or carry the producer's products, but help to sell these to customers by negotiating prices and sales terms and conditions on the supplier's behalf. Other **intermediaries** – transport companies, independent warehouses, finance companies, banks – perform a range of channel functions to facilitate the flow of goods or services from producer to user.

WHOLESALERS. Wholesalers render important services to producers and resellers. Wholesalers' sales forces help manufacturers reach any small customers at a low cost. The wholesaler has more contacts and is often more trusted by the buyer than the distant manufacturer. Wholesalers can select items and build assortments needed by their customers, thereby saving the consumers a considerable amount of work. They save their customers money by buying in huge lots and breaking bulk (breaking large lots into small quantities). Wholesalers hold inventories, thereby reducing the inventory costs and risks of suppliers and customers. Wholesalers can provide quicker delivery to buyers because they are closer than the producers. They finance their customers by giving credit, and they finance their suppliers by ordering early and paying bills on time. Wholesalers absorb risk by taking title and bearing the cost of theft, damage, spoilage and obsolescence. They give information to suppliers and customers about competitors, new products and price developments. Wholesalers also provide management services and advice – they often help retailers train their sales assistants, improve store layouts and displays, and set up accounting and inventory control systems.

There are many types of wholesaler. They are classified according to the breadth and depth of their product/service lines and the range of services they offer. **Full-service wholesalers** provide a full set of services, such as carrying stock, using a sales force, offering credit, making deliveries and providing technical advice and management assistance. They are either *wholesale merchants* or *industrial distributors*. Wholesale merchants sell mostly to retailers. *General merchandise wholesalers* carry several lines of goods – for example, hardware, cosmetics, detergents, non-perishable foods and household goods – to meet the needs of both general-merchandise retailers and single-line retailers. *Limited-line wholesalers* carry one or two lines of goods, but offer a greater depth of assortment. Examples are hardware wholesalers, drug wholesalers and clothing wholesalers. Some *speciality-line-wholesalers* carry only part of a line in great depth, such as health-food wholesalers, seafood wholesalers and automotive parts wholesalers. They offer customers deeper choice and greater product knowledge.

Industrial distributors sell mainly to producers rather than to retailers. They provide inventory, credit, delivery, technical advice and other services. They may handle a wide, limited or special line of products. Industrial distributors concentrate on lines such as maintenance and operating supplies, original-equipment goods (such as ball bearings and motors) and equipment (such as power tools and forklift trucks).

Limited-service wholesalers perform a limited number of functions and offer fewer services to their suppliers and customers. There are several types of limited-service wholesaler. **Cash-and-carry wholesalers** have a limited line of fast-moving goods, such as groceries, toys, household goods, clothes, electrical supplies, office supplies and building materials. They sell to small retailers and industrial firms for cash and normally do not deliver. A small fish-store retailer, for example, normally drives at dawn to a cash-and-carry fish wholesalers and buys several crates of fish, pays on the spot, drives the merchandise back to the store and unloads it. Cash-and-carry wholesalers are important to some small retailers and industrial customers that are not served by the bigger wholesalers. They may not benefit from the services that full-service wholesalers can offer, but they do get lower-priced merchandise and immediate access to goods. An example of a cash-and-carry wholesaler is Makro, although Makro is a hybrid operator, servicing both individual consumers and small retailers.

Truck wholesalers (also called *truck jobbers*) perform a selling and delivery function. They carry a limited line of goods (such as milk, bread or snack foods) that they sell for cash as they make their rounds of supermarkets, small groceries, hospitals, restaurants, factory cafeterias and hotels. *Drop shippers* operate in bulk industries such as coal, oil, chemicals, lumber and heavy equipment. They do not carry inventory or handle the product. They receive orders from retailers, industrial buyers or other wholesalers and then forward these to producers, which ship the goods directly to the customer. The drop shipper takes title and risk from the time the order is accepted to the time it is delivered to the customer. Because drop shippers do not carry inventory, their costs are lower and they can pass on some savings to customers. *Rack jobbers* serve grocery and general merchandise retailers, mostly in the area of branded non-food items, such as books, magazines, toys, stationery, housewares, health and beauty aids, and hardware items. These retailers do not want to order and maintain displays of hundreds of non-food items. Rack jobbers send delivery trucks to stores and the delivery person sets up display racks for the merchandise. They price the goods, keep them fresh and maintain inventory records. Rack jobbers sell on consignment – they retain title to the goods and bill the retailers only for the goods sold to consumers. Thus they provide services such as delivery, shelving, inventory and financing. They do little promotion because they carry many branded items that are already highly advertised.

Other limited-service wholesalers include *producers' co-operatives*, owned by farmer-members, who assemble farm produce to sell in local markets, and

limited-service wholesalers
Those who offer only limited services to their suppliers and customers.

cash-and-carry wholesalers
Wholesalers that stock a limited line of fast-moving goods – such as groceries, toys, household goods, clothes, electrical supplies and building materials – and that sell to small retailers and industrial firms for cash and normally do not provide a delivery service.

mail-order wholesalers, which use catalogues to sell to retail, industrial and institutional customers and give discounts for large orders. Their main customers are businesses located in small outlying areas. They have no sales forces to call on customers and provide very few services. The orders are filled and goods are sent to customers by mail, truck or other means.

Although wholesalers play an important channel role, **retailers** are also critical intermediaries as they provide the final link between the consumer and provider.

RETAILERS.   Retail stores come in all shapes and sizes, and new retail types keep emerging. Generally, they can be distinguished by the amount of service they offer, the product line and relative price emphasis.

Different products require *different amounts of service* and *customer service preferences* vary. **Self-service retailers** cater for customers who are willing to perform their own 'locate-compare-select' process to save money. Today, self-service is the basis of all discount operations and is typically used by sellers of grocery and convenience goods (e.g. supermarkets) and nationally branded, fast-moving shopping goods (e.g. discount stores). **Limited-service retailers**, such as department stores, provide more sales assistance because they carry more shopping goods about which customers need information. They also offer additional services such as credit and merchandise return not usually offered by low-service stores. Their increased operating costs, however, result in higher prices. **Full-service retailers**, such as speciality stores and first-class department stores, assist customers in every phase of the shopping process. They usually carry more speciality goods and slower-moving items, such as cameras, jewellery and fashions, for which customers like to be 'waited on'. They provide more services, resulting in much higher operating costs, which are invariably passed along to customers as higher prices.

Retailers vary in the *length and breadth of their product assortments*. A **speciality store** carries a narrow product line with a deep assortment within that line. Examples are stores selling outdoor leisure garments, furniture, books, cosmetics, jewellery, electronics, flowers or toys (e.g Rohan, Hennes & Mauritz, Benetton, Foyles, Interflora). Today, speciality stores are flourishing for several reasons. The increasing use of market segmentation, market targeting and product specialization has resulted in a greater need for specialist stores that focus on specific products and segments. Because of changing consumer lifestyles and the increasing number of two-income households, many consumers have greater incomes but less time to spend shopping. They are attracted to speciality stores that provide high-quality products, convenient locations, excellent service and quick entry and exit.

A **department store** carries a wide variety of product lines – typically, clothing and fashion accessories, cosmetics, home furnishings and household goods – each operated as a separate department managed by specialist buyers or merchandisers. Examples of well-known department stores are Harrods and Harvey Nicholls (in the United Kingdom), Sogo, Takashimaya and Isetan (in Japan and south-east Asia), Saks Fifth Avenue and Bloomingdale (in the United States), El Corte Ingles (in Spain), Galeries Lafayette (in France) and Karlstadt (in Germany). **Variety stores** tend to be low-cost, self-service stores. They specialize in a wider range of goods than specialist stores, but have a narrower range compared to department stores and are more basic in terms of the level of extra amenities offered. Woolworth, for example, sells a variety of products – compact discs, records, cassettes, household goods, children's clothes and confectionery – but, except for a café/restaurant, does not offer the extra facilities and services provided by a huge department store. However, some variety stores like Marks &

---

self-service retailers
Retailers that provide few or no services to shoppers; shoppers perform their own locate-compare-select process.

self-service retailers
Retailers that provide few or no services to shoppers; shoppers perform their own locate-compare-select process.

limited-service retailers
Retailers that provide only a limited number of services to shoppers.

full-service retailers
Retailers that provide a full range of services to shoppers.

speciality store
A retail store that carries a narrow product line with a deep assortment within that line.

department store
A retail organization that carries a wide variety of product lines - typically clothing, home furnishings and household goods; each line is operated as a separate department managed by specialist buyers or merchandisers.

variety store
Self-service store that specializes in a wide range of merchandise. It offers a wider range than specialist stores, but a narrower variety than department stores.

Cité Europe: a testing ground for new shopping concepts in Europe.

Spencer, which sells clothing and accessories, food, cosmetics, household goods, home furnishing and financial services, have not only focused on quality, but also differentiated themselves from the competition by providing extra services for customers, including store cards, special events and mail order. **Convenience stores** are small stores that carry a limited line of high-turnover convenience goods – essential groceries, toiletries, cigarettes and newspapers. Examples are Happy Shopper, Spar, Mace and VG stores. These locate near residential areas and remain open for long hours, seven days a week. They satisfy an important consumer need in a niche segment – shoppers in this segment use convenience stores for emergency or 'fill-in' purchases outside normal hours or when time is short, and they are willing to pay for the convenience of location and opening hours.

Supermarkets are large, low-cost, low-margin, high-volume, self-service stores that carry a wide variety of food, laundry and household products. Their growth in Europe, since the 1960s, and more recently in industrializing Asian markets, has been phenomenal. Many of these supermarkets were located in town or city-centre high streets with ample car parking and, for a while, offered a good range and value-for-money to consumers. However, with town and city centres becoming increasingly congested and car ownership rising fast in the 1980s and 1990s, people were keen to shop outside towns and cities. Many supermarkets started to close unprofitable high-street stores and build big edge-of-town stores. These **superstores** typically occupy 2,000–4,000 square metres and sell everything from baked beans to fine wines, aspirins to ankle socks. They also offer a range of services such as dry cleaning, post offices, film developing and photo finishing, cheque cashing, petrol forecourts and self-service car-washing facilities. Many are cutting costs, establishing more efficient and effective operations through rigid quality control, centralized distribution and electronic technologies, and lowering prices in order to compete more effectively with discount stores, such as the German Aldi, Norma and Lidl, the Danish Netto and the French Carrefour, which have expanded aggressively across Europe in recent years. These **discount stores** regularly sell national brands at lower prices by accepting lower margins and selling higher volume.

Superstores are well developed in many parts of Europe, where they account for a sizeable share of total retail sales. Most are located out-of-town, frequently in

convenience store
A small store located near a residential area that is open long hours seven days a week and carries a limited line of high-turnover convenience goods.

supermarkets
Large, low-cost, low-margin, high-volume, self-service stores that carry a wide variety of food, laundry and household products.

superstore
A store almost twice the size of a regular supermarket that carries a large assortment of routinely purchased food and non-food items and offers such services as dry cleaning, post offices, film developing, photo finishing, cheque cashing, petrol forecourts and self-service car-washing facilities.

discount store
A retail institution that sells standard merchandise at lower prices by accepting lower margins and selling at higher volume.

category killers
A modern 'breed' of exceptionally aggressive 'off-price' retailers that offer branded merchandise in clearly defined product categories at heavily discounted prices.

hypermarkets
Huge stores that combine supermarket, discount and warehouse retailing; in addition to food, they carry furniture, appliances, clothing and many other products.

cash-and-carry retailers
Large, 'no-frills' stores that sell an extensive assortment of goods, and are noted particularly for their bulk discounts.

retail parks, with vast free car parks. In recent years, non-grocery retailers, such as the US Toys 'Я' Us, the UK Specialist Computer Holdings (SCH) and IKEA, have also opened superstores in out-of-town sites. SCH sells leading hardware and software brands such as IBM, Toshiba, Compaq, Apple, Microsoft, Lotus and Borland, and offers finance, training and maintenance packages. Analysts report that superstores will account for more than 40 per cent of computer sales by the mid-1990s.[11]

The latter group of retailers are also known as **category killers**. They are a new breed of exceptionally aggressive discounters, offering a wide range of branded products in a clearly defined category. Their predatory pricing strategy – pile them high, sell them cheaper than the competition – and ability to decimate much of the competition in their sector explains their name. Their price advantage is generally based on scale economies, bulk buying power and a rigorous attention to costs. Category killers have, in recent years, been one of the most dynamic growth sectors in retailing. Leading US and European category killers have been successful in penetrating overseas markets, with long-term growth potential predicted for the format as well as for its leading players (see Table 21.1). Importantly, the American market is near saturation, and Europe is now a focus for expansion for many more of those leading players – K Mart, T J Maxx, Blockbuster Video, Staples and Sports Authority, to name but a few (see Marketing Highlight 21.2).

Hypermarkets are even bigger than superstores. A typical hypermarket occupies about 10,000 square metres of space, almost as big as six football fields. They carry more than just routinely purchased goods, for they also sell furniture, appliances, clothing and many other things. The hypermarket operates like a *warehouse*. Products in wire 'baskets' are stacked high on metal racks; forklifts move through aisles during selling hours to restock shelves. The store gives discounts to customers who carry their own heavy appliances and furniture out of the store. Examples are the French Carrefour and Casino, and Savacentre which is owned by the British Sainsbury's. Hypermarkets have been successful in world markets. For example, Carrefour, the large French retailer, successfully operates hundreds of these giant stores in Europe, South America and Asia. There is a continuing trend towards large-scale retail development, particularly in south-east Asia, Japan and South America.[12] Other retail stores that feature low prices include cash-and-carry stores, warehouse clubs and catalogue showrooms. **Cash-and-carry retailers** are large stores (around 3,000–4,000 square metres) selling an extensive assortment of goods, ranging from groceries to office furniture. For example, Makro, the Dutch-based retailer, whose European self-service cash-and-carry outlets were sold to the Metro retailing group of Germany in 1997, operates vast warehouses across Europe, selling food, beverages, wines and spirits, confectionery, household goods, clothes and other assortments to a dual customer base – consumers and trade (resellers/retailers). It has also expanded rapidly in Asian markets.

{Channel Design Decisions ● 915}

Table 21.1 Forecast number of category killers in selected markets in the year

| | NUMBER OF STORES | | | |
	TOYS AND GAMES	DIY	ELECTRICALS/CONSUMER ELECTRONICS/HOME FURNISHINGS	OFFICE SUPPLIES
Australia	20	41	29	25
Austria	5	8	6	6
Belgium	6	8	7	5
Brazil	20	30	25	20
Canada	45	40	35	35
Denmark	5	8	7	6
France	27	33	30	30
Germany	56	84	69	60
Indonesia	20	–	–	–
Italy	27	44	35	30
Japan	117	200	153	140
Mexico	30	45	40	40
Netherlands	14	17	15	15
Norway	4	4	4	4
Philippines	10	–	–	–
Portugal	3	3	3	3
South Korea	40	–	–	–
Spain	35	50	42	40
Sweden	4	6	5	5
Switzerland	5	5	5	5
Taiwan	15	–	–	–
Thailand	10	–	–	–
United Kingdom	45	60	55	55

NOTE: Based on current category killer sectors.
SOURCE: *Euromonitor*.

Makro opened its cash-and-carry store (the size of about two football fields) in Bangkok, Thailand in 1989. It is heaped from floor to ceiling with discounted goods of every kind. Open from 6 a.m. to 10 p.m. every day, it is packed with shoppers wheeling giant trolleys filled with an eclectic assortment of goods, ranging from office furniture and TV sets to soft drinks and live eels. It has been the trail-blazer in bulk discount retailing in Asia. It now has six stores in Thailand and continues to spread to other parts of Asia, including Taiwan, Indonesia and Malaysia, South Korea and China. Makro's success in Thailand was helped by its alliance with Charoen Pokphand, a powerful local conglomerate, which opened doors to Thai manufacturers. Makro was also helped by demand from small shopkeepers, its main customers. Makro gives these small buyers the chance not just to by-pass the traditional distributors and buy their own selection of merchandise, but to do so in bulk and at lower prices.[13]

Invasion of the Retail Giants: Coming to Terms with the Global Marketplace

Marketing Highlight 21.2

Store retailing is a business worth over $5 trillion a year worldwide, but one that once proved difficult to transfer across national frontiers. However, as the major retailers have consolidated into corporate giants and found that their domestic markets have become ever more crowded, the big stores are crossing borders for growth opportunities.

Large retailers are spreading out in all directions: east, west, north, south. Dutch retailer Ahold has bought 11 supermarkets in the Czech Republic; Germany's Obi, the do-it-yourself chain and part of the Tengelmann Group, has targeted Italy, Hungary and the Czech Republic. After making its mark in the UK, with the discount chain Ed and the warehouse club Costco, Carrefour is looking beyond Europe and targeting the emerging markets of Latin America and the Far East. Indeed Ahold, Aldi and Tengelmann, Belgium's Delhaize and Carrefour are among those with more than 30 per cent of sales coming from outside their domestic markets. The United Kingdom's Tesco operates the Catteau chain of supermarkets in northern France, while Sainsbury's, through acquisitions, has become the eleventh-largest grocer in the United States. Migros, the Swiss grocery retailer, until recently active only in Switzerland, now operates in France, Germany and Austria, where it is committed to taking a leading position. French fashion chains like Pimkie, Promod, Camieu and Naf Naf have made a substantial impact on the Belgian market; Sweden's fashion retailer Hennes & Mauritz has taken the German market by storm; so has Marks & Spencer in French, Spanish and Far Eastern markets. To this list can be added fashion and furnishing chains whose international businesses are already well advanced – the Dutch C & A (arguably the oldest retail chain in Europe), Italy's Benetton, the Swedish IKEA and America's McDonald's, Gap (clothing) and Toys 'Я' Us. And the global march continues, as seen in the recent acquisition of Germany's Wertkauf hypermarket chain by the world's largest retailer, the US Wal-Mart Stores – a deal that has sent a shockwave through the European retail industry.

The extent of cross-border retailing is highlighted by research conducted by the Oxford Institute of Retail Management (UK). The study reported that retailers made 530 international moves between 1991 and 1993, of which 381 or 72 per cent involved European firms expanding into other European countries. A further 676 moves were made in Europe by non-European, including US, retailers. The move to eastern European countries was also very popular, with the Czech Republic, Slovakia, Poland and Hungary being the most favoured destinations outside the EU. Another study published by market analyst Corporate Intelligence in Retail (CIR) reinforced the unsettling pace of internationalization by retailers, reporting that European retailers made 610 cross-border moves in the first four years of the 1990s, compared with 611 cross-border deals in the whole of the 1980s.

Asian retailers with international ambitions are also emerging. Japanese store groups, such as Sogo, Mitsukoshi, Takashimaya, Isetan and Yaohan, have spread across Japan, Singapore, Hong Kong and Thailand. Isetan has stores in Europe. Yaohan is set to open 170 department stores in China, Hong Kong and Macau by the end of the decade. Hong Kong's Bossini and Giordano have spread to Malaysia, Taiwan and Singapore, and are making the running in China. Similarly, Asia's industrializing countries have attracted western retailers, which have been scrambling to meet the increasingly sophisticated demands of consumers eager to buy products ranging from deodorants and frozen food to luxury accessories and designer fashion brands. Leading retailers that have set up stores across the region include Carrefour, Galeries Lafayette, Makro, Marks & Spencer, IKEA, Toys 'Я' Us, The Body Shop, K-Mart and Wal-Mart.

In 1990 Japan's 'Large Scale Retail Law', which controlled planning consent for new stores

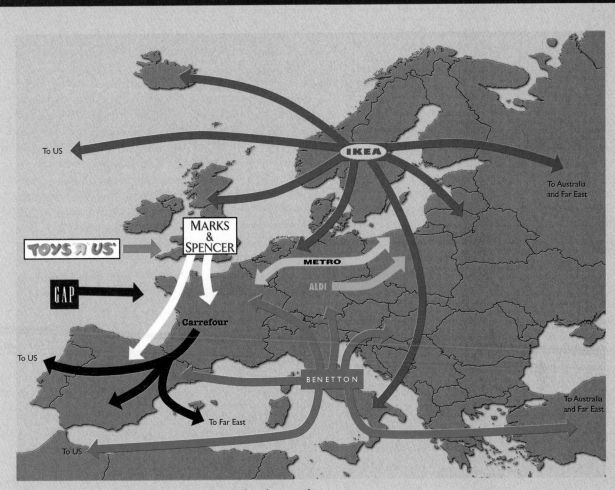

Retail giants tapping the rewards in cross-border retailing

and opening hours in order to protect small retailers from new high-street competitors, was deregulated. This has created new opportunities for superstore retailers, which can now open stores with floor space of up to 1,000 square metres without the approval of the Ministry of International Trade and Industry. Retailing law reforms have also enabled foreign retailers to break the links between the manufacturers and the high-street stores. Toys 'Я' Us bypassed the intricate web of wholesalers to deal directly with one of its suppliers, Nintendo, the video game maker, and was thus able to undercut Japanese toy prices. Large supermarket chains with bulk purchasing power are also bypassing the traditional multilayered wholesale network that has kept prices high, and are procuring merchandise direct from manufacturers or producers. Stronger antitrust laws in Japan have overturned manufac-

turers' grip on retail prices. Large manufacturers had controlled retail prices and prevented discounting of their products by threatening to stop supplies. Now retailers can discount prices without fear of losing supply contracts. More importantly, deregulation in Japan is making the market more accessible to foreign retailers.

According to a report by Braxton Associates, the global strategy arm of Deloitte and Touche Consulting, those that do cross frontiers must fulfil *six criteria* that are critical for international retailer planning. First, the successful internationalist must have *a strong corporate philosophy*. Like IKEA or Hennes & Mauritz, they must bring a strong corporate identity, brand image or style that they can implant or adapt in international markets. Second, they must provide something that does not currently exist in the market – *offering something genuinely new* to consumers is a tedious truism of business, yet it is frequently forgotten when retailers take their concepts overseas. Third, they must select *an appropriate format* for export. Braxton Associates suggests several alternative formulae:

(a) The high-end luxury retailer such as Gucci and LVMH, whose brands are strong products in their own right. M & S outlets in mainland Europe, with a slightly up-market positioning, sit at the lower edge of this category.

(b) The second exportable format is the category killer that has carved a place in a single sector, such as Toys 'Я' Us and IKEA.

(c) High-quality speciality retailers are also eminently exportable, as seen in the fashion and cosmetics brands of Benetton, Gap and The Body Shop.

(d) The final format is discount retailing. Discounters such as Carrefour, Aldi and Metro-Gruppe are appealing to the lowest common denominator force in consumerism – value at low cost – and thus have a universal appeal.

Fourth, retailers using whatever format must *identify a clear target market*. Arguably, young, affluent, internationally oriented, as a broad group, defines the market of most successful international retailers from Benetton to Body Shop to Virgin Megastores. Fifth, international expansion has to be backed by the *commitment and hands-on attention of senior executives*. Finally, *short-termism* is the kiss of death for international retailers. IKEA waited eight years until its US store eventually went into profit, just as M & S took a long time to get its format right in the French market. By persevering and taking a long-term view of international expansion, these companies reaped rewards from their initial investments.

The future shape of European and indeed global retailing is still evolving. The long-term view required to make it happen means that the single European high street will not happen overnight. But one thing is certain. The winners will be retailing groups which are prepared to play the long game. Isetan in Volgograd or Migros in Shanghai may still be years away. Nonetheless, one of the world's biggest but most localized industries – retailing – is finally coming to terms with the global marketplace. And, of course, even those companies with no ambition to cross borders cannot be complacent. One retailer's domestic market is another's foreign opportunity.

SOURCES: Neil Buckley, 'Retailers' global shopping spree', *Financial Times* (12 October 1994), p. 25; Clive Branson, 'Find what the customer likes before opening doors abroad', *The European* (18–24 March 1994), p. 22; Wilf Altman, 'Customers pick up rewards from cross-border retailing', *The European* (18–24 February 1994), p. 20; Richard Halstead, 'Let competition commence', *BusinessAge Magazine* (July 1994), pp. 84–6; Bronwyn Cosgrave, 'France fills the T-shirt gap', *The European élan* (6–12 May 1994), p. 14; Neil Herndon, 'Wal-Mart goes to Hong Kong, looks at China', *Marketing News*, **28**, 24 (21 November 1994), p. 2; Guy de Jonquières, 'Temptations along the eastern aisle', *Financial Times* (6 April 1994), p. 19; 'Japanese industry: inefficient structure', *Financial Times* (6 December 1994), p. IV; William Dawkins, 'Japanese industry: progress will be painfully slow', *Financial Times* (6 December 1994), p. VI; 'Japanese retailing', *The Economist* (25 January 1997), pp. 92, 95; Simon Watkins, 'Invasion of the retail giants', *The European* (30 October–5 November 1997), pp. 26–7; Richard Tomkins, 'Wal-Mart makes foray into Europe with Wertkauf buy', *Financial Times* (19 December 1997), p. 21.

Warehouse club (wholesale club, membership warehouse)
Off-price retailer that sells a limited selection of brand-name grocery items, appliances, clothing and a hodgepodge of other goods at deep discounts to members who pay annual membership fees.

Warehouse clubs (also known as *wholesale clubs* or *membership warehouses*) sell huge volumes of a narrow range of goods – typically, brand-name grocery items, appliances and clothing – at rock-bottom prices from low-cost, edge-of-town, warehouse-like facilities to customers, mainly small retailers, which pay an annual membership fee.

An example is Costco. Because its margins are so low, Costco relies on bulk buying and the annual membership fee for profit. It selects its target customers carefully – individuals are allowed to join provided they are professionals, operate their own business and have an above-average income and stable employment. Costco goes for doctors and solicitors with Volvos and big houses to store things in; the ABs looking for bargains. Lower social groups are catered for by discount supermarkets such as Kwik Save and Netto.[14]

A **catalogue showroom** sells a wide selection of high-mark-up, fast-moving, brand-name goods at discount prices. Catalogue showrooms make their money by cutting costs and margins to provide low prices that will attract a higher volume of sales. Products on sale are all listed in catalogues, which are placed on counters in the store. Consumers fill in order forms for goods they want and pass these to sales assistants, who complete the transaction. The customer collects the merchandise from the sales assistants or picks it up from a collection point in the store. Argos and Index are examples of catalogue retailers that operate on British high streets.

We have looked at the types of retailer. Next, let us address brokers and agents.

BROKERS AND AGENTS. **Brokers** and **agents** differ from merchant wholesalers in two ways: they do not take title to goods, and they perform only a few functions. Their main function is to help in buying and selling, and for these services they earn a commission on the selling price. Like merchant wholesalers, they generally specialize by product line or customer type. Because they are specialists, they can offer valuable sales advice and expertise to clients.

A broker brings buyers and sellers together and assists in negotiation. Brokers are employed temporarily and paid by the parties hiring them. They do not carry inventory, get involved in financing, or assume risk. The most familiar examples are food brokers, real estate brokers, insurance brokers and security brokers. Agents represent buyers or sellers on a more permanent basis. There are several types:

Manufacturers' agents or *representatives* are the most common type of agent. They represent two or more manufacturers of related lines. They have a formal agreement with each manufacturer, covering prices, territories, order-handling procedures, delivery, warranties and commission rates. They know each manufacturer's product line and use their wide contacts to sell the products. They do not, however, have much influence over prices and other marketing decisions, and provide limited, if any, technical, product or service support. Manufacturers' agents are used in lines such as clothing, furniture and electrical goods. Most manufacturers' agents are small businesses, with only a few employees who are skilled salespeople. They are hired by small producers that cannot afford to maintain their own field sales forces and by large producers that want to open new territories to sell in areas that cannot support a full-time salesperson. Manufacturers' agents therefore help producers to minimize selling costs for current and new products and market territories.

Selling agents contract to sell a producer's entire output – either the manufacturer is not interested in doing the selling or feels unqualified. The selling agent serves as a sales department and has considerable influence over prices, terms and conditions of sale, as well as packaging, product development, promotion and distribution policies. Unlike other manufacturers' agents, the selling agent normally has no territory limits. Selling agents are found in product areas such as textiles, industrial machinery and equipment, coal and coke, chemicals and metals.

Purchasing agents generally have a long-term relationship with buyers. They make purchases for buyers and often receive, inspect, warehouse and ship goods to the buyers. One type of purchasing agent is a *resident buyer* in big clothing markets – purchasing specialists who look for apparel lines that can be carried by small retailers located in small cities. They know a great deal about their product lines, provide helpful market information to clients, and can also obtain the best goods and prices available.

Commission merchants (or *houses*) are agents that take physical possession of products, grade, store and transport them, and negotiate sales with buyers in the market. They are normally not used on a long-term basis. They are used most

catalogue showroom
A retail operation that sells a wide selection of high mark-up, fast-moving, brand-name goods at discount prices.

broker
A wholesaler who does not take title to goods and whose function is to bring buyers and sellers together and assist in negotiation.

agent
A wholesaler who represents buyers or sellers on a relatively permanent basis, performs only a few functions, and does not take title to goods.

often in agricultural marketing by farmers who do not want to sell their own output and who do not belong to co-operatives. Typically, the commission merchant will take a truckload of farm products to a central market, sell it for the best price, deduct expenses and a commission, and pay the balance to the farmer. Commission merchants have more power than the small producer over prices and terms of sale. Not only do they obtain the best price possible in the market for the producer, but they may also offer planning and financial assistance.

We have discussed the types of channel member. Next we look at decisions concerning the number of channels to use.

● *Number of Marketing Intermediaries*

Companies must also decide on *channel breadth*: that is, how extensive their market coverage should be and, therefore, the number of channel members to use at each level. Three strategies are available: intensive distribution, exclusive distribution and selective distribution.

Producers of convenience products and common raw materials typically seek **intensive distribution** – a strategy whereby they stock their products in as many outlets as possible. These goods must be available where and when consumers want them. For example, sweets, chewing gum, disposable razors, soft drinks, batteries, camera film and other similar items are sold in myriad outlets to provide maximum brand exposure and consumer convenience. Bic, Coca-Cola, Nestlé, Duracell, Fuji, Kodak and many consumer-goods companies distribute their products in this way.

By contrast, some producers purposely limit the number of intermediaries handling their products. The extreme form of this practice is **exclusive distribution**, in which the producer gives only a limited number of dealers the exclusive rights to distribute its products in their territories. Exclusive distribution is often found in the distribution of luxury cars (e.g. Rolls-Royce, Lexus) and prestige clothes for men and women (e.g. Giorgio Armani, Hugo Boss, Yves St Laurent, Christian Dior). By granting exclusive distribution, the manufacturers gain strong selling support from the outlet and more control over dealer prices, promotion, credit and services. Exclusive distribution also enhances brand image and allows for higher mark-ups.

Between intensive and exclusive distribution lies **selective distribution** – the use of more than one, but fewer than all of the intermediaries that are willing to carry a company's products. Many electronics and other small household ap-

intensive distribution
Stocking the product in as many outlets as possible.

exclusive distribution
Giving a limited number of dealers the exclusive right to distribute the company's products in their territories.

selective distribution
The use of more than one, but less than all of the intermediaries that are willing to carry the company's products.

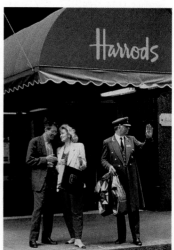

Convenience goods are sold through every available outlet. Prestige goods are sold exclusively through a limited number of stores.

pliance brands are distributed in this manner. For example, Philips-Whirlpool, Braun, Electrolux and Hoover sell their major appliances through dealer networks and selected large retailers. By using selective distribution, they do not have to spread their efforts over many outlets, including many marginal ones. They can develop good working relationships with selected channel members and expect a better-than-average selling effort. Selective distribution gives producers good market coverage with more control and less cost than does intensive distribution.

● *Responsibilities of Channel Members*

The producer and its intermediaries need to agree on the terms and responsibilities of each channel member. The producer should establish a list price and a fair set of discounts for intermediaries. It must define each channel member's territory, and it should be careful about where it places new resellers. Mutual services and duties need to be spelled out carefully, especially in franchise and exclusive distribution channels. For example, McDonald's provides franchisees with promotional support, a record-keeping system, training and general management assistance. In turn, franchisees must meet company standards for physical facilities, co-operate with new promotion programmes, provide requested information, and buy and supply specified food products.

Evaluating the Main Alternatives

Suppose a company has identified several channel alternatives and wants to select the one that will best satisfy its long-run objectives. The firm must evaluate each alternative against *economic*, *control* and *adaptive* criteria.

Using economic criteria, the company compares the likely profitability of different channel alternatives. It estimates the sales that each channel would produce and the costs of selling different volumes through each channel. The company must also consider control issues. Using intermediaries usually means giving them some control over the marketing of the product, and some intermediaries take more control than others. Other things being equal, the company prefers to keep as much control as possible. Finally, the company must apply adaptive criteria. Channels often involve long-term commitments to other firms and loss of flexibility, making it hard to adapt the channel to a changing marketing environment. The producer wants to keep the channel as flexible as possible. It must therefore assess the level of risk attached to selecting a channel system. For example, a company using a sales agency may have to offer a five-year contract. During this period, other means of selling, such as a company sales force, may become more effective, but the company cannot drop the sales agency. To be considered, a channel involving long-term commitment should be greatly superior on economic or control grounds.

Designing International Distribution Channels

International marketers face many additional complexities in designing their channels. Each country has its own unique distribution system that has evolved over time and changes very slowly. These channel systems can vary widely from country to country. The relative significance of different members or elements of a channel system – for example, the role of wholesalers versus retailers or shopkeepers – can vary significantly across countries. For instance, in food and drinks retailing, contract distributors play a far more important role in the delivery of goods from producer to retailer in the United Kingdom than in other EU countries like Germany, France, Spain and Italy. Also, multiple retailer dominance of the grocery market is more pervasive in the United Kingdom than in the latter countries. Intercountry variations are partly due to history, tradition, legal conditions and economic reasons behind effectiveness and efficiency. Thus global marketers must usually adapt their channel strategies to the existing structures within each country.

In some markets, the distribution system is complex and hard to penetrate, consisting of many layers and large numbers of intermediaries. Consider Japan:

> The Japanese distribution system stems from the early seventeenth century when cottage industries and a [quickly growing] urban population spawned a merchant class … Despite Japan's economic achievements, the distribution system has remained remarkably faithful to its antique pattern … [It] encompasses a wide range of wholesalers and other agents, brokers and retailers, differing more in number than in function from their European or American counterparts. There are myriad tiny retail shops. An even greater number of wholesalers supplies goods to them, layered tier upon tier, many more than most executives in other country markets would think necessary. For example, soap may move through three wholesalers plus a sales company after it leaves the manufacturer before it ever reaches the retail outlet. A steak goes from rancher to consumers in a process that often involves a dozen middle agents … The distribution network … reflects the traditionally close ties among many Japanese companies … [and places] much greater emphasis on personal relationships with users … Although [these channels appear] inefficient and cumbersome, they seem to serve the Japanese customer well … Lacking much storage space in their small homes, most Japanese homemakers shop several times a week and prefer convenient [and more personal] neighbourhood shops.[15]

Many western firms have had great difficulty breaking into the closely knit, tradition-bound Japanese distribution network. Foreign companies have often found this a major barrier to setting up shop in Japan, although more recently, channel changes within the Japanese market have enabled fast-footed multinationals to secure a foothold in this unwieldy market. Marketing Highlight 21.2 draws attention to changes in Japan's Large-Scale Retail Store Law, and shows how large western retailers have sought to breaking into Japan's famously restrictive and overregulated retailing industry.

At the other extreme, distribution systems in developing countries may be scattered and inefficient, or altogether lacking. For example, China and India are huge markets, each containing hundreds of millions of people. In reality, however, these markets are much smaller than the population numbers suggest. Because of inadequate distribution systems in both countries, most companies can profitably access only the small portion of the population that is located in each country's most affluent cities.[16]

Thus international marketers face a wide range of channel alternatives. Designing efficient and effective channel systems between and within various country markets poses a difficult challenge.

Channel Management Decisions

Channel management calls for selecting and motivating individual channel members and evaluating their performance over time.

Selecting Channel Members

Producers vary in their ability to attract qualified marketing intermediaries. Some producers have no trouble signing up channel members. For example, Toyota had no trouble attracting new dealers for its Lexus line. In fact, it had to turn down many would-be resellers. In some cases, the promise of exclusive or selective distribution for a desirable product will draw plenty of applicants.

At the other extreme are producers that have to work hard to line up enough qualified intermediaries. When Reckitt & Coleman first launched its new 'green' detergent brand, Down to Earth, in the UK market in 1990, access was restricted to one supermarket chain – Tesco's. The Belgian firm Ecover managed to acquire sole rights for distribution in Asda stores, and in Sainsbury's, Safeway and the Co-op when it launched its radical 'green' detergents at the height of green consumerism in the United Kingdom. A rival green brand, Ark, was launched in 1989 and secured distribution in specialist retail outlets, but since then, declining sales have meant an erosion of the brand to the extent that it is no longer able to secure distribution at all except through its mail-order network. Similarly, many small food and grocery producers that own marginal brands often have difficulty getting retailers to carry their products.

When selecting intermediaries, the company should determine what characteristics distinguish the better ones. It will want to evaluate the channel members' years in business, other lines carried, growth and profit record, level of co-operation and reputation. If the intermediaries are sales agents, the company will want to evaluate the number and character of other lines carried and the size and quality of the sales force. If the intermediary is a retail store that wants exclusive or selective distribution, the company will want to evaluate the store's customers, location and future growth potential.

Motivating Channel Members

Channel members must be continuously motivated to do their best. The company must sell not only *through* the intermediaries, but *to* them. Most producers see gaining intermediary co-operation as the primary problem. They can use the 'carrot-and-stick' approach. At times, they offer *positive* motivators such as higher margins, special deals, premiums, co-operative advertising allowances, display allowances and sales contests. At other times they use *negative* motivators, such as threatening to reduce margins, to slow down delivery or to end the relationship altogether. A producer using this approach has usually failed to do a good job of studying the needs, problems, strengths and weaknesses of its channel members.

More advanced companies try to forge long-term partnerships with their distributors. This involves building a planned, professionally managed, vertical marketing system that meets the needs of both the manufacturer *and* the distributors.[17] Thus, manufacturers such as P & G are working together with grocery retailers to create superior value for final consumers. They jointly plan merchandising goals and strategies, inventory levels and advertising and promotion plans. By working closely, as opposed to coercively, with these outlets, branded goods manufacturers can increase their chances of successfully selling their company's products. The challenge for companies lies in their ability to convince distributors that they can make their money by being part of an advanced vertical marketing system.

Evaluating and Controlling Channel Members

The producer must regularly monitor the channel's performance against agreed targets such as sales quotas, average inventory levels, customer delivery time, treatment of damaged and lost goods, co-operation in company promotion and training programmes, and services to the customer. The company should recognize and reward intermediaries that are performing well. Those which are underperforming should be helped, remedial actions should be taken or, as a last resort, the intermediary should be replaced. The firm must periodically 'requalify' its intermediaries and prune the weak performers, allowing only the best ones to carry its products.

Finally, manufacturers need to be sensitive to their dealers. Those which treat their dealers lightly risk not only losing their support, but also confronting legal problems. Disputes with dealers are counterproductive and create bottlenecks that can frustrate a company's growth. The experience of the brewery group Anheuser-Busch is insightful.

If you ask for a Budweiser in a bar in America or Asia, you will get a light beer from Anheuser-Busch, the world's largest brewer. Ask the same question in a European bar and you are likely to be served a stronger, hoppier beer from the Czech Republic's Budêjovicky Budvar brewery. If you want the American version, you will have to ask for a 'Bud', unless you are in the United Kingdom, where both variants share the Budweiser name. But Budvar has now started selling its own Bud in the Czech Republic, an extra strong lager, which it hopes also to sell to big-drinking Germans. However, it will have to win the right to use the name Bud in Germany, a privilege also denied to the American brewer Anheuser-Busch, which sells its beer in the country as plain 'B'. Anheuser-Busch, began selling Budweiser beer in 1876, some 19 years before Budêjovicky Budvar, the Czech brewer was established. Following an agreement in 1911, Budvar won exclusive rights to use the Budweiser name throughout most of Europe, while Anheuser-Busch gained the rights in North America, South America and most of Asia. Currently, Budvar has the exclusive rights to use the name Budweiser in 42 countries, in addition to the UK, while Anheuser-Busch sells under that name in 11 European countries, and the name Bud in a further 9. Budvar, however, had registered the name Bud in 1950 in a few countries, including the former Soviet Union, Czechoslovakia, Hungary and Austria. Both brewers are keen to expand sales of their Budweiser/Bud brand in Europe, especially the big drinking markets like Germany. After the Velvet Revolution in 1989, Anheuser-Busch started a concerted campaign to gain a 34 per cent stake in Budvar and resumed trademark negotiations. Anheuser-Busch, however, had to divorce the purchase of the stake in Budvar from a resolution of the trademark dispute, which was hampering the brewer's plans to market Budweiser in other important European markets. Jack Purnell, chairman and chief executive of Anheuser-Busch International, said he hoped that separation of the investment from the trademark dispute would advance progress in both issues. The delicate relations between Budvar and Anheuser-Busch have made the Czech government procrastinate with privatization, originally scheduled for the end of 1996. So, while the government would eventually decide on how Budvar should be privatized, Anheuser-Busch pursued further negotiations on reaching trademark agreements elsewhere. The American brewer terminated negotiations in September 1996 after securing favourable trademark rulings in Spain, Greece, Sweden, Finland, Norway, Lithuania and Latvia. Meanwhile, Anheuser-Busch is prepared to appeal against any unfavourable decisions (e.g. if Budvar succeeds in its claim to the Bud name in Germany) which hampers the development of its Budweiser business in Europe.[18]

The key to profitable channel management lies in creating win-win outcomes for all in the channel system – a symbiotic relationship that yields co-operation, not conflict, among channel participants will invariably result in higher channel performance.

Physical Distribution and Logistics Management

In today's global marketplace, selling a product is sometimes easier than physically getting it to customers. Companies must decide on the best way to store, handle and move their products and services, so that they are available to customers in the right assortments, at the right time and in the right place. Logistics effectiveness will have a significant impact on both customer satisfaction and company costs. A poor distribution system can destroy an otherwise good marketing effort. Here we consider the nature and importance of *marketing logistics*, goals of the *logistics system*, *major logistics functions*, *choosing transportation modes* and the importance of *international logistics*.

Nature and Importance of Physical Distribution and Marketing Logistics

To some managers, physical distribution means only trucks and warehouses. But modern logistics is much more than this. **Physical distribution** or **marketing logistics** involves planning, implementing and controlling the physical flow of materials, final goods and related information from points of origin to points of consumption to meet customer requirements at a profit. In short, it involves getting the right product to the right customer in the right place at the right time.

Traditional physical distribution has typically started with products at the plant and tried to find low-cost solutions to get them to customers. However, *marketing logistics* thinking starts with the marketplace and works backwards to the factory. Logistics addresses the problem of outbound distribution (moving products from the factory to customers) and that of inbound distribution (moving products and materials from suppliers to the factory). It involves the management of entire *supply chains*, value-added flows from suppliers to final users, as shown in Figure 21.6. Thus the logistics manager's task is to co-ordinate the whole channel physical distribution system – the activities of suppliers, purchasing agents, marketers, channel members and customers. These activities include forecasting, purchasing, production planning, order processing, inventory management, warehousing and transportation planning.

Companies today are placing greater emphasis on logistics for several reasons:

● Customer service and satisfaction have become the cornerstones of marketing strategy in many businesses, and distribution is an important

physical distribution *(marketing logistics) The tasks involved in planning, implementing and controlling the physical flow of materials and final goods from points of origin to points of use to meet the needs of customers at a profit.*

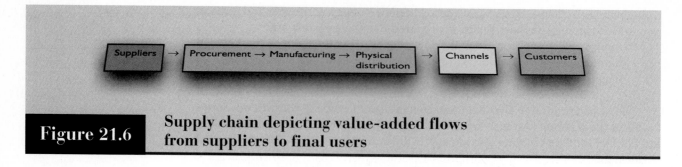

Figure 21.6

Supply chain depicting value-added flows from suppliers to final users

customer service element. Companies are finding that they can win and keep more customers by giving faster delivery, better service or lower prices through more effective logistics. On the other hand, companies may lose customers when they fail to supply the right products on time.

● Logistics is a major cost element for most companies. About 15 per cent of an average product's price is accounted for by shipping and transport alone. Companies that do not take advantage of modern decision tools for co-ordinating inventory levels, transportation modes, and plant, warehouse and store locations make poor logistics decisions that result in higher costs. Improvements in physical distribution efficiency can yield tremendous cost savings for both the company and its customers.

● The explosion in product variety has created a need for improved logistics management. For example, in the early part of the twentieth century, the typical grocery store carried only 200–300 items. The store manager could keep track of this inventory on about ten pages of notebook paper stuffed in a shirt pocket. Today, the average store carries a bewildering stock of thousands of items. Ordering, shipping, stocking and controlling such a variety of products presents a sizeable logistics challenge.

● Finally, developments in information technology have created opportunities for positive gains in distribution efficiency. The increased use of computers, electronic point-of-sale scanners, uniform product codes, satellite tracking, electronic data interchange (EDI) and electronic funds transfer (EFT) has allowed companies to create advanced systems for order processing, inventory control and handling, and transportation routing and scheduling. These recent technological advances benefit not only manufacturers, but also members at other levels of the channel. Take EDI, for example: it speeds up the sending of business information, such as invoices and orders. With the need for fast response time, a retailer connected up to its suppliers could ensure that the lead time between order and supply is shortened as far as is possible. The manufacturers or suppliers have up-to-date information on retailer stocking levels and needs, and can respond faster than by using traditional manual methods. Consumers further down the line gain in that they can buy what they want at the right time and the right place. Indeed, in some industry sectors, such as retailing, certain companies are demanding EDI connections as a condition of trading.

Goals of the Logistics System

The starting point for designing a marketing logistics system is to study the service needs of customers. They may want several distribution services from suppliers: fast and efficient order processing, speedy and flexible delivery, presorting and pretagging of merchandise, order-tracking information, and a willingness to take back or replace defective goods.

Unfortunately, few companies can achieve the logistic objective of *both* maximizing customer service *and* minimizing distribution costs. Maximum customer service implies rapid delivery, large inventories, flexible assortments, liberal returns policies and a host of other services – all of which raise distribution costs. In contrast, minimum distribution cost implies slower delivery, small inventories and larger shipping lots – which represent a lower level of overall customer service.

Instead, the goal of the marketing logistics system should be to provide *a targeted level of customer service at the least cost* by identifying the importance of various distribution services that customers require and then setting desired service levels for each segment, taking into account the level of service offered by competitors. The ultimate objective is to maximize *profits*, not sales. Therefore, the company must weigh the benefits of providing higher levels of service against the costs. Some companies offer less service than their competitors and charge a lower price. Other companies offer more service and charge higher prices to cover higher costs.

Major Logistics Functions

The major logistics functions are order processing, warehousing, inventory management and transportation.

● *Order Processing*

The logistics process starts with the firm getting an order from the customer. Orders can be submitted in many ways – by mail or telephone, through salespeople, or via computer and electronic data interchange (EDI). Once received, orders must be processed quickly and accurately. The order-processing system prepares invoices and sends order information to those who need it. The appropriate warehouse receives instructions to pack and dispatch the ordered items. Products out of stock are back-ordered. Shipped items are accompanied by shipping and billing documents, with copies going to various departments.

Both the company and its customers benefit when the order-processing steps are carried out efficiently. Ideally, salespeople send in their orders daily, often using online computers. The order department immediately processes these orders and the warehouse sends the goods out on time. Bills or invoices go out as soon as possible. Most companies now use computerized order-processing systems to speed up the order–shipping–billing cycle. Such modern computing systems enable firms to reduce distribution costs, while speeding up activities and increasing the level of service to customers.

● *Warehousing*

Every company must store its goods while they wait to be sold. To ensure it can meet orders speedily, it must have stock available. A storage function is needed because production and consumption cycles rarely match. For example, a lawn mower manufacturer must produce all year long and store up its products for the heavy spring and summer buying season. The storage function overcomes differences in needed quantities and timing.

A company must decide on *how many* and *what types* of warehouses it needs, and *where* they will be located. The more warehouses the company uses,

ONE SITE HAS

MORE THAN 20%

OF ALL HIGH BAY

WAREHOUSING

IN THE U.K.

Photograph shows the IBD warehouse at Magna Park, Lutterworth, Europe's largest dedicated distribution centre. The park has over 700,000 square metres (200 hectares) of which 350,000 square metres is already occupied.

the more quickly goods can be delivered to customers and the higher the service level. However, more locations mean higher warehousing costs. The company, therefore, must balance the level of customer service against distribution costs.

Some company stock is kept at or near the production plant, with the rest located in warehouses around the country. The company might own private warehouses, rent space in public warehouses, or both. Companies have more control over owned warehouses, but that ties up their capital and is less flexible if desired locations change. In contrast, public warehouses charge for the rented space and provide additional services (at a cost) for inspecting goods, packaging them, shipping them and invoicing them. By using public warehouses, companies also have a wide choice of locations and warehouse types.

distribution centre
A large, highly automated warehouse designed to receive goods from various plants and suppliers, take orders, fill them efficiently, and deliver goods to customers as quickly as possible.

Companies may use **distribution centres**, which are designed to move goods rather than just store them. They are large and highly automated warehouses designed to receive goods from various plants and suppliers, take orders, fill them efficiently, and deliver goods to customers as quickly as possible. In the European market, producers of industrial and consumer goods are having not only to make trade-offs between customer service level and costs, but also to consider the feasibility of incorporating pan-European distribution networks to provide consistently high standards of service and flexibility. For example, British Steel, in the face of stiff competition in mainland European markets, set up regional distribution centres to be closer to customers, while also developing information-technology links between production plants, distribution operators and customers in an attempt to improve service efficiency.[19]

Newer, single-storey *automated warehouses* with advanced materials-handling systems under the control of a central computer are increasingly replacing older, multistorey warehouses with outdated materials-handling methods In these warehouses, only a few employees are necessary. Computers read orders and direct lift trucks, electric hoists or robots to gather goods, move them to loading docks and issue invoices. The modern high-tech warehouse – with high bay storage, using narrow aisle trucks and more stacker cranes, backed by multilevel picking or sorting systems – is a growing trend in Europe. Such warehouses have reduced worker injuries, labour costs, theft and breakage, and have improved inventory control. Producers, however, do not necessarily have to

Automated warehouses: this sophisticated Compaq computer distribution centre can ship any of 500 different types of Compaq computer and options within four hours of receiving an order.

make heavy capital investments to secure such high-tech warehousing – increasingly, the advanced software and warehousing solutions are being provided by specialist distribution companies, which are taking over large sections of firms' in-house warehousing and distribution functions.

● *Inventory*

Inventory levels also affect customer satisfaction. The major problem is deciding how much stock should be held. Logistics managers have to decide on how to maintain the delicate balance between carrying too much inventory and carrying too little. Carrying too much inventory results in higher-than-necessary inventory carrying costs and stock obsolescence. Carrying too little may result in stock-outs, costly emergency shipments or production, customer dissatisfaction or, worse, lost sales as unserved customers defect to a competitor. In making inventory decisions, management must balance the costs of carrying larger inventories against resulting sales and profits.

Inventory decisions involve knowing both *when* to order and *how much* to order. In deciding when to order, the company balances the risks of running out of stock against the costs of carrying too much. In deciding how much to order, the company needs to balance order-processing costs against inventory carrying costs. Larger average-order size means fewer orders and lower order-processing costs, but it also means larger inventory carrying costs.

During the past decade, many companies have greatly reduced their inventories and related costs through *just-in-time* (JIT) logistics systems. Through such systems, producers and retailers carry only small inventories of parts or merchandise, often only enough for a few days of operations. New stock arrives at the factory or retail outlet exactly when needed, rather than being stored in inventory until being used. JIT systems require accurate forecasting along with fast, frequent and flexible delivery, so that new supplies will be available when needed. However, these systems result in substantial savings in inventory carrying and handling costs. By keeping the flow in the pipeline – raw materials, work-in-progress, finished goods – to a minimum, suppliers can enhance logistics efficiency, while ensuring that customer service objectives are regularly met.

Sophisticated distribution providers, operating in today's global markets, integrate transportation and computer-based technologies to ensure that they deliver the highest level of service to customers.

● *Transportation*

Transportation decisions have a critical impact on logistics costs. The choice of transportation carriers affects the pricing of products, delivery performance and condition of the goods when they arrive – all of which will ultimately affect customer satisfaction.

In shipping goods to its warehouses, dealers and customers, the company can choose among five transportation modes: road, rail, water, pipeline and air.

ROAD. Trucks are highly flexible in their routing and time schedules. They are efficient for short hauls of high-value merchandise. In the EU, the bulk of goods traded is moved by road vehicles. The Conference of European Transport Ministers (CEMT) reported that transport volumes in the EU have risen by more than 50 per cent in the last 20 years. The bulk of this growth has been in road transport, which accounts for over 74 per cent of European freight transport.[20] Haulage rates for different cargo loads over different distances among EU member nations do, however, vary – Greek domestic rates are the lowest, followed by UK rates; German haulage costs are the highest, with France and Italy close behind in the high end of the rate spectrum.[21] The gradual deregulation and removal of restrictive practices in the road transport market in the EU is expected to increase intra-EU haulage competition, with a downward pressure on rates. Also, there will be greater freedom for international hauliers to transport goods between destinations within one country, thereby raising the efficiency in use of trucks.

RAIL. Railroads are one of the most cost-effective modes for shipping large amounts of bulk products – coal, sand, minerals, farm and forest products – over long distances. In Europe, rail accounts for just over 17 per cent of total freight traffic. Ongoing developments, such as the Channel Tunnel and its associated freight links, together with the EU's efforts to speed up the development of rail freight and combined road/rail transport services throughout Europe – including the opening up of networks in eastern Europe – are pushing rail transport much more firmly into the general distribution spotlight:

A European 'rail renaissance' will cost a staggering ecu300 billion. The importance given to railways is apparent from the European Commission's list of two dozen or more priority transport projects. Nine of them are high-speed rail links, including the Brenner rail tunnel through the Austrian Alps and the Fehnmarn Belt Baltic fixed link running between Denmark and Germany. However, real collaboration and standardization among Europe's railways is indispensable for reinforcing rail's presence on main cross-border routes. While there is some evidence that Europe's new railways are attracting passengers back, the revitalization of rail freight may take some time. There is optimism in the air as authorities and politicians alike agree that it is not a simple question of road versus rail – Europe must have both.[22]

WATER.   In countries favourably served by coastal and inland waterways, a large amount of goods can be moved by ships and barges. On the one hand, the cost of water transportation is very low for shipping bulky, low-value, non-perishable products such as sand, coal, grain, oil and metallic ores – a single coaster or ro-ro (roll on, roll off) ship can carry the same cargo as dozens of trains or hundreds of trucks. On the other hand, water transportation is the slowest transportation mode and is sometimes affected by the weather. Again, producers and suppliers have to make choice decisions based on trade-offs between speed, security and costs of transportation.

In the EU, waterways' share of freight transport volume is around 8 per cent – low compared to rail and roads. Its full potential, however, cannot be realized without harmonization of European shipping and port policies and pricing systems, and the removal of existing restrictive and unnecessary legislation. German operators, for example, have been set against traditional cheaper rivals in Holland, Belgium and France. Despite the problems, the EU and member governments are set on pushing ahead with ambitious plans to upgrade Europe's waterway network, with hopes pinned on a healthier waterway freight industry in the future.[23]

PIPELINE.   Pipelines are a specialized means of shipping raw commodities such as petroleum, natural gas and chemicals from sources to markets. Pipeline shipment of petroleum products costs less than rail shipment, but more than water shipment. Most pipelines are used by their owners to ship their own products.

AIR.   Although the use of air carriers tends to be restricted to low-bulk goods, they are becoming more important as a transportation mode. Air-freight rates are much higher than rail or truck rates, but air freight is ideal when speed is needed or distant markets have to be reached. Among the most frequently air-freighted products are perishables (fresh fish, cut flowers) and high-value, low-bulk items (technical instruments, jewellery). Companies find that air freight also reduces inventory levels, packaging costs and the number of warehouses needed.

Choosing Transportation Modes

In choosing a transportation mode for a product, shippers consider as many as five criteria, as shown in Table 21.2. Thus, if a shipper needs speed, air and truck are the prime choices. If the goal is low cost, then water or pipeline might be best. Trucks appear to offer the most advantages. In practice, firms may rely on a combination of transportation methods which would best enable them to meet logistics objectives cost effectively.

Table 21.2	**Ranking of transportation modes**

	SPEED (DOOR-TO-DOOR) DELIVERY TIME	DEPENDABILITY (MEETING SCHEDULES ON TIME)	CAPABILITY (ABILITY TO HANDLE VARIOUS PRODUCTS)	AVAILABILITY (NO. OF GEOGRAPHIC POINTS SERVED)	COST (PER TON-MILE)
Rail	3	4	2	2	3
Water	4	5	1	4	1
Truck	2	2	3	1	4
Pipeline	5	1	5	5	2
Air	1	3	4	3	5

NOTE: 1 = highest rank.
SOURCE: Carl M. Guelzo, *Introduction to Logistics Management* (Englewood Cliffs, NJ: Prentice Hall, 1986), p. 46.

International Logistics

International logistics is a critical area for more and more global businesses, whose inbound supply movements are shifting from domestic sources to global ones, and whose outbound supplies undergo an equally international trade flow. Sophisticated computer-based technologies, such as computer-integrated logistics (CIL), are being used to enable international companies and logistics service providers to manage the supply chain and specific logistics functions.

International logistics place even greater demands on good integration of logistics operations and systems between supplier/manufacturer and others involved in moving supplies or goods along the supply chain across national borders. In the European market, increasing competitive pressures and the continuing drive for greater efficiency have forced distribution service providers, in the first instance, to focus more heavily on service quality improvement or risk losing out on invitations to bid for new business. Manufacturers and distribution operators alike have sought to set up pan-European distribution networks, although with mixed results.[24] To be effective, international logistics must be planned and co-ordinated to achieve desired cost advantages while meeting customer service needs.

Channel Trends

We have examined the major channel and logistics decisions facing managers. Finally, let us look at the major changes occurring in distribution channels.

Integrated Logistics Management

integrated logistics management
A physical distribution concept that recognizes the need for a firm to integrate its logistics system with those of its suppliers and customers. The aim is to maximize the performance of the entire distribution system.

Today, companies are increasingly adopting the concept of **integrated logistics management**. This concept recognizes that providing better customer service and trimming distribution costs require *teamwork*, both inside the company and among all the marketing channel organizations. Inside the company, the various functional departments must work closely together to maximize the company's own logistics performance. The company must also integrate its logistics system with those of its suppliers and customers to maximize the performance of the entire distribution system. Where firms recognize that particular logistics functions are not their area of core competence, they have these activities carried out by specialists that will achieve greater effectiveness and efficiency.

● *Cross-Functional Teamwork Inside the Company*

In most companies, responsibility for various logistics activities is assigned to many different functional units – marketing, sales, finance, manufacturing, purchasing. Too often, each function tries to optimize its own logistics performance without regard for the activities of the other functions. However, transportation, inventory, warehousing and order-processing activities interact, often in an inverse way. For example, lower inventory levels reduce inventory carrying costs. But they may also reduce customer service and increase costs from stock-outs, backorders, special production runs and costly fast-freight shipments. Because distribution activities involve strong trade-offs, decisions by different functions must be co-ordinated to achieve superior overall logistics performance. Thus the goal of integrated logistics management is to harmonize all of the company's distribution decisions. Close working relationships among functions can be achieved in several ways.

Some companies have created permanent logistics committees made up of managers responsible for different physical distribution activities. These committees meet often to set policies for improving overall logistics performance.

Companies can also create management positions that link the logistics activities of functional areas. Many companies have created 'supply managers', who manage the full supply chain activities for each of the company's product categories.[25] Some have a head of logistics with cross-functional authority. In fact, according to one logistics expert, three-quarters of all large wholesalers and retailers and a third of the big manufacturing companies have senior logistics officers at top management level.[26] The location of the logistics functions within the company is a secondary concern. The important thing is that the company coordinates its logistics and marketing activities to create high market satisfaction at a reasonable cost.

● *Building Channel Partnerships*

The members of a distribution channel are linked closely in delivering customer satisfaction and value. One company's distribution system is another company's supply system. The success of each channel member depends on the performance of the entire supply chain. For example, a big supermarket can charge the lowest prices at retail only if its entire supply chain – consisting of thousands of merchandise suppliers, transport companies, warehouses and service providers – operates at maximum efficiency.

Companies must do more than improve their own logistics. They must also work with other channel members to improve whole-channel distribution. This would enable everyone involved to enhance total customer satisfaction. For example, it makes little sense for a clothing manufacturer to ship finished apparel to its own warehouses, then from these warehouses to a department store's warehouses, from which they are then shipped to the department store. If the two companies can work together, the apparel producer might be able to ship much of its merchandise directly to the department store, saving time, inventory and shipping costs for both. Today, clever companies are co-ordinating their logistics strategies and building strong partnerships with suppliers and customers to improve customer service and reduce channel costs.[27]

These channel partnerships can take many forms. Many companies have created *cross-functional, cross-company teams*. Other companies partner through *shared projects*. For example, many larger retailers are working closely with suppliers on in-store programmes. Some retailers even allow key suppliers to use their stores as a testing ground for new merchandising programmes. The suppliers spend time at the stores watching how their product sells and how customers relate to it. They then create programmes specially tailored to the store and its customers. In this way, both supplier and customer benefit from such partnerships.

Channel partnerships may also take the form of *information sharing* and *continuous inventory replenishment* systems. Companies manage their supply chains through information. Suppliers link up with customers through EDI systems to share information and co-ordinate their logistics decisions. The recent success of America's big drug wholesalers or Pharmacy Benefit Managers has been, in part, due to their ability to supply such information services to retailers and bulk buyers of medicines. Benetton, the Italian company, has also gained competitive advantage through its management of total supply or throughput time. It uses direct feedback from its franchised outlets to monitor sales trends, links this information into its computer-aided design and manufacturing system and, making use of its highly flexible manufacturing processes, quickly produces (even small quantities) to order.[28]

Today, as a result of such partnerships, many companies have switched from *anticipatory-based distribution systems* to *response-based distribution systems*.[29] In anticipatory distribution, the company produces the amount of goods called for by a sales forecast, holding stocks at various supply points such as the plant, distribution centres and retail outlets. Each supply point reorders automatically when its order point is reached. When sales are slower than expected, the company tries to reduce its inventories by offering discounts, rebates and promotions.

A response-based distribution system, in contrast, is *customer-triggered*. The producer continuously builds and replaces stock as orders arrive. It produces what is currently selling. For example, Japanese car makers take orders for cars, then produce and ship them within four days. Some large appliance manufacturers, such as Philips-Whirlpool, are moving to this system. And Benetton uses a *quick-response system* – it dyes its sweaters and garments in grey, so that these can be swiftly re-dyed in the new 'in' colours for the season, instead of trying to guess long in advance which colours people will want. Producing for order rather than for forecast substantially cuts down inventory costs and risks.

Partnerships in logistics are expected to grow in importance in the years ahead. Furthermore, some companies are outsourcing more and more of their logistics functions to third-party logistics providers (e.g. FedEx Logistics, Emory Global Logistics) that they believe can do the jobs more efficiently, leaving them free to focus more intensely on their core business. Finally, managers argue that integrated logistics companies understand increasingly complex logistics environments. For example, companies distributing in Europe can gain a complete pan-European distribution system without incurring the costs, delays and risks associated with setting up their own system, given the bewildering array of environmental restrictions that affect logistics – from product packaging standards, truck size and weight limits to noise and pollution controls.

The purpose of external logistics partnerships and outsourcing logistics must ultimately be to improve service delivery to customers and enhance customer

Marketing Highlight 21.3

The Attraction of Logistics Partnership

The trend towards globalization means that more and more multi-national businesses have cut their number of factories in Europe and concentrated production in fewer countries. Many such companies have also subcontracted their transport and warehousing services to a single outside provider of logistics services.

A recent study carried out jointly by McKinsey, the management consultancy, and the Centre for European Logistics examined logistics alliances between 50 customer companies and 20 logistics specialists across five northern European countries. The study's main conclusion was that most of the companies' outsourcing of logistics activities was excessively driven by *cost reduction* with insufficient focus on *improving service quality* to customers.

The study showed that logistics alliances were being set up rapidly in both industrial and consumer product sectors. So far, most involved the stocking, handling and transporting of finished goods. Less than 50 per cent of firms studied also developed alliances for handling the inflow of goods, parts and materials. The study highlighted two main motives for creating logistics alliances:

1. To specialize production across national borders.
2. To focus on the firm's core competences, such as production, product development, marketing and selling.

Thus it was deemed better to outsource logistics to a specialist provider.

The study showed that pioneers like the photocopier maker Rank Xerox and the Dutch transport company Frans Maas have maintained an evolving relationship for over ten years, with periodic increases in the scope and value added by the arrangement. It takes a great deal of time to build this level of relationship. Almost half the arrangements studied which involved international flows were taken by freight forwarders such as Sweden's ASG and Germany's Kuehne & Nagel. If national alliances were included, the leaders were warehousing specialists, such as Nedlloyd's Districenters and NFC's Excel.

For the majority of logistics deals, the relationship would best be described as 'contract logistics', not a mature alliance. Companies tended to choose logistic service providers on the basis of hard, competitive cost bidding, with only one in seven of the customer companies opting to negotiate with an existing service provider on a 'sole-source' basis. The excessive focus on cost cutting and the lamentably low emphasis given to service improvement was largely due to the fact that the main stimulus behind many of the alliances was corporate restructuring.

The McKinsey consultants stress that such cost-oriented thinking underlying alliance negotiations inhibits a successful outcome. Rather, customer companies should prioritize delivery service. If this can be improved then, arguably, cost reduction will occur through improved methods and co-operation between the alliance partners.

Furthermore, to set up successful logistics partnerships, companies must nurture their relationship with service providers. For the relationship to flourish, there must be information sharing and a desire to explore means of extending the scope of the arrangement: for example, subcontracting management control of all or part of the company's inward and outward logistics, or supply chain.

Logistics alliances are a means of achieving competitive advantage in the supply chain. However, companies must balance cost pressures (efficiencies) against the pursuit of longer-run benefits, such as service delivery improvements and customer satisfaction. Ultimately, only by taking a more customer-driven approach will companies' logistics deals deliver.

SOURCES: Peter van Laarhoven and Graham Sharman, 'Logistics alliances: the European experience', *McKinsey Quarterly*, 1 (1994); Christopher Lorenz, 'A deal that aims to deliver', *Financial Times* (1 June 1994), p. 19.

satisfaction. Too often, however, logistics alliances are focused too much on cost reduction and too little on achieving real improvements in delivery performance and customer satisfaction (see Marketing Highlight 21.3).

Retailing and Wholesaling Trends

● *Retailing Trends*

A number of general trends affect the retailing industry worldwide. During the 1980s, retail sales in real terms grew in most European countries, the United States and Japan. Many retailers expanded their operations quickly, often using borrowed money. During the 1990s, a combination of sluggish consumer spending – as recession hit harder in these countries – rising interest rates and overcapacity led to many casualties:

> A host of American department stores, including Bloomingdales and Bon Marché, filed for bankruptcy; the United States' most famous store, Sears Roebuck, had been reduced to offering everyday low prices; bankruptcy also hit the British speciality fashion retailer, Sock Shop International; Harvey Nicholls, a fashionable London department store, was sold by its owner, the Burton Group, to Dickson Concepts, the Hong Kong-based retailing and wholesaling group; Aquascutum and Daks-Simpson fashion groups were taken over by Japanese companies; banks came to the rescue of Germany's Co-op, having agreed to write off loans of $1 billion; Germany's two largest store groups, Karstadt and Hartie, merged; Benetton gave up its financial services business and sought to refocus its efforts on its fashion business. In Japan, small shopkeepers were panicking as the Large-Scale Store Law which unfairly protected their trade was to be repealed.[30]

Most exposed to the retailing difficulties were stores that grew too fast and/or borrowed too much during the 1980s. However, other retailers and retailing approaches – mail-order companies, discounters, warehouses, hypermarket chains and the large and out-of-town 'category killers' – have become more prominent.[31]

Another trend that impacts on retailers is the increasing *internationalization* of the industry. For many domestic retailers, the opportunities for expansion in the home territory are drying up. Growth will have to come from winning share from competitors in existing markets. But greater competition and new types of retailer make it harder to improve market shares. As a result, more big retailers are now looking overseas for earnings growth. They must develop an awareness of international retailing developments and develop the skills for international retailing. To remain competitive, retailers must adjust to a tougher trading climate in the late 1990s. They must do several things well:

● They must choose target segments carefully and position themselves strongly.

● Retailers have to find new ways to boost sales. To do this, they must stress good value for money, respond to demographic trends and strive to deliver products that consumers want. Good service will also be paramount for success. The latter means more than just smiling sales staff; it means efficient stock control, quality assurance, logical store layouts and convenient access, including good opening hours to encourage shoppers to spend more in the shops.

● Quickly rising costs will make more efficient operation and smarter buying essential to successful retailing. Controlling costs will be vital. As a result, retail technologies are growing in importance as competitive tools. As mentioned earlier, progressive retailers and producers alike are using computers to produce better forecasts, reduce and control inventory costs, order electronically from suppliers, communicate between stores, and even sell to consumers within stores. They are adopting checkout scanning systems, in-store television, online transaction processing and electronic funds transfer. The key to lasting success is *efficient consumer response (ECR)* – slicing time out of the entire supply process and working in partnership with their suppliers to deliver goods consumers want whenever and wherever they want them.[32]

Many retailing innovations are partially explained by the **wheel of retailing** concept. According to this concept, many new types of retailing forms begin as low-margin, low-price, low-status operations. They challenge established retailers that have become 'fat' by letting their costs and margins increase. The new retailers' success leads them to upgrade their facilities, carry higher-quality merchandise and offer more services. In turn, their costs increase, forcing them to increase their prices. Eventually, the new retailers become like the conventional retailers they replaced. The cycle begins again when still newer types of retailer evolve with lower costs and prices. The wheel of retailing concept seems to explain the initial success and later troubles of department stores, supermarkets and discount stores, and the recent success of off-price and no-frills retailers.[33] Thus retailers can no longer sit back with a successful formula. To remain successful, they must keep adapting and reshaping their business accordingly.

While the wheel of retailing explains the evolution and development of new types of retail store, the concept of the **retailing accordion** can be used to explain the intermittent changes in the depth of retailers' merchandise or the breadth of their operations. Typically, retailers begin by selling a wide assortment of products. They are followed by retailers offering a narrower or more specialized range of products, which in turn are eventually superseded by broad-line mass merchandisers. The theory suggests that retailers pass through a *general–specific–general cycle*. It adequately tapped the evolution of the American retail scene, where the nineteenth-century general stores gave way to the twentieth-century specialist retailers, which were then superseded by the postwar mass merchandisers. The accordion concept may be used to describe the more recent *specific–general–specific* cycle of retailing observed in some sectors.

For instance, some retailers begin by selling a narrow range or special type of goods, as in a grocery store that carries mainly food, drinks and convenience items. As sales expand, the store manager tends to add new merchandise, such as household goods, stationery, cosmetics and non-prescription drugs, to his or her portfolio. As it grows further, extra services and amenities – for example, delicatessen, fresh-fish-and-seafood counter, in-store bakery, credit card and cheque facilities – are added. This is the path reflected by large supermarkets in the United Kingdom, which started as narrow-line high-street grocery retailers, stretching out, over the 1980s, into broad-line superstores. More recently, as further growth in edge-of-town superstores is slowing down and out-of-town shopping centres are reaching saturation point, the United Kingdom's

wheel of retailing
A concept of retailing which states that new types of retailer usually begin as low-margin, low-price, low-status operations, but later evolve into higher-priced, higher-service operations, eventually becoming like the conventional retailers they replaced.

retailing accordion
A phenomenon describing how the width of retailers' product assortment or operations shifts over time: there tends to be a general–specific–general cycle. However, it is possible that many retailing businesses evolve along a specific–general–specific cycle.

Pharmaceutical Wholesalers: Global Trends

Marketing Highlight 21.4

Traditionally, pharmaceutical wholesalers are local operators, with no single company operating worldwide, in marked contrast to the pharmaceutical company, which tends to be global. Generally, drug wholesalers tend to be fragmented, with few firms serving an entire national territory. The majority are family-owned firms and most of the large ones grew from small operations. Globally, there are no standard channel structures and systems differ from country to country. However, many are affected by common operational and regulatory conditions. In countries where the wholesalers plays a dominant role in supply, the traditional channel system bears the following features and trends:

● Wholesalers tend to consolidate goods from all manufacturers and deliver them to a specific group of clients (primarily pharmacies, hospitals and other bulk buyers of medicines). In the principal developed economies, the majority of pharmaceutical products reach patients through the wholesaler–pharmacy route. On average, about 80 per cent of pharmaceutical products flow to retailers through wholesalers; however, the figures for individual countries vary, as shown in Table 1.

Manufacturers continue to use wholesalers because of the high 'value added' they contribute to the manufacturer's product, their provision of customer service, and their sophisticated level of operation and potential efficiencies. The number of drug wholesalers varies from country to country: for example, there is one, the state-owned distributor, operating in Norway; two in Sweden; three in Finland; between 5 and 280 in the other European countries; 180 in the United States; and over 7,000 in Japan.

● In most countries, the pharmaceuticals industry, as part of the healthcare industry, faces strong pressure to lower prices. Wholesalers in this industry are invariably affected by these conditions, and margins (at lower than 5 per cent) are already being squeezed due to pressure for cost containment by governments, private healthcare insurance programmes and increased competition in many markets.

● Increased automation of logistics systems, as in the use of electronic data processing, invoicing and inventory control, has helped wholesalers to streamline operations and reduce costs, with most of the savings being passed to customers. They are placing more emphasis on market information and intelligence. Those, like the big US distributors, that have lots of timely data are able to service key customers more effectively than others. And they use this valuable asset to tie up manufacturers that supply them with the merchandise.

● More consolidation is expected to occur in the drug wholesaling industry, resulting in fewer, but financially stronger, companies. An Economist Intelligence Unit (EIU) study reports that, with the exception of Italy, Japan and Spain, the drug wholesalers sector in most countries is dominated by just two operators (e.g. the top two wholesalers have 45 per cent share of the market in Germany, 55 per cent in France, 65 per cent in Canada, 67 per cent in the United Kingdom, 41 per cent in the United States and 80 per cent in the Netherlands).

● Increasingly, wholesalers are trying to diversify and to expand into new geographic markets. Recently, many national wholesalers have attempted to 'Europeanize' their operations through acquisitions or alliances: CERP Rouen (France) acquired SA Defraene (Belgium) and three other Spanish wholesalers; ERP (France) and the Italian Alleanza took stakes in the Portuguese SIF; CERP Lorraine (France) bought Leige Pharma and Promephar of Belgium, while

TABLE 1 PERCENTAGE OF DRUGS GOING THROUGH WHOLESALERS (1992)

COUNTRY	PERCENTAGE
United States	60
Japan	80
United Kingdom	72
Germany	80
France	82
Belgium	90
Netherlands	91
Spain	85
Italy	79
Scandinavia	100

the German Schulz acquired France's Chafer and Brocaceph of the Netherlands. Tredimed was formed as a result of the alliance between OCP (France), AAH (UK) and GEHE (Germany); the PAG alliance includes Unichem (UK), OPG (Netherlands), Anzag and Egwa-Wiweda (both from Germany); FPN is formed by companies from 13 countries, while Alliance Santé was formed by Italy's Alleanza FCA and France's IFP and ERPI. By the turn of the century, drug wholesaling in Europe may well be dominated by five or six large European organizations.

- Vertical integration is another trend. Some wholesalers have started manufacturing or retailing operations. For example, the Dutch OPG runs Pharmachemie, which produces ethical drugs, SAN makes OTC (over-the-counter) medicines and operates the retail outlet Apoteck Extra. Unichem, in the United Kingdom, manufacturers own-label OTC medicines as well as running the Moss retail outlets.

The pharmaceutical industry worldwide is affected by the general trend towards higher cost, increasing competition and the pressures of internationalization. Wholesalers play a critical role in dictating the flow of products from producer to end-user in this sector. To sustain their channel position, they must adapt to the current state of continuous flux that has created new competition and fresh challenges for all in the industry.

SOURCES: 'Wholesale changes', *SCRIP Magazine* (June 1992), pp. 38–40; Barrie James, 'The global pharmaceutical industry in the 1990s: the challenge of changes', The Economist Intelligence Unit (November 1990); Richard Platford, 'Changing distribution channel strategy', Coopers & Lybrand (1992); William Goests, 'Wholesalers', International Federation of Pharmaceutical Wholesalers (1990); Peter O'Donnell, *Pharmaceutical Wholesaling World-Wide: A study of present practice and future issues* (London: PJO Publications, 1986).

largest supermarkets are contemplating moving back into the high streets. Sainsbury's and Tesco have recently reintroduced small town-centre formats, Metro and Central respectively, which they are able to trade more profitably now than they could ten years ago because they have already secured increased buying power and efficiency.[34]

Trends in Wholesaling

Progressive wholesalers constantly watch for better ways to meet the changing needs of their suppliers and target customers. They recognize that, in the long run, their only reason for existence comes from increasing the efficiency and effectiveness of the entire marketing channel. However, rising costs on the one hand, and the demand from business customers and retailers for increased services on the other, will put the squeeze on wholesaler profits. Wholesalers that do not find efficient ways to deliver value to their customers will soon fall by the wayside.

The distinction between large retailers and large wholesalers continues to blur. Many retailers now operate formats such as wholesale clubs and hypermarkets that perform many wholesale functions. In return, many large wholesalers are setting up their own retailing operations. A prime example of this type of *hybrid* operator is the cash-and-carry self-service wholesaler, Makro, which, in one sense, is a limited-service wholesaler, selling primarily to the trade – that is, to small shopkeepers/retailers. In another sense, Makro is also a large retailer in that many of the 'trade visitors' who purchase goods from its warehouse are not resellers but individuals bulk-buying for personal consumption. Furthermore, Makro stores do not fit the traditional notion of the frills-free 'pile 'em high, sell 'em cheap' shed operators. Their depots are neither dowdy nor devoid of amenities and services. Indeed, carefully controlled store designs and layouts, well-trained staff, customer service and ongoing customer-relationship building are hallmarks of the Makro operation. Makro's regular newsletter also keeps customers (trade members who own a Makro card) informed of store developments, promotions and other news.[35]

Finally, facing slow growth in their domestic markets and the trend towards globalization, many large wholesalers are now going global, thus creating new challenges for the wholesaling industry worldwide (see Marketing Highlight 21.4). To survive, players must learn to adapt to their changing environment. Like their customers – the resellers or retailers, whose success relies on their ability to capture and retain customers by offering better value than the competition can – wholesalers must consistently add to that value-creation process. For all channel partners, wholesalers and retailers alike, nothing happens until a sale takes place, until customers buy. And there are no long-term rewards unless these customers come back for more!

Summary

Marketing channel decisions are among the most complex and challenging decisions facing the firm. A company's channel decisions directly affect every other marketing decision. Each channel system creates a different level of revenues and costs, and reaches a different segment of target customers. Most producers try to forge a *distribution channel* – a set of interdependent organizations involved in the process of making a product or service available for use or consumption by the consumer or business user. Marketing channels perform many key functions: *information gathering and dissemination*; *promotion*; *contact work*; *matching offers to buyers' needs*; *negotiation*; *physical distribution*; *financing*; and *risk taking*

Each firm needs to identify alternative ways to reach its market. Available means vary from direct marketing channels to using one, two, three or more intermediary *channel levels*. Marketing channels face continuous and sometimes dramatic change. Three of the most important trends are the growth of *vertical*, *horizontal* and *hybrid marketing systems*. These trends affect channel co-operation, conflict and competition.

Channel design begins with assessing customer channel-service needs and company channel objectives and constraints. The company then identifies the main channel alternatives in terms of the *types* of intermediary, the *number* of intermediaries and the *channel responsibilities* of each.

There are many types of channel intermediary, ranging from wholesalers, brokers and agents to retailers. *Wholesaling* includes all the activities involved in selling goods or services to those who are buying for the purpose of resale or for business use. Wholesalers perform many functions, including selling and promoting, buying and assortment building, bulk-breaking, warehousing, transporting, financing, risk bearing, supplying market information and providing management services and advice. Wholesalers fall into two groups. First, *merchant wholesalers* take possession of the goods. They include *full-service wholesalers* (wholesale merchants, industrial distributors) and *limited-service wholesalers* (cash-and-carry wholesalers, trucks wholesalers, drop shippers, rack jobbers, producers' co-operatives and mail-order wholesalers). Second, *manufacturers' sales branches and offices* are wholesaling operations conducted by non-wholesalers to bypass the wholesalers. *Agents* and *brokers* do not take possession of the goods, but are paid a commission for facilitating buying and selling. *Retailers* perform activities involved in selling goods and services directly to final consumers for their personal use. There are many types of retailer, which differ in the *amount of service* they provide (e.g. self-service, limited service or full service); *product line sold* (e.g. speciality store, department store, supermarket, convenience store, superstore, hypermarket); and their *relative price emphasis* (e.g. discount store, category killer, cash-and-carry warehouse, warehouse club and catalogue showroom).

Each channel alternative must be evaluated according to economic, control and adaptive criteria. Channel management calls for selecting qualified intermediaries and motivating them. Individual channel members must be evaluated periodically. Companies operating in different geographic markets can apply the key principles of channel management, but must adapt approaches to the conditions in individual markets.

More business firms are now paying attention to *physical distribution* or *marketing logistics*. Logistics is an area of potentially high cost savings and improved customer satisfaction. Better logistics management can provide a significant source of competitive advantage for companies. Marketing logistics involves co-ordinating the activities of the entire *supply chain* to deliver maximum value to customers. No logistics system can both maximize customer service and minimize distribution costs. Instead, the goal of logistics management is to provide a targeted level of service at the least cost. The primary logistics functions include *order processing*, *warehousing*, *inventory management* and *transportation*.

Increasingly, companies are adopting the *integrated logistics concept*, recognizing that improved logistics requires teamwork in the form of close working relationships across functional areas inside the company, and across various organizations in the supply chain. Companies can achieve logistics harmony among functions by creating cross-functional logistics teams, integrative supply manager positions and senior-level logistics executives with cross-functional authority. Channel partnerships can take the form of cross-company teams, shared projects and information-sharing systems. Through such partnerships, many companies have switched from *anticipatory-based distribution systems* to customer-triggered *response-based distribution systems*. Today, some companies are outsourcing their logistics functions to third-party logistics providers to reduce costs, increase efficiency and gain faster and more effective access to global markets. The trends – higher cost pressures, increasingly demanding customers, globalization and the rising impact of technologies – affect not just the way producers must think about, and manage, channel activities, but also how channel intermediaries, such as wholesalers and retailers, should adapt their services to meet target customer needs. All members in the entire supply and value-adding chain must be aware of channel developments and their impact on the future of their industry. They must adapt their products or services to satisfy the needs of target customers and seek cost-effective methods of doing business in an increasingly competitive and international environment.

Key Terms

Administered VMS 904
Agent 919
Broker 919
Cash-and-carry retailers 914
Cash-and-carry wholesalers 911
Catalogue showroom 918
Category killers 914
Channel conflict 900
Channel level 897
Contractual VMS 902
Convenience store 913
Conventional distribution channel 900
Corporate VMS 902
Department store 912
Direct-marketing channel 897
Discount store 913

Distribution centre 928
Distribution channel (marketing channel) 895
Exclusive distribution 920
Franchise 902
Full-service retailers 912
Full-service wholesalers 910
Horizontal marketing system 905
Hybrid marketing channels 906
Hypermarket 914
Integrated logistics management 932
Intensive distribution 920
Limited-service retailers 912
Limited-service wholesalers 911
Physical distribution (marketing logistics) 925

Retailers 912
Retailer co-operatives 905
Retailing accordion 937
Selective distribution 920
Self-service retailers 912
Speciality store 912
Supermarket 913
Superstore 913
Variety store 912
Vertical marketing system (VMS) 900
Warehouse club (wholesale club, membership warehouse) 918
Wheel of retailing 937
Wholesaler 910

Discussing the Issues

1. Describe the channel service needs of: (a) consumers buying a computer for home use; (b) retailers buying computers to resell to individual consumers; (c) purchasing agents buying computers for company use. What channels would a computer manufacturer design to satisfy these different needs?

2. What are the advantages accruing to firms that have developed vertical marketing systems? Contrast the advantages and limitations of the three major types of vertical marketing system – corporate, contractual and administered.

3. Why have horizontal marketing arrangements become more common in recent years? Suggest several pairs of companies that you think could have successful horizontal marketing programmes.

4. Which distribution channel strategies – intensive, selective or exclusive – are used for the following products and why? (a) Piaget watches; (b) Lexus cars; (c) Yamaha motor cycles; (d) Kit Kat chocolate bars; (e) Häagen-Dazs ice cream.

5. When planning desired inventory levels, what consequences of running out of stock need to be considered? How should retailers ensure no stock-outs?

6. 'Category killers' and discounters provide tough price competition to other retailers. Will large retailers' growing power in channels of distribution affect manufacturers' willingness to sell to category killers and other discounters? What policy should Sony have regarding selling to these retailers?

Applying the Concepts

1. Discount houses and category killers have been increasing in popularity in recent years. If you have one of these outlets nearby, visit it and study the retailers. What sort of merchandise is sold in these stores? Do these stores compete with the retailers normally used by manufacturers? What are the pros and cons of operating through discount stores?

2. Go through a camera or computer magazine and pay special attention to large advertisements for mail-

order retailers. Look for ads for brand-name products that use selective distribution, such as Nikon cameras or Compaq computers. Can you find an ad that is from an authorized dealer and one that appears not to be? How can you judge which channel is legitimate? Are there price differences between the legitimate and the unauthorized dealers? If so, are they what you would expect?

References

1. Ian Roger, 'Sealed with innovation', *Financial Times* (3 August 1993), p. 10.

2. Report on distribution operations by retailers and manufacturers in the United Kingdom, compiled by Corporate Development Consultants Ltd (1988); see also 'Managing the European supply chain', NFC Contract Distribution Report (1989), p. 6.

3. Louis Stern and Adel I. El-Ansary, *Marketing Channels*, 4th edn (Englewood Cliffs, NJ: Prentice Hall, 1992), p. 3.

4. For alternative levels of definition of a channel of distribution, see Michael J. Baker, *Macmillan Dictionary of Marketing and Advertising*, 2nd edn (London: Macmillan, 1990), pp. 47–8.

5. Kevin Done, 'Ford to increase stake in Hertz to 54%', *Financial Times* (15 February 1994), p. 23.

6. 'Furnishing the world', *The Economist* (19 November 1994), pp. 101–2; John Thornhill, 'IKEA logs furniture sales of 2.7 times industry average', *Financial Times* (18 May 1992), p. 10; John Thornhill, 'IKEA's logic furnishes a market riddle', *Financial Times* (20 October 1992), p. 27.

7. This has been called 'symbiotic marketing'. For further reading, see Lee Adler, 'Symbiotic marketing,' *Harvard Business Review* (November–December 1966), pp. 59–71; P. 'Rajan' Varadarajan and Daniel Rajaratnam, 'Symbiotic marketing revisited', *Journal of Marketing* (January 1986), pp. 7–17; Gary Hamel, Yves L. Doz and C.D. Prahalad, 'Collaborate with your competitors and win', *Harvard Business Review* (January–February 1989), pp. 133–9.

8. See Allan J. Magrath, 'Collaborative marketing comes of age again', *Sales and Marketing Management* (September 1991), pp. 61–4; Lois Therrien, 'Café au lait, à croissant and trix', *Business Week* (24 August 1992), pp. 50–1.

9. See Louis W. Stern and Frederick D. Sturdivant, 'Customer-driven distribution systems', *Harvard Business Review* (July–August 1987), p. 35.

10. See Martin Christopher, *Logistics and Supply Management: Strategies for reducing costs and improving services* (London: Pitman, 1992), pp. 184–208; Colin Egan, 'Spread the word', *Marketing Business* (December–January 1991–2), pp. 32–5.

11. Andrew Adonis, 'Computer seller sets up UK "superstores"', *Financial Times* (2 August 1993), p. 15.

12. 'Norma and Carrefour invade UK', *Marketing Week* (22 January 1993), p. 6; 'Killing off the competition', *Marketing Business* (April 1994), pp. 11–14; *Category Killers: Prospects for the year 2000* (London: Euromonitor, 1994); Alex Spillius, 'Invasion of the category killers', *Observer Life* (27 February 1994), pp. 6–7.

13. 'Retailing in Asia: Makro-economics', *The Economist* (25 September 1993), pp. 100, 105; 'Asian retailing: teach me shopping', *The Economist* (18 December 1993), pp. 78–9; Barbara Smit, 'Unravelling a family empire: Dutch-based SHV is selling its European cash-and-carry stores', *Financial Times* (21 July 1997), p. 22.

14. John Thornhill, 'Silent enemy poised for attack', *Financial Times* (5 March 1992), p. 11; David Nicholson-Lord, 'Britain targeted as springboard for retail "attack"', *Independent* (31 January 1994), p. 5.

15. Subhash C. Jain, *International Marketing Management*, 3rd edn (Boston: PWS-Kent Publishing, 1990), pp. 489–91; see

16. also Emily Thornton, 'Revolution in Japanese retailing', *Fortune* (7 February 1994), pp.143–7.

16. See Philip Cateora, *International Marketing*, 7th edn (Homewood, IL: Irwin, 1990), pp. 570–1; Mark L. Clifford and Nicole Harris, 'Coke pours into Asia', *Business Week* (28 October 1996), pp. 72–6; Dexter Roberts, 'Blazing away at foreign brands', *Business Week* (12 May 1997), p. 58.

17. See Jan B. Heide, 'Interorganizational governance in marketing channels', *Journal of Marketing* (January 1994), pp. 71–85; Nirmalya Kumar, 'The power of trust in manufacturer–retailer relationships', *Harvard Business Review* (November–December 1996), pp. 92–106; James, A. Narus and James C. Anderson, 'Rethinking distribution', *Harvard Business Review* (July–August 1996), pp. 112–20.

18. Vincent Boland, 'Anheuser-Busch seeks decision on Czech brewer', *Financial Times* (13 October 1994), p. 34; Jeff Lovitt, 'A Bud by any other name would taste bitter', *The European* (31 July–6 August 1997), p. 28.

19. Michael Terry, 'Drive for greater efficiency', *Financial Times* (3 September 1992), p. IV.

20. Tom Todd, 'The new ground rules', *EuroBusiness* (May 1994), pp. 43–4.

21. E.J. Gubbins and P. Hancox, 'Cabotage and the single European market', *European Business Review* (1990), pp. 2, 14.

22. 'Rays of hope and prophesies of doom', *EuroBusiness* (May 1994), pp. 46–7.

23. 'Taking arms against a sea of troubles' and 'Bright future, present problems', *Eurobusiness* (May 1994), pp. 48–51 and 56–9 respectively.

24. Phillip Hastings, 'Efficiency and quality rule', *Financial Times* (3 September 1992), p. I.

25. Anderson Consulting, 'Managing logistics in the 1990s', in id., *Logistics Perspectives* (Cleveland, OH: Anderson Consulting, July 1990), pp. 1–6.

26. Shlomo Maital, 'The last frontier of cost reduction', *Across the Board*, **31**, 2 (February 1994), pp. 51–2.

27. See D. Shipley, 'What British distributors dislike about manufacturers', *Industrial Marketing Management*, **16** (1987), pp. 153–62; Robert D. Buzzell and Gwen Ortmeyer, 'Channel partnerships streamline distribution', *Sloan Management Review* (22 March 1995), p. 85.

28. Martin Christopher, 'From logistics to competitive advantage', *Marketing Business* (August 1989), pp. 20–1.

29. For a general discussion of improving supply chain performance, see Marshall L. Fisher, 'What is the right supply chain for your product?', *Harvard Business Review* (March–April 1997), pp. 105–16.

30. Clive Branson, 'Out-of-town shopping set to reach saturation', *The European* (29 July–4 August 1994), p. 30; 'Tough on the streets', *The Economist* (24 February 1990), pp. 81–2; John Thornhill, 'Burton sells Harvey Nicholls and Angus Foster' and 'Niche market success for Hong Kong businessman', *Financial Times* (16 August 1991), pp. 1 and 15 respectively; Laura Zinn, 'Retailing: who will survive?', *Business Week* (26 November 1990), p. 134; Peggy Hollinger, 'Harvey Nicholls suffer as sales growth slows', *Financial Times* (12 December 1997), p. 22.

31. 'No frills please', *The Economist* (20 July 1991), pp. 31–2.

32. Alan Mitchell, 'Serving up a logistical philosophy', *Marketing*

Week (24 May 1996), pp. 26–7. For more on retailing trends, see John Fernie, 'Distribution strategies of European retailers', *European Journal of Marketing*, **26**, 8/9 (1992), pp. 35–47; Francis J. Mulhern, 'Retail marketing: from distribution to integration', *International Journal of Research in Marketing*, **14** (1997), pp. 103–24.

33. See Malcolm P. McNair and Eleanor G. May, 'The next revolution of the retailing wheel', *Harvard Business Review* (September–October 1978), pp. 81–91; Eleanor G. May, 'A retail odyssey', *Journal of Retailing* (Fall 1989), pp. 356–67; Stephen Brown, 'The wheel of retailing: past and future',

Journal of Retailing (Summer 1990), pp. 143–9; Sachiko Sakamaki, 'Simple success', *Far Eastern Economic Review* (21 August 1997), p. 75.

34. S.C. Hollander, 'Notes on the retail accordion', *Journal of Retailing*, **42**, 2 (1966), p. 24; Neil Buckley, 'Still shopping as the margins drop', *Financial Times* (4 August 1994), p. 15; Clive Branson, 'Out-of-town shopping set to reach saturation point', *The European* (29 July–4 August 1994), p. 30.

35. Various Makro (UK) Newsletters (Leeds: Makro self-service wholesalers, 1995, 1996, 1997); see also *Cash and Carry Outlets* (Hampton, Middx.: Key Note Publications, 1992).

Case 21

Pieta Luxury Chocolates

PETER ABEL, THE YOUNG MANAGING director of his family's firm, was pleased with the way he had revitalized the firm after he took over in 1989. Since formed in 1923, Pieta had sold its luxury Belgian chocolates through its own small shops. It had a high reputation within the trade and many devoted customers. It was the country's largest luxury chocolate manufacturer, but until Peter took over, the company had stagnated. In his opinion, Pieta should be more like other leading family firms such as Cadbury, Ferrero and Mars.

When he took over, he launched the company into new ventures. Franchising widened distribution to some small shops which now had corners devoted to Pieta's range. He felt these did not compete with Pieta's own shops because the franchisees were CTNs (confectioners, tobacconists and newsagents), where people made many impulse purchases. These contrasted with Pieta's shops, which people visited to make purchases for a special occasion or as an indulgence. Other distribution channels that were developed included own-label to Marks & Spencer in the United Kingdom, direct mailing for special occasions and exporting (see Exhibit 21.1).

There were some new Pieta shops and 20 per cent of the old ones were refurbished. The refurbishment rate was slower than he would have liked, for he knew that many of the shops were poorly located, cluttered and over-crowded. The well-sited shops often had queues trailing out of the their doors when they were busy, but most did not do so well. The company had not kept pace with changes in shopping and geodemographics. Most of Pieta's shops were on secondary sites in declining industrial towns. Other new channel opportunities, such as 'shop-in-shop' outlets and international expansion, had also been largely ignored.

However, the product range was now wider. The chocolate market was seasonal, so the shops sold ice creams to help summer sales. The outlets also carried a range of greetings cards and Pieta gift vouchers to make them more of a one-stop shop. Soon he would be introducing countlines aimed at the mass market.

With more and more competitors now following Dell's successful strategy of direct selling, the company is not standing still. Dell is taking its direct marketing formula a step further. It is selling PCs on the Internet. Now, by simply clicking the 'Buy a Dell' icon at Dell's Web site (www.dell.com), customers can design and price customized computer systems electronically. Then, with a click on the 'purchase' button, they can submit an order, choosing from online payment options that include a credit card, company purchase order or corporate lease. Dell dashes out a digital confirmation to customers within 5 minutes of receiving the order. After receiving confirmation, customers can check the status of the order online at any time.

The Internet is a perfect extension of Dell's direct marketing model. Customers who are already comfortable buying direct from Dell now have an even more powerful way to do so. 'The Internet', says Michael Dell, 'is the ultimate direct model. [Customers] like the immediacy, convenience, savings and personal touches that the [Internet] experience provides. Not only are some sales done completely online, but people who call on the phone after having visited Dell.com are twice as likely to buy.'

If initial sales are any indication, it looks as though Dell has once again rewritten the book on successful direct marketing. The direct marketing pioneer now sells more than $2 million worth of computers daily from its Web site, and Internet sales are growing at 20 per cent each month. Some 225,000 browsers visit Dell's site each week, and buyers range from individuals purchasing home computers to large business users buying high-end $30,000 servers. Michael Dell sees online marketing as the next great conquest in the company's direct marketing crusade. 'The Internet is like a booster rocket on our sales and growth,' he proclaims. 'Our vision is to have *all* customers conduct *all* transactions on the Internet, globally.'

This time, competitors are not scoffing at Michael Dell's vision of the future. It is hard to argue with success, and Michael Dell has been very successful. By following his hunches, he has built one of the world's hottest computer companies. In the process, he has amassed a personal fortune exceeding $4.3 billion.[1]

QUESTIONS

1. Taking the case of Dell Computer Corporation, outline the major advantages of direct marketing for: (a) the manufacturer and (b) the customer.

2. Dell has pioneered mail-order selling of PCs. What other methods of direct selling might the firm use?

3. Identify the organizational and operational factors that govern successful implementation of direct methods of selling products such as PCs.

4. Dell is taking advantage of new technologies such as the Internet to market its products. What might be the advantages and limitations of Internet or online marketing?

5. How might advances in communications technology affect the marketing methods used by firms such as Dell and other computer manufacturers towards the twenty-first century?

6. Suggest an integrated direct marketing strategy for Dell, showing how it will help the company to create and sustain a competitive advantage.

Introduction

Dell forces us to think about the role that direct marketing methods play in achieving market performance. In this chapter, we look at the nature of direct marketing and how it can be used by organizations to reach target customers more effectively and efficiently.

Many of the marketing tools we examined in previous chapters were developed in the context of *mass marketing*: targeting broadly with standardized messages and marketing offers. Today, however, with the trend towards more narrowly targeted or one-to-one marketing, more and more companies are adopting *direct marketing*, as a primary marketing approach or as a supplement to other approaches. Increasingly, companies are turning to direct marketing in an effort to reach carefully targeted customers more efficiently and to build stronger, more personal, one-to-one relationships with them.

In this chapter, we examine the nature, role and growing applications of direct marketing and its newest form, online marketing. We address the following questions: What is direct marketing? What are its benefits to companies and their customers? How do customer databases support direct marketing? What channels do direct marketers use to reach individual prospects and customers? What marketing opportunities do online channels provide? How can companies use integrated direct marketing to create a competitive advantage? What public and ethical issues do direct and online marketing raise?

What is Direct Marketing?

Once, all marketing was of the direct sort: the salesperson confronted customers face to face, one 'doorstep' at a time. This technique was steadily replaced by mass marketing, whereby mass marketers spread a standard message to millions of buyers through the mass media – newspapers, magazines, radio and then television. Thus, companies typically promoted products with a single message, hoping that millions nationwide would learn the message and buy the brand. They did not need to know their customers' names or anything specific about them, only that they have certain needs that their products might help to fulfil. Most marketing communications consisted of one-way communication directed *at* consumers, not two-way communication *with* them.

direct marketing
Marketing through various advertising media that interact directly with consumers, generally calling for the consumer to make a direct response.

With the rising number of TV channels and new rivals, such as the Internet, mass audiences are dwindling and firms are having to target potential customers more precisely. **Direct marketing** consists of direct communications with carefully targeted individual customers, often on a one-to-one, interactive basis, to obtain an immediate response. Firms closely match their marketing offers and communications to the needs of narrowly defined segments or even individual buyers. And beyond brand and image building, they usually seek a direct, immediate and measurable consumer response. For example, Dell Computer interacts directly with customers, by telephone or through its Web page, to design systems that meet their individual needs. Buyers order directly from Dell, which then quickly and efficiently delivers the new computers to their homes or offices.

Early direct marketers – catalogue companies, direct mailers and telemarketers – gathered customer names and sold their goods mainly through the post and by telephone. Today, improved database technologies and new media –

computers, modems, fax machines, e-mail, the Internet and online services – permit more sophisticated direct marketing. Their availability and reasonable costs have greatly enlarged direct marketing opportunities.

Today, most direct marketers see direct marketing as playing an even broader role than simply selling products and services. They see it as an effective tool for interacting with customers to build long-term customer relationships. Thus, catalogue companies send birthday cards, information on special events or small gifts to select members of their customer bases. Airlines, hotels and other businesses build strong customer relationships through frequency award programmes (for example, frequent-flyer miles) and club programmes. Company Web sites provide ways for customers to 'visit' companies, learn about their products and services, interact with company personnel and participate in entertaining events and activities. In this way, direct marketing becomes *direct relationship marketing*.

Growth and Benefits of Direct Marketing

Reflecting the trend towards more targeted and one-to-one marketing, direct marketing is now the fastest-growing form of marketing. In this section, we discuss the benefits of direct marketing to customers and sellers, and the reasons for its rapid growth.

The Benefits of Direct Marketing

Direct marketing benefits customers in many ways. First, home shopping is convenient and hassle-free. It saves time and introduces consumers to a larger selection of merchandise. They can do comparative shopping by browsing through mail catalogues and online shopping services, then order products for themselves or others. Industrial customers can learn about available products and services without waiting for and tying up time with salespeople.

Direct marketers also benefit. They can buy mailing lists containing names of almost any group, from millionaires and new parents, to left-handed people or recent university graduates. They can then personalize and customize their messages. With today's technology, a direct marketer can select small groups or even individual consumers, customize offers to their special needs and wants, and promote these offers through individualized communications.

The direct marketer can build a continuous relationship with each customer. For example, Nestlé's baby food division maintains a database of new parents and mails them six personalized packages of gifts and advice at key stages in the baby's life. Direct marketing can also be timed to reach prospects at just the right moment. And because they reach more interested consumers at the best times, direct marketing materials receive higher readership and response. Direct marketing also permits easy testing of alternative media and messages. Finally, direct marketing provides privacy – the direct marketer's offer and strategy are less visible to competitors.

The Growth of Direct Marketing

Sales through traditional direct marketing channels (catalogues, direct mail and telemarketing) have been growing rapidly. A recent survey on worldwide marketing expenditure suggests not only that direct marketing has been a huge and growing activity in the past five years, but that the annual rate of growth in spending on conventional direct marketing channels (e.g. direct mail) will continue to outstrip that for mass-marketing channels in the next five years.[2]

Internet (the Net)
A vast global computer network that enables computers, with the right software and a modem (a telecommunications device that sends data across telephone lines), to be linked together so that their users can obtain or share information and interact with other users.

While direct marketing through traditional channels is growing rapidly, online marketing is growing explosively. The creation of the 'information super-highway' or **Internet** promises to revolutionize commerce. According to a recent survey by the US company Network Wizards, there were some 9,472,000 computer connections to the Internet worldwide in 1996, up from 4,852,000 in January 1995. The number of Internet connections is doubling each year. Internet penetration statistics produced by the Réseaux IP Européens (RIPE) Network Co-ordination Centre's DNS Hostcount (http://www.ripe.net) show that there are currently over 3 million computers connected to the Internet in Europe. Although there is no accurate count of the actual number of users of the Internet, which is estimated to be around 30–5 million, or higher, user penetration is rising and the trend is forecast to continue over the next few years.[3] Previously dominated by technically oriented, young, male users, the Internet is now attracting more females and more users in the 25–35 age group. While still some way from becoming the dominant promotion medium for businesses and other organizations, its use is growing and few companies can ignore its potential as a cost-effective global marketing tool. For example, the Internet search company Yahoo! had limited resources which precluded the use of mass advertising to promote its brand name. Instead it made use of the global reach of the Internet. Yahoo! grew out of a list of favourite Web sites maintained by two Stanford University students. Although theirs was one of hundreds of similar Web navigation services, at the time, it attracted many newcomers to the Internet with its contemporary style and catchy name, while also providing a service that users regarded as a friendly 'home base' among the confusion of the Web. Yahoo! relied on strategically placed 'hyperlinks' on other Web sites, such as the home page of Netscape Communications, the world's leading supplier of Web browser software, to attract users at minimal cost. And then, it relied on users to spread the word to attract new users to the service. Only recently has Yahoo! begun to advertise on TV and radio to encourage 'near surfers' who are not yet online, but are interested in 'taking the plunge', to use its services. An estimated 5 million computer users go to Yahoo!'s pages every day. At a market capitalization of $2.3 billion, Yahoo! is currently the most highly valued Internet company.[4]

Over 100,00 companies around the world have launched Web sites during the past year and the number is rising. In business-to-business marketing alone, annual revenues on the Internet amount to $600 million, and that number could go as high as $66 billion by the year 2000.[5] We will examine online marketing in greater detail later in this chapter.

What are the factors that are driving the growth in direct marketing? In the consumer market, the extraordinary growth of direct marketing is a response to the new marketing realities discussed in previous chapters. Market 'demassification' has resulted in an ever-increasing number of market niches with distinct preferences. Direct marketing allows sellers to focus efficiently on these micro-markets with offers that better match specific consumer needs.

Fragmentation of the television audience – and the increasing cost of reaching consumers *en masse* – is another driver. The soaring value of commercial slots in a diminishing number of TV programmes that pull in the big audiences means that many advertisers, under pressure to show a return on advertising investment, are turning to direct marketing methods.

Other trends have also fuelled the rapid growth of direct marketing in the consumer market. Higher costs of driving, traffic congestion, parking headaches,

Table 22.1	Mass marketing versus One-to-One Marketing

MASS MARKETING	ONE-TO-ONE MARKETING
Average customer	Individual customer
Customer anonymity	Customer profile
Standard product	Customized market offering
Mass production	Customized production
Mass distribution	Individualized distribution
Mass advertising	Individualized message
Mass promotion	Individualized incentives
One-way message	Two-way messages
Economies of scale	Economies of scope
Share of market	Share of customer
All customers	Profitable customers
Customer attraction	Customer retention

SOURCE: Adapted from Don Peppers and Martha Rogers, *The One-to-One Future* (New York: Doubleday/Currency, 1993).

lack of time, a shortage of retail sales help and long queues at checkout counters all encourage at-home shopping. Consumers are responding favourably to direct marketers' freephone numbers, their willingness to accept telephone orders 24 hours a day, seven days a week, and their growing commitment to customer service. The growth of 24-hour and 48-hour delivery via express carriers such as Federal Express, UPS, DHL and others has made direct shopping fast and easy. Finally, the growth of affordable computer power and customer databases has enabled direct marketers to single out the best prospects for any product they wish to sell.

Direct marketing has also grown rapidly in business-to-business marketing, partly in response to the ever-increasing costs of reaching business markets through the sales force. When personal sales calls cost several hundred pounds per contact, they should be made only when necessary and to high-potential customers and prospects. Lower cost-per-contact media – such as telemarketing, direct mail and the newer electronic media – often prove more cost-effective in reaching and selling to more prospects and customers.[6]

Customer Databases and Direct Marketing

Table 22.1 lists the main differences between mass marketing and so-called *one-to-one marketing*.[7] Companies that know about individual customer needs and characteristics can customize their offers, messages, delivery modes and payment methods to maximize customer value and satisfaction. Today's companies have a very powerful tool for accessing the names, addresses, preferences and other pertinent information about individual customers and prospects: the customer database.

customer database
An organized collection of comprehensive data about individual customers or prospects, including geographic, demographic, psychographic and buying behaviour data.

Successful direct marketing begins with a good customer database. The **customer database** is an organized collection of comprehensive data about individual customers or prospects, including geographic, demographic, psychographic and buying behaviour data. The database can be used to locate good potential customers, tailor products and services to the special needs of targeted consumers, and maintain long-term customer relationships. *Database marketing* is the process of building, maintaining and using customer databases and other databases (products, suppliers, resellers) for the purpose of contacting and transacting with customers.

Although many companies are now building and using customer databases for targeting marketing communications and selling efforts at the individual customer, data protection regulations in some countries may slow down growth in database marketing practices. For example, usage in the United States and the United Kingdom is far more widespread, with data laws being much more open compared to the rest of Europe. But the international race is on to exploit database marketing and few businesses can afford to ignore this important vehicle for competitive success. As Tom Peters comments in *Thriving on Chaos*, 'A market has never bought things. Customers buy things. That's why database marketing's ability to target the individual customer in the crowded marketplace is so valuable.'[8]

Many companies confuse a customer mailing list with a customer database. A customer mailing list is simply a set of names, addresses and telephone numbers. A customer database contains much more information. In business-to-business marketing, the salesperson's customer profile might contain information such as the products and services that the customer has bought; past volumes and prices; key contacts (and their ages, birthdays, hobbies and favourite foods); competitive suppliers; status of current contracts; estimated customer expenditures for the next few years; and assessments of competitive strengths and weaknesses in selling and servicing the account. In consumer marketing, the customer database might contain a customer's demographics (age, income, family members, birthdays), psychographics (activities, interests and opinions), buying behaviour (past purchases, buying preferences) and other relevant information. Companies must distinguish between *transaction-based* and *custom-built* marketing databases. Transactional databases are put in by an accounts department for the purpose of sending invoices/bills out and getting money back. By contrast, custom-built databases focus on what the firm's marketing people need to know to serve and satisfy customers profitably and better than the competition can – for example, the most cost-effective way to reach target customers, the net worth of a transaction, customers' requirements and lifetime values, lapsed customers and why they departed, why competitors are making inroads and where.

Business-to-business marketers and service retailers (e.g. hotels, banks and airlines) are among the most frequent users of database marketing. Increasingly, however, consumer packaged-goods companies and other retailers are also employing database marketing. Armed with the information in their databases, these companies can identify small groups of customers to receive fine-tuned marketing offers and communications (see Marketing Highlight 22.1).

As more companies move into database marketing, the nature of marketing will change. Mass marketing and mass retailing will continue, but their prevalence and power may diminish as more buyers turn to non-retail shopping. More consumers will use electronic shopping to search for the information and products they need. Online services will provide more objective information about the comparative merits of different brands. Consequently, marketers will need to think of new ways to create effective online messages, as well as new channels for delivering products and services efficiently.

Forms of Direct Marketing

The major forms of direct marketing include face-to-face selling, direct mail marketing, catalogue marketing, telemarketing, direct-response television (DRTV) marketing and online shopping. These forms of marketing can be used as communications tools to convey messages to target customers – as well as non-store retail channels – to elicit sales. Many of these techniques were first developed in the United States, but in recent times they have become increasingly popular in Europe. In the EU, some forms of direct marketing – notably direct mail and telemarketing – are forecast to grow. In practice, however, the impact of a unified Europe has been limited by the labyrinth of legislation across the Union, which means that certain direct marketing techniques are feasible in some countries but not others.

> For example, telemarketing is widely practised in some countries, but virtually illegal in Germany. Differences in postal systems, standards and rates for different countries pose problems for pan-European direct-mailing programmes. Direct mail is strong in countries with efficient and inexpensive postal systems (e.g. the UK, Sweden) and weak where the post is slow and delivery unreliable (e.g. Spain, Italy). Until EU-wide uniformity of postal prices and standards is achieved, the growth of pan-European direct marketing will be restricted.[9] Even etiquette is a problem. The bright, brash American-style direct-mail methods used in the United Kingdom would be considered anything but courteous in France. On the other hand, the flowery phrases of a formal letter in France would definitely be *de trop* on the other side of the channel.

Face-to-Face Selling

The original and oldest form of direct marketing is the sales call, which we examined in Chapter 20. Most business-to-business marketers rely heavily on a professional sales force to locate prospects, develop them into customers, build lasting relationships and grow the business. Or they hire manufacturers' representatives and agents to carry out the direct selling task. Many consumer companies also use a direct selling force to reach final consumers. *Door-to-door selling*, which started centuries ago with roving pedlars, has grown into a huge industry today. The image of door-to-door selling improved greatly when Avon Cosmetics entered the industry with its Avon representative – the homemaker's friend and beauty consultant. In the UK, Avon leads in the face-to-face selling and direct-to-door distribution of cosmetics and personal care products. Vacuum cleaners manuacturer Electrolux has a direct sales business in Europe. Betterware, a British direct-selling household products company, has seen strong sales growth in recent years and has expanded its operations into continental European countries, such as France. Others, notably Tupperware, Ladybird Books and Oriflame Cosmetics, have also helped to popularize home selling, through home-sales parties or *party plans*, in which several friends and neighbours attend a party at a private home where products are demonstrated and sold directly to a group of people. Tupperware has been particularly successful in a number of countries across Europe and in Asian markets, notably Japan. Indeed, Japan represents the world's largest direct sales market with sales estimated at over $20 billion a year.[10]

Database Marketing: A Question of Extracting Gold from the Informational Ore

Marketing Highlight 22.1

Databases are at the heart of contemporary direct marketing. The latter has been boosted by improvements in computer technology, which help businesses to develop bigger, more complex databases containing vast amounts of information about their customers. Collecting data is one thing, using it profitably is quite a different matter. More retailers and manufacturers are now learning how to extract gold from the informational ore.

They do so in a number of ways.

Forming Relationships and Deepening Customer Loyalty

Database marketers track individual customers and work out what marketing stimuli they might respond to next. The aim is to form a 'relationship' with the target customer. Loyalty schemes run by airlines, supermarkets and retail stores are good examples. They identify the most profitable customers and pamper them! Companies can also build customers' interest and enthusiasm by remembering their preferences and by sending appropriate information, gifts or other materials. For example, Mars, a market leader in pet food as well as confectionery, maintains an exhaustive pet database. In Germany, the company has compiled the names of virtually every German family that owns a cat. It obtained these names by contacting veterinarians and by offering the public a free booklet entitled *How to Take Care of Your Cat*. People who request the booklet fill out a questionnaire, providing their cat's name, age, birthday and other information. Mars then sends a birthday card to each cat in Germany each year, along with a new cat-food sample and money-saving coupons for Mars brands. The result is a lasting relationship with the cat's owner.

Pattern Spotting

A second use for databases is to find patterns of behaviour across large groups of customers. Neural networks and massively parallel computers are used to crunch huge amounts of data that are common to attractive customers. Lands' End uses a technique known as 'data mining' to identify different groups of catalogue clothing purchasers; at the last count, it had identified 5,200 different segments! In Belgium, American Express is using its customer database to test a system that links cardholder spending patterns with postal zone data. If a new restaurant opens, for example, the company might offer a special discount to cardholders who live within walking distance and who eat out a lot. Good pattern spotting can help firms to replace conventional advertising altogether. When Land Rover launched its new luxury Range Rover in the United Kingdom, it spent nothing on mass marketing, but instead splashed out some £30 a head on quirky gifts (seashells, chrysanthemums, maple leaves) to 11,000 people whom it had identified as prime prospects. The strategy paid off: 85 per cent of the targets visited Range Rover's showroom to see the new model, compared with a 1–2 per cent response rate for conventional mass advertising.

What works for a £42,000 Range Rover also works for a 42p can of baked beans. In 1994 Heinz abandoned conventional advertising for its ketchup and baked beans, and adopted consumer database marketing instead. Using its database of 1 million names, gathered from people who had responded to an earlier promotion, plus lists bought from brokers, Heinz built a database of 4.6 million consumers to whom the company sent a copy of a free magazine, *At Home*, which contained recipes and promotions of Heinz products. Heinz claims the strategy has paid off.

Deciding Which Customers Should Receive a Particular Offer

Companies identify the profile of an ideal customer for an offer. Then they search their databases for individuals most closely resembling the ideal type. By tracking individual responses, the company can improve its targeting precision over time. Following a sale, it can set up an automatic sequence of activities: one week later, send a thank-you note; five weeks later, send a new offer; ten weeks later (if the customer has not responded), phone the customer and offer a special discount. One clothing catalogue company that specializes in clothes for large people has 21 million names on its database, which can be grouped into 75 different segments. The firm adjusts its catalogues accordingly. It uses pink dresses on the cover for one group; blue trousers for another; free credit for frequent buyers; overnight delivery for the impatient but high-spending, valued customers and so forth.

Reactivating Customer Purchases

The database can help a company make attractive offers of product replacements, upgrades or complementary products just when customers might be ready to act. One information service company, Firefly, uses data about people's personal tastes – their likes and dislikes – to suggest new films, books and music.

Database 'miners' have to learn how best to use all the data they have extracted. In the past, the reputation of direct marketers has been tarnished by supper-time interruptions by telemarketers and the notion that direct mail is 'junk'. Then there is the threat to consumer privacy that marketers' databases present. Supporters of database marketing argue that the whole point of collecting facts is to learn when not to telephone

– and what not to shove through the letterbox! Yet most people are not opposed to giving information about themselves providing they get something in return, be this a tailored product, a discount for goods and services, or even a fee. Thus, database marketers of the future may have to learn how to reward consumers for the privilege of being able to sell to them.

Like many other marketing tools, database marketing requires a special investment. Companies must invest in computer hardware, database software, analytical programmes, communication links and skilled personnel. The database system must be user friendly and available to various marketing groups, including those in product and brand management, new-product development, advertising and promotion, direct mail, telemarketing, field sales, order fulfilment and customer service. A well-managed database should lead to sales gains that will more than cover its costs.

SOURCES: 'How to turn junk mail into a gold mine', *The Economist* (1 April 1995), p. 51; Weld F. Royal, 'Do databases really work?', *Sales and Marketing Management* (October 1995), pp. 66-74; 'Hi ho, hi ho, down the data mine we go', *The Economist* (23 August 1997), pp. 55–6; Jonathan Berry, 'A potent new tool for selling: database marketing', *Business Week* (5 September 1994), pp. 56–62; Richard Cross and Janet Smith, 'Customer bonding and the information core', *Direct Marketing Magazine* (February 1995), p. 28.

The advantages of door-to-door selling are consumer convenience and personal attention. However, the high costs of hiring, training, paying and motivating the sales force often result in higher prices. Although some door-to-door companies are still thriving, door-to-door selling has a somewhat uncertain future. The increase in the number of single-person and working-couple households decreases the chances of finding a buyer at home. Home-party companies are having trouble finding non-working women who want to sell products part-time. Besides, door-to-door selling does have an image problem, which, although inaccurate, has stuck. And, with recent advances in interactive direct marketing technology, the door-to-door salesperson may well be replaced in the future by the household telephone, television or home computer.

Direct-Mail Marketing

Direct-mail marketing involves mailings of letters, ads, samples, fold-outs and other 'salespeople on wings' sent to prospects on mailing lists. The mailing lists

direct-mail marketing
Direct marketing through single mailings that include letters, ads, samples, fold-outs, and other 'sales-people on wings' sent to prospects on mailing lists.

Door-to-door retailing: selling door to door, office to office, or at home-sales parties.

are developed from customer lists or obtained from mailing-list houses that provide names of people fitting almost any description – the superwealthy, mobile-home owners, veterinarians, pet owners, the typical catalogue purchaser and many, many others.

Direct mail is well suited to direct, one-on-one communication. It permits high target-market selectivity, can be personalized, is flexible and allows easy measurement of results (the firm can count the responses it gets and the value of those responses to the business). Whereas the cost per thousand people reached is higher than with mass media such as television or magazines, the people who are reached are much better prospects, since direct-mail marketers target individuals according to their personal suitability to receive particular offerings and promotions. Direct mail has proved very successful in promoting and selling books, magazine subscriptions, insurance and financial products. Increasingly, it is being used to sell novelty and gift items, clothing, gourmet foods, consumer packaged goods and industrial products. Direct mail is also used heavily by charities, such as Oxfam and Action Aid, which rely on correspondence selling to persuade individuals to donate to their charity.

Within the EU, direct mail is worth over ecu12 billion. Direct mail in Europe represents around 60 per cent of Europe's total spend on direct marketing. Over the past decade, expenditure on direct mail has grown faster than expenditure by organizations on other advertising media. However, a number of barriers must be overcome to assure direct mail's future. These include: EU legislation that prejudices its use; differences in postal standards, systems and prices; and 'cowboy' operators, whose indiscriminate mass mailings earn direct mail the 'junk mail' tag. In the case of junk mail, the cowboys' efforts can effectively be strangled through compulsory observation of industry standards or a code of practice, and linkages with national and international regulatory authorities to expose these operators. Users of direct mail and the direct-mail industry, in general, agree that the way forward must be to seek balanced consumer protection with a mixture of statutory and self-regulatory controls.[11]

The direct-mail industry constantly seeks new methods and approaches. For example, videocassettes have become one of the fastest-growing direct-mail media. Some direct marketers even mail out computer diskettes. For example, Ford sends a computer diskette called 'Disk Drive Test Drive' to consumers responding to its ads in computer publications. The diskette's menu provides technical specifications and attractive graphics about Ford cars, and answers frequently asked questions.

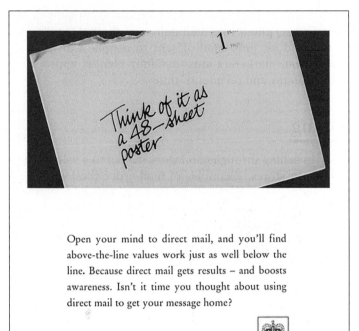

Open your mind to direct mail, and you'll find above-the-line values work just as well below the line. Because direct mail gets results – and boosts awareness. Isn't it time you thought about using direct mail to get your message home?

Royal Mail offers a unique direct marketing service for its customers.

Until recently, all direct mail was paper-based and handled by postal and tele-graphic services and other mail carriers. Recently, however, three new forms of mail delivery have become popular:

● *Fax mail.* Fax machines allow delivery of paper-based messages over telephone lines. Fax mail has one major advantage over regular mail: the message can be sent and received almost instantaneously. Marketers now routinely send fax mail announcing offers, sales and other events to prospects and customers with fax machines. Fax numbers of companies and individuals are now available through published directories. However, some prospects and customers resent receiving unsolicited fax mail, which clutters their machines and consumes their paper.

● *E-mail.* E-mail (i.e. *electronic mail*) allows users to send messages or files directly from one computer to another. Messages arrive almost instantly and are stored until the receiving person retrieves them. Many marketers now send sales announcements, offers, product information and other messages to e-mail addresses – sometimes to a few individuals, sometimes to large groups. As people begin to receive more e-mail messages, including unimportant ones, they may look for an 'agent' software programme to sort out the more important messages from those than can be ignored or discarded.

● *Voice mail.* Voice mail is a system for receiving and storing oral messages at a telephone address. Telephone companies sell this service as a substitute for answering machines. The person with a voice mail account can check messages by dialling into the voice mail system and punching in a personal code. Some marketers have set up programmes that will dial a large number of telephone numbers and leave the selling messages in the recipients' voice mailboxes.

These new forms deliver direct mail at incredible speeds, compared to the post office's 'snail mail' pace. Yet, much like mail delivered through traditional channels, they may be resented as 'junk mail' if sent to people who have no interest in them. For this reason, marketers must carefully identify appropriate targets to avoid wasting their money and recipients' time.

Catalogue Marketing

catalogue marketing
Direct marketing through catalogues that are mailed to a select list of customers or made available in stores.

Catalogue marketing involves selling through catalogues mailed to a select list of customers or made available in stores. Examples of mail-order catalogue operators are Freemans, GUS, Index, Otto Versand, La Redoute and Trois Suisses. Buying from a mail-order catalogue used to be popular among isolated populations or less affluent, older married women. The image of catalogue marketing, however, has been transformed by some retailers. Consider the following example:

> Trois Suisses, the French mail-order giant, has distanced itself from the old-fashioned catalogue image. One of its recent catalogues featured nothing less than a pair of sensuous lips. Its catalogues now feature a range of products by the leading textiles designers such as Vivienne Westwood and Elizabeth de Senneville, as well as household articles designed by Starck and André Putman. The new style is a far cry from the first catalogue sent out when the company was founded in 1932. It was the first major catalogue to aim for the glossy high-fashion market when, back in 1992, it featured the American model Cindy Crawford on a catalogue cover.
>
> Trois Suisses stresses that the traditional rural clientele is giving way to young working women who are busy and under pressure. The catalogue's up-market repositioning reflects these changes. The company's market research suggests that over a quarter of the regular clients who place orders six or more times a year are women under the age of 24; new catalogues must be a fashion and media event. Trois Suisses is described as an aggressive direct marketer, sending out more than 8 million catalogues a year and keeping its best clients in touch with follow-up literature every two weeks. Trois Suisses also operates in Belgium, the Netherlands, the UK, Austria, Germany, Italy, Spain and Portugal. To support its up-market repositioning, the firm has streamlined operations and improved performance (staff spend on average not more than three and a half minutes on each order). It offers a 24-hour delivery service on most items. Sales are processed in one large three-storey depot. There is one vast room dedicated to express sales, where each regular client is allotted a location within the section earmarked for his or her town. Over a kilometre of conveyor belts carry the items round the complex and out to the delivery vans.
>
> Trois Suisses' recent repositioning strategy has paid off, and it has turned a lack-lustre catalogue business into a profitable venture during the 1990s.[12]

Catalogues are increasingly used by store retailers, which see them as an additional medium for cultivating sales.

Most consumers enjoy receiving catalogues and will sometimes even pay to get them. Many catalogue marketers are now even selling their catalogues at book stores and magazine stands. Advances in technology are enabling retailers and

Quick.

Slow.

WANT HELP? PHONE THE SMOKELINE ON 0800 84 84 84. YOU CAN DO IT. WE CAN HELP.

This award-winning direct response advertising campaign run by the Scottish Health Education Board, drew tremendous responses from smokers seeking counselling, showing what communication can achieve when advertisers get it right.

manufacturers to experiment with multiple forms of media, such as videotapes, computer discs, CD-ROMs and Internet catalogues. The revolution has already begun in the United States in the case of Royal Silk, a clothing company, which sells a 35-minute video catalogue to its customers for $5.95. The tape contains a polished presentation of Royal Silk products, tells customers how to care for silk and provides ordering information. Soloflex uses a video brochure to help sell its in-home exercise equipment. The 22-minute video shows an attractive couple demonstrating the exercises possible with the system. Soloflex claims that almost half of those who view the video brochure later place an order via telephone, compared with only a 10 per cent response from those receiving regular direct mail.[13] Many business-to-business marketers also rely heavily on catalogues. Whether in the form of a simple brochure, three-ring binder or book, or encoded on a videotape or computer disc, catalogues remain one of today's indispensable sales tools.

Telemarketing

Telemarketing uses the telephone to sell directly to consumers. It has become a primary direct marketing tool. Marketers use *outbound* telephone marketing in a proactive way to generate and qualify sales leads, and sell directly to consumers and businesses. Calls may also be for research, testing, database building or appointment making, as a follow-up to a previous contact, or as part of a motivation or customer-care programme.

Marketers use *inbound* freephone numbers to receive orders from customers. These calls are usually made in response to an advertisement in the press, on radio or television, in a door drop or direct mailing, in catalogues or via a mixture of these media. Marketers also use the telephone in a reactive way for inbound calls involving customer enquiries and complaints.

The use of telemarketing has grown in recent years, particularly in the United States. One study suggests that the average household receives 19 telephone sales calls each year and makes 16 calls to place orders. During 1990, AT & T logged more than 7 billion 800-number calls. In 1995 marketers spent an estimated $54.1 billion on outbound calls to consumers and businesses, generating an estimated $385 billion in sales. Some industry analysts boldly predict that by the turn of the century, half of all retail sales will be completed by telephone.[14]

telemarketing
Using the telephone to sell directly to consumers.

Other marketers use telemarketing to sell consumers information, entertainment or the opportunity to voice an opinion. For example, for a charge, Nintendo offers game players assistance with the company's video games. Ronald McDonald House Charities uses telemarketing to raise funds. Similarly, consumers can obtain weather forecasts from American Express; pet care information from Quaker Oats; advice on snoring and other sleep disorders from Somnus; or golf lessons from Golf Digest.

In the UK, the growth of inbound telemarketing may be linked to BT's introduction of the 0800 Linkline in 1985. Prospects, once converted to a customer, use the 0345 number, which charges only a local rate. Thousands of companies have used these lines since, with over 10,000 calls an hour passing through them. In the rest of Europe, telemarketing is more established in the Netherlands than in Germany, which has the toughest telemarketing laws. For example, telemarketing in Germany is impossible because the consent of the prospects or consumers is needed before they can be contacted. If someone buys a shovel from a garden centre in winter, even if they gave their name and telephone number, the centre cannot telephone them in the spring with a special offer on bulbs because that would be illegal. Contrast the situation in Holland, where, for example, before an election, political parties are permitted to ring voters to gain their support.[15]

Not surprisingly, the rise in unsolicited telephone marketing annoys customers who object to 'junk phone calls' that pull them away from the dinner table or clog up their answering machines. Laws or self-regulatory measures have been introduced in different countries in response to complaints from irate customers. At the same time, consumers can appreciate many of the genuine and well-presented offers they receive by telephone. When properly designed and targeted, telemarketing provides many benefits, including purchasing convenience and increased product and service information.[16]

Direct-Response Television Marketing

direct-response television marketing (DRTV)
The marketing of products or services via television commercials and programmes which involve a responsive element, typically the use of a freephone number that allows consumers to phone for more information or to place an order for the goods advertised.

Direct-response television marketing (DRTV) takes one of two main forms. The first is *direct-response advertising*. Direct marketers air television spots, 30–60 seconds long, that persuasively describe a product or service and give customers a freephone number for ordering. DRTV is essentially mass marketing of a product or service, but with a responsive element – the freephone number which gives the consumer the autonomy and authority to make the decision as to whether or not to buy the product. Direct-response television advertising can also be used to build brand awareness, convey brand/product information, generate sales leads and build a customer database. For example, biscuit manufacturer McVitie's ran an eight-week DRTV campaign offering consumers the opportunity to call in and request a free sample pack of biscuits. Not only did the activity provide a means of collecting the names and addresses of consumers for follow-up purposes, but it also allowed the company to consult and interact with consumers who respond, in a way that conventional advertising has never done before. McVitie's believes that it will be better able to target future mailings and marketing activity using the data gathered.

Television viewers may encounter longer advertising programmes, or 'infomercials', for a single product. An infomercial is a themed TV programme, typically 30 minutes long, during which the features or virtues of a product – say, an exercise machine or multipurpose kitchen device – are discussed by 'experts' before an audience. These are selling programmes which are presented in an entertaining manner to attract the target audience. In Europe, infomercials are broadcast on existing pan-European satellite stations such as NBC Super Channel and Eurosport. The infomercial industry is expanding, with companies such as Quantum International and TV Shop airing programmes across countries in Europe.

Direct-response advertising is growing in popularity. For example, in the United Kingdom, some 20 per cent of commercials on television carry a telephone response number, a growth of 46 per cent in the last three years. According to the Direct Marketing Association, spend in DRTV grew by 68 per cent during 1995 alone. Companies ranging from mail order (e.g. Sounds Direct), leisure (e.g. Scandinavian Seaways) and financial services (e.g. Direct Line, AA Insurance Services) to cars (e.g. Daewoo, Fiat) and fast-moving consumer goods (e.g. Britvic, Martini, McVitie's) are spending on DRTV today. Direct-response television marketing has also been successfully used by charities and specific fund-raising campaigners to persuade viewers to offer donations or volunteer services. The 'Live Aid' campaign that captured the imagination of millions of people across the globe, 'Children in Need' and many other international fund-raising events have used direct-response advertising to good effect. DRTV recruitment campaigns have also been successfully employed by the British army for a number of years: a recent campaign reported one in four enquiries converted into a volunteer.[17]

Home-shopping channels, another form of direct-response television marketing, are TV programmes or entire channels dedicated to selling goods and services. Television home shopping is already a massive phenomenon in the United States, with more than half of all US homes having access to home-shopping channels such as Quality Value Channel (QVC), HSN and Value Club of America. European consumers seem likely to follow suit.

> In the United States, home-shopping channels, such as the Quality Value Channel (QVC) and the Home Shopping Network (HSN), broadcast 24 hours a day. QVC's live shows run not just 24 hours a day, but 364 days a year, and it processes well over 130,000 phone calls every day. On HSN, the programme's hosts offer bargain prices on products ranging from jewellery, lamps, collectible dolls and clothing, to power tools and consumer electronics – usually obtained by the home-shopping channel at close-out prices. The use of multimedia techniques means that the presentation of products is upbeat and a theatrical atmosphere is created, often with the help of celebrity guests, and up-to-date information can be given on product availability, creating further buying excitement. Viewers call an 800 number to order goods. At the other end of the operation, hundreds of operators handle more than 1,200 incoming lines, entering orders directly into computer terminals. Orders are shipped within 48 hours.
>
> QVC and other US-spawned TV shopping channels are already operating in Europe and consumers are waking up to the benefits of TV shopping. By far the largest electronic home-shopping business owned by Europeans is TV Shop. TV Shop is active in 19 European countries, of which Germany is the biggest market, and it is now expanding into Asia, particularly China. TV Shop is 94 per cent owned by the MTG Group, itself part of steel and paper group Kinnevik, which operates radio stations, television stations – TV3, TV1000, TV6 and ZTV – and digital and cellular systems telephone networks in Scandinavia as well as cellular systems in South America, eastern Europe, Asia and Africa. While infomercials account for some 60 per cent of the firm's turnover, its activities are wide ranging. It is Scandinavia's largest producer of commercial videos and short-form commercials. It puts together TV programmes, operates TVG, its own Swedish shopping channel, runs

sales operations through the Internet in 14 countries and has an established electronic shopping mall in Europe. It has its own computerized order-processing system and runs a growing chain of retail outlets.

So far access to TV shopping channels has been restricted to homes with satellite or cable TV. In Europe, Germany, Sweden and the Netherlands lead in terms of household penetration of cable systems. However, over the next few years, marketers believe that the reach of TV shopping channels will increase as the cable and satellite market grows. TV shopping channel operators believe that countries such as the United Kingdom, France, Spain and Italy, with less than 20 per cent satellite and cable penetration, have great potential for growth. Many experts think that advances in two-way, interactive television will make video shopping one of the major forms of direct marketing by the end of the century. The recent launch of the Philips Web TV Box means that consumers need to own a TV and one of these boxes to make sales on the Internet – if you have an electric plug and access to a phone line, you can surf the Internet on your TV screen without buying a computer.[18]

Online Marketing and Electronic Commerce

The most recent and fastest-growing form of direct marketing involves online channels and electronic commerce. We discuss these channels in detail in the next section.

Online marketing is conducted through interactive online computer systems, which link consumers with sellers electronically. A modem connects the consumer's computer or TV set-top 'Web machine' with various services through telephone lines. There are two types of online marketing channel: commercial online services and the Internet.

Commercial online services offer online information and marketing services to subscribers who pay a monthly fee. The best-known online services are America Online, CompuServe and Prodigy, with more than 8,000,000, 2,500,000 and 1,000,000 subscribers respectively.[19] These online services provide subscribers with information (news, libraries, education, travel, sports, reference), entertainment (fun and games), shopping services, dialogue opportunities (bulletin boards, forums, chat boxes) and e-mail. With a few clicks of the mouse button at their home PCs, subscribers can order thousands of products and services electronically from dozens of major stores and catalogues. They can also do their banking with local banks; buy and sell investments through discount brokerage services; book airline, hotel and car-rental reservations; play games, quizzes and contests; check *Consumer Reports* ratings of various products; receive the latest sports scores and statistics; obtain weather forecasts; and exchange e-mail messages with other subscribers around the country.

After growing rapidly through the mid-1990s, the commercial online services are now being overtaken by the Internet as the primary online marketing channel. In fact, all of the online service firms now offer Internet access as a primary service. The Internet is a vast and burgeoning global web of computer networks. It was created by the US Defense Department during the 1960s, initially to link government labs, contractors and military installations. Today, this huge, public computer network links computer users of all types all around the world. Anyone with a PC, a modem and the right software can browse the Internet to obtain or share information on almost any subject and to interact with other users.[20]

online marketing
A form of direct marketing conducted through interactive on-line computer services, which provide two-way systems that link consumers with sellers electronically.

commercial online services
Companies that offer online information, entertainment, shopping and other marketing services to subscribers who pay the company a monthly fee. They make use of their own dedicated networks and operate their own computers which are connected to the Internet, thus offering somewhat better security than the Internet.

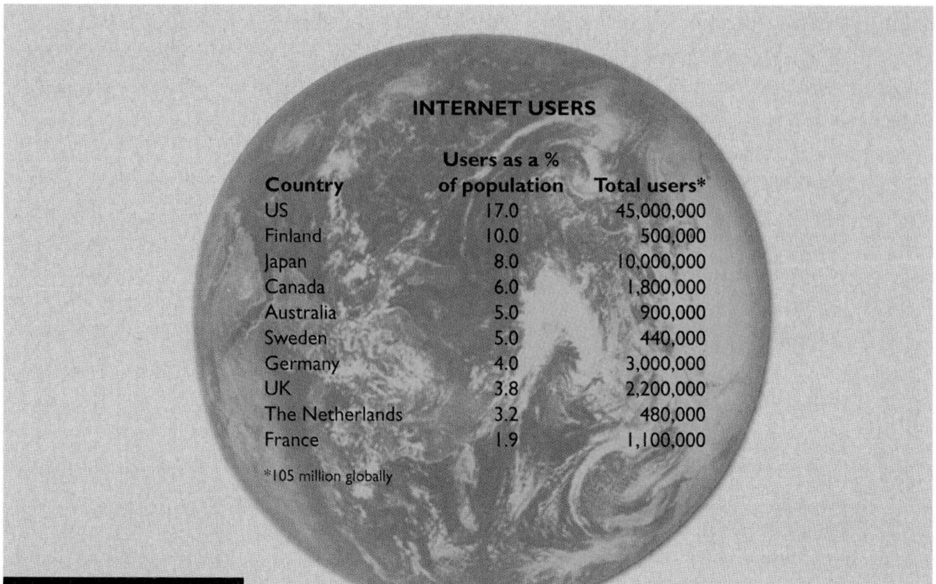

INTERNET USERS

Country	Users as a % of population	Total users*
US	17.0	45,000,000
Finland	10.0	500,000
Japan	8.0	10,000,000
Canada	6.0	1,800,000
Australia	5.0	900,000
Sweden	5.0	440,000
Germany	4.0	3,000,000
UK	3.8	2,200,000
The Netherlands	3.2	480,000
France	1.9	1,100,000

*105 million globally

Figure 22.1 **Internet Users**

Internet usage has surged with the recent development of the user-friendly **World Wide Web** access standard and Web browser software such as Netscape Navigator, Microsoft Internet Explorer and Mosaic. Now, even novices can surf the Net with fully integrated text, graphics, images and sound. Users can send e-mail, exchange views, shop for products, and access news, food recipes, art and business information. The Internet itself is free, although individual users must usually pay a commercial access provider to be hooked up to it.

World Wide Web (WWW or the Web) *A part of the Internet that uses a standard computer language to allow documents containing text, images, sound and video to be sent across the Internet.*

● *Rapid Growth of Online Marketing*

In recent years, several large Internet marketing systems have failed because of a lack of subscribers or too little use, or because consumers found the buying procedures baffling and returned to the familiarity of conventional buying channels. The online information and shopping services industry has its roots in the United States. Although still in their infancy, Internet usage and online marketing are growing explosively. According to a recent study, 23 per cent of people 16 or older in the United States and Canada – more than 50 million people – have used the Internet in the last month, up from just 1 million people in late 1994. An additional 12 per cent of adults use commercial online services such as America Online and CompuServe. Currently, there are some 105 million Internet users globally. Figure 22.1 shows Internet usage (users as a percentage of population) for the top ten countries in the world. Internet usage is estimated to be increasing at a rate of 12,000 new users per day, and some analysts predict that there will be more than a billion users, with Internet transactions totalling $50 billion, by the year 2000.

Although most of the world's online marketing takes place in the United States and the Internet is still some way from becoming a major promotion medium, European marketers can no longer ignore the technology.[21] There may now be as many as 4 to 6 million Web sites worldwide, and this number is growing by as many as 400 new sites each week.[22] Figure 22.2 shows that Internet users go online for a number of reasons, ranging from browsing, work and education to entertainment, and not just for buying things. In time, the biggest opportunity will

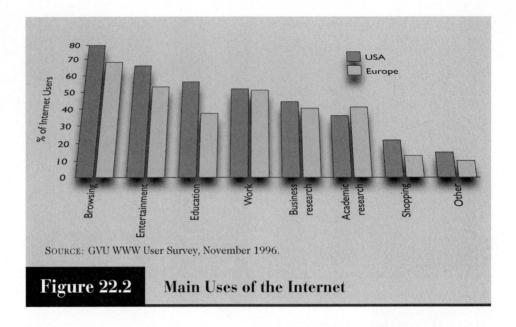

SOURCE: GVU WWW User Survey, November 1996.

Figure 22.2   **Main Uses of the Internet**

be for sales or service delivery across national borders. For example, 27 per cent of the sales of the US Internet bookshop Amazon.com are abroad, frequently to customers who would otherwise be unable to find the book they were looking for.[23] Virgin Radio, which launched Europe's first online radio station, offers a live audio-feed direct to the computers of Internet users visiting the radio station's Web site. The service (www.virginradio.co.uk) is a live relay of Virgin via the Internet, which can be accessed from anywhere in the world. It uses state-of-the-art RealAudio software, which allows the users to download free from the Virgin Radio site. But instead of downloading the file to the computer and then replaying it, using RealAudio allows them to hear the material played to them direct over the Net.[24]

Just as television burst on to the media scene and dramatically revolutionized marketing 40 years ago, so the explosion of Internet usage heralds the dawning of a new world of *electronic commerce*. **Electronic commerce** is the general term for a buying and selling process that is supported by electronic means. *Electronic markets* are 'market spaces' in which sellers offer their products and services electronically, and buyers search for information, identify what they want and place orders using a credit card or other means of electronic payment. For example, a reporter wants to buy a 35 mm camera. She turns on her computer, logs on to the Shopper's Advantage Web site, clicks on cameras, then clicks on 35 mm cameras. A list of all the major brands appears, along with information about each brand. She can retrieve a photo of each camera and reviews by experts. Finding the camera she wants, she places an order by typing in her credit card number, address and preferred shipping mode.

The electronic commerce explosion is all around us, as more and more businesses begin to recognize the vast potential of electronic technology (see Marketing Highlight 22.2). A recent study found that 39 per cent of all Net users have searched for product information online prior to making a purchase. Fifteen per cent of Net users have purchased a product or service online, and the percentage is growing daily. Early attempts to develop online shopping and electronic shopping malls had been held back by consumers' concerns about security, fraud and missing or damaged products. But consumer confidence is expected to grow, as improvements in technologies, standards and services are being achieved to make online transactions a mainstay of twenty-first century commerce.[25]

electronic commerce
A general term for a buying and selling process that is supported by electronic means.

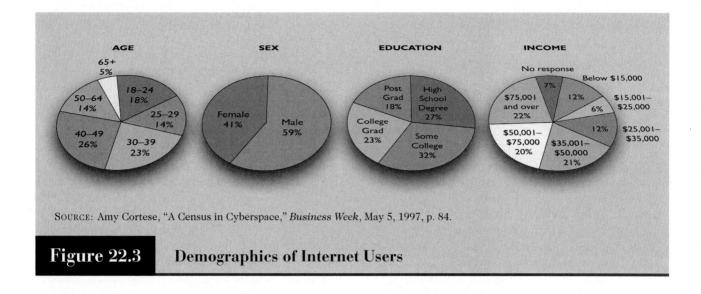

SOURCE: Amy Cortese, "A Census in Cyberspace," *Business Week*, May 5, 1997, p. 84.

Figure 22.3   **Demographics of Internet Users**

● *The Online Consumer*

When people envision the typical Internet user, many mistakenly imagine a pasty-faced computer nerd or 'cyberhead'. Others imagine a young, technically-minded, up-scale male professional. Although such stereotypes are sadly outdated, the Net population does differ demographically from the general population. Figure 22.3 summarizes the demographics of Internet users.

As a whole, Internet users remain an elite group. The Net population is younger, more affluent, better educated and more male than the general population.[26] However, as more and more people find their way on to the Net, the cyberspace population is becoming more mainstream. Increasingly, the Internet provides online marketers with access to a broad range of demographic segments. The proportion of female Net users has doubled in the past two years to 41 per cent. Although more than half of all users are professionals or managers, this percentage is decreasing.

Net users come from all age groups. For example, the population of more than 4 million 'Net kids' (predicted to reach almost 20 million by the year 2000) has attracted a host of online marketers. America Online offers a Kids Only area featuring homework help and online magazines along with the usual games, software and chat rooms. The Microsoft Network site carries Disney's Daily Blast, which offers kids games, stories, comic strips with old and new Disney characters and current events tailored to preteens. Ten of the leading girls' entertainment software publishers have joined forces to launch a special web site (at www.just4girls.com) that promotes stories, games, dolls and accessories targeted at 8–12-year-old girls.[27]

Although Internet users are younger on average than the population as a whole, 45 per cent are 40 years of age or older. Whereas younger groups are more likely to use the Internet for entertainment and socializing, older Net surfers go online for more serious matters. For example, 24 per cent of 50–64-year-olds use the Net for investment purposes, compared with only 3 per cent of those between 25 and 29. And although only 5 per cent of consumers over 65 use the Internet, 42 per cent of those users have purchased something online.

Internet users also differ psychographically from the general consumer population. SRI, creator of the VALS 2 lifestyle typology discussed in Chapter 7, is now developing an iVALS typology, which focuses on the attitudes, preferences

Music Cyberstores: 'Now' Plays a Global Song

Marketing Highlight 22.2

Jason and Matthew Olims' vain search for an obscure Miles Davis album led to the birth of CDnow. The twin brothers borrowed $20,000 and set up their Internet record store, which they operated from their parents' home in Philadelphia. Three years later, the brothers Olims filed for an initial public offering in New York to raise $60 million to expand their business. Many start-up Internet record stores like CDnow owed their origin to entrepreneurial enthusiasm, but the future winners are those players that have learnt to compete in an aggressive and expensive market. Until recently, specialists such as CDnow and Music Boulevard, owned by N2K, the US Internet entertainment group, dominated the market. Several US retailers, including Tower Records and Camelot Music, have started selling music and videos over the Internet, as have Sony and Bertelsmann. More recent entrants include the United Kingdom's Virgin and HMV, a subsidiary of the entertainment group EMI.

The global online music market, though still small, is expected to grow from $47 million in 1997 to $1.64 billion – or 7.5 per cent of global record sales – by 2002 as Internet access increases, according to research consultancy Jupiter. Traditional record labels and retailers were initially sceptical about the Internet, but the success of upstarts like CDnow and N2K has changed the industry's attitudes towards the Net.

Now the race is on. Both CDnow and N2K are trying hard to ward off online competition from traditional retailers by investing heavily in marketing. They are both spending more on advertising both on and off the Internet. They have negotiated exclusive placement rights with Internet sites or search engines, whereby users click on their logos to visit the Music Boulevard and CDnow sites. N2K expects to pay $18 million for a placement agreement with commercial online service provider America Online. CDnow's deals with search engine companies Yahoo! and Excite cost some $5.5 million. Although both companies have tended to concentrate their marketing efforts on North America in the past, they now give greater attention to Asian and European markets, which are expanding rapidly as Internet use increases. Already, locally bred specialist Internet record and entertainment stores have sprung up in these regions. N2K, however, is keen to turn Music Boulevard into a worldwide chain of virtual music and video stores. But, it must establish its overseas operations before the local competition strengthens. As such, N2K is launching a Japanese-language version of Music Boulevard in Japan in 1998, followed by similar operations in Germany, the UK and other countries in Europe by the end of 1998. To compete in the international online music market, a global network of Internet record subsidiaries is essential. At present it supplies consumers outside the United States by airmail or courier. Local operations would help it tailor product ranges to suit local needs, and to increase sales by offering faster, cheaper delivery. Then there are the challenges presented by software advances. Newcomers such as Virgin Net are offering secure shopping guarantees built around a secure electronic transaction (SET) standard to ensure that transactions over the Internet are secure and tamper free. They are also marketing low-cost set-top boxes which would cost about £200 and provide users with Internet access via their television sets. Others are making substantial investments in software to deliver albums and singles directly to consumers' computers as digital signals, rather than sending compact discs by the post.

WORLDWIDE SALES, ESTIMATED	
	$m
1997	47
1998	110
1999	240
2000	505
2001	958
2002	1,640

SOURCE: Jupiter Communications, USA

The upbeat tempo may not be music to all ears. The cost of Internet placement deals, expansion and software advances is proving too much for smaller companies. Meanwhile, N2K and CDnow are intent on battling it out, making substantial investments from their flotation proceeds to keep the business rolling in cyberspace.

SOURCES: Alice Rawthorn, '"Chain" of online stores planned' and 'Internet music retailers hear an upbeat tempo', *Financial Times* (5 December 1997), p. 27; Paul Taylor, 'Virgin Group to launch Internet shopping service', *Financial Times* (18 November 1997), p. 47; Louise Kehoe, 'Intel tries to net TV', *Financial Times* (10 December 1997), p. 22.

and behaviours of online service and Internet users. SRI's Web site (www.future.sri.com) allows visitors to take the VALS 2 questionnaire and get immediate feedback on their VALS 2 type. Fully 50 per cent of those who have visited this site so far are Actualizers, the stereotypical up-scale, technically oriented academics and professionals. Only 10 per cent of the general population belongs to this segment.[28]

Finally, Internet consumers differ in their approaches to buying and in their responses to marketing. They are empowered consumers who have greater control over the marketing process.[29] People who use the Net place greater value on information and tend to respond negatively to messages aimed only at selling. Whereas traditional marketing targets a somewhat passive audience, online marketing targets people who actively select which Web sites they will visit and which ad banners they will click on. They decide which marketing information they will receive about which products and services and under what conditions. Thus, in online marketing, the consumer, not the marketer, controls the interaction.

Internet 'search engines', such as Yahoo!, Infoseek and Excite – with huge databases containing searchable details about most Internet sites and the pages within those sites – give consumers access to varied information sources. This helps to make them better informed and more discerning shoppers. In fact, online buyers are increasingly creators of product information, not just consumers of it. As greater numbers of consumers join Internet interest groups that share product-related information, 'word of Web' is joining 'word of mouth' as an important buying influence. Thus, the new world of electronic commerce will require new marketing approaches.

● *The Benefits of Online Marketing*

Why have online services become so popular? The recent expansion of Internet marketing can be attributed to a number of benefits that both consumers and marketers gain from using the medium.

● *Benefits to Consumers*

Online buying provides the same basic benefits to consumers as other forms of direct marketing. It is *convenient*: customers don't have to battle with traffic, find a parking space, and walk through seemingly countless stores and aisles to find and examine products. They can compare brands, check out prices and order merchandise 24 hours a day from any location. Online buying is *easy* and *private*: customers face fewer buying hassles and do not have to face salespeople or open themselves up to persuasion and emotional pitches.

Online buying offers consumers some additional advantages. The commercial online services and the Internet give consumers access to an abundance of comparative *information* – about companies, products and competitors. In addition, online buying is *interactive* and *immediate*. Consumers can often interact with the seller's site to find exactly the information, products or services they desire, then order or download them on the spot.

● *Benefits to Marketers*

Online marketing also yields many benefits to marketers. Because of its one-to-one, interactive nature, online marketing is a good tool for *customer relationship building*. It brings companies and their customers closer together. Companies can interact with customers to learn more about specific customer needs and wants, and to build customer databases. In turn, online customers can ask questions and volunteer feedback. Based on this ongoing interaction, companies can increase customer value and satisfaction through product and service refinements. They can also tailor their communications and offers to the requirements of specific customers. George Fisher, CEO of Eastman Kodak Company, sums it up this way: 'Online activity gives us a way to meet customer needs and desires that is unparalleled since the days of the door-to-door salesman.'[30]

Online marketing can *reduce costs* and *increase efficiency*. Online marketers avoid the expense of maintaining a store and the accompanying costs of rent, insurance and utilities. Because customers deal directly with sellers, online marketing often results in lower costs and improved efficiencies for channel and logistics functions such as order processing, inventory handling, delivery and trade promotion. Finally, communicating electronically often costs less than communicating on paper through the post. For instance, a company can produce digital catalogues for much less than the cost of printing and mailing paper ones. The relatively low costs of setting up an online marketing operation mean that both small and large firms can afford it. For example, it generally costs less to set up an effective Web site than it does to purchase 30 seconds of commercial time on prime-time network TV.

Online marketing also offers greater *flexibility*, allowing the marketer to make continuous adjustments to its offers and programmes. For example, once a paper catalogue is mailed, the products, prices and other catalogue features are fixed until the next catalogue is sent. However, an online catalogue can be adjusted continuously, adapting product assortments, prices, and promotions to match changing market conditions.

Finally, the Internet is a truly *global* medium that allows buyers and sellers to click from one country to another in seconds. A Web surfer from Paris or Istanbul can access a Lands' End catalogue as easily as someone living on 1 Lands' End Lane in Dodgeville, Wisconsin, the direct retailer's home town. Thus, even small online marketers find that they have ready access to global markets. Despite these many benefits, however, online marketing is not for every company or for every product. Careful thought has to be given to if, when and how it should be done.

● *Online Marketing Channels*

Marketers can conduct online marketing in four ways: by creating an electronic storefront; placing ads online; participating in Internet forums, news groups or 'Web communities'; or using online e-mail or Webcasting. Let us take a look at these channels next.

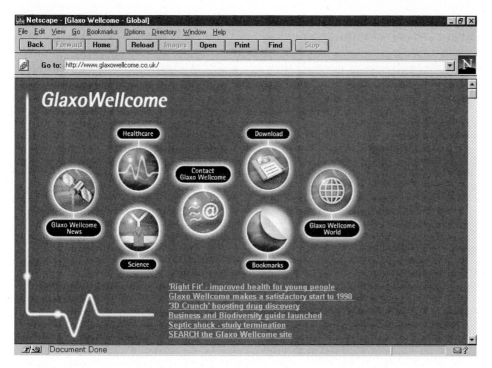

More and more companies are launching Web-sites, recognizing the Internet's vast potential as a global communications tool.

• *Creating an Electronic Storefront*

In opening an electronic storefront, a company has two choices: it can buy space on a commercial online service or it can open its own Web site. Buying a location on a commercial online service involves either renting storage space on the online service's computer or establishing a link from the company's own computer to the online service's shopping mall. A retailer, for example, can link to America Online, CompuServe and Prodigy, gaining access to the millions of consumers who subscribe to these services. The online services typically design the storefront for the company and introduce it to their subscribers. For these services, the company pays the online service an annual fee plus a small percentage of the company's online sales.

In addition to buying a location on an online service, or as an alternative, thousands of companies have now created their own Web sites. These sites vary greatly in purpose and content. The most basic type is a **corporate Web site**.[31] These sites are designed to handle interactive communication *initiated by the consumer*. They seek to build customer good will and to supplement other sales channels rather than to sell the company's products directly. Corporate Web sites typically offer a rich variety of information and other features in an effort to answer customer questions, build closer customer relationships and generate excitement about the company. Corporate Web sites generally provide information about the company's history, its mission and philosophy, and the products and services that it offers. They might also tell about current events, company personnel, financial performance and employment opportunities. Many corporate Web sites also provide exciting entertainment features to attract and hold visitors. Finally, the site might also provide opportunities for customers to ask questions or make comments through e-mail before leaving the site.

Other companies create a **marketing Web site**. These sites are designed to engage consumers in an interaction that will move them closer to a purchase or

corporate Web site
A site set up by a company on the Web, which carries information and other features designed to answer customer questions, build customer relationships and generate excitement about the company, rather than to sell the company's products or services directly. The site handles interactive communication initiated by the consumer.

marketing Web site
A site on the Web created by a company to interact with consumers for the purpose of moving them closer to a purchase or other marketing outcome. The site is designed to handle interactive communication initiated by the company.

other marketing outcome. With a marketing Web site, communication and inter-action are *initiated by the marketer*. Such a site might include a catalogue, shopping tips and promotional features such as coupons, sales events or contests. Companies aggressively promote their marketing Web sites in print and broadcast advertising, and through 'banner-to-site' ads that pop up on other Web sites.

> For example, Toyota operates a marketing Web site at www.toyota.com. Once a potential customer clicks in, the car maker wastes no time trying to turn the enquiry into a sale. The site offers plenty of entertainment and useful information, from cross-country trip guides and tips for driving with kids, to golf and outdoor events. But the site is also loaded with more serious selling features, such as detailed descriptions of current Toyota models and information on dealer locations and services, complete with maps and dealer Web links. Visitors who want to go further can fill out an online order form (supplying name, address, phone number and e-mail address) for brochures and a free interactive CD-ROM that shows off the features of Toyota models. The chances are good that before the CD-ROM arrives, a local dealer will call to invite the prospect in for a test drive.[32]

Business-to-business marketers also make good use of marketing Web sites. For example, corporate buyers can visit Sun Microsystems' Web site (www.sun.com), select detailed descriptions of Sun's products and solutions, request sales and service information and interact with staff members. Customers visiting GE Plastics' Web site can draw on more than 1,500 pages of information to get answers about the company's products any time and from anywhere in the world. And FedEx's Web site (www.fedex.com) allows customers to schedule their own shipments, request a courier and track their packages in transit.

Creating a Web site is one thing; getting people to *visit* the site is another. The key is to create enough value and excitement to get consumers to come to the site, stick around and come back again. This means that companies must constantly update their sites to keep them fresh and exciting. Doing so involves time and expense, but the expense is necessary if the online marketer wishes to cut through the increasing online clutter.

For some types of product, attracting visitors is easy. Consumers buying new cars, computers or financial services will be open to information and marketing initiatives from sellers. Marketers of lower-involvement products, however, may face a difficult challenge in attracting Web-site visitors. As one veteran notes: 'If you're shopping for a computer and you see a banner that says, "We've ranked the top 12 computers to purchase", you're going to click on the banner. [But] what kind of banner could encourage any consumer to visit dentalfloss.com?'[33] For such low-interest products, the company should create a corporate Web site to answer customer questions and build good will, using it only to supplement selling efforts through other marketing channels.

Next, let us take a look at how advertisements are placed online.

● *Placing Advertisements Online*

online advertising
Placing advertisements on the Internet in special sections offered by commercial online services, as banner ads that pop up while computer subscribers are surfing online services or Web sites, or in Internet news groups that have been set up for commercial purposes.

Companies can place online advertisements in any of three ways. First, they can place *classified ads* in special sections offered by the major commercial online services. The ads are listed according to when they arrived, with the latest ones heading the list. Second, ads can be placed in certain Internet *newsgroups* that are set up for commercial purposes. Finally, the company can buy **online ads** that *pop up* while subscribers are surfing online services or Web sites. Such ads include banner ads, pop-up windows, 'tickers' (banners that move across the

Advertising online: banner ads like these may be used in addition to setting up a company Web-site.

screen) and 'roadblocks' (full-screen ads that users must pass through to get to other screens they wish to view). For example, a Web user or America Online subscriber who is looking up airline schedules or fares might find a flashing banner on the screen exclaiming 'Rent a car from Alamo and get up to 2 days free!' To attract visitors to its own Web site, Toyota sponsors Web banner ads on other sites, ranging from major Internet publisher sites like ESPNet SportZone (www.espn.com) to Parent Soup (www.parentsoup.com), a kind of online coffee klatch through which mums and dads exchange views.

Web advertising is on the increase. However, many marketers still question its value as an effective advertising tool. Costs are reasonable compared with those of other advertising media and it is relatively easy to create a site: as little as $300 a year will buy an Internet address, create a site with a few pages and launch it. Web advertising on more popular sites such as ESPNet SportsZone, which attracts more than 500,000 Web surfers and 20 million 'hits' – the number of times the site is accessed – per week, costs about $300,000 per year. Netscape, the popular Web-browser site, charges about $360,000 per year and delivers an estimated 1 million impressions. Still, Web surfers can easily ignore these banner ads, and often do. Ad Web locations that sell advertising space are still working to develop good measures of advertising impact. Thus, although many firms are experimenting with Web advertising, it still plays only a minor role in their promotion mixes. For example, the Internet is estimated to have attracted about $200 million in total ad revenue over 1996, primarily in buying banners, with the majority of it originating in the United States. This can be put into perspective when we consider that a company such as Procter & Gamble spent over $150 million on advertising in the United Kingdom alone over the same period.[34]

● *Participating in Forums, Newsgroups and Web Communities*

Companies may decide to participate in or sponsor Internet forums, newsgroups and bulletin boards that appeal to specific special interest groups. Such activities may be organized for commercial or non-commercial purposes. *Forums* are discussion groups located on commercial online services. A forum may operate a library, a 'chat room' for real-time message exchanges and even a classified ad directory. For example, America Online boasts some 14,000 chat rooms, which account for a third of its members' online time. It recently introduced 'buddy lists', which alert members when friends are online, allowing them to exchange instant messages.[35] Most forums are sponsored by interest groups. Thus, as a major musical instruments manufacturer, Yamaha might start a forum on classical music.

Newsgroups are the Internet version of forums. Unlike commercial forums, newsgroups are made up of groups of people posting and reading messages on a specified topic of interest to them, rather than managing libraries or conferencing. Internet users can participate in newsgroups without subscribing. The discussions are like a telephone conference call, only everything is typed on-screen and people can come and go at any time over a period of days and might not even 'say' anything at all. There are thousands of newsgroups dealing with every imaginable topic, from healthy eating, home repairs and caring for your Bonsai tree to collecting antique cars or exchanging views on the latest soap opera happenings. For example, one newsgroup, rec.autos.vw, on a section of the Internet called usenet, hosted a discussion about the reliability of different versions of one model of Volkswagen car. Newsgroups carry a lot of information about customers, and companies can take advantage of the chance to 'meet' potential customers by participating in the discussions. However, firms must beware when joining the forum. People organizing newsgroups have a distinct aversion to the hard sell of businesses – after all, they set up their groups deliberately outside the normal arenas of commercial influence.[36]

Bulletin board systems (BBSs) are specialized online services that centre on a specific topic or group. These deal with a wide range of topics, from holidays and health to computer games and property. Marketers might want to identify and participate in newsgroups and BBSs that attract subscribers who fit their target markets. However, like newsgroups, BBS users often resent commercial intrusions on their Net space, so the marketer must tread carefully, participating in subtle ways that provide real value to participants.

The popularity of forums and newgroups has resulted in a rash of commercially sponsored Web sites called *Web communities*. Such sites provide a place where members can congregate online and exchange views on issues of common interest. They are 'the cyberspace equivalent to the bar, where everybody knows your e-mail address'.[37] For example, Women's Wire is a Web community where career-oriented women can engage in discussion forums and celebrity chats on women's issues. Tripod is an online hangout for twenty-somethings, offering chat rooms and free home pages for posting curriculum vitae. And Parent Soup is an online community of more than 200,000 parents who spend time online gathering parenting information, chatting with other parents about kid-related issues and linking with other related sites.

Visitors to these Net neighbourhoods or *cyberhoods* develop a strong sense of community. Such communities are attractive to advertisers because they draw consumers with common interests and well-defined demographics. For example, Parent Soup provides an ideal environment for the Web ads of Johnson & Johnson and other makers of children's products. Moreover, cyberhood consumers visit frequently and stay online longer, increasing the chance of meaningful exposure to the advertiser's message.

● *Using e-mail and Webcasting*

A company can encourage prospects and customers to send questions, suggestions and complaints to the company via e-mail. Customer service representatives can quickly respond to such messages. The company may also develop Internet-based electronic mailing lists of customers or prospects. Such lists provide an excellent opportunity to introduce the company and its offerings to new customers and to build ongoing relationships with current ones. Using the lists, online marketers can send out customer newsletters, special product or promotion offers based on customer purchasing histories, reminders of service requirements or warranty renewals, or announcements of special events.

Companies can also sign on with any of a number of **Webcasting** services, which automatically download customized information to recipients' PCs. For a monthly fee, subscribers to these services can specify the channels they want – news, company information, entertainment and others – and the topics they're interested in. Then, rather than spending hours scouring the Internet, they can sit back while the Webcaster automatically delivers information of interest to their desktops.

Webcasting, also known as 'push' programming, affords an attractive channel through which online marketers can deliver their Internet advertising or other information content. Instead of waiting for Web surfers to stumble on to their sites and banner ads, marketers can send animated ads directly to the desktops of target customers. Companies can use such in-your-face methods to notify subscribers of promotions and even send them order forms.[38]

US Webcasting services such as PointCast and Ifusion are growing fast and attracting an ever increasing number of advertisers. The major commercial online services are also beginning to offer Webcasting to their members. For example, America Online has added a feature called Driveway that will fetch information, Web pages and e-mail based on members' preferences and automatically deliver it to their PCs. However, as with other types of online marketing, companies must be careful that they do not cause resentment among Internet users who are already overloaded with 'junk e-mail'. Warns one analyst, 'there's a fine line between adding value and the consumer feeling that you are being intrusive'.[39]

Webcasting (push programming)
Process whereby the online marketer sends advertisements or information over the Internet directly to the desktops of target customers. Companies can also sign on with Webcasting service providers, which automatically download customized information to the personal computers of subscribers to their services.

● *The Promise and Challenges of Online Marketing*

Online marketing offers great promise for the future. Its most ardent supporters envision a time when the Internet and electronic commerce will replace magazines, newspapers and even stores as sources for information and buying. Yet despite all the hype and promise, online marketing may be years away from realizing its full potential. And even then, it is unlikely to fulfil such sweeping predictions. Instead, eventually, online marketing will become another important tactical tool, much like the television or telephone, and should work alongside other tactical elements in a fully integrated marketing mix.

Although novel and exhilarating, online marketing has yet to carve out a central role in consumers' lives. For most online marketers, the Web is still not a money-making proposition – according to one report, money-losers exceed money-winners by more than 2 to 1.[40] Here are just some of the challenges that online marketers face:

● *Limited consumer exposure and buying.* Although expanding rapidly, online marketing still reaches only a limited market-space. Even in affluent countries such as the United States, 98 per cent of the population owns a TV, whereas less than 10 per cent have Internet access. In Europe Internet connections lag behind the United States, although the gap is narrowing. Moreover, Web users appear to do more window browsing than actual buying. Only an estimated 10–20 per cent of Web surfers actually use the Web regularly for shopping or to obtain commercial services such as travel information (see Figure 22.2).[41]

● *Skewed user demographics and psychographics.* Online users tend to be more upscale and technically oriented than the general population. This makes online marketing ideal for marketing computer hardware and software, consumer electronics, financial services and certain other classes of product. However, it makes online marketing less effective for selling mainstream products.

● *Chaos and clutter.* The Internet offers up millions of Web sites and a staggering volume of information. Thus, navigating the Internet can be frustrating, confusing and time consuming for consumers. In this chaotic and cluttered environment, many Web ads and sites go unnoticed or unopened. Even when they are noticed, marketers will find it difficult to hold consumer attention. One study found that a site must capture Web surfers' attention within eight seconds or lose them to another site. That leaves very little time for marketers to promote and sell their goods. By contrast, TV commercials and infomercials offer a narrative that the Internet cannot, and the marketer is able to control the pace and sequence of the advertisement.

● *Security.* Consumers worry that unscrupulous snoopers will eavesdrop on their online transactions or intercept their credit card numbers and make unauthorized purchases. In turn, companies doing business online fear that others will use the Internet to invade their computer systems for the purposes of commercial espionage or even sabotage. Online marketers are developing solutions to such security problems. However, there appears to be a 'never-ending competition between the technology of security systems and the sophistication of those seeking to thwart them'.[42]

● *Ethical concerns.* Privacy is a primary concern. Marketers can easily track Web-site visitors, and many consumers who participate in Web-site activities provide extensive personal information. This may leave consumers open to information abuse if companies make unauthorized use of the information in marketing their products or exchanging electronic lists with other companies. There are also concerns about segmentation and discrimination. The Internet currently serves up-scale consumers well. However, poorer consumers have less access to the Net, leaving them increasingly less informed about products, services and prices.[43]

Despite these challenges, companies large and small are quickly integrating online marketing into their marketing mixes. More than the latest fad, towards the twenty-first century, online marketing will prove to be a powerful tool for building customer relationships, improving sales, communicating company and product information, and delivering products and services more efficiently and effectively.

Integrated Direct Marketing

integrated direct marketing
Direct marketing campaigns that use multiple vehicles and multiple stages to improve response rates and profits.

Although direct marketing and online marketing have boomed in recent years, many companies still relegate them to minor roles in their marketing and promotion mixes. Many direct marketers use only a 'one-shot' effort to reach and sell to a prospect, or a single vehicle in multiple stages to trigger purchases. For example, a magazine publisher might send a series of four direct-mail notices to a household to get a subscriber to renew before giving up. A more powerful approach is **integrated direct marketing**, which involves using multiple-vehicle, multiple-stage campaigns. Such campaigns can greatly improve response. Whereas a direct-mail piece alone might generate a 2 per cent response, adding a freephone number can raise the response rate by 50 per cent. A well-designed outbound telemarketing effort might lift response by another 500 per cent. Suddenly a 2 per cent response has grown to 15 per cent or more by adding interactive marketing channels to a regular mailing.[44]

More elaborate integrated direct-marketing campaigns can be used. Consider the following multimedia, multistage marketing campaign:

Paid ad with a → Direct → Outbound → Face-to-face
response channel   mail   telemarketing   sales call

Here, the paid ad to target customers creates product awareness and stimulates enquiries. The company immediately sends direct mail to those who enquire. Within a few days, the company follows up with a phone call seeking an order. Some prospects will order by phone; others might request a face-to-face sales call. In such a campaign, the marketer seeks to improve response rates and profits by adding media and stages that contribute more to additional sales than to additional costs.

Consider the following examples:

Flying Flowers is a UK flowers-by-post business. The 17-acre Jersey-based carnation nursery now offers a postal pack service to most northern European countries. Its strong sales have been achieved through direct-response advertising and by mailing to an increasingly large customer database. The firm's progressive involvement with retail chains, mail-order companies and credit card operators has also generated additional sales. It also became an Air Miles promoter. In special promotions such as for Valentine's Day and Mother's Day, Air Miles members who got Flying Flowers to dispatch a bouquet of flowers would get up to 35 Air Miles awards. All the consumer had to do was order by phone, quoting his/her Air Miles membership number, credit card details, bouquet code and Air Miles promotion reference number. Easy! It is clear that Flying Flowers uses multiple direct marketing channels, while also taking advantage of its expanding marketing database to maintain a consistent sales growth record.

The French mail-order giant, Trois Suisses, integrates its existing mail-order format with other direct retailing approaches. It takes orders by post, telephone and the French interactive information network, Minitel, which is installed in more than 3 million houses. It is linked with a shopping programme on the French RTL-TV and is taking the step into television shopping. Trois Suisses believes that the online revolution could strengthen its foothold in the new shopping environment of the future.[45]

Public Policy and Ethical Issues in Direct Marketing

Direct marketers and their customers usually enjoy mutually rewarding relationships. Occasionally, however, a darker side emerges. The aggressive and sometimes shady tactics of a few direct marketers can bother or harm consumers, giving the entire industry a black eye. Abuses range from simple excesses that irritate consumers to instances of unfair practices or even outright deception and

Remember Your Netiquette, Please

Marketing Highlight 22.3

The Internet offers many exciting commercial opportunities to companies. It enables a direct two-way contact with users, which allows multimedia communications and which reaches consumers around the globe. There are rewards for businesses as long as they respect the culture of the Internet. Users may not want 'in-your-face' advertising on-screen, but those who are interested in a company's product or service will access the company's Web pages. Businesses will do well to take on board the implications of the Internet's unwritten code. Here are some dos and don'ts of Netiquette.

Electronic Mail

- Do not send a commercial e-mail message to an Internet user who has not asked for it. However, if an Internet user sends an enquiry to an organization, it should be acceptable for the recipient to respond to the user using e-mail.

- If an Internet user requests information from companies within a specific category – for example, scuba diving – the companies within this category should be able to send this user relevant information. The company may offer the user the option to be added to its list server – an Internet convention allowing people interested in a particular topic to subscribe to an ongoing electronic conference on that topic.

- Enquiries to commercial list servers should not result in an automatic subscription. Organizations should not add the user's name to a mailing list to which he or she has not subscribed. All list servers must respect the Internet's 'unsubscribe' command and refrain from sending further e-mail messages when this command is received.

- Internet users who choose to put their personal details such as addresses or phone numbers in their electronic signatures should be able to do so with the knowledge that marketers will not use this information to make unsolicited contact by telephone, regular mail or fax.

Customer Data

- Internet data should remain the private property of the user. If a user has expressed interest in, say, scuba diving, through the Internet, the behavioural data of the user should not be resold to a company that wishes to use it to target divers without the permission of that user.

- If a list server subscriber list is to be released, only the addresses of those subscribers who have expressly approved the release of their details should be included.

Advertising

- Advertisers should avoid commercial advertising to newsgroups and list server conferences that are unrelated to the newsgroup or conference topic.

Communications Software

- Under no circumstances should marketers use communications software to gather data from users without the knowledge or permission of the user.

- No data should be sent or collected using the Internet without the express permission and knowledge of the person who owns the data.

Information gathering without an individual's permission is both an invasion of privacy and illegal.

Market Research

- Only conduct consumer research as long as participating consumers are made fully aware of the consequences of answering the questionnaire.

- Internet users should have ready and easy access to information detailing the uses and implications of participating in the market research survey.

Promotions and Direct Selling

● Promotions should be self-selected by an Internet user and potential customer of the product, service or promotion.

● Internet users should be made fully aware of the guidelines, rules and parameters of the event or offer before they commit to responding to the promotion.

As consumers become more literate in the ways of direct marketing, whatever their form, online or offline, they can easily see through the 'spams', false offers and acts of impropriety. Companies that attempt to lure the naive do no one, least of all themselves, any favours. Code breakers risk consumer backlash, blacklisting, even the threat of legislative extinction, which would restrict growth of the industry. Where the Internet is concerned, the obstacles to sales – privacy, consumer protection and product liability – are yet to be solved. Governments worldwide are responding to OECD initiatives to address problems and to seek agreement on ways to dismantle the barriers to global electronic commerce. Meanwhile, code makers are already working their way towards creating a cyberworld of better business netiquette!

SOURCES: Jack Schofield, 'Untangling the Web', *Marketing Business* (March 1995), pp. 10–13; 'The Internet: spam, spam, spam, spam', *The Economist* (1 November 1997), p. 123; Martin Croft, 'Clean-up operation', *Marketing Week* (8 March 1996), pp. 61–3; Richenda Wilson, 'Security alarm', *Marketing Week* (26 January 1996), pp. 49–53.

fraud. During the past few years, the direct marketing industry has also faced growing concerns about invasion of privacy.[46]

Irritation, Unfairness, Deception and Fraud

Direct marketing excesses sometimes annoy or offend consumers. Most of us dislike direct-response TV commercials that are too loud, too long and too insistent. Especially bothersome are dinner-time or late-night phone calls. Beyond irritating consumers, some direct marketers have been accused of taking unfair advantage of impulsive or less sophisticated buyers. TV shopping shows and programme-long 'infomercials' seem to be the worst culprits. They feature smooth-talking hosts, elaborately staged demonstrations, claims of drastic price reductions, 'while they last' time limitations, and unequalled ease of purchase to inflame buyers who have low sales resistance.

Worse yet, 'heat merchants' design mailings and write copy intended to mislead buyers. Other direct marketers pretend to be conducting research surveys when they are actually asking leading questions to screen or persuade consumers. Fraudulent schemes, such as investment scams or phoney collections for charity, have also multiplied in recent years. Crooked direct marketers can be hard to catch: direct marketing customers often respond quickly, do not interact personally with the seller, and usually expect to wait for delivery. By the time buyers realize that they have been duped, the thieves are usually somewhere else, plotting new schemes.

Invasion of Privacy

Invasion of privacy is perhaps the toughest public policy issue now confronting the direct marketing industry. These days, it seems that almost every time consumers order products by mail or telephone, enter a sweepstake, apply for a credit card or take out a magazine subscription, their names are entered into some company's already bulging database. Using sophisticated computer technologies, direct marketers can use these databases to 'microtarget' their selling efforts. Yes, consumers often benefit from such database marketing – they receive more offers that are closely matched to their interests. However, many critics worry that marketers may know *too* much about consumers' lives, and that they may use this knowledge to take unfair advantage of consumers. At some point, they claim, the extensive use of databases intrudes on consumer privacy. For example, they ask, should telecom network operators be allowed to sell marketers the names of customers who frequently call the free (e.g.0800) numbers of, say, catalogue companies? Is it right for credit bureaux to compile and sell lists of people who have recently applied for credit cards – people who are considered prime direct marketing targets because of their spending behaviour? Or is it right for government agencies to sell the names and addresses of driver's licence holders, along with height, weight and gender information, allowing clothing retailers to target tall or overweight people with special offers?

In their drives to build databases, companies sometimes get carried away. For example, Microsoft caused substantial privacy concerns when it introduced its Windows 95 software. It used a 'Registration Wizard' which allowed users to register their new software online. However, when users went online to register, without their knowledge, Microsoft took the opportunity to 'read' the configurations of their PCs. Thus, the company gained instant knowledge of the major software products running on each customer's system. When users learned of this invasion, they protested publicly. The enraged outcry led Microsoft to abandon such snooping. However, such actions have spawned a quiet but determined 'privacy revolt' among consumers and public policy makers.[47]

The direct marketing industry in a number of countries is addressing issues of ethics and public policy. For example, in the United Kingdom, faced with the threat of legislation, including wider EU directives, the industry has adopted stringent self-regulation measures to restrain unsavoury practices and to bring the 'cowboys' into line. Similarly, in the case of the Internet, there is rising user concern about malpractice, ranging from the flood of unsolicited 'junk cybermail' to intrusion of privacy. So, while the Internet offers vast potential as a multimedia, global communication channel to marketers, firms should seek to police themselves, operating within acceptable codes of practice (see Marketing Highlight 22.3). Direct marketers know that, left untended, such problems will lead to increasingly negative consumer attitudes, lower response rates, and calls for more restrictive legislation. More importantly, most direct marketers want the same things that consumers want: honest and well-designed marketing offers targeted only towards consumers who will appreciate and respond to them. Direct marketing is just too expensive to waste on consumers who don't want it.

Mass marketers have typically tried to reach millions of buyers with a single product and a standard message communicated via the mass media. Consequently, most mass-marketing communications were one-way communications directed *at* consumers rather than two-way communications *with* consumers. Today, many companies are turning to direct marketing in an effort to reach carefully targeted customers more efficiently and to build stronger, more personal, one-to-one relationships with them.

Summary

We discussed the benefits of direct marketing to customers and companies, and the trends fuelling its rapid growth. Customers benefit from direct marketing in many ways. For consumers, home shopping is fun, convenient and hassle free, saves time and gives them a bigger selection of merchandise. It allows them to compare shop offers using mail catalogues and online shopping services, then to order products and services without dealing with salespeople. Sellers also benefit. Direct marketers can buy mailing lists containing names of nearly any target group, customize offers to special wants and needs, and then use individualized communications to promote these offers. Direct marketers can also build a continuous relationship with each customer; time offers to reach prospects at the right moment, thereby receiving higher readership and response; and easily test alternative media and messages. Finally, direct marketers gain privacy because their offer and strategy are less visible to competitors.

Various trends have led to the rapid growth of direct marketing. Market 'demassification' has produced a constantly increasing number of market niches with specific preferences. Direct marketing enables sellers to focus efficiently on these minimarkets with offers that better match particular consumer wants and needs. Other trends encouraging at-home shopping include higher costs of driving, traffic congestion, parking headaches, lack of time, a shortage of retail sales help and long lines at checkouts. Consumers like the convenience of direct marketers' freephone numbers, their acceptance of orders round the clock and their commitment to customer service. The growth of quick delivery via express carriers has also made direct shopping fast and easy. The increased affordability of computers and customer databases has allowed direct marketers to single out the best prospects for each of their products. Finally in business-to-business marketing, lower cost-per-contact media have proven more cost-effective in reaching and selling to more prospects and customers than if a sales force were used.

We also looked at the ways companies use databases in direct marketing. A *customer database* is an organized collection of comprehensive data about individual customers or prospects, including geographic, demographic, psychographic and behavioural data. Companies use databases to identify prospects, form relationships with target customers and deepen customer loyalty, decide which customers should receive a particular offer and reactivate customer purchases.

Next we addressed the main forms of direct marketing including *face-to-face selling, direct-mail marketing, catalogue marketing, telemarketing, direct-response television marketing* and *on-line marketing*. Most companies today continue to rely heavily on *face-to-face selling* through a professional sales force, or they hire manufactures' representatives and agents. *Direct-mail marketing* consists of the company sending an offer, announcement, reminder or other item to a person at a specific address. Recently, three new forms of mail delivery have become popular – *fax mail, e-mail* and *voice mail*. Some marketers rely on *catalogue marketing*, or selling through catalogues mailed to a select list of customers or made available in stores. *Telemarketing* consists of using the telephone to sell directly to consumers. *Direct-response television marketing* has two forms: (1) *direct-response advertising* or *infomericials* and (2) *home-shopping channels*. *Online marketing* involves online channels and electronic commerce, and is usually conducted through interactive online computer systems, which electronically link consumers with sellers.

We examined the two types of online marketing channel – *commercial online services* and the *Internet* – and explained the effect of the Internet on electronic commerce. *Commercial online services* provide online information and marketing services to subscribers for a monthly fee. The *Internet* is a vast global and public web of computer networks. In contrast to commercial online services, use of the Internet is free – anyone with a PC, a modem and the right software can 'surf' the Internet to obtain or share information on almost any subject and to interact with other users.

The explosion of Internet usage has created a new world of *electronic commerce*, a term that refers to the buying and selling process that is supported by electronic means. In this process, *electronic markets* become 'marketspaces' in which sellers offer products and services electronically, while cyberbuyers search for information, identify their wants and needs, and then place orders using a credit card or other form of electronic payment.

The growth in online marketing can be appreciated when we examine the benefits of Internet technology. For consumers, online marketing is beneficial for many reasons. It is *interactive* and *immediate*, and provides access to an abundance of comparative *information* about products, companies and competitors. Marketers also benefit from online marketing. For them, it helps *consumer relationship building*, *reduces costs*, *increases efficiency*, provides more *flexibility*, and is, in the form of the Internet, a *global* medium that enables buyers and sellers in different countries to interact with each other in seconds. Marketers can conduct online marketing by creating an electronic storefront, placing ads online, participating in Internet forums, newsgroups or 'Web communities, or using online e-mail or Webcasting.

Finally, there is growing pressure on direct marketers to address a variety of public policy and ethical issues. Direct marketers and their customers have typically forged mutually rewarding relationships. However, there remains a potential for customer abuse, ranging from irritation and unfair practices to deception and fraud. In addition, there have been growing concerns about invasion of privacy, perhaps the most difficult public policy issue currently facing the direct marketing industry.

Key Terms

Catalogue marketing 960
Commercial online services 964
Corporate Web site 971
Customer database 954
Direct marketing 950
Direct-mail marketing 957

Direct-response television marketing (DRTV) 962
Electronic commerce 966
Integrated direct marketing 976
Internet (the Net) 952
Marketing Web site 971

Online advertising 972
Online marketing 964
Telemarketing 961
Webcasting 975
World Wide Web (WWW or the Web) 965

Discussing the Issues

1. Name a record or book club that has successfully marketed its products by mail. Why do so few record labels or publishers sell their offerings by mail themselves? How might mail-order clubs compete successfully against established retailers?

2. Make a list of products or services that you have purchased via direct marketing channels. What were the factors that influenced your decision to buy direct? If these products or services could also be purchased from a reseller or retail outlet, would the buying experience be different? How?

3. Identify some organizations that have used direct-response television advertising to promote their offering. What types of response are typically sought by the advertisers? What are some of the key issues concerning response handling that users of DRTV must consider to ensure an effective outcome for the campaign?

4. Take a retailer that offers a loyalty scheme such as club membership and a storecard for registered members. Through the scheme, the retailer manages to develop a vast consumer database to help direct its marketing activities. Discuss how the consumer database might be used to develop an effective marketing strategy.

5. Consider the example of Virgin Radio online. How might online marketing enable Virgin to attract more listeners and visitors to its radio stations on- and offline?

6. What do you understand by 'integrated direct marketing'? Suggest ways in which the concept enables the following to reach target customers effectively and create satisfying relationships: a grocery retailer; a mail-order company; an educational institution; a charity; a pharmaceuticals company.

Applying the Concepts

1. Collect as many catalogues as you can that you have received in the mail recently.

   ● Sort them by type of product category. Is there some pattern to the types of direct marketer that are targeting you?

   ● Where do you think the catalogue companies got your name?

   ● How would you think a company that was selling your name and address to a direct marketer would describe your buying habits?

2. Watch a satellite or cable television shopping channel or tune into a television shopping show. Where feasible, you might surf the Internet and 'tour' a specialist retailer's site. Or you might sample Virgin's radio station by clicking on icons, accessing features such as playlists and DJ biographies.

   ● How are the TV shows attempting to reach target buyers? Do they mix product lines (e.g. fine china with sports equipment) or do they target more carefully?

   ● How do online communications attempt to reach target buyers?

   ● What are the main differences in the way the TV shopping channels and Internet retailers attempt to evoke a response from target consumers?

References

1. Quotes from Gary McWilliams, 'Whirlwind on the Web', *Business Week* (7 April 1997), pp. 132–6; Bill Robbins and Cathie Hargett, 'Dell Internet sales top $1 million a day', press release, Dell Computer Corporation (4 March 1997). See also 'Dell PC sales via Internet doubling', Reuters Ltd (18 June 1997); Eryn Brown, 'Could the very best PC maker be Dell Computer?', *Fortune* (14 April 1997), pp. 26–7; 'Michael Dell's plan for the rest of the decade', *Fortune* (9 June 1997), p. 138; Andrew E. Serwer, 'The hottest stock of the '90s', *Fortune* (8 September 1997), p. 16.

2. 'Hi ho, hi ho, down the data mine we go', *The Economist* (23 August 1997), pp. 55–6.

3. Zenith Media, 'Satellite watch', *Marketing Week* (5 April 1996), p. 16; John Shannon, 'Building brands on the Internet', *Marketing Week* (3 May 1996), p. 22.

4. Louise Kehoe and Nick Denton, 'Accidental advertising campaigns', *Financial Times* (17 October 1997), p. 12.

5. James Champy, 'The cyber-future is now', *Sales and Marketing Management* (September 1997), p. 28.

6. David Reed, 'Write to reply', *Marketing Week* (13 December 1996), pp. 35–8.

7. See Don Peppers and Martha Rogers, *The One-to-Future* (New York: Doubleday/Currency, 1993).

8. Tom Peters, *Thriving on Chaos* (New York: Knopf, 1987).

9. Alena Hola, 'Can the EC deliver postal harmony?', *Marketing Business* (February 1994), pp. 24–8.

10. Richard Berry, 'Doorstepping', *Marketing Business* (November 1992), pp. 43–5.

11. Tony Coad, 'Distinguishing marks', *Marketing Business* (October 1992), pp. 12–14.

12. Ian Harding, 'Trois Suisses change the image of mail-order', *The European* (2–8 December 1994), p. 28.

13. Richard L. Benchin, 'Telefocus: telemarketing gets synergized', *Sales and Marketing Management* (February 1992), pp. 49–57.

14. 'Telemarketing cited as chief form of direct marketing', *Marketing News* (1 January 1996), p. 1.

15. Burnside, 'Calling the shots', *Marketing* (25 January 1990),

p. 40; Anne Massey, 'Ring my bell', *Marketing Business* (June 1992), pp. 35–9; Kevin R. Hopkins, 'Dialing into the future', *Business Week* (28 July 1997), p. 90.

16. See Michael Steven, *The Handbook of Telemarketing* (London: Kogan Page, 1992); Martin Everett, 'Selling by telephone', *Sales and Marketing Management* (December 1993), pp. 75–9; John F. Yarbrough, 'Dialing for dollars', *Sales and Marketing Management* (January 1997), pp. 61–7.

17. See Martin Croft, 'Right to reply', *Marketing Week* (12 April 1996), pp. 37–42; Paul Gander, 'Tele vision', *Marketing Week* (23 August 1996), pp. 29–34; David Reed, 'Double vision', *Marketing Week* (17 April 1997), pp. 59–62.

18. See Frank Rose, 'The end of TV as we know it', *Fortune* (23 December 1996), pp. 58–68; Elizabeth Lesly and Robert D. Hof, 'Is digital convergence for real?', *Business Week* (23 June 1997), pp. 42–3; Torin Douglas, 'A case of sofa not so good', *Marketing Week* (30 September 1994), p. 17; David Short, 'QVC loses out in UK screen test', *The European* (9–15 September 1994), p. 21; Miroslav Cerovic, 'Sofa so good for home shopping', *Marketing Week* (16 August 1996), p. 24; Hale Richards, 'Europe turns on to TV shopping', *The European* (2–8 January 1997), p. 19.

19. See Michael H. Martin, 'What's online: how to get on the Net without AOL', *Fortune* (14 April 1997), p. 174; Catherine Arnst and Peter Elstrom, 'CompuServe: too little, too late?', *Business Week* (19 May 1997), p. 118G.

20. For more on the basics of using the Internet, see Raymond D. Frost and Judy Strauss, *The Internet: A new marketing tool* (Upper Saddle River, NJ: Prentice Hall, 1997).

21. Richenda Wilson, 'Security alarm', *Marketing Week* (26 January 1996), pp. 49–53; Amy Cortese, 'Census in cyberspace', *Business Week* (5 May 1997), p. 84. For the most recent statistics, check the results of an ongoing survey of Internet usage conducted by CommerceNet and Nielsen Media Research, ww.commerce.net/nielsen/. See also Edith Coron, 'Le web: Jospin orders the French to log on', *The European* (26 January–1 February 1998), p. 22.

22. See John Deighton, 'The future of interactive marketing', *Harvard Business Review* (November–December 1996), pp. 151–62; Philip Kotler, Gary Armstrong, Peggy H. Cunningham and Robert Warren, *Principles of Marketing*, 3rd Canadian edn (Scarborough, Ontario: Prentice Hall Canada, 1996), p. 525.

23. 'But in the physical world', *The Economist* (1 November 1997), p. 100.

24. 'Virgin starts Europe's first live on-line radio', *Marketing Week* (15 March 1996), p. 15.

25. 'The once and future mall', *The Economist* (1 November 1997), pp. 92, 97; 'Startling increase' in Internet shopping reported in *New CommerceNet/Nielsen Media Research Survey*, CommerceNet press release, www.commerce.net/nielsen/press-97.html (12 March 1997).

26. Amy Cortese, 'A census in cyberspace', op. cit., p. 84; James Champy, 'The cyber-future is now', *Sales and Marketing Management* (September 1997), p. 28.

27. Yovovich, 'Girls in cyberspace', *Marketing News* (8

December 1997), pp. 8, 12; Paul M. Eng, 'Cibergiants see the future and it's Jack and Jill', *Business Week* (14 April 1997), p. 44.

28. See Rebecca Piirto Heath, 'The frontiers of psychographics', *American Demographics* (July 1996), pp. 38–43.

29. Kotler, Armstrong, Cunningham and Warren, op. cit., pp. 526–7.

30. Deighton, op. cit., pp. 151–62.

31. Ibid., p. 154.

32. See Kathy Rebello, 'Making money on the Net', *Business Week* (23 September 1996), pp. 104–18.

33. Deighton, op. cit., p. 154.

34. See Frank Harrison, 'Net performs to a limited public', *Marketing Week* (14 February 1997), p. 32; Roger Baird, 'Microsoft invests in multimedia future', *Marketing Week* (12 July 1996), pp. 14–15; Nzong Xiong, 'Web advertising beyond banners', *The New York Times* (28 July 1997), p. D6.

35. Robert D. Hof, 'Internet communities', *Business Week* (5 May 1997), pp. 64–80.

36. Malcolm Laws, 'How firms miss out on the Internet', *The European* (7–13 December 1995), p. 19.

37. Hof, op. cit., p. 66.

38. Amy Cortese, 'It's called Webcasting, and it promises to deliver the info you want, straight to your PC', *Business Week* (24 February 1997), pp. 95–104; Mary J. Cronin, 'Using the Web to push key data to decision makers', *Fortune* (29 September 1997), p. 254.

39. Cortes, 'It's called Webcasting', p. 98. See also Hoag Levins, 'Growing impact of e-mail', *Editor and Publisher* (1 March 1997), pp. 26–7.

40. Kathy Rebello, 'Making money on the Net', pp. 104–18.

41. Deighton, op. cit., p. 156; CNN Headline News (9 June 1997).

42. Ibid., p. 158. See also Wilson, 'Security alarm'.

43. See Ira Teinowitz, 'Internet privacy concerns addressed', *Advertising Age* (16 June 1997), p. 6; Teinowitz, 'Net privacy debate spurs self-regulation', *Advertising Age* (9 June 1997), p. 36.

44. See Ernan Roman, *Integrated Direct Marketing* (New York: McGraw-Hill, 1988), p. 108; Mark Suchecki, 'Integrated marketing: making it pay', *Direct* (October 1993), p. 43.

45. Gary Evans, 'Valentine boom for Flying Flowers', *Financial Times* (15 February 1994), p. 22; *Air Miles Members' Newsletter*, Air Miles Travel Promotions Ltd (Winter 1995); Ian Harding, 'Trois Suisses change the image of mail order', *The European* (2–8 December 1994), p. 28.

46. Parts of this section are based on Terrence H. Witkowski, 'Self-regulation will suppress direct marketing's downside', *Marketing News* (24 April 1989), p. 4. See also Katie Muldoon, 'The industry must rebuild its image', *Direct* (April 1995), p. 106.

47. 'Hi ho, hi ho, down the data mine we go', op. cit.; John Hagel III and Jeffrey F. Rayport, 'The coming battle for customer information', *Harvard Business Review* (January–February 1997), pp. 53–65.

Case 22

Virgin Direct – Personal Financial Services

Dr Susan Bridgewater[*]

The Virgin Brand

You bought the record, you drank the cola, you took the aeroplane to New York. Richard Branson's Virgin empire is more than a casual assortment of consumer goods; in marketing terms, it is a whole way of life. But Branson's baby boomers are about to grow up. With all the pre-publicity of a Hollywood film premiere, Virgin is set to enter its least glamorous market: the personal equity plan.[1]

Ask any member of the Virgin Direct team why Richard Branson was interested in the financial services market and you will get the answer 'If an industry needs "sorting out", Richard Branson is interested in doing so.' The brand image of good service, good value for money and challenging the status quo has led Richard Branson's Virgin Group to diversify into a variety of seemingly unrelated sectors. If the customers' needs could be met better, then there is a challenge for the Virgin brand. In the words of Jayne-Anne Gadhia, operations director of Virgin Direct:

> The Virgin brand is about taking on the rest of the industry. It is a brand with personality. Richard Branson is seen by the public as a customers' champion, who is allowed to question how to do things better and differently.

Virgin Direct

In March 1995, the Virgin Group set up a joint venture with Norwich Union to enter the financial services market using the telephone as its distribution method. On entry into the market, Virgin stated its aims:

> to advertise itself as the friendly face in a world of financial cowboys. The combination of easy-to-understand products and low initial charges will soon be applied to pensions and life insurance, where public faith has been shaken by accusations of mis-selling and over-charging.[2]

The Virgin Personal Equity Plan (PEP) was Richard Branson's attempt to attract new customers into a market that he felt to be overcomplicated. With its initial product, Virgin made innovative use of index tracking, a technique of investment which shadows the performance of the All Share stock market index, rather than using fund managers who pick and choose the companies in which they invest. At the time of its launch this was the lowest-priced PEP, with no entry and exit charges.[3] By July 1997, Virgin Direct managed

* Warwick Business School, Coventry, UK.

over £1 billion on behalf of its 200,000 customers and the Virgin Growth PEP had established itself as the UK's most popular PEP. Virgin's entry into this market forced established firms to review their charges and brought a number of other non-financial services firms into the 'no-frills' sector.

Building on its early success, in June 1996 Virgin launched life insurance, health and critical illness plans and, on 1 November 1996, entered the pensions market. The introduction of these new, more complex financial products was a significant step. Virgin's PEP products were initially sold on an execution-only basis; customers made their own decisions about the suitability of the product based on the information provided. With a core product range in place, Virgin Direct introduced a service to advise customers about the best financial choices for their own particular circumstances. Although it is early days to judge the success of the move into life insurance and pensions, Virgin received 6,000 phone calls a day during the launch of its pensions and has over twice the industry conversion rate from interest into purchase.

Communication

Virgin Direct's target market can be broadly described as aged 35+, ABC1 adults. The company has a wide appeal and, while viewed as a young brand, has been particularly successful in attracting the older age groups. The opportunity created by an often ill-served customer cuts right across the demographic groups.

The managing director of Virgin Direct, Rowan Gormley, regards traditional financial services as product-oriented. They are concerned with creating clever products that are expensive and ineffective in meeting customers' needs. Virgin Direct's approach to financial services is that of a virtuous circle. Identify a genuine customer need, then design products which meet that need, offered by a company that can be trusted. In this way the maxim that financial services must be sold, because they are not voluntarily bought, can be broken.

Contact with the customer is direct, via the telephone. Use of high-tech alternatives, such as modems, was felt to exclude a proportion of the market that Virgin wished to reach. Virgin Direct has two main communication rules. The first is about what is said. Everything must be about the customer or for the customer. Statements of fact should be used, not claims. The second is about the way things are said: clear and straightforward, not patronizing, witty, surprising and different. Television has played a key role in communicating the Virgin message; however, a major challenge is that the target audience are light viewers of television. Therefore the thrust of advertising has been through poster campaigns and in the national press. Messages include: 'Beware of the charges of the light fingered brigade' and 'Choose the wrong pension and you might be condemned to an extra eighteen months of hard labour.'

Part of Virgin Direct's strategy is to put customers firmly in control by giving them information they need. If a customer rings to ask about PEPs, an information pack will be sent with a simplified application form, which has already been filled in with as many details as possible to reduce the time required to complete it. A follow-up call will check that the pack has arrived, but the customer will never be chased to return an application. This is part of Virgin's 'no pester promise' – a response to the hard-sell tactics traditionally associated with the industry. In its simplicity and clarity, Virgin Direct literature differs markedly from the complex financial formulae usually found and is one of the major tools in showing Virgin's different approach to the business.

The Call Centre

The Call Centre is where the customers come into contact with the 'Virgin Experience'. The systems are designed to be user friendly and to offer quick quotes to customers. Every contact with the customer is important and is carefully thought through. When the caller gives his or her postcode, a database is called forward which provides details of any previous transactions with the firm. Virgin undertakes not to supply this database to anyone else.

It is quite usual in life insurance to have to go through several stages of form filling before a quote can be given. At this stage, the customer has already invested significant time and effort, but might eventually discover that he or she cannot be insured. Should the customer need to claim, the definitions of what is covered are so vague that it might take a long time to establish whether he or she is eligible. So, for life and health insurance, Virgin Direct has introduced an expert system which allows the telephone operator to fill in the answers to a series of basic questions. In the majority of cases, this will result in an immediate quotation, although if there are some pre-existing medical conditions, this may be provisional pending a medical examination. Here again, Virgin has taken an innovative approach. Rather than telling the customer to go away, have a medical and then begin the process again, Virgin has a 'nurse on a motorbike'. If a medical is necessary, a date can be agreed there and then with the customer, and someone will come to him or her to carry it out.

The real challenge for Virgin Direct lies in its success. On television advertising evenings, the Call Centre is organized to have the maximum number of telephone operators available to handle calls. Communication activity aims to achieve the right volume of calls. The business has already grown to take over the entire building in which it is based. Maintaining the informality of communication, cross-functional teams and service excellence of operators may be a challenge as numbers increase further.

QUESTIONS

1. What advantages does Virgin's direct marketing approach to financial services offer customers of PEPs, life insurance and pensions?
2. Identify the factors that influence the success of its direct marketing operation.
3. Critically assess the role that communications play in building and sustaining the Virgin brand name in financial services.
4. Evaluate Virgin's ability to compete against retail banks.
5. What are the major challenges facing Virgin Direct?
6. Recommend a strategy for Virgin Direct, showing how it will enable the company to sustain a differential advantage in an increasingly competitive market.

REFERENCES

1. Richard Wolffe, 'Weekend money: putting the pop into PEPs', *Financial Times* (11 February 1995), p. 1.
2. Tony Wood, Virgin Direct marketing director, quoted in ibid., p. 1.
3. 'Midweek money: Branson competes on price – Bond Peps/Smart Money', *Financial Times* (4 October 1995).

Freixenet *Cava*: bubbles down a new way

*Roberto Alvarez del Blanco and Jeff Rapaport**

THE SPANISH COMPANY FREIXENET IS the world's largest producer and exporter of *cava* (sparkling wines). In September 1985, management needed to decide a new distribution strategy for the US market. There was much concern and uncertainty regarding the decision. Freixenet had enjoyed spectacular growth from 1983 to 1985 and the management questioned the wisdom of implementing far-reaching changes so soon.

The Freixenet management team had two main responsibilities for the US market. These were the distribution system, and the development of strategies to market and advertise the brand. International wine and liquor producers that export to the American market typically choose one company, usually in New York, as a national importer. This distribution company buys the goods from the international supplier and then sells to a network of wholesalers located in each state or territory. The margin typically charged by these importers was 15 per cent of the US-landed price. Under this system, a brand manager employed by the import company usually heads the marketing of brands. He or she is responsible for the annual advertising and promotional budget allocated by the brand owner and the supplier.

The Company

Freixenet, SA is a family-run business located at Sant Sadurni d'Anoia in the Region del Cava (the sparkling wine region), about 35 kilometres south-east of Barcelona in Catalonia, Spain. Freixenet's annual sales in 1985 were about Pta17,100 million, 28 per cent of which are from exports. Freixenet's products sold in 40 countries; it had commercial branches in the United Kingdom, Germany and the United States, and production facilities in Spain, Mexico and California.

The Product

Cava-type sparkling wine is produced by the *méthode champenoise*, where the second stage of the fermentation process occurs in the original bottle. Only

* University of California Berkeley Haas School of Business, USA.

sparkling wines produced by the *méthode champenoise* in the Champagne region of France could bear the name 'champagne'. Wines produced outside the region can only use *méthode champenoise* on their label. However, a decision by the EU forbade the use of this description and established a transitional period of eight years.

Another method of producing sparkling wines is the *granvas* method (sometimes called the *cuve-close* method), in which the second stage of fermentation is in large tanks instead of the original bottle. It is faster and less expensive than the *champenoise* method, but yields a lower-quality wine. Freixenet produces five *cavas*: Carta Nevada, Cordon Negro, Brut Nature, Brut Barroco and Brut Rose. Each *cava* has a distinctive quality resulting from its production process.

Expanding Internationally

At the end of World War II, Freixenet began significant international expansion. José Ferrer, president and general manager, travelled to various European countries searching for opportunities to sell his products. Fellow *cava* producers did not share his eagerness for international expansion. José Ferrer remembered: 'One day, at a *cava* producers' meeting, a colleague … stated, "This business of exports is a joke. What you like is to travel. Forget this business – outside of Spain you won't sell a single bottle."'

The country initially targeted for export was the United Kingdom because of its high champagne consumption and need to import due to its lack of vineyards and local brands. Unfortunately, Freixenet met with difficulties resulting from a British bias towards French products and the poor image of Spanish products. José Ferrer explained:

> We believed it necessary to join forces with a British company to distribute our products because no one wanted to buy from a Spanish distributor. After two years, the British company became tired of losing money and was replaced by two other associates who also became tired of the business. At this point we took over the whole operation.

The new British company was named Direct Wine Supply. Freixenet's hopes for the British market were overinflated. In 1984 the Freixenet group sold only about 45,000 cases of its product in the United Kingdom (25,000 Freixenet and the remainder Freixenet's Castellblanch brand). These results were poor considering the eight years of work invested in developing the brand. José Ferrer further explained:

> Direct Wine Supply was essentially a deadweight. We should have dropped them, but we haven't done it yet because we believe that in the end it will work out when we implement a more dynamic and creative management team instead of the conservative one which we had for eight years. If this doesn't work, we might sell the company to some of the 'admirers' who recognize our success domestically and internationally. If we do this, we can recoup the £200,000 to £300,000 that we have already invested.

The first phase of international expansion lasted over 30 years, during which Direct Wine Supply (DWS) began to export to several European countries. In the United States, Freixenet hired a representative in New Jersey to import products and market them nationally. This distribution system, which employs only one import representative for the whole country, followed the system that Freixenet used in Europe.

The second phase of international expansion began during the early 1980s with the establishment of two commercial branches, one in the United States and the other in Germany. Freixenet's exports to the United States had grown slowly during the 1960s and early 1970s. Management realized that one representative located on the east coast could not adequately cover the whole country because of diverse regional markets. In 1978 the company decided to hire a wine consultant to help the representative establish distribution to untapped states and to increase sales in states where distribution was already established. In 1980 the contract with this representative expired. Instead of renewing it, Freixenet opened a US branch in New Jersey called Freixenet USA, Inc. The new national distribution system emphasized decentralization by assigning roughly one import-distributor to each state. This structure allowed the company to establish a significantly more active presence in each market by having a more concentrated market focus through each distributor. Freixenet USA provided marketing support for these importer-distributors. Ramon Masia, the export manager of the Freixenet group of companies, described the work of Freixenet USA:

> The office helps the importer-distributors by solving problems related to advertising, shipments and internal logistics. It provides support for advertising in four ways. First, it negotiates national advertising contracts. Second, it co-ordinates these advertising campaigns with regional distributors. Third, it manages all of the co-operative advertising that Freixenet USA uses with direct distributors. Fourth, it develops point-of-sale materials. The office also manages stock between distributors and does follow-up work for Freixenet, SA.

Twelve Americans currently work in the subsidiary. The annual cost of running this office, including personnel and regional agents' salaries, is approximately $600,000. This amount does not include advertising and promotional expenses.

The third phase of international expansion began with setting up two production facilities: one in Mexico and one in the United States. The first bottles produced in Mexico would be available for sale in 1986. The operation included about 50 hectares of vineyards and a production plant with a 1 million bottle capacity. The total investment was Pta500 million. This facility supplied the Mexican and Latin American market. The rationale for this investment in Mexico was that the Mexican market had been closed to foreign sparkling wines for more than 20 years.

The American production facility, Freixenet Sonoma Champagne Caves, opened at the beginning of 1985. This facility was in the Carneros area of Napa Valley, just north of San Francisco. It consisted of 180 acres considered to have the best vineyards and had a 1 million bottle capacity. Completed in 1986, it required an initial investment of $6 million. The wine produced here would be a Californian *cava*, named Gloria Ferrer, in honour of José Ferrer's wife.

Export manager, Ramon Masia, headed the international Freixenet branch. He supervised the export managers of Castellblanch and Segura Viudas, as well as the managers for the US, German and British DWS commercial branches. The Mexican and US facilities were not under his management.

Establishing Joint Ventures and Subcontracting

Freixenet wished to explore new ways of expanding its business through joint-venture and subcontracting opportunities. It also bought two businesses from the well-known Spanish company Rumasa, which included an immediately available idle production facility in Sant Sadurni d'Anoia. Freixenet used this plant to produce wine for an American company that owned the Paul Cheneau brand. José Ferrer described this subcontracting operation:

> They began to entrust its production to Freixenet, but they soon told us that they liked neither our product nor our price and they looked for other subcontractors. After a while, they came back to Freixenet under the same conditions.

In 1984 Freixenet was contacted by Domecq, a large Spanish producer of wines and brandies, which had 19 sales representatives and distributors in the United States. Domecq's sales force sold well-known Spanish and Mexican brands of wine and liqueurs. They soon discovered that they needed more products to sell and hoped to form a joint venture with Freixenet. The two companies created a new French brand name, 'Lembey', and equally shared marketing expenses and profits. Freixenet produced this *cava* in Sant Sadurni. The brand had a successful start in the United States and was forecast to achieve a sales volume of over 80,000 cases in 1985. José Ferrer commented on the joint ventures:

> The experience with 'Paul Cheneau' demonstrated the dangers of subcontracting. In a market with established surplus capacity, the subcontractor is totally at the mercy of his client, who can constantly pressure him on prices. On the other hand, with a brand joint venture, the first-year promotional expenses correspond to the second-year price discount involved in subcontracting. The difference is that in a joint venture you own 50 per cent of the brand and if business has been good, this investment will have gained in value.

International Market for Sparkling Wines

In 1984 the world production of sparkling wines was about 120 million cases, an increase of 16.8 per cent from 1979. The main producers were France (25 per cent), Germany (17 per cent), USSR (17 per cent), Italy (13 per cent) and Spain (8 per cent). These six countries controlled 91 per cent of the total world production and the latter four countries showed a large increase in their production compared to 1979. The top sparkling-wine exporting countries were France with 13 million cases a year, Italy with 10 million and Spain with 2.9 million. The top importing countries were the United States with 7 million cases a year, Germany with 6.8 million and the United Kingdom with 2 million. The industrialized production methods (the 'cuve-close' and 'transfer' methods) accounted for most of the total production.

Germany's market was the largest with 28 million cases sold per year, followed by the United States with 17 million cases, France with 16 million cases and the USSR with 15 million cases. Germany also led with a per capita consumption of 5.5 bottles per year, followed by the United States' 3.7, France's 2.3 and the USSR's 1.7.

The US Market for Sparkling Wines

The United States is one of the main world producers, consumers and importers of sparkling wines. Although per capita consumption is not high, it shows regular and rapid increases, especially in the large urban areas of California, the East Coast and Texas. Between 1978 and 1982, annual per capita consumption increased from 1.75 to 2.69 bottles in the District of Columbia and from 1.31 to 1.77 in California. Between 1975 and 1984, consumption of sparkling wine increased from 7.1 million to almost 16.3 million cases. The top ten states accounted for almost three-quarters of the total consumption in the United States.

Sales by month reveal an interesting pattern. October was the top month in 1984, with 18.2 per cent of the year's sales. November and December had more than 12.0 per cent and May registered 10.1 per cent. February was the lowest sales month of the year with only 4.2 per cent. This data pattern shows a strong seasonality that is typical for this industry.

The US sparkling wine market had four price segments. American preference is clearly for wines costing less than $4. Spanish and Italian wines dominated the $4–9 segment; Italian and Californian dominated the $9–15 segment and French champagnes dominated the over $15 segment. The first two segments, those costing less than $9, represented 86 per cent of market share.

American sales of sparkling wine increased noticeably between 1979 and 1984. Italian sparkling wines, especially Asti Spumante, took first place for imports in 1984 with 50.1 per cent of total sparkling wines. French champagnes followed with 24.5 per cent and Spanish *cavas* with 21.9 per cent. Total imported brands with the highest sales in 1984 were Freixenet, Tosti and Martini & Rossi.

Freixenet Marketing in the United States

Starting in 1973, Freixenet's sales to the United States grew explosively. From 1980 onwards, Freixenet's average sales increased by over 50 per cent per year. For 1985, the US market represented more than 70 per cent of Freixenet's exports. This figure included the sale of Freixenet brands and joint ventures, Paul Cheneau and Lembey.

Five types of distributor operated in the American market: nation-wide importers; regional importers; 'brokers' or brand-representatives; wholesale distributors; and retailers. Retail trade has three categories; retailers that specialize in wines and liquors; supermarkets and small retail shops; and 'clubs' patronized by wine connoisseurs. Two large distribution channels handled Freixenet's products in the United States. Approximately 75 per cent of sales were to supermarkets and liquor stores, known as 'off premises'. The other 25 per cent of sales were to restaurants, bars and hotels, known as 'on premises'.

According to a Freixenet executive, advertising was one of the principal components of Freixenet USA's marketing strategy. For 1985, Freixenet budgeted $4 million to promote its products to the American market and $1 million for the remainder of the export markets. Of the $4 million that would be invested in the United States, $1 million was for television commercials in the 12 main regional markets, $2 million for national magazine advertisements, $500,000 for co-operative advertising (the same amount being invested by the importers-distributors), $300,000 for public relations, $100,000 for a gigantic blimp that travels throughout the country, and $100,000 for the yearly importers' convention.

Other imported sparkling wines had smaller budgets. Among these, the most popular French champagne sold in the United States is Moët et Chandon, which had a $1 million budget for public relations involving social events and benefit projects and a $1 million budget for print and television advertising.

A key reason for success in the United States was the design of the Freixenet bottle. Ramon Masia explained:

> We did marketing research on Cordon Negro, the most popular sparkling wine sold in the US. The research indicated that Cordon Negro's black bottle exerts an immediate attraction for people. Americans perceive it as an indicator of high prestige and since it sells for only $6, they see it as a great bargain. Since the word 'Freixenet' is difficult to pronounce, Americans ask for it by asking for the black bottle.

The president of Freixenet USA, Inc., Bill Kroesing, summarized some of the most important factors regarding the company's strategy:

> The success achieved in the US is due to the bottle, the promotion, the distribution system and the proper quality/price relationship. Regarding the latter factor, Freixenet has filled the void left by the French and the American producers.

Ramon Masia added:

> We realized that there were four markets for *cava* in the US. The first market is for a sparkling wine with low quality and price, the second is for an average wine, the third is for a wine with high quality and price, and the fourth is the super-high-quality market. American producers who, like Gallo, produce a low-quality *granvas* wine, supply the low-price national segment. The higher-price segment is controlled by California producers and the highest-quality segment by French champagnes. There was no participant positioned for the middle segment and this is where we entered with Carta Nevada and Cordon Negro and we now dominate this segment of the market.

Low labour and material costs allowed the Spanish producers to be more price competitive than the French, Italians and Californians. The price of 1 kg of grapes in the *cava* region was Pta25–30. In contrast, 1 kg of grapes in the Champagne region costs Ffr23 (there are about 25pta to Ffr1). In the United States, the prices of French champagnes fluctuated between $15 and $20, prices of Spanish *cavas* between $4 and $5 a bottle and the Cordon Negro between $6 and $7 a bottle. Both use 750 ml bottles. The American tariffs on Spanish *cava* imports were 15–20 per cent of the landed-price, varying from state to state. Of the total cost of Freixenet products, 60 per cent consisted of raw materials, labour and production. The remaining 40 per cent covered administration and marketing activities. Freixenet was not content with the budget's allocation.

Management felt that they were not getting a good return for their advertising dollar. Armando Gavidia, the vice-president for the north-east region of Freixenet USA, who had a big portion of the co-operative budget to invest, was not satisfied with the service he was getting from the advertising and public relations companies. He suggested to José Ferrer that Freixenet should create its own advertising and public relations company to service all the Freixenet brands in the US market. His reasoning was as follows:

> Our advertising and public relations budgets are small for the big advertising and PR companies, so they assign junior account executives to our accounts who do not know the wine market and business. They also have a high personnel turnover rate. Whenever one of these people gets familiar with our company and the wine business, he or she jumps to another company and we have to start from scratch again and again.
> If we hire a couple of advertising managers, we could create our own advertising 'shop'. The creative part will be handled by freelancers. The media buying will be performed by one of the well-known media buying services and then we will assign our own people to create and maintain our own database for public relations. In this way, we will get the proper return for the money we allocate. Our people will be more concerned with the small brands, like Segura Viudas, and they will ensure that they get the service and attention each deserves to maximize each brand's potential.

Entering the US High-Price Segment

Freixenet decided to launch the Gloria Ferrer brand in the US high-price segment. This positioned *cava* against the California producers. Even though the *cava* would not be available until 1986, Californian producers made a small amount that was sold in 1984. The Gloria Ferrer brand sold for $13–16 a bottle. José Ferrer explained the decision to produce a California *cava*:

> We expect that our distributors will be able to offer the whole range of products that the market requires and there is a large market for California *cava*. There are restaurants and bars that sell only California wines. This includes some California *cavas* which sell for higher prices than French *cavas* … We could have entered the lower-price (under $4) segment with Dubois, but we did not want to risk devaluing the image of Spanish champagne … We have set up our own vineyards and production facilities to promote and improve our image. This helps our sales efforts in the US. All of the prestigious wineries have their own vineyards in California … Furthermore, producing in California protects us from any increases in the American import restrictions from the EU.

Gloria Ferrer was sold through the same importers who distributed the *cava* brought from Spain. These distributors sold a wide range of products and some had separate sales forces to sell to 'off premises' and 'on premises' locations.

The New Distribution System

In September 1985, Freixenet USA needed to set up a new US distribution system. The new proposed structure employed no national 'agent', 'broker' or brand-assigned nominee. Freixenet would retain all rights of administrative co-ordination, marketing and advertising. This system also extended certain responsibilities to the primary US importers. These importers would be not only distributors, but also Freixenet's representatives in their respective marketing areas.

This new import-distribution system aimed to eliminate the 'national importer' and create one wholesaler per state, acting as the direct importer, brand representative and wholesaler for his or her territory. The Freixenet USA office would assist the national network of direct importers by sending their orders to Spain and communicating with the winery regarding shipments and transport problems.

The Freixenet USA office would also handle the national marketing budget for advertising and public relations and assist the local importers in developing their regional and local advertising and promotional campaigns. This system also established a co-operative advertising budget in which Freixenet USA would match each local importer's investment. Armando Gavidia explained:

> With this new distribution structure, Freixenet will get more involvement with the brand from the importers and they will create their own local advertising and promotions. This will motivate these managers to achieve better results. The beauty is that this co-operative investment programme will not cost Freixenet any extra money because it will be funded by the 15 per cent profit margin that would have been paid to the national importer.

A new contract had an explicit description of the Freixenet primary importers' obligations and rights. If implemented, each primary importer would sign this contract. Under the terms of the contract, the importers had a number of obligations:

1. The primary importer must have current licences to service its assigned territories.

2. The primary importer must solicit and distribute all brands throughout assigned territories.

3. The primary importer must order sufficient stock of all basic items to ensure adequate inventory to service expected demand for a minimum of 90 days.

4. Cheques must be sent with each order.

5. The primary importer must give Freixenet immediate notice of its selection of wholesaler distributor(s). Importers must also notify Freixenet of any sales made by a distributor to wholesalers or retailers located outside the importer's assigned territory.

6. The primary importer must provide Freixenet with monthly depletion reports.

7. The primary importer must perform operational supervision of the distributor(s), including personal visits as necessary.

8. The primary importer must agree always to apply 'its very best' efforts on an equal basis to all of Freixenet SA's brands.

9. The primary importer must co-ordinate marketing and promotional programmes with the Freixenet USA Marketing Office and advertising with Freixenet's Advertising Agency.

10. The 'basic six' Freixenet sparkling wines must be inventoried and offered for sale by all distributors.

11. The primary importers' advertising and marketing must be in reasonable conformity with Freixenet's international and national programme and trademark protection interests. Product segmentation is an important part of this – this is why Carta Nevadas is available in two bottle sizes.

12. At least every six months, the primary importer must provide a copy of its posting or price list and that of the distributor(s) for Freixenet brands to Freixenet USA and to all regional vice-presidents.

13. Primary importers must not provide false or misleading information to Freixenet or the regional vice presidents. Freixenet must receive 60 days' notice of the planned or actual sale of the primary importer's company.

According to its proponents, this strategy would eliminate a layer of management and reduce costs significantly. With the savings, Freixenet would offer a 'managerial service performance allowance' to reimburse each importer as a brand representative and to pay for brand-management costs incurred by each importer/marketing representative.

Proponents of the new distribution system expected it to be well received by the national wholesale network. They believed that, with this system, all importers would feel more involved with the brand than in the past. They would appreciate the allocation of the marketing budget according to their local market needs. The proponents believed that the importers would consider Freixenet's strategy a big improvement on the other brands' systems that used national importers. This was largely because the national brand managers in New York never really understood the local needs of each market. This was the key reason that proponents expected everyone in the network to be pleased with this new strategic distribution design.

Proponents also hoped to have a National Importer Convention in Lanzarote, Spain in May 1986, and planned a special recognition ceremony for the following achievements: no. 1 importer of the year, best promotion of the year, best local advertising of the year, and best on-premises promotion of the year (promotions related to restaurants and bars). During this convention, each importer would present and explain his or her accomplishments and results to the rest of the network. It would give each importer the chance to share different strategies and policies that were effective in different markets. Another important objective was to create a 'family' feeling among the distribution network members. Armando Gavidia explained:

> I expect that most of our distributors will become friends with each other and also will develop a very positive attitude towards the brand. This will create many positive feelings and generate loyalty to the company. This will help our future growth and increase the speed for expanding our market share in the USA.

However, critics of the plan had serious misgivings:

1. Freixenet did not currently have enough managers with adequate experience to implement the system.
2. The financial risk would be significantly greater because the company would have to ship to 50 different companies in the United States and the risk involved would be very difficult to assess.
3. The money that would be saved by eliminating the importers would be spent in the organization of Freixenet USA.
4. The new system would not be well received by the wholesalers, which are used to the 'old boy' network.
5. If the implementation of the new distribution strategy failed, it could permanently damage the US marketing operation.

QUESTIONS

1. Contrast Freixenet's entry into the US and UK markets.
2. What went wrong in the UK market?
3. Identify the different sorts of distribution and relationship that Freixenet used in the US market.
4. What are the advantages of each?
5. Is it wise for Freixenet to change its distribution system? What is the case for and against the existing and proposed distribution systems?
6. How do Freixenet's relationship and controls change with the move from the existing to the proposed system?

Glossary

Accessibility   The degree to which a market segment can be reached and served.

Actionability   The degree to which effective programmes can be designed for attracting and serving a given market segment.

Actual product   A product's parts, quality level, features, design, brand name, packaging and other attributes that combine to deliver core product benefits.

Adapted marketing mix   An international marketing strategy for adjusting the marketing-mix elements to each international target market, bearing more costs but hoping for a larger market share and return.

Administered VMS   A vertical marketing system that co-ordinates successive stages of production and distribution, not through common ownership or contractual ties, but through the size and power of one of the parties.

Adoption   The decision by an individual to become a regular user of the product.

Adoption process   The mental process through which an individual passes from first hearing about an innovation to final adoption.

Advertising   Any paid form of non-personal presentation and promotion of ideas, goods or services by an identified sponsor.

Advertising objective   A specific communication task to be accomplished with a specific target audience during a specific period of time.

Advertising specialities   Useful articles imprinted with an advertiser's name, given as gifts to consumers.

Affordable method   Setting the promotion budget at the level management thinks the company can afford.

Age and life-cycle segmentation   Dividing a market into different age and life-cycle groups.

Agent   A wholesaler who represents buyers or sellers on a relatively permanent basis, performs only a few functions, and does not take title to goods.

Allowance   (1) Reduction in price on damaged goods. (2) Promotional money paid by manufacturers to retailers in return for an agreement to feature the manufacturer's product in some way.

Alternative evaluation   The stage of the buyer decision process in which the consumer uses information to evaluate alternative brands in the choice set.

Annual plan   A short-term plan that describes the company's current situation, its objectives, the strategy, action programme and budgets for the year ahead and controls.

Approach   The step in the selling process in which the salesperson meets and greets the buyer to get the relationship off to a good start.

Aspirational group   A group to which an individual wishes to belong.

Atmospheres   Designed environments that create or reinforce the buyer's leanings towards consumption of a product.

Attitude   A person's consistently favourable or unfavourable evaluations, feelings and tendencies towards an object or idea.

Augmented product   Additional consumer services and benefits built around the core and actual products.

Available market   The set of consumers who have interest, income and access to a particular product or service.

Balance sheet   A financial statement that shows assets, liabilities and net worth of a company at a given time.

Barter transaction   A marketing transaction in which goods or services are traded for other goods or services.

Basing-point pricing   A geographic pricing strategy in which the seller designates some city as a basing point and charges all customers the freight cost from that city to the customer location, regardless of the city from which the goods are actually shipped.

Behavioural segmentation   Dividing a market into groups based on consumer knowledge, attitude, use or response to a product.

Belief   A descriptive thought that a person holds about something.

Benchmarking   The process of comparing the company's products and processes to those of competitors or leading firms in other industries to find ways to improve quality and performance.

Benefit segmentation   Dividing the market into groups according to the different benefits that consumers seek from the product.

Brand   A name, term, sign, symbol or design, or a combination of these, intended to identify the goods or services of one seller or group of sellers and to differentiate them from those of competitors.

Brand equity   The value of a brand, based on the extent to which it has high brand loyalty, name awareness, perceived quality, strong brand associations, and other assets such as patents, trademarks and channel relationships.

Brand extension   Using a successful brand name to launch a new or modified product in a new category.

Brand image   The set of beliefs that consumers hold about a particular brand.

Break-even pricing (target profit pricing)   Setting price to break even on the costs of making and marketing a product; or setting price to make a target profit.

Broker   A wholesaler who does not take title to goods and whose function is to bring buyers and sellers together and assist in negotiation.

Business analysis   A review of the sales, costs and profit projections for a new product to find out whether these factors satisfy the company's objectives.

Business buying process   The decision-making process by which business buyers establish the need for purchased products and services, and identify, evaluate and choose among alternative brands and suppliers.

Business market All the organizations that buy goods and services to use in the production of other products and services, or for the purpose of reselling or renting them to others at a profit.

Business portfolio The collection of businesses and products that make up the company.

Buyer The person who makes an actual purchase.

Buyer-readiness stages The stages that consumers normally pass through on their way to purchase, including awareness, knowledge, liking, preference, conviction and purchase.

Buyers People in an organization's buying centre with formal authority to select the supplier and arrange terms of purchase.

Buying centre All the individuals and units that participate in the business buying-decision process.

By-products Items produced as a result of the main factory process, such as waste and reject items.

By-product pricing Setting a price for by-products in order to make the main product's price more competitive.

Capital items Industrial goods that partly enter the finished product, including installations and accessory equipment.

Captive-product pricing Setting a price for products that must be used along with a main product, such as blades for a razor and film for a camera.

Cash-and-carry retailers Large, 'no-frills' stores that sell an extensive assortment of goods, and are noted particularly for their bulk discounts.

Cash-and-carry wholesalers Wholesalers that stock a limited line of fast-moving goods – such as groceries, toys, household goods, clothes, electrical supplies and building materials – and that sell to small retailers and industrial firms for cash and normally do not provide a delivery service.

Cash cows Low-growth, high-share businesses or products; established and successful units that generate cash that the company uses to pay its bills and support other business units that need investment.

Cash discount A price reduction to buyers who pay their bills promptly.

Cash refund offers (rebates) Offers to refund part of the purchase price of a product to consumers who send a 'proof of purchase' to the manufacturer.

Catalogue marketing Direct marketing through catalogues that are mailed to a select list of customers or made available in stores.

Catalogue showroom A retail operation that sells a wide selection of high mark-up, fast-moving, brand-name goods at discount prices.

Category killers A modern 'breed' of exceptionally aggressive 'off-price' retailers that offer branded merchandise in clearly defined product categories at heavily discounted prices.

Causal research Marketing research to test hypotheses about cause-and-effect relationships.

Channel conflict Disagreement among marketing channel members on goals and roles – who should do what and for what rewards.

Channel level A layer of intermediaries that performs some work in bringing the product and its ownership closer to the final buyer.

Closed-end questions Questions that include all the possible answers and allow subjects to make choices among them.

Closing The step in the selling process in which the salesperson asks the customer for an order.

Co-branding The practice of using the established brand names of two different companies on the same product.

Cognitive dissonance Buyer discomfort caused by postpurchase conflict.

Commercial online services Companies that offer online information, entertainment, shopping and other marketing services to subscribers who pay the company a monthly fee. They make use of their own dedicated networks and operate their own computers which are connected to the Internet, thus offering somewhat better security than the Internet.

Commercialization Introducing a new product into the market.

Communication adaptation [to come]

Company and individual brand strategy A branding approach that focuses on the company name and individual brand name.

Comparison advertising (knocking copy) Advertising that compares one brand directly or indirectly to one or more other brands.

Competitions, sweepstakes, lotteries, games Promotional events that give consumers the chance to win something – such as cash, trips or goods – by luck or through extra effort.

Competitive advantage An advantage over competitors gained by offering consumers greater value, either through lower prices or by providing more benefits that justify higher prices.

Competitive-parity method Setting the promotion budget to match competitors' outlays.

Competitive strategies Strategies that strongly position the company against competitors and that give the company the strongest possible strategic advantage.

Competitor analysis The process of identifying key competitors; assessing their objectives, strategies, strengths and weaknesses, and reaction patterns; and selecting which competitors to attack or avoid.

Competitor-centred company A company whose moves are mainly based on competitors' actions and reactions; it spends most of its time tracking competitors' moves and market shares and trying to find strategies to counter them.

Complex buying behaviour Consumer buying behaviour in situations characterized by high consumer involvement in a purchase and significant perceived differences among brands.

Concentrated marketing A market-coverage strategy in which a firm goes after a large share of one or a few submarkets.

Concept testing Testing new product concepts with a group of target consumers to find out if the concepts have strong consumer appeal.

Confused positioning A positioning error that leaves consumers with a confused image of the company, its product or a brand.

Consumer buying behaviour The buying behaviour of final consumers – individuals and households who buy goods and services for personal consumption.

Consumer market All the individuals and households who buy or acquire goods and services for personal consumption.

Consumer-oriented marketing A principle of enlightened marketing which holds that a company should view and organize its marketing activities from the consumers' point of view.

Consumer product A product bought by final consumers for personal consumption.

Consumer promotion Sales promotion designed to stimulate consumer purchasing, including samples, coupons, rebates, prices-off, premiums, patronage rewards, displays, and contests and sweepstakes.

Consumer relationship-building promotions Sales promotions that promote the product's positioning and include a selling message along with the deal.

Consumerism An organized movement of citizens and government agencies to improve the rights and power of buyers in relation to sellers.

Continuity Scheduling ads evenly within a given period.

Contract manufacturing A joint venture in which a company contracts with manufacturers in a foreign market to produce the product.

Contractual VMS A vertical marketing system in which independent firms at different levels of production and distribution join together through contracts to obtain more economies or sales impact than they could achieve alone.

Convenience product A consumer product that the customer usually buys frequently, immediately, and with a minimum of comparison and buying effort.

Convenience store A small store located near a residential area that is open long hours seven days a week and carries a limited line of high-turnover convenience goods.

Conventional distribution channel A channel consisting of one or more independent producers, wholesalers and retailers, each a separate business seeking to maximize its own profits even at the expense of profits for the system as a whole.

Copy testing Measuring the communication effect of an advertisement before or after it is printed or broadcast.

Core product The problem-solving services or core benefits that consumers are really buying when they obtain a product.

Core strategy The 'hub' of marketing strategy. It has two parts: the identification of a group of customers for whom the firm has a differential advantage; and then positioning itself in that market.

Corner shop A small store, usually owned and managed by a person who lives in the local neighbourhood. It is

typically a grocery store, a convenience store or a confectioner-tobacconist-newsagent (CTN). It serves the immediate neighbourhood.

Corporate brand strategy A brand strategy whereby the firm makes its company name the dominant brand identity across all of its products.

Corporate licensing A form of licensing whereby a firm rents a corporate trademark or logo made famous in one product or service category and uses it in a related category.

Corporate VMS A vertical marketing system that combines successive stages of production and distribution under single ownership – channel leadership is established through common ownership.

Corporate Web site A site set up by a company on the Web, which carries information and other features designed to answer customer questions, build customer relationships and generate excitement about the company, rather than to sell the company's products or services directly. The site handles interactive communication initiated by the consumer.

Cost of goods sold The direct costs allocated to goods sold. These include variable cost items such as raw materials and labour used in making a product.

Cost-plus pricing Adding a standard mark-up to the cost of the product.

Countertrade International trade involving the direct or indirect exchange of goods for other goods instead of cash. Forms include barter compensation (buyback) and counterpurchase.

Coupons Certificates that give buyers a saving when they purchase a product.

Critical success factors The strengths and weaknesses that most critically affect an organization's success. These are measured relative to competition.

Cultural empathy An understanding of and true feeling for a culture.

Cultural environment Institutions and other forces that affect society's basic values, perceptions, preferences and behaviours.

Cultural universals Cultural characteristics and attributes that are found in a wide range of cultures: that is, features that transcend national cultures.

Culture The set of basic values, perceptions, wants and behaviours learned by a member of society from family and other important institutions.

Current marketing situation The section of a marketing plan that describes

the target market and the company's position in it.

Customer-centred company A company that focuses on customer developments in designing its marketing strategies and on delivering superior value to its target customers.

Customer database An organized collection of comprehensive data about individual customers or prospects, including geographic, demographic, psychographic and buying behaviour data.

Customer delivered value The difference between total customer value and total customer cost of a marketing offer – 'profit' to the customer.

Customer lifetime value The amount by which revenues from a given customer over time will exceed the company's costs of attracting, selling and servicing that customer.

Customer sales force structure A sales force organization under which salespeople specialize in selling only to certain customers or industries.

Customer satisfaction The extent to which a product's perceived performance matches a buyer's expectations. If the product's performance falls short of expectations, the buyer is dissatisfied. If performance matches or exceeds expectations, the buyer is satisfied or delighted.

Customer value The consumer's assessment of the product's overall capacity to satisfy his or her needs.

Customer value analysis Analysis conducted to determine what benefits target customers value and how they rate the relative value of various competitors' offers.

Customer value delivery system The system made up of the value chains of the company and its suppliers, distributors and ultimately customers, who work together to deliver value to customers.

Cycle The medium-term wavelike movement of sales resulting from changes in general economic and competitive activity.

Decider The person who ultimately makes a buying decision or any part of it – whether to buy, what to buy, how to buy, or where to buy.

Deciders People in the organization's buying centre who have formal or informal powers to select or approve the final suppliers.

Decision-and-reward system Formal and informal operating procedures that guide planning, targeting, compensation and other activities.

Decision-making unit (DMU)   All the individuals who participate in, and influence, the consumer buying-decision process.

Decline stage   The product life-cycle stage at which a product's sales decline.

Deficient products   Products that have neither immediate appeal nor long-term benefits.

Demand curve   A curve that shows the number of units the market will buy in a given time period, at different prices that might be charged.

Demands   Human wants that are backed by buying power.

Demarketing   Marketing to reduce demand temporarily or permanently – the aim is not to destroy demand, but only to reduce or shift it.

Demographic segmentation   Dividing the market into groups based on demographic variables such as age, sex, family size, family life cycle, income, occupation, education, religion, race and nationality.

Demography   The study of human populations in terms of size, density, location, age, sex, race, occupation and other statistics.

Department store   A retail organization that carries a wide variety of product lines – typically clothing, home furnishings and household goods; each line is operated as a separate department managed by specialist buyers or merchandisers.

Derived demand   Business demand that ultimately comes from (derives from) the demand for consumer goods.

Descriptive research   Marketing research to better describe marketing problems, situations or markets, such as the market potential for a product or the demographics and attitudes of consumers.

Desirable products   Products that give both high immediate satisfaction and high long-run benefits.

Differential advantage   A sustainable internal or external strength that an organization has over its competitors.

Differentiated marketing   A market-coverage strategy in which a firm decides to target several market segments and designs separate offers for each.

Direct investment   Entering a foreign market by developing foreign-based assembly or manufacturing facilities.

Direct-mail marketing   Direct marketing through single mailings that include letters, ads, samples, fold-outs and other

'salespeople on wings' sent to prospects on mailing lists.

Direct marketing   Marketing through various advertising media that interact directly with consumers, generally calling for the consumer to make a direct response.

Direct-marketing channel   A marketing channel that has no intermediary levels.

Direct-response television marketing (DRTV)   The marketing of products or services via television commercials and programmes which involve a responsive element, typically the use of a freephone number that allows consumers to phone for more information or to place an order for the goods advertised.

Discount   A straight reduction in price on purchases during a stated period of time.

Discount store   A retail institution that sells standard merchandise at lower prices by accepting lower margins and selling at higher volume.

Dissonance-reducing buying behaviour   Consumer buying behaviour in situations characterized by high involvement but few perceived differences among brands.

Distribution centre   A large, highly automated warehouse designed to receive goods from various plants and suppliers, take orders, fill them efficiently, and deliver goods to customers as quickly as possible.

Distribution channel (marketing channel)   A set of interdependent organizations involved in the process of making a product or service available for use or consumption by the consumer or industrial user.

Diversification   A strategy for company growth by starting up or acquiring businesses outside the company's current products and markets.

Dogs   Low-growth, low-share businesses and products that may generate enough cash to maintain themselves, but do not promise to be large sources of cash.

Door-to-door retailing   Selling door to door, office to office, or at home-sales parties.

Durable product   A consumer product that is usually used over an extended period of time and that normally survives many uses.

Economic environment   Factors that affect consumer buying power and spending patterns.

Electronic commerce   A general term for a buying and selling process that is supported by electronic means.

Embargo   A ban on the import of a certain product.

Emotional appeals   Message appeals that attempt to stir up negative or positive emotions that will motivate purchase; examples are fear, guilt, shame, love, humour, pride and joy appeals.

Emotional selling proposition (ESP)   A non-functional attribute that has unique associations for consumers.

Engel's laws   Differences noted over a century ago by Ernst Engel in how people shift their spending across food, housing, transportation, health care, and other goods and services categories as family income rises.

Enlightened marketing   A marketing philosophy holding that a company's marketing should support the best long-run performance of the marketing system; its five principles are consumer-oriented marketing, innovative marketing, value marketing, sense-of-mission marketing and societal marketing.

Environmental management perspective   A management perspective in which the firm takes aggressive actions to affect the publics and forces in its marketing environment rather than simply watching it and reacting to it.

Environmentalism   An organized movement of concerned citizens and government agencies to protect and improve people's living environment.

Events   Occurrences staged to communicate messages to target audiences; examples are news conferences and grand openings.

Exchange   The act of obtaining a desired object from someone by offering something in return.

Exchange controls   Government limits on the amount of its country's foreign exchange with other countries and on its exchange rate against other currencies.

Exclusive distribution   Giving a limited number of dealers the exclusive right to distribute the company's products in their territories.

Experience curve (learning curve)   The drop in the average per-unit production cost that comes with accumulated production experience.

Experimental research   The gathering of primary data by selecting matched groups of subjects, giving them different treatments, controlling related factors and checking for differences in group responses.

Exploratory research   Marketing research to gather preliminary information that will help better to define problems and suggest hypotheses.

Export department A form of international marketing organization that comprises a sales manager and a few assistants whose job is to organize the shipping out of the company's goods to foreign markets.

Exporting Entering a foreign market by sending products and selling them through international marketing intermediaries (indirect exporting) or through the company's own department, branch, or sales representatives or agents (direct exporting).

External audit A detailed examination of the markets, competition, business and economic environment in which the organization operates.

Fads Fashions that enter quickly, are adopted with great zeal, peak early and decline very fast.

Family life cycle The stages through which families might pass as they mature over time.

Fashion A currently accepted or popular style in a given field.

Financial intermediaries Banks, credit companies, insurance companies and other businesses that help finance transactions or insure against the risks associated with the buying and selling of goods.

Fixed costs Costs that do not vary with production or sales level.

FOB-origin pricing A geographic pricing strategy in which goods are placed free on board a carrier; the customer pays the freight from the factory to the destination.

Focus group A small sample of typical consumers under the direction of a group leader who elicits their reaction to a stimulus such as an ad or product concept.

Follow-up The last step in the selling process, in which the salesperson follows up after the sale to ensure customer satisfaction and repeat business.

Forecasting The art of estimating future demand by anticipating what buyers are likely to do under a given set of conditions.

Fragmented industry An industry characterized by many opportunities to create competitive advantages, but each advantage is small.

Franchise A contractual association between a manufacturer, wholesaler or service organization (a franchiser) and independent businesspeople (franchisees) who buy the right to own and operate one or more units in the franchise system.

Franchise organization A contractual vertical marketing system in which a channel member, called a franchiser, links several stages in the production-distribution process.

Freight-absorption pricing A geographic pricing strategy in which the company absorbs all or part of the actual freight charges in order to get the business.

Frequency The number of times the average person in the target market is exposed to an advertising message during a given period.

Full-service retailers Retailers that provide a full range of services to shoppers.

Full-service wholesalers Wholesalers that provide a full set of services such as carrying stock, using a sales force, offering credit, making deliveries and providing management assistance.

Functional discount (trade discount) A price reduction offered by the seller to trade channel members that perform certain functions, such as selling, storing and record keeping.

Gatekeepers People in the organization's buying centre who control the flow of information to others.

Gender segmentation Dividing a market into different groups based on sex.

General need description The stage in the business buying process in which the company describes the general characteristics and quantity of a needed item.

Geodemographics The study of the relationship between geographical location and demographics.

Geographic segmentation Dividing a market into different geographical units such as nations, states, regions, counties, cities or neighbourhoods.

Geographical pricing Pricing based on where customers are located.

Global firm A firm that, by operating in more than one country, gains R & D, production, marketing and financial advantages in its costs and reputation that are not available to purely domestic competitors.

Global industry An industry in which the strategic positions of competitors in given geographic or national markets are affected by their overall global positions.

Global marketing Marketing that is concerned with integrating or standardizing marketing actions across different geographic markets.

Global organization A form of international organization whereby top corporate management and staff plan worldwide manufacturing or operational facilities, marketing policies, financial flows and logistical systems. The global operating unit reports directly to the chief executive, not to an international divisional head.

Going-rate pricing Setting price based largely on following competitors' prices rather than on company costs or demand.

Government market Governmental units – national and local – that purchase or rent goods and services for carrying out the main functions of government.

Gross margin The difference between the direct cost of products and what they are sold for.

Gross sales The total amount charged to customers over a period.

Growth-share matrix A portfolio-planning method that evaluates a company's strategic business units (SBUs) in terms of their market growth rate and relative market share. SBUs are classified as stars, cash cows, question marks or dogs.

Growth stage The product life-cycle stage at which a product's sales start climbing quickly.

Habitual buying behaviour Consumer buying behaviour in situations characterized by low consumer involvement and few significant perceived brand differences.

Handling objections The step in the selling process in which the salesperson seeks out, clarifies and overcomes customer objections to buying.

Horizontal marketing systems A channel arrangement in which two or more companies at one level join together to follow a new marketing opportunity.

Human need A state of felt deprivation.

Human want The form that a human need takes as shaped by culture and individual personality.

Hybrid marketing channels Multichannel distribution, as when a single firms sets up two or more marketing channels to reach one or more customer segments. A variety of direct and indirect approaches are used to deliver the firm's goods to its customers.

Hypermarkets Huge stores that combine supermarket, discount and warehouse retailing; in addition to food, they carry furniture, appliances, clothing and many other products.

Idea generation The systematic search for new-product ideas.

Idea screening Screening new-product ideas in order to spot good ideas and drop poor ones as soon as possible.

Implausible positioning Making claims that stretch the perception of the buyers too far to be believed.

Income segmentation Dividing a market into different income groups.

Individual marketing Tailoring products and marketing programmes to the needs and preferences of individual customers.

Industrial product A product bought by individuals and organizations for further processing or for use in conducting a business.

Industry A group of firms which offer a product or class of products that are close substitutes for each other. The set of all sellers of a product or service.

Inelastic demand Total demand for a product that is not much affected by price changes, especially in the short run.

Influencer A person whose views or advice carries some weight in making a final buying decision; they often help define specifications and also provide information for evaluating alternatives.

Influencers [to come]

Information search The stage of the buyer decision process in which the consumer is aroused to search for more information; the consumer may simply have heightened attention or may go into active information search.

Informative advertising Advertising used to inform consumers about a new product or feature and to build primary demand.

Initiator The person who first suggests or thinks of the idea of buying a particular product or service.

Innovation An idea, product or technology that has been developed and marketed to customers who perceive it as novel or new. It is a process of identifying, creating and delivering new-product service values that did not exist before in the marketplace.

Innovative marketing A principle of enlightened marketing which requires that a company seek real product and marketing improvements.

Institutional market Schools, hospitals, nursing homes, prisons and other institutions that provide goods and services to people in their care.

Integrated direct marketing Direct marketing campaigns that use multiple vehicles and multiple stages to improve response rates and profits.

Integrated logistics management A physical distribution concept that recognizes the need for a firm to integrate its logistics system with those of its suppliers and customers. The aim is to maximize the performance of the entire distribution system.

Integrated marketing communications The concept under which a company carefully integrates and co-ordinates its many communications channels to deliver a clear, consistent, and compelling message about the organization and its products.

Intensive distribution Stocking the product in as many outlets as possible.

Interactive marketing Marketing by a service firm that recognizes that perceived service quality depends heavily on the quality of buyer-seller interaction.

Intermediaries Distribution channel firms that help the company find customers or make sales to them, including wholesalers and retailers that buy and resell goods.

Internal audit An evaluation of the firm's entire value chain.

Internal marketing Marketing by a service firm to train and effectively motivate its customer-contact employees and all the supporting service people to work as a team to provide customer satisfaction.

Internal records information Information gathered from sources within the company to evaluate marketing performances and to detect marketing problems and opportunities.

International division A form of international marketing organization in which the division handles all of the firm's international activities. Marketing, manufacturing, research, planning and specialist staff are organized into operating units according to geography or product groups, or as an international subsidiary responsible for its own sales and profitability.

International market Buyers in other countries, including consumers, producers, resellers and governments.

Internet (the Net) A vast global computer network that enables computers, with the right software and a modem (a telecommunications device that sends data across telephone lines), to be linked together so that their users can obtain or share information and interact with other users.

Introduction stage The product life-cycle stage when the new product is first distributed and made available for purchase.

Invention A new technology or product that may or may not deliver benefits to customers.

Joint ownership A joint venture in which a company joins investors in a foreign market to create a local business in which the company shares joint ownership and control.

Joint venturing Entering foreign markets by joining with foreign companies to produce or market a product or service.

Key account managers Managers whose primary responsibility is to orchestrate the company's relationship with a major customer or prospective customer in order to achieve lasting and mutually beneficial exchange between the two parties.

Leading indicators Time series that change in the same direction but in advance of company sales.

Learning Changes in an individual's behaviour arising from experience.

Licensed brand A product or service using a brand name offered by the brand owner to the licensee for an agreed fee or royalty.

Licensing A method of entering a foreign market in which the company enters into an agreement with a licensee in the foreign market, offering the right to use a manufacturing process, trademark, patent, trade secret or other item of value for a fee or royalty.

Life-cycle segmentation Offering products or marketing approaches that recognize the consumer's changing needs at different stages of their life.

Lifestyle A person's pattern of living as expressed in his or her activities, interests and opinions.

Limited-service retailers Retailers that provide only a limited number of services to shoppers.

Limited-service wholesalers Those who offer only limited services to their suppliers and customers.

Line extension Using a successful brand name to introduce additional items in a given product category under the same brand name, such as new flavours, forms, colours, added ingredients or package sizes.

Long-range plan A plan that describes the principal factors and forces affecting the organization during the next several years, including long-term objectives, the chief marketing strategies used to attain them and the resources required.

Macroenvironment The larger societal forces that affect the whole microenvironment – demographic, economic, natural, technological, political and cultural forces.

Management contracting A joint venture in which the domestic firm supplies the management know-how to a foreign company that supplies the capital; the domestic firm exports management services rather than products.

Manufacturer's brand (national brand) A brand created and owned by the producer of a product or service.

Market The set of all actual and potential buyers of a product or service.

Market-build-up method A method used mainly by business products firms to estimate the market potential of a city, region or country based on determining all the potential buyers in the market and estimating their potential purchases.

Market-centred company A company that pays balanced attention to both customers and competitors in designing its marketing strategies.

Market challenger A runner-up firm in an industry that is fighting hard to increase its market share.

Market development A strategy for company growth by identifying and developing new segments and markets for current company products.

Market-factor index method A method used mainly by consumer products firms to estimate the market potential for consumer products.

Market follower A runner-up firm in an industry that wants to hold its share without rocking the boat.

Market leader The firm in an industry with the largest market share; it usually leads other firms in price changes, new product introductions, distribution coverage and promotion spending.

Market nicher A firm in an industry that serves small segments that the other firms overlook or ignore.

Market penetration A strategy for increasing sales of current products to current market segments. This is achieved by winning over competitors' customers, acquiring a competitor and/or increasing product usage rate.

Market-penetration pricing Setting a low price for a new product in order to attract large numbers of buyers and a large market share.

Market positioning Arranging for a product to occupy a clear, distinctive and desirable place relative to competing products in the minds of target consumers. Formulating competitive positioning for a product and a detailed marketing mix.

Market segment A group of consumers who respond in a similar way to a given set of marketing stimuli.

Market segmentation Dividing a market into distinct groups of buyers with different needs, characteristics or behaviour, who might require separate products or marketing mixes.

Market-skimming pricing Setting a high price for a new product to skim maximum revenues layer by layer from the segments willing to pay the high price; the company makes fewer but more profitable sales.

Market targeting The process of evaluating each market segment's attractiveness and selecting one or more segments to enter.

Marketing A social and managerial process by which individuals and groups obtain what they need and want through creating and exchanging products and value with others.

Marketing audit A comprehensive, systematic, independent and periodic examination of a company's environment, objectives, strategies and activities to determine problem areas and opportunities, and to recommend a plan of action to improve the company's marketing performance.

Marketing budget A section of the marketing plan that shows projected revenues, costs and profits.

Marketing concept The marketing management philosophy which holds that achieving organizational goals depends on determining the needs and wants of target markets and delivering the desired satisfactions more effectively and efficiently than competitors do.

Marketing control The process of measuring and evaluating the results of marketing strategies and plans, and taking corrective action to ensure that marketing objectives are attained.

Marketing database An organized set of data about individual customers or prospects that can be used to generate and qualify customer leads, sell products and services, and maintain customer relationships.

Marketing environment The actors and forces outside marketing that affect marketing management's ability to

develop and maintain successful transactions with its target customers.

Marketing implementation The process that turns marketing strategies and plans into marketing actions in order to accomplish strategic marketing objectives.

Marketing information system (MIS) People, equipment and procedures to gather, sort, analyze, evaluate and distribute needed, timely and accurate information to marketing decision makers.

Marketing intelligence Everyday information about developments in the marketing environment that helps managers prepare and adjust marketing plans.

Marketing intermediaries Firms that help the company to promote, sell and distribute its goods to final buyers; they include physical distribution firms, marketing-service agencies and financial intermediaries.

Marketing management The analysis, planning, implementation and control of programmes designed to create, build and maintain beneficial exchanges with target buyers for the purpose of achieving organizational objectives.

Marketing mix The set of controllable tactical marketing tools – product, price, place and promotion – that the firm blends to produce the response it wants in the target market.

Marketing process The process of (1) analyzing marketing opportunities; (2) selecting target markets; (3) developing the marketing mix; and (4) managing the marketing effort.

Marketing research The function that links the consumer, customer and public to the marketer through information – information used to identify and define marketing opportunities and problems; to generate, refine and evaluate marketing actions; to monitor marketing performance; and to improve understanding of the marketing process.

Marketing services agencies Marketing research firms, advertising agencies, media firms, marketing consulting firms and other service providers that help a company to target and promote its products to the right markets.

Marketing strategy The marketing logic by which the business unit hopes to achieve its marketing objectives.

Marketing strategy statement A statement of the planned strategy for a new product that outlines the intended target market, the planned product positioning, and the sales, market share and profit goals for the first few years.

Marketing Web site   A site on the Web created by a company to interact with consumers for the purpose of moving them closer to a purchase or other marketing outcome. The site is designed to handle interactive communication initiated by the company.

Mark-up/mark-down   The difference between selling price and cost as a percentage of selling price or cost.

Mass customization   Preparing individually designed products and communication on a large scale.

Mass marketing   Using almost the same product, promotion and distribution for all consumers.

Materials and parts   Industrial products that enter the manufacturer's product completely; including raw materials and manufactured materials and parts.

Maturity stage   The stage in the product life cycle where sales growth slows or levels off.

Measurability   The degree to which the size, purchasing power and profits of a market segment can be measured.

Media   Non-personal communications channels including print media (newspapers, magazines, direct mail); broadcast media (radio, television); and display media (billboards, signs, posters).

Media impact   The qualitative value of an exposure through a given medium.

Media vehicles   Specific media within each general media type, such as specific magazines, television shows or radio programmes.

Membership groups   Groups that have a direct influence on a person's behaviour and to which a person belongs.

Merchant wholesalers   Independently owned businesses that take title to the merchandise they handle.

Message source   The company, the brand name, the salesperson of the brand, or the actor in the ad who endorses the product.

Microenvironment   The forces close to the company that affect its ability to serve its customers – the company, market channel firms, customer markets, competitors and publics.

Micromarketing   A form of target marketing in which companies tailor their marketing programmes to the needs and wants of narrowly defined geographic, demographic, psychographic or behavioural segments.

Mission statement   A statement of the organization's purpose – what it wants to accomplish in the wider environment.

Modified rebuy   A business buying situation in which the buyer wants to modify product specifications, prices, terms or suppliers.

Monetary transaction   A marketing transaction in which goods or services are exchanged for money.

Monopolistic competition   A market in which many buyers and sellers trade over a range of prices rather than a single market price.

Moral appeals   Message appeals that are directed to the audience's sense of what is right and proper.

Motive (drive)   A need that is sufficiently pressing to direct the person to seek satisfaction of the need.

Multibrand strategy   A strategy under which a seller develops two or more brands in the same product category.

Multiple niching   Adopting a strategy of having several independent offerings that appeal to several different subsegments of customer.

Natural environment   Natural resources that are needed as inputs by marketers or that are affected by marketing activities.

Need recognition   The first stage of the buyer decision process in which the consumer recognizes a problem or need.

Net profit   The difference between the income from goods sold and all expenses incurred.

New product   A good, service or idea that is perceived by some potential customers as new.

New-product development   The development of original products, product improvements, product modifications and new brands through the firm's own R & D efforts.

New task   A business buying situation in which the buyer purchases a product or service for the first time.

Niche marketing   Adapting a company's offerings to more closely match the needs of one or more subsegments where there is often little competition.

Non-durable product   A consumer product that is normally consumed in one or a few uses.

Non-personal communication channels   Media that carry messages without personal contact or feedback, including media, atmospheres and events.

Non-tariff trade barriers   Non-monetary barriers to foreign products, such as

biases against a foreign company's bids or product standards that go against a foreign company's product features.

Objective-and-task method   Developing the promotion budget by (1) defining specific objectives; (2) determining the tasks that must be performed to achieve these objectives; and (3) estimating the costs of performing these tasks. The sum of these costs is the proposed promotion budget.

Observational research   The gathering of primary data by observing relevant people, actions and situations.

Occasion segmentation   Dividing the market into groups according to occasions when buyers get the idea to buy, actually make their purchase, or use the purchased item.

Oligopolistic competition   A market in which there are a few sellers that are highly sensitive to each other's pricing and marketing strategies.

Online advertising   Placing advertisements on the Internet in special sections offered by commercial online services, as banner ads that pop up while computer subscribers are surfing online services or Web sites, or in Internet news groups that have been set up for commercial purposes.

Online marketing   A form of direct marketing conducted through interactive on-line computer services, which provide two-way systems that link consumers with sellers electronically.

Open-end questions   Questions that allow respondents to answer in their own words.

Operating control   Checking on-going performance against annual plans and taking corrective action.

Operating statement (profit-and-loss statement or income statement)   A financial statement that shows company sales, cost of goods sold and expenses during a given period of time.

Opinion leaders   People within a reference group who, because of special skills, knowledge, personality or other characteristics, exert influence on others.

Optional-product pricing   The pricing of optional or accessory products along with a main product.

Order-routine specification   The stage of the business buying process in which the buyer writes the final order with the chosen suppliers(s), listing the technical specifications, quantity needed, expected time of delivery, return policies and warranties.

Overpositioning A positioning error referring to too narrow a picture of the company, its product or a brand being communicated to target customers.

Packaging The activities of designing and producing the container or wrapper for a product.

Packaging concept What the package should be or do for the product.

Patronage rewards Cash or other awards for the regular use of a certain company's products or services.

Penetrated market The set of consumers who have already bought a particular product or service.

Percentage-of-sales method Setting the promotion budget at a certain percentage of current or forecast sales or as a percentage of the sales price.

Perception The process by which people select, organize and interpret information to form a meaningful picture of the world.

Perceptual maps A product positioning tool that uses multidimensional scaling of consumers' perceptions and preferences to portray the psychological distance between products and segments.

Performance review The stage of the business buying process in which the buyer rates its satisfaction with suppliers, deciding whether to continue, modify or drop them.

Personal communication channels Channels through which two or more people communicate directly with each other, including face to face, person to audience, over the telephone, or through the mail.

Personal influence The effect of statements made by one person on another's attitude or probability of purchase.

Personal selling Oral presentation in a conversation with one or more prospective purchasers for the purpose of making sales.

Personality A person's distinguishing psychological characteristics that lead to relatively consistent and lasting responses to his or her own environment.

Persuasive advertising Advertising used to build selective demand for a brand by persuading consumers that it offers the best quality for their money.

Physical distribution (marketing logistics) The tasks involved in planning, implementing and controlling the physical flow of materials and final goods from points of origin to points of use to meet the needs of customers at a profit.

Physical distribution firms Warehouse, transportation and other firms that help a company to stock and move goods from their points of origin to their destinations.

Place All the company activities that make the product or service available to target customers.

Planned obsolescence A strategy of causing products to become obsolete before they actually need replacement.

Pleasing products Products that give high immediate satisfaction, but may hurt consumers in the long run.

Point-of-purchase (POP) promotions Displays and demonstrations that take place at the point of purchase or sale.

Political environment Laws, government agencies and pressure groups that influence and limit various organizations and individuals in a given society.

Portfolio analysis A tool by which management identifies and evaluates the various businesses that make up the company.

Postpurchase behaviour The stage of the buyer decision process in which consumers take further action after purchase based on their satisfaction or dissatisfaction.

Potential market The set of consumers who profess some level of interest in a particular product or service.

Preapproach The step in the selling process in which the salesperson learns as much as possible about a prospective customer before making a sales call.

Premiums Goods offered either free or at low cost as an incentive to buy a product.

Presentation The step in the selling process in which the salesperson tells the product 'story' to the buyer, showing how the product will make or save money for the buyer.

Price The amount of money charged for a product or service, or the sum of the values that consumers exchange for the benefits of having or using the product or service.

Price elasticity A measure of the sensitivity of demand to changes in price.

Price packs Reduced prices that are marked by the producer directly on the label or package.

Primary data Information collected for the specific purpose at hand.

Primary demand The level of total demand for all brands of a given product or service – for example, the total demand for motor cycles.

Private brand (middleman, distributor or store brand) A brand created and owned by a reseller of a product or service.

Problem recognition The first stage of the business buying process in which someone in the company recognizes a problem or need that can be met by acquiring a good or a service.

Product Anything that can be offered to a market for attention, acquisition, use or consumption that might satisfy a want or need. It includes physical objects, services, persons, places, organizations and ideas.

Product adaptation Adapting a product to meet local conditions or wants in foreign markets.

Product-bundle pricing Combining several products and offering the bundle at a reduced price.

Product concept The idea that consumers will favour products that offer the most quality, performance and features, and that the organization should therefore devote its energy to making continuous product improvements.

Product development A strategy for company growth by offering modified or new products to current market segments. Developing the product concept into a physical product in order to ensure that the product idea can be turned into a workable product.

Product idea An idea for a possible product that the company can see itself offering to the market.

Product image The way consumers perceive an actual or potential product.

Product innovation charter (PIC) A new-product strategy statement formalizing management's reasons or rationale behind the firm's search for innovation opportunities, the product/market and technology to focus upon, and the goals and objectives to be achieved.

Product invention Creating new products or services for foreign markets.

Product life cycle (PLC) The course of a product's sales and profits over its lifetime. It involves five distinct stages: product development, introduction, growth, maturity and decline.

Product line A group of products that are closely related because they function in a similar manner, are sold to the same customer groups, are marketed through the same types of outlet, or fall within given price ranges.

Product line filling Increasing the product line by adding more items within the present range of the line.

Product line pricing Setting the price steps between various products in a product line based on cost differences between the products, customer evaluations of different features, and competitors' prices.

Product line stretching Increasing the product line by lengthening it beyond its current range.

Product mix (product assortment) The set of all product lines and items that a particular seller offers for sale to buyers.

Product position The way the product is defined by consumers on important attributes – the place the product occupies in consumers' minds relative to competing products.

Product quality The ability of a product to perform its functions; it includes the product's overall durability, reliability, precision, ease of operation and repair, and other valued attributes.

Product sales force structure A sales force organization under which salespeople specialize in selling only a portion of the company's products or lines.

Product specification The stage of the business buying process in which the buying organization decides on and specifies the best technical product characteristics for a needed item.

Product-support services Services that augment actual products.

Production concept The philosophy that consumers will favour products that are available and highly affordable, and that management should therefore focus on improving production and distribution efficiency.

Promotion Activities that communicate the product or service and its merits to target customers and persuade them to buy.

Promotion mix The specific mix of advertising, personal selling, sales promotion and public relations that a company uses to pursue its advertising and marketing objectives.

Promotional allowance A payment or price reduction to reward dealers for participating in advertising and sales-support programmes.

Promotional pricing Temporarily pricing products below the list price, and sometimes even below cost, to increase short-run sales.

Proposal solicitation The stage of the business buying process in which the buyer invites qualified suppliers to submit proposals.

Prospecting The step in the selling process in which the salesperson identifies qualified potential customers.

Psychographic segmentation Dividing a market into different groups based on social class, lifestyle or personality characteristics.

Psychographics The technique of measuring lifestyles and developing lifestyle classifications; it involves measuring the chief AIO dimensions (activities, interests, opinions).

Psychological pricing A pricing approach that considers the psychology of prices and not simply the economics; the price is used to say something about the product.

Public Any group that has an actual or potential interest in or impact on an organization's ability to achieve its objectives.

Public relations Building good relations with the company's various publics by obtaining favourable publicity, building up a good 'corporate image', and handling or heading off unfavourable rumours, stories and events. Major PR tools include press relations, product publicity, corporate communications, lobbying and counselling.

Publicity Activities to promote a company or its products by planting news about it in media not paid for by the sponsor.

Pull strategy A promotion strategy that calls for spending a lot on advertising and consumer promotion to build up consumer demand. If the strategy is successful, consumers will ask their retailers for the product, the retailers will ask the wholesalers, and the wholesalers will ask the producers.

Pulsing Scheduling ads unevenly, in bursts, over a certain time period.

Purchase decision The stage of the buyer decision process in which the consumer actually buys the product.

Pure competition A market in which many buyers and sellers trade in a uniform commodity – no single buyer or seller has much effect on the going market price.

Pure monopoly A market in which there is a single seller – it may be a government monopoly, a private regulated monopoly or a private non-regulated monopoly.

Push strategy A promotion strategy that calls for using the sales force and trade promotion to push the product through channels. The producer promotes the product to wholesalers, the wholesalers promote to retailers, and the retailers promote to consumers.

Qualified available market The set of consumers who have interest, income, access and qualifications for a particular product or service.

Qualitative research Exploratory research used to uncover consumers' motivations, attitudes and behaviour. Focus-group interviewing, elicitation interviews and repertory grid techniques are typical methods used in this type of research.

Quality The totality of features and characteristics of a product or service that bear on its ability to satisfy stated or implied needs.

Quantitative research Research which involves data collection by mail or personal interviews from a sufficient volume of customers to allow statistical analysis.

Quantity discount A price reduction to buyers who buy large volumes.

Quantity premium A surcharge paid by buyers who purchase high volumes of a product.

Question marks Low-share business units in high-growth markets that require a lot of cash in order to hold their share or become stars.

Quota A limit on the amount of goods that an importing country will accept in certain product categories; it is designed to conserve on foreign exchange and to protect local industry and employment.

Range branding strategy A brand strategy whereby the firm develops separate product range names for different families of product.

Rational appeals Message appeals that relate to the audience's self-interest and show that the product will produce the claimed benefits; examples are appeals of product quality, economy, value or performance.

Reach The percentage of people in the target market exposed to an ad campaign during a given period.

Reference groups Groups that have a direct (face-to-face) or indirect influence on the person's attitudes or behaviour.

Reference prices Prices that buyers carry in their minds and refer to when they look at a given product.

Relationship marketing The process of creating, maintaining and enhancing strong, value-laden relationships with customers and other stakeholders.

Reminder advertising Advertising used to keep consumers thinking about a product.

Resellers The individuals and organizations that buy goods and services to resell at a profit.

Retailer co-operatives Contractual vertical marketing systems in which retailers organize a new, jointly owned business to carry on wholesaling and possibly production.

Retailers Businesses whose sales come primarily from retailing.

Retailing All activities involved in selling goods or services directly to final consumers for their personal, non-business use.

Retailing accordion A phenomenon describing how the width of retailers' product assortment or operations shifts over time: there tends to be a general-specific-general cycle. However, it is possible that many retailing businesses evolve along a specific- general-specific cycle.

Role The activities a person is expected to perform according to the people around him or her.

Sales force management The analysis, planning, implementation and control of sales force activities. It includes setting sales force objectives; designing sales force strategy; and recruiting, selecting, training, supervising and evaluating the firm's salespeople.

Sales force promotion Sales promotion designed to motivate the sales force and make sales force selling efforts more effective, including bonuses, contests and sales rallies.

Sales promotion Short-term incentives to encourage purchase or sales of a product or service.

Sales quotas Standards set for salespeople, stating the amount they should sell and how sales should be divided among the company's products.

Salesperson An individual acting for a company by performing one or more of the following activities: prospecting, communicating, servicing and information gathering.

Salutary products Products that have low appeal but may benefit consumers in the long run.

Sample A segment of the population selected for marketing research to represent the population as a whole.

Samples Offers to consumers of a trial amount of a product.

Sealed-bid pricing Setting price based on how the firm thinks competitors will price rather than on its own costs or demand – used when a company bids for jobs.

Seasonal discount A price reduction to buyers who buy merchandise or services out of season.

Seasonality The recurrent consistent pattern of sales movements within the year.

Secondary data Information that already exists somewhere, having been collected for another purpose.

Segment marketing Adapting a company's offerings so they more closely match the needs of one or more segments.

Segmented pricing Pricing that allows for differences in customers, products and locations. The differences in prices are not based on differences in costs.

Selective attention The tendency of people to screen out most of the information to which they are exposed.

Selective demand The demand for a given brand of a product or service.

Selective distortion The tendency of people to adapt information to personal meanings.

Selective distribution The use of more than one, but less than all of the intermediaries that are willing to carry the company's products.

Selective retention The tendency of people to retain only part of the information to which they are exposed, usually information that supports their attitudes or beliefs.

Self-concept Self-image, or the complex mental pictures that people have of themselves.

Self-service retailers Retailers that provide few or no services to shoppers; shoppers perform their own locate-compare-select process.

Selling concept The idea that consumers will not buy enough of the organization's products unless the organization undertakes a large-scale selling and promotion effort.

Selling process The steps that the salesperson follows when selling, which include prospecting and qualifying, preapproach, approach, presentation and demonstration, handling objections, closing and follow-up.

Sense-of-mission marketing A principle of enlightened marketing which holds that a company should define its mission in broad social terms rather than narrow product terms.

Sequential product development A new-product development approach in which one company department works individually to complete its stage of the process before passing the new product along to the next department and stage.

Served market (target market) The part of the qualified available market that the company decides to pursue.

Service Any activity or benefit that one party can offer to another which is essentially intangible and does not result in the ownership of anything.

Service inseparability A major characteristic of services – they are produced and consumed at the same time and cannot be separated from their providers, whether the providers are people or machines.

Service intangibility A major characteristic of services – they cannot be seen, tasted, felt, heard or smelled before they are bought.

Service perishability A major characteristic of services – they cannot be stored for later sale or use.

Service variability A major characteristic of services – their quality may vary greatly, depending on who provides them and when, where and how.

Services Activities, benefits or satisfactions that are offered for sale.

Shopping product A consumer product that the customer, in the process of selection and purchase, characteristically compares with others on such bases as suitability, quality, price and style.

Simultaneous product development An approach to developing new products in which various company departments work closely together, overlapping the steps in the product development process to save time and increase effectiveness.

Single-source data systems Electronic monitoring systems that link consumers' exposure to television advertising and promotion (measured using television metres) with what they buy in stores (measured using store checkout scanners).

Social classes Relatively permanent and ordered divisions in a society whose members share similar values, interests and behaviours.

Societal marketing A principle of enlightened marketing which holds that a company should make marketing decisions by considering consumers' wants, the company's requirements, consumers' long-run interests and society's long-run interests.

Societal marketing concept   The idea that the organization should determine the needs, wants and interests of target markets and deliver the desired satisfactions more effectively and efficiently than competitors in a way that maintains or improves the consumer's and society's well-being.

Speciality product   A consumer product with unique characteristics or brand identification for which a significant group of buyers is willing to make a special purchase effort.

Speciality store   A retail store that carries a narrow product line with a deep assortment within that line.

Specialized industry   An industry where there are many opportunities for firms to create competitive advantages that are huge or give a high pay-off.

Stalemate industry   An industry that produces commodities and is characterized by a few opportunities to create competitive advantages, with each advantage being small.

Standardized marketing mix   An international marketing strategy for using basically the same product, advertising, distribution channels and other elements of the marketing mix in all the company's international markets.

Stars   High-growth, high-share businesses or products that often require heavy investment to finance their rapid growth.

Statistical demand analysis   A set of statistical procedures used to discover the most important real factors affecting sales and their relative influence; the most commonly analyzed factors are prices, income, population and promotion.

Status   The general esteem given to a role by society.

Straight product extension   Marketing a product in a foreign market without any change.

Straight rebuy   A business buying situation in which the buyer routinely reorders something without any modifications.

Strapline   A slogan often used in conjunction with a brand's name, advertising and other promotions.

Strategic business-planning grid   A portfolio planning method that evaluates a company's strategic business units using indices of industry attractiveness and the company's strength in the industry.

Strategic business unit (SBU)   A unit of the company that has a separate mission and objectives and that can be planned independently from other company businesses. An SBU can be a company division, a product line within a division, or sometimes a single product or brand.

Strategic control   Checking whether the company's basic strategy matches its opportunities and strengths.

Strategic focus   A strategic planning tool to help marketers identify ways of achieving sales and profit growth. Two routes – productivity increases and volume expansion – form the basis of analysis.

Strategic group   A group of firms in an industry following the same or a similar strategy.

Strategic plan   A plan that describes how a firm will adapt to take advantage of opportunities in its constantly changing environment, thereby maintaining a strategic fit between the firm's goals and capabilities and its changing market opportunities.

Strategic planning   The process of developing and maintaining a strategic fit between the organization's goals and capabilities and its changing marketing opportunities. It relies on developing a clear company mission, supporting objectives, a sound business portfolio and co-ordinated functional strategies.

Style   A basic and distinctive mode of expression.

Subculture   A group of people with shared value systems based on common life experiences and situations.

Substantiality   The degree to which a market segment is sufficiently large or profitable.

Supermarkets   Large, low-cost, low-margin, high-volume, self-service stores that carry a wide variety of food, laundry and household products.

Superstore   A store almost twice the size of a regular supermarket that carries a large assortment of routinely purchased food and non-food items and offers such services as dry cleaning, post offices, film developing, photo finishing, cheque cashing, petrol forecourts and self-service car-washing facilities.

Supplier search   The stage of the business buying process in which the buyer tries to find the best vendors.

Supplier selection   The stage of the business buying process in which the buyer reviews proposals and selects a supplier or suppliers.

Suppliers   Firms and individuals that provide the resources needed by the company and its competitors to produce goods and services.

Supplies and services   Industrial products that do not enter the finished product at all.

Survey research   The gathering of primary data by asking people questions about their knowledge, attitudes, preferences and buying behaviour.

SWOT analysis   A distillation of the findings of the internal and external audit which draws attention to the critical organizational strengths and weaknesses and the opportunities and threats facing the company.

Systems buying   Buying a packaged solution to a problem and without all the separate decisions involved.

Target costing   A technique to support pricing decision, which starts with deciding a target cost for a new product and works back to designing the product.

Target market   A set of buyers sharing common needs or characteristics that the company decides to serve.

Target marketing   Directing a company's effort towards serving one or more groups of customers sharing common needs or characteristics.

Target profit pricing   See **Break-even pricing**.

Tariff   A tax levied by a government against certain imported products. Tariffs are designed to raise revenue or to protect domestic firms.

Team selling   Using teams of people from sales, marketing, production, finance, technical support, and even upper management to service large, complex accounts.

Technological environment   Forces that create new technologies, creating new product and market opportunities.

Telemarketing   Using the telephone to sell directly to consumers.

Television marketing   Direct-response television marketing (DRTV).

Territorial sales force structure   A sales force organization that assigns each salesperson to an exclusive geographic territory in which that salesperson carries the company's full line.

Test marketing   The stage of new-product development where the product and marketing programme are tested in more realistic market settings.

Time-series analysis Breaking down past sales into its trend, cycle, season and erratic components, then recombining these components to produce a sales forecast.

Total costs The sum of the fixed and variable costs for any given level of production.

Total customer cost The total of all the monetary, time, energy and psychic costs associated with a marketing offer.

Total customer value The total of all of the product, services, personnel and image values that a buyer receives from a marketing offer.

Total market demand The total volume of a product or service that would be bought by a defined consumer group in a defined geographic area in a defined time period in a defined marketing environment under a defined level and mix of industry marketing effort.

Total quality management (TQM) Programmes designed to constantly improve the quality of products, services, and marketing processes.

Trade-in allowance A price reduction given for turning in an old item when buying a new one.

Trade (or retailer) promotion Sales promotion designed to gain reseller support and to improve reseller selling efforts, including discounts, allowances, free goods, co-operative advertising, push money, and conventions and trade shows.

Transaction A trade between two parties that involves at least two things of value, agreed-upon conditions, a time of agreement and a place of agreement.

Trend The long-term, underlying pattern of sales growth or decline resulting from basic changes in population, capital formation and technology.

Two-part pricing A strategy for pricing services in which price is broken into a fixed fee plus a variable usage rate.

Underpositioning A positioning error referring to failure to position a company, its product or brand.

Undifferentiated marketing A market-coverage strategy in which a firm decides to ignore market segment differences and go after the whole market with one offer.

Uniform delivered pricing A geographic pricing strategy in which the company charges the same price plus freight to all customers, regardless of their location.

Unique selling proposition (USP) The unique product benefit that a firm aggressively promotes in a consistent manner to its target market. The benefit usually reflects functional superiority: best quality, best services, lowest price, most advanced technology.

Unsought product A consumer product that the consumer either does not know about or knows about but does not normally think of buying.

User The person who consumes or uses a product or service.

Users Members of the organization who will use the product or service; users often initiate the buying proposal and help define product specifications.

Value analysis An approach to cost reduction in which components are studied carefully to determine if they can be redesigned, standardized or made by less costly methods of production.

Value-based pricing Setting price based on buyers' perceptions of product values rather than on cost.

Value chain A major tool for identifying ways to create more customer value.

Value marketing A principle of enlightened marketing which holds that a company should put most of its resources into value-building marketing investments.

Value pricing Offering just the right combination of quality and good service at a fair price.

Variable costs Costs that vary directly with the level of production.

Variety-seeking buying behaviour Consumer buying behaviour in situations characterized by low consumer involvement, but significant perceived brand differences.

Variety store Self-service store that specializes in a wide range of merchandise. It offers a wider range than specialist stores, but a narrower variety than department stores.

Vertical marketing system (VMS) A distribution channel structure in which producers, wholesalers and retailers act as a unified system. One channel member owns the others, has contracts with them, or has so much power that they all co-operate.

Volume industry An industry characterized by few opportunities to create competitive advantages, but each advantage is huge and gives a high pay-off.

Warehouse club (wholesale club, membership warehouse) Off-price retailer that sells a limited selection of brand-name grocery items, appliances, clothing and a hodgepodge of other goods at deep discounts to members who pay annual membership fees.

Webcasting (push programming) Process whereby the online marketer sends advertisements or information over the Internet directly to the desktops of target customers. Companies can also sign on with Web-casting service providers, which automatically download customized information to the personal computers of subscribers to their services.

Wheel of retailing A concept of retailing which states that new types of retailer usually begin as low-margin, low-price, low-status operations, but later evolve into higher-priced, higher-service operations, eventually becoming like the conventional retailers they replaced.

Wholesaler A firm engaged primarily in selling goods and services to those buying for resale or business use.

Word-of-mouth influence Personal communication about a product between target buyers and neighbours, friends, family members and associates.

Workload approach An approach to setting sales force size, whereby the company groups accounts into different size classes and then determines how many salespeople are needed to call on them the desired number of times.

World Wide Web (WWW or the Web) A part of the Internet that uses a standard computer language to allow documents containing text, images, sound and video to be sent across the Internet.

Zone pricing A geographic pricing strategy in which the company sets up two or more zones. All customers within a zone pay the same total price; the more distant the zone, the higher the price.

Subject Index